Contemporary Authors®

NEW REVISION SERIES

ISSN 0275-7176

REF
Z
1224
.C6
NRS
v.126

Contemporary Authors®

A Bio-Bibliographical Guide to Current Writers in Fiction, General Nonfiction, Poetry, Journalism, Drama, Motion Pictures, Television, and Other Fields

80892

CONCORDIA COLLEGE LIBRARY
BRONXVILLE, NEW YORK 10708

NEW REVISION SERIES
volume 126

Detroit • New York • San Diego • San Francisco • Cleveland • New Haven, Conn. • Waterville, Maine • London • Munich

Contemporary Authors, New Revision Series, Vol. 126

Project Editor
Tracey Watson

Editorial
Katy Balcer, Shavon Burden, Sara Constantakis, Natalie Fulkerson, Michelle Kazensky, Julie Keppen, Joshua Kondek, Jenai A. Mynatt, Lisa Kumar, Mary Ruby, Lemma Shomali, Susan Strickland, Maikue Vang

Research
Michelle Campbell, Tracie A. Richardson, Robert Whaley

Permissions
Margaret Chamberlain, Jacqueline Key, Sue Rudolph

Imaging and Multimedia
Randy Bassett, Dean Dauphinais, Leitha Etheridge-Sims, Lezlie Light, Michael Logusz, Dan Newell, Christine O'Bryan, Kelly A. Quin

Composition and Electronic Capture
Kathy Sauer

Manufacturing
Lori Kessler

© 2004 by Gale. Gale is an imprint of The Gale Group, Inc., a division of Thomson Learning, Inc.

Gale and Design™ and Thomson Learning™ are trademarks used herein under license.

For more information, contact
The Gale Group, Inc.
27500 Drake Rd.
Farmington Hills, MI 48331-3535
Or you can visit our internet site at
http://www.gale.com

ALL RIGHTS RESERVED
No part of this work covered by the copyright herein may be reproduced or used in any form or by any means—graphic, electronic, or mechanical, including photocopying, recording, taping, Web distribution, or information storage retrieval systems—without the written permission of the publisher.

This publication is a creative work fully protected by all applicable copyright laws, as well as by misappropriation, trade secret, unfair competition, and other applicable laws. The authors and editors of this work have added value to the underlying factual material herein through one or more of the following: unique and original selection, coordination, expression, arrangement, and classification of the information.

For permission to use material from the product, submit your request via the Web at http://www.gale-edit.com/permissions, or you may download our Permissions Request form and submit your request by fax or mail to:

Permissions Department
The Gale Group, Inc.
27500 Drake Rd.
Farmington Hills, MI 48331-3535
Permissions Hotline:
248-699-8006 or 800-877-4253, ext. 8006
Fax 248-699-8074 or 800-762-4058

Since this page cannot legibly accommodate all copyright notices, the acknowledgments constitute an extension of the copyright notice.

While every effort has been made to secure permission to reprint material and to ensure the reliability of the information presented in this publication, the Gale Group neither guarantees the accuracy of the data contained herein nor assumes any responsibility for errors, omissions or discrepancies. Gale accepts no payment for listing; and inclusion in the publication of any organization, agency, institution, publication, service, or individual does not imply endorsment of the editors or publisher. Errors brought to the attention of the publisher and verified to the satisfaction of the publisher will be corrected in future editions.

LIBRARY OF CONGRESS CATALOG CARD NUMBER 81-640179

ISBN 0-7876-6718-8
ISSN 0275-7176

Printed in the United States of America
10 9 8 7 6 5 4 3 2 1

Contents

Indexing note: All *Contemporary Authors* entries are indexed in the *Contemporary Authors* cumulative index, which is published separately and distributed twice a year.

As always, the most recent Contemporary Authors cumulative index continues to be the user's guide to the location of an individual author's listing.

Preface

Contemporary Authors (*CA*) provides information on approximately 115,000 writers in a wide range of media, including:

- Current writers of fiction, nonfiction, poetry, and drama whose works have been issued by commercial publishers, risk publishers, or university presses (authors whose books have been published only by known vanity or author-subsidized firms are ordinarily not included)
- Prominent print and broadcast journalists, editors, photojournalists, syndicated cartoonists, graphic novelists, screenwriters, television scriptwriters, and other media people
- Notable international authors
- Literary greats of the early twentieth century whose works are popular in today's high school and college curriculums and continue to elicit critical attention

A *CA* listing entails no charge or obligation. Authors are included on the basis of the above criteria and their interest to *CA* users. Sources of potential listees include trade periodicals, publishers' catalogs, librarians, and other users.

How to Get the Most out of *CA*: Use the Index

The key to locating an author's most recent entry is the *CA* cumulative index, which is published separately and distributed twice a year. It provides access to *all* entries in *CA* and *Contemporary Authors New Revision Series* (*CANR*). Always consult the latest index to find an author's most recent entry.

For the convenience of users, the *CA* cumulative index also includes references to all entries in these Gale literary series: *Authors and Artists for Young Adults, Authors in the News, Bestsellers, Black Literature Criticism, Black Literature Criticism Supplement, Black Writers, Children's Literature Review, Concise Dictionary of American Literary Biography, Concise Dictionary of British Literary Biography, Contemporary Authors Autobiography Series, Contemporary Authors Bibliographical Series, Contemporary Dramatists, Contemporary Literary Criticism, Contemporary Novelists, Contemporary Poets, Contemporary Popular Writers, Contemporary Southern Writers, Contemporary Women Poets, Dictionary of Literary Biography, Dictionary of Literary Biography Documentary Series, Dictionary of Literary Biography Yearbook, DISCovering Authors, DISCovering Authors: British, DISCovering Authors: Canadian, DISCovering Authors: Modules* (including modules for Dramatists, Most-Studied Authors, Multicultural Authors, Novelists, Poets, and Popular/Genre Authors), DISCovering Authors 3.0, *Drama Criticism, Drama for Students, Feminist Writers, Hispanic Literature Criticism, Hispanic Writers, Junior DISCovering Authors, Major Authors and Illustrators for Children and Young Adults, Major 20th-Century Writers, Native North American Literature, Novels for Students, Poetry Criticism, Poetry for Students, Short Stories for Students, Short Story Criticism, Something about the Author, Something about the Author Autobiography Series, St. James Guide to Children's Writers, St. James Guide to Crime & Mystery Writers, St. James Guide to Fantasy Writers, St. James Guide to Horror, Ghost & Gothic Writers, St. James Guide to Science Fiction Writers, St. James Guide to Young Adult Writers, Twentieth-Century Literary Criticism, 20th Century Romance and Historical Writers, World Literature Criticism,* and *Yesterday's Authors of Books for Children.*

A Sample Index Entry:

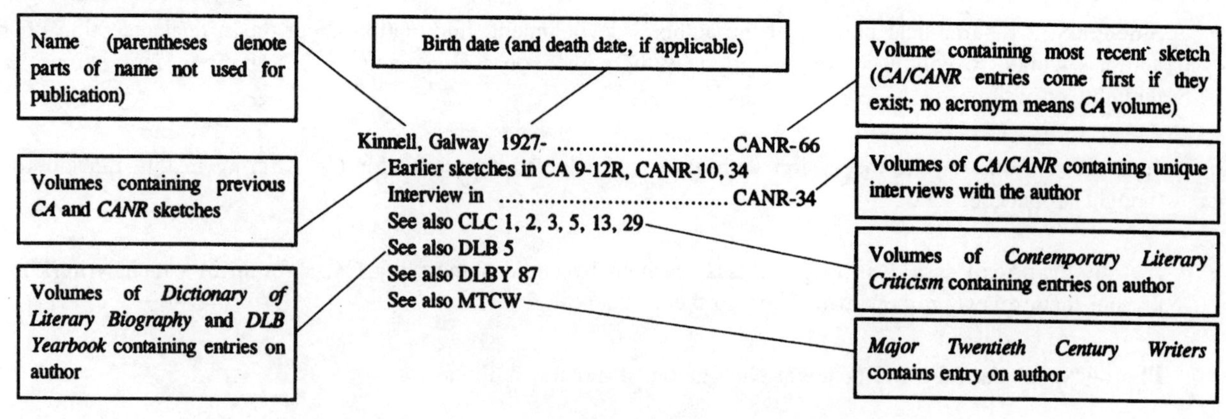

How Are Entries Compiled?

The editors make every effort to secure new information directly from the authors; listees' responses to our questionnaires and query letters provide most of the information featured in *CA*. For deceased writers, or those who fail to reply to requests for data, we consult other reliable biographical sources, such as those indexed in Gale's *Biography and Genealogy Master Index,* and bibliographical sources, including *National Union Catalog, LC MARC,* and *British National Bibliography.* Further details come from published interviews, feature stories, and book reviews, as well as information supplied by the authors' publishers and agents.

An asterisk (*) at the end of a sketch indicates that the listing has been compiled from secondary sources believed to be reliable but has not been personally verified for this edition by the author sketched.

What Kinds of Information Does An Entry Provide?

Sketches in *CA* contain the following biographical and bibliographical information:

- **Entry heading:** the most complete form of author's name, plus any pseudonyms or name variations used for writing

- **Personal information:** author's date and place of birth, family data, ethnicity, educational background, political and religious affiliations, and hobbies and leisure interests

- **Addresses:** author's home, office, or agent's addresses, plus e-mail and fax numbers, as available

- **Career summary:** name of employer, position, and dates held for each career post; resume of other vocational achievements; military service

- **Membership information:** professional, civic, and other association memberships and any official posts held

- **Awards and honors:** military and civic citations, major prizes and nominations, fellowships, grants, and honorary degrees

- **Writings:** a comprehensive, chronological list of titles, publishers, dates of original publication and revised editions, and production information for plays, television scripts, and screenplays

- **Adaptations:** a list of films, plays, and other media which have been adapted from the author's work

- **Work in progress:** current or planned projects, with dates of completion and/or publication, and expected publisher, when known

- **Sidelights:** a biographical portrait of the author's development; information about the critical reception of the author's works; revealing comments, often by the author, on personal interests, aspirations, motivations, and thoughts on writing

- **Interview:** a one-on-one discussion with authors conducted especially for *CA*, offering insight into authors' thoughts about their craft

- **Autobiographical essay:** an original essay written by noted authors for *CA*, a forum in which writers may present themselves, on their own terms, to their audience

- **Photographs:** portraits and personal photographs of notable authors

- **Biographical and critical sources:** a list of books and periodicals in which additional information on an author's life and/or writings appears

- **Obituary Notices** in *CA* provide date and place of birth as well as death information about authors whose full-length sketches appeared in the series before their deaths. The entries also summarize the authors' careers and writings and list other sources of biographical and death information.

Related Titles in the *CA* Series

Contemporary Authors Autobiography Series complements *CA* original and revised volumes with specially commissioned autobiographical essays by important current authors, illustrated with personal photographs they provide. Common topics include their motivations for writing, the people and experiences that shaped their careers, the rewards they derive from their work, and their impressions of the current literary scene.

Contemporary Authors Bibliographical Series surveys writings by and about important American authors since World War II. Each volume concentrates on a specific genre and features approximately ten writers; entries list works written by and about the author and contain a bibliographical essay discussing the merits and deficiencies of major critical and scholarly studies in detail.

Available in Electronic Formats

GaleNet. *CA* is available on a subscription basis through GaleNet, an online information resource that features an easy-to-use end-user interface, powerful search capabilities, and ease of access through the World-Wide Web. For more information, call 1-800-877-GALE.

Licensing. *CA* is available for licensing. The complete database is provided in a fielded format and is deliverable on such media as disk, CD-ROM, or tape. For more information, contact Gale's Business Development Group at 1-800-877-GALE, or visit us on our website at www.galegroup.com/bizdev.

Suggestions Are Welcome

The editors welcome comments and suggestions from users on any aspect of the *CA* series. If readers would like to recommend authors for inclusion in future volumes of the series, they are cordially invited to write the Editors at *Contemporary Authors*, Gale Group, 27500 Drake Rd., Farmington Hills, MI 48331-3535; or call at 1-248-699-4253; or fax at 1-248-699-8054.

Contemporary Authors Product Advisory Board

The editors of *Contemporary Authors* are dedicated to maintaining a high standard of excellence by publishing comprehensive, accurate, and highly readable entries on a wide array of writers. In addition to the quality of the content, the editors take pride in the graphic design of the series, which is intended to be orderly yet inviting, allowing readers to utilize the pages of *CA* easily and with efficiency. Despite the longevity of the *CA* print series, and the success of its format, we are mindful that the vitality of a literary reference product is dependent on its ability to serve its users over time. As literature, and attitudes about literature, constantly evolve, so do the reference needs of students, teachers, scholars, journalists, researchers, and book club members. To be certain that we continue to keep pace with the expectations of our customers, the editors of *CA* listen carefully to their comments regarding the value, utility, and quality of the series. Librarians, who have firsthand knowledge of the needs of library users, are a valuable resource for us. The *Contemporary Authors* Product Advisory Board, made up of school, public, and academic librarians, is a forum to promote focused feedback about *CA* on a regular basis. The seven-member advisory board includes the following individuals, whom the editors wish to thank for sharing their expertise:

- **Anne M. Christensen,** Librarian II, Phoenix Public Library, Phoenix, Arizona.
- **Barbara C. Chumard,** Reference/Adult Services Librarian, Middletown Thrall Library, Middletown, New York.
- **Eva M. Davis,** Youth Department Manager, Ann Arbor District Library, Ann Arbor, Michigan.
- **Adam Janowski, Jr.,** Library Media Specialist, Naples High School Library Media Center, Naples, Florida.
- **Robert Reginald,** Head of Technical Services and Collection Development, California State University, San Bernadino, California.
- **Stephen Weiner,** Director, Maynard Public Library, Maynard, Massachusetts.

International Advisory Board

Well-represented among the 115,000 author entries published in *Contemporary Authors* are sketches on notable writers from many non-English-speaking countries. The primary criteria for inclusion of such authors has traditionally been the publication of at least one title in English, either as an original work or as a translation. However, the editors of *Contemporary Authors* came to observe that many important international writers were being overlooked due to a strict adherence to our inclusion criteria. In addition, writers who were publishing in languages other than English were not being covered in the traditional sources we used for identifying new listees. Intent on increasing our coverage of international authors, including those who write only in their native language and have not been translated into English, the editors enlisted the aid of a board of advisors, each of whom is an expert on the literature of a particular country or region. Among the countries we focused attention on are Mexico, Puerto Rico, Spain, Italy, France, Germany, Luxembourg, Belgium, the Netherlands, Norway, Sweden, Denmark, Finland, Taiwan, Singapore, Malaysia, Thailand, South Africa, Israel, and Japan, as well as England, Scotland, Wales, Ireland, Australia, and New Zealand. The sixteen-member advisory board includes the following individuals, whom the editors wish to thank for sharing their expertise:

- **Lowell A. Bangerter,** Professor of German, University of Wyoming, Laramie, Wyoming.
- **Nancy E. Berg,** Associate Professor of Hebrew and Comparative Literature, Washington University, St. Louis, Missouri.
- **Frances Devlin-Glass,** Associate Professor, School of Literary and Communication Studies, Deakin University, Burwood, Victoria, Australia.
- **David William Foster,** Regent's Professor of Spanish, Interdisciplinary Humanities, and Women's Studies, Arizona State University, Tempe, Arizona.
- **Hosea Hirata,** Director of the Japanese Program, Associate Professor of Japanese, Tufts University, Medford, Massachusetts.
- **Jack Kolbert,** Professor Emeritus of French Literature, Susquehanna University, Selinsgrove, Pennsylvania.
- **Mark Libin,** Professor, University of Manitoba, Winnipeg, Manitoba, Canada.
- **C. S. Lim,** Professor, University of Malaya, Kuala Lumpur, Malaysia.
- **Eloy E. Merino,** Assistant Professor of Spanish, Northern Illinois University, DeKalb, Illinois.
- **Linda M. Rodríguez Guglielmoni,** Associate Professor, University of Puerto Rico—Mayagüez, Puerto Rico.
- **Sven Hakon Rossel,** Professor and Chair of Scandinavian Studies, University of Vienna, Vienna, Austria.
- **Steven R. Serafin,** Director, Writing Center, Hunter College of the City University of New York, New York City.
- **David Smyth,** Lecturer in Thai, School of Oriental and African Studies, University of London, England.
- **Ismail S. Talib,** Senior Lecturer, Department of English Language and Literature, National University of Singapore, Singapore.
- **Dionisio Viscarri,** Assistant Professor, Ohio State University, Columbus, Ohio.
- **Mark Williams,** Associate Professor, English Department, University of Canterbury, Christchurch, New Zealand.

CA Numbering System and Volume Update Chart

Occasionally questions arise about the *CA* numbering system and which volumes, if any, can be discarded. Despite numbers like "29-32R," "97-100" and "218," the entire *CA* print series consists of only 272 physical volumes with the publication of *CA* Volume 219. The following charts note changes in the numbering system and cover design, and indicate which volumes are essential for the most complete, up-to-date coverage.

***CA* First Revision**

- 1-4R through 41-44R (11 books)
  Cover: Brown with black and gold trim.
  There will be no further First Revision volumes because revised entries are now being handled exclusively through the more efficient *New Revision Series* mentioned below.

***CA* Original Volumes**

- 45-48 through 97-100 (14 books)
  Cover: Brown with black and gold trim.
  101 through 219 (119 books)
  Cover: Blue and black with orange bands.
  The same as previous *CA* original volumes but with a new, simplified numbering system and new cover design.

***CA* Permanent Series**

- *CAP*-1 and *CAP*-2 (2 books)
  Cover: Brown with red and gold trim.
  There will be no further Permanent Series volumes because revised entries are now being handled exclusively through the more efficient *New Revision Series* mentioned below.

***CA* New Revision Series**

- CANR-1 through CANR-126 (126 books)
  Cover: Blue and black with green bands.
  Includes only sketches requiring significant changes; **sketches are taken from any previously published CA, CAP, or CANR volume.**

If You Have:	You May Discard:
CA First Revision Volumes 1-4R through 41-44R and *CA Permanent Series* Volumes 1 and 2	*CA* Original Volumes 1, 2, 3, 4 and Volumes 5-6 through 41-44
CA Original Volumes 45-48 through 97-100 and 101 through 219	**NONE:** These volumes will not be superseded by corresponding revised volumes. Individual entries from these and all other volumes appearing in the left column of this chart may be revised and included in the various volumes of the *New Revision Series.*
CA New Revision Series Volumes *CANR*-1 through *CANR*-126	**NONE:** The *New Revision Series* does not replace any single volume of *CA*. Instead, volumes of *CANR* include entries from many previous *CA* series volumes. All *New Revision Series* volumes must be retained for full coverage.

A Sampling of Authors and Media People Featured in This Volume

Charles Frazier
Frazier taught early American literature before publishing his award-winning first novel *Cold Mountain.* The 1997 book concerns a soldier's three-hundred-mile-long journey home to the North Carolina mountains and the woman he loves. Well received by critics and fans, *Cold Mountain* received the 1997 National Book Award. In 2003 the book was made into a film of the same title and released by MGM and Mirimax, starring Jude Law, Nicole Kidman, and Renee Zellweger.

Virginia Hamilton
Hamilton, a prolific novelist and children's book author, helped launch a new era in the portrayal of African Americans in children's literature. Hamilton, recognized as a gifted and demanding storyteller, is author of such works as *The House of Dies Drear, The Planet of Junior Brown, Sweet Whispers, Brother Rush* and the novel *M. C. Higgins, the Great,* which was the first work ever to win both the National Book Award and the Newbery Medal. Hamilton has won every major award in her field, including the 1995 Laura Ingalls Wilder Award for lifetime achievement. *Time Pieces: The Book of Time,* Hamilton's final novel, was published posthumously in 2002.

V. S. Naipaul
Naipaul, the 2001 Nobel Prize winner for literature, is frequently referred to as a writer of the world due to his disassociation of region and tradition. Born in Trinidad to descendants of Hindu immigrants from northern India and later being educated at Oxford University are factors supporting the author's argument that he contentedly exists without ancestors or heritage. As a result many of his books, including *The Mystic Masseur, The Suffrage of Elvira,* and *Miguel Street* deal with people who seek to belong in societies that they are ostensibly part of, but cannot relate to. In 2003 he published *Literary Occasions: Essays,* which includes his Nobel Prize lecture.

Anna Quindlen
Quindlen, a journalist and best selling novelist, received national attention along with a loyal fan base as a syndicated newspaper columnist at the *New York Times* and as a contributor to *Newsweek* magazines's "Last Word" column. Noted by critics for her unaffected style of column writing and her proud, outspoken expression of feminist leanings, Quindlen received the Pulitzer Prize for commentary in 1992. She expanded her penchant to fiction penning best selling novels *Object Lessons, Black and Blue,* and 2000's *A Short Guide to a Happy Life.* Her 2002 offering, *Blessings,* centers around an elderly woman haunted by memories from the past.

Arundhati Roy
An outspoken activist, novelist, and screenplay writer, Roy created an international sensation with her first novel *The God of Small Things.* The book garnered her the 1997 Booker Prize, setting the precedent for the first citizen of India to win that award. The author remained in the limelight due to public displays of social activism concerning globalization, which many times resulted in imprisonment. Roy expressed her opinions about the topic in many essays, including those collected in *The Cost of Living* and *Power Politics.* Other works published by Roy include, *The Greater Common Good, War Talk,* and 2004's *Globalization Dissent: Conversations with Arundhati Roy,* with David Barsamian.

Dan Simmons
Simmons has written in several genres, from fantasy to science fiction and horror to mystery. He has been awarded for his efforts in these categories receiving Hugo, Locus, and Bram Stoker awards. Noted by critics for his accurate research and intellectual sophistication, Simmons's first series of science fiction books, stories of the "Hyperion" received substantial and favorable critical attention. He introduced another science fiction series in 2003, with the novel *Illium* inspired by Homer's *Iliad.*

Neil Simon
Renowned playwright Neil Simon's comedies have dominated the Broadway stage since 1959. Many of them have been adapted as popular films as well. Some of his most noted works include, *Barefoot in the Park, The Odd Couple,* and *The Sunshine Boys.* Though Simon's plays are characterized by their humor, critics note the onset of more serious works beginning in 1982 with the autobiographical trilogy *Brighton Beach Memoirs, Biloxi Blues,* and *Broadway Bound.* Recipient of numerous awards,

including Emmy, Tony, and lifetime achievement awards, Simon won the prestigious Pulitzer Prize in 1991 for *Lost in Yonkers.* His 2003 play *Rose and Walsh* concerns a writer dealing with the loss of her husband and a falling career.

Quincy Troupe

Poet and creative writing instructor Troupe writes about jazz, sports and street life according to critics. He received an American Book Award for his second volume of poetry *Snake-back Solos.* Since then his poetic penchant and scholarly interests led him to publish *Giant Talk: An Anthology of Third World Writings* with Rainer Schulte and the popular *The Inside Story of TV's "Roots"* in 1978 with David L. Wolper. His acclaim spread further with the collaboration of jazz icon Miles Davis on *Miles: The Biography,* which earned him another American Book Award in 1990. In 2002 Troupe was named California's first Poet Laureate. A scandal involving falsified academic credentials eventually led Troupe to resign from his lucrative teaching position despite protests from students and colleagues. He also in turn stepped down from his honorary Poet Laureate position.

Acknowledgments

Grateful acknowledgment is made to those publishers, photographers, and artists whose work appear with these authors' essays. Following is a list of the copyright holders who have granted us permission to reproduce material in this volume of *CA*. Every effort has been made to trace copyright, but if omissions have been made, please let us know.

Photographs/Art

Arnold Adoff: Arnold, photograph by Virginia Hamilton Adoff. Reproduced by permission of Arnold Adoff.

George Ancona: Ancona, photograph by Marina Ancona. Reproduced by permission.

James Edward Arnosky: Arnosky, photograph by Deanna Arnosky. Reproduced by permission.

Molefi Kete Asante: Asante, photograph. Courtesy of Molefi Kete Asante. Reproduced by permission.

Natalie Babbitt: Babbitt, photograph by Steve Adams Photography. Reproduced by permission.

Lidia Matticchio Bastianich: Bastianich, photograph. James Leynse/Corbis. Reproduced by permission.

Madeline Blais: Blais, photograph. Bettman/Corbis. Reproduced by permission.

Megan Chance: Chance, photograph by Jerry Bauer. Reproduced by permission.

Andrew Clements: Clements, photograph by Bill Crofton. Bill Crofton/Motophoto. Reproduced by permission.

Jayne Cortez: Cortez, photograph. Christopher Felver/Corbis. Reproduced by permission.

Anita Diamant: Diamant, photograph. © Jerry Bauer. Reproduced by permission.

Berlie Doherty: Doherty, photograph. Reproduced by permission.

Diane Duane: Duane, photograph. Reproduced by permission.

Douglas Dunn: Dunn, photograph. © Jerry Bauer. Reproduced by permission.

Bret Easton Ellis: Ellis, photograph. © Jerry Bauer. Reproduced by permission

Buchi Emecheta: Emecheta, photograph by Jerry Bauer. © Jerry Bauer. Reproduced by permission.

Eve Ensler: Ensler, photograph. Jim Spellman/WireImage.com. Reproduced by permission.

Tom Eyen: Eyen, photograph. AP/Wide World Photos. Reproduced by permission.

Susan Faludi: Faludi, photograph. AP/Wide World Photos. Reproduced by permission.

Naomi Foner: Foner, photograph. Getty Images. Reproduced by permission.

Charles Frazier: Frazier, photograph by Marion Ettlinger. AP/Wide World Photo. Reproduced by permission.

Ernest J. Gaines: Gaines, photograph by Alex Brandon. AP/Wide World Photos. Reproduced by permission.

Celia Godkin: Godkin, photograph. Reproduced by permission.

Mike Gordon: Gordon, photograph. Reproduced by permission.

David Guterson: Guterson, photograph by Jill Sabella. Reproduced by permission of Jill Sabella.

Virginia Hamilton: Hamilton, photograph. Reproduced by permission.

Lawson Fusao Inada: Inada, photograph by Paul Schraub. Reproduced by permission of Lawson Fusao Inada.

Eartha Kitt: Kitt, photograph. AP/Wide World Photos, Inc. Reproduced by permission.

Helen Lester: Lester, photograph. Reproduced by permission.

Alice McDermott: McDermott, photograph by Jerry Bauer. © Jerry Bauer. Reproduced by permission.

Czeslaw Milosz: ilosz, photograph. Getty Images. Reproduced by permission.

V. S. Naipaul: Naipaul, photograph by Jerry Bauer. © Jerry Bauer. Reproduced by permission.

Leonard Nimoy: Nimoy, photograph. AP/Wide World. Reproduced by permission.

Kenzaburo Oe: Oe, photograph by Itsuo Inouye. AP/Wide World Photos. Reproduced by permission.

Marie Osmond: Osmond, photograph by Reed Saxon. AP/Wide World Photos. Reproduced by permission.

Gary Paulsen: Paulsen, photograph. Reproduced by permission.

Terry Pratchett: ratchett, photograph. © Rune Hellestad/Corbis. Reproduced by permission.

Anna Quindlen: Quindlen, photograph. AP/Wide World Photos. Reproduced by permission.

Arundhati Roy: oy, photograph. © Karen Kapoor/Corbis. Reproduced by permission.

Lola M. Schaefer: Schaefer, photograph. Reproduced by permission.

Will Self: Self, photograph by Mark Gerson. Reproduced by permission of Mark Gerson.

Olive Senior: Senior, photograph by Maria LaYacona. Reproduced by permission.

Dan Simmons: Simmons, photograph. Bassouls Sophie/Corbis Sygma. Reproduced by permission.

Neil Simon: Simon, photograph. AP/Wide World Photos. Reproduced by permission.

William Styron: Styron, photograph. AP/Wide World Photos. Reproduced by permission.

Qunicy Troupe: Troupe, photograph by Christopher Felver/Corbis. Reproduced by permission.

Fred Willard: Willard, 1981, photograph. AP/Wide World Photos. Reproduced by permission.

Jane Yolen: Yolen, photograph by Jason Stemple. Copyright © 2000 Jason Stemple. Reproduced by permission.

A

** Indicates that a listing has been compiled from secondary sources believed to be reliable, but has not been personally verified for this edition by the author sketched.*

ADKINS, Jan 1944-

PERSONAL: Born November 7, 1944, in Gallipolis, OH; son of Alban Blakemore (a sheet-metal contractor) and Dixie Lee (Ellis) Adkins; married Deborah Kiernan, September 14, 1968 (died, June, 1976); married Dorcas Sheldon Peirce, December, 1977 (marriage ended); married Deborah Fenning (marriage ended); children: (first marriage) Sally, Samuel Ulysses, Robbie (stepchild). *Ethnicity:* "Caucasian; Welsh, German, Scots." *Education:* Ohio State University, B.A., 1969. *Politics:* "Skeptic." *Hobbies and other interests:* Tennis, hiking, sailing, singing, bicycling, cooking for friends.

ADDRESSES: *Office*—Jan Adkins Studio, 25 Wildwood Ln., Novato, CA 94947. *Agent*—Writer's House, 21 West 26th St., New York, NY 10010. *E-mail*—j.adkins@verizon.net.

CAREER: Author and illustrator. Ireland & Associates Architects, Columbus, OH, architectural designer, 1963-66; writer, graphic designer, and illustrator, 1969—; math and science teacher in Mattapoisett, MA, 1969-70; Buzzard Inc. (advertising agency), Marion, MA, vice president and art director, 1974-76; *National Geographic* magazine, Washington, DC, associate art director, 1980-88; Design Lab, Providence, RI, art director, 1995-96. Teacher of illustration at Rhode Island School of Design and Maryland Institute College of Art, 1990-96. Consultant to art museums, zoos, and natural history and science museums.

MEMBER: Society of Children's Book Writers and Illustrators.

AWARDS, HONORS: Brooklyn Museum Art citations, 1972, 1973, and 1974; Lewis Carroll Shelf Award, University of Wisconsin, and National Book Award nomination, both 1972, both for *The Art and Industry of Sandcastles: Being an Illustrated Guide to Basic Constructions along with Divers Information;* Children's Book Showcase awards, Children's Book Council, 1974, for *Toolchest,* and 1976, for *Inside: Seeing beneath the Surface;* Children's Science Book Award, New York Academy of Sciences, 1981, for *Moving Heavy Things;* Best Science Book, American Society of Science Teachers, 1985, for *Workboats;* Silver Addy Award for Design, Orlando Art Directors; Gold Medal for Best Essay of 1999, International Regional Magazine Association; Elementary & Early Childhood Award, Bridgewater State College, 2001, for contributions to literacy in young readers; Gold Medal for Best Editorial Illustration, San Francisco Society of Illustrators, 2001; Author of the Year, Naval Institute, 2002, for contributions to young people's naval history; Nonfiction Honor List selection, *Voice of Youth Advocates,* 2003, for *Bridges: From My Side to Yours;* numerous design and illustration awards from Society of Illustrators, Art Directors Clubs of Metropolitan Washington and New York, *Communication Arts,* and others.

WRITINGS:

SELF-ILLUSTRATED, EXCEPT WHERE NOTED

The Art and Industry of Sandcastles: Being an Illustrated Guide to Basic Constructions along with Divers Information, Walker (New York, NY), 1971, reprinted, 1994.

The Craft of Making Wine, Walker (New York, NY), 1971.

How a House Happens, Walker (New York, NY), 1972.

The Craft of Sail, Walker (New York, NY), 1972.

Toolchest, Walker (New York, NY), 1973.

Small Garden, Big Surprise, Ginn (Lexington, MA), 1974.

The Bakers: A Simple Book about the Pleasures of Making Bread, Scribner (New York, NY), 1975.

Inside: Seeing beneath the Surface, Walker (New York, NY), 1975.

Luther Tarbox (children's fiction), Scribner (New York, NY), 1977.

Moving On: Stories of Four Travelers, Scribner (New York, NY), 1978.

Symbols: A Silent Language, Walker (New York, NY), 1978.

Wooden Ship, Houghton Mifflin (Boston, MA), 1978.

The Art and Ingenuity of the Woodstove, Everest House (New York, NY), 1978.

Moving Heavy Things, Houghton Mifflin (Boston, MA), 1980.

The Wood Book: An Entertaining, Interesting, and Even Useful Compendium of Facts, Notions, Opinions, and Sentiments about Wood and Its Growing, Cutting, Working, and Burning, Little, Brown (Boston, MA), 1980.

Heavy Equipment, Scribner (New York, NY), 1980.

Letterbox: The Art and History of Letters, Walker (New York, NY), 1981.

A Storm without Rain (young adult novel), Little, Brown (Boston, MA), 1983, reprinted, Beech Tree Books (New York, NY), 1993.

Workboats, Macmillan (New York, NY), 1985.

String: Tying It Up, Tying It Down, Scribner (New York, NY), 1992.

Machines in Our Garden ("Collections for Young Scholars" series), Open Court Publishers (Chicago, IL), 1995.

The Wonder of Light, Newbridge Communications (New York, NY), 1997.

Bridges: From My Side to Yours, Roaring Book Press (Brookfield, CT), 2002.

John Adams, Young Revolutionary, illustrated by Merle Henderson, Aladdin (New York, NY), 2002.

What If You Meet a Pirate?, Roaring Brook Press (Brookfield, CT), 2003.

OTHER

(Illustrator) Laurence Pringle, *Chains, Webs, and Pyramids: The Flow of Energy in Nature,* Crowell (New York, NY), 1975.

Cookie (mystery novel), Harper (New York, NY), 1988.

Deadline for Final Art (adult mystery novel), Walker (New York, NY), 1990.

Solstice: A Mystery of the Season (young adult novel), Walker (New York, NY), 1990.

(Editor and illustrator) *The Ragged Mountain Portable Wilderness Anthology,* Ragged Mountain Press (Camden, ME), 1993.

(Illustrator) Bill Pinkney, *Captain Bill Pinkney's Journey* ("Collections for Young Scholars" series), Open Court Publishers (Chicago, IL), 1995.

(Illustrator) Dean Torges, *Hunting the Osage Bow: A Chronicle of Craft* (originally published in *Traditional Bowhunter* magazine), Gilliland Press (Arkansas City, KS), 1998.

(Author of text) *Dream Spinner: The Art of Roy Andersen,* Settlers West (Tucson, AZ), 2000.

Contributor to periodicals, including *Air and Space, Island Journal, Chesapeake Bay, Harper's, Mother Earth News, Sail, Smithsonian,* and *WoodenBoat.* Contributing editor to magazines, including *Cricket, Smithsonian, Muse,* and *Click.* Contributor of short fiction to anthologies, including *Unusual Suspects.* Author of scripts for television documentaries, including works for the *Nova* series and the Discovery Channel. Adkins's books have been published in Braille editions, as well as in Swedish and Danish.

WORK IN PROGRESS: Villains; Red Rover Comes Over; Kinky Wang's Disappearing Zoo; Gold Rush, a young adult novel; *The Browning of Greenville; Lt. Kijé.*

SIDELIGHTS: An award-winning author and illustrator whose detailed drawings involve and inspire young readers, Jan Adkins has created books on subjects as diverse as sand castles, baking bread, and sailing, each inspired by his curiosity, his own desire to learn about a certain subject, and his enthusiasm for sharing that knowledge with others. In addition to nonfiction titles such as *How a House Happens, The Wonder of Light,* and *Moving Heavy Things,* he has also penned fiction for both teens and adults.

Born in Ohio and raised across the river in Wheeling, West Virginia, Adkins inherited both his creativity and his ability to figure things out from his parents, whom he describes on his *Jan Adkins Studio* Web site as "a sheet-metal contractor who invented clever devices and could fix anything" and "a loopy, beautiful woman with wit and a lyric Welsh soprano." After graduating from high school in Ohio, he studied architecture at Ohio State University, but ultimately changed his major to English literature and creative writing. Meanwhile, Adkins apprenticed as an architectural designer, developing his illustration skills and his ability to present technical objects in clear, easy-to-understand diagrams. In 1980, he was invited to join the staff of *National Geographic,* where he worked as an associate art director, teaming up with authors, illustrators, and researchers to create the illustrated texts for which the magazine is noted. The recipient of numerous design awards from professional organizations and others for his books, magazine work, and exhibitions, Adkins cites his favorite job as writing nonfiction for young people.

Adkins's first book, 1971's *The Art and Industry of Sandcastles: Being an Illustrated Guide to Basic Constructions along with Divers Information,* is a whimsical illustrated guide to building with wet sand. More than that, it also provides readers with an introduction to the history and structure of actual castles as well as to life in medieval times. Illustrated with detailed drawings of historical castles and their sand counterparts, the book was favorably reviewed by critics, several of whom remarked on the author's unusual presentation. *Scientific American* contributors Philip Morrison and Phylis Morrison dubbed the work "a small tour de force" and a "loving study of medieval life and times," while in *School Library Journal,* Ruth M. McConnell called *The Art and Industry of Sandcastles* "an instructive, fun ramble on sandcastle building that is doubtless the definitive work on the subject."

Adkins has brought the same combination of skillful drawing, lucid explanation, and novelty to bear on each of the subjects he has tackled since, claim reviewers, including a discussion of the tools, materials, and terminology involved in each topic. While some reviewers have expressed concern that such technical information might be unappreciated by younger readers, Adkins once commented in an interview with Norma Bagnall published in *Language Arts:* "I don't want children to understand everything; I want them to read the book. . . . If children understand everything the first time around, they'll throw the book away, and they ought to."

In his 1992 title *String: Tying It Up, Tying It Down,* Adkins presents a knot primer that details techniques from the half-hitch to the square knot, with practical uses ranging from boat-docking to necktie-tying. "Using fun illustrations and text," the book "shows how to securely tie everything from shoes to ships," explained W. E. Butterworth IV in his review for *Boy's Life,* while in *Booklist,* Deborah Abbott praised Adkins for creating "a text that reads like a novel—smooth flowing, carefully woven, precise, lively." While noting that the text might be too advanced for younger readers, *Voice of Youth Advocates* contributor Sherry Hoy nonetheless praised *String* as "an esoteric, eclectic blend of lore." Commending the author/illustrator for his "detailed black-and-white pencil drawings," *School Library Journal* contributor Carole B. Kirkpatrick found the book to be "more practical and far-reaching in scope" than its title would imply; "that it's enjoyable just to read through is a pleasant bonus."

Other nonfiction titles by Adkins include *The Art and Ingenuity of the Woodstove, Moving Heavy Things, The Craft of Sail, Letterbox: The Art and History of Letters,* and *Bridges: From My Side to Yours.* Reviewing *Letterbox,* Barbara Elleman commented in *Booklist* that the work contains Adkins's "well-known precision, wit, and attentive style," while in *Kirkus Reviews,* a contributor cited it as one of the author's "earnestly high-toned, craft-looking anomalies" that contains "lots of fine calligraphy" intermixed with such a wealth of extraneous details that the book becomes a kind of "cultural collage." The more focused *Bridges* presents a 10,000-year history of bridge construction from the days of the Roman Empire to the present. Mixing stories about engineering advances and the people who made them, Adkins reveals a "fascination with his subject," according to *Horn Book* reviewer Mary M. Burns, and "his knowledge of history is as dazzling as his understanding of engineering principles." In addition, "fascinating human interest tidbits add historical context," Mary Ann Carcich wrote in her *School Library Journal* review, praising *Bridges* as well-illustrated and a useful volume for "a wide audience."

In addition to writing nonfiction, Adkins has found success as a fiction writer. His first self-illustrated picture book, 1977's *Luther Tarbox,* follows a lobsterman as he pulls in his traps in a dense New England fog, his work hastened by the novice boaters nearby who hope he will lead them back to shore. In her *Horn*

Book review, Charlotte W. Draper praised the humorous tale for its "rich and rhythmic" language, while in *Bulletin of the Center for Children's Books,* Zena Sutherland dubbed *Luther Tarbox* "a brisk and salty tale" that "conveys the appeal of the sea" to young listeners.

The sea also figures in 1990's *Solstice: A Mystery of the Season,* as Charlie and his father travel by motorboat to an island off the Maine coast for Christmas. When their boat engine fails, the two are taken in by a lobsterman and his family who teach them some simple lessons about family, but their hosts ultimately turn out to be ghosts from the distant past. A reviewer for *Publishers Weekly* called the book "slender but hypnotic," and noted that Adkins's "almost mystical novel captures the intensity of the holiday season in both its promise and its pain."

For adult readers, Adkins's *Deadline for Final Art* is a "taut mystery/thriller," according to a *Publishers Weekly* contributor. In the novel, an associate art director for *National Geographic* magazine finds himself in the center of Cold War espionage involving a highly sensitive missile defense system, resulting in what the *Publishers Weekly* reviewer described as "a brisk, savvy thriller, spiced with Washington and magazine-publishing details."

Adkins ventures into sci-fi territory with *A Storm without Rain.* Set in eastern Massachusetts and drawing on its author's knowledge of shipbuilding and sailing, the young adult novel follows the adventures of fifteen-year-old Jack Carter, who begins a short sailing trip in 1981 and ends up in 1904. In his family's shipyard, Jack meets his own grandfather, then a teen himself, and together the two boys try to find a way to help Jack return to his own time. Writing in the *New York Times Book Review,* Jane Langton commended Adkins for including details about turn-of-the-twentieth-century Massachusetts that bring Jack's plight to life for young readers. She also hailed Adkins's "memorable" illustrations, which with the text create "an authentic background." The critic concluded, "The reader puts down the book with admiration for craftsmanship—for that of the boatbuilders . . . and for that of the writer, who honed his fanciful tale so authentically."

BIOGRAPHICAL AND CRITICAL SOURCES:

BOOKS

Children's Literature Review, Volume 7, Gale (Detroit, MI), 1984, pp. 17-28.

Something about the Author Autobiography Series, Volume 19, Gale (Detroit, MI), 1992.

PERIODICALS

American Biology Teacher, July, 1998, Teri Clark, review of *The Wonder of Light,* p. 550.

Appraisal, fall, 1973, p. 5; fall, 1981, review of *Moving Heavy Things* and *Heavy Equipment,* pp. 8-9.

Backpacker, April, 1994, Nancy Humes, review of *The Ragged Mountain Portable Wilderness Anthology,* p. 102.

Booklist, July 15, 1971, review of *The Art and Industry of Sandcastles: Being an Illustrated Guide to Basic Constructions along with Divers Information,* p. 913; October 1, 1973, review of *The Craft of Sail,* p. 168; February 1, 1976, Barbara Elleman, review of *Inside: Seeing beneath the Surface,* p. 763; February 1, 1979, Barbara Elleman, review of *Symbols: A Silent Language,* p. 862; September 1, 1981, Barbara Elleman, review of *Letterbox: The Art and History of Letters,* p. 40; April 15, 1983, Barbara Elleman, review of *A Storm without Rain,* p. 1089; April 15, 1992, Deborah Abbott, review of *String: Tying It Up, Tying It Down,* p. 1524; July, 2002, Gillian Engberg, review of *Bridges: From My Side to Yours,* p. 1838.

Boy's Life, December, 1992, W. E. Butterworth IV, review of *String,* p. 19.

Bulletin of the Center for Children's Books, June, 1971, Zena Sutherland, review of *The Art and Industry of Sandcastles,* p. 149; September, 1972, Zena Sutherland, review of *How a House Happens,* p. 1; January, 1974, Zena Sutherland, review of *The Craft of Sail,* p. 73; April, 1974, Zena Sutherland, review of *Toolchest,* p. 121; April, 1976, Zena Sutherland, review of *Inside,* p. 121; May, 1976, Zena Sutherland, review of *The Bakers: A Simple Book about the Pleasures of Making Bread,* p. 137; February, 1978, Zena Sutherland, review of *Luther Tarbox,* p. 89.

Christian Science Monitor, October 23, 1978, William Jaspersohn, review of *Wooden Ship,* p. B2.

Cricket, May, 1977, p. 54.

Horn Book, February, 1978, Charlotte W. Draper, review of *Luther Tarbox,* p. 42; October, 1978, Karen M. Klockner, review of *Wooden Ship,* pp. 512-513; April, 1979, Kate M. Flanagan, review of *Symbols,* pp. 203-204; February, 1981, Karen Jameyson, review of *Heavy Equipment,* p. 65;

August, 1983, Mary M. Burns, review of *A Storm without Rain,* pp. 448-449; March-April, 1986, p. 215; July-August, 2002, Mary M. Burns, review of *Bridges,* p. 481.

Kirkus Reviews, May 15, 1973, review of *The Craft of Sail,* p. 569; November 15, 1973, p. 1266; November 15, 1975, review of *Inside,* p. 1289; February 1, 1976, review of *The Bakers,* pp. 135-136; February 1, 1979, p. 127; August 1, 1980, review of *Moving Heavy Things,* p. 980; January 1, 1981, review of *Heavy Equipment,* p. 9; September 1, 1981, review of *Letterbox,* pp. 1084-1085.

Kliatt, September, 1993, Jody K. Hanson, review of *A Storm without Rain,* p. 15.

Language Arts, May, 1980, Norma Bagnall, interview with Jan Adkins, pp. 560-566.

Library Journal, August, 1973, p. 2326.

New York Times Book Review, November 4, 1973, Lavinia Russ, "How to Make Almost Everything," p. 62; November 16, 1975, Louise Armstrong, review of *Inside,* p. 46; May 2, 1976, Craig Claiborne, review of *The Bakers,* p. 41; October 30, 1977, Joyce Milton, review of *Luther Tarbox,* p. 34; December 10, 1978, Rex Benedict, "Trains and Boats," review of *Wooden Ship,* pp. 77, 91; September 13, 1981, pp. 49-50; September 18, 1983, Jane Langton, review of *A Storm without Rain,* p. 39.

Publishers Weekly, July 5, 1971, review of *The Art and Industry of Sandcastles,* p. 50; June 24, 1983, review of *A Storm without Rain,* p. 58; February 19, 1988, p. 77; June 22, 1990, review of *Deadline for Final Art,* pp. 46-47; November 30, 1990, review of *Solstice: A Mystery of the Season,* p. 70.

Reading Teacher, May, 1979, review of *Toolchest,* p. 945.

School Library Journal, September, 1971, Ruth M. McConnell, review of *The Art and Industry of Sandcastles,* p. 147; October, 1972, Barbara Gibson, review of *How a House Happens,* pp. 108-109; October, 1973, Don Reaber, review of *The Craft of Sail,* p. 111; March, 1976, review of *The Bakers,* p. 98; October, 1978, Phyllis Ingram, review of *Wooden Ship,* p. 152; January, 1979, Daisy Kouzel, review of *Symbols,* p. 50; August, 1981, Lorraine Douglas, review of *Letterbox,* p. 61; October, 1983, p. 155; April, 1986, p. 81; October, 1990, p. 33; June, 1992, Carole B. Kirkpatrick, review of *String,* p. 127; July, 2002, Mary Ann Carcich, review of *Bridges,* p. 128.

Scientific American, December, 1971, Philip Morrison and Phylis Morrison, review of *The Art and Industry of Sandcastles,* p. 112; December, 1973, p. 134; December, 1980, review of *Moving Heavy Things,* pp. 47-48; December, 1986, p. 32.

Voice of Youth Advocates, August, 1992, Sherry Hoy, review of *String,* p. 180.

Washington Post Book World, February 12, 1984, Michael Dirda, review of *Toolchest,* pp. 10-11.

ONLINE

Jan Adkins Studio, http://www.janadkins.com/ (June 10, 2003).

* * *

ADOFF, Arnold 1935-

PERSONAL: Born July 16, 1935, in New York, NY; son of Aaron Jacob (a pharmacist) and Rebecca (Stein) Adoff; married Virginia Hamilton (a writer), March 19, 1960 (died, February 19, 2002); children: Leigh Hamilton (daughter), Jaime Levi (son). *Education:* City College of New York (now City College of the City University of New York), B.A., 1956; graduate studies at Columbia University, 1956-58; attended New School for Social Research, 1965-67. *Politics:* "Committed to change for full freedom for all Americans." *Religion:* "Freethinking pragmatist." *Hobbies and other interests:* History, music.

ADDRESSES: Home—Yellow Springs, OH. *Office*—Arnold Adoff Agency, P.O. Box 293, Yellow Springs, OH 45387. *E-mail*—arnoldadoff@aol.com.

CAREER: Poet, writer of fiction and nonfiction, and anthologist. Teacher in New York City public schools, 1957-69; Arnold Adoff Agency, Yellow Springs, OH, literary agent, 1977—. Instructor in federal projects at New York University, Connecticut College, and other institutions; visiting professor, Queens College, 1986-87. Lecturer at colleges throughout the United States; consultant in children's literature, poetry, and creative writing. Member of Yellow Springs planning commission. *Military service:* Served with New York National Guard.

AWARDS, HONORS: Children's Books of the Year citation, Child Study Association of America, 1968, for *I Am the Darker Brother,* 1969, for *City in All*

Arnold Adoff

Directions, and 1986, for *Sports Pages;* Best Children's Books, *School Library Journal,* 1971, for *It Is the Poem Singing into Your Eyes,* and 1973, for *Black Is Brown Is Tan;* Notable Children's Trade Book citation, National Council for the Social Studies/Children's Book Council (NCSS/CBC), 1974, and Children's Choice citation, International Reading Association/ Children's Book Council (IRA/CBC), 1985, both for *My Black Me: A Beginning Book of Black Poetry;* Art Books for Children Award for *MA nDA LA,* 1975; Books for the Teen Age citation, New York Public Library, 1980, 1981, and 1982, all for *It Is the Poem Singing into Your Eyes;* Jane Addams Children's Book Award special recognition, 1983, for *All the Colors of the Race;* Parents' Choice Award (picture book), 1988, for *Flamboyan;* National Council of Teachers of English Award in Excellence in Poetry for Children, 1988; American Library Association (ALA) notable book citation, for *Street Music;* ALA Best Book for Young Adults citation, for *Slow Dance Heartbreak Blues;* Blue Ribbon Award, *Bulletin of the Center for Children's Books,* for *Love Letters;* Children's Book of Distinction award, *Riverbank Review,* for *Love Letters.*

WRITINGS:

POETRY; FOR CHILDREN

MA nDA LA, illustrated by Emily Arnold McCully, Harper (New York, NY), 1971.

Black Is Brown Is Tan, illustrated by Emily Arnold McCully, Harper (New York, NY), 1973, reprinted, 2002.

Make a Circle Keep Us In: Poems for a Good Day, illustrated by Ronald Himler, Delacorte (New York, NY), 1975.

Big Sister Tells Me That I'm Black, illustrated by Lorenzo Lynch, Holt (New York, NY), 1976.

Tornado!, illustrated by Ronald Himler, Delacorte (New York, NY), 1977.

Under the Early Morning Trees, illustrated by Ronald Himler, Dutton (New York, NY), 1978.

Where Wild Willie, illustrated by Emily Arnold McCully, Harper (New York, NY), 1978.

Eats, illustrated by Susan Russo, Lothrop (New York, NY), 1979.

I Am the Running Girl, illustrated by Ronald Himler, Harper (New York, NY), 1979.

Friend Dog, illustrated by Troy Howell, Lippincott (Philadelphia, PA), 1980.

OUTside/INside Poems, illustrated by John Steptoe, Lothrop, Lee & Shepard (New York, NY), 1981.

Today We Are Brother and Sister, illustrated by Glo Coalson, Lothrop, Lee & Shepard (New York, NY), 1981.

Birds, illustrated by Troy Howell, Lippincott (Philadelphia, PA), 1982.

All the Colors of the Race, illustrated by John Steptoe, Lothrop, Lee & Shepard (New York, NY), 1982.

The Cabbages Are Chasing the Rabbits, illustrated by Janet Stevens, Harcourt (New York, NY), 1985.

Sports Pages, illustrated by Steven Kuzma, Lippincott (Philadelphia, PA), 1986.

Greens, illustrated by Betsy Lewin, Morrow (New York, NY), 1988.

Flamboyan, illustrated by Karen Barbour, Harcourt (New York, NY), 1988.

Chocolate Dreams, illustrated by Turi MacCombie, Lothrop, Lee & Shepard (New York, NY), 1988.

Hard to Be Six, illustrated by Cheryl Hanna, Lothrop, Lee & Shepard (New York, NY), 1990.

In for Winter, out for Spring, illustrated by Jerry Pinkney, Harcourt (New York, NY), 1991.

The Return of Rex and Ethel, illustrated by Catherine Deeter, Harcourt (New York, NY), 1993.

Street Music: City Poems, illustrated by Karen Barbour, HarperCollins (New York, NY), 1995.

Slow Dance Heart Break Blues, illustrated by William Cotton, Lothrop, Lee & Shepard (New York, NY), 1995.

Touch the Poem, illustrated by Bill Creevy, Scholastic (New York, NY), 1996.

Love Letters, illustrated by Lisa Desimini, Scholastic (New York, NY), 1997.

The Return of Rex and Ethel, illustrated by Catherine Deeter, Harcourt (New York, NY), 2000.

Touch the Poem, illustrated by Lisa Desimini, Blue Sky Press (New York, NY), 2000.

The Basket Counts, illustrated by Michael Weaver, Simon & Schuster (New York, NY), 2000.

Daring Dog and Captain Cat, illustrated by Joe Cepada, Simon & Schuster (New York, NY), 2001.

EDITOR

I Am the Darker Brother: An Anthology of Modern Poems by Negro Americans, illustrated by Benny Andrews, Macmillan (New York, NY), 1968, revised edition, introduction by Rudine Sims Bishop, foreword by Nikki Giovanni, Simon & Schuster (New York, NY), 1997.

Black on Black: Commentaries by Negro Americans, Macmillan (New York, NY), 1968.

City in All Directions: An Anthology of Modern Poems, illustrated by Donald Carrick, Macmillan (New York, NY), 1969.

Black Out Loud: An Anthology of Modern Poems by Black Americans, illustrated by Alvin Hollingsworth, Macmillan (New York, NY), 1970.

Brothers and Sisters: Modern Stories by Black Americans, Macmillan (New York, NY), 1970.

It Is the Poem Singing into Your Eyes: An Anthology of New Young Poets, Harper (New York, NY), 1971.

The Poetry of Black America: An Anthology of the Twentieth Century, introduction by Gwendolyn Brooks, Harper (New York, NY), 1973.

My Black Me: A Beginning Book of Black Poetry, Dutton (New York, NY), 1974.

Celebrations: A New Anthology of Black American Poetry, Follett (New York, NY), 1977.

OTHER

Malcolm X (children's nonfiction), illustrated by John Wilson, Crowell (New York, NY), 1970, illustrated by Rudy Gutierrez, HarperTrophy (New York, NY), 2000.

Contributor of articles and reviews to periodicals.

WORK IN PROGRESS: Jazzicals, a collection of poetry.

SIDELIGHTS: An accomplished poet, biographer, and anthologist as well as a respected educator, Arnold Adoff is recognized as one of the first—and finest—champions of multiculturalism in American juvenile literature. Described by Jeffrey S. Copeland in *Speaking of Poets* as "a writer on a mission," Adoff, whose works most often reflect the African-American experience, is among the first authors to consistently, accurately, and positively portray black subjects and concerns in a manner considered both specific and universal; several of his books, most notably the anthologies *I Am the Darker Brother* and *City in All Directions,* the illustrated biography *Malcolm X,* and the picture book *Black Is Brown Is Tan,* are acknowledged as groundbreaking titles in their respective genres. During a career that has spanned over three decades, noted Copeland, Adoff "has been influencing how young readers view such matters as equality of races, sex-role stereotyping, individual rights, and ageism. . . . [He] has spent his writing career expounding the strength of family, both in terms of the individual family structure and the family of humanity." Writing in *Twentieth-Century Children's Writers,* Marilyn Kaye stated that a "constant factor in Adoff's work is the imaginative expression of faith in people and their spirit. Each work, in its own way, salutes the human condition and its ability to triumph." *New York Times Book Review* contributor Ardis Kimzey called Adoff "one of the best anthologists in the world," and concluded, "With his taste and ear, it stands to reason that he should have turned to writing poetry himself, and done it well."

As a poet, Adoff characteristically utilizes free verse, vivid images, and unusual structures and sounds to express warm, affectionate family portraits; the intimate thoughts and feelings of children; and a variety of moods and tones. His poetry is noted for its invention and innovation as well as for its idiosyncratic use of capitalization and punctuation, elements Adoff believes have a strong effect on the movement and rhythm of a poem. He seeks to visually represent the meaning of the words in his poetry by including variations of line length, type size, and letter arrangement; he uses punctuation and rhyme sparingly and sometimes incorporates black English into his verse. His collections of original poetry consist of books on a particular subject, such as eating, tornadoes, sports, or birds; poems from the viewpoint of a particular character; and combinations of poetry and poetic prose that often focus on the duality of the fantastic and the realistic; he has also included some autobiographical material in his collections. Praised for the depth and range of subjects of his poetry as well as for its sensitivity, insight, musicality, structure, and control, Adoff is perceived as a poet whose skill with language and unexpected variances of meaning and rhythm help make his works especially distinctive. Writing in *Twentieth-Century Young Adult Writers,* Myra Cohn Livingston maintained that Adoff "strives to present a poetry of 'shaped speech' that is colloquial, that is relevant, short, and exciting." She claimed that each of Adoff's books "promises and delivers something new, fresh, and challenging. . . . [Always] he fulfills his own code, the 'need of the poet to help mold a complete reality through control of technique and imagination.'"

As an anthologist, Adoff is acknowledged for creating carefully selected poetry and prose collections that feature African-American writers and focus on themes of survival, transcendence, and hope. Directing these books to young adults, Adoff includes works by such writers as Langston Hughes, Lucille Clifton, Paul Laurence Dunbar, Gwendolyn Brooks, Arna Bontemps, and Nikki Giovanni, as well incorporating entries by talented but lesser-known contributors, many of whose works were unpublished prior to their appearance in Adoff's collections.

Adoff was born in New York City and grew up in a mixed working-class neighborhood in the South Bronx. His father, who operated a pharmacy, immigrated to the United States from a town near the Polish-Russian border. "In our home, as in so many others, the emphasis was on being American with a keen sense of Jewish," Adoff once told *CA.* Members of the Adoff family, especially the women, were deeply concerned with social justice, and lively discussions were common. "There was a tradition of liberal, free-thinking females in the family," he recalled. The Adoff family was well read, and numerous magazines and newspapers could be found around the house, the exception being comics, which Adoff's grandmother strictly forbade as too lowbrow.

Around age ten Adoff attended a neighborhood Zionist school, where he studied the Old Testament, Zionism, and other facets of his Jewish heritage. As a teen he read works by Shakespeare, Balzac, Dos Passos, Steinbeck, and Maupassant; in addition, he was exposed to the writings of Havelock Ellis and the works of psychologists such as Menninger, Steckel, and Horney, as well as a great deal of poetry by Dylan Thomas, e. e. cummings, Rainer Maria Rilke, Marianne Moore, Gwendolyn Brooks, and Robert Hayden. Adoff attended high school with an early goal of becoming a doctor, but instead developed an intense interest in jazz, an area in which his family had an influence. At age sixteen he began writing poetry; he also began sneaking into New York City jazz clubs, becoming familiar with such jazz legends as Dizzy Gillespie, Charlie Parker, and Sarah Vaughan. Jazz demonstrated to Adoff, as he remarked to *CA,* that "what was called 'American culture' most often did not include black or Latino culture."

Adoff enrolled at the Columbia University School of Pharmacy, but withdrew to major in history and literature at New York's City College. He wrote for the college newspaper and literary magazine and was politically active, participating in protests for civil liberties. At college, Adoff was introduced to writers such as James Joyce and Gertrude Stein who were especially gifted with language and wordplay. He was also greatly influenced by jazz artist Charles Mingus, who lectured before the jazz club of which Adoff was president. "Without a doubt, he was the most impressive person I had ever met," Adoff commented to *CA.* "From then on, I went to see him wherever he played, and we got to know each other. In time, he would become my spiritual father." In later years he became Mingus's manager and maintained "running chronicles of the Village club scene."

Adoff attended graduate school at Columbia University; although he finished the required coursework for a Ph.D. in American history, he left before completing his dissertation. While at graduate school, Adoff began teaching seventh-grade social studies at a *yeshiva* in the Brownsville section of Brooklyn. After leaving college he moved to Greenwich Village and began substitute teaching in New York City public schools; he spent the remainder of his time writing and going to jazz clubs in the Village. Through Mingus, Adoff met his future wife, African-American children's writer Virginia Hamilton, in 1958. The couple were married in 1960 and shortly thereafter they moved to Spain and France to work on writing projects. During their stay in Europe, the civil rights movement was intensifying in the United States and they decided to return. "Virginia is black, our children brown—we felt somehow it would be wrong to stay," Adoff once explained. "Besides, it all seemed very exciting and we didn't want to be removed from the action. So we returned to New York, where we threw ourselves into our work and as much political work as we could handle."

In New York Adoff began teaching students in Harlem and on Manhattan's Upper West Side. In addition, he expanded the collection of black literature he had begun in the late 1950s. Adoff began to realize that there was a paucity of written materials appropriate for use in the classroom that reflected black students' lives. In his preface to the anthology *The Poetry of Black America* Adoff describes the exchange that resulted: "As a teacher I had students who wanted life in those dusty classrooms. They wanted pictures of themselves inside themselves. . . . I was the dealer. The pusher of poems and stories. Plays and paintings. Jazz and blues. And my students began to push on me. To deal their sounds and write their poems. And I was made to become serious about myself. To get my head together and attempt to go beyond the classrooms and students and schools. To go beyond the racist textbooks and anthologies that were on the shelves and in the bookstores."

Adoff began to assemble some of the poems he had collected and shared with his students. His first anthology, *I Am the Darker Brother: An Anthology of Modern Poems by Negro Americans,* was published by Macmillan in 1968, launching a number of subsequent anthologies of black poetry and prose. His 1973 anthology, *The Poetry of Black America: An Anthology of the Twentieth Century,* was one of the largest anthologies of black poetry ever published in the United States. Adoff told *CA* that the volume, which contains an introduction by poet Gwendolyn Brooks, "contains 600 poems, although my manuscript consisted of 3.000 poems that richly deserved to be included. The final choices were among the most agonizing selections I have ever had to make."

In an interview with Lee Bennett Hopkins in *More Books by More People,* Adoff commented that his objective in producing black literature anthologies is to portray a truer cultural picture of literary America. "I want . . . to make Black kids strong in their knowledge of themselves and their great literary heritage—give them facts and people and power. I also want these Black books of mine to give knowledge to White kids around the country, so that mutual respect and understanding will come from mutual learning. . . . Children have to understand that the oversimplifications they get in classrooms, along with the token non-White artists represented, are not the true American literature. . . . But for those who want the truth, for themselves and for their students, using an anthology is the first step to discovery. The anthology then leads to individual works of the writers." Regarding his inclusion criteria, Adoff remarked to *Top of the News* that in all of his books, "the material selected must be the finest in literary terms as well as in content/message/racial vision"; he added, "If I can lay Malcolm and Du Bois on top of Sambo and Remus, will they finally die and disappear?"

Adoff faced another formidable selection task with the anthology *It Is the Poem Singing into Your Eyes,* for which the editor solicited work from young poets across the country and received over 6,000 submissions. "The tragedy . . . is that I was allowed to publish only one hundred poems," he recalled. "There were many, many, many poems that were absolutely superb. . . . The title of the volume was suggested by one of my young correspondents. I loved her statement 'a poem truly does sing into your eyes and then on into your mind and soul.'" Among the young poets included in this collection was August Wilson, who would later become a Pulitzer Prize-winning playwright. In addition to his poetry anthologies, Adoff has compiled several collections of fiction and commentary by black writers.

While Adoff focused on his compilations, he also continued to write poetry. Shortly after returning from Europe in 1965, he enrolled in a class at New York's New School for Social Research that was taught by

Filipino-American poet Jose Garcia Villa. Garcia Villa "became my second spiritual father," Adoff told *CA*. "He talked about creating a poetry that was as pure as music. . . . His extremism based on an exhaustive knowledge of the art and craft of poetry set him apart." Adoff decided to create poetry in which "form and physical shape . . . should serve to promote its message." In 1971 he published his first book of poetry for children, *MA nDA LA*. A story poem using only words containing the sound "ah," *MA nDA LA* relates the cycle of African family life in a small village. Writing in *Twentieth-Century Children's Writers*, Marilyn Kaye described Adoff's "sing-song verse" in *MA nDA LA* as "a simple compilation of sounds which evoke a sense of celebration." As Adoff noted to *CA*, "Ideally, each poem should be read three times: for meaning; for rhythm; for technical tricks. My poems demand active participation."

Throughout the 1970s and 1980s Adoff published several volumes of poetry for young people that display his characteristic use of free verse, vivid sensory images, striking word pictures, and lively rhythms while offering sensitive portrayals of family life and interior emotions. *Black Is Brown Is Tan*, which is based on the poet's own family, is one of the first few children's books to depict interracial families; according to Kaye, it "extends the focus beyond color to encompass a family's delight in each other." In *All the Colors of the Race* Adoff explores the emotions of a girl with a black mother and a white father; "contemplative, jubilant, and questioning, the upbeat verses stress the young person's humanity in terms of gifts received from her forebears," wrote Ruth M. Stein in *Language Arts*. Praising the 2002 edition, which features updated illustrations by Emily Arnold McCully, *School Library Journal* contributor Dorothy N. Bowen commended Adoff for painting a "picture of an interracial home in which there is fun, security, and plenty of love."

In *Where Wild Willie*, which Stein called "Adoff's paean to independence" in another review in *Language Arts*, the poet describes a child who temporarily leaves her family to go on her own adventure of learning. The poem recounts the girl's journey and is interspersed with the encouraging words of her parents. Zena Sutherland wrote in the *Bulletin of the Center for Children's Books* that *Where Wild Willie* "describes with lilting fluency Willie's rambles and then the voices from home speak for themselves, an antiphonal arrangement in which the two draw closer until Willie comes home." Adoff's favorite book is *OUTside/INside Poems*, a poem cycle that recreates a day in the life of a small boy and expresses his range of feelings. Adoff called this work "a great vehicle for teaching young readers to write poetry. Also, this is the one that really has the greatest element of reality/fantasy."

Adoff considers *Sports Pages*, a book of poetry for middle graders, to be "a breakthrough [because I] worked in a longer form of a combination of poetic prose and poetry and dealt with some autobiographical material using individual voice in the midst of organized activity." A reviewer in the *Bulletin of the Center for Children's Books* called it "one of his best collections," while a *Kirkus* reviewer suggested that *Sports Pages* might "easily lure the adolescent" who will enjoy Adoff's "sensitivity and acuity."

With *Flamboyan* Adoff again uses poetic prose in a picture-book fantasy about a Puerto Rican girl who longs to fly with the birds circling high above her yard. Called "a magical story of a girl's yearning to be outside her own life" by a reviewer in *Publishers Weekly*, *Flamboyan* will "appeal to all who long to go beyond the ordinary." Illustrated by Karen Barbour, the book contains an unusual typographic device, a red leaf that appears in the text to provide directions for reading aloud. Ruth K. MacDonald in *School Library Journal* called *Flamboyan* a "dazzling combination of both text and illustration."

Adoff's next book, *Chocolate Dreams*, collects original poems on one of many readers' favorite subjects: food. Described by Betsy Hearne in the *Bulletin of the Center for Children's Books* as a "rich confection of wordplay, rhythms, and unexpected twists of rhyme and meaning from a poet in his element," the poems, contended Hearne, reveal Adoff's ability to combine "invention and control, depth and delight."

In 1995 Adoff published *Street Music: City Poems*, a collection of jazzy poems in free verse that celebrates the vibrancy of city life, and *Slow Dance Heart Break Blues*, a collection about the thoughts and experiences of adolescence that is intended for readers in their early teens. *Slow Dance Heart Break Blues*, according to a *Kirkus* reviewer, "is laden with empathy," while Sharon Korbeck concluded in *School Library Journal* that the volume contains "a great deal of depth" and challenged readers to question what poetry is and to reexamine "who and where they are in light of today's fast-moving issues and society." Writing in *Horn Book,* Robert D. Hale stated, "If the word gets out, *Slow Dance Heart Break Blues* will become a best seller. Arnold Adoff knows what teenagers are thinking and feeling, which is evident in this collection of on-target poems."

In *Love Letters,* a volume of poetry illustrated by Lisa Desimini, Adoff presents primary graders with twenty valentines written as anonymous notes. Dulcy Brainard in *Publishers Weekly* claimed that "much of the pleasure" comes from the author's and illustrator's "abilities to evoke not only . . . everyday feelings but the more complicated sense of privacy and mystery they summon." Writing in the *Bulletin of the Center for Children's Books,* Elizabeth Bush suggested, "When it's got to be sweet, but it can't be saccharine, drop one of these on a desktop or into a booktalk and wait for the sparks to fly."

In February of 2002, Adoff's wife, Virginia, passed away, leaving him alone in the home the couple built on the Hamilton family's land in Yellow Springs, Ohio. He continues to write for young people, seeing a link with his concerns for social justice. "I began writing for kids," Adoff once told *CA,* "because I wanted to effect a change in American society. I continue in that spirit. By the time we reach adulthood, we are closed and set in our attitudes. The chances of a poet reaching us are very slim. But I can open a child's imagination, develop his appetite for poetry, and most importantly, show him that poetry is a natural part of everyday life. We all need someone to point out that the emperor is wearing no clothes. That is the poet's job." In an interview with Jeffrey S. Copeland in *Speaking of Poets,* Adoff added another perspective: "I'm still attempting to influence kids one way or another, whether it is the way they view the color of skin or reality and fantasy. I hope always to be considered perhaps controversial, perhaps dangerous, to the status quo. . . . It is a struggle to create something you hope is art. I work long and hard at my craft. I like to feel I have good instincts when it comes to language. All in all, I am very proud of what I've done."

BIOGRAPHICAL AND CRITICAL SOURCES:

BOOKS

Adoff, Arnold, *The Poetry of Black America: An Anthology of the Twentieth Century,* Harper (New York, NY), 1973.

Children's Literature Review, Volume 7, Gale (Detroit, MI), 1984.

Copeland, Jeffrey S., *Speaking of Poets: Interviews with Poets Who Write for Children and Young Adults,* National Council of Teachers of English, 1993.

Hopkins, Lee Bennett, *More Books by More People: Interviews with Sixty-five Authors of Books for Children,* Citation Press, 1974.

St. James Guide to Children's Writers, 5th edition, St. James Press (Detroit, MI), 1999.

Something about the Author Autobiography Series, Volume 15, Gale (Detroit, MI), 1993.

Twentieth Century Young-Adult Writers, St. James Press (Detroit, MI), 1994, pp. 4-5.

PERIODICALS

Booklist, January 1, 1997, Ilene Cooper, review of *Love Letters,* p. 863; February 15, 1997, Hazel Rochman, review of *I Am the Darker Brother: An Anthology of Modern Poems by African Americans,* p. 1013; February 1, 2000, Gillian Engberg, review of *The Basket Counts,* p. 1017; February 15, 2000, Hazel Rochman, review of *Malcolm X,* p. 1103; March 15, 2000, Ilene Cooper, review of *Touch the Poem,* p. 1378; October 1, 2001, Annie Ayres, review of *Daring Dog and Captain Cat,* p. 322; April 15, 2002, Hazel Rochman, review of *Black Is Brown Is Tan,* p. 76.

Bulletin of the Center for Children's Books, March, 1979, p. 109; June, 1986, p. 181; November, 1989, p. 49; March, 1997, p. 239.

Horn Book, November-December, 1995, p. 770.

Kirkus Reviews, May 1, 1986, p. 721; July 1, 1995, p. 942.

Language Arts, September, 1979, pp. 690-691; April, 1983, pp. 483-484.

New York Times Book Review, April 25, 1982, p. 37.

Publishers Weekly, August 26, 1988, p. 88; December 2, 1997; January 10, 2000, review of *The Basket Counts,* p. 68; April 17, 2000, review of *Touch the Poem,* p. 80; May 15, 2000, review of *The Return of Max and Ethel,* p. 118; September 24, 2001, review of *Daring Dog and Captain Cat,* p. 93.

Reading Teacher, May, 1998, review of *Love Letters,* p. 684.

School Library Journal, October, 1988, p. 114; September, 1995, p. 221; March, 1997, Carolyn Angus, review of *Love Letters,* p. 195; May, 1997,

Carrie Scadle, review of *I Am the Darker Brother* p. 141; February, 2000, Nina Linsdsay, review of *The Basket Counts,* p. 128; June, 2000, Margaret Bush, review of *The Return of Max and Ethel,* p. 100; September 2001, Nina Lindsay, review of *Daring Dog and Captain Cat,* p. 182; July, 2002, Dorothy N. Bowen, review of *Black Is Brown Is Tan,* p. 76.

Top of the News, January, 1972, pp. 153-55.*

* * *

ANCONA, George 1929-

George Ancona

PERSONAL: Born Jorge Efrain Ancona, December 4, 1929, in New York, NY; son of Efrain José (an accountant and amateur photographer) and Emma (a seamstress; maiden name, Diaz) Ancona; married Patricia Apatow, March 4, 1951 (divorced, 1966); married Helga Von Sydow (a journalist), June 20, 1968; children: (first marriage) Lisa, Gina, Tom; (second marriage) Isabel, Marina, Pablo. *Ethnicity:* Mexican-American. *Education:* Attended Academia San Carlos, 1949-50, Art Students League, 1950-51, and Cooper Union, 1951-52. *Politics:* Democrat.

ADDRESSES: *Home*—35 Calle Enrique, Santa Fe, NM 87507. *E-mail*—geoancona@cybermesa.com.

CAREER: *Esquire* magazine, New York, NY, art director, 1951-53; *Seventeen* magazine, New York, NY, head of promotion department, 1953-54; Grey Advertising, New York, NY, art director, 1954-57; Daniel & Charles, New York, NY, art director, 1957-61; George Ancona, Inc., New York, NY, photographer and filmmaker, 1961—. Instructor at Rockland Community College, School of Visual Arts, and Parsons School of Design in New York, NY; lecturer on film, design photography, and books.

MEMBER: Authors' Guild.

AWARDS, HONORS: Art Director's Show awards, 1959, 1960, 1967; Cine Golden Eagle Awards, Council on Non-Theatrical Events, 1967, for film "Reflections," and 1972, for film "Cities of the Web;" awards from American Institute of Graphic Arts, 1967, 1968, 1974; Cindy Award, Industry Film Producers Association, 1967; Nonfiction Younger Honor, Science Book Awards, New York Academy of Sciences, 1975, for *Handtalk: An ABC of Finger Spelling and Sign Language,* and 1988, for *Turtle Watch;* Golden Kite Award, Society of Children's Book Writers and Illustrators, 1980, for *Finding Your First Job;* Junior Literary Guild selection, c. 1984, for *Monster Movers;* American Library Association Notable Book, and Notable Children's Trade Book in the Field of Social Studies, National Council for the Social Studies/Children's Book Council (NCSS/CBC), 1986, both for *Sheep Dog;* Best Illustrated Children's Books of the Year citation, *New York Times,* 1987, for *Handtalk Birthday;* Carter G. Woodson Book Award for Outstanding Merit, NCSS, 1987, for *Living in Two Worlds;* Junior Literary Guild selection, for *Turtle Watch;* Notable Children's Trade Book in the Field of Social Studies, NCSS/CBC, c. 1989, for *Spanish Pioneers of the Southwest;* Texas Blue Bonnet Award, c. 1989, for

The American Family Farm; Notable Children's Trade Book in the Field of Social Studies, NCSS/CBC, c. 1990, for *Riverkeeper* and *Mom Can't See Me;* Pick of the Lists citation, American Booksellers Association, 1991, for *The Aquarium Book;* Children's Book of the Year citation, Bank Street College, 1993, for *Pablo Remembers: The Fiesta of the Day of the Dead;* Best 100 Children's Books citation, New York Public Library, 1993, for *Powwow;* John Burroughs List of Nature Books for Young Readers, 1993, for *Earth Keepers,* by Joan Anderson; Parents' Choice Award, 1994, for *The Piñata Maker/El Piñatero;* Children's Book of the Year citation, Bank Street College, 1994, for *Twins on Toes;* Golden Duck Award for excellence in children's science fiction, 1994, for *Richie's Rocket;* Outstanding Science Trade Book for Children citation, National Science Teachers Association/Children's Book Council, 1995, for *The Golden Lion Tamarin Comes Home;* Americas Award for Children's and Young Adult Literature, Consortium of Latin American Studies Programs, 1998, and Pura Belpré Honor Book, Association for Library Service to Children/National Association to Promote Library and Information Services to Latinos and the Spanish Speaking, 2000, both for *Barrio: José's Neighborhood; Washington Post*/Children's Book Guild Nonfiction Award, for body of work, 2002.

WRITINGS:

AND PHOTOGRAPHER

Monsters on Wheels, Dutton (New York, NY), 1974.
And What Do You Do?, Dutton (New York, NY), 1976.
I Feel: A Picture Book of Emotions, Dutton (New York, NY), 1977.
Growing Older, Dutton (New York, NY), 1978.
It's a Baby!, Dutton (New York, NY), 1979.
Dancing Is . . . , Dutton (New York, NY), 1981.
Bananas: From Manolo to Margie, Clarion (New York, NY), 1982.
Teamwork: A Picture Essay about Crews and Teams at Work, Crowell (New York, NY), 1983.
Monster Movers, Dutton (New York, NY), 1983.
Freighters, Crowell (New York, NY), 1985.
Sheep Dog, Lothrop (New York, NY), 1985.
Helping Out, Clarion (New York, NY), 1985.
Turtle Watch, Macmillan (New York, NY), 1987.
Riverkeeper, Macmillan (New York, NY), 1990.
The Aquarium Book, Clarion (New York, NY), 1991.
Man and Mustang, Macmillan (New York, NY), 1992.
My Camera, Crown (New York, NY), 1992.
Pablo Remembers: The Fiesta of the Day of the Dead, Lothrop (New York, NY), 1993.
Powwow, Harcourt (San Diego, CA), 1993.
Ser util, Scholastic (New York, NY), 1993.
The Golden Lion Tamarin Comes Home, Macmillan (New York, NY), 1994.
The Piñata Maker/El Piñatero, Harcourt (San Diego, CA), 1994.
Ricardo's Day/El Dia de Ricardo, Scholastic (New York, NY), 1995.
Fiesta U.S.A., Dutton (New York, NY), 1995.
Stone Cutters, Carvers and the Cathedral, Lothrop (New York, NY), 1995.
Earth Daughter: Alicia of Acoma Pueblo, Simon & Schuster,(New York, NY) 1995.
In City Gardens, Celebrations Press (Glenview, IL), 1996.
Mayeros: A Yucatec Maya Family, Lothrop (New York, NY), 1997.
Let's Dance!, Morrow/Avon (New York, NY), 1998.
Fiesta Fireworks, Lothrop (New York, NY), 1998.
Barrio: José's Neighborhood, Harcourt (San Diego, CA), 1998.
Carnaval, Harcourt (San Diego, CA), 1999.
Charro: The Mexican Cowboy, Harcourt (San Diego, CA), 1999.
Cuban Kids, Marshall Cavendish (Tarrytown, MD), 2000.
Harvest, Marshall Cavendish (Tarrytown, MD), 2001.
Come and Eat, HarperCollins (New York, NY), 2001.
Murals, Walls That Sing, Marshall Cavendish (Tarrytown, MD), 2003.

Turtle Watch was published in Portuguese as *Tartarugas marinhas: Uma Especie em extincao,* Salamandra Consultoria Editorial (Rio de Janeiro, Brazil), 1987; *Pablo Remembers: The Fiesta of the Day of the Dead* was published in Spanish as *Pablo recuerda,* Lothrop (New York, NY), 1993; and *Barrio: José's Neighborhood* was published in Spanish as *Barrio: El Barrio de José,* Harcourt (San Diego, CA), 1998.

"VIVA MEXICO!" SERIES; AND PHOTOGRAPHER

The Fiestas, Marshall Cavendish (Tarrytown, MD), 2002.
The Folk Arts, Marshall Cavendish (Tarrytown, MD), 2002.

The Past, Marshall Cavendish (Tarrytown, MD), 2002.

The People, Marshall Cavendish (Tarrytown, MD), 2002.

The Foods, Marshall Cavendish (Tarrytown, MD), 2002.

"HANDTALK" SERIES; AND PHOTOGRAPHER

(With Remy Charlip and Mary Beth Miller) *Handtalk: An ABC of Finger Spelling and Sign Language,* Parents' Magazine Press (New York, NY), 1974.

(With Remy Charlip and Mary Beth Miller) *Handtalk Birthday: A Number and Story Book in Sign Language,* Four Winds Press (New York, NY), 1987.

(With Mary Beth Miller) *Handtalk Zoo,* Four Winds Press (New York, NY), 1989.

(With Mary Beth Miller) *Handtalk School,* Four Winds Press (New York, NY), 1991.

PHOTOGRAPHER

Barbara Brenner, *A Snake-Lover's Diary,* Scott Young Books, 1970.

Barbara Brenner, *Faces,* Dutton (New York, NY), 1970.

Barbara Brenner, *Bodies,* Dutton (New York, NY), 1973.

Louise Jackson, *Grandpa Had a Windmill, Grandma Had a Churn,* Parents' Magazine Press (New York, NY), 1977.

Jean Holzenthaler, *My Feet Do,* Dutton (New York, NY), 1979.

Louise Jackson, *Over on the River,* Lothrop (New York, NY), 1980.

Sue Alexander, *Finding Your First Job,* Dutton (New York, NY), 1980.

Howard Smith, *Balance It,* Four Winds Press (New York, NY), 1982.

Maxine B. Rosenberg, *My Friend Leslie: The Story of a Handicapped Child,* Lothrop (New York, NY), 1983.

Joan Anderson, *First Thanksgiving Feast,* Clarion (New York, NY), 1984.

Maxine B. Rosenberg, *Being Adopted,* Lothrop (New York, NY), 1984.

Joan Anderson, *Christmas on the Prairie,* Clarion (New York, NY), 1985.

Maxine B. Rosenberg, *Being a Twin, Having a Twin,* Lothrop (New York, NY), 1985.

Joan Anderson, *The Glorious Fourth at Prairietown,* Morrow (New York, NY), 1986.

Maxine B. Rosenberg, *Making a New Home in America,* Lothrop (New York, NY), 1986.

Maxine B. Rosenberg, *Living in Two Worlds,* Lothrop (New York, NY), 1986.

Joan Anderson, *Pioneer Children of Appalachia,* Clarion (New York, NY), 1986.

Floreva G. Cohen, *My Special Friend,* Board of Jewish Education (New York, NY), 1986.

Sam and Beryl Epstein, *Jackpot of the Beagle Brigade,* Macmillan (New York, NY), 1987.

Joan Anderson, *Joshua's Westward Journal,* Morrow (New York, NY), 1987.

Maxine B. Rosenberg, *Artists of Handcrafted Furniture at Work,* Lothrop (New York, NY), 1988.

Maxine B. Rosenberg, *Finding a Way: Living with Exceptional Brothers and Sisters,* afterword by Stephen Greenspan, Lothrop (New York, NY), 1988.

Joan Anderson, *From Map to Museum: Uncovering Mysteries of the Past,* introduction by David Hurst Thomas, Morrow Junior Books (New York, NY), 1988.

Joan Anderson, *A Williamsburg Household,* Clarion (New York, NY), 1988.

Joan Anderson, *The American Family Farm: A Photo Essay,* Harcourt (San Diego, CA), 1989.

Marcia Seligson, *Dolphins at Grassy Key,* Macmillan (New York, NY), 1989.

Joan Anderson, *Spanish Pioneers of the Southwest,* Dutton (New York, NY), 1989.

Shirley Climo, *City! New York,* Macmillan (New York, NY), 1990.

Shirley Climo, *City! San Francisco,* Macmillan (New York, NY), 1990.

Joan Anderson, *Harry's Helicopter,* Morrow (New York, NY), 1990.

Sally Hobart Alexander, *Mom Can't See Me,* Macmillan (New York, NY), 1990.

Joan Anderson, *Pioneer Settlers of New France,* Dutton (New York, NY), 1990.

Maxine B. Rosenberg, *Brothers and Sisters,* Clarion (New York, NY), 1991.

Joan Anderson, *Christopher Columbus: From Vision to Voyage,* Dial (New York, NY), 1991.

Shirley Climo, *City! Washington, D.C.,* Macmillan (New York, NY), 1991.

Christine Loomis, *My New Baby-Sitter,* Morrow (New York, NY), 1991.

Bonnie Larkin Nims, *Just Beyond Reach and Other Riddle Poems,* Scholastic (New York, NY), 1992.

Sally Hobart Alexander, *Mom's Best Friend,* Macmillan (New York, NY), 1992.

Joan Anderson, *Earth Keepers,* Gulliver Green/Harcourt (San Diego, CA), 1993.

Mildred Leinweber Dawson, *Over Here It's Different: Carolina's Story,* Macmillan (New York, NY), 1993.

Joan Anderson, *Richie's Rocket,* Morrow (New York, NY), 1993.

Joan Anderson, *Twins on Toes: A Ballet Debut,* Lodestar (New York, NY), 1993.

Joan Anderson, *Sally's Submarine,* Morrow (New York, NY), 1995.

Joan Anderson, *Cowboys: Roundup on an American Ranch,* Scholastic (New York, NY), 1996.

Barbara Beasely Murphy, *Miquel Lost and Found in the Palace,* Museum of New Mexico Press (Santa Fe, NM), 2002.

Faces was translated into Spanish by Alma Flor Ada as *Caras,* Dutton (New York, NY), 1977.

OTHER

Also author of filmscripts, including "Doctor" and "Dentist," two short films for *Sesame Street;* "Faces" and "The River," for children; "Getting It Together," a documentary film about the Children's Television Workshop and Neighborhood Youth Corps; "Cities of the Web," produced by Macmillan; "Looking for Pictures," "Looking for Color," and "Seeing Rhythm," a series; "Reflections," produced by American Crafts Council; "The Link," produced by Orba Corporation; and "Expansion," produced by Diamond International Corporation.

WORK IN PROGRESS: A dual language series called "Somos Latinos" for Children's Press, which will include *Mi Casa/My House, Mis Amigos/My Friends, Mi Barrio/My Neighborhood, Mis Fiestas/My Holidays, Mis Bailes/My Dances, Mi Escuela/My School,* and *Mi Familia/My Family.*

SIDELIGHTS: George Ancona is renowned for his vivid photo essays that allow children to immerse themselves in new ideas and cultures, to appreciate labor that so often goes unnoticed behind the scenes of daily life, and to accept themselves as well as others. Ancona's numerous photo essays and writings have also celebrated his own Mexican heritage and the Spanish language. Ancona keeps the interests of his readers in mind while he works. As he wrote in *Something about the Author Autobiography Series* (*SAAS*), he attempts to convey "the same feeling I had when my father would show me . . . big ships. It's like seeing something awe-inspiring and you just have to say, 'WOW.'"

Ancona once told *CA* about his childhood: "My parents had come from Yucatan in Mexico, and I was raised a Mexican, learning to speak Spanish first. My father wanted me to grow up in the American way so we never lived in a Latin barrio. Instead I grew up the only Latin in an Italian neighborhood. There I acquired my English, work skills, street wisdom, and a godfather.

"Growing up in Coney Island, my world consisted of the contrast between the fantasies of the amusement rides and the limitless space of the sea. Summers were spent in a bathing suit running with a pack of boys through the streets to the beach, swimming out beyond the third barrel, straining the sands for coins, and sneaking into the amusement parks. From the age of twelve, I worked weekends and summers for a variety of craftsmen. An auto mechanic, a carpenter, and in the amusement parks. I would, also, make money with a friend by collecting junk and scrap paper in an old push cart. When loaded with newspaper it took both of us to raise it on its two big wheels and push it to the junk dealer. This way we always had money for the movies and a hot dog."

Ancona began to express his creativity as an artist while he was still young. "My father's hobby was photography and it was my first introduction to the making of images. . . . It was at home that I began to draw by copying photographs." Later, at Mark Twain Junior High School, Ancona began "to take an active interest in drawing and design. It was the sign-painting teacher who got me interested in lettering and painting the sets for the dramatic performances. When I graduated, I was given the Sign Painting Medal. In Lincoln High School, I had the good fortune of studying design with Mr. Leon Friend, who had organized an extracurricular group called the Art Squad," Ancona recalled. He excelled under the direction of the Art Squad and its alumni, and won a scholarship to the Art Students League in New York City. He also met Rufino Tamayo, a renowned Mexican artist, who invited Ancona to visit him in Mexico.

Ancona accepted Tamayo's invitation, and Tamayo arranged for Ancona to spend six months painting at the Academy of San Carlos in Mexico. There, Ancona met José Clemente Orozco, a famous Mexican muralist, Igor Stravinsky, the composer, Diego Rivera, another great Mexican muralist, and Rivera's wife Frida Kahlo, a painter and artist in her own right. Ancona also journeyed to Merida, in the Yucatan, to meet relatives from both sides of his family. Traveling further into the Yucatan, he spent the night at the Mayan ruins of Chichen Itza.

When his money ran out, Ancona returned to the United States to attend the Art Students League. He stayed for the duration of his scholarship, nine months, and then went to work as an artist's apprentice. Although he tried to attend school at Cooper Union at night, a new job in the promotion department at the *New York Times* left him exhausted. He decided to forgo school and concentrate on work. Around the same time, he also decided to marry his first wife, Patricia Apatow. Ancona went on to work as a staff designer at *Esquire* magazine, as an art director for *Apparel Arts* magazine, and then as art director of the promotion department for *Seventeen* magazine. Ancona recalled in his *SAAS* essay that the job at *Seventeen* "gave me my first taste of advertising. I enjoyed the challenge of blending images with words to create forceful messages."

Ancona moved on again to become an art director for the NBC television and radio networks, to work in fashion photography, and to try his hand at filmmaking. "The film experiences and my early attempts at photography seemed to be leading me into a different career direction. Having started out as someone who loved to draw and paint, I was spending more and more time with film and still cameras." At thirty years old, Ancona felt he had to make a decision about his career: "It was now or never so I took the plunge," he wrote in *SAAS.* He quit his job and began his career as a freelance photographer by taking photographs for *Vogue Children.* In addition, he made a film for *Sesame Street* and filmed the children's series *Big Blue Marble.* As he worked, he traveled to Brazil, Pakistan, Hong Kong, Japan, Iceland, Tunisia, and Switzerland. It was during this time that Ancona and his first wife divorced. Ancona's three children, Lisa, Gina, and Tomas, stayed with him, and he later married Helga Von Sydow. With Von Sydow, Ancona had three more children, Isabel, Marina, and Pablo.

Ancona created his first children's book photographs in 1970. "My introduction to children's books was totally unexpected," Ancona revealed. Barbara Brenner, Ancona's friend and an established writer, asked Ancona if he would be interested in making photographs to illustrate one of her books. "Since I had never done a children's book, I said yes." *Faces, Bodies,* and *A Snake-Lover's Diary* resulted. Later, when the editor of Brenner and Ancona's books suggested that he write the text as well as illustrate a book, Ancona "gulped hard" and said he "would try." Ancona's interest in "watching construction sites and huge machinery" and "several months photographing" led to the creation of his first book, *Monsters on Wheels.* This detailed book describes machines that "push, lift, crush, and haul," from cranes to the Lunar Roving Vehicle that explored the moon. John S. Radosta, writing in the *New York Times Book Review,* characterized the book as "excellent."

Monster Movers features sixteen machines, from a walking dragline to a clamshell bucket loader, that move mountains of coal, grain, and cargo over land, onto ships, and off ships. One of these machines, a crawler-transporter, is pictured moving the Space Shuttle. "Once again Ancona has mixed striking photographs, a lucid text and a fascinating subject with winning results," Connie Tyrrell Burns of *School Library Journal* commented. Like *Monsters on Wheels* and *Monster Movers, Freighters* presents various machines that help people work. Yet in *Freighters* Ancona focuses on the people who control the machines as well as on the machines; with his camera, Ancona follows the qualifications, training, and daily routine of a freighter crew. Many of Ancona's books are entirely devoted to workers and the jobs they perform. Even *Sheep Dog,* which features a very intelligent breed of dogs, is about an important kind of work: guarding and herding sheep.

According to *School Library Journal* reviewer Andy Ward, *And What Do You Do?* presents twenty-one jobs, including carpenter, costume designer, dental assistant, barber, and nurse with "outstanding photographs" and a "lucid writing style." Denise M. Wilms of *Booklist* noted that the photographs feature "men and women of varying racial and ethnic backgrounds" and that there is a "conscious attempt to avoid stereotyping." *Teamwork: A Picture Essay about Crews and Teams at Work* follows the team efforts of mountain climbers, a nursing crew, a sailing crew, a film crew, and other workers. As in *And What Do You Do?,* women and men in *Teamwork* are not cast in stereotypical roles.

Ancona has also made photo essays on specific jobs. *Man and Mustang* shows how feral horses are captured, transported, and tamed by prison inmates for the Bureau of Land Management. *Stone Cutters, Carvers and the Cathedral* illuminates an esoteric and fascinating profession. With black-and-white photographs and text, *Riverkeeper* follows John Cronin, the riverkeeper of the Hudson River in New York who protects the water, plants, and wildlife. Ancona demonstrates that Cronin cannot protect the water from pollution from the seat of his powerboat, named *Riverkeeper;* as a representative of the Hudson River Fishermen's Association, he must deal with corporate polluters and a host of government agencies to ensure its cleanliness. According to Mary M. Burns in *Horn Book,* Ancona provides a "balanced, rational presentation" which "speaks directly to our times in a manner as informative as it is appealing." Betsy Hearne of the *Bulletin of the Center for Children's Books* concluded that *Riverkeeper* "will energize kids" to view its subject "in the light of ecological responsibility."

Looking forward to a satisfying career and an understanding of the world of work is just one aspect of childhood. Ancona has dealt with a variety of other childhood concerns and interests in his work. *Helping Out,* according to a *Publishers Weekly* critic, is based on a "stimulating" idea—children can help out (washing cars, planting seeds, doing chores) to the satisfaction of all. The children featured in Ancona's black-and-white pictures smile and, as the reviewer noted, "show clearly that they like what they're doing."

Children are fascinated with babies, as the nursery school teachers who told Ancona that they needed a book that would discuss babies and explain how they grow must have known. Ancona met this need by staying home to photograph the first twelve months in the life of Pablo, his third child with Helga. Ancona said in a *Junior Literary Guild* article that the text of *It's a Baby!* "grew out of the questions children would ask" about Pablo when they saw him. This book shows Pablo nursing, playing, climbing, and taking his first steps. In *Horn Book,* Kate M. Flanagan described the black-and-white photographs as "exquisite."

Ancona's photographs have also helped children learn to accept themselves and others by bringing life to books featuring physically challenged children and adults. *Mom Can't See Me* and *Mom's Best Friend,* both by Sally Hobart Alexander, show how a blind woman lives a fulfilling life; *Finding a Way: Living with Exceptional Brothers and Sisters,* by Maxine B. Rosenberg, demonstrates how children can help physically-challenged siblings in a caring, positive manner. The "Handtalk" series has been especially popular. In *Handtalk Zoo,* the third book by Ancona and Mary Beth Miller, children visit the zoo and communicate in sign language. Ancona's color photographs clearly show the signs the children make, as well as capturing hands in rapid movement. As Hanna B. Zeiger observed in *Horn Book,* some "photos of signs capture very clearly the essence of the animal" the children are viewing. In the words of *School Library Journal* contributor Susan Nemeth McCarthy, *Handtalk Zoo* introduces children to sign language vocabulary in a "creative and exuberant manner."

Ancona's travels to countries around the world have provided him with alternate settings to explore his favorite topics—machines, working and occupations, and nature. Ancona was inspired to write *Bananas: From Manolo to Margie* while visiting a Honduran village. This book demonstrates how the bananas are cultivated on a Honduran plantation, picked by plantation workers, and sent on a two-week trip to a grocery store in the United States, where Margie and her mother buy some. The mostly black-and-white photos focus on the equipment used in the process of picking and transporting as well as on the people who operate it. They also feature the families of the plantation workers. These photos in *Bananas* are "fair: workers live poorly and work hard," as Terry Lawhead noted in *School Library Journal.* Zena Sutherland of the *Bulletin of the Center for Children's Books* observed that information about the plantation workers is offered, although the text does not really discuss the "personal lives" of Margie and the transportation and marketing workers.

Turtle Watch follows the efforts of oceanographers attempting to replenish the sea turtle population in northeastern Brazil. During nesting season, oceanographers and the people of Praia do Forte alike have important responsibilities. The local people, especially fishermen, must encourage one another to leave the eggs and turtles they find instead of selling them. Oceanographers must observe female turtles laying eggs, recover the eggs for safe hatching, and then, after the baby turtles emerge from their eggs, help them make their way to the ocean. According to Karey Wehner, writing in *School Library Journal,* "Ancona conveys some of the excitement and wonder scientists must feel when observing animals firsthand, in the field." Ancona said in *Junior Literary Guild* that photographing the turtles was difficult. "We would arrive either too early or too late to see them emerge from the sea." Although it took a long time for Ancona to finally get his photos, he remarked that he did not mind much. "Brazil is a wonderful place to be stranded in." Ancona returned to Brazil to research and take photos for a book on the Golden Lion Tamarin monkey.

Pablo Remembers: The Fiesta of the Day of the Dead features a Mexican family as they prepare for and enjoy the festival of the Day of the Dead. As Ancona wrote in *SAAS,* "It is a time for family reunions, meals, and an evening spent in the cemetery among flowers and candles on the decorated tombs of departed relatives." He continued, "In the streets, people parade in costume and recite satiric poems in front of their neighbors' houses." During the festival's three days (All Hallows Eve, All Saints Day, and All Souls Day), which honor the dead in a combination of Aztec and Catholic traditions, altars are decorated, children eat candy skulls, and Pablo takes time to remember his deceased grandmother. According to *Bulletin of the Center for Children's Books* contributor Roger Sutton, the "photography has the intimacy of high-quality family snapshots." Margaret A. Bush concluded in *Horn Book* that the "beautiful book" serves as a fitting "tribute to Mexican home life."

The Piñata Maker/El Piñatero also focuses on life in Mexico, but its text is written in both Spanish and English. Ancona follows Don Ricardo Nunez Gijon, better known as Tio Rico in the village, as he carefully crafts fantastic, delightful piñatas. Ancona's photos demonstrate how Tio Rico makes a paste out of old newspapers and paper bags, and then shapes the paste into the form of a carrot, swan, star, or other figure. The next series of photos demonstrates how Daniela, a young girl, chooses a piñata for her birthday party, and how her guests crack it open and spill the candy. "Ancona has created an authentic, detailed account of one aspect of Mexican culture which has particularly wide appeal to children," wrote Maeve Visser Knoth in *Horn Book.* According to Ann Welton in *School Library Journal,* the "balance between text and illustration is masterful."

One problem Ancona had once he had created *Pablo Remembers* and *The Piñata Maker,* as he wrote in *SAAS,* was saying good-bye to the friends he had made. "The departure is very sad for me because these people have become part of my life and I don't know if I will ever see them again. . . . Someday I would like to take as much time as it would take to visit all the people I have gotten to know through my travels and books."

Ancona did not have to travel far to meet the people he photographed for *Powwow.* With color photographs and a thoughtful introduction, Ancona provides what *School Library Journal* reviewer Lisa Mitten described as an "exquisite kaleidoscope of Native-American music, customs, and crafts." The Crow Fair in Montana provides an opportunity for people from various tribes, including the Crow, Lakota, Cheyenne, Cree, and Ojibwa, to dance Traditional, Fancy, Grass, and Jingle-dress dances competitively. Ancona follows the celebration as it progresses from parade to dance; he focuses his camera on the people watching the dances as well as the dancers themselves. As Bush noted in *Horn Book,* Ancona's camera records "the ironies of traditional cultural practice in the modern setting." Objects like Diet Pepsi, cars, and telephone wires, according to Sutton in another *Bulletin of the Center for Children's Books* article, "[give] the old ways—in new forms—the breath of continuing relevance." Importantly, as Bush concluded, Ancona "conveys the universal appeal of spectacle and celebration" in *Powwow.*

Ancona returned to Mexican-American themes with *Fiesta U.S.A.,* a book dealing with four of the holidays most celebrated by Latinos in North America, showing both "color and passion" in food, dance, and music, according to Elizabeth S. Watson in the *Horn Book Guide.* Featured holidays include El Dia de los Muertos, or Day of the Dead, Los Matachines, celebrated on New Year's Day, La Fiesta de los Reyes Magos, or Three Kings' Day, and Los Posadas, a reenactment of Mary and Joseph's hunt for accommodations in Bethlehem. Ancona takes readers to a New Mexican pueblo in *Earth Daughter: Alicia of Acoma Pueblo,* an "attractive photo-essay," according to *Booklist*'s Stephanie Zvirin. Young Alicia, who is learning to throw pottery, introduces readers to the simple life of her small town that dates to the Spanish conquest. Traveling farther south to the Yucatan Peninsula and his own heritage, Ancona features Mayan culture in

Mayeros: A Yucatec Maya Family, with color photographs of not only people of the region, but also of their ancient artwork and temples. "Ancona ably interweaves the history of . . . the ancient Mayeros with the daily life of their descendants," claimed Karen Morgan in *Booklist.* Frances E. Millhouser, writing in *School Library Journal,* praised Ancona's "involving text" as well as the manner in which he "seamlessly interspersed" more factual information into the narrative of the present day family. Millhouser concluded, "Ancona provides a unique perspective on the vibrant survival of an enduring way of life."

More Hispanic themes are served up in *Fiesta Fireworks,* in which Ancona follows Caren and her family of fireworks makers in Tultepec, a town near Mexico City, as they create the fireworks display for the annual festival of San Juan de Dios, a local patron saint. *Booklist*'s Carolyn Phelan found that the book "captures the excitement of a fiesta," while *School Library Journal*'s Selene S. Vasquez called it "an informative tribute to an enduring Mexican tradition." Ancona deals with a year in the life of a Mexican-American youth in San Francisco's Mission District in *Barrio: José's Neighborhood.* José strolls through this barrio and enjoys sights from a soccer game to a colorful mural as well as the traditional celebrations that mark the year. Annie Ayres, writing in *Booklist,* called the book "a fond and fascinating photo-essay focusing on the richness of the Latino experience." Similarly, Dina Sherman of *School Library Journal* observed that the "title successfully captures images of a particular place as seen through the eyes of a child." *Charro: The Mexican Cowboy* is set in Guadalajara, Mexico, on the day of a local rodeo, or charreada. Ancona focuses on the riding and roping skills of the cowboys who take part in the event, and his color photographs also highlight the scene, complete with mariachi bands and the fancy dress of both men and women. Helen Rosenberg of *Booklist* felt that Ancona's book is "beautiful and informative," and that it "will satisfy any reader interested in the ways of today's cowboys." A reviewer for *Publishers Weekly* praised Ancona's "energetic" photographs, while Ruth Semrau, writing in *School Library Journal,* similarly noted that "Ancona's pictures just keep getting better and better." Reviewing the book in the *Bulletin of the Center for Children's Books,* Deborah Stevenson concluded that "young buckaroos who enjoy a rodeo will be intrigued by this southern alternative."

Ancona also deals with themes from festivals to Caribbean children to Mexican field workers in *Carnaval, Cuban Kids,* and *Harvest.* In *Carnaval,* he documents these celebrations in the Brazilian town of Olinda in an "appealing picture-book format" with "accessible, lively text," according to *Booklist*'s Chris Sherman. Similarly, a contributor for *Hungry Mind Review* noted that "full-page photographs bring all the wonder and energy of carnival to life." Paul Kelsey, writing in *School Library Journal,* concluded that *Carnaval* is "an excellent introduction in an inviting and visually pleasing format." Ancona illustrates life in Cuba through his photos of students in *Cuban Kids,* "a very fine portrait of modern Cuba," according to *Booklist*'s Denia Hester, who also praised the "well-written text." Marilyn Long Graham of *School Library Journal* felt the book was "upbeat and positive." With *Harvest,* "Ancona puts a face on Mexican migrant workers," explained Ilene Cooper in a *Booklist* review. With photos and text, he shows the hard work these people do, picking produce on various West Coast farms. At the same time, the author/illustrator also introduces young readers to a wide variety of crops and to the work of labor organizer Cesar Chavez.

Ancona subsequently travels from the farm to the world of art in *Murals, Walls That Sing.* He focuses on wall paintings from prehistoric times in France to Mexican church murals to modern graffiti in Harlem. He not only deals with the use of materials in the execution of these very public works of art, but through a combination of close-up and wide-angle shots, lets readers see the work in relation to the architecture they adorn. Once again, Ancona's work elicited praise from reviewers. Susannah Price, writing in *School Library Journal,* called the title an "eye-catching book [that] just might whet the appetite of budding artists." *Booklist*'s Gillian Engberg also felt that "the beautiful, sharp color photos and the unusual subject will attract plenty of browsers." And a contributor for *Kirkus Reviews* concluded, "A unique chronicle of our country's diversity and an engaging look at the connection between the arts and activism."

Ancona has also celebrated Mexico in the five-volume set, "Viva Mexico!," whose titles include *The Fiestas, The Folk Arts, The Foods, The Past,* and *The People.* Blending clear color photos with his typical incisive text, Ancona views these various aspects of contemporary Mexican life in works that provide a "visual feast," as *Booklist*'s Annie Ayres commented about the series. Reviewing *The Past, The Foods,* and *The People* in *School Library Journal,* Coop Renner called the books "breezy and upbeat," while Mary Elam, writing in the same journal, found "The Fiestas" and *The Folk Arts* "beautifully illustrated volumes," and ones that "contain a wealth of information."

Aspiring photographers who admire Ancona's work may enjoy *My Camera,* which demonstrates how to use a 35mm camera like the one Ancona uses. He describes how to compose pictures, how to use the flash, and how to put together albums, photo essays, and storyboards. Ancona also includes a diagrammatic and textual explanation of how a camera works. "Evidence of Ancona's photographic talent and teaching ability radiates from every page," remarked Nancy E. Curran in *School Library Journal.*

A thorough understanding of the technical issues involved in photography is just one aspect of any photographer's success. Ancona once revealed the character trait that has stimulated his achievements for *CA* readers: "Curiosity is the biggest element in my work. . . . I think people are fascinating and I love to find myself in strange places, meeting people, getting to know them, and learning about them. This helps me to learn about myself. Photographing, filming, or writing about someone or someplace is my way of feeling alive and in touch with the world around me. I believe that work does this for many people. Whether it is baking bread, building a house, driving a truck, or singing a song, people reach each other each in their own way. I think that's what living is all about." And in an interview with Rosalinda B. Barrera for *Language Arts,* Ancona elaborated on his career in creating children's books: "If I weren't doing books, I'd probably be in school teaching. I like kids, and I love watching them develop and explore. They are a wonderful community to photograph." He further explained: "So, doing children's books keeps me in touch and I can still apply my craft, my love for imagery, and share it with others."

BIOGRAPHICAL AND CRITICAL SOURCES:

BOOKS

Ancona, George, *Monsters on Wheels,* Dutton (New York, NY), 1974.

St. James Guide to Children's Writers, 5th edition, St. James Press (Detroit, MI), 1999.

Something about the Author Autobiography Series, Volume 18, Gale (Detroit, MI), 1994, pp. 1-18.

PERIODICALS

Booklist, July 1, 1976, Denise M. Wilms, review of *And What Do You Do?,* p. 1525; April 15, 1982, p. 1091; October 1, 1995, Annie Ayres, review of *Fiesta U.S.A.,* pp. 305-306; October 15, 1995, Stephanie Zvirin, review of *Earth Daughter: Alicia of Acoma Pueblo,* p. 397; April 15, 1997, Karen Morgan, review of *Mayeros: A Yucatec Maya Family,* p. 1420; April, 1998, Carolyn Phelan, review of *Fiesta Fireworks,* p. 1323; September 1, 1998, Ellen Mandel, review of *Let's Dance!,* p. 121; December 1, 1998, Annie Ayres, review of *Barrio: José's Neighborhood,* p. 662; May 15, 1999, Helen Rosenberg, review of *Charro: The Mexican Cowboy,* p. 1689; November 15, 1999, Chris Sherman, review of *Carnaval,* p. 617; December 15, 2000, Denia Hester, review of *Cuban Kids,* p. 811; January 1, 2002, Ilene Cooper, review of *Harvest,* pp. 846-847; March 1, 2002, review of "Viva Mexico!" series, pp. 1121-1132; October 1, 2002, Stephanie Zvirin, *Awards and Prizes,* p. 317; April 15, 2003, Gillian Engberg, review of *Murals, Walls That Sing,* p. 1467.

Bulletin of the Center for Children's Books, January, 1983, Zena Sutherland, review of *Bananas,* p. 81; November, 1989, p. 49; July-August, 1990, Betsy Hearne, review of *Riverkeeper,* p. 259; May, 1993, Roger Sutton, review of *Powwow,* p. 276; December, 1993, Roger Sutton, review of *Pablo Remembers: The Fiesta of the Day of the Dead,* p. 114; May, 1999, Deborah Stevenson, review of *Charro,* pp. 306-307.

Horn Book, February, 1980, Kate M. Flanagan, review of *It's a Baby!,* p. 7; November-December, 1989, Hanna B. Zeiger, review of *Handtalk Zoo,* p. 775; May-June, 1990, Mary M. Burns, review of *Riverkeeper,* p. 345; May-June, 1993, Margaret A. Bush, review of *Powwow,* p. 343; March-April, 1994, Margaret A. Bush, review of *Pablo Remembers,* pp. 213-214; July-August, 1994, Maeve Visser Knoth, review of *The Piñata Maker/El Piñatero,* p. 469; November-December, 1995, Elizabeth S. Watson, review of *Fiesta U.S.A.,* pp. 728-729; May-June, 1998, Margaret A. Bush, review of *Fiesta Fireworks,* pp. 353-354.

Horn Book Guide, spring, 1992, p. 100; fall, 1996, Elizabeth S. Watson, review of *Fiesta U.S.A.,* p. 318.

Hungry Mind Review, fall, 1999, review of *Carnaval,* p. 34.

Junior Literary Guild, September, 1979; October, 1987-March, 1988, review of *Turtle Watch,* p. 25.

Kirkus Reviews, May 1, 1976, p. 537; March 15, 2003, review of *Murals, Walls That Sing,* p. 458.

Language Arts, October, 1997, Rosalinda B. Barrera, "Profile—George Ancona: Photographer and Writer," pp. 477-481.

New York Times Book Review, January 19, 1975, John S. Radosta, review of *Monsters on Wheels,* p. 8.

Publishers Weekly, July 19, 1985, review of *Helping Out,* p. 53; June 7, 1999, review of *Charro,* p. 85; December 20, 1999, review of *Carnaval,* p. 82.

School Library Journal, September, 1976, Andy Ward, review of *And What Do You Do?,* p. 109; November, 1977, p. 43; January, 1983, Terry Lawhead, review of *Bananas,* pp. 69-70; February, 1984, Connie Tyrrell Burns, review of *Monster Movers,* p. 65; October, 1987, Karey Wehner, review of *Turtle Watch,* p. 131; April, 1992, p. 128; October, 1989, Susan Nemeth McCarthy, review of *Handtalk Zoo,* pp. 99-100; February, 1993, Nancy E. Curran, review of *My Camera,* p. 95; April, 1993, Lisa Mitten, review of *Powwow,* pp. 125-126; April, 1994, Ann Welton, review of *The Piñata Maker/El Piñatero,* p. 116; November, 1995, Rose Zertuche Trevino, review of *Fiesta U.S.A.,* p. 136; December, 1995, Darcy Schild, review of *Earth Daughter,* p. 94; June, 1997, Frances E. Millhouser, review of *Mayeros: A Yucatec Maya Family,* p. 105; March, 1998, Selene S. Vasquez, review of *Fiesta Fireworks,* p. 191; November, 1998, Kit Vaughan, review of *Let's Dance!,* p. 101; December, 1998, Dina Sherman, review of *Barrio: José's Neighborhood,* p. 99; June, 1999, Ruth Semrau, review of *Charro,* p. 110; February, 2000, Paul Kelsey, review of *Carnaval,* p. 107; January, 2001, Marilyn Long Graham, review of *Cuban Kids,* p. 112; February, 2002, Mary Elam, review of *The Folk Arts* and *The Fiestas,* pp. 138-139; March, 2002, Coop Renner, review of *The Foods, The Past,* and *The People.* pp. 240-241; April, 2002, Louise L. Sherman, review of *Harvest,* p. 162; May, 2003, Susannah Price, review of *Murals, Walls That Sing,* p. 161.

ONLINE

Scholastic Author Studies Homepage, http://www2.scholastic.com/ (May 22, 2003), "George Ancona's Interview Transcript."*

ARNOSKY, James Edward 1946-
(Jim Arnosky)

PERSONAL: Born September 1, 1946, in New York, NY; son of Edward J. (a draftsman) and Marie (Telesco) Arnosky; married Deanna L. Eshleman, August 6, 1966; children: Michelle L., Amber L. *Hobbies and other interests:* Leisurely walking, growing food, fishing, fly-tying, watching wildlife.

ADDRESSES: *Home*—South Ryegate, VT 05069. *Agent*—c/o Author Mail, Putnam's Publicity, 345 Hudson St., New York, NY 10014.

CAREER: Draftsman in Philadelphia, PA, 1964; Braceland Brothers (printers), Philadelphia, PA, art trainee, 1965-66, creative artist, 1968-72; freelance illustrator and writer, 1972—. *Military service:* U.S. Navy, 1966-72.

AWARDS, HONORS: Outstanding Science Book Award, American Association of Science Teachers, 1978, for *Possum Baby;* Christopher Award, 1984, for *Drawing from Nature;* Nonfiction Award, *Washington Post*/Children's Book Guild, 1988; Orbis Pictus Award Honor Book, National Council of Teachers of English, 2001, for *Wild and Swampy: Exploring with Jim Arnosky.*

WRITINGS:

UNDER NAME JIM ARNOSKY; SELF-ILLUSTRATED CHILDREN'S BOOKS

I Was Born in a Tree and Raised by Bees, Putnam (New York, NY), 1977.

Outdoors on Foot, Coward (New York, NY), 1977.

Nathaniel, Addison-Wesley (New York, NY), 1978.

Crinkleroot's Book of Animal Tracks and Wildlife Signs, Putnam (New York, NY), 1979, revised edition published as *Crinkleroot's Book of Animal Tracking,* Bradbury Press, 1989.

A Kettle of Hawks, Coward (New York, NY), 1979.

Mudtime and More Nathaniel Stories, Addison-Wesley (New York, NY), 1979.

Drawing from Nature, Lothrop (New York, NY), 1982.

Freshwater Fish and Fishing, Four Winds (New York, NY), 1982.

James Edward Arnosky

Mouse Numbers and Letters, Harcourt, 1982.
Secrets of a Wildlife Watcher, Lothrop (New York, NY), 1983.
Mouse Writing, Harcourt, 1983.
Drawing Life in Motion, Lothrop (New York, NY), 1984.
Watching Foxes, Lothrop (New York, NY), 1984.
Deer at the Brook, Lothrop (New York, NY), 1986.
Flies in the Water, Fish in the Air: A Personal Introduction to Fly Fishing, Lothrop (New York, NY), 1986.
Raccoons and Ripe Corn, Lothrop (New York, NY), 1987.
Sketching Outdoors in Spring, Lothrop (New York, NY), 1987.
Sketching Outdoors in Summer, Lothrop (New York, NY), 1988.
Sketching Outdoors in Autumn, Lothrop (New York, NY), 1988.
Sketching Outdoors in Winter, Lothrop (New York, NY), 1988.
Gray Boy, Lothrop (New York, NY), 1988.
Come Out, Muskrats, Lothrop (New York, NY), 1989.
In the Forest, edited by Dorothy Briley, Lothrop (New York, NY), 1989.
Crinkleroot's Guide to Walking in Wild Places, Bradbury Press, 1990.
Fish in a Flash!: A Personal Guide to Spin-Fishing, Macmillan (New York, NY), 1991.
Otters under Water, Putnam (New York, NY), 1992.
Long Spikes: A Story, Clarion Books (New York, NY), 1992.
Crinkleroot's Guide to Knowing the Trees, Macmillan (New York, NY), 1992.
Crinkleroot's Guide to Knowing the Birds, Macmillan (New York, NY), 1992.
Sketching Outdoors in All Seasons, Countryman Press, 1993.
Crinkleroot's Twenty-five Fish Every Child Should Know, Macmillan (New York, NY), 1993.
Crinkleroot's Twenty-five Birds Every Child Should Know, Macmillan (New York, NY), 1993.
Every Autumn Comes the Bear, Putnam (New York, NY),1993.
All Night near the Water, Putnam (New York, NY), 1994.
Crinkleroot's Twenty-five Mammals Every Child Should Know, Macmillan (New York, NY), 1994.
Crinkleroot's Twenty-five More Animals Every Child Should Know, Macmillan (New York, NY), 1994.
All about Alligators, Scholastic (New York, NY), 1994.
All about Owls, Scholastic (New York, NY), 1995.
I See Animals Hiding, Scholastic (New York, NY), 1995.
Little Champ, Putnam (New York, NY), 1995.
Crinkleroot's Guide to Knowing Butterflies and Moths, Simon & Schuster (New York, NY), 1996.
Nearer Nature, Lothrop (New York, NY), 1996.
All about Deer, Scholastic (New York, NY), 1996.
Rabbits and Raindrops, Putnam (New York, NY), 1997.
Bug Hunter, Random House (New York, NY), 1997.
Animal Tracker, Random House (New York, NY), 1997.
Bird Watcher, Random House (New York, NY), 1997.
Bring 'Em Back Alive!: Capturing Wildlife on Home Video: A Guide for the Whole Family, Little, Brown (Boston, MA), 1997.
Shore Walker, Random House (New York, NY), 1997.
Crinkleroot's Guide to Knowing Animal Habitats, Simon & Schuster (New York, NY), 1997.
Watching Water Birds, National Geographic Society (Washington, DC), 1997.
All about Rattlesnakes, Scholastic (New York, NY), 1997.
Little Lions, Putnam (New York, NY), 1998.

Watching Desert Wildlife, National Geographic Society (Washington, DC), 1998.

Crinkleroot's Visit to Crinkle Cove, Simon & Schuster (New York, NY), 1998.

All about Turkeys, Scholastic (New York, NY), 1998.

Mouse Letters: A Very First Alphabet Book, Clarion Books (New York, NY), 1999.

Mouse Numbers: A Very First Counting Book, Clarion Books (New York, NY), 1999.

Big Jim and the White-Legged Moose, Morrow (New York, NY), 1999.

Crinkleroot's Nature Almanac, Simon & Schuster (New York, NY), 1999.

Arnosky's Ark, National Geographic Society (Washington, DC), 1999.

All about Turtles, Scholastic (New York, NY), 2000.

Rattlesnake Dance, Putnam (New York, NY), 2000.

A Manatee Morning, Simon & Schuster (New York, NY), 2000.

Beaver Pond, Moose Pond, National Geographic Society (Washington, DC), 2000.

Wild and Swampy, Morrow (New York, NY), 2000.

Wolves, National Geographic Society (Washington, DC), 2001.

Mouse Colors: A Very First Book, Clarion Books (New York, NY), 2001.

Mouse Shapes: A Very First Book, Clarion Books (New York, NY), 2001.

Raccoon on His Own, Putnam (New York, NY), 2001.

All about Frogs, Scholastic (New York, NY), 2002.

Turtle in the Sea, Putnam (New York, NY), 2002.

Field Trips: Birdwatching, Animal Tracking, Bug Hunting, and Shore Walking with Jim Arnosky, HarperCollins (New York, NY), 2002.

Wild Ponies, National Geographic Society (Washington, DC), 2002.

Armadillo's Orange, Putnam (New York, NY), 2003.

All about Sharks, Scholastic (New York, NY), 2003.

Following the Coast, HarperCollins (New York, NY), 2004.

Beachcombing, Dutton (New York, NY), 2004.

All about Lizards, Scholastic (New York, NY), 2004.

Coyote Raid in Cactus Canyon, Putnam (New York, NY), in press.

UNDER NAME JIM ARNOSKY; ILLUSTRATOR

Melvin Berger and Gilda Berger, *Fitting In: Animals in Their Habitats,* Coward (New York, NY), 1976.

Miska Miles, *Swim, Little Duck,* Atlantic Monthly Press (Boston, MA), 1976.

Miska Miles, *Chicken Forgets,* Atlantic Monthly Press (Boston, MA), 1976.

Miska Miles, *Small Rabbit,* Atlantic Monthly Press (Boston, MA), 1977.

Marcel Sislowitz, *Look: How Your Eyes See,* Coward (New York, NY), 1977.

Berniece Freschet, *Porcupine Baby,* Putnam (New York, NY), 1978.

Berniece Freschet, *Possum Baby,* Putnam (New York, NY), 1978.

Berniece Freschet, *Moose Baby,* Putnam (New York, NY), 1979.

Eloise Jarvis McGraw, *Joel and the Magic Merlini,* Knopf (New York, NY), 1979.

(With Lydia Dabcovich and Charles Mikolaycak) Richard Kennedy, *Delta Baby and Two Sea Songs,* Addison-Wesley (New York, NY), 1979.

Kaye Starbird, *The Covered Bridge House and Other Poems,* Four Winds (New York, NY), 1979.

Ann E. Weiss, *What's That You Said?: How Words Change,* Harcourt (New York, NY), 1980.

Michael New, *The Year of the Apple,* Addison-Wesley (New York, NY), 1980.

Betty Boegehold, *Bear Underground,* Doubleday (New York, NY), 1980.

Margaret Bartlett and Preston Bassett, *Raindrop Stories,* Four Winds (New York, NY), 1980.

Anne Rockwell, *Up a Tall Tree,* Doubleday (New York, NY), 1981.

A. R. Swinnerton, *Rocky the Cat,* Addison-Wesley (New York, NY), 1981.

Joan Hiatt Harlow, *Shadow Bear,* Doubleday (New York, NY), 1981.

Berniece Freschet, *Black Bear Baby,* Putnam (New York, NY), 1981.

Betty Boegehold, *Chipper's Choices,* Coward (New York, NY), 1981.

Honore de Balzac, *A Passion in the Desert,* Creative Education, 1983.

Berniece Freschet, *Wood Duck Baby,* Putnam (New York, NY), 1983.

Berniece Freschet, *Raccoon Baby,* Putnam (New York, NY), 1984.

Dale H. Fife, *The Empty Lot,* Little, Brown (Boston, MA), 1991.

ADAPTATIONS: The "Crinkleroot" books were adapted for television as the *Backyard Safari* series, Public Broadcasting System (PBS).

SIDELIGHTS: James Edward Arnosky's children's books about animals and the natural world have elicited praise for their competent integration of enlightening factual detail and attractive drawings. His character Crinkleroot, a woodsy outdoorsman whose stories teach children about wild animals, has been featured in a number of bestselling books as well as in a television series.

The "Crinkleroot" books feature an outdoorsman wearing a pith helmet whose walks through the wild include tips on what to look out for, information about the habits of animals, birds, and insects, and what Linda Perkins in *Booklist* called a "characteristic enthusiasm." In the books in this series, children learn such things as what the tracks of various animals look like, the meanings of words like "habitat" and "pollinate," and the natural changes the forest undergoes with the change of seasons. Projects, songs, and games are also included.

Other books by Arnosky range from general nature guides to looks at specific animals. The nature guide *Field Trips: Bug Hunting, Animal Tracking, Birdwatching, Shore Walking,* for example, gives young naturalists helpful suggestions as to what to look for on a nature walk, what to collect, and how to keep proper notes. Danielle J. Ford, writing in *Horn Book,* noted: "A walk through the woods or along the shore takes on new meaning with the advice provided for novice naturalists in this first-rate guide." Among Arnosky's books on specific animals is *Turtle in the Sea,* in which he focuses on the life of the female sea turtle. A *Kirkus* reviewer found that "Arnosky's gentle combination of lesson and beautiful artwork will serve to capture the nature-lover in every child."

Critics have expressed appreciation for Arnosky's ability to combine well-presented facts with clear and imaginative illustrations. "*Secrets of a Wildlife Watcher* . . . is more than just a collection of useful hints and attractive illustrations," wrote Francja C. Bryant in a review of this 1983 book for *Christian Science Monitor.* "It is an ardent attempt to nourish a child's interest in the world around him." Norma Bagnell, in *Appraisal,* similarly acclaimed Arnosky's *Freshwater Fish and Fishing,* calling it "an information book for young children that not only presents facts accurately but also uses our language with skill and appreciation." The critic also praised Arnosky's black-and-white illustrations, which "are integrated skillfully into the text so that instructions are easy to follow and techniques are made clear." A critic for *Kirkus Reviews* concluded that Arnosky "really is unmatched in his approach to sharing nature with young children."

With many self-illustrated books to his credit, Arnosky has established himself as a consistent producer of quality children's literature. Becoming an author/illustrator of children's books, however, was not necessarily by design. As Arnosky once told *CA:* "I had no formal art training but learned a great deal about drawing from my dad who is a skillful patent draftsman. With this training at home I began working in the art field as a trainee. . . . It wasn't until I had been on my own, freelancing in illustration for nearly five years, that I was introduced to the writing end of books. . . . Like solid, well-written poetry, writing for children emphasizes structure and the need for every word to count."

The discretion he considers necessary for children's writing seems rooted in the way Arnosky gathers his subject matter—with the keen observational eye of a naturalist. Reviewing *Secrets of a Wildlife Watcher* for *Appraisal,* Douglas B. Sands wrote, "When we have a skilled artist imbued with a naturalist's discerning eye, the result is a rare book—enjoyable from cover to cover by any lover of the out-of-doors. Jim Arnosky's notes on nature are accurate, lacking the flaws so common in many so-called nature books. Here is a writer who obviously knows and understands his natural surroundings." Arnosky's knowledge of nature, however, is not merely the product of detached research. He told *CA:* "I have always had a deep connection with the natural world and find its rhythm close to my own. I think of myself as an artist/naturalist. Most of my close friends are working naturalists, teachers, writers, photographers, farmers, and woodsmen. For four and a half years my wife, my two daughters, and I lived in a tiny cabin at the base of Hawk Mountain in Pennsylvania. There I matured as a writer and illustrator of natural subjects. . . . We have made our home in the hills of northern Vermont because its natural pace of life fits our needs best as a family and mine as a writer and illustrator."

BIOGRAPHICAL AND CRITICAL SOURCES:

BOOKS

Children's Literature Review, Volume 15, Gale (Detroit, MI), 1988.

PERIODICALS

Appraisal, fall, 1982; winter, 1984.

Booklist, December 1, 1998, review of *Little Lions,* p. 676; August, 1999, Susan Dove Lempke, review of *Big Jim and the White-Legged Moose,* p. 2062; September 1, 1999, Linda Perkins, review of *Crinkleroot's Nature Almanac,* p. 135; November 1, 1999, Susan Dove Lempke, "Crinkleroot's Nature Guides," p. 534; November 15, 1999, Shelle Rosenfeld, review of *Arnosky's Ark,* p. 630; February 1, 2000, Kay Weisman, review of *All about Turtles,* p. 1024; October 15, 2000, Carolyn Phelan, review of *A Manatee Morning,* p. 444; November 1, 2000, Denia Hester, review of *Wild and Swampy,* p. 528; January 1, 2001, Stephanie Zvirin, review of *Beaver Pond, Moose Pond,* p. 966; February 1, 2002, Carolyn Phelan, review of *All about Frogs,* p. 942; September 1, 2002, John Peters, review of *Turtle in the Sea,* p. 136; July, 2003, Carolyn Phelan, review of *All about Sharks,* p. 1893; August, 2003, Dianne Foot, review of *Armadillo's Orange,* p. 1986.

Childhood Education, winter, 2002, Amy Easter, review of *All about Frogs,* p. 108.

Christian Science Monitor, April 6, 1984.

Horn Book, November, 1998, Margaret A. Bush, review of *Watching Desert Wildlife,* p. 751; March-April, 2002, Betty Carter, review of *All about Frogs,* p. 226; July-August, 2002, Danielle J. Ford, review of *Field Trips: Bug Hunting, Animal Tracking, Bird-watching, Shore Walking,* p. 482.

Kirkus Reviews, January 1, 2002, review of *All about Frogs,* p. 42; March 15, 2002, review of *Field Trips,* p. 405; July 1, 2002, review of *Turtle in the Sea,* p. 948; September 1, 2002, review of *Wild Ponies,* p. 1302.

Publishers Weekly, May 31, 1999, review of *Big Jim and the White-Legged Moose,* p. 92; August 2, 1999, review of *Otters under Water,* p. 87; August 9, 1999, "Natural Wonders," p. 354; June 11, 2001, review of *Raccoon on His Own,* p. 87; November 12, 2001, review of *Mouse Shapes,* p. 61; April 29, 2002, reviews of *Watching Desert Wildlife* and *Watching Water Birds,* p. 73; May 20, 2002, review of *Field Trips, Shore Walking,* p. 69.

Reading Today, August, 2001, "NCTE Names Orbis Pictus Winner," p. 21.

St. Louis Post-Dispatch, June 18, 2001, Michelle Richardson, review of *Raccoon on His Own,* p. D3.

School Library Journal, June, 1999, Barbara Elleman, review of *Big Jim and the White-Legged Moose,* p. 110; October, 1999, Arwen Marshall, review of *Crinkleroot's Nature Almanac,* p. 131; April, 2000, Patricia Manning, review of *All about Turtles,* p. 118; June, 2000, Ruth Semrau, review of *Rattlesnake Dance,* p. 100; September, 2000, Joy Fleishhacker, review of *A Manatee Morning,* p. 184; October, 2000, Arwen Marshall, review of *Wild and Swampy,* p. 144; November, 2000, Ellen Heath, review of *Beaver Pond, Moose Pond,* p. 139; May, 2001, Lee Bock, review of *Raccoon on His Own,* p. 108; March, 2002, Ellen Heath, review of *All about Frogs,* p. 206; June, 2002, review of *Field Trips,* p. 118; August, 2002, Ellen Heath, review of *Turtle in the Sea,* p. 146; October, 2002, Patricia Manning, review of *Wild Ponies,* p. 140; July, 2003, Grace Cliff, review of *Armadillo's Orange,* p. 86.

Tampa Tribune, November 22, 1998, review of *All about Turkeys,* p. 5.

Teacher Librarian, January, 1999, Jessica Higgs, review of *Watching Water Birds,* p. 50.

ONLINE

Jim Arnosky Web site, http://www.jimarnosky.com/ (February 12, 2003).

* * *

ARNOSKY, Jim
See ARNOSKY, James Edward

* * *

ASANTE, Molefi Kete 1942-
(Molefi K. Asante, Arthur L. Smith)

PERSONAL: Born Arthur Lee Smith, Jr., August 14, 1942, in Valdosta, GA; name legally changed, 1973; son of Arthur L. and Lillie B. (Wilkson) Smith; married second wife, Kariamu Welsh; children: Kasina Eka, Daahoud Ali, Molefi Khumalo. *Education:* Southwestern Christian College, A.A., 1962; Oklahoma Christian College, B.A. (cum laude; communication), 1964; Pepperdine College (now Pepperdine Univer-

Molefi Kete Asante

sity), M.A. (communication), 1965; University of California, Los Angeles, Ph.D. (communication), 1968; Université Catholique de l'Ouest, diploma in French, 2002. *Politics:* Democrat. *Religion:* Ancestralism. *Hobbies and other interests:* Poetry, painting, gardening, basketball, astronomy.

ADDRESSES: Home—P.O. Box 30004, Elkins Park, PA 19027-0304. *Office*—Department of African-American Studies, Gladfelter Hall 025-26, Temple University, 1115 West Berks Mall, Philadelphia, PA 19122. *E-mail*—masante@temple.edu.

CAREER: Educator, author, and activist. California State Polytechnic College (now California State Polytechnic University), Pomona, instructor, 1966-67; San Fernando Valley State College (now California State University, Northridge), instructor, 1967; Purdue University, Lafayette, IN, assistant professor of communication, 1968-69; University of California, Los Angeles, assistant professor, 1969-70, associate professor of speech, 1971-73, director of Center for Afro-American Studies, 1969-73; State University of New York at Buffalo, professor of communications, 1973-82, chair of department of communications, 1973-82, chair of department of Black studies, 1977-79; Temple University, Philadelphia, PA, professor of African-American studies, 1984—, chair of department, 1984-96. Visiting professor, Florida State University, 1972, and Howard University, 1979-80, 1995; Fulbright professor, Zimbabwe Institute of Mass Communication, 1981-82. President, Trans-Cultural Education/Communication Foundation, 1971-81; vice president, National Council of Black Studies, 1988-90; founder and president, National Afrocentric Institute, 1989-91; president and chair, African Writers Endowment, 2000—; president, African Writers Endowment Foundation, 2000—; director, Institute for the Study of Intercultural Communication. Developer of Asante Imprint Books, Peoples Publishing Group, for Afrocentric Infusion, 1993-2000. Indiana State Civil Rights Commission on Higher Education and the Afro-American, chair, 1968-69; member of selection committee, Martin Luther King and Woodrow Wilson fellowships, 1970-72; board member, Project Daytime Television. Consultant to Zimbabwe Institute for Mass Communication, 1981-82, United Nations University, 1985-86, and publishers, including Chandler, Macmillan, Sage Publications, Allyn & Bacon, Prentice-Hall, McGraw-Hill, Peoples Publishing, Harper & Row, and Curriculum Press. Host of radio programs for WHAT, 1994-2000, and WURD, 2001—.

MEMBER: International Communication Association (vice president, 1978-80), National Communication Association, Association of Nubian Kemetic Heritage (president, 1995-2003), Association for the Study of Classical African Civilizations, African Heritage Studies Association, American Studies Association, African Studies Association, American Education Research Association, American Academy of Political and Social Sciences, Modern Language Association, Society for Intercultural Education, Training and Research (president, 1975-76).

AWARDS, HONORS: Christian Education Guild Writer's Award, 1965; D.H.L., University of New Haven, 1976; named Outstanding Community Scholar, Jackson State University, 1980; D.H.L., Sojourner-Douglass College, 1989; outstanding scholar, National Council of Black Studies, 1990; Pan-African Society Excellence Award, 1992; Outstanding Communication Scholar in America, Howard University, 1992; Education and Community Service Award, Howard University, 1994; College of Arts and Sciences Award for Distinguished Academic Service, Morgan State University, 1995; Nguzo Saba Award, NAKO, 2000, for scholarly initiative; Philadelphia '76ers and Philadelphia Tribune Community Service Award, 2002; Carter Woodson and Cheikh Anta Diop Award, West Virginia University, 2002, for lifetime achievement in African studies research and scholarship; Douglas Ehninger Award, National Communication Association, 2002, for distinguished rhetorical scholarship.

WRITINGS:

UNDER NAME MOLEFI K. ASANTE UNLESS NOTED

African and Afro-American Communication Continuities, State University of New York at Buffalo Center for International Affairs (Buffalo, NY), 1975.

(With Eileen Newmark) *Intercultural Communication: Theory into Practice,* Speech Communication Association (Alexandria, VA), 1976.

(With Jerry K. Frye) *Contemporary Public Communication,* Harper (New York, NY), 1976.

(Editor, with Mary B. Cassata) *The Social Uses of Mass Communication,* Communication Research Center, State University of New York at Buffalo (Buffalo, NY), 1977.

(With Jerry K. Frye) *Contemporary Public Communication: Applications,* Harper (New York, NY), 1977.

Epic in Search of African Kings, Amulefi Publishing (Buffalo, NY), 1978.

(With Mary B. Cassata) *Mass Communication: Principles and Practices,* Macmillan (New York, NY), 1979.

(With wife, Kariamu Welsh) *A Guide to African and African-American Art and Antiquities,* Museum of African and African-American Art, 1979.

(Editor, with Eileen Newmark and Cecil A. Blake, and contributor) *Handbook of Intercultural Communication,* Sage Publications (Thousand Oaks, CA), 1979.

Afrocentricity: The Theory of Social Change, Amulefi Publishing (Buffalo, NY), 1980, 4th expanded edition, African American Images (Chicago, IL), 2003.

(Editor, with Abdulai S. Vandi, and contributor) *Contemporary Black Thought: Alternative Analyses in Social and Behavioral Science,* Sage Publications (Thousand Oaks, CA), 1980.

Research in Mass Communication: Guide to Practice, Zimbabwe Institute of Mass Communications (Harare, Zimbabwe), 1982.

African Myths: New Frames of Reference, Zimbabwe Institute of Mass Communications (Harare, Zimbabwe), 1982.

(With others) *Media Training Needs in Zimbabwe,* Mass Media Trust and Friedrich Naumann Foundation (Harare, Zimbabwe), 1982.

(Editor, with Kariamu Welsh Asante, and contributor) *African Culture: The Rhythms of Unity,* Greenwood Press (Westport, CT), 1985.

The Afrocentric Idea, Temple University Press (Philadelphia, PA), 1987, revised and expanded edition, 1998.

Umfundalai: Afrocentric Rite of Passage, National Afrocentric Institute (Philadelphia, PA), 1989.

(Editor, with William B. Gudykunst and Eileen Newmark) *Handbook of Intercultural and International Communication,* Sage Publications (Thousand Oaks, CA), 1989.

Kemet, Afrocentricity, and Knowledge, Africa World Press (Trenton, NJ), 1990.

(With Mark Mattson) *Historical and Cultural Atlas of African Americans,* Macmillan (New York, NY), 1991, revised edition published as *The African-American Atlas: Black History and Culture,* 1998.

The Book of African Names, Africa World Press (Trenton, NJ), 1991.

(With Dhyana Ziegler) *Thunder and Silence: The Mass Media in Africa,* Africa World Press (Trenton, NJ), 1991.

(Author of foreword) Duane Smith, *The Nubian,* Azimuth Press, 1992.

Classical Africa (high school textbook), Peoples Publishing (Saddle Brook, NJ), 1993.

Malcolm X As Cultural Hero, and Other Afrocentric Essays, Africa World Press (Trenton, NJ), 1993.

Mfecane (novel), 1984.

Fury in the Wilderness, Scribner (New York, NY), 1994.

(Editor, with Abu Abarry) *The Sources of the African Tradition,* Temple University Press (Philadelphia, PA), 1994.

African American History: A Journey of Liberation, Peoples Publishing (Saddle Brook, NJ), 1995, 2nd edition, 2001.

(Editor, with Abu Abarry) *African Intellectual Heritage: A Book of Sources,* Temple University Press (Philadelphia, PA), 1996.

(Under name Molefi Kete Asante) *Love Dance,* Sungai Press (Trenton, NJ), 1996.

(With Augusta Mann) *Activity Book for African American History,* Peoples Publishing Group (Maywood, NJ), 1997.

(Editor, with Charmaine Harris-Stewart and Augusta Mann) *Teacher's Guide for African American History,* Peoples Publishing Group (Maywood, NJ), 1997, 2nd edition, with Charmaine Harris-Stewart, Theresa Flynn-Nason, and David J. Glunt, 2001.

(With Renee Muntaqim) *The African-American Book of Names and Their Meanings,* Peoples Publishing Group (Maywood, NJ), 1999.

The Painful Demise of Eurocentrism: An Afrocentric Response to Critics, Africa World Press (Trenton, NJ), 1999.

(Under name Molefi Kete Asante) *Scream of Blood: Desettlerism in Southern Africa,* Sungai Books (Princeton, NJ), 1999.

The Egyptian Philosophers: Ancient African Voices from Imhotep to Akhenaten, African American Images (Chicago, IL), 2000.

(Editor, with Eungjun Min) *Socio-Cultural Conflict between African American and Korean American,* University Press of America (Lanham, MD), 2000.

(Editor, with Charmaine Harris-Stewart, Theresa Flynn-Nason, and David J. Glunt) *Worktext for African American History,* 2nd edition, Peoples Publishing Group (Maywood, NJ), 2001.

(With Judylynn Mitchell) *Discovery Essays for Teachers,* Ankh Publishers (Philadelphia, PA), 2001.

(Editor, with Virginia H. Milhouse and Peter O. Nwosu) *Transcultural Realities: Interdisciplinary Perspectives on Cross-cultural Relations,* Sage Publications (Thousand Oaks, CA), 2001.

One Hundred Greatest African Americans: A Biographical Encyclopedia, Prometheus Books (Amherst, NY), 2002.

Culture and Customs of Egypt, Greenwood Press (Westport, CT), 2002.

Scattered to the Wind (fiction), Sungai Books (Princeton, NJ), 2002.

(Editor, with Ama Mazama) *Egypt, Greece, and the American Academy,* African American Images (Chicago, IL), 2002.

Erasing Racism: The Survival of the American Nation, Prometheus Books (Amherst, NY), 2003.

(Editor, with Maulana Karenga) *Handbook of Black Studies,* Sage Publications (Thousand Oaks, CA), 2003.

(Editor, with Ama Mazama) *Encyclopedia of Black Studies,* Sage Publications (Thousand Oaks, CA), 2003.

UNDER NAME ARTHUR L. SMITH

The Break of Dawn (poetry), Dorrance (Philadelphia, PA), 1964.

The Rhetoric of Black Revolution, Allyn & Bacon (Boston, MA), 1969.

(With Andrea Rich) *Rhetoric of Revolution: Samuel Adams, Emma Goldman, Malcolm X,* Moore Publishing (Durham, NC), 1970.

Toward Transracial Communication, Afro-American Studies Center, University of California, Los Angeles (Los Angeles, CA), 1970.

(Editor, with Stephen Robb) *The Voice of Black Rhetoric,* Allyn & Bacon (Boston, MA), 1971.

(With Anne Allen and Deluvina Hernandez) *How to Talk with People of Other Races, Ethnic Groups, and Cultures,* Transcultural Educational Foundation (Los Angeles, CA), 1971.

Language, Communication, and Rhetoric in Black America, Harper (New York, NY), 1972.

Transracial Communication, Prentice-Hall (Englewood Cliffs, NJ), 1973.

Also editor of unpublished book *In Their Faces: Situating Alternatives to Afrocentricity,* 1994. Contributor to books, including *Topics in Afro-American Studies,* edited by Henry Richards, Black Academy Press, 1971; *Return to Vision,* Houghton Mifflin, 1971; *Speech Communication Behavior,* edited by L. Barker and R. Kibler, Prentice-Hall, 1971; *America in Controversy,* edited by DeWitte Holland, W. C. Brown, 1973; *Black Communication,* edited by Jack Daniel, Speech Communication Association, 1974; *Education in the Eighties,* edited by Gus Friedrich, NEA-SCA, 1981; *International Communication Theory,* edited by William B. Gudykunst, Sage Publications, 1982; *Television and the Socialization of the Minority Child,* edited by Gordon Berry and Claudia Mitchell-Kernan, Academic Press, 1982; *Black Male,* edited by Lawrence Gary, Sage Publications, 1982; *Blacks in Science: Ancient and Modern,* edited by Ivan Van Sertima, Transaction Books, 1983; *Kemet and the African Worldview,* edited by Maulana Karenga and Jacob Carruthers, University of Sankore Press, 1986; *Colored, on White Campus: The Education of a Racial World,* MARS Productions, 1992; *The African-German Experience: Critical Essays,* edited by Aisha Blackshire-Belay, Greenwood Press, 1997; *Conversation in America: Changing Rules, Hidden Dimensions,* edited by William F. Eadie and Paul E. Nelson, Sage Publications, 2000; *Black Identity in the Twentieth Century: Expressions of the U.S. and U.K. African Diaspora,* edited by Mark Christian, Hansib, 2002; *The Anthology of African-American Social and Political Thought,* Oxford University Press, 2003; *Under-*

standing African-American Rhetoric: Classical Origins to Contemporary Innovations, edited by Ronald Jackson and Elaine Richardson, Routledge, 2003; and *Déraison, esclavage, et droit: Les fondements ideologiques et juridiques de la traite négrière et de l'esclavage,* by Isabel Castro Henriques and Louis Sala-Molins, Editions UNESCO, 2003.

Contributor to journals, including *African Centred Review, Black Scholar, Academe, Educational Leadership, World and I, American Scholar, Journal of Negro Education, Black Collegian, Southern Communication Journal, Critical Social Issues, African Concord, Dissent, Communication Quarterly, Journal of Black Studies, Journal of African Civilization, International Journal of Intercultural Relations, Journal of Popular Culture, Review of Afro-American Issues and Cultures, Language Artist, Palestine Review, Western Journal of Black Studies, Colorado Journal of Educational Research, Speech Abstracts, Language Quarterly, Today's Speech, Quarterly Journal of Black Speech,* and *Urban Research;* contributor to newspapers and magazines, including *Utne Reader, Philadelphia New Observer, Philadelphia Tribune, Philadelphia Daily News, Buffalo Challenger,* and the *Los Angeles Times.*

Editor, "African Dissertation Series," Routledge, Taylor & Francis, 2001—. Member of board of editors, "Black Men in America" reprint series, 1969-70; founding editor, *Journal of Black Studies,* 1969—; editorial associate, *Speech Teacher,* 1970-73; contributing editor, *Encore,* 1970-72; advisory editor, *Imhotep;* also associate editor of *Nigerian Journal of Political Economy, Afrodiaspora, Afrique Histoire, Africa and the World, Urban African Quarterly,* and *Journal of African Civilization.* Book reviewer, *Journal of Communication,* 1970-72; reviewer for scholarly books, *UNESCO,* 1985. Member of advisory board, *Black Law Journal,* 1971-73, and *Race Relations Abstract,* 1973-76.

SIDELIGHTS: Molefi Kete Asante is considered the founder of the Afrocentricity movement, which he defines in his book *The Afrocentric Idea* as "literally placing African ideals at the center of any analysis that involves African culture and behavior." With an educational background in communications and both modern and ancient languages, Asante has worked as both an educator and a writer to help people understand the importance of African people as agents of history and culture. "Asante seeks pluralism without hierarchy," explained Alex Boyd and Catherine J. Lenix-Hooker in *Library Journal.* He believes that "Afrocentrism should take its place not above but alongside other cultural and historical perspectives." Many of Asante's books concentrate on communication and Afrocentricity, and provide reference sources on the historical contributions made by people of African descent.

Born Arthur Lee Smith, Jr. and raised in the American South during the 1940s and 1950s, Asante experienced the pain of racial prejudice firsthand. While attending Nashville Christian Institute, a black boarding school, he worked in the tobacco and cotton fields during school breaks. At the age of twelve, he got a job as a shoeshine boy, but quit after his first day when a white man spat on him. Fortunately, he gained emotional support from his father and mother, who, although they had only an elementary education, encouraged their son to improve himself intellectually. Asante also developed a strong work ethic, thanks to the influential president of his boarding school, Marshall Keeble, and was also inspired by his high school teacher Frank Tharp as well as by a fellow student, Fred Gray, who later became an attorney representing Martin Luther King, Jr. Another important influence was a Nigerian named Essien Essien, whom Asante met while attending Southwestern Christian College. Essien encouraged the young man to learn more about his African heritage. This he did energetically, while also studying European languages and cultures. And his studies of both European and African classic languages and cultures brought him to a fuller understanding of how the two have clashed and interrelated to each other in American society.

Asante's first published book to focus on the African-American experience was *The Rhetoric of Black Revolution,* and he first addressed cross-cultural communication in his *Transracial Communication*—both books were published under his given name. He was prompted to change his name legally to Molefi Kete Asante in 1973 by an incident that occurred while he was visiting the University of Ghana. A librarian there told him that he assumed *The Rhetoric of Black Revolution* had been written by a white man; Asante decided then and there to embrace an African name that better represented his heritage.

A few years later, in 1980, Asante released his landmark book concerning his concept of Afrocentricity: *Afrocentricity: The Theory of Social Change,* which has been revised several times since. As he told a *Newsweek* writer, "Afrocentricity believes that in order to have a stable society, we must always have a society that respects difference." Slavery and racism, while practiced in the United States, have not respected such differences; thus they have denied a large percentage of American citizens their own sense of identity.

Asante's 1987 title *The Afrocentric Idea* explores his argument that cultural ethics originating in Africa have a direct effect on speech and behavior in black communities in the Western Hemisphere. Aware of the way in which speech has at times been used to perpetuate racial division, "Asante stresses the significance of rhetoric and rhythm in black life," according to Andrew Hacker in the *New York Review of Books.* Asante also emphasizes the prominence in black culture of oral dialogue over the written word. Moreover, the heritage of African Americans is manifest in the achievements of blacks in music and sports, according to Asante.

Some reviewers, such as Hacker, noted that Asante's listing of many blacks from the sports and entertainment fields "to show that their talents derive from African culture are certainly suggestive." However, Hacker added, "the problem is that this African emphasis supports a more insidious aspect of white racism" by not emphasizing intellectual achievements. However, Melvin Dixon added in the *New York Times Book Review* that Asante makes the Afrocentric perspective an ideal crucial not only to an enriched awareness but also to any noteworthy analysis of the lives of blacks. "Asante's discussion ends by promoting spiritual balance as the key to an Afrocentric ideal in America," Dixon concluded. "Such balance is crucial to our African-American identity; neither Africa nor Europe alone provides sufficient scope for our collective experience."

A revised and expanded edition of *The Afrocentric Idea* published in 1998 represents Asante's efforts to respond to some of the critics of the original book. "His method," as Maulana Karenga noted in *Black Issues in Higher Education,* "is to outline and identify critical weaknesses in cherished Eurocentric conceptions, dismiss them, and then introduce alternative pathways to pursue in the ongoing engagement with the products and processes of the Afrocentric project." Karenga concluded in his review that "Asante's works are clearly in the vanguard of this intellectual and cultural thrust toward African centering. Thus, . . . one cannot honestly deny that both his work and our dialogue with him has expanded the intellectual horizon and enriched the discourse of the discipline of Black studies."

As with his earlier *Rhetoric of Black Revolution,* Asante's 2003 book *Erasing Racism: The Survival of the American Nation* deals directly with the tension between whites and African Americans. Among other things, the author argues in support of the payment of reparations to blacks for the centuries of slavery imposed on them in the United States. He feels that such payments would go a long way toward healing the rift between whites and blacks and would be in the spirit of "patriotism" in which all citizens of a nation work to help one another. "Anyone who has struggled to understand race relations in America. . . ," asserted a *Publishers Weekly* contributor, "will glean something valuable from this book."

Part of Asante's efforts to foster understanding among African Americans with regard to their cultural heritage has been to publish a number of educational resources that are especially suited for researchers in high school and undergraduate school. One of these, *Historical and Cultural Atlas of African Americans,* which has since been revised as *The African-American Atlas: Black History and Culture,* is a chronological history of black history extending from African origins forward in time to the present. In his book Asante provides several resources for the reader, including charts, lists of important dates to remember, statistical data, highlights of selected events, brief biographies of important people, and a practical atlas format. R. C. Dickey, writing in *Choice,* described the *Historical and Cultural Atlas of African Americans* as a "helpful overall view of black American history." Another reference work by Asante, *One Hundred Greatest African Americans: A Biographical Encyclopedia,* offers brief biographies of important African Americans based on criteria established by Asante that include how much the person contributed to the advancement of racial equality in America, personal sacrifices made and risks taken, and achievements that can serve to inspire other African Americans. While *Reference and User Services Quarterly* reviewer M. Elaine Hughes felt that the author's selection of listees is, not surprisingly, somewhat subjective, she praised Asante's encyclopedia for being "very well researched and written."

Asante's concern for U.S. public-school education is evident not only in the books he has written but also in his service as a curricula consultant to various urban school districts. He has encouraged schools to design courses that incorporate Afrocentric principles which help students feel more connected to their coursework. In both his efforts to help educate school children and his academic work, Asante has dedicated much of his life to breaking down communications barriers between European and African Americans and helping connect blacks with their heritage in order that they might better understand where they stand in contemporary U.S. society.

BIOGRAPHICAL AND CRITICAL SOURCES:

BOOKS

Contemporary Black Biography, Volume 3, Gale (Detroit, MI), 1992.

PERIODICALS

Atlanta Journal, June 16, 1991.

Black Issues in Higher Education, June 11, 1998, Maulana Karenga, review of *The Afrocentric Idea,* p. 25.

Booklist, April 15, 1999, Mary Ellen Quinn, review of *The African-American Atlas: Black History and Culture,* p. 1548; February 15, 2003, Donna Seaman, review of *Erasing Racism: The Survival of the American Nation,* p. 1037.

Book Report, November-December, 1991, Marie A. Ramsey, review of *Historical and Cultural Atlas of African Americans,* p. 59.

Chicago Tribune, April 23, 1989.

Choice, September, 1991, p. 51.

Chronicle of Higher Education, April 18, 1997, Denise K. Magner, "Deep Rifts Divide Faculty in Temple U.'s Afrocentric Ph.D. Program," p. A12.

Ebony, June, 1981, review of *Contemporary Black Thought: Alternative Analyses in Social and Behavioral Science,* p. 26.

Journal of Black Studies, November, 2000, Kwame Okoampa-Ahoofe, review of *Scream of Blood: Desettlerism in Southern Africa,* p. 247; July, 2002, Diane D. Turner, "An Oral History Interview: Molefi Kete Asante," p. 711; May, 2003, Daryl Zizwe Poe, review of *The Egyptian Philosophers: Ancient African Voices from Imhotep to Akhenaten,* pp. 704-705.

Library Journal, July, 1991, Kenneth F. Kister, review of *Historical and Cultural Atlas of African Americans,* p. 86; November 1, 1992, pp. 46-49; September 1, 1996, Anthony O. Edmonds, review of *African Intellectual Heritage: A Book of Sources,* p. 191.

Newsweek, September 23, 1991.

New York Review of Books, March 3, 1988, Andrew Hacker, review of *The Afrocentric Idea,* pp. 36-41.

New York Times Book Review, January 7, 1990, p. 35.

Publishers Weekly, March 3, 2003, review of *Erasing Racism,* p. 60.

Reference and User Services Quarterly, summer, 1999, Eva Lautemann, review of *The African-American Atlas,* p. 406; summer, 2003, M. Elaine Hughes, review of *One Hundred Greatest African Americans: A Biographical Encyclopedia,* p. 356.

School Library Journal, May, 1999, Janet Woodward, review of *The African-American Atlas,* p. 148.

Wilson Library Bulletin, September, 1991, James Rettig, review of *Historical and Cultural Atlas of African Americans,* pp. 123-124.

ONLINE

Molefi Kete Asante Web site, http://www.asante.net/ (January 14, 2004).*

B

BABBITT, Natalie (Zane Moore) 1932-

PERSONAL: Born July 28, 1932, in Dayton, OH; daughter of Ralph Zane (a business administrator) and Genevieve (Converse) Moore; married Samuel Fisher Babbitt (vice president of Brown University), June 26, 1954; children: Christopher Converse, Thomas Collier II, Lucy Cullyford. *Education:* Smith College, B.A., 1954. *Politics:* Democrat. *Hobbies and other interests:* Needlework, piano, word puzzles.

ADDRESSES: *Home*—26 Benefit St., Apt. 4, Providence, RI 02904; and 63 Seaside Ave., Dennis, MA 02638. *Office*—81 Benefit St., Providence, RI 02904.

CAREER: Children's book writer and illustrator.

MEMBER: Authors Guild, Authors League of America, PEN (American Center).

AWARDS, HONORS: Best Book of 1969 for Children Ages Nine to Twelve citation, *New York Times,* for *The Search for Delicious;* American Library Association (ALA) Notable Book citation, 1970, Newbery Honor Book citation, 1971, and *Horn Book* Honor citation, all for *Kneeknock Rise; Book World* Children's Spring Book Festival Honor Book citation, 1971, Children's Book Council Showcase title, 1972, and *School Library Journal* Honor List citation, all for *Goody Hall;* ALA Notable Book citation, *School Library Journal* Best Book of the Year citation, *Horn Book* Honor List citation, and National Book Award nomination, all 1974, all for *The Devil's Storybook;*

Natalie Babbitt

ALA Notable Book citation, *Horn Book* Honor List citation, and Christopher Award for juvenile fiction, all 1976, and International Reading Association choices list citation, U.S. Honor Book citation, and Congress of the International Board on Books for Young People citation, all 1978, all for *Tuck Everlasting;* ALA Notable Book citation, 1977, for *The Eyes of the Amaryllis;* George C. Stone Center for Children's Books award, 1979; Hans Christian Andersen Medal nomination, 1981; Best Books of 1982 citation, *New York Times,* for *Herbert Rowbarge;* Children's Literature Festival Award, Keene State College, 1993, for body of work; Blue Ribbon Book, *Bulletin of the Center for Children's Books,* 1998, ALA Notable Book citation, 1999, and Audie Award, 2001, all for *Ouch!*

WRITINGS:

SELF-ILLUSTRATED; VERSE

Dick Foote and the Shark, Farrar, Straus (New York, NY), 1967.
Phoebe's Revolt, Farrar, Straus (New York, NY), 1968.

SELF-ILLUSTRATED; FICTION

The Search for Delicious, Farrar, Straus (New York, NY), 1969.
Kneeknock Rise, Farrar, Straus (New York, NY), 1970.
The Something, Farrar, Straus (New York, NY), 1970.
Goody Hall, Farrar, Straus (New York, NY), 1971.
The Devil's Story Book, Farrar, Straus (New York, NY), 1974.
Tuck Everlasting, Farrar, Straus (New York, NY), 1975.
The Eyes of the Amaryllis, Farrar, Straus (New York, NY), 1977.
Herbert Rowbarge, Farrar, Straus (New York, NY), 1982.
The Devil's Other Storybook, Farrar, Straus (New York, NY), 1987.
Nellie: A Cat on Her Own, Farrar, Straus (New York, NY), 1989.
Bub; or, The Very Best Thing, HarperCollins (New York, NY), 1994.
Elsie Times Eight, Hyperion Books for Children (New York, NY), 2001.

ILLUSTRATOR

Samuel Fisher Babbitt, *The Forty-ninth Magician,* Pantheon (New York, NY), 1966.
Valerie Worth, *Small Poems,* Farrar, Straus (New York, NY), 1972.
Valerie Worth, *More Small Poems,* Farrar, Straus (New York, NY), 1976.
Valerie Worth, *Still More Small Poems,* Farrar, Straus (New York, NY), 1978.
Valerie Worth, *Curlicues: The Fortunes of Two Pug Dogs,* Farrar, Straus (New York, NY), 1980, published as *Imp and Biscuit: The Fortunes of Two Pugs,* Chatto & Windus (London, England), 1981.
Valerie Worth, *Small Poems Again,* Farrar, Straus (New York, NY), 1985.
Valerie Worth, *Other Small Poems Again,* Farrar, Straus (New York, NY), 1986.
Valerie Worth, *All the Small Poems,* Farrar, Straus (New York, NY), 1987.
Valerie Worth, *All the Small Poems and Fourteen More,* Farrar, Straus (New York, NY), 1994.
Valerie Worth, *Peacock and Other Poems,* Farrar, Straus (New York, NY), 2002.

OTHER

(Reteller) *Ouch!: A Tale from Grimm,* illustrated by Fred Marcellino, Harper Collins (New York, NY), 1998.

Contributor to *Tikvah: Children's Book Creators Reflect on Human Rights,* North-South Books, 2001. Contributor to periodicals, including *Redbook, Publishers Weekly, Horn Book, New York Times Book Review, Cricket, School Library Journal, USA Today,* and *Washington Post Book World.*

Babbitt's books have been translated into several languages, including Spanish.

ADAPTATIONS: Kneeknock Rise was made into a filmstrip, Miller-Brody Productions, 1975, and recorded on audiocassette, American School Publishers, 1987; *The Search for Delicious* was recorded on audiocassette, Listening Library; *Ouch!* was recorded on audiocassette with teacher's guide, Live Oak Media, 2000. *Tuck Everlasting* was recorded on audiocassette, Audio Bookshelf, 1995, and made into a motion picture, Walt Disney Productions, 2001.

SIDELIGHTS: A man who has lost his identical twin, a family who has discovered the secret to eternal life, and a boy who must save his kingdom from evil are all subjects of novels written by Natalie Babbitt. Although primarily known as a children's book writer, she is also appreciated by older readers as a gifted storyteller. In entertaining narratives, her characters confront many basic human needs, including the need to be loved, the need for growth, change, and independence, the need to overcome fear, and the need to believe in something unexplainable. Her originality, sense of humor, and courage in focusing on challenging themes has also established her reputation as an important children's book author. Since its publication in 1975, her award-winning novel *Tuck Everlasting* has become a classic of children's literature and has also been adapted for film.

Babbitt's mother encouraged her two daughters' early interest in art and reading. Genevieve Moore read children's books aloud to her daughters, and they decided Natalie would become an artist and her sister a writer. Impressed with Brazilian artist Luis de Vargas's airbrushed figures of glamorous women popular during the second World War, the young artist imitated them using colored pencils. Discouraged by the difference between Vargas's finished drawings and her own, she was inspired by Sir John Tenniel's illustrations in *Alice in Wonderland* to work with pen and ink, which became her specialty.

Babbitt received brief training in a summer fashion-illustration course at the Cleveland School of Art. There she realized she enjoyed creative drawing more than drawing sketches of alligator bags. Later, in art classes at Smith College, where she competed with other artists for the first time in her life, she saw that success as an illustrator required more than creativity. In *Something about the Author Autobiography Series* (*SAAS*), Babbitt explained, "It was . . . the best lesson I learned in four years of college: to wit, you have to work hard to do good work. I had always done what came easily, and what came easily had always been good enough. It was not good enough at Smith, and would never be good enough again."

While at Smith, she met Samuel Babbitt, whom she married in 1954. She kept busy working and raising a family of three children while her husband, an aspiring writer, wrote a novel. The many hours alone with the novel did not suit him, however, and he went back to work as a college administrator. Her sister also produced a comic novel, for which Babbitt supplied illustrations, but abandoned the project when an editor asked for a substantial rewriting. "I learned three valuable things from observing what happened to my mother, sister and husband with their forays into the writer's world," she explained in her autobiographical essay. "You have to give writing your full attention, you have to like the revision process, and you have to like to be alone. But it was years before I put any of it to good use." After reading Betty Freidan's *The Feminine Mystique,* she realized that while her career as a homemaker had been successful, she had neglected to develop her other talents. After discussions with other women making similar discoveries, Babbitt decided to pursue a second career as an illustrator.

In 1966 *The Forty-ninth Magician,* written by Babbitt's husband, was published with her illustrations, thanks to the help of Michael di Capua at Farrar, Straus & Giroux. Di Capua's encouragement helped Babbitt to continue producing children's books even after her husband became too busy to write the stories. She subsequently wrote *Dick Foote and the Shark* and *Phoebe's Revolt,* two picture books in which the stories are told in rhyming poetry.

Babbitt's ideas for books sometimes start with her meditations on a single image, such as a mountain and what can be found behind it, or on a single word. While thinking about the image or the word, she imagines characters whose personalities allow her to develop dialogue and plots for each story. The final result is often very different from her first idea. For example, *Goody Hall* started with Babbitt's thinking about the word "smuggler," yet it became a conversation with her mother. Her Grandmother Converse was a woman who supported herself and a daughter by dressmaking. In *SAAS,* Babbitt wrote, "I loved my Grandma Converse. . . . I doubt she ever had an ambitious thought in her life. But my mother not only wanted things, she knew what to want—what, that is, in terms of a Great American Dream of wealth, accomplishment, and social acceptability. . . . Like the heroes of Horatio Alger, my mother was never afraid of hard work, and many of the things she wanted were worth wanting. . . . She died when I was twenty-four and not yet mature enough to have figured it all out and discussed it with her. So I put it all into my story *Goody Hall* instead."

Goody Hall is a Gothic mystery set in the English countryside. A large Victorian house decorated with ornate wood carvings belongs to Midas Goody, whose disappearance spurs a young tutor to investigate. His encounters with an empty tomb, a hollow statue stuffed with precious stones, a gypsy, a rich youngster and his eccentric mother, and other surprises lead to a happy ending where confusing disguises are abandoned and the Goody family is reunited. Though the plot, like the old house with its hints of secret passageways and hidden closets, can frighten and bewilder, "in the end we feel the way the Goodys did about their house," Jean Fritz remarked in the *New York Times Book Review.*

In *The Devil's Storybook,* the title character is a trickster who is fooled as often as he tries to fool others. For example, he gives the power of speech to a goat who then annoys the devil with his constant complaining. In another story, the devil sneaks into the bedroom of a pretty lady who outwits him. Babbitt's devil is middle-aged and pot-bellied and often fails to reach his goal of causing trouble for others. In light of this, his continued meddling in others' lives makes the stories interesting to read, wrote Selma G. Lanes in *Horn Book.* The sequel, *The Devil's Other Story Book,* also pits the devil against animals and humans who leave the trickster in the dust. There is a moral lesson even in the stories where the devil gives "hell, literally, to those who deserve it," Laurel Graeber remarked in the *New York Times Book Review,* adding that "Babbitt's ethical lessons . . . rarely undermine her narrative gifts."

In *Tuck Everlasting,* a family who has discovered a secret spring that makes the drinkers immortal finds out that living forever without ever growing or changing is not very pleasant; this is explained to a ten-year-old girl, Winnie, who discovers the family by accident. Winnie falls in love with Tuck, but it is a romance the pair realize cannot last because Winnie is not immortal. Tuck's explanation of the role of mortality in the cycle of nature "is one of the most vivid and deeply felt passages in American children's literature," *Ms.* reviewer Michele Landsberg asserted. In an article for *Children's Literature in Education,* Kim Aippersbach, considering the novel's themes and symbolism, remarked: "A ten-year-old may not be able to formulate hypotheses concerning the nature of life and death and the importance of interrelationships within the human community, but she can sense the joy that is the other side of sadness that illuminates this story. And, in the end, that is all any of us can do."

When the Walt Disney motion picture version of *Tuck Everlasting* appeared in cinemas in 2001, it gave Babbitt's tale a wider audience and encouraged moviegoers to read the book as well. *Horn Book*'s Tim Wynne-Jones predicted that even in another hundred years *Tuck Everlasting* "will still have something essential to say about the human condition. And how well it does so, with flawless style, in words that are exact and simple and soothing and right."

In addition to illustrating the works of others, particularly verse collections by Valerie Worth, Babbitt has illustrated most of her own texts with her delicate watercolor paintings. Among her own picture books are the fairy tales *Bub; or, The Very Best Thing* and *Elsie Times Eight.* The former tells the story of a prince named Bub whose parents hold different ideas about child-rearing. After Bub's parents take a poll of the castle occupants and come no closer to a conclusion, the cook's daughter asks the toddler prince his opinion. He replies "Bub," a term of endearment. Finally all understand that "love is the very best thing." Reviewers gave the work qualified praise. Because *Bub* does not contain much action, *Booklist*'s Ilene Cooper decided its appeal rests with the author's artwork, and Betsy Hearne, writing in the *Bulletin of the Center for Children's Books,* found the watercolor scenes photographically realistic yet sometimes "flat," with the prince's dog stealing the show. Also believing the "royal dog and toy dragon steal the show" was Hanna B. Zeiger, who nonetheless concluded in *Horn Book* that the author-illustrator's "elegant writing style and totally engaging characterizations in her illustrations combine to create a memorable picture book."

In her 2001 offering *Elsie Times Eight,* which *Commonweal* contributor Daria Donnelly described as a "very funny, smart new picture book," Babbitt portrays what happens when a hard-of-hearing fairy godmother goes into action. She clones eight Elsies, and havoc ensues as Elsie's parents try to cope. Eventually they locate the godmother, who puts things to rights. Among the book's enthusiasts was Joanna Rudge Long of *Horn Book,* who praised Babbitt's "lively compositions" and "cheerful narration, with its funny, unexpected turns," and a *Kirkus Reviews* contributor, who predicted that the book's premise is "sure to appeal to youngsters." Others held less-laudatory opinions. For example, Grace Oliff, writing in *School Library Journal,* likened Babbitt's pastel watercolors to those of classic Mother Goose tales and complimented her "inimitable prose style," yet dubbed the story "thin." Although *Booklist* critic Ilene Cooper also found the premise "slight," she complimented Babbitt for her energetic and "edgy" telling and her ink-and-watercolor illustrations, which contain some "delightful moments."

In *Ouch! A Tale from Grimm* Babbitt uses her "fine, comfortable storyteller's voice," to quote a *Kirkus Reviews* critic, to retell the Brothers Grimm tale "The Devil with the Three Golden Hairs." This story revolves around a boy who is born with a crown-shaped birthmark and who is predicted to marry the princess of the kingdom. After some time and after surmounting several challenges, he does marry the princess, only to be ordered by his new father-in-law to pull three hairs from the devil's head. The prince succeeds, thus creating the exclamation of the title. Graced with Frank Marcellino's Renaissance-style illustrations, this book appealed to a *Publishers Weekly* reviewer, who praised Babbitt for her "intelligent retelling, mixed with a dash of sly humor." *Ouch!* also turned out to be an award winner.

Babbitt believes that writers do not always have an audience of a specific age group in mind. "The source of any book is a writer's sense of urgency that something needs to be said in print," she said in a 1987 PEN symposium and published in the *PEN Newsletter.* "The choice to write either for children or for adults comes more from a writer's temperament, or is suggested by the age of the main character," she added. She once told *CA,* "I write for children because I am interested in fantasy and the possibilities for experience of all kinds before the time of compromise. I believe that children are far more perceptive and wise than American books give them credit for being."

In a *Horn Book* essay, however, Babbitt also expressed her concern about the final effect of fantasy stories on impressionable minds: "On a recent school visit a fifth-grader asked me if the magic spring water in *Tuck Everlasting* . . . was real. 'No,' I said, 'it isn't real.' 'But,' said the fifth-grader, 'didn't you ever think that when you described it so well, as if it was real, we might believe you?' I have lain awake over that question. Are we somehow implying in our books that the unreal, the impossible, is more greatly to be desired than the real and the possible? Are we maybe whispering that there are instant metamorphoses to be had somewhere, that everyone can and should be a hero? I am only trying to say that we had better tread lightly." In an age when television characters and glamorous celebrities are the most visible role models, the author continued, writers need to be aware of how children's view of themselves can plummet when they compare themselves to fictional wizards and beauty queens: "It is absolutely true that in America anyone can grow up to be president, but the word is *can,* not *will.* We'd better be sure our children know that while luck is always a factor in how things turn out, there will be no magic, no fairy godmother, no hag on the road with her basket of charms." Babbitt believes young readers also need to be reminded that in the real world, growth and change can take a long time to achieve.

Looking back on her published work, Babbitt recognizes that many of her own childhood memories are embedded within her stories. The childhood experiences woven into Babbitt's books remain meaningful into adulthood. Anita Moss commented in the *Dictionary of Literary Biography* that her books remain enjoyable for readers of all ages. A *Horn Book* reviewer summarized, "Babitt's infectious sense of humor, her wisdom and perspective on life, and her ability not to take herself too seriously—but to take what she writes and her audience very seriously—have shaped a magnificent body of work."

BIOGRAPHICAL AND CRITICAL SOURCES:

BOOKS

Children's Literature Review, Volume 2, Gale (Detroit, MI), 1976, pp. 5-8.

Dictionary of Literary Biography, Volume 52: *American Writers for Children since 1960: Poets, Writers, Illustrators, and Nonfiction Authors,* Gale (Detroit, MI), 1987, pp. 22-29.

Hopkins, Lee Bennett, *More Books by More People,* Citation Press, 1974, pp. 24-29.

Levy, Michael M., *Natalie Babbitt,* Twayne Publishers (Boston, MA), 1991.

St. James Guide to Children's Writers, 5th edition, Gale (Detroit, MI), 1999.

Something about the Author Autobiography Series, Volume 5, Gale (Detroit, MI), 1988, pp. 41-52.

PERIODICALS

Booklist, October 15, 1989, Ilene Cooper, review of *Nellie: A Cat on Her Own,* pp. 447-448; February 15, 1994, Ilene Cooper, review of of *Bub; or, The*

Very Best Thing, pp. 1091-1092; January 15, 1995, Hazel Rochman, review of *All the Small Poems and Fourteen More,* p. 933; April 15, 1995, review of *Goody Hall,* p. 1502; November 15, 1997, Barbara Elleman, review of *The Eyes of the Amaryllis,* p. 546; November 15, 1998, review of *Ouch!: A Tale from Grimm,* p. 582; March 15, 1999, review of *Ouch!,* p. 1302; November 15, 2001, Ilene Cooper, review of *Elsie Times Eight,* pp. 579-580; August, 2002, Carolyn Phelan, review of *Peacock and Other Poems,* p. 1963.

Books, spring, 2002, review of *Tuck Everlasting,* p. 23.

Bulletin of the Center for Children's Books, June, 1994, Betsy Hearne, review of *Bub,* pp. 312-313; January, 1999, review of *Ouch!,* p. 159; December, 2001, review of *Elsie Times Eight,* p. 129.

Children's Book Review Service, March, 1994, review of *Bub,* p. 85; January, 1999, review of *Ouch!,* p. 49.

Children's Bookwatch, September, 1998, review of *The Something* p. 5.

Children's Literature in Education, June, 1990, Kim Aippersbach, "*Tuck Everlasting* and the Tree at the Center of the World," pp. 83-97.

Commonweal, November 23, 2001, Daria Donnelly, "Wanted: Hobbits, Fairies and Wind-up Toys," p. 22.

Cricket, April, 1974.

Entertainment Weekly, April 8, 1994, review of *Bub,* p. 69.

Five Owls, May, 1995, review of *Tuck Everlasting,* p. 100.

Horn Book, August, 1969, p. 407; June, 1970, p. 295; August, 1971, pp. 380-381; February, 1978, Mary M. Burns, review of *The Eyes of the Amaryllis,* pp. 42-43; November, 1984, pp. 779-783; July, 1987, pp. 509-511; September, 1987, pp. 607-608; May, 1988, pp. 329-331; September, 1988, Natalie Babbitt, "Metamorphosis" pp. 582-589; March, 1989, pp. 133-134; November, 1989, pp. 728-731; May, 1994, Hanna B. Zeiger, review of *Bub,* p. 305; March-April, 1995, Nancy Vasilakis, review of *All the Small Poems and Fourteen More,* p. 212; January-February, 1999, review of *Ouch!,* p. 73; November, 2000, Tim Wynne-Jones, review of *Tuck Everlasting,* p. 720; January-February, 2002, Joanna Rudge Long, review of *Elsie Times Eight,* p. 66; July-August, 2002, Mary M. Burns, review of *Peacock and Other Poems,* p. 481.

Instructor, January, 1993, reviews of *Nellie, The Search for Delicious,* and *Tuck Everlasting,* p. 57.

Kirkus Reviews, February 1, 1994, review of *Bub,* p. 137; November 1, 1998, review of *Ouch!,* p. 1596; August 15, 2001, review of *Elsie Times Eight,* p. 1206; March 1, 2002, review of *Peacock and Other Poems,* p. 349.

Learning, January, 1995, review of *The Search for Delicious,* p. 16.

Library Journal, May 15, 1969, p. 2096; June 15, 1970, p. 2306; October, 1974, Jane Abramson, review of *The Devil's Storybook,* p. 102; November 1, 2001, review of *Tuck Everlasting,* p. 160.

Ms., May 11, 1990, Michele Landsberg, review of *Tuck Everlasting,* p. 74.

New Advocate, fall, 1994, review of *Bub,* p. 284.

New Statesman, November, 1968.

New Yorker, December 4, 1971, p. 199.

New York Times Book Review, July 2, 1967, p. 16; November 9, 1969, p. 62; May 2, 1971, p. 18; July 28, 1974, p. 8; November 16, 1975, p. 32; November 13, 1977, p. 37; November 14, 1982, pp. 44, 54; November 1, 1987, p. 36; June 19, 1994, review of *Bub,* p. 28; March 14, 1999, review of *Ouch!,* p. 31; January 20, 2002, review of *Elsie Times Eight,* p. 15.

PEN Newsletter, September, 1988, pp. 16-26.

Publishers Weekly, January 3, 1994, review of *Bub,* p. 80; November 2, 1998, review of *Ouch!,* p. 80; October 1, 2001, review of *Elsie Times Eight,* p. 60; February 11, 2002, review of *Peacock and Other Poems,* p. 184.

Quill & Quire, October, 1993, review of *Tuck Everlasting,* p. 18.

Reading Teacher, September, 1999, review of *Ouch!,* p. 83.

Redbook, December, 1971.

School Library Journal, April, 1994, review of *Bub,* p. 96; June, 1995, review of *Tuck Everlasting* (audio version), p. 71; May, 1996, review of *The Search for Delicious* (audio version), p. 76; April, 1997, review of *Kneeknock Rise* (audio version), p. 82; December, 1998, review of *Ouch!,* p. 100; February, 1999, review of *Bub,* p. 68; February, 2001, Teresa Bateman, review of *Ouch!* (audiobook review), p. 61; November, 2001, Kathleen Isaacs, "*Tikvah*: Children's Book Creators Reflect on Human Rights," p. 198; November, 2001, Grace Oliff, review of *Elsie Times Eight,* p. 110; May, 2002, Nicole Lindsay, review of *Peacock and Other Poems,* p. 145.

Time, December 7, 1998, review of *Ouch!,* p. 219.

Times Literary Supplement, April 4, 1975, p. 365; July 16, 1976, p. 882; March 25, 1977, p. 348; June 29, 1984, p. 737; August 31, 1984, p. 977.

Top of the News, summer, 1987, pp. 376-382.
Washington Post Book World, December 12, 1982, p. 8; April 3, 1994, Michael Dirda, review of *Bub,* p. 10; November 1, 1998, review of *Ouch!,* p. 8; December 9, 2001, review of *Elsie Times Eight,* p. 8.
Writer, June, 1971.

OTHER

"A Visit with Natalie Babbitt," *Tuck Everlasting,* DVD special feature, Walt Disney Home Video, 2003.*

* * *

BANG, Garrett
See BANG, Molly Garrett

* * *

BANG, Molly Garrett 1943-
(Garrett Bang)

PERSONAL: Born December 29, 1943, in Princeton, NJ; daughter of Frederik Barry (a research physician) and Betsy (a translator and scientist; maiden name, Garrett) Bang; married Richard H. Campbell (an acoustics engineer), September 27, 1974; children: Monika. *Education:* Wellesley College, B.A., 1965; University of Arizona, M.A., 1969; Harvard University, M.A., 1971.

ADDRESSES: *Home*—89 Water St., Woods Hole, MA 02543.

CAREER: Author, illustrator, and translator. Doshisha University, Kyoto, Japan, teacher of English, 1965-67; Asahi Shimbun, New York, NY, interpreter of Japanese, 1969; *Baltimore Sun,* Baltimore, MD, reporter, 1970. Editor of *Woods Hole Passage*; member of Woods Hole Community Association (trustee). Illustrator and consultant for UNICEF, Johns Hopkins Center for Medical Research and Training, and Harvard Institute for International Development.

AWARDS, HONORS: Notable book award, American Library Association, 1977, for *Wiley and the Hairy Man,* and 1980, for *The Grey Lady and the Strawberry Snatcher; Boston Globe/Horn Book* honor award for illustration, 1980, for *The Grey Lady and the Strawberry Snatcher,* 1984, for *Dawn,* and 1986, for *The Paper Crane;* Caldecott Honor Book awards, 1981, for *The Grey Lady and the Strawberry Snatcher,* 1983, for *Ten, Nine, Eight,* and 2000, for *When Sophie Gets Angry—Really, Really Angry;* Kate Greenaway honor, Library Association, 1983; Hans Christian Andersen Award nomination, 1988, for *The Paper Crane;* Charlotte Zolotow Award, 2000, for *When Sophie Gets Angry—Really, Really Angry;* nominee (with Monika Bang-Campbell), *Boston Globe-Horn Book* Award in picture book category, 2002, for *Little Rat Sets Sail;* Giverny Book Award for best children's science picture book, for *Common Ground: The Water, Earth, and Air We Share.*

WRITINGS:

FOR CHILDREN; ALL SELF-ILLUSTRATED

(Compiler) *The Goblins Giggle, and Other Stories* (folk tales), Scribner (New York, NY), 1973.
(As Garrett Bang; translator and compiler) *Men from the Village Deep in the Mountains, and Other Japanese Folktales,* Macmillan (New York, NY), 1973.
(Adaptor) *Wiley and the Hairy Man* (folktale), Macmillan (New York, NY), 1976.
(Editor) *The Buried Moon and Other Stories* (tales from China, Japan, England, and India), Scribner (New York, NY), 1977.
The Grey Lady and the Strawberry Snatcher, Four Winds Press (New York, NY), 1980.
(Adaptor) *Tye May and the Magic Brush* (Chinese folktale), Greenwillow (New York, NY), 1981.
Ten, Nine, Eight, Greenwillow (New York, NY), 1983.
(Adaptor) *Dawn* (Japanese folktale), Morrow (New York, NY), 1983.
(Adaptor) *The Paper Crane* (Chinese folktale), Greenwillow (New York, NY), 1985.
Delphine, Morrow (New York, NY), 1988.
Picture This: Perception and Composition, foreword by Rudolf Arnheim, Little, Brown (New York, NY), 1991.
Yellow Ball, Morrow (New York, NY), 1991.
One Fall Day, Greenwillow (New York, NY), 1994.
Sunshine's Book, Greenwillow (New York, NY), 1994.
Chattanooga Sludge, Harcourt (New York, NY), 1996.
Goose, Blue Sky Press (New York, NY), 1996.

Common Ground: The Water, Earth, and Air We Share, Blue Sky Press (New York, NY), 1997.

When Sophie Gets Angry—Really, Really Angry, Blue Sky Press (New York, NY), 1999.

Picture This: How Pictures Work, SeaStar Books (New York, NY), 2000.

(Coauthor) *Nobody Particular: One Woman's Fight to Save the Bays,* Henry Holt (New York, NY), 2000.

Line in the Water, Henry Holt (New York, NY), 2000.

Tiger's Fall, Henry Holt (New York, NY), 2001.

My Light, Blue Sky Press (New York, NY), 2004.

ILLUSTRATOR

Betsy Bang, translator and editor, *The Old Woman and the Red Pumpkin: A Bengali Folktale,* Macmillan (New York, NY), 1975.

Betsy Bang, translator and editor, *The Old Woman and the Rice Thief,* Morrow (New York, NY), 1978.

Betsy Bang, translator and editor, *Tuntuni, the Tailor Bird,* Greenwillow (New York, NY), 1978.

Betsy Bang, translator and editor, *The Demons of Rajpur,* Greenwillow (New York, NY), 1980.

Judith Benet Richardson, *David's Landing,* Woods Hole Historical Collection (Woods Hole, MA), 1984.

Sylvia Cassedy and Suetake Kunihirs, translators, *Red Dragonfly on My Shoulder* (haiku), Harper (New York, NY), 1992.

(With others) Amy Cohn, editor, *From Sea to Shining Sea: A Treasury of American Folklore and Folk Songs,* Scholastic (New York, NY), 1993.

Robert and Warren Heydenberk, *When I Get Angry,* Blue Sky Press (New York, NY), 1999.

Star Livingstone, *Harley,* SeaStar Books (New York, NY), 2001.

Monika Bang-Campbell, *Little Rat Sets Sail,* Harcourt (New York, NY), 2002.

Monika Bang-Campbell, *Little Rat Rides,* Harcourt (New York, NY), 2004.

SIDELIGHTS: Author and illustrator Molly Garrett Bang is noted for bringing an international flavor to her sometimes humorous, sometimes poignant retellings of folktales from many lands that are replanted in modern times. A world traveler—she lived for a time in Japan, India, and Mali, and is fluent in Japanese—Bang is interested in a wide variety of cultures, prompting her to gather stories and legends containing universally understood messages and, often with the professional help of her mother, translator Betsy Bang, adapt them for a U.S. audience. Bang has also written and published a number of her own stories; among these award-winning self-illustrated children's books are *The Grey Lady and the Strawberry Snatcher* and *Ten, Nine, Eight,* the latter published in 1983.

A story without words, *The Grey Lady and the Strawberry Snatcher* depicts an elderly black woman who is chased through a swamp by a scary, goblin-like being swathed in a flowing green cape who desires the strawberries the old woman has in her possession. "The skillfully executed, impressionistic illustrations, so full of meticulous, often startling details, offer an exciting visual treat to . . . readers," wrote Patricia Jean Cianciolo in *Picture Books for Children. Ten, Nine, Eight* is a counting book for bedtime that critics found unusual at the time of its publication because Bang depicted both the young girl preparing to go to bed and her father as non-Caucasian. Noting that the "simplicity" of Bang's illustrations adds to the meaning of the text, *School Library Journal* reviewer Sharon McElmeel called *Ten, Nine, Eight* "a delightfully satisfying book."

Among the folktales and legends collected by Bang is *Wiley and the Hairy Man,* which has its roots in the U.S. South, as a boy and his mother attempt to outwit a scary creature known only as the Hairy Man. Oriental traditions are reflected in Bang's writings from 1985, *The Paper Crane, Tye May and the Magic Brush,* and *Men from the Village Deep in the Mountains, and Other Japanese Folktales.* Stories from France, China, Japan, Ireland, and Germany are collected in *The Goblins Giggle, and Other Stories.* Reviewing *The Paper Crane* for *Horn Book,* contributor Hanna B. Zeiger noted, "In a world in which we use the word *gentle* to describe everything from laxatives to scouring powder, Molly Bang has restored dignity to the word with her truly gentle tale. . . .The book successfully blends Asian folklore themes with contemporary Western characterization."

Nobody Particular tells the story of shrimper Diane Wilson, who waged a single-handed fight to stop pollution of the East Texas bays where she and her family fished for a living. Bang notes in the book's introduction that she wrote the book because she wanted to present stories about people who make a difference in the world, and Wilson fit that category. As Linc Bedrosian wrote in *National Fisherman,* the book is inspiring: "You might think you're nobody in particular, but Wilson's story demonstrates that one person does have the power to make a particularly great difference."

Common Ground and *Chattanooga Sludge* express Bang's concern for the environment. *Common Ground* shows how the activities of a simple farming village affect the land, through increased livestock grazing, overpopulation, and poor land use. Bang makes clear that polluting the land and then leaving it to continue polluting somewhere else is not the answer, as land and wildlife are limited resources that cannot be replaced when they are gone. *Chattanooga Sludge* recounts the true story of John Todd, a scientist who worked to clean up one of the most polluted waterways in the United States, using natural cleansers such as toxin-eating bacteria and green plants. He was only partially successful, showing that pollution is easier to create than to remove.

Bang is also an advocate for literacy and for poor children having more access to books. She once commented, "If [children] only have flimsy paperbacks, they never experience the feel of a real book. Because they are less available to people who are poor, books become less relevant. In the midst of all this self-congratulation we have to think about that."

BIOGRAPHICAL AND CRITICAL SOURCES:

BOOKS

Children's Literature Review, Volume 8, Gale (Detroit, MI), 1985.

Cianciolo, Patricia Jean, *Picture Books for Children,* American Library Association (New York, NY), 1981.

St. James Guide to Children's Writers, 5th edition, St. James Press (Detroit, MI), 1999.

Silvey, Anita, editor, *Children's Books and Their Creators,* Houghton Mifflin (New York, NY), 1995.

PERIODICALS

Booklist, May 1, 1996, Carolyn Phelan, review of *Chattanooga Sludge,* p. 1500; September 15, 1996, Hazel Rochman, review of *Goose,* p. 239; October 1, 1997, Susan Dove Lempke, review of *Common Ground: The Water, Earth, and Air We Share,* p. 330; February 1, 1999, Stephanie Zvirin, review of *When Sophie Gets Angry—Really, Really Angry,* p. 978; February 1, 2001, Michael Cart, review of *Nobody Particular: One Woman's Fight to Save the Bays,* p. 1050; November 1, 2001, Hazel Rochman, review of *Tiger's Fall,* p. 474; April 1, 2002, Kathy Broderick, review of *Little Rat Sets Sail,* p. 1326.

Childhood Education, Doris Burkhart, review of *Harley,* p. 172.

Horn Book, January, 1986, p. 45; September-October, 1988, p. 612; June, 1981, p. 295; July-August, 1992, p. 462; January-February, 1995, Lolly Robinson, review of *One Fall Day,* p. 47; November-December, 1997, Ellen Fader, review of *Common Ground,* p. 692; January, 2001, review of *Nobody Particular,* p. 106; July, 2001, review of *Harley,* p. 456.

Kirkus Reviews, September 15, 2001, review of *Tiger's Fall,* p. 1352; February 1, 2002, review of *Little Rat Sets Sail,* p. 176.

National Fisherman, May, 2002, Linc Bedrosian, review of *Nobody Particular,* p. 9.

New York Times Book Review, May 3, 1992, p. 31.

Publishers Weekly, June 24, 1988, p. 110; March 22, 1991, p. 79; August 8, 1994, p. 428; April 22, 1996, review of *Chattanooga Sludge,* p. 72; October 28, 1996, review of *Goose,* p. 80; September 22, 1997, review of *Common Ground,* p. 81; January 1, 1999, p. 337; January 18, 1999, review of *When Sophie Gets Angry—Really, Really Angry,* p. 337; December 11, 2000, review of *Nobody Particular,* p. 86; February 26, 2001, review of *Harley,* p. 87; January 7, 2002, p. 65; July 15, 2002, review of *Little Rat Sets Sail,* p. 75.

School Arts, December, 2000, Kent Anderson, review of *Picture This: How Pictures Work,* p. 56.

School Library Journal, May, 1983, p. 56; October, 1994, Joy Fleishhacker, review of *One Fall Day,* p. 85; August, 1996, Melissa Hudak, review of *Chattanooga Sludge,* p. 148; November, 1996, Jane Claes, review of *Goose,* p. 76; October, 1997, Margaret Bush, review of *Common Ground,* p. 88; January, 1999, Marianne Saccardi, review of *When Sophie Gets Angry—Really, Really Angry,* p. 79; January, 2001, Kathy Piehl, review of *Nobody Particular,* p. 138; July, 2000, Ginny Harrell, review of *Wiley and the Hairy Man,* p. 55; June, 2001, Kathleen Kelly MacMillan, review of *Harley,* p. 125; December, 2001, Caroline Ward, review of *Tiger's Fall,* p. 132; June, 2002, Lynda S. Poling, review of *Little Rat Sets Sail,* p. 80.

Washington Post Book World, October 9, 1983, pp. 10-11.

Whole Earth, spring, 1998, review of *Chattanooga Sludge,* p. 11.*

* * *

BARAHENI, Reza 1935-

PERSONAL: Born April 7, 1935, in Tabriz, Iran; immigrated to the United States, 1974; son of Mohammad-Taghi (a worker) and Zahrasoltan (Shokoohetaze) Baraheni; married Angela Marangozidi, 1959 (divorced, June 22, 1966); married Sanaz Sihhati (a teacher), September 24, 1971; children: Aleca, Oktay-Mohammad. *Education:* University of Tabriz, B.A., 1957; University of Istanbul, Ph.D., 1960. *Religion:* "Born to a Moslem family."

ADDRESSES: Office—Centre for Comparative Literature, Isabel Bader Theatre, University of Toronto, 93 Charles St. W, 3rd Floor, Toronto, Ontario M5S 1K9, Canada; fax: 905-787-1367. *E-mail*—baraheni@yahoo.com.

CAREER: University of Tehran, Tehran, Iran, lecturer, 1961-62, assistant professor, 1964-68, associate professor of English literature, 1968-74, dean of students, 1965-68, department chair for correspondence faculty, 1974; University of Iowa, Iowa City, poet in residence for International Writing Program, 1974; Indiana University—Bloomington, visiting professor of creative writing, 1975; Bard College, Annandale-on-Hudson, NY, associate professor of English, 1977; University of Maryland—Baltimore, professor of creative writing, 1977-79; University of Tehran, professor of English and comparative literature, 1979-82; Fiction and Poetry Workshop, Tehran, director and instructor, 1983-96; University of Toronto, Toronto, Ontario, Canada, visiting instructor, 1997, writer in exile at Massey College, 1997-98, visiting professor of English, 1998-99, visiting professor at Centre for Comparative Literature, 1998—. American University in Cairo, distinguished visiting professor, 1971; University of Texas—Austin, visiting associate professor, 1972; University of Utah, visiting associate professor, 1973; Oxford University, Persian fellow at St. Antony's College, 1992. Lecturer in Iran and the United States; has given poetry readings and appeared at writers' festivals; guest on media programs in the United States and abroad, including the *Today Show* and the *David Susskind Show.* Committee for Artistic and Intellectual Freedom in Iran (honorary cochair, 1975-79); member of Council of Latin American Human Rights and Mustafa Zjemilev Committee. *Military service:* Iranian Army, 1960-62.

MEMBER: International PEN (president of Canadian branch, 2001).

AWARDS, HONORS: Overseas Press Club of America Award, 1977, for international reporting in any medium that demonstrates a concern for humanity; Scholars at Risk Program Award, University of Toronto, 2000; award from International Freedom to Publish Committee, Association of American Publishers, 2000.

WRITINGS:

IN ENGLISH

Play No Play (one-act play), first produced in Salt Lake City, UT, at Salt Lake City Public Auditorium, 1973.

Zillulah, Abjad Publications (New York, NY), 1975, translation by the author published as *God's Shadow: Prison Poems,* Indiana University Press (Bloomington, IN), 1976.

The Crowned Cannibals: Writings on Repression in Iran, introduction by E. L. Doctorow, Vintage (New York, NY), 1977.

TRANSLATOR INTO PERSIAN

William Shakespeare, *Richard III,* Amir Kabir (Tehran, Iran), 1963.

Ivo Andric, *The Bridge over Drina,* Franklin Pocket Books, 1963, 3rd edition, Nil Publications (Tehran, Iran), 1977.

Maxim Rodinson, *Israel and the Arabs,* Kharazmi Publications (Tehran, Iran), 1969, 3rd edition, 1973.

David Caute, *Franz Fanon,* Kharazmi Publications (Tehran, Iran), 1973.

OTHER

Khayyam and Fitzgerald within the Framework of the Victorian Era, University of Istanbul Publications (Istanbul, Turkey), 1960.

Ahovan-e bagh (poetry; title means "The Deer of the Garden"), Bamdad (Tehran, Iran), 1962.

Jangal-o-shahr (poem; title means "The Jungle and the City"), Bamdad (Tehran, Iran), 1963.

Shabi az nimrooz (poetry; title means "Night—Starting from Midday"), Bamdad (Tehran, Iran), 1965.

Tala dar mes (criticism; title means "Gold in Copper"), Chehr House (Tehran, Iran), 1965, 2nd edition, Zaman (Tehran, Iran), 1970.

Quesseh-nevisi (title means "The Writing and Theory of Fiction"), Ashraf Publications (Tehran, Iran), 1965.

Mosibati zir-e afetab (poetry and prose; title means "An Evil under the Sun"), Amir Kabir Publications (Tehran, Iran), 1970.

Gol bar gostare-ye mah (poetry; title means "A Flower upon Moon—Moonflower"), Zaman (Tehran, Iran), 1970.

Roozegar-e doozakhi-ye agha-ye Ayyaz (novel, first volume of a trilogy; title means "The Infernal Life of Aqa-ye Ayyaz"), Amirkabir Publications (Tehran, Iran), 1971.

Safar-e Mesr (title means "Journey into Egypt"), Pindar (Tehran, Iran), 1972.

Tarikh-e mozakkar: Resale-i piramoon-e tashattot-e farhang dar Iran (title means "Masculine History: A Manifesto on the Causes of Cultural Disintegration in Iran"), Pindar (Tehran, Iran), 1973.

Jonoone neveshtan (title means "The Insanity of Writing"), Iranmehr (Tehran, Iran), 1973.

Do baradar akhar-e khat dar yek khat (novel; title means "Two Brothers on the Same Line at the End"), Neguin (Tehran, Iran), 1974.

Chah be chah (novel; title means "From One Well to Another"), Nashr-i Naw (New York, NY), 1976.

Persia sin Mascara, Editorial Argos Vergara (Barcelona, Spain), 1978.

Dar inqil-ab-i Iran chih shudah ast va chih khv-ahad shud, Kit-ab-i Zam-an (Tehran, Iran), 1979.

What Happened after the Wedding (novel), Nashr-i Naw (Tehran, Iran), 1983.

Av-az-i kushtig-an, Nashr-i Naw (Tehran, Iran), 1983.

Our Grand Griefs: Requiems (poetry), Avval Publications (Tehran, Iran), 1983.

The Song of the Slain (novel), Nashr-i Naw (Tehran, Iran), 1983.

Gham'h-a-yi buzurg-i m-a: Mar-a-s-i, Nashr-i Naw (Tehran, Iran), 1984.

Esmael (poem), Nashr-i Murgh-i Am-in (Tehran, Iran), 1984.

Alchemy and Dust (criticism), Nashr-i Murgh-i Am-in (Tehran, Iran), 1985.

Hunar va adab-iy-at-i imr-uz, Kit-absar-a-yi B-abil (Tehran, Iran), 1986.

Ism-a-il: Yak shi r-i buland, Nashr-i Murgh-i Am-in (Tehran, Iran), 1987.

R-az'h-a-yi sarzam-in-i m-an, Nashr-i Murgh-i Am-in (Tehran, Iran), 1987.

Come to the Window (poetry), Nashr-i Murgh-i Am-in (Tehran, Iran), 1987.

Jun-un-i nivishtan, Shirkat-i Intish-ar-at-i-i Rass-am (Tehran, Iran), 1988.

The Mysteries of My Land, two volumes, Moghan Press (Tehran, Iran), 1988.

The Insanity of Writing, Rassam Publications (Tehran, Iran), 1989.

Y-ar khvush ch-iz-i ast: Shir'h-a-yi taghazzul-i, 1336-68, Shirkat-i Nashr va Pakhsh-i Vays (Tehran, Iran), 1990.

The Loved One, a Miracle: Selected Lyrical Poems, 1957-1989, Veys Publications (Tehran, Iran), 1990.

Tal-a dar mis, R. Bar-ahin-i, (Tehran, Iran), 1992.

Khit-ab bih parv-anah'h-a (shir), v Chir-a man d-igar sh-a 'ir-i N-im-a-i n-istam (bah-s-i dar sh-air-i) (poetry; title means "Accosting the Butterflies"), Nashr-i Markaz (Tehran, Iran), 1995.

Buhr-an-i rahbar-i-i naqd-i adab-i, Intish-ar-at-i V-ist-ar, (Tehran, Iran), 1996.

Scheherazade and Dr. Sharifie's Private Auschwitz (Our Lady of Scribes) (novel), Baran Publications (Stockholm, Sweden), 1996.

Leadership Crisis of Literary Criticism in Iran, Vistar Publications (Tehran, Iran), 1996.

The Autobiography of Reza Baraheni, Iranian Society of Sweden (Sweden), 1996.

The Vigilant Vision (nonfiction), Qatreh Publications (Tehran, Iran), 1997.

Report to Tomorrow's Ageless Generation (essays), Markaz Publications (Tehran, Iran), 1998.

Persona non Grata (poetry), [Stockholm, Sweden], 1998.

Les Saisons en enfer du jeune Ayyaz (novel), Pauvert/Fayard (Paris, France), 2000.

(With others) *Making Meaning,* Art Gallery of Ontario (Toronto, Canada), 2000.

Work represented in anthologies, including *City Lights Anthology,* edited by Lawrence Ferlinghetti, City

Lights (San Francisco, CA), 1974; *New Writings from the Middle East,* New American Library (New York, NY), 1978; *Voices of Conscience: Poetry from Oppression,* edited by Hume Cronyn, Richard McKane, and Stephen Watts, Iron Press (London, England), 1995; *This Prison Where I Live: The PEN Anthology of Imprisoned Writers,* edited by Siobhan Dowd, Cassell (London, England, 1996; and *Literatures of Asia, Africa, and Latin America,* edited by Willis Barnstone and Tony Barnstone, Prentice-Hall (Tappan, NJ), 1999. Contributor of more than a hundred articles, poems, and translations to scholarly journals and popular magazines, including *Penthouse, Iowa Review,* and *American Poetry Review.*

Some of Baraheni's full-length manuscripts were published serially in Iranian periodicals. Editor-in-chief of *Jahane No* (title means "Modern World"), 1966; literary editor of *Ferdowsi,* 1964-70.

Baraheni's works have been published in Arabic, Armenian, French, German, Polish, Russian, Spanish, and Turkish.

SIDELIGHTS: The writer as witness may have emerged as one of the most characteristic artists of the twentieth century, and Reza Baraheni, a well-known writer and chronicler of tortures in Iran, is among the most important, according to E. L. Doctorow, writing in *Harper's.*

Some critics believe that politics makes bad art; some subscribe to the aesthetic dogma that denies the writer any other function than to place words in pleasing patterns. For the writer-witnesses, such as Baraheni, Doctorow found that the major problem is "how to communicate to those who insulate themselves in literature the terrible inadequacy of aesthetic criteria as applied to human suffering." Baraheni may have resolved this problem, since critics report that his works are successful both aesthetically and as eloquent statements of the human condition.

Baraheni's chronicles may be of special interest to Americans, for they are involved, indirectly or directly, in the support of a repressive Iranian government. *New York Times* contributor John Leonard said of Baraheni's writing: "And if his documentation of SAVAK terror, his prison memoirs, his compendium of tortures—names, dates, devices, sound familiar, we ought to remind ourselves that the Gulag seems to be the preeminent form of modern architecture, a franchise built of human bones, and that in this case, with the Shah, we are responsible."

Baraheni once told *CA*: "Since 1974, I have appealed directly to the American public and through them to the world at large. I have spoken and read my poetry and prose on more than fifty American campuses and talked to the people on almost all the major news media. My aims have been: first, to expose the Shah's dictatorial regime and the U.S. government's complicity with that regime; second, to force the Shah to open his jails and release all the political prisoners of Iran and to let the people take their own destiny in their own hands; next, to prevent the Shah, the Pentagon, and the Central Intelligence Agency (CIA) from arming our people to the teeth through the help of multinational corporations, and to allow our people to use their natural wealth the way they see fit; fourth, to force the Shah to stop harassing Iranian dissidents and students in the United States and to force SAVAK (the Iranian secret police) out of this country; and finally, to stop the Shah from extending his dictatorship to American universities through his attempts to bribe the academic community here.

"Since 1953, Americans have been directly responsible for the dictatorship in Iran. The legally elected government of Dr. Mohammad Mossadeq was overthrown by the CIA in that year and the Shah who had run away earlier was brought back and reinstalled on the throne. The American-trained SAVAK came to existence in 1957. The number of Americans in Iran is estimated at 30,000, with most of them involved in the training of the army, the police and the gendarmerie, or acting as representatives and employees of American corporations.

"Americans should ask their government to open the files of the CIA, the Federal Bureau of Investigation, and the State Department on Iran. They should force their government to stop selling arms to the Shah, and to stop supporting his dictatorial rule. Public opinion in the United States should openly voice its opposition to the President's silence on the miserable situations of human rights in Iran.

"The people of Iran have come to the realization that they, and only they, should decide what form of government they want for their future. Whatever the form of that government, it will not be genuine unless the underprivileged majority of the people have the representation they rightly deserve. I can imagine that representation being achieved before we are through with the last decade of this century."

In a discussion of his literary influences, Baraheni wrote: "If I hadn't read the works of Rumi, the great Iranian poet, I wouldn't have known the meaning of poetry. My learning from the West taught me how to rationalize about the irrational (hence, my literary criticism). I have learned from Marx, Lenin, and Trotsky, as well as many others who were not revolutionaries socially: Proust, Joyce, Mann, Yeats, and Charles Olson. But at heart I am deeply rooted in the culture of the Middle East. My knowledge of Persian, Turkish, and Arabic, as well as French and English, is my window to the world."

Baraheni, who is considered by some to be the founder of modern literary criticism in Iran, was imprisoned and tortured by Iranian secret police for 102 days in 1973. His release was due to public pressure generated by the American branch of PEN, Amnesty International, and the Committee for Artistic and Intellectual Freedom in Iran.

BIOGRAPHICAL AND CRITICAL SOURCES:

BOOKS

Ferlinghetti, Lawrence, editor, *City Lights Anthology,* City Lights (San Francisco, CA), 1974.
Harriri, Nasser, *Contemporary Art and Literature* (interviews), Babolsar Publishing House (Babol, Iran), 1986.
Yar-Shater, Ehsan, *Iran Faces the Seventies,* Praeger (New York, NY), 1970.

PERIODICALS

Harper's, May, 1977, article by E. L. Doctorow.
Index on Censorship, spring, 1976.
New York Times, December 16, 1973; June 17, 1977, article by John Leonard; June 20, 1977.
Village Voice, March 3, 1975; February, 1976.
Washington Post, September 4, 1977, article by Richard Sale.

BARRETT, James Lee 1929-1989

PERSONAL: Born November 19, 1929, in Charlotte, NC; died of cancer, October 15, 1989, in Templeton, CA; son of James Hamlin and Anne (Blake) Barrett; married Merete Engelstoft, June, 1960; children: Jessica, Penelope, Birgette, Christian David. *Education:* Attended Anderson Junior College, Furman University, Pennsylvania State University, and Art Students League.

CAREER: Screenwriter, producer, and journalist. Television work includes series producer and executive consultant, *In the Heat of the Night,* 1988-94. Actor as Sonny Boy in film *Fools' Parade,* 1971. *Military service:* U.S. Marine Corps, 1950-52.

AWARDS, HONORS: Antoinette Perry Award for Book of a Musical, 1975, for *Shenandoah.*

WRITINGS:

SCREENPLAYS

The D.I. (also known as *The Drill Instructor*), Warner Bros., 1957.
The Truth about Spring (adapted from the novel *Satan* by Henry de Vere Stackpoole), Universal, 1964.
(With George Stevens) *The Greatest Story Ever Told,* United Artists, 1965.
Shenandoah, Universal, 1965.
Bandolero! (adapted from a story by Stanley L. Hough), Twentieth Century-Fox, 1968.
(With Kenneth B. Facey) *The Green Berets* (adapted from the novel by Robin Moore), Warner Bros., 1968.
The Undefeated, Twentieth Century-Fox, 1969.
(And producer) *. . . Tick . . . Tick . . . Tick,* Metro-Goldwyn-Mayer, 1970.
(And executive producer) *The Cheyenne Social Club,* National General Pictures, 1970.
(And producer) *Fools' Parade* (adapted from the novel by Davis Grubb), Columbia, 1971.
(And producer) *Something Big,* National General Pictures, 1971.
Smokey and the Bandit, Universal, 1977.
Wild Horse Hank (based on the novel *The Wild Horse Killers* by Melvin Richard Ellis), Vestron, 1979.

Also uncredited scriptwriter for *On the Beach,* produced in 1959.

TELEVISION SCREENPLAYS

The Awakening Land (miniseries), 1978.
Stubby Pringle's Christmas, 1978.
Mayflower: The Pilgrims' Adventure, 1979.
The Day Christ Died, 1980.
Belle Starr, 1980.
The Defiant Ones, 1986.
Stagecoach, 1986.
Vengeance: The Story of Tony Cimo, 1986.
The Quick and the Dead, 1987.
Poker Alice, 1987.
April Morning (based on the novel of the same name by Howard Fast), 1988.
Jesse, 1988.
Ruby Jean and Joe, 1996.
Warden of Red Rock, 2001.

Author of scripts for television series, including *Checkmate,* 1960, *Our House,* 1986-88, and *In the Heat of the Night,* 1988.

OTHER

(With Peter Udell and Philip Rose) *Shenadoah* (stage play; based on Barrett's screenplay), produced at Goodspeed Opera House, East Haddam, CT, 1975; produced on Broadway, 1975.

SIDELIGHTS: James Lee Barrett is remembered as the author of a number of screenplays for both motion pictures and television movies as well as two television series. His works include the popular western *Shenandoah,* starring James Stewart, and two John Wayne vehicles: the western *The Undefeated* and the war film *The Green Berets.* Also written by Barrett is the popular 1977 action comedy *Smokey and the Bandit,* which starred Burt Reynolds and Sally Field. In addition, Barrett penned the religious classic *The Greatest Story Ever Told,* which recounts the life, death, and resurrection of Jesus Christ.

In his work for television, Barrett recreated such historical events as the voyage of the Pilgrims to the New World and the taming of the West, and his scripts often provide female actresses with starring roles. He also portrayed racial tension between African Americans and whites in the series *In the Heat of the Night,* which ran for six years and for which he served as producer.

Barrett was born and raised in Charlotte, North Carolina. He served in the U.S. Marine Corps during the Korean War and soon afterward put his military experience to use in writing the screenplay for the motion picture *The D.I,* also known as *The Drill Instructor.* With the assistance of Colonel Kenneth B. Facey, Barrett also wrote the screenplay for the 1968 Vietnam War film *The Green Berets.*

Although he worked in several genres, Barrett returned most often to the western. His motion-picture screenplay *Bandolero!* deals with a brother rescuing another from a life of crime, and *The Undefeated* portrays former U.S. Civil War colonels from both the North and South resolving their differences in order to save their charges from Mexican bandits and revolutionaries in the Southwest. *The Cheyenne Social Club,* a western comedy starring James Stewart and Henry Fonda, follows the two cowboys as they take charge of a high-class brothel, which John (Stewart) has inherited from an uncle. *Wild Horse Hank,* based on the novel *Wild Horse Killers* by Melvin Richard Ellis, stars a teenage Linda Blair, who plays a young woman determined to drive a herd of wild horse to the safety of a refuge to prevent them from being captured and turned into dog food.

Perhaps Barrett's most enduring film, 1967's *Shenandoah* captures life in the post-Civil War South. James Stewart plays a farmer whose land is located in the middle of the Shenandoah Valley of Virginia. Although he tries to remain neutral during the war, he is forced into action when his youngest son is taken prisoner by Union forces. In 1975, ten years after its screen debut, Barrett joined several other writers in adapting *Shenandoah* as a stage musical of the same name. Produced in New York City, it won the Antoinette Perry Award for best book of a musical for that year, and was revived on Broadway in the mid-1980s.

Beginning in the mid-1970s Barrett became increasingly involved in writing for television, creating pilot episodes for series and screenplays for made-for-television movies while also working as a producer.

Several of these films were in the western genre, among them a remake of the John Ford film *Stagecoach,* which showcases the talents of country-and-western singers Johnny Cash, Kris Kristofferson, Willie Nelson, and Waylon Jennings, and *The Quick and the Dead,* based on Louis L'Amour's novel of the same name and starring Sam Elliott. Several of his westerns feature strong women heroines: In *Belle Starr* a female bandit has her way, while in *Poker Alice* a New England woman addicted to gambling wins a bordello in a poker game while traveling west by train with her brother.

Although Barrett wrote many westerns for television, he also created several works that focus on other periods in America's past. The 1978 television miniseries *The Awakening Land,* starring Hal Holbrook and Elizabeth Montgomery, revolves around a frontierswoman's struggle to settle in the Western Reserve Territory (now Ohio) during the early 1800s. The following year *Mayflower: The Pilgrim's Adventure* aired, chronicling the decisions and vicissitudes faced by the Pilgrims during their voyage to the New World. A decade later, Barrett adapted Howard Fast's *April Morning,* a juvenile novel about the American Revolutionary War, into a made-for-television movie of the same name.

In 1970 he wrote the motion picture screenplay . . . *Tick . . . Tick . . . Tick . . . ,* which focuses on racial tension between whites and African Americans by dealing with the repercussions caused when a black man is elected sheriff in a small southern town. Interestingly, Barrett would return to this topic when he proposed and produced the television series *In the Heat of the Night,* which portrays a crusty southern sheriff and his African-American lieutenant as they investigate crimes in their racially charged community. This series, starring Carroll O'Connor and Howard E. Rollins, Jr., frequently explored the causes of racial tension during its run from 1988 to 1994.

Barrett's last work to be aired before his death from cancer in 1989 was the legal drama *Jesse.* However, several of his screenplays have been produced since his death, among them the 1996 television film *Ruby Jean and Joe,* about an aging rodeo rider and a young female hitchhiker. Dedicated in Barrett's memory is his television movie *Warden of Red Rock.* In this historical film, set in Arizona at the turn of the twentieth century, prison warden John Flinders is surprised to find an old friend incarcerated and now under his supervision. When this friend escapes the prison, Flinders is forced to decided between friendship and duty.

In 1970, responding to a letter from a student and former neighbor, Barrett gave some advice about screenwriting. Along with counseling discipline and knowledge of a wide variety of fields of endeavor, he stressed becoming "accustomed to loneliness. Writing is the loneliest occupation there is," he wrote in the letter, which is posted on the University of South Carolina Manuscript Collection's Web site. "I am only the middle man between my characters and the paper they come to life on," he continued. "I don't know from one second to the next what a character is going to say or do. I keep them within certain bounds because I know where they have to go. I like for my characters to entertain me. If the characters and their story entertain me, my ego is sufficient to allow me to believe they will entertain others as well." In many instances, Barrett's judgment proved to be correct, for his films continue to entertain movie viewers thanks to the wide distribution of classic films on videotape.

BIOGRAPHICAL AND CRITICAL SOURCES:

PERIODICALS

Christian Science Monitor, August 15, 1989, John Beaufort, review of *Shenandoah,* p. 10.
New York, August 21, 1989, John Simon, review of *Shendoah,* pp. 134-135.
New York Times, September 11, 1986, p. C25.
Variety, May 30, 1984, review of *You Are the Jury,* p. 38; May 21, 1986, review of *Stagecoach,* p. 80; June 3, 1987, review of *Poker Alice,* p. 86; May 4, 1988, review of *April Morning,* pp. 534-535.

ONLINE

University of South Caroline Manuscript Collections, http://www.sc.edu/ (August 9, 2003), "James Lee Barrett Letter, February 1970, Los Angeles, CA, to Miss Becky Stuart."

OBITUARIES:

PERIODICALS

Variety, October 25, 1989, p. 83.*

BASTIANICH, Lidia Matticchio 1947-

Lidia Matticchio Bastianich

PERSONAL: Born February 21, 1947, in Pula, Italy; naturalized U.S. citizen; daughter of Vittorio (a mechanic) and Erminia (a schoolteacher; maiden name, Motika) Matticchio; married Felice Bastianich (divorced, 1998); children: Joseph, Tanya Bastianich Manual. *Ethnicity:* "Italian." *Education:* Attended Hunter College and Queens College, both of the City University of New York. *Hobbies and other interests:* Gardening, singing.

ADDRESSES: *Office*—Felidia Restaurant, 243 East 58th St., New York, NY 10022; fax 212-935-7687. *Agent*—Jane Dystel, Jane Dystel Literary Management, 1 Union Sq. W, New York, NY 10003. *E-mail*—lidia@lidiasitaly.com.

CAREER: Chef and cook-book author. Buonavia Restaurant, Forest Hills, NY, owner, 1972-81; Felidia Restaurant, New York, NY, owner, 1981—. Villa Secondo, Fresh Meadows, NY, owner, 1979-81; Becco Restaurant, New York, NY, co-owner, 1993—; Frico Bar and Restaurant, co-owner, 1995—; Lidia's Kansas City, Kansas City, MO, co-owner, 1998—; Lidia's Pittsburgh, Pittsburgh, PA, co-owner, 2001—; Lidia's Flavors of Italy, partner. Esperienze Italian Travel, president, 1997—. Host of Public Broadcasting Service (PBS) television shows *Lidia's Italian-American Kitchen* and *Lidia's Italian Table.* Guest on television programs, including guest chef for *Julia Child's Cooking with Master Chefs,* PBS, 1994. UNICEF, chairperson of Roman Holidays fund-raising benefit, 1991, member of advisory board, 1994, cochairperson of Celebration of Women charity event, 1998, and member of New York metropolitan committee. Founder of nonprofit Lidia Matticchio Bastianich Foundation, 1999.

MEMBER: International Italian Guild of Professional Restaurateurs, Distinguished Restaurants of North America, American Academy in Rome, American Institute of Wine and Food, Culinary Institute of America, National Organization of Italian-American Women, James Beard Foundation, Women Chefs and Restaurateurs (cofounder; member of board of directors, 1997), Dames d'Escoffier, Caterina de Medici Society, New York State Restaurant Association.

AWARDS, HONORS: Best Pasta in America Award, National Pasta Association, 1986; Innovation Award and named woman of the year in restaurant category, Women's Institute of the Center for Food and Hotel Management, 1987; Grand Award, Restaurant Wine List, 1988; Emmy Award nomination, Academy of Television Arts and Sciences, 1994, for *Julia Child's Cooking with Master Chefs;* Felidia Restaurant listed among Top Ten Italian Restaurants, *Wine Spectator,* 1997; Mayor Vincent A. Cianci, Jr. Award, 1998; award from New York Association of Cooking Teachers, 1998; named America's best chef, James Beard Foundation, 2002.

WRITINGS:

(With Jay Jacobson) *La Cucina di Lidia: Distinctive Regional Cuisine from the North of Italy,* Doubleday (New York, NY), 1990, published as *La Cucina di Lidia: Recipes and Memories from Italy's Adriatic Coast,* Broadway Books (New York, NY), 2003.

Lidia's Italian Table: More Than 200 Recipes from the First Lady of Italian Cooking, Morrow (New York, NY), 1998.

Lidia's Italian-American Kitchen, Knopf (New York, NY), 2001.

(With Mario Batali) *Vino Italiano: The Regional Wines of Italy,* Clarkson-Potter (New York, NY), 2002.

Editor of column "A Celebration of Life," in *New York Times Magazine,* 1991-98.

WORK IN PROGRESS: Lidia's Italian Table with Friends and Family.

SIDELIGHTS: Lidia Matticchio Bastianich was born in Italy and spent her early years there, coming to the United States with her family when she was twelve years old. Her formative years gave her rich memories of her grandparents' restaurant, where most of the food they prepared was also grown on their farm; they also produced their own oil, wine, and cured meats. As an adolescent Bastianich learned more about cooking by putting dinner on her family's table while her parents worked. By the age of twenty-four she had opened her first restaurant in Queens, New York; another opened nearby a few years later.

In 1981 Bastianich broke into the stylish Manhattan restaurant scene with Felidia, where her traditional Italian cuisine was a resounding success. Other restaurants followed, including another in New York City, one in Pittsburgh, and another in Kansas City. Bastianich's fame was spread further by her two PBS television shows, *Lidia's Italian-American Kitchen* and *Lidia's Italian Table.* She has also diversified her food business to include prepared sauces.

Bastianich's books include recipes and her personal thoughts and memories. She is both "a beguiling storyteller and a no-nonsense guide," concluded a *Publishers Weekly* reviewer after reading *Lidia's Italian-American Kitchen.* Despite the title, which may suggest that the book includes typical restaurant-style dishes, the cuisine featured in the book is mostly classic Italian. Reviewing *Lidia's Italian Table: More Than 200 Recipes from the First Lady of Italian Cooking,* Mark Knoblauch predicted in his *Booklist* review that the simplicity of the recipes and the popularity of Italian food will bring "a wide audience of enthusiastic followers" to this book.

Bastianich once told *CA:* "Through the years I have collected a multitude of information on the culture of Italian cuisine, and writing is a way for me to record and maintain my Italian heritage. I feel this need to record my life experiences for myself and my family, and then to share the record with the interested public. My work is influenced by M. K. Fisher, James Beard, Marcella Hazan, Julia Child, and Anna Gossetti. Dumas and Jane Davidson are also authors whose work I admire and enjoy. For me, to share a recipe is to share history and culture. Food is life and must be shared among people, not just in recipes. I continuously collect recipes, through my work, restaurants and cooking, my travels and friends, both familial and professional. I add cultural, scientific, and personal experiences in a narrative form to the list of recipes and techniques. In the narrative, my passion and sentiments for the subject flow freely."

BIOGRAPHICAL AND CRITICAL SOURCES:

PERIODICALS

Booklist, July, 1998, Mark Knoblauch, review of *Lidia's Italian Table: More Than 200 Recipes from the First Lady of Italian Cooking,* p. 1846; November 15, 2001, Mark Knoblauch, review of *Lidia's Italian-American Kitchen,* p. 534.

Library Journal, October 15, 2001, Judith C. Sutton, review of *Lidia's Italian-American Kitchen,* p. 102.

People, June 17, 2002, Mike Neill, "Now That's Italian: Top Chef Lidia Bastianich Invites the World inside Her Grandmother's Kitchen," p. 131.

Publishers Weekly, July 20, 1998, review of *Lidia's Italian Table,* p. 213; October 1, 2001, review of *Lidia's Italian-American Kitchen,* p. 53, Natalie Danford, interview with Bastianich, p. 55.

Restaurant Business, July 15, 1998, Elizabeth Bernstein, "Westward, Ho!," p. 41.

ONLINE

Lidia's Italy, http://www.lidiasitaly.com/ (January 19, 2004).*

* * *

BERNARD, Jami 1956-

PERSONAL: Born August 10, 1956, in New York, NY; daughter of Sam and Gloria (Weiss) Bernard. *Education:* Columbia University, B.A., 1978.

ADDRESSES: Office—c/o *New York Post,* 450 West 33rd St., New York, NY 10001. *E-mail*—jamiebern@aol.com.

CAREER: Journalist, reviewer, and author. *New York Post,* New York, NY, reporter, columnist, and editor, 1978-94, assistant entertainment editor, 1985-87, film critic, 1986-94; *New York Daily News,* New York, NY, film critic, 1994—. Judge for film festivals. Frequent guest on national television and radio programs.

MEMBER: New York Film Critics Circle (chair, 1991), National Society of Film Critics.

AWARDS, HONORS: Pulitzer Prize nomination, 1991.

WRITINGS:

Bantam's Caribbean, Bantam (New York, NY), 1991.
First Films: Illustrious, Obscure, and Embarrassing Movie Debuts, Citadel (Secaucus, NJ), 1993.
Total Exposure: The Movie Buff's Guide to Celebrity Nude Scenes, Citadel (Secaucus, NJ), 1995, revised and updated edition, Carol Publishing Group (Secaucus, NJ), 1999.
Quentin Tarantino: The Man and His Movies, HarperCollins (New York, NY), 1995.
Chick Flicks: A Movie Lover's Guide to the Movies Women Love, Carol Publishing Group (Secaucus, NJ), 1996.
Breast Cancer, There and Back: A Woman-to-Woman Guide, Warner Books (New York, NY), 2001.

Contributor of film reviews to periodicals, including *Video Review* and *Video* magazine.

SIDELIGHTS: Jami Bernard's *First Films: Illustrious, Obscure, and Embarrassing Movie Debuts* explores the screen debuts of over one hundred well-known actors and directors, including Sylvester Stallone, Whoopi Goldberg, William Shatner, Sharon Stone, Kevin Costner, and Julia Roberts. Bernard discusses each personality and his or her subsequent career development, generally with quotes from each subject profiled. David C. Tucker remarked in *Library Journal* that "Bernard's research is generally excellent, and she writes with the infectious enthusiasm of the true buff."

In 1995 Bernard published a biography of actor/director/screenwriter Quentin Tarantino, who rose to fame following the release of his film *Pulp Fiction. Quentin Tarantino: The Man and His Movies,* is for the casual reader rather than the avid fact-seeker, according to Maria Simson in *Publishers Weekly.* Noting the abundance of biographical information, Simson characterized the book's details as ranging in value from "choice" to "numbing." The reviewer concluded that, despite her reservations about the actual importance of some of the material, Bernard's opus "does earn the inside track" on the popular director's work. Patrick Goldstein, a reviewer for the *Los Angeles Times,* called the book "evenhanded, observant, gracefully written and adorned with the most disarming anecdotes."

Bernard again writes about the film world in her 1997 publication *Chick Flicks: A Movie Lover's Guide to the Movies Women Love.* The author begins by stating the common notion that men prefer war dramas such as *The Dirty Dozen* while women derive emotional satisfaction from more emotion-driven dramas such as *An Affair to Remember.* Almost immediately, she makes clear that she does not really believe in such simplistic gender lines, but then goes on to lightheartedly explore dozens of films that qualify as "chick flicks," or movies with particular appeal for women. Recommending the book in the Newark *Star-Ledger,* Harry Haun commented, "The fun part in this book is watching Bernard stiltwalk her way through the genre without letting any of the inherent goo get on her. No mean achievement, that and further indication why she's the best film critic now at work in New York City newspapers, with fewer pretensions and less attitude than her peers. Who else would jump in there and address the market so frontally?"

Bernard further endeared herself to pop-culture mavens with *Total Exposure: The Movie Buff's Guide to Celebrity Nude Scenes,* which delivers exactly what its subtitle advertises: a beacon—to the exact digital counter location on a videotape—for locating celebrity skin in films. The book is arranged alphabetically by actor name, with each entry offering a list of films in which a thespian exposes him/herself and a brief description of the visible body parts.

In 1996 Bernard was diagnosed with breast cancer, and underwent surgical treatment, radiation, and chemotherapy during the course of her cure. Her book

Breast Cancer, There and Back: A Woman-to-Woman Guide is a practical guide to managing the troubling side effects often experienced during traditional cancer treatments, including irritated skin, hair loss, lethargy, and loss of appetite. Keeping a humorous tone, she discusses clothing, cosmetics and skin care, wig use, coping skills, and healthful eating. The wealth of information provided will be helpful in encouraging a sense of "staying in control of one's life," commented a *Publishers Weekly* reviewer. The book is also "knee-slapping, wet-your-pants funny," warned Bette-Lee Fox in *Library Journal,* concluding: "This is a terrific book, with solid information presented in a warm and very accessible manner."

BIOGRAPHICAL AND CRITICAL SOURCES:

PERIODICALS

Booklist, March 1, 1993, p. 1147.
Entertainment Weekly, July 16, 1993, p. 62.
Library Journal, March 1, 1993, p. 79; September 1, 2001, Bette-Lee Fox, review of *Breast Cancer, There and Back: A Woman-to-Woman Guide,* p. 222.
Los Angeles Times, February 25, 1996, Patrick Goldstein, review of *Quentin Tarantino: The Man and His Movies,* p. 5.
New York Times Book Review, March 3, 1996, p. 21.
Publishers Weekly, October 23, 1995, p. 61; September 3, 2001, review of *Breast Cancer, There and Back,* p. 75.
Star-Ledger (Newark, NJ), April 20, 1997, Harry Haun, review of *Chick Flicks: A Movie Lover's Guide to the Movies Women Love,* p. 7.
USA Today, June 3, 1993, p. 8D.*

* * *

BISHOP, Gavin 1946-

PERSONAL: Born February 13, 1946, in Invercargill, New Zealand; son of Stanley Alan (a railway employee) and Doris Hinepau (McKay) Bishop; married Vivien Carol Edwards (a teacher and artist), August 27, 1966; children: Cressida, Charlotte, Alexandra. *Ethnicity:* "I am of European and Maori extraction." *Education:* University of Canterbury (New Zealand), Diploma of Fine Arts (with honors), 1967; Christchurch Teachers' College, diploma (with distinction), 1968. *Politics:* Liberal. *Hobbies and other interests:* Reading, movies, gardening (in fits and starts), traveling, food.

ADDRESSES: *Home*—11 Cracroft Terrace, Christchurch 8002, New Zealand. *Agent*—Ann Tobias, 520 East 84th St., Suite 4L, New York, NY 10028. *E-mail*—gavinbishop@netaccess.co.nz.

CAREER: Illustrator, author, educator. Linwood High School, Christchurch, New Zealand, art teacher and department chair, 1969-89; Christ's College, Christchurch, New Zealand, head of art department, 1989-1999; Rhode Island School of Design, Providence, RI, professor, 1996. UNESCO children's literature workshop leader in China, 1992, and Indonesia, 1997; judge for Noma Concours, Tokyo, Japan, 2003. *Exhibitions:* Bratislava Biennale, 1985, Premi Catalonia D' Illustracio, 1986, 1988.

MEMBER: New Zealand Society of Authors (PEN New Zealand Inc.), New Zealand Illustrators' Guild, Christchurch Book Festival Trust.

AWARDS, HONORS: Russell Clark Medal for Illustration, New Zealand Library Association, 1982, for *Mrs. McGinty and the Bizarre Plant;* New Zealand Children's Picture Book of the Year, New Zealand Government Publishers and New Zealand Literary Fund, 1983, for *Mr. Fox;* Grand Prix, Noma Concours, UNESCO and Kodansha International, 1984, for illustrations in *Mr. Fox;* Russell Clark Medal for Illustration finalist, New Zealand Library Association, 1988, for *A Apple Pie,* and 1991, for *Katarina;* AIM Award for Children's Picture Book of the Year, 1994, for *Hinepau;* New Zealand *Post* Picture Book of the Year shortlist, 1997, for *Maui and the Sun: A Maori Tale,* 2000, for *The Video Shop Sparrow,* 2001, for *Stay Awake, Bear!,* and 2002, for *Tom Thumb: The True History of Sir Thomas Thumb;* New Zealand *Post* Picture Book of the Year, New Zealand Children's Book of the Year, and Spectrum Print Award, all 2000, all for *The House That Jack Built: Being the Account of Jack Bull, Esq., Who Sailed There from These Shores to a Land Far Away to Live There and Trade with the Natives of That Said Land Twelfth Day of*

September 1798; Margaret Mahy Lecture Award, New Zealand Book Council, 2000; New Zealand *Post* Children's Book of the Year Award, 2003, for *Weaving Earth and Sky: Myths and Legends of Aotearoa;* grant from the Arts Council of New Zealand.

WRITINGS:

FOR CHILDREN; SELF-ILLUSTRATED

Mrs. McGinty and the Bizarre Plant, Oxford University Press (Auckland, New Zealand), 1981.

Bidibidi, Oxford University Press (Auckland, New Zealand), 1982.

(Reteller) *Mr. Fox,* Oxford University Press (Auckland, New Zealand), 1982.

(Reteller) *Chicken Licken,* Oxford University Press (Auckland, New Zealand), 1984.

The Horror of Hickory Bay, Oxford University Press (Auckland, New Zealand), 1984.

(Reteller) *Mother Hubbard,* Oxford University Press (Auckland, New Zealand), 1986.

A Apple Pie, Oxford University Press (Auckland, New Zealand), 1987.

(Reteller) *The Three Little Pigs,* Ashton Scholastic (Auckland, New Zealand), 1989.

Katarina, Random House (Auckland, New Zealand), 1990.

Hinepau, Ashton Scholastic (Auckland, New Zealand), 1993.

Maui and the Sun: A Maori Tale, North-South Books (New York, NY), 1996.

Little Rabbit and the Sea, North-South Books (New York, NY), 1997.

(Reteller) *Maui and the Goddess of Fire,* Scholastic (Auckland, New Zealand), 1997.

(Reteller) *The House That Jack Built: Being the Account of Jack Bull, Esq., Who Sailed There from These Shores to a Land Far Away to Live There and Trade with the Natives of That Said Land Twelfth Day of September 1798,* Scholastic (Auckland, New Zealand), 1999.

(Reteller) *The Wolf in Sheep's Clothing,* Shortland (Auckland, New Zealand), 1999, Shortland (Denver, CO), 2000.

Stay Awake, Bear!, Orchard Books (New York, NY), 2000.

(Reteller) *Tom Thumb: The True History of Sir Thomas Thumb,* Random House (Auckland, New Zealand), 2001.

(Reteller) *Three Billy-Goats Gruff,* Scholastic (Auckland, New Zealand), 2003.

EARLY READERS

The Cracker Jack, illustrated by Jill Allpress, Wendy Pye (Auckland, New Zealand), 1995.

Spider, illustrated by Peter Stevenson, Wendy Pye (Auckland, New Zealand), 1995.

There Is a Planet, illustrated by Andrew Trimmer, Wendy Pye (Auckland, New Zealand), 1995.

Cabbage Caterpillar, illustrated by Jim Storey, Wendy Pye (Auckland, New Zealand), 1996.

(Self-illustrated) *Good Luck Elephant,* Wendy Pye (Auckland, New Zealand), 1996.

The Secret Lives of Mr and Mrs Smith, illustrated by Korky Paul, Wendy Pye (Auckland, New Zealand), 1996.

I Like to Find Things, illustrated by Neil Vesey, Wendy Pye (Auckland, New Zealand), 1997.

(Illustrator) Joy Cowley, *The Bears' Picnic,* Shortland (Auckland, New Zealand), 1997.

Jump into Bed, illustrated by Craig Brown, Shortland (Auckland, New Zealand), 1997.

It Makes Me Smile, illustrated by Emanuela Carletti, Wendy Pye (Auckland, New Zealand), 1998.

Mice Like Rice, illustrated by Astrid Matijasevic, Wendy Pye (Auckland, New Zealand), 1998.

(Self-illustrated) *Rhymes with Ram,* Lands End (Auckland, New Zealand), 1998.

Lucky Grub, illustrated by Jim Storey, Wendy Pye (Auckland, New Zealand), 1999.

ILLUSTRATOR

Katherine O' Brien, *The Year of the Yelvertons,* Oxford University Press (Auckland, New Zealand), 1981.

Kathleen Leverich, *The Hungry Fox,* Houghton Mifflin (Boston, MA), 1986.

Joy Watson, *Pets,* Department of Education (Wellington, New Zealand), 1988.

Beverley Dietz, *The Lion and the Jackal,* Simon & Schuster (New York, NY), 1991.

Jeffrey Leask, *Little Red Rocking Hood,* Ashton Scholastic (Auckland, New Zealand), 1992.

Philip Bailey, reteller, *The Wedding of Mistress Fox,* North-South (New York, NY), 1994.

Kana Riley, *A Moose Is Loose,* Brown Publishing Network (Wellesley, MA), 1994.

Joy Cowley, *The Video Shop Sparrow,* Boyds Mills Press (Honesdale, PA), 1999.

Joy Cowley, *Pip the Penguin,* Scholastic (Auckland, New Zealand), 2001.

Robert Sullivan, *Weaving Earth and Sky: Myths and Legends of Aotearoa,* Random House (Auckland, New Zealand), 2002.

Joy Cowley, *The Nice Little Tractor,* Scholastic (Auckland, New Zealand), 2004.

Author of libretto for *Terrible Tom,* a ballet commissioned by Royal New Zealand Ballet Company, 1985, and *Te Maia and the Sea-Devil,* a ballet, Royal New Zealand Ballet Company, 1986; author of scripts for TVNZ television series *Bidibidi,* broadcast November and December, 1990, and *Bidibidi to the Rescue,* broadcast November and December, 1991, both based on his book *Bidibidi.*

WORK IN PROGRESS: Text and illustrations for a *Magicbook* in collaboration with the HIT lab at Canterbury University.

SIDELIGHTS: Gavin Bishop is one of the most prolific and highly honored illustrator/authors in New Zealand. The winner of numerous awards for several of his forty-plus picture books and beginning readers in his native country, Bishop is noted for his attention to background details in pictures that augment, often humorously, the stories they accompany. In addition to providing illustrations that are considered colorful and lively, Bishop has made a name for himself as an effective reteller of such traditional tales as *The Three Little Pigs, Mr. Fox, The House That Jack Built: Being the Account of Jack Bull, Esq., Who Sailed There from These Shores to a Land Far Away to Live There and Trade with the Natives of That Said Land Twelfth Day of September 1798,* and *Tom Thumb: The True History of Sir Thomas Thumb.* Additionally, he has also established himself as an original storyteller, dealing in narratives that highlight the native Maori culture of his New Zealand homeland, such as *Katarina* and *Maui and the Sun,* and in pleasant animal tales for young readers, including the award-winning *Little Rabbit and the Sea* and *Stay Awake, Bear!*

Born in Invercargill, the southernmost city in New Zealand, Bishop lived with his parents in his grandmother's little house "with a big rhododendron in front," as Bishop once told *CA.* He started school when the family moved to Kingston, "a tiny collection of houses at the end of the railway line from Invercargill," where they lived until he was eight. "At the single-teacher school in Kingston, there were only eleven pupils, and I was the only one in my class. Some days I got a ride to school on the back of a huge horse with two other kids. We had to climb the school gate to get onto its back," Bishop once recollected. "I had a dog called Smudge and a cat called Calla Callutsa, which was given to us by some Greek neighbors when they shifted to Wellington."

"In Kingston, we had no electricity or telephone, and we didn't have a car," Bishop continued. "Our radio ran on a car battery, but reception was poor because of the surrounding mountains. The *Southland Times* arrived spasmodically on the freight train from Lumsden. It was the *Auckland Weekly* news, though, that excited us all, with the pictures of the young Queen Elizabeth's coronation in 1953—the pageantry and the crown jewels."

At the age of eight, Bishop returned with his family to Invercargill, where he discovered the joys of a free library system and joined the public library. He was introduced to J. R. R. Tolkien's *The Hobbit* through an extract in a magazine when he was nine. "I have read it several times since and still find it a source of inspiration," Bishop once noted. Bishop knew since he was a small child that he would someday be an illustrator. "For as long as I can remember I've liked pictures and stories," Bishop told Barbara Murison in an interview reprinted on Bishop's Web site. "I knew that I wanted to be an artist from a very early age, and luckily I was encouraged by my parents and teachers to hold onto this idea. Books have always been a part of my life and I was read and sung to by my mother and grandmother when I was little."

At the age of eighteen, he enrolled at the Canterbury University School of Fine Arts in Christchurch to study painting. "I was fortunate to be a student there when Russell Clark, a well-known New Zealand illustrator, taught there," Bishop once recalled. Bishop has also noted, however, that his art school training caused a breach with a love of drawing representative objects which he has had since childhood. "When I went to art school I had to suspend that interest in drawing things—objects—animals, people, all those sorts of things, because it wasn't fashionable to draw anything in particular in art school," Bishop explained to Doreen

Darnell in a *Talespinner* interview. "We had to paint abstract paintings—in fact, to paint anything that looked as though it had any sort of subject matter was called illustrative. And we were told very firmly to get rid of that from our school work, so it wasn't until some years after leaving art school that I found the courage to leave the abstract painting behind me and start painting images again. The basics are all much the same. It's just that I now allow myself to draw images."

After graduating with honors in painting in 1967, he spent a year at the Christchurch Secondary Teachers' College, and for the next thirty years, Bishop earned much of his living teaching art, twenty years at a high school in Christchurch, New Zealand, and the final ten years at Christ's College in that same city. "From early in my life, I wanted to be an art teacher," Bishop once reflected. The two interests which have remained constant throughout his life, Bishop has noted, are his love of teaching and children's literature. "Books, stories, and pictures have provided a lifelong fascination for me. Children's picture books in particular, with their intertwined rhythms of pictures and words combining to tell a story in an often deceptively simple way, have always interested me."

Bishop's first self-illustrated children's book, *Mrs. McGinty and the Bizarre Plant,* won the Russell Clark Medal for Illustration from the New Zealand Library Association. In this story, the butt of the neighborhood children's jokes becomes a local hero of sorts when the plant she buys at the store grows to enormous proportions, eventually attracting the attention of a team of botanists, who airlift the giant plant for their collection. Zena Sutherland of the *Bulletin of the Center for Children's Books* found this an "amusing" plot, but offered greater praise for Bishop's illustrations, calling them "boldly designed, usually dramatically composed, nicely detailed." A critic for *Junior Bookshelf* similarly singled out Bishop's artwork, stating that he "most effectively and subtly depicts the transformation of Mrs. McGinty's character and outlook." "I love gardening and growing things," the author once admitted. "My wife and I have times when we talk and read about nothing else. On other occasions, however, we avoid the garden for months on end."

Bishop followed this first effort with adaptations of traditional stories for children as well as original tales. His illustrations for *Mr. Fox* drew comparisons to Maurice Sendak from Marcus Crouch in *Junior Bookshelf,* and Margery Fisher of *Growing Point* likewise noted that Bishop's "idiosyncratic illustrations" add an element of "implied social satire" to the story that "lifts the folk-tale far away from its simple origins." *Mr. Fox* is based on an old Massachusetts chain story and tells the tale of Mr. Fox who is out walking one day and finds a bumblebee which he puts in his bag. He deposits this bag, in turn, with a woman and tells her not to open it. But of course she does, and once it is opened the bumblebee flies out and is promptly eaten by a red rooster. Mr. Fox continues his walk and visits various houses until he finally meets his match with another woman.

Bidibidi is an original tale about a high country sheep in New Zealand who grows tired and bored with her uneventful life and diet of mountain grass. Following the rainbow in search of adventure, she has excitement galore. Similarly, the "vigor and humor" of Bishop's illustrations steal the show, according to a reviewer for the *Bulletin of the Center for Children's Book,* in the author's retelling *Chicken Licken,* the tale of a chick who thinks the sky is falling when an acorn lands on her head. "The traditional tale may be slight," wrote Ralph Lavender in *School Librarian,* "but the superbly autumnal pictures make it into something which is quite special." A review of Bishop's *Mother Hubbard* garnered the following comment from Marcus Crouch of *Junior Bookshelf:* "Gavin Bishop's distinguishing mark, apart from his brilliant technique, is his attention to detail. . . . These pictures are for reading." And a *Kirkus Reviews* commentator, who began by noting that there is little need for another version of the story of *The Three Little Pigs,* concluded the review of Bishop's rendering by remarking, "Why not another version, if it's this good?"

Original tales are served up in several other Bishop offerings. *The Horror of Hickory Bay* takes place on a quiet summer day on Christmas in the Southern Hemisphere. While the grownups rest after a holiday meal, a monster emerges from the sea. But young India Brown—modeled on Bishop's youngest daughter, Alexandra—and Uncle Atho and the dog Smudge team up to defeat the sea creature. *A Apple Pie* is a traditional English alphabet book based on an early Victorian rhyming version that follows one animal character after the other in pursuit of a slice of apple pie. With *Katarina,* Bishop tells a story closer to home. Based on the life of his great aunt, Katarina McKay, the picture book tells the story of a young Maori woman who, in the winter of 1861, leaves her tribal home in the North Island of New Zealand to travel and meet up with her Scottish husband on the South Island. A short time later, the white settlers begin to attack the Maori homeland in the North Island to win more land for European settlers, cutting off the woman's contact with her family. Only when her brother arrives does Katarina learn what happened to her people.

Bishop further explores the New Zealand and Maori experience in titles such as *Hinepau, Maui and the Sun,* and *Maui and the Goddess of Fire.* "*Hinepau* is a legend-like story that I named after my mother whose family were Maori/Scots," Bishop once explained to *CA.* The tale features a Maori woman with red hair and green eyes who is a weaver, but all of her weaving comes out backwards or inside out. Her tribe thinks she is a witch, and she is sent away to a lonely hut where she weaves all day. As if in punishment for this, the villagers are stricken by threat of death by starvation and thirst when a volcano covers all the surrounding countryside in ash. Hinepau then saves her villagers, however, making the ultimate sacrifice. In *Maui and the Sun* and *Maui and the Goddess of Fire,* Bishop adapts Maori legends about a trickster. In *Maui and the Sun,* the trickster always plays jokes on his older brothers, but nothing could equal the time he tries to capture the sun. *Booklist*'s Julie Corsaro found the tale "simple and lively." Maui makes a return in *Maui and the Goddess of Fire,* in which the mischief-maker brings fire to his people. Indeed, this playful trickster was also responsible, according to legend, for inventing the barbed fishing hook, an eel trap, and strong rope. "I would in the future like to produce more work of a bicultural nature," Bishop once told *CA.* "New Zealand children should know and feel comfortable with their Maori heritage. Besides creating a better understanding of Maori-Pakeha values, a knowledge of Taha-Maori would provide a richer and more stimulating country in which to live."

Focusing on animal characters is the 1997 *Little Rabbit and the Sea,* the tale of a little bunny who has never seen the sea. All day long he thinks about the water, and at night he dreams he is sailing on a little boat in the midst of the big blue sea. Asking various relatives what the sea is like, he gets different answers from each. His curiosity grows and grows until one day a seagull takes him for a flight to see for himself. A reviewer for *Publishers Weekly* found this story to be "a poignant and affirming tribute to the powers of imagination" whose illustrations "radiate a lustrous quality reminiscent of ceramic glaze."

Bishop commented to Murison that he still finds the "picture book format fascinating and [I] know that I will never exhaust all the ideas for books I would like to try." He further noted, "I'm very interested in seeing how far the traditional shape of a thirty-two page picture book can be pushed. I am also interested in using subject matter that is unexpected in this kind of book." Speaking with Doreen Darnell, he responded to a question of whether story or picture should come first in his books: "I've found through experience that you can get yourself into a lot of difficulties if you don't have a pretty definite shape of the story before you get started on the illustrations." Bishop further explained, "I might have a few ideas for some of the pictures, but I spend a lot of time on the story and once that's in a pretty finished state, then I can start playing around with the design of the book, and the illustrations. But if you get to a stage where you are still changing and working on the story, you can create a lot of extra work for yourself." Bishop also once explained to *CA* that he has drawn from personal experience for some of his projects. "I have become more and more interested in sifting through the memories of my own childhood in search of useful material for stories and ideas for pictures. The ballet libretto for *Terrible Tom,* commissioned by the Royal New Zealand Ballet in 1985, is loosely based on incidents from my early years in Invercargill."

Bishop has traveled extensively, not only throughout New Zealand, but also to many countries overseas—England, France, Italy, Germany, Australia, Greece, Holland, Canada, and Malaysia. He has been to Japan four times, and in 1990, he and his youngest daughter took part in a cultural exchange on the island of Sakhalin in the Soviet Far East. In 1992, he went to Beijing and Shanghai at the invitation of UNESCO to give lectures and run workshops on children's literature. In 1997, he went to Indonesia to work again for UNESCO. He has visited the United States several times and in the spring of 1996 taught at the Rhode Island School of Design in Providence.

It was while teaching in the United States that Bishop came up with the idea for *The House That Jack Built.* Because of its distinctive New Zealand theme, however, New York editors felt the book would do better in New Zealand. When he returned to New Zealand from his year at the Rhode Island School of Design, he showed an editor the idea and sold it immediately. One of his most popular books, *The House That Jack Built* gives this traditional rhyme a colonial flavor, by setting the action in New Zealand in 1798. Also, in Bishop's take on the tale, the tension between native Maori and the newcomers from Europe plays a central part in the action. *The House That Jack Built* went on to win several awards in New Zealand, including the New Zealand *Post* Picture Book of the Year and Book of the Year.

Working specifically for the American market, Bishop created *Stay Awake, Bear!,* the story of a bear who decides not to waste all his time hibernating. To stay awake, he turns up the radio, makes jam tarts, and watches videos. But when summer comes, the bear is so tired that he sleeps all through the season. A reviewer for *Publishers Weekly* felt that this title "lacks the depth of imagination" of *Little Rabbit and the Sea,* but that it still "conveys a cozy mood with autumnal watercolor hues." *School Library Journal* critic Kathleen M. Kelly MacMillan, however, found the tale "lively," predicting it would appeal to children who find napping "a waste of time." MacMillan also praised Bishop's artwork for expressing the "jovial characters" and their "delight in winter camaraderie."

Bishop told Murison that the work he does for the American market is different than what he creates for the New Zealand market. According to Bishop, "The American market . . . is a much more conservative one than ours." Speaking with Doreen Darnell, he noted that publishing in the United States is important to his career. "From a financial point of view, it can make being a writer and illustrator possible, because the print runs are much bigger and the potential income from those books is much greater."

Bishop has also had a go at retelling the Brothers Grimm tale *Tom Thumb: The True History of Sir Thomas Thumb.* In Bishop's version, he "has added episodes of his own which appeal more to the modern child's need for action," according to Margaret Kedian, writing in *Magpies.* Kedian lauded the book, calling the artwork "stunning," and further remarking that "Bishop has . . . excelled himself with the text" in this, his "best book so far."

"I like to think that books are such an efficient and convenient unit that they will always be around," Bishop concluded to Murison on the future of picture books. "They are so simple and mobile. . . . The act of nursing a child and reading a much loved picture book seems to me to be such a natural human thing to do that something extraordinary will be needed to replace it."

BIOGRAPHICAL AND CRITICAL SOURCES:

BOOKS

Dunkle, Margaret, editor, *The Story Makers,* Oxford University Press (Melbourne, Australia), 1987.

Gaskin, Chris, *Picture Book Magic,* Reed Publishing (Auckland, New Zealand), 1996.

Marantz, Sylvia and Kenneth Marantz, *Artists of the Page,* McFarland (Jefferson, NC), 1992.

PERIODICALS

Booklist, May 1, 1996, Julie Corsaro, review of *Maui and the Sun,* p. 1508; December 1, 1999, John Peter, review of *The Video Shop Sparrow,* p. 709; August, 2000, Isabel Schon, review of *Little Rabbit and the Sea,* p. 2154.

Bulletin of the Center for Children's Books, May, 1983, Zena Sutherland, review of *Mrs. McGinty and the Bizarre Plant,* p. 163; April, 1985, review of *Chicken Licken,* p. 141.

Faces: People, Places, and Cultures, January, 2001, review of *Maui and the Sun,* p. 46.

Growing Point, May, 1983, Margery Fisher, review of *Mr. Fox,* p. 4080; July, 1987, p. 4837.

Junior Bookshelf, August, 1982, review of *Mrs. McGinty and the Bizarre Plant,* pp. 128-129; June, 1983, Marcus Crouch, review of *Mr. Fox,* p. 107; February, 1988, Marcus Crouch, review of *Mother Hubbard,* p. 18.

Kirkus Reviews, January 15, 1990, review of *The Three Little Pigs,* pp. 101-102.

Magpies, September, 1999; March, 2002, Margaret Kedian, review of *Tom Thumb: The True History of Thomas Thumb,* p. 6.

Publishers Weekly, November 28, 1994, review of *The Wedding of Mistress Fox,* p. 61; October 20, 1997, review of *Little Rabbit and the Sea,* p. 74; March 20, 2000, review of *Stay Awake, Bear!,* p. 90.

School Librarian, June, 1985, Ralph Lavender, review of *Chicken Licken,* p. 133.

School Library Journal, November, 1985, p. 66; March, 1990, p. 188; December, 1994, Marilyn Taniguchi, review of *The Wedding of Mistress Fox,* pp. 122-123; July, 1996, Pam Gosner, review of *Maui and the Sun,* p. 77; December, 1997, Maura Bresnahan, review of *Little Rabbit and the Sea,* p. 81; December, 1999, Lisa Gangeni Krapp, review of *The Video Shop Sparrow,* p. 90; March, 2000, Kathleen M. Kelly MacMillan, review of *Stay Awake, Bear!,* p. 178.

Talespinner, September, 1999, Doreen Darnell, "An Interview with Gavin Bishop," pp. 22-29.

ONLINE

Gavin Bishop Home Page, http://www.gavinbishop.com/ (May 20, 2003), Barbara Murison, "An E-mail Interview with Gavin Bishop."

New Zealand Book Council, http://www.bookcouncil.org.nz/ (March 4, 2003), "Bishop, Gavin."

* * *

BLAIS, Madeleine 1947-

PERSONAL: Born August 25, 1947, in Chicopee, MA; daughter of Raymond Joseph (a doctor) and Maureen (a teacher; maiden name, Shea) Blais; married John Strong Miner Katzenbach (a writer), May 10, 1980. *Education:* College of New Rochelle, B.A., 1969; Columbia University, M.S., 1970.

ADDRESSES: Office—Tropic Magazine, Miami Herald, 1 Herald Plaza, Miami, FL 33101.

CAREER: Journalist and nonfiction writer. University of Massachusetts, Amherst, faculty member, 1987. Worked as reporter for *Trenton Times,* Trenton, NJ, and *Boston Globe,* Boston, MA; freelance journalist; *Miami Herald,* Miami, FL, feature writer for *Tropic* (Sunday magazine), 1979—.

AWARDS, HONORS: Nieman fellowship, Harvard University, 1986; second place in Ernie Pyle feature competition; Pulitzer Prize for feature writing, 1980; National Book Critics Circle Award in nonfiction, 1995, for *In These Girls, Hope Is a Muscle.*

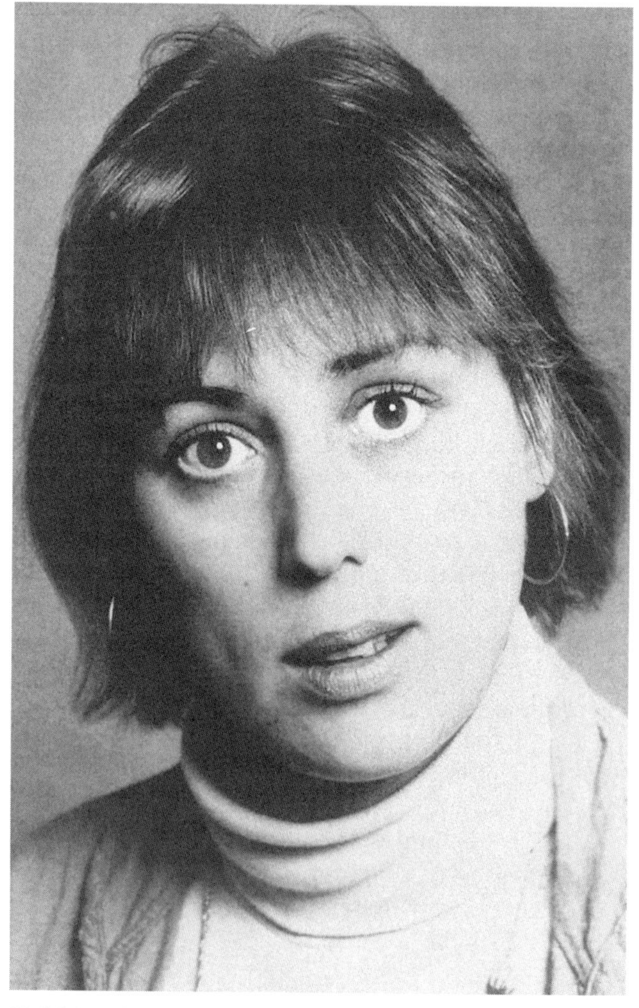

Madeleine Blais

WRITINGS:

They Say You Can't Have a Baby: The Dilemma of Infertility, Norton (New York, NY), 1979.

The Heart Is an Instrument: Portraits in Journalism, foreword by Geneva Overholser, University of Massachusetts Press (Amherst, MA), 1992.

In These Girls, Hope Is a Muscle, Atlantic Monthly Press (New York, NY), 1995.

Uphill Walkers: Memoir of a Family, Atlantic Monthly Press (New York, NY), 2001.

Contributor of articles to newspapers and periodicals, including *Chicago Tribune* and *Miami Herald.*

SIDELIGHTS: Madeleine Blais portrays the joy of women's sports in her book *In These Girls, Hope Is a Muscle,* which focuses on the girls' basketball team at a regional high school in Amherst, Massachusetts. The New England-based team, known as the Lady Hurricanes, captured the state championship in 1993. In one sense, the book is simply a play-by-play description of one season for the team, and it can be read as a thrilling sports story on that level. Yet, noted Steve Gietschier in the *Sporting News,* "there is so much more here to savor and absorb. The young women who give themselves so completely to their team's quest are extraordinary each in her own way. Burdened with the pains of adolescence, the duties that high school imposes and, in some cases, the tough circumstances of families rent asunder, they learn from one another how to dig deep to find the resources they need to reach their goal." *In These Girls* proves "that women's sports can be an astoundingly fulfilling and moving experience." Ruth Conniff, writing in the *Progressive,* noted that Blais's writing bogs down occasionally, yet still highly recommended the book, stating that it is "worth reading for the last chapter" alone, which describes the climactic final game of the 1993 basketball season. Conniff enthused, "Blais's description of that fateful night, from the pre-game locker-room talk to the bus ride home, is beautiful. She evokes exactly the feeling of time crystallized on those rare, clear moments. . . . I admit I had tears in my eyes."

Blais draws on her own life in *Uphill Walkers: A Memoir of a Family,* published in 2001. The author was born into a large Irish-American family in western Massachusetts, and her childhood was fairly typical until the death of her father. Her mother was pregnant at the time, and the family entered a period of hard times as the widowed mother struggled to keep her children's lives as unchanged as possible, despite financial strain and the increasing problems with a brother's mental illness. The memoir is "involving and beautifully written," approved a *Booklist* contributor. A *Publishers Weekly* writer found *Uphill Walkers* occasionally marred by overwriting but enlivened by "flashes of brilliance."

BIOGRAPHICAL AND CRITICAL SOURCES:

PERIODICALS

Austin American-Statesman, May 13, 2001, Mary Alice Davis, review of *Uphill Walkers: Memoir of a Family,* p. K6.

Booklist, December 1, 1994, Wes Lukowsky, review of *In These Girls, Hope Is a Muscle,* p. 650; May 15, 2001, Mary Carroll, review of *Uphill Walkers: A Memoir of a Family,* p. 1712.

Chicago Tribune, May 27, 1979.

Library Journal, July, 1992, Judy Solberg, review of *The Heart Is an Instrument: Portraits in Journalism,* p. 94; October 15, 1994, Kathy Ruffle, review of *In These Girls, Hope Is a Muscle,* p. 64; May 15, 2001, Nancy R. Ives, review of *Uphill Walkers,* p. 132.

Milwaukee Journal Sentinel, May 13, 2001, Geeta Sharma Jensen, "In Town: Madeleine Blais," p. 7.

New York Times Book Review, March 19, 1995, Gail Shister, review of *In These Girls, Hope Is a Muscle,* p. 45.

Progressive, January, 1995, Ruth Conniff, review of *In These Girls, Hope Is a Muscle,* p. 45.

Publishers Weekly, November 7, 1994, review of *In These Girls, Hope Is a Muscle,* p. 56; April 9, 2001, review of *Uphill Walkers,* p. 64.

School Library Journal, November, 1995, Frances Reiher, review of *In These Girls, Hope Is a Muscle,* p. 8.

Sporting News, May 15, 1995, Steve Gietschier, review of *In These Girls, Hope Is a Muscle,* p. 8.

Washington Post, June 3, 2001, Reeve Lindbergh, review of *Uphill Walkers,* p. T5.*

* * *

BRYANT, Christopher G. A. 1944-

PERSONAL: Born April 14, 1944, in Epsom, England; son of Gordon and Edna Mollie Bryant; married Elizabeth Peters, February 17, 1967; children: two. *Ethnicity:* "English." *Education:* University of Leicester, B.A., M.A.; University of Southampton, Ph.D. *Hobbies and other interests:* Dining with friends, travel, watching soccer.

ADDRESSES: *Office*—Dean's Office, Faculty of Arts, Media, and Social Sciences, University of Salford, Salford, Greater Manchester M5 4WT, England; fax: +44-161-295-4128. *E-mail*—c.g.a.bryant@salford.ac.uk.

CAREER: University of Salford, Greater Manchester, England, professor of sociology and dean of Faculty of Arts, Media, and Social Sciences, former director of Institute for Social Research.

WRITINGS:

NONFICTION

Sociology in Action: A Critique of Selected Conceptions of the Social Role of a Sociologist, Wiley (New York, NY), 1976.

Positivism in Social Theory and Research, St. Martin's Press (New York, NY), 1985.

Practical Sociology: Post-empiricism and the Reconstruction of Theory and Application, Blackwell (Cambridge, MA), 1995.

EDITOR

(With Henk A. Becker) *What Has Sociology Achieved?,* St. Martin's Press (New York, NY), 1990.

(With David Jary) *Giddens' Theory of Structuration: A Critical Appreciation,* Routledge (New York, NY), 1991.

(With Edmund Mokrzycki) *The New Great Transformation? Change and Continuity in East-Central Europe,* Routledge (New York, NY), 1994.

(With Edmund Mokrzycki) *Democracy, Civil Society and Pluralism in Comparative Perspective: Poland, Great Britain and the Netherlands,* IFiS Publishers (Warsaw, Poland), 1995.

(With David Jary) *Anthony Giddens: Critical Assessments,* four volumes, Routledge (New York, NY), 1997.

(With David Jary) *The Contemporary Giddens: Social Theory in a Globalizing Age,* Palgrave (New York, NY), 2001.

SIDELIGHTS: British sociologist Christopher G. A. Bryant has devoted much of his attention over the years to changes within the theory of sociology itself. In his 1985 book, *Positivism in Social Theory and Research,* he provides "a concise but comprehensive overview of the debates and controversies that the term 'positivism' has inspired," according to Jonathan H. Turner in *Social Forces.* Positivism, to paraphrase reviewer Stephan Nowak in the *American Journal of Sociology,* is the theory of social science as empirical science, in which only phenomena—the facts of experience—are relevant, and statements about values are irrelevant. Bryant presents a historical survey of three national traditions in positivist philosophy and sociology: the French, the German, and the American; these surveys were "the real meat," for Turner, of a book that "should be essential reading for those concerned about the problems and prospects of scientific sociology." Nowak, on the other hand, had reservations about Bryant's analysis of American "instrumental positivism," but he asserted that, overall, "one reads Bryant's book with intellectual satisfaction. It is a real pleasure to read a competent, precise, and evenhanded analysis of such a 'hot' issue in contemporary sociology."

Reviewer Russell Hanson, in *Contemporary Sociology,* declared that Bryant's chapter on American sociology laid out the beginnings of an "important, sweeping indictment of American sociology," but that the requisite evidence for such an indictment was not marshaled. In contrast to Turner, Hanson felt that the treatment of French positivism was cursory rather than concise. Hanson held that the book was too "schematic" to fulfill its purpose of placing positivism in context. However, Hanson added, "In other respects, the point of the book is well taken and well made. Bryant's style is remarkably lean and efficient, and he intelligently covers almost two hundred years of Western sociology in a few [214] pages."

In 1995, Bryant published *Practical Sociology: Post-empiricism and the Reconstruction of Theory and Application,* a book discussing the major change in sociology which reviewer J. Daniel Schubert, in the *American Journal of Sociology,* called "the linguistic turn." Positivism, although still holding sway in the public imagination and among policymakers, no longer ruled the academy. Instead, linguistically oriented theories such as post-structuralism had supplanted the empiricism of the past, spurning the assumption of a strict dichotomy between the sphere of facts and the sphere of values. Bryant calls the new style of inquiry "postempiricism." Schubert remarked: "For Bryant, postempiricism is a practical sociology that works politically and socially." Such a science, Schubert commented, would be scientific and rational, moral and empowering all at once. Schubert felt, however, that Bryant devoted so much of the 190-page book to a review of existing literature that he shortchanged his own original contributions: "Bryant's strength is also occasionally his weakness."

Offering a similar view was Martin Parker in the *Sociological Review,* who argued that although Bryant was "the right person for the job" of setting forth a new, practical sociology, this particular book hadn't done the job completely. Parker wished for fuller treatment of the post-structuralists Derrida, Foucault, and Lyotard, as well as for more explanation of "what (if anything) [Bryant] would change about British sociology at the moment in order to make it more 'practical.'" Nevertheless, Parker added: "I find Bryant's aims laudable and his book charming. . . . I do want to stress that this is a nice book to read, knowledgeably written with some excellent sketches of theorists and some bitingly accurate observations."

Bryant has also coedited volumes of essays on various sociological issues. In 1990, he and Henk A. Becker edited *What Has Sociology Achieved?* Their overall answer—given in fourteen "generally well written and often very enlightening" essays by twelve authors—was "quite optimistic and reasonable," in the view of Ragnvald Kalleberg in *Contemporary Sociology.*

In 1991, Bryant and David Jary edited *Giddens' Theory of Structuration: A Critical Appreciation.* Anthony Giddens, founder of structuration theory, and general editor of the "Theoretical Traditions in the Social Sciences" series, which had included *Positivism in Social Theory and Research,* was one of the more thoroughly discussed voices in contemporary British sociology. Ira J. Cohen argued in *Contemporary Sociology:* "The Bryant-Jary collection includes exceptionally fresh and provocative—albeit occasionally more speculative than secure—readings of Giddens on structuration theory." Cohen wrote that Bryant, in his own essay among the six in the book, "approaches Giddens more sympathetically than other authors yet still develops one of the most compelling contributions to the volume," Cohen pronounced.

The New Great Transformation? Change and Continuity in East-Central Europe, edited with Polish social scientist Edmund Mokrzycki, deals with a specific regional issue in another part of the world: the changes occurring in Eastern Europe during and after 1989. The book was, for Jozsef Borocz in *Contemporary Sociology,* "a selection of essays, at various levels of theoretical abstraction and acuity, about the complex, menacing uncertainty in which these societies found themselves a few years after the collapse of state socialism." Although Borocz claimed that the book "radiates a sense of disorientation, uncertainty, or, indeed . . . liminality," he found several of its contributions, including Bryant's, to be, "clearly, high-quality, refreshing readings." Borocz applauded the editors for their recognition of a major limiting factor in Western sociologists' analyses of Eastern Europe. The critic argued: "the study of 'communism' from the outside has always been, to a large extent, an exercise in self-reification and -reinforcement." One of the strengths of the collection, Borocz maintained, is that Bryant and his coeditor were "resigned" enough to be ambivalent about Western sociology's ability to fully understand the changes in Eastern Europe.

Bryant told *CA:* "I write because my contract as an academic obliges me, among other things, to research and publish. But writing has also always been a challenge and a pleasure. It has been a challenge because, when I started in the late 1960s, social scientists were routinely charged with over-using jargon and writing badly. I did not think there was any need for this, as Robert Merton, the American sociologist, had demonstrated. It was a pleasure because I had excelled at English in school without displaying any talent for creative writing. Now I could treat writing English as a craft and let it serve my career as a social scientist. This it has done ever since. On occasions I have been praised for expressing complex ideas lucidly, even elegantly. Nothing has given me greater pleasure. I am also mindful that, like most Britons, I am not fluent in any other language than English. With over ninety percent of the world literature in sociology in English, this has not mattered too much. I have, however, visited Eastern Europe often, and I know how hard social scientists there have to work to achieve proficiency in English. The very least that English native speakers like me can do for them is take the trouble to write as well as they can."

BIOGRAPHICAL AND CRITICAL SOURCES:

PERIODICALS

American Journal of Sociology, May, 1986, pp. 1499-1503; November, 1996, pp. 864-865.
British Book News, May, 1987, p. 284.
Contemporary Sociology, January, 1987, pp. 129-130; July, 1991, pp. 644-645; March, 1992, pp. 280-282; July, 1995, pp. 357-358.
Reference & Research Book News, June, 1990, p. 18.
Social Forces, December, 1986, pp. 567-569.
Sociological Review, February, 1986, p. 201; May, 1992, p. 377; November, 1996, pp. 761-764.

BUSCH, Lawrence (Michael) 1945-

PERSONAL: Born March 27, 1945, in New York, NY; son of Raymond and Carol Busch; married Karen Hagberg, December 30, 1966; children: Lisa, Rachel. *Ethnicity:* "Caucasian." *Education:* Hofstra University, B.A., 1965; Cornell University, M.S., 1971, Ph.D., 1974.

ADDRESSES: *Home*—5291 Hidden Lake Dr., East Lansing, MI 48823. *Office*—Department of Sociology, 316 Berkey Hall, Michigan State University, East Lansing, MI 48824-1111; fax: 517-432-2856. *E-mail*—lawrence.busch@ssc.msu.edu.

CAREER: U.S. Peace Corps, Washington, DC, volunteer in Labe, Guinea, 1965-66, and Lome, Togo, 1967-68; Volunteers in Service to America (VISTA), Washington, DC, supervisor of Community Action Council in Rose Hill, NC, 1968-70; University of Kentucky, Lexington, assistant professor, 1974-79, associate professor, 1979-84, professor of sociology, 1984-89; Michigan State University, East Lansing, MI, professor of sociology, 1990-96, University Distinguished Professor, 1997—. University of Trondheim, visiting professor, 1994, 1995, 1996. International Grain Sorghum/Pearl Millet Collaborative Research Support Program, vice chair, 1980-81; French Institute of Scientific Research for Development and Cooperation (ORSTOM), Paris, director of research, 1988-89; Center of International Cooperation and Agronomic Research for Development, Paris, member of scientific council, 1990-96; Council for Agricultural Science and Technology, member of board of directors, 1990-93. Guest on television and radio programs in the United States and Canada, including *Nova.*

MEMBER: International Sociological Association (chair of Research Committee on the Sociology of Agriculture, 1986-90), American Association for the Advancement of Science (fellow), American Sociological Association, Rural Sociological Society (chair of Social Organization of Agriculture Research Group, 1978-79; president, 1997-98), Society for Social Studies of Science, Society for Agriculture, Food, and Human Values (president, 1988-89), Association for the Study of Food and Society.

AWARDS, HONORS: Certificate of appreciation, U.S. Department of Agriculture, 1987; Thome Poe Cooper Award, 1988; award from Rural Sociological Society, 1990; E. A. Southee traveling scholar, University of Western Sydney, 1991; award for professional excellence, American Agricultural Economics Association, 1992; grants and fellowships from National Agricultural Research, National Science Foundation, U.S. Department of Agriculture, Embassy of Canada, Ford Foundation, and U.S. Agency for International Development.

WRITINGS:

(Editor and contributor) *Science and Agricultural Development,* Allanheld, Osmun (Montclair, NJ), 1981.

(With W. B. Lacy) *Science, Agriculture, and the Politics of Research,* Westview Press (Boulder, CO), 1983.

(Editor, with W. B. Lacy, and contributor) *Food Security in the United States,* Westview Press (Boulder, CO), 1984.

(Editor, with W. B. Lacy) *The Agricultural Scientific Enterprise: A System in Transition,* Westview Press (Boulder, CO), 1986.

(With W. B. Lacy, L. R. Lacy, and J. Burkhardt) *Plants, Power, and Profit: Social, Economic, and Ethnical Consequences of the New Biotechnologies,* Basil Blackwell (Cambridge, MA), 1991.

(Editor, with W. H. Friedland, F. H. Buttel, and A. Rudy) *Toward a New Political Economy of Agriculture,* Westview Press (Boulder, CO), 1991.

(Editor, with W. H. Friedland, A. Bonanno, and others) *From Columbus to Conagra: The Globalization of Agriculture,* University Press of Kansas (Lawrence, KS), 1994.

(With W. B. Lacy, J. Burkhardt, and others) *Making Nature, Shaping Culture: Plant Biodiversity in Global Context,* University of Nebraska Press (Lincoln, NE), 1995.

The Eclipse of Morality: Science, State, and Market, Aldine de Gruyter (New York, NY), 2000.

Contributor to books, including *The Impact of Biotechnology on Food Production and Processing,* edited by Dietrich Knorr, Marcel Dekker (New York, NY), 1986; *Biotechnology and the New Agricultural Revolution,* edited by Joseph J. Molnar and Henry Kinnucan, Westview Press (Boulder, CO), 1988; *The Future of Rural America: Anticipating Policies for Constructive Change,* edited by Kenneth E. Pigg, Westview Press (Boulder, CO), 1991; *Visions of American Agriculture,* edited by W. Lockeretz, Iowa State University Press, 1997; and *The Privatization of Information and Agricultural Industrialization,* edited by Steven A. Wolf, CRC Press (Boca Raton, FL), 1997. Contributor to numerous academic journals, including *Diversity, BioScience, Urban Life, Public Opinion Quarterly, Sociological Practice, Socioeconomic Planning Practices, Sociological Focus, Science and Public Policy, Journal of Sustainable Agriculture,* and *Policy Studies Journal.* Editor, *Agrarian Questions,* 1987-91; associate editor, *Rural Sociology,* 1981-85, *Agriculture and Human Values,* 1984—, and *Nature, Sciences, Societies,* 1991—; member of scientific board,*Science Tribune,* 1996—; advisory editor, *Sociological Quarterly,* 1986-88.

SIDELIGHTS: Lawrence Busch once told *CA:* "Most of my work revolves around agriculture and agricultural research. Although I was born in New York City, three-and-a-half years in West Africa in the Peace Corps convinced me of the importance of food and agriculture to all of us. I am particularly interested in ethical issues associated with the growth of a global agriculture. However, I put that into the context of the last 300 years of Western civilization, including both the values of the Enlightenment and the tragedies of colonialism and world wars. I see myself as pulled by philosophy, history, and social theory on one side, while concerned about practical issues of hunger and malnutrition on the other. Thus, my work has taken me to West Africa, India, China, Brazil, Norway, and France, among other places.

"My most recent project is a book on what I see as the three great themes of modernity—science, state, and market—as initially described by Bacon, Hobbes, and Smith respectively. I argue that in our search for social order, we have used these three themes as justifications for relieving individuals of moral responsibility. Only by expanding our understanding and application of democracy to include spheres currently defined as outside the political—science, education, health care, the workplace, the family—can we recapture the moral responsibility we have inappropriately delegated to others."

C

CASTEL, Robert 1933-

PERSONAL: Born March 27, 1933, in Brest, France. *Education:* University of Strasbourg, Licence de Philosophie; Sorbonne, University of Paris, Agrégation des Philosophie and Doctorat d'Etat de Lettres et Sciences Humaines.

ADDRESSES: *Home*—8 rue Falguiere, 75015 Paris, France. *Office*—Centre d'Études des Mouvements Sociaux, Ecole des Hautes Etudes en Sciences Sociales, 54 bd. Raspail, 75006 Paris, France; fax: 00-33-14-954-2670. *E-mail*—cemes@ebess.fr.

CAREER: University of Lille, Lille, France, associate professor of philosophy, 1962-67; University of Paris, Sorbonne, Paris, France, associate professor of sociology, 1967-68; University of Paris VIII, Paris, associate professor, 1968-72, professor of sociology, 1973-90, director of studies at École des Hautes Études en Sciences Sociales, 1990—, and director of Centre d'Études du Centre des Mouvements Sociaux. Mission interministerielle Recherche-experimentation, president of scientific council.

MEMBER: Societe internationale de sociologie de langue française, Societe international de sociologie, Societe française de sociologie.

AWARDS, HONORS: Officier des Palmes académiques, 1995; D.H.C., University of Lausanne, 1996, and University of Buenos Aires, 1999

WRITINGS:

Le Psychanalysme, Editions Maspero (Paris, France), 1973.

L'Ordre psychiatrique et le pouvoir, Editions de Minuit (Paris, France), 1976, translation by D. W. Halls published as *The Regulation of Madness,* Polity Press (Cambridge, England), 1988.

La Societe psychiatrique avancée, Grasset (Paris, France), 1979, translation by Arthur Goldhammer published as *The Psychiatric Society,* Columbia University Press (New York, NY), 1982.

La Gestion des risques, Editions de Minuit (Paris, France), 1981.

(With others) *Le Parler frais d'Erving Goffman: Colloque de Cerisy,* Editions de Minuit (Paris, France), 1989.

(With J. F. Lae) *Le Revue minimum d'insertion: Une Dette sociale,* L'Harmattan (Paris, France), 1991.

Les Metamorphoses de la question sociale: Une Chronique du salariat, Fayard (Paris, France), 1995.

(With C. Haroche) *Propriété privee, propriété sociale, propriété de soi,* Fayard (Paris, France), 2000.

BIOGRAPHICAL AND CRITICAL SOURCES:

PERIODICALS

Times Literary Supplement, June 18, 1982.

* * *

CHACONAS, Dori

See CHACONAS, D(oris) J.

* * *

CHACONAS, D(oris) J. 1938-
(Dori Chaconas)

PERSONAL: Born March 11, 1938, in Milwaukee, WI; daughter of Paul (a factory worker) and Kathryn (a homemaker; maiden name, Baratka) Kozak; married Nick Chaconas (in sales), October 12, 1957; children: Stacy DeKeyser, Stephanie Mielke, Michaela, Nicki. *Ethnicity:* "Slovenian." *Religion:* Catholic. *Hobbies and other interests:* Needlework.

ADDRESSES: *Home*—Germantown, WI. *Agent*—c/o Author Mail, Viking, 375 Hudson St., New York, NY 10014. *E-mail*—DJC719@aol.com.

CAREER: Writer.

MEMBER: Society of Children's Book Writers and Illustrators, Council for Wisconsin Writers.

AWARDS, HONORS: Archer/Eckblad Children's Picture Book Award, Council for Wisconsin Writers (CWW), 2000, for *On a Wintry Morning;* Betty Ren Wright Picture Book Award, CWW, 2002, for *One Little Mouse.*

WRITINGS:

A Hat for Lily, illustrated by Betsy Warren, Steck-Vaughn (Austin, TX), 1967.

In a Window on Greenwater Street, illustrated by Carroll Dolezal, Steck-Vaughn (Austin, TX), 1970.

(As Doris J. Chaconas) *The Way the Tiger Walked,* illustrated by Frank Bozzo, Simon & Schuster (New York, NY), 1970.

Danger in the Swamp (originally published in *Jack and Jill* magazine), illustrated by Haris Petie, Lantern Press (Mount Vernon, NY), 1971.

AS DORI CHACONAS

On a Wintry Morning, illustrated by Stephen Johnson, Viking (New York, NY), 2000.

One Little Mouse, illustrated by LeUyen Pham, Viking (New York, NY), 2002.

Goodnight, Dewberry Bear, illustrated by Florence S. Davis, Abingdon Press (Nashville, TN), 2003.

Momma, Will You?, illustrated by Steve Johnson and Lou Fancher, Viking (New York, NY), 2004.

That Blessed Christmas Night, illustrated by Deborah Perez-Stable, Abingdon Press (Nashville, TN), 2004.

WORK IN PROGRESS: "Cork and Fuzz" easy-to-read series, illustrated by Lisa McCue, for Viking (New York, NY); *Street Horses,* illustrated by Ted Lewin, for Peachtree Publishers (Atlanta, GA), due in 2005; *Coriander, the Contrary Hen,* illustrated by Marsha Gray Carrington, for Carolrhoda (Minneapolis, MN), due in 2005; *The Winter Mouseling,* illustrated by Susan Kathleen Hartung, for Viking (New York, NY), due in 2005; *Dancing with Katrina,* for Peachtree Publishers (Atlanta, GA).

SIDELIGHTS: In the 1960s, D. J. Chaconas published several children's books and numerous stories for children in magazines before taking up needlework design and giving up writing for thirty years. Then, inspired by questions from one of her adult daughters, who had become interested in writing for children, Chaconas rediscovered her desire to write. She joined a writers' support group on the Internet and revived her former career.

While cleaning her basement one day, she found the draft for the story that became *One Little Mouse,* brushed it up a bit, and sold it to a publisher within a month. The second book she sold, *On a Wintry Morning,* became her first to appear in bookstores after her nearly three-decade hiatus. Like her others, *On a Wintry Morning* is a simple story told in rhymes that delighted reviewers. Chaconas's lyrics describe a little girl and her father spending a winter morning together. They bundle up to go out in the snow where they sled, hunt for animal tracks, go for a sleigh ride, and buy a puppy at the market. Later they return home to dry off, warm up, and the little girl falls asleep to the sound of her father's humming voice. The story is "by turns exuberant and soothing," *School Library Journal* critic Jane Marino observed, and "celebrates the small moments that a father and toddler share." Likewise, a contributor to *Publishers Weekly* noted the quiet, nostalgic tone of the story, which bypasses the drama of plot, "but compensates with a cornucopia of child-pleasing images." This reviewer concluded by calling *On a Wintry Morning* "as nourishing as hearty winter soup."

One Little Mouse sports a jauntier manner, and is both a counting book and a story told in rhyme about a little mouse who goes out in search of a roomier place to live. In the meadow he encounters two moles, three frogs, and so on, up to ten, finding that he is just not comfortable in the homes of these other creatures. Finally, he makes his way home again, past the homes of all his animal friends, and counting down from ten to one until he makes his way to his own home. The result is "a charming counting book that will appeal especially to the read-aloud set," predicted Cathie E. Bashaw in *School Library Journal.* Chaconas's facility with telling a story in rhyme was again the subject of praise. When interviewer Julia Durango of the Web site *By the Book* asked the author: "Do you have any deep, dark secrets for writing such wonderful rhyme?," Chaconas replied: "I think I was born with a small clock ticking in my brain. I've always liked rhythms of any kind . . . music . . . poetry . . . sleet clicking on the window, or whatever. I think I remember every nursery rhyme and song I ever learned as a child, because I loved them so much. I'm lucky to have an ear for rhythms."

BIOGRAPHICAL AND CRITICAL SOURCES:

PERIODICALS

Booklist, September 15, 2000, Shelley Townsend-Hudson, review of *On a Wintry Morning,* p. 247; September 1, 2002, Kathy Broderick, review of *One Little Mouse,* p. 136.

Horn Book Guide, spring, 2001, Nell Beram, review of *On a Wintry Morning,* p. 13.

Publishers Weekly, October 23, 2000, review of *On a Wintry Morning,* p. 74.

School Library Journal, November, 2000, Jane Marino, review of *On a Wintry Morning,* p. 112; August, 2002, Cathie E. Bashaw, review of *One Little Mouse,* p. 148.

ONLINE

By the Book, http://www.geocities.com/juliadurango/ (February 13, 2001), Julia Durango, "Dori Chaconas Warms up Winter."

Cynthia Leitich Smith: Children's Literature Resources, http://www.cynthialeitichsmith.com/ (June 12, 2003), "The Story behind the Story: Dori Chaconas on *One Little Mouse*" and "The Story behind the Story: Dori Chaconas on *On a Wintry Morning.*"

Kezi Matthews Late Bloomers Page, http://kezimatthews.com/ (June 12, 2003), "Dori Chaconas."

* * *

CHANCE, Megan 1959-

PERSONAL: Born December 31, 1959, in Columbus, OH; daughter of C. William (an education consultant) and Anita (a registered nurse) Chance; married; children: two. *Education:* Western Washington University, B.A., 1983. *Politics:* Democrat. *Religion:* Protestant. *Hobbies and other interests:* Cooking, reading, history.

ADDRESSES: Agent—Marcy Posner, Marcy Posner Literary Agency, 85 John St., New York, NY 10038. *E-mail*—meganchance@meganchance.com.

CAREER: Romance novelist. Television news photographer, Seattle, WA, 1983-86; special events coordinator, Seattle, WA, 1987-89; commercial studio manager, 1988-95; full-time fiction writer, 1995—.

MEMBER: Romance Writers of America.

AWARDS, HONORS: Named Speech Graduate of the Year, Western Washington University, 1983; Reviewer's Choice Award for Best First Historical Novel, *Romantic Times,* 1993, and RITA Award for excellence in Romantic Fiction, 1994, both for *A Candle in the Dark;* Reviewer's Choice Certificate of Excellence for Historical Novel, *Romantic Times,* 1994, for *After the Frost,* and 1995, for *The Portrait;* Reviewer's Choice nomination for Best Victorian Romance, *Romantic Times,* 1996, for *A Heart Divided;* Emerald City Keeper Award for Best Historical Romance, 1997, for *Fall from Grace;* Reviewer's Choice nomination for Best Innovative Romance, *Romantic Times,* 1997, for *The Way Home;* Career Achievement nomination in Innovative Romance, *Romantic Times,* 1997.

WRITINGS:

A Candle in the Dark, Dell (New York, NY), 1993.
After the Frost, Dell (New York, NY), 1994.

Megan Chance

The Portrait, Dell (New York, NY), 1995.
A Heart Divided, Dell (New York, NY), 1996.
Fall from Grace, HarperMonogram (New York, NY), 1997.
The Way Home, HarperPaperbacks (New York, NY), 1997.
The Gentleman Caller, Harper (New York, NY), 1998.
A Season in Eden, Harper (New York, NY), 1999.
Susannah Morrow, Warner Books (New York, NY), 2002.
An Inconvenient Wife, Warner Books (New York, NY), 2004.

SIDELIGHTS: Romance novelist Megan Chance has won praise for her willingness to challenge the often rigid conventions of the genre with unusual twists on character stereotypes and on standard plot lines. According to critics and reviewers, her ability to write convincingly about the inner lives and complex relationships of her characters emerged clearly in her first book, *A Candle in the Dark,* which won the 1992-93 *Romantic Times* Reviewers' Choice Award for Best First Historical Novel.

After the Frost, Chance's second novel, tells the story of Belle Sault, who returns to the rural Ohio community of her upbringing from exile in New York. She is in search of her daughter, Sarah, whose illegitimate conception forced Belle to flee years earlier. Belle rediscovers her roots while negotiating new relationships with her reputation-conscious mother and her stepbrother Rand, Sarah's father.

The Portrait features a pair of unlikely romance protagonists. Imogene Carter is an awkward, passive, and not especially striking woman haunted by a sense of inferiority to her dead sister. A flamboyant personality and talented artist, Jonas Whitaker suffers severely from bipolar affective disorder in an age with little understanding of the condition (the nineteenth century). Jonas reluctantly takes Imogene as a student, and despite early friction in their relationship, each finds in the other someone capable of recognizing and encouraging the inner qualities others overlook.

Chance explores the conflicting claims of love and revenge in *A Heart Divided.* Pinkerton agent Conor Roarke finds himself in a sod house in Beaver Creek, Colorado, with Sarilyn Travers, an Irish immigrant with whom he had an affair some years earlier while investigating the Molly Maguires. Sari's brother, Michael, murdered Conor's adoptive father in retribution, and Conor hopes to use Sari to bring him to justice. Meanwhile, Sari struggles with her attraction to a man who manipulated her and whose prior activities led to the death of her husband. The characters are torn between their feelings for each other and their perceived duties to others.

Fall from Grace brings to life another atypical hero-and-heroine duo. Raised from the age of twelve by her parents' murderers, the outlaw Sharpe gang, Lily Tremaine takes vengeance a dozen years later by betraying the Sharpes and taking flight. When her husband, Texas (another member of the gang), tracks her down, Lily tries to kill him, at which point Texas determines to hand her over to his father, Hank, the gang's leader. On the way to Lily's doom they stop in with Texas's half-sister, Josie, whose hopelessly romantic notions about the outlaw life give her great faith in and admiration for the pair. This in turn instills a sense of responsibility in Lily and Texas, and, although they never fully leave behind their lawbreaking ways, they begin to envision a new life together.

Chance again uses the nineteenth-century West as a backdrop in her sixth novel, *The Way Home.* Eliza

Beaudry yearns to escape the sharecropping life of her parents. Rather than marry a local man of her father's choice, she becomes pregnant by a gambler passing through town. Cole Wallace has the good looks and devil-may-care attitude of the classic romance hero but is not interested in marrying Eliza, and when her father forces the issue, Cole volunteers his shy, outcast brother, Aaron, in his place. Though socially clumsy and a stutterer, Aaron is also caring and thoughtful, and his poet's soul at last wins Eliza over.

After successes with *The Gentleman Caller* and *A Season in Eden*, Chance's 2002 effort, *Susannah Morrow,* is more of a straight historical novel than a romance. The title character is only one of three narrators, and the story is set during the Salem witch trials of the late seventeenth century. Susannah Morrow arrives in Salem from England to see her sister, Judith, who is married to a Puritan. Judith already has a teenaged daughter, Charity, when she dies giving birth to another daughter. Susannah's attempts to help her sister's survivors are met with suspicion in a town completely opposed to her freethinking ways, and she is eventually caught up in the madness of the witch trials. Elsa Gaztambide, reviewing the novel for *Booklist*, concluded that "Chance is superb at bringing to life a gray world dominated by the Bible and rooted in the seeds of fear."

Chance once told *CA:*" My primary motivation in writing is the need to exorcise my own demons. I tend to write for myself—in the process, the reader rarely, if ever, enters my consciousness. I write to try to understand the world around me. Writing is my own personal therapy, if you will.

"My early influences were great romantic suspense and historical romance writers: Mary Stewart, Anya Seton, Susan Howatch, and Norah Lofts, as well as fantasy authors J. R. R. Tolkien and Anne McCaffrey, and historical novelists Taylor Caldwell and Leon Uris. Gothics, especially historical gothic romances, were probably the books that most made me want to be a writer. In college my greatest influences were the romantic poets: Byron, Shelley, Coleridge, and especially Robert Browning. Later, Walt Whitman and Theodore Roethke. Poetry has been, and continues to be, a major influence on my writing. Though I have written poetry, the more interesting challenge for me is in applying its lessons to storytelling in prose.

"My writing process begins with an idea. It could be something I heard on the radio or television, or something I read. A dream, a feeling, a snippet on artist's colonies in the nineteenth century, an interesting characterization. For every book, it's different. I usually make a note of it, and then let the idea settle in while I'm working on something else. By the time the idea has a hold on me, it's usually evolved into something more solid. Usually, it suggests a time and place for itself. At this point, with the most nebulous hold possible on character and motivation, I begin researching the setting.

"Research for me is very intensive, and hugely enjoyable. I'll research for several months, and during this process, the rest of the story begins to suggest itself to me. Without the research, I would have no idea where to go or what to say. When the research is finished, the story finally has bones. Then it's just a matter of filling in the blanks: Who is the character? Where does he come from? What does he want? The theme of the book begins to come clear, as does the structure and the technique I want to use to tell the story. I'll work on an outline, and by the time I sit down to write, I have a pretty good idea where the book is going to go, if not always how I'll get there. I like to leave characters a little vague and let them tell their own stories as the book progresses. The writing of a book, from start to finish, usually takes me about a year. I rewrite and edit constantly and ruthlessly.

"At the beginning of my writing career I'd written six unpublished manuscripts, and though I was getting 'good' rejections, I'd come to a crisis point where I had to ask myself: If I never published, would I keep on writing? The answer was yes. I'd written stories my entire life; I couldn't stop if I tried. The answer was extraordinarily freeing. Finally, I could write the book I really wanted to read. I wrote about characters I was told I 'couldn't' write about. That book was *A Candle in the Dark,* my first published romance.

"I write historical novels because I love history, but also because my vision of the world fits so well within an historical setting. People had the same problems they do today, but the social perception of those problems was crude and unsympathetic. There were few cures. There were no twelve-step programs or lithium. There was no therapy. You either dealt with your problems and went on, or you died. The adaptability of the human spirit is such an incredible thing, and historical novels allow me to really explore that in a way that is personally satisfying and life-affirming.

"Both *A Candle in the Dark* and *The Portrait* were written along this theme. Both books explore inner demons—of an alcoholic and an artist with bipolar illness, respectively. Both end with the characters learning to adapt and go on. With *Fall from Grace,* I especially wanted to deal with the reality of the outlaw West. The era is so romanticized, and I wanted to explore the real human emotions and motivations of a person who was, essentially, a sociopath. At some point in our lives, we all must come face to face with who we are and what we've become. What happens if those things include murder and robbery? That was the motivation behind *Fall from Grace.* Essentially, I write about flawed people who are forced to take responsibility for the choices they have made in their lives. If there was a central theme to my work, I imagine that would be it."

BIOGRAPHICAL AND CRITICAL SOURCES:

PERIODICALS

Affaire de Coeur, October, 1995.

Booklist, August, 2002, Elsa Gaztambide, review of *Susannah Morrow,* p. 1917.

Kirkus Reviews, August 15, 2002, review of *Susannah Morrow,* p. 1158.

Library Journal, September 15, 2002, Kim Rutter, review of *Susannah Morrow,* p. 88.

Publishers Weekly, September 5, 1994, p. 107; June 3, 1996, p. 81; September 2, 2002, review of *Susannah Morrow,* p. 53.

Romantic Times, September, 1993, p. 42; October, 1995; February, 1997.

ONLINE

Official Megan Chance Web site, http://www.meganchance.com/ (October 28, 2003).

Romance Reader Web site, http://www.theromancereader.com/ (October 21, 2003), reviews of *Susannah Morrow, A Season in Eden, Fall from Grace, The Gentleman Caller,* and *The Way Home.*

* * *

CLEMENTS, Andrew 1949-
(Andrew Elborn)

Andrew Clements

PERSONAL: Born May 29, 1949, in Camden, NJ; son of William Denney, Jr. (an insurance executive) and Doris (Kruse) Clements; married Rebecca Pierpont (an actress and homemaker), December 16, 1972; children: John, Nathaniel, George, Charles. *Education:* Northwestern University, B.A. (English literature), 1971; National Louis University, M.A. (elementary education), 1972.

ADDRESSES: *Home*—Westborough, MA. *Agent*—Writers House, 21 West 26th St., New York, NY 10010.

CAREER: Writer, editor, and educator. Sunset Ridge School, Northfield, IL, fourth-grade teacher, 1972-74; Wilmette Junior High School, Wilmette, IL, eighth-grade teacher, 1974-77; New Trier High School, Winnetka, IL, English teacher, 1977-79. Allen D. Bragdon Publishers, New York, NY, editor, 1980-82; Alphabet Press, Natick, MA, sales and marketing manager and editor, 1982-85; Keller Graduate School of Management, Chicago, IL, director, 1985-87; Picture Book Studio, Ltd., Saxonville, MA, vice president and editorial director, 1987-93; Houghton Mifflin, School Division, Boston, MA, editor, 1994-95; Christian Science Publishing Society, Boston, MA, editor, 1997-98. Member of executive board, Children's Book Council, 1983-85; frequent speaker in schools and at writing and education conferences.

AWARDS, HONORS: New York Public Library One Hundred Titles for Reading and Sharing listee, 1996, *Horn Book* Fanfare Book designation, Parents' Choice Honor Book designation, Christopher Award, and Judy Lopez Memorial Honor Book Award, all 1997, Great Stone Face Book Award, 1997-98, Chicago Public Library Best of the Best listee, *Family Fun* Best Kid's Book designation, and Rhode Island Children's Book Award, all 1998, William Allen White Children's Book Award, 1999, and nominations for Dorothy Canfield Fisher Book Award and others, all for *Frindle.*

WRITINGS:

FOR CHILDREN

Bird Adalbert, Picture Book Studio (Saxonville, MA), 1985.

Big Al (miniature book), illustrated by Yoshi, Picture Book Studio (Saxonville, MA), 1987.

Santa's Secret Helper, illustrated by Debrah Santini, Picture Book Studio (Saxonville, MA), 1990.

(As Andrew Elborn) *Noah and the Ark and the Animals,* illustrated by Ivan Gantschev, Picture Book Studio (Saxonville, MA), 1991.

Temple Cat, illustrated by Alan Marks, Picture Book Studio (Saxonville, MA), 1991, illustrated by Kate Kiesler, Clarion (New York, NY), 1996.

Mother Earth's Counting Book, illustrated by Lonni Sue Johnson, Picture Book Studio (Saxonville, MA), 1992.

Billy and the Bad Teacher, illustrated by Elivia Savadier, Picture Book Studio (Saxonville, MA), 1992.

Who Owns the Cow?, illustrated by Joan Landis, Clarion (New York, NY), 1995.

Bright Christmas: An Angel Remembers, illustrated by Kate Kiesler, Clarion (New York, NY), 1996.

Frindle (middle-grade novel), illustrated by Brian Selznick, Simon & Schuster (New York, NY), 1996.

(Adaptor) *Philipp's Birthday Book,* illustrated by Hanne Turk, North-South Books (New York, NY), 1996.

Riff's BeBop Book, Simon & Schuster (New York, NY), 1996.

Real Monsters Go for the Mold!, illustrated by Matthew Stoddart, Simon & Schuster (New York, NY), 1997.

Things That Go Eek on Halloween, illustrated by George Ulrich, Simon & Schuster (New York, NY), 1997.

Real Monsters Stage Fright, illustrated by Matthew Stoddart, Simon & Schuster (New York, NY), 1997.

Music Time, Any Time!, illustrated by Tom Leigh, Simon & Schuster (New York, NY), 1997.

Double Trouble in Walla Walla, illustrated by Salvatore Murdocca, Millbrook Press (New York, NY), 1997.

Workshop, illustrated by David Wisniewski, Clarion (New York, NY), 1998.

Gromble's Haunted Halloween, Simon & Schuster (New York, NY), 1998.

Where the Moon Lives, North-South Books (New York, NY), 1998.

Hey Dad, Could I Borrow Your Hammer?, illustrated by Jackie Snider, Millbrook Press (New York, NY), 1999.

The Landry News (middle-grade novel), Simon & Schuster (New York, NY), 1999.

The Janitor's Boy, Simon & Schuster (New York, NY), 2000.

Circus Family Dog, illustrated by Sue Truesdell, Clarion (New York, NY), 2000.

Ringo Saves the Day!, illustrated by Donald Cook, Simon & Schuster (New York, NY), 2001.

The Publishing Club, illustrated by Brian Selznick, Simon & Schuster (New York, NY), 2001.

Jake Drake, Bully Buster, Simon & Schuster (New York, NY), 2001.

Jake Drake, Know-It-All, Simon & Schuster (New York, NY), 2001.

Jake Drake, Teacher's Pet, Simon & Schuster (New York, NY), 2001.

The School Story (middle-grade novel), Simon & Schuster (New York, NY), 2001.

Brave Norman: A True Story, Simon & Schuster (New York, NY), 2001.

The Jacket, Simon & Schuster (New York, NY), 2001.

Things Not Seen, Philomel Books (New York, NY), 2002.

Dolores and the Big Fire: A True Story, Simon & Schuster (New York, NY), 2002.
Jake Drake, Class Clown, Simon & Schuster (New York, NY), 2002.
Big Al and Shrimpy, Simon & Schuster (New York, NY), 2002.
A Week in the Woods, Simon & Schuster (New York, NY), 2002.
Tara and Tiree: Fearless Friends, a True Story, illustrated by Ellen Beier, Simon & Schuster (New York, NY), 2002.
The Report Card, Simon & Schuster (New York, NY), 2003.
Because Your Daddy Loves You, illustrated by R. W. Alley, Clarion (New York, NY), 2004.

READING PROGRAM BOOKS FOR SCHOOLS

Karen's Island, Houghton Mifflin (Boston, MA), 1995.
Three Wishes for Buster, Houghton Mifflin (Boston, MA), 1995.
Bill Picket: An American Original, Texas Style, Houghton Mifflin (Boston, MA), 1996.
Hurricane Andrew, Houghton Mifflin (Boston, MA), 1998.
Ham and Eggs for Jack, Houghton Mifflin (Boston, MA), 1998.
Life in the Desert, Steck-Vaughn (Austin, TX), 1998.
Desert Treasure, illustrated by Wayne Anthony Still, Steck-Vaughn (Austin, TX), 1998.
Inventors: Making Things Better, Steck-Vaughn (Austin, TX), 1998.
Milo's Great Invention, illustrated by Johnansen Newman, Steck-Vaughn (Austin, TX), 1998.

Also translator and/or adaptor of more than a dozen picture books for Picture Book Studio and North-South Books, including *Where Is Mr. Mole?, The Christmas Teddy Bear, Brave As a Tiger, The Beast and the Boy, Little Pig, Bigger Trouble, A Dog's Best Friend,* and *Where the Moon Lives.*

ADAPTATIONS: Things Not Seen was adapted as an audiobook, Listening Library, 2002.

WORK IN PROGRESS: Circus Family Dog, a picture book for Clarion, and *Razzle Dazzled in Walla Walla,* a picture book for Millbrook Press; a four-book series of middle grades novels for Simon & Schuster.

SIDELIGHTS: Andrew Clements has all the bases covered in the field of children's books. An avid reader as a child, he later taught the joys of reading to students in elementary and high school, then went on to the world of publishing, acquiring, editing, marketing, and developing quality children's books for several publishing houses. In 1985 he decided to contribute his own work to that market, beginning with his first picture book, *Bird Adalbert.* The author of the award-winning *Frindle,* a book about the power of words that a *Kirkus* reviewer called "something of a classic," Clements has also attracted a wide readership for his picture books, including the popular *Big Al, Santa's Secret Helper, Temple Cat, Bright Christmas,* and his "Real Monsters" books.

"I've got a special place in my heart for libraries and librarians," Clements once commented. "As a kindergartner in Oaklyn, New Jersey, I confess that I was something of a showoff. I was already a good reader, and I didn't mind who knew about it." With parents who were compulsive readers themselves and who passed on the love of books to their children, it was no surprise at home that Clements should be such an early reader. At school, however, it was a different story. On his first trip to the school library, Clements chose a thick book on myths. The next day he asked his teacher if he could take it back to the library. "'Is it too hard, dear?' she asked sympathetically," Clements recalled. The teacher's eyebrows shot up when Clements informed her that it was not the difficulty of the book that was the problem. He had already finished it and wanted more. "That event created for me an open invitation to head to the library just about any old time I wanted to. And the librarian was a gem. She kept me well stocked."

Clements made his way through the classics, from A. A. Milne to Robert Louis Stevenson, and from Robin Hood to King Arthur. Later loves included Sherlock Holmes and the Hardy Boys, *Robinson Crusoe, The Swiss Family Robinson,* works by Alexandré Dumas and Jack London, as well as adventure stories and biographies. "I loved owning books. And I will always love that librarian at my elementary school, because she made me feel like I was the owner of every book. That's one of the greatest things about reading a book—read it, and you own it forever."

Clements attended Northwestern University and then earned a master's degree in education at National Louis University. For the next seven years he taught school, both at the grade-school level and high school. "I liked it," Clements related. "The kids and I laughed a lot. I enjoyed the hundreds of little conversations every day, the running jokes—I even liked the noise and the craziness of a Friday afternoon right before Christmas vacation. And I loved reading good books with kids—the kids at school and also the four boys my wife and I had at home. As a teacher, it was a thrill to read a book aloud, and see a whole class listen so carefully to every word, dying to know what would happen next. And I was amazed at the wonderful discussions a good book can spark. Good books make good things happen in real life. They can make a big difference. So when I was given the chance to start writing for children, I jumped at it."

That chance began, initially, as an editor of children's books at various publishers, including Alphabet Press and Picture Book Studio, where he not only acquired titles but also helped translate and adapt European picture books for the U.S. market. "I didn't start writing books until I was about thirty-five years old," Clements commented. "But I began writing a long time before that. And the way I really got started writing was by reading. Before too long I found myself reading something good and saying to myself, 'I wish I had written that!' I think the more good books you read, the better you learn what good writing sounds like and feels like. Every good writer I know started off as a good reader."

One of Clements's most popular titles is his second picture book, *Big Al,* a "simple story about the need for friendship," as Gratia Banta described the book in *School Library Journal.* Big Al of the title is a rather ugly and scary-looking fish who desperately tries to be liked by the smaller fish. When Big Al saves the lives of the little fish, he accomplishes his mission, becoming their fast friend. Noting the illustrator Yoshi's use of silk batik and painting, Banta wrote that the "magnificence" of the illustrations matched "Clements's international story of friendship. . . . The book offers a welcome sense of something other than western culture."

Other picture books followed. Illustrated by Debrah Santini, *Santa's Secret Helper* features Mrs. Santa as a stand-in for her exhausted husband, dressed just like Santa and filling stockings with great care. Back at the North Pole, she gets a big hug from her husband. "This story is appealing in its simplicity," noted *Booklist*'s Ilene Cooper, who gave high praise to the artwork which keeps the helper's identity a secret until the very end. Another holiday title is Clements's *Bright Christmas: An Angel Remembers,* the story of the Nativity told from the point of view of an angel. A contributor to *Publishers Weekly* remarked that in "the voice of a seasoned spinner of yarns, Clements imagines a heavenly perspective on the birth of Jesus." Writing in *Booklist,* Shelley Townsend-Hudson described the book as a "lovely blend of words and pictures" which "attempt to explain the idea of eternity." A *School Library Journal* reviewer noted that the book is told "in spare, tempered, and reverent prose," and concluded that *Bright Christmas* "is a fine combination of text and illustration that tells a familiar story."

Clements has explored themes ranging from strengthening counting skills to accepting differences to the concept of ownership in his ambitious picture books. A simple task such as learning how to count is transformed by Clements into an exploration "of the diverse wonders of our planet," as Steven Engelfried described *Mother Earth's Counting Book* in a *School Library Journal* review. The seven continents and four oceans of this planet all figure into Clements's counting scheme. *Billy and the Bad Teacher* tells a story of acceptance that "will have students and teachers rolling out of their chairs," according to Jeanne Marie Clancy in *School Library Journal.* Neat and compulsive Billy is initially horrified when he gets the unorthodox Mr. Adams for his new teacher, but slowly comes to love this teacher who makes long division fun and reads *The Swiss Family Robinson* to the class each day. "The story makes a nice point about accepting the foibles of others without hitting readers over the head with it," concluded Clancy.

The concept of ownership comes under scrutiny in *Who Owns the Cow?,* a story about a cow, a farmer, and the many people who come into contact with both. A little girl thinks of the cow when she hears its bell; a milkman earns a living by delivering its milk; an artist paints it. So who really owns it? While several reviewers felt this question of ownership might be too philosophical for most young readers, Deborah Stevenson of the *Bulletin of the Center for Children's Books* maintained that *Who Owns the Cow?* is an "offbeat book with an appealing style" that "will puzzle some and become the favorite of others." Relationships also figure in *Temple Cat,* the story of an ancient Egyptian feline who is the lord of a temple but is tired of being pampered. The cat longs simply to be loved, and finds such love in the arms of two children after it has run away. Susan Middleton, writing in *School Library Journal,* asserted that "this endearing tale is sure to find favor wherever cat stories are in demand," while a *Kirkus Reviews* critic remarked that "Clements pens a tale for consummate cat enthusiasts or lovers of antiquity."

A further adventure in the picture-book format is *Double Trouble in Walla Walla.* Young Lulu is sent to the principal's office when she cannot stop speaking in a sort of hyphenated slang, in a book that Barbara McGinn in *School Library Journal* dubbed "side-splitting fun." "In this breathlessly verbose tale, a rash of compound nonsense words infects an elementary school," commented a *Publishers Weekly* reviewer, who concluded that "children with a fondness for wordplay may delight in this dizzying romp."

More such wordplay is served up in Clements's first novel for middle graders, *Frindle.* The book was inspired by comments Clements once made when talking to students at a Rhode Island school, "teaching them a little about the way words work," as the author later recalled. "I was trying to explain to them how words only mean what we decide they mean. They didn't believe me when I pointed to a fat dictionary and told them that ordinary people like them and like me had made up all the words in that book—and that new words get made up all the time." To illustrate his point, Clements pulled a pen from his pocket and told the students that they could change the name of this instrument from pen to anything they made up. Clements chose a made-up word, "frindle," and challenged students to start calling it by that name instead of "pen" to see if such a name would stick. "The kids loved that story, and for a couple of years I told that same story every time I went to talk at a school or a library. Then one day in 1990 as I was sifting through my life, looking for a story idea, I wondered what would happen if a kid started using a new word, and other kids really liked it, but his English teacher didn't. So the idea for the book was born."

In the novel, Nick, who always stays one step ahead of his teachers, can usually manage to sidetrack the teacher from assigning homework. However, when he meets Mrs. Granger, his new fifth-grade language-arts teacher, this simple ruse breaks down. To irritate her, he invents the word "frindle" for pen and convinces other kids in the school to use the neologism. Soon the word spreads to the city, the state, the nation, and ten years later "frindle" has even made it into the dictionary. And only then does Nick realize that Mrs. Granger has secretly been rooting for him and his new word all the time. "The chesslike sparring between the gifted Nicholas and his crafty teacher is enthralling," commented a *Kirkus Reviews* critic, who concluded that "this is a captivating tale—one to press upon children, and one they'll be passing among themselves." A *Publishers Weekly* commentator remarked that "dictionary lovers will cotton to this mild classroom fantasy, while readers who have a hard time believing that one person could invent a word out of thin air will be surprised to learn that the word 'quiz' was invented the same way." *Booklist*'s Kay Weisman concluded her review of *Frindle* by noting that the book is sure to be "popular with a wide range of readers [and] will make a great read-aloud as well." Elizabeth S. Watson of *Horn Book* remarked that Clements "has created a fresh imaginative plot that will have readers smiling all the way through, if not laughing out loud." Award committees agreed with the critics: *Frindle* garnered more than thirty award nominations, and won the 1997 Christopher Award.

In *The Landry News* Clements tells of Cara Landry, a bright student who wants to become a journalist someday. When she begins to publish her own newspaper, the *Landry News,* she runs into trouble with the school principal over her claims that a particular teacher does no teaching at all. Issues of censorship, teacher incompetence, and administrative coverup come to the fore in this novel. A critic for *Publishers Weekly* claimed that "the affecting conclusion brings triumph for both teacher and students, and will elicit cheers from readers," while a *Horn Book* reviewer dubbed *The Landry News* a "terrific school story."

Jack Rankin undergoes persistent teasing from his classmates in *The Janitor's Boy* because his father works as the school janitor. When Jack rebels against his father, the punishment—that he must assist his father in his duties—drags him into his father's world and an understanding develops between the two. William McLoughlin in the *School Library Journal* found that many readers will "identify with the beleaguered Jack and his struggle to make peace with his father and with himself." According to Kay Weisman in

Booklist, "Clements's strength is his realistic depiction of public schools, both from the child and the adult point of view."

In addition to stand-alone novels, Clements has written several novels featuring fourth-grader Jake Drake. In *Jake Drake, Bully Buster* Jake recounts how he comes to terms with Link Baxter, a boy who has bullied him for years. When the two boys are assigned to work on a Thanksgiving project, Jake finds that Link is good at making models. He also discovers that Link is scared to speak before the class. Jake agrees to do the talking for the pair when they present their project, thereby earning Link's respect and gratitude. "While the tone of the book is light and humorous," Elaine E. Knight noted in *School Library Journal,* "it is a realistic look at a common problem." In *Jake Drake, Know-It-All* Jake enters a science-fair contest to win a computer, but he refuses to work with his friend Willie because he wants the prize all to himself. When Jake realizes he is becoming someone he does not like, he changes his mind, works with Willie, and the pair win second prize. Pat Leach, writing in *School Library Journal,* felt that in recounting his story, Jake "sounds like a regular fourth grader as he describes his teachers and classmates. But he also digs deep to reveal the character-building lessons in everyday events." Linda Perkins in *Booklist* found that "Clements portrays a common, annoying classroom situation, resolves it in an upbeat way, and inserts a little practical advice."

In *Jake Drake, Teacher's Pet* Jake finds that for several days, he is everybody's favorite, a situation he does not enjoy because the other kids resent him. Leach noted: "Jake embodies the average boy who seldom draws attention to himself, but who is quietly observing and tries to do the right thing." *Jake Drake, Class Clown* finds the boy being a little too funny for his own good when a substitute teacher comes to his classroom. Kay Bowes in a review for *School Library Journal* called Jake "an endearing boy who uses his head to sort out appropriate conclusions to bad situations."

In *A Week in the Woods* young Mark's family has just moved to New Hampshire where the boy, knowing his inattentive parents plan to soon ship him to a distant private academy, refuses to fit in at his temporary school. When he is wrongly accused by his teacher, Mr. Maxwell, of bringing a knife to a school nature outing, Mark hides in the forest, gets lost, and must survive in the rugged terrain on his own. "The story explores both Mark's and Mr. Maxwell's point of view," Jean Gaffney noted in *School Library Journal,* "and the final resolution of their conflict is effective." "Clements's compassionate character studies are realistic and hopeful," added Francisca Goldsmith in *Booklist.*

Clements continues his commitment to the world of children's books with classroom appearances and the writing and/or illustrating of early readers, picture books, and more novels for middle graders. "There has been a lot of talk in recent years about the decline of reading," he once commented, "the overpowering influence of the television and multi-media screens, even a national descent into illiteracy. Everyone is so upset when these ideas are voiced, and everyone feels sure that reading and books are important—but why? Apart from the basic skill of functional or task-related reading, why is there a universal conviction that books and literature are indispensable? I think it's because when we read, we're in charge. That's probably the most significant difference between pagetime and screentime. When we read, we decide when, where, how long, and about what. One of the few places on earth that it is still possible to experience an instant sense of freedom and privacy is anywhere we open up a good book and begin to read."

Clements told *CA:* "Most of my characters are fairly normal people who are dealing with the basics of everyday life—getting along with others, finding a place in the world, discovering talents, overcoming challenges, trying to have some wholesome fun along the way, and getting into some scrapes and a little mischief now and then too. I guess I hope my readers will be able to see bits and pieces of themselves in the stories, particularly the novels that take place in and around school. School is a rich setting because schools and education are at the very heart of every community. The stories that are set in school seem to resonate with kids, teachers, parents, librarians—readers of all ages. Everyone's life has been touched by school experiences. And I also hope, of course, that kids and others will enjoy reading, enjoy the uses of language, and enjoy the storytelling.

"I'm often asked "Among your works, of which are you most proud?" I know people mean of which *book* am I most proud, but I choose to hear the question literally. Of all my works, the one I'm proudest of is the fact that I've been able to keep living a fairly normal life and still manage to carve out some creative accomplishments. When I visited a school recently a boy asked, "Mr. Clements, is writing your whole life?" And the answer is quite simply, no. Sometimes writing and the surrounding responsibilities of that career would try to become a person's whole life. Writing is hard, solitary work—work that is not helped along by continual interruptions. But the fact is, I am many other things before I am a writer. I am a son; I am a brother; I am a church member; I am a neighbor and a citizen. And then somewhere along the way and in the midst of that life, I am also a writer. I would not be the writer I am without these 'interruptions' that collectively comprise the work of which I am most proud.

"Regarding the books I've written, I couldn't pick out one as a favorite. But taken together, I'm glad that my school stories might give kids and parents some insights into how much unselfish care and thought and love teachers pour into their work every day. It's an extraordinarily difficult job to do well, and teachers rarely get either the recognition or the compensation they deserve.

"Looking to the future, I'd like to keep finding ideas that are worth exploring, and I think every good idea is worth exploring, and I think there is no shortage of good ideas. So that sounds like a recipe for full employment."

BIOGRAPHICAL AND CRITICAL SOURCES:

PERIODICALS

Booklist, February 15, 1985, p. 842; December 15, 1990, pp. 860-861; September 1, 1996, pp. 125, 136; December 15, 1996, p. 734; March 1, 2000, Kay Weisman, review of *The Janitor's Boy,* p. 1243; June 1, 2000, Ilene Cooper, review of *Circus Family Dog,* p. 1905; December 1, 2000, Elaine Hanson, review of *The Janitor's Boy,* p. 740; June 1, 2001, Chris Sherman, review of *The School Story,* p. 1879; November 1, 2001, Linda Perkins, review of *Jake Drake, Know-It-All,* p. 474, and Gillian Engberg, review of *The School Story,* p. 478, and Gillian Engberg, review of *Brave Norman,* p. 486; January 1, 2002, Catherine Andronik, review of *Jake Drake, Teacher's Pet,* p. 856; March 1, 2002, Hazel Rochman, review of *The Jacket,* p. 1136; April 15, 2002, Hazel Rochman, review of *Things Not Seen,* p. 1412; June 1, 2002, Ilene Cooper, review of *Dolores and the Big Fire,* p. 1733; October 1, 2002, Francisca Goldsmith, review of *A Week in the Woods,* p. 324.

Bookseller, January 18, 2002, Wendy Cooling, review of *Frindle,* p. 48.

Bulletin of the Center for Children's Books, October, 1995, p. 49; February, 1996, p. 186; October, 1996, pp. 51-52.

Childhood Education, mid-summer, 2002, Susan L. Angstadt, review of *The School Story,* p. 306.

Horn Book, November-December, 1996, Elizabeth S. Watson, review of *Frindle,* p. 732; July, 1999, review of *The Landry News,* p. 462; July, 2000, review of *The Janitor's Boy,* p. 454; July, 2001, review of *The School Story,* p. 448; March-April, 2002, Roger Sutton, review of *Things Not Seen,* p. 210.

Instructor, January-February, 2003, Judy Freeman, review of *A Week in the Woods,* p. 79.

Kirkus Reviews, July 1, 1995, p. 944; July 1, 1996, p. 965; October 1, 1996, p. 1475; November 1, 2001, review of *Jake Drake, Teacher's Pet,* p. 1546; February 1, 2002, review of *The Jacket,* p. 177, and review of *Things Not Seen,* p. 178; July 1, 2002, review of *Big Al and Shrimpy,* p. 951; August 1, 2002, review of *A Week in the Woods,* p. 1124.

New York Times Book Review, March 16, 1997, p. 26.

Publishers Weekly, September 14, 1994, p. 31; July 15, 1996, p. 74; September 30, 1996, p. 90; October 6, 1997, p. 50; October 13, 1997, p. 74; April 27, 1998, review of *Where the Moon Lives,* p. 66; March 29, 1999, review of *Workshop,* p. 104; June 7, 1999, review of *The Landry News,* p. 83; May 1, 2000, review of *The Janitor's Boy,* p. 71; August 21, 2000, review of *The Landry News,* p. 75; May 28, 2001, review of *The School Story,* p. 88; October 29, 2001, review of *Jake Drake, Teacher's Pet,* p. 66; December 17, 2001, review of *The Jacket,* p. 91; January 28, 2002, review of *Things Not Seen,* p. 291; April 1, 2002, Sally Lodge, interview with Andrew Clements, p. 25; August 12, 2002, review of *A Week in the Woods,* p. 301.

School Library Journal, June, 1989, p. 86; July, 1990, p. 59; June, 1993, p. 72; January, 1994, p. 87; October, 1994, p. 39; December, 1995, p. 73; March, 1996, p. 167; October, 1996, p. 34; November, 1996, p. 87; January, 1998, p. 81; July,

1998, Rosalyn Pierini, review of *Where the Moon Lives,* p. 74; May, 1999, Shirley Wilton, review of *Workshop,* p. 104; July, 1999, Anne Knickerbocker, review of *The Landry News,* p. 95; May, 2000, William McLoughlin, review of *The Janitor's Boy,* p. 170; August, 2000, Wanda Meyers-Hines, review of *Circus Family Dog,* p. 146; May, 2001, Elaine E. Knight, review of *Jake Drake, Bully Buster,* p. 114; June, 2001, Terrie Dorio, review of *The School Story,* p. 144; September, 2001, Maura Bresnahan, review of *Ringo Saves the Day!,* p. 212; November, 2001, Pat Leach, review of *Jake Drake, Know-It-All,* p. 113; February, 2002, Holly T. Sneeringer, review of *Brave Norman,* p. 117; March, 2002, Lucinda Snyder Whitehurst, review of *The Jacket,* p. 226, and Saleena L. Davidson, review of *Things Not Seen,* p. 226; April, 2002, review of *Jake Drake, Teacher's Pet,* p. 102; May, 2002, Jessica Snow, review of *Dolores and the Big Fire,* p. 135; July, 2002, Brian E. Wilson, review of *The School Story,* p. 64, and Kay Bowes, review of *Jake Drake, Class Clown,* p. 86; November, 2002, Kathleen Simonetta, review of *Big Al and Shrimpy,* p. 119, and Jean Gaffney, review of *A Week in the Woods,* p. 160; March, 2003, Maria Tanaguchi, review of *Tara and Tiree: Fearless Friends,* p. 179.

Stone Soup, January-February, 2003, Jill Giornelli, review of *The School Story,* p. 12.

ONLINE

Houghton Mifflin Education Place Web site, http://www.eduplace.com/kids/ (November 10, 2003).

Official Frindle Web site, http://www.frindle.com/ (November 10, 2003).

Read-In Foundation Web site, http://www.readin.org/ (November 10, 2003).

* * *

CORTEZ, Jayne 1936-

PERSONAL: Born May 10, 1936, in Fort Huachuca, AZ; married Ornette Coleman (a jazz musician), 1954 (divorced, 1964); married Melvin Edwards (a sculptor), 1975; children: (first marriage) Denardo Coleman. *Ethnicity:* "African American." *Education:* Compton Junior College, Los Angeles, CA; studied drama at Ebony Showcase, Los Angeles.

Jayne Cortez

ADDRESSES: *Agent*—c/o Author Mail, Bola Press, Box 96, Village Station, New York, NY 10014.

CAREER: Poet and performance artist. Watts Repertory Theatre Company, Los Angeles, CA, cofounder, 1964, artistic director, 1964-70; Bola Press, New York, NY, founder, 1972; Livingston College of Rutgers, writer-in-residence, 1977-83. Was active in black voter registration drives in Mississippi, 1963-64; has lectured and read her poetry alone and with musical accompaniment at universities, including Dartmouth College, Howard University, Queens College, Wesleyan University, University of Ibadan, and throughout Europe, Africa, Latin America, and the Caribbean at UNESCO and other events; appeared at Berlin Jazz Festival; appeared at Fourth World Conference on Women in Beijing, China; has released several recordings with band the Firespitters; poem "I Am New York City" appeared in episode of Fox Television series *Tribeca.*

MEMBER: Poetry Society of America (board member), PEN American Center, Coordinating Council of Literary Magazines (board member), Organization of Women Writers of Africa (cofounder), Poet's House (board member).

AWARDS, HONORS: Rockefeller Foundation grant, 1970; Creative Artists Public Service poetry award, New York State Council on the Arts, 1973, 1981; National Endowment for the Arts fellowship in creative writing, 1979-80, 1986; American Book Award, 1980, for *Mouth on Paper*; New York Foundation for the Arts Award, 1987; Fannie Lou Hamer Award, 1994; Afrikan Poetry Theatre tribute and award, 1994; International African Festival Award; Arts International award, 1996; Langston Hughes Medal, City College of New York, 2001.

WRITINGS:

POETRY

Pissstained Stairs and the Monkey Man's Wares, Phrase Text (New York, NY), 1969.

Festivals and Funerals, drawings by husband, Mel Edwards, Bola Press (New York, NY), 1971.

Scarifications, drawings by Mel Edwards, Bola Press (New York, NY), 1973.

Mouth on Paper, Bola Press (New York, NY), 1977.

Firespitter, drawings by Mel Edwards, Bola Press (New York, NY), 1982.

Coagulations: New and Selected Poems, Thunder's Mouth Press (New York, NY), 1984.

Poetic Magnetic, drawings by Mel Edwards, Bola Press (New York, NY), 1991.

Somewhere in Advance of Nowhere, Serpent's Tail (London, England), 1997.

A Jazz Fan Looks Back, Hanging Loose Press (Brooklyn, NY), 2002.

OTHER

Celebrations and Solitudes: The Poetry of Jayne Cortez (sound recording), Strata-East Records, 1975.

Unsubmissive Blues (sound recording), Bola Press (New York, NY), 1980.

There It Is (sound recording), Bola Press (New York, NY), 1982.

War against War (performance piece), UNESCO (Paris, France), 1982.

Poetry in Motion (film), Sphinx Productions (Toronto, Ontario, Canada), 1983.

Maintain Control (sound recording), Bola Press (New York, NY), 1986.

Everywhere Drums (sound recording), Bola Press (New York, NY), 1991.

Mandela Is Coming (music video), Globalvision, 1991.

Cheerful & Optimistic (sounding recording), with band the Firespitters, 1994.

Taking the Blues Back Home (sound recording), with band the Firespitters, Harmolodic/Verve, 1997.

Borders of Disorderly Time (sound recording), with band the Firespitters, Bola Press (New York, NY), 2003.

Contributor to anthologies, including *We Speak As Liberators,* edited by Orde Coombs, Dodd, 1970; *The Poetry of Black America,* edited by Arnold Adoff, Harper, 1972; *Hommage à Leon Gontran Damas,* Présence Africaine, 1979; *Black Sister,* edited by Erlene Stedson, Indiana University Press, 1981; *Women on War,* edited by Daniela Gioseffi, Simon & Schuster, 1988; and *Daughters of Africa,* Pantheon, 1992.

Contributor to numerous periodicals, including *Free Spirits, Mother Jones, UNESCO Courier, Black Scholar, Heresies, Mundus Artium, Post Modern American Poetry, Surrealist Women,* and *Women on War.* Guest editor, *Black Scholar,* 1988, and *Drumvoices Revue,* 1994; contributor to *Poetry in Motion,* 1983, a video anthology of contemporary avant-garde American poets. Director of film, *Yari Yari: Black Women Writers and the Future,* 1999. Author's works have been translated into numerous languages.

SIDELIGHTS: Poet and performance artist Jayne Cortez began her creative explorations as an actress, publishing her first volume of poetry, *Pissstained Stairs and the Monkey Man's Wares,* in 1969. Her work, which reflects the politics and culture of African Americans, has been translated into twenty-eight languages and is characterized by a dramatic intensity. D. H. Melhem noted in an introduction to an interview with Cortez published in *Heroism in the New Black Poetry:* "Her fine ear for music, her dynamic imagery, and her disposition to orchestrate in a broad cultural span, both African and American, have led her social and political concerns into unique and risk-taking forms." She records and performs her poetry around the world, often accompanied by jazz musicians, including her own band, the Firespitters, in which her son, Denardo Coleman, plays drums. Barbara T. Christian, writing in *Callaloo,* commented: "Cortez has forged connections . . . that help us see how our histories . . . whether we live in Chile, Harlem or Nigeria, are related. The result is a poetry as wide in its scope as it is compelling in its craft."

In a review for *Negro Digest* of *Pissstained Stairs and the Monkey Man's Wares,* the poet Nikki Giovanni remarked: "We haven't had many jazz poets who got inside the music and the people who created it. We poet about them, but not of them. And this is Cortez's strength. She can wail from Theodore Navarro and Leadbelly to Ornette [Coleman, Cortez's first husband] and never lose a beat and never make a mistake. She's a genius and all lovers of jazz will need this book—lovers of poetry will want it." The book phonically portrays the love lives of such great jazz performers as Billie Holiday, Charlie Parker, and Bessie Smith.

Cortez's second book of poetry, *Festivals and Funerals,* reaches out through the jazz theme into ideology and political concerns for African Americans, with poems like "I Am a Worker," which is written in the voice of an oppressed garment worker. These poems also deal with the themes of colonialism, African nationalism, and the artist as revolutionary. In an in-depth study of Cortez's work for *African American Review,* Tony Bolden commented that her poetry "operates as a sort of antibiotic that attacks the false consciousness in the colonized psyche," encouraging readers who have been victims of colonization "to revise the terms in which they view themselves, so that they can move, at least psychologically, from margin to center."

Her third work, *Scarifications,* whose title refers to the African practice of ritual scarring, takes up the cause of peace during the Vietnam War and digs deeply into urban strife. Tom Lavazzi, writing in the *Encyclopedia of World Literature,* said the poems "are a praxis, a performed knowledge of the relationship among beauty, social status, and pain."

Cortez's 1977 work, *Mouth on Paper,* winner of a 1980 American Book Award, continues to follow the jazz and African-American themes of her first three books, but these poems are much more performance pieces, or "linguistic improvisations," as Lavazzi called them. They honor the work of such jazz masters as Duke Ellington (with the poem "Rose Solitude") and Miles Davis (with "A Miles Davis Trumpet"), recreating the moods that these artists were able to evoke and contributing to what Leon Lewis, writing in the *Encyclopedia of American Literature,* called "an ethos evocative of their playing." Cortez owes some of her rhythms here to the Beat poets, including Allen Ginsberg, Ted Joans, and Bob Kaufman. Jon Woodson, writing in the *Dictionary of Literary Biography* about the jazz elements threaded throughout Cortez's body of work, remarked that she remains "a creative artist uniquely able to reach audiences for whom books of poetry have little appeal."

Although the influence of music is readily evident in Cortez's work, the poet also pointedly seeks to convey a message. She does so, beginning with her second book; her 1982 collection, *Firespitter* (named for a type of African mask), continues this trend, further developing the surreal qualities introduced in *Pissstained Stairs,* with an emphasis on feminism. Her poem "If the Drum Is a Woman" conveys an African folk custom of castigating men who are abusive to women they supposedly love. Others, such as "Rape" and "He Got She Got," draw on the fiery strength gained from women's experiences. Bolden found that "If the Drum Is a Woman" also evokes Ellington when Cortez and her band perform the piece. An answer to Ellington's suite titled "A Drum Is a Woman," the poem "challenges male listeners to question their conceptualizations of gender roles," according to Bolden. At the same time, it shows how the colonized become a reflection of the colonizer and in turn victimize others, said Bolden.

Reviewing the 1984 collection *Coagulations,* Barbara Christian stated: "it is eminently clear . . . that Jayne Cortez is a blatantly political poet—that her work intends to help us identify those who control our lives and the devastating effects such control has on our lives, and she rouses us to do something about it. . . . Like the poets and warriors whose words and actions it celebrates, Jayne Cortez's *Coagulations* is a work of resistance."

Bolden said the poem "In the Morning," which draws upon African rhythms brought by early slaves to America, "reenacts the rocking emotional energy reflected in the syncopation, hand clapping, foot stomping, and suggestive gyrations of the ring shout." He thought the poem "You Know," the counterpart to "In the Morning," is perhaps her best. Patterned on the familiar phrase "you know," repeated in conversation by working-class African Americans, the poem "does not concern music so much as it does blues poetics. . . . [It] both describes and exemplifies Cortez's ability to merge script and sound and thereby incarnate secular priesthood," observed Bolden.

Citing influences such as Amiri Baraka, Langston Hughes, Aimé Césaire, Gwendolyn Brooks, Margaret Walker, and Pablo Neruda, John F. Roche noted in an essay in *Contemporary Women Poets* that Cortez's free verse is characterized by its "impassioned crescendo," as well as the use of anaphora, repetition, alliteration, and modulated spoken tones. "She often combines African iconology, American colloquialisms, and leftist political themes with surrealist body imagery," explained Roche, adding that her more recent verse explores the patterned typesetting characteristic of the concrete poetry of the 1960s. Lewis commented on Cortez's fascination with surrealism, on her "intertwining of elaborate, unusual juxtapositions of objects, ideas, emotions and graphic images with the rhythms and sonic effects of blues variants."

Cortez's 1991 book *Poetic Magnetic,* one of several illustrated by her husband, Melvin Edwards, creates what Lavazzi called a "verbal-visual collage." The collaboration is characteristic of Cortez's need to "get beyond the page to reach the largest possible audience and keep in touch with the increasingly audio-visual rhythms of African-American culture," Lavazzi observed.

Commenting on Cortez's 1997 collection, *Somewhere in Advance of Nowhere,* a *Publishers Weekly* contributor praised Cortez's ability to write in a manner that remains rhythmic while providing "an unflinching glimpse at life's ugliness" that nonetheless ends with the ability to survive. "This resilience animates Cortez's work and supports the unwavering and compelling directness with which she confronts the world," the reviewer added. Leon Lewis found that the last poem in the collection contains lines that might be indicative of the values Cortez supports: "Find your own voice & use it / use your own voice & find it."

In an interview with Melhem in *Heroism in the New Black Poetry,* Cortez outlined what she believes to be the responsibilities inherent in her craft: "I think that poets have the responsibility to be aware of the meaning of human rights, to be familiar with history, to point out distortions, and to bring their thinking and their writing to higher levels of illumination." An acknowledgement of Cortez's success at meeting these standards was made in 1994, when she received the Fannie Lou Hamer award for her "outstanding contribution through her poetry to the struggle for justice, equality, and the freedom of the human spirit."

In addition to her work as a published author, Cortez has distinguished herself as an internationally acclaimed performance artist. She has several recorded performances to her credit, including *Everywhere Drums, Cheerful & Optimistic,* and *Taking the Blues Back Home.* Commenting on *Unsubmissive Blues,* a 1980 recording of the poet reading her works accompanied by jazz musicians Bill Cole, Joe Daley, Bern Nix, and Cortez's son, Denardo Coleman, Warren Woessner wrote in the *Small Press Review* that the record "is the most accomplished collaboration between a poet and jazz group that I've listened to in recent years." He continued: "*Unsubmissive Blues* is an unqualified success. The sum of this collaboration is always greater than its individual pieces."

Tony Bolden wrote that Cortez's ability to rehearse and perform with her own band "allows her to fine-tune her use of tonal semantics in her interactions with band members," often employing "vocal techniques that simulate those of blues singers and/or instrumentalists." Bolden also commented, "Cortez's poetic style exemplifies blues music's propensity for syncretism. She often blends surrealistic imagery with rhythms that riff on—that is, revise—the black sermon form," particularly the "call and response," which originated in Africa.

With her 2002 book of poetry, *A Jazz Fan Looks Back,* Cortez makes what a *Publishers Weekly* contributor called "an erudite and sensual homage to global jazz culture" as she touches on African, Brazilian, American, and Afro-Spanish jazz in her sixty-six poems, in progress since the 1960s.

Bolden concluded in his study that "Cortez's version of blues poetry constitutes a profound challenge to literary conventions, and demonstrates the eloquence of contemporary blues poetics. As such, it affirms Raymond Williams's suggestion that it is possible to create literature for a colonized audience. Yet the hallmark of her achievement is her production of a syncretized form that blends oral forms like blues music and the sermon with the notion of literature as script. While many African-American poets have experimented with vernacular forms, Cortez adds a new dimension to literary history by incarnating the black performer." Leon Lewis wrote that, while Cortez's blend of blues and surrealism has perhaps kept her work at the fringes of American literary awareness, it has also led to a remarkable collection that "will remain striking when more conventional writing has begun to seem bland and muted."

BIOGRAPHICAL AND CRITICAL SOURCES:

BOOKS

American Women Writers: From Colonial Times to the Present, Volume 5, Continuum (New York, NY) 1994.

Contemporary Women Poets, St. James Press (Detroit, MI), 1997.

Dictionary of Literary Biography, Volume 41: *Afro-American Poets since 1955,* Gale (Detroit, MI), 1985.

Directory of American Poets and Fiction Writers, 2001-2002 edition, Poets & Writers (New York, NY), 2001.

Encyclopedia of American Literature, Continuum (New York, NY), 1999.

Encyclopedia of World Literature in the 20th Century, St. James Press (Detroit, MI), 1999.

Melhem, D. H., *Heroism in the New Black Poetry,* University Press of Kentucky (Lexington, KY), 1990.

PERIODICALS

African American Review, spring, 2001, Tony Bolden, "All the Birds Sing Bass: The Revolutionary Blues of Jayne Cortez," p. 61.

American Book Review, May, 1985, review of *Coagulations: New and Selected Poems,* p. 11.

Black Scholar, March, 1981, review of *Scarifications,* p. 88, review of *Mouth on Paper,* p. 87; July, 1985, review of *Coagulations,* p. 65.

Black World, March, 1975.

Callaloo, winter, 1986, Barbara T. Christian, review of *Coagulations,* pp. 235-39.

Choice, January, 1985, review of *Coagulations,* p. 679.

Essence, October, 1984, review of *Coagulations,* p. 62.

Georgia Review, spring, 1985, review of *Coagulations,* p. 169.

Greenfield Review, summer-fall, 1983.

Library Journal, July, 1984, review of *Coagulations,* p. 1330.

MELUS, spring, 1996, pp. 71-79.

Nation, December, 25, 1982, review of *Firespitter,* p. 694.

Negro Digest, December, 1969, Nikki Giovanni, review of *Pissstained Stairs and the Monkey Man's Wares.*

Publishers Weekly, June 8, 1984, review of *Coagulations,* p. 61; June 3, 1996, review of *Somewhere in Advance of Nowhere,* p. 74; April 29, 2002, review of *A Jazz Fan Looks Back,* p. 66.

Small Press Review, March, 1981, Warren Woessner, review of *Unsubmissive Blues.*

Sulfur, fall, 1997, review of *Somewhere in Advance of Nowhere,* p. 199.

ONLINE

Academy of American Poets Web site, http://www.poets.org/ (August 4, 2002), "Jayne Cortez."

D

DEITZ, Tom 1952-

PERSONAL: Born Thomas Franklin Deitz, 1952; raised in Young Harris, Georgia. *Education:* University of Georgia, B.A. and M.A. in medieval literature.

ADDRESSES: *Home*—Georgia. *Agent*—c/o Author Mail, Avon Books, 1350 Avenue of the Americas, New York, NY 10019. *E-mail*—tdeitz@yhc.edu.

CAREER: Writer.

MEMBER: Society for Creative Anachronism (cofounder of local chapter).

WRITINGS:

FANTASY NOVELS; "DAVID SULLIVAN" SERIES

Windmaster's Bane, Avon (New York, NY), 1986.
Fireshaper's Doom, Avon (New York, NY), 1987.
Darkthunder's Way, Avon (New York, NY), 1989.
Sunshaker's War, Avon (New York, NY), 1990.
Stoneskin's Revenge, Avon (New York, NY), 1991.
Ghostcountry's Wrath, AvoNova (New York, NY), 1995.
Dreamseeker's Road, AvoNova (New York, NY), 1995.
Landslayer's Law, AvoNova (New York, NY), 1997.
Warstalker's Track, AvoNova (New York, NY), 1999.

FANTASY NOVELS; "SOULSMITH SERIES"

Soulsmith, AvoNova (New York, NY), 1991.
Dreambuilder, AvoNova (New York, NY), 1992.
Wordwright, AvoNova (New York, NY), 1993.

FANTASY NOVELS; "TALES OF ERON"

Bloodwinter: A Tale of Eron, Bantam Spectra (New York, NY), 1999.
Springwar: A Tale of Eron, Bantam Books (New York, NY), 2000.
Summerblood: A Tale of Eron, Bantam Books (New York, NY), 2001.
Warautumn, Bantam Spectra (New York, NY), 2002.

FANTASY NOVELS

The Gryphon King, Avon (New York, NY), 1989.
Above the Lower Sky, AvoNova (New York, NY), 1994.
The Demons in the Green, AvoNova (New York, NY), 1996.

SIDELIGHTS: Tom Deitz grew up in the mountains of northern Georgia, which also happens to be the setting for most of his fantasy novels. He received his master's degree in medieval literature, the closest, he has said, that he could come to majoring in J. R. R. Tolkien, the author of the *Lord of the Rings*. Deitz has written several novels, most of which are based on either Celtic or Native American mythology, especially those stories told by southeastern U.S. tribes. Many of his books have recurring characters and are published in a particular sequence, such as his "David Sullivan" series, which includes nine separate novels and his first four published books. Deitz continues to live in the mountains and has also stated, in a brief biography on the *Dragon Con* Web site, that he would like to build a small castle some day.

The character David Sullivan first appears in the initial novel of a nine-book series, with the title *Windmaster's Bane*, written in 1986. Teenaged Sullivan is somewhat alienated from his peers because he is not impressed with pop culture and would rather spend his time reading books, especially those that are based on ancient legends. One day, to his surprise, he finds that he has been gifted with Second Sight and is able to peer into an overlapping reality, that of the Faerie from Tir-Nan-Og. When the faeries discover that a mortal is watching them, Sullivan's real adventures begin as he and two of his friends are brought into the other world and into the faeries' battles between the Light and the Dark masters. Sullivan is the protagonist of these stories, but he is not a one-sided hero. He often makes mistakes, and he not incapable of crumpling into an emotional mess of tears throughout the entire nine novels. The series ends with *Warstalker's Track*, published in 1999, and in which Sullivan finds himself in the middle of a war. He must help rescue the deposed Faerie king in order to save not only Tir-Nan-Og but also his own land in his own reality.

Deitz has written another sequential collection of books referred to as the "Soulsmith" Series, which includes the titles *Soulsmith*, *Dreambuilder*, and *Wordwright*. These three novels are also set in the woods of Georgia, but the protagonist this time is Ronny Dillon, a young man who finds himself welcomed into the mysterious family that lives in a magnificent estate called Cardalba. The family has roots in Wales and reportedly also has the gift of magic. In the first of the series, Dillon's foster parents die, and the master of Cardalba takes the young protagonist under his care. Once inside the confines of the estate, Dillon learns of the dark secrets and powers of the Welch family.

The second book begins with Dillon far from Cardalba. He has left that part of his life behind. But his half-brother suddenly appears and urges him to return home. Dillon finally relents, and thus begins yet another adventure of magic and illusion in which Dillon faces the challenges of both love and loss. He leaves, once again, but in the third book, after being told of his half-brother's death, Dillon must once again return to Cardalba in an attempt to reclaim his legacy, the power of magic.

Deitz's next series, "The Tales of Eron," includes the titles *Bloodwinter: A Tale of Eron*, *Springwar: A Tale of Eron*, *Summerblood: A Tale of Eron*, and *Warautumn*. This collection is based in what *Library Journal* contributor Jackie Cassada described as "an exotic world ruled by rituals and steeped in ancient traditions." Eron has been all but destroyed by a plague and in the first book is just starting to recover. One of the main characters of this series, Avail, a metalsmith, discovers a magical gem that contains the power, as related by a *Publishers Weekly* reviewer, "to link minds across distances," when those minds are focused on the magical stone. In the next book, the gem takes Eron to the brink of war as jealousies and schemes of revenge ravage the land. Cassada praised the writing of this tale for its "intelligent, realistic characters." And *Booklist* reviewer Roland Green wrote that Deitz upholds his "reputation for intelligent, action-packed fantasy."

In *Summerblood*, the war continues with Avail, who has become the king. Avail is intensely focused on mastering the powers of the gems, but his enemies have other plans. *Booklist* reviewer Roland Green stated that Deitz keeps his readers' interest because of his well-developed characters who must face "compelling internal and external dilemmas," while Cassada found that it was Deitz's ability to put "a fresh look at how magic works" that enlivened this series.

The fourth book in this series, *Warautumn*, features the culmination of the war in Eron. A cult-like religious group has taken over Eron, but King Avail prevails. Once again, critics wrote of Deitz's ability to create realistic and complex characters. More fantasy writers should follow Deitz's writing style, Green stated in his review of *Summerblood*. "There aren't enough fantasy writers like him."

BIOGRAPHICAL AND CRITICAL SOURCES:

PERIODICALS

Booklist, July, 2000, Roland Green, review of *Springwar: A Tale of Eron,* p. 2015; March 1, 2001, Roland Green, review of *Summerblood: A Tale of Eron,* p. 1232; August, 2002, Roland Green, review of *Warautumn,* p. 1936.

Kirkus Reviews, February 1, 1999, review of *Bloodwinter: A Tale of Eron,* p. 182; February 1, 2001, review of *Summerblood,* p. 149.

Library Journal, March 15, 1999, Jackie Cassada, review of *Bloodwinter,* p. 112; July, 2000, Jackie Cassada, review of *Springwar,* p. 147; April 15, 2001, Jackie Cassada, review of *Summerblood,* p. 137; August, 2002, Jackie Cassada, review of *Warautumn,* p. 152.

Publishers Weekly, March 29, 1999, review of *Bloodwinter,* p. 96; April 2, 2001, review of *Summerblood,* p. 45.

Science Fiction Chronicle, April, 2001, review of *Summerblood,* p. 36.

Voice of Youth Advocates, October, 2001, review of *Summerblood,* p. 288.

ONLINE

Dragon Con Web site, http://www.dragoncon.org/people/deitzt.html/ (February 22, 2003), "Thomas F. Deitz".*

* * *

DENZIN, Norman K(ent) 1941-

PERSONAL: Born March 24, 1941, in Iowa City, IA; son of Kenneth F. (a naval captain) and Betty Townsley (maiden name, Campbell) Denzin; married Katherine E. Ryan; children: Johanna, Rachel, Nathan. *Education:* University of Iowa, A.B., 1963, Ph.D., 1966. *Hobbies and other interests:* Trout fishing, reading mystery novels, jazz.

ADDRESSES: *Home*—107 South Prospect Ave., Champaign, IL 61820-4624. *Office*—Institute of Communication Research, University of Illinois, Urbana-Champaign, Urbana, IL 61801. *E-mail*—n-denzin@uiuc.edu.

CAREER: University of Illinois, Urbana-Champaign, assistant professor of sociology, 1966-69; University of California, Berkeley, assistant professor of sociology, 1969-71; University of Illinois, Urbana-Champaign, associate professor, 1971-73, professor of sociology, 1973-80, College of Communications, research communications scholar, distinguished professor of sociology, criticism and interpretive theory professor, 1981-94, distinguished research professor of communications, 1995—. Referee on grant applications, National Foundation on the Arts and Humanities, 1970—.

MEMBER: International Sociological Association (secretary-treasurer of social psychology section, 1978-80), American Anthropological Association, American Psychological Association, American Association for Public Opinion Research, Society for the Study of Symbolic Interaction (vice president, 1975-76; president, 1993-95), Society for the Sociological Study of Social Problems, Society for the Psychological Study of Social Issues, Society for the Study of Applied Anthropology, Pacific Sociological Society, Midwest Sociological Society (president, 1987-89).

AWARDS, HONORS: Charles Horton Cooley Award, 1987; George Herbert Mead Award, 1997.

WRITINGS:

The Research Act: A Theoretical Introduction to Sociological Methods, Aldine (Hawthorne, NY), 1970, 3rd edition, Prentice-Hall (Englewood Cliffs, NJ), 1989.

(With others) *Social Relationships,* Aldine (Hawthorne, NY), 1970.

(With Alfred R. Lindesmith and A. R. Strauss) *Readings in Social Psychology,* 2nd edition (Denzin was not associated with previous edition), Holt (New York, NY), 1975, 8th edition, Sage Publications (Beverly Hills, CA), 1997.

Childhood Socialization, Jossey-Bass (San Francisco, CA), 1977.

On Understanding Emotion, Jossey-Bass (San Francisco, CA), 1984.

The Alcoholic Self, Sage Publications (Newbury Park, CA), 1987.

The Recovering Alcoholic, Sage Publications (Newbury Park, CA), 1987.

Treating Alcoholism: An Alcoholics Anonymous Approach, Sage Publications (Newbury Park, CA), 1987.

(With Alfred R. Lindesmith and A. R. Strauss) *Social Psychology,* 6th edition (Denzin was not associated with previous editions), Prentice-Hall (Englewood Cliffs, NJ), 1988.

Interpretive Interactionism, Sage Publications (Newbury Park, CA), 1989, 2nd edition, 2001.

Interpretive Biography, Sage Publications (Newbury Park, CA), 1989.

Hollywood Shot by Shot: Alcoholism in American Cinema, A. de Gruyter (New York, NY), 1991.

Images of Postmodern Society: Social Theory and Contemporary Cinema, Sage Publications (Newbury Park, CA), 1991.

Symbolic Interactionism and Cultural Studies: The Politics of Interpretation, Blackwell (Oxford, England), 1992.

The Alcoholic Society: Addiction and Recovery of the Self, Transaction (New Brunswick, NJ), 1993.

The Cinematic Society: The Voyeur's Gaze, Sage Publications (Thousand Oaks, CA), 1995.

Interpretive Ethnography: Ethnographic Practices for the 21st Century, Sage Publications (Thousand Oaks, CA), 1997.

(With others) *Social Psychology,* Sage Publications (Thousand Oaks, CA), 1999.

Reading Race: Hollywood and the Cinema of Racial Violence, Sage Publications (Thousand Oaks, CA), 2002.

Performance Ethnography: Critical Pedagogy and the Politics of Culture, Sage (Thousand Oaks, CA), 2003.

EDITOR

(And contributor, with Stephen P. Spitzer) *The Mental Patient: Studies in the Sociology of Deviance,* McGraw-Hill (New York, NY), 1968.

(And contributor) *Sociological Methods: A Sourcebook,* Aldine (Hawthorne, NY), 1970, 2nd edition, McGraw-Hill (New York, NY), 1977.

(And contributor) *The Values of Social Science,* Aldine (Hawthorne, NY), 1970, 2nd edition, Dutton (New York, NY), 1973.

Children and Their Caretakers, Dutton (New York, NY), 1973.

Studies in Symbolic Interaction: A Research Annual, JAI Press (Greenwich, CT), 1978—.

(With Yvonna S. Lincoln) *Handbook of Qualitative Research,* Sage Publications (Newbury Park, CA), 1994, 2nd edition, 2000.

(With Yvonna S. Lincoln) *Collecting and Interpreting Qualitative Materials,* Sage Publications (Thousand Oaks, CA), 1998, 2nd edition, 2003.

(With Yvonna S. Lincoln) *The Landscape of Qualitative Research: Theories and Issues,* Sage Publications (Thousand Oaks, CA), 1998, 2nd edition, 2003.

(With Yvonna S. Lincoln) *Strategies of Qualitative Inquiry,* Sage Publications (Thousand Oaks, CA), 1998, 2nd edition, 2003.

(With Yvonna S. Lincoln) *The American Tradition in Qualitative Research,* Sage Publications (London, England; Thousand Oaks, CA), 2001.

(With Yvonna S. Lincoln) *The Qualitative Inquiry Reader,* Sage Publications (Thousand Oaks, CA), 2002.

(With Yvonna S. Lincoln) *Turning Points on Qualitative Research: Tying Knots in a Handkerchief,* AltaMira Press (Walnut Creek, CA), 2003.

(With Yvonna S. Lincoln) *9-11 in American Culture,* AltaMira Press (Walnut Creek, CA), 2003.

Also author of *Performance Narratives,* 1997. Contributor to numerous periodicals, including *Social Forces, Journal of Health and Social Behavior, Mental Hygiene, Sociological Quarterly, Social Problems, American Sociological Review, American Sociologist, American Journal of Sociology, Word, Quest,* and *Slavic Review. Trans-action,* special issue editor, June-July, 1971; *Sociological Quarterly,* associate editor, 1972-82, editor, 1992—; *Urban Life,* associate editor, 1972—; *Contemporary Sociology,* associate editor, 1978-81; *Qualitative Inquiry,* coeditor, 1994—; *Cultural Studies: A Research Annual,* editor, 1995—; *American Journal of Sociology,* editorial referee.

SIDELIGHTS: Noted sociologist and educator Norman K. Denzin is the author or editor of more than fifty books and a contributor to dozens of professional journals. Several of his books are concerned with alcoholism and American culture, especially cinema, which he also writes about in relation to race and violence. Denzin and coeditor Yvonna S. Lincoln have edited several volumes on the value of qualitative research in sociology.

Denzin once told *CA:* "[My] basic position is that human conduct can only be understood by grasping the historical and cultural perspectives, languages and points of view of those we study. Instrumental works have been by G. H. Mead, C. H. Cooley, H. Blumer, C. Peirce, W. James, J. Dewey, A. Smith, E. Husserl, M. Scheler, S. Freud, Karl Marx, Martin Heidegger, and Jean-Paul Sartre. [The] basic question guiding my work is: How is meaning constructed and lived in the lives of ordinary people and how may we, as interpretive scholars, ground our understandings in the spoken prose of the people we study?"

Such are the questions answered by *The Handbook of Qualitative Research.* Because qualitative research—as opposed to the facts and figures of quantitative research—has been documented from the time of ancient civilizations, reviewer Marie Miller-Whitehead of the Tennessee Valley Educators for Excellence described the book's second edition as "a handbook of contemporary qualitative research." Divided into six parts, with some fifty-six contributing authors, the book discusses (1) the historical, political, and ethical aspects of qualitative studies; (2) feminist, racial, ethnic, and sexual studies that have influenced current trends in qualitative research; (3) the current approaches to qualitative study, such as ethnography, life histories, case studies, and clinical research; (4) the collection and analysis of data in qualitative research; (5) the interpretation and evaluation of this data; and (6) the future of qualitative research. Part VI is "ever mindful," as Miller-Whitehead pointed out, "of what the editors describe as 'the structural processes that make race, gender and class potentially repressive presences in daily life.'" Miller-Whitehead observed, "The reader gains a feel for the evolution of the field and the boundaries it has set for itself. . . . [The editors delineate] the often blurred lines that divide areas of qualitative research, such as those that differentiate the study of folklore from ethnography, semiotics from symbolism, and the literary critic's *explication de texte* from Denzin's 'Practices and Politics of Interpretation.'"

Denzin and Lincoln coedited five subsequent books about qualitative research following publication of the *Handbook. Strategies of Qualitative Inquiry* contains Part III of the *Handbook*: "Strategies of Inquiry." The book begins with a discussion of the ways to organize and design a qualitative study, continues to paradigm or perspective, and then covers empirical research. The history of qualitative studies is accessed, as are the various ways of conducting qualitative interviews. The book *Collecting and Interpreting Qualitative Materials* contains Parts IV and V of the *Handbook*: "Methods of Collecting and Analyzing Empirical Materials" and "The Art of Interpretation, Evaluation, and Presentation."

The Qualitative Inquiry Reader contains a wide variety of the best articles from the Sage Publications journal *Qualitative Inquiry.* It is divided into five sections: "Reflexive Ethnography, Autoethnography, Poetics, Performance Narratives," and "Assessing the Text." The book is geared toward helping scholars and students evaluate the way narratives have been used in the best qualitative research and learn the newest techniques in the field.

Interpretive Ethnography: Ethnographic Practices for the 21st Century uses "postmodern" writings, including journalism, crime fiction, performance texts, narrative, and poetry, to form a theory of the type of ethnography arising from postmodernism. *Sociology* contributor Martyn Hammersley stated, "For me, the value of this book is primarily as a portrayal of the various forms of writing characteristic of 'ethnographic postmodernists.'. . . It does not provide an effective discussion of postmodernist ideas for newcomers or for those not already convinced." Hammersley called Denzin "a true believer in postmodernism," but said he "does not engage with the viewpoints of his opponents; he simply denounces them, for example as 'voyeurs'."

Denzin's works on cinema include *The Cinematic Society: The Voyeur's Gaze* and *Reading Race: Hollywood and the Cinema of Racial Violence.* In *The Cinematic Society,* Denzin answers four questions about film watching and how it has defined what is acceptable in modern society. He relates the "voyeur's gaze" to class, gender, and ethnicity and discusses the need to watch films and the cost to society. He also discusses film in terms of postmodernism. Marijean Levering of *Film Quarterly* felt Denzin is "most lucid and insightful when critiquing and explaining the undercurrents of a film," but she thought the book would have been more effective had the author "narrowed his theoretical focus."

Reading Race is concerned with film's relationship to race and culture, with Denzin arguing that film does not adequately portray diversity and multiculturalism, which it should honor. Divided into four parts, the book contains discussions of race, segregation, and discrimination; women and violence; weapons; "Boyz N Girlz in the Hood, Zoot Suits and Homeboys (and Girls);" and filmmaker Spike Lee.

BIOGRAPHICAL AND CRITICAL SOURCES:

PERIODICALS

American Anthropologist, June, 1998, Ivan Brady, review of *Interpretive Ethnography: Ethnographic Practices for the 21st Century,* p. 510.

American Journal of Sociology, March, 1980, review of *Childhood Socialization,* p. 1278; September, 1985, review of *On Understanding Emotion,* p.

439; January, 1989, reviews of *Treating Alcoholism: An Alcoholics Anonymous Approach, The Recovering Alcoholic,* and *The Alcoholic Self,* p. 864; May, 1992, review of *Hollywood Shot by Shot: Alcoholism in American Cinema,* p. 1788; March, 1993, review of *Images of Postmodern Society: Social Theory and Contemporary Cinema,* p. 1208.

Book World, July 28, 1991, review of *Hollywood Shot by Shot,* p. 13.

Choice, October, 1984, review of *On Understanding Emotion,* p. 345; January, 1988, reviews of *The Recovering Alcoholic* and *The Alcoholic Self,* p. 803; December, 1991, review of *Hollywood Shot by Shot,* p. 674; October, 1995, review of *The Cinematic Society: The Voyeur's Gaze,* p. 301; September, 2000, T. N. Smalley, review of *Handbook of Qualitative Research,* 2nd edition, p. 106.

Contemporary Psychology, September, 1985, review of *On Understanding Emotion,* p. 731; January, 1990, review of *Interpretive Interactionism,* p. 86.

Contemporary Sociology, September, 1985, review of *On Understanding Emotion,* p. 552; July, 1990, review of *Interpretive Interactionism,* p. 626; March, 1991, review of *Interpretive Biography,* p. 328; March, 1992, review of *Hollywood Shot by Shot,* p. 262; November, 1993, review of *Images of Postmodern Society,* p. 883; January, 1994, review of *Symbolic Interactionism and Cultural Studies: The Politics of Interpretation,* p. 125; May, 1995, review of *Handbook of Qualitative Research,* p. 416; September, 1997, Patricia A. Adler and Peter Adler, "Ethnography and Human Development: Context and Meaning in Social Inquiry," review of *Interpretive Ethnography,* p. 654; July, 1998, Carolyn Ellis, review of *Interpretive Ethnography,* p. 422; January, 2001, review of *Cultural Studies: A Research Annual,* Volume 5, p. 98.

Film Quarterly, fall, 1992, review of *Images of Postmodern Society,* p. 38; fall, 1992, review of *Hollywood Shot by Shot,* p. 55; spring, 1998, Marijean Levering, review of *The Cinematic Society,* p. 66.

Harvard Educational Review, winter, 1996, review of *Handbook of Qualitative Research,* p. 890.

Journal of Communication, winter, 1993, review of *Hollywood Shot by Shot,* p. 168; spring, 1994, review of *Images of Postmodern Society,* p. 172.

Journal of Economic Literature, September, 2001, review of *Studies in Symbolic Interaction: A Research Annual,* Volume 24, p. 1056.

JQ: Journalism Quarterly, summer, 1992, review of *Hollywood Shot by Shot,* p. 513; summer, 1993, reviews of *Symbolic Interactionism and Cultural Studies* and *Images of Postmodern Society,* p. 468.

Quarterly Journal of Speech, February, 1998, Leslie H. Jarmon, review of *Interpretive Ethnography,* p. 117.

Reference & Research Book News, August, 1992, review of *Hollywood Shot by Shot,* p. 36; May, 1994, review of *Handbook of Qualitative Research,* p. 17; May, 1997, review of *Interpretive Ethnography,* p. 42.

Sight and Sound, December, 1991, review of *Hollywood Shot by Shot,* p. 35.

Social Forces, September, 1992, reviews of *Images of Postmodern Society* and *Hollywood Shot by Shot,* p. 252.

Social Science Quarterly, September, 1992, review of *Hollywood Shot by Shot,* p. 719.

Social Service Review, December, 1994, review of *The Alcoholic Society: Addiction and Recovery of the Self,* p. 613.

Sociological Review, November, 1990, reviews of *Interpretive Interactionism* and *Interpretive Biography,* p. 797; August, 1993, review of *Images of Postmodern Society,* p. 593; February, 1994, review of *Symbolic Interactionism and Cultural Studies,* p. 154.

Sociology, November, 1997, Martyn Hammersley, review of *Interpretive Ethnography,* p. 811.

ONLINE

Qualitative Social Research Forum Web site, http://qualitative-research.net/fqs/ (August 5, 2002), "Editorial Board: Norman K. Denzin."

Tennessee Valley Educators for Excellence Web site, www.ed.asu.edu/edrev/ (January 21, 2002), Marie Miller-Whitehead, review of *Handbook of Qualitative Research,* 2nd edition.*

* * *

DESAI, Meghnad 1940-

PERSONAL: Born July 10, 1940, in Baroda, India; son of Jagdish Chandra (a civil servant) and Mandakini (a homemaker; maiden name, Majmundar) Desai; married Gail Graham Wilson, June 27, 1970; children: Tanvi, Nuala, Sven. *Education:* University of Bombay, B.A., 1958, M.A., 1960; University of Pennsylvania, Ph.D., 1964. *Politics:* Socialist.

ADDRESSES: Home—51 Ellington St., London N7 8PN, England. *Office*—London School of Economics and Political Science, University of London, Houghton St., Aldwych, London WC2, England. *E-mail*—m.desai@lse.ac.uk.

CAREER: University of California, Berkeley, associate specialist in agricultural economics, 1963-65; London School of Economics and Political Science, London, England, lecturer, 1965-76, senior lecturer, 1977-79, reader, 1980-82, professor of economics, 1983—; director of the Centre for the Study of Global Governance, member of university senate. Past chairman of Holloway Labour Ward, Islington, London; consultant to United Nations Food and Agriculture Organization, World Bank, and University of Algeria.

MEMBER: Association of University Teachers in Economics, Royal Economic Society, Econometric Society, Economic History Society, Society for Economic Dynamics and Control, American Economic Association.

WRITINGS:

Marxian Economic Theory, Gray-Mills (Oxford, England), 1974.

Applied Econometrics, Philip Allan (Oxford, England), 1976.

Marxian Economics, Rowan & Littlefield (Totowa, NJ), 1979.

Testing Monetarism, St. Martin's Press (New York, NY), 1982.

Hayek, Wheatsheaf Books (London, England), 1988.

The Economic Policy of the BJP, National Centre for South Asian Studies (Melbourne, Australia), 1994.

The Selected Essays of Meghnad Desai, Volume 1: *Macroeconomics and Monetary Theory,* Volume 2: *Poverty, Famine and Economic Development,* E. Elgar (Aldershot, Hants, England), 1995.

India's Triple By-pass: Economic Liberalisation, the BJP, and the 1996 Elections, National Centre for South Asian Studies (Melbourne, Australia), 1996.

Marx's Revenge: The Resurgence of Capitalism and the Death of Statist Socialism, Verso (New York, NY), 2002.

(With Yahia Said) *Global Governance and Financial Crises,* Routledge (New York, NY), 2003.

EDITOR

(With Dharma Kumar) *The Cambridge Economic History of India,* Volume 2: c. 1757 - c. 1970, Cambridge University Press (Cambridge, England), 1983.

(With Susanne Hoeber Rudolph and Ashok Rudra) *Agrarian Power and Agricultural Productivity in South Asia,* University of California Press (Berkeley, CA), 1984.

(And author of introduction) Vladimir Il'ich Lenin, *Lenin's Economic Writings,* Lawrence & Wishart (London, England), 1988, Humanities Press International (Atlantic Highlands, NJ), 1989.

(And author of introduction) Denis Sargan, *Lectures on Advanced Econometric Theory,* Blackwell (Oxford, England), 1988.

(With Paul Redfern) *Global Governance: Ethics and Economics of the World Order,* Pinter (London, England), 1995.

LSE on Equality: A Centenary Anthology, Transaction (New Brunswick, NJ), 1997.

(With Philip Arestis and Sheila Dow) *Essays in Honour of Victoria Chick,* Routledge (London, England), 2001.

Also author of *Leave All Things to Me,* 1989, and *Trahisons des Proletariat,* 1989. Contributor to economic journals.

SIDELIGHTS: Meghnad Desai is a professor of economics at the London School of Economics and Political Science and a respected consultant on matters of economics worldwide. Desai once told *CA:* "I have always been interested in ideas. I hope ultimately to absorb in my work influences from a broad range of social sciences and history. In a sense, all social science provides a way to write history, if only in a more ugly and jargon-ridden way than historians manage. History is a key to change, and it is my wish to be able to harness ideas to changing society so that more people can indulge in the luxury of a concern with ideas."

Desai has written several books concerning Marxian economics and socialism and is a noted researcher in international economics, especially in the areas of the inequality of income that results from capitalism, famine and poverty and their costs to society as a whole, and the economies of South Asia and Europe.

He has also edited a number of essay collections, as well as a history of Indian economics and the writings of Lenin. One of the collections edited by Desai is *LSE on Equality: A Centenary Anthology,* published in 1995 on the centenary of the London School of Economics. The anthology contains ten essays by various economists. One essay, written by Hugh Dalton, is on measuring income as an indicator of individual economic welfare and covers several economic principles. Six of the collection's essays "support inequality by arguing against equality," according to William M. Dugger in a review for the *Journal of Economic Issues.* Such authors as William Letwin, John Charvet, and James Woodburn argue that equality of incomes, and therefore social status, in a society cannot work, for a variety of reasons. Dalton and R. H. Tawney wrote the remaining three essays, favoring equality. Although outnumbered by the authors promoting inequality, Dalton and Tawney (particularly Tawney) stand their ground, observed Dugger. He wrote, "Although more of the anthology is devoted to essays that attack equality, the power of the three egalitarian essays makes up for it. R. H. Tawney . . . was a master rhetorician. . . . I would not hesitate to assign the anthology as a whole to a good student." However, Dugger found one final point to make about the collection: "After reading all of the essays, most of the usual issues of the equality/inequality debate seem to have been covered in one or more of them. However, none of the essays is written from an instrumentalist point of view. So none of them develops the idea that equality could be instrumental, could make the poor and the deprived more efficient by making them healthier, more ambitious, longer-lived, less obsequious, less servile, less frustrated, more intelligent, and more inquiring. Equality could then speed up the evolution of new and improved technology by bringing more people actively into the life process. This is the argument that institutionalists could contribute to the debate."

In his 2002 book *Marx's Revenge,* Desai presents a revisionist commentary on Karl Marx's economic writings, a subject on which Desai wrote a textbook in 1979. In the new book, Desai maintains that Marx knew that capitalism would prevail as a successful economic system after socialism was dead. He bases his theories on Marx's writings in Volumes 2 and 3 of his major work *Das Kapital. Marx's Revenge* contains chapters on: the writings and principles of economists Adam Smith, Hegel, Keynes, Schumpeter, and Hayek, in addition to Marx; war and revolution; war and imperialism; the years between the two world wars; the rise and fall of socialism; the global order; the golden age of capitalism; and capitalism's future. Desai shows how Marx's original theories on capitalism and socialism were displaced by a "Marxist" movement, which Faisal Islam, in a review for the *London Observer,* said was a "reductive Bolshevism that emerged in the last century, shaped by Lenin's pamphlet on imperialism and these days incorporating a wide span of belief, including the fringes of fascism." Those who adopted this theory, said Islam, selectively read Marx's comments in Volume 1 of *Das Kapital* that a falling profit rate would bring about the end of capitalism. They also ignored Marx's surplus profit exploitation equilibrium models, Islam commented. The reviewer wrote that the book's importance lies in its audience. "Nobody in Wall Street or the City of London will care that Marx is now on their side," Islam commented. "But for those who still express moral indignation at pronounced and prolonged inequality and poverty, the market is the most likely rescue route. . . . As Desai points out, the market is a tool for eliminating scarcity. It is departures from the free market, such as big subsidies for agriculture in rich countries, that are doing most to solidify poverty."

In a review of *Marx's Revenge* for the London *Sunday Telegraph,* Michael Prowse wrote, "Some books are more than the sum of their parts; others are less. Unhappily, *Marx's Revenge* falls into the latter category." Prowse thought that Desai's argument that globalization of trade and the lifting of tariffs and other barriers will eventually lead to the collapse of capitalism and the natural implementation of socialism was "not rigorous." Prowse wrote that Marx "could neither identify the process whereby capitalism would fail, nor even sketch how a post-capitalist society would function." However, Prowse thought that the individual chapters in Desai's book were "entertaining and instructive" and that readers will "learn much from his analysis of two centuries of economic history."

BIOGRAPHICAL AND CRITICAL SOURCES:

PERIODICALS

British Book News, May, 1982, review of *Testing Monetarism,* p. 292.

Choice, December, 1982, review of *Testing Monetarism,* p. 623.
Economica, August, 1989, L. G. Godfrey, review of *Lectures on Advanced Econometric Theory,* p. 405.
Economic Books: Current Selections, fall, 1990, review of *Lenin's Economic Writings,*
Economic Journal, September, 1989, Hedley Rees, review of *Lectures on Advanced Econometric Theory,* p. 863; January, 1996, *The Selected Essays of Meghnad Desai,* Volume 2: *Poverty, Famine and Economic Development,* p. 291; November, 1996, review of *The Selected Essays of Meghnad Desai,* Volume 1: *Macroeconomics and Monetary Theory,* p. 1835.
International Affairs, October, 1996, Tony Evans, review of *Global Governance: Ethics and Economics of the World Order,* p. 797.
Journal of Asian Studies, May, 1987, review of *Agrarian Power and Agricultural Productivity in South Asia,* p. 427.
Journal of Economic Issues, December, 1998, William M. Dugger, review of *LSE on Equality: A Centenary Anthology,* p. 1165.
Journal of Economic Literature, December, 1995, review of *The Selected Essays of Meghnad Desai,* Volume 1, p. 2054, and *The Selected Essays of Meghnad Desai,* Volume 2, p. 2079; March, 1998, review of *LSE on Equality,* p. 307.
Kyklos, spring, 1996, Amitrajeet A. Batabyal, review of *The Selected Essays of Meghnad Desai,* Volume 2: *Poverty, Famine and Economic Development,* p. 76.
New Statesman, January 31, 1997, "Destiny, Not Defeat," p. 11.
Observer (London, England), May 19, 2002, Faisal Islam, "Can You Hear Marx Tittering in Highgate?," review of *Marx's Revenge: The Resurgence of Capitalism and the Death of Statist Socialism.*
Pacific Affairs, fall, 1986, review of *Agrarian Power and Agricultural Productivity in South Asia,* p. 515.
Slavic Review, spring, 1991, Alfred Evans, Jr., review of *Lenin's Economic Writings,* p. 190.
Sunday Telegraph (London, England), April 21, 2002, Michael Prowse, "Marx in the Marketplace: This Paean for Market Economies by an Ex-Marxist Does Little for the Cause of Capitalism, Says Michael Prowse," review of *Marx's Revenge.*
Times Literary Supplement, June 10, 1983.

ONLINE

London School of Economics Web site, http://econ.lse.ac.uk/staff/mdesai/ (August 6, 2002).*

DIAMANT, Anita 1951-

PERSONAL: Born June 27, 1951; daughter of Maurice and Helene Diamant; married Jim Ball (in public relations), June 12, 1983; children: Emilia. *Education:* Washington University, St. Louis, MO, B.A. (comparative literature), 1973; State University of New York at Binghamton, M.A. (English), 1975.

ADDRESSES: *Agent*—c/o Author Mail, Scribner, 27500 Drake Rd., Farmington Hills, MI 48075. *E-mail*—anitaweb@aol.com.

CAREER: Writer. *Equal Times,* editor, 1977-78; *Boston Phoenix,* columnist and staff writer, 1980-83; *Boston,* senior staff writer, 1986-88; WBUR-FM Radio, commentator, 1981-82; *New England Monthly,* contributing editor, 1984-86; *Boston Globe* magazine, columnist, 1988—; *Parenting,* columnist, 1993-95; Radcliffe College, honorary visiting scholar at Schlesinger Library, 1994-95; Brandeis University, visiting scholar in Women's Studies Department, 1995-96.

MEMBER: Phi Beta Kappa.

AWARDS, HONORS: Clarion Award, 1981; New England Women's Press Association, Best Columnist Award, 1982, Award of Excellence, 1983; awards from Massachusetts Division, American Cancer Society, 1987, 1988; fellow, Casey Journalism Center for Children and Families, 1994; Boston Author's Club Book of the Year award, 1988, Significant Jewish Book of the Year, *Reform Judaism* magazine, 1999, and Booksense Book of the Year, 2001, all for *The Red Tent;* Literary Light award, Boston Public Library, 2003.

WRITINGS:

The New Jewish Wedding, Simon & Schuster (New York, NY), 1985, revised edition, 2001.
The Jewish Baby Book, Simon & Schuster (New York, NY), 1988, published as *The New Jewish Baby Book: Names, Ceremonies, Customs—A Guide for Today's Families,* Jewish Lights Publishing (Woodstock, VT), 1994.
What to Name Your Jewish Baby, Simon & Schuster (New York, NY), 1989.

Anita Diamant

(With Howard Cooper) *Living a Jewish Life,* HarperCollins (New York, NY), 1991.

Bible Baby Names: Spiritual Choices from Judeo-Christian Tradition, Jewish Lights Publishing (Woodstock, VT), 1996.

Choosing a Jewish Life: A Handbook for People Converting to Judaism and for their Family and Friends, Schocken Books (New York, NY), 1997.

The Red Tent, St. Martin's Press (New York, NY), 1997.

Saying Kaddish: How to Comfort the Dying, Bury the Dead, and Mourn As a Jew, Schocken Books (New York, NY), 1998.

(With Karen Kushner) *How to be a Jewish Parent: A Practical Handbook for Family Life,* Schocken Books (New York, NY), 2000.

Good Harbor: A Novel, Scribner (New York, NY), 2001.

Pitching My Tent: On Marriage, Motherhood, Friendship, and Other Leaps of Faith, Scribner (New York, NY), 2003.

Contributor to periodicals, including *New England Monthly, Sesame Street Parents, Yankee, Hadassah,* and *McCall's.*

WORK IN PROGRESS: A third novel.

SIDELIGHTS: Anita Diamant had penned several well-received nonfiction books about issues in modern Jewish culture before she found great word-of-mouth success with her first novel, 1997's *The Red Tent.* The book adds great dimension to the Biblical story of Dinah, overlooked half-sister to the founders of the twelve tribes of Israel, who is known only to have been raped in the book of Genesis. Diamant imagines the story in Dinah's own words, from her youth with her mother and her aunts, all married to the Biblical patriarch Jacob, to the willing relationship with a Canaanite prince that her brothers term "rape," to her subsequent life as a midwife in Egypt. The initial hardcover printing of *The Red Tent* sold modestly, and many copies of it were scheduled for destruction by the publisher, when Diamant presented them with a list of Reform Reconstructionist rabbis to whom she felt they should send the surplus copies. Her strategy worked; many such recipients of her book talked about it with their congregations, who went out and bought the novel, then recommended it to their friends and fellow book club members. Diamant's publisher repeated this tactic with a list of female clergy, who also frequently talked about and recommended the novel. As Judith Rosen reported in a 2001 article for the *Writer,* "*The Red Tent*'s momentum keeps on going." Diamant followed *The Red Tent* with another novel, *Good Harbor,* in 2001, and a book of personal anecdotes entitled *Pitching My Tent* two years later.

Among Diamant's factual works about Judaism is *Choosing a Jewish Life: A Handbook for People Converting to Judaism and for Their Family and Friends.* This volume had personal resonance for Diamant because her husband converted to Judaism before their marriage. Ilene Cooper, reviewing *Choosing a Jewish Life* in *Booklist,* noted that "Diamant's discussion is both informative and wide-ranging." Diamant collaborated with Karen Kushner on *How to Be a Jewish Parent: A Practical Handbook for Family Life,* which a *Publishers Weekly* critic praised as an "easy-to-read guide" while mentioning that the volume is aimed at "the liberal Jewish community." Of the author's *Saying Kaddish: How to Comfort the Dying, Bury the Dead, and Mourn As a Jew,* George Cohen concluded that "this comprehensive guide answers many of the questions that contemporary Jews may have in a time of grief." Diamant's *The New Jewish Wedding* has proved so successful with readers that she issued a revised version of it in 2001.

The Red Tent met with even better critical reception than Diamant's nonfiction. "The best fiction writers create a world and bathe us in it," began Jane Redmont, reviewing the novel in *National Catholic Reporter,* "its sounds and sights, its language and climate, the intricate relationships among its inhabitants. Anita Diamant has performed this wonderous craft." Cooper also reviewed *The Red Tent* for *Booklist,* and stated that "Diamant makes readers see there's not so very much difference between people across the eons, at least when it comes to trial and tragedy, happiness and love." According to Susannah Meadows in *Newsweek,* the novel's popularity has a great deal to do with its emphasis on the female bonding that goes on in the eponymous "tent," which is where the women go when they are ill, menstruating, or giving birth—and where they also share their stories and culture. "With its trinity of woman empowerment, God and quivering thighs, the commercial appeal of the book seems obvious," she maintained.

Though fans of *The Red Tent* have urged Diamant to take on other female figures of the Bible, she switched to a contemporary setting for 2001's *Good Harbor.* In it, two Jewish women—one a convert from Catholicism—meet in a harbor town in Massachusetts. Kathleen is in her fifties and battling breast cancer; Joyce is in her forties and battling a teenage daughter and an indifferent husband. Critics did not respond quite as well to *Good Harbor* as to *The Red Tent,* but a *Publishers Weekly* reviewer felt that the author "does make a smooth entry into the arena of contemporary women's fiction with this graceful story."

Diamant told *CA:* "I can identify five main ingredients that are part of my creative process. The first is ego. For most of my childhood, I wanted to be an actress, to get up in front of a group of people. As a columnist, that's precisely what I do. When editors tell me I have a strong 'voice,' what they are really saying is 'Boy, do you have a healthy ego!' I inherited my ego from my mother. Another ingredient is my father, who read Jack London to me as a kid. The literary part of me is my patrimony.

"The third ingredient is poetry. The first thing I published was a poem—a rather mediocre few lines about basketball playoffs. It was my first byline and, once I saw my name in print, my career as a poet was preempted by journalism. Nevertheless, of all my literary influences, Walt Whitman is at the top of the list. My other all-time favorite poet is the Chilean, Pablo Neruda, who wrote a series of extraordinary odes to things as ordinary and elemental as a pair of wool socks, salt, and watermelon.

"When I began writing essays in 1977, I began reading essayists. Russell Baker and Calvin Trillin are constant sources of pleasure, but my idol, and the fourth ingredient in my creative soup, is Mary Frances Kennedy Fisher. She wrote, often for the *New Yorker,* about her life, her travels, and exquisitely about food. She wrote very elegantly and simply about things that matter. I like to write about food. I even spent a couple of years as a food writer for the late, lamented *New England Monthly* magazine.

"The fifth and final ingredient is feminism and, for me, feminism flows straight out of M. F. K. Fisher's explanation that the elemental truths of our lives (hunger, love, children, neighborhood) are the primary locus of power, struggle, despair, happiness—life and art. I am a product and creature of that ongoing revolution in consciousness, which shifted the world off its social axis forever.

"My career as a book author began in 1983, when I was both casting around for a book idea and planning a wedding. The books that were available on Jewish weddings did not begin to address the spiritual and cultural riches of Jewish tradition, and they were not addressed to grooms, who wanted egalitarian goals reflected in the ceremony. After my first book was published, I swore I would write no more Jewish books, but I did. Each time, I felt that a similar gap on the bookshelf needed to be filled.

"My [nonfiction] books are all about contemporary Jewish practice. Indeed, they are 'how-to' books of a sort. What makes them different from other books of this nature is the quality of the writing and an approach that is respectful of tradition, yet also respectful of the realities and insights of the present—which include, of course, the transformed status of women."

BIOGRAPHICAL AND CRITICAL SOURCES:

PERIODICALS

Book, November-December, 2001, conversation between Anita Diamant and James Carroll, pp. 44-48.

Booklist, April 15, 1997, Ilene Cooper, review of *Choosing a Jewish Life: A Handbook for People Converting to Judaism and for Their Family and Friends,* p. 1366; October 1, 1997, Ilene Cooper, review of *The Red Tent,* p. 284; September 15, 1998, George Cohen, review of *Saying Kaddish: How to Comfort the Dying, Bury the Dead, and Mourn As a Jew,* p. 175.

Christian Science Monitor, October 11, 2001, Merle Rubin, "Women Who Shelter Each Other," p. 20.

Commentary, December, 1998, Jon D. Levenson, review of *Saying Kaddish,* p. 74.

Daily Telegraph (London), November 16, 2002, Charlotte Moore, "Her Mother's Lover, and Her Brother's."

Guardian (London), March 30, 2002, Alex Clark, interview with Anita Diamant, p. 11.

Los Angeles Times, April 24, 2000, Emily Dwass, "A Biblical Woman's Tale That Won Readers' Hearts," p. E1.

National Catholic Reporter, May 22, 1998, Jane Redmont, review of *The Red Tent,* p. 28.

Newsweek, February 5, 2001, Susannah Meadows, "Meeting under a Big 'Tent': How a Biblical Tale Became a Word-of-Mouth Phenom," p. 61.

Publishers Weekly, September 11, 2000, review of *How to Be a Jewish Parent: A Practical Handbook for Family Life,* p. 87.

Writer, April, 2001, Judith Rosen, "Anita Diamant's Red Tent Turns to Gold," p. 30.

ONLINE

Anita Diamant Home Page, http://www.anitadiamant.com/ (April 29, 2003).

Lilith Magazine, http://www.lilithmag.com/ (April 29, 2003), review of *The Red Tent.*

Lucy's Books, http://www.lucysbooks.com/ (April 29, 2003) review of *The Red Tent.*

* * *

DOHERTY, Berlie 1943-

PERSONAL: Surname is pronounced "*Dor*-ty"; born November 6, 1943, in Liverpool, England; daughter of Walter Alfred (a railway clerk) and Peggy (Brunton) Hollingsworth; married Gerard Doherty, 1966; children: Janna, Tim, Sally. *Education:* University of Durham, B.A. (with honors), 1965; University of Liverpool, postgraduate certificate in social science, 1966; University of Sheffield, postgraduate certificate in education, 1978. *Hobbies and other interests:* Music, walking, tennis, travel, and theater.

ADDRESSES: *Agent*—David Higham Associates, 5-8 Lower John St., Golden Square, London W1R 4HA England. *E-mail*—dha@davidhigham.co.uk.

CAREER: Leicestershire Child Care Services, Leicester, England, child care officer, 1966-67; homemaker, 1967-78; teacher in Sheffield, England, 1978-80; schools broadcaster for British Broadcasting Corp. (BBC) Radio, Sheffield, 1980-82; full-time writer, 1983—. Writer-in-residence at Calderdale Libraries, 1985; chair of Arvon Foundation at Lumbank, 1989—; member of Yorkshire Arts Literature Panel.

AWARDS, HONORS: Carnegie Medal, 1986, Burnley/National Provincial Children's Book of the Year Award, 1987, and *Boston Globe-Horn Book* Honor Book, 1988, all for *Granny Was a Buffer Girl;* award from Television and Film Awards, New York, 1988, for "White Peak Farm"; Carnegie Medal, 1991, and Sankei Award, both for *Dear Nobody;* Children's Book Award for *Snowy;* National Association for Special Educational Needs (NASEN) Award, 1995, for *The Golden Bird;* Carnegie Medal, 1995, for *Willa and Old Miss Annie;* Oppenheim Gold Seal Award, for *The Magical Bicycle;* Writers Guild of Great Britain Award, 1997, for *Daughter of the Sea;* Talkies Award, 1999, for *The Water Babies;* honorary doctorate, University of Derby, 2002.

Berlie Doherty

WRITINGS:

Requiem, M. Joseph (London, England), 1991.

The Vinegar Jar, St. Martin's Press (New York, NY), 1996.

FOR YOUNG READERS

How Green You Are!, Methuen (London, England), 1982.

The Making of Fingers Finnigan, Methuen (London, England), 1983.

White Peak Farm, Methuen (London, England), 1984, reprinted as *Jeannie of White Peak Farm,* Puffin (New York, NY), 2003.

Tilly Mint Tales, Methuen (London, England), 1984.

Children of Winter, Methuen (London, England), 1985.

Granny Was a Buffer Girl, Methuen (London, England), 1986.

Tough Luck, Hamish Hamilton (London, England), 1988.

Paddiwack and Cosy, Methuen (London, England), 1989.

Tilly Mint and the Dodo, Methuen (London, England), 1989.

Spellhorn, Hamish Hamilton (London, England), 1989.

Dear Nobody, Orchard Books (New York, NY), 1992.

Old Father Christmas, based on a story by Juliana Horatia Ewing, illustrated by Maria Teresa Meloni, Barron's (New York, NY), 1993.

Snowy, pictures by Keith Bowen, Dial Books (New York, NY), 1993.

Willa and Old Miss Annie, illustrated by Kim Lewis, Candlewick Press, (Cambridge, MA), 1994.

Street Child, Orchard Books (New York, NY), 1994.

The Magic Bicycle, illustrated by Christian Birmingham, Crown Publishers (New York, NY), 1995.

The Golden Bird, Heinemann (London, England), 1995.

The Snake-Stone, Orchard Books (New York, NY), 1996.

Walking on Air, Collins (London, England), 1996.

Daughter of the Sea, illustrated by Sian Bailey, DK Publishing (New York, NY), 1997.

Bella's Den, Heinemann (London, England), 1997.

Tales of Wonder and Magic, Candlewick Press (Cambridge, MA), 1997.

The Midnight Man, Candlewick Press (Cambridge, MA), 1998.

Fairy Tales, Candlewick Press (Cambridge, MA), 2000.

The Famous Adventures of Jack, Hodder (London, England), 2000.

The Forsaken Merman, Hodder (London, England), 2000.

The Sailing Ship Tree, Puffin (New York, NY), 2000.

The Snow Queen, Scholastic (New York, NY), 2000.

Holly Starcross, Greenwillow (New York, NY), 2001.

Zzaap and the Word Master, BBC Publications (London, England), 2001.

The Nutcracker, Doubleday (New York, NY), 2002.

Blue John, Puffin (New York, NY), 2003.

Coconut Comes to School, Collins (London, England), 2003.

Deep Secret, Puffin (New York, NY), 2003.

TELEVISION AND RADIO PLAYS

The Drowned Village, BBC-Radio 4, 1980.

Requiem, BBC-Radio 4, 1983.

A Case for Probation, BBC-Radio 4, 1983.

The White Bird of Peace, BBC-Radio 4, 1983.

Miss Elizabeth, BBC-Radio 4, 1984.

Fuzzball, BBC-TV 4, 1985.
Sacrifice, BBC-Radio 4, 1985.
The Mouse and His Child (adapted from Russell Hoban's work of the same title), BBC-Radio 4, 1986.
White Peak Farm (serial), BBC-TV 1, 1988.
Children of Winter, BBC-Radio 4, 1988.
Dream of Unicorns, BBC-Radio 4, 1988.
Granny Was a Buffer Girl, BBC-Radio 4, 1990.
There's a Valley in Spain, BBC-Radio 4, 1990.
Dear Nobody, BBC-Radio 5, 1993.
Children of Winter, BBC-TV 4, 1994.
The Snow Queen, BBC-Radio 4, 1994.
Heidi, BBC-Radio 4, 1996.
The Water Babies (radio play), 1999.
Zzaap and the Word Master, BBC-TV 2, 2001.

STAGE PLAYS

Howard's Field (one-act), produced in Sheffield, England, 1980.
Smells and Spells (two-act), produced in Sheffield, England, 1980.
A Growing Girl's Story (one-act), produced in Hartlepool, England, 1982.
Rock 'n' Roll Is Here to Stay (one-act), produced in Sheffield, England, 1984.
The Amazing Journey of Jazz O'Neill, produced in Hull, England, 1984.
Return to the Ebro (one-act), produced in Manchester, England, 1985.
Tilly Mint and the Dodo, produced in Doncaster, England, 1986.
A Case for Probation, published in *Studio Scripts,* edited by David Self, Hutchinson (London, England), 1986.
A Growing Girl's Story, produced in Yorkshire, England, 1989.
Memories, produced in Halifax, Nova Scotia, Canada, 1992.
The Sleeping Beauty, produced in Stoke-on-Trent, England, 1993.
Who Wants Gold (two-act), produced in Newcastle-under-Lyme, England, 1993.

Also author of short stories for British Broadcasting Corp. (BBC) Radio 4 and BBC-Radio Sheffield; author of numerous series for local radio. Work represented in anthologies, including *School Poems,* Oxford University Press, 1986; *How Green You Are!,* published in *Drama 1,* edited by John Foster, Macmillan (London, England), 1987; *Matthew, Come Home,* published in *Drama 2,* edited by John Foster, Macmillan (London, England), 1987; *Tribute to Tom,* published in *Drama 3,* edited by John Foster, Macmillan (London, England), 1988; *Home,* published in *Stage Write,* edited by Gervase Phinn, Unwin Hyman (London, England), 1988; *Best Short Stories 1989.* Contributor to magazines and newspapers, including *Arts Yorkshire, Times Educational Supplement, Stand,* and *Critical Quarterly.*

WORK IN PROGRESS: Daughters of the Sea: Opera Libretto, and Oxford Book of Bible Stories.

SIDELIGHTS: Berlie Doherty's works range from picture books such as *Paddiwak and Cosy* to adult novels like *Requiem* and *The Vinegar Jar.* However, she is probably best known for her award-winning books for young adults. Doherty has twice received Great Britain's prestigious Carnegie Medal, in 1986 for *Granny Was a Buffer Girl,* a generational portrait of a family living near Sheffield, England, and in 1991 for *Dear Nobody,* about the way two teenagers react to an unplanned pregnancy. *Magpies* contributor Agnes Nieuwenhuizen, in an interview with the author, listed some of the major themes in Doherty's books: "Unlocking the secrets of the past, family and family connections, colour, landscape, domestic detail, the inner life, the search for identity and the precise nature of the bond between mother and child." A critic for *Kirkus Reviews* commented: "Everything Doherty writes is fresh and enchanting: exquisite language, brimming with love, telling stories all readers want to hear."

Doherty's relationship with her parents provided inspiration for some of her books. She was born in Liverpool, England, on November 6, 1943—in the middle of World War II. Her father worked as a railway clerk and maintained a close relationship with the younger of his two daughters. The author's mother was a more distant figure. "She was nearly forty when I was born, and often ill," Doherty wrote in her *Something about the Author Autobiography Series* (*SAAS*) entry. "She died in her mid-seventies, and I always regret the fact that I never really talked to her." "If I have inherited anything from her," the author declared, "it is my love of daydreaming. She loved to sit in the firelight and watch the flickering of flames and the shadows they made on the walls. Years later she gazed at the television set in the same way, watching the flickering patterns there, for hours on end, daydreaming." "My mother was very shy of strangers," Doherty continued, "and would sometimes cross the road rather than have to talk to people when she was out shopping. Yet, as a young woman, she had been an exhibition ballroom dancer. My father put a stop to that because, as she put it, he had two left feet, and the only dancing I ever saw her doing was round the kitchen when she was in a good mood. An old man who had known her as a young woman told me recently that she had always been the life and soul of the party."

"From my father I inherited stories," Doherty explained in *SAAS*. Although he spent his life as a railway clerk, Walter Alfred Hollingsworth was also a frustrated writer. "When I was a child I remember my father writing," Doherty once recalled in an interview. "He loved writing poetry and short stories so it was always a very familiar and comforting thing to see him typing away on the typewriter in the corner of the room." "My father used to type out my stories and send them in for me (though very soon I learnt how to type for myself)," she concluded in her *SAAS* entry. "He wanted success for me . . . he was a writer too, in the sense that he loved writing and was compelled to do it."

Doherty spent her earliest years in a public school, but in the 1950s she won a scholarship to a private, Catholic convent school. "At school I was a relatively poor child among many very rich girls," Doherty stated in *SAAS*. "I had to lose my Liverpool accent in order to survive. I had to keep my nails clean, and have my hair tied back in plaits. And at night, instead of playing out, I had homework to do. To my friends in the street, who all went to a local school, it was the ultimate betrayal. They never forgave me for it." "I loved the chapel," Doherty added, "with its sweet smells of polish and incense and flowers, and the jewelled patterns of light cast by the stained glass windows, the tiptoeings of the nuns as they came and went, the susurrations of their prayers. I must have spent hours there, at peace with myself and daydreaming, and I understand now that it must have looked like prayer, and that my natural love of solitude and introspection must have made me seem a very holy child."

"It must have soon become very clear that I had no vocation to be a nun, because the matter was never referred to again," she continued. "My commitment was to other things." After she was "invited to join the choir, and became the soloist," the author explained, "from then on singing and music became my passion." "I wanted to write, and I wanted to sing," Doherty concluded. "My life has turned out in such a way that it has been possible to do both, and I know how lucky I am, though I never became the singer of my dreams, and my writing had to wait a long time before I put my mind to it properly." Doherty drew on her experiences in the convent school for several books, most notably *Requiem, How Green You Are!* and *The Making of Fingers Finnigan.*

Doherty completed her primary education in Liverpool and launched herself on a career as a musician. "I sang as a duo then with a boyfriend and we performed as floor singers in some of the famous Liverpool folk clubs, haunting the footsteps of the Spinners and Liverpool/Irish groups," she stated in *SAAS*. "This was in the sixties, when folk music was at its height." Even when she went off to the University of Durham she stayed extremely active in music, singing light opera, madrigals, and in choirs. It was at the University of Durham that she met her future husband Gerard Doherty, who shared her interest in music. "We got married when he was still a student in his fourth year. I had gone from Durham to Liverpool to do a postgraduate course," Doherty recalled, "then came to Leicester as a social worker." "We spent every minute of our spare time arranging, learning, rehearsing, and sometimes composing songs," she remembered. "It seems now like another life, something that happened to somebody else."

"And now my life took a huge revolution," Doherty revealed. "I struggled to make independence work, to learn to be an individual." Her marriage to Gerard Doherty in 1966 was followed by a year with Leicester Child Care Services as a child care officer. In 1967 she retired to work at raising her three children. Over the next ten years her marriage began to suffer, and she and her husband eventually separated. "It was the darkest period of my life," Doherty recalled, "and I deeply sympathise with anyone who enters the same black waters. I had months of counseling, and emerged from all that as a writer." "I needed a career, and I needed it to fit in with my children's school hours," she explained. "Teaching was the only thing I could think of." Doherty earned a postgraduate certificate in education in 1978 and began teaching in a Sheffield school system.

Doherty's education certificate revived her interest in writing, and "was interested to see that there was an option to do some creative writing. The tutor asked us to write a 1,500-word story, and he said the subject was to be Black and White. My thoughts flew to the black-and-white habits that the nuns at school had worn." Drawing on her experience in the Catholic girls' school, Doherty "wrote a short story called 'Requiem,' about the death of the nun who had taught singing at my convent school." "Writing it had unlocked something in me, and it was a kind of emotional truth," she revealed. "The story was about coming through a psychological barrier; so had the writing of it been. But also what was important about it was the joy I had felt when I was writing it, as if I was touching some arcane part of my inner life."

The composition of "Requiem" opened new vistas for the author. "The tutor liked the story, and recommended I should try to sell it," Doherty stated. "I was very excited. I showed it to a friend, a playwright, and he said, whatever you do, don't push this back in a drawer." "I had no idea where to send it," she confessed, "but I knew they sometimes broadcast stories on our local radio station, so I took it there." The producer, a man named Dave Sheasby, bought the broadcast rights to the story and requested that Doherty write ten more stories for radio broadcast. "Nothing, in the whole of my writing career, seeing my work on television and on the stage, winning two Carnegie Medals," she concluded, "nothing has given me more joy than that first letter of acceptance gave me."

In 1980 Doherty left the classroom and took the position of schools radio broadcaster. "The two years I spent as a seconded teacher to BBC-Radio Sheffield, for school broadcasts, were invaluable," she once told *CA.* The stories that she wrote for broadcast were collected in her first two books, *How Green You Are!* and *The Making of Fingers Finnigan.* Both are set near Liverpool on Britain's west coast and feature a group of four average teenagers—Bee, Julia, Kevin, and Marie—who live fairly ordinary lives. "Each chapter of [*How Green You Are!*] is a separate episode," wrote A. Thatcher in the *Junior Bookshelf,* "but it interlinks into a vividly written and strongly characterized picture of their lives, their friends and relatives, people who live in the street, and their schools."

In the title story of *How Green You Are!,* Julie repeats Doherty's own experience by winning a scholarship to a rich "snob" Catholic school for girls. At first her friends are angry—they mock her green school uniform—but soon, stated Thatcher, "they find out that she has not changed." In *The Making of Fingers Finnigan,* the friends join with adults "in an attempt to save the decrepit swimming pool," declared *Junior Bookshelf* reviewer R. Baines, "and fund raising activities for this project continue intermittently throughout the book." The title episode tells how Julie's little brother Robert gets locked in a local movie house and has to be set free by Finnigan, a local small-time crook. "Bee, Kevin, Julie and the rest of their friends," stated Lucinda Fox in the *School Librarian,* "could easily be the children you might expect to meet in your own neighborhood."

"Writing for radio determined my style and it is still my favourite medium," Doherty said in a *Magpies* interview with Nieuwenhuizen. "I learned that each chapter has to work on its own and has to be satisfying as a unit. Clear, strong voices are important too. I started off by asking myself what young people want to find when they go through the door into the secret garden that a writer creates. I decided that maybe what they most wanted to find was themselves, or someone very like themselves, doing the kind of things that they do, or would love to do if they had the chance." In radio, she once revealed, "the writer can go anywhere and so can the listener. The world inside your head is perhaps the greatest—it is obviously the greatest imaginative world there is . . . as long as the language is strong enough and vivid enough that you're going to take your reader with you, you're going to invoke an emotional response and you're going to create the color."

The experiences of young people growing up form the basis for her next two books, *White Peak Farm* and *Children of Winter.* They share other elements in common as well. "*White Peak Farm* is set in nearby Derbyshire, which I love," the author once told *CA,* "as is *Children of Winter,* a story of the plague year." Like *How Green You Are!* and *The Making of Fingers Finnigan, White Peak Farm* consists of a series of interrelated stories about a farm family. Jeannie Tanner, the young narrator, tells the story of how her family copes with the rhythms of the farm and the problems that arise from everyday life. Jeannie's experiences lead her to the realization "that it is not permanence that is the heart of life," explained a *Publishers Weekly* reviewer, "but rather a steady stream of changes, big and small."

"Much of the life of the stories," wrote *Times Educational Supplement* contributor Geoff Fox, "stems from the tension between the emerging young people and the claims of both the land and a brooding patriarch of a father (not a stock character)." Jeannie's grandmother moves to a hospice for the terminally ill, her sister Kathleen elopes with the son of a neighbor, and her brother Martin chooses art school over the family farm. Finally, Mr. Tanner himself is permanently crippled in an accident involving a tractor and has to surrender control of the farm to his wife. "In the end," concluded Trev Jones in the *School Library Journal,* "all is not-so-neatly resolved through love and family bonding." The novel, stated Nancy Vasilakis in *Horn Book,* "is a bittersweet meditation on the effects of people and place on the individual." "The richness of the novel's imagery and thematic content and the finely textured ambiguities of its characterizations," she concluded, "will leave readers with sweet, lingering memories."

Children of Winter differs from *White Peak Farm* in that it incorporates the fantasy element of time travel. In the story, a family hiking through the countryside is caught in a storm and seeks shelter in an old barn where centuries earlier a couple had sheltered their children to save them from the effects of the plague. When the modern-day children, Catherine, Patsy, and Andrew, are left alone by their parents, time is altered. "The time-slip is made possible," wrote Margery Fisher in *Growing Point,* "because Catherine Tebbutt is a sensitive, dreamy girl, ready to respond to the influence of the old barn where they shelter from the storm and to the spirit of an earlier Catherine Tebbutt." Catherine and her small brother and sister "emerge to join a sadly depleted village group in celebrating the end of the terror." "The book may serve a two-fold purpose," stated Lucinda Fox in the *School Librarian:* "for escape reading, or as a vivid picture of what might have happened to a family in plague-stricken England." Doherty also mixes fantasy elements in several later volumes, including her young adult novel *Spellhorn* and her books for younger readers *Tilly Mint Tales* and *Tilly Mint and the Dodo.*

"*Granny Was a Buffer Girl* reflects the loss of the steel industry of Sheffield, my adopted city," Doherty once told *CA,* "but is more importantly a book for teenagers about aspects of love: a difficult and essential subject to explore." Like *White Peak Farm,* it is an intergenerational family story, but the family in question is urban rather than rural. The narrator, Jess, is about to leave home for a year of study in France. She brings her family together and listens to their stories about their love for each other. "In each generation there is love rewarded and love betrayed," wrote a *Kirkus Reviews* critic: "the contrasts and parallels enrich the meaning of all." Her grandparents Bridie and Jack defy their religious differences when they fall in love and marry in spite of their parents' opposition. Her own parents have to confront the slow sickness and death of Jess's brother Danny, who suffered from a wasting disease.

"Not expecting her to understand him, Grandad Albert tells seventeen-year-old Jess that Love doesn't have much to do with kissing and cuddling," stated *School Librarian* contributor Dorothy Atkinson. "What it does have to do with is the substance of this story: family loyalties, disappointments, great griefs, and brief, vivid happiness." Her grandmother Dorothy recalls how she worked in Sheffield's world-famous cutlery industry as a "buffer girl," cleaning and polishing silverware. She reveals that, although the factory owner's son had been a suitor, she chose her husband Albert—a common steelworker—because of the timing of his proposal. "Such pieces of distant family folklore, and the more recent death of her young brother," explained a *Publishers Weekly* reviewer, "give Jess the courage to embrace changes in her life head-on." The British Library Association honored *Granny Was a Buffer Girl* with a Carnegie Medal in 1986.

Street Child and *Tough Luck* return readers to the world of schoolchildren. *Street Child* is reminiscent of the novels of nineteenth-century novelist Charles Dickens, according to a *Publishers Weekly* contributor, who noted: "Homelessness is the central topic of this grim and gripping novel set in Victorian England." The book tells the story of Jim Jarvis, an orphan condemned by poverty to wander the streets of London in the 1860s. "Unlike Dickens, Doherty doesn't romanticize Jim's hard times," wrote a *Kirkus Reviews* critic. "His trials are soberingly realistic, his encounters with those who wish they could help him poignantly brief." Jim's story has a happy ending, however: he is adopted by Thomas John Barnardo, a wealthy Irishman who founded and maintained schools and homes for destitute children in Victorian London. *Tough Luck* is set in a modern classroom and looks at the problems of several teenage students. The problems are as varied as the student body: Twagger, whose mother is missing and who consistently skips school as a consequence; Sprat, whose mother left home after an unexpected pregnancy; and Nasim, a Pakistani student who had begun to settle in when she was summoned home to complete an arranged marriage. Doherty "refuses to make her adults into easy caricatures," declared Geoff Fox in the *Times Educational Supplement.* A *Junior Bookshelf* reviewer praised *Tough Luck,* noting that the novel, "rooted in experience, is told straightforwardly and with truth."

Doherty won her second Carnegie Medal for *Dear Nobody,* about two teenagers, Helen and Chris, who conceive a child. The story is told largely from Chris's point of view. He wants to marry Helen, but she has other plans. "I wanted to look seriously and genuinely at love because that's a major part of what being a teenager is about," Doherty once told an interviewer. Helen and Chris learn about themselves and their families in the turmoil that follows. As her pregnancy advances, Helen withdraws from Chris and begins to concentrate on her unborn child, to whom she addresses a series of letters—the "dear nobody" of the title. Chris encounters the mother who deserted him years before; Helen learns that her own mother was born out of wedlock. The two teenagers are reunited after the birth of their daughter. Helen and Chris, Doherty explained, "never totally separate . . . it's a journey towards their own parents. It's a way for them to find out as much as they can about their own parents—to come to an understanding about what parenthood means."

Doherty chose a distinctly individual approach to a problem theme. "I wanted it to speak directly to teenagers about something that is very important to them: love," she stated in *SAAS.* "Most of all, I wanted to speak to boys. If there is any justification at all in writing and selling books for teenagers it is that it gives them a place to find themselves, the inner, emotional self, taking that exciting and bewildering and sometimes distressing journey towards adulthood." "The subject matter is one that every teenager wonders and worries about," Doherty told Nieuwenhuizen. "How to step away from the familiar territory of childhood and strike out alone. I wanted to write a love story, not a romance. Helen needs to make her own decision. To reach this point, she needs to face a number of trials, overcome a number of obstacles. She was my version of the hero. Her journey is not a cosmic one, but a personal one."

Critics largely celebrated Doherty's accomplishment in *Dear Nobody.* "Told as a flashback, in some of the loveliest, most lyrical prose to be found in YA fiction," stated *School Library Journal* contributor Alice Casey Smith, "Helen and Chris narrate the consequences of one night's unprotected passion that changes the course of their lives forever." "Doherty's excellent writing, combined with the unusual dual point of view from the narration and the letters," declared a reviewer in the *Bulletin of the Center for Children's Books,* "makes this a richly nuanced examination of a familiar situation." "Doherty realistically depicts two nice young people who care for each other as they struggle to cope with the consequences of their incaution," *Booklist* reviewer Stephanie Zvirin stated. "While the story outline is all too familiar, Doherty sets her version of it apart by plunging into her characters' emotions in a way that will move you to tears."

Doherty turns to fantasy in the books *Daughter of the Sea* and *The Midnight Man.* In *Daughter of the Sea,* Jannet and Munroe Jaffray find a baby floating in a basket in the sea. But the baby belongs to the seal-folk, and her people want her back. Barbara Harrison in *Horn Book* found that "the atmosphere comes to life in Doherty's poetic text." *The Midnight Man* finds a boy and his dog waking each night to follow the Midnight Man, a mysterious stranger who rides horseback through town as he flings the stars into the sky. The stranger leads the pair far out onto the moors, where the moon finds them sleeping and gently carries them to bed. A critic for *Publishers Weekly* called *The Midnight Man* "an enigmatic bedtime fantasy," while GraceAnne A. DeCandido in *Booklist* labeled the story "a magical tale."

In *Holly Starcross* Doherty tells of a fourteen-year-old girl whose mother has remarried and moved the family from the farm to the big city. Holly must take care of her three step-siblings and try to satisfy her demanding mother. She hates her new life, until her father returns after eight years to take her back. Hazel Rochman in *Booklist* found that "Doherty writes with urgency and intimate detail about family love and distance, and tension builds to the very last chapter." "Holly's unique voice and her interactions with both parents are touching and memorable," according to a critic for *Publishers Weekly.* Joanna Rudge Long in *Horn Book* concluded of the novel: "The relationships here are so nuanced, and the balance between Holly's drastically different worlds so finely tuned, that the outcome remains in doubt until the last page."

"Don't concentrate on one kind of writing," Doherty advised aspiring writers in her *Magpies* interview, "and write a little bit every day. Writing is rather like learning an instrument. You need to limber up, perhaps by writing in a diary. You need to keep the 'word muscles' going. Every day, something happens that is worth writing about—jot it down." People who want to be authors, she later explained to an interviewer, ought to "write and write and to love writing. To write about anything and everything. To keep a notebook, to make writing part of their daily life whether or not they call it a diary or a journal. To just pour everything out, to keep going back to things. To take an idea that they've written about and bring it out again and rework it—never to think of something as being finished." "I want children to be fascinated or excited or moved by what I write," Doherty stated on her Web site. "But I also want to write about something that matters both to them and to me." "Sometimes children say to me, 'What would you do if you didn't write?' and the answer, now, is that I don't know," Doherty declared in *SAAS*. "I can't imagine doing anything else."

BIOGRAPHICAL AND CRITICAL SOURCES:

BOOKS

Carter, James, editor, *Talking Books: Children's Authors Talk about the Craft, Creativity, and Process of Writing,* Routledge (London, England), 1999.

Children's Literature Review, Volume 21, Gale (Detroit, MI), 1990.

Rosen, Michael, and Jill Burridge, editors, *Treasure Islands 2,* BBC Publications (London, England), 1993.

Something about the Author Autobiography Series, Volume 16, Gale (Detroit, MI), 1993.

Twentieth-Century Children's Writers, 3rd edition, St. James Press (Detroit, MI), 1989.

PERIODICALS

Booklist, October 1, 1992, Stephanie Zvirin, review of *Dear Nobody,* p. 329; May 15, 1998, Julie Corsaro, review of *Tales of Wonder and Magic,* p. 1625; February 15, 1999, GraceAnne A. DeCandido, review of *The Midnight Man,* p. 1074; August, 1999, Shelley Townsend-Hudson, review of *Paddiwak and Cozy,* p. 2063; November 15, 2000, Hazel Rochman, review of *Fairy Tales,* p. 640; October 1, 2001, GraceAnne A. DeCandido, review of *The Famous Adventures of Jack,* p. 318; November 1, 2002, Hazel Rochman, review of *Holly Starcross,* p. 484.

Books for Keeps, June, 1987, p. 3; July, 1987, p. 11.

British Council News, July-August, 2002, Don Watson, "The Sound of Enjoyment."

Bulletin of the Center for Children's Books, March, 1988, p. 133; January, 1993, review of *Dear Nobody,* p.143; March, 1996, p. 224.

Growing Point, May, 1985, Margery Fisher, review of *Children of Winter,* p. 4432.

Horn Book, August, 1987, p. 177; May-June, 1988; July-August, 1990, Nancy Vasilakis, review of *White Peak Farm,* pp. 461-462; May-June, 1996, p. 339; November-December, 1997, Barbara Harrison, review of *Daughter of the Sea,* p. 679; September-October, 2002, Joanna Rudge Long, review of *Holly Starcross,* p. 569.

Junior Bookshelf, December, 1983, R. Baines, review of *The Making of Fingers Finnigan,* p. 242; December, 1984, p. 254.

Kirkus Reviews, January 1, 1988, review of *Granny Was a Buffer Girl,* p. 53; August 15, 1992, p. 1059; October 15, 1994, review of *Street Child,* p. 1406; August 15, 2002, review of *Holly Starcross,* p. 1221.

Publishers Weekly, January 29, 1988, review of *Granny Was a Buffer Girl,* p. 431; March 30, 1990, review of *White Peak Farm,* p. 63; September 7, 1992, p. 97; September 19, 1994, review of *Street Child,* p. 71; June 24, 1996, p. 46; December 14, 1998, review of *The Midnight Man,* p. 75; March 27, 2000, review of *Daughter of the Sea,* p. 83; September 25, 2000, review of *Fairy Tales,* p. 117; September 30, 2002, review of *Holly Starcross,* p. 72.

School Librarian, December, 1984; November, 1989, p. 159; November, 1993, p. 162.

School Library Journal, March, 1990, Trev Jones, review of *White Peak Farm,* pp. 234-235; October, 1992, Alice Casey Smith, review of *Dear Nobody,* p. 140; July, 1998, Pam Gosner, review of *Tales of Wonder and Magic,* p. 104; November 1, 1998, John Peters, review of *The Midnight Man,* p. 83; October, 1999, Kathleen Staerkel, review of *Paddiwak and Cozy,* p. 112; October, 2000, Nina Lindsay, review of *Fairy Tales,* p. 182; September, 2001, Diane Balodis, review of *The Famous Adventures of Jack,* p. 73; January, 2002, Susan

M. Moore, review of *The Famous Adventures of Jack,* p. 117; August, 2002, Connie Tyrrell Burns, review of *Holly Starcross,* p. 183.
Spectator, December 11, 1993, pp. 45-46.
Times Educational Supplement, September 7, 1984, Geoff Fox, review of *White Peak Farm,* p. 29; January 18, 1985; February 13, 1987, p. 48; November 11, 1988; September 1-7, 1989, p. 957.
Times Literary Supplement, December 16, 1988, p. 1406; September 1, 1989.
Voice of Youth Advocates, June, 1988, p. 84; October, 1990, p. 216; June, 1996, pp. 94-95.

ONLINE

Berlie Doherty Web site, http://www.berliedoherty.com/ (November 7, 2003).

* * *

DUANE, Diane (Elizabeth) 1952

Diane Duane

PERSONAL: Born May 18, 1952, in New York, NY; daughter of Edward David (an aircraft engineer) and Elizabeth Kathryn (Burke) Duane; married Robert Peter Smyth (a writer under pseudonym Peter Morwood), February 15, 1987. *Hobbies and other interests:* Collecting recipes and cookbooks, traveling, gardening, astronomy.

ADDRESSES: *Home*—Ireland; c/o Sloane Club, 52 Lower Sloane St., London SW1W 8BS, England. *Agent*—Donald Maass Literary Agency, 64 West 84th St., Apt. 3-A, New York, NY 10024; Meg Davis, MBA Agency, 45 Fitzroy St., London W1P 5HR, England.

CAREER: Novelist and television writer. Pilgrim State Hospital, Brentwood, NY, registered nurse, 1974; Payne Whitney Clinic, New York Hospital-Cornell Medical Center, New York, NY, psychiatric nurse, 1974-76; writer's assistant, 1976-78; freelance writer, 1978—; Filmation Studios, Reseda, CA, staff writer, 1983-84. -

AWARDS, HONORS: Best Books selection, *School Library Journal,* 1985, and Best Science Fiction and Fantasy Titles for Young Adults selection, *Voice of Youth Advocates,* 1986, both for *Deep Wizardry;* Best Science Fiction and Fantasy Titles for Young Adults selection, *Voice of Youth Advocates,* 1986, for *The Door into Shadow;* Books for the Teen Age citation, New York Public Library, 1994, for *Dark Mirror,* and 2003, for *A Wizard Alone;* special commendation, Anne Spencer Lindbergh Prize in Children's Literature, Charles A. and Anne Morrow Lindbergh Foundation, for "Young Wizards" series.

WRITINGS:

"MIDDLE KINGDOM" SERIES

The Door into Fire (also see below), Dell (New York, NY), 1979.
The Door into Shadow (also see below), Bluejay Books (New York, NY), 1984.
The Door into Sunset, Tor Books (New York, NY), 1993.
The Tale of the Five: The Sword and the Dragon (includes *The Door into Fire* and *The Door into Shadow*), Meisha Merlin Books (Decatur, GA), 2002.

"YOUNG WIZARDS" SERIES

So You Want to Be a Wizard (also see below), Delacorte (New York, NY), 1983.
Deep Wizardry (also see below), Delacorte (New York, NY), 1985.
High Wizardry (also see below), Delacorte (New York, NY), 1990.
Support Your Local Wizard (contains *So You Want to Be a Wizard, Deep Wizardry,* and *High Wizardry*), Guild American (New York, NY), 1990.
A Wizard Abroad, Corgi (London, England), 1993, Harcourt (San Diego, CA), 1997.
The Wizard's Dilemma, Harcourt (San Diego, CA) 2002.
A Wizard Alone, Harcourt (San Diego, CA) 2003.
Wizard's Holiday, Harcourt (San Diego, CA), 2003.

"CAT WIZARDS" SERIES

The Cats of Grand Central, Warner Books (New York, NY), 1997.
The Book of Night with Moon, Warner (New York, NY), 1997.
On Her Majesty's Wizardly Service, Hodder & Stoughton (London, England), 1998, published as *To Visit the Queen,* Aspect/Warner Books (New York, NY), 1999.

SCIENCE-FICTION NOVELS; BASED ON "STAR TREK" TELEVISION SERIES

The Wounded Sky, Pocket Books (New York, NY), 1983.
Spock's World, Pocket Books (New York, NY), 1988.
Doctor's Orders, Pocket Books (New York, NY), 1990.
The Next Generation: Dark Mirror, Pocket Books (New York, NY), 1993.
The Next Generation: Intellivore, Pocket Books (New York, NY), 1997.

"RIHANNSU" SERIES; BASED ON "STAR TREK" TELEVISION SERIES

My Enemy, My Ally, Pocket Books (New York, NY), 1984.
(With Peter Morwood) *The Romulan Way,* Pocket Books (New York, NY), 1987.
Swordhunt, Pocket Books (New York, NY), 2000.
Honor Blade, Pocket Books (New York, NY), 2000.
The Empty Chair, Pocket Books (New York, NY), in press.

"SPACE COPS" SERIES; WITH PETER MORWOOD

Mindblast, Avon (New York, NY), 1991.
Kill Station, Avon (New York, NY), 1992.
High Moon, Avon (New York, NY), 1992.

MARVEL COMICS' "SPIDER-MAN" SERIES

The Venom Factor, illustrated by Ron Lim, Byron Preiss Multimedia/Putnam (New York, NY), 1994.
The Lizard Sanction, illustrated by Darick Robertson and Scott Koblish, Byron Preiss Multimedia/Putnam (New York, NY), 1995.
The Octopus Agenda, illustrated by Darick Robertson, Byron Preiss Multimedia/Putnam (New York, NY), 1996.

"STARDRIVE: THE HARBINGER" TRILOGY

Starrise at Corrivale, TSR (Lake Geneva, WI), 1998.
Storm at Eldala, TSR (Renton, WA), 1999.
Nightfall at Algemron, TSR (Renton, WA), 2000.

"TOM CLANCY'S NET FORCE" SERIES; BASED ON THE CONCEPT BY TOM CLANCY AND STEVE PIECZENIK

Deathworld, Berkley (New York, NY), 2000.
Safe House, Berkley (New York, NY), 2000.
Runaways, Berkley (New York, NY), 2001.
Death Match, Berkley (New York, NY), 2003.

OTHER

(With Peter Morwood) *Keeper of the City* (fantasy), Bantam (New York, NY), 1989.
(Adapter, with Peter Morwood) *SeaQuest DSV: The Novel* (based on the Steven Spielberg television program), Ace (New York, NY), 1993.
X-COM UFO Defense (science-fiction novel; based on the computer game), Prima (New York, NY), 1995.
Raetian Tales: A Wind from the South, Badfort Press (Dublin, Ireland), 1995.
Marvel Comics' X-Men: Empire's End, Byron Preiss Multimedia/Putnam (New York, NY), 1997.

Stealing the Elf-King's Roses, Warner Books (New York, NY), 2002.

Also coauthor, with Michael Reaves, of "Where No One Has Gone Before," for the early episodes of *Star Trek: The Next Generation.* Contributor to *Star Trek: The Kobayashi Alternative* computer game, Simon & Schuster Interactive (New York, NY), 1985. Also contributor to *Wizards at Large.* Author, story editor, and consultant for television programs, including work for Fox Children's Television, Walt Disney Productions, Warner Brothers Animation, British Broadcasting Corporation, Electronic Arts, Marvel Productions, and Hanna-Barbera Productions.

Work represented in anthologies, including *Flashing Swords! 5,* edited by Lin Carter, Dell (New York, NY), 1981; *Sixteen: Short Stories by Outstanding Young Adult Writers,* edited by Donald R. Gallo, Delacorte (New York, NY), 1984; *Dragons and Dreams: A Collection of New Fantasy and Science Fiction Stories,* edited by Jane Yolen and others, Harper (New York, NY), 1986; *Xanadu Two,* edited by Jane Yolen, Tor (New York, NY), 1994; and *On Crusade: More Tales of the Knights Templar,* edited by Katherine Kurtz, Warner Books (New York, NY), 2003. Contributor to periodicals, including *Fantasy Book* and *Amazing.*

ADAPTATIONS: *Spock's World* was released on audiocassette in 1989. Several titles in the "Wizardry" series have been adapted for audiocassette by Recorded Books. *So You Want to Be a Wizard, Deep Wizardry,* and *High Wizardry* have been adapted into books for younger readers, Harcourt (San Diego, CA), 2003.

WORK IN PROGRESS: *The Door into Starlight,* Meisha Merlin Books (Decatur, GA), fourth and final volume of "The Middle Kingdom" series; *Wizards at War,* for Harcourt (San Diego, CA), eighth volume in the "Young Wizards" series.

SIDELIGHTS: Best known for her young-adult science-fiction and fantasy series "Young Wizards," prolific novelist Diane Duane has penned dozens of novels for both adults and children since her 1979 debut. A versatile author, she writes both series and stand-alone titles, creates screenplays, writes as a stable author for established series, and with her husband, writer Peter Morwood, has plans for establishing a publishing imprint. Duane plans each of her books far in advance and dedicates a great deal of time to researching her science-based plots. Called "not only highly talented but highly unpredictable," by Jessica Yates in *Twentieth-Century Young Adult Writers,* Duane is known for her diverse output characterized by imaginative plots, strong, well-rounded male and female characters, and a firm grounding in such time-honored virtues as beauty, heroism, and loyalty.

Raised in Roosevelt, Long Island, in the suburbs of New York City, Duane experienced a childhood that was "essentially quite boring and sometimes rather unhappy," the author once told *CA,* "but the unhappiness was tempered with a great love of books and writing in general. I have been writing for almost as long as I've been reading. This started out as an expression of discontent . . . the library simply didn't stock enough of the kinds of books that I wanted to read, so I began to write my own, occasionally illustrating them (usually in crayon). When I left high school, I went on to study astronomy (something else I had loved greatly from a young age), didn't do too well at that, and then on a friend's recommendation went on to study nursing, which I did much better at. But the writing, for my own enjoyment, went on all the time." Duane's nursing career led her to a staff position as a psychiatric nurse at the Payne Whitney Clinic of the New York Hospital-Cornell Medical Center. By 1976, however, she finally decided to give writing a serious attempt, and moved to California for a time, where she made her first sale of a novel, *The Door into Fire,* the initial volume of "The Middle Kingdom" series. She also began writing for the screen while in California, then moved to Pennsylvania for a time, and in 1987, married the Northern Irish writer Peter Morwood and moved with him to County Wicklow in the Republic of Ireland.

Duane's first book, *The Door into Fire,* introduces five characters, some human, some not, whose adventures span several volumes in the "Middle Kingdom" series. These adult fantasies, which include *The Door into Shadow* and *The Door into Sunset,* encompass an epic battle between good and evil hinging on the paranormal abilities and growth of each character. In *The Door into Shadow,* for instance, a young woman named Segnbora vows to support the fugitive Prince Frelorn's Ferrant in his attempt to regain the throne of the kingdom of Arlen against the usurpation of his greedy half-brother, Cillmod, whose rule is guided by the ancient Shadow. In opposition to the Shadow's evil powers stands the Goddess, the creator of life in Duane's mythical world. In *The Door into Sunset,* still supported by Segnbora, who has focused her magic powers and now rallies dragons to Frelorn's cause, and Queen Eftgan d'Arienn and her troops from the neighboring kingdom of Darthan, the Prince engages in a war of absolutes in a novel that a *Publishers Weekly* reviewer deemed an "intelligent and exhilarating Swords and Sorcery adventure." The series is scheduled for completion with the title *The Door into the Starlight.*

Despite the fact that their settings are products of the author's vivid imagination, Duane's fantasy books require extensive background research—"a great deal of reading in myths and legends of all countries, comparative religions, folklore, fairy tales, and (every now and then) other people's fantasy novels," she once explained to *CA.* "One wants to see what the colleagues are up to! But I find the oldest material the most useful for my purposes. Fraser's *Golden Bough* and the *Larousse Encyclopedia of Mythology* have been two major helps to my fantasy work: the old themes, the Jungian 'archetypes,' are what makes fantasy work best in any time and place it's set—ancient Greece or modern Manhattan."

With her book *So You Want to Be a Wizard,* Duane began her popular series of teen novels about the fantastic exploits of two modern teenagers in an alternate Earth. From reading a book in the local library, twelve-year-old Kit Rodriguez and thirteen-year-old Nita Callahan learn to harness the powers of magic as a defense against several neighborhood bullies. However, instead of simplifying their lives, the magic complicates things, as they suddenly find themselves in an alien and alternate New York City inhabited by machines that attack living creatures. They enter this realm through Worldgates in locations such as Rockefeller Center. Given the task of rescuing a magical book from a dragon's lair, the children incur the wrath of the evil Starsnuffer, who follows them back into their own world and snuffs out the light of the Sun. Using their powers and magical incantations from the book to vanquish their foe, the children are also aided by Fred, a "white hole" from the edge of the galaxy. Praising *So You Want to Be a Wizard* as "outstanding" and "original," *Horn Book* reviewer Ann A. Flowers added that the novel "stands between the works of Diane Wynne Jones, in its wizardry and spells, and those of Madeleine L'Engle, in its scientific concepts and titanic battles between good and evil." Writing in *Five Owls,* Judy Rosenbaum noted that "Duane makes brilliant use of the Manhattan setting to give her fantasy real individuality." Rosenbaum further praised the "Young Wizards" series, which this title inaugurated, as "one of the most gripping, exhilarating, and inventive fantasy series for young people."

Further novels in the "Young Wizards" series include *Deep Wizardry, High Wizardry,* and *A Wizard Abroad.* In *Deep Wizardry,* Nita and Kit must come to the rescue again, this time to help an injured Whale wizard named S'reee prevent the evil Lone Power from coaxing a dormant volcano beneath Manhattan into unleashing its power and destroying the city. Nita's eleven-year-old sister, Dairine, a budding computer hacker, finds a way to incorporate the ancient laws of wizardry with modern technology in *High Wizardry.* Programming the family's laptop computer to transport her across the Universe, Dairine is followed by caretakers Nita and Kit as she is initiated into wizardom by confronting the malevolent Lone One. Reviewing the third title in the series, a *Publishers Weekly* critic called it a "rollicking yarn," and further noted that "Duane is tops in the high adventure business." Margaret A. Chang, writing in *School Library Journal,* felt that the novel was "audacious in theme," and that it paid "homage to the science fiction of the 1950s, particularly [Robert] Heinlein." *A Wizard Abroad* finds the teens in Ireland where they rally the country's wizards to help battle the ghostly Fomori, an army of ancient invaders that are the pawns of the Lone One. *Booklist*'s Chris Sherman noted that Duane "weaves the heroes and demons of Irish legends" in this fourth installment, a tale "equally satisfying" as the first three. According to *Science Fiction Chronicle*'s Don D'Ammassa, the book is an "exceptional work of children's fantasy." Of the "Young Wizards" series, Jessica Yates commented in *School Librarian* that Duane "has succeeded in writing an exciting and moral fantasy which doesn't preach, and her style . . . lives up to the challenge of her cosmic theme."

The series continues with the 2002 *The Wizard's Dilemma.* Here Nita is putting her feet up after the adventures she had in Ireland, but there is little rest for her. It becomes apparent that Kit is growing away from her, and then her mother develops brain cancer. The only way Nita can save her is to go to the alternate universe to search for a cure. There the Lone One offers her a Faustian bargain: her mother's life for the power she, Nita, possesses. Meanwhile, Kit faces his own inner demons as he must decide whether or not he will retreat within himself or continue to battle evil. Sally Estes, reviewing the title in *Booklist,* felt this was a novel for "stalwart fans" of the saga. Beth Wright of *School Library Journal* praised the "well-crafted plot, occasional dry humor, and appealing main characters," while a critic for *Kirkus Reviews* also commended this fifth installment, concluding that it was "powerful and satisfying on many levels." Writing for the *Green Man Review,* Michael M. Jones commented that with *The Wizard's Dilemma* Nita and Kit's "adventures take on both macro levels, as they explore a panoply of strange new universes, and micro levels, as they discover that we are each our own universe." The same reviewer also felt that it "just goes to remind us that long before Harry Potter made his debut, 'The Young Wizards' series was exploring some of the same ground, and a lot of new territory."

Indeed, with the growing popularity of J. K. Rowling's "Harry Potter" books, Duane's series was increasingly hailed as a fine alternative or another source of magic for those who recently discovered the genre. Comparing the two series in *January* magazine, Monica Stark commented that "Duane's magic is, if anything, more scientifically based than that which Rowling creates." Stark went on to note that "Duane's young wizards are competent and powerful, especially since, in her mythology, wizards enjoy their greatest strength while immature. The wisdom and focus they attain as they grow older makes up for the loss of early power." And writing on the *SFF* Web site, Victoria Strauss observed, "Long before Harry Potter . . . , Diane Duane's Young Wizards were working to master the ways of magic, and fulfill the wizard's charge of fighting the forces of entropy that threaten to overtake the universe." Strauss further commented, "It's a deservedly popular series, combining page-turning adventure, likeable characters, imaginative world building, and intelligent themes into books that are as thought-provoking as they are entertaining."

Book six in "Young Wizards," *A Wizard Alone,* finds Nita mourning the death of her mother and closing off herself to her friend Kit. At the same time, Kit is involved in a life-and-death struggle to save a young wizard in training, Darryl, an autistic boy. When Kit and his dog become trapped in Darryl's world, Nita finally comes out of herself in order to save her friend. Lisa Prolman, reviewing the novel in *School Library Journal,* felt that "the incorporation of Darryl's autism is seamless and drives the plot forward," while *Booklist*'s GraceAnne A. DeCandido, called the book "a fine fantasy." DeCandido also noted that Duane "expertly weaves" the manner in which Nita and Kit have explained their wizardry to their families and "integrated wizard training into urban teen life."

Though best known for her "Young Wizards" series, Duane has also written several other series and in numerous other genres, from fantasy to horror to science fiction. In 1983, Duane published the first of her "Star Trek" novels. Based on the characters from the original television series, *The Wounded Sky* would be followed by many more books, including several, such as *Dark Mirror,* based on the cast of characters familiar to viewers of television's *Star Trek: The Next Generation.* In *My Enemy, My Ally,* Captain Kirk and the crew of the starship *Enterprise* join a Romulan commander in a brief peace, during which time the two commanders team up to stop Romulan scientists from channeling Vulcan mind powers into weaponry. A political debate on whether the planet Vulcan should secede from the Federation is the subject of *Spock's World,* while "Bones" McCoy becomes the central character in *Doctor's Orders.* With Kirk gone on a routine mission to a newly discovered planet, Dr. McCoy is left as acting captain and must confront an aggressive attack by a Klingon spaceship with designs on the unclaimed planet. Praising Duane for staying close to the facts set out in the original series, a *School Library Journal* reviewer dubbed *Doctor's Orders* "a fast-paced, well-written adventure."

About writing science fiction, Duane once explained to *CA,* "I would say that nearly half the time I spend in 'writing' a book is spent in research—especially in the sciences. Science fiction is worthless without a good solid grounding in the sciences that underlie it, though you would be surprised how many people try to write it without studying, and then fail miserably, and don't understand why. These people typically think that writing science fiction should be easy 'because you're making it all up.' Nothing could be further from the truth. I spend at least one day a week rummaging in the local library, or reading *New Scientist* or *Science News* to keep up on the latest developments. So many of these have suggested ideas for new projects that it seems unlikely I'll run out of ideas for novels before the middle of the next century or so . . .

since any new discovery brings with it the question, 'How will people react to this?' And people are the heart of good science fiction."

While many of her books are suitable for a teen audience, Duane never consciously decided to write with that age group in mind. "I always wrote what pleased me," Duane once admitted to *CA,* "and was rather shocked when it began to sell (though the shock was very pleasant). Occasionally I find I'm writing a story which younger readers would probably appreciate more thoroughly than older ones, or rather, it would take older readers of taste and discernment to have fun with a story that younger readers would have no problem with at all. I let my publishers label or target the markets for my books, and I myself sit home and get on with the storytelling."

"It took several years of uneven output to get used to the fact that I was going to be able to make my living as a writer," Duane previously noted to *CA,* ". . . for it's hard to go smoothly from a job where you 'punch the clock' to one where you are the only judge of how much work you do each day. I don't consider writing 'work'—at least not when it's coming easily. When I'm having to write something I don't care for (or don't care for at the moment), the situation sometimes looks different. But this rarely lasts."

In addition to her popular "Wizards" and "Star Trek" books for YA readers, Duane is the author of several novels featuring the Marvel comic book character Spider-Man. These books have been praised for mixing modern-day reality with super hero fantasy in an entertaining and believable fashion. Reviewing her *Spider-Man: The Venom Factor* in *Booklist,* Dennis Winters concluded, "Great Literature it ain't, but it's fun, which, after all, is what it's supposed to be." Along with her husband, a writer under the name Peter Morwood, she has also written several books featuring the pair's "Space Cop" heroes.

Duane's "Cat Wizards" series employs concepts and characters from "Young Wizards" in tales that feature magical felines. In *The Book of Night with Moon,* she "chronicles the adventures of an elite corps of human and animal sorcerers in league against the Lone Power," according to a contributor for *Publishers Weekly.* Four cats, Rhiow, Saash, Urruah, and Arhu, who guard the gates between worlds at Grand Central station, are forced to enter the world of Lone Power to avoid an invasion by the creatures of Downside. In the course of the telling, Duane also supplies minutiae of the cat civilization she has created, including their language and customs. A *Publishers Weekly* reviewer concluded that Duane's story "purrs with charms that even ailurophobes will find irresistible." Similarly, Rita M. Fontinha, writing in *Kliatt,* thought that "cat lovers who also enjoy fantasy will delight in this well-constructed tale." Likewise, Susan Allen, writing in *Voice of Youth Advocates,* noted, "The reader need only be a cat lover or fantasy reader to delve into the surreal worlds that are described."

In *To Visit the Queen,* originally published as *On Her Majesty's Wizardly Service,* the cats are in action again, traveling back in time to Victorian London to stop the assassination of Queen Victoria. Their mission is complicated when the felines of London resent the assistance of ones from the United States. Allen, writing again in *Voice of Youth Advocates,* felt that "there is something for most readers in this delightful fantasy." A contributor for *Publishers Weekly* also thought "even those who don't fancy felines should enjoy this purr of a tale." Jackie Cassada, reviewing the second title in the series in *Library Journal,* called it a "whimsical adventure," and *Booklist*'s Sally Estes thought the book was "fun fare for fantasy and cat lovers."

Despite her continued versatility of subject, Duane retains similar themes in all her books. "But they're subject to change without notice," she once told *CA,* "and in any case I don't care to spell them out. I prefer to let the reader find them, if he or she cares to. If the themes aren't obvious, so much the better—a book made primarily for entertainment purposes is not the place for a writer to shout. People who are listening hard enough will hear even the whispers, the rest shouldn't be distracted from being entertained, which in itself is a noble thing, in this busy, crazy world. My only and daily hope is that my readers feel they're getting their money's worth."

BIOGRAPHICAL AND CRITICAL SOURCES:

BOOKS

St. James Guide to Science Fiction Writers, 4th edition, St. James Press (Detroit, MI), 1996.

Twentieth-Century Young Adult Writers, St. James Press (Detroit, MI), 1994, pp. 191-192.

PERIODICALS

Analog, October, 1984, pp. 146-147.

Booklist, August, 1984, pp. 1596-1597; February 15, 1993, p. 10; October 15, 1993, p. 195; October 15, 1994, Dennis Winters, review of *Spider-Man: The Venom Factor,* p. 405; October 1, 1997, Chris Sherman, review of *A Wizard Abroad,* p. 319; March 1, 1999, Sally Estes, review of *To Visit the Queen,* p. 1160; March 15, 1999, Barbara Baskin, review of *So You Want to Be a Wizard* (audiobook), p. 1349; February 1, 2001, Lolly Epson, review of *High Wizardry* (audiobook), p. 1063; June 1, 2001, Sally Estes, review of *The Wizard's Dilemma,* p. 1862; November 15, 2002, GraceAnne A. DeCandido, review of *A Wizard Alone,* p. 588.

Five Owls, January-February, 2001, Judy Rosenbaum, review of *So You Want to Be a Wizard,* p. 63.

Horn Book, December, 1983, Ann A. Flowers, review of *So You Want to Be a Wizard,* p. 716; May-June, 1985, p. 311.

Kirkus Reviews, October 15, 1993, p. 1297; June 1, 2001, review of *The Wizard's Dilemma,* p. 800.

Kliatt, March, 1998, Rita M. Fontinha, review of *The Book of Night with Moon,* p. 18.

Library Journal, February 15, 1999, Jackie Cassada, review of *To Visit the Queen,* p. 188.

Magazine of Fantasy and Science Fiction, June, 1998, Charles de Lint, review of *The Book of Night with Moon,* pp. 37-38; March, 2002, Michelle West, review of *The Wizard's Dilemma,* pp. 34-39.

New York Times Book Review, November 6, 1988.

Publishers Weekly, March 9, 1984, p. 111; April 13, 1990, review of *High Wizardry,* p. 67; January 4, 1993, review of *The Door into Sunset,* p. 62; October 3, 1994, review of *Spider-Man: The Venom Factor,* p. 54; September 22, 1997, p. 74; November 10, 1997, review of *The Book of Night with Moon,* pp. 59-60; January 25, 1999, review of *To Visit the Queen,* p. 77; November 18, 2002, "Out of the Box," p. 63.

School Librarian, August, 1992, Jessica Yates, reviews of *So You Want to Be a Wizard, Deep Wizardry,* and *High Wizardry,* p. 113; February, 1994.

School Library Journal, March, 1985, p. 176; March, 1990, Margaret A. Chang, review of *High Wizardry,* pp. 216-217; December, 1990, review of *Doctor's Orders,* p. 140; December, 1998, Susan McCaffrey, review of *So You Want to Be a Wizard* (audiobook), p. 65; August, 2001, Beth Wright, review of *The Wizard's Dilemma,* p. 178; July, 2002, Celeste Steward, review of *The Wizard's Dilemma* (audiobook), pp. 64-75; February, 2003, Lisa Prolman, review of *A Wizard Alone,* p. 140.

Science Fiction Chronicle, June, 1998, Don D'Ammassa, review of *A Wizard Abroad,* pp. 42-43; February, 2003, Lisa Prolman, review of *A Wizard Alone,* p. 140.

Voice of Youth Advocates, February, 1984, p. 342; February, 1990, p. 371; December, 1990, p. 296; April, 1992, p. 42; October, 1993, pp. 225-226; October, 1995, pp. 207-208; April, 1998, Susan Allen, review of *The Book of Night with Moon,* p. 54; August, 1999, Susan Allen, review of *To Visit the Queen,* p. 190.

Washington Post Book World, May 12, 1985, p. 8.

Xignals, August-September, 1988, pp. 1-3, 16.

ONLINE

Diane Duane Home Page, http://www.owlsprings.com/ (June 18, 2003).

Green Man Review, http://www.greenmanreview.com/ (September 1, 2003), Michael M. Jones, review of *The Wizard's Dilemma.*

January, http://www.januarymagazine.com/ (September, 2001), Monica Stark, review of *The Wizard's Dilemma.*

Out of Ambit: Diane Duane Weblog, http://www.outofambit.blogspot.com/ (September 1, 2003).

SFF, http://www.sff.net/ (September 1, 2003), Victoria Strauss, review of *The Wizard's Dilemma.*

Young Wizards on the Web, http://www.youngwizards.net/ (September 1, 2003).*

* * *

DUNN, Douglas (Eaglesham) 1942-

PERSONAL: Born October 23, 1942, in Inchinnan, Renfrewshire, Scotland; son of William Douglas (a factory worker) and Margaret (McGowan) Dunn; married Lesley Balfour Wallace (a senior keeper of an art gallery), November 26, 1964 (died, March 13, 1981); married Lesley Jane Bathgate (a graphic designer and artist), August 10, 1985; children: one son. *Education:*

Douglas Dunn

Attended University of Glasgow; Scottish School of Librarianship, A.L.A., 1962; University of Hull, B.A. (English; with first class honors), 1969.

ADDRESSES: *Office*—School of English, University of St. Andrews, St. Andrews, Scotland. *Agent*—Pat Kavanagh, A. D. Peters and Co. Ltd., 10 Buckingham St., London WC2N 6BU, England. *E-mail*—ded@st-andrews.ac.uk.

CAREER: Renfrew County Library, Renfrewshire, Scotland, junior library assistant, 1959-62; University of Strathclyde, Glasgow, Scotland, library assistant at Andersonian Library, 1962-64; Akron Public Library, Akron, OH, assistant librarian, 1964-66; University of Glasgow, librarian at Chemistry Department Library, 1966; University of Hull, Hull, England, assistant librarian at Brynmor Jones Library, 1969-71, writer-in-residence, 1974-75; University of St. Andrews, St. Andrews, Scotland, professor of English language and literature, 1991—, and director of St. Andrews Scottish Studies Institute. Poet and freelance writer; writer-in-residence at University of New England in Australia, 1984, and Duncan of Jordanstone College of Art, Dundee District Library, 1986-88; University of Dundee, writer-in-residence, 1981-82, honorary visiting professor, 1987-89. Member of Scottish Arts Council.

MEMBER: Royal Society of Literature (fellow), Scottish PEN, Society of Authors.

AWARDS, HONORS: Society of Authors Eric Gregory Award, 1968, for manuscript collection, and Somerset Maugham Award, 1972, for *Terry Street;* Scottish Arts Council publication awards, 1970, for *Terry Street,* and 1975, for *Love or Nothing;* Geoffrey Faber Memorial Prize, 1976, for *Love or Nothing;* Hawthornden Prize, 1982, for *St. Kilda's Parliament;* Whitbread Literary Awards for poetry and for book of the year, 1985, both for *Elegies;* honorary LL.D., University of Dundee, 1987.

WRITINGS:

POETRY

Terry Street, Faber & Faber (London, England), 1969, Chilmark House (Washington, DC), 1973.

Backwaters, The Review, 1971.

The Happier Life, Faber & Faber (London, England), 1972, Chilmark House (Washington, DC), 1973.

Love or Nothing, Faber & Faber (London, England), 1974.

Barbarians, Faber & Faber (London, England), 1979.

Europa's Lover, Bloodaxe Books (Newcastle upon Tyne, England), 1982.

St. Kilda's Parliament, Faber & Faber (London, England), 1982.

Elegies, Faber & Faber (London, England), 1985.

Selected Poems: 1964-1983, Faber & Faber (London, England), 1986.

Northlight, Faber & Faber (London, England), 1988.

New and Selected Poems, 1966 to 1988, Ecco Press (New York, NY), 1989.

Dante's Drum-Kit, Faber & Faber (Boston, MA), 1993.

This Year's Afternoon, Faber & Faber (Boston, MA), 2000.

The Donkey's Ears: Politovsky's Letters Home, Faber & Faber (Boston, MA), 2000.

New Selected Poems, 1964-1999, Faber & Faber (London, England), 2003.

EDITOR

New Poems, 1972-73: The P.E.N. Anthology, Hutchinson (London, England), 1973.

A Choice of Lord Byron's Verse, Faber & Faber (London, England), 1974.

Two Decades of Irish Writing, Carcanet Press (Manchester, England), 1975.

What Is to Be Given: Selected Poems of Delmore Schwartz, Carcanet Press (Manchester, England), 1976.

The Poetry of Scotland, Batsford, 1979.

Poetry Book Society Supplement, Poetry Book Society, 1979.

A Rumoured City: New Poets from Hull, Bloodaxe Books (Newcastle upon Tyne, England), 1982.

To Build a Bridge, Lincolnshire and Humberside Arts Association, 1982.

(And author of introduction) *The Essential Browning,* Ecco Press (New York, NY), 1990.

The Faber Book of Twentieth-Century Scottish Poetry, Faber & Faber (Boston, MA), 1992.

Scotland: An Anthology, Fontana (London, England), 1992.

The Oxford Book of Scottish Short Stories, Oxford University Press (New York, NY), 1995.

RADIO AND TELEVISION SCRIPTS

Scotsmen by Moonlight (play), BBC-Radio, 1977.

(Author of verse commentary) *Running,* BBC-TV, 1977.

Ploughman's Share (play), BBC-TV, 1979.

Wedderburn's Slave, BBC-Radio Scotland, 1980.

(Author of verse commentary) *Anon's People,* BBC-TV Scotland, 1984.

The Telescope Garden, BBC-Radio, c. 1985.

OTHER

Secret Villages (short stories), Dodd, Mead (New York, NY), 1985.

Under the Influence: Douglas Dunn on Philip Larkin, Edinburgh University Press, 1987.

(Translator) Jean Racine, *Andromache: A Version of Racine's "Andromaque,"* Faber & Faber (London, England), 1990.

Boyfriends and Girlfriends (short stories), Faber & Faber (London, England), 1995.

Contributor to periodicals, including *New Statesman, Poetry Nation, Times Literary Supplement, New Yorker, Punch, London, New Review,* and *Listener.* Poetry reviewer, *Encounter,* beginning 1971; special editor, *Antaeus,* Volume 12, 1973.

Dunn's manuscripts are collected at the Brynmor Jones Library, University of Hull, Hull, England.

SIDELIGHTS: With the publication of *Elegies* in 1985, Scottish writer Douglas Dunn became "established as one of Britain's most important contemporary poets," according to Bernhard O'Donoghue of the *Times Literary Supplement.* A *Stand* contributor called Dunn "a poet of passionate decency who reminds us that decorum, decoration and decency have a common core," while Adam Thorpe wrote in the *Observer,* "Dunn's stated task as a poet is to risk feeling, to preserve the sweet and true, 'to be life's accomplice.'" Dunn has been praised for his form in both his poetry and short stories. A recurring theme in his writings is Scotland and its people.

In a review of *Dante's Drum-Kit,* James Wood suggested in the *London Review of Books* that the volume "will be a great disappointment to those readers who have admired Dunn's earlier verse [because] from somewhere, most traceably Larkin, Dunn has got the idea that poetry must be wise. Typically, he dispenses this wisdom with much colloquialism, in lines that are as loose as sacking: they seem almost to fall off the page." However, in the *Times Literary Supplement,* Don Paterson praised the poet's transition: "Dunn's ability to transform himself from one kind of poet to another from book to book is due, in part, to the small number of personal effects he has to check through the barrier each time; his style resides more in an effortlessly graceful syntax and a naturally rich vocabulary than the usual battery of tricks and tropes. . . . His technique alone is almost enough to prevent him from writing a bad poem." Paterson concluded, "*Dante's Drum-Kit* contains more than enough vintage Dunn to fill an average collection."

In his short-story collection *Boyfriends and Girlfriends* Dunn displays his knack for writing dialog and experimenting with the short-story form. The stories, mainly set in Scotland, feature mostly middle-aged, middle-class, lowbrow Scots undergoing transformations. Frances Partridge remarked in the

Spectator that Dunn's "gift for dialogue at once catches the attention," adding that the writer's "plots are inventive . . . original, quiet and subtle rather than over dramatic," and "many . . . contain as much meat as a full-length novel." O'Donoghue wrote, "Dunn's general subject [is] the crudeness of power-politics with its hierarchies and condescensions," and his "stories, like his public poems, are severe in their strictures against any easy political judgments." Carter Kaplan explained in a review of *Boyfriends and Girlfriends* for *World Literature Today:* "Dispassion is clearly Dunn's goal . . . and the stark directness of his voice superbly reflects the bleak and wounded landscapes which occupy him." Noted Kaplan: "Dunn ignores literary and philosophical traditions." O'Donoghue concluded, "The collection is a riveting amalgam of opinion and humour and elegance, and there isn't a dull page in it."

For *Scotland: An Anthology* Dunn collected pieces about Scotland written by twentieth-century writers, including foreigners. Maurice Lindsay remarked in the *Times Literary Supplement:* "Retrospectively, it adds up to more of an argument than a celebration; but, with such an end in view, the prose and the poetry are cleverly counterpointed, and nearly everything included is aptly chosen. It is, however, a fairly grim Scotland that Dunn depicts; plenty of politics and passion, but not much humour." John Jolliffe asserted in the *Spectator* that "one of the great merits of this anthology is that it gives some idea of how and why [the Scots'] shortcomings have arisen, as well as illustrating the splendid qualities" they possess.

"That there is such a thing as Scottish poetry distinct from the body of English literature is the argument of Dunn's well-reasoned introduction" to *The Faber Book of Twentieth-Century Scottish Poetry,* maintained Peter Meinke in the *Spectator.* The compilation includes representative writers in the Gaelic, Scots, and English languages whom Dunn thinks are distinctively Scottish. However, Dunn excludes samples of his own poetry. "Dunn surely does his anthology a disservice by his modest self-exclusion. Dunn . . . has moved from being the ambivalently detached poet of working-class English life to being one of the few in contemporary Scottish poetry . . . to re-invent and meditate on a significant number of Scottish historical occasions and animating motifs," commented Neil Corcoran in the *Times Literary Supplement.*

BIOGRAPHICAL AND CRITICAL SOURCES:

BOOKS

Contemporary Literary Criticism, Gale (Detroit, MI), Volume 6, 1976, Volume 40, 1986.

Crawford, Robert, and David P. Kinloch, *Reading Douglas Dunn,* Edinburgh University Press (Edinburgh, Scotland), 1992.

Dictionary of Literary Biography, Volume 40: *Poets of Great Britain and Ireland since 1960,* Gale (Detroit, MI), 1985.

Haffenden, John, *Viewpoints: Poets in Conversation with John Haffenden,* Faber & Faber (London, England), 1981.

PERIODICALS

Booklist, November 1, 1995, Ray Olson, review of *The Oxford Book of Scottish Short Stories,* p. 454.

Library Review, June, 1994, review of *The Faber Book of Twentieth-Century Scottish Poetry,* p. 63.

Listener, August 9, 1973.

London Review of Books, July 9, 1992, review of *The Faber Book of Twentieth-Century Scottish Poetry,* p. 10; March 24, 1994, James Wood, review of *Dante's Drum-Kit,* p. 22; June 21, 2001, David Wheatley, "Dialect with Army and Navy," p. 40.

Los Angeles Times Book Review, July 28, 1985.

New Statesman, June 16, 1972; December 6, 1974.

New Statesman & Society, August 7, 1992, review of *The Faber Book of Twentieth-Century Scottish Poetry,* p. 41; March 10, 1995, review of *Boyfriends and Girlfriends,* p. 36.

Observer (London, England), July 2, 1972; October 20, 1974; January 3, 1993, review of *The Faber Book of Twentieth-Century Scottish Poetry,* p. 36; April 3, 1994, review of *Dante's Drum-Kit,* p. 18; January 22, 1995, review of *Boyfriends and Girlfriends,* p. 20; January 21, 1996, review of *Boyfriends and Girlfriends,* p. 16.

Oxford Poetry, Volume 2, number 2, 1985.

Parnassus, fall, 1993, Bill Marx, "Things to Translate and Other Poems," p. 100.

Spectator, July 22, 1972; January 4, 1975; August 10, 1991, review of *Scotland: An Anthology,* p. 30; July 18, 1992, David Wright, review of *The Faber Book of Twentieth-Century Scottish Poetry,* p. 33; February 11, 1995, Frances Partridge, review of *Boyfriends and Girlfriends,* p. 34.

Stand, summer, 1993, review of *The Faber Book of Twentieth-Century Scottish Poetry,* p. 22; spring, 1995, review of *Dante's Drum-Kit,* p. 57.

Times Educational Supplement, August 23, 1991, Brian Morton, review of *Scotland,* p. 21; May 29, 1992, Kate Chisholm, review of *Scotland,* p. 31; June 26, 1992, review of *The Faber Book of Twentieth-Century Scottish Poetry,* p. 28; December 10, 1993, review of *The Faber Book of Twentieth-Century Scottish Poetry,* p. 28.

Times Literary Supplement, June 9, 1972; January 31, 1975; October 2, 1981; January 7, 1983; August 19, 1983; May 31, 1985; April 5, 1985; October 21-27, 1988; August 16, 1991, Maurice Lindsay, review of *Scotland,* p. 21; July 31, 1992, Neil Corcoran, review of *The Faber Book of Twentieth-Century Scottish Poetry,* p. 21; February 4, 1994, Don Paterson, review of *Dante's Drum-Kit,* p. 22; January 27, 1995, Bernard O'Donoghue, review of *Boyfriends and Girlfriends,* p. 22; May 26, 1995, Andrew Biswell, review of *The Oxford Book of Scottish Short Stories,* p. 22; December 19, 1997, Sean O'Brien, review of *Selected Poems: 1964-1983,* p. 24; June 9, 2000, Roger Caldwell, review of *The Donkey's Ears: Politovsky's Letters Home,* p. 25.

Virginia Quarterly Review, spring, 1975.

Washington Post Book World, August 20, 1995, review of *The Oxford Book of Scottish Short Stories,* p. 12.

World Literature Today, autumn, 1995, Carter Kaplan, review of *Boyfriends and Girlfriends,* p. 794.

ONLINE

National Library of Scotland Write Stuff Web site, http://www.nls.uk/writestuff/ (July 24, 2003), "Douglas Dunn."*

E

ELBORN, Andrew
See CLEMENTS, Andrew

* * *

ELISHA, Ron 1951-

PERSONAL: Born December 19, 1951, in Jerusalem, Israel; son of David (a builder) and Haya (Bash) Elisha; married Bertha Rita Rubin (an administrator), December 6, 1981; children: Raphael, Abby. *Ethnicity:* "Israeli." *Education:* University of Melbourne, M.B., B.S., 1975. *Politics:* "None (tending to anarchy)." *Religion:* "Atheist." *Hobbies and other interests:* Music, carpentry.

ADDRESSES: Home and office—2 Malonga Ct., North Caulfield, Victoria 3161, Australia; fax: 03-9576-1967. *Agent*—Sandy Wagner, 12/44A Bayswater Rd., Kings Cross, New South Wales 2011, Australia. *E-mail*—relisha@bigpond.net.au.

CAREER: General practitioner of medicine, Melbourne, Australia, 1977—.

MEMBER: Australian Writers Guild.

AWARDS, HONORS: Awgie Awards, Australian Writers Guild, 1982, 1984 and 1992; Gold Award, best screenplay, Houston International Film Festival, 1990.

WRITINGS:

PLAYS

In Duty Bound, Yackandandah Playscripts (Montmorency, Australia), 1983.
Two, Currency Press (Sydney, Australia), 1985.
Einstein, Penguin (Ringwood, Australia), 1986.
The Levine Comedy, Yackandandah Playscripts (Montmorency, Australia), 1987.
Safe House, Currency Press (Sydney, Australia), 1989.
Esterhaz, Currency Press (Sydney, Australia), 1990.
Pax Americana, Yackandandah Playscripts (Montmorency, Australia), 1990.
Choice, Currency Press (Sydney, Australia), 1994.
Unknown Soldier, Playbox Theater Company, 1996.
The Goldberg Variations, Currency Press (Sydney, Australia), 2000.

OTHER

Pigtales (children's book), illustrated by Craig Smith, Random House Australia, 1994.
Too Big (children's book), illustrated by Cathy Netherwood, Random House Australia, 1997.

Contributor to periodicals, including *Medical Observer.*

WORK IN PROGRESS: One children's book, *Ferry Tales;* several plays, including *Jesus's Blood, Acts of Dog, Affairs of the Heartless, Wandering Gentile, A Tree, Falling, Renaissance, Answers, Wrongful Life, The Capgras Delusion,* and *The Stayman Convention;* three novels, *The Hangman's Table, Paris,* and *Paper Cuts;* several screenplays, including *Money, Seven Hills to Happiness, Saviours, Critters, Star Quality, Star Crossed, Help Wanted, Boomers, November,* and *Duty of Care.*

SIDELIGHTS: Ron Elisha once commented: "My main motivation in writing for children is to create something that adults and children can read together, without boring the pants off either.

"I believe that it's never too early for children to be introduced to the concept of irony, a sorely undervalued commodity in writing for the young. I don't believe that endings need necessarily be either neat or happy, nor do I feel that children should be led to believe that the world is just or makes sense.

"I *do* believe that we should avoid the dumbing-down of children's literature that is being forced upon us by frightened editors. It's time that we, as writers, did our part to ensure that those who come after us are provided with the equipment they will need to express themselves. True expression requires precision. Precision requires both vocabulary and grammar. A child doesn't attain either without being stretched by the books he or she reads."

BIOGRAPHICAL AND CRITICAL SOURCES:

BOOKS

Contemporary Dramatists, 5th edition, St. James Press (Detroit, MI), 1993.

PERIODICALS

Magpies, March, 1995, p. 24.

* * *

ELLIOT, Alistair 1932-

PERSONAL: Born October 13, 1932, in Liverpool, England; son of James Adam and Gladys (Haynes) Elliot; married Barbara Demaine, 1956; children: William, Matthew. *Education:* Christ Church, Oxford, B.A., 1955, M.A., 1958.

ADDRESSES: Home and office—27 Hawthorn Rd., Newcastle upon Tyne, Tyne and Wear NE3 4DE, England. *E-mail*—alistair.elliot@btinternet.com.

CAREER: English Children's Theatre, London, England, actor and stage manager, 1957-59; Kensington Public Library, Kensington, England, library assistant, 1959-61; University of Keele, Keele, England, assistant cataloging librarian, 1961-65; Pahlavi University, Shiraz, Iran, assistant acquisitions librarian, 1965-67; University of Newcastle upon Tyne, Newcastle upon Tyne, England, special collections librarian, 1967-82; translator and writer, 1983—.

AWARDS, HONORS: Fellow, Arts Council of Great Britain, 1979; Prudence Farmer Award, *New Statesman,* 1983 and 1991; fellow of Ingram Merrill Foundation and Djerassi Foundation, both 1983; Cholmondeley Award, Society of Authors, 2000.

WRITINGS:

POETRY

Contentions, Ceolfrith Press (London, England), 1977.
Kisses: Poems, Ceolfrith Press (London, England), 1978.
Talking Back, Secker & Warburg (London, England), 1982.
Talking to Bede (poem, with annotations), Mid Northumberland Arts Group (Ashington, England), 1982.
On the Appian Way, Secker & Warburg (London, England), 1984.
My Country: Collected Poems, Carcanet Press (Manchester, England), 1989.
Turning the Stones, Carcanet Press (Manchester, England), 1993.
Facing Things, Carcanet Press (Manchester, England), 1997.

TRANSLATIONS

Euripides, *Alcestis,* Chandler Publishing, 1965.
Heinrich Heine, *The Lazarus Poems,* Carcanet Press (Manchester, England), 1979.
Paul Verlaine, *Femmes/Hombres: Women/Men,* Anvil Press (London, England), 1979.
French Love Poems, Bloodaxe Books (Tarset, Northumberland, England), 1991.
Euripides, *Medea* (play; produced in London, England, at Almeida Theatre, 1992, then on Broadway, Longacre Theatre, 1994), Oberon Books (London, England), 1993.
Italian Landscape Poems, Bloodaxe Books (Tarset, Northumberland, England), 1993.

(And author of notes) Paul Valery, *La Jeune Parque,* Bloodaxe Books (Tarset, Northumberland, England), 1997.

Roman Food Poems, Prospect Books (England), 2003.

OTHER

(Compiler, with others) *Short-title List of the Sandes Library (Kendal Grammar School) Deposited in Newcastle University Library,* Library, University of Newcastle-upon-Tyne (Newcastle-upon-Tyne, England) 1969.

(Compiler) *Poems by James I and Others: From a Manuscript Miscellany in Newcastle University Library,* Eagle Press, 1970.

(Editor) Virgil, *The Georgics,* translated by John Dryden, Mid Northumberland Arts Group (Ashington, England), 1981.

BIOGRAPHICAL AND CRITICAL SOURCES:

PERIODICALS

Times Literary Supplement, October 21, 1977; September 30, 1983; August 22, 1997.

* * *

ELLIS, Bret Easton 1964-

PERSONAL: Born March 7, 1964, in Los Angeles, CA; son of Robert Martin (a real estate investment analyst) and Dale (a homemaker; maiden name, Dennis) Ellis. *Education:* Bennington College, B.A., 1986. *Hobbies and other interests:* Piano, playing keyboards in bands, reading.

ADDRESSES: Agent—Amanda Urban, International Creative Management, 40 West 57th St., New York, NY 10019.

CAREER: Writer; appeared in the documentary film *This Is Not an Exit: The Fictional World of Bret Easton Ellis,* First Run Features, 2000.

MEMBER: Authors Guild, PEN, Writers Guild (West).

Bret Easton Ellis

WRITINGS:

Less Than Zero (novel), Simon & Schuster (New York, NY), 1985.

The Rules of Attraction (novel), Simon & Schuster (New York, NY), 1987, Vintage (New York, NY), 1998.

American Psycho (novel), Vintage (New York, NY), 1991.

Informers (short stories), Knopf (New York, NY), 1994.

Glamorama (novel), Knopf (New York, NY), 1999.

Contributor of articles to periodicals, including *Rolling Stone, Vanity Fair, Wall Street Journal,* and *Interview.*

ADAPTATIONS: Less Than Zero was adapted as a film, produced by Twentieth Century Fox, 1987. *American Psycho* was adapted as a film, released by Lions Gate Films, 2000. *The Rules of Attraction* was adapted as a film, released by Lions Gate Films, 2002.

SIDELIGHTS: In 1985, twenty-one-year-old Bret Easton Ellis jolted the literary world with his first novel,

Less Than Zero. Many reviewers' reactions to the book echoed that of *Interview* magazine's David Masello, who called it "startling and hypnotic." Eliot Fremont-Smith of the *Voice Literary Supplement* pronounced the book "a killer"—and, like other critics, was impressed not only with the novel itself but also with its author's youth. "As a first novel, [*Less Than Zero*] is exceptional," John Rechy declared in the *Los Angeles Times Book Review*; it is "extraordinarily accomplished," a *New Yorker* critic concurred. *Less Than Zero,* wrote Larry McCarthy in *Saturday Review,* "is a book you simply don't forget." A college undergraduate at the time of the novel's publication, Ellis has been hailed by more than one critic as the voice of his generation. Upon the publication of his third novel, *American Psycho,* Ellis again attracted attention, this time for writing a story so disturbing and violent that Matthew Tyrnauer of *Vanity Fair* called Ellis "the most reviled writer in America, the Salman Rushdie of too much, too fast."

The somewhat-autobiographical *Less Than Zero* grew out of a writing project Ellis began at Bennington College under his professor, writer Joe McGinniss. Comprised of vignettes, the book centers on Clay, an eighteen-year-old freshman at an eastern college who returns to Los Angeles for Christmas vacation. Drugs, sex, expensive possessions, and an obsession with videotapes, video games, and music videos fill the lives of Clay and his jaded peers. Events others might find horrifying—hardcore pornography, a corpse in an alley, and a girl who is kidnapped, drugged, and raped—become passive forms of entertainment for this group.

The novel's grim subject matter is related in a detached, documentary-style prose, leading *New York Times* reviewer Michiko Kakutani to state that *Less Than Zero* was "one of the most disturbing novels [she had] read in a long time." *Time* magazine's Paul Gray asserted that "Ellis conveys the hellishness of aimless lives with economy and skill," while Alan Jenkins of the *Times Literary Supplement* found that "at times [the novel] reproduces with numbing accuracy the intermittent catatonic lows of a psychophysical system artificially stimulated beyond normal human endurance."

Some critics drew comparisons between *Less Than Zero* and J. D. Salinger's *Catcher in the Rye,* the 1950s classic of disaffected youth. But Anne Janette Johnson, writing in the *Detroit Free Press,* explained that such comparisons could not extend "beyond the fact that both [novels] concern teenagers coming of age in America. Salinger's [Holden Caulfield] had feelings—anger, self-pity, desire. The youths in [*Less Than Zero*] are merely consuming automatons, never energetic enough to be angry or despairing." For some critics, the novel brought to mind Jack Kerouac and similar "beat generation" writers of the 1950s. And Kakutani found echoes of Raymond Chandler, Joan Didion, and Nathanael West in Ellis's evocation of Los Angeles. Ellis himself has admitted to the influence that Didion has had on his work. He told an interviewer for the Random House Web site that "Didion's essays and fiction appealed to the Southern Californian side of me and I think as a prose writer she's a genius. And I completely ripped her off when I wrote *Less Than Zero,* and I'm proud of it."

Ellis's second novel, *The Rules of Attraction,* continued in the vein of *Less Than Zero*; as R. Z. Sheppard of *Time* magazine noted, "the village of the damned goes East." *Rules* is set at Camden College, a fictional East Coast school which bears a striking similarity to Bennington College in Vermont, where Ellis earned his degree. Despite the academic setting, many reviewers noted the absence of the usual rigors of higher education. Richard Eder announced in the *Los Angeles Times Book Review* that "we actually catch a glimpse of one professor . . . and he is asleep on his office couch and reeks of pot." What is present, however, are "drunken parties, drugs, sex, shoplifting, [and] pop music," according to Campbell Geeslin in *People.* The three main characters, Paul, Sean, and Lauren, are involved in a frustrating love triangle: Paul, a homosexual, desires the bisexual Sean; Sean meanwhile longs to deepen his involvement with Lauren, who is pining after someone else. *New York Times Book Review* contributor Scott Spencer stated that these characters "live in a world of conspicuous and compulsive consumption—consuming first one another, and then drugs, and then anything else they can lay their hands on."

Spencer praised Ellis for "portraying the shallowness of [his characters'] desires," but objected to what he deemed the author's gratuitous use of brand names which he felt served no function in the narrative. Spencer also surmised that Ellis is a potentially adept satirist, but that in *The Rules of Attraction* "his method of aping the attitudes of the burnt-out works against him. . . . One closes the book feeling that this time out the author has stumbled over the line separating cool from cold. Where we ought to be saying, 'Oh my God, no,' we are, instead, saying, 'Who cares?'" *Newsweek* reviewer David Lehman also found Ellis's authorial skill to be somewhat deficient, and he concluded that "like *Less Than Zero, The Rules of Attraction* is more effective as a sociological exhibit than as a work of literary art." One unlikely proponent of the book was Gore Vidal, whom Tyrnauer quoted as remarking, "I thought it was really rather inspired. . . . These nutty characters, each on his own track—and the tracks keep crossing. It was a wonderfully comic novel." When Roger Avary directed the film version of *The Rules of Attraction,* which appeared on theater screens in 2002, he updated the tale to contemporary times rather than the 1980s.

A minor character from *The Rules of Attraction*—Sean's older brother, Patrick—became the central figure in Ellis's third novel, *American Psycho.* Like Ellis's other protagonists, Patrick Bateman is young, greedy, wealthy, and devoid of morals. A Wall Street executive who shops at the most expensive stores and dines at the trendiest restaurants, Patrick also enjoys torturing, mutilating, and murdering people at random, mostly from New York City's underclass. His crimes are described in the same emotionless detail that he devotes to his observations on food, clothing, and stereo equipment. Though he drops many hints of his covert activities to friends and authorities, he is never caught, and none of the victims seems to be missed.

Ellis has stated that he intended *American Psycho* to be a satirical black comedy about the lack of morality in modern America, and some critics believe that he achieved this aim. Other commentators, however, accused him of pandering to readers' most base desires by producing a novel with all the artistic worth of a low-budget horror movie. Man, woman, child, and animal all meet grisly ends at the hands of Bateman, and the book's violence toward women in particular prompted one chapter of the National Organization for Women to organize to boycott not only the book itself, but all books by its publisher, Vintage, and its parent company, Random House. The novel generated controversy from the very beginning, however. Ellis's first publisher, Simon & Schuster, refused to carry through on their agreement to publish it, even though they had already given the author a $300,000 advance.

Some critics saw little literary merit in the book. In a *Washington Post* review, Jonathan Yardley called *American Psycho* "a contemptible piece of pornography, the literary equivalent of a snuff flick" and urged readers to forego the experience. Andrew Motion echoed Yardley's sentiments in the London *Observer,* calling the book "deeply and extremely disgusting . . . . Sensationalist, pointless except as a way of earning its author some money and notoriety." Similarly, Albert Manguel of *Saturday Night* also reported that his reaction to the book was not as the author intended: "not intellectual terror, which compels you to question the universe, but physical horror—a revulsion not of the senses but of the gut, like that produced by shoving a finger down one's throat." John Leonard of the *Nation,* however, argued that "There is no reason this couldn't have been funny: if not Swiftian, at least a sort of *Bonfire of the Vanities* meets *The Texas Chainsaw Massacre.* . . . Ellis has an ear for the homophobic and misogynistic fatuities of his social set. . . . When Patrick tells people that he's 'into murders and executions,' what they hear him say is 'mergers and acquisitions.'"

Director David Cronenberg considered making a film version, and author Michael Tolkin argued, as Tyrnauer reported: "There was a massive denial about the strengths of the book. . . . People scapegoated the violence, but that wasn't his sin. He made a connection between the language of fashion writing and serial murder." The film was eventually made in 2000, however, and after actor Leonardo DiCaprio first agreed and then declined to take on the role of Patrick Bateman, it went to Christian Bales. Several critics lauded the work of director Mary Harron, including Gavin Smith in *Film Comment,* who noted that "she and screenplay collaborator-actress Guinevere Turner . . . have done an exemplary job of adaptation—distilling, sharpening, and fleshing out the malignant essence of the novel," and that "the result is a mordantly funny and agreeably blatant satire with genuinely subversive bite." Similarly, Richard Corliss in *Time* felt that "Harron and . . . Turner do understand the book, and they want their film to be understood as a period comedy of manners."

The debate over Ellis's style continued with his 1994 publication, *The Informers.* A book of short stories constructed from loosely related short pieces which take place once again in Los Angeles and concern rich and beautiful college students, the book displays the deadpan prose and scenes of horror on which Ellis's reputation has been built. The book contains graphic depictions of vampirism and murder on a par with those in *American Psycho,* but violence is not the book's focus. A multitude of friends and acquaintances, mostly tan, blonde, and sleeping with each other, find their lives uprooted by several random murders and mutilations of their relatives and peers. As it turns out, two of these young trendy types, Dirk and Jamie, are vampires. But once again Ellis focuses on the emptiness of the 1980s and on characters consumed with style and materialism who have contempt for any real analysis of their lives. "The *Informers* is full of scintillating chitchat," wrote Leonard in the *Nation.* "What Ellis has digitized, instead of a novel, is a video. He channel-surfs—from bloody bathroom to bloodier bedroom; from herpes to anorexia," he continued. For Neal Karlen, reviewer for the *Los Angeles Times Book Review, The Informers* represented "a further slide down for an author who long ago had it." Karlen dismissed the book as full of "a rancid phoniness" and characterized all of Ellis's later work as being "opaque and bitter, devoid of both humanity and meaning" because "Ellis apparently has not learned the lesson of empathy, either on the page or in life." Conversely, for *New York Times Book Review* contributor George Stade, *The Informers* was "spare, austere, elegantly designed, telling in detail, coolly ferocious, sardonic in its humor." Stade concluded that Ellis himself was "a covert moralist and closet sentimentalist, the best kind, the kind who leaves you space in which to respond as your predispositions nudge you, whether as a commissar or hand-wringer or, like me, as an admirer of his intelligence and craft."

Ellis published his fourth novel, *Glamorama,* in 1999. As he explained on the Random House Web site, *Glamorama* differs from his previous work because, "to put it bluntly, it has a plot, or at least an identifiable narrative that my other novels really don't have." In it, protagonist and senator's son Victor Ward is a male model who leaves his shallow milieu to become unwittingly involved in a European terrorist ring. Ellis further observed, "I think the connection I'm making has to do with the tyranny of beauty in our culture and the tyranny of terrorism. Of course that's a metaphor and the idea of models actually blowing up hotels and airlines is farfetched." After quoting a particularly gruesome passage of *Glamorama* in a critique for the *National Review,* however, James Panero asked, "Now did the tyranny of beauty ever make you feel that uneasy?" Panero also presented another question about Ellis in discussing *Glamorama*: "The plot is nihilistic; the characters, depraved. And page after page is filled with horrible, graphic violence. So why do I get the feeling Ellis is a closet conservative?" A reviewer from *Esquire* was less impressed, stating that while Ellis "may even be said to succeed at rendering a certain world whole, in its squirming, teeming entirety," the author "neglects to . . . make the world of his choosing interesting." Likewise, an *Entertainment Weekly* critic felt that the novel's "overly complicated plot drags on and on." Robert Plunket in the *Advocate,* however, praised *Glamorama* as "sick, twisted, and possibly brilliant," commenting further that the book "secures [Ellis's] reputation as the Jeffrey Dahmer of novelists—dangerous and deranged. . . . Clearly, here is a man who is doing what he is born to do."

In Tyrnauer's interview with Ellis, he noted that "a certain slangy level of ironic detachment informs even his most serious statements—and not everybody gets it. 'I am an incredibly moralistic person. . . . A lot of people totally mistake the books in some cases as advocating a certain behavior or as glorifying a certain form of behavior." Commenting on his role as a spokesperson for his generation, Ellis told *CA* that "I . . . don't believe that there's one or two spokespeople for a generation, one collective voice who's going to speak for the whole lot. . . . What you have to do . . . is just feel safe enough about your own opinion and go ahead and state it."

BIOGRAPHICAL AND CRITICAL SOURCES:

BOOKS

Authors and Artists for Young Adults, Volume 43, Gale (Detroit, MI), 2002.

Contemporary Literary Criticism, Gale (Detroit, MI), Volume 39, 1986, Volume 71, 1992.

Contemporary Novelists, 7th edition, St. James Press (Detroit, MI), 2001.

St. James Encyclopedia of Popular Culture, St. James Press (Detroit, MI), 2000.

PERIODICALS

Advocate, February 2, 1999, Robert Plunket, review of *Glamorama,* p. 65.

Chicago Tribune, September 13, 1987.

Current Biography, November, 1994, p. 23.
Detroit Free Press, August 18, 1985.
Detroit News, August 11, 1985.
Entertainment Weekly, August 19, 1994; January 22, 1999, "Glitter Haughty," p. 95.
Esquire, October, 1994, p. 158; February, 1999, "Bret Easton Ellis Plays Tom Wolfe," p. 26.
Film Comment, December, 1985; March, 2000, Gavin Smith, review of *American Psycho,* p. 72.
Guardian, January 9, 1999, "Leader of the Bret Pack."
Hollywood Reporter, October 7, 2002, Frank Scheck, review of *The Rules of Attraction,* pp. 10-11.
Interview, June, 1985; January, 1991, p. 54.
Library Journal, January, 1991; July, 1994.
Los Angeles Times Book Review, May 26, 1985; September 13, 1987.
Mademoiselle, June, 1986.
Nation, April 1, 1991, p. 426; September 5, 1994, p. 238.
National Review, February 14, 1986; June 24, 1991; September 12, 1994, p. 86; June 17, 1996, p. 56; March 8, 1999, James Panero, "Ellis's Island," p. 53.
New Republic, June 10, 1985; September 5, 1994, p. 46.
New Statesman, November 11, 1994, p. 40; January 15, 1999, Scott Reyburn, review of *Glamorama,* p. 49.
Newsweek, July 8, 1985; September 7, 1987; March 4, 1991, p. 58.
New Yorker, July 29, 1985; October 26, 1987, p. 142.
New York Review of Books, May 29, 1986.
New York Times, June 8, 1985; January 5, 1999, Michiko Kakutani, "Fashion Victims Take Terrorist Chic Seriously," p. E8.
New York Times Book Review, June 16, 1985; June 22, 1986; September 13, 1987, p. 14; December 16, 1990, p. 3; September 18, 1994, p. 14; January 24, 1999, Daniel Mendelsohn, "Lesser Than Zero," p. 8.
Observer, April 21, 1991, p. 61; January 3, 1999, Andrew Motion, "What Do You Give a Man with Two Girlfriends? A Really Hard Time."
People Weekly, July 29 1985; September 28, 1987.
Playboy, July, 1991, p. 26.
Publishers Weekly, June 13, 1994.
Rolling Stone, September 26, 1985.
Saturday Night, July-August, 1991, pp. 46-47, 49.
Saturday Review, July-August, 1985.
Time, June 10, 1985; October 19, 1987; March 18, 1991, p. 14; April 17, 2000, Richard Corliss, "A Yuppie's Killer Instinct," p. 78.
Times Literary Supplement, February 28, 1986.
USA Today Magazine, July, 2000, Christopher Sharrett, "American Psychosis," p. 67.
Vanity Fair, April, 1994, p. 108; August, 1994, p. 94.
Voice Literary Supplement, May, 1985.
Washington Post, February 27, 1991, pp. B1, B3; April 28, 1991, pp. C1, C4.
Writer's Digest, December, 1986.

ONLINE

Good Reports, http://www.goodreports.net/glaell.htm/ (March 6, 1999), review of *Glamorama.*
Random House, http://www.randomhouse.com/ (May 2, 2003), "An Interview with Bret Easton Ellis."

OTHER

This Is Not an Exit: The Fictional World of Bret Easton Ellis (film), First Run Features, 2000.*

* * *

EMECHETA, (Florence Onye) Buchi 1944-

PERSONAL: Born July 21, 1944, in Yaba, Lagos, Nigeria; daughter of Jeremy Nwabudike (a railway worker and molder) and Alice Ogbanje (Okwuekwu) Emecheta; married Sylvester Onwordi, 1960 (separated, 1966); children: Florence, Sylvester, Jake, Christy, Alice. *Education:* University of London, B.Sc. (with honors), 1972, Ph.D., 1991. *Religion:* Anglican. *Hobbies and other interests:* Gardening, attending the theatre, listening to music, reading.

ADDRESSES: Home—7 Briston Grove, Crouch End, London N8 9EX, England.

CAREER: British Museum, London, England, library officer, 1965-69; Inner London Education Authority, London, youth worker and sociologist, 1969-76; community worker, Camden, NJ, 1976-78. Writer and lecturer, 1972—. Visiting professor at several universities throughout the United States, including Pennsylvania State University, University of California, Los Angeles, and University of Illinois at Urbana-Champaign, 1979; senior resident fellow and visiting

Buchi Emecheta

professor of English, University of Calabar, Nigeria, 1980-81; lecturer, Yale University, 1982, London University, 1982—; fellow, London University, 1986. Proprietor, Ogwugwu Afor Publishing Company, 1982-83. Member of Home Secretary's Advisory Council on Race, 1979—, and of Arts Council of Great Britain, 1982-83.

AWARDS, HONORS: Jock Campbell Award for literature by new or unregarded talent from Africa or the Caribbean, *New Statesman,* 1978; selected as the Best Black British Writer, 1978, and one of the Best British Young Writers, 1983.

WRITINGS:

In the Ditch, Barrie & Jenkins (London, England), 1972.

Second-Class Citizen (novel), Allison & Busby (London, England), 1974, Braziller (New York, NY), 1975.

The Bride Price: A Novel, Braziller (New York, NY), 1976, also published as *The Bride Price: Young Ibo Girl's Love; Conflict of Family and Tradition.*

The Slave Girl: A Novel, Braziller (New York, NY), 1977.

The Joys of Motherhood: A Novel, Braziller (New York, NY), 1979.

Destination Biafra: A Novel, Schocken (New York, NY), 1982.

Naira Power (novelette), Macmillan (London, England), 1982.

Double Yoke (novel), Schocken (New York, NY), 1982.

The Rape of Shavi (novel), Ogwugwu Afor (Ibuza, Nigeria), 1983, Braziller (New York, NY), 1985.

Adah's Story: A Novel, Allison & Busby (London, England), 1983.

Head Above Water (autobiography), Ogwugwu Afor (Ibuza, Nigeria), 1984, Collins (London, England), 1986.

The Family (novel), Braziller (New York, NY), 1990.

Gwendolen (novel), Collins (London, England), 1990.

Kehinde, Heinemann (Portsmouth, NH), 1994.

The New Tribe, Heinemann (Portsmouth, NH), 2000.

JUVENILE

Titch the Cat (based on story by daughter Alice Emecheta), Allison & Busby, 1979.

Nowhere to Play (based on story by daughter Christy Emecheta), Schocken (New York, NY), 1980.

The Moonlight Bride, Oxford University Press (Oxford, England), 1981.

The Wrestling Match, Oxford University Press (Oxford, England), 1981, Braziller (New York, NY), 1983.

Family Bargain (publication for schools), British Broadcasting Corp. (London, England), 1987.

OTHER

(Author of introduction and commentary) Maggie Murray, *Our Own Freedom* (book of photographs), Sheba Feminist (London, England), 1981.

A Kind of Marriage (teleplay; produced by BBC-TV), Macmillan (London, England), 1987.

Also author of teleplays *Tanya, a Black Woman,* produced by BBC-TV, and *The Juju Landlord.* Contributor to journals, including *New Statesman, Times Literary Supplement,* and *Guardian.*

SIDELIGHTS: Although Buchi Emecheta has resided in London since 1962, she is "Nigeria's best-known female writer," commented John Updike in the *New Yorker.* "Indeed, few writers of her sex . . . have arisen in any part of tropical Africa." Emecheta enjoys great popularity in Great Britain, and she has gathered an appreciative audience on this side of the Atlantic as well. Although Emecheta has written children's books and teleplays, she is best known for her historical novels set in Nigeria, both before and after independence. Concerned with the clash of cultures and the impact of Western values upon agrarian traditions and customs, Emecheta's work is strongly autobiographical; and, as Updike observed, much of it is especially concerned with "the situation of women in a society where their role, though crucial, was firmly subordinate and where the forces of potential liberation have arrived with bewildering speed."

Born to Ibo parents in Yaba, a small village near Lagos, Nigeria, Emecheta indicates that the Ibos "don't want you to lose contact with your culture," wrote Rosemary Bray in the *Voice Literary Supplement.* Bray explained that the oldest woman in the house plays an important role in that she is the "big mother" to the entire clan, said Bray: "She was very old and almost blind," Buchi recalls, "And she would gather the young children around her after dinner and tell stories to us." The stories the children heard were about their origins and ancestors; and, according to Bray, Emecheta recalls: "I thought to myself 'No life could be more important than this.' So when people asked me what I wanted to do when I grew up I told them I wanted to be a storyteller—which is what I'm doing now."

In the Ditch, her first book, originally appeared as a series of columns in the *New Statesman.* Written in the form of a diary, it "is based on her own failed marriage and her experiences on the dole in London trying to rear alone her many children," stated Charlotte and David Bruner in *World Literature Today.* Called a "sad, sonorous, occasionally hilarious . . . extraordinary first novel," by Adrianne Blue of the *Washington Post Book World,* it details her impoverished existence in a foreign land, as well as her experience with racism, and "illuminates the similarities and differences between cultures and attitudes," remarked a *Times Literary Supplement* contributor, who thought it merits "special attention."

Similarly autobiographical, Emecheta's second novel, *Second-Class Citizen,*"recounts her early marriage years, when she was trying to support her student-husband—a man indifferent to his own studies and later indifferent to her job searches, her childbearing, and her resistance to poverty," observed the Bruners. The novel is about a young, resolute and resourceful Nigerian girl who, despite traditional tribal domination of females, manages to continue her own education; she marries a student and follows him to London, where he becomes abusive toward her. "Emecheta said people find it hard to believe that she has not exaggerated the truth in this autobiographical novel," reported Nancy Topping Bazin in *Black Scholar.* "The grimness of what is described does indeed make it painful to read." Called a "brave and angry book" by Marigold Johnson in the *Times Literary Supplement,* Emecheta's story, however, "is not accompanied by a misanthropic whine," noted Martin Levin in the *New York Times Book Review.* Alice Walker, who found it "one of the most informative books about contemporary African life" that she has read, observed in *Ms.* that "it raises fundamental questions about how creative and prosaic life is to be lived and to what purpose."

"Emecheta's women do not simply lie down and die," observed Bray. "Always there is resistance, a challenge to fate, a need to renegotiate the terms of the uneasy peace that exists between them and accepted traditions." Bray added that "Emecheta's women know, too, that between the rock of African traditions and the hard place of encroaching Western values, it is the women who will be caught." Concerned with the clash of cultures, in *The Bride Price: A Novel,* Emecheta tells the story of a young Nigerian girl "whose life is complicated by traditional attitudes toward women," wrote Richard Cima in *Library Journal.* The young girl's father dies when she is thirteen; and, with her brother and mother, she becomes the property of her father's ambitious brother. She is permitted to remain in school only because it will increase her value as a potential wife. However, she falls in love with her teacher, a descendant of slaves; and because of familial objections, they elope, thereby depriving her uncle of the "bride price." When she dies in childbirth, she fulfills the superstition that a woman would not survive the birth of her first child if her bride price had not been paid; and Susannah Clapp maintained in the *Times Literary Supplement,* that the quality of the novel "depends less on plot or characterization than on the information conveyed about a set of customs and the ideas which underlay them." Calling it "a captivating Nigerian novel lovingly but unsentimentally written, about the survival of ancient marriage customs in modern Nigeria," Valerie Cunningham added in *New Statesman* that this book "proves Buchi Emecheta to be a considerable writer."

Emecheta's *Slave Girl: A Novel* is about "a poor, gently raised Ibo girl who is sold into slavery to a rich African marketwoman by a feckless brother at the turn of the century," wrote a *New Yorker* contributor. Educated by missionaries, she joins the new church where she meets the man she eventually marries. In *Library Journal,* Cima thought that the book provides an "interesting picture of Christianity's impact on traditional Ibo society." Perceiving parallels between marriage and slavery, Emecheta explores the issue of "freedom within marriage in a society where slavery is supposed to have been abolished," wrote Cunningham in the *New Statesman,* adding that the book indicts both "pagan and Christian inhumanity to women." And although a contributor to *World Literature Today* suggested that the "historical and anthropological background" in the novel tends to destroy its "emotional complex," another contributor to the same journal believed that the sociological detail has been "unobtrusively woven into" it and that *The Slave Girl* represents Emecheta's "most accomplished work so far. It is coherent, compact and convincing."

"Emecheta's voice has been welcomed by many as helping to redress the somewhat one-sided picture of African women that has been delineated by male writers," according to *A New Reader's Guide to African Literature.* Writing in *African Literature Today,* Eustace Palmer indicated that "the African novel has until recently been remarkable for the absense of what might be called the feminine point of view." Because of the relatively few female African novelists, "the presentation of women in the African novel has been left almost entirely to male voices . . . and their interest in African womanhood . . . has had to take second place to numerous other concerns," continued Palmer. "These male novelists, who have presented the African woman largely within the traditional milieu, have generally communicated a picture of a male-dominated and male-oriented society, and the satisfaction of the women with this state of things has been . . . completely taken for granted." Palmer added that the emergence of Emecheta and other "accomplished female African novelists . . . seriously challenges all these cozy assumptions. The picture of the cheerful contented female complacently accepting her lot is replaced by that of a woman who is powerfully aware of the unfairness of the system and who longs to be else's appendage." For instance, Palmer noted that *The Joys of Motherhood: A Novel* "presents essentially the same picture of traditional society . . . but the difference lies in the prominence in Emecheta's novel of the female point of view registering its disgust at male chauvinism and its dissatisfaction with what it considers an unfair and oppressive system."

The Joys of Motherhood is about a woman "who marries but is sent home in disgrace because she fails to bear a child quickly enough," wrote Bazin. "She then is sent to the city by her father to marry a man she has never seen. She is horrified when she meets this second husband because she finds him ugly, but she sees no alternative to staying with him. Poverty and repeated pregnancies wear her down; the pressure to bear male children forces her to bear child after child since the girls she has do not count." Palmer observed that "clearly, the man is the standard and the point of reference in this society. It is significant that the chorus of countrymen say, not that a woman without a child is a failed woman, but that a woman without a child *for her husband* is a failed woman." Bazin observed that in Emecheta's novels, "a woman must accept the double standard of sexual freedom: it permits polygamy and infidelity for both Christian and non-Christian men but only monogamy for women. These books reveal the extent to which the African woman's oppression is engrained in the African mores."

Acknowledging that "the issue of polygamy in Africa remains a controversial one," Palmer stated that what Emecheta stresses in *The Joys of Motherhood* is "the resulting dominance, especially sexual, of the male, and the relegation of the female into subservience, domesticity and motherhood." Nonetheless, despite Emecheta's "angry glare," said Palmer, one can "glean from the novel the economic and social reasons that must have given rise to polygamy. . . . But the author concentrates on the misery and deprivation polygamy can bring." Palmer praised Emecheta's insightful psychological probing of her characters' thoughts: "Scarcely any other African novelist has succeeded in probing the female mind and displaying the female personality with such precision." Blue likewise suggested that Emecheta "tells this story in a plain style, denuding it of exoticism, displaying an impressive, embracing compassion." Calling it a "graceful, touching, ironically titled tale that bears a plain feminist message," Updike added that "in this compassionate but slightly distanced and stylized story of a life that comes to seem wasted, [Emecheta] sings a dirge for more than African pieties. The lives within *The Joys of Motherhood* might be, transposed into a different cultural key, those of our own rural ancestors."

Emecheta's "works reveal a great deal about the lives of African women and about the development of feminist perspectives," observed Bazin, explaining that one moves beyond an initial perspective of "personal experience," to perceive "social or communal" oppression. This second perspective "demands an analysis of the causes of oppression within the social mores and the patriarchal power structure," added Bazin. Finding both perspectives in Emecheta's work, Bazin thought that her descriptions reveal "what it is like to be for" millions of black African women. Although her feminist perspective is anchored in her own personal life, said Bazin, Emecheta "grew to understand how soon preference, bride price, polygamy, menstrual taboos, . . . wife beating, early marriages, early and unlimited pregnancies, arranged marriages, and male dominance in the home functioned to keep women powerless." The Bruners wrote that "obviously Emecheta is concerned about the plight of women, today and yesterday, in both technological and traditional societies, though she rejects a feminist label." Emecheta told the Bruners: "The main themes of my novels are African society and family; the historical, social, and political life in Africa as seen by a woman through events. I always try to show that the African male is oppressed and he too oppresses the African women. . . . I have not committed myself to the cause of African women only. I write about Africa as a whole."

Emecheta's *Destination Biafra: A Novel* is a story of the "history of Nigeria from the eve of independence to the collapse of the Biafran secessionist movement," wrote Robert L. Berner in *World Literature Today.* The novel has generated a mixed critical response, though. In the *Times Literary Supplement,* Chinweizu felt that it "does not convey the feel of the experience that was Biafra. All it does is leave one wondering why it falls so devastatingly below the quality of Buchi Emecheta's previous works." Noting, however, that Emecheta's publisher reduced the manuscript by half, Berner suggested that "this may account for what often seems a rather elliptical narrative and for the frequently clumsy prose which too often blunts the novel's satiric edge." Finding the novel "different from any of her others . . . larger and more substantive," the Bruners stated: "Here she presents neither the life story of a single character nor the delineation of one facet of a culture but the whole perplexing canvas of people from diverse ethnic groups, belief systems, levels of society all caught in a disastrous civil war." Moreover, the Bruners felt that the "very objectivity of her reporting and her impartiality in recounting atrocities committed by all sides, military and civilian, have even greater impact because her motivation is not sadistic."

At about the same time that Emecheta published *Destination Biafra,* her novel *Double Yoke* also saw print. *Double Yoke* details the difficulties facing African women in the academic world; though at first, the heroine Nko's boyfriend seems progressive, he later repudiates her for allowing him to have sex with her before marriage. Nko must also deal with a professor who extorts sexual favors from her under the threat of preventing her from receiving her degree. According to Jewelle Gomez in *Black Scholar,* "Here, as in Emecheta's other novels, she speaks with an undeniably Nigerian voice; makes clear the Nigerian woman's circumscribed position in society and her skillful adaptation to it."

The Rape of Shavi represents somewhat of a departure in that "Emecheta attempts one of the most difficult of tasks: that of integrating the requirements of contemporary, realistic fiction with the narrative traditions of myth and folklore," wrote Somtow Sucharitkul in the *Washington Post Book World.* Roy Kerridge described the novel's plot in the *Times Literary Supplement:* "A plane crashes among strange tribespeople, white aviators are made welcome by the local king, they find precious stones, repair their plane and escape just as they are going to be forcibly married to native girls. The king's son and heir stows away and has adventures of his own in England." Called a "wise and haunting tale" by a *New Yorker* contributor, *The Rape of Shavi* "recounts the ruination of this small African society by voracious white interlopers," said Richard Eder in the *Los Angeles Times.* A few critics suggested that in *The Rape of Shavi,* Emecheta's masterful portrayal of her Shavian community is not matched by her depiction of the foreigners. Eder, for instance, called it a "lopsided fable," and declared: "It is not that the Shavians are noble and the whites monstrous; that is what fables are for. It is that the Shavians are finely drawn and the Westerners very clumsily. It is a duet between a flute and a kitchen drain." However, Sucharitkul thought that portraying the Shavians as "complex individuals" and the Westerners as "two dimensional, mythic types" presents a refreshing, seldom expressed, and "particularly welcome" point of view.

Although in the *New York Times* Michiko Kakutani called *The Rape of Shavi* "an allegorical tale, filled with ponderous morals about the evils of imperialism and tired aphorisms about nature and civilization," Sucharitkul believed that "the central thesis of [the novel] is brilliantly, relentlessly argued, and Emecheta's characters and societies are depicted with a bittersweet, sometimes painful honesty." The critic also praised Emecheta's "persuasive" prose: "It is prose that appears unusually simple at first, for it is full of the kind of rhythms and sentence structures more often found in folk tales than in contemporary novels. Indeed, in electing to tell her multilayered and often very contemporary story within a highly mythic narrative framework, the author walks a fine line between the pitfalls of preciosity and pretentiousness. By and large, the tightrope act is a success."

Following *The Rape of Shavi,* Emecheta seemed to be more concerned with discussing the lives of African immigrants to England and other western countries. The title character of *Gwendolen* is a young Jamaican girl whose parents move to England in search of a better life, leaving her in the care of her grandmother. Her grandmother's boyfriend molests her, and when she eventually rejoins her parents in England, her own father rapes her. Despite these troubles, and her father's suicide, she eventually finds happiness. "This modern ending," in the words of Kirsten Holst Peterson in the *Concise Dictionary of World Literary Biography,* "rests on a new set of relationships formed on the basis of personal choice rather than on blind acceptance of the established pattern of race and family relationships." Peterson concluded that "there seems to be an implicit suggestion that this alternative mode of social organization might avoid a repeat of the experiences of the main character."

In 1994's *Kehinde,* the heroine is Kehinde Okolo, whom Emecheta's entry in *Contemporary Black Biography* described as "a thirty-five-year-old Londoner of Nigerian descent with a management position in international banking." She is happy and successful in England, but when her husband wishes to return home to his village in Nigeria, where his social status is greatly increased, she follows him. She has stayed in London to sell their home, however, and by the time she arrives in Nigeria, he has taken another wife who has provided him with children, and her own social status is greatly lowered. Emecheta takes the stand that even African men are better off in Western countries in her 2000 novel, *The New Tribe.* Chester, a boy of Nigerian descent, is adopted by a white British family, but as an adult travels to Nigeria to get in touch with his ethnic origins. There, he is "tricked out of his passport and his money," as Bruce King reported in *World Literature Today,* and becomes "disillusioned by the corruption, violence, filth, and unhealthy environment," which causes him to contract malaria. His black English girlfriend comes to rescue him and take him back to England, which he now "accepts . . . as home," in King's words.

"Emecheta has reaffirmed her dedication to be a full-time writer," said the Bruners. Her fiction is intensely autobiographical, drawing on the difficulties she has both witnessed and experienced as a woman, and most especially as a Nigerian woman. Indicating that in Nigeria, however, "Emecheta is a prophet without honor," Bray added that "she is frustrated at not being able to reach women—the audience she desires most. She feels a sense of isolation as she attempts to stake out the middle ground between the old and the new." Remarking that "in her art as well as in her life, Buchi Emecheta offers another alternative," Bray quoted the author: "What I am trying to do is get our profession back. Women are born storytellers. We keep the history. We are the true conservatives—we conserve things and we never forget. What I do is not clever or unusual. It is what my aunt and my grandmother did, and their mothers before them."

BIOGRAPHICAL AND CRITICAL SOURCES:

BOOKS

Allan, Tuzyline Jita, *Womanist and Feminist Aesthetics: A Comparative Review,* Ohio University Press (Athens, OH), 1995.

Concise Dictionary of World Literary Biography, Volume 3, Gale (Detroit, MI), 1999.

Contemporary Black Biography, Gale (Detroit, MI), 2001.

Contemporary Literary Criticism, Gale (Detroit, MI), Volume 14, 1980, Volume 28, 1984.

Contemporary Novelists, 7th edition, St. James Press (Detroit, MI), 2001.
Fishburn, Katherine, *Reading Buchi Emecheta: Cross-Cultural Conversations,* Greenwood Press (Westport, CT), 1995.
Umeh, Marie, *Emerging Perspectives on Buchi Emecheta,* Africa World Press (Trenton, NJ), 1995.
Zell, Hans M., and others, *A New Reader's Guide to African Literature,* 2nd revised and expanded edition, Holmes & Meier, 1983.

PERIODICALS

African Literature Today, number 3, 1983.
Atlantic, May, 1976.
Black Scholar, November-December, 1985, Jewelle Gomez, review of *Double Yoke,* p. 51; March-April, 1986.
International Fiction Review, January, 2002, Teresa Derrickson, "Class, Culture, and the Colonial Context: The Status of Women in Buchi Emecheta's *The Joys of Motherhood,*" pp. 40-52.
Library Journal, September 1, 1975; April 1, 1976; January 15, 1978; May 1, 1979; May 15, 1994, p. 98.
Listener, July 19, 1979.
Los Angeles Times, October 16, 1983; March 6, 1985; January 16, 1990.
Ms., January, 1976; July, 1984; March, 1985.
New Statesman, June 25, 1976; October 14, 1977; June 2, 1978; April 27, 1979.
New Yorker, May 17, 1976; January 9, 1978; July 2, 1979; April 23, 1984; April 22, 1985.
New York Times, February 23, 1985; June 2, 1990.
New York Times Book Review, September 14, 1975; November 11, 1979; January 27, 1980; February 27, 1983; May 5, 1985; April 29, 1990.
School Library Journal, September, 1994, p. 255.
Times Literary Supplement, August 11, 1972; January 31, 1975; June 11, 1976; February 26, 1982; February 3, 1984; February 27, 1987; April 20, 1990.
Voice Literary Supplement, June, 1982.
Washington Post Book World, May 13, 1979; April 12, 1981; September 5, 1982; September 25, 1983; March 30, 1985.
World Literature Today, spring, 1977; summer, 1977; spring, 1978; winter, 1979; spring, 1980; winter, 1983; autumn, 1984; spring, 2001, Bruce King, review of *The New Tribe,* p. 310.*

ENSLER, Eve 1953-

PERSONAL: Born May 25, 1953, in New York, NY; married Richard McDermott, September 15, 1979; children: one stepson. *Education:* Middlebury College, B.A.

ADDRESSES: Home—16 West 16th St., 14 SN, New York, NY 10011. *Agent*—Deborah Skelly, William Morris Agency, Inc., 1325 Avenue of the Americas, New York, NY 10019.

CAREER: Writer. Editor, *Central Park Magazine.* Director, *Word of Mouth* (one-act monologue), Promenade Theater, New York, 1995. Founder of V-Day, a day devoted to raising funds and awareness to end violence against women.

AWARDS, HONORS: Art of Peace award, poetry, 1984; Obie Award, 1997, Guggenheim Fellowship Award, 1999, Berilla-Kerr Award for Playwriting, Jury Award for Theater, 2000, from the U.S. Comedy Festival, and Creative Vision for Women's Justice Award, 2002, from Pace Women's Justice Center, all for *The Vagina Monologues.*

WRITINGS:

PLAYS

Floating Rhoda and the Glue Man, produced at the HERE Theatre, New York, 1995.
The Vagina Monologues (one-woman show; produced in New York City, c. 1996) Villard (New York, NY), 1998.
Necessary Targets, produced at the Helen Hayes Theatre, 1996, and at the Variety Arts Theater in New York, NY, March, 2002.

OTHER

Acting You (teaching aid), Girls Clubs of America, 1983.

Also author of the plays *When I Call My Voices,* 1979, *Rendezvous,* 1983, *Lemonade,* and *The Good Body.* Contributor to numerous magazines, including *Chicago Review, Win, Third Wind, Marie Claire.* Contributor to *Peace or Perish: A Crisis Anthology.*

Eve Ensler

ADAPTATIONS: The Vagina Monologues was filmed for HBO.

SIDELIGHTS: Eve Ensler is a playwright whose works take on issues of women's relationships with their own bodies and with men. In her 1995 play *Floating Rhoda and the Glue Man,* a woman in her thirties meets a man at an art gallery and the two start a fitful relationship, hindered by their involvement with others and by their own neuroses. Occasionally, Ensler's characters step outside of themselves in order to discuss their feelings and thoughts while other actors continue on in their places. *Variety* reviewer Greg Evans likened this technique to the scene in Woody Allen's film *Annie Hall* in which Annie steps outside of herself to smoke while making love. Evans noted that the objects of Ensler's parody in *Floating Rhoda*—including her protagonist, an "overly 'therapized' New York Jewish intellectual," whose current lover is involved in the type of overtly masculine therapy that the book *Iron John* made infamous, and the trendy, New York art scene of her would-be lover—occasionally "[seem] more than a little dated." Evans's biggest complaint, however, was that Ensler's characters lacked the depth to carry the big issues her parodies raise: "They're stick figures designed solely to represent notions, and some of the notions are pretty trite."

An initial production of Ensler's *Necessary Targets* received more favorable notice. In this 1996 drama, an American psychiatrist travels to Yugoslavia with her translator in order to interview female victims in the Bosnian refugee camps and returns to her former life utterly transformed by what she has heard. Debuting at the Helen Hayes Theatre in New York City as a benefit performance, this production was directed by Ensler and attracted the talents of actresses Meryl Streep and Angelica Huston, among others. The combination made for a performance with "powerful impact," according to Robert Brustein in the *New Republic.* In particular, Brustein credited the actresses who performed this production with "[managing] to turn what otherwise might have been an inspirational movie of the week into a deeply affecting experience." Robert L. King, discussing *Necessary Targets* in the *North American Review* had high praise for the work. "Like other intelligent political plays," he maintained, "*Necessary Targets* tests the value of language as instrument for knowing a harsh reality and dealing with it insightfully." The published version of the play met with positive response as well; for instance, Jack Helbig in *Booklist* stated that "Ensler's portrayals avoid the easy clichés of quick-hit news stories and convey human experience in all its painful complexity." Similarly, Laura A. Ewald in the *Library Journal* concluded that "*Necessary Targets* tells an important story of survival and coping that will move readers and audiences alike."

Ensler interviewed hundreds of women about their opinions on and experiences concerning their vaginas in preparation for *The Vagina Monologues,* an award-winning piece she wrote and performed in 1996, and which provided the material for a 1998 book of the same title. In the performance and in the book, Ensler provides excerpts from these interviews, occasionally retaining the question-and-answer format of the original interviews, as when she poses the question "If your vagina could talk, what would it say?" and supplies the humorous response "Where's Brian?" The author also describes the experience of a rape, and, in the performance, imitates the sound of twenty different types of moans of pleasure made by women during intercourse. Helbig, in another review for *Booklist,* commented favorably on the translation from performance piece to book: "Ensler is first and foremost a storyteller and has fashioned her material into a highly readable script." Although *New York* theater critic John Simon expressed reservations about the content of some of Ensler's monologues, a contributor to *Kirkus Reviews* concluded: "You might have to be a woman to appreciate the humor and poignancy here, but women will." The play was adapted for television by HBO in 2002.

Ensler is also the author of *Acting You,* a series of pamphlets—published in 1983—designed to help teachers, youth counselors, and young people to utilize theater techniques to learn to recognize emotions and resolve conflicts in a nonthreatening manner. She has also given away the performance rights to *The Vagina Monologues* to any theater company who is willing to donate the profits from its staging to causes dedicated to preventing violence against women. From this practice, Ensler has moved to re-naming Valentine's Day as V-Day, and promoting it as an international day devoted to ending mysogynistic violence—not only rape and domestic abuse, but also the practice of female circumcision. In cities and on college campuses that participate in V-Day, *The Vagina Monologues* is often staged as a fund raiser.

Before the terrorist attacks on the World Trade Center and the Pentagon on September 11, 2001, focused attention on the nation of Afghanistan, Ensler was writing about the plight of women in that country under the rule of the Taliban. She herself wore a burka—the long black garment that covers a woman's entire body insisted upon by the Taliban—to enter Afghanistan and report on conditions there. Though she was intensely moved by the courage of Afghan women who risked death by execution in order to pursue forbidden education, she did not support the U.S. backing of the Northern Alliance in that country. She told Janelle Brown during an interview for *Salon.com* in 2001: "Wouldn't it be ideal if the Northern Alliance marched into Kabul and Kandahar and all these different groups lived peacefully? But I think we're on the verge of a civil war."

Ensler, according to Andrea Lewis in the *Progressive,* "has a new one-woman show, *The Good Body,*" which "addresses the ways women around the world feel compelled to conform to society's standard of beauty." The playwright told Lewis: "I went around the world for four months and interviewed women in fourteen different countries." She also confided: "After I finished *The Vagina Monologues,* my self-hatred moved into my stomach. . . . And I thought, 'Oh, no! Now I'm obsessed with my stomach!' I started thinking, 'Why are we so obsessed with our bodies?' So that has begun this new adventure."

BIOGRAPHICAL AND CRITICAL SOURCES:

PERIODICALS

Advocate, February 4, 1997, p. 69.

Booklist, February 1, 1998, p. 893; February 1, 2001, Jack Helbig, review of *Necessary Targets,* p. 1034.

Hollywood Reporter, February 14, 2002, Ray Richmond, review of *The Vagina Monologues,* pp. 12-13; March 6, 2002, Frank Schock, review of *Necessary Targets,* p. 57.

Kirkus Reviews, December 1, 1997, p. 1768.

Library Journal, January 1, 2001, Laura A. Ewald, review of *Necessary Targets,* p. 106.

Nation, December 2, 2002, Jennifer Baumgardner, "When in Rome," p. 22.

New Republic, December 16, 1996, p. 32.

New York, November 4, 1996, p. 88.

New Yorker, March 11, 2002, Nancy Franklin, "War Stories: Revisiting the Ruins of Bosnia," pp. 90-91.

North American Review, March-April, 2002, Robert L. King, "New Plays and a Modern Master," pp. 45-51.

Progressive, March, 2001, Andrea Lewis, "All about Eve," p. 39.

Time, October 25, 1999, Richard Zoglin, review of *Necessary Targets,* p. 123.

Variety, May 15, 1995, p. 234; September 18, 1995, p. 92; March 4, 2002, Charles Isherwood, review of *Necessary Targets,* pp. 42-43.

Voice of Youth Advocates, December, 1983, pp. 291-292.

Westchester County Business Journal, October 7, 2002, "Pace Women's Justice Center," p. 33.

ONLINE

Official Vagina Monologues Web site, http://www.vaginamonologues.co.uk/ (November 8, 2003).

Salon.com, http://www.salon.com/ (November 26, 2001), Janelle Brown, "Eve Ensler: 'Afghanistan Is Everywhere.'"*

* * *

EYEN, Jerome
See EYEN, Tom

* * *

EYEN, Tom 1941-1991
(Jerome Eyen, Roger Short, Jr.)

PERSONAL: Born August 14, 1941, in Cambridge, OH; died of a heart attack, May 26, 1991, in Palm Beach, FL; son of Abraham and Julia (Farhad) Eyen; married Liza Giraudoux (divorced); children: Jacque, David, Christopher. *Education:* Ohio State University, B.A., 1961; attended the American Academy of Dramatic Arts, 1961-62.

CAREER: Playwright and director. Had own repertory company, Theatre of the Eye, part of the La Mama complex. Sometimes directed own plays under the names Jerome Eyen and Roger Short, Jr. Former publicity agent; drama teacher at Metropolitan Television Arts, New York, NY, scriptwriter for the syndicated television series, *Mary Hartman, Mary Hartman,* beginning 1976.

AWARDS, HONORS: Rockefeller Foundation grant, 1967-68; *Show Business* Best Playwright Off-Off-Broadway Grand Award, 1969, for *4 No Plays* and *The White Whore and the Bit Player*; Guggenheim fellowship, 1970; Tony Award, American Theatre Wing, and Grammy Award, National Academy of Recording Arts and Sciences, both 1982, and NAACP Award, 1983, all for *Dreamgirls.*

WRITINGS:

PLAYS

(And director and producer) *Tour de Four,* first produced in New York, 1963.

Tom Eyen

Frustrata, the Dirty Little Girl with the Paper Rose Stuck in Her Head Is Demented!, first produced in New York, 1964, produced in London, 1970.

The White Whore and the Bit Player (also see below; produced Off-Broadway at Cafe La Mama, 1964), Hill & Wang, 1969.

Sarah B. Divine! and Other Plays (contains: *My Next Husband Will Be a Beauty!,* produced in New York, 1964; *The White Whore and the Bit Player*; *Three Sisters from Springfield, Illinois,* produced Off-Broadway at Cafe La Mama; *Why Hannah's Skirt Won't Stay Down,* produced in New York, 1965; *Grand Tenement/November 22nd,* produced in New York, 1967; *Sarah B. Divine!,* first produced in Spoleto, Italy, 1967, produced in London, 1973; *The Death of Off-Broadway,* produced in New York; *The Kama Sutra,* produced in New York, 1968; *Who Killed My Bald Sister Sophie?,* produced in New York, 1968; *What Is*

Making Gilda So Gray?, produced Off-Off Broadway at La Mama Experimental Theatre Club, 1969; *Aretha in the Ice Palace: Or, the Fully Guaranteed F—- Me Doll,* produced Off-Off Broadway at the Extension Theatre, January, 1970), Winter House, 1971.

Court, produced Off-Broadway at Cafe La Mama, 1965.

Can You See a Prince, produced in New York, 1965.

The Last Great Cocktail Party, produced in New York, 1965.

The Demented World of Tom Eyen, produced in New York, 1965.

Cinderella Revisited, produced in New York, 1965.

Give My Regards to Off-Off Broadway (Part I and II), produced Off-Broadway, 1966.

When Johnny Comes Dancing Home Again, produced in New York, 1968.

Alice through the Glass Lightly, produced in New York, 1968.

(Editor) *New American Plays,* Volume II, Hill & Wang, 1968.

(Editor) *Michael Smith Anthology of Plays,* Bobbs-Merrill, 1968.

4 No Plays (a program consisting of four short plays, *Paradise Later, Fantasies and Smaller Peaces, Frankenstein's Wife,* and *Antigone Meets Dionysus for Lunch*), produced Off-Off-Broadway at La Mama Experimental Theatre Club, January, 1969.

(And director) *Caution: A Love Story,* produced Off-Off Broadway at La Mama Experimental Theatre Club, January, 1969.

(And director) *Lana Got Laid in Lebanon,* produced Off-Off Broadway at La Mama Experimental Theatre Club January, 1970.

Gertrude Stein and Other Great Men, produced Off-Off Broadway at La Mama Experimental Theatre Club, January, 1970.

(And director) *The Dirtiest Show in Town,* first produced Off-Off Broadway at La Mama Repertory Theatre, spring, 1970; produced Off-Broadway at Astor Place Theatre, June, 1970; produced on West End at Duchess Theatre, 1971.

Why Hanna's Skirt Won't Stay Down (produced Off-Broadway at the Village Gate, June, 1974), Samuel French (New York, NY), 1971.

Women behind Bars (first produced Off-Off Broadway at the New York Theatre Ensemble, 1974; produced Off-Broadway at Astor Place Theatre, 1975), Samuel French, 1975.

(Author of book and lyrics) *Dreamgirls,* produced on Broadway at Imperial Theater, December 20, 1981.

(And director) *Kicks: The Showgirl Musical,* 1986.

(And director) *Dangerous Music,* 1988.

Also author of *The Dirtiest Musical,* 1975, "2008 1/2 (A Spaced Odyssey)," 1976, and "Milliken Breakfast Shows," 1977-78.

Also author of script for "'Ole Redhead Is Back!" a National Broadcasting Co. (NBC-TV) special starring Bette Midler.

ADAPTATIONS: The White Whore and the Bit Player was filmed by Cannon Films, 1969.

SIDELIGHTS: Tom Eyen had a score of Off-Broadway plays to his credit—including the critically acclaimed *Why Hannah's Skirt Won't Stay Down* and *Women behind Bars*—when in 1981 he wrote the book and lyrics for perhaps his most well-known effort, and one of the biggest Broadway successes of the 1980s, *Dreamgirls. Dreamgirls* follows the rise, fall, and rebirth of a 1960s-era black female trio as they move from appearances at the Apollo Theatre in Harlem to a niche in "mainstream" pop music. Sexual politics, betrayals, and ruthless ambition earmark the progress of the main characters as they struggle for individual identities in a business that would package them as a disposable product. Though Eyen died of a heart attack in 1991, *Dreamgirls* remains a viable property, with a new soundtrack album released in 2001, and a full stage revival scheduled for 2004. The playwright will also be remembered for his contribution to the offbeat 1970s television series, *Mary Hartman, Mary Hartman.*

Eyen's Off-Broadway work *Why Hannah's Skirt Won't Stay Down* is, according to Michael T. Smith in *Contemporary Dramatists,* "set in the funhouse at Coney Island, where Hannah gets her thrills by standing over the airhole." Smith went on to report that the character of Hannah shows up in several of Eyen's subsequent plays, including *Who Killed My Bald Sister Sophie?* and *What Is Making Gilda So Gray?* Eyen began experimenting with the musical form before *Dreamgirls,* and, as Smith put it, "won some commercial viability" with *The Dirtiest Show in Town,* which the critic described as "a satirical response to the sex-oriented shows featuring nude actors that were the fad in New York."

"It's the nature of that ruthlessness that gives *Dreamgirls* its bite," noted Frank Rich in a *New York Times* review of the musical. "Instead of just providing the usual white villains, Tom Eyen's libretto also suggests that the black characters betray themselves as they pursue an empty white American dream." "Presumably, [*Dreamgirls*] is telling us that the entertainment industry is populated by sharks with pearly cuff links, that greed and ambition prevail and that performers are molded into best-selling artists only to be tossed aside once their earning power declines," said *Washington Post* critic David Richards. "But its cynicism is a pose. It really believes you can pick yourself up, dust yourself off and climb right back up the charts again. The heavies get their comeuppance. The others get comebacks."

That Eyen, whose Off-Broadway work is characterized by counter-cultural themes and outrageous characters, was involved in as commercial a project as *Dreamgirls* surprised some. As the author related to Sondra Lowell in a *Los Angeles Times* article, "One of my old friends said, 'You wrote that? But it's so sensitive, so real.' I said, 'I beg your pardon.' How dare they?" But, according to Lowell, Eyen saw a continuity in his work: "*Dreamgirls*," said the playwright, "has a large lady who's very unhappy and against the system. *Women behind Bars* also has a large lady. I always have a large lady in some abstract situation who's the villain. I think my basic theme is the freak against society."

BIOGRAPHICAL AND CRITICAL SOURCES:

BOOKS

Contemporary Dramatists, 4th edition, St. James Press (Chicago, IL), 1988.

PERIODICALS

American Theatre, May, 2002, Lenora Inez Brown, reveiw of *Dreamgirls in Concert*, p. 68.

Back Stage, December 21, 1990, Ira J. Bilowit, "Struggling to Produce *Dreamgirls*," p. 28.

Los Angeles Times, March 12, 1982, January 6, 1983, April 2, 1983, August 14, 1986.

Newsweek, April 28, 1969.

New York, June 6, 1970.

New York Times, May 2, 1970, December 21, 1981, September 23, 1983; April 25, 2003, Jesse McKinley, "On Stage and Off," p. E2.

St. Louis Post-Dispatch, November 6, 1997, Judith Newmark, review of *Dreamgirls*, p. C6.

San Francisco Chronicle, March 31, 2002, Steven Winn, "*Dreamgirls* Better Second Time Around," p. 44.

Saturday Review, April 19, 1969.

Washington Post, April 26, 1986.

OBITUARIES:

PERIODICALS

Chicago Tribune, May 28, 1991.

Los Angeles Times, May 28, 1991.

New York Times, May 28, 1991.

Time, June 10, 1991.

Washington Post, May 29, 1991.*

F

FABRIZIO, Timothy C(harles) 1948-

PERSONAL: Born June 9, 1948, in Schenectady NY; son of Felix Charles (an engineer) and Kathleen (a teacher's aide; maiden name, Della Rocco) Fabrizio; married Jane Kray (divorced, 1984); married Claire Heffernan, June 16, 1990. *Ethnicity:* "Italian/Irish." *Education:* Boston University, B.F.A., 1970. *Politics:* "Eclectic." *Religion:* "Eclectic." *Hobbies and other interests:* History of recorded sound and motion pictures.

ADDRESSES: *Home*—Rochester, NY. *Office*—Terra Firma Books and Antiques, P.O. Box 10307, Rochester, NY 14610. *E-mail*—phonophan@aol.com.

CAREER: National Pantomime Theater, Boston, MA, actor and technician, 1968-71; Lift Bridge Book Shops, Brockport, NY, co-owner, 1972-84; Terra Firma Books and Antiques, Rochester, NY, owner, 1985—. Library of Congress, consultant in music machine and record acquisition.

MEMBER: Association for Recorded Sound Collections, Musical Box Society International.

AWARDS, HONORS: Award for Excellence, Association for Recorded Sound Collections, 1998, for *The Talking Machine.*

WRITINGS:

(With George F. Paul) *The Talking Machine,* Schiffer (Atglen, PA), 1997.

(With George F. Paul) *Antique Phonograph: Gadgets, Gizmos, and Gimmicks,* Schiffer (Atglen, PA), 1999.

(With George F. Paul) *Discovering Antique Phonographs,* Schiffer (Atglen, PA), 2000.

(With George F. Paul) *Phonographs with Flair: A Century of Style in Sound Reproduction,* Schiffer (Atglen, PA), 2001.

WORK IN PROGRESS: Designer Phonographs, 1920-1970; *More Gadgets, Gizmos, and Gimmicks*; research on recordings of the Spanish-American War.

SIDELIGHTS: Timothy C. Fabrizio told *CA:* "I have always been driven to sift through historical details in order to remove the facts from any traces of subsequent manipulation. As a young man I devoured all the written material I could find regarding the history of recorded sound. Yet, as I began to do my own research, I came to understand that the authors I had read with such devotion had not always done their duty to the reader. Inconsistencies, inaccuracies, and misinterpretations abounded. Furthermore, there seemed to be a general feeling that the history of recorded sound was a 'pop' field, and not worthy of the time it would take to represent it properly. It became my goal to take the time.

"I have been primarily influenced by nonfiction. Even as a boy, historical works interested me more than *The Hardy Boys.* Yet I read fiction, and I think one may find the influences of this in my prose style."

FALUDI, Susan 1959-

PERSONAL: Born April 18, 1959, in New York, NY; daughter of Steven (a photographer) and Marilyn Lanning (an editor) Faludi. *Education:* Harvard University, B.A. (summa cum laude), 1981.

ADDRESSES: *Home*—San Francisco, CA. *Agent*—Sandra Dijkstra, Sandra Dijkstra Literary Agency, 1155 Camino del Mar, Suite 515, Del Mar, CA 92014.

CAREER: Journalist. *New York Times,* New York, NY, copy clerk, 1981-82; *Miami Herald,* Miami, FL, reporter, 1983; *Atlanta Constitution,* Atlanta, GA, reporter, 1984-85; *West* magazine, San Jose, CA, staff writer, 1985-89; *Mercury News,* San Jose, reporter, 1986-88; Institute for Research on Women and Gender, Stanford University, staff member, 1989-91; *Wall Street Journal,* San Francisco bureau, staff writer, 1990-92; contributing editor to *Newsweek.*

AWARDS, HONORS: Robert F. Kennedy Memorial Journalism Award citation, 1989; John Hancock Award, 1991; Pulitzer Prize, Columbia University Graduate School of Journalism, 1991, for *Wall Street Journal* article on the leveraged buyout of Safeway supermarkets; National Book Critics Circle Award nomination, 1992, for *Backlash: The Undeclared War against American Women.*

WRITINGS:

Backlash: The Undeclared War against American Women, Crown (New York, NY), 1991.

Stiffed: The Betrayal of the American Man, Morrow (New York, NY), 1999.

Contributor of articles to periodicals, including *Mother Jones, California Business,* and *Ms.*

ADAPTATIONS: *Backlash* was adapted as an audio cassette read by the author, Publishing Mills, 1992.

WORK IN PROGRESS: A book about the goals of contemporary American women, for Holt.

Susan Faludi

SIDELIGHTS: Pulitzer Prize-winning journalist Susan Faludi gained nationwide attention with her first book, *Backlash: The Undeclared War against American Women,* in which the author investigates the attacks-she observed on feminism and women's social, economic, and political progress during the 1980s. From advertisements for plastic surgery that term small breasts a "disease" to blue-collar men who harass their few female coworkers, and from right-wing preachers who denounce feminists as "witches" and "whores" to Hollywood films that depict single career women as desperate and crazed, Faludi found a "backlash" against women virtually everywhere. The culmination of four years of research, *Backlash* drew praise and stirred controversy, with some critics maintaining that Faludi essentially claims society conspires to keep women oppressed. "So much of the criticism [of *Backlash*] seems to be about a book I didn't write," Faludi told a *Time* magazine contributor. "I'm charged with saying there's a male conspiracy out there to put women down. Anyone who says that can't possibly have read the book. . . . This is not a book about hating men." Indeed, Faludi tried to show that her arguments apply just as much to men as they do to women when she released her second book, *Stiffed: The Betrayal of the American Man.*

Faludi, who served as an editor of both her high school and college newspapers, is no stranger to controversy. In high school she wrote about school meetings of born-again Christian students and teachers, gatherings that, by virtue of being held on public-school grounds, did not maintain the separation of church and state and were therefore unconstitutional. As an undergraduate at Harvard University, she penned a story about ongoing sexual harassment on campus. Though a guilty professor and the dean tried to convince her not to print it, the story appeared in the paper and the university subsequently asked the professor to take a leave of absence.

After graduating from college, Faludi worked as a copy clerk for the *New York Times,* and while there and at her succeeding positions she gained a reputation as "a superb crusading journalist, attacking injustice with a rare passion," according to Carol Pogash in *Working Woman.* She wrote about how former President Ronald Reagan's budget cuts affected poor children, how companies in California's Silicon Valley were replacing older employees with younger, more cost-effective workers, and about the human impact of Safeway Stores' leveraged buyout. Faludi received a Pulitzer Prize for the last story, which appeared in the *Wall Street Journal.* "Then as now," Pogash observed, "her stories were laden with research and punch-in-the-gut images—the writer, part academian, part assassin."

Faludi was inspired to write *Backlash* by a 1986 marriage study that made national headlines. The study, which was then being conducted by researchers at Harvard and Yale universities, stated that college-educated, thirty-year-old women had only a twenty-percent chance of ever getting married, and by age thirty-five the odds dropped to five percent. After one of the researchers talked to a reporter about the unpublished study's findings, newspapers, popular magazines, and talk shows began running stories about the "marriage crunch" and "man shortage" in America. Women who postponed marriage in favor of educations and careers, the researchers reasoned, would have difficulty finding a husband. "I hadn't been worrying about marriage," Faludi recalled to Kim Hubbard in *People* magazine, "but suddenly I felt morose and grouchy."

Skeptical of the researchers' statistics, Faludi contacted the U.S. Census Bureau and other sources and learned that the methodology used to generate the marriage study was flawed and that the report's conclusions were suspect. She and other journalists wrote articles about this discovery, but their input was virtually ignored by the national media. "What was remarkable to me," Faludi told Hubbard, "was that there was so little interest in finding out whether the study was true or false. The story simply fit the notion of where women were at that point in history."

Faludi points out in *Backlash* that many accepted ideas about women's status in the 1980s were also myths. In addition to the nationally trumpeted marriage study, the author discredits other media trend stories in her book, including accounts of professional women abandoning the work force in large numbers to care for their homes and children, and reports of single and career women suffering from depression, nervous breakdowns, and burnout in epidemic proportions. Upon examining these claims, Faludi discovered that they had no empirical basis. A number of studies comparing working and non-working women, for example, concluded that women who work are actually mentally and physically healthier than their non-working counterparts. According to Faludi, myths about single and working women are "the chisels of a society-wide backlash. They are part of a relentless whittling-down process—much of it amounting to outright propaganda—that has served to stir women's private anxieties and break their political wills."

Though conventional wisdom suggests that the women's movement had achieved its aims by the late twentieth century, Faludi notes in *Backlash* that women still receive mixed messages about equality. She explains that the media and politicians often present women's liberation as the source of women's problems. Feminists, for instance, are often portrayed as women who are unable to attract men, working women are depicted as poor mothers, and independent single women are shown to be desperate to marry and bear children. The moral of these stories, Faludi maintains, is that "it must be all that equality that's causing all that pain. Women are unhappy precisely *because* they are free."

Faludi challenges this conclusion in her book by detailing how the backlash against women's rights continued to be perpetuated by newspapers, magazines, television programs, movies, the fashion and beauty industry, popular psychology, anti-abortion activists, and national politics. She also cites an array of statistics that give a different and, she argues, more accurate picture of women's progress. According to Faludi, women still struggle for equality in politics, the workplace, and at school and home, and this is truly the cause of the unhappiness they express. The author observes in *Backlash,* for instance, that by 1990 the average female college graduate earned less than the average man with a high school diploma, and that American women "face the worst gender-based pay gap in the developed world." The lack of child care and family leave policies, Faludi asserts, also undermines women's equality in the workplace. At home, women "still shoulder 70 percent of the household duties. . . . Furthermore, in thirty states, it is still generally legal for husbands to rape their wives; and only ten states have laws mandating arrest for domestic violence—even though battering was the leading cause of injury of women in the late '80s."

In what some critics consider *Backlash*'s most effective section, Faludi profiles a number of notable antifeminists, including George Gilder, a speechwriter for former President Ronald Reagan and author of *Wealth and Poverty;* Allen Bloom, author of *The Closing of the American Mind,* a book that decries feminism's influence in higher education; Robert Bly, a founder of the men's movement and author of *Iron John;* and Sylvia Ann Hewlett, author of *A Lesser Life: The Myth of Women's Liberation in America.* She also interviews philosophy professor Michael Levin, who wrote *Feminism and Freedom,* a book denouncing feminism as an "antidemocratic, if not totalitarian, ideology," Faludi notes. Levin also claims that men are naturally better at math and that women prefer to take on household duties such as cooking. During her interview with Levin, Faludi learned that Levin's wife, Margarita, is a professor of the philosophy of mathematics, that the Levins split child care and household tasks equally, and that cooking is the favorite activity of one of their young sons. Gayle Greene remarked in a *Nation* review that "Faludi must be a crackerjack interviewer, letting subjects babble on until they blurt out marvelously self-incriminating revelations, offering up the real reasons they hate and fear feminists—motives that are self-serving, silly, often sinister—which Faludi simply, deadpan, recounts."

Published in 1991, *Backlash* quickly became a bestseller. Though the response from critics was generally favorable, some reviewers found the book to be overlong or disagreed that a backlash against women's progress exists. *Business Week* writer Walecia Konrad commented that, "even for committed feminists, Faludi's analysis is an eye-opener. But her relentless presentation of facts, figures, anecdotes, polls, and interviews is so dense that at times the book is hard to read." In *Commentary* Charlotte Allen opined that *Backlash* has "none of the sustained theorizing or distanced observation that we might expect from a work of cultural criticism." In contrast, however, *Newsweek* contributor Laura Shapiro compared Faludi's book to Simone de Beauvoir's *The Second Sex* and Betty Friedan's *The Feminine Mystique* and described *Backlash* as "less visionary than theirs but just as gripping. She's not a theorist, she's simply a reporter."

Backlash was described by other admirers, Hubbard reported, as "feminism's new manifesto." Greene noted that the "book offers a rich compendium of fascinating information and an indictment of a system losing its grip and reeling from changes it does not begin to understand." Konrad called *Backlash* "a thinking person's book. Instead of spoon-feeding answers, Faludi offers compelling and disturbing evidence that some of the toughest battles for women are still to come." And Shapiro reported that "once you've read this hair-raising but meticulously documented analysis, you may never read a magazine or see a movie or walk through a department store the same way again."

Backlash's success soon made Faludi a sought-after guest on talk shows and the subject of a *Time* magazine cover story with noted feminist Gloria Steinem. But despite the attention she received, she remained reluctant to promote herself as feminism's new spokeswoman. "It's strange, since in my book I'm fairly critical of instant experts," Faludi told Hubbard. "I don't want to set myself up as a sort of seer." The author remarked to Pogash in *Working Woman:* "To the extent that *Backlash* arms women with information and a good dose of cynicism, I think it will have served its purpose." She added, "It's also very large, so it can be thrown at misogynists."

After completing *Backlash,* Faludi felt that her first work did not answer the question of why men were resisting the feminist movement in the first place. She therefore spent six years interviewing men in all sorts of occupations to get at the heart of the matter. But while the original question for her was why men seemed to be so disturbed by the prospects of female empowerment, her research led her to an entirely different question: Why are men allowing themselves to be subjugated by a shallow, materialistic, appearance-obsessed society, and why are they not doing anything to fight against it? The result of her studies is the book *Stiffed: The Betrayal of the American Man.* Here she examines the lives of men living a wide variety of lifestyles, including cadets at the Citadel, laid-off blue-collar workers, Christian Promise Keepers, astronauts, male porn stars, and street gang members, rounding out her survey with a thirty-page examination of actor Sylvester Stallone, who serves as a model of ideal manhood. She found that the men of the 1990s, especially those of the Baby Boomer generation, felt disconnected and disempowered because they grew up with emotionally distant fathers and because they found themselves locked in an "ornamentalist" culture that demands good looks over substance, for men just as much as for women.

Faludi blames rampant capitalism, which has laid off so many working-class people in favor of beefing up stock prices, for leaving many men feeling emasculated because they cannot earn enough to support their families or fulfill a sense of purpose in their lives. "Interestingly," observed Cathy Young in *Reason,* "unlike many feminists, Faludi does not equate traditional masculinity with abusive, egotistical dominance. Rather, she notes that cultural concepts of manhood have always been based on care-taking, social responsibility, and productivity." The author further discovered that the ability of men to be productive was not necessarily tied to a strong economy. "I found that as the economy improved," she told Sue Halpern in *Mother Jones,* "the men I was talking to were still stricken with a sense that they had been betrayed, and that the betrayal went much deeper than a paycheck. It had to do with loyalty and a social pact that they had been led to believe was bedrock and part of being a man."

The solution to modern American men's dilemma, however, remains elusive, according to Faludi. As *New Republic* contributor James Wolcott explained in his review of *Stiffed,* all the author can offer is "the prospect of men joining like-minded women to create 'a new paradigm of human progress.'" As she commented in a *Newsweek* interview, however, Faludi is somewhat optimistic that the post-Baby Boom generation will fare better than their fathers: "The one bright light in this otherwise pretty bleak story is that the younger generation are more open, caring fathers. That's largely the result of the women's movement—that men need to have a full life by having a meaningful domestic life."

A number of reviewers of Faludi's *Stiffed* argued with her portrayal of men facing a "bleak" world. For one thing, several critics pointed out that the author's sampling of men avoids including those who are content and successful in their lives. "The polls tell us that there are many men in America who are generally satisfied with their lot," commented Midge Decter in the *National Review.* Writing in *Progressive,* Laura Flanders also noted that Faludi's sampling of men is misleading as supporting evidence for her conclusions. "Faludi's study of gender gets mixed up with class because she focuses almost exclusively on men who fit the stereotypical image of masculinity—brawny laborers and evangelical/militaristic macho types (and Sylvester Stallone). . . . If she'd interviewed some affluent traders making pots of money in the market or business executives or Silicon Valley nerds, she could have filled a crucial gap. And plenty of men are doing just fine, thank you, with the traditional model."

Adding that "the author's failure to choose a representative sample of men is not her book's most serious shortcoming," Decter said that in trying to find out what is troubling men Faludi "has finally achieved little more than to raise the volume on that most tiresome and least enlightening form of human expression. I am referring to the Whine." The critic went on to write that "what men need above all is the simple recognition of their full and necessary value in the lives of women. Such a recognition would go a very long way toward the healing understanding that this book and its author claim to seek"; yet in failing to address this, Faludi's "researches will have virtually nothing to teach us." Rebecca Abrams, writing in the *New Statesman,* similarly felt that Faludi is not exactly saying anything new in *Stiffed.* "The disappointing aspect of this book," according to Abrams, "is that although Faludi appears to be breaking new ground, in a sense all she actually does is graft accepted feminist 'truths' on to male experience. After all, feminism pioneered mother-blame decades ago. Compared to the battle that daughters were waging—consciously or unconsciously—on the dire influence of their mothers, patriarchy was always something of a picnic."

Despite these criticisms, however, a number of reviewers found *Stiffed* to be, as Abrams put it, "a rewarding read. Faludi is a meticulous and sensitive interviewer, and her compendium of American men . . . grows into a gallery of compelling and detailed portraits." Other critics also found that Faludi's reporting, compared to her concluding arguments, is the strong point of the book. "Her reporting is stellar," asserted Flanders, "as it was in *Backlash.*" An *Economist* writer found the author's retelling of men's personal accounts of their disappointments in life to be "often fascinating. *Stiffed* displays Ms. Faludi's formidable research skills and her keen journalistic nose"; and the reviewer added that "in her explorations of different male subcultures, Ms. Faludi is always alert and almost never dull." Although *Library Journal* contributor Rebecca Miller felt that Faludi's conclusions "won't surprise anyone," the critic concluded that "this important book is sure to spark dialog."

In the end, as Faludi told Halpern, her point is that men and women should overcome the dictates of American culture and work together so as not to "be judged according to superficial and ephemeral and impossible-to-attain objectives." Although she feels the solution to creating this kind of change is "not obvious . . . we need to start at square one and figure out what the forces are and respond to them."

BIOGRAPHICAL AND CRITICAL SOURCES:

BOOKS

Faludi, Susan, *Backlash: The Undeclared War against American Women,* Crown (New York, NY), 1991.

PERIODICALS

American Enterprise, June, 2000, Evan Gahr, review of *Stiffed: The Betrayal of the American Man,* p. 59.

Atlantic, December, 1991, pp. 123-126.

Business Week, November 4, 1991, Walecia Konrad, review of *Backlash,* pp. 12, 17.

Christian Century, December 1, 1999, Mary Stewart Van Leeuwen, review of *Stiffed,* p. 1166.

Commentary, February, 1992, Charlotte Allen, review of *Backlash,* pp. 62-64.

Economist, November 13, 1999, "American Men: What Do They Really Want?," p. 5.

Entertainment Weekly, October 15, 1999, Lisa Schwarzbaum, "Men Overboard: In Her Provocative New Book, *Stiffed,* Susan Faludi Makes a Strong Case That Macho America Ain't What It Used to Be," p. 72.

Forbes, March 16, 1992, Gretchen Morgenson, "A Whiner's Bible," p. 152; November 29, 1999, Virginia Postrel, "Who's in Charge? You Are," p. 112.

Fortune, November 22, 1999, Albert Mobilio, "Angry White Knuckleheads," p. 86.

Insight on the News, June 5, 1995, Suzanne Fields, "Invasion of the Neoclassical Feminist Body-Snatchers," p. 40; November 15, 1999, Suzanne Fields, "Betrayal of the American Woman," p. 48.

Library Journal, October 15, 1999, Rebecca Miller, review of *Stiffed,* p. 90.

Maclean's, November 1, 1999, Anthony Wilson-Smith, "Gender Armistice: A Leading Feminist Argues That Men Are Victims, Too," p. 70.

Mother Jones, September-October, 1999, Sue Halpern, "Susan Faludi: The Mother Jones Interview."

Nation, February 10, 1992, Gayle Greene, review of *Backlash,* pp. 166-170.

National Review, March 30, 1992, Maggie Gallagher, review of *Backlash,* p. 41; October 25, 1999, Midge Decter, "Guy Talk," p. 58.

New Republic, March 16, 1992, pp. 30-34; November 15, 1999, James Wolcott, "The Male Eunuch," p. 36.

New Statesman, November 1, 1999, Rebecca Abrams, "Pity the Boys," p. 56.

New Statesman and Society, April 3, 1992, pp. 44-45.

Newsweek, October 21, 1991, Laura Shapiro, review of *Backlash,* pp. 41-44; September 13, 1999, "This Time, a Backlash for Guys: What's a Nice Feminist Like Susan Faludi Doing Writing a Book about Men?," p. 59.

New Yorker, December 23, 1991, p. 108.

New York Times Book Review, October 27, 1991, pp. 1, 36.

People, November 11, 1991, pp. 138-140; October 25, 1999, "Male-ady: Feminist Author Susan Faludi Says American Men Must Be Liberated from Superficial Values That Have Long Bedeviled Women," p. 143.

Progressive, June, 1993, Ruth Conniff, "Susan Faludi," p. 35; November, 1999, Laura Flanders, review of *Stiffed,* p. 41.

Publishers Weekly, May 25, 1992, Gayle Feldman, "Faludi's New Book on Men Goes to Morrow/ Avon," p. 18; July 6, 1992, review of *Backlash*

(sound recording), p. 23; September 13, 1999, review of *Stiffed,* p. 69.
Reason, December, 1999, Virginia Postrel, "Reactionary Running Mates," p. 4; March, 2000, Cathy Young, "The Man Question," p. 64.
Tikkun, March, 2000, Janna Malamud Smith, "Where Have All the Fathers Gone?," p. 73.
Time, March 9, 1992, pp. 56-57; October 4, 1999, Elizabeth Gleick, "Men on the Edge: Feminist Susan Faludi Comes to the Defense of the American Male," p. 100; October 25, 1999, Joel Stein, "The Emasculation Proclamation," p. 46.
Times (London, England), March 26, 1992.
Working Woman, April, 1992, pp. 64-67, 104.*

* * *

FERNIE, Eric (Campbell) 1939-

PERSONAL: Born June 9, 1939, in Edinburgh, Scotland; son of Sidney Robert (an engineer) and Catherine (Reid) Fernie; married Margaret Lorraine French (a sculptor), November 28, 1964; children: Lyndall Kathleen, Jessica Ann, Ivan Robert. *Education:* University of the Witwatersrand, B.A. (with honors), 1960; University of London, postgraduate diploma in History of Art, 1963.

ADDRESSES: Home—Flat 10, 8 Northburgh St., London EC1V 0AY, England.

CAREER: University of the Witwatersrand, Johannesburg, South Africa, lecturer in art history, 1964-67; University of East Anglia, Norwich, England, 1967-84, began as lecturer, became senior lecturer in art history and dean of school of Fine Art and Music; University of Edinburgh, Edinburgh, Scotland, Watson Gordon Professor of Fine Art, 1984-95, and dean of faculty, 1989-92; University of London, London, England, director of Courtauld Institute of Art, 1995—. Chair, Ancient Monuments Board, Scotland, 1989-95. Trustee of National Galleries of Scotland, 1991-97, Scotland Inheritance Fund, 1992—, and Samuel Courtauld Trust, 1995—.

MEMBER: Association of Art Historians, Royal Commission on the Historical Monuments of England, British Archaeological Association, Royal Archaeological Institute, Society for Medieval Archaeology, Society of Antiquaries of Scotland, Norfolk and Norwich Archaeological Society, Society of Antiquaries of London (vice president, 1992-95).

AWARDS, HONORS: Named Commander of the British Empire, 1995.

WRITINGS:

The Architecture of the Anglo-Saxons, Batsford (London, England), 1983.
(Editor, with Paul Crossley) *Medieval Architecture and Its Intellectual Context: Studies in Honor of Peter Kidson,* Hambledon Press (London, England), 1990.
An Architectural History of Norwich Cathedral, Oxford University Press (New York, NY), 1993.
(Author of selection and commentary) *Art History and Its Methods: A Critical Anthology,* Phaidon Press (London, England), 1995.
(Editor, with others) *Norwich Cathedral: Church, City and Diocese, 1096-1996,* Hambledon Press (London, England), 1996.
The Architecture of Norman England, Oxford University Press (New York, NY), 2000.

Contributor to art and archaeology journals.

SIDELIGHTS: Art historian Eric Fernie writes on the architecture of Anglo-Saxon and medieval times. His study *The Architecture of Norman England* ties the design elements of the post-Norman Conquest to the period's "social and political agendas," according to Simon Pepper in the *Times Literary Supplement.* Indeed, Pepper continued, "Norman architecture was highly political. . . . The Romanesque style that developed in the Duchy of Normandy was closely identified with the French-influenced modernizing policies of the newly established Norse regime." Many buildings took on the dual roles of "residence and fortress," said Pepper, and Fernie "takes the discussion a stage further by asking whether the military elements—thick walls, narrow windows. . .—were primarily for military purposes or primarily for display."

A millennium's worth of history is included in *Norwich Cathedral: Church, City and Diocese, 1096-1996.* Fernie coedited this work, whose theme is the cathedral's "uneasy relationship with the laity," in the words of *Journal of Ecclesiastical History* contributor Diarmaid MacCulloch. "With so many lavishly endowed baronial monastic houses throughout the diocese, Norwich enjoyed little major patronage from the secular nobility." Few laypersons chose Norwich as a burial site, the reviewer added; the monument was also the object of a struggle "between city and cathedral over jurisdiction," leading to damage during a 1272 riot. Norwich's fall from secular grace ended in the twentieth century, when the cathedral "really [came] into its own in the affections of the diocese," as MacCulloch commented. The historic structure today runs under the auspices of the Friends of the Cathedral organization, "a happy climax for a story of a magnificent building, here magnificently told."

For a more general readership, Fernie produced *Art History and Its Methods: A Critical Anthology.* The book takes a chronological approach to its subject, beginning with the Renaissance and wrapping up with Oguibe, an artist born in 1964. *Choice* critic P. Emison found that "each selection is equipped with a pungent but not propagandistic introduction by Fernie." *Library Journal* reviewer Joan Levin praised the author for his "insightful comments . . . and helpful glossary [providing] a substantial framework for the erudite writings."

BIOGRAPHICAL AND CRITICAL SOURCES:

PERIODICALS

Antiquaries Journal, winter, 1990, review of *Medieval Architecture and Its Intellectual Context: Studies in Honor of Peter Kidson,* p. 158.

Burlington, August, 1994, review of *An Architectural History of Norwich Cathedral,* p. 556; September, 1993, review of *Medieval Architecture and Its Intellectual Context,* p. 643.

Choice, February, 1996, P. Emison, review of *Art History and Its Methods: A Critical Anthology,* p. 940.

Contemporary Review, March, 2001, review of *The Architecture of Norman England,* p. 184.

Journal of Ecclesiastical History, July, 1997, Diarmaid MacCulloch, review of *Norwich Cathedral: Church, City and Diocese, 1096-1996,* p. 545.

Library Journal, December, 1995, Joan Levin, review of *Art History and Its Methods,* p. 98.

Speculum: A Journal of Medieval Studies, January, 1995, Lawrence Hoey, review of *An Architectural History of Norwich Cathedral,* p. 139; April, 1998, Lisa Reilly, review of *Norwich Cathedral,* p. 458.

Times Literary Supplement, October 5, 2001, Simon Pepper, review of *The Architecture of Norman England,* p. 21.*

* * *

FILES, Meg 1946-

PERSONAL: Born 1946; married.

ADDRESSES: *Office*—Department of English, Pima Community College, 2202 West Anklam Rd., Tucson, AZ 85709-0001; fax: 520-572-0620. *Agent*—Victoria Sanders, P.O. Box 853394, Tuczon, AZ 85754. *E-mail*—megfiles@compuserve.com.

CAREER: Pima Community College, Tucson, AZ, began as director of Writing Lab, c. 1988, presently chair of Department of English. Ohio State University, Thurber House writer in residence.

WRITINGS:

Meridian 144 (novel), Soho Press (New York, NY), 1991.

Home Is the Hunter, and Other Stories, J. Daniel (Santa Barbara, CA), 1996.

Write from Life, Writer's Digest Books, 2002.

Contributor of short stories and articles to periodicals, including *Crazyhorse* and *Oxford.*

SIDELIGHTS: Meg Files's novel *Meridian 144* blends an apocalyptic science-fiction scenario with one woman's forced journey of self-discovery. As the novel begins, Catherine "Kit" Manning is scuba-diving underneath the surface of the Pacific Ocean with her Air Force captain boyfriend when a nuclear strike occurs. She survives and makes it back to the island, breathing through her scuba equipment while she scavenges for food, finds her dog, and does battle with the more sociopathic elements who have also survived.

She also contemplates her life in flashback: a difficult childhood, unresolved conflicts with her mother, and an unhappy marriage recently ended.

A *Booklist* reviewer noted that while a chronicle of protagonist Manning's misspent life is "crushingly sad, her current situation is nothing less than hellish." As *Meridian 144* progresses, she eventually comes across like-minded survivors, who band together and resolve to re-create civilization. *School Library Journal* contributor Carolyn E. Gecan indicated that Manning's journey of "self-redemption" had put her in the position to take on an Eve-like role in a contemporary Genesis creation story and termed Files's debut "grisly and poetic in turn." Gecan noted that the novel "ends with a glimmer of realistic hope."

Files is also the author of a collection of short stories of loss and redemption in which these themes are connected to water and submersion. In "The Living Desert" a woman comes to terms with the drowning of her father years before. "The Mill Pond" chronicles the moments in which a couple cannot rescue both themselves and their children from their vehicle, which has just careened into a body of water. Perry Glasser noted in the *North American Review* that the author "writes with considerable skill and a touch of poetry in her prose."

BIOGRAPHICAL AND CRITICAL SOURCES:

PERIODICALS

Booklist, October 15, 1991, review of *Meridian 144,* p. 406.

Cosmopolitan, October, 1991, p. 48.

Kirkus Reviews, August 1, 1991, review of *Meridian 144,* p. 950.

North American Review, March-April, 1997, Peggy Glasser, review of *Home Is the Hunter, and Other Stories,* pp. 43-45.

Publishers Weekly, August 16, 1991, p. 47.

School Library Journal, April, 1992, Carolyn E. Gecan, review of *Meridian 144,* p. 163.

Writer's Digest, June, 1995, pp. 80-81.

* * *

FINCH, Christopher (Robin) 1939-

PERSONAL: Born 1939, in England.

ADDRESSES: *Agent*—c/o Author Mail, Abbeville Press, 116 W. 23rd St., Suite 500, New York, NY 10011.

CAREER: Writer. Walker Art Center, Minneapolis, MN, curator, 1968-69.

WRITINGS:

Pop Art: Object and Image, Studio Vista, 1968.

Image As Language: Aspects of British Art, 1950-1968, Penguin (New York, NY), 1968.

Patrick Caulfield (part of "Penguin New Art" series), Penguin (New York, NY), 1971.

The Art of Walt Disney: From Mickey Mouse to the Magic Kingdoms, with special essay by Peter Blake, Abrams (New York, NY), 1973, 2nd edition, 1975.

Rainbow: The Stormy Life of Judy Garland, designed by Will Hopkins, Grosset & Dunlap (New York, NY), 1975.

Norman Rockwell's America, Abrams (New York, NY), 1976.

(Author of introduction) *Fifty Norman Rockwell Favorites,* Crown (New York, NY), 1977.

Walt Disney's America, Abbeville Press (New York, NY), 1978.

(Author of introduction) *102 Favorite Paintings by Norman Rockwell,* Crown (New York, NY), 1978.

(With Linda Rosenkrantz) *Gone Hollywood: The Movie Colony in the Golden Age,* Doubleday (New York, NY), 1979.

(Author of introduction) *Norman Rockwell: 332 Magazine Covers,* Abbeville Press (New York, NY), 1979.

Norman Rockwell, Artabras (New York, NY), 1979.

Of Muppets and Men: The Making of "The Muppet Show," Knopf (New York, NY), 1981.

The Making of "The Dark Crystal": Creating a Unique Film, Holt (New York, NY), 1983.

Special Effects: Creating Movie Magic, Abbeville Press (New York, NY), 1984.

American Watercolors, Abbeville Press (New York, NY), 1986.

Twentieth-Century Watercolors, Abbeville Press (New York, NY), 1988.

Beer: A Connoisseur's Guide to the World's Best, Abbeville Press (New York, NY), 1989.

(With Charles S. Finch) *Highways to Heaven: The Auto Biography of America,* HarperCollins (New York, NY), 1992.

Jim Henson: The Works: The Art, the Magic, the Imagination, Random House (New York, NY), 1993.

(With W. Scott Griffiths) *America's Best Beers,* Little, Brown (Boston, MA), 1994.

The Art of the Lion King, foreword by James Earl Jones, Hyperion (New York, NY), 1994.

(With Scott Griffiths) *Famous Chefs (and Other Characters) Cook with Beer,* Doubleday (New York, NY), 1996.

(With Linda Rosenkrantz) *Sotheby's Guide to Animation Art,* Holt (New York, NY), 1998.

(As Christopher Robin Finch) *Disney's Winnie the Pooh: A Celebration of the Silly Old Bear,* Disney Editions (New York, NY), 2002.

In the Market: The Illustrated History of the Financial Markets, foreword by John M. Angelo, Abbeville Press (New York, NY), 2001.

Also author of guides to exhibitions of the works of such artists as Peter Phillips, David Hockney, Chuck Close, and Joe Tilson.

SIDELIGHTS: English art critic Christopher Finch has written a variety of books, choosing primarily as his focus the personalities, paintings, and films that have dominated American popular culture. The art of Norman Rockwell and Patrick Caulfield, figures such as Walt Disney and Judy Garland, and movies including *The Dark Crystal* have provided a wealth of visual material around which Finch inscribes textual frameworks. His love of fine art is incorporated into several art books and criticisms, including *Image As Language: Aspects of British Art, 1950-1968, American Watercolors,* and *Twentieth-Century Watercolors.* Finch is also the author of several books about beer, including *Famous Chefs (and Other Characters) Cook with Beer,* a cookbook reflecting yet another of his many enthusiasms.

American Watercolors is a historical survey of the art of watercolor painting, from the gouache tradition of Victorian artists, in which colors were used opaquely, through the development of the translucent technique that found its way across the Atlantic Ocean from England near the turn of the twentieth century. "Finch has chosen his examples well," noted Peter S. Prescott of *Newsweek,* commending the book for the historical perspective which it presents using the works of such artists as John Singer Sargent, James Abbott McNeill Whistler, Winslow Homer, John Cheri Marin, Charles Ephraim Burchfield, and Charles Demuth.

Finch provides a colorful look at some of the most famous American animated characters in *The Art of Walt Disney: From Mickey Mouse to the Magic Kingdoms.* Designed as a pictorial history rather than a critical study, the book provides readers with an overview of the development of the Disney "style" that culminated not only in the many feature-length films produced by Walt Disney's studio, but also in the theme parks which bear his name and the imprint of his vision. Finch assembled a lavish collection of illustrations tracing the development of the style characteristic of Disney Studios, and of the many artists who contributed to it. "Like a visual Bumstead of a sandwich," commented critic R. O. Blechman in the *New York Times Book Review,* "packaged with the greatest care and lavishness (and yes, love!), the choices range from the banal to the exotic, from the unbearably sweet and the faintly moldy to the rich and meaty. It's all here." Blechman praised the visual aspects of *The Art of Walt Disney* but questioned the absence of a discussion of the philosophy and motivation underlying the creations of Walt Disney, aspects of the man that have been the subject of debate and discussion. Blechman wrote, "It's not that he doesn't criticize Disney. It's that he does it with such respect; he praises with faint damning. The author's attitude toward him is not unlike Disney's attitude toward the public. Careful, upbeat and unfailingly polite."

The Art of the Lion King is a coffee-table book in which Finch dedicates his full attention to the one Disney film. "It recounts the story line in leaden, portentous prose, but who'll stop to read that pseud-mystical text when the gorgeously reproduced illustrations speak so swell for themselves? Smartly varied, they map the exhaustive preparatory steps that go into a Disney 'toon movie," wrote *Entertainment Weekly* critic Steve Daly.

With Linda Rosenkrantz, Finch wrote *Gone Hollywood: The Movie Colony in the Golden Age,* a collection of short essays and anecdotes on the everyday events in the motion picture studios of Hollywood during the reign of such major studios as Universal and Metro-Goldwyn-Mayer. *Village Voice* writer M. T. Nera described it as "ably written, researched, and illustrated." *Gone Hollywood* has been recommended for both students of American film and the general film buff. Finch's earlier *Rainbow: The Stormy Life of Judy Garland* received praise from critic Walter Clemons in *Newsweek* for its "sustained effort to examine

Garland as an artist." Clemons added that "within the space limitations of writing a text for a lavish pictorial biography [Finch] produces a cogent bio-critical essay" and commended *Rainbow* as "one of the most intelligent [books] so far" about the famous entertainer. *New York Times Book Review* writer Julia Whedon regarded the book as an "evocative biography," noting that "by acknowledging her talent and letting go of the legend imposed upon and created by the woman, [Finch] restores to her a certain dignity called reality."

Embarking upon new territory, Finch examines the history of financial markets with *In the Market.* Critic Richard Drezen noted that "Finch has produced a sumptuous book with a narrative that guides the reader from century to century, accompanied by lavish illustrations and a timeline of historic events."

BIOGRAPHICAL AND CRITICAL SOURCES:

PERIODICALS

Booklist, September 1, 1994, Gordon Flagg, review of *The Art of the Lion King,* p. 15.

Choice, March, 1994, C. R. Hannum, review of *Jim Henson: The Works: The Art, the Magic, the Imagination,* p. 1120.

Entertainment Weekly, July 15, 1994, Steve Daly, review of *The Art of the Lion King,* p. 57.

Library Journal, December, 1995, Janice Zlendich, review of *The Art of Walt Disney: From Mickey Mouse to the Magic Kingdoms,* p. 102; January, 2002, Richard Drezen, review of *In the Market: The Illustrated History of the Financial Markets,* p. 119.

Los Angeles Times, July 21, 1996, Kevin Baxter, review of *Beer: A Connoisseur's Guide to the World's Best,* p. 5.

Los Angeles Times Book Review, November 16, 1986, p. 10.

New Republic, December 22, 1973, pp. 22-24.

Newsweek, October 15, 1973, pp. 101-102; June 9, 1975, pp. 79-80; December 8, 1986, p. 89.

New York Review of Books, May 16, 1974, pp. 3-7.

New York Times Book Review, December 2, 1973, pp. 55, 58, 62-63; December 7, 1975, p. 86; January 4, 1976, pp. 3, 16.

Professional Geographer, August, 1993, Peter L. Russell, review of *Highways to Heaven: The Auto Biography of America,* p. 371.

Publishers Weekly, September 20, 1999, review of *The Art of Walt Disney,* p. 68.

Technology and Culture, January, 1995, Joseph J. Corn, review of *Highways to Heaven: The Auto Biography of America,* p. 192.

Time, December 22, 1975, p. 67; December 14, 1981, p. 87.

Times (London, England), January 27, 1987.

Times Literary Supplement, November 27, 1969, p. 1354; August 13, 1971, p. 962.

Village Voice, April 21, 1980, p. 44.*

* * *

FONER, Naomi 1950 (?)-

PERSONAL: Born c. 1950 in New York, NY; married Stephen Gyllenhaal (a film director); children: Maggie, Jake. *Education:* Barnard College, B.A. in English; Columbia University, M.A. in Developmental Psychology.

ADDRESSES: Home—Los Angeles, CA. *Agent*—c/o Stephen Gyllenhaal, 32 Ocean View Farm Rd., Chilmark, MA 02535.

CAREER: Served as media director of Eugene McCarthy's campaign for president, 1968; Public Broadcasting Service (PBS), production assistant and researcher on staff of *Sesame Street,* beginning 1968; creator and coproducer of television series *The Best of Families;* screenwriter and film producer, 1986—.

AWARDS, HONORS: Academy Award nomination for best original screenplay, Golden Globe Award for best screenplay, Hollywood Foreign Press Association, PEN West Screenplay Award, all 1989, all for *Running on Empty.*

WRITINGS:

SCREENPLAYS

Violets Are Blue, Columbia, 1986.

Running on Empty, Warner Bros., 1988.

A Dangerous Woman (based on a novel by Mary McGarry Morris), Universal, 1993.

Naomi Foner

Losing Isaiah (based on a novel by Seth Margolis), Paramount, 1995.

Also the author of teleplay "Blackout," for PBS series *Visions*; wrote the screenplay for *Paris Underground* (based on the novel by Etta Shiber) and the screenplay for *Bee Season* (based on the novel by Myla Goldberg), both to be released.

WORK IN PROGRESS: Working on a film, tentatively titled "Pilgrim's Progress," for Paramount.

SIDELIGHTS: Naomi Foner has held several interesting positions in the media. She began her career as the media director of Senator Eugene McCarthy's campaign for the presidency in 1968, then later that year she went to work for the Public Broadcasting System (PBS). While at PBS, Foner served with the acclaimed children's series *Sesame Street,* and played a role in developing other children's programming, including *The Electric Company.* Foner's first screenplay to become a film, *Violets Are Blue,* reached movie audiences in 1986. She followed this with other successful scripts, including the screenplay for the 1988 film *Running on Empty,* which garnered her an Academy Award nomination, a Golden Globe Award, and a PEN West Screenplay Award for her writing. Foner served as producer for her two later screenplays, 1993's *A Dangerous Woman* and 1995's *Losing Isaiah.* Both of these films were directed by her husband, Stephen Gyllenhaal.

Violets Are Blue brings to the screen the story of two former lovers who meet again. The man is locked into his family's newspaper business, and has a wife and children. The woman has had an adventurous life as a photojournalist, and when the two rekindle their affair, she attempts to persuade him to abandon his responsibilities for a more exotic existence at her side. Sissy Spacek and Kevin Klein play the lead characters. Richard Schickel in *Time* observed the feminist aspects of the film, but felt *Violets Are Blue* needed more of a sense of "fun and frolic" to be successful.

Running on Empty, which was more widely reviewed than her previous films, focuses on a couple, the Popes, who have been in hiding from the FBI since they bombed a napalm plant in protest during the 1960s. The Popes thought that the building was empty, but a janitor had been present and was blinded. Flash forward twenty years, and the couple have two adolescent boys; their sons' lives have been considerably disrupted by having to move every time the FBI got too close to their parents. The oldest boy, Danny, has a talent for piano and a chance to go to the famous Juilliard School, but his parents fear they will again have to run while he is there studying and they will never see him again. The adult Popes are played by Christine Lahti and Judd Hirsch, while Danny is portrayed by the late River Phoenix.

Though David Denby, reviewing *Running on Empty* for *New York* magazine, felt the film was "insincere," he also conceded that it "has more than a little charm." Stuart Klawans, discussing *Running on Empty* in the *Nation,* cited two of his favorite scenes—one of Annie Pope's birthday party in which the whole family dances around the living room, the other of Annie and Danny performing a piano duet—and proclaimed: "At a time when filmmaking seems to be dominated by theme-park pictures such as *Die Hard,* or well-meaning but relentlessly programmed ones such as *Eight Men Out,* it is a blessed relief to come upon scenes such as these two." He explained that the scenes "respect the audience enough to let them understand and feel on their own." In the *Los Angeles Times,* Kevin Thomas remarked that "*Running on Empty* is remarkably successful in playing its taut portrayal of 1960s radicals still on the run against a warm evocation of family life and first love."

Foner adapted *A Dangerous Woman* from a novel by Mary McGarry Morris. In the film, a somewhat odd and naive woman, Martha, is living under the care of her aunt, Frances, who is the mistress of a state politician. The title character is dangerous because she doesn't know how to lie. Though Martha is portrayed as a social, and possibly even mental, misfit, a handyman who comes to work at Frances's house sexually awakens her. Debra Winger acts the part of Martha, while Barbara Hershey performs the role of her relatively young aunt. Like much of Foner's work, *A Dangerous Woman* met with mixed reviews. Anthony Lane in the *New Yorker* believed the film to be "nicely set up and . . . ready to go, but somehow, apart from one great scene involving a kitchen knife, it fails to take off." Ty Burr in *Entertainment Weekly* found the relationship between Martha and the handyman "intriguing," but disliked what he saw as "a precious vagueness" in the script. Jonathan Romney in the *New Statesman and Society,* however, gave *A Dangerous Woman* a glowing write-up, pronouncing it "a small, smart miracle of a film" and especially praising "a beautifully ambivalent ending that's one in the eye for the very concept of the 'feel-good' movie."

Losing Isaiah, which stars Jessica Lange and Halle Berry, is the story of a white social worker, Margaret Lewin, who adopts a black baby found in the garbage. When his biological mother conquers her drug addiction, she wants him back, but Margaret refuses. A legal struggle over custody of the child, Isaiah, ensues. Denby, in yet another *New York* review, described *Losing Isaiah* as "a decent, upright piece of work" in which "the two women fight for the child with logic and emotion, and the movie holds both forces in balance."

Next, Foner adapted *Paris Underground,* a novel by Etta Shiber, as a screenplay. According to Charles Lyons in *Variety,* the story "centers on two women, one American, one French, who team up during World War II to save . . . Allied soldiers . . . behind enemy lines." The film stars actresses Julianne Moore and Winona Ryder, and was directed by Hunt Lowry and Casey La Scala. Foner also told *Screenwriters Online* that she is working on the script for yet another film, *Pilgrim's Progress,* but that it has no relation to John Bunyan's spiritual classic of the same name. She is slated to be the picture's director as well.

BIOGRAPHICAL AND CRITICAL SOURCES:

BOOKS

Contemporary Theatre, Film and Television Volume 21, Gale (Detroit, MI), 1999.

PERIODICALS

Cosmopolitan, November, 1990, pp. 294-97.
Entertainment Weekly, December 3, 1993, pp. 47, 50.
Los Angeles Times, September 9, 1988.
Nation, October 31, 1988, p. 434.
New Republic, October 10, 1988, pp. 26-27.
New Statesman and Society, May 20, 1994, pp. 32, 34.
New York, September 26, 1988, pp. 110, 114, 116; April 3, 1995, p. 59.
New Yorker, December 13, 1993, p. 125.
Time, April 14, 1986, p. 104.
Variety, August 26, 1988; October 30, 2000, Charles Lyons, "Foner Making 'Paris' Journey," p. 61.

ONLINE

Internet Movie Database, http://www.imdb.com/ (February 4, 2004).
Screenwriters Online, http://screenwriter.com/insider/NaomiAOL.html/ (May 3, 2003).*

* * *

FOX, William L. 1953-

PERSONAL: Born December 16, 1953, in Takoma Park, MD; son of William Lloyd (a historian) and Lynn G. (a bookkeeper) Fox; married Lynn Smith (a director of public affairs), August 1, 1981; children: Hallie. *Education:* St. Lawrence University, B.A.,

1975; Harvard University, M.Div., 1978; George Washington University, Ph.D., 1989. *Hobbies and other interests:* Canoeing, golf, bicycling.

ADDRESSES: Home—3526 Woodbine St., Chevy Chase, MD 20815. *Office*—Goucher College, 1021 Dulaney Valley Rd., Baltimore, MD 21204; fax: 410-337-6533. *E-mail*—wfox@goucher.edu.

CAREER: Senior minister of Congregational church in Pomona, CA, 1988-92; Universalist National Memorial Church, Washington, DC, senior minister, 1993-98; Goucher College, Baltimore, MD, special assistant to the president, 1999—. Howard University, adjunct professor, 1992-99.

MEMBER: American Society of Church History, Organization of American Historians, Cosmos Club.

WRITINGS:

Willard L. Sperry: Quandaries of a Liberal Protestant Mind, Peter Lang (New York, NY), 1991.

Lodge of the Double-Headed Eagle: Two Centuries of Scottish Rite Freemasonry in America's Southern Jurisdiction, University of Arkansas Press (Fayetteville, AR), 1997.

Valley of the Craftsman: A Pictorial History of Scottish Rite Freemasonry, 1801-2001, University of South Carolina Press (Columbia, SC), 2001.

General editor, "Church History Series," Peter Lang (New York, NY).

SIDELIGHTS: William L. Fox told *CA:* "I write with the aim of producing biographical narrative on several levels. I have it in mind to explain and interpret large events through the experience and thought of an individual. Similarly, a portrayal of group biography, such as American liberal Protestants or the Order of Freemasons, must somehow reflect a single person's perspective on that group for it to come fully alive. The audiences I try to reach simultaneously include the specialist scholar—in intellectual, cultural, Southern, or religious history—and the general reader for whom cultural reference points frame a reassuring context and also the surprise of learning new connections to surrounding social arrangements."

FRASER, Gordon 1943-

PERSONAL: Born February 23, 1943, in Glasgow, Scotland; married Gillian Harbinson, October 16, 1975; children: Nathalie, Benjamin. *Education:* Imperial College of Science and Technology, London, B.Sc. (with first class honors), 1964, Ph.D., 1967. *Hobbies and other interests:* Languages, crossword puzzles.

ADDRESSES: Home—14 La Chataigneraie, Crassy, 01220 Divonne-les-Bains, France. *E-mail*—gordon.fraser@wanadoo.fr.

CAREER: IPC Business Press, London, England, journalist, 1970-72; self-employed publicist, London, England, 1972-75; Rutherford Laboratory, Chilton, England, information officer, 1975-77; *CERN Courier,* Geneva, Switzerland, editor, 1977-2002; Cambridge University Press, Cambridge, England, editor in chief of *New Physics,* 2001—. Visiting lecturer in science communication at British universities.

WRITINGS:

(Coauthor) *Search for Infinity,* Facts on File (New York, NY), 1995.

The Quark Machines, IOP Publishing (Philadelphia, PA), 1997.

(Editor) *The Particle Century,* IOP Publishing (Philadelphia, PA), 1998.

Antimatter—the Ultimate Mirror, Cambridge University Press (Cambridge, England), 2000.

SIDELIGHTS: Gordon Fraser once told *CA:* "As a physicist-turned-popular science writer, I aim to convey the difficult concepts of modern physics without compromising the underlying science. While working for my doctorate in theoretical physics in the mid-1960s, I wrote short stories as a hobby. By 1970 it was clear to me that I was not cut out for scientific research, and I spun together two very different strands of interest by becoming a reporter for a weekly British newspaper for the computer industry. I returned to science as an in-house editor at major laboratories, and I became the editor of the *CERN Courier,* the monthly magazine of the international high-energy physics community."

FRAZIER, Charles 1950-

PERSONAL: Born November 4, 1950, in Asheville, NC; son of Charles O. (a high school principal) and Betty (a school librarian and administrator) Frazier; married, c. 1976; wife's name Katherine (an accounting professor); children: Annie. *Education:* University of North Carolina-Chapel Hill, B.A., 1973, University of South Carolina, Ph.D., 1976; graduate study at Appalachian State University.

ADDRESSES: *Home*—A farm near Raleigh, NC. *Agent*—Amanda Urban, International Creative Management, Inc., 40 West 57th St., New York, NY 10019.

CAREER: Writer, university professor, and horse breeder. University of Colorado, Boulder, instructor in early American literature; taught literature at a college in North Carolina, prior to 1990; freelance writer, 1990—. Raises horses on farm near Raleigh, North Carolina.

AWARDS, HONORS: National Book Award for fiction, from the National Book Foundation, 1997, for *Cold Mountain.*

WRITINGS:

(With Donald Secreast) *Adventuring in the Andes: The Sierra Club Travel Guide to Ecuador, Peru, Bolivia, the Amazon Basin, and the Galapagos Islands* (nonfiction), Sierra Club Books (San Francisco, CA), 1985.

Cold Mountain (novel), Atlantic Monthly Press (New York, NY), 1997.

Also author of the introduction to a paperback edition of *The Book of Job.*

ADAPTATIONS: *Cold Mountain* was adapted for film by MGM and Miramax in 2003, directed by Anthony Minghella and starring Jude Law, Nicole Kidman, and Renee Zellweger.

WORK IN PROGRESS: Another novel, about a one hundred-year-old white man who grew up with the Cherokees in North Carolina, and who was found in a North Carolina psychiatric hospital near the turn of the century.

Charles Frazier

SIDELIGHTS: Before publishing his award-winning first novel, *Cold Mountain,* in 1997, Charles Frazier taught early American literature, first at the University of Colorado and later in his native North Carolina. He also traveled extensively in South America, his experiences becoming the basis for a book written in collaboration with Donald Secreast that appeared in 1985, *Adventuring in the Andes: The Sierra Club Travel Guide to Ecuador, Peru, Bolivia, the Amazon Basin, and the Galapagos Islands.* Around 1990, he left academic life to focus on the story that would become *Cold Mountain.* Frazier's first novel brought him considerable critical acclaim, winning a National Book Award and reaching the top of the *New York Times* bestseller list.

Adventuring in the Andes contains a variety of knowledge useful to anyone planning a vacation near the South American mountain range—from people who want strenuous hiking to those who merely want a comfortable hotel stay in an exotic location. The volume discusses one hundred hiking trails, including the Inca trail to Machu Picchu; it also describes the cuisine available in each region. In addition, Frazier and his coauthor warn readers of the various types of disease and other medical complications they might encounter during their travels in South America. John Brosnahan noted in *Booklist* that "The book supplies a generous amount of . . . information." A *Kliatt* reviewer called *Adventuring in the Andes* "excellent" and "invaluable," while Harold M. Otness in the *Library Journal* summed it up as "a fine choice for travel collections."

Frazier has also hiked extensively in the North Carolina mountains, not coincidentally the setting of *Cold Mountain.* He got the idea for the novel from the life of one of his ancestors, a great-great uncle named W. P. Inman who, after being wounded, deserted from the Confederate Army during the War between the States. Frazier tells the story of Inman's three-hundred-mile-long journey home to the woman and the mountain he loves, evading troops from the North as well as Southern Home Guard patrols bent on capturing and executing deserters as he winds his way through the mountains. Frazier alternates Inman's chapters with others written from the viewpoint of Inman's sweetheart Ada, a genteel Southern woman from Charleston whose life has been changed drastically by the war and by her father's death. Another interesting character featured in Ada's chapters is Ruby, a more practical woman who helps Ada homestead a farm. More importantly, perhaps, Ruby teaches Ada how to be self-sufficient, and steeps her in the old Appalachian folklore that guides her in her interactions with the natural world surrounding Cold Mountain.

Critics have been as quick to praise *Cold Mountain* as readers have been in sending it to the bestseller list. Mel Gussow in the *New York Times* asserted that the novel "is filled with flavorful details: language (tools like maul and froe, spurtle, fleam and snath), crops, food, books and Cherokee legends," and went on to note that "Mr. Frazier is a stickler for authenticity." The difference, Gussow noted, between this and other popular novels about the Civil War is that in this one, "the war is in the background." Frazier told Gussow that he was aiming at "an *Odyssey* rather than an *Iliad.*" Civil War historian Shelby Foote read the book and liked it, in part, according to Gussow, because Frazier "did not presume to step inside historical characters." A reviewer for *Publishers Weekly* lauded *Cold Mountain* as "rich in evocative physical detail and timeless human insight." Likewise, David A. Berona in the *Library Journal* proclaimed it both "a remarkable effort" and a "monumental novel." Malcolm Jones, Jr. in *Newsweek* cited Frazier's acknowledgment in which he apologizes for not being completely true to the facts of his ancestor's life and to "the geography surrounding Cold Mountain," and concluded: "One must assume that he is merely being polite. This writer owes apologies to no one." One of the few voices of dissent came from Greil Marcus, reviewing the novel in *Esquire.* "I was halfway through *Cold Mountain* . . . when I realized it was only going to get worse," the critic remarked. Marcus went on to maintain that "*Cold Mountain* is a ridiculous book. Not for its story, which is merely picaresque when it's Inman's and uplifting when it's Ada's, but for its language: denatured, tangled, squeamish."

Frazier discussed with Gussow his feelings about the ways *Cold Mountain* compares with other novels about the Civil War. "When you grow up in the South," he told the reporter, "you get this concept of the war as this noble, tragic thing, and when I think about my own family's experience, it doesn't seem so noble in any direction." He added, "These people were sort of duped by a kind of war-fever hysteria. To go off and fight for a cause they had not much relation to: that's the part I see as tragic." Speaking of Civil War novels such as Stephen Crane's *The Red Badge of Courage* and Michael Shaara's *The Killer Angels,* Frazier told Gussow: "I felt those battle books had been done and in many cases done well. What I was interested in was the old lost culture of the southern Appalachians." To Jones, Frazier asserted what is perhaps his answer to Marcus's criticism. "I want the diction of the book to make people understand this is a different world," he stated.

Frazier worked for approximately seven years on *Cold Mountain* before it was ready for publication, and has frequently acknowledged the roles that family members and friends played in its creation. His daughter read drafts of the novel aloud for him, and Frazier told Michelle Green in *People* that "it really helped to hear it in somebody else's voice and to see if she was getting the rhythm of the sentences." The author also revealed his gratitude to his wife Katherine to Green, saying "I don't know many wives who would have said to a forty-year-old man, 'Sure, honey, quit your job. Write that novel.'" Also, one of the members of the Fraziers' parental car pool who took turns driving the neighborhood children to activities turned out to be novelist Kaye Gibbons. Frazier showed a draft of *Cold Mountain* to Gibbons, who in turn encouraged him to show it to agents and publishers.

Though Frazier's accomplishment of selling *Cold Mountain* to Atlantic Monthly Press for a six-figure advance on the basis of the first one hundred pages of his draft is impressive, he has since sold his follow-up book for over eight million dollars on the basis of a one-page outline. Several sources have reported that the subject of Frazier's next novel comes "from research he had come across while writing *Cold Mountain,*" as an article about the author in *Newsmakers* put it. "Around 1900," the piece continued, "a North Carolina state psychiatric hospital housed a 100-year-old man who sometimes refused to speak any language but Cherokee. He was not a Native American, but rather had grown up among the Cherokee in North Carolina, and represented them in Washington for a time." Frazier has already sold the film rights to the story. *Cold Mountain,* on the other hand, has been made into a film directed by Anthony Minghella and starring Jude Law, Nicole Kidman, and Renee Zellweger. Zellweger's performance earned her an Oscar in 2004 for best actress in a supporting role.

BIOGRAPHICAL AND CRITICAL SOURCES:

BOOKS

Authors and Artists for Young Adults, Volume 34, Gale (Detroit, MI), 2000.

Contemporary Southern Writers, St. James Press (Detroit, MI), 1999.

Newsmakers, Issue 2, Gale (Detroit, MI), 2003.

PERIODICALS

Atlanta Journal-Constitution, April 5, 1998, Bo Emerson, "Author Deals with a Mountain of Success," p. M1; September 27, 1998, Greg Changnon, "The Reading Room," p. L11.

Booklist, September 1, 1985, p. 23.

Entertainment Weekly, September 26, 1997, pp. 46-47.

Esquire, November, 1998, Greil Marcus, "The Maiden Takes Her Easement," pp. 70-72.

Guardian (London), April 9, 1998, Roger Clarke, "American Odyssey," p. 16.

Kliatt, fall, 1985, p. 57.

Library Journal, June 1, 1985, p. 127; May 15, 1997, p. 100.

Mississippi Quarterly, spring, 1999, Bill McCarron and Paul Knoke, "Images of War and Peace: Parallelism and Antithesis in the Beginning and Ending of *Cold Mountain,*" p. 273; winter, 2001, Terry Gifford, "Terrain, Character, and Text: Is *Cold Mountain* by Charles Frazier a Post-Pastoral Novel?," pp. 87-96.

New Statesman, April 29, 2002, Jason Cowley, "Books Diary," p. 53.

Newsweek, June 23, 1997, p. 73; July 28, 1997, Malcom Jones, Jr., interview with Charles Frazier, pp. 64-65; April 15, 2002, Malcom Jones, "Publishing: King of the Mountain," p. 54.

New York Times, August 27, 1997, pp. B1, B7.

People, February 23, 1998, Michelle Green, interview with Charles Frazier, p. 107.

Publishers Weekly, May 5, 1997, pp. 196-197.

San Francisco Chronicle, October 6, 1998, Jon Carrol, "Five Thoughts on *Cold Mountain,*" p. B10.

Variety, April 8, 2002, Jonathan Ding, "'Mountain' Man Books $11 Mil for Next Novel," pp. 1-2.

ONLINE

Cold Mountain Official Web site, http://www.miramax.com/cold_mountain/ (November 8, 2003).*

G

GAINES, Ernest J(ames) 1933-

PERSONAL: Born January 15, 1933, in Oscar, LA; son of Manuel (a laborer) and Adrienne J. (Colar) Gaines; married Dianne Saulney (an attorney), 1993. *Education:* Attended Vallejo Junior College; San Francisco State College (now University), B.A., 1957; graduate study at Stanford University, 1958-59. *Hobbies and other interests:* Listening to music ("Bach to Coltrane"), watching television, reading, spending time in the gym.

ADDRESSES: Office—128 Buena Vista Blvd., Lafayette, LA, 70503-2059; and Department of English, University of Southwestern Louisiana, P.O. Box 44691, Lafayette, LA 70504-0001. *Agent*—JCA Literary Agency, Inc., 242 West 27th St., New York, NY 10001.

CAREER: Novelist. Denison University, Granville, OH, writer-in-residence, 1971; Stanford University, Stanford, CA, writer-in-residence, 1981; University of Southwestern Louisiana, Lafayette, professor of English and writer-in-residence, beginning 1983. Whittier College, visiting professor, 1983, writer-in-residence, 1986. *Military service:* U.S. Army, 1953-55.

AWARDS, HONORS: Wallace Stegner fellow, Stanford University, 1957; Joseph Henry Jackson Award, San Francisco Foundation, 1959, for "Comeback" (short story); National Endowment for the Arts award, 1967; Rockefeller grant, 1970; Guggenheim fellow, 1971; Black Academy of Arts and Letters award, 1972; fiction gold medal, Commonwealth Club of California, 1972, for *The Autobiography of Miss Jane Pittman,* and 1984, for *A Gathering of Old Men;* Louisiana Library Association award, 1972; honorary doctorate of letters from Denison University, 1980, Brown University, 1985, Bard College, 1985, Whittier College, 1986, and Louisiana State University, 1987; award for excellence of achievement in literature, San Francisco Arts Commission, 1983; American Academy

Ernest J. Gaines

and Institute of Arts and Letters literary award, 1987; MacArthur Foundation fellowship, 1993; National Book Critics Circle Award for Fiction, 1993, for *A Lesson before Dying;* made Commander of the Order of Arts and Letters (France), 1996; inducted into Literary Hall of Fame for Writers of African Descent, Chicago State University, 1998; Emmy Award for Best Television Movie, 1999, for adaptation of *A Lesson before Dying;* National Humanities Medal, National Endowment for the Humanities, 2000.

WRITINGS:

FICTION

Catherine Carmier (novel), Atheneum (New York, NY), 1964.

Of Love and Dust (novel), Dial (New York, NY), 1967.

Bloodline (short stories; also see below), Dial (New York, NY), 1968, reprinted, Vintage Contemporaries (New York, NY), 1997.

A Long Day in November (originally published in *Bloodline*), Dial (New York, NY), 1971.

The Autobiography of Miss Jane Pittman (novel), Dial (New York, NY), 1971.

In My Father's House (novel), Knopf (New York, NY), 1978.

A Gathering of Old Men (novel), Knopf (New York, NY), 1983.

A Lesson before Dying (novel), Knopf (New York, NY), 1993.

OTHER

Conversations with Ernest Gaines, edited by John Lowe, University Press of Mississippi (Jackson, MS), 1995.

Gaines's works have been translated into other languages, including German and French.

ADAPTATIONS: The Autobiography of Miss Jane Pittman, adapted from Gaines's novel, aired on the Columbia Broadcasting System (CBS-TV), 1974, and won nine Emmy Awards. "The Sky Is Gray," a short story originally published in *Bloodline,* was adapted for public television in 1980. *A Gathering of Old Men,* adapted from Gaines's novel, aired on CBS-TV, 1987. *In My Father's House* was adapted for audiocassette. *A Lesson before Dying* was filmed for Home Box Office, 1999, and was adapted for the stage by Romulus Linney, 2001.

SIDELIGHTS: The fiction of Ernest J. Gaines, including his 1971 novel *The Autobiography of Miss Jane Pittman* and his 1993 novel *A Lesson before Dying,* is deeply rooted in the African-American culture and storytelling traditions of rural Louisiana where the author was born and raised. His stories have been noted for their convincing characters and powerful themes presented within authentic, often folk-like, narratives that tap into the complex world of the rural South. Gaines depicts the strength and dignity of his black characters in the face of numerous struggles: the dehumanizing and destructive effects of racism; the breakdown in personal relationships as a result of social pressures; and the choice between secured traditions and the sometimes radical measures necessary to bring about social change. Although the issues presented in Gaines's fiction are serious and often disturbing, "this is not hot-and-breathless, burn-baby-burn writing," Melvin Maddocks pointed out in *Time;* rather, it is the work of "a patient artist, a patient man." Expounding on Gaines's rural heritage, Maddocks continued: Gaines "sets down a story as if he were planting, spreading the roots deep, wide and firm. His stories grow organically, at their own rhythm. When they ripen at last, they do so inevitably, arriving at a climax with the absolute rightness of a folk tale."

Gaines's experiences growing up on a Louisiana plantation provide the foundation upon which much of his fiction is based. Particularly important, he told Paul Desruisseaux in the *New York Times Book Review,* were "working in the fields, going fishing in the swamps with the older people, and, especially, listening to the people who came to my aunt's house, the aunt who raised me." Although Gaines moved to California at the age of fifteen and subsequently went to college there, his fiction has been based in an imaginary Louisiana plantation region called Bayonne, which a number of critics have compared to William Faulkner's fictional Yoknapatawpha County. Gaines has acknowledged looking to Faulkner, in addition to Ernest Hemingway, for language, and to such French writers as Gustave Flaubert and Guy de Maupassant for style. A perhaps greater influence, however, have been the writings of nineteenth-century Russian authors.

Gaines's first novel, *Catherine Carmier,* is "an apprentice work more interesting for what it anticipates than for its accomplishments," noted William E. Grant in the *Dictionary of Literary Biography.* The novel chronicles the story of a young black man, Jackson Bradley, who returns to Bayonne after completing his education in California. Jackson falls in love with Catherine, the daughter of a Creole sharecropper who refuses to let members of his family associate with anyone darker than he, believing Creoles to be racially and socially superior. The novel portrays numerous clashes of loyalty: Catherine is torn between her love for Jackson and for her father; Jackson is caught between a bond to the community he grew up in and the experience and knowledge he has gained in the outside world. "Both Catherine and Jackson are immobilized by the pressures of [the] rural community," noted Keith E. Byerman in the *Dictionary of Literary Biography,* which produces "twin themes of isolation and paralysis [that] give the novel an existential quality. Characters must face an unfriendly world without guidance and must make crucial choices about their lives." The characters in *Catherine Carmier*—as in much of Gaines's fiction—are faced with struggles that test the conviction of personal beliefs. Winifred L. Stoelting explained in the *CLA Journal* that Gaines is concerned more "with how [his characters] . . . handle their decisions than with the rightness of their decisions—more often than not predetermined by social changes over which the single individual has little control."

Gaines sets *Catherine Carmier* in the time of the U.S. civil rights movement, yet avoids making it a primary force in the novel. "In divorcing his tale from contemporary events," Grant commented, "Gaines declares his independence from the political and social purposes of much contemporary black writing. Instead, he elects to concentrate upon those fundamental human passions and conflicts which transcend the merely social level of human existence." Grant found Gaines "admirable" for doing this, yet also believed Jackson's credibility is marred because he remains aloof from contemporary events. For Grant, the novel "seems to float outside time and place rather than being solidly anchored in the real world of the modern South." Byerman held a similar view, stating that the novel "is not entirely successful in presenting its major characters and their motivations." Nonetheless, he pointed out that in *Catherine Carmier,* "Gaines does begin to create a sense of the black community and its perceptions of the world around it. Shared ways of speaking, thinking, and relating to the dominant white society are shown through a number of minor characters."

Gaines's next novel, *Of Love and Dust,* is also a story of forbidden romance, and, as in *Catherine Carmier,* a "new world of expanding human relationships erodes the old world of love for the land and the acceptance of social and economic stratification," wrote Stoelting. *Of Love and Dust* is the story of Marcus Payne, a young black man bonded out of prison by a white landowner and placed under the supervision of a Cajun overseer, Sidney Bonbon. Possessed of a rebellious and hostile nature, Marcus is a threat to Bonbon, who in turn does all that he can to break the young man's spirit. In an effort to strike back, Marcus pays special attention to the overseer's wife; the two fall in love and plot to run away. The novel ends with a violent confrontation between the two men in which Marcus is killed. After the killing, Bonbon claims that to spare Marcus would have meant his own death at the hands of other Cajuns. Grant noted a similarity between *Of Love and Dust* and *Catherine Carmier* in that the characters are "caught up in a decadent social and economic system that determines their every action and limits their possibilities." Similarly, the two novels are marked by a "social determinism [that] shapes the lives of all the characters, making them pawns in a mechanistic world order rather than free agents."

Of Love and Dust demonstrates Gaines's development as a novelist, offering a clearer view of the themes and characters that have come to dominate his work. Stoelting noted that "in a more contemporary setting, the novel . . . continues Gaines's search for human dignity, and when that is lacking, acknowledges the salvation of pride," adding that "the characters themselves grow into a deeper awareness than those of [his] first novel. More sharply drawn . . . [they] are more decisive in their actions." Byerman remarked that the novel "more clearly condemns the economic, social, and racial system of the South for the problems faced by its characters." Likewise, the first-person narrator in the novel—a coworker of Marcus—"both speaks in the idiom of the place and time and instinctively asserts the values of the black community."

Gaines turns to a first-person narrator again in his next novel, *The Autobiography of Miss Jane Pittman,* which many consider to be his masterwork. Miss Jane Pittman—well over 100 years old—relates a personal history that spans the time from the U.S. Civil War and slavery up through the civil rights movement of the 1960s. "To travel with Miss Pittman from adolescence to old age is to embark upon a historic journey, one staked out in the format of the novel," wrote Addison Gayle, Jr. in *The Way of the World: The Black Novel in America.* "Never mind that Miss Jane Pittman is fictitious, and that her 'autobiography,' offered up in the form of taped reminiscences, is artifice," added Josh Greenfield in *Life,* "the effect is stunning." Gaines's gift for drawing convincing characters is clearly demonstrated in *The Autobiography of Miss Jane Pittman.* "His is not . . . an 'art' narrative, but an authentic narrative by an authentic ex-slave, authentic even though both are Gaines's inventions," Bryant commented. "So successful is he in *becoming* Miss Jane Pittman, that when we talk about her story, we do not think of Gaines as her creator, but as her recording editor."

The character of Jane Pittman could be called an embodiment of the black experience in America. "Though Jane is the dominant personality of the narrative—observer and commentator upon history, as well as participant—in her odyssey is symbolized the odyssey of a race of people; through her eyes is revealed the grandeur of a people's journey through history," maintained Gayle. "The central metaphor of the novel concerns this journey: Jane and her people, as they come together in the historic march toward dignity and freedom in Sampson, symbolize a people's march through history, breaking old patterns, though sometimes slowly, as they do." The important historical backdrop to Jane's narrative—slavery, Reconstruction, the civil rights era, segregation—does not compromise, however, the detailed account of an individual. "Jane captures the experiences of those millions of illiterate blacks who never had a chance to tell their own stories," Byerman explained. "By focusing on the particular yet typical events of a small part of Louisiana, those lives are given a concreteness and specificity not possible in more general histories."

In his fourth novel, *In My Father's House,* Gaines focuses on a theme that appears in varying degrees throughout his fiction: the alienation between fathers and sons. As the author told Desruisseaux, "In my books there always seems to be fathers and sons searching for each other. That's a theme I've worked with since I started writing. Even when the father was not in the story, I've dealt with his absence and its effects on his children. And that is the theme of this book." *In My Father's House* tells of prominent civil rights leader Reverend Phillip Martin, who, at the peak of his career, is confronted with a troubled young man named Robert X. Although Robert's identity is initially a mystery, eventually he is revealed to be one of three offspring from a love affair Martin had in an earlier, wilder life and then abandoned. Robert arrives to confront and kill the father whose neglect he sees as responsible for the family's disintegration: his sister has been raped, his brother imprisoned for the murder of her attacker, and his mother alone and reduced to poverty. Although the son's intent to kill his father is never carried out, Martin is forced "to undergo a long and painful odyssey through his own past and the labyrinthine streets of Baton Rouge to learn what really happened to his first family," wrote William Burke in the *Dictionary of Literary Biography Yearbook.* Larry McMurtry, in the *New York Times Book Review,* noted that as the book traces the lost family, "we have revealed to us an individual, a marriage, a community and a region, but with such an unobtrusive marshaling of detail that we never lose sight of the book's central thematic concern: the profoundly destructive consequences of the breakdown of parentage, of a father's abandonment of his children and the terrible and irrevocable consequences of such an abandonment."

A Gathering of Old Men, Gaines's fifth novel, presents a cast of aging Southern black men who, after a life of subordination and intimidation, make a defiant stand against injustice. Seventeen of them, together with the thirty-year-old white heiress of a deteriorating Louisiana plantation, plead guilty to murdering Beau Boutan, a member of a violent Cajun clan. While a confounded sheriff and vengeful family wait to lynch the black they've decided is guilty, the group members—toting recently fired shotguns—surround the dead man and "confess" their motives. "Each man tells of the accumulated frustrations of his life—raped daughters, jailed sons, public insults, economic exploitation—that serve as sufficient motive for murder," wrote Byerman. "Though Beau Boutan is seldom the immediate cause of their anger, he clearly represents the entire white world that has deprived them of their dignity and manhood. The confessions serve as ritual purgings of all the hostility and self-hatred built up over the years." Over a dozen characters—white, black, and Cajun—advance the story through individual narrations, creating "thereby a range of social values as well as different perspectives on the action," Byerman noted. *New York Times Book*

Review contributor Reynolds Price noted that the black narrators "are nicely distinguished from one another in rhythm and idiom, in the nature of what they see and report, especially in their specific laments for past passivity in the face of suffering." The accumulated effect, observed Elaine Kendall in the *Los Angeles Times Book Review,* is that the "individual stories coalesce into a single powerful tale of subjugation, exploitation and humiliation at the hands of landowners."

Another theme of *A Gathering of Old Men,* according to *America*'s Ben Forkner, is "the simple, natural dispossession of old age, of the traditional and well-loved values of the past, the old trades and the old manners, forced to give way to modern times." Sam Cornish commented in the *Christian Science Monitor* that the novel's "characters—both black and white—understand that, before the close of the novel, the new South must confront the old, and all will be irrevocably changed. Gaines portrays a society that will be altered by the deaths of its 'old men,' and so presents an allegory about the passing of the old and birth of the new."

A Lesson before Dying, issued ten years after *A Gathering of Old Men,* continues the author's historical reflections on the South. The setting is a characteristic one: a plantation and jail in Bayonne during a six-month span in 1948. The unlikely hero is Jefferson, a scarcely literate, twenty-one-year-old man-child who works the cane fields of the Pichot plantation. Trouble finds the protagonist when he innocently hooks up with two men; they then rob a liquor store and are killed in the process along with the shop's proprietor, leaving Jefferson as an accomplice. The young man's naivete in the crime is never recognized as he is brought to trial before a jury of twelve white men and sentenced to death. Jefferson's defense attorney ineffectively attempts to save his client by presenting him as a dumb animal, as "a thing that acts on command. A thing to hold the handle of a plow, a thing to load your bales of cotton." When Jefferson's godmother learns of this analogy, she determines that her nephew will face his execution as a man, not as an animal. Thus, she enlists the help of young teacher Grant Wiggins, who is initially resistant but works to help Jefferson to resolutely shoulder his fate in his final days.

According to Sandra D. Davis in the *Detroit Free Press,* "*A Lesson before Dying* begins much like many other stories where racial tension brews in the background." Yet, as in Gaines's other works, the racial tension in this novel is more of a catalyst for his tribute to the perseverance of the victims of injustice. Unexpectedly, pride, honor, and manhood in a dehumanizing environment emerge as the themes of this novel. Through Wiggins, the young narrator and unwilling carrier of the "burden" of the community, and his interaction with the black community, as represented by Jefferson's godmother and the town's Reverend Ambrose, Gaines "creates a compelling, intense story about heroes and the human spirit," contended Davis. Ironically, Jefferson and Reverend Ambrose ultimately emerge as the real teachers, showing Wiggins that, as Davis asserted, "education encompasses more than the lessons taught in school." Wiggins is also forced to admit, according to Jonathan Yardley in the *Washington Post Book World,* "his own complicity in the system of which Jefferson is a victim." *Commonweal* critic Madeline Marget likened Jefferson's ordeal to the crucifixion of Jesus Christ: "*A Lesson before Dying* is Gaines's retelling of the Passion—a layered and sensual story of a suffering man and his life-changing struggle," one that Gaines explores "through a narrative of tremendous velocity."

Of that community which yields the lessons of Gaines's fiction and his relation to it, Alice Walker wrote in the *New York Times Book Review:* Gaines "claims and revels in the rich heritage of Southern Black people and their customs; the community he feels with them is unmistakable and goes deeper even than pride . . . Gaines is mellow with historical reflection, supple with wit, relaxed and expansive because he does not equate his people with failure." The novelist has been criticized by some, however, who feel his writing does not more directly focus on problems facing blacks. Gaines responded to Desruisseaux that he feels "too many blacks have been writing to tell whites all about 'the problems,' instead of writing something that all people, including their own, could find interesting, could enjoy." Gaines has also remarked that more can be achieved than strictly writing novels of protest. In an interview for *San Francisco,* the author stated: "So many of our writers have not read any farther back than [Richard Wright's] *Native Son.* So many of our novels deal only with the great city ghettos; that's all we write about, as if there's nothing else." Gaines continued: "We've only been living in these ghettos for 75 years or so, but the other 300 years—I think this is worth writing about."

In *Conversations with Ernest Gaines,* the author reveals to editor John Lowe some of the factors behind his popularity and critical acclaim. "While a notable consistency in themes and setting is evident within the body of his writing," stated critic Valerie Babb, writing about *Conversations with Ernest Gaines* in the *African American Review,* "in novel ways this talented writer consistently re-envisions and reworks the material that inspires him. . . . The best commentary is Gaines's own . . . as he assesses his art." "Critiques of racial essentialism are many," Babb concluded, "and there is increased scholarly emphasis on finding voice and telling story, two elements that imbue Gaines's works with their own unique pyrotechnics. With greater appreciation of how small details make great fiction, it seems our critical age is indeed ready to appreciate the fiction of Ernest Gaines."

Gaines's output has been slow but steady, and his focus remains restricted to Louisiana's past. "I can write only about the past," he explained to Jerome Weeks of the *Knight Ridder/Tribune News Service.* "I let it sink into me for a long time, let it stay there. I can't write about something that happened last week." Although his works number less than a dozen, their influence has been widespread. His novels have become part of the mainstay of high school and college literature courses because his characters struggle to define themselves within themselves, their communities, society, and humanity. "We must all try to define ourselves. It's a human struggle," he told Weeks.

BIOGRAPHICAL AND CRITICAL SOURCES:

BOOKS

Babb, Valerie-Melissa, *Ernest Gaines,* Twayne (Boston, MA), 1991.

Beavers, Herman, *Wrestling Angels into Song: The Fictions of Ernest J. Gaines and James Alan McPherson,* University of Pennsylvania Press (Philadelphia, PA), 1995.

Bruck, Peter, editor, *The Black American Short Story in the Twentieth Century: A Collection of Critical Essays,* B. R. Gruner (Amsterdam, Netherlands), 1977.

Carmean, Karen, *Ernest J. Gaines: A Critical Companion,* Greenwood Press (Westport, CT), 1998.

Children's Literature Review, Gale (Detroit, MI), Volume 62, 2002.

Concise Dictionary of American Literary Biography: Broadening Views, 1968-1988, Gale (Detroit, MI), 1989.

Contemporary Literary Criticism, Gale (Detroit, MI), Volume 3, 1975, Volume 11, 1979, Volume 18, 1981.

Conversations with Ernest Gaines, University Press of Mississippi (Jackson, MS), 1995.

Dictionary of Literary Biography, Gale (Detroit, MI), Volume 2: *American Novelists since World War II,* 1978, Volume 33: *Afro-American Fiction Writers after 1955,* 1984.

Dictionary of Literary Biography Yearbook: 1980, Gale (Detroit, MI), 1981.

Estes, David C., *Critical Reflections on the Fiction of Ernest J. Gaines,* University of Georgia Press (Athens, GA), 1994.

Gaudet, Marcia, and Carl Wooton, *Porch Talk with Ernest Gaines: Conversations on the Writer's Craft,* Louisiana State University Press (Lafayette, LA), 1990.

Gayle, Addison, Jr., *The Way of the New World: The Black Novel in America,* Doubleday (New York, NY), 1975.

Hicks, Jack, *In the Singer's Temple: Prose Fictions of Barthelme, Gaines, Brautigan, Piercy, Kesey, and Kosinski,* University of North Carolina Press (Chapel Hill, NC), 1981.

Hudson, Theodore R., *The History of Southern Literature,* Louisiana State University Press (Lafayette, LA), 1985.

Lowe, John, editor, *Conversations with Ernest Gaines,* University Press of Mississippi (Jackson, MS), 1995.

O'Brien, John, editor, *Interview with Black Writers,* Liveright (New York, NY), 1973.

PERIODICALS

African American Review, fall, 1994, p. 489; February, 1998, p. 350.

America, June 2, 1984.

Atlanta Journal-Constitution, October 26, 1997; July 28, 2002, Teresa K. Weaver, "National Black Arts Festival: The Importance of Reading Ernest (Gaines)," p. L1.

Black American Literature Forum, Volume 11, 1977; Volume 24, 1990.

Black Issues Book Review, May, 2002, review of *In My Father's House* (audio version), p. 26.

Booklist, June 1, 1999, review of *A Lesson before Dying,* p. 1796; November 15, 2001, review of *Catherine Carmier,* p. 555.

Callaloo, Volume 7, 1984; Volume 11, 1988; winter, 1999, Keith Clark, "Re-(w)righting Black Male Subjectivity: The Communal Poetics of Ernest Gaines's *A Gathering of Old Men,*" p. 195; winter, 2001, review of *A Lesson before Dying,* p. 346.

Chicago Tribune Book World, October 30, 1983.

Christian Science Monitor, December 2, 1983.

Chronicle of Higher Education, May 11, 1994, p. A23.

CLA Journal, March, 1971; December, 1975.

Commonweal, June 16, 2000, Madeline Marget, review of *A Lesson before Dying,* p. 23.

Detroit Free Press, June 6, 1993, p. 7J.

Essence, August, 1993, p. 52.

Globe and Mail (Toronto, Ontario, Canada), June 12, 1999, review of *A Lesson before Dying,* p. D4.

Guardian (London, England), March 18, 2000, Nick Hasted, "Nick Hasted Ghosthunts with Ernest Gaines in Altered Southern States," p. 11.

Iowa Review, winter, 1972.

Knight Ridder/Tribune News Service, February 28, 2001, Jerome Weeks, "Author Ernest J. Gaines Mines His Rich Southern Past," p. K882.

Library Journal, May 15, 2001, Nancy Pearl, review of *A Lesson before Dying,* p. 192.

Life, April 30, 1971.

Los Angeles Times, March 2, 1983.

Los Angeles Times Book Review, January 1, 1984.

MELUS, Volume 11, 1984; spring, 1999, Wolfgang Lepschy, "Ernest J. Gaines" (interview), p. 197.

Mississippi Quarterly, spring, 1999, Jeffrey J. Folks, "Communal Responsibility in Ernest J. Gaines's *A Lesson before Dying,*" p. 259.

Nation, February 5, 1968; April 5, 1971; January 14, 1984.

Negro Digest, November, 1967; January, 1968; January, 1969.

New Orleans Review, Volume 1, 1969; Volume 3, 1972; Volume 14, 1987.

New Republic, December 26, 1983.

New Statesman, September 2, 1973; February 10, 1984; May 29, 2000, Nicola Upson, review of *A Gathering of Old Men,* p. 57.

Newsweek, June 16, 1969; May 3, 1971.

New Yorker, October 24, 1983.

New York Times, July 20, 1978.

New York Times Book Review, November 19, 1967; May 23, 1971; June 11, 1978; October 30, 1983; May 22, 1999, Ron Wertheimer, review of *A Lesson before Dying,* p. B15; September 19, 2000, Bruce Weber, "Last-Minute Lessons for a Condemned Prisoner in the Jim Crow South," p. E1.

Observer (London, England), February 5, 1984.

Publishers Weekly, March 21, 1994, p. 8.

San Francisco, July, 1974.

Sojourners, September-October, 2002, Dale Brown, "A Lesson for Living," pp. 30-33.

Southern Review, Volume 10, 1974; Volume 21, 1985.

Studies in Short Fiction, summer, 1975.

Studies in the Humanities, June-December, 2001, Lorna Fitzsimmons, "*The Autobiography of Miss Jane Pittman:* Film, Intertext, and Ideology," pp. 94-109.

Time, May 10, 1971; December 27, 1971.

Times (London, England), March 18, 2000, Paul Connolly, review of *A Gathering of Old Men,* p. 21.

Times Literary Supplement, February 10, 1966; March 16, 1973; April 6, 1984.

Voice Literary Supplement, October, 1983.

Wall Street Journal, September 20, 2000, Amy Gamerman, review of *A Lesson before Dying,* p. A24.

Washington Post, January 13, 1976; May 22, 1999, Ken Ringle, review of *A Lesson before Dying,* p. C01.

Washington Post Book World, June 18, 1978; September 21, 1983; March 28, 1993, p. 3; May 23, 1993.

Writer, May, 1999, p. 4.

ONLINE

NewOrleans, http://www.neworleans.com/lalife/ (summer, 1997), Faith Dawson, "A Louisiana Life: Ernest J. Gaines."

OTHER

Louisiana Stories: Ernest Gaines (television film), WHMM-TV, 1993.*

* * *

GARBUS, Martin 1934-

PERSONAL: Born August 8, 1934, in Brooklyn, NY; son of Solomon and Doris Garbus; married Ruth Streifer, November 13, 1964; children: Cassandra and Elizabeth. *Education:* Hunter College (now Hunter College of the City University of New York), B.A., 1955; New York University, J.D., 1959; attended Columbia University.

ADDRESSES: Office—Davis & Gilbert, L.L.P., 1740 Broadway, New York, NY 10018. *E-mail*—mgarbus@dglaw.com.

CAREER: Admitted to the Bar of New York State, 1960, and the Bar of the U.S. Supreme Court, 1962. General counsel to Committee to Abolish Capital Punishment, 1964; Columbia University, New York, NY, director of Center on Social Welfare Policy and Law, 1968; associate director of American Civil Liberties Union, 1969; Yale University, New Haven, CT, lecturer in law, 1974; Frankfurt, Garbus, Klein & Selz, New York, NY, law partner, 1977-2003. Davis & Gilbert, New York, NY, law partner, 2003—. Lecturer, Tsinghau University, Beijing, China, 2004.

MEMBER: Communications and Media Law Committee, Association of the Bar of the State of New York.

WRITINGS:

Ready for the Defense, Farrar, Straus (New York, NY), 1970.

Traitors and Heroes: A Lawyer's Memoir, Atheneum (New York, NY), 1987.

(With Stanley Cohen) *Tough Talk: How I Fought for Writers, Comics, Bigots, and the American Way,* Times Books (New York, NY), 1998.

Courting Disaster: The Supreme Court and the Dangerous Unmaking of American Law, Times Books (New York, NY), 2002.

Contributor to newspapers and law journals.

SIDELIGHTS: Trial lawyer Martin Garbus is well known as a defender of civil liberties and an expert on the freedoms covered by the First Amendment. He has written about his career and his many famous clients, who have included comedian Lenny Bruce, author Salman Rushdie, and Czech president Vaclav Havel; he also has written a book critiquing the U.S. Supreme Court.

Traitors and Heroes: A Lawyer's Memoir deals with Garbus's work for human rights. He supported the dissidents persecuted in the former Soviet Union, sneaking a letter from one of them, Andrei Sakharov, out of the country and into the hands of former U.S. President Jimmy Carter in the late 1970s, leading Carter to speak out about human rights violations by the Soviet government.Garbus also was an observer of the trials in 1974 of Chileans who opposed Augusto Pinochet's military regime and those conducted in 1977 in South Africa of antiapartheid activists.

"Garbus offers a moving and rare inside glimpse at the legal systems of all three nations," related William Blum in the *Los Angeles Times Book Review.* The book, he added, "is much more than an engaging personal saga. It is also a thoughtful reflection on the nature and evolution of the high crime of treason." Some nations, Garbus points out, have made the accusation of treason against those who have merely criticized their government; meanwhile, the United States has had a less-than-perfect record of tolerating dissent. Herbert Mitgang, reviewing for the *New York Times,* noted that Garbus "maintains that Americans ought to be concerned with the personal rights of individuals in foreign countries to speak and write freely." Mitgang termed *Traitors and Heroes* "admirable," and Blum summed it up as "superb."

Garbus recounts many of his high-profile cases in *Tough Talk: How I Fought for Writers, Comics, Bigots, and the American Way.* These included working with Daniel Ellsberg on the release of the Pentagon Papers during the Vietnam War; defending comedian Lenny Bruce when he was accused of obscenity; attempting to persuade Iranian Islamic fundamentalists to end their death threats against author Salman Rushdie; and handling actor Robert Redford's lawsuit against a tobacco company that wanted to appropriate his name for a cigarette brand. His devotion to free speech for all has also led him to defend the rights of neo-Nazis to march in the heavily Jewish Chicago suburb of Skokie and of physicist William Shockley to appear on college campuses to discuss his belief in white superiority. What's more, Garbus is critical of some feminists' attempts to suppress pornographic material. "Garbus is deeply disturbed by those on both the right and the left who would restrain speech in the hope of improving human conduct," reported Anthony Day in the *Los Angeles Times.*

Garbus also describes how he came by his views. He grew up in poverty in the Bronx, the son of Jewish immigrants who had fled persecution in Poland. His mother died in a fire when he was three; his father ran a candy store, where Martin figured he would make his career, until he entered college almost as an afterthought. But he became passionate about the law and free speech while serving in the Korean War, when he was court-martialed for including controversial subjects in a current events class he conducted for fellow soldiers.

"Part memoir, part polemic, *Tough Talk* is consistently entertaining and often thought-provoking," commented Seth Bloom in the *American Lawyer.* To Eric Alterman, writing in the *New York Times Book Review,* "Reading Martin Garbus's memoir is like sitting in a bar . . . and listening to the guy on the stool next to you regale you with story after story, each better than the last, about the cases he has worked on in the course of a long career." Alterman expressed some reservations about the book, saying, "While almost all of these episodes are fascinating in isolation, Garbus could have used a stronger editorial hand to force him to draw his stories into a larger narrative." Bloom had a similar criticism, feeling the book needed "a broader perspective on the First Amendment and its impact on society." Alterman also thought Garbus "extremely stingy with personal information." Day, however, found that "Garbus's tale of how he became a lawyer is as interesting as the cases he handled" and that this "splendid book . . . gives us a lively tour of the state of free speech in America over the last forty years." *Columbia Journalism Review* contributor Ellen Alderman, meanwhile, dubbed *Tough Talk* "a lively chronicle of Garbus's eventful life and career."

Courting Disaster: The Supreme Court and the Dangerous Unmaking of American Law concentrates on Garbus's professional opinion of the highest U.S. court. He argues that since the 1980s, the court has become not an impartial dispenser of justice but an active maker of national policy—and that policy generally favors and implements conservative ideas. The court, he says, has weakened protections for civil rights and liberties, including abortion rights, and has undermined affirmative action and other social programs. For what he sees as the court's right-wing bias, he blames Chief Justice William Rehnquist and the justices appointed by presidents Ronald Reagan and George H. W. Bush. He predicts that George W. Bush will nominate ultraconservatives to the lower federal courts and, if the opportunity arises, to the Supreme Court, and he calls on his readers to oppose these nominees.

"Garbus has advanced impassioned and provocative arguments to buttress his position," commented L. Peter Parcher and Partha Chattoraj in the *New York Law Journal.* They noted that he "confesses his own biases" toward a reading of the Constitution that favors liberal ideas, but added that "this informative, important and controversial book is well worth reading, regardless of one's personal, social or political views." Steve Weinberg, writing in *Legal Times,* thought Garbus had not quite proved his case. "He demonstrates that the Court's majorities are increasingly illiberal," remarked Weinberg, who said he was still unconvinced that the conservative justices were "allied in a well-designed cabal to destroy individual liberties." Weinberg continued, "Perhaps that is so, but invective is not the same as evidence." Parcher and Chattoraj, however, observed that Garbus "cites case after case" to illustrate "many ways in which this vast change in American law is being accomplished." A *Kirkus Reviews* contributor called *Courting Disaster* "an openly liberal polemic, but nevertheless a brilliant summary of the important legal trends of the last twenty years." A *Publishers Weekly* reviewer related that "Garbus's writing is clear and comprehensible" and that "sympathetic—that is, liberal—readers will find his message chilling."

BIOGRAPHICAL AND CRITICAL SOURCES:

PERIODICALS

American Lawyer, October, 1998, Seth Bloom, review of *Tough Talk: How I Fought for Writers, Comics, Bigots, and the American Way.*

Columbia Journalism Review, Ellen Alderman, review of *Tough Talk,* p. 83.

Kirkus Reviews, July 15, 2002, review of *Courting Disaster: The Supreme Court and the Dangerous Unmaking of American Law,* p. 1007.

Los Angeles Times, August 28, 1998, Anthony Day, "Defending Our Right to Speak Our Minds," section E, p. 2.

Los Angeles Times Book Review, July 26, 1987, William Blum, review of *Traitors and Heroes: A Lawyer's Memoir,* p. 1.

New York Law Journal, October 8, 2002, L. Peter Parcher and Partha Chattoraj, review of *Courting Disaster,* features section, p. 2.

New York Times, August 20, 1987, Herbert Mitgang, "Champion of the Individual," section C, p. 25.

New York Times Book Review, August 9, 1998, Eric Alterman, "Expletive Included," p. 17.

Publishers Weekly, July 8, 2002, review of *Courting Disaster,* p. 39.

ONLINE

Davis & Gilbert L.L.P., http://www.dglaw.com/biographies/mGarbus_bio.html/ (November 8, 2003), author biography.*

* * *

GARLAND, Sherry 1948-
Lynn Lawrence

PERSONAL: Born July 24, 1948, in McAllen, TX; daughter of Joseph (a farmer and carpenter) and Desla (a homemaker) Allison; married Clyde L. Garland, July 4, 1971. *Education:* University of Texas at Arlington, B.A. (with honors), 1970, graduate studies, 1970-71.

ADDRESSES: *Home*—Central TX. *Office*—c/o Author Mail, Harcourt & Co., 525 B Street, Suite 1900, San Diego, CA 92101.

CAREER: Texas A & M University, College Station, TX, librarian in oceanography/meteorology department, 1972-75; secretarial work for various home-builders in Houston, TX, 1976-89; lecturer and writer.

AWARDS, HONORS: Work-in-progress grant, Society of Children's Book Writers and Guilded Quill Award in juvenile fiction, both 1990, both for *Song of the Buffalo Boy;* ABC Children's Booksellers Choice Award; Best Book for Young Adults, Notable Picture Book, and Best Book for Reluctant Readers citations, American Library Association; American Booksellers Association Pick of the List citation; California Young Reader's Medal, for *Shadow of the Dragon*; Notable Children's Trade Book in the Field of Social Studies citations, National Council for the Social Studies/Children's Book Council; Parents' Choice Honor Book; Lamplighter Award, National Christian Schools Association, for *The Silent Storm*; Best Books for the Teen Age citation, New York Public Library; Orbis Pictus recommended nonfiction book, for *Voices of the Alamo*; Cuffy Award, *Publishers Weekly*; Reading Rainbow featured book, for *The Lotus Seed*; numerous "readers' choice" citations from individual states; Texas Bluebonnet Master List, for *The Lotus Seed*; Texas Lone Star Reading List; Texas Institute of Letters Award for juvenile fiction; Spur Award from Western Writers of America for juvenile fiction; Honor Book, Society of School Librarians International, 2002, for *In the Shadow of the Alamo.*

WRITINGS:

FOR CHILDREN

Vietnam: Rebuilding a Nation (nonfiction), Dillon/Macmillan (New York, NY), 1990.
Where the Cherry Trees Bloom (novel), [Germany], 1991.
Best Horse on the Force (novel), Holt (New York, NY), 1991.
Song of the Buffalo Boy (novel), Harcourt (San Diego, CA), 1992.
The Lotus Seed (picture book), illustrated by Tatsuro Kiuchi, Harcourt (San Diego, CA), 1993.
Why Ducks Sleep on One Leg (picture book), illustrated by Jean and Mou-sien Tseng, Scholastic (New York, NY), 1993.
The Silent Storm (novel), Harcourt (New York, NY), 1993.
Shadow of the Dragon (novel), Harcourt (New York, NY), 1993
I Never Knew Your Name (picture book), illustrated by Sheldon Greenberg, Houghton Mifflin (Boston, MA), 1994.
Summer Sands, illustrated by Robert J. Lee, Harcourt (New York, NY), 1995.
Indio, Harcourt (New York, NY), 1995.
Cabin 102, Harcourt (New York, NY), 1995.
Letters from the Mountain, Harcourt (New York, NY), 1996.
The Last Rainmaker, Harcourt (New York, NY), 1997.
A Line in the Sand: The Alamo Diary of Lucinda Lawrence ("Dear America" series), Scholastic (New York, NY), 1998.
My Father's Boat (picture book), illustrated by Ted Rand, Scholastic (New York, NY), 1998.
Voices of the Alamo (picture book), illustrated by Ronald Himler, Scholastic (New York, NY), 2000.
Children of the Dragon: Selected Tales from Vietnam, illustrated by Trina Schart Hyman, Harcourt (New York, NY), 2001.

In the Shadow of the Alamo, Harcourt (New York, NY), 2001.

Valley of the Moon: The Diary of Maria Rosalia de Milagros ("Dear America" series), Scholastic (New York, NY), 2001.

FOR ADULTS

(Under pseudonym Lynn Lawrence) *The Familiar Touch,* Berkley (New York, NY), 1982.

(Under pseudonym Lynn Lawrence) *Deep in the Heart,* Berkley (New York, NY), 1983.

Writing for Young Adults, Writer's Digest Books (Cincinnati, OH), 1998.

ADAPTATIONS: A Line in the Sand has been adapted as a movie for Home Box Office (HBO).

SIDELIGHTS: Sherry Garland has combined her interest in many cultures and her love of storytelling into a successful career as an author of books for young readers. With several picture books to her credit, Garland has also authored novels for both beginning readers and teens, including *Shadow of the Dragon, Indio,* and *A Line in the Sand.* Garland is a lifelong resident of Texas, and her love for the state's history and wildlife informs her work. She has also traveled widely and has come to know people of other cultures and backgrounds, so many of her books are set in foreign countries, especially Vietnam. Whatever their setting, her novels and stories offer meditations on such universal themes as loneliness, searching for identity, and love of nature.

Born in Texas's Rio Grande Valley into a large family, Garland grew up the youngest child of tenant farmers. Shy and often residing in isolated locations, she grew up telling herself stories and observing the many animals on the farm and in the fields. She began writing in secret but was encouraged by a high school teacher who praised her efforts and challenged her to enter contests. After graduating from college with a degree in French, Garland worked a series of jobs and had almost given up on writing until a dream inspired her to write a novel. She published two adult romance novels before turning to work for younger readers and publishing her first juvenile book, *Vietnam: Rebuilding a Nation,* in 1990.

A number of Garland's books are about Vietnam because she has many friends and acquaintances from that nation. By happenstance, some Vietnamese refugees moved into her neighborhood in Houston after the Vietnam War had ended, and she helped them to assimilate. In return they introduced her to their culture and their stories. An editor at a 1990 writer's conference mentioned to Garland she was looking for Asian folk tales, and Garland's response was to create *Why Ducks Sleep on One Leg.* A light-hearted story, the book contains a great deal of insight into Vietnamese traditions. Vietnamese culture also figures in the plot of her 1998 picture book *My Father's Boat,* which focuses on Vietnamese-American shrimpers working along the Gulf Coast. Dubbed a "thoughtful and loving family story" by *School Library Journal* contributor Carol Schene, *My Father's Boat* features a boy and his father working aboard their boat. The father tells tales of fishing in the South China Sea and vows that the two will one day experience that together. Garland "welds telling details of the sea, sky, and fishing life into a powerful narrative," according to a *Publishers Weekly* reviewer, while Schene praised a prose style that "flows effortlessly."

In addition to *My Father's Boat,* other works by Garland concerning Vietnamese themes include *Song of the Buffalo Boy, The Lotus Seed, Shadow of the Dragon,* and *Children of the Dragon: Selected Tales from Vietnam.* In *Song of the Buffalo Boy,* the Amerasian protagonist runs away from an arranged marriage but finds herself ostracized in Saigon because her father was an American serviceman. The heroine of *The Lotus Seed* is an elderly immigrant who carries with her a lotus seed she took from the emperor's garden in Vietnam. She plants the lotus seed in America and grows new seeds for her grandchildren. The stories collected in *Children of the Dragon* reveal the common concerns of Vietnamese and American children, from discovering the "why" in animal behavior to earning the rewards of frugality and hard work. In *School Library Journal,* Margaret A. Chang wrote that readers would enjoy *Children of the Dragon* for its "smooth writing and appealing format." Carolyn Phelan in *Booklist* called the collection a "beautiful volume."

Garland's books set in America often reveal her love of animals both wild and tame. She once told *CA* that one of her earliest projects was based upon her love for horses. "One day I met a . . . mounted policeman and his horse at a city park," she said. "After hearing him explain how special these horses are and how they are trained to tolerate crowds and loud noises, and after learning that at one time teenagers did volunteer work at the stables, I knew I had the ingredients for a unique story." Garland's *Best Horse on the Force,* published in 1991, proved to be one of her most popular books and generated a great deal of fan mail.

Garland continued to draw on her personal experiences in *The Silent Storm,* published in 1993. Recalling 1983, the year Hurricane Alicia hit Houston, she was inspired to write a story showing the fury of a hurricane. "I just *had* to name the character Alyssa, in honor of that storm," Garland told *CA.* The author combined the storm with a stable of sturdy ponies and a heroine unable to speak due to the trauma of witnessing her parents killed at sea, and created a complex, challenging novel. From her extensive research in preparation for writing *The Silent Storm,* Garland learned a great deal about hurricanes, the life of shrimp harvesters, and the history of Galveston Island, a region prone to hurricane damage.

Other books combining Garland's interest in history, her curiosity, and her insight into human nature include *Indio,* a young adult novel about Southwestern Indians and Spanish conquistadors, and her books for the popular "Dear America" series, *A Line in the Sand: The Alamo Diary of Lucinda Lawrence* and *Valley of the Moon: The Diary of Rosalia de Milagros.* Featuring a thirteen-year-old protagonist who witnesses the events leading up to the Battle of the Alamo in 1836, *A Line in the Sand* was hailed by *School Library Journal* critic Phyllis Graves as "carefully researched and historically accurate." The critic added that Garland's attention to detail adds "interest and give[s] a clear picture of the many hardships and simple joys of early Texas farm life." In *Valley of the Moon,* hardworking Rosalia writes secretly of her never-ending chores and the changes coming to California with the arrival of new Anglo settlers. *Booklist* correspondent Jean Franklin noted that Rosalia's love for her rural home "infuses her story with a strong sense of place."

After twenty-two years of living in or near Houston, Garland has relocated to a smaller town in central Texas that reminds her of her childhood home. Having once won a contest with an essay that began: "I've never seen the Alamo," she is now the author of three books on the siege of the Alamo, including the popular picture book *Voices of the Alamo.* To quote GraceAnne A. DeCandido in *Booklist,* Garland's works on the Alamo "will make vivid for readers this period of American history."

BIOGRAPHICAL AND CRITICAL SOURCES:

PERIODICALS

Booklist, April 1, 1992, p. 1438; November 15, 1993, p. 621; June 1, 1997, p. 1675; March 1, 1999, GraceAnne A. DeCandido, review of *A Line in the Sand: The Alamo Diary of Lucinda Lawrence,* p. 1213; April 1, 2001, Jean Franklin, review of *Valley of the Moon: The Diary of Rosalia de Milagros,* p. 1482; July, 2001, Carolyn Phelan, review of *Children of the Dragon: Selected Tales from Vietnam,* p. 2010.

Bulletin of the Center for Children's Books, July, 1992, p. 294; April, 1995, p. 274; September, 1998, p. 13; October 15, 2001, Shelle Rosenfeld, review of *In the Shadow of the Alamo,* p. 389.

Horn Book, fall, 1993, p. 298; fall, 1998, p. 292; November-December, 2001, Betty Carter, review of *In the Shadow of the Alamo,* p. 747.

Kirkus Reviews, March 1, 1990, p. 341; March 15, 1992, p. 393; May 15, 1998, p. 737.

Publishers Weekly, February 17, 1992, p. 64; June 1, 1998, review of *My Father's Boat,* p. 48; August 27, 2001, review of *Children of the Dragon,* p. 85.

School Library Journal, July, 1993, p. 60; December, 1995, p. 104; June, 1997, p. 117; July, 1998, Carol Schene, review of *My Father's Boat,* p. 74; January, 1999, Phyllis Graves, review of *A Line in the Sand,* p. 127; June, 2000, Ruth Semrau, review of *Voices of the Alamo,* p. 164; April, 2001, Carolyn Janssen, review of *Valley of the Moon,* p. 140; October, 2001, Margaret A. Chang, review of *Children of the Dragon,* p. 139; December, 2001, Lana Miles, review of *In the Shadow of the Alamo,* p. 133.

Voice of Youth Advocates, October, 1992, p. 223; December, 1993, p. 290; December, 1995, p. 300; August, 1997, p. 183.

ONLINE

Sherry Garland Home Page, http://www.sherrygarland.com/ (October 13, 2003).

GODKIN, Celia (Marilyn) 1948-

PERSONAL: Born April 15, 1948, in London, England; daughter of Geoffrey Maxwell (a pharmacist) and Olive Mary (a teacher; maiden name, Oakey) Godkin; married Brude Dodds, 1981 (divorced, 1984); partner of Olney John Hawkins. *Ethnicity:* "English." *Education:* University of London, B.Sc. (with honors; zoology), 1969; Ontario College of Art, A.O.C.A., 1983; University of Toronto, M.Sc. (zoology), 1983. *Hobbies and other interests:* Gardening, painting, cycling, reading, classical music.

ADDRESSES: Home—680 Queen's Quay W, Unit 411, Toronto, Ontario M5V 2Y9, Canada. *Office*—Division of Biomedical Communications, University of Toronto, Medical Sciences Bldg., 1 King's College Circle, Toronto, Ontario M5S 1A8, Canada. *E-mail*—celia.godkin@utoronto.ca.

CAREER: Worked as biologist and teacher, 1969-76; University of Toronto, Toronto, Ontario, Canada, instructor in natural science illustration, 1981-82, assistant professor of biomedical communications (formerly "art as applied to medicine"), 1987—, department program supervisor, 1988-89, instructor for school of continuing studies, 1988—; Wilfrid Laurier University, Waterloo, Ontario, Canada, presented weekend workshops in biological illustration, 1983-85. Arts and crafts instructor, Riverdale Community Action Centre, 1973-78; instructor, Network for Learning, 1985, and Royal Ontario Museum, 1985-90. Reptile Breeding Foundation, herpetologist, 1974-76; Glenora Fisheries Station, Ontario Ministry of Natural Resources, fisheries biologist, summers, 1976-81; Ministry of the Environment, biological consultant, 1985-86. Illustrator, Assiniboine Park Zoo, 1983. *Exhibitions:* Godkin's work has appeared at Gallery 76, Slusser Gallery, Royal Ontario Museum, Taiwan Museum, Bancroft Art Gallery, Gallery 503, York University, Bologna Fiere, Toose Art Gallery, Arcadia Art Gallery, and Civic Garden Centre.

MEMBER: Canadian Society of Children's Authors, Illustrators, and Performers, Writer's Union of Canada.

AWARDS, HONORS: Information Book Award, Children's Literature Roundtables of Canada, 1990, for *Wolf Island;* Honour Book, Children's Literature Roundtables of Canada, 1995, for *Ladybug Garden.*

Celia Godkin

WRITINGS:

SELF-ILLUSTRATED; FOR CHILDREN

Wolf Island, Fitzhenry & Whiteside (Markham, Ontario, Canada), 1989, Scientific American Books for Young Readers (New York, NY), 1993.

Ladybug Garden, Fitzhenry & Whiteside (Markham, Ontario, Canada), 1995, published as *What about Ladybugs?,* Sierra Club Books (San Francisco, CA), 1995.

Sea Otter Inlet, Fitzhenry & Whiteside (Markham, Ontario, Canada), 1997.

Flying Lessons, Fitzhenry & Whiteside (Markham, Ontario, Canada), 1999.

When the Giant Stirred: Legend of a Volcanic Island, Fitzhenry & Whiteside (Markham, Ontario, Canada), 2002.

ILLUSTRATOR

Clive Roots, *Endangered Species: Canada's Disappearing Wildlife,* Fitzhenry & Whiteside (Markham, Ontario, Canada), 1987.

Shirley E. Woods, *Black Nell: The Adventures of a Coyote,* Douglas & McIntyre (Toronto, Ontario, Canada), 1998.

Shirley E. Woods, *Kit: The Adventures of a Raccoon,* Douglas & McIntyre (Toronto, Ontario, Canada), 1999.

Shirley E. Woods, *Jack: The Story of a Beaver,* Fitzhenry & Whiteside (Markham, Ontario, Canada), 2002.

Shirley E. Woods, *Amber: The Story of a Fox,* Fitzhenry & Whiteside (Markham, Ontario, Canada), 2004.

Illustrator of high school textbooks. Contributor of articles and illustrations to scientific journals, including *Bulletin of Marine Science, Canadian Journal of Fisheries and Aquatic Science, Environmental Biology of Fishes,* and *Guild of Natural Science Illustrators Newsletter.*

WORK IN PROGRESS: Illustrating *Tooga: The Story of a Polar Bear,* written by Shirley E. Woods.

SIDELIGHTS: Celia Godkin spent her childhood in Brazil, her adolescence in England, and her adulthood in Canada. An illustration job preparing signs for the Winnipeg Zoo led to her first book, a collaboration with zoo director Clive Roots on *Endangered Species: Canada's Disappearing Wildlife.* Godkin eventually went on to write and illustrate her own stories, which feature fact-filled plots and strong ecological themes. While some of these stories are considered more successful than others, Godkin's illustrations are almost universally admired for their evocative coloring and true-to-life details.

Godkin's first solo effort, *Wolf Island,* tells the story of the impact on an island ecosystem when its wolves are accidentally taken away to the mainland. The promise of a return to balance appears when a natural ice bridge allow the wolves to return to the island. Although Godkin's illustrations were praised by most reviewers, "the ecological message is heavy-handed," wrote Stephanie Loer in *Horn Book Guide.* Writing in *Science Books and Films,* Eugene A. Oshima remarked that Godkin "does provide an excellent opportunity for the introduction" of a number of complex biological ideas that parents and teachers can easily build upon.

Ladybug Garden, published in the United States as *What about Ladybugs?,* is an ecological morality tale about a farmer who sprays his garden with pesticide to rid himself of the bugs he does not want, and as a consequence also rids himself of the insects his garden needs to thrive. When a neighbor helps him solve the puzzle of why his garden is failing, the farmer returns some ladybugs to his garden, bringing it back to balance with nature. "The text is simple and brief and is laced with just the right amount of biological information to teach children without losing their interest," wrote Patricia Hickman in *Quill & Quire.* "Narrative and illustrations effectively demonstrate how each creature and plant plays a vital role," remarked Diane Nunn in a *School Library Journal* review of *What about Ladybugs?* While *Books in Canada* reviewer Rhea Tregebov objected to the strongly moral flavor of Godkin's story, complaining, "I don't know whether this is particularly good ecology; it certainly isn't good literature," *Emergency Librarian* reviewer Shirley Lewis cited *Ladybug Garden* on a list of "Best Canadiana," calling it "a marvelous picture book."

For her next book, *Sea Otter Inlet,* Godkin tells the story of how hunters destroy the otter population of a remote inlet and change its ecology. Once the otters are gone, the sea urchin population explodes, no longer being fed upon by the otters. Consequently, the kelp bed the urchins feed upon soon becomes destroyed by the overpopulated urchins. This leaves the creatures that hide in the kelp bed vulnerable to their predators, and a domino effect of destruction is wrought. When a pair of sea otters returns to the inlet, however, to feed upon the abundant sea urchins, the inlet begins to return to its natural state. "This nonfiction book leaves readers surprisingly moved, if not teary-eyed, at the end," remarked Paul Kropp in *Quill & Quire.* Godkin's illustrations were also the subject of lavish praise. "The charmingly drawn otters pull readers in, but the other residents of the kelp bed have their own appeal as well," claimed Arwen Marshall in *School Library Journal.* In this book, as in some of her others, Godkin's storytelling seems equal to her artistic abilities, according to reviewers. *Canadian Book Review Annual* reviewer Steve Pitt concluded: "Godkin's elegant prose and lovely pictures tell her story as a lyrical yet scientific equation."

Godkin ventured into the realm of early readers with her story *Flying Lessons,* which tells the tale of a family of robins as the youngsters hatch out of their eggs and then learn how to fly. The author creates suspense in her illustrations as the youngest bird, reluctant to leave the nest, is compelled to fly when a predatory cat climbs up the tree to his nest. "The story is simple, suspenseful, and even educational," wrote Terri L. Lyons in *Canadian Book Review Annual,* though she found the language a bit complex for the target audience.

Animals are not the main focus of *When the Giant Stirred: Legend of a Volcanic Island,* which represents a departure for Godkin. Here she tells the story of the gentle people who inhabit an island overshadowed by a rumbling volcano that finally forces them to leave their homes when it erupts, destroying all the life on the island. At the book's closing, the author offers a view of the island as, over the years, life begins to return to the lava-scarred terrain. "The text is clear, as well as poetic, and describes the original beauty of the island in perfect evocative detail," wrote Isobel Lang in *Resource Links.* Others noted the author's lushly-colored illustrations, which some considered reminiscent of Paul Gauguin's famous paintings of Tahiti. The resulting book is "a lyrical yet dramatic portrait of nature's cycle," according to a contributor to *Publishers Weekly.*

Godkin has also illustrated several informational stories about animals, written by Shirley Woods, including *Jack: The Story of a Beaver, Kit: The Adventures of a Raccoon,* and *Black Nell: The Adventures of a Coyote.*

Godkin once recalled, "Writing has always been for me a means of communicating an idea, and I think of myself as an educator or as an illustrator rather than a writer. Most important ideas are fundamentally simple, though in many cases their ramifications are not. For this reason, I like to present the idea in its simplest form and suggest some of the ramifications, without laboring over them, so that the reader is encouraged to think through the implications themselves. One advantage of being a Jill-of-all-trades is that there is complete agreement between the scientist, writer, designer, and artist, since they are all housed in the same person. As a result, my text can be purposely spare because I know any embellishment required will be picked up by the illustrations."

BIOGRAPHICAL AND CRITICAL SOURCES:

BOOKS

Science Explorations 10, Wiley (Toronto, Ontario, Canada), 1987.

The Storymakers: Illustrating Children's Books, Canadian Children's Book Centre/Pembroke Publishers (Markham, Ontario, Canada), 1999.

PERIODICALS

Appraisal, autumn, 1995, review of *What about Ladybugs?,* p. 20.

Booklist, November 1, 2002, GraceAnne A. DeCandido, review of *When the Giant Stirred: Legend of a Volcanic Island,* p. 507; January 1, 2003, John Peters, review of *Jack: The Story of a Beaver,* p. 894.

Books in Canada, May, 1995, Rhea Tregebov, review of *Ladybug Garden,* p. 50.

Canadian Book Review Annual, 1997, Steve Pitt, review of *Sea Otter Inlet,* pp. 569-570; 1999, Terri L. Lyons, review of *Flying Lessons,* p. 495.

Emergency Librarian, March, 1991, Shirley Lewis, review of *Wolf Island,* p. 22; March, 1996, Shirley Lewis, review of *Ladybug Garden,* p. 24.

Horn Book Guide, spring, 1994, Stephanie Loer, review of *Wolf Island,* p. 34.

Kirkus Reviews, April 1, 1995, review of *What about Ladybugs?,* p. 467; September 15, 2002, review of *When the Giant Stirred,* p. 1390.

Nature Canada, summer, 1988, Bob Waldon, review of *Endangered Species: Canada's Disappearing Wildlife,* p. 49.

Publishers Weekly, October 21, 2002, review of *When the Giant Stirred,* p. 76.

Quill & Quire, October, 1993, Scott Anderson, review of *Wolf Island,* p. 19; May, 1995, Pamela Hickman, review of *Ladybug Garden,* p. 50; February, 1998, Paul Kropp, "Kids' Nonfiction Has Come a Long Way," review of *Sea Otter Inlet,* p. 44.

Resource Links, December, 2002, Isobel Lang, review of *When the Giant Stirred,* p. 5; February, 2003, Stephanie Olson, review of *Jack: The Story of a Beaver,* p. 21.

School Library Journal, June, 1995, Diane Nunn, review of *What about Ladybugs?,* p. 100; January, 1999, Arwen Marshall, review of *Sea Otter Inlet,* p. 115; December, 2002, Harriet Fargnoli, review of *When the Giant Stirred,* p. 96.

Science Books and Films, March, 1994, Eugene A. Oshima, review of *Wolf Island,* p. 48.

Teacher Librarian, November, 1998, Jessica Higgs, review of *Sea Otter Inlet,* p. 52.

Toronto Star, December 9, 1989.

GOGOL, Sara 1948-

PERSONAL: Born June 4, 1948, in Chicago, IL; daughter of Sam (a teacher) and Rose (a teacher; maiden name, Edelstein) Gogol. *Education:* University of Illinois, B.A., 1971; Portland State University, M.A. *Politics:* "Left-leaning democrat." *Religion:* Jewish.

ADDRESSES: *Home*—Portland, OR. *Office*—c/o Author Mail, Lerner Publications Co., 241 1st Ave. N, Minneapolis, MN 55401. *E-mail*—sgogol@pcc.edu.

CAREER: Portland Community College, Portland, OR, instructor in English. Formerly taught English as second language.

AWARDS, HONORS: First prize in nonfiction, Kay Snow Writing Contest, 1991, for "A Bridge across the River."

WRITINGS:

Vatsana's Lucky New Year, Lerner (Minneapolis, MN), 1992.
The Message Writer, Royal Fireworks Press (Unionville, NY), 1996.
A Mien Family, Lerner Publications (Minneapolis, MN), 1996.
Playing in a New League: The Women of the American Basketball League's First Season, Masters Press (Indianapolis, IN), 1998.
Katy Steding: Pro-Basketball Pioneer, Lerner Publications (Minneapolis, MN), 1998.
Hard Fought Victories: Women Coaches Making a Difference, Wish Publishing (Indianapolis, IN), 2002.

SIDELIGHTS: Sara Gogol told *CA*: "I've been writing about fifteen years—stories, articles, story-like essays, novels for children. I'm 'hooked' on writing, also on reading. I read mysteries, nonfiction, biographies, assorted novels, many books for children, etc.

"Other interests include hiking, kayaking, dog training, and gardening. My two dogs, a border terrier and a golden retriever, enjoy outings to the parks with me. We've all adapted to the frequent rain in Oregon.

"I'm a strong opponent of any form of censorship, and I support strong rights protection for *everyone.* I like to see books available that deal with the diversity of human experience both within the country and worldwide. I'm pleased with the current interest in multicultural children's books."

BIOGRAPHICAL AND CRITICAL SOURCES:

PERIODICALS

Booklist, February 15, 2002, David Pitt, review of *Hard Fought Victories: Women Coaches Making a Difference,* p. 983.
Library Journal, March 15, 2002, Kathy Ruffle, review of *Hard Fought Victories,* p. 87.
Publishers Weekly, December 14, 1992, review of *Vatsana's Lucky New Year,* p. 57.
School Library Journal, February, 1993, Diane S. Marton, review of *Vatsana's Lucky New Year,* p. 93; January, 1997, Linda Greengrass, review of *A Mien Family,* p. 125; December, 1998, Bard Lawlor, review of *Katy Steding: Pro Basketball Pioneer,* p. 136.*

* * *

GORDON, Mike 1948-

PERSONAL: Born March 16, 1948, in Manchester, England; son of Frederick (an aircraft fitter) and Gladys (present surname, Jones) Gordon; divorced; former wife's name Maria (a writer); children: Carl, Lucy, Kimberley, Jay. *Education:* Attended Rochdale College of Art, Lancashire, England.

ADDRESSES: *Office*—P.O. Box 91818, Santa Barbara, CA 93190-1818. *E-mail*—mike@gordonillustration.com.

CAREER: Illustrator and cartoonist, 1983—; greeting card designer; creator of promotional cartoons, including designs for Post-It Notes, 1989. Work represented in exhibitions, including Showcase of the Federation of European Cartoonists Organisations.

MEMBER: Cartoonists Club of Great Britain, British Cartoonists Association, American National Cartoonists Society.

Mike Gordon

AWARDS, HONORS: Named Berol Cartoonist of the Year, 1988; runner-up, International Cartoonist Public Prize, Italy's "Trento Fra Realto e Follia," 1989; German Silver Quill Award nomination, 1991; Best Illustrator Award nomination, American National Cartoonists Society, 1995.

WRITINGS:

FOR CHILDREN; AND ILLUSTRATOR

(With Maria Gordon) *Haunted House,* MacDonald (London, England), 1989, Simon & Schuster (New York, NY), 1990.

(With Maria Gordon) *Kids Corner Literacy Stories,* Sundance, 2000.

ILLUSTRATOR; "ANIMAL TALES" SERIES

Rod Hunt, *Hippo Learns His Name,* Century Hutchinson (London, England), 1986.

Rod Hunt, *Mole Wins a Prize,* Century Hutchinson (London, England), 1986.

Rod Hunt, *Piglet Goes to the Rescue,* Century Hutchinson (London, England), 1986.

Rod Hunt, *Worm Plans a Great Escape,* Century Hutchinson (London, England), 1986.

ILLUSTRATOR; "PLAY WITH ME" SERIES

Gerald Hawksley, *Hello, I'm Mouse: Play with Me,* Century Hutchinson (London, England), 1987.

Gerald Hawksley, *Hello, I'm Bear: Play with Me,* Century Hutchinson (London, England), 1987.

Gerald Hawksley, *Hello, I'm Rabbit: Play with Me,* Century Hutchinson (London, England), 1987.

Gerald Hawksley, *Hello, I'm Frog: Play with Me,* Century Hutchinson (London, England), 1987.

ILLUSTRATOR; "SHARP EYE STARTER" SERIES

Martin Waddell, *All about Me,* Ginn (Aylesbury, England), 1989.

Martin Waddell, *Super School,* Ginn (Aylesbury, England), 1989.

Martin Waddell, *Super Me,* Ginn (Aylesbury, England), 1989.

Martin Waddell, *Your Monster's Feelings,* Ginn (Aylesbury, England), 1989.

(With Sheila Ratcliffe) Chris Buckton, *Zoo Do,* Ginn (Aylesbury, England), 1989.

ILLUSTRATOR; "MINI BOO PRESCHOOL PUZZLERS" SERIES

Richard Powell, *Farm Friends,* Victoria House (Portland, OR), 1990.

Richard Powell, *Forest Friends,* Victoria House (Portland, OR), 1990.

Richard Powell, *Zoo Friends,* Victoria House (Portland, OR), 1990.

Illustrator of one other title in the series.

ILLUSTRATOR; "I'M ALIVE" SERIES

Mandy Suhr, *How I Breathe,* Wayland (Hove, England), 1991, Carolrhoda (Minneapolis, MN), 1992.

Mandy Suhr, *I Can Move,* Wayland (Hove, England), 1991, Carolrhoda (Minneapolis, MN), 1992.

I Am Growing, Wayland (Hove, England), 1991, Carolrhoda (Minneapolis, MN), 1992.

When I Eat, Wayland (Hove, England), 1991, Carolrhoda (Minneapolis, MN), 1992.

ILLUSTRATOR; "FAVOURITE FOODS" SERIES

Brian Moses, *Milkshake,* Wayland (Hove, England), 1992.
Brian Moses, *Chocolate,* Wayland (Hove, England), 1992.
Brian Moses, *Ice Cream,* Wayland (Hove, England), 1992.
Brian Moses, *Chips,* Wayland (Hove, England), 1992.
Brian Moses, *Pizza,* Wayland (Hove, England), 1992.
Brian Moses, *Cake,* Wayland (Hove, England), 1993.

ILLUSTRATOR; "MY PET" SERIES

Nigel Taylor and John Yates, *Pony and Horse,* Wayland (Hove, England), 1992.
Nigel Taylor and John Yates, *Guinea Pig,* Wayland (Hove, England), 1992.
Nigel Taylor and John Yates, *Fish,* Wayland (Hove, England), 1992.
Nigel Taylor and John Yates, *My Pocket Pets,* Wayland (Hove, England), 1992.
Nigel Taylor and John Yates, *Dog,* Wayland (Hove, England), 1992.
Nigel Taylor and John Yates, *Cat,* Wayland (Hove, England), 1992.
Nigel Taylor and John Yates, *Rabbit,* Wayland (Hove, England), 1992.
Nigel Taylor and John Yates, *Hamster,* Wayland (Hove, England), 1992.
Nigel Taylor and John Yates, *Mini Pets,* Wayland (Hove, England), 1992.

ILLUSTRATOR; "YOUR EMOTIONS" SERIES

Brian Moses, *I Feel Angry,* Wayland (Hove, England), 1993.
Brian Moses, *I Feel Frightened,* Wayland (Hove, England), 1993.
Brian Moses, *I Feel Jealous,* Wayland (Hove, England), 1993.
Brian Moses, *I Feel Sad,* Wayland (Hove, England), 1993.

ILLUSTRATOR; "YOUR SENSES" SERIES

Mandy Suhr, *I Can Taste,* Wayland (Hove, England), 1993.
Mandy Suhr, *I Can Hear,* Wayland (Hove, England), 1993, published as *Hearing,* Lerner Publications (Minneapolis, MN), 1994.
Mandy Suhr, *Sight,* Lerner Publications (Minneapolis, MN), 1994.
Mandy Suhr, *Smell,* Lerner Publications (Minneapolis, MN), 1994.
Mandy Suhr, *Touch,* Lerner Publications (Minneapolis, MN), 1994.
Mandy Suhr, *Taste,* Lerner Publications (Minneapolis, MN), 1994.

ILLUSTRATOR; "SIMPLE SCIENCE" SERIES; BY MARIA GORDON, EXCEPT WHERE INDICATED

Sound, Wayland (Hove, England), 1994.
Heat, Wayland (Hove, England), 1994, published as *Fun with Heat,* Thomson Learning (New York, NY), 1995.
Light, Wayland (Hove, England), 1994, published as *Fun with Light,* Thomson Learning (New York, NY), 1995.
Color, Wayland (Hove, England), 1994, published as *Fun with Color,* Thomson Learning (New York, NY), 1995.
Float and Sink, Wayland (Hove, England), 1994, Thomson Learning (New York, NY), 1995.
Air, Wayland (Hove, England), 1994.
Caroline Rush, *Wheels and Cogs,* Wayland (Hove, England), 1994, Steck-Vaughn (Austin, TX), 1997.
Day and Night, Wayland (Hove, England), 1994, Thomson Learning (New York, NY), 1995.
Push and Pull, Wayland (Hove, England), 1994, Thomson Learning (New York, NY), 1995.
Electricity and Magnetism, Wayland (Hove, England), 1994, Thomson Learning (New York, NY), 1996.
Rocks and Soil, Wayland (Hove, England), 1994, Thomson Learning (New York, NY), 1996.
Skeletons and Movement, Wayland (Hove, England), 1994, Thomson Learning (New York, NY), 1996.
Caroline Rush, *Levers,* Wayland (Hove, England), 1994, Steck-Vaughn (Austin, TX), 1996.
Materials, Wayland (Hove, England), 1994, published as *Fun with Materials,* Thomson Learning (New York, NY), 1996.
Caroline Rush, *Pulleys,* Steck-Vaughn (Austin, TX), 1997.
Caroline Rush, *Slopes,* Steck-Vaughn (Austin, TX), 1997.

ILLUSTRATOR; "YOUR FEELINGS" SERIES

Brian Moses, *I Feel Bored,* Wayland (Hove, England), 1996, published as *I'm Bored,* 1997.

Brian Moses, *I'm Lonely,* Wayland (Hove, England), 1997.

Brian Moses, *It's Not Fair,* Wayland (Hove, England), 1997.

Brian Moses, *I'm Worried,* Wayland (Hove, England), 1997.

ILLUSTRATOR; "VALUES" SERIES

Brian Moses, *Manners,* Wayland (Hove, England), 1996.

Brian Moses, *"It Wasn't Me": Learning about Honesty,* Wayland (Hove, England), 1996.

Brian Moses, *"Excuse Me": Learning about Politeness,* Wayland (Hove, England), 1997.

Brian Moses, *"I'll Do It": Learning about Responsibility,* Wayland (Hove, England), 1997.

Brian Moses, *"I Don't Care!": Learning about Respect,* Wayland (Hove, England), 1997.

"LEARNING TOGETHER" SERIES

Let's Write, Letts Educational, 1997.

Let's Read, Letts Educational, 1997.

Let's Count, Letts Educational, 1997.

ILLUSTRATOR; FOR CHILDREN

Andrew Pennycock, *The Indoor Games Book,* Faber (London, England), 1973, revised edition published as *The Puffin Book of Indoor Games,* Puffin (London, England), 1985.

Adrian Rumble, editor, *Sit on the Roof and Holler* (poems), Bell & Hyman (London, England), 1984.

Shari Lewis, *Abracadabra,* Puffin (London, England), 1984.

Lift and Look Books, four volumes, Colourmasters, 1984.

Marlow and Davies, *Cooking,* Purnell, 1985.

Cooking Pack, Purnell, 1985.

Robotman and the Stolen Ring, Ravette, 1986.

A. J. Wood, *Sunny Stories,* four volumes, Templar, 1987.

Thick and Thin, Ginn (London, England), 1987.

William Shepherd, *Buttons,* Ginn (London, England), 1987.

William Shepherd, *Colours,* Ginn (London, England), 1987.

Boy Scouts Cook Book, Peter Campbell, 1987.

Jumble of Jungly Jokes, Arrow (Canton, MA), 1987.

Wendy Body and Pat Edwards, *Animal Antics,* Longman (London, England), 1988.

The Adventures of Henry Hound, Macdonald (London, England), 1988.

Vera Southgate, *The Magic Porridge Pot: Based on a Traditional Folk Tale,* Ladybird (Loughborough, England), 1989.

Charlie Fann, *The Supermarket,* Ginn (London, England), 1989.

Colin Gumbrell, *Puzzlers A to Z,* Puffin (London, England), 1989.

Eddie McGee, *The Outdoors Handbook,* Beaver Books, 1989.

Ian Souter, *Twenty Pounds and All That Nonsense,* Ginn (London, England), 1989.

David Smith and Sue Cassin, *Fascinating Facts about Animals: A Flap Book Full of Surprises,* Collins (London, England), 1989.

David Smith and Sue Cassin, *Fascinating Facts about Your Body: A Flap Book Full of Surprises,* Collins (London, England), 1989.

David Smith and Sue Cassin, *Fascinating Facts about Dinosaurs: A Flap Book Full of Surprises,* Collins (London, England), 1989.

David Hawcock and Maria Gordon, *Griffin,* Simon & Schuster (New York, NY), 1990.

David Hawcock and Maria Gordon, *Dragon,* Simon & Schuster (New York, NY), 1990.

The Ladybird Christmas Book, Ladybird (Loughborough, England), 1990.

Lesley Newson, *Down the Drain,* Simon & Schuster (New York, NY), 1990.

Lesley Newson, *A Load of Rubbish,* Simon & Schuster (New York, NY), 1990.

John Grant, *Storytime for Seven-Year-Olds,* Ladybird (Loughborough, England), 1990.

John Drinkwater, *Exploring Maths,* Ladybird (Loughborough, England), 1990.

John Drinkwater, *Fun with Maths,* Ladybird (Loughborough, England), 1990.

Brough Girling, *The Green and Scaly Book,* Puffin (London, England), 1991.

Anita Ganeri, *The Green Activity Book,* Ladybird (Loughborough, England), 1991, published as *The Ladybird Green Book,* 1992.

Neil Morris and Ting Morris, *Funtime for Seven-Year-Olds,* Ladybird (Loughborough, England), 1991.

Lesley Newson, *Stopping the Rot,* Simon & Schuster (New York, NY), 1991.

David Hawcock and Maria Gordon, *Space Tank,* Simon & Schuster (New York, NY), 1991.

David Hawcock and Maria Gordon, *Robot,* Simon & Schuster (New York, NY), 1991.

Moira Harvey, *Spooky Dice Games,* Teeney Books, 1992.

Moira Harvey, *Dinosaur Dice Games,* Teeney Books, 1992.

Jana Novotny Hunter, *Hector the Spectre,* Puffin (London, England), 1992.

Gymnastics, Wayland (Hove, England), 1992.

Maria Gordon, *The Fancy Dress Party Book,* Hamlyn (London, England), 1993.

Jana Novotny Hunter, *Hector's Hoax,* Puffin (London, England), 1994.

Pancake Day, Ginn (London, England), 1994.

Animal Adventures, Joshua Morris, 1994.

Star Science, Ginn (London, England), 1995.

Fascinating Facts, two volumes, Teeney Books, 1995.

Music Machine, Joshua Morris, 1995.

Funny Animal Songs, Joshua Morris, 1995.

Gillian Cross, *Posh Watson,* Walker (London, England), 1995.

Pat Thompson, *Superpooch,* HarperCollins (New York, NY), 1995.

Pat Thompson, *Superpooch and the Missing Sausages,* HarperCollins (New York, NY), 1996.

The Gross Joke Book, Daniel Weiss (New York, NY), 1996.

Free the Whales, Walker Books (New York, NY), 1996.

Debbie Dadey, *Bobby and the Great Green Booger,* Willowisp (St. Petersburg, FL), 1997.

Debbie Dadey, *Bobby and the Big, Blue Bulldog,* Willowisp (St. Petersburg, FL), 1998.

Susan Hood, *Let's Jump In!,* Reader's Digest Children's Books (New York, NY), 1999.

Brian Moses and others, *Kids Corner Kid-to-Kid Books,* Sundance, 1998-2000.

Harriet S. Mosatche and Karen Unger, *Too Old for This, Too Young for That!: Your Survival Guide for the Middle-School Years,* Free Spirit, 2000.

Amy Imbody, *Snug As a Bug?,* Zonderkidz (Grand Rapids, MI), 2001.

Jen Green, *Where's My Present?,* Wayland (Hove, England), 2001.

Cynthia Copeland, *What Are You Waiting For?,* Millbrook (Brookfield, CT), 2002.

Carmela LaVigna Coyle, *Do Princesses Wear Hiking Boots?,* Rising Moon (Flagstaff, AZ), 2003.

Margaret McNamara, *The Counting Race,* Aladdin Paperbacks (New York, NY), 2003.

Margaret McNamara, *One Hundred Days (Plus One),* Aladdin Paperbacks (New York, NY), 2003.

Margaret McNamara, *The Pumpkin Patch,* Aladdin Paperbacks (New York, NY), 2003.

Margaret McNamara, *Too Many Valentines,* Aladdin Paperbacks (New York, NY), 2003.

Thera S. Callahan, *All Wrapped Up,* Children's Press (New York, NY), 2003.

Margaret McNamara, *The Playground Problem,* Aladdin Paperbacks (New York, NY), 2004.

Diane Namm, *My Best Friend,* Children's Press (New York, NY), 2004.

Illustrator of "Lift and Learn Series," published by Silver Burdett (Morristown, NJ), including the titles *Colors, Counting, Opposites,* and *Shapes.* Illustrator of numerous textbooks.

FOR ADULTS

(Illustrator) Kim Durdant-Hollamby and Martyn Forrester, *Breaking Wind,* Arrow Books (Canton, MA), 1984.

(Illustrator) Cas Clarke, *Grub on a Grant,* Columbus (London, England), 1985.

The Duffer's Guide to Coarse Fishing, Columbus (London, England), 1985.

The Duffer's Guide to Snooker, Columbus (London, England) 1986.

The Duffer's Guide to D.I.Y., Columbus (London, England) 1986.

The Duffer's Guide to Horse Racing, Columbus (London, England) 1986.

(Illustrator) Kevin Goldstein-Jackson, *Jokes for Telling,* 1986.

(Illustrator) Kevin Goldstein-Jackson, *The Right Joke for the Right Occasion,* 1986.

The Duffer's Guide to Squash, Columbus (London, England) 1987.

(Illustrator) Cas Clarke, *Protein Power,* Columbus (London, England) 1987.

(Illustrator) Maryon Stewart, *How to Beat PMT through Diet,* Ebury Press, 1987.

William Cooke, *Howlers,* F. Muller (London, England), 1988.

The Duffer's Guide to Cycling, Columbus (London, England) 1988.

(Illustrator) James Oram, *Hogan,* Columbus (London, England) 1988.

The Duffer's Guide to Boxing, Columbus (London, England) 1989.

(Illustrator) David Smith, *Phallic Thimbles: The Illustrated Guide to Sexual Trivia,* Firebird (Poole, England), 1989.

(Illustrator) Maureen Miller, *Double Income, No Kids . . . Yet,* Grapevine, 1989.

(Illustrator) David Smith, *Strange but True Facts about Sex: The Illustrated Book of Sexual Trivia,* Firebird (Poole, England), 1993.

(Illustrator) Steve Barlow and Steve Skidmore, *Stone Me!,* Ginn (London, England), 1993.

(Illustrator) *Food in a Flash,* Headline (London, England, 1994.

(Illustrator) *Family Feasts,* Headline (London, England), 1994.

(Illustrator) Russell Ash, editor, *Tall Stories,* Aurum (London, England), 1994.

(Illustrator) *Vegetarian Grub,* Headline (London, England), 1995.

(Illustrator) *Soft Toy,* Russ Berrie, 1996.

(Illustrator) *Nursery Nosh,* Headline (London, England), 1997.

ILLUSTRATOR; "LITTLE INSTRUCTION BOOK" SERIES

Baby's, HarperCollins (New York, NY), 1995.
Office Life, HarperCollins (New York, NY), 1995.
Driver's, HarperCollins (New York, NY), 1995.
Scotsman's, HarperCollins (New York, NY), 1995.
Gardeners, HarperCollins (New York, NY), 1995.
Fishermen's, HarperCollins (New York, NY), 1995.
Cat-a-logue, HarperCollins (New York, NY), 1995.
Golfers, HarperCollins (New York, NY), 1995.

Illustrator language teaching books for adults. Also illustrator of "Fat Cat and House Mouse," a cartoon strip, *Patches,* 1986-87; and "Barry the Beetle," a cartoon strip, *Crown,* 1989-91. Contributor of illustrations to magazines, including *Junior Education, Flying Pages, Buster and Jackpot, Riding, National Geographic, Humpty Dumpty,* and *Puffin News.*

WORK IN PROGRESS: Four books for "Feelings" series, Wayland; four books for "Health" series, Wayland; illustrating "My Dog Can't Read," a four-volume series by Maria Gordon, Wayland; *Bobby and the Stinky Brown Shoes,* for Pages Publishing.

SIDELIGHTS: Mike Gordon is a prolific illustrator by any standard, turning out pictures for children's and adult books as well as greeting cards and online animation. One key to his success is the help he receives from computer software programs for coloration. Gordon and his son Carl have collaborated on fine-tuning these programs to give Gordon's drawings their vibrant color faster. The father-son collaboration has been done in Gordon's home in California as well as through the Internet when Carl Gordon returns to his own studio in England. Examples of Gordon's illustrations and animation can be seen on his web site.

Gordon once commented: "I was born in 1948 in Manchester, England. In 1963 I attended Rochdale College of Art, but with sound advice from my parents, I soon settled into a 'real' job as an engineer. It wasn't until 1983 that I started my freelance career as an illustrator. In that year I created over a hundred greeting cards. Now, just over a decade later, much to my surprise, I have completed over two hundred children's and adults' books and many hundreds of humorous cards.

"In 1993 I escaped the gray climes of England and moved to California, where I work harder than ever, providing for my four hungry kids and complaining about my poor, pale body which never sees the light of day. I am faced with many deadlines which keep me on my toes, producing works such as *Hector the Spectre, Superpooch, Strange but True Facts about Sex,* and *Funny Animal Songs!* Thoroughly confused, doing Christmas cards in July and Valentines in December, I live California life to the full, with help from my therapist."

BIOGRAPHICAL AND CRITICAL SOURCES:

PERIODICALS

Christian Parenting Today, May, 2001, Jennifer Mangan, review of *Snug As a Bug?,* p. 60.

School Library Journal, March, 1993; December, 1994; September, 2000, Leslie Ann Lacika, review of *Too Old for This, Too Young for That!: Your Survival Guide for the Middle-School Years,* p. 253.

Sunday Telegraph (London, England), April 8, 2001, Dinah Hall, "So Where Is the Bunny?"

ONLINE

Gordon Illustration, http://www.gordonillustration.com/ (January 29, 2003), Mike Gordon's Web site; animation, greeting cards, and biographies of Gordon and his son.*

* * *

GRAFF, Gerald (Edward) 1937-

PERSONAL: Born June 28, 1937, in Chicago, IL; son of David R. and Mollie (Newman) Graff. *Education:* University of Chicago, A.B., 1959; Stanford University, Ph.D., 1963. *Politics:* "Left-radical." *Religion:* Jewish.

ADDRESSES: *Office*—Department of English, University of Illinois at Chicago, 410 University Hall, 601 South Morgan St., Chicago, IL 60607-7104. *E-mail*—ggraff@uic.edu.

CAREER: University of New Mexico, Albuquerque, assistant professor of English, 1963-66; Northwestern University, Evanston, IL, assistant professor, 1966-70, associate professor, 1970-78, professor of English, 1978-91, chairman of department, 1977-82; University of Illinois at Chicago, George M. Pullman Distinguished Service Professor of English and Education, 1991—. Formerly director of Northwestern University Press.

MEMBER: Modern Language Association, Teachers for Democratic Culture (cofounder).

AWARDS, HONORS: American Book Award, Before Columbus Foundation, and Frederic W. Ness Award, Association of American Colleges and Universities, both 1993, both for *Beyond the Culture Wars: How Teaching the Conflicts Can Revitalize American Education*; fellow, Harvard University Center for Literary and Cultural Studies; awards from Illinois Arts Council, National Endowment for the Humanities, and John Simon Guggenheim Foundation.

WRITINGS:

Poetic Statement and Critical Dogma, Northwestern University Press (Evanston, IL), 1970.

(Editor, with Barbara Heldt Monter) W. B. Scott, *Chicago Letter and Other Parodies,* Ardis (Ann Arbor, MI), 1978.

Literature against Itself: Literary Ideas in Modern Society, University of Chicago Press (Chicago, IL), 1979, reprinted, I. R. Dee (Chicago, IL), 1995.

(Editor, with Reginald Gibbons) *Criticism in the University,* Northwestern University Press (Evanston, IL), 1985.

(Editor, with Barbara Heldt Monter) Scott, *Parodies, Etc. and So Forth,* Northwestern University Press (Evanston, IL), 1985.

Professing Literature: An Institutional History, University of Chicago Press (Chicago, IL), 1987.

(Editor, with Michael Warner) *The Origins of Literary Studies in America: A Documentary Anthology,* Routledge (London, England), 1988, Routledge (New York, NY), 1989.

Beyond the Culture Wars: How Teaching the Conflicts Can Revitalize American Education, Norton (New York, NY), 1992.

(Coeditor) *Adventures of Huckleberry Finn: A Case Study in Critical Controversy,* Bedford/St. Martin's Press (New York, NY), 1995.

(Coeditor) *The Tempest: A Case Study in Critical Controversy,* Bedford/St. Martin's Press (New York, NY), 2000.

Clueless in Academe: How Schooling Obscures the Life of the Mind, Yale University Press (New Haven, CT), 2003.

Contributor to literary journals. Member of editorial boards, *TriQuarterly, Salmagundi, Works and Days,* and *American Literary History.*

SIDELIGHTS: Gerald Graff started his career as a literary critic in the early 1970s, and since then has gone on to write several influential books about theories ranging from modern poetics and postmodern discourses to curricular reform in education. His 1987 book *Professing Literature: An Institutional History* marked his progression from being a pure theorist to an educational activist, and he has continued his calls for reform in the influential 1992 publication *Beyond the Culture Wars: How Teaching the Conflicts Can Revitalize American Education.* In this book Graff recommends solutions to many cultural, political, and ideological debates going on within the world of the humanities in American universities. Underlying his commentaries is the strong belief that disagreement is only dangerous when it is masked, and that teaching conflicting ideas can actually develop students' ability to comprehend various points of view. "The impressive variety and consistent focus of Graff's work have earned him one of the broadest audiences in literary studies and education and have made him one of the most important voices in American criticism over the last quarter of the twentieth century," claimed Luchen Li in a *Dictionary of Literary Biography* essay.

Graff's first major work, *Poetic Statement and Critical Dogma,* was based on his doctoral dissertation. In it, he discusses poetic assertion and meaning as defined by theorists including Cleanth Brooks, Northrop Frye, and I. A. Richards. He points out that the theories espoused by these writers do not provide "an adequate account of the concrete facts of poetic structure and meaning," according to Li. "Graff argues that propositional assertion and expository argument are important semantic and structural principles of poetry. He suggests that the reader transcend the either/or distinction between propositional theories of poetry and those theories that view poetry as a dramatic reenactment of the process of thought."

In *Literature against Itself: Literary Ideas in Modern Society,* Graff argues "that recent critical thought has been undermining belief in the power of language to connect us with the world," Harry Levin summarized in the *New York Times Book Review.* In his analysis of late twentieth-century literary criticism, Graff "offers a body of commentary the shrewdness and cogency of which are constantly arresting," noted *Virginia Quarterly Review* contributor N. A. Scott. While Graff's thesis—that current critics have trivialized the literature they examine—is occasionally "encumbered" by ideology, Scott concluded that *Literature against Itself* "does, nevertheless, what it principally sets out to do, conduct a wonderfully trenchant and illuminating inquiry."

Similarly, with *Professing Literature: An Institutional History,* "Graff attempts to undermine the present organization of the English department by a historical treatment of the institutionalized teaching of literature," observed Stacey D'Erasmo in the *Village Voice.* The author, whom *Times Literary Supplement* contributor Chris Baldick called "among the most perceptive observers of modern literary criticism," suggests that "institutional pressures and inertias . . . have generated the complex pattern of hostilities now entrenched between professors of literature," thus fragmenting literary scholarship into fields such as women's literature and Afro-American writing. *Professing Literature* "is a solidly researched and convincingly argued work," the critic continued, and while Graff "ventures too infrequently outside the campus, his fascinating account of the literary academy in the United States from the 1840s to the present day avoids inconsequential gossip and keeps its most pressing arguments continuously before the reader's attention." *Professing Literature* contains some "lively academic and cultural arguments," Kermit Vanderbilt concluded in *American Literature.* Graff "has given us a stimulating critique of our institutional literary research, criticism, theory, and pedagogy."

Beyond the Culture Wars is the summation of Graff's influential "Teach the Conflicts" philosophy, and the points he raises in this book also formed the basis for many speaking appearances, seminars, and talk-show appearances. He outlines the ways in which specialized literary theories deprive students of a cohesive experience of literature read during college. He states that in an increasingly diverse society, consensus becomes less possible all the time, making it increasingly important to understanding how to disagree. In practical terms, Graff offers specific techniques for drawing students into the dispute. *Change* reviewer Rosemary Park called *Beyond the Culture Wars* "a practical therapy for the struggling student whose intellectual interests can be awakened, the author believes, by a more direct experience of the actual, fundamental, and rich divergences" that characterize an increasingly multicultural student body.

Li concluded that although Graff's focus has shifted from literary criticism to educational pedagogy over the course of his career, his "notion of teaching the conflicts has always been coherent in its focus on how such an educational strategy may build a better learning community by involving a critique of those academic discourses from the perspective of students."

BIOGRAPHICAL AND CRITICAL SOURCES:

BOOKS

Cain, William E., editor, *Teaching the Conflicts: Gerald Graff, Curricular Reform, and the Culture Wars,* Garland (New York, NY), 1994.

Dictionary of Literary Biography, Volume 246: *Twentieth-Century American Cultural Theorists,* Gale (Detroit, MI), 2001.

PERIODICALS

American Literature, March, 1988.
Booklist, October 1, 1992, Mary Carroll, review of *Beyond the Culture Wars: How Teaching the Conflicts Can Revitalize American Education,* p. 219.
Change, November-December, 1992, Rosemary Park, review of *Beyond the Culture Wars,* p. 66.
Choice, June, 1993, p. 1680; November, 2003, J. F. Biter, review of *Clueless in Academe: How Schooling Obscures the Life of the Mind,* p. 594.
Christian Science Monitor, January 11, 1993, Laurel Shaper Walters, review of *Beyond the Culture Wars,* p. 13.
Contemporary Literature, spring, 1994, Michael Berube, review of *Beyond the Culture Wars,* p. 212.
Education Digest, December, 1992, Dudley Barlow, review of *Beyond the Culture Wars,* p. 77.
Library Journal, November 1, 1992, Shirley L. Hopkinson, review of *Beyond the Culture Wars,* p. 98.
Nation, February 8, 1993, Paul Levine, review of *Beyond the Culture Wars,* p. 13.
National Forum, winter, 1994, James Andrew Clark, review of *Beyond the Culture Wars,* p. 44.
New York Review of Books, February 11, 1993, Alan Ryan, review of *Beyond the Culture Wars,* p. 13.
New York Times, December 21, 1992, Christopher Lehmann-Haupt, review of *Beyond the Culture Wars,* p. B2.
New York Times Book Review, August 5, 1979; November 22, 1992, Nina Auerbach, review of *Beyond the Culture Wars,* p. 11.
Publishers Weekly, September 7, 1992, review of *Beyond the Culture Wars,* p. 82.
Reason, June, 1993, Cathy Young, review of *Beyond the Culture Wars,* p. 58.
Renaissance Quarterly, summer, 2000, review of *The Tempest: A Case Study in Critical Controversy,* p. 620.
Times Literary Supplement, November 6-12, 1987.
Village Voice, May 3, 1988.
Virginia Quarterly Review, autumn, 1979.
Wall Street Journal, May 27, 2003, Steven Lagerfield, "Shakespeare and the Spice Girls," p. D5.
Washington Post, April 4, 1993, Sara Mosle, review of *Beyond the Culture Wars,* p. ER23.*

* * *

GURTOV, Melvin 1941-

PERSONAL: Born September 2, 1941, in Brooklyn, NY; son of Bernard (an IRS revenue agent) and Sally (a homemaker; maiden name, Gruber) Gurtov; married Leigh Anne Fansler (a spiritual teacher), May 29, 1982; children: Ellene, Marci, Alia. *Education:* Columbia University, A.B., 1963, M.I.A. and certificate in international affairs and East Asian studies, 1965; attended Stanford University Inter-University Center, Taipei, Taiwan, 1965-66; University of California—Los Angeles, Ph.D., 1971.

ADDRESSES: *Home*—7335 Southeast 32nd Ave., Portland, OR 97202. *Office*—Division of Political Science, Hatfield School of Government, Portland State University, P.O. Box 751, Portland, OR 97207; fax: 503-725-8444. *E-mail*—mgurtov@aol.com.

CAREER: Rand Corp., Santa Monica, CA, research associate in social science, 1966-71; University of California—Riverside, Riverside, CA, associate professor, 1971-76, professor of political science, 1976-86, department chair, 1973-74; Portland State University, Portland, OR, professor of political science, 1986—, director of International Studies Program, 1986-92, director of Asia Programs, 1992-96. University of California—Davis, visiting professor, 1975; Waseda University, visiting scholar at Graduate School of Asia-Pacific Studies and Center for International Education, 2001; visiting lecturer at other institutions, including University of California—Santa Barbara, 1969, California Institute of Technology, 1971-72, and University of California—Berkeley, 1975. Portland-Suzhou Sister City Committee, member of board of directors, 1988-95; Oregon Peace Institute, member of board of directors, 1988-93; Northwest Regional China Council, board member, 1987-95, president, 1993-95; public speaker on international issues.

MEMBER: Association for Asian Studies, International Studies Association.

AWARDS, HONORS: Haynes Foundation fellow, 1972; Oregon Committee for the Humanities, grant, 1989, scholarship, 1990-93; senior Fulbright scholar in Korea, 1994; 50th Anniversary Research Award, Korea Fulbright Foundation, 1995-96; award from Asia Research Fund, 1999; grants from U.S. Department of State, Hyundai Motors of America, World Forestry Center, Japan Foundation, and Korean Foundation.

WRITINGS:

The First Vietnam Crisis: Chinese Communist Strategy and United States Involvement, 1953-1954, Columbia University Press (New York, NY), 1967.

Problems and Prospects of United States Policy in Southeast Asia, Rand Corp. (Santa Monica, CA), 1969.

Southeast Asia Tomorrow: Problems and Prospects for U.S. Policy, Johns Hopkins University Press (Baltimore, MD), 1970.

China and Southeast Asia—The Politics of Survival: A Study of Foreign Policy Interaction, D. C. Heath (Lexington, MA), 1971.

The United States against the Third World: Antinationalism and Intervention, Praeger (New York, NY), 1974.

(Editor, with Sudershan Chawla and Alain-Gerard Marsot, and contributor) *Southeast Asia under the New Balance of Power,* Praeger, 1974.

(Editor, with Jae Kyu Park, and contributor) *Southeast Asia in Transition: Regional and International Politics,* Institute for Far Eastern Studies (Seoul, South Korea), 1977.

Making Changes: The Politics of Self Liberation, Harvest Moon Books (Oakland, CA), 1979.

(With Byong-Moo Hwang) *China under Threat: The Politics of Strategy and Diplomacy,* Johns Hopkins University Press (Baltimore, MD), 1980.

(With Ray Maghroori) *The Roots of Failure: United States Policy in the Third World,* Greenwood Press (Westport, CT), 1984.

(With Dariush Haghighat) *Global Politics in the Human Interest,* Lynne Rienner (Boulder, CO), 1988, 4th edition, 1999.

(Editor and contributor) *The Transformation of Socialism: Perestroika and Reform in the Soviet Union and China,* Westview Press (Boulder, CO), 1990.

(Editor, with Devorah Lieberman, and contributor) *Revealing the World: An Interdisciplinary Reader for International Studies,* Kendall/Hunt (Dubuque, IA), 1992.

(With Byong-Moo Hwang) *China's Security: The New Roles of the Military,* Lynne Rienner (Boulder, CO), 1998.

Pacific Asia? Prospects for Security and Cooperation in East Asia, Rowman & Littlefield, 2001.

Contributor to books, including *Vietnam and American Foreign Policy,* edited by John Boettiger, D. C. Heath (Lexington, MA), 1968; *The Cultural Revolution in China,* edited by T. Robinson, University of California Press (Berkeley, CA), 1971; *Indochina in Conflict: A Political Assessment,* edited by J. J. Zasloff and A. E. Goodman, D. C. Heath (Lexington, MA), 1972; *The Changing Order in Northeast Asia and the Korean Peninsula,* edited by Manwoo Lee and Richard Mansbach, Institute for Far Eastern Studies, 1993; and *Korea's Amazing Century: From Kings to Satellites,* Korean Fulbright Foundation/Korean-American Educational Commission, 1997. Contributor of articles and reviews to periodicals in the United States and abroad, including *Pacific Affairs, China Quarterly, World Development, Journal of East Asian Affairs, Current History, Contemporary China, Nation, Studies in Comparative Communism, Southeast Asia Record,* and *Oregonian.* Editor in chief, *Asian Perspective,* 1994—.

Gurtov's books have been published in Chinese, Japanese, Korean, and Spanish.

SIDELIGHTS: Political scientist, academic, and author Melvin Gurtov worked for a few years as a research associate for the Rand Corporation beginning in the mid-1960s. He prepared several books and monographs for Rand before leaving the company in 1971 to take a professorial position at the University of California at Riverside. One of the last projects Gurtov completed under the auspices of Rand, *China and Southeast Asia, the Politics of Survival: A Study of Foreign Policy Interaction,* would become controversial after its author supported Pentagon Papers leaker Daniel Ellsberg's denunciation of U.S. policy in regard to the Vietnam War. As Henry Raymont phrased it in the *New York Times,* Gurtov and Ellsberg both asserted that U.S. government policy in Southeast Asia was "designed to deceive the American public." Following Gurtov's decision to second Ellsberg's criticism, Rand requested his resignation as a consultant and asked that Rand's name be dropped from copies of *China and Southeast Asia.* Long respected as an authority on matters concerning politics in Southeast Asia, Gurtov has since penned, edited, or collaborated on several other titles.

Gurtov's first major book-length work, however, was *The First Vietnam Crisis: Chinese Communist Strategy and United States Involvement, 1953-1954.* In this book, he discusses the roots of United States involvement in the Vietnam War. He tells of French mistakes in dealing with its former colonial territories in Southeast Asia, and of a treaty signed by the United States during the administration of President Dwight D. Eisenhower that promised the French air support for its military operations against the Vietminh—the forerunner of the Vietcong. The French requested American help in its battle for the Vietnamese city of Dienbienphu, but at that time the federal government feared that air support would lead to troop commitment—a fear that became reality during the following decade, after the French pulled out of Vietnam in defeat. Harvey G. Simmons, reviewing *The First Vietnam Crisis* in *Canadian Forum,* praised the work as "one of the most important books published on the Vietnam problem in the past few years." The critic also asserted that its "fascination . . . lies in the author's recounting of the forces brought to bear on Eisenhower convincing him that . . . the projected American air strike against Vietminh positions around Dienbienphu . . . was unwise."

In 1974 Gurtov published *The United States against the Third World: Antinationalism and Intervention.* This volume puts forth the idea that American foreign policy with regard to Third World nations operates on the assumption that international stability is more beneficial to the United States than small, national revolutions—even if those revolutions lead to greater freedom for Third World citizens, rather than to communism. Gurtov asserts that even if the guiding ideology of a Third World nation's revolution is communism or socialism, that nation should still be allowed self-determination without interference from the United States. Applauding *The United States against the Third World* as "a forceful critique," a *Choice* reviewer concluded that the book "should be of interest to all college and public libraries." A *Library Journal* critic labeled it a "well-documented account of U.S. adventures abroad from the Eisenhower through the Nixon years."

Gurtov teamed with one of his graduate students, Byong-Moo Hwang, to write *China under Threat: The Politics of Strategy and Diplomacy.* In this book Gurtov and Hwang argue that the policies of communist China, rather than being aimed toward world domination as long believed by many within the United States government, have been formulated and implemented with the sole purpose of protecting the ongoing communist revolution within that country's own borders. The authors illustrate their point through discussion of China's role in the Korean war during the early 1950s, the Taiwan Strait crisis of 1958, a 1962 border conflict with India, the Vietnam War, and border conflicts with the then-Soviet Union in 1969.

Critical opinion of *China under Threat* varied. M. L. Baron suggested in the *Political Science Quarterly* that its authors were too easy on the Chinese government. Baron cited what he described as the way in which "during the 1950s and 1960s, analysts of Chinese foreign policy stressed Peking's aggressive, warlike ways," and judged that "Gurtov and Hwang thereby inadvertently reverse the studies of the 1950s." "Instead of the Chinese being the permanent aggressors," Baron continued, "they are now to be viewed as the permanently aggrieved. No doubt the truth lies somewhere in between." A *Choice* reviewer expressed the reservation that Gurtov and Hwang exaggerated the role of Chinese leader Mao Zedong in that nation's policy, while D. D. Buck in the *Library Journal* hailed the collaborative effort as "a challenging new interpretation," and concluded that the authors "present their case ably and argue it well."

For *The Roots of Failure: United States Policy in the Third World,* Gurtov teamed up with Ray Maghroori. Though, like many of Gurtov's other volumes, *The Roots of Failure* discusses Vietnam, it also examines United States foreign policy with regard to the nations of Iran and Nicaragua. With Maghroori, Gurtov asserts that the policy of the United States toward all three of these countries has been similar—and similarly flawed. Though both authors outline a possible substitute foreign policy, which they label a "global-humanist alternative," they express the belief that neither their proposal nor any other radically different plan is likely to be adopted by the United States government. "For alternative courses of action even to be put on the decision-makers' agenda and debated as 'live options' requires radical alterations of their ideology, values, and attitudes," warn Gurtov and Maghroori. "It also requires major changes in the way foreign-policy bureaucrats perceive and act upon problems." Keeping this declaration in mind, Paul W. Van Der Veur in the *Annals of the American Academy of Political and Social Science* questioned the efficacy of *The Roots of Failure,* but nevertheless commended it as "an interesting and stimulating work." B. W. Jentleson in *Choice* praised the volume as well, calling it "one of the more forcefully argued yet still empirically based critiques" within his realm of experience.

Gurtov once told *CA:* "As my sense of injustice and abuses of power sharpened in the 1960s and 1970s, my teaching and research interests in international affairs changed. I teach and write with the hope of promoting social justice, peaceful resolution of conflict, and protection of the environment; and my perspective is that of a global citizen rather than a United States citizen wedded to the 'national interest.' Respect for the great diversity of human life and compassion for those less fortunate are values I learned in childhood and try to take seriously in and outside my work."

BIOGRAPHICAL AND CRITICAL SOURCES:

BOOKS

Gurtov, Melvin, and Ray Maghroori, *The Roots of Failure: United States Policy in the Third World,* Greenwood Press (Westport, CT), 1984.

PERIODICALS

Annals of the American Academy of Political and Social Science, March, 1986, Paul W. Van Der Veur, review of *The Roots of Failure,* p. 158.

Canadian Forum, February, 1968, Harvey G. Simmons, review of *The First Vietnam Crisis: Chinese Communist Strategy and United States Involvement, 1953-1954.*

Choice, March, 1975, review of *The United States against the Third World: Antinationalism and Intervention,* p. 142; May, 1981, review of *China under Threat: The Politics of Strategy and Diplomacy,* p. 1325; May, 1985, B. W. Jentleson, review of *The Roots of Failure,* p. 1405.

Library Journal, October 1, 1974, review of *The United States against the Third World,* p. 2464; January 15, 1981, D. D. Buck, review of *China under Threat,* p. 134.

New York Times, September 24, 1971, article by Henry Raymont.

New York Times Book Review, June 4, 1967, p. 3.

Political Science Quarterly, fall, 1981, M. L. Baron, review of *China under Threat,* p. 517.

Times Literary Supplement, May 25, 1967, p. 431.

* * *

GUSTAFSON, Susan E(lizabeth) 1959-

PERSONAL: Born May 21, 1959, in Albany, GA; married Gary P. Gustafson, May, 1980. *Education:* Attended University of Minnesota—Duluth, 1977-80; University of Minnesota—Twin Cities, B.A. (summa cum laude), 1981; attended University of California—Davis, 1981-82; Stanford University, M.A., 1982, Ph. D., 1987; attended University of Bonn, 1983-84. *Hobbies and other interests:* Bicycling, movies.

ADDRESSES: *Office*—Department of Modern Languages and Cultures, La Himore 402, University of Rochester, Rochester, NY 14627. *E-mail*—sgfn@db1.cc.rochester.edu.

CAREER: University of Cincinnati, Cincinnati, OH, Charles Taft postdoctoral fellow, 1986-87; University of Rochester, Rochester, NY, assistant professor, 1987-94, associate professor of German and comparative literature and women's studies, 1994—. Susan B. Anthony Research Institute, associate, 1988—; lecturer at colleges and universities, including Cornell University, University of Pennsylvania, University of Minnesota—Twin Cities, University of Texas—Austin, and University of Delaware.

MEMBER: International Comparative Literature Association, Goethe Society of North America, Modern Language Association of America, American Comparative Literature Association, German Studies Association, Women in German, Lessing Society, ECS.

AWARDS, HONORS: Fulbright fellow, 1983-84; Alexander von Humboldt research fellow in Bonn, Germany, 1991-92; shared Florence Howe Award for Feminist Scholarship, 1992; grant from National Endowment for the Humanities, 1995.

WRITINGS:

(With Jonathan B. Conant) *Beginning German,* Volumes I-II, University of Minnesota Press (Minneapolis, MN), 1982.

Absent Mothers and Orphaned Fathers: Narcissism and Abjection in Lessing's Aesthetic and Dramatic Production, Wayne State University Press (Detroit, MI), 1995.

Men Desiring Men: The Poetry of Same-sex Identity and Desire in German Classicism, Wayne State University Press (Detroit, MI), 2002.

Contributor to books, including *Images, Bodies, and Texts in the Eighteenth Century,* edited by Dorothea von Muecke and Veronica Kelly, Stanford University Press (Stanford, CA), 1994; and *Outing Goethe and His Age,* edited by Alice Kuzniar, Stanford University Press (Stanford, CA), 1996. Contributor of articles and reviews to periodicals in the United States and Germany, including *Poetics Today, PMLA, Seminar: Journal of Germanic Studies,* and *Eighteenth-Century Studies.*

WORK IN PROGRESS: Research on contemporary best-sellers by women authors in Germany.

* * *

GUTERSON, David 1956-

PERSONAL: Born May 4, 1956, in Seattle, WA; son of Murray Bernard (a criminal defense attorney) and Shirley (Zak) Guterson; married Robin Ann Radwick, January 1, 1979; children: Taylor, Travis, Henry, Angelica. *Education:* University of Washington, B.A., 1978, M.A., 1982. *Hobbies and other interests:* Hiking, hunting.

ADDRESSES: *Agent*—Georges Borchardt, Inc., 136 East 57th St., New York, NY 10020.

CAREER: Writer. High school English teacher in Bainbridge Island, WA, 1984-94.

AWARDS, HONORS: PEN/Faulkner Award for Fiction, Folger Shakespeare Library, Barnes & Noble Discovery Award, and Pacific Northwest Booksellers Award, all 1995, all for *Snow Falling on Cedars.*

David Guterson

WRITINGS:

The Country ahead of Us, the Country Behind (stories), Harper (New York, NY), 1989.

Family Matters: Why Homeschooling Makes Sense, Harcourt Brace (New York, NY), 1992.

Snow Falling on Cedars, Harcourt Brace (San Diego, CA), 1994.

East of the Mountains, Harcourt Brace (San Diego, CA), 1999.

Our Lady of the Forest, Knopf (New York, NY), 2003.

Contributor to periodicals, including *Harper's, Sports Illustrated,* and *Gray's Sporting Journal.*

Snow Falling on Cedars has been translated into twenty-one languages.

ADAPTATIONS: *Snow Falling on Cedars* was adapted as a motion picture starring Max Von Sydow and Ethan Hawke, Universal, 2000, and as an audiobook by

Random House Audiobooks, 1995. Selections from *The Country ahead of Us, the Country Behind* were recorded by Random House Audiobooks (New York, NY), 1996. *East of the Mountains* was adapted as an audiobook, BDD Audio, 1999.

SIDELIGHTS: Although David Guterson made his literary debut in 1989 with the collection of short stories *The Country ahead of Us, the Country Behind,* it was not until his first novel, *Snow Falling on Cedars,* was published five years later that the world took notice of the clean-living English teacher from the Pacific Northwest. The debut novel, which recounts the trial of a Japanese man for the alleged killing of a Caucasian fisherman in 1954, became a phenomenal best-seller and winner of the prestigious PEN/Faulkner Award. It sold more than two million copies in the United States alone, was translated into twenty-one languages, and resulted in a motion picture of the same title, starring Ethan Hawke and Max Von Sydow. Guterson's more recent novels, *East of the Mountains* and *Our Lady of the Forest,* have further demonstrated the depth of his talent and his ongoing concern for addressing universal and timeless moral issues in his writing.

The son of a criminal defense attorney and a homemaker, Guterson and his two brothers and two sisters grew up on the north end of Seattle, Washington. Guterson spoke fondly of the region to Bill Donahue of *Book:* The woods nearby were like "Valhalla, the land of the giants. We'd go into them, my friends and I, and get completely lost. Or we'd eat blackberries and wander around with stains on our faces." He and his friends were also active in the Boy Scouts, though their popular name for the den was "Plastered Plums," which reflected their long hair and countercultural bent. Although as a child Guterson liked to read, he did not consider becoming a writer until his junior year of college, after he was inspired by the teacher of a short-story writing class. There his teacher "emphasized that stories really matter, that when people read stories they are transfigured by them. That spoke to me," the novelist told John DiConsiglio in an interview in *Literary Cavalcade.* One day Guterson "went to the library and after an hour of working on this story," he recalled to Donahue, "I thought 'This is fun.' And I knew that it was also meaningful, useful. I knew from my own life as a reader how powerful stories are—how they shape human values." During summers Guterson had worked with the Forest Service fire-fighting crew, and he at first planned to become a firefighter, but as his interest in writing grew, he decided to become an English teacher and writer because he felt the work of teaching would enrich his writing efforts.

Shortly after his wife, Robin, gave birth to the first of their four children, Guterson and his family moved to an old bungalow on Bainbridge Island in Puget Sound, which then was home to some 8,000 people, but by 2000 would boast an upscale population of 20,000. For a decade Guterson taught English at Bainbridge Island High School and wrote in the early mornings after walking his dog. Writing in an eclectically decorated study, Guterson was happy if he managed to write 250 words per day. This desire to pen *le mot juste,* he explained to Donahue, "goes back to 'In the beginning was the word.' We constitute our world using words, and the more accurate the words are, the more clarified the world is. Getting it right feels almost like a holy act."

Guterson's first published fiction is contained in *The Country ahead of Us, the Country Behind,* a collection of short stories; his first nonfiction work is *Family Matters: Why Homeschooling Makes Sense,* a profile of the homeschooling movement with a discussion of the impetus for its growth. The couple home-schooled their own four children, gradually transitioning them into the public schools. Guterson does not see homeschooling as right for everyone, but he believes that people should have the option.

He wrote his debut novel, *Snow Falling on Cedars,* over a decade, stopping midway to pen *Family Matters.* Among his inspirations for the novel were a photographic exhibit depicting the one-hundred-year history of the Japanese-American community of Bainbridge Island, including their deportation and internment in California camps during World War II. "I was quite moved by the photo exhibit, in particular by seeing in those photos the faces of people I knew, which gave history a real face, which made history come alive, which made history real," he told Bob Edwards in a radio interview published on the National Public Radio Web site. Another was Harper Lee's classic novel *To Kill a Mockingbird,* which Guterson presented each year to his high school students. One reason Guterson's novel required ten years to complete was his effort to maintain historical accuracy.

With much of its action taking place during the 1940s, *Snow Falling on Cedars* tells the story of Caucasian teen Ishmael's enduring love for a Japanese girl, Hatsue, on the fictional island of San Piedro in Puget Sound. The format of a later courtroom drama in which Hatsue's husband, Kabuo, is accused of murdering a Caucasian fisherman over a land dispute is the jumping off point for numerous omniscient flashbacks that tell a nuanced story of love in spite of prejudice, the internment of the Japanese, the horrors of World War II in the Pacific, and the recurrent struggle to do what is right. In the process, Ishmael comes to terms both with his losses and with his father's legacy of high moral standards.

By all accounts, Guterson's efforts paid off handsomely, bringing him fame and critical acclaim, and making him a millionaire through books sales and the sale of movie rights. Reviewers praised his characterizations, courtroom scenes, historical accuracy, and lyrical descriptions of the Pacific Northwest. *Time* reviewer Pico Iyer called the novel a "beautifully assured and full-bodied story" that is also "unusually lived in, focused and compassionate." Several critics voiced qualified praise, including Tom Deignan of the *World and I,* who wrote that while *Snow Falling on Cedars* is "often long-winded, . . . Guterson had a lush, rugged landscape and good old courtroom drama to serve as the book's sturdy spine." In the opinion of William Swanson, writing in *Mpls-St. Paul* magazine, Guterson "provides one of the most vividly realized physical settings this side of McCarthy's Tex-Mex landscapes. His development of the book's large cast is equally exhaustive, but not so effective." *Booklist* reviewer Dennis Dodge praised the novel as "compellingly suspenseful on each of its several levels."

After the success of *Snow Falling on Cedars,* Guterson felt some pressure to produce another best-selling literary novel: "When it comes time to sit down and write the next book, you're deathly afraid that you're not up to the task," he told Alden Mudge for *BookPage.* "That was certainly the case with me after *Snow Falling on Cedars.*"

By now Guterson had quit his teaching job to devote himself full-time to writing. When the once athletic writer began suffering from back trouble while still in his mid-thirties, he began to grapple with issues surrounding aging, and these thoughts led to his next work of fiction. *East of the Mountains* is an older man's tale, a mythic journey in the ancient concept of romance as quest. In it readers follow the story of retired physician and widower Ben, who, suffering from colon cancer, plans to commit suicide while on a hunting trip and make his death appear to be an accident. During his three-day journey to the semiarid steppe desert of eastern Washington State, Ben encounters challenges and meets strangers who make him reconsider both his grief and his choice to end his life. "Guterson's prose is spare and powerful," Tony Freemantle remarked of the 1999 novel in the *Houston Chronicle.*

Like *Snow Falling on Cedars, East of the Mountains* employs numerous flashbacks to add depth to the storyline. Using this technique, Guterson "manages in a few words to paint a vivid picture of the physical and moral landscape through which Ben travels and, in a series of flashbacks seamlessly woven into the narrative, of the path through life he has already navigated," explained Freemantle. Instead of snow, the main symbolism in *East of the Mountains* pertains to apples, a famous produce crop for Washington state as well as a recurring symbol in literature, including King Arthur's legend, the Judeo-Christian story of the Fall from Grace, and the golden apple of Greek mythology's Trojan War.

The setting of *East of the Mountains* is a desert-like landscape that recalls the biblical tradition of the Christian hermits. "When Guterson is at his best, the story and the landscape nearly become one," wrote *New York Times* critic Robert Sullivan. The critic went on to praise the author's "smooth and pleasing and often sensual" prose and favorably compared his combination of story and setting to that of Wallace Stegner. For his part, Guterson explained to Mudge that in formulating his novels he starts with a "love of place, which seeks expression, which wants to use me to express itself. . . . It's almost as if I'm compelled to sing these places."

While some critics found *East of the Mountains* less engaging than Guterson's debut novel, others recognized a development in the author's style. In *East of the Mountains* Guterson intentionally cultivated a leaner prose style because he believed it more in keeping with the novel's themes and subject matter. Calling Guterson a "prodigious storyteller," *Quadrant* reviewer Sarah Barnett noted: "Guterson words his pages sparsely, evoking emotions economically. He is able to weave a sort of eloquent beauty into suffering. The very humanness of loving and losing, the bittersweet sense of being parted from a soulmate, is captured on the pages of *East of the Mountains.*" Bennett concluded, "Its simplicity makes it no less rich in the writing and no less rewarding in the reading" than *Snow Falling on Cedars.*

Continuing to explore the novel format, in 2003 Guterson published *Our Lady of the Forest.* The novel focuses on Ann, a runaway teenager, who is one of four main characters in the story. When the troubled teen has a vision of the Blessed Virgin Mary while picking mushrooms in a Pacific Northwest forest, her vision sets in motion a chain of events that transforms the area around North Fork, Washington, into an unflattering portrait of modern U.S. society. According to a *Kirkus Reviews* critic, *Our Lady of the Forest* is a "witty fable of faith, greed, purity, and hope" told in a manner that is "sharp and incisive without a trace of cynicism or credulity." A *Publishers Weekly* reviewer predicted that the "gloominess of this uncompromising novel" might put off some readers, but that Guterson's story would conversely attract others because of its "intensity." In *Time* Pico Iyer voiced appreciation for this gloom, seeing in it a return to the traditions of American fiction embodied in the works of Nathaniel Hawthorne and Ralph Waldo Emerson. *Our Lady of the Forest* presents "an unflinching picture of Hawthorne's descendants in the wake of [rock star] Kurt Cobain," Iyer noted. "More than that, it shows Guterson to be a serious and searching craftsman, very much in the American grain and determined to take himself further."

Guterson once told *CA:* "I write because something inner and unconscious forces me to. That is the first compulsion. The second is one of ethical and moral duty. I feel responsible to tell stories that inspire readers to consider more deeply who they are." Although his life changed in a material sense as a result of the success of *Snow Falling on Cedars,* he has taken those changes in stride. His status as a well-known author "doesn't matter. It might be entertaining for my fifteen minutes, but I'm ephemeral," he told *Book* interviewer Donahue. "What lasts I hope, are my books. Stories will always matter—stories that present human beings in crisis, deciding how to confront their struggles, how to be fully human. Stories deliver us the heroes of the common people. Without them, we wouldn't have culture. We wouldn't know who we are."

BIOGRAPHICAL AND CRITICAL SOURCES:

BOOKS

Contemporary Novelists, 7th edition, St. James Press (Detroit, MI), 2001.

PERIODICALS

Antioch Review, winter, 2000, Carolyn Maddux, review of *East of the Mountains,* p. 116.

Atlanta Journal-Constitution, April 18, 1999, Diane Roberts, review of *East of the Mountains,* p. L11; May 30, 1999, Don O'Briant, "Seeds of 'Cedars': Guterson Deals with Fallout of Success," p. K12.

Book, May, 1999, review of *East of the Mountains,* p. 77; March-April, 2000, Bill Donahue, "Living in His Landscape, the Northwesterner Looks East of the Mountains with His New Novel"; November, 2000, p. 10.

Booklist, September 1, 1992, Denise Perry Donavin, review of *Family Matters: Why Homeschooling Makes Sense,* p. 14; August, 1994, Dennis Dodge, review of *Snow Falling on Cedars,* p. 2022; January 1, 1999, review of *East of the Mountains,* p. 792; June 1, 1999, review of *East of the Mountains,* p. 1797; September 15, 2000, Karen Harris, review of *Snow Falling on Cedars* (audio version), p. 262.

Books, summer, 1999, review of *East of the Mountains,* p. 20.

Christian Science Monitor, May 6, 1999, Kendra Nordin, review of *East of the Mountains,* p. 20.

Economist (United Kingdom), June 19, 1999, review of *East of the Mountains,* p. S14.

English Journal, October, 1997, Donna C. Neumann, review of *Snow Falling on Cedars,* p. 112; March, 1999, John Manear, review of *The Country ahead of Us, the Country Behind,* pp. 118-119.

Entertainment Weekly, December 29, 1995, Dave Karger, "David Guterson," p. 55; April 23, 1999, review of *East of the Mountains,* p. 56.

Gentleman's Quarterly, May, 1999, Thomas Mallon, review of *East of the Mountains,* pp. 112-115.

Globe and Mail (Toronto, Ontario, Canada), April 24, 1999, review of *East of the Mountains,* p. E4.

Guardian (London, England), June 2, 1999, Nick Wroe, review of *East of the Mountains,* p. T16.

Houston Chronicle (Houston, TX), May 16, 1999, Tony Freemantle, review of *East of the Mountains,* p. 22.

Hungry Mind Review, winter, 1999, review of *Snow Falling on Cedars,* p. 11.

Kirkus Reviews, January 15, 1999, review of *East of the Mountains,* p. 88; July 15, 2003, review of *Our Lady of the Forest,* p. 927.

Library Journal, July, 1989, Francis Poole, review of *The Country ahead of Us, the Country Behind,* p. 109; September 1, 1992, Hilma F. Cooper, review of *Family Matters,* p. 186; August, 1994, Sheila Riley, review of *Snow Falling on Cedars,* p. 129; February 15, 1999, review of *East of the Mountains,* p. 183; September 15, 2001, review of *Snow Falling on Cedars,* p. 140; June 1, 2003, Rebecca Stuhr, review of *Our Lady of the Forest,* p. 166.

Literary Cavalcade, January, 1998, John DiConsiglio, "Mountain Main" (interview), pp. 4-5.

Los Angeles Times, May 9, 1999, Jonathan Levi, review of *East of the Mountains,* p. 2; December 12, 1999, Patrick Goldstein, "*Snow Falling on Cedars* Was No Simple Screenplay," p. E1.

Maclean's, June 21, 1999, review of *East of the Mountains,* p. 52.

Mpls-St. Paul, April, 1996, William Swanson, "When 'Snow' Turns to Gold," pp. 30-32.

New Republic, February 8, 1993, Alan Wolfe, review of *Family Matters,* pp. 25-32.

Newsweek, December 18, 1995, Malcolm Jones, Jr., "*Snow* on Top," p. 72.

New Yorker, May 17, 1999, Joyce Carol Oates, "Off the Road: A Strange Journey through the Pacific Northwest," pp. 89-91.

New York Times, April 9, 1999, Michiko Kakutani, "Distracting Detours in the Hunt for a Final Exit," p. E47; December 22, 1999, Stephen Holden, "Prejudice Lingers in the Land of Mists," p. E5.

New York Times Book Review, September 3, 1989, Lois E. Nesbitt, review of *The Country ahead of Us, the Country Behind,* p. 14; October 16, 1994, Susan Kenney, review of *Snow Falling on Cedars,* p. 12; May 9, 1999, Robert Sullivan, review of *East of the Mountains,* p. 16.

New York Times Upfront, November 15, 1999, "No Snow in Texas," p. 7.

Observer (London, England), June 6, 1999, review of *East of the Mountains,* p. 11.

People, March 13, 1995, Joanne Kaufman, review of *Snow Falling on Cedars,* p. 31; March 4, 1996, Kim Hubbard, "Out of the Woods" (interview), pp. 89-90.

Publishers Weekly, May 26, 1989, Sybil Steinberg, review of *The Country ahead of Us, the Country Behind,* pp. 54-55; July 13, 1992, review of *Family Matters,* p. 42; August 1, 1994, review of *Snow Falling on Cedars,* p. 70; January 11, 1999, review of *East of the Mountains,* p. 51; April 5, 1999, John Blades, "David Guterson: Stoic of the Pacific Northwest," pp. 215-216; May 3, 1999, review of *East of the Mountains,* p. 35; July 28, 2003, review of *Our Lady of the Forest,* p. 75.

Quadrant, December, 1999, Sarah Barnett, review of *East of the Mountains,* p. 85+.

Spectator, May 8, 1999, Katie Grant, review of *East of the Mountains,* pp. 34-35.

Time, September 26, 1994, Pico Iyer, review of *Snow Falling on Cedars,* p. 79; April 26, 1999, review of *East of the Mountains,* p. 98; November 10, 2003, Pico Iyer, review of *Our Lady of the Forest,* p. 93.

Time Canada, May 3, 1999, Pico Iyer and Andrea Sachs, review of *East of the Mountains,* p. 57.

Times Literary Supplement, June 11, 1999, Bill Brown, review of *East of the Mountains,* p. 23.

Wall Street Journal, April 23, 1999, David Byers, review of *East of the Mountains,* p. W7.

Washington Post Book World, May 2, 1999, review of *East of the Mountains,* p. 3.

Woman's Journal, June, 1999, review of *East of the Mountains,* p. 16.

World and I, September, 1999, reviews of *East of the Mountains,* p. 242, Tom Deignan, "A Farewell," p. 256.

ONLINE

BookPage, http://www.bookpage.com/ (May 10, 2003), Alden Mudge, "Guterson Offers a Moving Story of One Man's Final Pilgrimage."

National Public Radio Web site, http://www.npr.org/ (January 3, 2002), Bob Edwards, transcript of *Morning Edition* interview with Guterson.

Printed Matter, http://www.dcn.ca.us/ (November 12, 1995), Elisabeth Sherwin, "New Writer Thanks Harper Lee for Leading the Way."*

H

HAMILTON, Virginia (Esther) 1936-2002

PERSONAL: Born March 12, 1936, in Yellow Springs, OH; died of breast cancer, February 19, 2002, in Dayton, OH; daughter of Kenneth James (a musician) and Etta Belle (Perry) Hamilton; married Arnold Adoff (an anthologist and poet), March 19, 1960; children: Leigh Hamilton, Jaime Levi. *Education:* Studied at Antioch College, 1952-55, Ohio State University, 1957-58, and New School for Social Research, 1958-60.

CAREER: Novelist and author of children's books.

AWARDS, HONORS: Notable Children's Book citation, American Library Association (ALA), 1967, and Nancy Block Memorial Award, Downtown Community School Awards Committee, New York, both for *Zeely;* Edgar Allan Poe Award for best juvenile mystery, Mystery Writers of America, 1969, for *The House of Dies Drear;* Ohioana Literary Award, 1969; John Newbery Honor Book Award, 1971, for *The Planet of Junior Brown;* Lewis Carroll Shelf Award, *Boston Globe-Horn Book* Award, 1974, John Newbery Medal, and National Book Award, both 1975, and Gustav-Heinemann-Friedinspreis für kinder und Lugendbucher, 1991, all for *M. C. Higgins, the Great;* John Newbery Honor Book Award, Coretta Scott King Award, *Boston Globe-Horn Book* Award, and American Book Award nomination, all 1983, all for *Sweet Whispers, Brother Rush*; *Horn Book* Fanfare Award in fiction, 1985, for *A Little Love;* Coretta Scott King Award, *New York Times* Best Illustrated Children's Book citation, Children's Book Bulletin Other Award,

Virginia Hamilton

and *Horn Book* Honor List selection, all 1986, all for *The People Could Fly: American Black Folktales; Boston Globe-Horn Book* Award, 1988, and Coretta Scott King Award, 1989, both for *Anthony Burns: The Defeat and Triumph of a Fugitive Slave;* John Newbery Honor Book Award, 1989, for *In the Beginning: Creation Stories from around the World;* D.H.L., Bank St. College, 1990; Regina Medal for lifetime achievement, Catholic Library Association, 1990; Hans Christian Andersen Award, U.S. nominee, 1992, for body of work; Laura Ingalls Wilder Award for lifetime achievement, ALA, 1995; MacArthur Foundation grant, 1995; Coretta Scott King Award, 1996, for *Her Stories;* LL.D., Wright State University; honorary doctorate, Ohio State University, Kent State University, 1996; an annual grant for graduate students at Kent State University College of Education and School of Library Science was created in Hamilton's name, 2004.

WRITINGS:

FICTION FOR CHILDREN

Zeely, illustrated by Symeon Shimin, Macmillan (New York, NY), 1967.

The House of Dies Drear, illustrated by Eros Keith, Macmillan (New York, NY), 1968.

The Time-Ago Tales of Jahdu, Macmillan (New York, NY), 1969.

The Planet of Junior Brown, Macmillan (New York, NY), 1971.

Time-Ago Lost: More Tales of Jahdu, illustrated by Ray Prather, Macmillan (New York, NY), 1973.

M. C. Higgins, the Great, Macmillan (New York, NY), 1974, published with teacher's guide by Lou Stanek, Dell (New York, NY), 1986, published with short stories, poems, and memoirs by various writers, as *M. C. Higgins, the Great: With Connections,* Holt, Rinehart (Austin, TX), 1998.

Arilla Sun Down, Greenwillow (New York, NY), 1976.

Illusion and Reality, Library of Congress (Washington, DC), 1976.

Justice and Her Brothers (first novel in "Justice" trilogy), Greenwillow (New York, NY), 1978.

Jahdu, illustrated by Jerry Pinkney, Greenwillow (New York, NY), 1980.

Dustland (second novel in "Justice" trilogy), Greenwillow (New York, NY), 1980.

The Gathering (third novel in "Justice" trilogy), Greenwillow (New York, NY), 1981.

Sweet Whispers, Brother Rush, Philomel (New York, NY), 1982.

The Magical Adventures of Pretty Pearl, Harper (New York, NY), 1983.

Willie Bea and the Time the Martians Landed, Greenwillow (New York, NY), 1983.

A Little Love, Philomel (New York, NY), 1984.

Junius over Far, Harper (New York, NY), 1985.

The People Could Fly: American Black Folktales, illustrated by Leo and Diane Dillon, Knopf (New York, NY), 1985, published with cassette, 1987.

The Mystery of Drear House: The Conclusion of the Dies Drear Chronicle, Greenwillow (New York, NY), 1987.

A White Romance, Philomel (New York, NY), 1987.

In the Beginning: Creation Stories from around the World, Harcourt (San Diego, CA), 1988.

Anthony Burns: The Defeat and Triumph of a Fugitive Slave, Knopf (New York, NY), 1988.

Bells of Christmas, illustrated by Lambert Davis, Harcourt (San Diego, CA), 1989.

The Dark Way: Stories from the Spirit World, illustrated by Lambert Davis, Harcourt (San Diego, CA), 1990.

Cousins, Putnam (New York, NY), 1990.

The All-Jahdu Storybook, illustrated by Barry Moser, Harcourt (San Diego, CA), 1991.

Drylongso, illustrated by Jerry Pinkney, Harcourt, Brace (San Diego, CA), 1992.

Many Thousand Gone: African Americans from Slavery to Freedom, illustrated by Leo and Diane Dillon, Knopf (New York, NY), 1992.

Plain City, Blue Sky/Scholastic (New York, NY), 1993.

Her Stories: African-American Folktales, Fairy Tales, and True Tales, Scholastic (New York, NY), 1995.

Jaguarundi, Blue Sky Press (New York, NY), 1995.

When Birds Could Talk and Bats Could Sing: The Adventures of Bruh Sparrow, Sis Wren, and Their Friends, illustrated by Barry Moser, Blue Sky Press (New York, NY), 1995.

A Ring of Tricksters: Animal Tales from America, the West Indies, and Africa, Blue Sky Press (New York, NY), 1997.

Second Cousins, Scholastic (New York, NY), 1998.

Bluish: A Novel, Blue Sky Press (New York, NY), 1999.

The Girl Who Spun Gold, illustrated by Leo and Diane Dillon, Blue Sky Press (New York, NY), 2000.

Wee Winnie Witch's Skinny: An Original Scare Tale for Halloween, illustrated by Barry Moser, Blue Sky Press (New York, NY), 2001.

Time Pieces: The Book of Times, Blue Sky Press (New York, NY), 2002.

Bruh Rabbit and the Tar Baby Girl, illustrated by James Ransome, Blue Sky Press (New York, NY), 2003.

OTHER

W. E. B. Du Bois: A Biography (for children), Crowell (New York, NY), 1972.

Paul Robeson: The Life and Times of a Free Black Man (for children), Harper (New York, NY), 1974.
(Editor) W. E. B. Du Bois, *The Writings of W. E. B. Du Bois,* Crowell (New York, NY), 1975.
(Author of introduction) Martin Greenberg, editor, *The Newbery Award Reader,* Harcourt (New York, NY), 1984.

ADAPTATIONS: The House of Dies Drear was adapted for the Public Broadcasting Service series *Wonderworks* and released on videocassette, Public Media Video (Chicago, IL), 1984, and on audiocassette by Recorded Books (Frederick, MD), 1995. *The People Could Fly* was adapted for the *Reading Rainbow* television series. *M. C. Higgins, the Great* was released on audiodisc, Recorded Books (Frederick, MD), 1993. *The Planet of Junior Brown* was adapted as the film *Junior's Groove,* PIX Entertainment, 1999.

SIDELIGHTS: During a career that spanned more than three decades, Virginia Hamilton helped launch a new era in the portrayal of African Americans in children's literature, at the same time setting a new standard of quality in the genre. Not only have many of her works received awards such as the National Book Award, but her novel *M. C. Higgins, the Great* was the first work ever to win both the National Book Award and the Newbery Medal. Hamilton, winner of every major award in her field, including the 1995 Laura Ingalls Wilder Award for lifetime achievement, is widely recognized as a gifted and demanding storyteller. As Ethel L. Heins wrote in *Horn Book:* "Few writers of fiction for young people are as daring, inventive, and challenging to read—or to review—as Virginia Hamilton. Frankly making demands on her readers, she nevertheless expresses herself in a style essentially simple and concise." Her "rare ability to combine storytelling with scholarly research allowed her to rescue and retell important narratives that would otherwise have remained lost," Bonnie Verbug added in an article for *Black Issues Book Review.*

Hamilton's vision was deeply influenced by her background. Her mother's side of the family was descended from a fugitive slave, Levi Perry, who settled in the southern Ohio Miami valley town of Yellow Springs. The Perry family grew and prospered by farming the rich Ohio soil. "I grew up within the warmth of loving aunts and uncles, all reluctant farmers but great storytellers," Hamilton once recalled in a *Horn Book* article by Lee Bennett Hopkins. "I remember the tales best of all. My own father, who was an outlander from Illinois, Iowa, and points west, was the finest of the storytellers besides being an exceptional mandolinist. Mother, too, could take a slice of fiction floating around the family and polish it into a saga."

While attending Antioch College on a scholarship, Hamilton majored in writing and composed short stories. One of her instructors liked her stories enough to encourage the young student to leave college and test her skills in New York City. Hamilton was eager to experience the excitement of city life, and so in 1955 she began spending her summers in New York, working as a bookkeeper. Later, she moved to the city permanently. "I don't have a clear recollection of the day I officially left home to go to New York," she once told an interviewer. "My plan was to find a cheap apartment, a part-time job, write and have a good time. And it all came together."

An important influence on the creation of *Zeely* came after Hamilton married poet and anthologist Arnold Adoff, whom she met not long after arriving in New York City. The two newlyweds traveled to Spain and then to northern Africa. "Going to Africa had been an enduring dream of Hamilton's," according to *Dictionary of Literary Biography* contributor Jane Ball, "and the land of dark-skinned people had 'a tremendous impression' on her . . . even though her stay was brief. The impact is apparent on her first book." According to John Rowe Townsend in his *A Sounding of Storytellers: New and Revised Essays on Contemporary Writers for Children, Zeely* exemplifies the type of writing Hamilton produced throughout her career: there "is not taint of racism in her books. . . . All through her work runs an awareness of black history, and particularly of black history in America. And there is a difference in the furniture of her writing mind from that of most of her white contemporaries: dream, myth, legend and ancient story can be sensed again and again in the background of naturalistically-described present-day events."

Zeely is about a girl called Geeder who, fascinated by a tall, regal-looking woman she sees tending pigs on a farm, obsessively imagines the woman to be a Watusi queen. By the end of the tale, Zeely convinces Geeder she is nothing of the sort, "and with the aid of a parable she helps Geeder [accept herself for who she is.]

. . . She is not a queen; and perhaps there is an implication that for black Americans to look back towards supposed long-lost glories in Africa is unfruitful."

In Hamilton's "Jahdu" tales, including *The Time-Ago Tales of Jahdu, Time-Ago Lost: More Tales of Jahdu, Jahdu,* and *The All-Jahdu Storybook,* Hamilton took an approach that mimics the style of the traditional folk tale. These works tell of the fantastic adventures of Jahdu and his "encounters [with] the allegorical figures Sweetdream, Nightmare, Trouble, Chameleon, and others," wrote Marilyn F. Apseloff in the *Dictionary of Literary Biography.* "These original tales have a timeless quality about them; in addition, they reveal racial pride, as Jahdu discovers in [*The Time-Ago Tales of Jahdu*] . . . that he is happiest when he becomes a part of a black family in Harlem." Similarly, in the collections *The People Could Fly: American Black Folktales, In the Beginning: Creation Stories from around the World,* and *The Dark Way: Stories from the Spirit World,* Hamilton retells old myths and folk tales from her own black ancestry—as well as many other cultures—in an attempt to restore pride in this diverse and rich literary heritage.

One ethnic group in particular, Native Americans, influenced Hamilton's writing in books like the Edgar Award-winning *The House of Dies Drear.* "The references to Indians in her books," observed Apseloff, "are probably the result of two factors: Hamilton knew that many Shawnees lived in the Yellow Springs area originally, with Cherokees further south, and her grandmother claimed to be part American Indian." Despite this element in the story, however, *The House of Dies Drear* is a mystery novel centered on the history of the Underground Railroad, the route fugitive blacks took to escape slavery in the South before the U.S. Civil War. It "is a taut mystery, one which youngsters gulp down quickly and find hard to forget," attested Hopkins. Hamilton called *The House of Dies Drear* one of her favorite books, "I think, because it is so full of all the things I love: excitement, mystery, black history, the strong, black family. In it I tried to pay back all those wonderful relatives who gave me so much in the past."

Hamilton's *M. C. Higgins, the Great* emphasizes the importance of family. The story portrays the Higginses, a close-knit family that resides on Sarah's Mountain in southern Ohio. The mountain has special significance to the Higginses, for it has belonged to their family since M. C.'s great-grandmother Sarah, an escaped slave, settled there. The conflict in the story arises when a huge spoil heap, created by strip mining, threatens to engulf the family home. M. C. is torn between his love for his home and his concern for his family's safety, and he searches diligently for a solution that will allow him to preserve both. *M. C. Higgins, the Great* was highly praised by critics, including poet Nikki Giovanni, who wrote in the *New York Times Book Review*: "Once again Virginia Hamilton creates a world and invites us in. *M. C. Higgins, the Great* is not an adorable book, not a lived-happily-ever-after kind of story. It is warm, humane and hopeful and does what every book should do—creates characters with whom we can identify and for whom we care."

Hamilton chronicles slavery in both *Anthony Burns: The Defeat and Triumph of a Fugitive Slave* and *Many Thousand Gone: African Americans from Slavery to Freedom.* In *Anthony Burns* she relates the true story of an escaped slave who was captured and tried under the Fugitive Slave Act. The trial triggered riots and ended with Burns's return to his former owner. Hamilton based her account on court records, newspaper reports, biographies, and other primary sources. "Told in an appropriately restrained, unadorned style, incorporating verbatim the speeches of counsel for both sides, *Anthony Burns* is a work of simple, but noble, eloquence," praised Elizabeth Ward in the *Washington Post Book World.* A reviewer for *Children's Book Review Service* also found the work compelling and remarked, "Black history comes alive in this striking, gripping, personalized account."

Based on information found in nineteenth-century archives and oral histories, *Many Thousand Gone* contains biographical profiles of celebrated and obscure individuals that reveal their personal experiences with slavery. The stories included provide insight on slavery in America from the early 1600s to its abolishment in 1865 with the ratification of the Thirteenth Amendment to the Constitution. "All of these profiles drive home the sickening realities of slavery in a personal way," asserted David Haward Bain in the *New York Times Book Review,* the critic adding that "many also show how the experiences of individuals in the legal system worked in the larger struggle for freedom." Michael Dirda concluded in the *Washington Post Book World* that "as a kind of portrait gallery of the brave and resourceful, *Many Thousand Gone* deserves many thousand readers."

Throughout the 1990s Hamilton continued to pen works dealing with folklore and strong female characters. In the *New York Times Book Review* Veronica Chambers characterized Hamilton's *Her Stories: African-American Folktales, Fairy Tales, and True Tales* as "possibly the first collection of such folk literature to focus exclusively on African-American women and girls." Hamilton recasts stories dealing with animals, fairy tales, the supernatural, folkways, and true experiences that were passed down through oral history and in several African languages, as well as Spanish and English. "Hamilton's retellings of these stories strike a nice balance between dialect and accessibility, modernizing just enough to make the stories easily readable without sacrificing the flavor of the originals," credited Jennifer Howard in a *Washington Post Book World* review.

Another tale with a strong heroine is Hamilton's retelling of the European Rumplestiltskin tale as *The Girl Who Spun Gold. School Library Journal*'s Carol Ann Wilson dubbed the 2000 book "charming and visually stunning" as well as "humorous and, at times, scary," while both *Horn Book* reviewer Robert Strang and *Booklist* critic Hazel Rochman remarked on how well the tale sounds. It is told in "immediate, colloquial style, with a rhythm just right for reading aloud," Rochman noted.

In addition to the folktales focusing on human characters, Hamilton also published animal-centered tales as *Jaguarundi, When Birds Could Talk and Bats Could Sing: The Adventures of Bruh Sparrow, Sis Wren, and Their Friends,* and *A Ring of Tricksters: Animal Tales from America, the West Indies, and Africa.* She also penned several realistic novels set in contemporary times, among them *Cousins,* its sequel *Second Cousins,* and *Bluish. Cousins* tells the story of cousins Cammy and Patty Ann, who do not get along at day camp, while the sequel tells what happens when a family reunion brings two sophisticated New York cousins into the picture. *Bluish* follows the efforts of the new girl at a Manhattan magnet school, ten-year-old Dreenie, to make friends, which she does, with Natalie, who has leukemia. "Spare prose expresses each stage of the girls' friendship," commented a *Publishers Weekly* reviewer of *Bluish,* and Dreenie comes to accept Natalie—nicknamed Bluish for her pale skin and prominent veins—illness and all. A *Horn Book* reviewer found Hamilton's portrayal of the fifth graders' speech and behavior "right on target." Among those portrayed is the emotionally needy Tuli, whose characterization in the capable hands of Hamilton *Booklist*'s Hazel Rochman called "funny," "touching," and one of the highlights of the novel.

Hamilton's final novel, *Time Pieces: The Book of Times,* was completed shortly before the author succumbed to breast cancer. Published posthumously, it is semiautobiographical and weaves together her childhood experiences and the family tales that made up part of her heritage. In it discerning readers can see many of the nuggets of family history around which Hamilton built her long works; as *Booklist*'s Hazel Rochman predicted: "Her fans will also be fascinated to see the seeds of so many books here." The stories included in *Time Pieces* are set into the framework of a contemporary tale about a girl named Valena who likes to hear her family's stories; while a *Publishers Weekly* contributor called the contemporary frame tale "sketchy" when contrasted with the richness of the family stories, in *School Library Journal* Lauralyn Persson praised the humor and suspense of the tales and the "simplicity and directness of the language," which qualities, she maintained, "serve the subject matter beautifully." In *Kirkus Reviews* a commentator concluded that *Time Pieces* "makes a loving, thoughtful addition" to Hamilton's "unique literary legacy."

BIOGRAPHICAL AND CRITICAL SOURCES:

BOOKS

Children's Literature Review, Gale (Detroit, MI), Volume 1, 1976, Volume 8, 1985, Volume 11, 1986, Volume 40, 1996.

Contemporary Literary Criticism, Volume 26, Gale (Detroit, MI), 1983.

Dictionary of Literary Biography, Gale (Detroit, MI), Volume 33: *Afro-American Fiction Writers after 1955,* 1984, Volume 52: *American Writers for Children since 1960: Fiction,* 1986.

Egoff, Sheila A., *Thursday's Child: Trends and Patterns in Contemporary Children's Literature,* American Library Association (Chicago, IL), 1981, pp. 31-65, 130-158.

Mikkelsen, Nina, *Virginia Hamilton,* Twayne (New York, NY), 1994.

St. James Guide to Young Adult Writers, 2nd edition, St. James Press (Detroit, MI), 1999.

Sims, Rudine, *Shadow and Substance: Afro-American Experience in Contemporary Children's Fiction,* National Council of Teachers of English, 1982, pp. 79-102.

Townsend, John Rowe, *A Sounding of Storytellers: New and Revised Essays on Contemporary Writers for Children,* Lippincott (Philadelphia, PA), 1979, pp. 97-108.

Wheeler, Jill C., *Virginia Hamilton,* Abdo & Daughters (Minneapolis, MN), 1997.

PERIODICALS

African American Review, spring, 1998, Roberta Seelinger Trites, "'I Double Ever Never Lie to My Chil'ren': Inside People in Virginia Hamilton's Narratives," pp. 146-156.

Best Sellers, January, 1983.

Black Issues Book Review, November, 1999, reviews of *Bluish* and *Bells of Christmas,* p. 72; September, 2000, Khafre Abif, review of *The Girl Who Spun Gold,* p. 80; July, 2001, review of *The Girl Who Spun Gold,* p. 74.

Book, January, 2001, Kathleen Odean, review of *The Girl Who Spun Gold,* p. 83.

Booklist, August, 1982, p. 1525; April 1, 1983, pp. 1034-1035; July, 1985, p. 1554; February 15, 1994, Ilene Cooper, review of *The Bells of Christmas,* p. 1095; April 1, 1994, p. 1464; December 15, 1994, p. 753; November 1, 1995, Hazel Rochman, review of *Her Stories,* p. 470; January 1, 1998, Julie Corsaro, review of *A Ring of Tricksters,* p. 802; September 15, 1999, Hazel Rochman, review of *Bluish,* p. 257; August, 2000, Hazel Rochman, review of *The Girl Who Spun Gold,* p. 2134; February 15, 2001, review of *The Girl Who Spun Gold,* p. 1152, review of *Sweet Whispers, Brother Rush,* p. 1149; July, 2001, review of *The Girl Who Spun Gold,* p. 2011.

Book Report, March, 1999, review of *Second Cousins,* p. 57; November, 1999, review of *Bluish,* p. 61.

Bulletin of the Center for Children's Books, September, 1978, p. 9; March, 1981, p. 134; July-August, 1982, p. 207; November, 1983, pp. 50-51; April, 1985, p. 148; June, 1988; November, 1998, Janice M. Del Negro, review of *Second Cousins,* pp. 97-98; October, 1999, Janice M. Del Negro, review of *Bluish,* p. 54; December 15, 2002, Hazel Rochman, review of *Time Pieces: The Book of Times,* p. 761.

Catholic Library World, September, 1999, review of *A Ring of Tricksters,* p. 33.

Childhood Education, summer, 2003, Jeanie Burnett, review of *Time Pieces,* p. 245.

Children's Book Review Service, April, 1985, p. 97; July, 1988, review of *Anthony Burns,* p. 146; October, 1992, p. 22; March, 1995, p. 90; October, 1995, p. 22; March, 1996, p. 91; October, 1999, review of *Bluish,* p. 189.

Children's Bookwatch, December, 1999, review of *Bluish,* p. 4.

Children's Literature Association Quarterly, fall, 1982, pp. 45-48; winter, 1983, pp. 10-14, 25-27; spring, 1983, pp. 17-20; fall, 1986, pp. 134-42; winter, 1995-96, pp. 168-174.

Children's Literature in Education, winter, 1983; summer, 1987, pp. 67-75.

Christian Science Monitor, May 4, 1972, p. B5; March 12, 1979, p. B4; May 12, 1980, p. B9; March 2, 1984, p. B7; August 3, 1984.

Detroit Free Press, January 27, 2002, review of *Many Thousand Gone,* p. 5E.

Horn Book, October, 1968, p. 563; February, 1970; February, 1972; October, 1972, p. 476; December, 1972, Lee Bennett Hopkins, "Virginia Hamilton," pp. 563-569; June, 1973; October, 1974, pp. 143-144; April, 1975; August, 1975, pp. 344-348; December, 1976, p. 611; December, 1978, pp. 609-619; June, 1980, p. 305; October, 1982, pp. 505-506; June, 1983; February, 1984, pp. 24-28; September-October, 1984, pp. 597-598; September-October, 1985, pp. 563-564; March-April, 1986, pp. 212-213; January-February, 1988, pp. 105-106; March-April, 1989, pp. 183-185; July-August, 1993, p. 437; September-October, 1993, p. 621; March-April, 1994, p. 204; July-August, 1995, pp. 436-445; September-October, 1996, Nancy Vasilakis, review of *When Birds Could Talk and Bats Could Sing,* p. 604; January-February, 1998, p. 83; January-February, 1999, p. 61; September-October, 2000, Robert Strang, review of *The Girl Who Spun Gold,* p. 586.

Instructor, January, 2001, Judy Freeman, "All You Need Is Love," p. 19; May, 2001, review of *The Girl Who Spun Gold,* p. 37.

Interracial Books for Children Bulletin, numbers 1 and 2, 1983, p. 32; number 5, 1984; Volume 15, number 5, 1984, pp. 17-18; Volume 16, number 4, 1985, p. 19.

Kirkus Reviews, July 1, 1974; October 15, 1980, pp. 1354-1355; April 1, 1983; October 1, 1985, pp. 1088-1089; March 1, 1996, p. 375; October 15,

1999, review of *Bluish,* p. 1643; November 1, 2002, review of *Time Pieces,* p. 1612.
Kliatt, July, 1999, review of *Plain City,* p. 4.
Language Arts, March, 2002, review of *The Girl Who Spun Gold,* p. 355.
Lion and the Unicorn, Volume 9, 1985, pp. 50-57; Volume 10, 1986, pp. 15-17.
Los Angeles Times Book Review, March 23, 1986; May 22, 1988, p. 11; December 17, 1989, p. 8; November 18, 1990, p. 8.
New York Times Book Review, October 13, 1968, p. 26; October 24, 1971, p. 8; September 22, 1974, p. 8; December 22, 1974, Nikki Giovanni, review of *M. C. Higgins, the Great,* p. 8; October 31, 1976, p. 39; December 17, 1978, p. 27; May 4, 1980, pp. 26, 28; September 27, 1981, p. 36; November 14, 1982, pp. 41, 56; September 4, 1983, p. 14; March 18, 1984, p. 31; April 17, 1985, p. 20; November 10, 1985, p. 38; November 8, 1987, p. 36; October 16, 1988, p. 46; November 13, 1988, p. 52; December 17, 1989, p. 29; November 11, 1990, p. 6; November 22, 1992, p. 34; February 21, 1993, David Haward Bain, review of *Many Thousand Gone,* p. 23; November 12, 1995, Veronica Chambers, review of *Her Stories,*. p. 23; September 22, 1996, review of *When the Birds Could Talk and Bats Could Sing,* p. 28; April 19, 1998, review of *A Ring of Tricksters,* p. 32; February 11, 2001, Linda Villarosa, review of *The Girl Who Spun Gold,* p. 27.
Publishers Weekly, January 18, 1993, p. 470; January 4, 1993, review of *Cousins,* p. 74; February 6, 1995, review of *Plain City,* p. 86; February 19, 1996, p. 214; October 6, 1997, p. 59; April 20, 1998, p. 69; October 25, 1999, review of *Bluish,* p. 81; November 4, 2002, review of *Time Pieces,* p. 85.
Reading Teacher, February, 1999, review of *A Ring of Tricksters,* p. 498; May, 2001, review of *The Girl Who Spun Gold,* p. 832.
School Library Journal, December, 1968, pp. 53-54; September, 1971, p. 126; December, 1978, p. 60; March, 1980, p. 140; April, 1981, p. 140; April, 1983, p. 123; August, 1985, p. 97; December, 1994, Karen K. Radtke, review of *Jaguarundi,* p. 75; January, 1995, p. 70; February, 1996, pp. 70-71; December, 1996, p. 29; November, 1999, Katie O'Dell, review of *Bluish,* p. 158; September, 2000, Carol Ann Wilson, review of *The Girl Who Spun Gold,* p. 217; December, 2002, Lauralyn Persson, review of *Time Pieces,* p. 140.
Times (London, England), November 20, 1986.
Times Literary Supplement, May 23, 1975; July 11, 1975, p. 766; March 25, 1977, p. 359; September 19, 1980, p. 1024; November 20, 1981, p. 1362; August 30, 1985, p. 958; February 28, 1986, p. 230; October 30, 1987, p. 1205; November 20, 1987, p. 1286; July 29, 1988, p. 841.
Tribune Books (Chicago, IL), November 10, 1985, pp. 33-34; October 16, 1988, p. 9; November 13, 1988, p. 6; February 26, 1989, p. 8; November 11, 1990; February 14, 1993.
Voice of Youth Advocates, August, 1980, pp. 31-32; October, 1983, p. 215; June, 1985, p. 130; October, 1988, p. 201; February, 1994, Alice F. Stern, review of *Plain City,* p. 267; August, 1997, p. 173; February, 1999, Joyce Sparrow, review of *Second Cousins,* p. 434.
Washington Post Book World, June 25, 1967, p. 12; November 10, 1974; November 7, 1976, p. G7; November 11, 1979; September 14, 1980, p. 6; November 7, 1982, p. 14; November 10, 1985; July 10, 1988, p. 11; April 8, 1990, p. 8; November 4, 1990, p. 19; December 9, 1990, p. 14; February 14, 1993, Michael Dirda, review of *Many Thousand Gone,* p. 10; December 5, 1993, Elizabeth Ward, review of *In the Beginning,* pp. 21, 26; December 10, 1995, Jennifer Howard, review of *Her Stories,* p. 17.

OBITUARIES:

PERIODICALS

Black Issues Book Review, March-April, 2003, pp. 71-73.
Horn Book, May-June, 2002, pp. 366-367.
New York Times, February 20, 2002, p. 19.*

* * *

HAMPSON, (Margaret) Daphne 1944-

PERSONAL: Born June 15, 1944, in Croydon, England. *Education:* University of Keele, B.A. (with first class honors), 1966; Oxford University, D.Phil., 1974; Harvard University, Th.M., 1976, Th.D., 1983; University of Warwick, M.A. (with distinction), 1994.

ADDRESSES: *Home*—14 Melbourne Pl., St. Andrews KY16 9EY, Scotland. *Office*—St. Mary's College, University of St. Andrews, St. Andrews KY16 9JU, Scotland; fax: +44-01-33-446-2852. *E-mail*—dh1@st-and.ac.uk.

CAREER: University of North Carolina—Greensboro, instructor in British history, 1970-71; University of Stirling, Stirling, Scotland, lecturer in the history of religious thought, 1974-76; University of St. Andrews, St. Andrews, Scotland, lecturer at St. Mary's College, 1977-94, senior lecturer, 1994-99, reader in systematic theology, 1999-2001, professor of post-Christian thought, 2001—. Cambridge University, visiting academic at King's College, 1997, 1999.

AWARDS, HONORS: Woodrow Wilson British exchange fellow, 1970-71; Knox fellow, Harvard University, 1971-72, 1974, 1976-77; Leverhulme research grant, 1988-89; Arts and Humanities Research Board Award, 2003.

WRITINGS:

Theology and Feminism, Basil Blackwell (Oxford, England), 1990.

After Christianity, SCM Press (London, England), 1996, revised edition, 2002, Trinity Press International (Valley Forge, PA), 1997.

(Editor) *Swallowing a Fishbone? Feminist Theologians Debate Christianity,* S.P.C.K., 1996.

Christian Contradictions: The Structures of Lutheran and Catholic Thought, Cambridge University Press (New York, NY), 2001.

WORK IN PROGRESS: Research on theology and recent continental philosophy.

* * *

HARSCH, Rick 1959-
(Carlos Oretti)

PERSONAL: Born 1959. *Education:* Attended University of Iowa. *Politics:* "Exiled therefrom." *Religion:* "Soon to be Hindu." *Hobbies and other interests:* Fencing, archery.

ADDRESSES: *Agent*—Warren Frazier, John Hawkins and Associates, Inc., 71 West 23rd St., Suite 1600, New York, NY 10010.

CAREER: Writer. Also works as a taxicab driver.

AWARDS, HONORS: Michener Copernicus Award, University of Iowa, 1997.

WRITINGS:

"DRIFTLESS" TRILOGY

Driftless Zone, Steerforth Press (South Royalton, VT), 1997.

Billy Verite, Steerforth Press (South Royalton, VT), 1998.

The Sleep of the Aborigines, Steerforth Press (South Royalton, VT), 2002.

Some writings appear under the pseudonym Carlos Oretti.

SIDELIGHTS: Rick Harsch is the author of the "Driftless" trilogy, which consists of *Driftless Zone, Billy Verite,* and *The Sleep of the Aborigines.* In the last book of the trilogy, the hero is Spleen—the twin brother of the protagonist of the first novel. Several other characters from the previous two books return as well, including a transvestite named Bette Davis and a bad mayor named Skunk Lane Forhension. The final book also features a dead writer named Rick Harsh, whose murder the second Spleen is bent on avenging—while mourning his wife's departure from their marriage to take a teaching job in Tennessee. A *Kirkus Reviews* critic concluded of *The Sleep of the Aborigines* that "the signature quirks and insouciance are all in place, making this an apt closer for a tough trio of stories from the bleeding heartland of losers."

Harsch told *CA:* "I have written primarily to avoid working, which I consider the lesser form of slavery. My work is influenced by an involuntary alembic that digests various styles and another alembic that digests various injustices and rages. The writing process is the distortion of these pure elements. I have never chosen a subject, nor has one ever chosen me."

BIOGRAPHICAL AND CRITICAL SOURCES:

PERIODICALS

Booklist, July, 2002, Frank Sennett, review of *The Sleep of the Aborigines*, p. 8282.

Kirkus Reviews, June 15, 2002, review of *The Sleep of the Aborigines,* p. 1826.

Publishers Weekly, July 29, 2002, review of *The Sleep of the Aborigines,* p. 54.*

* * *

HART, Carolyn G(impel) 1936-

PERSONAL: Born August 25, 1936, in Oklahoma City, OK; daughter of Roy William (an organ builder) and Doris (Akin) Gimpel; married Philip Donnell Hart (an attorney), June 10, 1958; children: Philip Donnell, Jr., Sarah Ann. *Ethnicity:* "Caucasian." *Education:* University of Oklahoma—Norman, B.A., 1958. *Religion:* Protestant.

ADDRESSES: Home and office—1705 Drakestone Ave., Oklahoma City, OK 73120. *Agent*—Deborah C. Schneider, Gelfman Schneider Agents Inc., 250 West 57th St., New York, NY 10107. *E-mail*—cghart1@earthlink.net.

CAREER: Norman Transcript, Norman, OK, reporter, 1958-59; *Sooner Newsmakers* (University of Oklahoma alumni news), editor, 1959-60; freelance writer, 1961-82, 1986—; University of Oklahoma, School of Journalism and Mass Communications, assistant professor, 1982-85.

MEMBER: Sisters in Crime (president, 1991-92), Mystery Writers of America (past national director), Authors Guild, Authors League of America, Phi Beta Kappa, Theta Sigma Phi, American Crime Writers League, International Association of Crime Writers USA.

AWARDS, HONORS: Calling All Girls Prize, Dodd, Mead, 1964, for *The Secret of the Cellars;* Agatha Award, Malice Domestic, 1989, for *Something Wicked,* and 1993, for *Dead Man's Island;* Anthony Award, Bouchercon, 1989, for *Something Wicked,* and 1990, for *Honeymoon with Murder;* Macavity Award, Mystery Readers International, 1990, for *A Little Class on Murder;* Macavity Award and Agatha Award nominations, both 1994, both for *Scandal in Fair Haven;* Pulitzer Prize nomination for fiction, Oklahoma Center for Poets and Writers at Oklahoma State University, 2003.

WRITINGS:

Flee from the Past, Bantam (New York, NY), 1975.

A Settling of Accounts, Doubleday (New York, NY), 1976.

(With Charles F. Long) *The Sooner Story, 1890-1980,* University of Oklahoma Foundation (Norman, OK), 1980.

Escape from Paris, R. Hale (London, England), 1982, St. Martin's Press (New York, NY), 1983.

The Rich Die Young, R. Hale (New York, NY), 1983.

Death by Surprise, R. Hale (New York, NY), 1983.

Castle Rock, R. Hale (New York, NY), 1983, Five Star (Unity, ME), 2000.

Skulduggery, R. Hale (New York, NY), 1984, Five Star (Unity, ME), 2000.

The Devereaux Legacy, Harlequin (Tarrytown, NY), 1986.

Brave Hearts, Pocket Books (New York, NY), 1987.

(Editor) *Crimes of the Heart,* Berkeley (New York, NY), 1995.

Crime on Her Mind: A Collection of Short Stories, Five Star (Unity, ME), 1999.

(Editor) *Love and Death,* Berkeley (New York, NY), 2001.

Secrets and Other Stories of Suspense, Five Star (Waterville, ME), 2002.

Motherhood Is Murder, Avon (New York, NY), 2003.

Letter from Home, Berkley (New York, NY), 2003.

"DEATH ON DEMAND" MYSTERIES

Death on Demand, Bantam (New York, NY), 1987.

Design for Murder, Bantam (New York, NY), 1988.

Something Wicked, Bantam (New York, NY), 1988.

Honeymoon with Murder, Bantam (New York, NY), 1989.

A Little Class on Murder, Doubleday (New York, NY), 1989.

Deadly Valentine, Doubleday (New York, NY), 1990.

The Christie Caper, Bantam (New York, NY), 1991.

Southern Ghost, Bantam (New York, NY), 1992.

Mint Julep Murder, Bantam (New York, NY), 1995.

Yankee Doodle Dead, Avon (New York, NY), 1998.

White Elephant Dead, Avon (New York, NY), 1999.

Sugarplum Dead, Morrow (New York, NY), 2000.

April Fool Dead, Morrow (New York, NY), 2002.

Engaged to Die, Morrow (New York, NY), 2003.

Murder Walks the Plank, HarperCollins (New York, NY), 2004.

"HENRIE O" MYSTERIES

Dead Man's Island, Bantam (New York, NY), 1993.
Scandal in Fair Haven, Bantam (New York, NY), 1994.
Death in Lovers' Lane, Avon (New York, NY), 1997.
Death in Paradise, Avon (New York, NY), 1998.
Death on the River Walk, Avon (New York, NY), 1999.
Resort to Murder, Morrow (New York, NY), 2001.

FOR CHILDREN

The Secret of the Cellars, Dodd (New York, NY), 1964.
Dangerous Summer, Four Winds (New York, NY), 1968.
Rendezvous in Vera Cruz, M. Evans (New York, NY), 1970.
No Easy Answers, M. Evans (New York, NY), 1970.
Danger! High Explosives!, M. Evans (New York, NY), 1972.

ADAPTATIONS: Dead Man's Island was made into a CBS television movie, starring Barbara Eden and William Shatner.

SIDELIGHTS: Carolyn G. Hart has won a loyal following for her "Death on Demand" and "Henrie O" mystery series. Set on a fictional South Carolina resort island, the "Death on Demand" series features an attractive, wealthy couple, Annie and Max Darling. They own a mystery bookshop, and also work together to solve the many real mysteries that come their way. "Henrie O" is short for Henrietta O'Dwyer Collins, a retired journalist who brings her investigative skills to bear on mysteries. *Armchair Detective* reviewer Charles L. P. Silet praised the Darling mysteries for their "delightful mix of old Southern charm, eccentric island characters, and crime fiction esoterica." Emily Melton of *Booklist* complimented Henrie's first outing in *Dead Man's Island,* declaring that "this book has the same kind of pleasantly entertaining appeal as the Miss Marple stories and should prove popular with Christie fans."

Henrie O is perhaps a reflection of Hart's youthful ambition to be a reporter. She majored in journalism at the University of Oklahoma, but marriage and a family kept her from pursuing that career. She began writing fiction instead, and eventually entered a contest that involved writing a mystery for young girls. Hart's winning manuscript was published in 1964 as *The Secret of the Cellars.* She wrote a few more novels for young readers, including *No Easy Answers,* about the Vietnam War, and *Danger! High Explosives!,* about a college torn over the question of a military presence on the campus. "There's a very definite distinction between mystery and suspense," Hart once told *CA.* "In a mystery novel the point of the book is to figure out who committed a crime. When you do that, what you're really exploring (especially in the case of murder, which is what mysteries are usually about) is what went wrong in the lives of these people. How did these relationships become so tortured that violence resulted? A suspense novel, on the other hand, tells the story of a person who is trying to accomplish something. It doesn't matter if it's getting to the top of the mountain, escaping from the Japanese during the war, or whatever—the suspense novel is built around a series of episodes where the character must continue to struggle to achieve a goal. It's a very different kind of story than a mystery."

After finishing *Danger! High Explosives* in 1972, Hart began writing for adults. "*The Devereaux Legacy* was written during a very desperate period in my career," she explained. "I couldn't sell anything. I was at a very low point, the point where I thought that maybe I should just give up writing. No one was buying mysteries by American women, but the romance novel was at the height of its popularity, and my agent said, 'There's just no point in writing mysteries. You've got to write romances.' I thought, 'Well, maybe I can do this. I suppose the question is not "Who Killed Roger Ackroyd?" but "Will She Win the Hero in the End?"' So I tried my hand at it. Basically what I did with *The Devereaux Legacy* was to take a mystery that I had written and recast it as a romance. It has a very southern background, and that's why it was bought by the Harlequin Gothic arm. *Southern Ghost* has elements of the gothic in it intentionally. My editor said 'Why don't you write a Southern Gothic?' and I said, 'Well, all right, I'll see what I can do with that.' It was a very fascinating and difficult book to write. I later realized that the reason why it was so stressful was because when you're writing a Southern Gothic you're writing about a family, and nothing is more distressing than destructive emotions in a family situation. In only one of my other books had there been a focus on a family rather than just a group of individuals. It was a challenge."

Hart hit on a winning formula with her "Death on Demand" series. The stories combine elements of romance, mystery fiction, and bibliophilia, and have proved tremendously popular with readers. Hart told Silet in an *Armchair Detective* interview that she hit upon the inspiration of the first novel in the series after a talk she gave to the Mystery Writers of America. "After this day-long talk about mysteries, I thought—I am going to write the mystery I have always wanted to write and if it doesn't go then I'm just going to quit—and I wrote *Death on Demand.*" Part of the fun of the series comes from Annie Laurance Darling's devoted customers, all of whom are fanatical mystery readers. The author reveals in the books a familiarity with esoteric mystery fiction that appeals to devotees of the genre. Susan L. Clark, writing in *Armchair Detective* about the third installment of the series, praised Hart's knowledge of the detective fiction genre and said, "Any reader who has ever perused the subject lists and maps in Golden Age detective fiction books . . . will thoroughly enjoy *Something Wicked.*" Jane Bakerman, writing for *Belles Lettres,* stated that in *Honeymoon with Murder,* Hart "as usual . . . stuffs her dialogue with allusions to other mysteries, and provides lots of fun for her readers."

Mint Julep Murder finds Annie hosting five authors and their children at the Dixie Book Festival. Trouble begins when publisher Kenneth Hazlitt threatens to expose delicate secrets about each of the authors. When Hazlitt turns up dead, Annie finds herself accused. She is "alternately indignant that anyone would see her as a killer and terrified that she'll take the rap," observed Emily Melton in *Booklist.* Annie sets out to clear her name and find the killer in a story that blends "genteel ambience, southern charm, a likeable heroine, and some wonderfully nasty characters into a pleasantly charming mystery," concluded Melton. A *Publishers Weekly* reviewer also recommended *Mint Julep Murder* as a "light tale in a deliciously inviting setting," which "offers mystery readers a winsome treat."

The close relationship between Max and Annie evolves throughout the series. "I was making a very deliberate statement" with Annie and Max's relationship, Hart told Silet. "I truly believe that happy marriages are quite possible. . . . I know that there are a great many women who have had difficult lives—they are estranged from people, they are divorced, they are unhappy. But you *can* have a good marriage, it really can exist, and that was what I wanted to celebrate with Max and Annie." "The traditional mystery, in my view, is a parable of life," she continued. "I think it has a reality which the hard-boiled private detective books don't. They, oddly enough, are the more truly romantic books because they are about the white knight on a quest. The private detective is trying to remain incorruptible in a corrupt world, and this is truly a romantic vision. In my view, what I write touches much more directly on reality."

The "Henri O" series features another of Hart's appealing sleuths. The author has admitted that Henrietta O'Dwyer Collins is a braver, idealized projection of herself. Henrietta is a widow, a journalist who has also worked as a journalism professor. Her investigative reporting skills come in handy when she is repeatedly faced with mysteries to solve as an amateur sleuth. In *Death in Lovers' Lane,* Henrietta must investigate the death of a student at the university where she teaches. The deceased was investigating a trio of older, unsolved deaths at the campus, and Henrietta wonders if there is a connection. There is a suggestion of Agatha Christie's "gift for plotting and suspense" in this "intricately wrought tale," noted Alan Moores in *Booklist. Death in Paradise* finds Henrietta challenged by an anonymous message stating that her late husband was murdered. To investigate the incident, she must visit Belle Ericcson, one of her late husband's closest friends. The action shifts to Hawaii, to a dramatic mountain locale. "Hart is at her award-winning best as she tightens the suspense and keeps the killer's identity out of focus until the cliffhanging finale." A *Publishers Weekly* writer mused, "This series has a deeper and darker emotional texture than Hart's more lively and lighthearted 'Death on Demand series,' but her fans will enjoy the complex plot, local color and vivid characters."

Hart told *CA:* "I grew up during World War II and very early understood that newspapers were hugely important and the bigger and blacker the headline, the more important the story. I was determined to be a reporter and focused on this throughout my school days. I majored in journalism at the University of Oklahoma. I ended up being a novelist, but I have never lost my fascination with news and newspaper reporting.

"I love writing the traditional mystery and take pride in books I have done. My favorite—*Letter from*

Home—is a book where the focus is not on the resolution of the crime but the effect of the crime upon the lives of the characters. Moreover it combines my fascination with the process of writing with my recollections of Oklahoma during World War II. It is my book about home.

Agatha Christie is a major influence on Hart's work. "She was and is and will always be the greatest writer of traditional mysteries. I believe in the importance of mysteries and their contribution to goodness. The world is best by evil and injustice but the traditional mystery will always offer a good, just and decent world to readers.

Hart told *CA* that the most important thing she has learned as a writer is "To trust the process. I am always terrified when I begin a book that I will not be able to finish. Every time I have to struggle and work and hope and every time the book is there to be found."

"I hope I will entertain readers, offer them a brief moment to rest in the sun, provide them respite from care."

BIOGRAPHICAL AND CRITICAL SOURCES:

BOOKS

St. James Guide to Crime and Mystery Writers, 4th edition, St. James Press (Detroit), 1996.

PERIODICALS

Armchair Detective, fall, 1989, p. 430; fall, 1993, pp. 46-49; winter, 1996, pp. 108-109.

Belles Lettres, summer, 1989, p. 33.

Booklist, August, 1993, p. 2039; August, 1995, Emily Melton, review of *Mint Julep Murder,* p. 1931; January 1, 1997, Alan Moores, review of *Death in Lovers' Lane,* p. 825; March 1, 1998, Emily Melton, review of *Death in Paradise,* p. 1097; September 1, 1998, John Rowen, review of *Yankee Doodle Dead,* p. 70; January 1, 1999, John Rowen, review of *Crime on Her Mind,* p. 837; February 15, 1999, Jenny McLarin, review of *Death on the River Walk,* p. 1045; August, 1999, review of *White Elephant Dead,* p. 2034; October 15, 2000, Whitney Scott, review of *The Rich Die Young,* p. 422; January 1, 2001, GraceAnne A. DeCandido, review of *Love and Death,* p. 925; October 1, 2001, Candace Smith, review of *Resort to Murder,* p. 342; April 1, 2002, John Rowen, review of *April Fool Dead,* p. 1309; October 1, 2002, Jenny McLarin, review of *Secrets and Other Stories of Suspense,* p. 304; February 15, 2003, Sue O'Brien, review of *Engaged to Die,* p. 1053.

Chattanooga Times, June 26, 1992, p. C6.

Clarion-Ledger (Jackson, MS), July 5, 1992.

Green Bay Press-Gazette, April 28, 2002, "Master of Mysteries Finds Herself in Demand," p. 5.

Island Packet (Hilton Head Island, SC), June 14, 1992.

Kirkus Reviews, June 15, 1991, p. 761; June 15, 1993, p. 753; September 1, 2003, review of *Letter from Home,* p. 1102.

Kliatt, September, 2003, Nola Theiss, review of *Engaged to Die* (audiobook), p. 50.

Library Journal, August, 1995, Rex E. Klett, review of *Mint Julep Murder,* p. 123; December, 1996, Juleigh Muirhead Clark, review of *Deadly Valentine,* p. 169; January, 1997, Rex E. Klett, review of *Death in Lovers' Lane,* p. 153; October 1, 1998, Rex E. Klett, review of *Yankee Doodle Dead,* p. 139; February 1, 1999, Rex E. Klett, review of *Crime on Her Mind,* p. 125; September 1, 1999, Rex E. Klett, review of *White Elephant Dead,* p. 236; September 1, 2000, Rex Klett, review of *Sugar Plum Dead,* p. 255; February 1, 2001, Rex E. Klett, review of *Love and Death,* p. 128; October 1, 2003, Rex Klett, review of *Letter from Home,* p. 121.

Nashville Banner, June 13, 1992.

New York Times Book Review, November 23, 2003, Marilyn Stasio, review of *Letter from Home.*

Pioneer Press (St. Paul, MN), July 15, 1992.

Publisher Weekly, June 19, 1995, review of *Mint Julep Murder,* p. 52; December 9, 1996, review of *Death in Lovers' Lane,* p. 62; July 27, 1998, review of *Yankee Doodle Dead,* p. 56; January 26, 1998, review of *Death in Paradise,* p. 72; August 9, 1999, review of *White Elephant Dead,* p. 347; January 25, 1999, review of *Death on the River Walk,* p. 75; October 2, 2000, review of *Sugar Plum Dead,* p. 62; November 13, 2000, review of *Love and Death,* p. 89; March 12, 2001, review of *Resort to Murder,* p. 66; March 18, 2002, review of *April Fool Dead,* p. 81; February 17, 2003, review of *Engaged to Die,* p. 60; September 8, 2003, review of *Letter from Home,* p. 58; January 12, 2004, Kay Brundidge, "Death on Demand for

Fun," interview with Carolyn G. Hart, and review of *Murder Walks the Plank.*

ONLINE

Carolyn Hart Home Page, http://www.carolynhart.com/ (February 14, 2002), interview with Carolyn Hart.*

* * *

HÉBERT, Anne 1916-2000

PERSONAL: Born August 1, 1916, in Sainte-Catherine-de-Fossambault, Quebec, Canada; died of cancer, January 22, 2000, in Quebec City, Quebec, Canada; daughter of Maurice-Lang (a literary critic) and Marguerite Marie (Tache) Hébert. *Education:* Attended College Saint-Coeur de Marie and College Notre Dame.

CAREER: Poet and novelist. Worked for Radio Canada, 1950-53, and for National Film Board, 1953-54, 1959-60.

MEMBER: Royal Society of Canada.

AWARDS, HONORS: Grants from Canadian government, 1954, Canadian Council of Arts, 1960 and 1961, Guggenheim Foundation, 1963, and Province of Quebec, 1965; Prix de la Province de Quebec, France Canada prize, and Duvernay prize, all 1958, all for *Les Chambres de bois;* Molson Prize, 1967; French booksellers prize, 1971; Governor General award, 1975, for *Les Enfants du sabbat,* and 1992, for *L'Enfant charge de songes;* Grand Prix de Monaco, 1975; French Academy award, 1975; Prix David (Quebec), 1978; Prix Femina, 1982, for *Les Fous de bassan;* D.Litt., University of Toronto, 1967, University of Quebec, 1979, McGill University, 1980, University of Laval, and University of Laurentienne; Giller Prize finalist, 1999, for *Am I Disturbing You?*

WRITINGS:

POETRY

Les Songes en equilibre (title means "Dreams in Equilibrium"), Éditions de l'Arbre (Montreal, Quebec, Canada), 1942.

Le Tombeau des rois (also see below), Institut Litteraire du Quebec, 1953, translation by Peter Miller published as *The Tomb of the Kings,* Contact Press (Toronto, Ontario, Canada), 1967.

Poemes (includes *Le Tombeau des rois*), Éditions du Seuil (Montreal, Quebec, Canada), 1960, translation by Alan Brown published as *Poems,* Musson (Don Mills, Ontario, Canada), 1975.

Saint-Denys Garneau and Anne Hébert (selected poetry), translation by F. R. Scott, Klanak Press (Vancouver, British Columbia, Canada), 1962, revised edition, 1978.

Eve: Poems, translation by A. Poulin, Jr., Quarterly Review of Literature, 1980.

Selected Poems, translation by A. Poulin, BOA Editions (Brockport, NY), 1987.

Oeuvres poetiques: 1950-1990, Boreál (Montreal, Quebec, Canada), 1992.

Le Jour n'a d'egal que la nuit, Boreál (Montreal, Quebec, Canada), 1992, published as *Day Has No Equal but Night,* translation by A. Poulin, BOA Editions (Brockport, NY), 1994.

Poemes pour la main gauche, Boreál (Montreal, Quebec, Canada), 1997.

NOVELS

Les Chambres de bois, Éditions du Seuil (Montreal, Quebec, Canada), 1958, translation by Kathy Mezei published as *The Silent Rooms,* Musson (Don Mills, Ontario, Canada), 1974.

Kamouraska, Éditions du Seuil (Montreal, Quebec, Canada), 1970, translation by Norman Shapiro, Crown (New York, NY), 1973.

Les Enfants du sabbat, Éditions du Seuil (Montreal, Quebec, Canada), 1975, translation by Carol Dunlop-Hébert published as *Children of the Black Sabbath,* Crown (New York, NY), 1977.

Heloise, Éditions du Seuil (Montreal, Quebec, Canada), 1980, translation by Sheila Fischman, Stoddart (Toronto, Ontario, Canada), 1982.

Les Fous de bassan, Éditions du Seuil (Montreal, Quebec, Canada), 1982, translation by Sheila Fischman published as *In the Shadow of the Wind,* Stoddart (Toronto, Ontario, Canada), 1983.

Le Premier jardin, Éditions du Seuil (Montreal, Quebec, Canada), 1988, translation published as *The First Garden,* Anansi (Concord, Ontario, Canada), 1990.

L'Enfant charge de songes (title means "The Child Filled with Dreams"), Éditions du Seuil (Montreal,

Quebec, Canada), 1992, translation published as *Burden of Dreams,* Anansi (Concord, Ontario, Canada), 1994.

Aurelien, Clara, Mademoiselle et le Lieutenant Anglais, translation by Sheila Fischman published as *Aurelien, Clara, Mademoiselle, and the English Lieutenant,* General Distribution Services, 1996.

Un Habit de lumiere, Éditions du Seuil (Montreal, Quebec, Canada), 1999, translation by Sheila Fischman published as *A Suit of Light,* Anansi (Toronto, Ontario, Canada), 2000.

OTHER

Le Torrent (short stories), Beauchemin, 1950, new edition published as *Le Torrent, suivi de deux nouvelles inedites,* Éditions HMH (Montreal, Quebec, Canada), 1963, translation by Gwendolyn Moore published as *The Torrent: Novellas and Short Stories,* Harvest House (Montreal, Quebec, Canada), 1973.

Les Invites au proces, le theatre du grand prix (radio play; produced by Radio-Canada, 1952), published in *Le Temps sauvage, La Merciere assassinee, Les Invites au proces: Theatre,* 1967.

(With others) *Trois de Quebec* (radio play), Radio-Canada, 1953.

Les Indes parmi nous (screenplay), National Film Board of Canada, 1954.

La Canne a peche (screenplay), National Film Board of Canada, 1959.

Saint-Denys Garneau (screenplay), National Film Board of Canada, 1960.

Le Temps sauvage (play; produced in Quebec, 1966), published in *Le Temps sauvage, La Merciere assassinee, Les Invites au proces: Theatre,* 1967.

Le Temps sauvage, La Merciere assassinee, Les Invites au proces: Theatre (plays), Éditions HMH, 1967.

(With F. R. Scott) *Dialogue sur la traduction,* edited by Jeanne Lapointe, Éditions HMH, 1970.

La Cage: L'Ile de la demoiselle (play), Boreál (Montreal, Quebec, Canada), 1990.

Est-ce que je te derange?, Éditions du Seuil (Montreal, Quebec, Canada), 1998, translation by Sheila Fischman published as *Am I Disturbing You?,* Anansi (Toronto, Ontario, Canada), 1998.

Also author of *Drole de mic-mac* and *Le Medecin du nord,* both 1954, and *Le Deficient mental,* 1960. Contributor of poems to literary journals.

SIDELIGHTS: French-Canadian poet and novelist Anne Hébert was acclaimed as one of her country's most distinguished literary stylists. Continuing from her first book of verse, 1942's *Les Songes en equilibre,* Hébert contributed novels, poems, and plays to the growing body of modern Canadian letters, winning the poet numerous awards for her work. Praised by critics for her originality, Hébert was particularly known for the novel *Kamouraska,* published in 1970, and the poetry cycle *Le Tombeau des rois,* translated as *The Tomb of the Kings* and first published in 1953.

Hébert was born in 1916 and raised in an intellectually stimulating environment. Her father, Maurice-Lang Hébert, was a distinguished literary critic; among his friends were some of the finest minds in Quebec. Due to a childhood illness Hébert was educated privately and spent most of her time at the family's country home in Sainte-Catherine-de-Fossambault. She began writing poetry in her adolescence with the advice and guidance of both her father and her cousin, poet Hector de Saint-Denys Garneau.

Unlike Saint-Denys Garneau, who remained in self-isolation until his death, Hébert emerged from the spiritual struggle described in her first two books of poetry. *Les Songes en equilibre,* her poetic debut, chronicles the experiences of a young woman who travels from carefree childhood to the renunciation of pleasure and the acceptance of a lonely life of spiritual and poetic duty. Hébert received strict Roman Catholic training as a child, and believed the obligation of a poet is to be a spiritual force in man's salvation.

In her second book of poetry, *The Tomb of the Kings,* Hébert reveals that the austere life she chose for herself had stifled her work. It is in this volume of her poetry that she emerges from a dark and deep spiritual struggle. Samuel Moon characterized *The Tomb of the Kings* as a work "closely unified by its constant introspection, by its atmosphere of profound melancholy, by its recurrent themes of a dead childhood, a living death cut off from love and beauty, suicide, the theme of introspection itself. Such a book would seem to be of more interest clinically than poetically, but the miracle occurs and these materials are transmuted by the remarkable force of Mlle. Hébert's imagery, the simplicity and directness of her diction, and the restrained lyric sound of her *vers libre.*"

Although known primarily as a poet, Hébert also wrote for the stage and television, and was the author of several published novels. Characteristic of her prose work is the theme of the inhibiting burden of the past, which binds any freedom for future actions. Many critics have noted that this theme is a French-Canadian phenomenon.

Hébert's first novel, *Les Chambres de bois,* appeared in 1958. Catherine, the novel's chief protagonist, is married to an artist who is repulsed by sex. She eventually abandons her husband for another man, and discovers happiness in this new relationship. According to an article in *Contemporary Literary Criticism, Les Chambres de bois* "was well received by critics who applauded Hébert's use of symbolist imagery." A contributor to *Books and Writers* commented that the "fantastic elements" found in *Les Chambres de bois* can also be found in Hébert's subsequent works.

Kamouraska, Hébert's second novel, was published seventeen years after *Les Chambres de bois,* and drew praise from both Canadian and U.S. critics. A *Choice* reviewer noted that the novel "conveys the same sense of mounting and almost unendurable excitement that one felt on first reading a Brontë novel—except that *Kamouraska* is modern in style and explicitness. The events are a stream-of-consciousness re-creation of a murder of passion that actually occurred in 1840. Hébert's poetic vision draws the thoughtful reader to be one with each of the frenzied characters." *Kamouraska* tells the story of Elisabeth d'Aulnieres, who conspires to slay her abusive spouse with the aid of her lover, Doctor George Nelson. Following the murder of Antoine Tassy, Nelson escapes to the United States, but Elisabeth is imprisoned for the crime. A *Canadian Forum* critic compared Hébert's "highly complex style and imagery" with that of writers Marcel Proust, Franz Kafka, and James Joyce, and stated that "the greatness of this work resides in the happy mixture of particularity and universality, unity and complexity, vitality and artistic originality, and, above all, in the way the author makes simplistic moral judgment of the characters impossible."

Mel Watkins in the *New York Times* called Hébert a "stylist of the first rank" in his review of *Children of the Black Sabbath,* a novel that deals with a young novice possessed by the devil. Watkins observed that Hébert "both complements and heightens this eerie, aphotic atmosphere with the verity and density of her minor characters and with the restrained elegance of her prose. The result is an impressionistic tale that moves smoothly. . . . The vitality of the prose, of itself, makes it one of the best of its kind." Suspense and atmosphere are keys to Hébert's later works, as well. *Heloise* recounts the tale of a Paris vampire, and *Les Fous de bassan* concerns the reactions of several people to a savage crime. For the latter work, Hébert received the Prix Femina, an award honoring novels penned by women.

Hébert's treatment of her characters in *Les Fous de bassan*—translated in 1984 as *In the Shadow of the Wind*—drastically departs from her previous books. While Hébert's other novels portray strong women who break down societal conventions, the cousins Nora and Olivia of *In the Shadow of the Wind* are at the mercy of their cruel cousin Stevens, and one is sexually abused by their uncle Reverend Jones. The story of the girls' murders is narrated at different times by Stevens, Reverend Jones, and Nora prior to her death as well as by Olivia thereafter. In the work, the cousins are depicted as "the source of temptation." As Lori Saint-Martin commented in *Women's Review of Books,* "Such a purely misogynistic vision is relatively rare today—especially among women writers. Coming from Anne Hébert, the turnaround is even more disturbing."

While such misogyny may have been a departure for Hébert, critics nonetheless praised *Les Fous de bassan.* A *Publishers Weekly* critic found the dark tale reminiscent of Edith Wharton's *Ethan Frome,* while C. D. B. Bryan in the *New York Times Book Review* termed it "haunting" and remarked that "The winds Anne Hébert stirs up in her readers' minds do not die down until long after the book has been closed." Despite such praise and receipt of the Prix Femina, the book was deemed flawed by Matthew Clark in *Quill and Quire:* "I find the language precious, the characterization thin, the situation conventionally Gothic, and the actions unmotivated."

Hébert's 1992 novel *L'Enfant charge de songes* received the Canadian Governor General Award for French fiction. Its English title, *Burden of Dreams,* aptly describes the protagonists of the novel who, according to Bettina L. Knapp in *World Literature Today,* are never "described as flesh-and-blood beings." Anne Denoon in *Books in Canada* noted that from the novel's "very first page the reader is acutely conscious of entering a strange, unruly and disquieting world." Knapp praised the novelist's imaginative plot, exclaiming: "More than a first-class storyteller, Hébert fuses supernatural and natural domains, the collective with the individual." Stephen Smith in *Quill and Quire* found that "the overwhelming impression that Anne Hébert's plangent novel leaves is of blurred edges: it's an impressionistic landscape, a story filtered through fevered sleep."

After an absence of nearly twenty years, Hébert returned to poetry with the 1994 publication *Day Has No Equal but Night.* The volume includes both previously published work and unpublished work, "adding," according to contributor J. Warwick in *Choice,* "a new political dimension . . . but not eclipsing her intensely personal themes." Translator A. Poulin, Jr. chose to include the poet's original French, with its English translation on the facing page. While Poulin had served as translator for Hébert's *Selected Poems,* published in 1988, reviewers were mixed in their opinion of the translator's literal treatment of Hébert's words in this work, Judy Clarence in *Library Journal* calling Poulin's effort "clunky and cumbersome." Acknowledging the difficulty in translating Hébert's imaginative writing, Sarah Lawall in *World Literature Today* maintained that Poulin "offers fluent, readable, and usually literal translations that also emulate the form of the original *vers libre.* Still there are some instances where the word choice seems either mistaken or else inattentive to indications in the text." Despite the translation, reviewers continued to be fascinated by Hébert's work. Pat Monaghan, reviewing *Day Has No Equal but Night* in *Booklist,* lauded Hébert as "a visionary descendant" of French poet Arthur Rimbaud.

In 1999 Hébert's final novel, *Un Habit de lumiere,* was published. Bettina L. Knapp noted in a *World Literature Today* article that this work is "reminiscent of some of [Hébert's] . . . previous writing," such as *L'Enfant charge de songes* and *Les Fous de Bassan,* which are also filled with "deeply troubled and troubling beings." The story in *Un Habit de lumiere* revolves around the strong fantasy lives of three members of a Spanish family residing in Paris. Hébert examines the inner lives of Rose-Alba, Rose's husband, and their son, Miguel, contrasting each person's dream worlds with the stifling reality of their everyday lives. Knapp concluded by saying that *Un Habit de lumiere* presents "a pitiful world of. . . . pitifully predictable solutions."

Three years prior to her death from cancer in 2000, Hébert returned from Paris to spend her final years in her native Quebec. In a *Maclean's* article, Sheila Fischman, who translated seven of Hébert's novels, stated that the late writer "used the French language like something fine and rare; her style is . . . luminous and pure. Every word she used was necessary and right. . . . Hébert's great achievement will be part of our human experience as long as fine writing is admired and read."

After Hébert's death, Marie-Claire Blais wrote appreciatively of Hébert in *Time International:* Hébert "was a poet for whom the beauty of the world was a vast source of inspiration and delight. . . . For future generations of writers and poets who will come after her, this great artist will continue to be an exemplary model of courage and perseverance in the way that she approached the act of writing."

BIOGRAPHICAL AND CRITICAL SOURCES:

BOOKS

Contemporary Literary Criticism, Gale (Detroit, MI), Volume 4, 1975, Volume 13, 1980, Volume 29, 1984.

Contemporary Women Poets, St. James Press (Detroit, MI), 1997.

Contemporary World Writers, St. James Press (Detroit, MI), 1993.

Dictionary of Literary Biography, Volume 68: *Canadian Writers, 1920-1959, First Series,* Gale (Detroit, MI), 1988.

Knight, Kelton, *Anne Hébert: In Search of the First Garden,* P. Lang (New York, NY), 1995.

Lewis, Paula Gilbert, editor, *Traditionalism, Nationalism, and Feminism: Women Writers of Quebec,* Greenwood Press (Westport, CT), 1985.

Mitchell, Constantina, *Shaping the Novel: Textual Interplay in the Fiction of Malraux, Hébert, Modiano,* Berghahn Books (Providence, RI), 1995.

Russell, Delbert W., *Anne Hébert,* Twayne (New York, NY), 1983.

PERIODICALS

American Review of Canadian Studies, fall, 1987.

Booklist, January 15, 1991, p. 1045; September 1, 1993, p. 43; March 15, 1994, p. 1323.

Books in Canada, April, 1990, p. 47; February, 1995, p. 35.
Canadian Forum, November-December, 1973; December, 1999, Suzette Mayr, review of *Am I Disturbing You?,* pp. 42-44.
Canadian Literature, Volume 58, 1973; spring, 1981; summer, 1985; autumn, 1991, p. 175; summer, 1992, p. 187; spring, 1994, p. 110; summer, 2000, Eva-Marie Kroller, pp. 5-9.
Choice, September, 1973; September, 1994, p. 117.
Essays on Canadian Writing, Volume 12, 1978; summer, 1983.
French Review, May, 1986; December, 1988, p. 363; February, 1991, p. 451; December, 1999, Patrice J. Proulx, review of *Est-ce que je te derange?,* pp. 380-381; December, 2000, Douglas L. Boudreau, "Anglophone Presence in the Early Novels of Anne Hébert," pp. 308-319; December, 2000, Karin Egloff, review of *Un Habit de lumiere,* pp. 398-399.
Journal of Canadian Fiction, Volume 2, number 1, 1972.
Library Journal, March 15, 1994, p. 74.
Los Angeles Times, January 26, 2000.
Modern Fiction Studies, summer, 1981.
New York Times, September 7, 1977.
New York Times Book Review, July 22, 1984, p. 7.
Poetry, June, 1968.
Publishers Weekly, May 18, 1984, p. 142; March 28, 1994, p. 91.
Quebec Studies, Volume 3, 1985; Volume 4, 1986; Volume 5, 1987; Volume 6, 1988; Volume 8, 1989.
Quill and Quire, November, 1983, p. 20; January, 1995, p. 35.
Studies in Canadian Literature, Volume 14, number 1, 1989.
Waves, spring, 1982.
Women's Review of Books, November, 1984.
World Literature Today, spring, 1993, p. 323; autumn, 1994, p. 781; winter, 2000, Bettina L. Knapp, review of *Un Habit de lumiere,* p. 104.
Yale French Studies, Volume 65, 1983.

ONLINE

Books and Writers, http://www.kirjasto.sci.fi/ (May 11, 2003).

OBITUARIES:

PERIODICALS

Los Angeles Times, January 26, 2000, p. A16.
Maclean's, February 7, 2000, p. 57.
New York Times, February 3, 2000, p. A23.
Time International, February 7, 2000, p. 56.*

* * *

HELLER, Joseph 1923-1999

PERSONAL: Born May 1, 1923, in Brooklyn, NY; died of a heart attack, December 12, 1999, in East Hampton, CT; son of Isaac (a truck driver) and Lena Heller; married Shirley Held, September 3, 1945 (divorced); married Valerie Humphries, 1987; children: (first marriage) Erica Jill, Theodore Michael. *Education:* Attended University of Southern California; New York University, B.A., 1948; Columbia University, M.A., 1949; graduate study, Oxford University, 1949-50.

CAREER: Novelist. Pennsylvania State University, University Park, instructor in English, 1950-52; *Time,* New York, NY, advertising writer, 1952-56; *Look,* New York, NY, advertising writer, 1956-58; *McCall's,* New York, NY, promotion manager, 1958-61; former teacher of fiction and dramatic writing at Yale University and University of Pennsylvania; City College of the City University of New York, Distinguished Professor of English, until 1975; full-time writer, 1975—. Worked in the theater, movies, and television. *Military service:* U.S. Army Air Forces, World War II; served as B-25 wing bombardier; flew sixty missions; became first lieutenant.

MEMBER: Phi Beta Kappa.

AWARDS, HONORS: Fulbright scholar, 1949-50; National Institute of Arts and Letters grant in literature, 1963; Prix Interallie (France) and Prix Medicis Étranger (France), both 1985, both for *God Knows;* Thomas Cooper Medal, University of South Carolina, 1996.

WRITINGS:

Catch-22 (novel; also see below; portions originally published in *New World Writing,* 1955), Simon & Schuster (New York, NY), 1961.

Something Happened (novel; portions originally published in *Esquire,* September, 1966), Knopf (New York, NY), 1974.
Good As Gold (novel), Simon & Schuster (New York, NY), 1979.
God Knows (novel), Knopf (New York, NY), 1984.
(With Speed Vogal) *No Laughing Matter* (autobiography), Putnam (New York, NY), 1986.
Picture This, Putnam (New York, NY), 1988.
Closing Time, Simon & Schuster (New York, NY), 1994.
Now and Then: From Coney Island to Here, Franklin Library, 1998.
Portrait of an Artist, As an Old Man, Simon & Schuster (New York, NY), 2000.
Catch As Catch Can: The Collected Stories and Other Writings, Simon & Schuster (New York, NY), 2003.

PLAYS

We Bombed in New Haven (two-act; first produced at Yale Repertory Theater, 1967, produced on Broadway, 1968), Knopf (New York, NY), 1968.
Catch-22: A Dramatization (one-act play; based on novel of same title; first produced in East Hampton, NY, 1971), Samuel French (New York, NY), 1971.
Clevinger's Trial (based on portion of *Catch-22;* produced in London, England, 1974), Samuel French (New York, NY), 1973.

SCREENPLAYS

(With David R. Schwartz) *Sex and the Single Girl* (based on the book by Helen Gurley Brown), Warner Bros., 1964.
(Uncredited) *Casino Royale* (based on the novel by Ian Fleming), Columbia Pictures, 1967.
(With Tom Waldman and Frank Waldman) *Dirty Dingus Magee* (based on the novel *The Ballad of Dingus Magee* by David Markson), Metro-Goldwyn-Mayer, 1970.
(Contributor) *Of Men and Women* (television drama), American Broadcasting Companies, Inc., 1972.

Also author, under pseudonym, of other television screenplays, c. 1960s. Contributor to books, including *Nelson Algren's Own Book of Lonesome Monsters,* Lancer, 1960; contributor of short stories to periodicals, including *Atlantic Monthly, Esquire,* and *Cosmopolitan*; contributor of reviews to periodicals, including *New Republic.*

ADAPTATIONS: Catch-22 was produced as a motion picture adapted by Buck Henry and directed by Mike Nichols, Paramount, 1970. *Now and Then: From Coney Island to Here* was adapted for audio cassette.

SIDELIGHTS: "There was only one catch . . . and that was Catch-22," Doc Daneeka informs Yossarian. As Yossarian, the lead bombardier of Joseph Heller's phenomenal first novel, soon learns, this one catch is enough to keep him at war indefinitely. After pleading with Doc Daneeka that he is too crazy to fly any more missions, Yossarian is introduced to Catch-22, a rule which stipulates that anyone rational enough to want to be grounded could not possibly be insane and therefore must return to his perilous duties. The novel *Catch-22* is built around the multifarious attempts of Captain John Yossarian to survive World War II, to escape the omnipresent logic of a regulation which somehow stays one step ahead of him.

At the time of its publication in 1961, Heller's antiwar novel met with modest sales and lukewarm reviews. But by the middle of its first decade it became a favored text of the counterculture. *Catch-22* "came when we still cherished nice notions about WW II," Eliot Fremont-Smith recalled in the *Village Voice.* "Demolishing these, it released an irreverence that had, until then, dared not speak its name." With more than ten million copies now in print by the end of the twentieth century, *Catch-22* became generally regarded as one of the most important novels of the postwar era. The title itself has become part of the language, and its "hero" Yossarian, according to Jack Schnedler of the *Newark Star-Ledger,* "has become the fictional talisman to an entire generation."

In the *New York Times Book Review,* Heller once cited three reasons for the success of *Catch-22:* "First, it's a great book. I've come to accept the verdict of the majority. Second, a whole new generation of readers is being introduced to it. . . . Third, and most important: Vietnam. Because this is the war I had in mind; a war fought without military provocation, a war in which the real enemy is no longer the other side but someone allegedly on your side. The ridiculous war I felt lurking in the future when I wrote the book." "There seems no denying that though Heller's macabre farce was written about a rarefied part of the raging war of the forties during the silent fifties," Josh Greenfeld wrote in a *New York Times Book Review* article, "it has all but become the chapbook of the sixties." Joseph Epstein likewise summarized in *Book World: Catch-22* "was a well-aimed bomb."

In his *Bright Book of Life,* Alfred Kazin found that "the theme of *Catch-22* . . . is the total craziness of war . . . and the struggle to survive of one man, Yossarian, who knows the difference between his sanity and the insanity of the system." After his commanding officer repeatedly raises the number of bombing missions required for discharge, Yossarian decides to "live forever or die in the attempt." "Yossarian's logic becomes so pure that everyone thinks him mad," Robert Brustein wrote in the *New Republic,* "for it is the logic of sheer survival, dedicated to keeping him alive in a world noisily clamoring for his annihilation." Brustein continued: "According to this logic, Yossarian is surrounded on all sides by hostile forces. . . . [He] feels a blind, electric rage against the Germans whenever they hurl flak at his easily penetrated plane; but he feels an equally profound hatred for those of his own countrymen who exercise an arbitrary power over his life."

"The urgent emotion in Heller's book is . . . every individual's sense of being directly in the line of fire," Kazin believed. In the *Dictionary of Literary Biography,* Inge Kutt viewed Pianosa, the fictional island in the Mediterranean Sea on which the novel is set, as a microcosm of "the postwar world which not only includes the Korean and Vietnam wars but also the modern mass society." "Heller's horrifying vision of service life in World War II is merely an illustration of the human condition itself," Jean E. Kennard asserted in *Mosaic.* "The world has no meaning but is simply there," and "man is a creature who seeks meaning," Kennard elaborated. "Reason and language, man's tools for discovering the meaning of his existence and describing his world, are useless."

Language, as presented in *Catch-22,* is more than useless; it is dangerous, a weapon employed by the authorities to enslave individuals in a world of institutionalized absurdity, a world where pilots lose their lives because their commanding officer wants to see prettier bombing patterns or his name in the *Saturday Evening Post.* Language, in the form of Catch-22, is the mechanism which transforms military doublethink into concrete reality, into commands which profoundly affect human life and death. Catch-22, as the novel states, is the rule "which specified that a concern for one's safety in the face of dangers that were real and immediate was the process of a rational mind. Or was crazy and could be grounded. All he had to do was ask; and as soon as he did, he would no longer be crazy and would have to fly more missions." As Jerry H. Bryant noted in his book *The Open Decision:* "Only the insane voluntarily continue to fly. This is an almost perfect catch because the law is in the definition of insanity. . . . The system is closed."

The acquiescence of men to language in *Catch-22,* Carol Pearson observed, is rooted in their failure to find any "transcendental comfort to explain suffering and to make life meaningful. . . . People react to meaninglessness by renouncing their humanity, becoming cogs in the machine. With no logical explanation to make suffering and death meaningful and acceptable, people renounce their power to think and retreat to a simple-minded respect for law and accepted 'truth.'" Writing in the *CEA Critic,* Pearson cited one of the book's many illustrations of this moral retreat: "The M.P.'s exemplify the overly law-abiding person who obeys law with no regard for humanity. They arrest Yossarian who is AWOL, but ignore the murdered girl on the street. By acting with pure rationality, like computers programmed only to enforce army regulations, they have become mechanical men." This incident, this "moment of epiphany," as Raymond M. Olderman described it in *Beyond the Waste Land,* symbolizes "much of the entire novel's warning—that in place of the humane, . . . we find the thunder of the marching boot, the destruction of the human, arrested by the growth of the military-economic institution."

In the novel, the character Milo Minderbinder is the personification of this military-economic system. An enterprising mess officer, Minderbinder creates a one-man international syndicate whose slogan, "What's good for MM Enterprises is good for the country," is used to justify a series of war-profiteering schemes. Minderbinder forms a private army of mercenaries available to the highest bidder, corners the market on food and makes enormous profits selling it back to army mess halls, and convinces the U.S. government that it must buy up his overstock of chocolate-coated cotton balls in the interest of national security. Milo's empire soon stretches across Europe and North Africa, and his ambitions culminate in one final economic boom. As Olderman observed: "The ultimate inversion comes when Milo bombs and strafes his own camp for the Germans, who pay their bills more promptly than some, and kills many Americans at an enormous profit. In the face of criticism, he reveals the overwhelming virtue of his profit." In the *Canadian Review of American Studies* Mike Franks concluded that "for Milo, contract, and the entire economic structure and ethical system it embodies and represents, is more sacred than human life."

"The military-economic institution rules, and the result is profit for some, but meaningless, inhuman parades for everyone else," Olderman wrote. Confronted with this "totally irrelevant and bureaucratic power that either tosses man to his death or stamps out his spirit," Yossarian must make a moral decision. Olderman surveyed Yossarian's alternatives: "He can be food for the cannon; he can make a deal with the system; or he can depart, deserting not the war with its implications of preserving political freedom, but abandoning a waste land, a dehumanized inverted, military-economic machine." As Bryant noted, "The only way that the circular justification of Catch-22 can be dealt with is by breaking out of the circle."

In the *Partisan Review,* Morris Dickstein commented: "The insanity of the system . . . breeds a defensive counter-insanity." Yossarian is "a protagonist caught up in the madness, who eventually steps outside it in a slightly mad way." Heller remarked in *Pages* that much of the humor in his novel arises out of his characters' attempts to escape, manipulate, and circumvent the logic of Catch-22. Before deserting, Yossarian tries to outwit Catch-22 in order to survive; he employs "caution, cowardice, defiance, subterfuge, stratagem, and subversion, through feigning illness, goofing off, and poisoning the company's food with laundry soap," Brustein wrote.

"Heller's comedy is his artistic response to his vision of transcendent evil, as if the escape route of laughter were the only recourse from a malignant world," Brustein stated. The novelist "is concerned with that thin boundary of the surreal, the borderline between hilarity and horror. . . . Heller often manages to heighten the macabre obscenity of war much more effectively through its gruesome comic aspects than if he had written realistic descriptions. And thus, the most delicate pressure is enough to send us over the line from farce to phantasmagoria." "Below its hilarity, so wild that it hurts, *Catch-22* is the strongest repudiation of our civilization, in fiction, to come out of World War II," Nelson Algren stated in the *Nation.*

Heller's subsequent novels continued this "war," extending the field of battle to governmental and corporate life. *Good As Gold,* Fremont-Smith noted in the *Village Voice,* is "touted . . . as doing for the White House what *Catch-22* did for the military," while the absurdity and alienation of the American business community is the focus of *Something Happened,* the story of Bob Slocum, a middle-level manager who describes himself as "one of those many people . . . who are without ambition already and have no hope."

In the *New Republic,* William Kennedy analyzed *Something Happened*'s restless protagonist: "Slocum is no true friend of anybody's. He is a woefully lost figure with a profound emptiness, a sad, absurd, vicious, grasping, climbing, womanizing, cowardly, sadistic, groveling, loving, yearning, anxious, fearful victim of the indecipherable, indescribable malady of being born human." John W. Aldridge described Slocum as "a man raging in a vacuum." Writing in the *Saturday Review/World,* Aldridge examined Slocum's plight: "He is haunted by the sense that at some time in the past something happened to him, something that he cannot remember but that changed him from a person who had aspirations for the future, who believed in himself and his work, who trusted others and was able to love, into the person he has since unaccountably become, a man who aspires to nothing, believes in nothing and no one, least of all himself, who no longer knows if he loves or is loved."

Slocum's loss of meaning is symbolized by the lost dreams of his youth. "As Yossarian kept flashing back to that primal, piteous scene in the B-25 where his mortally wounded comrade, Snowden, whimpered in his arms, so Slocum keeps thinking back, with impacted self-pity and regret, to the sweetly hot, teasing, slightly older girl in the insurance office where he worked after graduating from high school, whom he could never bring himself to 'go all the way' with," Edward Grossman wrote in *Commentary.* "He blew it," D. Keith Mano remarked in the *National Review,* "and this piddling missed opportunity comes to stand for loss in general. He makes you accompany him again and again, and again and again to the back staircase for a quiet feel that never matures." As Mano noted, "Slocum becomes semi-obsessed: telephones the insurance company to ascertain if his . . . girlfriend is still employed there, if *he* is still employed there. And he isn't." Instead, Slocum finds that this haunting figure of a girl, like his own spirit, has committed suicide.

In the *Atlantic Monthly,* Benjamin DeMott attributed Slocum's pain to the fact that "caring at levels deeper than these is beyond him." Melvin Maddocks pointed out that "it is not what has happened, but what has not happened to Slocum that constitutes his main problem." In a *Time* review, Maddocks described Slocum as "a weightless figure with no pull of gravity morally or emotionally" who can love only his nine-year-old son, and then only for "brief, affecting moments."

However much the circumstances of his life may conspire against Slocum, the real pressure is exerted from within. As Heller once commented in the *Newark Star-Ledger:* "All the threats to Bob Slocum are internal. His enemy is his own fear, his own anxiety." According to an *America* review, "Heller has replaced the buzzing, booming world of an army at war with the claustrophobic universe of Bob Slocum's psyche, where all the complications, contradictions and absurdities are generated from within. . . . Like Yossarian, Slocum always feels trapped—by his wife, by his children, but mostly by himself." Slocum, who giggles inwardly at the thought of rape and glances over his shoulder for sodomists, confesses, "Things are going on inside me I cannot control and do not admire." "Within and without, his world is an unregenerate swamp of rack and ruin," Pearl K. Bell asserted in a *New Leader* review. "Pathologically disassociated from himself, Slocum is a chameleon, taking on the gestures and vocabularies of whichever colleague he is with; even his handwriting is a forgery, borrowed from a boyhood friend." This disassociation is more than a middle-age malaise; it is symptomatic of a deeper affliction, a crippling of the spirit that leaves Slocum barely enough strength to lament, "I wish I knew what to wish."

According to *Playboy, Something Happened* "unleashed a fusillade of violently mixed reviews. . . . Nearly three quarters of the critics viewed Heller's looping, memory-tape narrative as a dazzling, if depressing, literary tour de force." Fremont-Smith, for instance, called *Something Happened* a "very fine, wrenchingly depressing" novel. "It gnaws at one, slowly and almost nuzzlingly at first, mercilessly toward the end. It hurts. It gives the willies." In his *New York Times Book Review* article, Kurt Vonnegut described the novel as "splendidly put together and hypnotic to read. It is as clear and hard-edged as a cut diamond." Melvin Maddocks, however, labeled Heller's second novel "a terrific letdown," while Grossman dubbed *Something Happened* "a painful mistake." He cited as a frequent criticism of the novel that Heller "indulges in overkill. When we have seen Bob Slocum suffer a failure of nerve (or a failure of common humanity) in a dozen different situations, we do not need to see him fail a dozen times more." Mano asserted that "you can start *Something Happened* on page 359, read through to the end, and still pass a multiple choice test in plot, character, style."

Heller's third novel "indicts a class of clerks," Leonard wrote in the *New York Times. Good As Gold* is a fictional exposé of the absurd workings of the machinery of government, of a politics reduced to public relations, of a president who spends most of his first year in office penning *My Year in the White House,* of an administrative aide who mouths such wisdom as "Just tell the truth . . . even if you have to lie" and "This President doesn't want yes-men. What we want are independent men of integrity who will agree with all our decisions after we make them." Into this world stumbles Bruce Gold, a professor of English who is called to public service after writing a favorable review of the Presidential book. Gold is rewarded for his kind words with a "spokesman" position but yearns for higher duty; specifically, he wants to be secretary of state, more specifically, he wants to be the first *real* Jewish secretary of state (Gold is convinced that Henry Kissinger, who prayed with Richard Nixon and "made war gladly," cannot possibly be Jewish). For his part, Gold chips in by coining such expressions as "You're boggling my mind" and "I don't know," phrases that enter the lexicon of the press conference and earn Gold the admiration of his superiors. As *Time*'s R. Z. Sheppard observed, Gold "is no stranger to double-think. A literary hustler whose interest in government is a sham, he does not even vote, a fact 'he could not publicly disclose without bringing blemish to the image he had constructed for himself as a radical moderate.'"

Good As Gold "is essentially about Jews, especially those like Gold, who wants to escape his identity while exploiting it, particularly by making a lot of money on a big book about Jews," Leonard Michaels commented in the *New York Times Book Review.* "Gold yearns to escape what he is so that he can become what he isn't, which is precisely what he hates. He nearly succeeds, nearly becomes a Washington non-Jewish Jew, a rich, powerful slave with a tall blonde wife." Gold, unlike other characters in the story, is very much aware of his moral degeneration; a passage from the book reads: "How much lower would he crawl to rise to the top? he asked himself with wretched self-reproval. Much, much lower, he answered in improving spirit, and felt purged of hypocrisy by the time he was ready for dinner."

In his *New York Times* article, Michaels elaborated on Gold's dilemma: "What is being proposed is that being brought up lower middle-class Jewish in this country means being humiliated by your own family; that you assimilate, by groveling, a vacuum and a lie; that you have masturbatory dreams of acquiring the power to exact revenge on the father who disdains you; that to acquire such power you will be willing to mortgage every morsel of your capacity for critical discrimination; that you lick the boots that specialize in stepping on you, and hate yourself in the morning."

Indeed, Heller's treatment of the "Jewish Experience in America"—particularly his attack on then-secretary of state Kissinger—aroused criticism, including accusations that *Good As Gold* was anti-Semitic. According to Sheppard, the book "is a savage, intemperately funny satire on the assimilation of the Jewish tradition of liberalism into the American main chance. It is a delicate subject, off-limits to non-Jews fearful of being thought anti-Semitic and unsettling to successful Jewish intellectuals whose views may have drifted to the right in middle age. Heller, who is neither a Gentile or a card-carrying intellectual, goes directly for the exposed nerve." In *Books and Bookmen,* Hayman pointed out that the Gentiles in Heller's satirical novel are "even more obnoxious" than the Jewish characters. "Both, fortunately, are extremely entertaining."

In the *New York Review of Books,* Thomas Edwards remarked that "*Good As Gold,* if hardly a perfect novel, is continuously alive, very funny, and finally coherent. . . . Like Heller's other novels, [it] is a book that takes large risks: it is sometimes rambling, occasionally self-indulgent, not always sure of the difference between humor and silliness. But this time the risks pay off. . . . Heller is among the novelists of the last two decades who matter." A *Hudson Review* contributor described it as a "big, ugly book," and Aram Bakshian, Jr. of the *National Review* called it "an embarrassing flop." Hayman found the novel flawed, but said that "nothing is unforgivable when a book makes you laugh out loud so often," and McPherson concluded: "When I didn't hate it, I loved it. Joseph Heller, of all people, would understand that." Finally, Mel Brooks in *Book World* rated *Good As Gold* "somewhere between *The Brothers Karamazov* and those dirty little books we used to read. . . . It's closer to *Karamazov.*"

Five years after publishing *Good As Gold* Heller produced *God Knows,* a satiric novel whose tone has been likened to that of a stand-up comedy routine. The narrator of *God Knows* is the Old Testament's David—the killer of Goliath, poet and singer for Biblical royalty, king of Israel, and father of the wise ruler Solomon—who is portrayed in the book as an idiot. Despite some critics' objections that the book lacks a unifying point, reviewers overwhelmingly proclaimed it, as did Stuart Evans in the London *Times,* "a very funny, very serious, very *good* novel." *Picture This,* published in 1988, is a reflection on such figures in Western history as Dutch painter Rembrandt, Greek philosophers Socrates and Plato, and several twentieth-century U.S. presidents. Similar in tone to *God Knows, Picture This* revels in anachronisms, mentioning the "freedom fighters" of the war between Athens and Sparta, for example, and of "police actions" in the fifth century B.C. A few of the author's main themes, according to Richard Rayner of the London *Times,* are that "power and intellect are incompatible, that politicians wage disastrous wars for no good reason, . . . and that humanity learns nothing from its mistakes." Rayner added, though, that "Heller does all this in *Picture This* and gets away with it most of the time, for the simple reason that he is funny. . . . He refuses to take institutions seriously; or rather, . . . he takes them *so* seriously they become hilarious."

While working on *God Knows* during the early 1980s, Heller was stricken with a nerve disease, Guillain-Barre syndrome, that left him paralyzed for several months. Though the author became too weak to move and almost too weak to breathe on his own, he eventually regained his strength and recovered from the often fatal disorder. After completing *God Knows,* Heller began writing his first memoir, *No Laughing Matter,* with Speed Vogel, a friend who helped him considerably during his illness. *No Laughing Matter* tells the story of Heller's convalescence and his friendship with Vogel in sections that are written alternately by the two men. Noting that Vogel's observations "provide comic relief to Mr. Heller's medical self-absorption," *New York Times* writer Christopher Lehmann-Haupt praised the book as both serious and comic. "It was indeed no laughing matter," Lehmann-Haupt observed. "And yet we do laugh, reading this account of his ordeal. We laugh because as well as being an astute observer of his suffering . . . Heller can be blackly funny about it." The reviewer added that "most of all, we laugh at the way Mr. Heller and his friends relate to each other. . . . [Their] interaction is not only richly amusing, it is positively cheering."

In 1994, thirty-four years after the publication of *Catch-22,* Heller published its sequel, *Closing Time.* The move astonished critics who felt a sequel was a gutsy undertaking considering the legendary status of the original novel. But *Closing Time* is not so much a sequel as it is a novel that involves a few of the characters from *Catch-22* in the 1990s. Those characters still have their quirks. John Yossarian still is in good health and still looking to be diagnosed with an ailment. Milo Minderbinder still runs MM Enterprises and has become a billionaire through questionable deals. The chaplain (renamed Albert Taylor Tapman) still is malleable. Of the characters carried over to *Closing Time,* Sammy Singer, a fainting unnamed gunner in *Catch-22,* has probably matured the most. A new protagonist is Giant Lew Rabinowitz, a childhood friend of Singer's who served in the infantry and succumbs to Hodgkin's disease during the course of the book.

About half of *Closing Time* is told in first-person narrative by Singer, Rabinowitz, and Rabinowitz's wife, Claire, after her husband's death. The second half of the book is told in the third person, referring to Yossarian. Employing black humor, Heller mixes sane tales with absurdities and phantasmagorias. The Port Authority Bus Terminal serves as the farcical scene for many events. When Yossarian and a policeman explore the subbasements of the building, they enter a hell inhabited by dead family members and other personages, and Yossarian sees a younger self at the Coney Island Steeplechase Park. The upper level of the Bus Terminal crawls with absurdity too, as misfits of every stripe inhabit it. Yet Minderbinder picks up on Yossarian's suggestion and holds his son's wedding and reception at the Bus Terminal, shipping the riffraff to shelters in New Jersey and hiring actors, who do a more credible job playing their parts. Meanwhile, instead of going to the wedding, the president stays home to play computer games and accidentally deploys the U.S. missile arsenal and attack bombers.

Critics gave *Closing Time* generally favorable reviews. Writing in the *New York Times Book Review,* William H. Pritchard remarked, "Although *Closing Time* won't astonish readers with its inventive brilliance and surprise, . . . it contains a richness of narrative tone and of human feeling lacking in the earlier book." According to Mark Jackson of *Books,* Heller confronts "mortality, monumental literature, war and the decline of civilisation before this wonderful and unforgettable novel draws to a close." In Chicago's *Tribune Books,* John W. Aldridge characterized *Closing Time* as "a different, not better book than *Catch-22.*" While it lacks a "central dramatic element" and its black humor sometimes "seems gratuitous," "on the whole and considering the daunting precedent of *Catch-22* looming behind it, this is an impressive performance."

"*Catch As Catch Can: The Collected Stories and Other Writings* is a wonderful testament to the mystery of literary creativity and to how much it often owes to a combination of dogged effort and serendipity," wrote Sean McCann in a *Book* review of this posthumous collection of Heller's work. Many of the pieces included in this volume were written during the author's university studies. Other pieces are related to his most famous work, *Catch-22.* In a *Los Angeles Times* article, David L. Ulin noted that the title of the collection "plays on both the serendipitous nature of the contents and their connection to the author's most iconic effort." Although he felt that the pieces are "uninspired," nevertheless *Catch As Catch Can* "does provide an interesting perspective on the author." *Library Journal* reviewer Edward B. St. John recommended this book as an addition to "most collections of postwar fiction." "Heller's *Catch As Catch Can* has some worthy entries," wrote Michael Upchurch of the Knight Ridder/Tribune News Service, citing in particular a reminiscence of Coney Island, as seen through the eyes of both the youthful and the ageing Heller.

Jeff Guinn of the *Knight Ridder/Tribune News Service* remarked that *Now and Then: From Coney Island to*

Here "reflects the absolute best of Heller as writer and human being." This autobiography, published a year before the author's death in 1999, focuses on Heller's childhood on Coney island and his experiences after World War II. "This nostalgic autobiography. . . . [is] not sentimental, but evocative," stated *Library Journal* reviewer Janice E. Braun. "The Coney Island scenes are the most vivid," added Jo Carr in a second *Library Journal* review. Daneet Steffens of *Entertainment Weekly* also praised the anecdotes about Coney Island. In a *People* article, Thomas Fields-Meyer mentioned that he appreciated the fact that Heller, unlike many writers, was able to pen a "memoir that dredges up [no] painful childhood traumas," instead focusing on "warmly recalled memories." A *Forbes* reviewer was delighted to encounter the actual people upon whom characters in *Catch-22* were based. Charles Glass concluded in the *New Statesman:* "You want to listen to the old man in the rocker . . . recalling unrelated incidents and people from childhood, because he is Joseph Heller. And Joseph Heller, one of the great postwar novelists, deserves respect."

Heller died of a heart attack in East Hampton, Connecticut, in 1999, and his last novel, *Portrait of an Artist, As an Old Man,* was published posthumously. Many critics viewed the book as autobiographical in nature, as it tells the story of an author who achieves literary success in his early years, and is thereafter considered a one-novel-wonder. The protagonist, Eugene Pota, is an author who experiences writer's block precisely at the point in his life when he would like to write just one more successful book before the end of his career.

Portrait of an Artist, As an Old Man "is a well-written, thoughtful and amusing depiction of a writer who . . . no longer has anything new to say yet still wants to say something," said *World Literature Today* critic Daniel Garrett. Robert McLaughlin, writing in the *Review of Contemporary Fiction,* felt that Heller penned "a smart, funny, bittersweet, personal novel . . . as a farewell gift" to the world of literature. "Although Heller clearly wanted to create a study of a soul in crisis. . . . it has only morbid interest," noted Stephen Amidon in a *Sunday Times* review of the novel, while *Book* reviewer Paul Evans praised Heller's ability to successfully describe every writer's ultimate dilemma. A *Publishers Weekly* writer considered the book to be "a pleasant reminder of the author's great charm and fluency." Donna Seaman of *Booklist* noted Heller's "impish pleasure in satirizing himself and literary ambition." "Though not a masterpiece, it has enough flashes of the old brilliance, the bawdy language and the caustic wit to enable him to end his literary career on an upbeat note," stated *Hindu* critic, M. S. Nagarajan.

In a *Knight Ridder/Tribune News Service* article written after Heller's death, Carolyn Alessio and Ron Grossman noted that Heller "was one of the few writers of this or any age to add a catch phrase to the English language." The writers concluded with comments that Heller made about his literary work: He "attributed his insights to lessons learned from the delicatessen philosophers of his Brooklyn youth. 'It gave me my literary voice,' he once said, 'a consistent one through my novels, that is divided, sentimental, sarcastic and critical.'"

BIOGRAPHICAL AND CRITICAL SOURCES:

BOOKS

A Dangerous Crossing, Southern Illinois University Press (De Kalb, IL), 1973.

Aichinger, Peter, *The American Soldier in Fiction, 1880-1963,* Iowa State University Press (Des Moines, IA), 1975.

American Novels of the Second World War, Mouton, 1969.

Authors and Artists for Young Adults, Volume 24, Gale (Detroit, MI), 1998.

Authors in the News, Volume 1, Gale (Detroit, MI), 1976.

Bergonzi, Bernard, *The Situation of the Novel,* University of Pittsburgh Press, 1970.

Bier, Jesse, *The Rise and Fall of American Humor,* Holt (New York, NY), 1968.

Bruccoli, Matthew J. and C. E. Frazer Clark, Jr., editors, *Pages: The World of Books, Writers, and Writing,* Gale (Detroit, MI), 1976.

Bryant, Jerry H., *The Open Decision: The Contemporary American Novel and Its Intellectual Background,* Free Press (New York, NY), 1970.

Burgess, Anthony, *The Novel Now: A Guide to Contemporary Fiction,* Norton (New York, NY), 1967.

Colmer, John, editor, *Approaches to the Novel,* Rigby (Adelaide, Australia), 1967.

Contemporary Literary Criticism, Gale (Detroit, MI), Volume 1, 1973, Volume 3, 1975, Volume 5, 1976, Volume 8, 1978, Volume 11, 1979, Volume 36, 1986, Volume 63, 1991.

Dictionary of Literary Biography, Gale (Detroit, MI), Volume 2: *American Novelists since World War II,* 1978, *Yearbook: 1980,* 1981, Volume 28: *Twentieth-Century American Jewish Fiction Writers,* 1984.

Encyclopedia of World Biography, 2nd edition, Volume 17, Gale (Detroit, MI), 1998.

Friedman, Bruce Jay, editor, *Black Humor,* Bantam (New York, NY), 1965.

Harris, Charles B., *Contemporary American Novelists of the Absurd,* College and University Press, 1971.

Harrison, Gilbert A., editor, *The Critic As Artist: Essays on Books, 1920-1970,* Liveright (New York, NY), 1972.

Hauck, Richard Boyd, *A Cheerful Nihilism: Confidence and the Absurd in American Humorous Fiction,* Indiana University Press, 1971.

Heller, Joseph, *Catch-22,* Simon & Schuster (New York, NY), 1961.

Heller, Joseph, *Something Happened,* Knopf (New York, NY), 1974.

Heller, Joseph, *Good As Gold,* Simon & Schuster (New York, NY), 1979.

Kazin, Alfred, *The Bright Book of Life: American Novelists and Storytellers from Hemingway to Mailer,* Little, Brown (Boston, MA), 1973.

Kiley, Frederick, and Walter McDonald, editors, *A Catch-22 Casebook,* Crowell (New York, NY), 1973.

Kostelanetz, Richard, editor, *On Contemporary Literature,* Avon (New York, NY), 1964.

Literary Horizons: A Quarter Century of American Fiction, New York University Press (New York, NY), 1970.

Littlejohn, David, *Interruptions,* Grossman, 1970.

Miller, James E., Jr., *Quests Surd and Absurd: Essays in American Literature,* University of Chicago Press (Chicago, IL), 1967.

Miller, Wayne Charles, *An Armed America, Its Face in Fiction: A History of the American Military Novel,* New York University Press (New York, NY), 1970.

Moore, Harry T., editor, *Contemporary American Novelists,* Southern Illinois University Press (De Kalb, IL), 1964.

Nagel, James, editor, *Critical Essays on Catch-22,* Dickenson, 1974.

Nelson, Gerald B., *Ten Versions of America,* Knopf (New York, NY), 1972.

Olderman, Raymond M., *Beyond the Waste Land: The American Novel in the Nineteen-Sixties,* Yale University Press (New Haven, CT), 1972.

Podhoretz, Norman, *Doings and Undoings: The Fifties and After in American Writing,* Farrar, Straus (New York, NY), 1964.

Potts, Stephen W., *From Here to Absurdity: The Moral Battlefields of Joseph Heller,* Borgo Press (San Bernardino, CA), 1995.

Richter, D. H., *Fable's End: Completeness and Closure in Rhetorical Fiction,* University of Chicago Press (Chicago, IL), 1974.

Scott, Nathan A., editor, *Adversity and Grace: Studies in Recent American Literature,* University of Chicago Press (Chicago, IL), 1968.

Scotto, Robert M., editor, *A Critical Edition of Catch-22,* Delta (New York, NY), 1973.

Tanner, Tony, *City of Words,* Harper (New York, NY), 1971.

Wallace, Ronald, *The Last Laugh,* University of Missouri Press, 1979.

Whitbread, Thomas B., editor, *Seven Contemporary Authors,* University of Texas Press (Austin, TX), 1966.

PERIODICALS

America, October 26, 1974; May 19, 1979.

American Heritage, June, 2001, review of *Something Happened,* p. 26.

Arizona Quarterly, winter, 1980.

Atlantic Monthly, January, 1962; October, 1974; March, 1979.

Book, September, 2000, Paul Evans, review of *Portrait of an Artist, As an Old Man,* p. 65; March-April, 2003, Sean McCann, review of *Catch As Catch Can: The Collected Stories and Other Writings,* pp. 71-72.

Book Digest, May, 1976.

Booklist, November 15, 1999, review of *Catch-22,* p. 601; May 1, 2000, Donna Seaman, review of *Portrait of an Artist, As an Old Man,* p. 1587.

Books, October, 1967; summer, 1995, p. 24; spring, 1998, review of *Now and Then,* p. 5.

Books and Bookmen, June, 1979.

Book Week, February 6, 1966.
Book World, October 6, 1974; March 11, 1979; December 9, 1979.
Canadian Review of American Studies, spring, 1976.
CEA Critic, November, 1974.
Chicago Tribune Book World, March 18, 1979.
Christian Science Monitor, October 9, 1974; March 28, 1979; April 9, 1979; October 4, 1994.
Commentary, November, 1974; June, 1979; February, 2000, Norman Podhoretz, "Looking Back at *Catch-22,*" p. 32.
Commonweal, December 5, 1974; May 11, 1979.
Contemporary Literature, winter, 1998, Charlie Reilly, interview with Joseph Heller, p. 507.
Critique, Volume 5, number 2, 1962; Volume 7, number 2, 1964-65; Volume 9, number 2, 1967; Volume 22, number 2, 1970; Volume 17, number 1, 1975; Volume 18, number 3, 1977.
Detroit Free Press, March 18, 1979.
Entertainment Weekly, October 14, 1994, p. 53; March 6, 1998, Daneet Steffens, review of *Now and Then: From Coney Island to Here,* p. 74; June 20, 2001, review of *Portrait of an Artist, As an Old Man,* p. 61.
Forbes, March 9, 1998, review of *Now and Then,* p. S164.
Guardian (London, England), March 27, 1999, Diane Armstrong, interview with Heller, p. 22.
Harper's, March, 1979.
Hudson Review, winter, 1979-80.
Insight on the News, November 7, 1994, p. 28.
Kirkus Reviews, January 1, 1998, review of *Now and Then,* p. 35; January 15, 2003, review of *Catch As Catch Can,* p. 113.
Knight Ridder/Tribune News Service, February 18, 1998, Jeff Guinn, review of *Now and Then,* p. 218K0932; December 14, 1999, p. K7920; June 21, 2000, Roger Moore, review of *Portrait of an Artist, As an Old Man,* p. K2527; March 26, 2003, Michael Upchurch, review of *Catch As Catch Can,* p. K3388.
Library Journal, March 15, 1998, Janice E. Braun, review of *Now and Then,* p. 65; June 1, 1999, Jo Carr, review of *Now and Then,* p. 207; February 15, 2003, Edward B. St. John, review of *Catch As Catch Can,* p. 139.
Life, January 1, 1968.
Listener, October 24, 1974; May 10, 1979.
London Review of Books, October 20, 1994, p.22.
Los Angeles Times Book Review, March 25, 1979; February 22, 1998, review of *Now and Then,* p. 9; March 30, 2003, David L. Ulin, review of *Catch As Catch Can,* p. R9.
Midstream, July, 2000, Sanford Pinsker, review of *Portrait of the Artist, As an Old Man,* p. 40.
Midwest Quarterly, winter, 1974.
Mosaic, fall, 1968; spring, 1971.
Motive, February, 1968.
Nation, November 4, 1961; October 19, 1974; June 16, 1979.
National Review, November 22, 1974; July 20, 1979.
Newark Star-Ledger, October 6, 1974.
New Leader, October 28, 1974; March 26, 1979.
New Republic, November 13, 1961; October 19, 1974; March 10, 1979.
New Statesman, October 25, 1974; October 7, 1994, p. 39; March 20, 1998, Charles Glass, review of *Now and Then,* p. 54.
Newsweek, October 14, 1974; December 30, 1974; March 12, 1979; October 3, 1994, p. 66; June 12, 2000, David Gates, review of *Portrait of an Artist, As an Old Man,* p. 74.
New York, September 30, 1974; September 12, 1994, p. 100.
New Yorker, December 9, 1961; November 25, 1974; April 16, 1979; October 10, 1994.
New York Review of Books, October 17, 1974; April 5, 1979; October 20, 1994, p. 20.
New York Times, October 23, 1961; December 3, 1967; December 7, 1967; June 19, 1970; October 1, 1974; March 5, 1979; September 19, 1984; February 13, 1986; September 1, 1988; February 24, 1998, Michiko Kakutani, review of *Now and Then,* p. E8; May 30, 2000, Michiko Kakutani, review of *Portrait of an Artist, As an Old Man,* p. B7.
New York Times Book Review, October 22, 1961; September 9, 1962; March 3, 1968; October 6, 1974; February 2, 1975; May 15, 1977; March 11, 1979; September 11, 1988; August 28, 1994, p. 3; September 25, 1994; February 15, 1998, Phillip Lopate, review of *Now and Then,* p. 32.
New York Times Sunday Magazine, March 4, 1979; January 12, 1986.
Observer (London, England), May 16, 1999, review of *Now and Then,* p. 14.
Paris Review, winter, 1974.
Partisan Review, Volume 43, number 2, 1976.
People, March 2, 1998, Thomas Fields-Meyer, review of *Now and Then,* p. 44.

Playboy, June, 1975; September, 1988.

Publishers Weekly, November 1, 1985; July 1, 1988; August 1, 1994; May 29, 2000, review of *Portrait of an Artist, As an Old Man,* p. 52.

Review of Contemporary Fiction, fall, 2000, Robert L. McLaughlin, review of *Portrait of an Artist, As an Old Man,* p. 144.

Rolling Stone, April 16, 1981.

San Francisco Chronicle, April 28, 1998, "*Catch-22* Author Denies He Plagiarized," p. A2.

Saturday Review, October 14, 1961; August 31, 1968; February 6, 1971.

Saturday Review/World, October 19, 1974.

Spectator, June 15, 1962; October 26, 1974; May 5, 1979.

Stand, Volume 16, number 3, 1975.

Studies in the Novel, spring, 1971; spring, 1972.

Sunday Times, (London, England), July 30, 2000, Stephen Amidon, review of *Portrait of an Artist, As an Old Man,* p. 46.

Time, October 27, 1961; February 1, 1963; June 15, 1970; October 14, 1974; March 12, 1979; October 3, 1994, p. 80.

Times (London, England), November 29, 1984; October 19, 1988; October 20, 1988; March 2, 2000, review of *Portrait of an Artist, As an Old Man,* p. 40.

Times Literary Supplement, October 25, 1974; March 20, 1998, review of *Now and Then,* p. 36; August 18, 2000, Lorna Sage, review of *Portrait of an Artist, As an Old Man, p. 22.*

Tribune Books (Chicago, IL), October 9, 1994, p. 1.

Twentieth Century Literature, January, 1967; October, 1973.

U.S. News and World Report, April 9, 1979.

Village Voice, March 5, 1979.

Vogue, January 1, 1963.

Wall Street Journal, June 9, 2000, Steve Barnes, review of *Portrait of an Artist, As an Old Man,* p. W9.

Washington Post, October 8, 1984; August 31, 1988; June 13, 2000, Steven Moore, review of *Portrait of an Artist, As an Old Man.*

World Literature Today, winter, 2001, Daniel Garrett, review of *Portrait of the Artist, As an Old Man,* p. 114.

Writer's Digest, March, 1987.

Yale Review, summer, 1975.

ONLINE

University of South Carolina Web site, http://www.sc.edu/ (May 11, 2003).*

* * *

HOOD, Mary 1946-

PERSONAL: Born September 16, 1946, in Brunswick, GA; daughter of William Charles (an aircraft worker) and Katherine (a teacher; maiden name, Rogers) Hood. *Education:* Georgia State University, Atlanta, A.B., 1967. *Politics:* Democrat. *Religion:* "Humming Quaker." *Hobbies and other interests:* Natural history, ornithology, wildflower gardening.

ADDRESSES: *Home*—Commerce, GA. *Agent*—Liz Darhansoff, Darhansoff, Verrill & Feldman, 236 West 26th St., Suite 802, New York, NY 10001. *E-mail*—maryhood@aol.com.

CAREER: Visiting author, University of Georgia, 1993; John and Renee Grisham Chair of Visiting Southern Writer, University of Mississippi, 1996; visiting writer, Centre College, 1999; writer in residence, Reinhardt College, 2001; writer.

AWARDS, HONORS: Flannery O'Connor Award for short fiction and *Southern Review*/Louisiana State University Short Fiction Award, both 1984, both for *How Far She Went;* National Magazine Award in fiction, Pushcart Prize, and Whiting Award, all 1986, all for short story "Something Good for Ginnie"; Lillian Smith Award, 1987, and Townsend Prize for Fiction, 1988, both for *And Venus Is Blue;* Georgia Writer of the Year citation from Dixie Council of Authors and Journalists, 1988; residency fellowship to Hambidge Center, 1992; named Writer of the Decade by Contemporary Literature and Writing Conference, Kennesaw State University, 1999.

WRITINGS:

How Far She Went (short stories), University of Georgia Press (Athens, GA), 1984.

And Venus Is Blue (novella and short stories), Ticknor & Fields (New York, NY), 1986.
Familiar Heat (novel), Knopf (New York, NY), 1995.

Work represented in anthologies, including *The Best American Short Stories, 1984,* edited by John Updike and Shannon Ravenal, Houghton Mifflin (Boston, MA), 1984; *The Editors' Choice: New American Short Stories,* Volume 1, compiled by George E. Murphy, Jr., Bantam (New York, NY), 1985.

Contributor of short stories and essays to *Georgia Review, Kenyon Review, Ohio Review, North American Review, Yankee, Harper's Magazine, Art and Antiques,* and *Southern Magazine*. Contributor to *The New Georgia Guide,* edited by Thomas G. Dyer and Stanley W. Lindberg, University of Georgia Press (Athens, GA), 1996; *Eudora Welty: Writers' Reflections upon First Reading Welty,* edited by Pearl Amelia McHaney, Hill Street Press (Athens, GA), 1999. Author of foreword, *Rosiebelle Lee Wildcat Tennessee,* by Raymond Andrews, University of Georgia Press (Athens, GA), 1988.

Some of the author's manuscripts are housed in the Watkins Collection at Robert W. Woodruff Library, Emory University.

WORK IN PROGRESS: A story collection, tentatively titled, *Survival, Evasion and Escape;* a novel, tentatively titled, *The Other Side of the River;* five novels that make up the "Bartram County Quintet": *One in a Row, Two for Tea, Three to Make Ready, Four & 20 Blackbirds,* and *Cinco de Mayo.*

SIDELIGHTS: In award-winning stories and an ambitious novel, Mary Hood chronicles the landscape and people of the modern American South. Born and raised in Georgia, Hood creates stories that are "dominated by the voices of strong women whose themes echo the traditional regional concern with family and community," to quote Dede Yow in the *Dictionary of Literary Biography.* Although some of Hood's work is recognizably Southern in its themes and characterization, she has also moved beyond the bounds of traditional Southern writing to include multiethnic characters and situations that reflect the South's transition into the twenty-first century. Family farms are rent by subdivision, Cuban refugees ply fishing boats, and if characters ruminate about God it may be from a Catholic perspective. As Yow put it, Hood's fiction "is likely to . . . illuminate an elemental truth of the heart: to be whole, people need a place, a past, and other people. Without these, life is as precarious as forest land in the suburbs."

In an essay titled "A Stubborn Sense of Place: Writers and Writing on the South," Hood declared herself to be the daughter of a New Yorker father and a Georgian mother who tempers her tendency toward Southern verbiage with a "Northern conscience . . . that stands ready, tapping its foot, jingling the car keys . . . wanting me to *get on with it,* asking with every turn and delay of plot, 'So?'" Hood added that she has always thought of herself as "American, blooming where planted—which happens to be with a Southern exposure." Nevertheless, Yow noted that, "Like Flannery O'Connor, Hood has a sharp eye and a tone-sensitive ear. The literary heritage of her characters' language is rooted in the local-color writing of the nineteenth-century South, and while she retains the integrity of the dialect and diction of northwest Georgia, she takes equal care with the diction of her omniscient narrator. Her goal—never to condescend to her characters—is reflected in the apparent seamless connections between narrative voice and characters."

How Far She Went, Hood's award-winning first collection of short stories, consists of nine tales set in rural Georgia, exploring particularly the twin modern ills of isolation and loneliness. In each narrative the characters are unable to communicate with one another, sometimes with disastrous results. In the story "Lonesome Road Blues," for example, a lonely widow invites an itinerant country-western singer back to her chantilly-lace flat between performances and attempts to seduce him, only to have him abandon her for a tryst with someone younger; in "Solomon's Seal" a wife discovers too late what her love of fine things has cost her; in "Inexorable Progress" an apparently happy housewife and mother slides into depression, and in the title story a grandmother and rebellious granddaughter come to terms with each other only as the result of a near-tragedy.

How Far She Went won the attention and praise of many critics, who described its stories as lush, rich, impressive, and memorable. Frederick Busch, writing in the *Georgia Review,* praised Hood for her "sure visions, firm craft, and a native wit" and dubbed her "a writer well worth reading now—and watching in the future." *West Coast Review of Books* contributor Randy S. Lavine recommended Hood's debut volume for its "extremely well-written, impassioned stories" in which the author "reaches to the core of human understanding."

In *And Venus Is Blue,* Hood's second collection of short stories, the author again recreates the people and places of backwoods Georgia—tough, determined characters who fight hard for what they want but who don't usually succeed. In many ways they seem uniquely Southern, but the problems they face, such as suicide, divorce, and old age, are universal. The long title story, for instance, explores the effects of a man's suicide on his daughter. Composed of a series of vignettes arranged chronologically, "And Venus Is Blue" takes place both in one day and in sixteen years. Notified by her family of her father's death, Delia and her husband, Tom, travel the daylong journey home. During the trip back, Delia daydreams about her life from age two to eighteen, each episode of which ends abruptly with news of her father's death. In "Finding the Chain," a story described by *New York Times Book Review* contributor Alice McDermott as both "wonderfully humorous" and "melancholy," a woman returns in search of things "that have meaning for her" in the abandoned cabin where her grandmother once lived. After her husband and children, who have accompanied her, "summarily ruin or lose or destroy much of what she had hoped to preserve," wrote McDermott, the granddaughter is about to conclude that the trip has been "one long erosion" until, according to the reviewer, the search for a missing chain from the old porch swing "suddenly unites them all in a tribute not so much to the land or the past but to one another and the fragile bonds that belong to the present alone."

Yow observed: "Routed by land clearing for subdivisions and golf courses, the humans and animals in *And Venus Is Blue* struggle to survive their dying world. The gradual destruction of Hood's own neighborhood is mirrored in these stories, in which new shopping centers, trailers, rental homes, and junkyards take over the countryside. The old folk were disappearing, being taxed off the land, and Hood wanted to honor these people who worked with their hands."

Some reviewers have invariably compared the South Hood portrays in her fiction with the familiar South of the literature of William Faulkner, Eudora Welty, and Flannery O'Connor, only to come to the conclusion that the settings are not at all the same. McDermott noted that for Hood's characters there is no respite in "that familiar Southern antidote, history and the land." Many of Hood's characters, explained the critic, are "without history—parents are absent or unknown, or sunk deeply enough into their own lives to be both—and the land, the rented apartments and mill towns and fields gone to sedge, has been drained of meaning." Similarly, Judith Kitchen, writing in *Georgia Review,* commented, "[Hood's] characters are a generation removed . . . from the concept of gentility and a sense of established tradition. . . . These characters are hard at work making their lives out of what might appear to be thin air. Something has failed them; even the fleeting world of their childhood has vanished, gone out to the malls at the edge of town along with the other comforts of the old town square." They are missing, Kitchen posited, "what the Old South might have supplied—a society with unshakeable values. Instead, they make up the rules as they go." Likewise, *Kenyon Review* contributor David Baker, noted, "[Hood's] is an unsentimental vision of the New South where front porches yield to shopping malls and Camaros outnumber cotton fields." Hood's South, he continued, "finds its families falling apart, its women stranded yet struggling individually to grow stronger, and its very past—the history and nostalgia so important to Southern tradition—vanishing or vanished."

McDermott began her review of *And Venus Is Blue* by describing it as "marvelous" and concluded with this series of compliments: "[Hood] is consummately honest. She does not fear the bleak conclusions of some lives or the quiet, fleeting triumphs of others. She believes that the hopes, the trials, the weariness of spirit and even the difficult loves of her characters, all unresolved, are well worthy of our attention, and in her capable hands a reader cannot help but believe the same." *Los Angeles Times Book Review* contributor Doris Betts described *And Venus Is Blue* as a "beautifully written" collection distinguished by a "calm but melodic prose about complex human beings" who "just happen to live in one of the Southern latitudes of the human condition." Kitchen, dismissing the "postmodern rush to entertain the intellect, to play with language, to create a clever text," praised Hood for "restor[ing] story to its rightful position and, at the same time, carv[ing] new territories for short prose as well." Hood's stories, pronounced Kitchen, are "fast-paced, filled with details of the here-and-now." By the same token, Baker called Hood "one of this country's finest young writers," extolling the author's language as "wonderful music, always precisely modulated, alternately soothing and disarming and funny." He reserved his highest compliment, however, for her "narrator's subtle control and generous presentation of characters," calling that Hood's "most remarkable achievement." Baker concluded, "Simply, the eight stories of *And Venus Is Blue* are some of the finest, most powerfully written and moving pieces of fiction I've read in a long time. Hood's fresh language redeems through its beauty. Her characters are memorably and graciously drawn in a generous narrative style rare these days. Her stylistic range . . . shows her talent to be immense, her project large. Even if Mary Hood's characters can't or won't see their own lives, moment by moment, we can. We see in them the beautiful struggles of our own."

Hood's first novel, *Familiar Heat,* was published in 1995. Set in a small Florida town, the story ranges widely through the lives of its characters, lingering longest on the tale of Faye Rios, who survives an atrocious act of violence only to fall victim to brain damage in the aftermath of an automobile accident. *Southern Review* contributor Dorothy M. Scura wrote, "Hood's story circles and retreats, eddies and surges, as it develops its portrait of a community bound together by pain, love, marriage, and God. Yet one is less startled by the guy wires and forces of form than by the panoply of characters whose stories are told here: the list includes (but is not limited to) Cubans, Vietnamese, Americans black and white, and Greeks." With her memory wiped clean, Faye struggles to differentiate between truth and falsehood both in the immediate circumstances of her life and in the larger Christian cosmology offered by the parish priest. Scura continued, "Hood has proven her storytelling gifts in two collections of short fiction, and with this first novel she shows that she is just as adept with a longer narrative. . . . With its deployment of a massive and diverse cast of characters, its intricate balancing of plots, and its narrative time shifts, *Familiar Heat* suggests that ambitious and worthy enterprises are being undertaken by southern women, whose fiction will develop, over time, in ways that tease the speculator." *America* contributor Patrick H. Samway found the book "first rate, showing keen insight, native wit and marvelous dialogue." Malcolm Jones, Jr. in *Newsweek* described the novel as a "serious work—subtle, moving, and often very funny [about] the horrors and triumphs of how our lives connect." Jones concluded: "This Georgia writer has made the leap to the longer form without ever looking winded."

BIOGRAPHICAL AND CRITICAL SOURCES:

BOOKS

Contemporary Southern Writers, St. James Press (Detroit, MI), 1999.

Dictionary of Literary Biography, Volume 234: *American Short-Story Writers since World War II, Third Series,* Gale (Detroit, MI), 2001, pp. 135-141.

Folks, Jeffrey J. and James Perkins, editors, *Southern Writers at Century's End,* University of Kentucky Press (Lexington, KY), 1997, pp. 21-31.

Ruppersburg, Hugh, editor, *After O'Connor,* University of Georgia Press (Athens, GA), 2003.

PERIODICALS

America, November 16, 1996, Patrick H. Samway, review of *Familiar Heat,* p. 21.

Atlanta Constitution, January 11, 1985.

Atlanta Journal, January 11, 1985.

Atlanta Journal-Constitution, January 4, 2001, Chris Reinolds, "To Classroom Again Is How Far Writer Went," p. JQ1.

Booklist, September 1, 1995, Alice Joyce, review of *Familiar Heat,* p. 39.

Georgia Review, spring, 1985, Judith Kitchen, "The Moments That Matter," pp. 209-214.

Gettysburg Review, 1988, Dan Pope, "The Post-Minimalist American Story or What Comes after Carver?," pp. 331-342.

Harper's, August, 1986, Mary Hood, "A Stubborn Sense of Place: Writers and Writing on the South," pp. 35-45.

Kenyon Review, fall, 1987.

Los Angeles Times Book Review, August 17, 1986.

Newsweek, November 20, 1995, Malcolm Jones, Jr., review of *Familiar Heat,* p. 86.

New Yorker, January 21, 1985.

New York Times Book Review, August 17, 1986; October 22, 1995, Kit Reed, review of *Familiar Heat,* p. 37.

Publishers Weekly, July 31, 1995, review of *Familiar Heat,* p. 70.
Southern Review, autumn, 1997, Dorothy M. Scura, review of *Familiar Heat,* p. 859.
USA Today, August 1, 1986.
West Coast Review of Books, March, 1985.
Women's Review of Books, June, 1985.

* * *

hooks, bell
See WATKINS, Gloria Jean

* * *

HORN, Stephen (McCaffrey Moore) 1931-

PERSONAL: Born May 31, 1931, in Gilroy, CA; son of John Stephen (a geologist) and Isabelle (McCaffrey) Horn; married Nini Moore, September 4, 1954; children: Marcia, Stephen. *Education:* Stanford University, A.B. (with great distinction), 1953, Ph.D., 1958; Harvard University, M.P.A., 1955. *Politics:* Republican. *Religion:* Protestant.

ADDRESSES: *Home*—3944 Pine Ave., Long Beach, CA 90807. *Office*—Suite 160, 4010 Watson Plaza Drive, Lakewood, CA 90712; 2331 Rayburn Building, Washington, DC 20515. *E-mail*—steve.horn@mail.house.gov.

CAREER: Department of Labor, Washington, DC, administrative assistant to the U.S. Secretary of Labor, 1959-60; Office of U.S. Senator Kuchel, Washington, DC, legislative assistant, 1960-66; Brookings Institution, Washington, DC, senior fellow, 1966-69; American University, Washington, DC, dean of graduate studies and research, 1969-70; California State University, Long Beach, president, 1970-88; California State University, trustee professor of political science, 1988-1992; host and senior consultant for Westinghouse Broadcasting Co. series, "Operation Government," 1967-69; U.S. Commission on Civil Rights, Washington, DC, vice-chair, 1969-82; public services chair of United Crusade, 1971-72; U.S. House Representative from California, 1992—. *Military service:* U.S. Army, Strategic Intelligence Reserve, 1954-62.

MEMBER: American Political Science Association, Western Political Science Association, California Historical Society, California Scholarship Federation (chapter president), Stanford Alumni Association (board member), Stanford Associates, Phi Beta Kappa, Pi Sigma Alpha, El Capitan Eating Club, founding member and chairman of National Institute of Corrections of the U.S. Department of Justice.

AWARDS, HONORS: Congressional fellow, American Political Science Association, 1958-59; Institute of Politics fellow, Harvard University, 1966-67; named one of the 100 most effective college presidents in the United States, 1986; Distinguished Federal Leadership Award from the Association of Government Accountants for unsurpassed commitment to excellence to improve accountability and management within the federal government, 2002.

WRITINGS:

The Cabinet and Congress, Columbia University Press (New York, NY), 1960, Octagon Books (New York, NY), 1982.
Unused Power: The Work of the Senate Committee on Appropriations, Brookings Institution (Washington, DC), 1970.
(With Edmund Beard) *Congressional Ethics: The View from the House,* Brookings Institution (Washington, DC), 1975.
(Editor, with Constance A. Morella) *Will Federal Government Computers be Ready for the Year 2000: Hearing before the Committee on Science, U.S. House of Representatives,* DIANE Publishing (Darby, PA), 1997.
(Editor, with Constance A. Morella) *Year 2000 Risks: What Are the Consequences of Information Technology Failure: Hearing before the Committee on Science, U.S. House of Representatives,* DIANE Publishing (Darby, PA), 1998.
(Editor) *H.R. 4007 and S. 1379, The Nazi War Crimes Disclosure Act: Hearing before the Committee on Government Reform and Oversight, U.S. House of Representatives,* DIANE Publishing (Darby, PA), 1998.

SIDELIGHTS: Stephen Horn, a native Californian, has been active in education and government for most of his professional career. Horn has enjoyed a long and successful career in Washington, D.C., first in the Eisenhower administration, during which time he was an administrative assistant to Secretary of Labor James P. Mitchell. Then he served as legislative assistant to Senator Thomas H. Kuchel, the Deputy Republican Leader of the U. S. Senate, which allowed him to be involved in the Civil Rights Acts of 1964, the Voting Rights Act of 1965, and the creation of Medicare. More recently, in 1992, Horn was elected to the House of Representatives and currently serves on the Committee on Transportation and Infrastructure, the Committee on Government Reform, and is chairman of the Subcommittee on Government Efficiency, Financial Management, and Intergovernmental Relations. He has several books to his credit, both as author and as editor.

All of Horn's books are focused on the topic of government. His first, *The Cabinet and Congress,* explores the powers and duties of the U.S. Congress as well as that of Cabinet officers and the executive powers of the presidency. His second book, *Unused Power: The Work of the Senate Committee on Appropriations,* explains how the Senate makes appropriations.

In 1975, Horn worked with Edmund Beard, to write *Congressional Ethics: The View from the House;* and later coedited two publications with Constance A. Morella, which covered Congressional hearings on the Y2K concerns at the turn of the century.

Horn retired from the U.S. House of Representatives at the end of his term in January, 2003.

BIOGRAPHICAL AND CRITICAL SOURCES:

ONLINE

United States House of Representatives, http://www.house.gov/ (November 20, 2002).*

I

INADA, Lawson Fusao 1938-

PERSONAL: Born May 26, 1938, in Fresno, CA; son of Fusaji and Masako (Saito) Inada; married Janet Francis, February 19, 1962; children: Miles Fusao, Lowell Masao. *Education:* Attended University of California—Berkeley, 1956-57; Fresno State College (now California State University, Fresno), B.A., 1959; University of Iowa, graduate study, 1960-62; University of Oregon, M.F.A., 1966.

ADDRESSES: Home—2320 Morada Lane, Ashland, OR 97520. *Office*—Department of English, Southern Oregon State College, Ashland, OR 97520. *E-mail*—inada@sou.edu.

CAREER: University of New Hampshire, Durham, instructor in English, 1962-65; Southern Oregon State College, Ashland, associate professor, 1966-77, professor of English, 1977—. Visiting lecturer at Lewis and Clark College, 1969, Eastern Oregon State College, 1975, and University of Hawaii, 1976; King/Parks Scholar-in-Residence at Wayne State University, 1987. Host of radio program, *Talk Story: The Written Word,* on KSOR-FM, Ashland, OR. Seminar leader at various poetry and creative writing workshops, including Asian-Americans for a Fair Media Conference, 1975, Siskiyou Writers Conference, 1977, and Iowa State Department of Education Conference, 1978. Judge, Coordinating Council of Literary Magazines College Contest, 1976. Chair, Council of Literary Magazines, 1982-84; site evaluator, National Endowment for the Arts, 1987—; member, Committee on Racism and Bias in the Teaching of English, 1988—. Member of board of directors, Southern Oregon Public Television, 1990—. Has given readings of his poetry at numerous universities and seminars, including University of California—Berkeley, University of California—Los Angeles, University of Michigan, University of Oregon, San Francisco State University, University of Washington, Oregon Poetry-in-the-Schools, Minnesota Poetry-in-the-Schools, Seattle Arts Commission Festival, and National Poetry Festival. Consultant to

Lawson Fusao Inada

literary organizations, including Third World Writers Festival, Central Washington State College, 1974, Society for the Study of Multi-Ethnic Literature of the United States, 1977, and Asian-American Writers Conference, 1978.

MEMBER: Japanese American Citizens League.

AWARDS, HONORS: University of Iowa Writers Workshop fellowship, 1960-62; National Endowment for the Arts creative writing fellowship, 1972; Pioneer Writers Award from Asian-American Writers Conference, 1975; Oregon State teaching excellence award, 1984; National Endowment for the Arts poetry fellowship, 1985; Arizona Commission for the Arts research fellowship, 1990; named Oregon State Poet of the Year, 1991; American Book Award, 1994, for *Legends from Camp.*

WRITINGS:

Three Northwest Poets: Drake, Inada, Lawder, Quixote Press (Madison, WI), 1970.

Before the War: Poems As They Happen, Morrow (New York, NY), 1971.

(Coeditor) *Aiiieeeee!: An Anthology of Asian-American Writers,* Howard University Press (Washington, DC), 1974.

(With Garrett Kaoru Hongo and Alan Chong Lau) *The Buddha Bandits down Highway 99,* Buddhahead Press (Mountain View, CA), 1978.

(With Patti Moran McCoy and Kathleen Bullock) *Hey Diddle Rock,* Kids Matter (Ashland, OR), 1986.

(With Patti Moran McCoy and Kathleen Bullock) *Hickory Dickory Rock,* Kids Matter (Ashland, OR), 1986.

(With Patti Moran McCoy and Kathleen Bullock) *Humpty Dumpty Rock,* Kids Matter (Ashland, OR), 1986.

(With Patti Moran McCoy and Kathleen Bullock) *Rock-a-doodle-doo,* Kids Matter (Ashland, OR), 1986.

(Coeditor) *The Big Aiiieeeee!: An Anthology of Chinese-American and Japanese-American Literature,* Penguin (New York, NY), 1990.

In This Great Land of Freedom: The Japanese Pioneers of Oregon, Japanese-American National Museum (Los Angeles, CA), 1993.

Legends from Camp, Coffee House Press (Minneapolis, MN), 1993.

Drawing the Line, Coffee House Press (Minneapolis, MN), 1997.

(Editor and author of introduction) *Only What We Could Carry: The Japanese-American Internment Experience,* Heyday Books/California Historical Society (Berkeley, CA), 2000.

(Author of introduction) Toshio Mori, *Unfinished Message: Selected Works of Toshio Mori,* Heyday Books (Berkeley, CA), 2000.

Consultant/writer, *The Boys of Heart Mountain* and *Moving Memories,* video-documentaries, Japanese-American National Museum. Work represented in numerous anthologies, including *Down at the Santa Fe Depot: Twenty Fresno Poets,* edited by David Kherdian, Giligia Press, 1970; *The Modern Idiom,* edited by Lio Hamalian, Crowell (New York, NY), 1972; *Settling America,* edited by David Kherdian, Macmillan (New York, NY), 1974; *Modern Poetry of Western America,* edited by William Stanfford, Brigham Young University Press (Provo, UT), 1975; *Focus on Forms,* edited by Philip J. McFarland, Houghton Mifflin (Boston, MA), 1977;*Dreamers and Desperadoes: Contemporary Short Fiction of the American West,* edited by Craig Lesley, Dell (New York, NY), 1993; and *Moment's Notice: Jazz in Poetry and Prose,* edited by Art Lange and Nathaniel Mackey, Coffee House Press (Minneapolis, MN), 1993. Contributor of poetry to periodicals, including *Amerasia Journal, Bridge, Carleton Miscellany, Chicago Review, Evergreen Review, Kayak, Massachusetts Review, English Journal, Mother Jones, Northwest Review, San Francisco Review,* and *Southwest Review.* Member of editorial board, *Directory of American Poets and Fiction Writers,* 1976—, and *Contemporary Poetry,* 1977—. Assistant editor, *Northwest Review,* 1965-66; editor, *Rogue River Gorge,* 1970—; contributing editor, *Dues: Third World Writing,* 1972-74; contributing editor, *Northwest Review,* 1987—; guest editor, *Hawaii Review,* summer, 1978.

SIDELIGHTS: Lawson Fusao Inada is a Japanese-American poet and editor. In addition to several children's books that are adaptations of Mother Goose rhymes, he has written extensively about his experiences in a Japanese internment camp after World War II. Inada spent a significant part of his childhood as a prisoner and was one of the youngest Japanese Americans in the camps.

Inada's first volume of poetry was *Before the War: Poems As They Happen.* In it, the writer reflects on his feelings of dispossession and traces themes from his childhood before and after his imprisonment. The poems have been applauded for the way they connect personal and social history, along with images of family. In an essay on Japanese-American literature in *Three American Literatures: Essays in Chicano, Native American, and Asian-American Literature for Teachers of American Literature,* the writers commented, "There is nothing quaint about Lawson Inada's poetry, no phony continuity between sigh-inspiring Oriental art and his tough, sometimes vicious language."

In 1993, Inada published *Legends from Camp,* a set of poems that reflects on life in the camps. With his first-hand experience, Inada "carries a reader into a child's world behind barbed wire," as R. C. Doyle explained in *Choice. Legends from Camp* won an American Book Award in 1994.

Legends from Camp is divided into five sections, beginning with Inada's time in the internment camp, then moving to "Fresno," "Jazz," "Oregon," and "Performance." As Andrew J. Dephtereos wrote in the *American Book Review,* the collection creates "a decidedly personal history of Inada, told in chapters that represent significant stages in his persona's life."

Inada's poems embody his conviction that poetry must be accessible to all readers, not just to those who are most knowledgeable about the genre. "Poetry happens—whenever, wherever it wants," Inada asserts in the preface to *Legends from Camp,* "and the poet simply has to be ready to follow through on the occasion." Reviewing the collection for *Amerasia Journal,* Lonny Kaneko explained that Inada "writes a kind of popular poem, built for the listener's ear, aware, like jazz, of the need to capture in sound the spirit of his theme, of letting it build and reverberate in repeated phrases, little riffs and refrains that play through the poems." While the critic for *Publishers Weekly* found Inada's work to be "unsophisticated in tone, technique and conceptual structure," Jessica Grim of the *Library Journal* judged the book to be "playful, full of life, and easy to understand, even when the subject is somber—as in the first section, 'Camp,' which recounts the author's experience as a boy in the Japanese internment camps." Doyle commented that the powerful "Camp" section "will add a fresh dimension to a growing body of literature that remembers, humanizes, and shares the Japanese-American internment experience for new generations."

In 1997, Inada published another collection of poetry, *Drawing the Line.* This book is a tribute to Inada's ancestors who survived the camps and he focuses on a main character, Yosh Kuromiya. The title is taken from a story about Yosh creating a line drawing of a nearby mountain, attempting to use art as an escape from the daily indignities and labor of the camp. Rapee Malinee Thongthiraj, a critic for *Amerasia Journal,* noted that in these poems Inada seems to be "facing the memories of his personal and collective past, [creating] his own strategy of survival and resistance by re-envisioning American history and producing poetry that can move and stimulate us all." Thongthiraj also commented that these poems force the reader to "capture the emotions deep within ourselves."

Much of Inada's poetry is often referred to as "jazz poetics," and he admits to being strongly influenced by jazz music and musicians. As Juliana Chang observed in her *Modern American Poetry* essay "Time, Jazz, and the Racial Subject: Lawson Inada's Jazz Poetics," "His jazz poetics of repetition and improvisation enable re-stagings and re-workings of a troubled past." Chang also added that while Inada is not the first Asian-American poet to use jazz characteristics in his poetry, his "stands out in its consistency and depth of engagement with jazz."

BIOGRAPHICAL AND CRITICAL SOURCES:

BOOKS

Baker, Houston A., editor, *Three American Literatures: Essays in Chicano, Native American, and Asian-American Literature for Teachers of American Literature,* Modern Language Association of America, 1972, pp. 197-228.

PERIODICALS

Amerasia Journal, winter, 1993, p. 167; winter, 1997-98, pp. 223-27.
American Book Review, December, 1993, p. 22.
Choice, May, 1993, p. 1465.

Kirkus Reviews, November 15, 1970, review of *Before the War,* p. 1275.
Library Journal, January, 1993, p. 121.
Los Angeles Times Book Review, September 5, 1993, p. 6.
Nation, August 28, 1995, p. 204.
Publishers Weekly, May 31, 1991, p. 67; November 16, 1992, p. 57.
Small Press, summer, 1993, p. 85.
Western American Literature, spring, 1994, p. 85.

ONLINE

University of Illinois, http://www.english.uiuc.edu/ (July 23, 2002), essays on Inada.

OTHER

I Told You So: Lawson Fusao Inada (documentary film), Visual Communications, 1975.*

* * *

IRVINE, Janice M. 1951-

PERSONAL: Born August 1, 1951, in Pittsburgh, PA; daughter of William and Elvera (Siket) Irvine. *Education:* Pennsylvania State University, B.A., 1973, M.Ed., 1975; Brandeis University, M.A., 1981, Ph.D., 1984; Boston University, M.P.H., 1992.

ADDRESSES: Home—25 Oak St., Watertown, MA 02172.

CAREER: Counselor of emotionally disturbed adolescent girls at a school in Philadelphia, PA, 1973; Juniata Valley Mental Health, Huntington, PA, assistant director of community residence, 1974-76; Preterm, Inc., Brookline, MA, assistant coordinator of counseling, 1976-77; University of Massachusetts, Boston, health education coordinator, 1978-80; Tufts University, Medford, MA, health and sexuality educator, 1984-87, instructor at Experimental College, 1985-87, lecturer in community health and internship coordinator, 1988—. Therapist, Gender Identity Service, Boston, 1976-80; director of rehabilitation, Merrimack Valley Rehabilitation, 1977-79; community educator, Quincy Family Planning, 1984; lecturer in women's studies, Wellesley College, 1985-88; coordinator of women's education and community education, AIDS Action Committee of Massachusetts, Inc., 1988; ethnographer, Nova/Project Warn, 1991—; consultant to Planned Parenthood League of Massachusetts, AIDS Action Committee of the National Institute of Mental Health, and Sexual Attitude Reassessment Workshops.

MEMBER: Society for the Scientific Study of Sex, Sex Information and Education Council of the United States, Phi Beta Kappa.

WRITINGS:

Disorders of Desire: Sex and Gender in Modern American Sociology, Temple University Press (Philadelphia, PA), 1990.
(Editor) *Sexual Cultures and the Construction of Adolescent Identities,* Temple University Press (Philadelphia, PA), 1994.
Talk about Sex: The Battles over Sex Education in the United States, University of California Press (Berkeley, CA), 2002.

Contributor to *Journal of Sex Research.*

SIDELIGHTS: Janice M. Irvine writes on the attitudes towards sex and adolescence in American culture. In *Sexual Cultures and the Construction of Adolescent Identities,* "Irvine has gathered writings that probe the experiential and subjective worlds of adolescent sexual cultures," according to Arlene Stein in *Signs.* Stein went on to note that the essays collected by Irvine "encompass a range of different topics, from cross-cultural considerations in sexuality education, to lesbian and gay adolescents, to sexuality in adolescent fiction." She concluded by praising "the careful, compassionate feminist scholarship" of the volume.

Irvine's 2002 work, *Talk about Sex,* laments the domination of sexual education dialogue by the forces of the religious right. She describes how this trend has evolved, from the 1960s through the more conservative 1980s, to the present day. A *Publishers Weekly* reviewer described *Talk about Sex* as a "closely observed analysis." Similarly, Martha Cornog in the *Library Journal* praised it as "indispensable for anyone concerned with sexual policy and for social history collections in public and academic libraries."

BIOGRAPHICAL AND CRITICAL SOURCES:

PERIODICALS

Library Journal, September 15, 2002, Martha Cornog, review of *Talk about Sex: The Battles over Sex Education in the United States,* p. 82.

Publishers Weekly, July 1, 2002, review of *Talk about Sex,* p. 66.

Signs, spring, Arlene Stein, review of *Sexual Cultures and the Construction of Adolescent Identities,* p. 857.*

* * *

IRVINE, Lucy 1956-

PERSONAL: Born February 1, 1956, in London, England; daughter of hotel proprietors; married Gerald Kingsland (a journalist), April, 1981 (separated); children: Laurie, Magnus, Joe, Benji. *Education:* Attended British schools until age twelve.

ADDRESSES: *Home*—Scotland. *Agent*—Hilary Rubinstein, A. P. Watt Ltd., 26/28 Bedford Row, London WC1R 4HL, England.

CAREER: Has worked variously as a monkey keeper, artist's model, charwoman, apprentice stonemason, pastry cook, concierge, waitress, and tax clerk; writer.

MEMBER: Mensa, Chelsea Arts Club.

WRITINGS:

Castaway: A Story of Survival (autobiography), Gollancz (London, England), 1983, Random House (New York, NY), 1984.

Runaway (autobiography), Viking (New York, NY), 1986.

One Is One (novel), Hodder & Stoughton (London, England), 1989.

Faraway, Doubleday (New York, NY), 2001.

ADAPTATIONS: *Castaway* was made into a film by Nicholas Roeg, starring Oliver Reed and Amanda Donohoe, released in 1987.

SIDELIGHTS: Lucy Irvine recounts her year on a deserted tropical island in *Castaway: A Story of Survival.* Answering a newspaper ad for a "wife" placed by fifty-year-old British journalist and adventurer Gerald Kingsland, the twenty-five-year-old Irvine eagerly anticipated a physical and emotional survival challenge in a tropical paradise. What she didn't expect was that she would actually have to marry her male companion (a demand of Australian immigration authorities) and that delayed government approval would woefully reduce the pair's funds and supplies. Their yearned-for arrival on the mile-long island of Tuin, in the Coral Sea north of Australia, was soon followed by a grisly fight for survival that included malnutrition, sickness, and despair. Furthermore, while Irvine married solely to realize her island dream, Kingsland expected "all the services of a wife"—and her refusal to become intimate brought hostility and abuse from her survival mate. "The physical dangers . . . seem slight compared with the psychological ordeal . . . Irvine endured," observed Stephanie Mansfield in a *Washington Post* interview with the author. Irvine elaborated: "When you get a man and a woman and a piece of land, you have all the problems in microcosm of humanity. Sex. Violence. Politics."

Still, despite the devastating hardships, Irvine's love for Tuin flourished and she began to take pleasure in her own strength and endurance—with Kingsland becoming, at times, irrelevant. Natives from the nearby island of Badu also aided the couple by offering food and medical supplies. Irvine even submitted to Kingsland sexually when he threatened to cut their adventure short, for she was determined to complete the project. Three hundred sixty-five days after first setting foot on Tuin, Irvine returned to "the soft textures of civilization" with much to think about. The year "cost me a lot, but it gave me more," she confessed to Mansfield, though "for a while I thought it was the other way around."

A best-seller in England, *Castaway* was well received in other countries as well. While Toronto *Globe and Mail* reviewer M. T. Kelly described Irvine's story "of all too familiar domestic chauvinism, insensitivity and ugliness" as "a cautionary tale about the necessity of feminism," more critics perceived it as an arresting and well-written adventure chronicle. "Irvine writes a clean, accomplished prose," complimented Jonathan Yardley in the *Washington Post Book World.* "Her descriptive powers are acute, she has a good ear for dialogue, and she takes a refreshing pleasure in laughing at herself. The result is a book that is frank, engrossing and considerably more moving than one might expect such a tale to be." A critic for the *New Yorker* commented that Irvine's "feeling for place, for the island flora and fauna, and her emotional and intellectual candor . . . give her book a warmth and vigor of integrity." And *Ms.* reviewer Cheryl Huff urged: "Read *Castaway* for great vicarious adventure or if you've ever fantasized about being one of the Swiss Family Robinson. Although the circumstances of Lucy's marriage are unique, the truths and traumas of her experience are universal."

After publishing her second volume of autobiography, *Runaway,* Irvine turned to fiction. Her first novel, *One Is One,* was described in *Publishers Weekly* as a "curious blend of the sublime and the pedestrian." It follows the stories of four misfit characters whose lives intersect after Hodge, an ex-convict, falls through the protagonist's skylight in a botched burglary attempt. Observing that the novel's tone is a bit too heavy, a reviewer for *Publishers Weekly* nevertheless praised Irvine's sensitive characterizations and "singular ability to draw details and dialogue."

Sixteen years after her experience on Tuin, Irvine returned to the South Pacific at the invitation of Diana Hepworth, an elderly British woman who had moved with her family to Pigeon Island, a tiny outpost in the outer Solomon Islands, in 1957. A former fashion model, Diana had sailed around the tropics for several years with her husband, Tom, before the couple decided to purchase Pigeon from the neighboring Reef Islanders as an idyllic setting in which to raise a family. They had a daughter, and then twin sons, who grew up on Pigeon. In 1999, Diana asked Irvine to spend a year with them on the island and to write about the family's history there. With her three sons, then aged thirteen, eleven, and nine, Irvine made the arduous journey, which culminated in an eight-hour canoe trip that almost killed them when a surprise squall blew up.

As Irvine recounts in *Faraway,* the Hepworths' "wonderful" life had indeed contained wonders but had also been fraught with dangers, tragedy, and cultural conflicts stemming from racial prejudice. Basing much of the book on the diaries of Tom Hepworth, who had died in 1994, Irvine writes that the settlers remained aloof from their Reef Island neighbors and lived like imperial bosses. Their daughter, Tasha, exhibited uncontrollable tantrums as a toddler and was later diagnosed as schizophrenic. Tasha was sexually assaulted at age five by a man from a nearby island; her parents' only recourse was to publicly shame him. The Hepworths did not enjoy a happy relationship with their sons, who began acting out as teenagers and were eventually estranged from their parents.

In addition to chronicling the Hepworths' story in *Faraway,* Irvine also writes about her own experiences and those of her sons during their year on Pigeon Island. Reviewers appreciated this personal and historical mix. The book, according to *Geographical* contributor Chris Martin, "gives a rather satisfying new depth to Irvine's continuing Castaway story" and "does surprising justice to both of these extraordinary women." *Guardian* reviewer Kirsty Scott described the "compelling" book as "part *Swiss Family Robinson,* part *Heart of Darkness.*" And *Booklist* writer David Pitt hailed the work as a "rich, detailed, often moving story" that "tickles the wanderer's imagination in all of us."

Irvine told *CA:* "Outside of what is published in my autobiographies, I wish to have my private life and interests kept as far as possible from the public eye."

BIOGRAPHICAL AND CRITICAL SOURCES:

PERIODICALS

Booklist, January 1, 2002, David Pitt, review of *Faraway,* p. 800.
Chicago Tribune, April 8, 1984.
Geographical, November, 2000, "Home and Far Away," p. 114; February, 2001, Chris Martin, review of *Faraway,* p. 96.
Globe and Mail (Toronto, Ontario, Canada), March 17, 1984.
Guardian (Manchester, England), November 6, 2000, Kirsty Scott, "What Lucy Did Next."
Library Journal, April 1, 1987, Judith Nixon, review of *Runaway,* p. 142.
Los Angeles Times Book Review, July 1, 1984.
Ms., July, 1984.
New Statesman, January 30, 1987, Helen Birch, review of *Runaway,* p. 30.
New Yorker, May 14, 1984.

New York Times Book Review, April 8, 1984; April 26, 1987, Ann Pringle Harris, review of *Runaway,* p. 25.

Publishers Weekly, February 6, 1987, review of *Runaway,* p. 82; June 29, 1990, review of *One Is One,* p. 86.

School Library Journal, December, 1987, review of *Runaway,* p. 40.

Sunday Times (London, England), November 12, 2000, Elizabeth Mahoney, "Castaway Who Never Returned to the Fold," p. 5.

Times Literary Supplement, June 16, 1989, Linda Taylor, review of *One Is One,* p. 669.

Village Voice, May 15, 1984.

Vogue, March, 1987, Francine Prose, review of *Runaway,* p. 314.

Washington Post, April 26, 1984.

Washington Post Book World, March 18, 1984.*

* * *

ISRAEL, Peter 1933-

PERSONAL: Born August 1, 1933, in New York, NY; son of J. Leon (an attorney) and Ruth L. Israel; married Peg Streep (an author), March 28, 1982; children: Elie, Alexandra. *Education:* Yale University, B.A., 1954.

ADDRESSES: *Agent*—Georges Borchardt, Inc., 136 East 57th St., New York, NY 10022.

CAREER: G. P. Putnam's Sons, New York, NY, began as editor, became editor in chief, 1959-65; Editions Albin Michel, Paris, France, director of foreign service, 1973-77; Putnam Publishing Group, New York, NY, president, 1978-86, chairman of board of directors, 1986-87; Peter Israel Enterprises, Montclair, NJ, book packager, 1988—.

MEMBER: Association of American Publishers (past director), Mystery Writers of America.

WRITINGS:

MYSTERY NOVELS

The Hen's House, Putnam (New York, NY), 1967.

Hush Money, Crowell (New York, NY), 1974.

The French Kiss, Crowell (New York, NY), 1976.

The Stiff Upper Lip, Crowell (New York, NY), 1978.

I'll Cry when I Kill You, Mysterious Press (New York, NY), 1988.

If I Should Die before I Die, Mysterious Press (New York, NY), 1989.

OTHER

(With Peg Streep) *The Kids' World Almanac Rhyming Dictionary: A Guide for Young Poets and Songwriters,* World Almanac (New York, NY), 1991.

(With Stephen Jones) *Others Unknown: The Oklahoma City Bombing Case and Conspiracy,* Public Affairs (New York, NY), 1998.

(With Arthur L. Liman) *Lawyer: A Life of Counsel and Controversy,* Public Affairs (New York, NY), 1998.

(With Kay Koplovitz) *Bold Women, Big Ideas: Learning to Play the High-Risk Entrepreneurial Game,* Public Affairs (New York, NY), 2002.

SIDELIGHTS: Peter Israel has written six mystery novels, but it is his nonfiction books that have gained the interest of critics. He first collaborated with his wife, Peg Streep, on a book for children, *The Kids' World Almanac Rhyming Dictionary: A Guide for Young Poets and Songwriters.* Then, seven years later, he coauthored a dramatically different book, *Others Unknown: The Oklahoma City Bombing Case and Conspiracy,* with Stephen Jones, Timothy McVeigh's chief defense counsel. McVeigh was tried for the 1995 bombing of the federal office building in Oklahoma City, which killed 168 people. Jones, however, believes that McVeigh was charged unfairly; and Israel helped Jones put together his thoughts about that trial. Jones believes McVeigh's trial was hindered by the judge, the government, the press, and a public audience that demanded swift justice. *Library Journal*'s Philip Young Blue, after reading the story, predicted that Israel's book was "bound to raise eyebrows"; while a *Publishers Weekly* reviewer went a step further, concluding that the book "does raise troubling questions." According to Jones, there was evidence which might have demonstrated that McVeigh was just a small member of a much larger group of terrorists, but that evidence was not allowed in the trial. He even claims there was a link between coconspirator Terry Nichols and Ramzi Yousef, a man indicted in the first New York World Trade Center bombing. Commenting on the book, *Newsweek*'s Peter Annin wrote, "Jones would have us believe that the case never got out of the shadows—that the country is still in the dark about what really happened on April 19, 1995."

The same year Israel collaborated with yet another lawyer, Arthur L. Liman, to write *Lawyer: A Life of Counsel and Controversy,* which *Library Journal*'s Philip Young Blue called, "an excellent book for both practicing attorneys and law students." With Israel's help, Liman recounts many of his high-profile cases, which include the investigation of Oliver North during the Iran-Contra Senate hearings in 1987 and the defense of Wall Street's notorious trader, Michael Milken. In the Iran-Contra hearings, Liman states, North caught the public's imagination and stole the show. Then when Limen defended Milken, Limen was publicly criticized because the media had demonized Milken. Through his stories about his cases, Liman demonstrates the power of public opinion but appeals to his fellow attorneys and all potential lawyers to stick to the principles of law and not allow public sentiment to sway them.

More recently, Israel switched from courtrooms to business offices when he worked with Kay Koplovitz on the book *Bold Women, Big Ideas: Learning to Play the High-Risk Entrepreneurial Game.* Koplovitz is a master when it comes to the entrepreneurial world, as she founded the cable television franchise, USA Networks. She also later put together a nonprofit organization to help pool venture capital, which would be granted to women who want to start up their own businesses. Springboard, as the organization is called, filled a big gap for entrepreneurial women, who previously had very few places they could turn to for financial support. Her book, with Israel's help, presents not only tips on how to create such essential tools as a clear business plan but it also offers inspiration. *Library Journal*'s Susan C. Awe found the book very businesslike but written with "glimmers of humor," through which, Awe believed, female entrepreneurs would learn and appreciate "how business works in today's economy." To do this, noted Joni Evans in *Publishers Weekly,* Koplovitz "offers readers a look into the psyche of today's venture capitalists and shares the business stories of other women."

BIOGRAPHICAL AND CRITICAL SOURCES:

PERIODICALS

Library Journal, October 1, 1998, Philip Young Blue, review of *Lawyer: A Life of Counsel and Controversy,* pp. 115-116; December 1998, Philip Young Blue, review of *Others Unknown: The Oklahoma City Bombing Case and Conspiracy,* p. 130; April 15, 2002, Susan C. Awe, review of *Bold Women, Big Ideas: Learning to Play the High-Risk Entrepreneurial Game,* pp. 100-101.

Newsweek, October 12, 1998, Peter Annin, "A Question of Conspiracy," p. 48.

Publishers Weekly, October 26, 1998, review of *Others Unknown: The Oklahoma City Bombing Case and Conspiracy,* p. 54; April 8, 2002, Joni Evans, review of *Bold Women, Big Ideas: Learning to Play the High-Risk Entrepreneurial Game,* p. 217.

Tribune Books, March 27, 1988.*

J

JACKSON, Marni 1946-

PERSONAL: Born May 1, 1946, in Winnipeg, Manitoba, Canada; daughter of Clyde (an engineer) and Olive (a homemaker; maiden name, Hay) Jackson; married Brian Johnson (senior writer at *Maclean's* magazine); children: Casey. *Hobbies and other interests:* Violin, canoeing.

ADDRESSES: *Home*—53 Seymour Ave., Toronto, Ontario M45 3T3, Canada. *Agent*—Lucinda Vardey Agency, Ltd., 10 St. Marys, Suite 510, Toronto, Ontario M4Y 1P9, Canada.

CAREER: Journalist and nonfiction writer. Host of the literary program *Imprint,* TVO network.

MEMBER: Writers guild.

AWARDS, HONORS: National Magazine Awards for humor and travel; shortlisted for the Stephen Leacock Humor Award, 1993; received honorary B.A. from Victoria College, University of Toronto.

WRITINGS:

The Mother Zone: Love, Sex and Laundry in the Modern Family, Macfarlane, Walter, & Ross (Toronto, Ontario, Canada), 1993.

Pain: The Fifth Vital Sign, Random House of Canada (Toronto, Ontario, Canada), 2002.

Also author of several plays produced in Canada. Contributor to anthologies, including *A Toronto Lampoon,* edited by Wayne Grigsby, Eden Press, 1984; *A.B.C. Lampoon,* edited by Jane O'Hara, Douglas & MacIntyre, 1985; *The Thinking Heart: Best Canadian Essays,* edited by George Galt, Quarry Press, 1993; *Local Colour,* edited by Carol Martin, Douglas & MacIntyre, 1994; and *Taking Risks: Literary Journalism from the Edge,* edited by Barbara Moon and Don Obe, Banff Centre Press, 1998. Columnist for *Toronto Life.*

WORK IN PROGRESS: *The Waiting Room,* a screenplay.

SIDELIGHTS: *The Mother Zone: Love, Sex, and Laundry in the Modern Family,* published in 1993, is Marni Jackson's personal account of motherhood, from conception and birth to caring for her child through to his adolescence. Throughout her account, Jackson examines the difficulties in resolving her child's sometimes overwhelming needs with her own need to maintain her sense of self. "There are some wonderfully wise insights along the way," wrote Heather Menzies in *Canadian Forum,* though the critic also noted areas of interest Jackson did not pursue completely. Such compelling topics as how she resolved her feelings toward her husband, whose autonomy remained intact after the birth of their child, and how she learned to relinquish what Menzies called "her gender-given monopoly of knowledge and expertise in the area of baby management," are introduced but not discussed in depth, according to Menzies. *Maclean's* contributor Brian Fawcett, on the other hand, praised Jackson's handling of her subject: "From the acquisition of her baby's father to the sometimes nasty realities of childbirth . . . she demystifies and entertains."

Despite her criticism, Menzies dubbed the book "a gem of an account of mothering." In *Booklist,* Denise Perry Donavin remarked on the "sharp sarcasm" with which Jackson describes her attempts to separate her own identity from her child's and the mixture of painful and pleasurable emotions that motherhood evokes, and called the result "fun to read." Genevieve Stuttaford of *Publishers Weekly* described *The Mother Zone* as "humorous, frank and passionate," and concluded: "Entertaining and gutsy, [Jackson's] account will warm and console parents." In *Maclean's,* Fawcett stated that "Jackson makes a major contribution towards restoring the dignity that mothering children deserves."

Pain: The Fifth Vital Sign examines the "social history of pain," wrote Martha E. Stone in *Library Journal,* who called the book "breezily readable." Jackson uses stories from various friends and relatives, as well as from professionals in the field. William Beatty, in *Booklist,* found the book to be "lively reading."

BIOGRAPHICAL AND CRITICAL SOURCES:

PERIODICALS

Booklist, January 1, 1993, p. 776; March, 2002, William Beatty, review of *Pain: The Fifth Vital Sign,* p. 1199.

Canadian Forum, April, 1993, pp. 41-43.

Globe and Mail (Toronto, Ontario, Canada), October 17, 1992, p. C24.

Library Journal, January, 1993; April 1, 2002, Martha E. Stone, review of *Pain,* p. 131.

Maclean's, October 19, 1992, p. 70.

Observer (Charlotte, NC), May 9, 1993.

Publishers Weekly, December 7, 1992, p. 50.

ONLINE

Marni Jackson Home Page, http://www.marnijackson.com/ (September 24, 2003).*

* * *

JASEN, David A(lan) 1937-

PERSONAL: Born December 16, 1937, in New York, NY; son of Barnet (a dentist) and Gertrude (Cohen) Jasen; married Susan Pomerantz (a registered nurse), December 30, 1963; children: Raymond Douglas. *Education:* American University, B. A., 1959; Long Island University, M. S., 1972.

ADDRESSES: Office—C. W. Post Center, Long Island University, Greenvale, NY 11548.

CAREER: Columbia Broadcasting System (CBS), New York, NY, supervisor of news videotape, 1959-66; American Educational Theatre Association, Washington, DC, administrative assistant, 1967; Florists' Transworld Delivery Association, Detroit, MI, field service representative, 1968-69; Reading Development Center, Inc., New York, NY, assistant to president, 1969-70; Long Island University, C. W. Post Center, Greenvale, NY, assistant professor, 1971-77, associate professor in School of Art, 1977—, professor of communication arts, 1982—, director of communication arts, 1975—, chairman of communication arts department, 1979—, director of Popular Music Archive, 1983—. Ragtime composer and pianist; record producer; public speaker.

MEMBER: American Library Association, Ragtime Society, Maple Leaf Club, Pi Delta Epsilon, Alpha Psi Omega.

AWARDS, HONORS: Scott Joplin Award, 1995, for contributions to the field of ragtime music.

WRITINGS:

Bibliography and Reader's Guide to the First Editions of P. G. Wodehouse, Archon (Hamden, CT), 1970, revised edition, Greenhill, 1986.

Recorded Ragtime, 1897-1958 (discography), Archon, 1973.

P. G. Wodehouse: A Portrait of a Master, Mason & Lipscomb, 1974, revised edition, Continuum (New York, NY), 1981.

(Editor) *The Uncollected Wodehouse,* Seabury (New York, NY), 1976.

(With Trebor Jay Tichenor) *Rags and Ragtime: A Musical History,* Seabury (New York, NY), 1978, revised edition, Dover (New York, NY), 1989.

(Editor) *Ragtime: 100 Authentic Rags* (music), Big 3 Music, 1979.

(Editor) P. G. Wodehouse, *The Swoop! and Other Stories,* Seabury (New York, NY), 1979.

The Theatre of P. G. Wodehouse, Batsford (London, England), 1979.

(Editor) *The Eighteen-Carat Kid, and Other Stories,* P. G. Wodehouse, Continuum (New York, NY), 1980.

(Editor) *Not George Washington: An Autobiographical Novel,* P. G. Wodehouse, Continuum (New York, NY), 1980.

(Editor) George Barr McCutcheon, *Brewster's Millions,* Continuum (New York, NY), 1980.

(Editor) Jerome K. Jerome, *Three Men in a Boat,* Continuum (New York, NY), 1980.

(Editor) *P. G. Wodehouse: Four Plays,* Methuen (New York, NY), 1983.

(Editor) *Alexander's Ragtime Band and Other Favorite Song Hits, 1901-1911,* Dover (Mineola, NY), 1987.

(Editor) *Scott Joplin: Complete Piano Rags,* Dover (Mineola, NY), 1988.

Tin Pan Alley, Fine (New York, NY), 1988.

(Editor) *For Me and My Gal and Other Favorite Song Hits, 1915-1917,* Dover (Mineola, NY), 1994.

(Editor) *A Pretty Girl Is Like a Melody and Other Favorite Song Hits, 1918-1919,* Dover (Mineola, NY), 1996.

(Editor) *Enter Jeeves: 15 Early Stories,* P. G. Wodehouse, Dover (Mineola, NY), 1997.

(Editor) *Ragtime Jubilee: 42 Piano Gems, 1911-21,* Dover (Mineola, NY), 1997.

(Editor) *Cakewalks, Two-Steps and Trots: For Solo Piano: 34 Popular Works from the Dance-Craze Era,* Dover (Mineola, NY), 1997.

(Editor) *35 Song Hits by Great Black Songwriters,* Dover (Mineola, NY), 1998.

(Editor) *Beale Street and Other Classic Blues: 38 Works, 1901-1921,* Dover (Mineola, NY), 1998.

(With Gene Jones) *Spreadin' Rhythm Around: Black Popular Songwriters, 1880-1930,* Schirmer (New York, NY), 1998.

(With Gene Jones) *That American Rag: The Story of Ragtime from Coast to Coast,* Schirmer (New York, NY), 1999.

(With Gene Jones) *Black Bottom Stomp: Eight Masters of Ragtime and Early Jazz,* Routledge (New York, NY), 2001.

A Century of American Popular Music (1899-1999): 2000 Best-Loved and Remembered Songs, Routledge (New York, NY), 2002.

RECORDINGS

Creative Ragtime, Euphonic Sound.

Fingerbustin' Ragtime, Blue Goose Records.

Rompin' Stompin' Ragtime, Blue Goose Records.

Rip-Roarin' Ragtime, Folkways.

Dave Jasen's Ragtime, Archive.

26 Happy Honky Tonk Memories, Special Music.

(Producer) *They All Played the Maple Leaf Rag,* Archive.

(Producer) *Zez Confrey Plays Zez Confrey,* Archive.

Also author of several ragtime pieces, included in his sound recordings. Contributor to *Ragtimer.*

SIDELIGHTS: In editing the collection *The Swoop! and Other Stories,* David A. Jasen "has performed a valuable service in combing through turn-of-the-century popular British periodicals . . . in search of pieces from the earliest years of [P. G.] Wodehouse's long career," remarked *New York Times Book Review* contributor Robert Kiely. "The result is a collection of fresh and delightful entertainments, many of which had been thought lost and none of which has been published in book form in this country." Jasen has edited several volumes of Wodehouse's work, and was the first to publish a biography of the great British humorist.

In addition to his work as an editor of Wodehouse fiction, Jasen is also a composer, performer, and producer of ragtime music. He has written and recorded several albums of ragtime, and has helped propogate the popularity of rags through concerts, radio shows, university classes, and books. His discography, *Recorded Ragtime, 1897-1958,* "is a landmark of ragtime scholarship," noted *Washington Post* writer Joseph McLellan. His historical work, *Rags and Ragtime,* written with fellow composer-performer Trebor Jay Tichenor, is "commendably lucid, accurate, detailed, and well-arranged, with interesting illustrations," commented McLellan. The critic added that the work helps "fill widespread needs which have begun to be felt only in the last generation and have reached their peak in the present decade."

Spreadin' Rhythm Around, which Jasen cowrote with Gene Jones, chronicles the struggles and successes of African-American songwriters between Reconstruction and the Great Depression. This was the period of Jim Crow laws, which cruelly restricted opportunities for blacks after the Civil War and deprived them of basic rights. Jasen and Jones, wrote Ann Sears in *American Music,* "bravely tackle the sensitive issues of racism and stereotypes wrapped up in the music" of this era, including minstrel show tunes and "coon" songs. "Jasen and Jones's explanations of the forces that shaped black composers' opportunities are thoughtful and worth pondering," concluded Sears.

Jasen and Jones collaborated again on *That American Rag: The Story of Ragtime from Coast to Coast,* a work that *Booklist* critic Alan Hirsch hailed as an "excellent reference for ragtime aficionados." In addition to outlines of the careers of major rag musicians such as Scott Joplin and Jelly Roll Morton, Jasen and Jones also discuss the role of ragtime publishers and describe the locations where the music was born. In *Black Bottom Stomp: Eight Masters of Ragtime and Early Jazz,* Jasen and Jones argue that ragtime played a crucial role in the development of early jazz. Critiquing music scholarship that dismisses ragtime as a relatively crude and minor predecessor to the more serious genre of jazz, Jasen and Jones, according to *Booklist* writer Ted Leventhal, "call for a more sophisticated, nuanced understanding of the relationship between the two popular music styles."

BIOGRAPHICAL AND CRITICAL SOURCES:

PERIODICALS

American Music, fall, 1999, Ann Sears, review of *Spreadin' Rhythm Around: Black Popular Songwriters, 1880-1930,* p. 357.

Booklist, August, 1998, Mike Tribby, review of *Spreadin' Rhythm Around,* p. 1949; November 1, 1999, Alan Hirsch, review of *That American Rag: The Story of Ragtime from Coast to Coast,* p. 498; November 15, 2001, Ted Leventhal, review of *Black Bottom Stomp: Eight Masters of Ragtime and Early Jazz,* p. 536.

Choice, May, 2000, D. R. De Lerma, review of *That American Rag,* p. 1659; May, 2002, C. M. Weisenberg, review of *Black Bottom Stomp,* p. 1595.

Library Journal, September 1, 1998, Dan Bogey, review of *Spreadin' Rhythm Around,* p. 172.

Los Angeles Times, June 1, 1980.

Melody Maker, September 1, 1973.

Mississippi Rag, June, 1979.

Newsday, October 22, 1972; January 15, 1992.

New Yorker, March 15, 1999, review of *Spreadin' Rhythm Around,* p. 20.

New York Times, November 14, 1971; February 10, 1985.

New York Times Book Review, July 1, 1979.

Publishers Weekly, July 13, 1998, review of *Spreadin' Rhythm Around,* p. 71.

Time, May 4, 1981.

Times Literary Supplement, September 27, 2002, John Postgate, review of *Black Bottom Stomp,* p. 20.

Washington Post, July 24, 1978.

Washington Post Book World, August 16, 1998, review of *Spreadin' Rhythm Around,* p. 13; December 5, 1999, review of *Spreadin' Rhythm Around,* p. 12.*

* * *

JENKINS, Mark 1958-

PERSONAL: Born November 22, 1958, in IA; son of Terry (a professor) and Sharon (Smehakken) Jenkins; married Susan Ibara (a professor); children: Addi Marquette. *Education:* University of Wyoming, B.A., and M.A.

ADDRESSES: *Home*—1102 Grand, Laramie, WY 82070. *Agent*—Carl D. Brandt, Brandt & Brandt Literary Agents, Inc., 1501 Broadway, New York, NY 10036.

CAREER: Freelance writer, 1983—; *Cross Country Skier,* Emmaus, PA, managing editor, 1988; *Adventure Travel,* managing editor, 1988; *Backpacker,* Emmaus, Rocky Mountain editor, beginning 1989; *Men's Health Magazine,* investigative editor, 1997—.

WRITINGS:

Off the Map: Bicycling across Siberia, Morrow (New York, NY), 1992.

To Timbuktu: A Journey down the Niger, Morrow (New York, NY), 1997.

The Hard Way: Stories of Danger, Survival, and the Soul of Adventure, Simon & Schuster (New York, NY), 2002.

SIDELIGHTS: When Mark Jenkins graduated from college with a degree in philosophy, it did not take him long to discover that there was not a big market for philosophers. He knew he wanted to be a writer, but the jobs he first applied for required a degree in journalism, so he continued to find himself unemployable in a field that interested him. So he and his girlfriend moved to Medicine Bowl, WY, where he skied all day and wrote all night, studying his craft. His break came when he was offered a position with *Cross Country Skiing Magazine,* a job that would teach him the insides of publishing. This experience, plus the skills he had honed in writing, and his love of travel and adventure have all successfully come together in a series of books.

Jenkins was only twelve years old when he first traveled to Europe. His father, a college professor, had taken a sabbatical from teaching, and the family spent a year in the Netherlands. Later, while still a young teen, he traveled to Africa, Russia, and other European countries. His adventures in other lands, since then, have just become more spectacular. He once commented that he is paid, however, not for the adventures, but for being able to distill the important details from the adventures to create interesting stories. A task that finds him up early in the morning, in his office basement.

His first book, *Off the Map: Bicycling across Siberia,* relates Jenkins's experience of being a member of a seven-person team that cycled from Vladivostok to Leningrad, a distance twice as long as the breadth of the United States. The feat has since been heralded in the *Guinness Book of World Records.* The journey was long and hard, but the book is not only about the difficulties of biking. Jenkins also writes about the people that he met along the way and the details of their sometimes-depraved lifestyles. David Newnham, for London's *Guardian,* noted that Jenkins's book is a departure from many other books about adventure and cycling. Jenkins gets into more than the equipment, Newnham found, as he shares his experiences both on and off the bike. Newnham also praised Jenkins's writing, which he likened to "a prose poem."

Jenkins's next trip took him to Mali, Africa, an adventure that is recorded in *To Timbuktu: A Journey down the Niger,* which relates a "riveting tale of travel," according to Mary Warner Marien for the *Christian Science Monitor.* The story recounts three separate tales, Warner Marien pointed out. One relates the misadventures of early European adventurers in Africa, and the other two describe two separate trips that Jenkins shared with his high school friend, Mike Moe. Their first trip to Mali occurred right after graduation from high school, as the two young teens sought out the legendary city of Timbuktu. They were terribly unprepared for their quest and had to give up after first being robbed and later realizing how tenuous their lives were when they found themselves stranded in the middle of the Sahara Desert. The two friends reunited, fifteen years later, determined to reach their earlier goal. Once in Africa, they set off in a canoe on the Niger River, seeking its source, which would eventually take them to Timbuktu. Along the way, they had to rely on maps that had not been revised since 1930 and share the river with crocodiles and hippos. David Schau, for *Library Journal,* called Jenkins's book an "excellent travel yarn"; while a *Publishers Weekly* reviewer referred to it as a "gripping adventure."

Jenkins's most recent book, *The Hard Way: Stories of Danger, Survival, and the Soul of Adventure,* is a collection of essays in which Jenkins reflects on almost two dozen different excursions that he has made into wild country. Whether he's on a glacier in Wyoming or climbing a mountain in Tibet, wrote a *Kirkus Reviews* critic, "there's no denying Jenkins's relish at being outdoors," especially if that particular place in the great outdoors has an element of danger. Most critics seem to agree that the unifying theme in Jenkins's adventures is his love of the unknown. He likes best to travel to places that he has read little or nothing about; places from which he does not know how or when he will return. It is this unknown element that sharpens his focus. *The Hard Way* includes trips to the Italian ridge of the Matterhorn, to battlefields in Turkey, to unexplored canyons in Australia, and the Simen Mountains in Ethiopia. In a review for *Booklist,* David Pitt remarked that he enjoyed Jenkins's books because of the way the author's writing style "invites" the reader to join in on the adventure.

BIOGRAPHICAL AND CRITICAL SOURCES:

PERIODICALS

Booklist, June 1, 1997, Benjamin Segedin, review of *To Timbuktu: A Journey down the Niger,* p. 1649; June 1, 2002, David Pitt, review of *The Hard Way: Stories of Danger, Survival, and the Soul of Adventure,* p. 1665.

Christian Science Monitor, September 25, 1997, Mary Warner Marien, review of *To Timbuktu,* p. B1.
Guardian (London, England), October 3, 1998, David Newhham, review of *Off the Map: Bicycling across Siberia,* p. 15.
Kirkus Reviews, May 1, 2002, review of *The Hard Way,* pp. 637-638.
Library Journal, May 15, 1997, David Schau, review of *To Timbuktu,* p. 91.
Los Angeles Times, December 14, 1997, Bill Berkeley, review of *To Timbuktu,* p. 6.
New York Times, June 25, 1997, Richard Bernstein, review of *To Timbuktu,* p. B7.
New York Times Book Review, October 12, 1997, Nina Sonenberg, review of *To Timbuktu,* p. 22.
Publishers Weekly, April 7, 1997, review of *To Timbuktu,* p. 78.
School Library Journal, October, 2002, review of *The Hard Way,* p. 197.*

* * *

JENNINGS, Kate 1948-

PERSONAL: Born 1948, in Australia. *Education:* University of Sydney, B.A. (with honors).

ADDRESSES: Home—NY. *Agent*—c/o Author Mail, Fourth Estate, 77-85 Fulham Palace Rd., London W6 8JB, England.

CAREER: Writer.

WRITINGS:

Come to Me My Melancholy Baby (poetry), Outback Press (Fitzroy, Victoria, Australia), 1975.
(Editor) *Mother, I'm Rooted: An Anthology of Australian Women Poets,* Outback Press (Fitzroy, Victoria, Australia), 1975.
Women Falling Down in the Street (short fiction), William Heinemann Australia (Port Melbourne, Victoria, Australia), 1990.
Snake (novel), Ecco Press (Hopewell, NJ), 1997.
Save Me, Joe Louis (autobiography), Penguin (Ringwood, Victoria, Australia), 1988.
Moral Hazard (novel), Fourth Estate (London, England), 2002.

Also the author of essays.

SIDELIGHTS: Australian expatriate Kate Jennings is well known in her native country for her poetry, essays, short stories, and novels. In 1997 the feminist writer gained recognition in the United States for *Snake,* a short novel composed of seventy-seven brief chapters that depict the disintegration of a family of four living in rural Australia during the 1950s. The first and last chapters are told in second person, the first addressed to Rex (the husband), and the final to Irene (the wife). The central part of this short novel is told in third person and describes the family's activities, including those of the children Girlie and Boy. Yet the book mainly focuses on wellborn Irene, who expected more of life and now finds herself consumed with anger at her situation. She has a desire to escape from her deadening existence on the farm.

Writing in *Booklist,* Mary Carroll described *Snake* as "a pointillistic portrait of a painfully dysfunctional family." Other commentators discussed Jennings's prose and use of reptile imagery, as literal and figurative snakes abound in the novel. Yvette Weller Olson, writing in *Library Journal,* called Jennings's writing style forceful and "sparse as the outback she describes, harsh yet beautiful." In *Publishers Weekly,* a critic termed *Snake* "lean" and "startling," declaring that "domestic dystopia has rarely been distilled into such concentrated literary form."

Jennings's second novel, *Moral Hazard,* is about Cath, an honest woman who goes to work on Wall Street in order to support her husband's Alzheimer's. As her husband deteriorates, Cath discovers just how ruthless and corrupt the bankers she works for are. Amanda Craig in the *New Statesman* wrote, "Jennings's crisp prose conveys pain beyond honesty." A *Publishers Weekly* reviewer remarked that Jennings "masterfully documents the culture of economic and corporate arrogance."

BIOGRAPHICAL AND CRITICAL SOURCES:

PERIODICALS

Australian Book Review, August, 1996, p. 45.
Book, July-August, 2002, Paul Evans, review of *Moral Hazard,* p. 83.

Booklist, April 1, 1997, p. 1281.
Kirkus Reviews, March 15, 2002, review of *Moral Hazard,* p. 359.
Library Journal, April 1, 1997, p. 127.
Los Angeles Times, June 13, 2002, Kai Maristed, review of *Moral Hazard,* p. E-4.
New Statesman, April 15, 2002, Amanda Craig, review of *Moral Hazard,* p. 53.
New York Times Book Review, May 11, 1997, p. 11; June 1, 1997, p. 37; June 30, 2002, Lisa Zeidner, review of *Moral Hazard,* p. 5.
O, The Oprah Magazine, June, 2002, review of *Moral Hazard,* p. 158.
Publishers Weekly, March 10, 1997, p. 50; April 8, 2002, review of *Moral Hazard,* p. 201.
Small Press, February, 1990, p. 50.
Time International, May 6, 2002, Michael Fitzgerald, review of *Moral Hazard,* p. 66.
Times Literary Supplement, March 29, 2002, Margaret Stead, review of *Moral Hazard,* p. 23.*

* * *

JOHNSTON, Joan 1948-

PERSONAL: Born September 18, 1948, in Little Rock, AR; daughter of George Robert (in U.S. Air Force) and Emogene Ruth (a music teacher; maiden name, Schaer) Mertens; married Hugh C. Johnston III, February 14, 1970 (divorced, April 5, 1986); children: Heather Lynne, Blake Delos. *Education:* Jacksonville University, B.A., 1970; University of Illinois at Urbana/Champaign, M.A., 1971; University of Texas at Austin, J.D. (with honors), 1980. *Hobbies and other interests:* Horseback riding, two-stepping, Dolphins football.

ADDRESSES: *Home*—Pembroke Pines, FL. *Agent*—Denise Marcil, Denise Marcil Literary Agency, Inc., 685 West End Ave., No. 9C, New York, NY 10025.

CAREER: *Weekly Herald,* San Antonio, TX, news editor and drama critic, 1971-73; Southwest Texas Junior College, Uvalde, director of theater, 1973-77; Hunton & Williams, Richmond, VA, attorney, 1980-83; Squire, Sanders & Dempsey, Miami, FL, attorney, 1983-85; Barry University, Miami Shores, FL, instructor, 1985-88; University of Miami, Coral Gables, FL, assistant professor, 1988-91; writer, 1991—. Broward County Chamber of Commerce, member of Cultural Affairs Committee; Florida Bar, member; Virginia Bar, associate.

MEMBER: Authors Guild, Novelists, Inc., Western Writers of America, Romance Writers of America, Order of Barristers.

AWARDS, HONORS: *Romantic Times* Awards, outstanding new western romance writer, 1987, for *Colter's Wife,* and best western series, 1989, for *Frontier Woman, Comanche Woman,* and *Texas Woman,* BookRak Award for Bestselling Historical Romance, 1991, for *Sweetwater Seduction,* Best Romance Award from *Romantic Times* Booksellers That Care, 1992, for *The Barefoot Bride.*

WRITINGS:

ROMANCE NOVELS

A Loving Defiance, Pocket Books (New York, NY), 1985.
Colter's Wife, Pocket Books (New York, NY), 1986.
Frontier Woman, Pocket Books (New York, NY), 1988.
Fit to Be Tied, Silhouette (New York, NY), 1988.
Comanche Woman, Pocket Books (New York, NY), 1989.
Texas Woman, Pocket Books (New York, NY), 1989.
Marriage by the Book, Silhouette (New York, NY), 1989.
Sweetwater Seduction, Dell (New York, NY), 1991.
Never Tease a Wolf, Silhouette (New York, NY), 1991.
A Wolf in Sheep's Clothing, Silhouette (New York, NY), 1991.
The Barefoot Bride, Dell (New York, NY), 1992.
A Little Time in Texas, Silhouette (New York, NY), 1992.
Honey and the Hired Hand, Silhouette (New York, NY), 1992.
Kid Calhoun, Dell (New York, NY), 1993.
Outlaw's Bride, Dell (New York, NY), 1993.
The Rancher and the Runaway Bride, Silhouette (New York, NY), 1993.
The Cowboy and the Princess, Silhouette (New York, NY), 1993.

The Wrangler and the Rich Girl, Silhouette (New York, NY), 1993.
The Cowboy Takes a Wife, Silhouette (New York, NY), 1994.
The Unforgiving Bride, Silhouette (New York, NY), 1994.
The Headstrong Bride, Silhouette (New York, NY), 1994.
The Inheritance, Dell (New York, NY), 1995.
The Disobedient Bride, Silhouette (New York, NY), 1995.
Maverick Heart, Dell (New York, NY), 1995.
Captive, Dell (New York, NY), 1996.
After the Kiss, Dell (New York, NY), 1997.
The Bodyguard, Dell (New York, NY), 1998.
The Bridegroom, Dell (New York, NY), 1999.
Hawkes Way Bachelors, Silhouette (New York, NY), 2000.
The Cowboy, Dell (New York, NY), 2000.
The Texan, Dell (New York, NY), 2001.
Hawkes Way Rogues, Silhouette (New York, NY), 2001.
The Loner, Dell (New York, NY), 2002.
Hawkes Way Grooms, Silhouette (New York, NY), 2002.
Sisters Found, Harlequin (New York, NY), 2002.
The Price, Pocket (New York, NY), 2004.

Contributor to anothologies, including *Untamed: Maverick Hearts,* Harlequin (Tarrytown, NY), 1993; *To Have and to Hold,* Avon (New York, NY), 1994; *A Christmas Together,* Avon, 1994; *Lonestar Christmas,* Silhouette (New York, NY), 1999.

SIDELIGHTS: Western romance writer Joan Johnston once told *CA:* "I was a reader before I was a writer. As an attorney with a major national firm, who had a six-year-old child and a six-week-old baby when I started practicing law, I found escape from stress in historical romance novels. I facilitated a sixty-three-million-dollar municipal bond closing on Wall Street and attended my first romance conference in New York the same weekend.

"I write about the West because I've lived there, in Wyoming and Texas, as the daughter of an Air Force staff sergeant. I learned to ride horseback when my father was stationed in Morocco, North Africa. I have an eclectic background: theater director, drama critic, newspaper news editor, college professor, and lawyer. That has helped me keep an open mind when I write. I write romance because it celebrates the best of life: love and happily-ever-after endings."

BIOGRAPHICAL AND CRITICAL SOURCES:

PERIODICALS

Booklist, March 15, 2001, Diana Tixier Herald, review of *The Texan,* p. 1359; November 15, 2002, Maria Hatton, review of *Comanche Woman,* p. 582; March 15, 2003, Maria Hatton, review of *The Price,* p. 73.

Publishers Weekly, July 1, 1988, Peggy Kaganoff, review of *Frontier Woman,* p. 73; March 10, 1989, Peggy Kaganoff, review of *Comanche Woman,* p. 80; November 30, 1990, Peggy Kaganoff, review of *Sweetwater Seduction,* p. 67; December 6, 1991, review of *The Barefoot Bride,* p. 67; October 11, 1993, review of *Outlaw's Bride,* p. 83; November 21, 1994, review of *The Inheritance,* p. 72; October 30, 1995, review of *Maverick Heart,* p. 57; March 25, 1996, review of *Captive,* p. 81; February 21, 2000, review of *The Cowboy,* p. 70; March 18, 2002, review of *The Loner,* p. 84; November 18, 2002, review of *Comanche Woman,* p. 47; March 17, 2003, review of *The Price,* p. 55.

ONLINE

Joan Johnston Home Page, http://www.joanjohnston.com/ (September 19, 2003).*

K

KEATES, Jonathan 1946-

PERSONAL: Born 1946, in Paris, France. *Education:* Attended Bryanston College and Magdalen College, Oxford.

ADDRESSES: *Agent*—c/o Author Mail, Chatto & Windus, Random House UK, 20 Vauxhall Bridge Rd., London SW1V 2SA, England.

CAREER: Writer. City of London School, London, England, teacher of English literature.

AWARDS, HONORS: James Tait Black Memorial Prize for Best Novel, and Hawthornden Prize, both 1983, both for *Allegro Postillions.*

WRITINGS:

The Companion Guide to the Shakespeare Country, Collins (London, England), 1979, Prentice-Hall (Englewood Cliffs, NJ), 1983.
(With Angelo Hornak) *Historic London,* Letts (New York, NY), 1979.
(With Angelo Hornak) *Canterbury Cathedral,* Summerfield (London, England), 1980, Prentice-Hall (Englewood Cliffs, NJ), 1983.
The Love of Italy, Crescent (New York, NY), 1980.
Allegro Postillions (short stories), Salamander Press (Edinburgh, Scotland), 1983, Braziller (New York, NY), 1985.
Handel: The Man and His Music, St. Martin's Press (New York, NY), 1985.
Tuscany, photographs by Charlie Waite, Salem House (Topsfield, MA), 1989.
Italian Journeys, Picador (London, England), 1992.
Venice, illustrated by John Lawrence, Sinclair-Stevenson (London, England), 1994.
Purcell: A Biography, Chatto & Windus (London, England), 1995, Northeastern University Press (Boston, MA), 1996.
Stendahl, Minerva (London, England), 1995, Carroll and Graf (New York, NY), 1997.
Soon to Be a Major Motion Picture (short stories), Chatto & Windus (London, England), 1997.
The Stranger's Gallery, Vintage (London, England), 1998.
Smile Please (novel), Chatto & Windus (London, England), 2000.

Also author of a commentary on William Bird's *Drawings and Sketches of Oxford,* Salamander Press (Edinburgh), 1983. Contributor of book reviews to periodicals.

SIDELIGHTS: Jonathan Keates is an author "in love with, or romantically most at ease in, the past," according to Andrew Barrow of the *Spectator.* Graceful prose, impressive scholarship, and a passion for history are the hallmarks of Keates's writings. These qualities are especially evident in his biographies and in the short stories collected in *Allegro Postillions* and *Soon to Be a Major Motion Picture,* most of which are set in the nineteenth or early twentieth century.

Although he has written nonfiction dating to the past, Keates's interest in the art, music, and literature of an earlier time finds its most creative expression in the short stories of *Allegro Postillions.* The four tales in this book are all set in Italy, but in the words of *Punch* contributor Mary Anne Bonney, Keates's Italy "is more an idea than a place." In *Books and Bookmen,* Justin Wintle called the collection a "dream object" and asserted that Keates is "an author for whom fiction matters." Wintle added that Keates's stories "explore their period through the period's own styles and conventions. There is no modernist intervention *à la French Lieutenant's Woman.* The action, and there is plenty of it, speaks nearly always for itself."

As in *Allegro Postillions,* most of the stories in *Soon to Be a Major Motion Picture* are set in the aristocratic Europe of grand hotels, maidservants, and fancy carriages that existed before World War I. A number of the stories explore gay themes. Barrow confessed in the *Spectator* that he had to turn to the book's blurb to understand the plot of the first story, but was quick to add that "the story and the collection as a whole rapidly gather momentum. Once you have got the hang of Mr. Keates's wonderfully fancy style and subject matter, everything goes swimmingly." Barrow also commented that although the rawness of some of the book's sexual material could have been "suffocating" if handled by a writer of lesser ability, Keates's "beautifully structured prose makes everything deeply enjoyable."

Keates's *Handel: The Man and His Music,* a study of eighteenth-century German composer George Frederick Handel, appeared in 1985. It was followed a decade later by a second biography, this time of Henry Purcell, the foremost English composer of the seventeenth century, and the volume's publication was timed to coincide with the tercentenary of Purcell's death. Larry A. Lipkis, writing in *Library Journal,* lauded *Purcell: A Biography* as "a marvel of insightful research and witty, elegant prose," and went on to remark that it presents "a vivid picture of Purcell's life and achievements." Keates's accomplishment, Lipkis added, is all the more impressive in light of the paucity of historical evidence concerning Purcell. In the *Times Literary Supplement,* Paul Griffiths declared that "Keates is vigorous, entertaining, flamboyant, proud: in a word, Purcellian, if at the expense of becoming himself, more than his cherished composer, the book's subject."

Keates's examination of the life of nineteenth-century French novelist Stendahl, which also appeared in 1995, likewise drew praise from several reviewers. Anita Brookner in the London *Observer* called it an "altogether admirable" biography and Rupert Christiansen in the *Spectator* praised Keates's "lucidity, wit and . . . military command over both the minutiae of the sources and the broader historical landscape in which Stendahl enacted his complex game with life." Roger Pearson in the *Times Literary Supplement* judged the biography to be "thoroughly researched, maturely conceived and elegantly written."

Keates's novel *Smile Please* is set among the gay community of contemporary London. Michael Arditti in the *Independent* explained that the plot revolves around "the romantic misadventures of a group of leisured, moneyed characters." The story centers on arts foundation staffer Adam and black actor Theo, gay flatmates, and their friends and relations, both married and unmarried, straight and gay. These include Frankie, an American choreographer, the sisters Daisy, Alice, and Serena, and the wealthy Guy. "Like a Restoration play," David Jays noted in the *Observer,* "*Smile Please* examines an affective but edgy clutch of friends, seen both on the urban range and marooned together for weekends in the country." "Keates charts all their wrong turnings, their play-acting and fancy footwork with glee," according to a critic for the London *Evening Standard.* "With its wit, graceful construction, snappy dialogue and slight whiff of narcissism," Arditti concluded, "*Smile Please* is a novel that Woody Allen might have written had he been a gay Londoner."

BIOGRAPHICAL AND CRITICAL SOURCES:

BOOKS

Contemporary Literary Criticism, Volume 34, Gale (Detroit, MI), 1985.

PERIODICALS

Atlantic Monthly, September, 1985, p. 115.

Books and Bookmen, January, 1985, pp. 34-35.

Evening Standard, February 7, 2000, review of *Smile Please,* p. 60.

Guardian Weekly, September 4, 1994, p. 28.

Herald, February 26, 2000, Kenneth Wright, review of *Smile Please,* p. 14.
History Today, June, 1985, p. 53.
Independent, February 26, 2000, Michael Arditti, review of *Smile Please.*
Library Journal, November 1, 1996, p. 69.
Listener, January 19, 1984, p. 26.
New Republic, June 15, 1998, Michael Ravitch, review of *Stendhal,* p. 37.
Observer (London, England), October 30, 1983, p. 32; January 24, 1993, p. 54; June 26, 1994, p. 16; July 10, 1994, p. 15; July 24, 1994, p. 17; July 30, 1995, p. 17; February 6, 2000, David Jays, review of *Smile Please,* p. 13.
Opera Quarterly, autumn, 1997, Malcolm S. Cole, review of *Purcell,* p. 118.
Publishers Weekly, December 20, 1993, p. 66; September 9, 1996, p. 73; February 10, 1997, p. 72.
Punch, November 30, 1983, p. 72.
Spectator, June 25, 1994, pp. 25-26; May 31, 1997, Andrew Barrow, review of *Soon to Be a Major Motion Picture,* pp. 42-43; February 5, 2000, Katie Grant, review of *Smile Please,* p. 34.
Times Educational Supplement, January 8, 1993, p. 10.
Times Literary Supplement, August 12, 1994, p. 8; September 15, 1995, pp. 3-4.
Wall Street Journal, March 25, 1997, p. A16.
World, October, 1991, p. S16.

ONLINE

Contemporary Writers in the UK, http://www.contemporarywriters.com/ (November 13, 2003).*

* * *

KENYON, Karen (Smith) 1938-

PERSONAL: Born September 4, 1938, in Oklahoma City, OK; daughter of Claude Emory Smith (an attorney) and Evelyn Grace Brown Smith Bass (a homemaker and pianist); married Richard Bertram Kenyon, February 14, 1963 (deceased); children: Richard Laurence, Johanna (deceased). *Ethnicity:* "Euro-American/Caucasian." *Education:* Attended University of New Mexico—Albuquerque, and University of Colorado; San Diego State University, B.A. (English and art), 1977, M.A. (creative writing and art), 1987. *Politics:* Democrat. *Hobbies and other interests:* Walking my dog, theater, and film.

ADDRESSES: *Home*—P.O. Box 12604, La Jolla, CA 92039. *Agent*—Danielle Egan-Miller, Multimedia Product Development, 410 South Michigan Ave., Ste. 460, Chicago, IL 60605. *E-mail*—kkenyon@ucsd.edu.

CAREER: Mira Costa College, Cardiff, CA, writing instructor, 1982—; San Diego State University—Extended Studies, San Diego, CA, writing instructor, 1985—; University of California, San Diego Extension, La Jolla, CA, writing instructor, 1983-93, and 2003—. Teacher of writing at Miramar College, 1992, at San Diego State University, 2001, and for the San Diego City Schools' Gifted and Talented Education program, 2002-03. Conductor of workshops at University of California—Los Angeles, University of California—Irvine, and The Writing Center. Guest on *The Lounge,* a production of PBS radio in San Diego, CA.

MEMBER: Society of Children's Book Writers and Illustrators, PEN, Brontë Society.

AWARDS, HONORS: Creativity Award, San Diego Institute for Creativity, 1974; Certificate of Merit, *Atlantic Monthly,* 1975, for poetry.

WRITINGS:

Sunshower (personal narrative), Richard Marek/Putnam (New York, NY), 1981.
(As Karen Smith Kenyon) *The Brontë Family: Passionate Literary Geniuses* (young-adult biography), Lerner Publications (Minneapolis, MN), 2002.

Also author of hundreds of articles, essays, and poems, published in periodicals, including *British Heritage, Writer, Boston Globe, Los Angeles Times, Christian Science Monitor, Ladies' Home Journal,* and others. Contributor of essay "Johanna Was a Sunshower" to *Redbook,* "A Survivor's Notes" to *Newsweek,* "The Pen That Heals" to *Writer's Digest,* and "Writing a Young Adult Biography," to *The Writer's Handbook, 2004.*

WORK IN PROGRESS: A young-adult biography on Charles Dickens; *Writing by Heart: Healing Our Lives with Our Pens,* "about how healing writing can be."

SIDELIGHTS: Karen Kenyon's first book offers a personal narrative that details the gradual recovery of her family from the death of Kenyon's husband by suicide. This shock followed the death of their infant daughter, eight years earlier, who was born with Down's Syndrome. Reeling with pain, Kenyon examines her nearly twenty-year relationship with her husband for clues to his suicidal impulse and concludes that he was not a man who could express his deepest feelings of sadness or despair. She sought the comfort of family, close friends, and writing. Kenyon titled her book *Sunshower* to accentuate the idea that the darkness of her grieving had also brought enlightenment, about the nature of love and family, especially. Priscilla Johnson called *Sunshower* "an honest and courageous book" in her *School Library Journal* review. For critic Tom Streissguth, writing in the Torrance, California, *South Bay Breeze,* Kenyon's story is ultimately about "how the human spirit can move out from the shadow of death and despair." "*Sunshower* is touching, affecting . . . and painfully valid," Streissguth concluded.

A freelance writer and college instructor, Kenyon penned hundreds of poems, essays, and articles in between the time her first and second books appeared in print. On her many trips to England, Kenyon became fascinated by the lives of the Brontës, a family of artists and writers whose short, often sad lives, produced work that continues to be appreciated more than a hundred years later. Out of this interest came Kenyon's young-adult biography *The Brontë Family: Passionate Literary Geniuses,* which begins with the early life of Charlotte, Emily, Anne, and Branwell Brontë, who lost their mother and two siblings to illness early in life. Growing up, the children nurtured each other's earliest artistic endeavors. The three sisters were writers, the brother a writer and painter. All died fairly young and tragically, though Charlotte lived to thirty eight, dying from complications of pregnancy. Critics of Kenyon's biography made much of the author's account of the necessity for Charlotte, Emily, and Anne to take on male pseudonyms in order for their writings to be taken seriously by publishers and critics in nineteenth-century England, and the literary furore caused by their unveiling. The Brontës' works were firmly rooted in their native Yorkshire, whose windswept heaths and moors they each memorably captured for generations to come. "Kenyon knows her subject well and draws readers into the Brontës' world," remarked Kathleen A. Nester in *School Library Journal,* praising the author's scrupulous research and fine writing style. The Brontës are often required reading for young adults, and the use of numerous illustrations in Kenyon's biography, as well as reference to contemporary film and television adaptations of their most famous works, should expand the book's interest for its intended audience, conjectured Mary Arnold in *Voice of Youth Advocates.* Arnold concluded: "The warm, accessible tone and format [of *The Brontë Family*] show how these women and their lives created 'classics' whose characters resonate with universal human emotions that are truly timeless."

"I am one of those people who have always liked to express myself in some creative way," Kenyon told *CA.* "My mother was a pianist and was often playing the piano and singing. As a child, I loved to sit next to her on the piano bench and experience the beauty and wonder of her playing, and the rapture of music. My father appreciated literature, and often quoted epic poems as we went for long car drives.

"When I was a child, I took dance lessons—tap and beginning ballet, piano lessons, and I was a very bad clarinetist in the junior high band! When I discovered art, I felt at home, and so in college at the University of New Mexico, I studied art for three years until I married. All during my life though, I had also been writing stories, poems, and once a little play. But I did not think of myself as a writer until, as happens with many people, I had something happen in my life which I felt drawn, almost compelled, to write about.

"In my case, it was the birth of a second child, seven years into my marriage. Our baby girl, Johanna, was a Down Syndrome baby. Her condition was a shock, as is always the case when your child is not healthy. We loved her, and cared for her, but suddenly, at six months of age, she died. I began to want to tell people about her and how she had changed our lives. The result is that I wrote 'Johanna Was a Sunshower,' an essay for *Redbook* (March, 1973).

"This article changed my life and set me on the path to writing. I started writing articles—on artists, and other interesting people. And I started going back to college, to finish my degree in writing. But a year after graduating, another difficult period of my life began. My husband, who was only thirty-eight years old, took his own life. There was no indication something like this might occur, except for what seemed to be some mild depression, which he had assured me he could handle.

"Our son was only twelve years old, and this event completely shocked us and altered our lives drastically. I thought I would never write about such a horrible, tragic, and difficult event. But my old friend writing was waiting for me, and in time, I started writing in my journal.

"Then one day I received a phone call from the husband of a woman acquaintance of mine. This woman was a writer, and she had had a baby boy around the time Johanna was born who was also a Down Syndrome baby. I had had lunch with her, and we spoke on the phone several times. She appeared to be a strong woman, in control of her life.

"Her husband had called me just four months after my husband's death to tell me that she too had taken her own life. I was stunned. Until my husband's death, I'd never known a person who had committed suicide.

"When I hung up the phone, a feeling which I could not dismiss filled me. I had to write about my husband's death. Because suicide happens, and no one ever says anything about it, I had to speak out. That night I wrote an essay which I called 'A Survivor's Notes,' which I sent to *Newsweek.* It was a magazine I always read, and I was familiar with their 'My Turn' column. The essay was published a mere ten days later. I received hundreds of wonderful letters from others who'd lost loved ones to suicide or other causes; from those who'd attempted taking their own lives, and then backed away from it; from doctors, psychiatrists; from a nun; from a prisoner. These letters overwhelmed me. I thought of Emily Dickinson's poem, 'This is my letter to the world, that never wrote to me. . . .' I too had written a letter to the world. But the world had answered my letter.

"Some of the letters asked if I planned to write a book. But at first I thought, 'How can I? It would be too painful.' But as I looked for books to help me, and found very few, and virtually no first-person account of a loss from suicide, I began to think I would begin such a book.

"That is how I came to write *Sunshower,* a personal narrative telling the story of my husband's and my marriage, our son, Richard, the loss of Johanna, and my husband's death, and how my son and I made it through this difficult journey. The book was published in 1981 by Richard Marek, through G. P. Putnam's Sons, in New York.

"During this time, also I finished my master's degree in English, with an emphasis in creative writing at San Diego State University. In addition, I started going to England after the loss of my husband, and with each trip have written articles on interesting sites—for example, Stonehenge and even on Liverpool and the Beatles; and also I began writing about visiting famous writers' homes—Charles Dickens, John Keats, Beatrix Potter. And then I visited the Brontë Parsonage in Northern England, the home of the Brontë sisters (Charlotte, Emily, and Anne). I saw not only the home where they lived but many of their belongings—Charlotte's wedding bonnet, the comb Emily is said to have dropped in the fire the day she died, a cross-stitch sampler made by their sister, Elizabeth, who died at age eleven, their father's desk, their brother Branwell's bed and his paintings. I walked out on the moors, the expanse of nature like a broken, angled meadow, where they roamed and played each day, where Catherine and Heathcliff lived out their dramatic and romantic fictional lives.

"When I came home, I wrote an article, and in 1994 when I returned, another. But I didn't feel finished with this amazing family of writers. I felt that in a way they had come home with me. I began to write a young-adult biography, because I realized that the teen years are when most people become acquainted with *Wuthering Heights* and *Jane Eyre* (still considered *the* coming-of-age story for girls).

"I used my first-person experience in and around their home, plus several years of reading almost every biography written about the Brontës, using the wonderful collection at the University of California—San

Diego. When I found conflicting facts in different biographies, I always consulted the assistant curator and librarian at the Brontë Parsonage Museum to clear it up. The high point of my later research was a trip to the Huntington Library in San Marino, where I was allowed to hold and read some of Charlotte Brontë's original letters. This book was published in 2003 by Lerner Publications Company, in Minneapolis.

"Today, I am beginning work on a new, long young-adult biography on Charles Dickens, for Lerner Publications, and am working on another book about how healing writing can be. The working title is *Writing by Heart: Healing Our Lives with Our Pens.*

"I believe there is a theme of creativity in my books and in my articles as well. I can't imagine life without writing, doing some art, and listening to music, going to plays. I hope to convey this enthusiasm to readers.

"I do not always write for a specific length of time every day, but try to make some progress, perhaps doing a little research, editing and retyping a chapter, contacting a publisher, doing an interview.

"I've been influenced by certain authors. Shakespeare probably comes first. No one else has so thoroughly covered the entire range of human emotion. On another level, of course, the Brontës, also Charles Dickens, contemporary poets, like Robert Bly, Mary Oliver, Jane Hirshfield, novelists John Fowles, Michael Ondaatje, Milan Kundera. Jane Yolen is an inspiring and incredible children's book author.

"My advice to aspiring authors is to follow your heart. Never write anything that you can turn away from. If you don't have to write it, you shouldn't, because passion must be part of it—as important as your pen. The ideas that call and beckon to us, that lure us, are showing us our path."

BIOGRAPHICAL AND CRITICAL SOURCES:

PERIODICALS

Chicago Tribune, October 30, 1981, Otto Scott, review of *Sunshower.*

Kirkus Reviews, August 1, 1981, review of *Sunshower.*

San Diego Union-Tribune, August 25, 2002, review of *The Brontë Family: Passionate Literary Geniuses.*

School Library Journal, December, 1981, Priscilla Johnson, review of *Sunshower,* p. 89; January, 2003, Kathleen A. Nester, review of *The Brontë Family,* p. 163.

South Bay Breeze (Torrance, CA), September 18, 1981, Tom Streissguth, review of *Sunshower.*

Voice of Youth Advocates, February, 2003, Mary Arnold, review of *The Brontë Family.*

ONLINE

Karen Kenyon Home Page, http://www.miracosta.edu/home/kkenyon/ (November 5, 2003).

* * *

KEPEL, Gilles 1955-

PERSONAL: Born June 30, 1955, in Paris, France. *Education:* Studied in Paris, France; earned Ph.D.

ADDRESSES: Home—4 Washington Square Village, Apt. 4C, New York, NY 10012.

CAREER: Centre National de la Recherche Scientifique, Paris, France, senior research fellow; Institut d'Etudes Politiques de Paris, professor; New York University, visiting professor, 1992; New York Consortium, visiting professor at New York University and Columbia University, 1995-96; lecturer at Harvard University, Princeton University, Universities of California, Berkeley and Los Angeles, and University of Chicago. Social Science Research Council, member of Committee for the Comparative Study of Muslim Societies, 1985-88.

WRITINGS:

Le Prophète et pharaon: Les Mouvements Islamistes dans l'Egypte contemporaine, La Découverte (Paris, France), 1984, translation by Jon Rothschild published as *Muslim Extremism in Egypt: The Prophet and Pharaoh,* University of California Press (Berkeley, CA), 1985, updated, with new preface, 2003.

Les Banlieues de l'Islam, Editions du Seuil (Paris, France), 1987.

(Editor, with R. Leveau) *Les Musulmans dans la societe Francaise,* Presses de la FNSP (Paris, France), 1988.

(Editor, with Y. Richard) *Intellectuels et militants de l'Islam contemporain,* Editions du Seuil (Paris, France), 1990.

La Revanche de Dieu: Chrétiens, Juifs et Musulmans à la reconquête du monde, Editions du Seuil (Paris, France), 1991, translation by Alan Braley published as *The Revenge of God: The Resurgence of Islam, Christianity, and Judaism in the Modern World,* Pennsylvania State University Press (University Park, PA), 1994.

(Editor) *Les Politiques de Dieu,* Editions du Seuil (Paris, France), 1993.

(Editor) *Exils et royaumes: Les Appartenances au monde Arabo-Musulman aujourd'hui,* Presses de la FNSP (Paris, France), 1994.

A l'ouest d'Allah, Editions du Seuil (Paris, France), 1994, translation by Susan Milner published as *Allah in the West: Islamic Movements in America and Europe,* Stanford University Press (Stanford, CA), 1997.

Jihad: Expansion et declin de l'Islamisme, Gallimard (Paris, France), 2000, translation by Anthony F. Roberts published as *Jihad: The Trail of Political Islam,* Belknap Press/Harvard University Press (Cambridge, MA), 2002.

Chronique d'une guerre d'orient (automne 2001): Suivi de brève chronique d'Israel et de Palestine (avril-mai 2001), Gallimard (Paris, France), 2002, translation by Pascale Ghazaleh published as *Bad Moon Rising: A Chronicle of the Middle East Today,* Saqi (London, England), 2003.

Kepel's works have been translated into numerous languages.

SIDELIGHTS: Gilles Kepel, described by *Times Literary Supplement* critic M. E. Yapp as a "prolific academic writer on modern Islam," attracted significant mainstream attention with the publication of *Jihad: The Trail of Political Islam.* In this book, originally published in French in 2000, Kepel argues that militant Islam, which enjoyed a surge of popular support in the late twentieth century, has been in decline since the late 1990s. Updating the book after the September 11, 2001, attack on the World Trade Center in New York City, Kepel states that "In spite of what hasty commentators contended in its immediate aftermath, the attack on the United States was a desperate symbol of the isolation, fragmentation and decline of the Islamist movement, not a sign of its strength and irrepressible might."

Kepel traces the rise of contemporary militant Islam to 1966, when the Egyptian government executed activist Sayyid Qutb. Through the 1970s the movement grew, aided by soaring population rates and increased literacy and urbanization in the Muslim world. The Iranian revolution in 1979 was a turning point; it was followed by Islamist uprisings in Afghanistan, Lebanon, Sudan, and the Balkans, as well as among the Palestinians. Yet, according to Kepel, these later episodes reveal the movement's ultimate failure to attract widespread support. Between 1996 and 1997, he writes, the "high season of jihad" began to wane. Two "entirely new phenomena" influenced this decline. The first, Kepel explains, "was the gradual opening of a gulf between the ideas of Islamist radicals and the needs of ordinary Muslims . . . Second, there began to emerge among those same ordinary Muslims a blueprint for a Muslim democratic society that went beyond the Islamist model. It was suggested that traditional Islamic culture could find a way to allow Muslims to embrace the modern world without betraying themselves."

Critics found Kepel's argument provocative, well-reasoned, and based on solid scholarship. *Jihad,* according to *New York Times Book Review* contributor Robin Wright, "is a compelling read that makes an appealing case." Similarly, Justin Wintle in the London *Sunday Times* found the book "deeply researched, deeply measured and deeply instructive." Some, however, did not find Kepel's thesis entirely convincing. In the *Atlantic Monthly,* Walter Laqueur observed, "It is to be hoped that reality catches up with Kepel's dream of a new dawn of freedom and democracy rooted in the great tradition of Muslim civilization. But it certainly won't happen soon." *Times Literary Supplement* reviewer M. E. Yapp also raised questions about Kepel's theory, pointing out that though it is sometimes persuasive, "the more one examines the situation in the contemporary Muslim world, the more the supposed common pattern seems to blur." Yet Yapp concluded that "*Jihad* is an excellent account of the development of radical Islam in the last quarter of the twentieth century, combining as it does a good knowledge of the recent history of several

Muslim countries, an understanding of Islamic thought and an ability to bring together historical events and longer-term social changes to afford a persuasive explanation of the phenomenon he is describing. Whether Gilles Kepel's optimism about the decline if Islamism is justified remains to be seen."

BIOGRAPHICAL AND CRITICAL SOURCES:

BOOKS

Kepel, Gilles, *Jihad: Expansion et declin de l'Islamisme,* Gallimard (Paris, France), 2000, translation by Anthony F. Roberts published as *Jihad: The Trail of Political Islam,* Belknap Press/ Harvard University Press (Cambridge, MA), 2002.

PERIODICALS

Atlantic Monthly, March, 2002, Walter Laqueur, "The Failure of Intelligence," p. 127.

Booklist, April 1. 2002, John Green, review of *Jihad,* p. 1284.

Choice, June, 2002, B. B. Lawrence, review of *The Revenge of God: The Resurgence of Islam, Christianity, and Judaism in the Modern World* and *Allah in the West: Islamic Movements in America and Europe,* p. SF7.

Economist, July 19, 1997, review of *Allah in the West,* p. S8.

International Affairs, October, 1997, Roger Hardy, review of *Allah in the West,* p. 821.

Journal of American Ethnic History, fall, 1999, Georges Sabagh, review of *Allah in the West,* p. 113.

Journal of Ecumenical Studies, winter, 1997, Yushua Sodiq, review of *The Revenge of God,* p. 150.

Journal of Intercultural Studies, December, 2001, Amandeep Sandhu, review of *Allah in the West,* p. 326.

Library Journal, March 15, 2002, Nader Entessar, review of *Jihad,* p. 96.

National Interest, winter, 1997, Herb Greer, review of *Allah in the West,* p. 94.

New Statesman, May 13, 2002, Mick Hume, review of *Jihad,* p. 50.

Newsweek International, May 8, 2000, "The Final Days of Jihad," p. 40.

New York Times Book Review, May 26, 2002, Robin Wright, review of *Jihad,* p. 10.

Partisan Review, summer, 2001, Walter Laqueur, "Fundamentalism," p. 499.

Publishers Weekly, March 4, 2002, review of *Jihad,* p. 68.

Sunday Telegraph (London, England), May 12, 2002, Efraim Karsh, review of *Jihad,* p. 15.

Sunday Times (London, England), June 23, 2002, Justin Wintle, review of *Jihad,* p. 41.

Times Higher Education Supplement, April 25, 1997, Shabbir Akhtar, review of *Allah in the West,* p. 26.

Times Literary Supplement, May 30, 1997, Malise Ruthven, review of *Allah in the West,* p. 3; June 28, 2002, M. E. Yapp, review of *Jihad,* p.

Wall Street Journal, March 29, 2002, Adrian Karatnycky, review of *Jihad,* p. W10.

Washington Times, May 21, 2002, Sol Schindler, review of *Jihad,* p. A21.*

* * *

KING, Mary (Elizabeth) 1940-

PERSONAL: Born July 30, 1940, in New York, NY; daughter of Luther Waddington (a Methodist minister) and Alba Iregui (a teacher of nursing) King; married Peter Geoffrey Bourne (a psychiatrist and author), November 9, 1974. *Ethnicity:* "Caucasian." *Education:* Ohio Wesleyan University, B.A., 1962; University of Wales—Aberystwyth, Ph.D., 1999. *Politics:* Democrat. *Religion:* Protestant.

ADDRESSES: *Office*—University for Peace, 2119 Leroy Pl. NW, Washington DC 20008-1848. *Agent*—Gerard F. McCauley, P.O. Box 844, Katonah, NY, 10536. *E-mail*—maryking@igc.org.

CAREER: National Student Young Women's Christian Association, Atlanta, GA, human relations specialist, 1962; Student Nonviolent Coordinating Committee, assistant director of communications in Atlanta, GA, and Jackson, MS, 1963-65; U.S. Office of Economic Opportunity, project officer, 1968-72; Mary King Associates, Inc., Washington, DC, president, 1972-76; ACTION (comprised of Peace Corps, Volunteers in Service to America, Foster Grandparents Program, and other U.S. national volunteer service corps programs), deputy director during Jimmy Carter administration,

1977-81; International Community Leadership Project, Washington, DC, administrator, 1981-83; Young Ideas, Inc., Washington, DC, executive director, 1983-85; U.S.-Iraq Business Forum, consultant on international trade and executive director, 1985-90; Albert Einstein Institution, Boston, MA, fellow, 1996-98; St. George's University, Grenada, professor of international politics, 1999-2001; University for Peace, Washington, DC, professor of peace and conflict studies and special advisor to the rector, 2001—. Wesley Theological Seminary, Washington, DC, member of board of governors, 1990-93; American University, visiting scholar at School of International Service, Center for Global Peace, 1997—. Political and civil rights worker, diplomat, expert on nonviolent struggle, peace and conflict studies, civil rights, civil society, and international affairs; Global Action, Inc., president, 1992—. Democratic National Convention, delegate from District of Columbia, 1976 and 1980; Jimmy Carter presidential campaign, chair of Health Policy Task Force, 1976; Committee of 51.3 Percent, national director, 1976; coordinator of mid-Atlantic presidential primary races, 1976; Member of United States delegations to United Nations world conferences, including delegations to the World Health Assembly in Geneva, Switzerland, 1977, Club des Amis du Sahel in Ottawa, Ontario, Canada, 1977, Organization for Economic Cooperation and Development in Paris, France, 1978, World Conference on Desertification in Nairobi, Kenya, 1978, World Conference on Agrarian Reform and Rural Development in Rome, Italy, 1979, United Nations High Commission on Refugees Pledging Conference in Geneva, Switzerland, 1979, and Mid-Decade World Conference on Women in Copenhagen, Denmark, 1980; special advisor to former president Jimmy Carter on the Middle East, 1984—; International Commission on Peace and Food, member, 1989-94; American Institute for Public Service, board of selectors for Jefferson Awards, 1993—; appointed advisor by the government of India, 1998—. Women's Action Alliance, member of board of directors, 1976—; Save the Children, member of board of directors, 1980-91; Arca Foundation, officer and member of board of directors, 1980—. AMIDEAST Educational and Testing Service, member of board of directors, 1989—.

MEMBER: National Association of Women Business Owners (cofounder; president, 1976-77), Women in International Security, Middle East Studies Association, Women's Foreign Policy Group, Authors Guild, Authors League of America.

AWARDS, HONORS: President's Award, National Association of Women Business Owners, 1975; Recognition of Achievement Award, Women's Equity Action League, 1977; one of the Robert F. Kennedy Memorial Book Awards of 1988, for *Freedom Song: A Personal Story of the 1960s Civil Rights Movement;* Distinguished Achievement Award, Ohio Wesleyan University, 1989; elected to National Women's Hall of Fame, 1992.

WRITINGS:

Freedom Song: A Personal Story of the 1960s Civil Rights Movement, foreword by Andrew Young, preface by Casey Hayden, afterword by Clayborne Carson, William Morrow (New York, NY), 1987.

(Editor, with Mary-Jane Deeb) *Hasib Sabbagh: From Palestinian Refugee to Citizen of the World,* University Press of America (Lanham, MD), 1996.

Mahatma Gandhi and Martin Luther King, Jr.: The Power of Nonviolent Action, UNESCO (Paris, France), 1999, 2nd edition, Mehta Publishers (New Delhi, India), 2002.

Contributor to books, including *Grand Mothers: Poems, Reminiscences, and Short Stories,* edited by Nikki Giovanni, Holt (New York, NY), 1994; and *Hands on the Plough,* edited by Faith Holsaert, Martha Prescod Norman, and others. Contributor of articles and reviews to periodicals, including *Christian Century, Journal of the American Public Health Association, Liberation, Los Angeles Times, Nation, Newsday, Sage Yearbook Series, Vogue, Washington Star,* and *Working Woman;* contributor to news services, including Knight-Ridder News Service and Scripps-Howard News Service.

SIDELIGHTS: Mary King struggled for years to find a publisher for her book *Freedom Song: A Personal Story of the 1960s Civil Rights Movement.* When the book was finally published in 1987, it received both critical acclaim and a Robert F. Kennedy Book Award. At the award ceremony, as reported by Elizabeth Kastor in the *Washington Post,* a tearful King told the audience of the heroism of little-known civil rights workers and criticized historians who only saw the more highly-publicized parts of the story. She said, "I really take the prize as an acknowledgment of an untold story."

King first came into contact with the civil rights movement as a senior at Ohio Wesleyan University. The daughter of a Methodist minister with Southern roots (and no relation to Martin Luther King, Jr.), King was working a senior project on race relations in the South and toured national headquarters of the Student Nonviolent Coordinating Committee (also known as SNCC), located in Atlanta, Georgia. SNCC was the more youthful and more militant alternative to older, mainstream civil rights organizations such as the National Association for the Advancement of Colored People (NAACP) and the Southern Christian Leadership Conference (SCLC).

Founded largely by idealistic young (mostly black) men in the early 1960s, SNCC ran voter registration drives and conducted sit-ins at segregated lunch counters in the South. During the tour, King met prominent civil rights figures Julian Bond, John Lewis, and James Forman. The experience galvanized King's imagination. As she wrote in *Freedom Song,* SNCC "was different in its dynamism and outlook from the other more staid civil rights groups I had encountered. In these SNCC workers I sensed high energy, self-assurance, impatience, and determination. I identified with them. I saw myself in them." SNCC had loose and consensual leadership practices rather than a rigid and hierarchical ruling structure. As King recalled in an interview with Barbara Gamarekian of the *New York Times,* "It was the most pure manifestation of democracy that I have ever encountered."

In *Freedom Song,* King recounts her experiences rooming with a young white Texan woman, Casey Hayden, who became one of her mentors in the intellectual side of the civil rights and feminist movements. King describes her various roles in SNCC during the heady early days. She worked for civil rights activist Ella Baker and in the communications arm of the organization, working for Julian Bond and writing press releases for James Forman and John Lewis. Nicknamed "Meticulous Mary" for her habit of keeping records, she amassed the materials that would later assist her—and, presumably, future historians—in writing about the movement.

The SNCC practice of leadership by consensus led to power struggles in which charismatic leaders, particularly Stokely Carmichael, increasingly imposed their views on the entire group. Tensions arose between white and black volunteers, between men and women, and between black women and white women. At one meeting, King and Hayden circulated, anonymously, a letter asking whether the movement would respond to the concerns of women in the organization. The letter stirred already-existing tensions and much discussion. The most memorable response allegedly came from Carmichael, who said, according to reviewer Juan Williams of the *Washington Post Book World,* that "the position of women in SNCC was 'prone.'" King, in *Freedom Song,* treats Carmichael's remark as a humorous quip, but Williams found it more serious and elaborated, "The reader wants more about the difficulties women faced and the sexual tension in SNCC."

A second King-Hayden document, titled "A Kind of Memo from Casey Hayden and Mary King to a Number of Other Women in the Peace and Freedom Movements," was an important stimulus for the late-1960s feminist movement, according to Susan Brownmiller in the *New York Times Book Review.* As King told Barbara Gamarekian in the *New York Times,* "It has been pretty well established that that manifesto served as a catalyst for a lot of the consciousness-raising groups that began meeting around the country."

Tensions within SNCC increased after a massive influx of white volunteers for the ambitious 1964 Summer Project, which King viewed ambivalently. The Summer Project led to 1,000 arrests, thirty beatings, thirty-five church bombings, thirty home bombings, and the killings of SNCC workers James Chaney, Andrew Goodman, and Michael Schwerner. It also led to the founding of the Freedom Democratic Party, and was a major focal point of publicity for the civil rights movement. It did not, however, strengthen SNCC internally. All whites, including King, were expelled from SNCC in 1965, but King's book expresses no bitterness. King remains lifelong friends with many of her former colleagues in the organization.

Critics considered *Freedom Song* to be a significant historical document about the American civil rights movement of the 1960s. Susan Brownmiller observed in the *New York Times Book Review* that "*Freedom Song* will stand as a monument to that wondrous time." Juan Williams, although commenting that King pulls punches on matters of intragroup conflict, said in the *Washington Post Book World* that "*Freedom Song* is most absorbing when it shows the details of post-adolescents running a civil rights group and the contradictions in their methods and actions." He stated that "the book works best when King writes about the romance of the movement and particularly her attraction to SNCC"; he also praised the "wonderful irony in her writing about the prejudice both black and white women faced in the male-dominated SNCC."

Harold Cruse, contributing to the *Los Angeles Times Book Review,* praised *Freedom Song* for its "quality of an extended diary," appearing as if it was "written in wistful retrospection" even though it does not adequately explain what caused the downfall of SNCC. According to a *New Yorker* reviewer, King's book does effectively memorialize what SNCC accomplished during its years of influence and does present a snapshot of American culture in the 1960s. The reviewer added that the book "commemorates the courage of young people who risked—or lost—their lives in the cause of conscience."

After leaving SNCC, King continued an active career in public service. In 1968 she became a project officer for the United States Office of Economic Opportunity, serving in that capacity for four years. In 1972, she joined a small group of people organizing Jimmy Carter's 1976 presidential campaign. During her affiliation with Carter, King attended the 1976 and 1980 Democratic National conventions as a delegate, coordinated a regional primary campaign, and convinced Carter of the importance of giving greater prominence to women in his organization. Simultaneously, she was president of a management consulting firm based in Washington, DC.

During the four-year Carter administration, King traveled extensively as a member of American delegations to international conferences on such subjects as food policy, agrarian reform, and the fight against hunger and poverty. A founder of the National Association of Women Business Owners, she became its president in 1976. She has also been an important figure in the work of the Save the Children Foundation and other public service groups.

King has worked with international as well as national interests. She has worked in international trade, with an emphasis on the Middle East, Central America, Africa, and Asia; she has spurred private initiatives on development, refugee issues, and improving international relations. From 1983 to 1985, she was the director of former Atlanta mayor and United States representative Andrew Young's nonprofit development organization called Young Ideas, Inc. From 1985 to 1990 she was the executive director of the U.S.-Iraq Business Forum, aimed at improving commercial relations between the two nations. Later, in the 1990s, King served as president of her own company, Global Action, Inc. Subsequently, she went on to become a global authority on nonviolent political movements and a professor of peace and conflict studies.

BIOGRAPHICAL AND CRITICAL SOURCES:

BOOKS

King, Mary, *Freedom Song: A Personal Story of the 1960s Civil Rights Movement,* foreword by Andrew Young, preface by Casey Hayden, and afterword by Clayborne Carson, William Morrow (New York, NY), 1987.

PERIODICALS

Los Angeles Times Book Review, August 2, 1987, Harold Cruse, review of *Freedom Song,* pp. 2, 9.

Ms., September, 1987, p. 30.

Nation, December 26, 1987-January 2, 1988, p. 794.

New Yorker, October 12, 1987, review of *Freedom Song,* pp. 145-146.

New York Times, August 31, 1987, article by Barbara Gamarekian.

New York Times Book Review, August 30, 1987, Susan Brownmiller, review of *Freedom Song,* pp. 12-13.

Washington Post, May 14, 1988, article by Elizabeth Kastor.

Washington Post Book World, July 19, 1987, Juan Williams, review of *Freedom Song,* pp. 10-11.

* * *

KITT, Eartha (Mae) 1928-

PERSONAL: Born January 26, 1928, in North, SC; daughter of William (a sharecropper) and Anna Mae (Riley) Kitt; married William McDonald, June, 1960 (divorced, 1965); children: Kitt McDonald Shapiro (daughter). *Education:* Educated in New York, NY.

Eartha Kitt

ADDRESSES: Home—New York, NY. *Office*—Eartha Kitt Productions, 888 Seventh Ave., Floor 37, New York, NY 10106-3799. *Agent*—Gurtman and Murtha Assoc., 162 West 56th St., New York, NY 10019. *E-mail*—eartha@earthakitt.com.

CAREER: Singer, dancer, actress, and nightclub performer. Toured United States, Mexico, and South America as a dancer and singer with Katherine Dunham dance troupe, 1944-49; European nightclub debut at Carroll's, Paris, France, 1949; played Helen of Troy in Orson Welles's production of *Faust,* Paris, 1951; American nightclub debut at La Vie en Rose, New York, NY. Stage performances include *New Faces,* 1952, *Mrs. Patterson,* 1954, *Shinbone Alley,* 1957, *Jolly's Progress,* 1959, and role of Princess-Sahleem-La-Lume, *Timbuktu,* 1978; touring performances include productions of *The Skin of Our Teeth, The Owl and the Pussycat,* and *Cinderella,* 2000-02. Motion picture performances include *New Faces,* 1954; *Accused,* 1957; *The Mark of the Hawk,* Universal, 1958; *Anna Lucasta,* Paramount, 1959; *Synanon,* 1965; *All by Myself,* 1982; *Ernest: Scared Stupid; Unzipped; Feast of All Saints,* 2000; and two French films. Television appearances include *Ed Sullivan Show, Colgate Comedy Hour, I Spy, Batman,* and *Police Woman.* Recordings include *At the Plaza,* 1965; *Bad but Beautiful,* 1976; *At Her Very Best,* 1982; *C'est si bon,* Polydor, 1983; *I Love Men,* Sunnyview, 1984; *St. Louis Blues,* 1985; *That Bad Eartha,* RCA, 1985; *Eartha Kitt with the Doc Cheatham Trio* (recorded 1950), Swing, 1986; *In Person at the Plaza* (recorded 1965), GNP Crescendo, 1987; *My Way: A Musical Tribute to Reverend Martin Luther King, Jr.,* Caravan of Dreams, 1987; *Eartha Kitt in Person at the Plaza,* 1988; *A Funny Dame,* 1988; *Diamond Series* (compilation), 1988; *I'm Still Here,* 1989; *Live in London,* 1990; *Best of Eartha Kitt* (compilation), MCA, 1990; *Miss Kitt to You,* RCA, 1992; *Primitive Man,* 1992; *Thinking Jazz,* ITM, 1992; *Back in Business,* 1995; *Love for Sale,* Capitol; and *The Romantic Eartha Kitt,* Capitol. Recorded dramatic readings include *Black Pioneers in American History: Nineteenth Century,* with Moses Gunn, Caedmon, 1968; and *Folk Tales of the Tribes of Africa,* Caedmon, 1968.

AWARDS, HONORS: Golden Rose First Place Award for best special of the year, Montreux Film Festival, 1962, for *This Is Eartha;* Woman of the Year Award, National Association of Black Musicians, 1968; three Tony Award nominations; Grammy Award nomination; Emmy Award nomination.

WRITINGS:

Thursday's Child (autobiography), Duell, Sloan & Pearce (New York, NY), 1956.

Alone with Me (autobiography), Regnery (Washington, DC), 1976.

I'm Still Here: Confessions of a Sex Kitten, Barricade Books (New York, NY), 1991.

Rejuvenate!: It's Never Too Late, Scribner (New York, NY), 2001.

ADAPTATIONS: Rejuvenate! was adapted as an audiobook, narrated by Kitt.

SIDELIGHTS: "In essence, I'm a sophisticated cotton picker," wrote vocalist and actress Eartha Kitt in her autobiography *Alone with Me.* Despite her childhood of poverty and instability, Kitt has achieved international recognition and success in one of show business's most unusual and poignant tales. From a humble background in the Deep South, Kitt rose to become the toast of Europe during the 1950s as a cabaret singer with a dynamic persona and memorable, throaty voice. Back in America, however, she faced criticism from the African-American community for being too "white," but later earned their support after speaking out against the Vietnam War in 1968. The media backlash over Kitt's remarks, combined with government harassment, effectively derailed Kitt's career in the United States for several years. Later, however, Kitt returned to both stage and screen and her recording career. She is one of the few performers to have earned nominations for Tony, Grammy, and Oscar awards in her lifetime.

Though Kitt is uncertain about her exact date of birth, she recalled a hardscrabble life in the sharecropping territory of South Carolina during the Great Depression. She, her mother, and younger sister moved from house to house while their mother did chores in exchange for room and board. The young Kitt routinely suffered taunts of "yella" because of her lighter skin; eventually her mother left her behind with one farm family when she married a man who rejected Kitt because of her mixed race. "My mother felt a man was more important than her daughter," Kitt told Richette Haywood in *Ebony.* "I would never have left my child," she added.

The young Kitt, who wore a dress made from a potato sack and did not own a pair of shoes, worked the fields and tended the animals. She was an outsider, and suffered for it. "Their children would put a sack on my head, tie me to a tree and throw stones," she remembered in an interview with *New York Times* contributor Michael T. Kaufman. In her autobiography *I'm Still Here: Confessions of a Sex Kitten,* she recalled accidentally allowing the farm's milk cow to stray near a patch of lima beans, poisonous to cows. The cow had a seizure and died before her eyes, but not before it bellowed terribly; across the field, its calf heard and replied in distress, and "the sound of her calf in answer brought me to sobs I cannot describe—afraid for the whipping I knew I would get and afraid for the calf who, like me, might be left without a mother."

Kitt's life changed when a distant relative from the North sent clothing and instructions to send the girl to New York City. She learned that this was her mother's sister, but has since suspected that this "aunt" was in reality her biological mother. Kitt arrived alone at Pennsylvania Station at the age of eight, and when brought to her aunt's apartment, saw electricity and an indoor toilet for the first time. Yet her aunt was abusive, and in many ways life in Spanish Harlem was no easier than it had been down South.

Nevertheless, Kitt quickly left behind her humble beginnings by exhibiting an aptitude for learning. She learned several languages while living in Spanish Harlem. She excelled in school, and also sang in a choir and took piano lessons. One day a sympathetic teacher gave Kitt bus fare and sent her to audition at New York's High School for the Performing Arts. Kitt was accepted, one of only six African Americans there at the time. Again, she excelled in her new and challenging setting, despite the sometimes precarious nature of her home life. Another kindly teacher gave her a ticket to a Broadway play and told her not to come to school the next day. Kitt was so moved by the experience she cried at the end.

As Kitt's situation at home deteriorated, she began to run away. She would stay with various friends or classmates, or sneak into apartment buildings and sleep on the roof. "When I see the homeless now, I empathize," she told Kaufman. "I know there but for the grace of God go I," she continued. Kitt managed to find work as a seamstress, and dropped out of her prestigious high school, though she was threatened with juvenile hall. One day, Kitt went to see a movie and was impressed by the famed Katherine Dunham Dance Company on screen, the first African-American corps de ballet. She decided she wanted to join it, and lucked into an audition not long afterward when one of the dancers happened to stop her in Harlem and ask for directions. Kitt won a spot—she was just sixteen—that paid a rich sum of $10 a week. With the Dunham troupe she toured Mexico, South America, and Europe and appeared in the movie *Casbah,* a musical adaptation of *Casablanca.* The prominence of belonging to such an acclaimed dance company afforded Kitt a wealth of opportunities, and she began dating playboys and celebrities. When the Dunham Company was performing in Paris in 1949, Kitt—by now a soloist—was offered a nightclub singing engagement. She was promptly fired from the company after giving two weeks' notice, but was a hit with her new audience at Carroll's, a swanky Paris nightclub.

Kitt became a Parisian sensation overnight. Critics raved about her sultry, unusual voice and slinky stage demeanor. Orson Welles cast her in his avant-garde stage production of *Faust* as the mythic beauty Helen of Troy. "I asked Orson at one point in the rehearsal who this character was," Kitt recalled in her autobiography. "What kind of woman is she? How old is she? 'Don't ask stupid questions, you stupid child,' Orson told me. 'I chose you to play this part because you are the most exciting woman in the world. You represent all women of all ages. You have no place or time.' This confused me more than ever," Kitt remembered, "so I just played myself."

Kitt's cabaret repertoire came to include several foreign-language songs, of which two—the French "C'est si bon" and "Usku Dara," a Turkish song, became her signature tunes. She also appeared in two French films. Still, her name was relatively unknown in the United States, and she hoped to conquer Broadway. She was selected as part of the revue *New Faces of 1952,* and the show was a hit. Again, she was the subject of a great deal of media attention, and with this success she began a recording career with RCA. Back in New York, she lived on her own for the first time in her life in a studio on Riverside Drive. The building had an unwritten "whites-only" rule, but two of Kitt's friends were tenants and signed over their lease in private to her when they moved.

Kitt's glamorous celebrity lifestyle continued uninterrupted in the United States. She dated a British aristocrat as well as Porfirio Rubirosa, the famed raconteur. At one point she was earning $3,000 a week, but that figure jumped to $10,000 after a scandal in the papers. It was claimed that Kitt had offended the royal family of Greece at a performance at Los Angeles's Mocambo nightclub, but it was simply a misunderstanding over another part of the show that had nothing to do with her. Headlines trumpeted the mayor's denunciation of Kitt. The star also faced the subtle disapproval of the African-American community, with whom her cosmopolitan cabaret act did not catch on. She was viewed as a bit over-sophisticated, someone who "acted white." Kitt's unusual act did not always find favor with industry types, either. The person who signed her to her first recording contract was fired because of it; it was said that Kitt's voice was "too weird to sell records," according to Ross Wetzsteon in the *Village Voice.*

Kitt sold many records on the RCA label despite that prediction. She performed nearly nonstop during this era, appearing back in Paris, in Las Vegas, and again on Broadway in such plays as *Shinbone Alley* and *Mrs. Patterson.* When she appeared on the *Ed Sullivan Show* the host instructed her to wear pants, saying, "Every time you wear a dress we get letters from the Catholics saying you are too sexy," Kitt remembered in her autobiography. During this era she fell in love with Arthur Loew, Jr., heir to the movie-theater chain, and the two lived together for a time. Gossip columnists treated the interracial relationship kindly—Loew's personality and drinking habits were said to have improved considerably under Kitt's watch—but he was the only Loew son and his mother was viciously opposed to the relationship.

Kitt also dated Sammy Davis, Jr. and Charles Revson, founder of Revlon—the lipstick shade "Fire and Ice" is rumored to be named for her—and was pals with actor James Dean. In 1960 she married Bill McDonald, a mentally unbalanced man she had dated casually; he had threatened to kill himself if she would not marry him, and she succumbed since she felt he would make a good father to the child she wanted so badly. She later described her daughter, Kitt, as "the only good thing" about her five-year marriage, she told a writer for *Ebony.* McDonald took over as Kitt's accountant, sold properties without her permission, and refused to pay child support after they separated. Kitt raised her daughter alone in Bel-Air and London.

In a long list of acknowledgments at the beginning of *Alone with Me,* Kitt included: "*My country,* which hasn't allowed me to work here but which takes a more than healthy chunk of my income because I refuse to be intimidated to leave it." The series of events which precipitated that sentiment began in January, 1968, with her participation, by the invitation of First Lady Mrs. Lyndon Johnson, in the first "Woman Doers' Luncheon" at the White House. The topic for discussion at the meeting was to be "Why is there so much juvenile delinquency in the streets of America?" It was a subject in which Kitt took a very personal interest. Over the years, she had helped organize numerous antipoverty and anticrime groups; she had visited ghettos and talked with their residents wherever she worked; she had formed dance workshops in Harlem and Watts. She accepted the White House invitation with "a grave sense of personal commitment," paying her own transportation expenses to attend.

Before she went, Kitt talked with a group called the Mothers of Watts about the discussion topic. Their feeling was that the war in Vietnam was a direct cause of street crime among the young in several ways: the drain on the economy, the disproportionate number of minorities being sent to war, and—worst of all—the fact that those with criminal records were deferred while the law-abiding young men were drafted. Kitt wanted to raise the issue of Vietnam, among many others, at the luncheon.

"But," as she said, "things got a little out of hand—to say the least." She described her growing chagrin at the lack of seriousness among many guests and the careful staging for a "surprise" visit by President Johnson. "I was most definitely getting upset," Kitt recalled. "I hadn't flown from Los Angeles to Washington, D.C., to watch a show." As she wrote in *Alone with Me:* "With God as my witness, I had no intention of launching a diatribe against the war in Vietnam. But the reaction to my statements precluded my saying much more." A writer for *Newsweek* quoted her remarks to Mrs. Johnson as follows: "I think we have missed the main point at this luncheon. We have forgotten the main reason we have juvenile delinquency . . . there's a war going on and America doesn't know why. Boys I know across the nation feel it doesn't pay to be a good guy. They figure that with a [crime] record they don't have to go off to Vietnam. . . . No wonder the kids rebel and take pot, and Mrs. Johnson, in case you don't understand the lingo, that's marijuana."

Kitt described the effect of this incident on her career. "After the White House luncheon and the press it received, I became persona non grata in my own country . . . club contracts were cancelled or 'lost' with the contractors refusing to draw up new ones. The television quiz show on which I was a semi-regular never invited me back and the phones stopped ringing." Finally, in 1974, she began once more to get nightclub bookings in the United States. In the *Washington Post,* Lon Tuck explained, in 1975 "Kitt learned through newspaper reports that an upshot of that incident was the assembling of a Secret Service dossier filled with gossip about her personal life, but concluding she was no immediate threat to the Republic." Later, when Jack Anderson's Washington, D.C., office disclosed the extent to which government intelligence agencies had investigated Kitt's activities, both before and after the 1968 luncheon, the recovery of her career was accelerated.

In the late 1970s Kitt returned to a recording career, cutting a disco record with Jacques Morali that launched her new status as a gay icon. During the 1980s she spent time on her extensive estate in Connecticut, where she tended to a large garden that kept the health-conscious dancer's kitchen well-stocked with fruits and vegetables. "I trust the dirt," Kitt told a writer for *Ebony.* "I don't trust diamonds and gold. I know how to survive in the dirt." In her book *Rejuvenate: It's Never too Late!,* she provides more of her philosophy of life, especially as it relates to women entering middle age.

Kitt returned to film in the early 1990s, appearing in *Ernest: Scared Stupid* and as a romantic interest in Eddie Murphy's *Boomerang.* She played herself in *Fatal Instinct,* a Carl Reiner spoof from 1993, and appeared in *Unzipped,* a documentary look at fashion designer Isaac Mizrahi. She released yet another album of songs, *Back in Business,* in 1995, and portrayed a homeless woman in a benefit play titled *Sam's Song,* performed at New York's All Souls Unitarian Church. Kitt also returned to the cabaret circuit, performing at Manhattan's Cafe Carlyle in 1993 and appearing in the one-woman show *Lady Day* at Emerson's Bar and Grill in 1996.

Tuck observed that throughout Kitt's conversations and writings there remains a strong consistency: "She describes her life as a success story, in which disaster, for a citizen of the world, has been only a temporary setback." In Kitt's own words: "Overall, I've had a very good life, a life of cotton and caviar. And the cotton years have made the caviar years far more savory than they would have been had my early life been an easy one."

BIOGRAPHICAL AND CRITICAL SOURCES:

BOOKS

Contemporary Black Biography, Volume 16, Gale (Detroit, MI), 1997.

Contemporary Musicians, Volume 9, Gale (Detroit, MI), 1993.

Kitt, Eartha, *Thursday's Child,* Duell, Sloan & Pearce, 1956.

Kitt, Eartha, *Alone with Me,* Regnery (Washington, DC), 1976.

Notable Black American Women, Gale (Detroit, MI), 1992.

PERIODICALS

Atlanta Journal-Constitution, March 21, 2001, Wendell Brock, "A Formidable Villainess Gets to Play Nice: An Interview with Eartha Kitt," p. G1.
Black Issues Book Review, May, 2001, Yasmain Broady-Soya, review of *Rejuvenate!: It's Never Too Late,* p. 61.
BlackLines, April, 1996.
Book, November-December, 2001, Kristin Kloberdanz, "A Purrfect Philosophy: For Eartha Kitt, Reading Is the Cat's Meow," p. 28.
Booklist, April 1, 2002, Whitney Scott, review of *Rejuvenate!,* p. 1347.
Chicago Defender Accent, November 18, 1978, p. 12.
Collier's, June 11, 1954, pp. 33-39.
Cue, November 27, 1954.
Detroit Free Press, September 17, 1978.
Detroit News, March 1, 2002, Lawrence B. Johnson, "Under Eartha's Spell, Kitt's Life Is Its Own 'Cinderella' Story," p. 1.
Ebony, December, 1957, pp. 83-92; October, 1993, pp. 112-16.
Essence, January, 1993, p. 56.
Good Housekeeping, October, 2000, "A Mom Is Just a Mom," p. 170.
Jet, January 16, 1995, p. 63.
Modern Maturity, March-April, 2001, Ponchitta Pierce, "Eartha, Moved," p. 28.
Negro History Bulletin, October 19, 1955, p. 10.
Newsweek, January 29, 1968.
New York Times, September 11, 1993, p. A25; January 8, 1995, p. WC11.
Outsmart, July, 2001, Blase DiStefano, "Eartha Kitt Purr-severes: The Feline Feminist Talks about Her Two Lives As the Child and the Woman."
Publishers Weekly, April 2, 2001, "Tip-Top and Long-Lasting," p. 61.
Time, February 13, 1978.
Village Voice, February, 1993, p. 92.
Washington Post, January 19, 1978.

ONLINE

Eartha Kitt Web site, http://www.earthakitt.com/ (November 13, 2003).

OTHER

All by Myself (documentary film), 1982.*

KOETHE, John (Louis) 1945-

PERSONAL: Surname is pronounced *Kay*-tee; born December 25, 1945, in San Diego, CA; son of John Louis (a naval career officer) and Sara (Mehrer) Koethe; married Susan Muench (a research immunologist), September 1, 1968. *Education:* Princeton University, A.B., 1967; Harvard University, Ph.D., 1973.

ADDRESSES: *Home*—2666 North Hackett Ave., Milwaukee, WI 53211. *Office*—Department of Philosophy, University of Wisconsin—Milwaukee, Milwaukee, WI 53211.

CAREER: University of Wisconsin—Milwaukee, assistant professor of philosophy, 1973—.

AWARDS, HONORS: Poet's Foundation Award, 1969; Frank O'Hare Award, 1973, for *Domes;* Kingsley Tufts Award, 1997, for *Falling Water.*

WRITINGS:

Blue Vents (poems), Audit/Poetry, 1969.
Domes (poems), Columbia University Press (New York, NY), 1973.
The Late Wisconsin Spring, Princeton University Press (Princeton, NJ), 1984.
The Continuity of Wittgenstein's Thought, Cornell University Press (Ithaca, NY), 1996.
Falling Water (poems), HarperPerennial (New York, NY), 1997.
The Constructor (poems), HarperFlamingo (New York, NY), 1999.
Poetry at One Remove (essays), University of Michigan Press (Ann Arbor, MI), 2000.
North Point North: New and Selected Poems, HarperCollins (New York, NY), 2002.

Contributor of poems and articles to *Poetry, Paris Review, Quarterly Review of Literature, Parnassus,* and *Art News.*

SIDELIGHTS: John Koethe has published several award-winning volumes of poetry. Many critics place him in the tradition of Wallace Stevens and John Ashbery, or, as Robert Huddleston noted in the *Chicago*

Review, "poets who used landscape as a figure or set-piece through which to address an array of concerns from the personal to the social." Koethe is also a professor of philosophy at the University of Wisconsin, and his works include *Domes, The Late Wisconsin Spring, Falling Water,* and *North Point North.* He has also authored a collection of essays about poetry, *Poetry at One Remove,* as well as the academically-oriented *The Continuity of Wittgenstein's Thought.*

Falling Water, which saw print in 1997, garnered Koethe the Kingsley Tufts Award and marked a widening of the poet's critical acclaim. The title poem of the collection takes its name from one of the famed buildings of architect Frank Lloyd Wright in Illinois. As Huddleston explained, "Wright's Prairie-style has affinities with Koethe's verse in its austere conventions, emphasis on horizontal . . . movement, . . . and in its tendency to go in multiple directions and explore the nuances of a shape." Huddleston went on to praise most of the other poems in *Falling Water* as well, noting that "when Koethe is on, and he often is in this new volume, he can show us as few other contemporary poets can into an oneiric world of magnificent austerity." Similarly, Janet St. John in *Booklist* observed that Koethe's poems "have much to offer the patient, careful reader." Huddleston concluded that the best of *Falling Water* "renovates the familiar in the collective social and personal landscape, exposing its particular histories, making it new, returning it to strangeness, which is the proper place for poetry."

Koethe followed *Falling Water* with *The Constructor* in 1999. A *Publishers Weekly* critic reviewing the volume noted that the poet's "sense of how imagination affects memory lends poignancy to his meditations." The title poem of *The Constructor* also appears in Koethe's 2002 collection, *North Point North. North Point North* also includes poetry from Koethe's previous collections, as well as several examples of new verse. Donna Seaman praised the volume in *Booklist* as "commodious and entrancing."

BIOGRAPHICAL AND CRITICAL SOURCES:

BOOKS

The Oxford Companion to Twentieth-Century Poetry in English, edited by Ian Hamilton, Oxford University Press (Oxford, England), 1994.

PERIODICALS

Booklist, September 1, 1997, Janet St. John, review of *Falling Water,* p. 53; July 2002, Donna Seaman, review of *North Point North,* pp. 1815-1816.

Chicago Review, fall, 1997, Robert Huddleston, review of *Falling Water,* pp. 158-160.

Publishers Weekly, March 29, 1999, review of *The Constructor,* p. 98; June 17, 2002, review of *North Point North,* p. 58.

ONLINE

OnMilwaukee, http://www.onmilwaukee.com/ (July 17, 2002), interview with John Koethe.*

* * *

KOGAWA, Joy Nozomi 1935-

PERSONAL: Born June 6, 1935, in Vancouver, British Columbia, Canada; daughter of Gordon Goichi (a minister) and Lois (a kindergarten teacher; maiden name, Yao) Nakayama; married David Kogawa, May 2, 1957 (divorced, 1968); children: Gordon, Deidre. *Education:* Attended University of Alberta, 1954, Anglican Women's Training College, 1956, Conservatory of Music, 1956, and University of Saskatchewan, 1968.

ADDRESSES: Home—25 The Esplanade, #1418, Toronto, Ontario M5E 1W5, Canada.

CAREER: Office of the Prime Minister, Ottawa, Ontario, staff writer, 1974-76; freelance writer, 1976-78; University of Ottawa, Ottawa, writer in residence, 1978; freelance writer, 1978—.

MEMBER: Writers Union of Canada, Order of Canada, 1986.

AWARDS, HONORS: Books in Canada First Novel Award, 1981, Canadian Authors Association Book of the Year Award, 1982, Before Columbus Foundation American Book Award, 1982, and American Library Association notable book citation, 1982, Periodical Distributors Best Paperback Fiction Award, 1983, all for *Obasan.*

WRITINGS:

NOVELS

Obasan (novel), Lester and Orphen Dennys (Toronto, Ontario, Canada), 1981, David Godine (New York, NY), 1982.

Naomi's Road (juvenile fiction), Oxford University Press (Toronto, Ontario, Canada), 1986.

Itsuka (sequel to *Obasan*), Viking Canada (Toronto, Ontario, Canada), 1992, Anchor Books (New York, NY), 1993.

The Rain Ascends, Knopf (Toronto, Ontario, Canada), 1995.

POETRY

The Splintered Moon, University of New Brunswick (St. John, New Brunswick, Canada), 1967.

A Choice of Dreams, McClelland & Stewart (Toronto, Ontario, Canada), 1974, Mosaic Press (Oakville, Ontario, Canada), 2003.

Jericho Road, McClelland & Stewart (Toronto, Ontario, Canada), 1977.

Woman in the Woods, Mosaic Press (Oakville, Ontario, Canada), 1985.

A Song of Lilith, Polestar Book Publishers (Vancouver, British Columbia, Canada), 2000.

A Garden of Anchors, Mosaic Press (Oakville, Ontario, Canada), 2003.

Contributor of poems to magazines in the United States and Canada, including *Canadian Forum, West Coast Review, Queen's Quarterly, Quarry, Prism International,* and *Chicago Review.*

SIDELIGHTS: Joy Nozomi Kogawa is best known for the novel *Obasan,* a fictionalization of her own experiences as a Japanese-Canadian during World War II. Like *Obasan*'s narrator, Kogawa was exiled into a detention camp in the Canadian wilderness. She published her first book of poetry, *The Splintered Moon,* in 1967. After two follow-up volumes, she received national acclaim for *Obasan.* With *Obasan,* wrote Gurleen Grewal in *Feminist Writers,* "Kogawa proved herself to be among the finest of feminist-humanist writers." Out of *Obasan* came the sequel, *Itsuka,* and *Naomi's Road,* a version of the story for children. In addition to pursuing her career as a writer, Kogawa has turned her attention to political work on behalf of Japanese-Canadian citizens.

Before turning to fiction, Kogawa was a "seasoned poet," wrote Grewal. Gary Willis observed in *Studies in Canadian Literature* that Kogawa's first three volumes of poetry are filled with "lyric verse" and poems that often "express feelings that emerge from a narrative context that is only partly defined." A poem from Kogawa's third collection, *Jericho Road,* for example, centers on "a striking surrealistic image" that never makes clear who the protagonist's enemies are. Kogawa explained to Janice Williamson in *Sounding Differences: Conversations with 17 Canadian Women Writers* that her poems often arise out of her dreams: "The practice of poetry," she says, "is the sweeping out of debris between the conscious and the unconscious." Grewal maintained that, "In fiction too, her endeavor is the same. Through protagonist Naomi Nakane's recollection of her painful childhood, *Obasan* lays bare the intergenerational pain of Japanese Canadians affected by the Canadian government's relocation and internment of its citizens during World War II."

Obasan was the first Canadian novel to deal with the internment of its citizens of Japanese heritage. The novel focuses on thirty-six-year-old Naomi. As young children, she and brother Stephen were separated from their loving parents during World War II. Their mother, visiting relatives in Japan, was not allowed to return to Canada, and their father was shipped to a labor camp. Naomi and Stephen were sent to a frontier town along with their Uncle Isamu and Aunt Obasan. When their parents never returned, they were raised by their aunt and uncle in a house filled with silence. One of the mysteries of Naomi's childhood was a yearly pilgrimage. As a child, Naomi continually asked "Why do we come here every year?" and as an adult, Naomi has lost the ability to communicate; as Kogawa writes, she is a victim of "the silence that will not speak." *Obasan* explores Naomi's search for the answer to her childhood question and shows her long-awaited acknowledgment of, as Grewal wrote, "life's imperative to heal."

At the beginning of the novel, Naomi's uncle has just died, and the rest of the novel, according to Erika Gottleib in *Canadian Literature,* "takes shape as a mourner's meditation during a wake, a framework well suited to the novel's central metaphor of a spiritual journey." Urged by her Aunt Emily, an activist seeking justice for internment victims, Naomi relives her past, thus enabling her to learn about the secrets long held by her family. Naomi reviews documents about the Japanese internment to understand what happened to her and her family. And at the end of the novel, Naomi learns the truth that has been kept from her, that her mother suffered and died in Nagasaki, a victim of the "other holocaust," as Grewal called it. Naomi, through her examination of the past and her examination of the truth, at last is free and learns to speak again.

Throughout the course of the novel, Naomi realizes her estrangement from mainstream Canadian society as well as from traditional Japanese culture. Kogawa explores the differences between these two groups. Observed Willis of *Obasan,* "[it is] expressive of a sensibility that wishes to define, in relation to each other, Japanese and Canadian ways of seeing, and even to combine these divergent perceptions in an integrated and distinctive vision." In one scene, Naomi muses on carpentry: "There is a fundamental difference in Japanese workmanship—to pull with control rather than push with force." The contrast between the "restrained" Japanese and the "forceful" Canadians is also apparent in the difference between the Issei—those born in Japan—and the Nisei—those born abroad, as represented by Naomi's two aunts. Neither of their models works for Naomi who "like Kogawa," writes Willis, "has roots in both traditions." By the end of the her own exploration, "Naomi blends a Japanese attention to silence with a Western attention to words. Indeed, it is this blending that gives rise to the distinctive beauties and subtleties of *Obasan.*"

Kogawa further enriches her text with documentation of this era of Canadian history. *Obasan* ends with the widely ignored memorandum sent by the Co-operative Committee on Japanese Canadians to the Canadian government in 1946, pointing out that the deportation of Japanese Canadians was "wrong and indefensible" and "an adoption of the methods of Nazism." Kogawa also includes among Aunt Emily's diaries and notes "a series of chilling nonfictional official papers and newspaper accounts," as Edmund M. White pointed out in the *Los Angeles Times Book Review.* These elements serve to emphasize what White called "systematic outrages inflicted by the Canadian government on its own citizens [which] echo the Nazi treatment of the Jews." Edith Milton in the *New York Times Book Review* wrote that *Obasan* "grows into a quietly appalling statement about how much hatred can cost when it is turned into a bureaucratic principle." White also found that "the novel, in turn, shares some of the tone of *The Diary of Anne Frank* in its purity of vision under the stress of social outrage."

Obasan's political implications have been noted by many critics, including Grewal who wrote, "This beautifully crafted novel with its moving resonances has done invaluable service to its varied readers. It has opened necessary dialogue; it has healed." Yet, *Obasan* always remains, according to Milton, "a tour de force, a deeply felt novel, brilliantly poetic in its sensibility." Willis noted that the message of Kogawa's poetry is more fully realized in *Obasan,* "an imaginative triumph over the forces that militate against expression of our inmost feelings." White pointed out that the novel has "a magical ability to convey suffering and privation, inhumanity and racial prejudice, without losing in any way joy in life and in the poetic imagination."

Itsuka is generally thought of as the sequel to *Obasan* but Sandra Martin commented in *Quill and Quire* that "Kogawa is not so much writing a sequel as reclaiming themes and characters from *Obasan.*" In *Itsuka,* Naomi goes to Toronto where she works on a multicultural journal and takes her first lover, Father Cedric, a French-Canadian priest. With his help, Naomi turns to activism in her desire to win redress for the victims of Canada's internment policies. In *Itsuka,* the political and erotic plots become intertwined. The book, using a similar technique as *Obasan,* closes with an apology from the Canadian government, in which it admits to instituting policies "influenced by discriminatory attitudes" toward Japanese Canadians and also to its own "unjust" actions.

Grewal maintained that *Itsuka* allows "the reader to witness Naomi's growth and personal fulfillment" and that it "openly bears the message of hope and trust implicit in *Obasan.*" Yet, Martin compared *Itsuka* unfavorably to the first novel, finding that "Kogawa seems too close to the partisan squabbling that accompanies any such [political] movement. She hasn't yet absorbed the facts and translated them into fiction." Janice Kulyk Keefer, writing in *Books in Canada,* also admitted to "a certain disappointment" with the book, one centering on "the absence in *Itsuka* of the kind of poetically charged language and intensity of perception that give *Obasan* its extraordinary power and beauty." But Keefer also noted that "it would be wrong to fault *Itsuka* for not being *Obasan Revisited.*" She wrote, "What Kogawa has done in her new novel is to move into a different kind of imaginative territory, exposing the politics of multiculturalism that has in may ways abetted rather than eradicated the racism that she presents as an institutionalized aspect of Canadian life." As Martin observed, Kogawa "has written poignantly about how innocent and loyal Japanese Canadian were stripped of their home and their possessions, interned, and dispersed." Grewal further sees a more universal message in Kogawa's work: an emphasis on "compassion and arduous work of healing."

Kogawa turned back to poetry after publication of her novels. The "insight found [in *Woman in the Woods*]," wrote Frank Manley in *Books in Canada,* "is enlightening." He also lauded the book's "passion for life" along with "its ability to say volumes with only a few words." A more recent poetic text, *A Song of Lilith,* takes as its theme the Biblical story of Adam's first companion, Lilith, who was created out of clay to be his equal. When this harmonious relationship is destroyed, Lilith escapes from Eden and is subsequently banished from earth. Yet she returns many generations later to comfort and help humanity in its distress. The poem was commissioned by theater director Kristine Bogyo as part of a multidisciplinary production incorporating poetry, projected paintings, and original music. The piece has been produced in Toronto, Vancouver, and other Canadian cities.

BIOGRAPHICAL AND CRITICAL SOURCES:

BOOKS

Cheung, King-Kok, *Articulate Silences: Hisaye Yamamoto, Maxine Hong Kingston, Joy Kogawa,* Cornell University Press (Ithaca, NY), 1993.

Contemporary Literary Criticism, Volume 78, Gale (Detroit, MI), 1994.

Feminist Writers, St. James Press (Detroit, MI), 1996.

Hogan, Robert and others, editors, *Memory and Cultural Politics: New Essays in American Ethnic Literatures,* Northeastern University Press (Boston, MA), 1996.

Kreiswirth, Martin and Mark A. Cheetham, editors, *Theory between the Disciplines: Authority/Vision/Politics,* University of Michigan Press (Ann Arbor, MI), 1990, pp. 213-229.

Ling, Amy and others, editors, *Reading the Literatures of Asian America,* Temple University Press (Philadelphia, PA), 1992.

Pearlman, Mickey, editor, *Canadian Women Writing Fiction,* University Press of Mississippi (Jackson, MS), 1993.

Williamson, Janice, *Sounding Differences: Conversations with 17 Canadian Women Writers,* University of Toronto Press (Toronto, Ontario, Canada), 1993.

PERIODICALS

Ariel, October, 1999, Laurie Kruk, "Voices of Stone: The Power of Poetry in Joy Kogawa's *Obasan,*" p. 75.

Booklist, January 1, 1994, p. 806.

Books in Canada, May, 1986, pp. 43-44; April, 1992, p. 35.

Canadian Forum, February, 1982, pp. 39-40; December, 1992, p. 38.

Canadian Literature, summer, 1986, pp. 34-53; spring, 1988, pp. 58-66, 68-82; winter, 1990, pp. 41-57.

Christianity and Literature, summer, 1999, Deborah Bowen, "Faithfully Reading Elie Weisel and Joy Kogawa, Two Generations After," p. 487.

Feminist Studies, summer, 1990, pp. 288-312.

Kunapipi, Volume 16, number 1, 1994.

Los Angeles Times Book Review, July 11, 1982. p. 3.

MELUS, fall, 1985, pp. 33-42; winter, 1999, Helena Grice, "Reading the Nonverbal: The Indices of Space, Time, Tactility and Taciturnity in Joy Kogawa's *Obasan,*" p. 93.

Mosaic: A Journal for the Interdisciplinary Study of Literature, spring, 1988, pp. 215-226; September, 2000, Apollo A. Amoko, "Resilient ImagiNations: No-No Boy, Obasan and the Limits of Minority Discourse," p. 35.

New York Times Book Review, September 5, 1982; March 13, 1994, p. 18.

Performing Arts & Entertainment in Canada, autumn, 2001, Sarah B. Hood, "A Loft with Lilith," p. 26.

Quill and Quire, March, 1992, p. 57.

Studies in Canadian Literature, Volume 12, number 2, 1987, pp. 239-249.

ONLINE

Voices from the Gaps, http://voices.cla.umn.edu/ (September 17, 2003), biography of Joy Kogawa.

L

LAWRENCE, Lynn
See GARLAND, Sherry

* * *

LECHLEIDNER, Mary L. 1947-
(Delia Parr)

PERSONAL: Born February 28, 1947, in Camden, NJ; children: Matthew J. Scheimer, Brett G. Scheimer, Elizabeth B. Scheimer. *Education:* Rutgers University, B.A., 1986, M.A., 1989. *Politics:* Independent. *Religion:* Christian.

ADDRESSES: *Agent*—Linda Kruger, The Fogelman Literary Agency, 7515 Greenville Ave., Suite 712, Dallas, TX 75231.

CAREER: High school social studies teacher, 1987—.

MEMBER: American Christian Romance Writers, Novelists, Inc.

WRITINGS:

ROMANCE NOVELS; UNDER PSEUDONYM DELIA PARR

Evergreen, St. Martin's Press (New York, NY), 1995.
The Fire in Autumn, St. Martin's Press (New York, NY), 1996.
By Fate's Design, St. Martin's Press (New York, NY), 1996.
The Ivory Duchess, St. Martin's Press (New York, NY), 1997.
The Minister's Wife, St. Martin's Press (New York, NY), 1998.
Sunrise, St. Martin's Press (New York, NY), 1999.

"TRINITY" SERIES; UNDER PSEUDONUM DELIA PARR

A Place Called Trinity, Thorndike Press (Waterville, ME), 2002.
Home to Trinity, Thorndike Press (Waterville, ME), 2003.

SIDELIGHTS: As Delia Parr, Mary L. Lechleidner creates nineteenth-century historical romance novels that are often set in the eastern United States. *By Fate's Design,* for example, takes place in a Shaker village in New Hampshire. That is where Sister Johanna Sims finds her planned life of celibate contemplation threatened by her "evil guardian—a mustache twirler if there ever was one," according to a *Publishers Weekly* reviewer. Sister Johanna must thwart the efforts of the guardian to sell her in an arranged marriage; along the way she encounters romantic temptation while nursing back to health the injured good-guy Michael Lawne. Another Parr romance, *The Ivory Duchess,* concerns Kate Baxter, a concert pianist touring Pennsylvania who, according to another *Publishers Weekly* critic, "escapes from her cruel manager with her valuable, trademark broach." Neither *The Ivory Duchess* nor *By Fate's Design* earned kudos from the *Publishers Weekly* reviewers, but romance readers quickly took these and other Parr books to heart.

The setting of *The Minister's Wife,* a 1998 release, is rural New York, where Emilee Clark decides to overcome the social stigma of being an illegitimate child by becoming "the most righteous of women—the minister's wife," in the words of a *Publishers Weekly* contributor. What Emilee did not count on was falling in love with Jared Burke, son of the previous minister. While the *Publishers Weekly* writer noted this novel's "sluggish" pacing and "morose" tone, *Library Journal* contributor Kristin Ramsdell found more to like in *The Minister's Wife.* Ramsdell cited "nicely handled sexual tension [and] several well-depicted secondary characters" in the story.

A Place Called Trinity, published in 2002, "will surely please [Parr's] fans," predicted Kathleen Hughes of *Booklist.* The first in the "Trinity" series, this book introduces Martha Cade, a midwife in 1830s Pennsylvania who leaves home for three months to search for her runaway daughter, Victoria. Returning to Trinity, Martha finds some disturbing changes, including a new doctor who may spell an end to her midwifery trade. Then there is the reappearance of Thomas Dillon, Martha's former beau who "is nearly untouched by the passing years," noted a *Kirkus Reviews* writer. Several interlocking subplots touch the narrative of *Trinity,* leading a *Kirkus Reviews* writer to describe the book as "well-meaning but meandering." But to Hughes, this book represents "a new artistic stretch" for the author. *Home to Trinity,* published in 2003, is the second book in the series.

Lechleidner once told *CA:* "With the release of my historical romance *Evergreen,* my dream of becoming a romance author came true. The publication of *The Fire in Autumn* is nothing short of wondrous. I have been a reader and fan of romances for many years. Now I have the ultimate joy: to write innovative stories about women and men who overcome tremendous obstacles to celebrate love, the greatest gift of all. Now, with a new inspirational series, I can explore the relationships between women, their neighbors, their families and friends, and God."

BIOGRAPHICAL AND CRITICAL SOURCES:

PERIODICALS

Booklist, February 1, 2002, Kathleen Hughes, review of *A Place Called Trinity,* p. 923.

Kirkus Reviews, December 15, 2001, review of *A Place Called Trinity,* p. 1712.

Library Journal, August, 1998, Kristin Ramsdell, review of *The Minister's Wife,* p. 73.

Publishers Weekly, August 19, 1996, review of *By Fate's Design,* p. 64; April 21, 1997, review of *The Ivory Duchess,* p. 69; July 6, 1998, review of *The Minister's Wife,* p. 57; July 19, 1999, review of *Sunrise,* p. 191; December 24, 2001, review of *A Place Called Trinity,* p. 42.

* * *

LEE, Gus 1946-

PERSONAL: Full name Augustus Samuel Mein-Sun Lee; born August 8, 1946, in San Francisco, CA; son of Tsung-Chi Lee (an engineer) and Da-Tsien Tsu (a storyteller); married Diane Elliott (a nurse educator); children: Jessica (deceased), Jena, Eric. *Education:* Attended United States Military Academy, West Point; University of California, Davis, B.A., 1969, J.D., 1976. *Religion:* Protestant. *Hobbies and other interests:* "Family."

ADDRESSES: Home—Colorado Springs, CO. *Agent*—Jane Dystel, Dystel & Goderich Literary Management, One Union Square W., Suite 904, New York, NY 10003.

CAREER: San Francisco Call-Bulletin and *News-Call-Bulletin,* San Francisco, CA, newsperson, 1955-60; Young Men's Christian Association (YMCA), San Francisco, CA, assistant gym instructor, lifeguard, and locker room clerk, 1955-64; University of California, Davis, assistant dean of students of Educational Opportunity Program and project coordinator of Asian American Studies, 1969-75; State of California, Department of Industrial Relations, law clerk, 1975-77; United States Army, Judge Advocate General's Corps, command judge advocate/general counsel and defense counsel, 1977-80; Sacramento County District Attorney, acting supervising deputy district attorney, lead attorney of Misdemeanor Trial Team, and police trainer, 1980-84; associate of Charles A. Murray and Associates, 1984-85; California District Attorneys Association, deputy director and director of training, 1985-89; State Bar of California, senior executive for Legal Education and Competence and director of Legal

Education, 1989-93; writer, 1991—. San Francisco Main Library Campaign, literary luminary, 1992—; member of board of directors, Boys and Girls Club; lecturer. *Military service:* United States Army, 1964-68; became drill sergeant and cadet corporal.

AWARDS, HONORS: Named Distinguished Military Graduate, University of California, Davis, 1974; Army Commendation Medal, 1980, for legal advising; Army Achievement Medal, 1983, for legal advising; Meritorious Service Medal and First Oak Leaf Cluster, 1978 and 1980, for criminal investigation and trial advocacy; Order of the Silk Purse, Sacramento County District Attorney, 1984, for trial advocacy; Outstanding Instructor Award, California District Attorneys Association, 1988; Meritorious Service Award, California District Attorneys Association, 1989; *China Boy* was named to the Top 100 list of the *New York Times* in 1991.

WRITINGS:

China Boy (novel), Dutton (New York, NY), 1991.

Honor and Duty (novel), Knopf (New York, NY), 1993.

Tiger's Tail (novel), Knopf (New York, NY), 1996.

No Physical Evidence (novel), Fawcett Columbine (New York, NY), 1998.

Chasing Hepburn: A Memoir of Shanghai, Hollywood, and a Chinese Family's Fight for Freedom, Harmony Books (New York, NY), 2002.

ADAPTATIONS: Honor and Duty was recorded as an audio book by Random House.

SIDELIGHTS: Gus Lee's unusual life has provided him with material for his fiction, including the novels *China Boy, Honor and Duty,* and *Tiger's Tail.* Each of his books have presented a Chinese-American protagonist, struggling to reconcile his Chinese heritage with life as an American citizen. Lee's parents were wealthy Chinese aristocrats who fled their country for the United States in 1945. They underwent a dramatic change of fortune, settling in a poor area of San Francisco known as the Panhandle. The Panhandle was primarily a black neighborhood with many street gangs. Lee's life there was made particularly difficult after his mother died and his father remarried a stern woman of Pennsylvania Dutch background. Her severe discipline and the terror of violence on the streets led him to take up boxing at the local YMCA. With the help of a coach there and a tough, caring friend, Lee learned to defend himself. At the urging of his father, he entered West Point, but was dismissed after failing an engineering course. He subsequently earned two degrees at the University of California at Davis. Lee later became a criminal defense lawyer for the U.S. Army, and, after leaving the service in 1979, he worked as a deputy district attorney in the state of California.

Over the course of his legal career, Lee had never entertained the notion of becoming a writer. His first novel, *China Boy,* began as a journal about his long-dead mother. Lee's young daughter had begun asking many questions about her grandmother, and Lee responded by writing down his memories about her, as well as additional information gleaned from other relatives. When he wrote about her death, he cried about it for the first time in his life. He continued writing, and the memoir about his mother transformed into the semiautobiographical novel, *China Boy,* which featured Lee's fictional alter ego, Kai Ting.

Kai Ting, who is seven when the novel opens, is the first American-born member of his family—who like Lee's real-life family, had fled China's Communist revolution in the 1940s to settle in San Francisco's Panhandle. Ting is spoiled by an affectionate mother who, although dazzled by American technology, is determined to pass the traditions of Chinese culture on to her children. When Ting is six years old, his mother dies. Soon thereafter, his father brings home a new wife, an attractive Pennsylvania Dutch woman named Edna, who wants to erase every Chinese custom from the family's life. She also begins to lock Ting out of the house after school and on weekends, where he is helpless to defend himself from neighborhood bullies, who call him the humiliating name "China Boy." Eventually, Ting finds allies—a street-fighting pal named Toussaint LaRue, a Chinese philosopher who is an old family friend, and a trio of coaches at a Young Men's Christian Association (YMCA) boxing program. Determined to make a place for himself in American life, Ting learns to defend himself and in the end he wins victories over both the local bully and his stepmother.

China Boy met with favorable reviews. In the *Los Angeles Times Book Review,* Bob Sipchen praised the book for providing "an engaging exploration of family dynamics and insight into a diversity of initiation rites" boys typically undergo in the process of becoming men. *Chicago Tribune* contributor Charles R. Larson commented, "Gus Lee's energetic first novel, *China Boy,* blends the West with Orientalism and in the process spins a compelling immigrant version of the American Dream." Writing in the *New York Times Book Review,* Kiki Olsen called Lee's book "a fascinating, evocative portrait of the Chinese community in California in the 1950s." And in the *Washington Post Book World,* author Walter Dean Myers lauded, "It is, on many levels, a pure delight."

Kai Ting's story continues in *Honor and Duty;* like his creator, he moves on to West Point. The novel mirrors the physical and emotional challenges its author faced when he attended the elite academy. Although Kai Ting occasionally comes up against racist attitudes, for the most part he finds the Army to be a more level playing field than the larger world. Once he has mastered the challenges issued to all new recruits, he feels accepted, and surrounded by a spirit of camaraderie. A major subplot in *Honor and Duty* involves cheating among students, and Kai Ting's response to it. Reviewing the book for the *New York Times Book Review,* Kathleen Norris noted that it "can be unwieldy," but added: "This story of the formation of a young man, as he struggles to honor his Chinese inheritance in an American context, is an important one." She pointed out that, like *China Boy, Honor and Duty* "reflects a fine comic sensibility." Both novels, she felt, are "honest in their account of the mean spirit that corrupts much human behavior," yet they "also reflect gratitude for the saving help that often comes from unlikely sources."

Lee replaces Kai Ting with another alter ego in *Tiger's Tail.* This story concerns Jackson Kan, a military lawyer struggling with conflicts between love and duty, and disturbing flashbacks to his term of service in Vietnam. The book shows much evidence of Lee's knowledge of the military world—-perhaps too much so, in the opinion of Scott Martelle, a reviewer for the *New York Times Book Review.* He found that Lee's "deep knowledge of both military affairs and Chinese mysticism" weighed down the plot, but he praised Lee's descriptive powers and the "tender affection for ancient Eastern Ways, as well as a deep respect for the power of love," that infused the story. *Booklist* reviewer Emily Melton called it "an odd, quixotic book that requires flexible, tenacious readers," but added that *Tiger's Tail* is "compelling, charming (despite the violence), and captivating." A reviewer for *Publishers Weekly* described *Tiger's Tail* as "a wise and wrenching novel, beautifully told," commenting that the author's exploration of the contrasts between American, Korean, and Chinese ways is "bold and revelatory." Lee, concluded the writer, possesses a vision that is "daring, deep and unflaggingly moral."

No Physical Evidence, Lee's next book, calls on the author's experience in the district attorney's office. Joshua Jin, the story's main character, is bereft after the loss of his wife and daughter. All Joshua has to live for is solving a sordid rape case with a thirteen-year-old victim who does not want to provide evidence to the authorities. The case seems unwinnable, but Joshua cannot let go of it; he has made a connection between winning justice for the girl and redeeming his own lost soul. *No Physical Evidence* differs from the standard courtroom drama, according to Wes Lukowsky in *Booklist;* rather than simply providing entertainment, this book is "a challenging, intellectually stimulating odyssey of the soul that concludes on a sobering, real-world note."

Lee once told *CA:* "I came to writing like I entered my boyhood—lacking patent skills and without a hint of eventual destination. *China Boy* began as a journal to answer our seven-year-old daughter's question about her missing *Bu-bu*—grandmother. This was my mother, who had immigrated to America before my birth and died when I was five. Embarrassed by my stark ignorance of her and her life, I quizzed my *tsiat-sia*—older sisters—as if preparing for trial: 'When did our mother get up in the morning? What'd she do first? What'd she wear, eat, say? Was she a morning person? Did she have a sense of humor? Who were her friends? How did she treat the servants in Shanghai?' This grilling, lacking, perhaps, only a bare light bulb suspended form the ceiling of a dank interrogation cell, went on for weeks.

"In order to coalesce my sisters' often differing accounts of our mother into a single story without narrative gaps, I inadvertently became a storyteller and a writer. When I reached our mother's death, I cried for her, for the first time. Without plan, I continued writing. It took the three months of the summer of 1989.

"I did not know that I would become a writer. I had never taken a creative writing course or participated in a writers workshop (which, to the discerning reader, may be obvious). And, as the years passed, novel reading became a quick victim to work and family, joining entities such as Sunday morning newspaper perusing, current cinema, sleeping in, dating my wife, and peace of mind in the rubble of child-raising and profession-serving.

"I recognize my opportunity to write as a blessing. It is a gift smaller than our children and less obvious than the generosity of friends, the love of family, and the magic of the nighttime sky, but it is a gift nonetheless. I have long been a rational, scientific man of little faith, seeking to control my world through effort, willpower, and strength, ever committed to the success of my professional cause and the growth of my career. But too many events, both wondrous and tragic, have occurred in my life and in the lives of my family to permit this attitude to persist.

"My writing appeared at a time that I was becoming increasingly aware of the importance of children, the crucial need for tolerant and attentive fathers, and the role of reverence and praise in a world too often driven by acquisition and selfishness. Even as I write these words, I am struck by their novelty to what I was, and the encouragement they represent to what I am seeking to be—a respectful father, a caring husband, a conscientious member of a larger society."

BIOGRAPHICAL AND CRITICAL SOURCES:

BOOKS

Notable Asian Americans, Gale (Detroit, MI), 1994.

PERIODICALS

Booklist, January 1, 1994, John Mort, review of *Honor and Duty,* p. 787; October 15, 1994, review of *China Boy,* p. 415; February 1, 1996, Emily Melton, review of *Tiger's Tail,* p. 899; August, 1998, Wes Lukowsky, review of *No Physical Evidence,* p. 1923; January, 1999, review of *No Physical Evidence* (audio version), p. 10.

Book World, April 7, 1996, review of *Tiger's Tail,* p. 3.

Chicago Tribune, May 26, 1991, Charles R. Larson, review of *China Boy,* p. 3.

English Journal, January, 1996, review of *China Boy,* p. 88.

Kirkus Reviews, February 1, 1996, review of *Tiger's Tail,* p. 165; August 1, 1998, review of *No Physical Evidence,* p. 1059.

Kliatt, November, 1992, Melinda D. Waugh, review of *China Boy,* p. 9.

Library Journal, April 1, 1991, review of *China Boy;* January, 1994, review of *Honor and Duty,* p. 162; March 15, 1996, review of *Tiger's Tail,* p. 96; August, 1998, Christine Perkins, review of *No Physical Evidence,* p. 132.

Los Angeles Times Book Review, June 16, 1991, Bob Sipchen, review of *China Boy,* pp. 2, 7; February 20, 1994, review of *China Boy,* p. 9; April 17, 1994, review of *Honor and Duty,* p. 6.

New York Times Book Review, July 21, 1991, p. 11; February 20, 1994, review of *Honor and Duty,* p. 8; February 5, 1995, review of *Honor and Duty,* p. 28; April 21, 1996, Scott Martelle, review of *Tiger's Tail,* p. 26.

Publishers Weekly, January 3, 1994, review of *Honor and Duty,* p. 70; January 23, 1995, review of *Honor and Duty,* p. 68; January 29, 1996, review of *Tiger's Tail,* p. 83; March 18, 1996, Judy Stone, interview with David Lee, p. 47; August 10, 1998, review of *No Physical Evidence,* p. 369; December 7, 1998, review of *No Physical Evidence* (audio version), p. 186.

Rapport, March, 1996, review of *Tiger's Tail,* p. 24.

Sewanee Review, summer, 1996, Gary Davenport, review of *Tiger's Tail,* pp. 461-467.

Time, June 3, 1991, Janice C. Simpson and Pico Iyer, "Fresh Voices above the Noisy Din," pp. 66-67; March 28, 1994, review of *Honor and Duty,* p. 66.

Tribune Books (Chicago, IL), March 13, 1994, review of *Honor and Duty,* p. 3; December 4, 1994, review of *Honor and Duty,* p. 1; February 19, 1995, review of *Honor and Duty,* p. 10; April 21, 1996, review of *Tiger's Tail,* p. 7.

Village Voice, October 1, 1991, review of *China Boy,* pp. 74-75.

Washington Post Book World, May 12, 1991, p. 7.

ONLINE

Metroactive, http://www.metroactive.com/ (April 20, 2002), Jordan Elgrably, review of *China Boy.*

MysteryGuide, http://www.mysteryguide.com/ (April 29, 2002), review of *Tiger's Tail.*

Mystery Reader, http://www.themysteryreader.com/ (April 29, 2002), Linda Mowery, review of *No Physical Evidence.**

* * *

LESTER, Helen 1936-

Helen Lester

PERSONAL: Born June 12, 1936, in Evanston, IL; daughter of William Howard (a businessman) and Elizabeth (Sargent) Doughty; married Robin Lester (a historian, teacher, and author), August 26, 1967; children: Robin Debevoise, James Robinson. *Education:* Bennett Junior College, A.A.S., 1956; Wheelock College, B.S., 1959. *Religion:* Protestant. *Hobbies and other interests:* Cooking, running, drawing, hiking.

ADDRESSES: *Home*—P.O. Box 64, Pawling, NY 12564.

CAREER: Writer. Elementary school teacher in Lexington, MA, 1959-62; Francis W. Parker School, Chicago, IL, teacher of second grade, 1962-69; Hamlin School, San Francisco, CA, teacher of first grade, 1987-89; Francis W. Parker School, teacher, 1989-92. Full-time school visitor and lecturer at teachers' conferences.

AWARDS, HONORS: Colorado Children's Book Award, 1990, California Young Reader Medal, 1991, and Nebraska Golden Sower Award, 1992, all for *Tacky the Penguin;* Montana Treasure State Award, 1997, for *Three Cheers for Tacky;* Blue Ribbon award, *Bulletin of the Center for Children's Books,* One Hundred Titles for Reading and Sharing, New York Public Library, Best Books of the Year selection, *Parenting* magazine, Notable Book for Children selection, *Smithsonian* magazine, Capitol Choices selection, and Notable Children's Book in the Language Arts, National Council of Teachers of English, all 1997, and Not Just for Children Anymore selection, Children's Book Council, 1998, all for *Author: A True Story;* Parents' Choice Gold Award and Best Books of the Year selection, *Parenting* magazine, both 1999, Notable Book for Children, American Library Association and Kentucky Bluegrass Award, both 2000, Wyoming Buckaroo and Indian Paintbrush Books Awards, Washington Children's Choice Picture Book and Sasquatch Reading Awards, Utah Beehive Award, Colorado Children's Book Award, Delaware Blue Hen Book Award, Maryland Children's Book Award, North Carolina Children's Book Award, North Dakota Flicker Tale Children's Book Award, all 2001, Arkansas Diamond Primary Book Award, California Young Reader Medal, Indiana Young Hoosier Book Award, Missouri Show Me Readers Award, Nevada Young Readers Award, South Carolina Children's Book Award, Tennessee Volunteer State Book Award, and Virginia Young Readers Program Award, all 2002, all for *Hooway for Wodney Wat.*

WRITINGS:

(And illustrator) *Cora Copycat,* Dutton (New York, NY), 1979.

The Wizard, the Fairy, and the Magic Chicken, illustrated by Lynn Munsinger, Houghton Mifflin (Boston, MA), 1983.

It Wasn't My Fault, illustrated by Lynn Munsinger, Houghton Mifflin (Boston, MA), 1985.

A Porcupine Named Fluffy, illustrated by Lynn Munsinger, Houghton Mifflin (Boston, MA), 1986.

Pookins Gets Her Way, illustrated by Lynn Munsinger, Houghton Mifflin (Boston, MA), 1987.

Tacky the Penguin, illustrated by Lynn Munsinger, Houghton Mifflin (Boston, MA), 1988.

The Revenge of the Magic Chicken, illustrated by Lynn Munsinger, Houghton Mifflin (Boston, MA), 1990.

Me First, illustrated by Lynn Munsinger, Houghton Mifflin (Boston, MA), 1992.

Pick a Pet, illustrated by Kevin Hawkes, Scott Foresman (Glenview, IL), 1993.

Lin's Backpack, illustrated by Lynn Munsinger, Scott Foresman (Glenview, IL), 1993.

Three Cheers for Tacky, illustrated by Lynn Munsinger, Houghton Mifflin (Boston, MA), 1994.

Katy's Pocket, illustrated by Paul Harvey, Newbridge Communications (New York, NY), 1994.

Hop to the Top, illustrated by Patrick Girouard, Newbridge Communications (New York, NY), 1994.

(With Robin Lester) *Wuzzy Takes Off,* illustrated by Miko Imai, Candlewick Press (Cambridge, MA), 1995.

Listen, Buddy, illustrated by Lynn Munsinger, Houghton Mifflin (Boston, MA), 1995.

The Four Getters and Arf, illustrated by Brian Karas, Addison-Wesley (New York, NY), 1995.

Help! I'm Stuck!, illustrated by Paulette Bogan, Celebration Press (Glenview, IL), 1996.

Wrong Way Reggie, illustrated by Timothy Foley, Celebration Press (Glenview, IL), 1996.

(With Robin Lester) *Roy Foy's Special Name,* illustrated by Diana Cain Blumenthal, Candlewick Press (Cambridge, MA), 1996.

Princess Penelope's Parrot, illustrated by Lynn Munsinger, Houghton Mifflin (Boston, MA), 1996.

The Shy People's Picnic, illustrated by Nadine Bernard Wescott, Celebration Press (Glenview, IL), 1996.

(And illustrator) *Author: A True Story,* Houghton Mifflin (Boston, MA), 1997.

Tacky in Trouble, illustrated by Lynn Munsinger, Houghton Mifflin (Boston, MA), 1998.

Hooway for Wodney Wat, illustrated by Lynn Munsinger, Houghton Mifflin (Boston, MA), 1999.

Tacky and the Emperor, illustrated by Lynn Munsinger, Houghton Mifflin (Boston, MA), 2000.

Score One for the Sloths, illustrated by Lynn Munsinger, Houghton Mifflin (Boston, MA), 2001.

Tackylocks and the Three Bears, illustrated by Lynn Munsinger, Houghton Mifflin (Boston, MA), 2002.

Something Might Happen, illustrated by Lynn Munsinger, Houghton Mifflin (Boston, MA), 2003.

Lester's books have been translated into Spanish, French, German, Hungarian, and Japanese, and many are available in the United Kingdom.

SIDELIGHTS: With her offbeat penguin protagonist Tacky, Helen Lester has created an icon of individuality and of going against the stream. Tacky is a waddling symbol of the humorous refusal to join in the sameness of things. Not that Tacky is a rebel; he displays what *Horn Book*'s Christine M. Heppermann described as a "sweet obliviousness" to the mainstream or of how things should be done, dressed in his tacky Hawaiian shirt instead of the prim tuxedo-like outfits of most penguins. In the course of several picture books in collaboration with illustrator Lynn Munsinger, Lester has established Tacky as a modern-day Don Quixote, accidentally battling windmills of conformity. And Tacky is just one of several characters Lester has created in her many well-received picture books for the three-to-six-year-old age group, stories which the author once typified in *CA* as "humorous approaches to a message." Often working with illustrator Munsinger, Lester writes of wizards, porcupines, penguins, chickens, pigs, rabbits, and loveable rats, as well as little boys and girls. Her stories explore themes such as cooperation, feelings of guilt, clumsiness—things that form the center of a childhood universe. "When I was a mother of young children I felt a need for more short but satisfying bedtime stories," Lester once told *CA*. "That need spurred me into writing. . . . Life's pretty serious sometimes, and I feel the heavier concepts are better received if given a lighter touch."

Born "sometime between the age of electricity and the age of television," as Lester humorously noted on the Houghton Mifflin Web site, the future author was brought up in Evanston, Illinois. As she further recalled, most of her early writing attempts were "thank-you notes at birthdays and Christmas . . . not a voluntary activity." Later, she began taking more pleasure in writing and joined in the family preoccupation with sending letters both humorous and "voluminous" to other family members. She developed, as she described it, a "sense of what fun could be had with the written word." Yet her ambitions were far from those of a professional writer; as a young woman coming of age in the 1950s, her one goal was to become a bride. "Since no one wanted to turn me into a bride, I became a teacher," she recalled.

During her ten years of teaching, she did marry and had two children. Taking a leave from teaching to care for her sons, she rediscovered the joy in words by reading them bedtime tales. Every once in a while one of these books would appeal to her as much as to her two boys, and she decided that "the world needed more books that would amuse both adults and children," as she wrote on the Houghton Mifflin Web site. Initially, Lester felt she could contribute to the world of books by illustrating them. She had always enjoyed illustration, and her early efforts with children's books centered on the pictures; her text was only secondary at that time. As a busy mother with two active children and a decade of teaching experience with all sorts of second-grade antics to draw from, Lester had ideas galore.

Publication was another matter, however. After receiving numerous rejections, her first book was finally published in 1979. With her first title, *Cora Copycat,* Lester presents a little girl whose copycat antics drive her family wild until one day a Wild Woolly Wurgal, freshly escaped from the zoo, cures her of this habit. Lester illustrated this first book herself, and a *Kirkus Reviews* critic noted both the "funny, comix-style cartoons" as well as Lester's "snappy text." However, with her next book, *The Wizard, the Fairy, and the Magic Chicken,* Lester—at the suggestion of her editor—teamed with Munsinger for the first time in a story of three sorcerers who are trying to outdo one another. Creating monsters, however, soon turns the sorcerers' competition into a need for cooperation. "Little kids will be all agog when they discover what happens next," concluded a *Publishers Weekly* reviewer. "A winner for kids and the adults who'll be reading it again and again," noted *Booklist*'s Ilene Cooper. This squabbling trio earned a reprise in Lester's *Revenge of the Magic Chicken,* which Cooper found "as zany as ever."

A little boy who refuses to accept blame forms the core of *It Wasn't My Fault.* Murdley Gurdson, while out for a walk one day, has an egg land on his head. When a round-robin of animals blames one another, Murdley is finally forced to admit that it is his fault. A *Kirkus Reviews* contributor found the story "deftly contrived, and comical without overstraining," while a *Bulletin of the Center for Children's Books* reviewer commented that it was "bright, sunnily nonsensical, capably structured and told." Names are at the center of *A Porcupine Named Fluffy,* and it is only when Fluffy meets a rhino named Hippo that things look brighter for the misnamed porcupine. A *Publishers Weekly* reviewer noted that Munsinger and Lester "tell a sweet story with joyful exuberance."

Ideas come to Lester from many sources: from her own career as a teacher, from her children as they were growing up, from jokes and nonsense rhymes. "I am usually moved to write a book when an idea pops into my head," Lester once told *CA.* "And an idea pops into my head usually when I'm in the middle of an unexciting task—doing such things as standing in bank lines or washing spinach. . . . Once an idea comes into my head it usually takes one or two months of misfires and charging up blind alleys until the story is completed."

Another little girl figured in *Pookins Gets Her Way,* a cautionary tale for children who must always have their own way. Pookins has ice cream for breakfast and practices roller-skating in the living room; in fact, the threat of her tantrums gets her anything she wants until she meets her match in a gnome from whom she demands three wishes. "It's extremely satisfying to see this rotten kid get her comeuppance," noted a reviewer for *Publishers Weekly.*

A pig, a parrot, and a rabbit are protagonists in a trio of books examining the consequences of selfishness, rudeness, and inattention. Greedy Pinkerton the pig mistakes a Sandwitch for a sandwich at a beach picnic in *Me First,* and is quickly up to his snout in trouble as the witch obliges him to do chores for her. "The Sandwitch is just the corny joke to amuse most children," Carolyn Jenks noted in *Horn Book.* Reviewing that same title, a contributor for *Publishers Weekly* felt it was "another successful joint effort," as well as a "funny, fetching tale." The birthday parrot in *Princess Penelope's Parrot* provides the comeuppance for the nasty little princess to whom it is given when the bird sputters all the rude remarks it has learned from her at a most inappropriate moment. Sally R. Dow, writing in *School Library Journal,* commented on the "delightfully droll humor" in the book as well as on Munsinger's "whimsical" illustrations. "Another small funny lesson in correct behavior from a well-known pair of collaborators," concluded *Horn Book* reviewer Ann A. Flowers. Also reviewing *Princess Penelope's Parrot,* a critic for *Publishers Weekly* felt that "Lester's storytelling calls to mind the dry wit of a Thurber," while *Booklist*'s Stephanie Zvirin noted that "the comical overlay makes the obvious message go down easily." Janice M. Del Negro, writing in *Bulletin of the Center for Children's Books,* called the same book "a great read-aloud." In *Listen, Buddy,* the eponymous bunny has trouble concentrating on what is said to him, despite his enormous ears. An adventure with Scruffy the Varmint helps Buddy to sharpen his listening skills in this "sprightly paced tale [which] amiably nudges kids whose direction-following skills need some honing," according to a reviewer for *Publishers Weekly.* Similarly, Hazel Rochman, writing in *Booklist,* felt that "kids will enjoy the slapstick and the word jokes." And Virginia Opocensky, reviewing the title in *School Library Journal,* concluded, "Sure to bring laughs at story time."

Lester and Munsinger turned their hands to the antics of a penguin with the award-winning *Tacky the Penguin* and its sequels, including *Three Cheers for Tacky.* Tacky is not your standard penguin; in fact, dressed in Hawaiian shirts and a purple bow tie, he hardly fits in with his other black-tie cousins. Though he does not blend well, it is Tacky who saves his friends from hunters in *Tacky the Penguin,* which Phillis Wilson, writing in *Booklist,* called a "perceptive text about being different." In *Three Cheers for Tacky,* the rumpled penguin is reprised in another title that "reinforces the message that there is nothing wrong—and quite a bit right—with being different," according to a contributor for *Publishers Weekly.* The same reviewer praised the "pithy" text and "winsome" illustrations in the "entertaining" title, which finds Tacky once again the nonconformist among his penguin pals, all attired in black-bow-tie penguin finery. Engaged in a cheering contest, Tacky once again finds himself hopelessly out of step and no competition for the other teams who are color coordinated and all cheer right on cue. But on the day of the competition, Tacky's bungling endears itself to the judges, who, completely bored by the sameness of the others, award Tacky and his team first prize, a new bow tie. Reviewing *Three Cheers for Tacky,* Ann A. Flowers concluded in *Horn Book* that the story is "a great comfort . . . to nonconformists." *Booklist*'s Kathryn Broderick also had praise for the book, noting that "Lester's clever writing and the slapstick humor of the story make this a funny, funny, picture book."

Tacky makes repeat performances in other titles from the collaborating duo of Lester and Munsinger. With *Tacky in Trouble,* Lester presents "Tacky's goofiest escapade yet," according to *Booklist*'s Stephanie Zvirin. Tacky's unerring sense for making mistakes once again comes to his rescue when he is blown off course while surfing as his Hawaiian shirt catches the wind and takes him far away from the iceberg his friends refuse to leave. He ends up on a tropical island where he mistakes an elephant for a big rock. In an effort to prove that he is a bird and not a big bouquet for the elephant (with his flowered shirt), Tacky engages in what should be typical penguin behavior, such as diving, and manages to destroy the elephant's tablecloth. However, he is saved at the last minute, because the elephant likes the mess Tacky has made. "The story will appeal to children who know that making a mess can cause trouble," commented Marty Abbott Goodman in *School Library Journal.* Pat Mathews, reviewing the third "Tacky" installment in *Bulletin of the Center for Children's Books,* thought that "Tacky is one nonconformist everyone will want to be like."

In *Tacky and the Emperor,* the penguins are busy getting things ready for the auspicious visit of the penguin emperor. Tacky's job is preparing the balloons, but of course he gets carried away—literally. He soars off with one of the balloons only to land near the emperor's palace. Tacky is unaware of his location; meanwhile, the emperor disrobes to take a dip in his pool. When Tacky stumbles onto the emperor's fancy clothes, he puts them on and returns home only to be amazed when all his friends greet him as the emperor. "Lester hits the mark again," commented Martha Link in *School Library Journal,* "tapping right into the humor of the primary set, and proving once more that it's cool to be tacky." Tim Arnold, writing in *Booklist,* had similar praise, concluding that the author and artist once again manufactured "a delightful Antarctic-of-the-imagination, where comfy conformity is the rule but a very funny misfit saves the day."

A school play forms the backdrop for the 2002 addition to the "Tacky" books, *Tackylocks and the Three Bears.* A critic for *Kirkus Reviews* observed that "pomposity gets one on the snoot" in this title. When the other "perfect" penguins decide to stage a school play, Tacky—an unwanted member—is cast as Goldilocks. After numerous rehearsals, the cast think they have the play ready and perform it in front of a class of younger penguins. When Tacky forgets his lines and eats all the porridge and then goes off to sleep in baby bear's bed, the others try to cover for him. But Tacky needs no such help; a pillow fight leads to unexpected audience participation and all the little penguins think this is the best play ever. A *Kirkus*

Review critic called this offering "another victory for oddfellows everywhere," while Marlene Gawron, writing in *School Library Journal,* thought that "this silliness will delight Tacky's loyal fans and win a lot of new devotees."

Lester and Munsinger turn to another character in their "celebrations of differences," as a reviewer for *Horn Book* wrote, in *Hooway for Wodney Wat.* Rodney Rat has a speech impediment and has trouble pronouncing his own name. Teased by his classmates, Rodney is so embarrassed that he hides inside his jacket. Rodney's status changes, however, when he is able to undo a new school bully with a game of Simon Says; his "w" for "r" substitution suddenly becomes his strength as he sends the bully to "wake the leaves" and "go west." A critic for *Publishers Weekly* felt that "Wodney's transformation from forlorn to triumphant will have children cheering." Likewise, *Booklist*'s Stephanie Zvirin noted that this "comical story . . . will not only make kids laugh but also hearten those who feel they'll be outsiders forever."

Another nonconformist takes center stage in *Score One for Sloths,* in which Sparky tries to put some oomph in her fellow students at Sleepy Valley Sloth School, with little effect. But, when a representative from the Society for Organizing Sameness visits, complaining of the low test scores and threatening to close the school, Sparky suddenly comes into her own. "Score one against rigid school standards," declared *Booklist*'s Hazel Rochman. A contributor for *Publishers Weekly* had further praise for the title, calling it a "comic caper with a subtly delivered moral."

Lester has also written a book about the writing life in her 1997 work *Author: A True Story.* "In the . . . years since I left teaching," Lester once told *CA,* "I've visited over two hundred schools, encouraging children to write. *Author: A True Story* is based on what I tell them during these visits. The enthusiasm for writing I encounter on these visits is most encouraging—both students and teachers are so much more involved than I was years ago." The book documents Lester's own difficulties as a child with learning disabilities as well as her persistence in getting published, overcoming multiple rejections. Self-illustrated, the book is at once "wry [and] funny," according to Hazel Rochman in *Booklist.* A contributor for *Publishers Weekly* found the autobiography a "lighthearted look at how [Lester] came to write children's books," and one that "will give aspiring authors of any age a lift." Similarly, *Horn Book*'s Ann A. Flowers found the title "disarming and very funny." Lester concluded on the Houghton Mifflin Web site, "How fortunate I am to have backed into this wonderful field."

In *Something Might Happen,* which came out in 2003, the wide-eyed lemur Twitchly Fidget is afraid of everything, including his sneakers (what if he gets them on the wrong feet and has to walk cross-legged for the rest of his life?). Ultimately he gets a "fixin" from his Aunt Bridget Fidget (who drops in for a "vidgit") and sets out with confidence to see the wonderful world. Lester told *CA*: "I wrote *Something Might Happen* in response to the events of 9/11 and dedicated it to our son Robin 'who chose to be there when something happened'—he volunteered on the site of Ground Zero for several days. His brother Jamie, to whom *Hooway for Wodney Wat* was dedicated, suggests that since Wodney has won so many awards perhaps *all* my future books be dedicated to him!"

BIOGRAPHICAL AND CRITICAL SOURCES:

BOOKS

Lester, Helen, *Hooway for Wodney Wat,* illustrated by Lynn Munsinger, Houghton Mifflin (Boston, MA), 1999.

PERIODICALS

Booklist, March 1, 1983, Ilene Cooper, review of *The Wizard, the Fairy, and the Magic Chicken,* p. 907; March 1, 1985, p. 985; April 15, 1986, p. 1223; April 15, 1987, p. 1290; April 1, 1988, Phillis Wilson, review of *Tacky the Penguin,* p. 1351; March 1, 1990, Ilene Cooper, review of *The Revenge of the Magic Chicken,* p. 1344; October 1, 1992, p. 336; February 15, 1994, Kathryn Broderick, review of *Three Cheers for Tacky,* p. 1092; October 15, 1995, Hazel Rochman, review of *Listen, Buddy,* p. 412; September 1, 1996, Stephanie Zvirin, review of *Princess Penelope's*

Parrot, p. 143; March 15, 1997, Hazel Rochman, review of *Author: A True Story,* p. 1246; April, 1998, Stephanie Zvirin, review of *Tacky in Trouble,* pp. 1331-1332; May 1, 1999, Stephanie Zvirin, review of *Hooway for Wodney Wat,* p. 1600; August, 2000, Tim Arnold, review of *Tacky and the Emperor,* p. 2148; August, 2001, Hazel Rochman, review of *Score One for the Sloths,* p. 2131; October 1, 2002, Kathy Broderick, review of *Tackylocks and the Three Bears,* p. 337.

Bulletin of the Center for Children's Books, June, 1985, review of *It Wasn't My Fault,* p. 188; April, 1988, p. 159; March, 1990, pp. 168-169; January, 1997, Janice M. Del Negro, review of *Princess Penelope's Parrot,* p. 179; May, 1998, Pat Matthews, review of *Tacky in Trouble,* p. 327.

Horn Book, September-October, 1986, p. 582; November-December, 1992, Carolyn K. Jenks, review of *Me First,* p. 717; October, 1994, Ann A. Flowers, review of *Three Cheers for Tacky,* p. 578; November-December, 1996, Ann A. Flowers, review of *Princess Penelope's Parrot,* p. 727; May-June, 1997, Ann A. Flowers, review of *Author,* p. 341; July-August, 1999, review of *Hooway for Wodney Wat,* p. 457; November-December, 2000, Christine M. Heppermann, review of *Tacky and the Emperor,* p. 748; September-October, 2001, Peter D. Sieruta, review of *Score One for the Sloths,* p. 576.

Junior Bookshelf, October, 1987, p. 218.

Kirkus Reviews, October 1, 1979, review of *Cora Copycat,* p. 1142; January 1, 1983, p. 4; March 1, 1985, review of *It Wasn't My Fault,* p. 8; July 15, 2002, review of *Tackylocks and the Three Bears,* p. 1037.

New York Times Book Review, April 6, 1986, p. 21.

Publishers Weekly, May 27, 1983, review of *The Wizard, the Fairy, and the Magic Chicken,* p. 68; April 25, 1986, review of *A Porcupine Named Fluffy,* p. 73; February 27, 1987, review of *Pookins Gets Her Way,* p. 163; August 3, 1992, review of *Me First,* p. 71; December 20, 1993, review of *Three Cheers for Tacky,* p. 71; July 24, 1995, review of *Listen, Buddy,* p. 64; October 7, 1996, review of *Princess Penelope's Parrot,* p. 74; February 3, 1997, review of *Author,* p. 105; April 19, 1999, review of *Hooway for Wodney Wat,* p. 72; July 30, 2001, review of *Score One for the Sloths,* p. 84.

School Librarian, August, 1993, p. 103.

School Library Journal, October, 1979, p. 142; August, 1983, p. 54; May, 1985, p. 78; August, 1986, p. 84; August, 1987, p. 70; April, 1988, p. 82; May, 1990, p. 88; February, 1992, p. 66; October, 1992, p. 91; May, 1994, p. 98; November, 1995, Virginia Opocensky, review of *Listen, Buddy,* p. 76; October, 1996, Sally R. Dow, review of *Princess Penelope's Parrot,* p. 101; May, 1998, Marty Abbott Goodman, review of *Tacky in Trouble,* pp. 119-120; November, 2000, Martha Link, *Tacky and the Emperor,* p. 126; October, 2001, Robin L. Gibson, review of *Score One for the Sloths,* pp. 123-124; September, 2002, Marlene Gawron, review of *Tackylocks and the Three Bears,* pp. 197-198; September, 2003, Be Astengo, review of *Something Might Happen,* p. 183.

Times Educational Supplement, April 2, 1993, p. 16.

ONLINE

Houghton Mifflin Home Page, http://www.houghtonmifflinbooks.com/ (June 11, 2002), "Helen Lester."*

* * *

LINCECUM, Jerry Bryan 1942-

PERSONAL: Born February 15, 1942, in Seale, TX; son of Jack (a farmer) and Mildred (Jones) Lincecum; married Etta Sanders, 1960 (divorced, 1985); married Peggy A. Redshaw (a professor of biology), September 28, 1985; children: David Bryan, Deborah Jensen, Stephen Douglas. *Education:* Texas A & M University, B.A. (magna cum laude), 1963; Duke University, M.A., Ph.D., 1967.

ADDRESSES: Home—608 North Cleveland, Sherman, TX 75090. *Office*—Department of English, Austin College, 900 North Grand Ave., Sherman, TX 75090; fax: 903-813-2368. *E-mail*—jlincecum@austincollege.edu.

CAREER: Austin College, Sherman, TX, began as assistant professor, became professor, 1967—, Henry L. and Laura H. Shoap Professor of English, 1997—. Telling Our Stories (autobiography writing project), director, 1990—.

MEMBER: National Council of Teachers of English, Texas Folklore Society, East Texas Historical Association.

AWARDS, HONORS: Named Piper Professor for Excellence in Teaching, Minnie Stevens Piper Foundation, 1980; Miss Ima Hogg Historical Achievement Award, Center for American History, University of Texas—Austin, and Ottis Lock Award, East Texas Historical Association, both 1998, for *Science on the Texas Frontier: Observations of Dr. Gideon Lincecum;* Homer P. Rainey award for Distinguished Service, Austin College, 2001.

WRITINGS:

(Editor, with Edward Hake Phillips) *Adventures of a Frontier Naturalist: The Life and Times of Dr. Gideon Lincecum,* Texas A & M University Press (College Station, TX), 1994.

(Editor, with Edward Hake Phillips and wife, Peggy A. Redshaw) *Science on the Texas Frontier: Observations of Dr. Gideon Lincecum,* Texas A & M University Press (College Station, TX), 1997.

(Coeditor) *Gideon Lincecum's Sword: Civil War Letters from the Texas Home Front,* University of North Texas Press (Denton, TX), 2001.

M

MacDONALD, Margaret Read 1940-

PERSONAL: Born January 21, 1940, in Seymour, IN; daughter of Murray Ernest (a builder) and Mildred (Amick) Read; married Robert Burns Ruff, August, 1962 (divorced, January, 1963); married James Bruce MacDonald (an employee of the Environmental Protection Agency), August 20, 1965; children: Jennifer Skye, Julie Liana. *Education:* Indiana University, A.B., 1962, Ph.D., 1979; University of Washington, Seattle, M.L.S., 1964; University of Hawaii, M.Ed. Ec., 1968.

ADDRESSES: *Office*—Bothell Regional Library, 18215 98th Ave. NE, Bothell, WA 98011.

CAREER: King County Library System, Seattle, WA, children's specialist, 1964-65; San Francisco Public Library, San Francisco, CA, children's librarian, 1966; Hawaii State Library, Honolulu, Oahu Bookmobile librarian, 1966-68; Singapore American School, storyteller, 1968-69; Fairfield Methodist Girl's School, Singapore, librarian, 1969; Mountain-Valley Regional Library System, Sacramento, CA, children's consultant, 1969-70; Montgomery County Library System, White Oak, MD, children's librarian, 1970-72; University of Washington, Seattle, visiting lecturer in librarianship, 1975- 79; King County Library System, children's specialist at Bothell Public Library, 1977—. Occasional adjunct professor of storytelling to Seattle Pacific University, Western Washington University, Pennisula College, and other northwestern U.S. colleges, 1983—.

MEMBER: American Library Association, Seattle Storyteller's Guild (board member, 1990-96; vice president, 1993-96), American Folklore Society (president, children's folklore section, 1993-94), Children's Literature Association, Association for Library Service to Children, National Storytelling Association (board member, 1992-95), Oral History Association, Washington Library Association, Washington State Folklife Council (board member, 1986-90; president, 1989-90), Youth Theatre Northwest (board member, 1988-91; president, 1989-90), Seattle Girl's Choir Parent Guild (president, 1986-87), International Board on Books for Young People, Washington Library Media Association, Society of Book Writers and Illustrators.

AWARDS, HONORS: *The Storyteller's Sourcebook: A Subject, Title, and Motif Index to Folklore Collections for Children* was named one of the outstanding reference sources of 1982 by American Library Association; Notable Children's Trade Book in the Field of Social Studies, National Council for the Social Studies/ Children's Book Council, 1992, for *Peace Tales: World Folktales to Talk About;* Fulbright Scholar, Mahasarakham University, 1995-97; Charlotte Zolotow Award highly commended book, 2002, for *Mabela the Clever.*

WRITINGS:

The Storyteller's Sourcebook: A Subject, Title, and Motif Index to Folklore Collections for Children, Gale (Detroit, MI), 1982.

Twenty Tellable Tales: Audience Participation Folktales for the Beginning Storyteller, H. W. Wilson (Bronx, NY), 1986.

Booksharing: 101 Programs for Preschoolers, Shoe String (Hamden, CT), 1988.

Scipio, Indiana: Threads from the Past, Ye Galleon (Fairfield, WA), 1988.

The Skit Book, Linnet Books (Hamden, CT), 1989.

Look Back and See: Twenty Lively Tales for Gentle Tellers, H. W. Wilson (Bronx, NY), 1991.

The Folklore of World Holidays, Gale (Detroit, MI), 1991.

Tom Thumb, Oryx (Phoenix, AZ), 1993.

The Storyteller's Start-up Book: Finding, Learning, Performing, and Using Folktales, August House (Little Rock, AR), 1993.

Celebrate the World: Twenty Tellable Folktales for Multicultural Festivals, H. W. Wilson (Bronx, NY), 1994.

Bookplay: 101 Creative Themes to Share with Young Children, Library Professional Publications (Hamden, CT), 1994.

A Parent's Guide to Storytelling, HarperCollins (New York City), 1995.

Ghost Stories from the Pacific Northwest, August House (Little Rock, AR), 1995.

Scipio Storytelling: Talk in a Southern Indiana Community, University Press of America (Lanham, MD), 1996.

FOR CHILDREN

When the Lights Go Out: 20 Scary Tales to Tell, H. W. Wilson (Bronx, NY), 1988.

The Skit Book: 101 Skits from Kids, Linnet Books (Hamden, CT), 1989.

Peace Tales: World Folktales to Talk About, Linnet Books (Hamden, CT), 1992.

(Editor) Supaporn Vathanaprida, reteller, *Thai Tales: Folktales of Thailand,* Libraries Unlimited (Englewood, CO), 1994.

Tuck-Me-In Tales: Bedtime Stories from Around the World, illustrated by Yvonne LeBrun Davis, August House (Little Rock, AR), 1996.

The Girl Who Wore Too Much: A Pu-Thai Folktale, illustrated by Davis, August House (Little Rock, AR), 1997.

Pickin' Peas, illustrated by Pat Cummins, HarperCollins (New York, NY), 1997.

(With Winifred Jaeger) *The Round Book,* illustrated by Davis, Linnet Books (Hamden, CT), 1997.

(With Supaporn Vathanaprida) *The Peacock and the Crow and Other Thai Animal Tales,* illustrated by Wilat Nirumsunsiri, Fulcrum (Golden, CO), 1997.

Slop! A Welsh Folktale, illustrated by Yvonne LeBrun Davis, Fulcrum (Golden, CO), 1997.

Earth Care: World Folktales to Talk About, Linnet (Hamden, CT), 1999.

Mabela the Clever, Albert Whitman (Morton Grove, IL), 2000.

Shake-it-Up Tales! Stories to Sing, Dance, Drum, and Act Out, August House (Little Rock, AR), 2000.

(Reteller) *Fat Cat: A Danish Folktale,* illustrated by Julie Paschkis, August House (Little Rock, AR), 2001.

Also author of *The Old Woman Who Lived in a Vinegar Bottle,* illustrated by Nancy Dunaway Fowlkes, 1995.

WORK IN PROGRESS: Collecting contributions for *Traditional Storytelling Today: An International Encyclopedia,* to be published by Garland Publishing. Also working with Brian Sturm on *The Tale-Finder: A Motif, Subject, and Title Index to Popular Folktale Collections,* to be published by H. W. Wilson.

SIDELIGHTS: Margaret Read MacDonald told *CA:* "My work is based mostly on the needs of the public libraries in which I work. Fortunately I can draw on my training in folklore at Indiana University to help me provide useful books for our school and public libraries. *The Storyteller's Sourcebook: A Subject, Title, and Motif Index to Folklore Collections for Children* gives access to folktales in 556 collections of folktales published for children, along with 389 folktale picture books. It uses the Stith Thompson motif-index schema to classify all of this material, and adds a subject index. Brian Sturm and I are now working on *The Tale-Finder: A Motif, Subject, and Title Index to Popular Folktale Collections* to be published by H. W. Wilson.

"For several years I have worked at retelling folktales for use by other storytellers. By telling these stories many times myself, I am able to put them down in a form which lends itself to oral retelling. I try to cite sources carefully so the next teller can retrace my steps to the original materials if they wish. *Look Back and See: Twenty Lively Tales for Gentle Tellers* is an example of this work.

"From my public library reference work come other needs which I fill with a new book now and then. For example, reference tools such as *The Folklore of World*

Holidays and *Traditional Storytelling Today: An International Encyclopedia* and accessible books for children such as *The Skit Book: 101 Skits from Kids* and *The Round Book.*

"Other books are prepared to help children's librarians by sharing my own programs. *Booksharing: 101 Programs for Preschoolers* and *Bookplay: 101 Creative Themes to Share with Young Children* were published to meet those needs. And I have produced several picture books which I hope read aloud well and give special pleasure when used with children in storytimes. The preparation of a fine picture book is a true marriage of art and language—a VERY difficult task. But when it succeeds—what a joy!

"I am especially proud of the work I have done in Scipio, Indiana. This is a small community in Southern Indiana in which my mother grew up. Well, I grew up right near there too. *Scipio, Indiana: Threads from the Past* documents the history of this tiny community, tracing its founders from Germany to Berks County, Pennsylvania, to Guilford, North Carolina, to Jennings County, Indiana. The work is carefully documented.

"And after spending ten years in taping and transcribing the storytelling of some older folks from Scipio, I finally published *Scipio Storytelling: Talk in a Southern Indiana Community.* Here I take an in-depth look at aspects of storytelling performance in this rural community. This is a book which perhaps only I could have written, since as a member of the community there were few barriers to my participant-observation.

* * *

MARGULIS, Lynn 1938-

PERSONAL: Born March 5, 1938, in Chicago, IL; daughter of Morris (a lawyer) and Leone (a travel agent; maiden name, Wise) Alexander; married Carl Sagan (an astronomer and writer), June 16, 1957 (divorced, 1963); married Thomas N. Margulis (a crystallographer), January 18, 1967; children: (first marriage) Dorion, Jeremy; (second marriage) Zachary, Jenny. *Education:* University of Chicago, A.B., 1957; University of Wisconsin—Madison, M.S., 1960; University of California—Berkeley, Ph.D., 1965. *Politics:* "Closet radical." *Religion:* "I reject them all."

ADDRESSES: Home—Gibbs St., Newton Centre, MA 02159. *Office*—Biology Department, Morrill South, University of Massachusetts, Box 35810, Amherst, MA 01003-5810.

CAREER: Boston University, Boston, MA, assistant professor, 1967-71, associate professor, 1971-76, professor of biology, 1976-88. Lecturer at international conferences in Mexico and in London, England; Paris, France; Montreal, Quebec, Canada; Barcelona, Spain; Ustaoset, Norway; Amsterdam, Netherlands; and Leningrad, Russia. Chairman of committee on planetary biology and chemical evolution, Space Science Board of the National Academy of Sciences, 1978-81. Director of Biology, Brandeis University Peace Corps Colombia Project, summers, 1965, 1966; member of African Primary Science Project, Akosomba, Ghana, 1967. Consultant to Educational Development Center, and to Instituto Brasileiro de Educacao, Ciencia e Cultura (Brazilian Institute of Education, Science, and Culture), Sao Paulo, Brazil, summer, 1970; Scripps Institute of Oceanography, visiting professor, 1980; California Institute of Technology, visiting professor, 1980; NASA, Ames Planetary biology and Microbial Ecology Summer Research Program, 1980, 1982, 1984; Autonomous University of Barcelona, visiting professor, 1986; University of Massachusetts, Amherst, professor, 1988-99.

MEMBER: International Society for the Study of the Origins of Life, American Society of Microbiology, American Institute of Biological Science, Society for Evolutionary Pristology.

AWARDS, HONORS: Boston University Shell Award, 1967; George Lamb Award, 1972; Sherman Fairchild fellow, California Institute of Technology, 1977; Guggenheim fellow, 1979; Public Service Award, NASA, 1981; National Medal of Science, 2000; Commonwealth Award for Interpretive Scientist (Massachusetts Cultural Council), 2001; Alexander von Humboldt Prize, 2002. Honorary degrees from Southeastern Massachusetts University, 1989, Westfield State College, 1989.

WRITINGS:

Origin of Eukaryotic Cells, Yale University Press (New Haven, CT), 1970.

Early Cells, Science Books International (Boston, MA), 1981.

(With K. V. Schwartz) *Phyla of the Five Kingdoms: An Illustrated Guide to the Kinds of Life on Earth,* W. H. Freeman (San Francisco, CA), 1981.

Symbiosis in Cell Evolution, W. H. Freeman (San Francisco, CA), 1981, 2nd edition, 1993.

Early Life, Science Books International (Boston, MA), 1982.

Five Kingdoms: An Illustrated Guide to the Phyla of Life on Earth, W.H. Freeman (New York, NY), 1982, 3rd edition, 1998.

Origins of Sex: Three Billion Years of Genetic Recombination, Yale University Press (New Haven, CT), 1986.

(With son, Dorion Sagan) *Microcosmos: Four Billion Years of Evolution from Our Microbial Ancestors,* Summit Books (New York, NY), 1986, University of California Press (Berkeley, CA), 1997.

(With Dorion Sagan) *The Microcosmos Coloring Book,* Harcourt Brace Jovanovich (Boston, MA), 1988.

(With Dorion Sagan) *Garden of Microbial Delights: A Practical Guide to the Subvisible World,* Harcourt Brace Jovanovich (Boston, MA), 1988.

Biospheres from Earth to Space, Enslow (Hillside, NJ), 1989.

(With Dorion Sagan) *Mystery Dance: On the Evolution of Human Sexuality,* Summit Books (New York, NY), 1991.

Diversity of Life: The Five Kingdoms, Enslow (Hillside, NJ), 1992.

The Illustrated Five Kingdoms: A Guide to Diversity of Life on Earth, HarperCollins College (New York, NY), 1994.

(With Dorion Sagan) *What Is Life?,* Simon & Schuster (New York, NY), 1995.

Gaia to Microcosm, Kendall Hunt (Dubuque, IA), 1996.

(With Dorion Sagan) *Slanted Truths: Essays on Gaia, Symbiosis, and Evolution,* Copernicus (New York, NY), 1997.

(With Dorion Sagan) *What Is Sex?,* Simon & Schuster (New York, NY), 1997.

Symbiotic Planet: A New Look at Evolution, Basic Books (New York, NY), 1998.

Diversity of Life: The Illustrated Guide to the Five Kingdoms, Jones & Bartlett (Boston, MA), 1999.

(With Dorion Sagan) *Acquiring Genomes: A Theory of the Origins of Species,* Basic Books (New York, NY), 2002.

(With Michael F. Dolan) *Early Life: Evolution on the Precambrian Earth,* Jones & Bartlett (Boston, MA), 2002.

EDITOR

Origins of Life, Volume I, Gordon & Breach (Newark, NJ), 1970, Volume II: *Cosmic Evolution, Abundance, and Distribution of Biologically Important Elements,* Gordon & Breach (Newark, NJ), 1971, Volume III: *Planetary Astronomy,* Springer Verlag (New York, NY), 1973, Volume IV: *Chemistry and Radioastronomy,* Springer Verlag (New York, NY), 1973.

(With C. Ponnamperuma) *Limits to Life,* Reidel (Boston, MA), 1980.

(With Mitchell B. Rambler and Rene Fester) *Global Ecology: Towards a Science of the Biosphere,* Academic Press (Orlando, FL), 1989.

(With others) *Handbook of Protoctista,* Jones & Bartlett (Boston, MA), 1990.

(With Rene Fester) *Symbiosis As a Source of Evolutionary Innovation,* MIT Press (Cambridge, MA), 1991.

(With Lorraine Olendzenski) *Environmental Evolution: Effects of the Origin and Evolution of Life on Planet Earth,* MIT Press, 1992, 2nd edition (with Clifford Matthews and Aaron Haselton), 2000.

(With Mark McMenmin) *Concepts of Symbiogenesis,* Yale University Press (New Haven, CT), 1992.

(With Heather I. McKhann and Lorraine Olendzenski) *Illustrated Glossary of Protoctista,* Jones & Bartlett (Boston, MA), 1993.

Also author of science booklets for children. Contributor of more than eighty articles and reviews to scientific journals. Editor of *Origins of Life, Journal of Molecular Evolution,* and *Bio Systems.*

WORK IN PROGRESS: A work of fiction, *Luminous Fish.*

SIDELIGHTS: Lynn Margulis, a microbiologist, has gained a reputation for her work in many different facets of science. She has put forth many theories during her career as a researcher, some of which were rejected at first, only to be accepted at a much later time, when science caught up with her conclusions. As a teacher, she has not only gained the honorary title of distinguished university professor at the University of Massachusetts in Amherst, but has helped to develop teaching materials for students from middle school through college. In 1981, she was honored with a NASA public service award for her involvement with their program to develop research strategies; and in 2000, President Clinton presented her with the National Medal of Science. In reference to her published works, which are numerous, she has gained recognition for her original concepts on the topics of cell biology and evolution.

Margulis was born on March 5, 1938, in Chicago, IL, and by the time she was ready to enter college, college was not quite ready for her. At the age of nineteen, she graduated from the University of Chicago with a degree in liberal arts because that was the only option open to her as a woman, despite her keen interest and abilities in science. It was also at the university that she met the famed astronomer, Carl Sagan, whom she would later marry upon obtaining her degree. After gaining their graduate degrees, the young couple moved to San Francisco. By the time that Margulis completed her doctorate, in 1965, she had mothered two sons and divorced Sagan. With her college education completed, Margulis moved to Massachusetts and began her long career as a university instructor and eventually as a professor. She married Thomas Margulis, a crystallographer, in 1967.

Margulis's main interest in science was the location of genes in the cell, which she believed, despite much criticism that she received from her colleagues, resided outside of the nucleus. Two of her earliest books, *Origin of Eukaryotic Cells* and *Symbiosis in Cell Evolution,* were written to more clearly explain her theory. Upon publication of the first, she lost credibility and found it difficult to obtain grants to help support further study. However, ten years later, when she wrote the second book, her theory found more welcoming responses.

Her next major project was to offer a new system for classifying living things. Toward this goal, she wrote a series of books: *Phyla of the Five Kingdoms: An Illustrated Guide to the Kinds of Life on Earth, Five Kingdoms: An Illustrated Guide to the Phyla of Life on Earth,* and *Diversity of Life: The Five Kingdoms.* Margulis based her new system on her studies in microbiology and named her classifications: cells without nuclei, cells with nuclei, funguses, plants, and animals. In the *Quarterly Review of Biology,* Francisco J. Ayala referred to *Five Kingdoms* as "fun to read," a conclusion that surprised Ayala. He added, "the prose is muscular but gracious, packed with useful information, instructive gee-whiz anecdotes, and learned references." Margulis's 1992 publication on the subject was written so children could better understand her theories.

Another controversial topic that has inspired Margulis is based on James E. Lovelock's concept referred to as the Gaia Theory, which proposes that all life (from animals to the Earth itself) are part of an all-encompassing symbiosis, or as various elements of one organism. Margulis's books on this topic include *Gaia to Microcosm,* and *Slanted Truths: Essays on Gaia, Symbiosis, and Evolution.*

Margulis has written several books with her son, Dorion Sagan. One of them, *Mystery Dance: On the Evolution of Human Sexuality,* like many of Margulis's books, has been met with some harsh criticism. In their study, Margulis and Sagan attempt to plot out the evolution of sexuality, which Paul S. Boyer, writing for *BioScience,* found to be riddled with "unbridled speculation." In contrast, a reviewer for *Publishers Weekly* found the book to be an "eloquent, stimulating exploration."

Margulis and her son also wrote *What Is Life?,* a study of life via the intricate study of a cell. Each cell contains hints of its evolutionary history and environmental influences, or as Gilbert Taylor, for *Booklist,* stated, each cell offers "a window to the past." Beginning with the most basic form of life, the two authors then move up the evolutionary ladder, explaining each complication along the way.

In 2002, the mother-and-son team published a new book, *Acquiring Genomes: A Theory of the Origins of Species.* In this study, the authors offer their theory for the source of inherited variation that underlies the development of a new species. Whereas the theory of random mutation has long been held as the basic cause for the birth of a new species, Margulis and Sagan believe that it is the acquisition of new genomes by symbiotic merger that is the real stimulus.

Margulis told *CA:* "Since my major social goal (the eradication of poverty and ignorance by population control and education) is hopeless, I spend my time deducing the early evolutionary history of life on earth."

BIOGRAPHICAL AND CRITICAL SOURCES:

PERIODICALS

BioScience, September, 1992, Paul S. Boyer, review of *Mystery Dance: On the Evolution of Human Sexuality,* pp. 633-634.

Booklist, September 1, 1995, Gilbert Taylor, review of *What Is Life?,* p. 23; October 15, 1998, Gilbert Taylor, review of *Symbiotic Planet: A New Look at Evolution,* p. 382; June 1, 2002, Gilbert Taylor, review of *Acquiring Genomes: A Theory of the Origins of Species,* p. 1655.
Kirkus Reviews, May 15, 2002, review of *Acquiring Genomes,* p. 718.
Nature, July 18, 2002, Axel Meyer, review of *Acquiring Genomes,* p. 275.
Publishers Weekly, June 14, 1991, review of *Mystery Dance,* p. 50; August 28, 1995, review of *What Is Life?,* p. 99; October 5, 1998, review of *Symbiotic Planet,* p. 67.
Quarterly Review of Biology, March 2001, Francisco J. Ayala, review of *Five Kingdoms: An Illustrated Guide to the Phyla of Life on Earth,* p. 63.
Science News, October 26, 2002, review of *Acquiring Genomes,* p. 271.
Tribune Books, October 23, 1988.*

* * *

MAUCH, Christof 1960-

PERSONAL: Born February 9, 1960, in Sindelfingen, West Germany (now Germany); son of Norbert A. and Elsbeth M. (Roller) Mauch; married Wendy Morgan Lower; children: Ian Maxwell, Alexander Morgan. *Education:* Attended King's College, London, and Leo Baeck College, London, 1983-84; University of Tübingen, Dr.Phil., 1990, Dr.Phil.Habil., 1998. *Hobbies and other interests:* Cooking, hiking, cycling, film, collecting clocks.

ADDRESSES: Office—German Historical Institute, 1607 New Hampshire Ave. NW, Washington, DC 20009; fax 202-483-3430. *E-mail*—mauch@ghi-dc.org.

CAREER: University of Tübingen, Tübingen, Germany, lecturer, 1990-94; University of Bonn, Bonn, Germany, lecturer, 1994-95; American University, Washington, DC, professorial lecturer, 1996; Georgetown University, Washington, DC, director of OSS Oral History Project, 1996-98; German Historical Institute, Washington, DC, deputy director, 1998-99, director, 1999—. Georgetown University, visiting scholar, 1993; University of Cologne, lecturer, 1994-95, professor, 2002.

AWARDS, HONORS: Grants from Volkswagen Foundation, 1989-92, American Council of Learned Societies, 1993, Roosevelt Institute, 1994, German Marshall Fund, 1995, and German Research Foundation, 1995-97; Offermann-Hergarten Book Prize, 2000, for *Schattenkrieg gegen Hitler: Das Dritte Reich im Visier der amerikanischen Geheimdienste, 1941-1945.*

WRITINGS:

(With E. Mauch) *Horologisches Lexikon/Horological Dictionary,* two volumes, Universitas Verlag Tübingen (Tübingen, Germany), 1984.
(Editor, with Jürgen Heideking) *American Intelligence and the German Resistance to Hitler,* Westview (Boulder, CO), 1996.
(Editor, with Birgit Zischke) *Research and Funding: A German-American Guide for Historians and Social Scientists,* German Historical Institute (Washington, DC), 1999.
Schattenkrieg gegen Hitler: Das Dritte Reich im Visier der amerikanischen Geheimdienste, 1941-1945, Deutsche Verlags-Anstalt (Stuttgart, Germany), 1999, translation by Jeremiah M. Riemer published as *The Shadow War against Hitler: The Covert Operations of America's Wartime Secret Intelligence Service,* Columbia University Press (New York, NY), 2003.
(Editor, with Thomas Reuther) *Americana in German Archives: A Guide to Primary Sources concerning the History of the United States and Canada,* German Historical Institute (Washington, DC), 2001.
(Editor, with Joseph Salmons) *German Jewish Identities in America,* Kade, Max Institute for German American Studies (Madison, WI), 2003.

IN GERMAN

(Editor) *Nicht aufs Kreuz gefallen,* Universitas Verlag Tübingen (Tübingen, Germany), 1986.
(With T. Brenner) *Für eine Welt ohne Krieg: Otto Umfrid und die Anfänge der Friedensbewegung,* G. A. Ulmer (Schönaich, Germany), 1987, 3nd edition, 1995.
(Editor) Kurt Marti, *Texte-Daten-Bilder,* Luchterhand Literaturverlag (Frankfurt, Germany), 1990.
(With U. Karbowiak) *Unsere Geldköpfe: Portraits der neuen Banknoten,* G. A. Ulmer (Schönaich, Germany), 1990, 3rd edition, 1995.

Poesie-Theologie-Politik: Studien zu Kurt Marti, Niemeyer (Tübingen, Germany), 1991.

TechtelMechtel: Was weiter gescah, das weiss keiner (limericks), Universitas Verlag Tübingen (Tübingen, Germany), 1993.

(Editor, with Jürgen Heideking) *Geheimdienstkrieg gegen Deutschland: Subversion, Propaganda, und politische Planungen des amerikanischen Geheimdienstes im Zweiten weltkrieg,* Vandenhök & Ruprecht (Göttingen, Germany), 1993.

(Editor, with Jürgen Heideking) *USA und deutscher Widerstand: Analysen und Operationen des amerikanischen Geheimdienstes im Zweiten Weltkrieg,* Francke (Tübingen, Germany), 1993.

(Editor, with Philipp Gassert) *Mrs. President: von Martha Washington bis Hillary Clinton,* Deutsche Verlags-Anstalt (Stuttgart, Germany), 2000.

(Editor, with Jürgen Heideking) *Die Präsidenten der USA,* [Munich, Germany], 2002.

(Editor, with Heike Bungert and Marc Frey) *Verfassung—Demokratie—Politische Kultur,* [Trier, Germany], 2002.

(With Jürgen Heideking) *Geschichte der USA,* [Tübingen, Germany], 2003.

Contributor to books. Contributor to academic journals and newspapers. Some of Mauch's writings have been translated into Czech and Estonian.

WORK IN PROGRESS: Nature in German History; Beyond the Windshield: Roads and Landscapes in Transatlantic Perspective, with Thomas Zeller; *Shades of Green: Global Environmentalism in Historical Perspective,* with Nathan Stoltzfus and Doug Weiner; *Berlin—Washington: Capital Cities, Cultural Representations, and National Identities, 1800-2000,* with Andreas Daum.

SIDELIGHTS: Christof Mauch once told *CA:* "A major focus of my writing has always been the history and culture of protest and resistance; for example, the pacifists' struggle before World War I and the protest against pietism and clerical language. An exploration into the history of the German opposition against Hitler led to my study of U.S. secret intelligence during World War II. Although I consider myself a scholarly writer, I have also written general interest books and articles."

* * *

McCLOSKEY, Deirdre N(ansen) 1942-
(Donald N. McCloskey)

PERSONAL: Original name, Donald Nansen McCloskey; born September 11, 1942, in Ann Arbor, MI; child of Robert Green (an academician) and Helen (a singer; maiden name, Stueland) McCloskey; married Joanne Comi (a nurse), June 19, 1965 (marriage ended); children: Daniel, Margaret. *Education:* Harvard University, B.A. (magna cum laude), 1964, Ph.D., 1970. *Politics:* Libertarian. *Hobbies and other interests:* Latin, Greek, folk music.

ADDRESSES: Office—College of Arts and Sciences, University Hall M/C 228, University of Illinois at Chicago, 601 South Morgan, Chicago, IL 60607-7104.

CAREER: University of Chicago, Chicago, IL, assistant professor, 1968-73, associate professor of economics, 1973-80, associate professor of history, 1979-80; University of Iowa, Iowa City, professor of history and economics, 1980-99; University of Illinois at Chicago, distinguished professor, liberal arts and sciences, 1999—. Erasmus University of Rotterdam, professor, 1997—; distinguished visiting faculty fellow, University of California at Riverside, 2000. Organizer of conferences, 1970-90; lecturer, 1985-94.

MEMBER: American Economic Association, American Economic History Association, Economic History Society (England).

AWARDS, HONORS: Guggenheim fellow, 1983; National Science Foundation grants.

WRITINGS:

UNDER NAME DONALD N. McCLOSKEY

Economic Maturity and Entrepreneurial Decline: British Iron and Steel, 1870-1913, Harvard University Press (Cambridge, MA), 1973.

Enterprise and Trade in Victorian Britain: Essays in Historical Economics, Allen & Unwin, 1981.

The Applied Theory of Price, Macmillan (New York, NY), 1982, 2nd edition, 1985.

The Rhetoric of Economics, University of Wisconsin Press (Madison, WI), 1985.

The Writing of Economics, Macmillan (New York, NY), 1987.

Econometric History, Macmillan (New York, NY), 1987.

If You're So Smart: The Narrative of Economic Expertise, University of Chicago Press (Chicago, IL), 1990.

(With George K. Hersh Jr. and others) *A Bibliography of Historical Economics to 1980,* Cambridge University Press (New York, NY), 1990.

Knowledge and Persuasion in Economics, Cambridge University Press (New York, NY), 1994.

Economics and the Historian, University of California Press (Berkeley, CA), 1996.

The Vices of Economists, the Virtues of the Bourgeoisie, Amsterdam University Press (Amsterdam, Netherlands), 1996.

The Rhetoric of Economics, University of Wisconsin Press (Madison, WI), 1998.

How to Be Human—Though an Economist, University of Michigan Press (Ann Arbor, MI), 2000.

EDITOR, UNDER NAME DONALD N. McCLOSKEY

Essays on a Mature Economy: Britain after 1840, Princeton University Press (Princeton, NJ), 1972.

(With Roderick Floud) *The Economic History of Britain since 1700,* Volume I: *1700-1860,* Volume II: *1860 to the 1970s,* Cambridge University Press (Cambridge, England), 1981, 2nd edition, 1994.

(With Allan Megill and John S. Nelson) *The Rhetoric of the Human Sciences: Language and Argument in Scholarship and Public Affairs,* University of Wisconsin Press (Madison, WI), 1987.

(With Arjo Klamer and Robert M. Solow) *The Consequences of Economic Rhetoric,* Cambridge University Press (New York, NY), 1988.

Second Thoughts: Myths and Morals of U.S. Economic History, Oxford University Press (New York, NY), 1993.

UNDER NAME DEIRDRE N. McCLOSKEY

The Vices of Economists, [MI], 1997.

Crossing: A Memoir, University of Chicago Press (Chicago, IL), 1999.

Measurement and Meaning in Economics: The Essential Deirdre McCloskey, edited by Stephen Thomas Ziliak, E. Elgar (Northampton, MA), 2001.

Contributor to professional journals. Editor, *Journal of Economic History,* 1981-85; associate editor, *Journal of Economic Perspectives;* contributing editor, *Critical Review* and *Reasoning.* Member of editorial boards of several professional journals.

WORK IN PROGRESS: Research on bourgeois virtue.

SIDELIGHTS: Deirdre N. McCloskey has taught both economics and the humanities at the university level; the author has combined these two seemingly disparate subjects in her 2000 work *How to Be Human—Though an Economist.* McCloskey's approach to "humanizing" a dry science has "allowed her to bridge a gap between economics and literary studies," according to *Reason* writer Nick Gillespie. When asked by Gillespie why it was so "hard for economists to be human," McCloskey replied that throughout economic history "the central argument . . . has been that prudence [is] the preeminent virtue." But prudence alone, she added, citing Adam Smith, "is not a complete account of human beings. So if we are going to be complete, we need to recognize other virtues, too."

It behooves budding economists to realize that, suggested critic Peter Boethke of *Humane Studies Review.* Economic studies "often devolve into academic showmanship rather than a mutual engagement with ideas," Boethke noted. "We value smarts, not necessarily wisdom. Somebody, therefore, has to fill in the missing gap as our moral teacher. In modern economics the wisest teacher of the public morality" is McCloskey. In the critic's view, "a young economist who learns and practices the fifteen rules McCloskey lays out [in *How to Be Human*] will not only become a good economist, but also practice her economics while being a decent human being." In this book, remarked *Times Literary Supplement* contributor David Throsby, McCloskey "argues that love alters economic behavior in ways that are understood by anthropologists, psychologists, theologians or poets, but not by economists. She suggests that taking account of love requires economic analysis, 'but an economic analysis of people, not of blackboard phantoms.'"

The author was already firmly established as an economist when the then-Donald McCloskey announced in 1995: "I am cross-gendered, and, at age 53, having been a good soldier for over four decades,

I am doing something about it. Not to startle you, but I am becoming a woman economist." McCloskey chronicled her transition from man to woman in both *How to Be Human* and in her 1999 memoir *Crossing.* More than 25,000 Americans have changed their gender, the book reveals; in McCloskey's case, the procedure included hair removal and was followed by "a tummy tuck and breast augmentation," Maxine Kumin wrote in a *New York Times Book Review* piece. "The facial reconstruction: reduction of the eyebrow ridge . . . , cheek and jaw surgery, an operation to reduce the nose, move the hairline forward, point the jaw, lift the eyebrows. The first voice operation was not successful, nor were subsequent ones." Kumin added that *Crossing,* beyond describing the arduous medical transformation of transgendering, focuses on "the gradual emotional evolution the writer experienced." Even after the procedure was complete, all was not well in McCloskey's life. "Sadly, his son, daughter and former wife turned away from this new person," noted Kumin. "But Deirdre McCloskey's mother and brother have been bulwarks of support, and her sister is moving toward reconciliation. She has finally stopped calling her 'Donald.'"

McCloskey told *CA* that, during the 1980s, she turned to "rhetoric" in economics and history. Her books in the "rhetoric of inquiry" have made her known throughout the social sciences and humanities. The author wrote: "My change of gender in 1996 corresponded with a turn toward ethical reflections. I am now a leader in bringing economics back to what I call 'the ethics of good old Adam Smith.'"

BIOGRAPHICAL AND CRITICAL SOURCES:

BOOKS

McCloskey, Deirdre, *Crossing: A Memoir,* University of Chicago Press (Chicago, IL), 1999.

PERIODICALS

American Historical Review, June, 1973; June, 1975.

Booklist, November 15, 1999, review of *Crossing,* p. 584.

Business History Review, autumn, 1972; summer, 1974.

Choice, March, 1974; November, 1998, review of *The Rhetoric of Economics,* 2nd edition, p. 569.

Journal of Economic History, September, 1974.

Journal of Economic Literature, December, 1997, review of *The Vices of Economists, the Virtues of the Bourgeoisie,* p. 2111; March, 1998, review of *The Vices of Economists, the Virtues of the Bourgeoisie,* p. 228; December, 1998, review of *The Rhetoric of Economics,* 2nd edition, p. 2212; June, 2001, review of *How to Be Human— Though an Economist,* p. 623; December, 2001, review of *How to Be Human—Though an Economist,* p. 1226.

Journal of Modern History, March, 1974.

Journal of Socio-Economics, November, 1999, Roger Frantz, review of *The Vices of Economists, the Virtues of the Bourgeoisie,* p. 777.

Kirkus Reviews, September 15, 1999, review of *Crossing,* p. 1477.

Library Journal, September 1, 1999, review of *Crossing,* p. 218.

New York Times Book Review, November 14, 1999, Maxine Kumin, "The Metamorphosis," p. 10.

Publishers Weekly, October 4, 1999, review of *Crossing,* p. 54.

Reason, May, 2001, Nick Gillespie, "Economical Humanism," p. 17.

Reference and Research Book News, August, 2001, review of *Measurement and Meaning in Economics: The Essential Deirdre McCloskey,* p. 76.

Times Literary Supplement, March 24, 1972; August 16, 1974; August 7, 1981; August 1, 1986; March 22, 2002, David Throsby, "Humans Can Apply," p. 28.

Washington Post Book World, May 17, 1987.

ONLINE

Humane Studies Review, http://www.humanestudies review.org/ (spring, 2002), Peter Boethke, "Being Human: What They Don't Teach in Graduate School."*

* * *

McCLOSKEY, Donald N.

See McCLOSKEY, Deirdre N(ansen)

McCRAW, Thomas K(incaid) 1940-

PERSONAL: Born September 11, 1940, in Corinth, MS; son of John Carey (an engineer) and Olive (Kincaid) McCraw; married Susan Morehead, September 22, 1962; children: Elizabeth, Thomas. *Education:* University of Mississippi, B.A., 1962; University of Wisconsin—Madison, M.A., 1968, Ph.D., 1970.

ADDRESSES: *Office*—Baker Library, Graduate School of Business Administration, Harvard University, Soldiers Field, Boston, MA 02163.

CAREER: University of Texas at Austin, assistant professor, 1970-74, associate professor of history, 1974-78; Harvard University, Graduate School of Business Administration, Boston, MA, professor of business administration, 1978—. Visiting associate professor of business administration, Harvard Business School, Harvard University, 1976-78. *Military service:* U.S. Navy, 1962-66; became lieutenant.

MEMBER: American Historical Association, Organization of American Historians.

AWARDS, HONORS: William P. Lyons Master's Essay Award from Loyola University of Chicago and Loyola University Press, 1969; Harvard-Newcomen resident fellowship in business history at Harvard University, 1973-74; Pulitzer Prize in history, 1985, for *Prophets of Regulation*.

WRITINGS:

Morgan vs. Lilienthal: The Feud within the TVA, Loyola University Press (Chicago, IL), 1970.

TVA and the Power Fight, 1933-1939, Lippincott (Philadelphia, PA), 1971.

(Editor) *Regulation in Perspective: Historical Essays*, Division of Research, Graduate School of Business Administration, Harvard University (Cambridge, MA), 1981.

Prophets of Regulation: Charles Francis Adams, Louis D. Brandeis, James M. Landis, Alfred E. Kahn, Belknap Press of Harvard University Press (Cambridge, MA), 1984.

(Editor) *America versus Japan*, Harvard Business School Press (Cambridge, MA), 1986.

(Editor) *The Essential Alfred Chandler: Essays Toward a Historical Theory of Big Business*, Harvard Business School Press (Cambridge, MA), 1991.

(Coauthor) *Management: Past and Present: A Casebook on the History of American Business*, South-Western College Publishing (Cincinnati, OH), 1996.

(Editor) *Creating Modern Capitalism: How Entrepreneurs, Companies, and Countries Triumphed in Three Industrial Revolutions*, Harvard University Press (Cambridge, MA), 1997.

(Coeditor) *The Intellectual Venture Capitalist: John H. McArthur and the Work of the Harvard Business School, 1980-1995*, Harvard Business School Press (Cambridge, MA), 1999.

American Business, 1920-2000: How It Worked, Harlan Davidson (Wheeling, IL), 2000.

Contributor to *The Progressive Era*, edited by Lewis L. Gould, Syracuse University Press, 1974; and *Fifty Years Later: The New Deal Evaluated*, edited by Harvard Sitkoff, Knopf (New York, NY), 1985. Contributor to scholarly journals and popular magazines, including *Business History Review, California Management Review, American Scholar, Journal of Policy Analysis and Management*, and *American Heritage*.

SIDELIGHTS: Thomas K. McCraw's Pulitzer Prize-winning book, *Prophets of Regulation*, profiles four men who were instrumental in the move for regulatory policy in the American marketplace. The working lives of these men—Charles Francis Adams, Louis D. Brandeis, James M. Landis, and Alfred E. Kahn—span the decades from the nineteenth-century railroad boom to the deregulation of the airline industry in the early 1980s. As Peter Schuck explained in the *Washington Post Book World*, "By tracing the careers and economic-political ideas of four central figures in the evolution of the administrative state . . . , McCraw hopes to illuminate some relationships between individuals and regulatory change, between ideas and regulatory techniques, that have previously been neglected and obscured."

Merin Wexler in the *New York Times Book Review* praised McCraw for his ability to explain "sophisticated economic theory in accessible terms." Schuck, appreciative of McCraw's "novel, stimulating approach," noted that McCraw's effort "to clarify the nature of regulation by carefully integrating biography, history of ideas and regulatory strategy pays handsome dividends." Eliot Janeway, commenting in the *Los Angeles Times Book Review*, reached a similar conclusion. "McCraw . . . has done an absorbing job of applying the Plutarchian art [of unfolding history in terms of trenchant personalities] to what might seem to be the tedious, Pecksniffian, barren subject of regulation in the United States," Janeway wrote. "*Prophets of Regulation* is a scholarly and provocative job of bringing Schumpeter's definition of economics as 'historical sociology' to life, presenting four regulators as role models in action."

In 1997 McCraw edited and wrote the introduction to *Creating Modern Capitalism: How Entrepreneurs, Companies, and Countries Triumphed in Three Industrial Revolutions,* which examines the evolution of capitalism in four industrial nations. Janet Knoedler, reviewing the book for *Journal of Economic Issues,* called it "an ambitious book, well-written and researched, comprehensive in its coverage and sweeping in its analysis."

BIOGRAPHICAL AND CRITICAL SOURCES:

PERIODICALS

Business History, April, 1999, Steven Tolliday, review of *Creating Modern Capitalism: How Entrepreneurs, Companies, and Countries Triumphed in Three Industrial Revolutions,* p. 165.

Business History Review,, summer, 1985, spring, 1998, W. Mark Fruin, review of *Creating Modern Capitalism,* p. 123.

Choice, December, 2000, R. L. Hogler, review of *American Business, 1920-2000: How It Worked,* p. 750.

Journal of Economic History, spring, 1985.

Journal of Economic Issues, December, 1998, review of *Creating Modern Capitalism,* p. 1170.

Los Angeles Times Book Review, October 28, 1984.

New York Times Book Review, October 21, 1984.

Washington Post Book World, October 7, 1984.*

* * *

McDERMOTT, Alice 1953-

Alice McDermott

PERSONAL: Born June 27, 1953, in Brooklyn, NY; daughter of William J. and Mildred (Lynch) McDermott; married David M. Armstrong (a research neuroscientist), June 16, 1979; children: three. *Education:* State University of New York, B.A., 1975; University of New Hampshire, M.A., 1978.

ADDRESSES: *Home*—Bethesda, MD. *Agent*—Harriet Wasserman Literary Agency, 137 East 36th St., New York, NY 10016.

CAREER: Writer. Lecturer in English at the University of New Hampshire, Durham, 1978-79; fiction reader for *Redbook* and *Esquire,* 1979-80; consulting editor of *Redbook*'s Young Writers Contest; lecturer in writing at the University of California, San Diego; teacher of writing workshops at American University; writer-in-residence, Virginia Center for the Creative Arts, 1995 and 1997; writer-in-residence, Johns Hopkins University, Baltimore, MD.

MEMBER: Writer's Guild, PEN, Associated Writing Programs, Poets and Writers.

AWARDS, HONORS: Whiting Writers Award, 1987; National Book Award nomination, 1987, and PEN/Faulkner Award for fiction nomination, 1988, both for

That Night; National Book Award, 1998, and American Book Award, Before Columbus Foundation, 1999, both for *Charming Billy.*

WRITINGS:

NOVELS

A Bigamist's Daughter, Random House (New York, NY), 1982.
That Night, Farrar, Straus (New York, NY), 1987.
At Weddings and Wakes, Farrar, Straus (New York, NY), 1991.
Charming Billy, Farrar, Straus (New York, NY), 1998.
Child of My Heart, Farrar, Straus (New York, NY), 2002.

Contributor of short stories to *Redbook, Mademoiselle,* Seventeen, and *Ms.*

ADAPTATIONS: Child of My Heart was adapted for audiocassette and CD and released by Audio Renaissance, 2002.

SIDELIGHTS: Award-winning novelist Alice McDer-
-
mottdeals with many aspects of love and family life in her novels, including a love affair between a cynical editor and a novelist, a romance between two teenagers in the early 1960s, and the many nuances of an Irish-American family. She infuses her works with inventiveness and originality and is praised for her storytelling skills, her lyrical writing, and her descriptive detail and imagery. Michael J. Bandler, writing in *Tribune Books,* noted: "McDermott is a spellbinder, adding a cachet of mystery and eloquence to common occurrences."

McDermott's first novel, *A Bigamist's Daughter,* concerns Elizabeth Connelly, a twenty-six-year-old editor at a vanity publisher. Her job consists of reading the summaries of books (instead of the entire manuscript), heaping enthusiasm and praise on the author, extracting payments of $5,000 or more from them, and then trying to explain why the book was never published. Two years of this kind of work at Vista Books has turned Elizabeth into a cynic, and it is at this point in her life that she meets and becomes involved with a southern client still in search of an ending for his novel about a bigamist. Consequently, Connelly ponders her own father's frequent absences from home as she was growing up. As Elizabeth's memories of her father begin to resurface, "she becomes more appealing; she loses the harshness and superficiality that initially alienate the reader," maintained Anne Tyler in the *New York Times Book Review.* LeAnne Schreiber, writing in the *New York Times,* praised the humor in *A Bigamist's Daughter:* "The laughter is wicked but not cruel." And Tyler concluded that the novel "is impressive," adding that at certain moments "McDermott sounds like anything but a first-time novelist. She writes with assurance and skill, and she has created a fascinatingly prismatic story."

A National Book Award finalist, McDermott's second novel, *That Night,* examines love and the loss of innocence through the story of two teenaged lovers and their separation. Set in suburbia during the early 1960s, the novel begins with the story of the night referred to in the title. Rick, one of the neighborhood boys, has been trying to get in touch with his girlfriend, Sheryl, for a number of days, only to be put off by her mother, who will not tell him where she is. His anxiety and rage finally culminate with a visit to Sheryl's house. Accompanied by a bunch of drunk friends, Rick pulls Sheryl's mother from the house, threatening her and demanding to see her daughter. The men in the neighborhood come to her rescue and a battle (in which no one is injured) ensues, with Rick ending up in jail. What Rick does not know is that a few days earlier Sheryl discovered she was pregnant and was whisked away to a cousin's house in a different state. All of this is recalled by a grown woman who was a child of ten during the time of Rick and Sheryl's romance. The incident becomes her initiation (and that of many others in the neighborhood) into the failures of love and the realities and many disappointments of the adult world.

That Night "is concerned not only with . . . [the] loss of innocence but also with the mundane disillusionments that go with adolescence and the rites of growing up," described Michiko Kakutani in the *New York Times.* Bandler maintained that McDermott "has taken as mundane a subject as one can find, a suburban teenage romance and pregnancy, and infused it with the power, the ominousness and the star-crossed romanticism of a contemporary Romeo and Juliet." What separates *That Night* "from the mass of literature that takes on the barely middle-class suburban experience is the almost baroque richness of . . . McDermott's sentences, the intellectual complexity of her moral vision and the explicit emotion of her voice," asserted David Leavitt in the *New York Times Book Review.* Leavitt added, "*That Night* gloriously rejects the notion that this betrayed and bankrupt world can be rendered only in the spare, impersonal prose that has become the standard of so much contemporary fiction, and the result is a slim novel of almost nineteenth-century richness, a novel that celebrates the life of its suburban world at the same moment that it mourns that world's failures and disappointments." Bandler concluded that through her descriptions of "suburban violence" and "loss by separation, McDermott has wrought a miracle, one that is enhanced even more in its telling."

In her 1991 novel *At Weddings and Wakes,* "McDermott's strategy is to use family gatherings to tell the tales of individual family members and the tale of the family as a whole," pointed out Catherine Petroski in *Tribune Books.* The family that McDermott presents is Irish-American and consists of four sisters, only one of whom—Lucy—is married and living with her own family in Long Island. The other three—May, an ex-nun; Agnes, a businesswoman; and Veronica, an introverted alcoholic—still live at home with their stepmother in Brooklyn. The wedding referred to in the title is between May and the mailman Fred, and the wake is also for May, who dies very suddenly just after her wedding. Through her presentation of such a fractured immigrant family, McDermott examines the many tensions that can arise, including the question of how their heritage should be honored. "Many of the Townes' antics are straight out of the prototypical dysfunctional family," observed Petroski. "Its members play their self-destructive and self-limiting roles; they deny the truth and themselves; they are often (usually unwittingly but sometimes not) as cruel to each other as they are tender." Petroski went on to conclude that "it is the actual words of this novel that I will remember—words that bring us a generously imagined, flawlessly realized, extraordinarily complex story of memorable characters whom otherwise we would never have known."

McDermott's fourth novel, *Charming Billy,* was a surprise winner of the 1998 National Book Award. The story is, on the surface, about the life of Billy Lynch, a charming Irish-American who dies from alcoholism at the age of sixty. Yet the novel also probes the whole Irish American culture and what happens to those who break away from it. Running back and forth in time, *Charming Billy* tells of the title character's return from World War II and his romance with a lovely Irish girl. He carefully saves money and sends it to her so that she can join him in America, but she is never heard from again. Billy's cousin tells him that she died of pneumonia, but in fact she simply took the money to open a gas station and marry another man. Brokenhearted, Billy spends the rest of his life mourning his lost love, even though he subsequently marries another woman. At his wake, Billy's friends discuss his life and the tragedy that marred it.

A *Publishers Weekly* reviewer called *Charming Billy* a "poignant and ironic story of a blighted life" and called attention to "dialogue so precise that a word or two conjures a complex relationship." Michiko Kakutani, reviewer for the *New York Times,* stated that "Ms. McDermott's people, unlike so many characters in contemporary American fiction, are defined largely by their relationships to other family members, relationships that are delineated with unusual understanding of how emotional debts and gifts are handed down, generation to generation, and how that legacy creates a sense of continuity and continuance, a hedge against the erasures of time. In *Charming Billy,* Ms. McDermott writes about such matters with wisdom and grace, refusing to sentimentalize her characters, even as she forces us to recognize their decency and goodness. She has written a luminous and affecting novel."

Commonweal writer Rand Richards Cooper pointed out that there is still more to the book than the story of Billy's life or his community. The narrator, though she is a rather ghostly figure, is also a very important one, for she represents the people who have broken free of the claustrophobic Irish-American communities to seek greater freedom and individual identity. In finding these things, Cooper suggested, she has also lost a great deal, for McDermott's book shows that "to shrug off the burdens of group identity is also to shrug off ferocious attachments; and McDermott's novels express doubt about whether, as ties attenuate and the old neighborhood sinks further into the past, anything as vivid and nourishing will take their place. The grand struggle to wrest one's self from the group delivers her protagonists to this deeply American paradox: that getting a life of your own brings a diminished sense of who you are."

In an interview for the *Irish Times* with Jocelyn McClurg, McDermott rejected the idea that her writing shows a preoccupation with death, yet she allowed: "If you're Irish-Catholic—emphasis on Catholic—you're taught to see the world in a certain way, to see life as brief and death as the thing to be prepared for." McClurg commented that "McDermott has developed a style that is completely her own, a multilayered approach to storytelling that effortlessly shifts between points of view, between present and past." McDermott responded: "I don't think our memories work chronologically. . . . Writing fiction is an attempt to make more sense than life makes."

In McDermott's next book, *Child of My Heart,* the author's main character is once again an Irish Catholic, and death—in this case, the death of both pets and humans—remains a seminal part of the story. Nevertheless, the novel is somewhat of a departure from her other books in that it is her first coming-of-age, loss-of-innocence story. "Certainly it's something I challenged myself to do consciously because I hadn't done it before," she told Molly McQuade in a *Booklist* interview. According to McQuade, McDermott called the book "her most heavily plotted fiction, and the most straightforwardly chronological."

The story revolves around the novel's fifteen-year-old narrator, Theresa, a budding Lolita-like beauty whose parents move to the upper-class realm of the Hamptons on Long Island in hopes that she will catch the eye of one of the rich scions and live happily ever after in the lap of luxury. True to at least part of her parents' wishes, Theresa is constantly ogled throughout the book; but the oglers are largely older, married men. When Theresa does decide to succumb and lose her virginity, it's to the advances of a septuagenarian artist already married to a woman much younger than himself. Much of the story focuses on Theresa's other obvious gifts, that is, as a nurturer and caretaker as she spends one summer in the early 1960s babysitting children and pets. In addition, she has invited her cousin Daisy to spend the summer with her. Unknown to anyone at the time, Daisy is dying. To her charges, including Daisy, Theresa is a heaven-sent angel who gives unconditional love to many who will ultimately face tragic loss and sorrow. Much of the novel also revolves around the seemingly mundane day-to-day life of Theresa, such as Theresa changing diapers and visiting the beach. "But McDermott's novel hangs upon that which roils under its surface—disease, adult corruption, the power of art and Theresa's burgeoning sexuality," Tom Deignan pointed out in a review in *America.* In an interview with Dave Weich on Powell's City of Books Web site, McDermott described her novel this way: "The story arises from the voice of a girl who refuses to be reconciled to some simple truths about relationships and how we live and die. The world as Theresa sees it is not acceptable to her. In her own way, she remakes it."

Writing in the *Weekly Standard,* reviewer John Podhoretz said that he had long admired McDermott's novels but concluded, "*Child of My Heart* is a cloying mess." He added, "McDermott tries but fails to infuse the day-to-dayness of ordinary life with mythical beauty." *Chicago Sun-Times* contributor Carolyn See commented that McDermott encounters a problem with her heroine in that she "does not resemble in any way a real adolescent girl." Nevertheless, See remarked, "the quality of the writing, and the exemplary sentiments that that writing expresses, should keep the minds of readers off that persistent problem." Another reviewer, writing in the *Economist,* remarked that McDermott "captures the world of a gorgeous fifteen-year-old girl to an impressive degree," adding that the only thing missing was the "squirm of rebellion" that most teenagers exhibit. Michelle Vellucci, writing in *People,* noted that McDermott "renders with subtlety and restraint an adolescent's blurry view of the adult world. In spare prose she paints deceptively simple pictures and allows the complex truths hidden within to slowly appear."

In her interview with Weich, McDermott remarked that she wrote *Child of My Heart* "very quickly" compared to her usual pace of writing and "without much planning" following the terrorist attacks in the United States on September 11, 2001. She also noted that, when she writes, she doesn't want to just tell a story. "We're bombarded with stories," said McDermott. "Everybody's got a good story. The six o'clock news has a good story just about every night. Oprah has lots of stories. Story is one thing, but that's not what I go to literature for. I go for that line-by-line, felicitous use of language to another end than simply telling me what happened to somebody at some time in their life."

BIOGRAPHICAL AND CRITICAL SOURCES:

BOOKS

Contemporary Literary Criticism, Volume 90, Gale (Detroit), 1996.

PERIODICALS

America, February 17, 2003, Tom Deignan, review of *Child of My Heart*, pp. 26-27.

Booklist, September 1, 2002, Molly McQuade, "Alice McDermott's Five-Finger Exercise," interview with McDermott, p. 56.

Chicago Sun-Times, Carolyn See, review of *Child of My Heart*, p. 17.

Commonweal, March 27, 1998, Rand Richards Cooper, "Charming Alice: A Unique Voice in American Fiction," p. 10; January 31, 2003, Margaret O'Brien Steinfels, review of *Child of My Heart*, pp. 28-29.

Economist (London, England), January 4, 2003, review of *Child of My Heart*, p. 68.

Irish Times, February 27, 1999, Jocelyn McClurg, interview with McDermott.

Newsweek, November 18, 2002, Malcom Jones, review of *Child of My Heart*, p. 80.

New York Times, February 1, 1982, LeAnne Schreiber, review of *A Bigamist's Daughter*, p. 13; March 28, 1987, Michiko Kakutani, review of *That Night*, p. 10; March 24, 1992, Michiko Kakutani, review of *At Weddings and Wakes*, p. C15; January 13, 1998, Michiko Kakutani, "The Ties That Bind and the Regrets That Strangle," p. E9; February 23, 2003, Ramin Ganeshram, "A Long-Ago Island Inspires Her Fiction," p. 16.

New York Times Book Review, February 21, 1982, Anne Tyler, review of *A Bigamist's Daughter*, pp. 1, 28-29; December 5, 1982, review of *A Bigamist's Daughter*, p. 36; April 19, 1987, David Leavitt, review of *That Night*, pp. 1, 29-31; April 12, 1992, Verlyn Klinkenborg, review of *At Weddings and Wakes*, p. 3; January 11, 1998, Alida Becker, review of *Charming Billy*, p. 8.

People, January 20, 2003, Michelle Vellucci, review of *Child of My Heart*, p. 54.

Publishers Weekly, March 30, 1992, Wendy Smith, "Alice McDermott," interview with McDermott, pp. 85-86; October 6, 1997, review of *Charming Billy*, p. 73; November 23, 1998.

Tribune Books (Chicago), April 30, 1987, Michael J. Bandler, "A Spellbinding Tale of Young Romance," p. 3; March 29, 1992, Catherine Petroski, "Life's Vital, Mysterious Family Rites: Alice Mcdermott Tells an Irish-American Story," pp. 1, 4.

Weekly Standard, December 9, 2002, John Podhoretz, review of *Child of My Heart*, pp. 31-33.

ONLINE

NPR: All Things Considered, http://www.npr.org/ (December 17, 2002), interview with Alice McDermott.

PBS, http://www.pbs.org/ (November 25, 2003), interview with Alice McDermott.

Powell's City of Books, http://www.powells.com/ (November 25, 2003), Dave Weich, "Alice McDermott, Child at Heart."*

* * *

MILOSZ, Czeslaw 1911-
(J. Syruc)

PERSONAL: Surname pronounced *Mee*-wosh; born June 30, 1911, in Szetejnie, Lithuania; defected to West, 1951; immigrated to United States, 1960; naturalized U.S. citizen, 1970; son of Aleksander (a civil engineer) and Weronika (Kunat) Milosz; married Janina Dluska, 1943 (died, 1986); married Carol Tigpen, 1992; children: (first marriage) Antoni, Piotr (sons). *Education:* University of Stephan Batory, M. Juris, 1934. *Religion:* Roman Catholic.

ADDRESSES: Office—Department of Slavic Languages and Literatures, University of California, 5416 Dwinelle Hall, Berkeley, CA 94720-0001.

CAREER: Poet, critic, essayist, novelist, and translator. Programmer with Polish National Radio, 1935-39; worked for Polish Resistance during World War II; cultural attache with Polish Embassy in Paris, France, 1946-50; freelance writer in Paris, 1951-60; University of California, Berkeley, visiting lecturer, 1960-61, professor of Slavic languages and literature, 1961-78, professor emeritus, 1978—.

MEMBER: American Association for the Advancement of Slavic Studies, American Academy and Institute of Arts and Letters, PEN.

AWARDS, HONORS: Prix Litteraire Europèen, 1953, for *La Prise du pouvoir;* Marian Kister Literary Award, 1967; Jurzykowski Foundation award for creative work, 1968; Institute for Creative Arts fellow, 1968;

Czeslaw Milosz

Polish PEN award for poetry translation, 1974; Wandycz Award, 1974; Guggenheim fellow, 1976; Litt. D., University of Michigan, 1977; Neustadt International Literary Prize for Literature, 1978; University Citation, University of California, 1978; Zygmunt Hertz literary award, 1979; Nobel Prize for literature, 1980; honorary doctorate, Catholic University, Lublin, 1981; honorary doctorate, Brandeis University, 1983; Bay Area Book Reviewers Association Poetry Prize, 1986, for *The Separate Notebooks;* Robert Kirsch Award for poetry, 1990; National Medal of Arts, 1990; nominee for National Book Critics Circle Award in poetry category, 2001, for *A Treatise on Poetry*; Gold Medal in poetry, California Book Award, 2001, for *New and Collected Poems, 1931-2001.*

WRITINGS:

Zniewolony umysl (essays), Instytut Literacki (Paris, France), 1953, translation by Jane Zielonko published as *The Captive Mind,* Knopf (New York, NY), 1953, reprinted, Octagon (New York, NY), 1981.

Traktat poetycki (title means "Treatise on Poetry"), Instytut Literacki (Paris, France), 1957, translation by Milosz and Robert Hass published as *A Treatise on Poetry,* Ecco Press (New York, NY), 2001.

Rodzinna Europa (essays), Instytut Literacki (Paris, France), 1959, translation by Catherine S. Leach published as *Native Realm: A Search for Self-Definition,* Doubleday (New York, NY), 1968.

Czlowiek wsrod skorpionow: Studium o Stanislawie Brzozowskim (title means "A Man among Scorpions: A Study of Stanislaw Brzozowski"), Instytut Literacki (Paris, France), 1962.

The History of Polish Literature, Macmillan (New York, NY), 1969, revised edition, University of California Press (Berkeley, CA), 1983.

Widzenia nad Zatoka San Francisco, Instytut Literacki (Paris, France), 1969, translation by Richard Lourie published as *Visions from San Francisco Bay,* Farrar, Straus (New York, NY), 1982.

Prywatne obowiazki (essays; title means "Private Obligations"), Instytut Literacki (Paris, France), 1972.

Moj wiek: Pamietnik nowiony (interview with Alexander Wat; title means "My Century: An Oral Diary"), edited by Lidia Ciolkoszowa, two volumes, Polonia Book Fund (London, England), 1977.

Emperor of the Earth: Modes of Eccentric Vision, University of California Press (Berkeley, CA), 1977.

Ziemia Ulro, Instytut Literacki (Paris, France), 1977, translation by Louis Iribarne published as *The Land of Ulro,* Farrar, Straus (New York, NY), 1984.

Ogrod nauk (title means "The Garden of Knowledge"), Instytut Literacki (Paris, France), 1980.

Dziela zbiorowe (title means "Collected Works"), Instytut Literacki (Paris, France), 1980.

Nobel Lecture, Farrar, Straus (New York, NY), 1981.

The Witness of Poetry (lectures), Harvard University Press (Cambridge, MA), 1983.

The Rising of the Sun, Arion Press (San Francisco, CA), 1985.

Unattainable Earth, translation from the Polish manuscript by Milosz and Robert Hass, Ecco Press (New York, NY), 1986.

Beginning with My Streets: Essays and Recollections (essays), translation by Madeline G. Levine, Farrar, Straus (New York, NY), 1992.

A Year of the Hunter, translation by Madeline G. Levine, Farrar, Straus (New York, NY), 1994.

Legendy nowoczesnosci: Eseje okupacyjne, Literackie (Krakow, Poland), 1996.

Szukanie ojczyzny, Znak (Krakow, Poland), 1996.

Traktat moralny: Traktat poetycki (interviews), Literackie (Krakow, Poland), 1996.

Striving toward Being: The Letters of Thomas Merton and Czeslaw Milosz, edited by Robert Faggen, Farrar, Straus (New York, NY), 1997.

Piesek przydroczny, Znak (Krakow, Poland), 1997, translation published as *Roadside Dog,* Farrar, Straus (New York, NY), 1998.

Zycie na wyspach (essays), Znak (Krakow, Poland), 1997.

Dar = Gabe, Literackie (Krakow, Poland), 1998.

Abecadlo Milosza, Literackie (Krakow, Poland), 1997.

Inne abecadlo, Literackie (Krakow, Poland), 1998.

Zaraz po wojnie: Korespondenczja z pisarzami, 1945-1950 (correspondence), Znak (Krakow, Poland), 1998.

Milosz's ABCs (selections from *Inne Abecadlo* and *Abecadlo Milosza*), translation by Madeline G. Levine, Farrar, Straus (New York, NY), 2001.

To Begin Where I Am: Selected Essays, edited by Bogadana Carpenter and Madeline G. Levine, Farrar, Straus (New York, NY), 2001.

POEMS

Poemat o czasie zastyglym (title means "Poem of the Frozen Time"),]Vilnius, Lithuania], 1933.

Trzy zimy (title means "Three Winters"), Union of Polish Writers, 1936.

(Under pseudonym J. Syruc) *Wiersze* (title means "Poems"), [Warsaw, Poland], 1940.

Ocalenie (title means "Salvage"), Czytelnik (Poland), 1945.

Swiatlo dzienne (title means "Daylight"), Instytut Literacki (Paris, France), 1953.

Kontynenty (title means "Continents"), Instytut Literacki (Paris, France), 1958.

Krol Popiel i inne wiersze (title means "King Popiel and Other Poems"), Instytut Literacki (Paris, France), 1962.

Gucio zaczarowany (title means "Bobo's Metamorphosis"), Instytut Literacki (Paris, France), 1965.

Lied vom Weltende (title means "A Song for the End of the World"), Kiepenheuer & Witsch, 1967.

Wiersze (title means "Poems"), Oficyna Poetow i Malarzy (London, England), 1969.

Miasto bez imienia (title means "City without a Name"), Instytut Literacki (Paris, France), 1969.

Selected Poems, Seabury Press (New York, NY), 1973, revised edition, Ecco Press (New York, NY), 1981.

Gdzie wschodzi slonce i kedy zapada (title means "From Where the Sun Rises to Where It Sets"), Instytut Literacki (Paris, France), 1974.

Utwory poetyckie (title means "Selected Poems"), Michigan Slavic Publications (Ann Arbor, MI), 1976.

The Bells in Winter, translation by Milosz and Lillian Vallee, Ecco Press (New York, NY), 1978.

Poezje, Instytut Literacki (Paris, France), 1981.

Traktat moralny, Krajowa Agencja Wydawnicza (Lublin, Poland), 1981.

Lud da sile swojemu poecie, Spoleczny Komitet Budowy Pomnika (Gdansk, Poland), 1981.

Hymn o Perle (title means "Hymn to the Pearl"), Michigan Slavic Publications (Ann Arbor, MI), 1982.

Ksiega psalmw, Katolicki Uniwersytet Lubelski (Lublin, Poland), 1982.

Swiadectwo poezji, Instytut Literacki (Paris, France), 1983.

The Separate Notebooks, translation by Robert Hass and Robert Pinsky, Ecco Press (New York, NY), 1984.

Ksiegi pieciu megilot, Katolicki Uniwersytet Lubelski (Lublin, Poland), 1984.

The Collected Poems, 1931-1987, Ecco Press (New York, NY), 1988.

Nieobjeta ziemia, Wydawn Literackie (Krakow, Poland), 1988.

(Author of text) Josef Koudelka, *Exiles,* Aperture Foundation (New York, NY), 1988.

Kroniki, Znak (Krakow, Poland), 1988.

The World, translation by Milosz, Arion Press, 1989.

Dalsze okolice, Znak (Krakow, Poland), 1991.

Provinces: Poems, 1987-1991, translation by Milosz and Robert Hass, Ecco Press (New York, NY), 1991.

Haiku, Znak (Krakow, Poland), 1992.

Na brzegu rzeki, Znak (Krakow, Poland), 1994.

Facing the River: New Poems, translation by Milosz and Robert Hass, Ecco Press (New York, NY), 1995.

Jakiegoz to goscia mielismy, Znak (Krakow, Poland), 1996.

Swiat: Poema naiwne (based on a 1943 manuscript), Literackie (Krakow, Poland), 1999.

Poezje, Literackie (Krakow, Poland), 1999.

Wyprawa w dwudziestolecie, Literackie (Krakow, Poland), 1999.

Wypisy z ksiag uzytecznych, Znak (Krakow, Poland), 2000.

New and Collected Poems, 1931-2001, Ecco Press (New York, NY), 2001.

Orfeusz i Eurydyka, Literackie (Krakow, Poland), 2002.

NOVELS

La Prise du pouvoir, translation by Jeanne Hersch, Gallimard (Paris, France), 1953, original Polish edition published as *Zdobycie wladzy,* Instytut Literacki (Paris, France), 1955, translation by Celina Wieniewska published as *The Seizure of Power,* Criterion (New York, NY), 1955, translation published as *The Usurpers,* Faber (London, England), 1955.

Dolina Issy, Instytut Literacki (Paris, France), 1955, translation by Louis Iribarne published as *The Issa Valley,* Farrar, Straus (New York, NY), 1981.

EDITOR

(With Zbigniew Folejewski) *Antologia poezji spolecznej* (title means "Anthology of Social Poetry"), [Vilnius], 1933.

Piesn niepodlegla (Resistance poetry; title means "Invincible Song"), Oficyna, 1942, Michigan Slavic Publications (Ann Arbor, MI), 1981.

Lettres inedites de O. V. de L. Milosz a Christian Gauss (correspondence), Silvaire, 1976.

(With Drenka Willen) *A Book of Luminous Things: An International Anthology of Poetry,* Harcourt (San Diego, CA), 1996.

TRANSLATOR

(And editor) Jacques Maritain, *Drogami Kleski,* [Warsaw, Poland], 1942.

(And editor) Daniel Bell, *Praca i jej gorycze* (title means "Work and Its Discontents"), Instytut Literacki (Paris, France), 1957.

(And editor) Simone Weil, *Wybor pism* (title means "Selected Works"), Instytut Literacki (Paris, France), 1958.

(And editor) *Kultura masowa* (title means "Mass Culture"), Instytut Literacki (Paris, France), 1959.

(And editor) *Wegry* (title means "Hungary"), Instytut Literacki (Paris, France), 1960.

(And editor) *Postwar Polish Poetry: An Anthology,* Doubleday (New York, NY), 1965, revised edition, University of California Press (Berkeley, CA), 1983.

(With Peter Dale Scott) Zbigniew Herbert, *Selected Poems,* Penguin (New York, NY), 1968.

Alexander Wat, *Mediterranean Poems,* Ardi, 1977.

Ewangelia wedlug sw. Marka (title means "The Gospel according to St. Mark"), Znak (Krakow, Poland), 1978.

Ksiega Hioba (title means "The Book of Job"), Dialogue (Paris, France), 1980.

Anna Swir, *Happy As a Dog's Tail,* Harcourt (San Diego, CA), 1985.

(With Leonard Nathan) Aleksander Wat, *With the Skin: Poems of Aleksander Wat,* Ecco Press (New York, NY), 1989.

Founder and editor, *Zagary* (literary periodical), 1931.

SIDELIGHTS: Czeslaw Milosz ranks among the most respected figures in twentieth-century Polish literature, as well as one of the most respected contemporary poets in the world, being awarded the Nobel Prize for literature in 1980. He was born in Lithuania, where his parents moved temporarily to escape the political upheaval in their native Poland. As an adult, he left Poland due to the oppressive Communist regime that came to power following World War II and has lived in the United States since 1960. Milosz's poems, novels, essays, and other works are written in his native Polish and translated by the author and others into English. Having lived under the two great totalitarian systems of modern history, national socialism and communism, Milosz writes of the past in a tragic, ironic style that nonetheless affirms the value of human life. While the faith of his Roman Catholic upbringing has been severely tested, it has remained intact. Terrence Des Pres, writing in the *Nation,* stated that "political catastrophe has defined the nature of our . . . [age], and the result—the collision of personal and public realms—has produced a new kind of writer. Czeslaw Milosz is the perfect example. In exile from a world which no longer exists, a witness to the Nazi devastation of Poland and the Soviet takeover of Eastern Europe, Milosz deals in his poetry with the central issues of our time: the impact of history upon moral being, the search for ways to survive spiritual ruin in a ruined world."

Born in Lithuania in 1911, Milosz spent much of his childhood in Czarist Russia, where his father worked as a civil engineer. After World War I the family returned to their hometown, which had become a part of the new Polish state, and Milosz attended local Catholic schools. He published his first collection of poems, *Poemat o czasie zastyglym* ("Poem of the Frozen Time"), at the age of twenty-one. Milosz was associated with the catastrophist school of poets during the 1930s. Catastrophism concerns "the inevitable annihilation of the highest values, especially the values essential to a given cultural system. . . . But it proclaims . . . only the annihilation of certain values, not values in general, and the destruction of a certain historical formation, but not of all mankind," Aleksander Fiut explained in *World Literature Today.* The writings of this group of poets ominously foreshadowed World War II.

When the war began in 1939, and Poland was invaded by Nazi Germany and Soviet Russia, Milosz worked with the underground Resistance movement in Warsaw, writing and editing several books published clandestinely during the occupation. One of these books, a collection titled *Wiersze* ("Poems"), was published under the pseudonym J. Syruc. Following the war, Milosz became a member of the new communist government's diplomatic service and was stationed in Paris, France, as a cultural attache. In 1951, he left this post and defected to the West.

The Captive Mind explains Milosz's reasons for defecting and examines the life of the artist under a communist regime. It is, maintained Steve Wasserman in the *Los Angeles Times Book Review,* a "brilliant and original study of the totalitarian mentality." Karl Jaspers, in an article for the *Saturday Review,* described *The Captive Mind* as "a significant historical document and analysis of the highest order. . . . In astonishing gradations Milosz shows what happens to men subjected simultaneously to constant threat of annihilation and to the promptings of faith in a historical necessity which exerts apparently irresistible force and achieves enormous success. We are presented with a vivid picture of the forms of concealment, of inner transformation, of the sudden bolt to conversion, of the cleavage of man into two."

Milosz's defection came about when he was recalled to Poland from his position at the Polish embassy. He refused to leave. Joseph McLellan of the *Washington Post* quoted Milosz explaining: "I knew perfectly well that my country was becoming the province of an empire." In a speech before the Congress for Cultural Freedom, quoted by James Atlas of the *New York Times,* Milosz declared: "I have rejected the new faith because the practice of the lie is one of its principal commandments and socialist realism is nothing more than a different name for a lie." After his defection Milosz lived in Paris, where he worked as a translator and freelance writer. In 1960 he was offered a teaching position at the University of California at Berkeley, which he accepted. He became an American citizen in 1970.

In *The Seizure of Power,* first published in France as *La Prise du pouvoir* in 1953, Milosz renders as fiction much of the same material found in *The Captive Mind.* The book is an autobiographical novel that begins with the Russian occupation of Warsaw at the close of World War II. As the Russian army approached the Nazi-held city, the Polish Resistance rose against the German occupation troops, having been assured that the Russians would join their fight once the uprising began. But instead, the Russians stood by a few miles outside of the city, allowing the Nazis to crush the revolt unhindered. When the uprising was over, the Russians occupied Warsaw and installed a communist regime. The novel ends with the disillusioned protagonist, a political education officer for the communists, immigrating to the West.

The Seizure of Power "is a novel on how to live when power changes hands," Andrew Sinclair explained in the London *Times.* Granville Hicks, in an article for the *New York Times Book Review,* saw a similarity between *The Captive Mind* and *The Seizure of Power.* In both books, "Milosz appeals to the West to try to understand the people of Eastern Europe," maintained Hicks. Told in a series of disjointed scenes meant to suggest the chaos and violence of postwar Poland, *The Seizure of Power* is "a novel of ineffable sadness, and a muffled sob for Poland's fate," wrote Wasserman. Michael Harrington, in a review for *Commonweal,* called *The Seizure of Power* "a sensitive, probing work, far better than most political novels, of somewhat imperfect realization but of significant intention and worth."

After living in the United States for a time, Milosz began to write of his new home. In *Native Realm: A Search for Self-Definition* and *Visions from San*

Francisco Bay, Milosz compares and contrasts the West with his native Poland. *Native Realm,* Richard Holmes wrote in the London *Times,* is "a political and social autobiography, shorn of polemic intent, deeply self-questioning, and dominated by the sense that neither historically nor metaphysically are most Westerners in a position to grasp the true nature of the East European experience since the First War." A series of personal essays examining events in Milosz's life, *Native Realm* provides "a set of commentaries upon his improbable career," as Michael Irwin maintained in the *Times Literary Supplement.* Milosz "has written a self-effacing remembrance composed of shards from a shattered life," observed Wasserman. "He tells his story with the humility of a man who has experienced tragedy and who believes in fate and in destiny. It is a work that reflects the stubborn optimism of his heart, even as it dwells on the pessimism of his intellect." Irving Howe, writing in the *New York Times Book Review,* found *Native Realm* "beautifully written." Milosz, Howe continued, "tries to find in the chaos of his life some glimmers of meaning."

In *Visions from San Francisco Bay* Milosz examines his life in contemporary California, a place far removed in distance and temperament from the scenes of his earlier life. His observations are often sardonic, and yet he is also content with his new home. Milosz "sounds like a man who has climbed up, hand over hand, right out of history, and who is both amazed and grateful to find that he can breathe the ahistorical atmosphere of California," Anatole Broyard stated in the *New York Times.* The opening words of the book are "I am here," and from that starting point Milosz describes the society around him. "The intention," noted Julian Symons in the *Times Literary Supplement,* "is to understand himself, to understand the United States, to communicate something singular to Czeslaw Milosz." Broyard takes this idea even further, arguing that Milosz "expresses surprise at 'being here,' taking this phrase in its ordinary sense of being in America and in its other, Heideggerian sense of being-in-the-world."

Although Milosz's comments about life in California are "curiously oblique, deeply shadowed by European experience, allusive, sometimes arch and frequently disillusioned," as Holmes pointed out, he ultimately embraces his adopted home. "Underlying all his meditations," commented Leon Edel in the *New York Times Book Review,* "is his constant 'amazement' that America should exist in this world—and his gratitude that it does exist." "He is fascinated," explained Symons, "by the contradictions of a society with enormous economic power, derived in part from literally nonhuman technical achievement, which also contains a large group that continually and passionately indicts the society by which it is maintained." Milosz, P. J. Kavanagh remarked in the *Spectator,* looks at his adopted country with "a kind of detached glee—at awfulness; an ungloomy recognition that we cannot go on as we are—in any direction. He holds up a mirror and shows us ourselves, without blame and with no suggestions either, and in the mirror he himself is also reflected." Edel believed that Milosz's visions "have authority: the authority of an individual who reminds us that only someone like himself who has known tyranny . . . can truly prize democracy."

The story of Milosz's odyssey from East to West is also recounted in his poetry. Milosz's "entire effort," Jonathan Galassi explained in the *New York Times Book Review,* "is directed toward a confrontation with experience—and not with personal experience alone, but with history in all its paradoxical horror and wonder." Speaking of his poetry in the essay collection *The Witness of Poetry,* Milosz stresses the importance of his nation's cultural heritage and history in shaping his work. "My corner of Europe," he states, "owing to the extraordinary and lethal events that have been occurring there, comparable only to violent earthquakes, affords a peculiar perspective. As a result, all of us who come from those parts appraise poetry slightly differently than do the majority of my audience, for we tend to view it as a witness and participant in one of mankind's major transformations." "For Milosz," Helen Vendler explained in the *New Yorker,* "the person is irrevocably a person in history, and the interchange between external event and the individual life is the matrix of poetry." Writing in *TriQuarterly,* Reginald Gibbons stated that Milosz "seems to wonder how good work can be written, no matter how private its subject matter, without the poet having been aware of the pain and threat of the human predicament."

Milosz sees a fundamental difference in the role of poetry in the capitalist West and the communist East. Western poetry, as Alfred Kazin wrote in the *New York Times Book Review,* is "'alienated' poetry, full of introspective anxiety." But because of the dictatorial nature of communist government, poets in the East cannot afford to be preoccupied with themselves. They are drawn to write of the larger problems of their society. "A peculiar fusion of the individual and the historical took place," Milosz wrote in *The Witness of Poetry,* "which means that events burdening a whole community are perceived by a poet as touching him in a most personal manner. Then poetry is no longer alienated."

For many years Milosz's poetry was little noticed in the United States, though he was highly regarded in Poland. Recognition in Poland came in defiance of official government resistance to Milosz's work. The communist regime refused to publish the books of a defector; for many years only underground editions of his poems were secretly printed and circulated in Poland. But in 1980, when Milosz was awarded the Nobel Prize for Literature, the communist government was forced to relent. A government-authorized edition of Milosz's poems was issued and sold a phenomenal 200,000 copies. One sign of Milosz's widespread popularity in Poland occurred when Polish workers in Gdansk unveiled a monument to their comrades who were shot down by the communist police. Two quotations were inscribed on the monument: one was taken from the Bible; the other was taken from a poem by Milosz.

The Nobel Prize also brought Milosz to the attention of a wider audience in the United States. After 1980 several of his earlier works were translated into English, while his new books received widespread critical attention. The poet's image also graced a postage stamp in Poland. Some of this public attention focused less on Milosz's work as poetry than "as the work of a thinker and political figure; the poems tend to be considered en masse, in relation either to the condition of Poland, or to the suppression of dissident literature under Communist rule, or to the larger topic of European intellectual history," as Vendler maintained. But most reviewers have commented on Milosz's ability to speak in a personal voice that carries with it the echoes of his people's history. Zweig explained that Milosz "offers a modest voice, speaking an old language. But this language contains the resources of centuries. Speaking it, one speaks with a voice more than personal. . . . Milosz's power lies in his ability to speak with this larger voice without diminishing the urgency that drives his words."

Because he lived through some of the great upheavals of twentieth-century Eastern Europe, and because his poetry fuses his own experiences with the larger events in his society, many of Milosz's poems concern loss, destruction, and despair. "There is a very dark vision of the world in my work," he told Lynn Darling of the *Washington Post.* And yet the writer went on to describe himself as "a great partisan of human hope" due to his religious convictions.

Milosz believes that one of the major problems of contemporary society—in both the East and the West—is its lack of a moral foundation. Writing in *The Land of Ulro,* he finds that modern man has only "the starry sky above, and no moral law within." Speaking to Judy Stone of the *New York Times Book Review,* Milosz stated: "I am searching for an answer as to what will result from an internal erosion of religious beliefs." Michiko Kakutani, reviewing *The Land of Ulro* for the *New York Times,* found that "Milosz is eloquent in his call for a literature grounded in moral, as well as esthetic, values. Indeed, when compared with his own poetry, the work of many Westerners—from the neurotic rantings of the Romantics to the cerebral mind games of the avant-gardists—seems unserious and self-indulgent."

Because of his moral vision Milosz's writings make strong statements, some of which are inherently political in their implications. "The act of writing a poem is an act of faith," Milosz claimed in *The History of Polish Literature,* "yet if the screams of the tortured are audible in the poet's room, is not his activity an offense to human suffering?" His awareness of suffering, wrote Joseph C. Thackery in the *Hollins Critic,* makes Milosz a "spokesman of the millions of dead of the Holocaust, the Gulags, the Polish and Czech uprisings, and the added millions of those who will go on dying in an imperfect world."

Milosz also warns of the dangers of political writing. In a PEN Congress talk reprinted in the *Partisan Review,* he stated: "In this century a basic stance of writers . . . seems to be an acute awareness of suffering inflicted upon human beings by unjust structures of society. . . . This awareness of suffering makes a writer open to the idea of radical change, whichever of many recipes he chooses. . . . Innumerable millions of human beings were killed in this century in the name of utopia—either progressive or reactionary, and always there were writers who provided convincing justifications for massacre."

In *The Witness of Poetry* Milosz argues that true poetry is "the passionate pursuit of the Real." He condemns those writers who favor art for art's sake or who think of themselves as alienated, and suggests, as Adam Gussow wrote in the *Saturday Review,* that poets may have "grown afraid of reality, afraid to see it clearly and speak about it in words we can all comprehend." What is needed in "today's unsettled world," Gussow explained, are poets who, "like Homer, Dante, and Shakespeare, will speak for rather than against the enduring values of their communities."

This concern for a poetry that confronts reality was noted by Thackery, who saw Milosz searching "for a poetry that will be at once harsh and mollifying, that will enable men to understand, if not to rationalize, the debasement of the human spirit by warfare and psychic dismemberment, while simultaneously establishing a personal *modus vivendi* and a psychology of aesthetic necessity." Des Pres also noted this unifying quality in Milosz's poetry, a trait he believed Milosz shares with T. S. Eliot. "The aim of both Milosz and Eliot," Des Pres stated, "is identical: to go back and work through the detritus of one's own time on earth, to gather up the worst along with the best, integrate past and present into a culminating moment which transcends both, which embraces pain and joy together, the whole of a life and a world redeemed through memory and art, a final restoration in spirit of that which in historical fact has been forever lost." Vendler wrote that "the work of Milosz reminds us of the great power that poetry gains from bearing within itself an unforced, natural, and long-ranging memory of past customs; a sense of the strata of ancient and modern history; wide visual experience; and a knowledge of many languages and literatures. . . . The living and tormented revoicing of the past makes Milosz a historical poet of bleak illumination."

With the publication in 1986 of *Unattainable Earth,* Milosz continued to show himself as a poet of memory and a poet of witness, for, in the prose footnote to "Poet at Seventy," he wrote of his continued "unnamed need for order, for rhythm, for form, which three words are opposed to chaos and nothingness." *Unattainable Earth* uses what Stanislaw Baranczak in *Threepenny Review* called, a "peculiar structure of a modern *silva rerum*" which "consists in including a number of prose fragments, notes, letters, verses of other poets." The book was the first of several lauded collaborative translations between the author and American poet Robert Hass.

A year later, *The Collected Poems, 1931-1987* was published, bringing together *Selected Poems, Bells in Winter, The Separate Notebooks,* and *Unattainable Earth* into one volume. The book contains 180 poems ranging in size from two lines to sixty pages. Forty-five poems appear for the first time in English, of which twenty-six are recently translated older poems and twenty are new poems. Warren W. Werner in *Southern Humanities Review* called the work "a big, varied, and important book . . . a feast of poetry." P. J. M. Robertson in *Queen's Quarterly* lauded the collection as "a gift to cherish, for it contains the song of a man . . . passionately affirming the daily miracle of life and its continuity even now on our battered earth." The critic affirmed that *The Collected Poems* "reveal Milosz's answer to the question of the role of poetry and of art in the twentieth century. . . . a responsibility to see and express beauty: that is, the truth about life in its miraculous complexity." *New York Times Book Review* contributor Edward Hirsch found the volume "one of the monumental splendors of poetry in our age." Baranczak believed that it is a book that can "finally give the English-speaking reader a fairly accurate idea of what [Milosz's] poetry really is, both in the sense of the largeness of its thematic and stylistic range and the uniqueness of his more than half-century-long creative evolution." Don Bogan of the *Nation* stated that "with its clarity, historical awareness and moral vision, *The Collected Poems* is among the best guides we have" to help remind us that "poetry can define and address the concerns of an age."

Milosz followed in 1991 with *Provinces: Poems, 1987-1991.* For Milosz, the life in each individual seems made up of provinces, and one new province which he must now visit is the province of old age. He explores getting older in the thirteen-part sequence titled, 'A New Province,' reporting that "not much is known about that country/ Till we land there ourselves, with no right to return." Hirsch found that these poems about old age have "a penetrating honesty" derived from "a powerful dialectical tension, a metaphysical dispute at work . . . about the conflicting claims of immanence and transcendence, the temporal and the eternal." Ben Howard, in *Poetry,* commented on the inclusion of Milosz's "abiding subjects—the loss of his native Lithuania, the suffering of Eastern Europe, the wrenching upheavals of a long and difficult life," and suggested that the poet through his verse is "asserting his affinity with the common people and his closeness to the soil." *New York Review of Books* contributor Helen Vendler called *Provinces* a collection of "many of Milosz's central themes—including the strangeness of human life (where in the blink of an eye absurdity can turn to bravery, or tranquillity to war), exile, sensuality, memory, Platonic idealism, and iron disbelief." Bill Marx in *Parnassus* described *Provinces* as "an inner landscape of clashing contraries and times. Valleys of sensuous admiration for the earth's delights are broken up by notched peaks of traumatic memory; deserts formed by perceptions of nature's indifference are dotted with oases rooted in intimations of the transcendent."

Beginning with My Streets: Essays and Recollections, published in 1992, is a collection of essays, philosophical meditations, literary criticism, portraits of friends and writers, and a genre that *Observer* reviewer Sally Laird identified as "'chatty narratives' in the Polish tradition." Donald Davie in the *New Republic* deemed the book "more a medley than a collection, with a deceptive air of being 'thrown together,'" made up, as Vendler pointed out, of essays in which Milosz "moves with entire naturalness from Swedenborg to Robinson Jeffers, from Lithuanian scenery to Meister Eckhart, from the Seven Deadly Sins to Polish Marxism." Laird praised in particular the essay "Saligia," in which Milosz takes on two multiple perspectives, that of poet and of engaged historian. The book contains accounts of the poet's childhood in Vilnius and closes with his 1980 Nobel lecture. *Washington Post Book World* contributor Alberto Manguel concluded, "Milosz excels in recounting, in finding the happy phrase for a scene or a concept. The invention of the past, the elusiveness of reality, the fluidity of time, the apparent banality or apparent importance of philosophical inquiries are traditional (some would say intrinsic) poetic fodder, and Milosz arranges the questions on the page with economy and elegance."

A Year of the Hunter, published in 1994, is a journal Milosz penned between August of 1987 and August of 1988. John Simon in the *Washington Post Book World* pointed out that these entries were "written on airplanes zooming to lecture engagements, poetry readings, literary congresses and the like." Ian Buruma praised the work in the *Los Angeles Times Book Review* as "a wonderful addition to [Milosz's] other autobiographical writing. The diary form, free-floating, wide-ranging . . . is suited to a poet, especially an intellectual poet, like Milosz," allowing for his entries to range from gardening to translating, from communism to Christianity, from past to present. Indeed, as Michael Ignatieff stated in the *New York Review of Books, A Year of the Hunter* is successful "because Milosz has not cleaned it up too much. Its randomness is a pleasure."

In 1995 Milosz produced the poetry collection *Facing the River: New Poems.* This volume includes verse that deals largely with Milosz's return to Vilnius, the city of his childhood, now the capital of the free republic of Lithuania. In returning, Ignatieff pointed out, Milosz found himself in an ironic circumstance: "Having been a poet of exile, he had now become the poet of the impossible return of the past." The poet recognized many streets, buildings, and steeples in his homeland, but the people from his past were gone. This left Milosz to "bring the absent dead back to life, one by one, in all their aching singularity," as Ignatieff stated. *Facing the River* is not just about Milosz's return to Lithuania and the people that he misses; it also addresses the poet's accomplishments and his views on life. In "At a Certain Age," Milosz declares that old men, who see themselves as handsome and noble, will find: "later in our place an ugly toad/ Half-opens its thick eyelid/ And one sees clearly: 'That's me.'" *Facing the River,* which ends with Milosz wondering, "If only my work were of use to people," left Ignatieff speaking for many readers of Milosz when he wrote: "Those like myself who see the world differently because of him hope he will continue to stand facing the river, and tell us what he sees."

In 1999, at age eighty-eight, Milosz published *Roadside Dog,* a collection "that at first encounter seems an invitation to revisit the remembered landscapes of his life," as Jaroslaw Anders noted in the *New Republic.* In "maxims, anecdotes, meditations, crumbs of worldly wisdom, introspections . . . [and] poems," Milosz takes readers on a trip through the sounds and images that have shaped his life as a poet. "Some of these morsels are perfectly finished," Anders found, "others appear sketchy, tentative, even commonplace: assertions in search of proof, thoughts that should become essays, plot lines that need to be tested in a novel. Is this the writer's scrap-book offered generously—but also a little self-indulgently—to his readers, the literary equivalent of a rummage sale?"

David S. Gross saw *Roadside Dog* differently. In his essay, part of a 1999 salute to Milosz published in *World Literature Today,* Gross admitted that it is "hard to say what these little pieces are. Prose poems, I suppose, after Baudelaire and others." Still, the work as a whole "constantly reexamines questions of politics, religion, the nature of poetry, issues of consciousness and meaning, and more, always toward the end of understanding, even reinventing, the self, in order to understand and reinvent the world." Again and again in *Roadside Dog,* said Gross, the poet "tries to get at that which links him with the suffering and the excluded, even though he has not for years had to suffer the same consequences."

Milosz remained active even as he advanced into his nineties. In 2001 he published *Milosz's ABCs,* a brief, alphabetical collection of entries illustrating his experiences and view on life. This may seem an odd approach to a life, but David Kipen stated in the *San Francisco Chronicle* that "in Milosz's hands it illuminates much of twentieth century literature and history and the muddled, tragic no-man's land where they've overlapped." Included are entries on old friends long dead, political movements, historical events, and spiritual matters. The book "derives its coherence from the Nobel Prize-winner's longstanding philosophical preoccupations: the impermanence of life in the face of 'the waters of oblivion,' and the paradox of Christian faith in the context of mass-scale human suffering," mused Kristen Case in the *New Leader.* Case added: "Parallel to the stream of personal recollections, crosscurrents of literary and philosophical thought gradually converge into something like a philosophical system: an understanding of life as a struggle between being and nothingness, creation and destruction. Many of the most compelling entries are those with abstract titles: 'Time,' 'Terror,' 'Curiosity.' Here Milosz grants himself some freedom from the minutiae of memory and engages the intellectual history of his nine decades." Reviewing the book for *Commonweal,* Harold Isbell called it "a remarkable testament to the place of memory in the definition of a conscious self. . . . In this book, the events of history become experience and, finally, art as Milosz turns the memory of experience back to elucidate the event." And John Kennedy recommended in *Antioch Review,* "This is a true 'companion' book; keep it close, for it is as much a gift of luminous moments as poems and parables are." Kennedy valued the book not only for its own sake, but also as a means of understanding its author: "If you want to know the man, if you want to know about the malleability of world consciousness, you must read this book. Milosz's pieces travel the geographies of emotions and tastes. It appears that nothing escapes him: not politics, partisanship, original sin, ethnicity, fear, love, or much else."

Also that year, Milosz published a translation of a work first published in 1957 in his native language: *A Treatise on Poetry.* This lengthy poetic work has four parts which ponder Europe at the turn of the twentieth century, Poland between the two world wars that devastated it, World War II, and the proper place of the poet in the world after the horror of World War II. It also serves as an historical survey of Polish poetry throughout those periods. It is a work that is "gripping, profound and beautiful," according to a writer for the *Economist.* Translated nearly fifty years after it was written, *A Treatise on Poetry* found an audience among a new generation of readers. Nicholas Wroe quoted Milosz in the *Guardian* as commenting: "It has been a great pleasure to see my poem apparently not getting old. . . . It is really a history of Polish poetry in the twentieth century, in connection to history and the problems of so-called historical necessity. And I am proud of having written a poem that deals with historical, political and aesthetic issues even though, of course, I know that for students, the parts of the poem where I deal with Hegelian philosophy and Marxism are, for them, completely exotic. They have such short memories." The year 2001 also saw the publication of another major collection of Milosz's poems, *New and Collected Poems, 1931-2001,* which inspired a *Publishers Weekly* reviewer to predict: "There are few superlatives left for Milosz's work, but this enormous volume, with its portentous valedictory feel, will have reviewers firing up their thesauri nationwide."

Milosz also published a collection of essays in 2001, titled *To Begin Where I Am: Selected Essays.* The subject matter is as varied as the poet's life experiences, and the essays stand as "testaments to a great philosophical mind and astonishing essayist"; they are written with "integrity, humility, and a vast knowledge of the major events and philosophies of Western civilization," advised John Kennedy in the *Antioch Review.* "The truths he extracts are particular, excavated out of the universal human struggles of various political and literary friends." In fact, the essays also form a kind of autobiography, beginning with an account of the poet's life on his grandparents' farm in Lithuania and proceeding on through the tumultuous decades that followed. *America* reviewer John Breslin commended the collection as well, singling out in particular the essay "If Only This Could Be Said," which offers his "fullest and most personal treatment of religion, an indispensable part of the human in his view." Milosz has frequently been pointed out as rather unusual in that he maintained his Catholic faith even through the horrors of two World Wars; many intellectuals who survived that time subsequently suffered crises of faith from which they never recovered. Wroe quoted him as explaining, however, that while he is a Catholic, he will not identify himself as a "Catholic writer," because "if you are branded as a Catholic, you are supposed to testify with every work of yours to following the line of the Church, which is not necessarily my case." Breslin concluded that Milosz's highly individual voice, with its call to faith and hope in the face of darkness, is one "we need to hear in our new and already deeply troubled century."

"Milosz's work is something so extraordinary in our epoch, that it seems to be a phenomenon that he has appeared on the surface of contemporary art from the mysterious depths of reality," declared Krzysztof Dybciak in *World Literature Today.* "At a time when voices of doubt, deadness, and despair are the loudest; when writers are outstripping each other in negation of man, his culture, and nature; when the predominant action is destruction . . . , the world built by the author of 'Daylight' creates a space in which one can breathe freely, where one can find rescue. It renders the world of surfaces transparent and condenses being. It does not promise any final solutions to the unleashed elements of nature and history here on earth, but it enlarges the space in which one can await the Coming with hope. Milosz does not believe in the omnipotence of man, and he has been deprived of the optimistic faith in the self-sufficiency of a world known only through empirical experience. He leads the reader to a place where one can see—to paraphrase the poet's own formula regarding time—Being raised above being through Being."

BIOGRAPHICAL AND CRITICAL SOURCES:

BOOKS

Contemporary Literary Criticism, Gale (Detroit, MI), Volume 5, 1976, Volume 11, 1979, Volume 22, 1982, Volume 31, 1985, Volume 56, 1989, Volume 82, 1994.

Czarnecka, Ewa, and Alexander Fiut, *Conversations with Czeslaw Milosz,* translation by Richard Lourie, Harcourt (San Diego, CA), 1988.

Czarnecka, Ewa, *Prdrozny swiata: Rosmowy z Czeslawem Miloszem, Komentane,* Bicentennial, 1983.

Czerni, Irena, *Czeslaw Milosz laureat literackiej nagrody Nobla 1980: Katalog wystawy,* Nakl. Uniwersytety Jagiellonskiego (Krakow, Poland), 1993.

Dictionary of Literary Biography, Volume 215: *Twentieth-Century Eastern European Writers, First Series,* Gale (Detroit, MI), 1999.

Dompkowski, Judith Ann, *Down a Spiral Staircase, Never-ending: Motion As Design in the Writing of Czeslaw Milosz,* P. Lang (New York, NY), 1990.

Dudek, Jolanta, *Gdzie wschodzi slonce i kedy zapada—europejskie korzenie poezji Czeslaw Milosza,* Nakl. Univwersytetu Jagiellonskiego, 1991.

Encyclopedia of World Biography, Gale (Detroit, MI), 1998.

European Writers, Scribner (New York, NY), 1990.

Fiut, Aleksander, *Rozmowy z Czeslawem Miloszem,* Wydawnictwo Literackie (Krakow, Poland), 1981.

Fiut, Aleksander, *The Eternal Moment: The Poetry of Czeslaw Milosz,* University of California Press (Berkeley, CA), 1990.

Gillon, A., and L. Krzyzanowski, editors, *Introduction to Modern Polish Literature,* Twayne (Boston, MA), 1964.

Goemoeri, G., *Polish and Hungarian Poetry, 1945 to 1956,* Oxford University Press (New York, NY), 1966.

Hass, Robert, *Twentieth-Century Pleasures: Prose on Poetry,* Ecco Press (New York, NY), 1984.

Malinowska, Barbara, *Dynamics of Being, Space, and Time in the Poetry of Czeslaw Milosz and John Ashbery,* P. Lang (New York, NY), 1997.

Milosz, Czeslaw, *The Captive Mind,* Knopf (New York, NY), 1953.

Milosz, Czeslaw, *The History of Polish Literature,* Macmillan (London, England), 1969, revised edition, University of California Press (Berkeley, CA), 1983.

Milosz, Czeslaw, *The Witness of Poetry,* Harvard University Press (Cambridge, MA), 1983.

Milosz, Czeslaw, *The Land of Ulro,* Farrar, Straus (New York, NY), 1984.

Mozejko, Edward, *Between Anxiety and Hope: The Poetry and Writing of Czeslaw Milosz,* University of Alberta Press (Edmonton, Alberta, Canada), 1988.

Nathan, Leonard, and Arthur Quinn, *The Poet's Work: An Introduction to Czeslaw Milosz,* Harvard University Press (Cambridge, MA), 1992.

Nilsson, Nils Ake, editor, *Czeslaw Milosz: A Stockholm Conference, September 9-11, 1991,* Kungl. Vitterhets (Stockholm, Sweden), 1992.

Volynska-Bogert, Rimma, and Wojciech Zaleswski, *Czeslaw Milosz: An International Bibliography 1930-80,* University of Michigan Press (Ann Arbor, MI), 1983.

PERIODICALS

America, December 18, 1982; December 15, 1984, p. 409; May 12, 1990, pp. 472-475; February 1, 1997, Robert Coles, "Secular Days, Sacred Moments," p. 6; January 21, 2002, John Breslin, review of *To Begin Where I Am: Selected Essays,* p. 25.

American Book Review, March, 1985, p. 22.

American Poetry Review, January, 1977.

American Scholar, winter, 2002, Minna Proctor, review of *To Begin Where I Am: Selected Essays,* p. 154.

Antioch Review, summer, 2002, John Kennedy, review of *To Begin Where I Am,* p. 529; winter, 2002, John Kennedy, review of *Milosz's ABCs,* p. 164.

Atlanta Journal-Constitution, April 2, 1989, p. N11; April 12, 1992, p. N11; April 23, 1995, p. M13; April 25, 1995, p. B7; April 26, 1995, p. D1.

Book, November-December, 2001, Stephen Whited, review of *Milosz's ABCs,* p. 64.

Booklist, April 15, 1988, p. 1387; November 1, 1991, p. 497; January 1, 1992, p. 806; March 1, 1992, p. 1191; November 1, 1998, Ray Olson, review of *Roadside Dog,* p. 465; December 15, 2000, Ray Olson, review of *Milosz's ABCs,* p. 780; October 15, 2001, Donna Seaman, review of *To Begin Where I Am,* p. 374.

Book Report, November 1988, p. 39.

Books Abroad, winter, 1969; spring, 1970; winter, 1973; winter, 1975.

Book Week, May 9, 1965.

Book World, September 29, 1968.

Boston Globe, October 16, 1987, p. 91; August 28, 1994, p. 62.

Canadian Literature, spring, 1989, pp. 183-184.

Chicago Tribune, October 10, 1980; September 6, 1987, p. 6; December 4, 1989, p. 2; March 15, 1992, p. 6; December 18, 1994, p. 5.

Christian Century, December 4, 2002, review of *New and Collected Poems, 1931-2001,* p. 31.

Christian Science Monitor, July 2, 1986, p. 21; October 5, 1990, p. 10; January 17, 1992, p. 14.

Commonweal, July 8, 1955; March 22, 1985, p. 190; November 6, 1992, p. 33-34; February 23, 2001, Harold Isbell, review of *Milosz's ABCs,* p. 20.

Denver Quarterly, summer, 1976.

Eastern European Poetry, April, 1967.

Economist, January 26, 2002, review of *A Treatise on Poetry.*

English Journal, January, 1992, p. 16.

Globe and Mail (Toronto, Ontario, Canada), March 16, 1985.

Guardian Weekly, October 2, 1988, p. 28; November 10, 2001, Nicholas Wroe, "A Century's Witness: Czeslaw Milosz," p. 6.

Harper's Weekly, April, 2002, Helen Vendler, review of *New and Collected Poems, 1931-2001,* p. 72.

Hollins Critic, April, 1982.

Hudson Review, autumn, 1992, p. 509.

Ironwood, number 18, 1981.

Journal of Religion, January, 1987, pp. 141-142.

Library Journal, November 15, 1984, p. 2114; April 15, 1986, p. 84; April 15, 1988, p. 83; January, 1989, p. 45; October 15, 1991, p. 80; September 15, 2001, Gene Shaw, review of *To Begin Where I Am,* p. 80; January, 2002, review of *To Begin Where I Am,* p. 50.

Los Angeles Times, January 14, 1987; September 13, 1987, p. 14.

Los Angeles Times Book Review, May 10, 1981; August 22, 1982; June 5, 1983; August 24, 1984; June 24, 1990, p. 12; November 4, 1990, p. 10; August 15, 1993, pp. 19-20; August 14, 1994, p. 3.

Modern Age, spring, 1986, p. 162.

Nation, December 30, 1978; June 13, 1981; December 22, 1984, p. 686; December 19, 1988, pp. 688-691.

New Leader, October 15, 1984, p. 14; September 19, 1988, p. 19; March 24, 1997, Phoebe Pettingell, review of *Striving toward Being: The Letters of Thomas Merton and Czeslaw Milosz,* p. 13; March, 2001, Kristen Case, review of *Milosz's ABCs,* p. 24.

New Perspectives Quarterly, fall, 1988, p. 55; spring, 1990, p. 44.

New Republic, May 16, 1955; August 1, 1983; October 3, 1988, pp. 26-28; March 16, 1992, pp. 34-37; April 12, 1999, Jaroslaw Anders, "Beauty and Certainty," p. 48.

New Statesman, October 24, 1980; December 17-24, 1982; August 30, 1985, p. 27; August 5, 1988, p. 38.

Newsweek, June 15, 1981; October 4, 1982.

New Yorker, November 7, 1953; March 19, 1984; October 24, 1988, p. 122; July 16, 1990, p. 80;

December 24, 2001, John Updike, review of *To Begin Where I Am,* p. 118.

New York Review of Books, April 4, 1974; June 25, 1981; February 27, 1986, p. 31; June 2, 1988, p. 21; August 13, 1992, pp. 44-46; August 11, 1994, p. 41; August 28, 1994, p. 9; May 11, 1995, p. 15; March 23, 1995, pp. 39-42; May 31, 2001, Helen Vendler, review of *A Treatise on Poetry,* p. 27; December 20, 2001, Charles Simic, review of *New and Collected Poems, 1931-2001,* p. 14.

New York Times, June 25, 1968; October 10, 1980; September 4, 1982; August 24, 1984; July 26, 1987; June 2, 1988, p. 21; February 18, 2001, Edward Hirsch, review of *Milosz's ABCs,* p. 10.

New York Times Book Review, April 17, 1955; July 7, 1974; March 11, 1979; February 1, 1981; June 28, 1981; October 17, 1982; May 1, 1983; September 2, 1984; October 20, 1985, p. 60; May 25, 1986, p. 2; July 6, 1986; June 2, 1988, p. 21; June 19, 1988, p. 6; December 8, 1988, p. 26; April 26, 1992, p. 20; May 17, 1992, p. 7; May 31, 1992, p. 22; August 28, 1994, p. 9; June 3, 2001, review of *Milosz's ABCs,* p. 26; December 2, 2001, Harvey Shapiro, review of *New and Collected Poems, 1931-2001,* p. 58; December 9, 2001, review of *New and Collected Poems, 1931-2001,* p. 30; December 16, 2001, review of *New and Collected Poems, 1931-2001,* p. 22; December 23, 2001, review of *New and Collected Poems, 1931-2001,* p. 14; January 27, 2002, Scott Veale, review of *Milosz's ABCs,* p. 24; June 2, 2002, review of *New and Collected Poems, 1931-2001,* p. 23.

New York Times Magazine, January 14, 1990, p. 22.

Observer (London, England), December 2, 1984, p. 19; August 11, 1985, p. 20; July 24, 1988, p. 42; November 22, 1992, p. 64; December 2, 2001, John Kinsella, review of *New and Collected Poems, 1931-2001,* p. 17.

Parnassus, fall, 1983, p. 127; 1989, p. 67; 1992, pp. 100-120.

Partisan Review, November, 1953; spring, 1977; fall, 1985, p. 448; 1986, pp. 177-119; 1990, p. 145.

Poetry, April, 1980; December, 1986, p. 168; January 1993, pp. 223-226; February, 1997, John Taylor, review of *Facing the River,* p. 293; August, 1999, Christian Wiman, review of *Roadside Dog,* p. 286; December, 2001, David Wohajn, review of *A Treatise on Poetry,* p. 161.

Progressive, March, 1985, p. 40.

Publishers Weekly, October 24, 1980; January 31, 1986, p. 362; February 26, 1988, p. 187; January 13, 1992, p. 37; June 6, 1994, p. 49; August 28, 1994, p. 48; September 28, 1998, p. 95; September 28, 1999, review of *Roadside Dog,* p. 95; November 13, 2000, review of *Milosz's ABCs,* p. 92; September 3, 2001, review of *New and Collected Poems, 1931-2001,* p. 82; September 10, 2001, review of *To Begin Where I Am,* p. 73.

Queen's Quarterly, winter, 1989, pp. 954-956.

Reflections, winter, 1985, p. 14.

Review of Contemporary Fiction, spring, 2002, David Seed, review of *Milosz's ABCs,* p. 150.

San Francisco Chronicle, February 4, 2000, p. C1; March 21, 2001, David Kipen, review of *Milosz's ABCs,* p. C1; March 30, 2002, "Milosz, Straight Win California Book Awards," p. D5.

San Francisco Review of Books, spring, 1985, p. 22.

Saturday Review, June 6, 1953; May-June, 1983.

Southern Humanities Review, fall, 1989, pp. 382-386.

Spectator, December 4, 1982.

Stand, summer, 1990, p. 12.

Theology Today, January, 1984.

Threepenny Review, summer, 1989, p. 23.

Times (London, England), July 16, 1981; January 6, 1983; May 19, 1983; February 9, 1985; May 27, 1987.

Times Literary Supplement, December 2, 1977; August 25, 1978; July 24, 1981; December 24, 1982; September 9, 1983; October 3, 1986, p. 1092; February 8, 1988, pp. 955-956; September 2, 1988, p. 955.

Tribune Books (Chicago, IL), May 31, 1981; March 15, 1992, p. 6; December 6, 1992, p. 13; December 18, 1994, p. 5.

TriQuarterly, fall, 1983.

Village Voice, May 2, 1974.

Virginia Quarterly Review, spring, 1975; autumn, 1991, p. 125; summer, 1992, p. 99.

Wall Street Journal, July 24, 1992, p. A10.

Washington Post, October 10, 1980; April 29, 1982; September 20, 1989, p. D1; April 26, 1995, p. C1.

Washington Post Book World, June 14, 1981; August 31, 1986, p. 8; December 22, 1991, p. 15; March 8, 1992, p. 9; October 9, 1994, p. 10.

World Literature Today, winter, 1978; spring, 1978, pp. 372-376; winter, 1985, p. 126; winter, 1987, p. 127; summer, 1987, p. 467; autumn, 1991, p. 735; winter, 1993, p. 210; autumn, 1999 (special Milosz issue), pp. 617-692; spring, 2002, Jerzy R. Krzyzanowski, review of *To Begin Where I Am,* p. 123.

Yale Review, spring, 1990, p. 467.*

N

NAIFEH, Steven Woodward 1952-

PERSONAL: Surname is pronounced "*Nay*-fee"; born June 19, 1952, in Tehran, Iran; U.S. citizen; son of George Amel (a consultant) and Marion (a professor; maiden name, Lanphear) Naifeh; life partner of Gregory White Smith (a writer). *Education:* Princeton University, A.B. (summa cum laude), 1974; Harvard University, J.D., 1977, M.A., 1978.

ADDRESSES: *Office*—Woodward/White, Inc., Suite F2, 1359 Silver Bluff Rd., Aiken, SC 29803. *Agent*—Connie Clausen, Connie Clausen Associates, 250 East 87th St., New York, NY 10028.

CAREER: National Gallery of Art, Washington, DC, staff lecturer, summer, 1976; Milbank, Tweed, Hadley & McCloy (law firm), New York, NY, associate, summer, 1976; Sabbagh, Naifeh & Associates, Inc. (consulting and public relations firm), Washington, DC, vice-president, beginning 1980; founder and president, with Gregory White Smith, of Woodward/White, Inc., Aiken, SC, 1981—; chair, Best Doctors, Inc., 1988—. Art exhibited in solo shows in the United States, United Arab Emirates, Nigeria, and Pakistan; lecturer in art.

MEMBER: Phi Beta Kappa.

AWARDS, HONORS: (With Gregory White Smith) National Book Award nomination for nonfiction, 1990, and Pulitzer Prize, 1991, both for *Jackson Pollock: An American Saga.*

WRITINGS:

Culture Making: Money, Success, and the New York Art World, Princeton University Press (Princeton, NJ), 1976.

WITH GREGORY WHITE SMITH

Moving Up in Style, St. Martin's Press (New York, NY), 1980.

Gene Davis, Arts Publisher, 1981.

(With Michael Morgenstern) *How to Make Love to a Woman,* C. N. Potter (New York, NY), 1982.

What Every Client Needs to Know about Using a Lawyer, Putnam (New York, NY), 1982.

The Bargain Hunter's Guide to Art Collecting, Morrow (New York, NY), 1982.

The Best Lawyers in America, Woodward/White (New York, NY), 1983, 8th edition, 2001.

Why Can't Men Open Up?: Overcoming Men's Fear of Intimacy, C. N. Potter (New York, NY), 1984.

The Human Animal, 1985.

The Mormon Murders: A True Story of Greed, Forgery, Deceit, and Death, Weidenfeld & Nicolson (New York, NY), 1988.

Jackson Pollock: An American Saga, C. N. Potter (New York, NY), 1989.

The Best Lawyers in America: Directory of Expert Witnesses, Woodward/White (New York, NY), 1990, revised edition, Woodward/White (Aiken, SC), 2002.

Final Justice: The True Story of the Richest Man Ever Tried for Murder, Dutton (New York, NY), 1993.

A Stranger in the Family: A True Story of Murder, Madness, and Unconditional Love, Dutton, (New York, NY), 1995.

On a Street Called Easy, in a Cottage Called Joye, Broadway Books (New York, NY), 1996.

Making Miracles Happen, Little, Brown (Boston, MA), 1997.

Also author, with Smith, of *The Best Doctors in America,* published by Best Doctors, Inc. (Arlington, VA). Contributor to *Arts, Art International,* and *African Arts.*

ADAPTATIONS: Jackson Pollock: An American Saga was adapted to film as *Pollock,* produced by Sony Pictures, 2000; film rights to *The Mormon Murders: A True Story of Greed, Forgery, Deceit, and Death* were sold.

WORK IN PROGRESS: Two "true crime" books for New American Library.

SIDELIGHTS: Exhaustive research and a highly readable style are the hallmarks of the most well-known and widely reviewed books by Steven Woodward Naifeh and his collaborator and domestic partner, Gregory White Smith. The two men met as students at Harvard University, where both were enrolled in the School of Law. Each of them graduated, but neither pursued a career as a lawyer. Naifeh's avocation, painting, led him to write his first book, *Culture Making: Money, Success, and the New York Art World,* a scholarly examination of the complex relationship between artists, the general public, and dealers in fine art. The art world also provided the basis for one of Naifeh and Smith's first collaborations, a short biography of the painter Gene Davis.

Finding that they worked well together, the two settled on a more ambitious subject: a definitive biography of the man some consider the greatest American artist of this century, Jackson Pollock. Pollock was a leader of the Abstract Expressionism movement of the 1940s and 1950s, and through his painting he sought to depict the inner landscape of the mind. He became known as an "action painter" due to his revolutionary technique of placing his canvases on the floor and splattering paint on them from above. Naifeh and Smith began researching Pollock's life in 1982, never dreaming that they would publish six other books before completing the biography.

The authors studied every Pollock canvas to which they could gain access, read everything previously written about him, and interviewed 2,500 people connected with the artist, including his widow, the painter Lee Krasner; his brothers; and many of his close friends. Their research yielded 40,000 single-spaced half-pages of notes. Interpreting and organizing such a mass of information was a formidable and lengthy task, and Naifeh and Smith supported themselves while working on it by publishing moneymaking titles such as *How to Make Love to a Woman* and consumer guides based on their backgrounds in law.

Their best-known collaboration published before the Pollock biography was *The Mormon Murders: A True Story of Greed, Forgery, Deceit, and Death.* This true-crime book details the strange case of Mark Hofmann, a master forger who, in October, 1985, was arrested for murder. Hofmann, raised in the Church of the Latter-day Saints (Mormon), had privately renounced his religion and then gone on to create false documents discrediting the church's founder, Joseph Smith. Mormon leaders found the forgeries so threatening that they were willing to pay huge sums in order to possess them, intending to hide them away in secret archives. When Hofmann's elaborate schemes began to crumble and it looked as though his forgeries might be exposed, he bombed the homes of two prominent Mormons in order to divert attention from himself, then seriously wounded himself with a third bomb.

Naifeh and Smith drew on court records, police investigations, and personal interviews to produce a book that was laden with forensic, financial, and legal details. Some reviewers faulted the authors for a somewhat sensationalistic style, but John Katzenbach, writing in the *New York Times Book Review,* praised Naifeh and Smith for their perceptive examination of Hofmann's youth and the bearing it had on his later actions; for their characterizations of the police officers who built the case against Hofmann; and for their delineation of the tangle of deception that surrounded the investigation.

Even when engaged in work on *The Mormon Murders* and other titles, the authors continued to research and speculate on the life of Jackson Pollock. "Pollock was our life," Smith told Judith Weintraub of the *Washington Post.* "We had no social life. We had to be obsessed with the material." Finally, after spending some $100,000 on research and travel and devoting ten hours a day, five days a week, for three full years to writing, the book was finished: 934 pages covering even the most minor details of Pollock's life and the authors' theories on the psychological underpinnings of his work. The result was as controversial as it was long. *Washington Post Book World* contributor William Drozdiak called *Jackson Pollock: An American Saga* "monumental and impressive," and he praised the authors for their efforts to "achieve nothing less than a full understanding of the complex social and psychological forces that lay behind the work of an artist considered by many to be America's greatest abstract painter." He further credited Naifeh and Smith with having "marshalled an exhaustive array of material to buttress their interpretation of Pollock's life."

On the other end of the critical spectrum, however, were reviewers such as Elizabeth Frank, who stated in the *New York Times Book Review* that the authors' collaborative style was "based on the kind of glib, reckless, off-the-rack psychobiography that is dazzling in its lack of speculative humility and intellectual caution. There are no questions in this book, only answers." Frank went on to add that Naifeh and Smith "proceed as if diving into the unconscious of a great artist were as easy as diving into a swimming pool. They are too literal, too positive, too contemptuous of Pollock and too ignorant of the ways in which the unconscious remains just that to explain his life or work in terms satisfactory from either an art-historical or a psychological perspective."

Speaking with *Los Angeles Times* writer Suzanne Muchnic, Naifeh and Smith explained that "an antibiographical bias in the art field" was the source of much of the negative reaction to their book. By delving into questions of Pollock's sexual orientation and exposing some of the less-attractive aspects of his life—such as his violent streak, his heavy drinking and his obsession with urinating in public—the authors broke many taboos of the art history world. "There's very little written about incredibly important artists," Naifeh told Muchnic. "And because it's never done, it seems unethical. Fifty percent of the people we talked to spent all of their spare time gossiping about everybody else's sex life, but the idea that you would actually talk about sex in a book, no matter how relevant that might be to the works of art, is somehow unseemly. . . . We knew we would get flak from certain quarters for writing a book that was readable. There's no jargon in it. . . . Someone writing about a literary figure would be excused the effort to make the product a literary experience in its own right, whereas the art world will not make such allowances."

Naifeh rejected the notion, advanced by some reviewers, that because he and Smith showed Pollock as somewhat uncontrolled and inarticulate, they did not respect the artist. "Some educated people have a hard time seeing that people can be intelligent without being verbal, without being articulate, without being logical, that there is an intelligence that is intuitive and emotional and visual without being translated into words," Naifeh told Muchnic. "What's wonderful about Jackson is the triumph over vulgarity of human life and his own desires and the coarseness and brutishness of his own life to create these incredible, lyrical, magical images. Jackson took the most tormented aspects of his daily life and worked them into his masterpieces."

Returning to the "true crime" genre characterized by *The Mormon Murders,* Naifeh and Smith followed *Pollock* with *Final Justice: The True Story of the Richest Man Ever Tried for Murder.* The book draws on the case of Cullen Davis, scion of a Texas millionaire who had amassed his fortune by "questionable means," as a *Publishers Weekly* contributor put it. A withdrawn adolescent who was abused by his father, Davis grew into what the reviewer called a "monstrous adult" who in 1976 was accused of the murder of the acquaintance and daughter of a friend of his estranged wife. Though Davis was also in court on subsequent murder-for-hire charges, he was never indicted, "thanks to a legal staff that eventually numbered thirty and the expenditure of perhaps $20 million," according to the reviewer.

The *Publishers Weekly* critic praised the authors' efforts in *Final Justice,* and similar notices accompanied the 1995 release of *A Stranger in the Family: A True Story of Murder, Madness, and Unconditional Love.* The titular stranger is Danny Starrett, who outwardly led a normal, middle-class life as a husband and father. But while his wife was away visiting her parents, Starrett engaged in violent sprees against young women in South Carolina and Georgia. After overwhelming evidence was brought against Starrett, he confessed to five rapes and one murder, the murder victim being a fifteen-year-old girl to whose body Starrett led the police. *Stranger* covers the events surrounding the crimes and the trials, particularly the efforts of Starrett's mother, Gerry, to spare her son from

Georgia's electric chair. It was Gerry who "gave [Naifeh and Smith] unlimited cooperation and access to her son and his prison journals," Pam Lambert pointed out in a *People* article.

Stranger in the Family uses prison interviews and diary excerpts to delve into the troubled past of the convicted murderer, plus the reactions of Starrett's relatives, who at first refused to believe that their loved one had committed such heinous crimes. In a review for *Entertainment Weekly,* Gene Lyons thought that by telling the story from the Starretts' point of view, the authors "paint themselves into a corner." But Lambert had another view, saying the case of a family man-turned-murderer is a "bizarre odyssey that makes for compelling reading." *Booklist*'s Sue-Ellen Beauregard thought that this account "lacks the punch" of *Final Justice,* but conceded that the excerpts from Starrett's diary "lend some insight into his disturbed mind." A *Publishers Weekly* contributor deemed the work "a powerful and perceptive study."

All the while Naifeh and Smith were producing *Pollock, Final Justice,* and other popular books, the authors were confronting a personal drama of their own. In 1986, Smith was diagnosed with an inoperable brain tumor; doctors gave him no more than six months to live. That prognosis didn't sit well with Smith, who embarked on a mission to find the doctor who would give him a better chance at survival. He searched worldwide until he found a neuroaudiologist in New York "whose experimental procedure shrank my [tumor] by half," as Smith related on the Best Doctors Web site. "That bought me the time I needed to search for still other specialists to provide me with the rest of the options and treatment I needed." Eleven years after being handed that initial death sentence, Smith and Naifeh published *Making Miracles Happen,* an account of Smith's medical journey. "With clarity, insight and no trace of self-pity," wrote a *Publishers Weekly* critic, the authors chronicle Smith's treatment and illustrate the stories of "other patients and physicians who struggle to obtain and provide innovative approaches to catastrophic illness or injury."

Their work in locating treatment for Smith's condition led the authors to found Best Doctors, Inc., a physician referral service dedicated to matching seriously ill patients with information on specialists who may be able to provide the best possible care; the organization also publishes a *Best Doctors* directory. In 1998, Best Doctors was the subject of an approving profile on the newsmagazine *60 Minutes.* In a similar vein, Naifeh and Smith publish the annual guide to *The Best Lawyers in America.*

BIOGRAPHICAL AND CRITICAL SOURCES:

PERIODICALS

Booklist, September 1, 1993, review of *Final Justice: The True Story of the Richest Man Ever Tried for Murder,* p. 15; May 15 1995, Sue-Ellen Beauregard, review of *A Stranger in the Family: a True Story of Murder, Madness, and Unconditional Love,* p. 1618; May 15, 1996, Margaret Flanagan, review of *On a Street Called Easy, in a Cottage Called Joye,* p. 1567; August, 1997, William Beatty, review of *Making Miracles Happen,* p. 1857.

Chicago Tribune, March 24, 1985.

Colonial Homes, June, 1996, Liesl Copland, review of *On a Street Called Easy, in a Cottage Called Joye,* p. 23.

Daily Business Review, February 16, 2001, "Making the List," p. B3.

Entertainment Weekly, June 9, 1995, Gene Lyons, review of *A Stranger in the Family,* p. 51; June 28, 1996, Nikki Amdur, review of *On a Street Called Easy, in a Cottage Called Joye,* p. 100.

Kirkus Reviews, July 1, 1993, review of *Final Justice,* p. 844; April 1, 1995, review of *A Stranger in the Family,* p. 449.

Library Journal, April 15, 1995, review of *A Stranger in the Family,* p. 99; July, 1997, Kay Hogan, review of *Making Miracles Happen,* p. 116.

Los Angeles Times, February 1, 1990.

New York Times, November 12, 1988; January 25, 1990.

New York Times Book Review, October 9, 1988; January 28, 1990.

People, November 20, 1995, Pam Lambert, review of *A Stranger in the Family,* p. 32.

Publishers Weekly, July 26, 1993, review of *Final Justice,* p. 54; May 1, 1995, review of *A Stranger in the Family,* p. 50; March 11, 1996, 50; June 2, 1997, review of *Making Miracles Happen,* p. 58.

Times (London, England), March 24, 1990.

Times Literary Supplement, November 25, 1977; June 9, 1989; March 16, 1990.

Washington Post, January 30, 1990.

Washington Post Book World, October 9, 1988; January 21, 1990; August 6, 1995, review of *A Stranger in the Family,* p. 13; August 13, 1995, review of *A Stranger in the Family,* p. 13.

ONLINE

Best Doctors, http://www.bestdoctors.com/ (October 9, 2002).*

* * *

NAIPAUL, V(idiadhar) S(urajprasad) 1932-

PERSONAL: Born August 17, 1932, in Chaguanas, Trinidad; son of Seepersad (a journalist and writer) and Dropatie (Capildeo) Naipaul; married Patricia Ann Hale, 1955 (marriage ended); married Nadira Khannum Alvi (a newspaper columnist). *Education:* Attended Queen's Royal College, Trinidad, 1943-48; University College, Oxford, B.A., 1953.

ADDRESSES: *Home*—Wiltshire, England. *Agent*—c/o Aitken & Stone Ltd., 29 Fernshaw Rd., London SW10 0TG, England.

CAREER: Writer. Also worked as a freelance broadcaster for British Broadcasting Corp. (BBC), 1954-56.

MEMBER: British Society of Authors, Royal Society of Literature (fellow).

AWARDS, HONORS: John Llewellyn Rhys Memorial Prize, 1958, for *The Mystic Masseur;* grant from government of Trinidad for travel in Caribbean, 1960-61; Somerset Maugham Award, 1961, for *Miguel Street;* Phoenix Trust Award, 1963; Hawthornden Prize, 1964, for *Mr. Stone and the Knights Companion;* W. H. Smith Award, 1968, for *The Mimic Men;* Booker Prize, 1971, for *In a Free State;* D. Litt, St. Andrew's College, 1979, Columbia University, 1981, Cambridge University, 1983, London University, 1988, and Oxford University, 1992; Bennett Award, *Hudson Review,* 1980; T. S. Eliot Award for Creative Writing, Ingersoll Foundation, 1986; knighted, 1990; David Cohen British Literature Award, 1993; Booker Prize nomination, 2001, for *Half a Life;* Nobel Prize for Literature, Swedish Academy, 2001.

V. S. Naipaul

WRITINGS:

The Mystic Masseur (also see below), Deutsch (London, England), 1957, Vanguard (New York, NY), 1959.

The Suffrage of Elvira (also see below), Deutsch (London, England), 1958.

Miguel Street (also see below), Deutsch (London, England), 1959, Vanguard (New York, NY), 1960.

A House for Mr. Biswas, Deutsch (London, England), 1961, McGraw-Hill (New York, NY), 1962, new edition, with an introduction by Ian Buruma, Penguin (New York, NY), 1992.

The Middle Passage: Impressions of Five Societies—British, French, and Dutch in the West Indies and South America (nonfiction), Deutsch (London, England), 1962, Macmillan (New York, NY), 1963.

Mr. Stone and the Knights Companion, Deutsch (London, England), 1963, Macmillan (New York, NY), 1964.

An Area of Darkness (nonfiction), Deutsch (London, England), 1964, Macmillan (New York, NY), 1965.
The Mimic Men, Macmillan (New York, NY), 1967.
A Flag on the Island (short stories), Macmillan (New York, NY), 1967.
The Loss of El Dorado: A History (nonfiction), Deutsch (London, England), 1969, Knopf (New York, NY), 1970, published as *The Loss of El Dorado: A Colonial History,* Vintage (New York, NY), 2003.
In a Free State (short stories), Knopf (New York, NY), 1971.
The Overcrowded Barracoon and Other Articles, Deutsch (London, England), 1972, Knopf (New York, NY), 1973.
Guerrillas, Knopf (New York, NY), 1975.
India: A Wounded Civilization (nonfiction), Knopf (New York, NY), 1977.
The Perfect Tenants and The Mourners, Cambridge University Press (Cambridge, England), 1977.
A Bend in the River, Knopf (New York, NY), 1979, with an introduction by Elizabeth Hardwick, Modern Library (New York, NY), 1997.
The Return of Eva Peron (nonfiction), Knopf (New York, NY), 1980.
A Congo Diary, Sylvester & Orphanos (Los Angeles, CA), 1980.
Among the Believers: An Islamic Journey, Knopf (New York, NY), 1981.
Three Novels (contains *The Mystic Masseur, The Suffrage of Elvira,* and *Miguel Street*), Knopf (New York, NY), 1982.
Finding the Center, Knopf (New York, NY), 1984.
The Enigma of Arrival, Knopf (New York, NY), 1987.
A Turn in the South, Knopf (New York, NY), 1989.
India: A Million Mutinies Now, Heinemann (London, England), 1990, Viking (New York, NY), 1991.
A Way in the World, Knopf (New York, NY), 1994.
(Author of text) Raghubir Singh, *Bombay: Gateway of India* (photographs), Aperture (New York, NY), 1994.
Beyond Belief: Islamic Excursions among the Converted Peoples, Random House (New York, NY), 1998.
Between Father and Son: Selected Correspondence of V. S. Naipaul and His Family, 1949-1953, edited by Gillon Aitken, Knopf (New York, NY), 2000.
Reading and Writing: A Personal Account, New York Review of Books (New York, NY), 2000.
Half a Life (novel), Picador (London, England), 2001, Knopf (New York, NY), 2002.
The Writer and the World, Knopf (New York, NY), 2002.
The Nightwatchman's Occurrence Book: And Other Comic Inventions (contains *The Suffrage of Elvira, Mr. Stones and the Knights Companion,* and *A Flag on the Island*), Vintage (New York, NY), 2002.
Literary Occasions: Essays, Knopf (New York, NY), 2003.
Vintage Naipaul, Vintage (New York, NY), 2004.

Contributor to *Island Voices: Stories from the West Indies,* edited by Andrew Salkey, Liveright (New York, NY), 1970. Contributor of book reviews to periodicals, including *New Statesman* and *New York Review of Books.*

ADAPTATIONS: The Mystic Masseur has been adapted as a film, produced by Ismail Merchant, in 2002.

SIDELIGHTS: V. S. Naipaul, considered one of the world's most gifted novelists, was awarded the 2001 Nobel Prize for literature. As a *New York Times Book Review* critic wrote: "For sheer abundance of talent there can hardly be a writer alive who surpasses V. S. Naipaul. Whatever we may want in a novelist is to be found in his books: an almost Conradian gift for tensing a story, a serious involvement with human issues, a supple English prose, a hard-edged wit, a personal vision of things. Best of all, he is a novelist unafraid of using his brains. . . . His novels are packed with thought, not as lumps of abstraction but as one fictional element among others, fluid in the stream of narrative. . . . [He is] the world's writer, a master of language and perception, our sardonic blessing."

Naipaul is frequently referred to as a writer of the world. He was born in Trinidad to the descendants of Hindu immigrants from northern India, and later educated at England's Oxford University. The idea of Naipaul as "the world's writer" comes largely, as he has pointed out himself, from his rootlessness. Unhappy with the cultural and spiritual poverty of Trinidad, distanced from India, and unable to relate to and share in the heritage of each country's former imperial ruler, Great Britain, Naipaul thought of himself as contentedly existing without ancestors or a heritage. As a result of this nonattachment to region and tradition, most of his work deals with people who, like himself, feel estranged from the societies they are ostensibly part of and who desperately seek ways to belong. The locales Naipaul chooses for his stories represent an extension of this same theme; most take place in emerging Third-World countries in the throes of creating new national identities from the remnants of native and colonial cultures.

Naipaul's early works explore the comic aspects of these themes. Essentially West Indian variations on the comedy of manners, these works present almost farcical accounts of an illiterate and divided society's shift from colonial to independent status, emphasizing the multiracial misunderstandings and rivalries and various ironies resulting from the sudden introduction of such democratic processes as free elections. In *The Mystic Masseur, The Suffrage of Elvira,* and *Miguel Street,* Naipaul exposes the follies and absurdities of Trinidadian society; his tone is detached yet sympathetic, as if he is looking back at a distant past of which he is no longer a part. The tragic aspects of the situation are not examined, nor is there any attempt to involve the reader in the plight of the characters. In his book *V. S. Naipaul,* Michael Thorpe described the prevailing tone of these early books as "that of the ironist who points up the comedy, futility and absurdity that fill the gap between aspiration and achievement, between the public image desired and the individual's inadequacies, to recognize which may be called the education of the narrator: *I had grown up and looked critically at the people around me.*"

A House for Mr. Biswas, published in 1961, marks an important turning point in Naipaul's work, his attention to psychological and social realism foreshadowing the intensive character studies of his later works. In addition, *A House for Mr. Biswas* has the universality of theme his earlier books lacked because of their emphasis on the particularities of Trinidadian society. As a consequence of these developments, many critics regard *A House for Mr. Biswas* as Naipaul's earliest masterpiece. Robert D. Hamner wrote in his biography *V. S. Naipaul* that the novel "is a vital embodiment of authentic West Indian life, but more than that, it transcends national boundaries and evokes universal human experiences. Mr. Biswas' desire to own his own house is essentially a struggle to assert personal identity and to attain security—thoroughly human needs."

A *New York Herald Tribune Books* reviewer noted that "Naipaul has a wry wit and an engaging sense of humor, as well as a delicate understanding of sadness and futility and a profound but unobtrusive sense of the tragi-comedy of ordinary living. . . . His style is precise and assured. In short, he gives every indication of being an important addition to the international literary scene. [*A House for Mr. Biswas*] is funny, it is compassionate. It has more than 500 pages and not one of them is superfluous." Paul Theroux admitted in the *New York Times Book Review* that "it is hard for the reviewer of a wonderful author to keep the obituarist's assured hyperbole in check, but let me say that if the silting-up of the Thames coincided with a freak monsoon, causing massive flooding in all parts of South London, the first book I would rescue from my library would be *A House for Mr. Biswas.*" Thorpe agreed that the novel is "a work of rare distinction," a "'novelist's novel,' a model work." In his *V. S. Naipaul* Thorpe commented that the popularity of *A House for Mr. Biswas* "must be largely due to its universality of subject and theme, the struggle of one ordinary man to climb—or cling on to—the ladder of life." In short, Thorpe concluded, "for West Indian literature *A House for Mr. Biswas* forged [the] connection [between literature and life] with unbreakable strength and set up a model for emulation which no other 'Third World' literature in English has yet equaled."

Since the success of *A House for Mr. Biswas,* Naipaul has increasingly sought broader geographic and social contexts in which to explore his themes. At the same time, his early lighthearted tone gradually has faded as the author examines the more tragic consequences of alienation and rootlessness through the eyes of various "universal wanderers." Noting that "Naipaul's writings about his native Trinidad have often enough been touched with tolerant amusement," Thomas Lask reported in the *New York Times* that the 1971 story collection *In a Free State* deals with the issue: "How does the expatriate fare after he leaves the island?" Noting that Naipaul's stories "focus on the failure of heart, on the animal-like cruelty man exhibits to other men and on the avarice that . . . is the root of all evil," Lask interpreted the fiction to say "that neither customs nor color nor culture seems able to quiet that impulse to destruction, that murderous wantonness that is so much part of our make-up." Characterizing Naipaul's style as "leaner than in the past and much more somber," the critic added: "There is virtually none of the earlier playfulness. He appears to have settled for precision over abundance. Each detail and each incident is made to carry its weight in the narrative. The effect is not small-scaled, for in the title story he has created an entire country. He has not tidied up every loose strand. . . . But there is nothing unfinished in these polished novellas." *In V. S. Naipaul: An Introduction to His Work,* Paul Theroux dubbed *In a Free State* "ambitious . . . a story-sequence brilliant in conception, masterly in execution, and terrifying in effect—the chronicles of a half-a-dozen self-exiled people who have become lost souls. Having abandoned their own countries (countries they were scarcely aware of belonging to), they have found themselves in strange places, without friends, with few loyalties, and with the feeling that they are trespassing. Worse, their lives have been totally altered; for them there is no going back; they have fled, each to his separate limbo, and their existence is like that of souls in a classical underworld." Comparing Naipaul to French author Albert Camus in his focus on "displacement," Theroux noted that "Naipaul is much superior to Camus, and his achievement—a steady advance through eleven volumes—is as disturbing as it is original. *In a Free State* is a masterpiece in the fiction of rootlessness."

The novel *Guerrillas* established Naipaul's reputation in the United States after its publication in 1975. Most reviewers commented on the novelist's somewhat grim outlook, Theroux calling it "a violent book in which little violence is explicit. . . . It is a novel, not of revolt, but of the play-acting that is frequently called revolt, that queer situation of scabrous glamour which Naipaul sees as a throw-back to the days of slavery. . . . *Guerrillas* is one of Naipaul's most complex books; it is certainly his most suspenseful, a series of shocks, like a shroud slowly unwound from a bloody corpse, showing the damaged—and familiar—face last. . . . This is a novel without a villain, and there is not a character for whom the reader does not at some point feel deep sympathy and keen understanding, no matter how villainous or futile he may seem. *Guerrillas* is a brilliant novel in every way, and it shimmers with artistic certainty. It is scarifying in the opposite way from a nightmare. One can shrug at fantasy, but *Guerrillas*—in a phrase Naipaul himself once used—is, like the finest novels, 'indistinguishable from truth.'"

Reviewing the novel in *Time,* Paul Gray contended that "perhaps no one but Naipaul has the inside and outside knowledge to have turned such a dispirited tale into so gripping a book. His island is built entirely of vivid descriptions and offhand dialogue. At the end, it has assumed a political and economic history, a geography and a population of doomed, selfish souls. . . . *Guerrillas* is not a polemic . . . but a Conradian vision of fallibility and frailty. With economy and compassion, Naipaul draws the heart of darkness from a sun-struck land." Noting that Naipaul takes a "hackneyed" theme—"incipient Black Power"—and manages to produce "a more significant treatment of it than most of his contemporaries with similar concerns," Charles R. Larson wrote in the *Nation* that *Guerrillas* "builds so slowly and so skillfully that . . . we are hardly aware of the necessary outcome of the events; it is only in retrospect that we see that the desultory action has in fact been charged with fate. . . . Written in a deliberately flat style, *Guerrillas* is a deeply pessimistic novel, telling us that we have seen about as much political change in the West Indian island republics as we are likely to see."

In *A Bend in the River,* Naipaul returns to the African backdrop of *In a Free State* and confirms his basic pessimism. John Leonard explained in the *New York Times* that the author "despises nostalgia for the colonial past, while at the same time heartlessly parodying . . . the African future." Calling *A Bend in the River* "brilliant and depressing," Leonard added: "It is no secret by now, certainly not since *Guerrillas* . . . that V. S. Naipaul is one of the handful of living writers of whom the English language can be proud, if, still, profoundly uneasy. There is no consolation from him, any more than there is sentiment. His wit has grown hard and fierce; he isn't seeking to amuse, but to scourge."

John Updike, writing in the *New Yorker,* asserted that *A Bend in the River* "proves once more that Naipaul is incomparably well situated and equipped to bring us news of one of the contemporary world's great subjects—the mingling of its peoples. . . . *A Bend in the River* is carved from the same territory [as *In a Free State*]—an Africa of withering colonial vestiges, terrifyingly murky politics, defeated pretensions, omnivorous rot, and the implacable undermining of all that would sustain reason and safety. . . . Rage . . . is perhaps the deepest and darkest fact Naipaul has to report about the Third World, and in this novel his understanding of it goes beyond that shown in *Guerrillas.* . . . Always a master of fictional landscape, Naipaul here shows, in his variety of human examples and in his search for underlying social causes, a Tolstoyan spirit, generous if not genial." In his *Newsweek* review, Walter Clemons described *A*

Bend in the River as "a hurtful, claustrophobic novel, very hard on the nerves, played out under a vast African sky in an open space that is made to feel stifling." Noting its political bent, Clemons added, "As an evocation of place, [the novel] succeeds brilliantly" and "confirms Naipaul's position as one of the best writers now at work." Irving Howe was equally laudatory, writing in the *New York Times Book Review* that "Naipaul has mastered the gift of creating an aura of psychic and moral tension."

For his 1987 novel *The Enigma of Arrival* Naipaul selected a new setting: Great Britain. John Thieme explained in the *Dictionary of Literary Biography* that in the years between the publication of *A Bend in the River* and *The Enigma of Arrival* the author "suffered from a serious illness and was deeply moved by the deaths of his younger sister and his brother, Shiva." *The Enigma of Arrival,* Thieme continued, reflects Naipaul's somber personal experience and "is pervaded by a sense of personal loss and fragility." The novel examines the impact of imperialism on a native English estate, slowly decaying along with its reclusive landlord, who is suffering from a degenerative disease. The decay of the manor house and its owner causes the novel's first-person narrator to ponder the inevitability of his own death. Calling *The Enigma of Arrival* "full of intimations of mortality," Thieme added that "ultimately it is as much a generalized lament for human transience and an expression of the writer's all-pervasive sense of vulnerability as an elegy for any particular person or community."

With *A Turn in the South* and *India: A Million Mutinies Now,* Naipaul turned to nonfiction. *A Turn in the South* tells of a journey the author took through the southern United States, ostensibly looking for similarities between his own Trinidadian culture and that of the American South. While the issue of race is "high on his agenda at the outset," Thieme noted that its importance decreases the further into the work the reader explores. Instead, Naipaul finds himself drawn deeper and deeper into a description of the culture of the modern American south, including country western music, strict, conservative Christianity, and the enduring fascination with Elvis Presley. *India: A Million Mutinies Now* represents Naipaul's third consideration of his ancestral homeland. Whereas Naipaul had formerly expressed pessimism about India's ability to overcome centuries of religious and ethnic strife, in this 1990 work he appears to "take . . . heart in what he sees," according to Thomas D'Evelyn in his appraisal of the book for the *Christian Science Monitor.* "As the details accumulate, the reader becomes more deeply involved in a growing appreciation for a life lived under extreme circumstances. Reading Naipaul," D'Evelyn concluded, "one becomes as optimistic about mankind as the author is about India." The author's "cautious optimism represents the primary value of the book," commented Douglas J. Macdonald in *America.* "Pessimism can too easily lead to inertia and despair. . . . Naipaul's message is that despite the problems, despite the obstacles, the Indians, and by extension the rest of us, must continue to try."

A Way in the World, published in 1994, is a collection of narratives that mix elements of fiction and nonfiction, merging Naipaul's Indian and West Indian heritage with the English history and culture he adopted when he immigrated to England at age eighteen. "His project is simultaneously to construct his own literary inheritance and the legacy he will leave to the world," explained Philip Gourevitch in *Commentary.* "The book . . . combines memoir, historical scholarship, and imaginative writing in a series of nine independent but thematically interlocking narratives. These narratives accumulate to form a dramatic portrait gallery of people—historical and fictionalized—whose lives have been formed and transformed by their encounters with Trinidad. And through the echo chamber of their stories there emerges a portrait of the artist, Naipaul himself, at the apex of his literary consciousness." "Now, near the end of his days," declared *New Republic* contributor Caryl Phillips, "Naipaul is clearly . . . deliberating over the question of whether he ever left home in the first place, for whatever else it is *A Way in the World* is a beautiful lament to the Trinidad he has so often denigrated."

Naipaul labels each of these early narratives "An Unwritten Story." He includes under that title tales about the sixteenth-century sea dog and explorer Sir Walter Raleigh traveling down a branch of the Orinoco River in Guyana in search of gold and not finding it, and an account of nineteenth-century South American revolutionary Francisco Miranda, who plotted a Venezuelan revolution that never materialized. Naipaul also traces the careers of other notables, such as the Trinidadian Marxist revolutionary he dubs "Lebrun," who served as advisor to several independence movements, but was discarded as irrelevant after the regimes were established. "Once in power," declared *Los Angeles Times Book Review* contributor Richard Eder, the nationalists "had no use for him; his ideology was good for building up their strength but they had no intention of actually setting up a Marxist regime." Instead, Lebrun found himself banished to the fringes of society, spending his life in exile, speaking to leftist groups in Great Britain and the United States.

"If there is one thing that unifies the chapters in [*A Way in the World*]," declared *Spectator* reviewer Amit Chaudhuri, "it is its attempt to explore and define the nature of the colonial's memory." Like other reviewers, Chaudhuri contrasted Naipaul's fiction with the work of Conrad, who often looked darkly at the spreading colonialism of Great Britain at the end of the nineteenth and the beginning of the twentieth centuries. The reviewer suggested that Naipaul retraces the colonialism Conrad depicted in his work and shows, in *A Way in the World,* how British imperialism created not just colonies but colonials: men and women with unique sensibilities and memories. "The river, in these 'stories,' no longer remains simply a Conradian image of Western exploration and territorial ambition," Chaudhuri concluded, "but becomes an emblem of the colonial memory attempting to return to its source."

Beyond Belief: Islamic Excursions among the Converted Peoples served as both a return to nonfiction and a sequel to Naipaul's 1981 work *Among the Believers: An Islamic Journey.* Discussing the earlier book with Jeffrey Myers of *American Scholar,* Naipaul described *Among the Believers* as "about people caught at a cultural hinge moment: a whole civilization is on the turn. . . . It seeks to make that change clear, and to make a story of it." *Beyond Belief,* like its predecessor, deals with Islamic countries that are non-Arabic: Indonesia, Iran, Pakistan, and Malaysia. Both books relate stories from individuals Naipaul encountered while traveling extensively through these countries. Comparing the two books, a *Booklist* reviewer observed that in *Beyond Belief* "Naipaul is more dispassionate, letting the people he meets take center stage as they express their struggles with family, religion, and nation." Meyers also observed this dispassionate quality, commenting, "The author of *Guerrillas* and *A Bend in the River* has done what I thought impossible: written a book as boring as its bland gray jacket." Meyers also found Naipaul's central thesis—that "everyone not an Arab who is a Muslim is a convert"—to be "radically flawed." Edward Said agreed, noting in the *Progressive:* "This ridiculous argument would suggest by extension that only a native of Rome can be a good Roman Catholic. . . . In effect, the 400-page *Beyond Belief* is based on nothing more than this rather idiotic and insulting theory. . . . The greater pity is that Naipaul's latest book will be considered a major interpretation of a great religion, and more Muslims will suffer and be insulted."

In support of his thesis, Naipaul points out how Islam came late to these nations and has since remained in conflict with older native traditions. He also shows how the revival of Islamic fundamentalism during the late twentieth century had a negative impact on these "converted" countries. Despite this argument, most critical response to the book expressed disagreement. Noted Jane I. Smith in a review for *Christian Century:* "Naipaul's picture of Islam among the converted peoples is not necessarily inaccurate; it is simply incomplete. And his presupposition that Muslims in the countries he visits have sacrificed their native traditions for a religion in which they can never fully share is a partial truth at best. The whole picture is both broader and considerably more hopeful than this artful but melancholy presentation might have us believe." While also questioning Naipaul's thesis and his generally negative views of Islam, L. Carl Brown in *Foreign Affairs* took a different slant on *Beyond Belief:* "In-depth interviews with a handful of the near-great and the obscure from each country produce brilliant writing and somber stories. . . . *Beyond Belief* is rewarding."

Between Father and Son: Selected Correspondence of V. S. Naipaul and His Family, 1949-1953 presents letters from Naipaul to his father, Seepersad Naipaul, and other members of his family during the time when Naipaul was studying in England on a scholarship. Longtime Naipaul readers will recognize Seepersad, a weary man struggling as a journalist, in the fictional title character in *A House for Mr. Biswas.* During the course of the correspondence, Naipaul's father suffers a heart attack, loses his job at a local newspaper, and dies at the age of forty-seven without having realized his dream of publishing his short stories. "A major theme of the letters is the conflict between devoting oneself to a future career, especially as a writer, and helping others in the family gain an education," noted Bruce King in *World Literature Today.* After his father's death, Vido—as Naipaul was known to his family—contemplates returning to Trinidad, but claims financial hardship in not doing so. Instead, his sister leaves India, where she is studying on scholarship, and returns to Trinidad to take care of family obligations. Naipaul remains in England, convinced that he can best help his family by continuing his studies and working toward his goal of becoming a published writer.

Even as a teenager studying abroad for the first time, Naipaul is concerned with many of the issues for which he will eventually become known. Among the themes familiar to readers of Naipaul's mature writing are "the enigma of arrival, the sadness of separation and exile, neocolonial ambition and the effort to find one's center," according to Abraham Verghese in the *New York Times Book Review.* Nevertheless, continued Verghese, "those who have formed the impression that Naipaul is arrogant and conceited will find little to change their beliefs." Noting that the letters document Naipaul's depression—or what the author himself characterized as a "nervous breakdown"—Joseph Epstein commented in *New Criterion* that Naipaul's literary vision is "hideously complicated"; *Between Father and Son* reminds readers "how little we really know about the workings of first-class literary minds."

In 2001 the Swedish Academy awarded Naipaul the Nobel Prize for Literature, in recognition of what they termed his "incorruptible scrutiny in works that compel us to see the presence of suppressed histories." Critics were nearly unanimous in their approval of the award, although some noted that Naipaul's strong views have been less than decorous throughout the years. "Few writers have offended their readers as regularly as V. S. Naipaul has," wrote Akash Kapur for *Salon;* he "has shown a staggering capacity for insensitivity and prejudice." Even while acknowledging Naipaul's hostility toward his native Trinidad, Caryl Phillips commented in the *Guardian* that the author's books "have been written in a sublime English, and with a ferocity of purpose unequaled by any of his contemporaries in the English language. His ability to synthesise, in almost equal part, his fiction and nonfiction—the one genre informing the other both structurally and thematically—has been both original in construction and fascinating to witness."

The Nobel announcement was made barely a month after Islamic fundamentalists seized international attention following the terrorist attacks on New York City and Washington, D.C., on September 11, 2001. Naipaul's often outspoken criticism of fundamentalism cast an air of irony over the Academy's choice. In his *Beyond Belief* Naipaul had dubbed fundamentalist Islam "the most uncompromising kind of imperialism," recalled *Salon.com* reviewer Gavin McNett. While *Los Angeles Times* contributor Tim Rutten cited the Nobel Prize honoree as maintaining, "I don't stand for any country," Rutten went on to note that Naipaul deplores the "calamitous effect" of some Islamic sects have had on their countries. Such controversy aside, David Pryce-Jones concluded in the London *Times* that "the Nobel Prize for Literature has gone to someone who deserves it. . . . His use of language is as precise as it is beautiful." Receipt of the Nobel Prize for Literature cemented Naipaul's status as one of the English language's most distinguished and perceptive contemporary writers.

The 2002 publication of *Half a Life* came on the heels of Naipaul's Nobel win. The novel recounts the first forty years of the life of Willie Chandran, the son of a local Hindu ascetic of some renown and his untouchable wife. Willie escapes an unremarkable youth in India to study in England where, confused by his sexual initiation and flustered by both his own heritage and the cultural shifts thrust upon him in 1960s England, he forgoes a budding literary career. Instead, Willie follows Ana, the first woman to express an interest in him, to a Portuguese-ruled African country. Willie remains there for eighteen years, doing nothing much except loathing the native population, enjoying the perks of Ana's wealth, and engaging in a liaison with Ana's best friend.

J. M. Coetzee praised Naipaul's prose in his review for the *New York Review of Books,* calling it "as clean and cold as a knife." While noting the self-righteousness of both Willie and his father—both men "believe they see through other people" but "are incapable of imagining anyone unlike themselves"—Coetzee added that neither character appears to grow during the course of the novel. "Willie's story ends not only without resolution but without any glimpse of what a resolution might look like," the critic commented. Willie's nihilistic tendencies prompted David Kipen to declare in the *San Francisco Chronicle* that "under everything lurks Naipaul's uncharitable treatment of his own characters, robbed of our sympathy through want of his." However, *Booklist* contributor Donna Seaman praised Naipaul for both his language and his "command of both the intimately personal and the sweepingly political," calling *Half a Life* "a psychological complex yet rapidly paced tale of a father and son who fail to fully engage with life." In the *New York Times* contributor Michiko Kakutani continued such praise, complimenting the author for his "uncommon elegance and acerbity," and dubbing the novel "a small masterpiece in its own right and . . . a potent distillation of the author's work to date, a book that recapitulates all his themes of exile, postcolonial confusion, third-world angst, and filial love and rebellion."

In Naipaul's 2002 essay collection *The Writer and the World,* he includes pieces about numerous elections around the world, including the 1984 American presidential campaign; the movement, led by Norman Mailer and Jimmy Breslin, to have New York City named the nation's fifty-first state; the influence of the Peron family on the country of Argentina; and the Black Power movements in America and the Caribbean. The book demonstrates the writer's "tragic view of history," stated Jason Cowley in the London *Observer,* which he has perhaps arrived at because "he has travelled so far and seen so much. He knows something of the world, its pitilessness and struggle, its indifference to human suffering." According to Cowley, after reading *The Writer and the World* one understands why Naipaul was compelled to stop writing in a comic vein. In his travels, the writer has sought to understand history, and his essays combine short biographies, cultural criticism, and historical narrative to arrive at his bleak analysis of the psychology of decolonized people. Sven Birkerts, in the *Washington Times,* similarly remarked that this book emanates an acerbic world view. "Naipaul is merciless and exacting in his fiction as well as his essays and documentary accounts, and many readers have concluded that he is scornful of his subjects, expending upon them a powerful private rage," Birkerts wrote. Yet he found that the essays collected in *The Writer and the World* must correct this misperception. "The more one reads these essays . . . the more clearly one sees that the point of his astringent reportage, his withering portraits of life in various unstable pockets of the Third World, is not to expose the deficits of the people or their culture—though it can certainly look that way—but rather to unmask the grandiose mythologies, the illusions, that flourish where the deeper continuities of civilization are lacking." In 2003 Naipaul published another essay collection, *Literary Occasions: Essays.* Included in this book is his Nobel Prize lecture, as well as essays on other writers of Indian extraction, memories of his childhood, even a foreword from the 1983 edition of his novel *A House for Mr. Biswas.*

Throughout Naipaul's career he has become increasingly well-accepted as "a writer with a world perspective, whose constantly evolving literary skill has few rivals in contemporary fiction," as an essayist for *Contemporary Novelists* pointed out. Yet his unique viewpoint has drawn critics who have accused him of "racism, chauvinism, and of displaying a nostalgic collaboration with imperialist ideology," reflected Stella Swain in the *Dictionary of Literary Biography.* On the other hand, Swain noted, those enthusiastic about his work generally praise it for its "aesthetic and philosophical considerations or from an appreciation of his honesty. Naipaul is lauded as a sophisticated artist whose refined and subtle prose represents the best of contemporary fiction in English." Swain conjectured that these two opposing views of the writer are difficult to reconcile, "except insofar as it could be said that the confusion he has caused in his reading public is simply an expression of anxieties and conflicts that already exist. In the sense that his work presses such tensions into articulation and dialogue, it is of great value."

BIOGRAPHICAL AND CRITICAL SOURCES:

BOOKS

Contemporary Literary Criticism, Gale (Detroit, MI), Volume 4, 1975, Volume 7, 1977, Volume 9, 1978, Volume 13, 1980, Volume 18, 1981, Volume 37, 1986, Volume 105, 1999.

Contemporary Novelists, 7th edition, St. James Press (Detroit, MI), 2001.

Dictionary of Literary Biography, Gale (Detroit, MI), Volume 125: *Twentieth-Century Caribbean and Black African Writers, Second Series,* 1993, Volume 204: *British Travel Writers, 1940-1997,* 1999, Volume 207: *British Novelists since 1960, Third Series,* 1999.

Dictionary of Literary Biography Yearbook: 1985, Gale (Detroit, MI), 1986.

Dissanayake, Wimal, *Self and Colonial Desire: Travel Writings of V. S. Naipaul,* P. Lang (New York, NY), 1993.

Gorra, Michael Edward, *After Empire: Scott, Naipaul, Rushdie,* University of Chicago Press (Chicago, IL), 1997.

Hamner, Robert D., *V. S. Naipaul,* Twayne (New York, NY), 1973.

Jussawalla, Feroza, editor, *Conversations with V. S. Naipaul,* University Press of Mississippi (Jackson, MI), 1997.

Kamra, Shashi, *The Novels of V. S. Naipaul: A Study in Theme and Form,* Prestige Books/Indian Society for Commonwealth Studies, 1990.

Khan, Akhtar Jamal, *V. S. Naipaul: A Critical Study,* Creative Books, 1998.

King, Bruce, *V. S. Naipaul,* St. Martin's Press (New York, NY), 1993.

Nixon, Rob, *London Calling: V. S. Naipaul, Postcolonial Mandarin,* Oxford University Press (New York, NY), 1992.

Theroux, Paul, *Sir Vidia's Shadow: A Friendship across Five Continents,* Houghton (Boston, MA), 1998.

Theroux, Paul, *V. S. Naipaul: An Introduction to His Work,* Deutsch (London, England), 1972.

Thorpe, Michael, *V. S. Naipaul,* Longmans (London, England), 1976.

Weiss, Timothy, *On the Margins: The Art of Exile in V. S. Naipaul,* University of Massachusetts Press (Amherst, MA), 1992.

PERIODICALS

Africa News Service, December 19, 2001, "Naipaul: The Writer Who Despises His Background."

America, June 15, 1991, pp. 656-657.

American Prospect, January 28, 2002, Amitava Kumar, *The Humor and the Pity,* p. 31.

American Scholar, winter, 1999, Jeffrey Meyers, review of *Beyond Belief,* p. 150.

Américas, March-April, 1998, Sandra Chouthi, "House of Worldly Treasures," p. 4.

Atlantic, May, 1970; January, 1976; July, 1977; June, 1979; February, 2002, Geoffrey Wheatcroft, "A Terrifying Honesty: V. S. Naipaul Is Certainly No Liberal and Herein Lies His Importance," p. 88; November, 2001, review of *Half a Life,* pp. 144-145.

Best Sellers, April 15, 1968.

Book, November-December, 2001, Paul Evans, review of *Half a Life,* p. 62.

Booklist, January 1, 1999, review of *Beyond Belief,* p. 777; August, 2001, Donna Seaman, review of *Half a Life,* p. 2051; May 1, 2002, Donna Seaman, review of *The Writer and the World,* p. 1442.

Books Abroad, winter, 1968; winter, 1969.

Books and Bookmen, October, 1967.

Boston Globe, March 15, 1987; January 22, 1989; December 23, 1990.

Chicago Sunday Tribune, July 12, 1959.

Chicago Tribune, November 14, 2001, Julia Keller, "Why Is V. S. Naipaul So Cranky?"

Choice, June, 1973.

Christian Century, September 9, 1998, Jane I. Smith, review of *Beyond Belief,* p. 835.

Christian Science Monitor, July 19, 1962; March 29, 1968; May 28, 1970; February 28, 1991, p. 11.

Commentary, August, 1994, pp. 27-31.

Commonweal, September 9, 1994, pp. 28-29.

Contemporary Literature, winter, 1968.

Economist (Great Britain), July 16, 1977.

Economist (U.S.), September 12, 1998, review of *Beyond Belief,* p. S7.

Europe Intelligence Wire, October 12, 2002, review of *The Writer and the World.*

Explicator, spring, 2002, Ervin Beck, "Naipaul's B. Wordsworth," p. 175.

Forbes, February 23, 1998, Richard C. Morais, "Tribal Tribulations," p. 149.

Foreign Affairs, September-October, 1998, L. Carl Brown, review of *Beyond Belief,* p. 162.

Guardian, September 1, 2001, Paul Theroux, "Into the Lion's Den"; October 12, 2001, Caryl Phillips, "Reluctant Hero."

Illustrated London News, May 20, 1967.

Kenyon Review, November, 1967.

Library Journal, May 15, 1998, James F. DeRoche, review of *Beyond Belief,* p. 91; June 15, 2002, Ravi Shenoy, review of *The Writer and the World,* p. 66; October 1, 2003, Michael Rogers, review of *India: A Wounded Civilization,* p. 123.

Listener, May 25, 1967; September 28, 1967; May 23, 1968.

London, May, 1967.

Los Angeles Times, May 9, 1980; March 15, 1989; October 15, 2001, Tim Rutten, "A Nod to Values We Embrace; People Can Take Heart in V. S. Naipaul's Recent Nobel Prize Win," p. E1.

Los Angeles Times Book Review, June 24, 1979; May 22, 1994, pp. 3, 11.

Modern Fiction Studies, spring, 2002, review of *The Return of Eva Peron,* p. 169.

Nation, October 9, 1967; October 5, 1970; December 13, 1975; July 2, 1977; June 30, 1979; Amitava Kumar, review of *Half a Life,* p. 32.

National Review, October 6, 1970; August 29, 1994, pp. 61-62; February 7, 2000, Francis X. Rocca, review of *Between Father and Son,* p. 48; December 31, 2001, David Pryce-Jones, "Nobility in the Novel"; April 8, 2002, David Pryce-Jones, "Indian War Drums: Rushdie, Naipaul, and the Subcontinent's Challenge."

New Criterion, March, 2000, Joseph Epstein, review of *Between Father and Son,* p. 58.

New Leader, May 4, 1998, Roger Draper, review of *Beyond Belief,* p. 13.

New Republic, July 9, 1977; June 9, 1979; June 10, 1991, pp. 30-34; June 13, 1994, pp. 40-45; July 13, 1998, Fouad Ajami, review of *Beyond Belief,* p. 27; November 5, 2001, James Wood, review of *Half a Life,* p. 31.

New Statesman, May 5, 1967; September 15, 1967; November 7, 1969; October 8, 1971; June 17, 1977; December 17, 2001, Lieve Joris, interview with V. S. Naipaul, p. 54.

Newsweek, December 1, 1975; June 6, 1977; May 21, 1979; June 13, 1994, p. 55.

Newsweek International, August 26, 2002, Ben Moser, review of *The Writer and the World,* p. 57.

New Yorker, August 4, 1962; August 8, 1970; June 6, 1977; May 21, 1979.

New York Herald Tribune Books, June 24, 1962.

New York Review of Books, October 26, 1967; April 11, 1968; December 30, 1971; May 31, 1979; February 14, 1991, pp. 3-5; November 1, 2001, J. M. Coetzee, "The Razor's Edge."

New York Times, December 16, 1967; December 25, 1971; August 17, 1977; May 14, 1979; March 13, 1980; May 17, 1994; October 12, 2001, Sarah Lyall, "Nobel in Literature Goes to Naipaul, an Explorer of Exile," p. A11; October 16, 2001, Michiko Kakutani, "A Young Man in a Strange Place at a Time That Can Never Be Right," p. E1.

New York Times Book Review, October 15, 1967; April 7, 1968; May 24, 1970; October 17, 1971; November 16, 1975; December 28, 1975; May 1, 1977; June 12, 1977; May 13, 1979; May 22, 1994, Brent Staples, "Con Men and Conquerors," pp. 1, 42-43; June 7, 1998, Michael Ignatieff, "In the Name of the Most Merciful"; January 5, 2000, Mel Gussow, "The Writer-to-Be and His Mentor"; January 16, 2000, Abraham Verghese, "The Family Business"; September 1, 2002, Daphne Merkin, review of *The Writer and the World,* p. 11.

New York Times Magazine, October 28, 2001, Adam Shatz, interview with Naipaul, p. 19.

Observer (London, England), April 30, 1967; September 10, 1967; October 26, 1969; September 22, 2002, Jason Cowley, review of *The Writer and the World,* p. 15.

PMLA, May, 2002, transcript of Naipaul's Nobel lecture, p. 479.

Progressive, November, 1998, Edward W. Said, review of *Beyond Belief,* p. 40.

Publishers Weekly, May 25, 1998, review of *Beyond Belief,* p. 82; November 29, 1999, review of *Between Father and Son,* p. 59; May 13, 2002, review of *The Writer and the World,* p. 58; June 23, 2003, review of *Literary Occasions: Essays,* p. 55.

Punch, May 10, 1967.

Rocky Mountain News, Ashley Simpson Shires, review of *Literary Occasions,* p. 29D.

St. Louis Post-Dispatch, August 25, 2002, Dale Singer, review of *The Writer and the World,* p. F9.

San Francisco Chronicle, October 17, 2001, David Kipen, "Unsatisfying 'Half' by Naipaul; Novelist Uncharitable to His Characters," p. E1.

Saturday Review, July 2, 1960; October 23, 1971; November 15, 1975.

Seattle Times, August 18, 2002, Michael Upchurch, review of *The Writer and the World,* p. K10.

Smithsonian, December, 2001, Paul Gray, *Any Other Year, Giving Reactionary Author V. S. Naipaul a Nobel Would Have Sparked Debate,* p. 106.

Spectator, September 22, 1967; November 8, 1969; May 14, 1994, p. 36.

Tennessean, October 12, 2003, Brian J. Buchanan, review of *Literary Occasions,* p. D38.

Time, May 25, 1970; December 1, 1975; June 20, 1977; May 21, 1979; May 30, 1994, p. 64; October 22, 2001, Robert Hughes, "Peace and Understanding," p. 84.

Time International, August 3, 1998, "Journey to Islam," p. 39; November 26, 2001, R. Z. Sheppard, review of *Half a Life,* p. 68.

Times (London, England), October 12, 2001, David Pryce-Jones, "Naipaul Is Truly a Nobel Man in a Free State."

Times Literary Supplement, May 31, 1963; April 27, 1967; September 14, 1967; December 25, 1969; July 30, 1971; November 17, 1972.

Transition, December, 1971.

Tribune Books (Chicago, IL), May 13, 1979; April 20, 1980.

Twentieth Century Literature, summer, 2000, Robert M. Greenberg, "Anger and the Alchemy of Literary Method in V. S. Naipaul's Political Fiction: The Case of *The Mimic Men,*" p. 214.

U.S. News & World Report, August 10, 1998, Jonah Blank, "Feuding Literary Titans," p. 39.

Washington Post, October 12, 2001, Linton Weeks, "A Winning Worldview: Globetrotting V. S. Naipaul Collects Nobel Prize for Literature," p. C01; October 26, 2003, Sudip Bose, review of *Literary Occasions,* p. B8.

Washington Post Book World, April 19, 1970; December 5, 1971; November 28, 1976; June 19, 1977; July 1, 1979; May 15, 1994, pp. 1, 14.

Washington Times, August 25, 2002, Sven Birkerts, review of *The Writer and the World,* p. B8.

Weekend Australian, December 28, 2002, Delia Falconer, review of *The Writer and the World,* p. B10.

World Literature Today, summer, 2000, Bruce King, review of *Between Father and Son,* p. 575; spring, 2002, Mervyn Morris, *Sir Vidia and the Prize,* p. 11; April-June, 2003, Bruce King, review of *Half a Life,* p. 90.

World Press Review, July, 1998, L. K. Sharma, "Faith and Neurosis," p. 41.

ONLINE

Salon.com, http://www.salon.com/ (January 18, 2000), Akash Kapur, review of *Between Father and Son;* (October 14, 2001), Gavin McNett, "The Black Sheep."*

* * *

NIMOY, Leonard 1931-

PERSONAL: Born March 26, 1931, in Boston, MA; son of Max and Dora (Spinner) Nimoy; married Sandra Zober, February 21, 1954 (divorced); married Susan Bay; children: (first marriage) Julie, Adam. *Education:* Boston College, B.A.; Antioch University, M.A.; studied drama at Pasadena Playhouse, Pasadena, CA, 1949-50. *Politics:* Democrat. *Religion:* Jewish. *Hobbies and other interests:* Black-and-white photography.

ADDRESSES: Home—Bel Air, CA. *Agent*—The Allen Agency, Inc., 23852 Pacific Coast Hwy., Suite 401, Malibu, CA 90265.

Leonard Nimoy

CAREER: Actor, producer, and director in television, films, and theatre; photographer; and author. Television roles include Mr. Spock on series *Star Trek,* National Broadcasting Companies, Inc. (NBC), 1966-69, and Paris on series *Mission Impossible,* Columbia Broadcasting System, Inc. (CBS), 1969-70; has also appeared in numerous other series, including *Sea Hunt, Kraft Theatre, Perry Mason, Twilight Zone, Bonanza,* and *Profiles in Courage*; host of television series *In Search Of . . . ,* 1976-80; producer-host of documentary *If the Mind Is Free.* Actor in stage plays, including *Full Circle,* 1973, *Dr. Faustus, Stalag 17, A Streetcar Named Desire, Cat on a Hot Tin Roof, Irma La Douce, Fiddler on the Roof, The King and I, My Fair Lady, Sherlock Holmes,* and *Equus.* Actor in films, including *Kid Monk Baroni,* 1952, *The Balcony,* 1963, *Deathwatch,* 1966, *The Invasion of the Body Snatchers,* 1978, *Star Trek,* 1979, and *Atlantis, the Lost Empire.* Producer of films, including *Deathwatch,* 1966, *Invasion of the Body Snatchers,* 1978, *Star Trek: The Wrath of Khan,* 1982, *Star Trek III: The Search for Spock,* 1984, *Star Trek IV: The Voyage Home,* and *Star Trek VI: The Undiscovered Country;* producer for theatre and television. Director of television shows

Night Gallery, The Powers of Matthew Star, and *T. J. Hooker*; director of films, including *Star Trek III: The Search for Spock,* 1984, *Star Trek IV: The Voyage Home,* 1986, *Three Men and a Baby,* 1987, *The Good Mother, Funny about Love,* and *Holy Matrimony.* Narrator of television specials and radio shows, including *Destiny in Space,* 1994, *Carpati: Fifty Miles, Fifty Years,* 1996, and *A Life Apart: Hasidism in America,* 1997; narrator, *The Illustrated Man* (sound recording), Caedmon, 1976, *The Martian Chronicles, War of the Worlds, The Green Hills of Earth,* and *Gentlemen, Be Seated.* Operated drama studio in North Hollywood, CA, 1962-65; teacher, Synanon, Santa Monica, CA, 1964-65; owner, Adajul Music Publishing Co. Member of advisory board, Parents for Peace (Western Los Angeles chapter). *Military service:* U.S. Army, 1954-56.

MEMBER: American Federation of Television and Radio Artists, Screen Actors Guild, Actors' Equity Association, American Civil Liberties Union.

AWARDS, HONORS: Three Emmy Award nominations for portrayal of Mr. Spock on *Star Trek*; given a star on the Hollywood Walk of Fame, 1985.

WRITINGS:

POETRY; SELF-ILLUSTRATED WITH PHOTOGRAPHS

You and I, Celestial Arts (Millbrae, CA), 1973.
Will I Think of You?, Celestial Arts (Millbrae, CA), 1974.
We Are All Children Searching for Love: A Collection of Poems and Photographs, Blue Mountain Press (Boulder, CO), 1977.
Come Be with Me, Blue Mountain Press (Boulder, CO), 1978.
These Words Are for You, Blue Mountain Press (Boulder, CO), 1981.
Warmed by Love, Blue Mountain Press (Boulder, CO), 1983.
A Lifetime of Love: Poems on the Passages of Life, Blue Mountain Press (Boulder, CO), 2002.

OTHER

I Am Not Spock (autobiography), Celestial Arts (Millbrae, CA), 1975.
(Coauthor) *Star Trek IV: The Voyage Home,* Simon & Schuster (New York, NY), 1986.
I Am Spock, Hyperion (New York, NY), 1995.
(Author of introduction and epilogue; and narrator) *Jewish Stories from the Old World to the New* (sound recording), KCRW-FM (Santa Monica, CA), 1999.
(With John de Lancie) *Star Trek: Spock vs. Q* (sound recording), Simon & Schuster (New York, NY), 2000.
Shekhina (collection of photographs), Umbrage Editions, 2002.

Contributor to *Bio-Cosmos,* by James Christian, 1975. Author of recordings, including *Leonard Nimoy Presents Mr. Spock's Music from Outer Space, Two Sides of Leonard Nimoy, The Way I Feel, The Touch of Leonard Nimoy,* and *The New World of Leonard Nimoy,* all for Dot.

ADAPTATIONS: I Am Spock was adapted as an audiobook, Brilliance (Grand Haven, MI), 1995.

SIDELIGHTS: Leonard Nimoy began his acting career at the age of nine and became world famous in 1966, when he created the role of Mr. Spock in the popular television series *Star Trek.* Spock, the science officer of the Starship *Enterprise,* is only half human; his father is of the unemotional, logical Vulcan race. The conflict between the two sides of Spock's nature intrigued many viewers, and Nimoy became strongly identified with the role. His 1975 autobiography was titled *I Am Not Spock,* but in a 1987 interview with *Chicago Tribune* contributor Philip Wuntch, Nimoy claimed, "I've made my peace with Spock. . . . I can't deny that Spock is an enormously important part of my life. At times I even find myself thinking . . . and talking like him. I can't deny what he has done for my career. I wouldn't even have a career if it weren't for Spock."

Born in Massachusetts, Nimoy took an early interest in acting and photography. At the age of eighteen he moved to California and began to study acting in earnest. After military service in 1956 he settled in Hollywood and began to appear in small roles in numerous television shows. When offered the role of Spock, he brought his own interpretation to the character, including his trademark Vulcan hand sign, which is actually a traditional Jewish greeting. When he created the role of Mr. Spock, Nimoy could hardly have foreseen that he would become so closely associated with the character. As the popularity of *Star Trek* skyrocketed, however, the actor discovered that being Spock was both blessing and curse. Although the exposure helped Nimoy win roles on Broadway and find venues for creative work as a poet, he was also prone to typecasting based on the emotionally reserved Spock.

It is perhaps not surprising, then, that Nimoy turned to directing films as one outlet for his creativity. After reprising the Spock character in the early installments of the successful "Star Trek" film series, he directed two of the films, *Star Trek III: The Search for Spock* and *Star Trek IV: The Voyage Home.* He is also given credit as producer of *Star Trek VI: The Undiscovered Country.* A *Time* film critic praised Nimoy's directorial work in *Star Trek III,* claiming that it has the effect of "beaming his film up onto a higher pictorial plane than either of its predecessors." David Denby also credited Nimoy, who began directing for television and theater in the 1950s, with upgrading the original "Star Trek." He wrote in a *New York* review of *Star Trek IV* that Nimoy "may be the first *Star Trek* director to provide the standard show-business virtue of pace, suspense, variety [to the series]. This *Star Trek* actually moves along smartly—an example of professionalism that some Trekkies will undoubtedly experience as a betrayal of the material's usual cardboard-and-mucilage approach to drama." Equally successful was Nimoy's directing of the box-office favorite *Three Men and a Baby,* starring Tom Selleck, Ted Danson, and Steve Guttenberg as bachelors who find a baby at their doorstep. *Three Men and a Baby* still ranks as one of the most successful comedy films of all time.

Nimoy's problematic relationship with his famous character is the subject of two autobiographies, *I Am Not Spock* and *I Am Spock.* Both books shed light on the experience of being a cast member in the original *Star Trek* television series, including the ways in which Nimoy influenced the character's evolution. Although *I Am Spock,* written twenty years after its predecessor, is meant to show how Nimoy has come to terms with the character, he still admits to having mixed feelings about this alien alter ego. A *Publishers Weekly* reviewer found *I Am Spock* to be "an intelligent and entertaining look at an actor's engagement with a character." Albert Kim in *Entertainment Weekly* noted that "the most compelling parts of *I Am Spock* are when Nimoy walks us through the vagaries of his own internalized angst. . . . During these moments of obsessive reflection, *I Am Spock* is genuinely absorbing."

In addition to his autobiographies, Nimoy is author of many volumes of poetry and a collection of art photographs titled *Shekhina.* The photographs are based on Nimoy's explorations of his Jewish heritage and the role of the divine feminine in Judaism. In a review of *Shekhina* for the Newark, New Jersey, *Star-Ledger,* Mitchell Seidel observed: "Even with his darkest images, Nimoy attempts to present an ethereal, other-worldly feel in his work. The prayer shawls, gauzy fabrics and longer exposures help to create a spiritual look of a being that is more light and imagination than flesh and blood."

Nimoy lives in Bel Air, California, and continues to be actively involved in film, photography, recording work, as well as motivational speaking.

BIOGRAPHICAL AND CRITICAL SOURCES:

BOOKS

Gerrold, David, *The World of Star Trek,* Ballantine (New York, NY), 1973.

Nimoy, Leonard, *I Am Not Spock,* Celestial Arts (Millbrae, CA), 1975.

Nimoy, Leonard, *I Am Spock,* Hyperion (New York, NY), 1995.

Whitefield, Stephen E., and Gene Roddenberry, *The Making of Star Trek,* Ballantine (New York, NY), 1973.

PERIODICALS

American Photo, September-October, 2002, "Leonard Nimoy: In a Down-to-Earth Interview, the Man Best Known in Our Galaxy As Mr. Spock Tells about His Life As an Art Photographer—and His New Portfolio of Nudes Based on Ancient Mysticism," p. 34.

Booklist, September 15, 1995, Ray Olson, review of *I Am Spock,* p. 115; September 15, 2000, Leah Sparks, review of *Star Trek: Spock vs. Q,* p. 259.

Chicago Tribune, December 13, 1987.

Entertainment Weekly, September 29, 1995, Albert Kim, review of *I Am Spock,* p. 54.
Library Journal, August, 1999, Meloday A. Moxley, review of *Jewish Stories from the Old World to the New,* p. 163.
Newsweek, February 23, 1976, December 1, 1986.
New York, June 11, 1984, December 8, 1986.
New Yorker, July 9, 1984; September 4, 1995, "Oy, Spock," p. 34.
New York Times, October 15, 1967, August 25, 1968.
New York Times Book Review, November 5, 1995, Anita Gates, review of *I Am Spock,* p. 22.
People, June 18, 1984.
Publishers Weekly, September 18, 1995, review of *I Am Spock,* p. 120.
San Francisco Chronicle, March 17, 2001, John McMurtrie, "Leonard Nimoy's Personal Quest," p. B3.
Saturday Review, June 17, 1967.
Star-Ledger (Newark, NJ), November 30, 2002, Mitchell Seidel, "Orthodox Jews Object to Nimoy's Images," p. 19.
Time, June 11, 1984, December 8, 1986.

ONLINE

Leonard Nimoy Fan Club Web site, http://www.nimoy.com/ (November 6, 2003).*

* * *

NIOSI, Jorge 1945-

PERSONAL: Born December 8, 1945, in Buenos Aires, Argentina; son of Salvador (in business) and Emilia (Farina) Niosi; married Graciela Ducatenzeiler (a university professor), November, 1971; children: Marianne, Laurence. *Ethnicity:* "Caucasian." *Education:* National University of Buenos Aires, license in sociology, 1967; Institut d'Études du Developpement Economique et Social, Paris, France, certificate in advanced studies in economics, 1970; École Pratique, Paris, Ph.D., 1973.

ADDRESSES: Home—4052 Marlowe, Montreal, Quebec H4A 3M2, Canada. *Office*—Inter-University Research on Science and Technology, University of Quebec—Montreal, P.O. Box 6192, Downtown Station, Montreal, Quebec H3C 4R2, Canada; fax: 514-987-3343. *E-mail*—niosi.jorge@uwam.ca.

CAREER: University of Quebec—Montreal, associate professor, 1970-74, aggregate professor, 1974-81, professor of sociology, 1981—, professor of administrative science, 1989—, director of Center for Research on the Development of Industry and Technology, 1986—. Statistics Canada, researcher, 1987-90.

MEMBER: International Sociological Association, International Management of Technology Association, European Association for Evolutionary Political Economy, Royal Society of Canada (fellow).

AWARDS, HONORS: John Porter Award, Canadian Sociological Association, 1983, for *Canadian Capitalism;* Fulbright fellow, 1995-96.

WRITINGS:

Los Empresarios y el estado Argentino (title means "Business and the Argentine State"), Siglo XXI, 1974.
The Economy of Canada, Black Rose Books (Montreal, Quebec, Canada), 1978.
Canadian Capitalism, Lorimer (Toronto, Ontario, Canada), 1981.
Canadian Multinationals, Garamond (Toronto, Ontario, Canada), 1985.
The Decline of the American Economy, Black Rose Books (Montreal, Quebec, Canada), 1988.
La Montee de l'ingenierie canadienne, Presses de l'Université de Montréal (Montréal, Québec, Canada), 1990.
Technology and National Competitiveness, McGill-Queen's University Press (Montreal, Quebec, Canada), 1991.
Flexible Innovation, McGill-Queen's University Press (Montreal, Quebec, Canada), 1995.
(Coeditor) *The Economic and Social Dynamics of Biotechnology,* Kluwer Academic Publishers (Norwell, MA), 2000.
Canada's National System of Innovation, McGill-Queen's University Press (Montreal, Quebec, Canada), 2000.

Also coauthor of *Biotechnologie et industrie au Québec,* Transcontinental (Montréal, Québec, Canada).

WORK IN PROGRESS: A book on Canada's regional system of innovation; research on Canadian technology transfer abroad.

SIDELIGHTS: Reflecting on his career, Jorge Niosi noted: "I started working on Canada with the idea of comparing it to Argentina. Both countries were similarly rich and successful fifty years ago. Why did Argentina fail when Canada succeeded? The comparison, however, never materialized.

"In Canada, I discovered that Canadian-owned large firms were much stronger and numerous than generally believed, that many of them were multinational corporations, and that their industrial base was much healthier than most of the literature had previously stated. The relative decline of American industry is not strongly affecting Canada's manufacturing industry, which is mostly based on energy- and resource-intensive strongholds like pulp and paper, metal refining, and petrochemicals.

"In 1982 I started studying Canadian innovation and technology. This is, and will remain, my main field of study. My main motivation for writing is pure curiosity."

* * *

NYE, Naomi Shihab 1952-

PERSONAL: Born March 12, 1952, in St. Louis, MO; daughter of Aziz (a journalist) and Miriam Naomi (a Montessori teacher; maiden name, Allwardt) Shihab; married Michael Nye (a lawyer and photographer), September 2, 1978; children: Madison Cloudfeather (son). *Ethnicity:* "Arab-American." *Education:* Trinity University (San Antonio, TX), B.A. (English and world religions; summa cum laude), 1974. *Politics:* Independent. *Religion:* "Ecumenical." *Hobbies and other interests:* Traveling, reading, cooking, gardening, bicycling, watching basketball.

ADDRESSES: Home—806 South Main Ave., San Antonio, TX 78204. *E-mail*—nshihab@aol.com.

CAREER: Freelance writer, editor, and speaker, 1974—; Texas Commission on the Arts' Writers in the Schools Project, affilate, 1974-86. Holloway Lecturer, University of California, Berkeley; visiting writer at University of Hawaii, 1991, University of Alaska, Fairbanks, 1994, and University of Texas at Austin, 1995 and 2001; U.S. Information Agency Arts America Program, traveling writer and workshop leader. Poetry editor for *Texas Observer*; translator for Project of Translation from Arabic Literature (PROTA). Member of national council, National Endowment for the Humanities. Featured on eight-part Public Broadcasting Service (PBS) television special *The Language of Life with Bill Moyers,* 1995, on PBS series *The United States of Poetry,* and on National Public Radio.

MEMBER: Poets and Writers, Radius of Arab-American Writers, Texas Institute of Letters, Phi Beta Kappa.

AWARDS, HONORS: Voertman Poetry Prize, Texas Institute of Letters, 1980, for *Different Ways to Pray,* and 1982, for *Hugging the Jukebox; Hugging the Jukebox* named a notable book of 1982, American Library Association (ALA); four Pushcart poetry prizes; I. B. Lavan Award, Academy of American Poets, 1988; Charity Randall Prize for Spoken Poetry (with Galway Kinnell), International Poetry Forum, 1988; Jane Addams Children's Book Award, and Honorary Book designation, National Association for Christians and Jews, both 1992, both for *This Same Sky;* Best Book citation, *School Library Journal,* and Pick of the List citation from American Booksellers Association, both 1994, and Notable Children's Trade Book in the Field of Social Studies citation, National Council for the Social Studies/Children's Book Council, and Jane Addams Children's Book Award, both 1995, all for *Sitti's Secrets;* Judy Lopez Memorial Award for children's literature, and Texas Institute of Letters Best Book for Young Readers, and Dorothy Canfield Fisher Children's Book Award Master List honoree, 1998, all for *Habibi;* Paterson Poetry Prize, for *The Tree Is Older Than You Are;* Guggenheim Fellowship, 1997; Witter Bynner Fellowship, U.S. Library of Congress, 2000; Lee Bennett Hopkins Poetry Award, 2000, for *Come with Me: Poems for a Journey;* National Book Award finalist in young people's literature category, 2002, for *Nineteen Varieties of Gazelle: Poems of the Middle East;* Lannan fellowship, 2003.

WRITINGS:

POETRY; EXCEPT AS NOTED

Different Ways to Pray, Breitenbush (Portland, OR), 1980.

On the Edge of the Sky, Iguana Press (Madison, WI), 1981.
Hugging the Jukebox, Dutton (New York, NY), 1982.
Yellow Glove, Breitenbush (Portland, OR), 1986.
Invisible, Trilobite (Denton, TX), 1987.
Mint (prose; also see below), State Street Press (Brockport, NY), 1991.
Red Suitcase, BOA Editions (Rochester, NY), 1994.
Words under the Words: Selected Poems, Far Corner Books (Portland, OR), 1995.
Fuel, BOA Editions (Rochester, NY), 1998.
Mint Snowball (prose; includes selections previously published in *Mint*), Anhinga Press (Tallahassee, FL), 2001.

POETRY FOR CHILDREN

(Editor) *This Same Sky: A Collection of Poems from around the World,* Four Winds Press (New York, NY), 1992.
(Editor) *The Tree Is Older Than You Are: Poems and Stories from Mexico,* Simon & Schuster (New York, NY), 1995.
(Editor, with Paul Janeczko) *I Feel a Little Jumpy around You: A Book of Her Poems and His Poems Collected in Pairs,* Simon & Schuster (New York, NY), 1996.
(With others) *The Space between Our Footsteps: Poems and Paintings from the Middle East,* Simon & Schuster (New York, NY), 1998, published as *The Flag of Childhood: Poems from the Middle East,* Aladdin (New York, NY), 2002.
(Selector) *What Have You Lost?* (young-adult poetry), with photographs by husband, Michael Nye, Greenwillow Books (New York, NY), 1999.
(Selector) *Salting the Ocean: 100 Poems by Young Poets,* illustrated by Ashley Bryan, Greenwillow Books (New York, NY), 2000.
Come with Me: Poems for a Journey, with images by Dan Yaccarino, Greenwillow Books (New York, NY), 2000.
Nineteen Varieties of Gazelle: Poems of the Middle East, Greenwillow Books (New York, NY), 2002.
Is This Forever, or What? Poems and Paintings from Texas, Greenwillow Books (New York, NY), 2004.
Sweet Sifter in Time: Poems for Girls, illustrated by Terre Maher, Greenwillow Books (New York, NY), 2005.

PICTURE BOOKS

Sitti's Secrets, illustrated by Nancy Carpenter, Macmillan (New York, NY), 1994.
Benito's Dream Bottle, illustrated by Yu Cha Pak, Simon & Schuster (New York, NY), 1995.
Lullaby Raft, illustrated by Vivienne Flesher, Simon & Schuster (New York, NY), 1997.
Baby Radar, illustrated by Nancy Carpenter, Greenwillow Books (New York, NY), 2003.

OTHER

Never in a Hurry (essays; for yung adults), University of South Carolina Press (Columbia, SC), 1996.
Habibi (novel; for young adults), Simon & Schuster (New York, NY), 1996.

Also author of chapbooks *Tattooed Feet,* 1977, and *Eye-to-Eye,* 1978. Contributor to *Texas Poets in Concert: A Quartet,* edited by Richard B. Sale, University of North Texas Press, 1990, and *Best American Essays 1991,* edited by Joyce Carol Oates. Contributor of poems, stories, and essays to periodicals, including *Atlantic, Iowa Review, Georgia Review, Ploughshares, Atlanta Review, Indiana Review, Hayden's Ferry Review, Virginia Quarterly Review, Southwest Review, Manoa, Houston Chronicle,* and *Austin Chronicle.*

Recordings include *Rutabaga-Roo* (songs), Flying Cat (San Antonio, TX), 1979; *Lullaby Raft,* Flying Cat (San Antonio, TX), 1981; and *The Spoken Page* (poetry reading), International Poetry Forum (Pittsburgh, PA), 1988.

WORK IN PROGRESS: A novel titled *Florrie Will Do It;* new poems, essays, and picture books.

SIDELIGHTS: Naomi Shihab Nye is known for award-winning poetry that lends a fresh perspective to ordinary events, people, and objects. "For me the primary source of poetry has always been local life, random characters met on the streets, our own ancestry sifting down to us through small essential daily tasks," Nye was quoted by Jane L. Tanner in an essay for the *Dictionary of Literary Biography.* Characterizing Nye's "prolific canon" in *Contemporary Women Poets,* Paul Christensen noted that Nye "is building a reputation . . . as the voice of childhood in America, the voice of the girl at the age of daring exploration." Nye's poetry is also informed by her Palestinian-American background, as well as by other cultures. In her work, according to Tanner, "Nye observes the business of living and the continuity among all the world's inhabitants. . . . She is international in scope and internal in focus."

Nye is also considered one of the leading figures in the poetry of the American Southwest, especially poetry expressing a woman's point of view. A contributor to *Contemporary Poets* wrote that she "brings attention to the female as a humorous, wry creature with brisk, hard intelligence and a sense of personal freedom unheard of" in the trying history of pioneer women.

Nye was born in St. Louis, Missouri, to a Palestinian father and an American mother of German and Swiss descent. As a young girl she read voraciously and listened to her father's stories about his homeland and family. She began writing poems at age six and had them published in a children's magazine at age seven. After spending much of her childhood in St. Louis, Nye moved with her family to Jerusalem, which was then part of Jordan. Nye attended a year of high school in Jordan before her family moved to San Antonio, Texas, where the poet continues to live with her husband and son. "My poems and stories often begin with the voices of our neighbors, mostly Mexican American, always inventive and surprising," Nye wrote in a press release for Four Winds Press. "I never get tired of mixtures." A contributor to *Contemporary Southern Writers* wrote that Nye's poetry "is playfully and imaginatively instructive, borrows from Eastern and Middle Eastern and Native American religions, and resembles the meditative poetry of William Stafford, Wallace Stevens, and Gary Snyder."

Nye's earliest published work includes a 1977 chapbook titled *Tattooed Feet;* another chapbook, *Eye-to-Eye,* followed in 1978. The early poems contained in these books, written in free verse, often reflect the theme of a journey or quest. According to Tanner, "What is remarkable is Nye's ability to draw clear parallels between the ordinary and the sublime."

Nye told *CA*: "I have always loved the gaps, the spaces between things, as much as the things. I love staring, pondering, mulling, puttering. I love the times when someone or something is late—there's that rich possibility of noticing more, in the meantime.

"Poetry calls us to pause. There is so much we overlook, while the abundance around us continues to shimmer, on its own."

In her first full-length collection, *Different Ways to Pray,* Nye explores the differences between, and shared experiences of, cultures from California to Texas, from South America to Mexico. In "Grandfather's Heaven," a child declares: "Grandma liked me even though my daddy was a Moslem." As Tanner observed, "with her acceptance of different 'ways to pray' is also Nye's growing awareness that living in the world can sometimes be difficult."

Nye followed *Different Ways to Pray* with *On the Edge of the Sky,* a slim volume printed on handmade paper, and *Hugging the Jukebox,* a full-length collection that also won the Voertman Poetry Prize. In *Hugging the Jukebox,* Nye continues to focus on the ordinary, on connections between diverse peoples, and on the perspectives of those in other lands. She writes: "We move forward, / confident we were born into a large family, / our brothers cover the earth." Nye creates poetry from everyday scenes in "The Trashpickers of San Antonio," where the trashpickers are "murmuring in a language soft as rags." The boy in the title poem "Hugging the Jukebox" is enthusiastic about the jukebox he adopts, singing its songs in a way that "strings a hundred passionate sentences in a single line."

Reviewers generally praised *Hugging the Jukebox,* noting Nye's warmth and celebratory tone. Writing in the *Village Voice,* Mary Logue commented that in Nye's poems about daily life, "sometimes the fabric is thin and the mundaneness of the action shows through. But, in an alchemical process of purification, Nye often pulls gold from the ordinary." According to *Library Journal* contributor David Kirby, the poet "seems to be in good, easy relation with the earth and its peoples." In Christensen's view, Nye "does not avoid the horrors of urban life, but she patches together the vision of simple nature struggling up through the cracks of the city."

Unlike her earlier work, the poems in *Yellow Glove* present a more mature perspective tempered by tragedy and sorrow. In this collection Nye considers the Palestinian-Israeli conflict in "Blood." She describes a café in combat-weary Beirut, bemoans "a world where no one saves anyone," and observes "The Gardener" for whom "everything she planted gave up under the ground." *Georgia Review* contributor Philip Booth declared that Nye brings "home to readers both how variously and how similarly all people live."

In addition to her poetry collections, Nye has produced fiction for children, poetry and song recordings, and poetry translations. She has also produced a book of essays, *Never in a Hurry,* published in 1996, and has edited several books of poems, including the award-winning anthology *This Same Sky.* In her introduction to *This Same Sky,* which represents the work of 129 poets from sixty-eight countries, Nye writes, "Whenever someone suggests 'how much is lost in translation!' I want to say, 'Perhaps—but how much is gained!'" A tremendous amount of work was involved in collecting these poems from around the world but, as Nye told a contributor to the *Children's Literature Review,* that "the poems ended up gathering themselves into sections that felt almost organic—related to family, or words and silences, or losses, or human mysteries. The sky seemed to occur surprisingly often as a universal reference point, which gave us the title."

Reviewers praised *This Same Sky,* which also includes country and poet indices as well as a map. These extras, according to Mary M. Burns in *Horn Book,* give "additional luster to a book which should prove invaluable for intercultural education." Although contributor Lauralyn Persson noted in *School Library Journal* that some of the poems in the collection would be better appreciated by adults, the reviewer added that the book is "brimming with much lovely material." Jim Morgan, in *Voice of Youth Advocates,* found the book's strongest characteristic to be its "sense of real human life behind the words" and a "universality of human concerns across cultures." *Booklist* critic Hazel Rochman called *This Same Sky* "an extraordinary anthology, not only in its global range . . . but also in the quality of the selections and the immediacy of their appeal."

Nye compiled and edited another anthology, *The Tree Is Older Than You Are,* which collects stories and poems from Nye's beloved Mexico, displaying them in both English and Spanish versions. Hazel Rochman, writing in *Booklist,* praised the "dreamy, lyrical writing with sudden leaps from the real to the magical." The 1996 collection *I Feel a Little Jumpy around You* combines 194 "his and her" poems, pairing a poem written by a man with one written by a woman for a lively poetic discussion of the differences between the genders and their perspectives on the world. Anthony Manna, in *Voice of Youth Advocates,* found the most intriguing aspect of the book to be "the degree to which the voices blend and gender boundaries give way to quests, quirks, and needs which signal the ties that bind us." The 1998 anthology *The Space between Our Footsteps* is a collection of the work of 127 contemporary Middle-Eastern poets and artists representing nineteen countries. Angela J. Reynolds in *School Library Journal* noted that "the universality of topics . . . gives insight into a culture and proves that differences are only skin deep."

Sitti's Secrets concerns an Arab-American child's relationship with her *sitti*—Arabic for grandmother—who lives in a Palestinian village. The child, Mona, recalls visiting Sitti in Palestine and how the two of them invented their own sign language to overcome the English-Arabic language barrier. When Mona returns to the United States, she sustains the bond with Sitti through her active imagination. Mona also writes a letter to the president of the United States, asking him for peace and informing him that she knows he would like her sitti a great deal if he were to meet her. Hazel Rochman, in *Booklist,* praised Nye for capturing the emotions of the "child who longs for a distant grandparent" as well as for writing a narrative that deals personally with Arabs and Arab Americans. A contributor to *Kirkus Reviews* asserted that Nye "deftly assembles particulars" of the relationship between grandmother and granddaughter and recounts incidents "with quiet eloquence."

Benito's Dream Bottle, a picture book for very young children, introduces the boy Benito, whose grandmother has stopped dreaming. He helps her fill up her "dream bottle," located between the stomach and the chest, with a world of sights and sounds so that she might dream again. Reviewers for *Publishers Weekly* and *Booklist* found the lists of images a bit overwhelming, but Judy Constantinides, in *School Library Journal,* called the book "inventive" and "lyrical."

In 1997 Nye published *Habibi,* her first young-adult novel. Readers meet Liyana Abboud, an Arab-American teen who moves with her family to her Palestinian father's native country during the 1970s, only to discover that the violence in Jerusalem has not yet abated. As Liyana notes, "in Jerusalem, so much old anger floated around . . . [that] the air felt stacked with weeping and raging and praying to God by all the different names." Autobiographical in its focus, *Habibi* was praised by Karen Leggett, who noted in the *New York Times Book Review* that the novel magnifies through the lens of adolescence "the joys and anxieties of growing up" and that Nye is "meticulously sensitive to this rainbow of emotion." Appraising *Habibi* in *Horn Book,* Jennifer M. Brabander agreed, saying, "The leisurely progression of the narrative matches the slow and stately pace of daily life" in Jerusalem "and the text's poetic turns of phrase accurately reflect Liyana's passion for words and language." As Nye explained to a *Children's Literature Review* contributor: "To counteract negative images conveyed by blazing headlines, writers must steadily transmit simple stories closer to heart and more common to everyday life. Then we will be doing our job."

What Have You Lost? contains 140 contemporary poems for young adults arranged by different themes of loss experienced over a person's lifetime. Written by mostly lesser-known poets, the poems, according to Jessica Roeder in *Riverbank Review,* take "a fresh look at this perennial theme," becoming "an exercise in expanding compassion." Hazel Rochman, in *Booklist,* pointed out that the book would be "a great stimulus for students' personal writing."

Come with Me: Poems for a Journey contains sixteen poems by Nye that are written for grade-school children and focus on journeys, both real and imaginary. A *Publishers Weekly* contributor found it "chock-full of unexpected images," and Shelle Rosenfeld, writing in *Booklist,* described *Come with Me* as ranging from "playful to pensive." Nina Lindsay, in *School Library Journal,* commented, "Each line exerts a pull like gravity."

Salting the Ocean is a collection of poems by children who have attended Nye's writing workshops over a twenty-five-year period. A contributor to *Horn Book* found that while some "occasionally catch fire," for the most part the poems are more imaginative word play than poetry. Linda Zoppa, in *School Library Journal,* said she enjoyed reading Nye's introduction in which the poet explained how she saved the poems over the years and eventually sought permission to print them from the adults who were once her students.

In her book of poetry *Nineteen Varieties of Gazelle,* Nye looks at the Middle East through her Palestinian-American poet's eye, recording the sights, sounds, smells, tastes, and people she encounters, especially in Jerusalem, in a time of terror and struggle. Brabander said that young-adult readers familiar with Nye's *Habibi* and *Sitti's Secrets* will recognize the people and "will feel they are reading the grown-up Liyana's poetry." Nye allows readers a view into the lives of the many innocent people in the Middle East in a post-September 11 world. A contributor to *Kirkus Reviews* said that reading the poems will "elicit a gasp of surprise, a nod of the head, a pause to reflect," while Hazel Rochman concluded in *Booklist,* that *Nineteen Variations of Gazelle* "will spark discussion and bring readers up close" to what war and vengeance really mean. Nina Lindsay, in *School Library Journal,* observed that Nye's book is "a celebration of her heritage, and a call for peace."

Nye told *CA:* "As a child I became crucially aware of that sweet sliver of day called *twilight.* I would stand on our little front porch in St. Louis, gazing into the softening light, feeling hugely nostalgic, wanting to hang onto everything. Don't go so soon, something inside me implored. Everything passes before we are ready for it to pass. I'm not done with this day! Please stay.

"Listening to poems read by my mother created a savory, magical atmosphere, suspended in time. Read it again, I would beg her. When I could read for myself, I found my eyes traveling up and down a poem, Langston Hughes, Emily Dickinson, Rabindranath Tagore, William Blake—taking time with each word and phrase, floating peacefully in the beautiful space around the words on the page. Naturally, if one loved to read so much, writing became the automatic 'next activity'—the thank-you letter for all that had been given.

"My advice to anyone who asks for it remains the same for many years: Read, read, then read some more. Find a way to engage in regular daily writing. Consider it parallel to physical fitness. Writing in small blocks of time keeps us flexible, responsive, in tone and tune with muscular, vivid, energetic words.

"Then, find some way to share your work. Become involved in local writing circles, attend readings by writers. Make a system, a notebook, for yourself—where you might send your work, along with a self-addressed stamped envelope, that magical detail. Keep track of what you send where.

"And don't let 'rejections' trouble you too much—they are utterly inevitable, part of the process. Look at your work with a fresh eye when it comes winging home to you. Is there any way you could make it better?

"There is no end to the writing/reading life. It always feels like a beautiful, wildly mysterious beginning. That is the gift we are given, to see again and again."

BIOGRAPHICAL AND CRITICAL SOURCES:

BOOKS

Children's Literature Review, Volume 59, Gale (Detroit, MI), 2000.

Contemporary Poets, 7th edition, St. James Press (Detroit, MI), 2001.

Contemporary Southern Writers, St. James Press (Detroit, MI), 1999.

Contemporary Women Poets, St. James Press (Detroit, MI), 1997.

Dictionary of Literary Biography, Volume 120: *American Poets since World War II,* Gale (Detroit, MI), 1992.

PERIODICALS

Book, September-October, 2002, review of *Nineteen Varieties of Gazelle: Poems of the Middle East,* p. 40.

Booklist, October 15, 1992, Hazel Rochman, review of *This Same Sky: A Collection of Poems from around the World,* p. 425; March 15, 1994, Hazel Rochman, review of *Sitti's Secrets,* p. 1374; May 1, 1995, Hazel Rochman, review of *Benito's Dream Bottle,* p. 1580; September 15, 1995, Hazel Rochman, review of *The Tree Is Older than You Are: Poems and Stories from Mexico,* p. 151; September 15, 1997, Hazel Rochman, review of *Habibi,* p. 224; March 15, 1999, review of *The Space between Our Footsteps: Poems and Paintings from the Middle East,* p. 1297; April 1, 1999, Hazel Rochman, review of *What Have You Lost?,* p. 1397; October 15, 2000, Shelle Rosenfeld, review of *Come with Me: Poems for a Journey,* p. 442; December 1, 2000, review of *Come with Me,* p. 693; March 15, 2001, review of *Salting the Ocean: 100 Poems by Young Poets,* p. 1393; April 1, 2002, Hazel Rochman, review of *Nineteen Varieties of Gazelle,* p. 1315.

BookPage, April, 2002, review of *Nineteen Varieties of Gazelle,* p. 26.

Book Report, September, 1999, review of *What Have You Lost?,* p. 75.

Books for Keeps, March, 2002, review of *The Space between Our Footsteps, Habibi,* and *Sitti's Secrets,* p. 4.

Bulletin of the Center for Children's Books, March, 1994, p. 228; March, 1999, review of *What Have You Lost?,* p. 251.

Catholic Library World, September, 1999, review of *Habibi,* p. 19.

Chelsea, June 7, 1999, review of *Fuel,* p. 188.

Children's Book & Play Review, January, 2001, review of *This Same Sky,* p. 4.

Detroit Free Press, April 14, 2002, review of *The Flag of Childhood: Poems from the Middle East,* p. E5.

Five Owls, March, 2001, review of *This Same Sky,* p. 78.

Georgia Review, spring, 1989.

Horn Book, March-April, 1993, Mary M. Burns, review of *This Same Sky,* p. 215; May-June, 1994, Maeve Visser Knoth, review of *Sitti's Secrets,* p. 317-18; November-December, 1996, p. 755; November-December, 1997, Jennifer M. Brabander, review of *Habibi,* pp. 683-684; March, 1999, review of *What Have You Lost?,* p. 218; July, 2000, review of *Salting the Ocean,* p. 472; September-October, 2002, Jennifer M. Brabander, review of *Nineteen Varieties of Gazelle,* p. 591.

Junior Bookshelf, April, 1995, Marcus Crouch, review of *Sitti's Secrets,* p. 65-66.

Kirkus Reviews, February 15, 1994, review of *Sitti's Secrets,* p. 231; April 1, 1998; February 15, 1999, review of *What Have You Lost?,* p. 303; April 15, 2002, review of *Nineteen Varieties of Gazelle,* p. 575.

Kliatt, May, 1999, review of *I Feel a Little Jumpy around You,* p. 31; September, 1999, review of *Habibi,* p. 19.

Library Journal, August, 1982.

MELUS, summer, 2002, Joy Castro, "Nomad, Switchboard, Poet: Naomi Shihab Nye's Multicultural Literature for Young Readers: An Interview," p. 225.

New York Times Book Review, November 16, 1997, Karen Leggett, review of *Habibi,* p. 50; November 23, 1997.

Poetry, March, 1999, review of *Fuel,* p. 357.

Publishers Weekly, April 24, 1995, review of *Benito's Dream Bottle,* p. 71; May 13, 1996, p. 77; September 8, 1997, p. 77; March 8, 1999, review of *What Have You Lost?,* p. 70; September 4, 2000, review of *Come with Me,* p. 108; April 16, 2001, review of *Mint Snowball,* p. 60; February 18, 2002, review of *The Flag of Childhood,* p. 99.

Reading Teacher, February, 1999, review of *Habibi,* p. 504; September, 1999, review of *The Space between Our Footsteps,* p. 85; May, 2001, review of *Come with Me,* p. 824.

Riverbank Review, spring, 1999, Jessica Roeder, review of *What Have You Lost?,* pp. 42-43.

School Library Journal, December, 1992, Lauralyn Persson, review of *This Same Sky,* p. 139; June, 1994, Luann Toth, review of *Sitti's Secrets,* p. 112; June, 1995, Judy Constantinides, review of *Benito's Dream Bottle,* p. 94; September, 1997, Kate McClelland, review of *Habibi,* pp. 223-224; May, 1998, Angela J. Reynolds, review of *The Space between Our Footsteps,* p. 159; April, 1999, review of *What Have You Lost?,* p. 152; July, 2000, Linda Zoppa, review of *Salting the Ocean,* p. 120; September, 2000, Nina Lindsay, review of *Come with Me,* p. 221; May, 2002, Nina Lindsay, review of *Nineteen Varieties of Gazelle,* p. 175.

Teacher Librarian, May, 1999, review of *What Have You Lost?,* p. 45; February, 2001, review of *Salting the Ocean,* p. 26.

Tribune Books (Chicago, IL), March 31, 2002, review of *Nineteen Varieties of Gazelle,* p. 5.

Village Voice, January 18, 1983, p. 37.

Voice of Youth Advocates, April, 1993, Jim Morgan, review of *This Same Sky,* p. 59; August, 1996, Anthony Manna, review of *I Feel a Little Jumpy around You,* p. 178; February, 1999, review of *The Space between Our Footsteps,* p. 413; August, 2001, review of *Salting the Ocean,* p. 171.

Washington Post Book World, May 13, 2001, review of *What Have You Lost?,* p. 5.

ONLINE

Academy of American Poets Web site, http://www.poets.org/ (August 28, 2002), "Naomi Shihab Nye."

Anhinga Press Web site, http://www.anhinga.org/ (February 11, 2003).

Harper/Collins Children's Books, http://www.harperchildrens.com/ (February 11, 2003).

NewPages, http://www.newpages.com/ (February 11, 2003), Denise Bazzett, review of *Mint Snowball.*

Voices from the Gaps Web site, http://voices.cla.umn.edu/ (April 9, 1999), Mindy S. Howie, "Naomi Shihab Nye."*

O

OE, Kenzaburo 1935-

PERSONAL: Surname is pronounced "*Oh*-ey"; born January 31, 1935, in Ehime, Shikoku, Japan; married; wife's name Yukari; children: Hikari Pooh, one other child. *Education:* Tokyo University, earned degree (French literature), 1959.

ADDRESSES: *Home*—585 Seijo-machi, Setagaya-Ku, Tokyo, Japan.

CAREER: Novelist and short story writer, 1952—.

AWARDS, HONORS: Akutagawa prize, Japanese Society for the Promotion of Literature, 1958, for novella *Shiiku;* Shinchosha literary prize, 1964; Tanizaki prize, 1967; Europelia Arts Festival Literary Prize, 1989; Nobel Prize for Literature, 1994; Order of Culture, Japanese government (declined), 1994.

WRITINGS:

IN ENGLISH

Shiiku (novella; title means "The Catch"), [Japan], 1958, translation by John Bester published in *The Shadow of Sunrise,* edited by Saeki Shoichi, [Palo Alto, CA], 1966.

Memushiri kouchi (fiction), [Japan], 1958, translation by Paul St. John Mackintosh and Maki Sugiyama published as *Nip the Buds, Shoot the Kids,* Marion Boyars (New York, NY), 1995.

Kenzaburo Oe

Kojinteki na taiken (fiction), [Japan], 1964, translation by John Nathan published as *A Personal Matter,* Grove (New York, NY), 1968.

Man'en gannen no futtoboru (fiction), [Japan], 1967, translation by John Bester published as *The Silent Cry,* Kodansha (New York, NY), 1974.

Pinchi ranna chosho (fiction), [Japan], 1976, translation by Michiko N. Wilson and Michael K. Wilson published as *The Pinch Runner Memorandum,* M. E. Sharpe (Armonk, NY), 1995.

Teach Us to Outgrow Our Madness (contains "The Day He Himself Shall Wipe My Tears Away," "Prize Stock," and "Aghwee the Sky Monster"), translation and introduction by John Nathan, Grove (New York, NY), 1977.

Hiroshima Notes (essays), translation by David L. Swain and Toshi Yonezawa, Marion Boyars (New York, NY), 1981, revised edition, 1995.

The Crazy Iris and Other Stories of the Atomic Aftermath, translation by Ivan Morris and others, Grove (New York, NY), 1984.

Japan, the Ambiguous, and Myself: The Nobel Prize Speech and Other Lectures, translation by Hisaaki Yamanouchi and Kunioki Yanagishita, Kodansha (New York, NY), 1995.

A Healing Family (essays), translation by Stephen Snyder, Kodansha International (New York, NY), 1996.

Shizuka na seikatsu, [Japan], translation by Kunioki Yanagishita and William Wetherall published as *A Quiet Life,* Grove (New York, NY), 1996.

Two Novels: Seventeen, J., translation by Luk Van Haute, introduction by Masao Miyoshi, Blue Moon Books (New York, NY), 1996.

Jinsei no shinseki, [Japan], 1989, translation by Margaret Mitusani published as *An Echo of Heaven,* Kodansha International (New York, NY), 1996.

Atarashii hito yo mezameyo, [Japan], 1986, translation by John Nathan published as *Rouse Up, O Young Men of the New Age!,* Grove (New York, NY), 2002.

Kaifuku-suru kazoku, Kodansha (Tokyo, Japan), 1995, translation by Stephen Snyder published as *A Healing Family,* illustrated by Yukari Oe, Kodansha International (New York, NY), 1996.

Chugaeri, [Japan] 1999, translation by Philip Gabriel published as *Somersault: A Novel,* Grove (New York, NY), 2003.

FICTION; IN JAPANESE

Warera no jidai (title means "Our Age"), [Japan], 1959.

Okurete kita seinen (title means "Born Too Late"), [Japan], 1961.

Sakebigoe (title means "Screams"), [Japan], 1962.

Nichijo seikatsu no boken, [Japan], 1971.

Kozui wa waga tamashii ni oyobi, [Japan], 1973.

Seinen no omei, [Japan], 1974.

M/T to mori no fushgi no monogatari (title means "M/T and the Wonders of the Forest"), Iwanami Shoten (Tokyo, Japan), 1990.

Sukuinushi ga nagurareru made (first novel of trilogy "The Flaming Green Tree"; title means "Until the 'Savior' Gets Socked,"), Shinchosha (Tokyo, Japan), 1993.

Yureugoku: "vashireshon" (second novel of trilogy "The Flaming Green Tree"; title means "Vacillating"), Shinchosha (Tokyo, Japan), 1994.

Aimaina Nohon no watakushi, Iwanami Shoten (Tokyo, Japan), 1995.

Oinaru hi ni (third novel of trilogy "The Flaming Green Tree"; title means "On the Great Day"), Shinchosha (Tokyo, Japan), 1995.

SHORT STORIES; IN JAPANESE

Oe Kenzaburo shu, [Japan], 1960.

Kodoku na seinen no kyuka, [Japan], 1960.

Seiteki ningen, [Japan], 1968.

Warera no hyoki o ikinobiru michi o oshieyo, [Japan], 1969, enlarged edition, 1975.

Oe Kenzaburo ("Gendai no bungaku" series), [Japan], 1971.

Mizukara waga namida o nugui-tamau hi, [Japan], 1972.

Sora no kaibutsu Agui, [Japan], 1972.

ESSAYS; IN JAPANESE

Jizokusuru kokorozashi, [Japan], 1968.

Kakujidai no sozoryoku, [Japan], 1970.

Kowaremono to shite no ningen, [Japan], 1970.

Okinawa noto, [Japan], 1970.

Kujira no shimetsusuru hi, [Japan], 1972.

Dojidai to shite no sengo, [Japan], 1973.

Jokyo e, [Japan], 1974.

Bungaku noto, [Japan], 1974.

Genshuku na tsunawatari, [Japan], 1974.

Kotoba no yotte, [Japan], 1976.

Sekai no wakamonotachi, [Japan], 1962.

Oe Kenzaburo zensakuhin, [Japan], 1966-67.

Oe Kenzaburo shu ("Shincho Nihon bungaku" series), [Japan], 1969.

(Editor) Mansaku Itami, *Itami Mansaku essei shu,* [Japan], 1971.

OTHER

(With Günter Grass) *Gestern, vor 50 jahren: Ein deutch-japanischer briefwechsel* (title means "Yesterday, 50 Years Ago: A German-Japanese Correspondence"), translation from the Japanese by Otto Putz, Steidl, 1995.

Also author of *The Perverts* (fiction), 1963, and *Adventures in Daily Life* (fiction), 1964.

SIDELIGHTS: Kenzaburo Oe became one of Japan's first authors ever to receive national recognition for his writing while still a university student. When he was awarded the prestigious Akutagawa prize in 1958 for his novella *Shiiku* ("The Catch"), the twenty-three-year-old became one of Japan's most popular writers. Now acclaimed as one of the greatest Japanese writers of the twentieth century, Oe won the 1994 Nobel Prize for Literature.

Oe was born in 1935 in the forested mountain region of Shikoku Island in southern Japan. His father died in 1944. He studied comparative literature at Tokyo University, taking a degree in French literature in 1959. A master of languages, he reads French, Russian, Chinese, English, and Russian, and has been particularly influenced by French and American authors—from Rabelais to Sartre and from Herman Melville and Mark Twain to Norman Mailer. It was from Rabelais, according to translator David Swain in the commentary included his translation of Oe's *Hiroshima Notes,* that Oe learned the image system of grotesque realism, "a mode of literary expression that has enabled Oe to eschew the traditional Japanese literary habits of indirection and suggestive innuendo and to develop instead a more universal style of dealing directly with reality as experienced yet without sacrificing subtlety."

Oe has been politically engaged since his student days when he led demonstrations against the reestablishment of the U.S.-Japan Security Treaty. He has consistently protested war, nuclear weapons, racism, even the nearly sacrosanct "Emperor system." Masao Miyoshi wrote in the *San Francisco Review of Books* that Oe's "passion for the underclass of the earth cannot be challenged." In *Portrait of a Postwar Generation,* Oe wrote movingly of hearing Emperor Hirohito, revered as an unseen and unheard god, announce over the radio on August 15, 1945, that Japan had surrendered: "How could we believe that an August presence of such awful power had become an ordinary human being on a designated summer day?" The cognitive dissonance of hearing that "ordinary" human voice has informed Oe's work: one is never quite sure when the bizarre, the grotesque, or the merely incredible will afflict the comfortable.

Western literature has greatly influenced Oe's writings. At Tokyo University he studied the existentialist philosophy of Jean-Paul Sartre, as well as the works of Blaise Pascal and Albert Camus. His favorite American authors are those whose heroes search for "personal freedom beyond the borders of safety and acceptance"—authors such as Herman Melville, William Faulkner, and Norman Mailer. Oe was most inspired by Mark Twain's character Huckleberry Finn, whom he used as a model for his own fictional hero.

Oe's interest in the political and the absurd are reflected in two of his earlier novels which have been more recently translated into English. *Nip the Buds, Shoot the Kids* is set on the island of Shikoku, Oe's "peripheral" birthplace. It takes place during World War II, as a group of juvenile delinquents are evacuated from a reformatory to a remote village. The boys are mistreated by hostile peasants until the villagers, fearing plague, abandon them. The adolescent narrator tells how the boys band together, caring for each other as well as an abandoned girl and a Korean boy. When the villagers return, they attempt to hush the boys about their abandonment at the hands of those meant to protect them. All but the narrator give in, and he is hounded and chased out of the village "insanely angry, tearful, shivering with cold and hunger." Julian Duplain of the *Times Literary Supplement* wrote: "As a story of misled innocents, Oe's novel draws clear parallels with imperialistic Japanese military policy in the Second World War, as well as providing a rallying cry for antiauthoritarian resistance. To Western readers, the directness of emotion—for example, the boys' honest esteem for one another—sometimes sounds simplistic." A *Kirkus Reviews* writer found *Nip the Buds, Shoot the Kids* to be "more shaded, more graphic, and angrier than *Lord of the Flies,* but the fierce anger is transmuted by Oe's art into literary gold—an anguished plea for tolerance more wrenching than any rant could ever be."

The pivotal event in Oe's life and work was the birth of his brain-damaged son Hikari ("Light") in 1963. As a strong bond developed between Oe and his son, the writer penned several partially autobiographical novels in which the protagonist is the father of a brain-damaged child. The first of these, *A Personal Matter,* is the story of a twenty-seven-year-old man nicknamed Bird, whose wife gives birth to a deformed baby. The boy, looking like a two-headed monster, appears to have a brain hernia, and the doctors tell Bird that the baby will probably die or be a vegetable for life. Bird is so horrified that he chooses to let the baby die rather than face life tied to a retarded son. While his wife and child are in the hospital, Bird runs off to the apartment of a young widow friend, where he escapes into a world of fantasy, sex, and alcohol. He loses his teaching job after being so hung over that he vomits during a lecture. Meanwhile, the baby, being fed only sugar water, refuses to die, so Bird takes him to an abortionist to have him killed. Suddenly, however, he changes his mind and returns the baby to the hospital. Doctors discover that the hernia is only a benign tumor and after successfully operating, they announce that the baby will be normal, though with a low IQ. Bird finds a new job and is reunited once more with his wife and child.

The novel is not as pretty as its ending might suggest. *Washington Post* reviewer Geoffrey Wolff remarked that *A Personal Matter* "reeks of vomit and spilled whisky. Its surreal characters are all vegetables, cut off from history and hope. They define themselves by their despair. They use sex to wound and humiliate one another. They trick themselves with hopeless dreams of a new life, far away." Alan Levensohn surmised that this representation of humanity is Oe's way of suggesting that "the stunted existence Bird's baby will probably have, if Bird allows him to live, comes to seem terribly close to the existence which Bird and the others are making for themselves." John Hearsum similarly commented, "The prose is hard and brittle, the images like tiny nightmares. . . . It communicates the full terror of such a predicament, and confronts the arbitrary horror of the universe without any recourse to fancy techniques."

In his own life, Oe, feeling much like Bird, went off on assignment to report on the international peace meeting in Hiroshima. His *Hiroshima Notes* records his views of the antinuclear movement from 1963 to 1965, focusing on the political bickering of the several factions and lashing out at their failure to recognize the real suffering of the victims of the atomic bombings. Oe drew strength from his encounters with the survivors, and particularly with Dr. Fumio Shigeto, whom Oe saw, according to Yoshio Iwamoto, as "the archetype of the authentic man of Hiroshima, a man who reclaims humanity out of the ashes of dehumanization." Oe's transforming experience in Hiroshima led him to approve the operation that saved Hikari's life, albeit with severe mental limitations. Virtually speechless, Hikari nevertheless later demonstrated a remarkable talent for music composition. Despite continuing health problems and his mental impairment, he released two CDs in Japan that have sold well.

The Pinch Runner Memorandum tells the story of a group of student radicals who construct their own atomic bomb. A brain-damaged boy and his father, a former nuclear physicist, work with Oe and his own son to avert disaster. "The invention of this 'pinch runner' double," Masao Miyoshi wrote in the *Nation,* "suggests the increasing complexity of a writer in positioning himself in his story—and the world." A critic for the *New Yorker* found that "Oe's writing is bold, savage, and often very funny. . . . This complicated book is above all a heartening display of the explosively constructive power of imagination."

Oe's *A Quiet Life,* published in Japan in 1990, is a semifictional account of three nearly adult children, one mentally disabled, who are left to cope alone when their parents move to the United States for eight months. A major theme of the novel is the anxiety of the caregivers over the feelings and needs of the mentally impaired family member, Eeyore, whose communication is rare and often ineffective. They consistently leap to the worst conclusions. When Eeyore writes a musical piece he calls "The Abandoned Child," his brother and sister immediately assume the reference is to Eeyore and his father, which Eeyore is only belatedly able to explain is not the case. "Yet," noted Lindsley Cameron in the *Yale Review,* "the question of the father's guilt is never really resolved. In fact, the novel is in a way a long exploration of that question, and some of its most strongly felt passages condemn the claims of exceptional individuals to exceptional privileges." The book has little plot, but is, said John David Morely, simply an account of the young people's daily life amid "an idiosyncratic set of family and friends, portraits drawn with affection, insight, and that wry humor . . . [that] is one of the defining qualities of [Oe's] talent."

The transformation of suffering is also the theme of Oe's novel *An Echo of Heaven,* which recounts the life of a Japanese woman, Marie Kuraki, whom Oe and the novel's narrator first knew as a teacher of foreign languages and literature in a Tokyo university. Marie marries and has two sons, one severely brain-damaged. As teenagers, the boys commit suicide together, and Marie's estranged husband turns into a drunken wastrel. The novel focuses on Marie's efforts to rise above these tragedies, as she works first with a theater troupe, then with a semi-Christian cult in California, and finally on a peasant commune in Mexico. The commune's leader, in a ploy to hold his project together, plans to transform Marie, a persistent unbeliever now dying of cancer in her late forties, into a saint to be revered by the peasants. Zia Jeffery, writing in the *Nation,* saw the novel as Oe's ironic backward glance at his own career as an artist being transformed from a man "into a martyr, then an image of a martyr and finally into kitsch."

Oe put the capstone on his autobiographical work about his son, Hiraki, with *Rouse Up, O Young Men of the New Age,* in which he traces the boy's development from childhood to young manhood. Employing images from nineteenth-century English poet William Blake, Oe "performs a kind of literary onanism," according to Andrew Irvin in the *Philadelphia Inquirer Online.* As Irvin further noted, with this work Oe "has looked inward and found the seeds of artistic invention in his own books." Again, Oe tells the tale of a famous Japanese author, known only as "K," and his mentally disabled son, nicknamed Eeyore. With his father away on a business trip, Eeyore acts erratically, becomes depressed and even violent. When K returns, he tries to get closer to his son to understand his mood swing; he finds succor and guidance in a strange place: the poetry of Blake. Adam Mars-Jones, writing in the *Guardian Online,* noted that "for most of this book, Oe takes from Blake the marvelous discovery that the most extreme expressions are sometimes the least distorted." Mars-Jones also found Oe's novel "fascinating and even rewarding," though he also noted "it isn't easy to take in." In a *Publishers Weekly* review, a contributor remarked that Oe writes with "depth and passion" about his relationship with his son. The same reviewer felt that Oe's book is "deceptively modest . . . [and] powerful," and that Oe is a "master at the height of his literary powers." Similarly, *Booklist*'s Ray Olson described the novel as "Oe at his best," in both an "intellectual treatise" and a "moving family memoir."

The winning of the Nobel Prize in 1994 marked the beginning of a new artistic era for Oe. His first novel after winning the prize, *Somersault,* "concerns an austere, embattled, and eventually self-destructive religious cult," according to a critic for *Kirkus Reviews.* Inspired by the 1995 events surrounding the Aum Shinrikyo cult, Oe moves away from the autobiographical stance of so many of his works featuring the relationship between him and his disabled son. In this book, artist and art professor Kizo, who is suffering from terminal cancer, falls in love with a boy, Ikuo, whom he met years earlier. Now the professor and his friend are enlisted in the effort to revive a religious cult discredited a decade earlier for terrorist plans. In the course of this work, they become involved with a strange girl, Dancer, who was earlier involved with Ikuo, as well as with a full panoply of characters inside the cult, all jockeying for power. Olson, writing in *Booklist,* called *Somersault* a "thick stew of sexual and more parareligious than religious incidents." Olson also felt that the novel resembles the work of "late Dostoevsky." Shirley N. Quan, reviewing the title for *Library Journal,* thought it "reads like a social/spiritual/religious commentary," and is a "highly literate piece." Commenting on the length of the work—576 pages—a reviewer for *Publishers Weekly* noted that Oe "has attempted to create a sprawling masterpiece, but American readers might decide there's more sprawl than masterpiece here." Similarly, the *Kirkus* reviewer found the first half of the novel "tedious." However, according to the same critic, the second half, detailing the reemergence of the thriving cult creates a "series of increasingly complex relationships and tensions." Interestingly, even in this nonautobiographical novel, Oe's son Hikari makes an appearance in the guise of a musical genius who has suffered brain damage.

In his acceptance speech for the Nobel Prize, Oe described how his son had once been "awakened by the voices of birds to the music of Bach and Mozart": "Herein I find the grounds for believing in the exquisite healing power of art. . . . As one with a peripheral, marginal, and off-center existence in the world, I would like to seek how. . . I can be of some use in a cure and reconciliation of mankind."

BIOGRAPHICAL AND CRITICAL SOURCES:

BOOKS

Cameron, Lindsley, *The Music of Light: The Extraordinary Story of Hikari and Kenzaburo Oe,* Free Press (New York, NY), 1998.

Contemporary Literary Criticism, Gale (Detroit, MI), Volume 10, 1979, Volume 36, 1986, Volume 86, 1995.

Dictionary of Literary Biography, Volume 182: *Japanese Writers since World War II,* Gale (Detroit, MI), 1997.

Dictionary of Literary Biography Yearbook: 1994, Gale (Detroit, MI), 1995.

Forest, Philippe, *Oe Kenzaburo: Legendes d'un romancier japonais,* Editions Plein Feux (Paris, France), 2001.

Literature Lover's Companion, Prentice Hall (Englewood, NJ), 2001.

Napier, Susan J., *Escape from the Wasteland: Romanticism and Realism in the Fiction of Mishima Yukio and Oe Kenzaburo,* Harvard University Press (Cambridge, MA), 1991.

Oe, Kenzaburo, *Hiroshima Notes* (essays), translation by David L. Swain and Toshi Yonezawa, Marion Boyars (New York, NY), 1981, revised edition, 1995.

Oe, Kenzaburo, *Japan, the Ambiguous, and Myself: The Nobel Prize Speech and Other Lectures,* translation by Hisaaki Yamanouchi and Kunioki Yanagishita, Kodansha (New York, NY), 1995.

Penguin International Dictionary of Contemporary Biography, Penguin Reference (New York, NY), 2001.

Reference Guide to Short Fiction, St. James Press (Detroit, MI), 1999.

Rubin, Jay, editor, *Modern Japanese Writers,* Scribner (New York, NY), 2000, pp. 277-293.

Short Story Criticism, Volume 20, Gale (Detroit, MI), 1995.

Wilson, Michiko N., *The Marginal World of Oe Kenzaburo: A Study in Themes and Techniques,* M. E. Sharpe (Armonk, NY), 1986.

PERIODICALS

Best Sellers, July 1, 1968; October, 1977.

Booklist, February 1, 2002, Ray Olson, review of *Rouse Up, O Young Men of the New Age!,* p. 908; March, 2003, Ray Olson, review of *Somersault,* p. 629.

Books Abroad, winter, 1969.

Boundary 2, fall, 1991; summer, 1993.

Christian Century, April 12, 1995, p. 382; December 24, 1997, p. 1226.

Christian Science Monitor, August 8, 1968; October 18, 1994, p. 13.

Critique, Volume 15, number 3, 1974.

Entertainment Weekly, March 22, 2002, review of *Rouse Up, O Young Men of the New Age!,* p. 104.

Hudson Review, autumn, 1968.

Japan Quarterly, July, 1996, p. 90; January, 1997, p. 102; October, 1997, p. 38.

Kirkus Reviews, March 1, 1995, review of *Nip the Buds, Shoot the Kids,* p. 261; February 1, 2002, review of *Rouse Up, O Young Men of the New Age!,* p. 134; February 1, 2003, review of *Somersault,* p. 172.

Library Journal, December, 2002, Shirley N. Quan, review of *Somersault,* p. 180.

Life, August 16, 1968.

Los Angeles Times, October 14, 1994, p. A1; October 19, 1994, p. B7.

Nation, August 5, 1968; May 15, 1995, Masao Miyoshi, review of *The Pinch Runner Memorandum* p. 696; September 30, 1996, Zia Jeffery, review of *An Echo of Heaven,* p. 34.

New Republic, August 17, 1968.

New Yorker, June 8, 1968; November 14, 1994, p. 147; February 6, 1995, p. 38; October 9, 1995, p. 91.

New York Review of Books, October 10, 1968.

New York Times, November 6, 1994, p. 5.

New York Times Book Review, July 7, 1968; September 8, 1985; June 19, 1995, p. 43; July 9, 1995, p.8.

Publishers Weekly, October 17, 1994, p. 17; March 27, 1995, pp. 48, 73; August 7, 1995, p. 438; April 8, 1996, p. 56; January 28, 2002, review of *Rouse Up, O Young Men of the New Age!,* p. 267; January 6, 2003, review of *Somersault,* p. 36.

Rain Taxi, summer, 2001, Jason Picone, review of *Rouse Up, O Young Men of the New Age!*

Review of Contemporary Fiction, fall, 2002, Amy Havel, review of *Rouse Up, O Young Men of the New Age!,* p. 145.

San Francisco Review of Books, March-April, 1995, pp. 8-9.

Studies in Short Fiction, fall, 1974.

Time, October 24, 1994, p. 64.

Times (London, England), May 16, 1995, p. 35.

Times Literary Supplement, October 26, 1984, p. 1227; April 28, 1989; May 12, 1995, Julian Duplain,

review of *Nip the Buds, Shoot the Kids,* p. 21; December 27, 1996, p. 32; October 31, 1997.
Voice Literary Supplement, October, 1982.
Washington Post, June 11, 1968, Geoffrey Wolff, review of *A Personal Matter.*
Washington Post Book World, August 25, 1968; September 11, 1977.
World Literature Today, spring, 1978; spring, 1985, p. 318; winter, 1995, pp. 5-16; spring, 1996, p. 475; autumn, 1996, p. 1033; summer, 1997, p. 653; winter, 1997, p. 229.
Yale Review, April, 1997, Lindsley Cameron, review of *A Quiet Life,* p. 150.

ONLINE

Guardian Online, http://www.guardian.co.uk/ (August, 4, 2002), Adam Mars-Jones, review of *Rouse Up, O Young Men of the New Age!*
Nobel e-Museum, http://www.nobel.se/ (1994), "Kenzaburo Oe—Biography."
Philadelphia Inquirer Online, http://www.philly.com/ (May 12, 2002), Andrew Ervin, review of *Rouse Up, O Young Men of the New Age!**

* * *

ORETTI, Carlos
See HARSCH, Rick

* * *

OSMOND, Marie 1959-

Marie Osmond

PERSONAL: Born Olive Marie Osmond, October 13, 1959, in Ogden, UT; daughter of George Viril and Olive (Davis) Osmond; married Stephen Craig, 1982 (marriage ended); married Brian Blosil, 1986; children: (first marriage) Stephen; (second marriage) Jessica, Rachael, Michael, Brandon, Brianna, Matthew. *Education:* Educated privately. *Religion:* Church of Jesus Christ of Latter-day Saints (Mormons).

ADDRESSES: *Agent*—William Morris Agency, One William Morris Pl., Beverly Hills, CA 90212.

CAREER: Member of family singing groupThe Osmonds, 1966-73; solo performer, beginning in 1973. Star of television programs, including *Donny and Marie,* 1976-79, *Marie,* 1980-81, *Ripley's Believe It or Not,* 1985-86, and *Donny and Marie,* 1998-2000; has appeared on numerous television specials, 1973—. Film credits include *Hugo the Hippo,* 1976, *Goin' Coconuts,* 1978, *The Velveteen Rabbit,* 1984, *Buster & Chauncey's Silent Night,* 1998, *Get Bruce,* 1999, and *I Married Wyatt Earp.* Stage appearances include *The Sound of Music,* 1994-95, and *The King and I,* 1997; also toured with annual Christmas musical variety show. Record albums include *Paper Roses,* 1973, *In My Little Corner of the World, Who's Sorry Now?, This Is the Way That I Feel, I Only Wanted You, Rose Petal Place, All in Love, Steppin' Stone, The Best of Marie Osmond, Marie Osmond—Twenty-five Hits,* and *There's No Stopping Your Heart,* 1985; (with Donny Osmond) *Make the World Go Away, I'm Leaving It All Up to You, Goin' Coconuts, New Season, Winning Combination, Donny and Marie Special,* and *Greatest Hits.* Co-owner of Marian (porcelain doll company), 2000—. Founder and spokesperson, Children's Miracle Network.

AWARDS, HONORS: Georgie Award (with others) for best vocal team, American Guild of Variety Artists, 1978; music award (with Dan Seals) for best country duo of the year, 1986, for song "Meet Me in Montana"; Roy Acuff Award, Country Music Foundation, 1989, for recognition of work on behalf of children.

WRITINGS:

(With Rochelle Reed) *Fun, Fame, and Family,* New American Library (New York, NY), 1973.

(With Julie Davis) *Marie Osmond's Guide to Beauty, Health, and Style,* Simon & Schuster (New York, NY), 1980.

(With Elizabeth Noble) *Marie Osmond's Exercises for Mothers-to-Be,* New American Library (New York, NY), 1985.

(With Marcia Wilkie) *Behind the Smile: My Journey out of Postpartum Depression,* Warner (New York, NY), 2001.

SIDELIGHTS: Marie Osmond has literally spent a lifetime entertaining audiences as a singer, actress, and talk-show host. Osmond began her performing career as a young teen alongside her brothers as part of the group The Osmonds, and then scored several top-ten hits in duet with her brother Donny. She has also gained recognition as a solo recording artist with hits such as "Paper Roses" and "Read My Lips." All of the Osmonds capitalized upon their religious upbringing and clean-cut appearances, and none more so than Marie, who once described herself in a song as "a little bit country." As Kate Coyne observed in *Good Housekeeping:* "In the late 1960s, the Osmonds served as America's Von Trapp family, a squeaky-clean lineup of eight Mormon brothers and their little sister." When fourteen-year-old Marie joined Donny in the *Donny and Marie Show* they were "nicknamed the 'One-Take Osmonds,' reflecting their determination to do everything right, the first time. Any pain or personal inconvenience—from working eighteen-hour days to performing with numerous injuries—was never spoken about."

Osmond recalls those years in the limelight in her book *Behind the Smile: My Journey out of Postpartum Depression.* The urge to be perfect at all times, to work hard without complaining, and to be ready to greet others with a big smile spilled over into Osmond's private life as she sought to maintain her busy schedule and raise seven children. A severe case of postpartum depression after the birth of her son Matthew forced Osmond to examine herself closely and to review not only her current personal and professional challenges but also the stresses inflicted during her unconventional childhood. *Behind the Smile* includes Osmond's candid reflections on the demands placed upon youthful pop sensations and her own varied means of dealing with the challenges of a career in entertainment.

In the late 1990s Donny and Marie Osmond hosted a daytime television talk show, and Marie also toured as a star of musical theater in such plays as *The Sound of Music* and *The King and I.* Marie Osmond has also become a successful entrepreneur with a line of personally designed porcelain dolls that are sold on television's QVC Network. She has been recognized for her work on behalf of disadvantaged children, most notably with the Children's Miracle Network, a major television fundraising initiative. Osmond told *Good Housekeeping:* "I'm a very strong person. I'm no wimp. I'm a survivor. People look at me and say, 'Oh, there's Marie, that goody goody.' But, you know what? You can't be in this business for as long as I have and be naïve. You can't not be tough."

BIOGRAPHICAL AND CRITICAL SOURCES:

BOOKS

Contemporary Theatre, Film, and Television, Volume 37, Gale (Detroit, MI), 2002.

Osmond, Donny, *Life Is What You Make It: My Life So Far,* 1999.

PERIODICALS

Good Housekeeping, April, 1978, p. 110; August, 1979, p. 44; September, 1983, pp. 156-157; May, 1985, p. 178; May, 2001, Kate Coyne, "Marie Osmond: Behind the Smile," p. 96.

Ladies' Home Journal, March, 1977, p. 52; October, 1979, pp. 65-66; November, 1985, p. 32.

McCalls, August, 1982, p. 32; May, 1984, p. 26; April, 1985, p. 38.

People, July 5, 1982, pp. 68-70; January 17, 1983, pp. 66-67; December 10, 1984, p. 60; January 31, 2000, "Behind the Smile: Only Weeks after Revealing Her Depression, Marie Osmond Splits from Husband," p. 52.

ONLINE

Marie Osmond Web site, http://www.osmond.com/marie/ (November 14, 2003).*

P

PAGE, Katherine Hall 1947-

PERSONAL: Born July 9, 1947, in NJ; daughter of William Kingman (a hospital administrator) and Alice (an artist; maiden name, Malmgreen) Page; married Alan Hein (a professor), December 6, 1975; children: Nicholas William. *Education:* Wellesley College, A.B., 1969; Tufts University, Ed.M., 1974; Harvard University, Ed.D., 1985.

ADDRESSES: *Home*—Lincoln, MA. *Agent*—Faith Hamlin, Sanford J. Greenburger Associates, Inc., 55 Fifth Ave., New York, NY 10022.

CAREER: Worked as a teacher of English and history, and as a director of programs for adolescents with special emotional needs, 1969-80; writer, 1980—. Educational consultant, 1985—.

MEMBER: Mystery Readers International, Authors Guild, Author's League of America, Mystery Writers of America, Sisters in Crime, International Crime Writers League, Boston Author's Club.

AWARDS, HONORS: Agatha Award for best first domestic mystery novel, 1990; Agatha Award for best short story, 2001, for "The Would-Be Widower."

WRITINGS:

"FAITH FAIRCHILD" MYSTERY NOVELS

The Body in the Belfry, St. Martin's Press (New York, NY), 1990.

The Body in the Kelp, St. Martin's Press (New York, NY), 1991.

The Body in the Bouillon, St. Martin's Press (New York, NY), 1991.

The Body in the Vestibule, St. Martin's Press (New York, NY), 1992.

The Body in the Cast, St. Martin's Press (New York, NY), 1993.

The Body in the Basement, St. Martin's Press (New York, NY), 1994.

The Body in the Bog, St. Martin's Press (New York, NY), 1996.

The Body in the Fjord, Morrow (New York, NY), 1997.

The Body in the Bookcase, Morrow (New York, NY), 1998.

The Body in the Big Apple, Morrow (New York, NY), 1999.

The Body in the Moonlight, Morrow (New York, NY), 2001.

The Body in the Bonfire, Morrow (New York, NY), 2002.

The Body in the Lighthouse, HarperCollins (New York, NY), 2003.

The Body in the Attic, Morrow (New York, NY), 2004.

"CHRISTIE AND COMPANY" YOUNG-ADULT MYSTERY NOVELS

Christie and Company, Avon (New York, NY), 1996.

Christie and Company Down East, Avon (New York, NY), 1997.

Christie and Company in the Year of the Dragon, Avon (New York, NY), 1997.

Bon Voyage, Christie and Company, Avon (New York, NY), 1999.

SIDELIGHTS: Katherine Hall Page is the author of two ongoing mystery series. The first of these revolves around Faith Fairchild, a Massachusetts caterer and minister's wife whose amateur crime investigations are laced with some of the recipes she puts to use in her catering business. The second of Page's mystery series is aimed at young readers and features three eighth-grade girls known as Christie and Company. The threesome's adventures include a healthy teenage concern for such things as hairstyles, boys, and clothing.

Writing in *Booklist,* Stuart Miller saw a strong parallel between Page's "Faith Fairchild" mysteries and the Miss Marple stories written by noted British writer Agatha Christie. Page's character "is probably closest in spirit to Miss Marple," Miller wrote, "especially since Page's style is an updated, Americanized version of the classic English village cozy—short on gruesome details and violence, long on local color and deduction." Faith also draws admiration because, like many of her female readers, she must juggle the demands of work, family, and marriage while still finding time to solve crimes. Emily Melton in *Booklist* described Faith as "a modern-day heroine" who "effectively mixes modern-day moral dilemmas with charm, warmth, and humor."

Typical of the series is *The Body in the Cast,* in which Faith is hired to cater the meals for a film crew working on a new film adaptation of Nathaniel Hawthorne's novel *The Scarlet Letter.* When a series of seeming pranks begins to plague the production, Faith starts to investigate, finding hidden links between the film crew's troubles and a particularly nasty local race for town council. A critic for *Publishers Weekly* praised the story for its "spirited characterization and energetic plotting."

Several of the "Faith Fairchild" books also feature Faith's neighbor, friend and part-time employee Pix Miller. In *The Body in the Basement,* Pix and her daughter visit the site of Faith's new summer home, under construction, to check up on the project's progress. When the pair discover that a body has been buried in the unfinished house's basement, Pix works to unravel the mystery, all the while keeping Faith informed of both the progress of her investigation and the progress of Faith's construction project. The mystery centers on a strange blue "X" stitched into the quilt wrapped around the murdered man's body. A *Publishers Weekly* reviewer called *The Body in the Basement* a "leisurely tale" and added that the "down-to-earth, eminently likable Pix . . . proves an enjoyable stand-in for Faith." Pix returns in *The Body in the Fjord,* this time journeying to Norway to see about the missing granddaughter of a close family friend. Pix finds that the granddaughter's fiancée has turned up dead, floating in a fjord, and the missing girl is tied to possible stolen artifacts. GraceAnne A. DeCandido in *Booklist* noted that the "real treat here is the detailed and totally engaging tour of the fjords of Norway," especially "the evocative descriptions of Norway's physical beauty and culinary triumphs."

Page's series about Christie and Company features Christie and her two school friends Maggie and Vicky. In the opening book of the series, the three sleuths work to uncover the identity of a thief who is stealing valuable items from the students at their Massachusetts boarding school. Calling the book "rather mild in the suspense department but impressive in its characterizations," a critic for *Publishers Weekly* praised how, "as the amiable heroines flex their sleuthing skills, Page deftly works into the plot details about their family backgrounds, shaping credible, distinct portraits of each girl." *Christie and Company Down East* takes the three girls to Maine for a month-long summer stay at an inn owned by Maggie's parents. While working at the inn as waitresses, the girls begin investigating "seemingly unrelated but progressively more serious events designed to ensure the resort's demise," as Susan DeRonne explained in *Booklist.* In the end, the girls "solve the mystery, and they patch up a few relationships along the way," DeRonne concluded.

Faith Fairchild's more recent appearances include a prequel, *The Body in the Big Apple,* that details Faith's life before her marriage and relocation to Massachusetts. The story involves a politician's wife who seeks Faith's help in thwarting a blackmail attempt. "New Yorkers and suburbanites alike should enjoy this fast-paced mystery," declared a *Publishers Weekly* reviewer. *The Body in the Bonfire* takes Faith to an exclusive boarding school, and *The Body in the Lighthouse* concerns the murder of a developer on a pristine Maine island. A *Publishers Weekly* critic called *The Body in the Lighthouse* "absorbing" and further commented that it is "an ideal beach read for cozy fans heading for the shore this summer."

On the HarperCollins Web site, Page had this to say about her "Faith Fairchild" novels: "When I think about the series, I imagine Faith standing by a pond, its surface a mirror perhaps reflecting some white birches or catching the flight of a heron. Everything looks quite perfect and serene, but if she takes a stick and pokes it beneath the surface, who knows what lies below—what secrets will emerge from the murky depths? The difference between what seems and what is, has been a theme throughout all the books. It's the tension between appearance and reality that taps into our greatest fears."

BIOGRAPHICAL AND CRITICAL SOURCES:

PERIODICALS

Booklist, March 15, 1996, p. 1243; December 1, 1996, p. 665; May 1, 1997, p. 1498; October 15, 1997, p. 392; November 15, 1998, Emily Melton, review of *The Body in the Bookcase,* p. 572; March 15, 2003, GraceAnne A. DeCandido, review of *The Body in the Lighthouse,* p. 1280.

Boston, April, 1996, p. 82.

Library Journal, November 1, 1997, p. 120; January, 2002, Rex Klett, review of *The Body in the Bonfire,* p. 158.

New York Times Book Review, January 9, 2000, Marilyn Stasio, review of *The Body in the Big Apple,* p. 24.

Publishers Weekly, October 11, 1993, p. 72; September 19, 1994, p. 54; April 15, 1996, p. 69; October 6, 1997, p. 77; October 5, 1998, review of *The Body in the Bookcase,* p. 84; October 25, 1999, review of *The Body in the Big Apple,* p. 54; March 17, 2003, review of *The Body in the Lighthouse,* p. 57.

ONLINE

HarperCollins Web site, http://www.harpercollins.com/ (April 16, 2003) "Katherine Hall Page."

Katherine Hall Page Mystery Writer, http://www.katherine-hall-page.org/ (February 4, 2004).*

PARR, Delia

See LECHLEIDNER, Mary L.

* * *

PATOSKI, Joe Nick 1951-

PERSONAL: Born June 6, 1951, in Allentown, PA; son of Victor Albert Patoski (an engineer) and Irene (Cassalias) Randall (a travel agent); married Kristine Anne Cummings (an artist), November 18, 1980; children: Jake, Andy. *Education:* Attended University of Texas at El Paso, University of Minnesota—Twin Cities, University of Texas at Austin, and Tarrant County Junior College.

ADDRESSES: *Office*—P.O. Box 1569, Austin, TX 78767-1569.

CAREER: *Texas Monthly,* Austin, senior editor, 1988—. Also worked as a radio broadcaster, taxi cab driver, and manager of rock-and-roll bands. Former reporter and columnist, *Austin American-Statesman.*

WRITINGS:

(With Bill Crawford) *Stevie Ray Vaughan: Caught in the Crossfire,* Little, Brown (Boston, MA), 1993.

Selena: Como la flor, Little, Brown (Boston, MA), 1996.

Texas Mountains, with photographs by Laurence Parent, University of Texas Press (Austin, TX), 2001.

Contributor to *The Rolling Stone Illustrated History of Rock and Roll.* Contributor to periodicals, including *Rolling Stone, Men's Journal, Spin,* and *Conde Nast Traveler.*

A collection of Patoski's papers are housed at the Albert B. Alkek Library, Texas State University, San Marcos.

SIDELIGHTS: Joe Nick Patoski, a senior editor at *Texas Monthly* magazine, is the author of two biographies of notable Texas musicians. *Stevie Ray Vaughan: Caught in the Crossfire,* which Patoski wrote with Bill

Crawford, details the artistry and tragic death of the notable blues guitarist. *Selena: Como la flor,* released on the anniversary of its subject's death, explores the brief life of Tejano pop star Selena Quintanilla-Perez. In both cases Patoski worked without the cooperation of the artists' family members, as they were planning their own books. Nevertheless he was able to reconstruct the lives of Vaughan and Selena while adding background on the musical styles each practiced. *Billboard* reviewer Trudi Miller Rosenblum found *Selena: Como la flor* "a thoughtful and extensively researched account of Selena's life." And David Browne, in *Entertainment Weekly,* wrote of *Stevie Ray Vaughan:* "The authors are clearly fans, and their clean, straightforward prose downplays the lurid aspects of Vaughan's addiction to cocaine and whiskey."

Texas Mountains is a natural-history volume with photographs and essays about the named mountain ranges that stretch over eight counties in western Texas. In *Library Journal,* Tim Markus noted that the book "will amaze readers who have never visited this vast and remote area as well as those few who have."

BIOGRAPHICAL AND CRITICAL SOURCES:

PERIODICALS

Billboard, March 16, 1996, Trudi Miller Rosenblum, review of *Selena: Como la flor,* p. 95.

Entertainment Weekly, May 21, 1993, David Browne, review of *Stevie Ray Vaughan: Caught in the Crossfire,* p. 42; March 29, 1996, Alanna Nash, review of *Selena,* p. 55.

Library Journal, May 1, 1996, James E. Ross, review of *Selena,* p. 96; February 15, 2002, Tim Markus, review of *Texas Mountains,* p. 175.

Publishers Weekly, April 5, 1993, review of *Stevie Ray Vaughan,* p. 60.*

* * *

PAULSEN, Gary 1939-

PERSONAL: Born May 17, 1939, in Minneapolis, MN; son of Oscar (an Army officer) and Eunice Paulsen; married third wife, Ruth Ellen Wright (an artist), May 5, 1971; children: (first marriage) two; (third marriage) James Wright. *Education:* Attended Bemidji College, 1957-58; and University of Colorado, 1976. *Religion:* "Spiritual progress."

Gary Paulsen

ADDRESSES: Home—New Mexico and on a boat in the Pacific. *Office*—c/o Children's Publicity, Bantam Dell Publishing Group, 1540 Broadway, New York, NY 10036. *Agent*—Flannery Literary, 1140 Wickfield Ct., Naperville, IL 60563-3300.

CAREER: Writer. Worked variously as a teacher, electronics field engineer, soldier, actor, director, farmer, rancher, truck driver, trapper, professional archer, migrant farm worker, singer, and sailor. *Military service:* U.S. Army, 1959-62; became sergeant.

AWARDS, HONORS: Central Missouri Award for Children's Literature, 1976; New York Public Library Books for the Teen Age selection, 1980, 1981, and 1982, for *The Green Recruit,* and 1982, for *Sailing: From Jibs to Jibing;* American Library Association Best Young-Adult Book designation, 1983, for *Dancing Carl,* and 1984, for *Tracker;* Society of Midland Authors Award, 1985, for *Tracker;* Parents' Choice Award, Parents' Choice Foundation, 1985; Child Study Association of America Children's Books of the Year designation, and Newbery Honor Book, both 1986, both for *Dogsong;* Newbery Honor Book, 1988, and Dorothy Canfield Fisher Children's Book Award, 1989, both for *Hatchet; Parenting* Reading-Magic Award, International Reading Association (IRA) Teachers' Choice Award, and *Learning* Best Book of the Year citation, all 1990, all for *The Voyage of the Frog;* Newbery Honor Book, Judy Lopez Memorial Award, and *Parenting* Best Book of the Year citation, all 1990, all for *The Winter Room;* Parents' Choice award, 1991, for *The Boy Who Owned the School;* ALAN Award, 1991; Western Writers of America Spur award, *Booklist* Editor's Choice citation, and Society of Midland Authors Book Award, all 1991, all for *Woodson;* Spur Award, 1993, for *The Haymeadow;* Children's Choice citation, IRA/Children's Book Council, 1994, for *Nightjohn and Dogteam;* PEN Center USA West Children's Literature Award finalist, 1994, for *Sisters/Hermanas;* Margaret A. Edwards Award for lifetime achievement, 1997; Young Adult Library Services Association Best Books for Young Adults designation, 1998, for *The Schernoff Discoveries.*

WRITINGS:

NOVELS

The Implosion Effect, Major Books (Canoga Park, CA), 1976.

The Death Specialists, Major Books (Canoga Park, CA), 1976.

The Foxman, Thomas Nelson (Nashville, TN), 1977.

Winterkill, Thomas Nelson (Nashville, TN), 1977.

Tiltawhirl John, Thomas Nelson (Nashville, TN), 1977.

C. B. Jockey, Major Books (Canoga Park, CA), 1977.

The Night the White Deer Died, Thomas Nelson (Nashville, TN), 1978.

Hope and a Hatchet, Thomas Nelson (Nashville, TN), 1978.

(With Ray Peekner) *The Green Recruit,* Independence Press (Independence, MO), 1978.

Meteorite-Track 291, Dell (New York, NY), 1979.

The Spitball Gang, Elsevier/Nelson (New York, NY), 1980.

The Sweeper, Harlequin (Tarrytown, NY), 1981.

Compkill, Pinnacle Books (New York, NY), 1981.

Clutterkill, Harlequin (Tarrytown, NY), 1982.

Popcorn Days and Buttermilk Nights, Lodestar (New York, NY), 1983.

Dancing Carl, Bradbury (Scarsdale, NY), 1983.

Tracker, Bradbury (Scarsdale, NY), 1984.

Dogsong, Bradbury (Scarsdale, NY), 1985.

The Crossing, Paperback Library (New York, NY), 1987.

Hatchet, Orchard Books (New York, NY), 1987, revised edition, Aladdin (New York, NY), 1999.

Murphy (western), Walker & Co. (New York, NY), 1987.

The Island, Orchard Books (New York, NY), 1988.

Murphy's Gold (western), Walker & Co. (New York, NY), 1988.

Murphy's Herd (western), Walker & Co. (New York, NY), 1989.

Night Rituals, Donald I. Fine (New York, NY), 1989.

The Boy Who Owned the School: A Comedy of Love, Orchard Books (New York, NY), 1990.

Canyons, Delacorte (New York, NY), 1990.

Kill Fee, Donald I. Fine (New York, NY), 1990.

Woodsong, illustrated by wife, Ruth Paulsen, Bradbury (Scarsdale, NY), 1990.

Murphy's War (western), Pocket Books (New York, NY), 1990.

The Cookcamp, Orchard Books (New York, NY), 1991.

Monument, Delacorte (New York, NY), 1991.

The River, Delacorte (New York, NY), 1991.

The Winter Room, Dell (New York, NY), 1991.

A Christmas Sonata, Delacorte (New York, NY), 1992.

Clabbered Dirt, Sweet Grass, paintings by Ruth Paulsen, Harcourt (New York, NY), 1992.

The Haymeadow, Doubleday (New York, NY), 1992.

Dogteam, Delacorte (New York, NY), 1993.

Murphy's Stand (western), Walker & Co. (New York, NY), 1993.

Nightjohn, Delacorte (New York, NY), 1993.

Sisters/Hermanas, Harcourt (New York, NY), 1993.

The Car, Harcourt (New York, NY), 1994.

Legend of Red Horse Cavern, Dell (New York, NY), 1994.

Rodomonte's Revenge, Dell (New York, NY), 1994.

Winterdance: The Fine Madness of Running the Iditarod, Harcourt (New York, NY), 1994.

Call Me Francis Tucket, Delacorte (New York, NY), 1995.

Danger on Midnight River, Delacorte (New York, NY), 1995.

Hook 'Em, Snotty!, Delacorte (New York, NY), 1995.

The Tent: A Tale in One Sitting, Harcourt (New York, NY), 1995.

The Rifle, Harcourt (New York, NY), 1995.

Murphy's Ambush (western), Walker & Co. (New York, NY), 1995.
The Tortilla Factory, Harcourt (New York, NY), 1995.
Murphy's Trail, Walker (New York, NY), 1996.
Brian's Winter, Delacorte (New York, NY), 1996.
Worksong, Harcourt (New York, NY), 1997.
Sarny: A Life Remembered, Bantam (New York, NY), 1997.
Tucket's Ride, Delacorte (New York, NY), 1997.
The Schernoff Discoveries, Delacorte (New York, NY), 1997.
Soldier's Heart: A Novel of the Civil War, Delacorte (New York, NY), 1998.
The Transall Saga, Delacorte (New York, NY), 1998.
Alida's Song, Delacorte (New York, NY), 1999.
Brian's Return, Delacorte (New York, NY), 1999.
Canoe Days, Doubleday (New York, NY), 1999.
Escape, Return, Breakout, Delacorte (New York, NY), 2000.
Tucket's Home, Delacorte (New York, NY), 2000.
The White Fox Chronicles, Delacorte (New York, NY), 2000.
The Glass Café; or, The Stripper and the State: How My Mother Started a War with the System That Made Us Kind of Rich and a Little Bit Famous, Wendy Lamb Books (New York, NY), 2003.
Brian's Hunt, Wendy Lamb Books (New York, NY), 2004.
Molly McGinty Has a Really Good Day, Wendy Lamb Books (New York, NY), 2004.
The Quilt, Wendy Lamb Books (New York, NY), 2004.

SHORT STORIES

Sentries, Bradbury (Scarsdale, NY), 1986.
The Madonna Stories, Van Vliet (Minneapolis, MN), 1989.
(Editor) *Shelf Life: Stories by the Book,* Simon & Schuster (New York, NY), 2003.

NONFICTION

(With Raymond Friday Locke) *The Special War,* Sirkay (Los Angeles, CA), 1966.
Some Birds Don't Fly, Rand McNally (Chicago, IL), 1969.
The Building a New, Buying an Old, Remodeling a Used, Comprehensive Home and Shelter Book, Prentice-Hall (New York, NY), 1976.
Puppies, Dogs, and Blue Northers: Reflections on Being Raised by a Pack of Sled Dogs, Harcourt (New York, NY), 1976.
Farm: A History and Celebration of the American Farmer, Prentice-Hall (Englewood Cliffs, NJ), 1977.
(With John Morris) *Hiking and Backpacking,* illustrated by Ruth Paulsen, Simon & Schuster (New York, NY), 1978.
Successful Home Repair: When Not to Call the Contractor, Structures (Farmington, MI), 1978.
(With John Morris) *Canoeing, Kayaking, and Rafting,* illustrated by John Peterson and Jack Storholm, Simon & Schuster (New York, NY), 1979.
Money-Saving Home Repair Guide, Ideals (State College, PA), 1981.
Beat the System: A Survival Guide, Pinnacle Books (New York, NY), 1983.
Eastern Sun, Winter Moon: An Autobiographical Odyssey, Harcourt (New York, NY), 1993.
Harris and Me: A Summer Remembered, Harcourt (New York, NY), 1993.
Father Water, Mother Woods: Essays on Fishing and Hunting in the North Woods, Delacorte (New York, NY), 1994.
Pilgrimage on a Steelride: A Memoir about Men and Motorcycles, Harcourt (New York, NY), 1997.
My Life in Dog Years, Bantam (New York, NY), 1998.
The Beet Fields: Memories of a Sixteenth Summer, Delacorte (New York, NY), 2000.
Caught by the Sea: My Life on Boats, Delacorte (New York, NY), 2001.
Guts: The True Stories behind "Hatchet" and the "Brian" Books, Delacorte (New York, NY), 2001.
How Angel Peterson Got His Name: And Other Outrageous Tales about Extreme Sports, Wendy Lamb Books (New York, NY), 2003.

FOR CHILDREN

Mr. Tucket, Funk & Wagnall (New York, NY), 1968.
(With Dan Theis) *Martin Luther King: The Man Who Climbed the Mountain,* Raintree (Milwaukee, WI), 1976.
The Small Ones, illustrated by K. Goff, photographs by W. Miller, Raintree (Milwaukee, WI), 1976.
The Grass Eaters: Real Animals, illustrated by K. Goff, photographs by W. Miller, Raintree (Milwaukee, WI), 1976.

Dribbling, Shooting, and Scoring Sometimes, Raintree (Milwaukee, WI), 1976.

Hitting, Pitching, and Running Maybe, Raintree (Milwaukee, WI), 1976.

Tackling, Running, and Kicking—Now and Again, Raintree (Milwaukee, WI), 1977.

Riding, Roping, and Bulldogging—Almost, Raintree (Milwaukee, WI), 1977.

The Golden Stick, Raintree (Milwaukee, WI), 1977.

Careers in an Airport, photographs by Roger Nye, Raintree (Milwaukee, WI), 1977.

The CB Radio Caper, illustrated by John Asquith, Raintree (Milwaukee, WI), 1977.

The Curse of the Cobra, illustrated by Asquith, Raintree (Milwaukee, WI), 1977.

Running, Jumping, and Throwing—If You Can, photographs by Heinz Kluetmeier, Raintree (Milwaukee, WI), 1978, revised with Roger Barrett as *Athletics,* Macdonald (Milwaukee, WI), 1980.

Forehanding and Backhanding—If You're Lucky, photographs by Heinz Kluetmeier, Raintree (Milwaukee, WI), 1978, revised with Roger Barrett as *Tennis,* Macdonald (Milwaukee, WI), 1980.

Downhill, Hotdogging, and Cross-Country—If the Snow Isn't Sticky, photographs by Willis Wood and Heinz Kluetmeier, Raintree (Milwaukee, WI), 1979, revised with Roger Barrett as *Skiing,* Macdonald (Milwaukee, WI), 1980.

Facing off, Checking, and Goaltending—Perhaps, photographs by Melchior DeGiacomo and Heinz Kluetmeier, Raintree (Milwaukee, WI), 1979, revised with Roger Barrett as *Ice Hockey,* Raintree (Milwaukee, WI), 1980.

Going Very Fast in a Circle—If You Don't Run Out of Gas, photographs by Heinz Kluetmeier and Bob D'Olivo, Raintree (Milwaukee, WI), 1979, revised with Roger Barrett as *Motor Racing,* Macdonald (Milwaukee, WI), 1980.

Launching, Floating High, and Landing—If Your Pilot Light Doesn't Go Out, photographs by Heinz Kluetmeier, Raintree (Milwaukee, WI), 1979, revised as *Full of Hot Air: Launching, Floating High, and Landing,* Delacorte (New York, NY), 1993.

Pummeling, Falling, and Getting Up—Sometimes, photographs by Heinz Kluetmeier and Joe DiMaggio, Raintree (Milwaukee, WI), 1979.

Track, Enduro, and Motocross—Unless You Fall Over, photographs by Heinz Kluetmeier and others, Raintree (Milwaukee, WI), 1979, revised with Roger Barrett as *Motor-cycling,* Macdonald (Milwaukee, WI), 1980.

(With Art Browne, Jr.) *TV and Movie Animals,* Messner (New York, NY), 1980.

Sailing: From Jibs to Jibing, illustrated by Ruth Paulsen, Messner (New York, NY), 1981.

Voyage of the Frog, Orchard Books (New York, NY), 1989.

"CULPEPPER ADVENTURES" SERIES; FOR CHILDREN

The Case of the Dirty Bird, Dell (New York, NY), 1992.

Dunc's Doll, Dell (New York, NY), 1992.

Culpepper's Cannon, Dell (New York, NY), 1992.

Dunc Gets Tweaked, Dell (New York, NY), 1992.

Dunc's Halloween, Dell (New York, NY), 1992.

Dunc Breaks the Record, Dell (New York, NY), 1992.

Dunc and the Flaming Ghost, Dell (New York, NY), 1992.

Amos Gets Famous, Dell (New York, NY), 1993.

Dunc and Amos Hit the Big Top, Dell (New York, NY), 1993.

Dunc's Dump, Dell (New York, NY), 1993.

Amos's Last Stand, Dell (New York, NY), 1993.

The Wild Culpepper Cruise, Dell (New York, NY), 1993.

Dunc's Undercover, Dell (New York, NY), 1993.

Dunc and Amos and the Red Tattoos, Dell (New York, NY), 1993.

Dunc and the Haunted House, Dell (New York, NY), 1993.

Cowpokes and Desperadoes, Dell (New York, NY), 1994.

Prince Amos, Dell (New York, NY), 1994.

Coach Amos, Dell (New York, NY), 1994.

Amos and the Alien, Dell (New York, NY), 1994.

Dunc and Amos Meet the Slasher, Dell (New York, NY), 1994.

Dunc and the Greased Sticks of Doom, Dell (New York, NY), 1994.

Amos's Killer Concert Caper, Dell (New York, NY), 1995.

Amos Gets Married, Dell (New York, NY), 1995.

Amos Goes Bananas, Dell (New York, NY), 1995.

Dunc and Amos Go to the Dogs, Dell (New York, NY), 1995.

Amos Binder, Secret Agent, Yearling Books (New York, NY), 1997.

"WORLD OF ADVENTURE" SERIES; FOR CHILDREN

Escape from Fire Mountain, Dell (New York, NY), 1995.

Rock Jockeys, Dell (New York, NY), 1995.

Captive!, Dell (New York, NY), 1996.

Skydive!, Yearling Books (New York, NY), 1996.

The Treasure of El Patron, Dell (New York, NY), 1996.

OTHER

Communications (one-act play), produced in New Mexico, 1974.

Together-Apart (one-act play), produced at Changing Scene Theater, 1976.

Also author of *The Winter Stories* and *The Meatgrinder* and of the screenplay *A Cry in the Wind.* Contributor of short stories and articles to periodicals.

ADAPTATIONS: Dogsong was adapted as a filmstrip with cassette, Random House/Miller-Brody, 1986. *Dancing Carl* was adapted as a narrative ballet for two dancers, original music by John Collins and choreography by Nancy Keller, and aired on Minnesota Public Television. Numerous books by Paulsen have been adapted as audiobooks.

SIDELIGHTS: Gary Paulsen has written prolifically in several genres, and is acclaimed as an author of powerful fiction for young-adult readers. Paulsen's books are frequently set in wilderness areas, where his protagonists deepen their self-awareness through their experiences in nature and often undergo challenging tests of their survival skills. Paulsen's expertise in this area is real: his life experiences include working as a government trapper in Minnesota and competing twice in the Alaskan Iditarod, a grueling dogsled race. His respect for and understanding of nature is evident in works such as *Tracker,* in which he tells the tale of a teen whose grandfather becomes ill, leaving the boy to hunt alone in order to supply meat for the family. In the novel, Paulsen evokes the mystical relationship between hunter and prey, and shows how the deer's death helps the boy come to grips with his grandfather's terminal illness. Writing in *Best Sellers,* Eugene J. Lineham praised the author's style, commenting, "There is poetic majesty in the descriptions without a touch of condescension to the young."

Paulsen's own childhood was riddled with many difficulties. His father was in the U.S. Army and the family moved often; both his parents were alcoholics, and his mother was also a drug addict who suffered from mental illness. Often left alone or in the care of relatives, Paulsen disliked school and was a poor student, more concerned with after-school jobs such as selling newspapers. Recalling that period in an interview with Leonard S. Marcus for *Publishers Weekly,* the author recalled: "I sold newspapers at night in bars, and I found that if I let the drunks get a little drunker, I could get a little more money for my papers. Instead of a dime, I could get a quarter." While waiting to make some sales one winter night, he entered the local library to warm up. "The librarian asked me if I would like a library card. I was a real cocky kid, and I said, 'Sure, why not.' So she gave me a card, and the most astonishing thing happened. This silly little card with my name on it gave me an identity I had not had. I felt I had become somebody." With the encouragement of the librarian, Paulsen became an avid reader.

At the age of fourteen, Paulsen ran away from home and began traveling with a carnival. Eventually his wandering led him to work as a migrant farm hand, a construction worker, a truck driver, a sailor, and an engineer. The picaresque adventures he had at this time have formed the basis of several autobiographical volumes, as well as providing material for fiction. His writing career was begun impulsively, and he worked at it steadily for some years, moving from California to Minnesota to New Mexico and Colorado. He sold a few adult novels and some how-to books, and had a respectable success with his young-adult book *Winterkill.* That book, however, was such a personal reminiscence that it sparked a libel suit. The ensuing legal battle, combined with mounting problems related to alcohol, caused Paulsen to give up writing altogether for about two years. He threw himself into the life of a dogsled racer, which consumed most of his waking life. When a medical condition forced him to sell his dog teams, he returned to writing with the same intensity he had applied to his canine endeavors. Dogs and sled-dog racing have figured prominently in many of his books.

Although Paulsen has written adult fiction, memoirs, and various types of nonfiction, it is his young-adult fiction for which he is best known. In his first success, *Winterkill,* the narrator looks back at his turbulent teen years, focusing on a policeman named Duda, who gave the youth some much-needed guidance and protection. Duda dies tragically, killed in the line of duty. In Paulsen's novel *Hatchet,* the pilot of a single-engine plane has a heart attack and dies, crashing his plane in the Canadian wilderness. Brian Robeson, the sole passenger, must put aside his troubled thoughts about his parents' divorce and try to survive, armed only with a hatchet his mother gave him as a parting gift. The tension surrounding Brian's struggle to survive is enhanced by Paulsen's "staccato, repetitive style," according to a *Kirkus Reviews* contributor, who called *Hatchet* a "plausible, taut, . . . [and] spellbinding account." Comparing Paulsen to best-selling authors Robert Cormier and Paula Fox, *Christian Science Monitor* contributor Stephen Fraser claimed that *Hatchet* "deserves special attention. Written in terse, poetic prose, it is an adventure story in the best tradition." Brian's story is continued in *Brian's Return* and *Brian's Winter,* which relate his difficulties in returning to everyday life following his wilderness experiences.

Dancing Carl deviates from Paulsen's adventure stories and focuses on interpersonal relationships. When two twelve-year-old boys first meet Carl, an enigmatic man in the flight jacket, they think he is an alcoholic and a bum. They quickly learn that Carl is much more than that; he takes over the skating rink with the power of his presence, and over the course of the winter becomes the topic of the whole town's conversations. With his dance-like movements he expresses his emotions, and the people who watch are made to feel things too, such as repentance for a violent act, happy memories of someone who just died, Carl's pain and terror of his war experience, and Carl's love for a woman. "Readers will come away with a sense of having met an intriguing person," wrote Jane E. Gardner in *School Library Journal.* "Filled with poetry and with life," *Dancing Carl* "is . . . an insightful, beautifully written story," declared Dorcas Hand in *Horn Book.*

Another book that touches on the subject of war and its effect on lives is *Sentries,* a collection of stories about four young people who are given the opportunity to make their lives a success during peacetime and three young men whose lives are destroyed by choices made during war. The peacetime tales relate the stories of a girl who chooses between her Native American heritage and the white world, a migrant worker who commits to working with beet harvesters, a daughter who proves herself as capable as any son, and a gifted rock musician who creates a new music. These stories are juxtaposed with tales expressed through four battle hymns set during World War II and the Vietnam War. The purpose of these veterans' tales of mental and physical suffering and the looming threat of nuclear war is to ensure that readers do not take their choices and opportunities for granted and to encourage them to be sentries to protect their rights and freedoms. The juxtaposition of the war and peacetime chapters "conveys, better than philosophizing, the interconnections of life," according to *New York Times Book Review* contributor Doris Orgel. Noting that *Sentries* "is strange [and] hard to pigeonhole," Orgel found that although the protaganists do not interact and the combined tales do not create a novel, the "stories produce a unified effect." *Voice of Youth Advocates* reviewer Evie Wilson hailed Paulsen for assembling a collection of stories that remind readers of the deadly potential of "the formidable human waste nuclear war promises."

In books like *Nightjohn* and *Mr. Tucket* Paulsen draws on history for literary inspiration. The twelve-year-old heroine of *Nightjohn* is a slave who awaits the day when she will be designated a "breeder" by her master. As Sarny tries to deal with this repugnant eventuality, she surreptitiously takes reading lessons from an older slave named John. John pays a high price for being Sarny's teacher—two of his toes are cut off—but he is eventually able to escape and establish an underground school. In *Mr. Tucket* fourteen-year-old Francis Tucket has a number of hair-raising adventures when he is captured by the Pawnee after wandering away from his family's Oregon-bound wagon train. After Francis escapes from the tribe, a one-armed fur trader named Jason Grimes continues the young teen's frontier education. Tucket's adventures are continued in several more books, including *Call Me Francis Tucket, Tucket's Ride,* and *Tucket's Home.*

Another of Paulsen's historical novels to win widespread acclaim is *Soldier's Heart,* which tells the story of a young boy named Charley Goddard who enlists in the Union army at the age of fifteen. Charley's term of service takes him through some of the most horrifying carnage of the U.S. Civil War, and when he returns to civilian life he is burdened by a condition known as "soldier's heart"—what is now known as post-traumatic stress syndrome. The book's gory details and the horror of seeing young Charley transformed into a battle-crazed killer make for some "fascinating and horrific" passages, stated Nancy Vasilakis in *Horn Book.* She added: "The level of realism conveyed in this brief but powerful novel is rarely seen in children's books about the Civil War." A *Publishers Weekly* reviewer commented, "Charley comes across fully human, both his vulnerabilities and strengths becoming more pronounced as the novel progresses. Warfare, too, emerges complexly—while a lesser writer might attempt to teach readers to shun war by dint of the protagonist's profound disgust, Paulsen compounds the horrors of the battlefield by demonstrating how they trigger Charley's own bloodlust."

The traumas that go hand-in-hand with coming of age are also present in *The Car,* Paulsen's 1994 novel about a teen who deals with emotional upheaval by working on a car kit. Terry pours the frustration and anger he feels about his parents' separation into long hours with his tools, building the convertible his father never finished. In his review of *The Car* for *School Library Journal,* Tim Rausch called the author's characters "interesting" and added that "the action is brisk."

Rosa and Traci of *Sisters/Hermanas* have little in common—at least on the surface. Rosa is an illegal immigrant who turns to prostitution in order to survive; Traci is a well-liked junior high schooler whose biggest concerns revolve around cheerleading tryouts and new clothes. Both teens, however, are deeply obsessed with beauty and its impact on their future happiness. The two young women's lives ultimately intersect at a mall, where both girls are forced to face some unpleasant realities. This tale of culture clash and youthful dreams is especially unique in that the entire text appears in both English and Spanish. Summing up the novel in the *Los Angeles Times Book Review,* Yvonne Sapia termed the work "brief, ambitious, and told quite poetically."

Paulsen's series of novels about the American West features Al Murphy, a New Yorker in his early thirties who heads west with the army following the U.S. Civil War and becomes a lawman. David Whitehead of *Twentieth-Century Western Writers* described Murphy: "Although he is a lawman's lawman, whose actions are dictated more by instinct than conscious thought, Murphy soon proves to be more than just another gunfast hero. In Paulsen's hands, he is as close to human—with all the foibles and contradictions that this entails—as any fictional character is likely to get." *Murphy* introduces the character as Paulsen's protagonist enforces the law in a Colorado town. When a girl is raped and murdered, Murphy's efforts to identify and capture the killer force him to consider his position in the community, which views him as a necessary evil. Murphy's hunches often amount to nothing, which, according to Whitehead, "serves only to make his dogged attempts at solving the crime all the more credible." Whitehead further praised the final resolution and the well-drawn cast of minor characters. The identity of the killer is revealed in *Murphy's Gold,* in which Murphy is still haunted by memories of the victim. The plot centers on the romantic possibilities between Murphy and Midge, a café owner, and Murphy's attempts to locate a Chinese woman's missing husband. In *Murphy's War,* Murphy has left the Colorado town and is keeping the peace in Fletcher, Wyoming. Tensions mount as he comes into conflict with a power-hungry storekeeper and a wealthy rancher intent on avenging the lynching death of his son.

Paulsen's own colorful life is the basis for his 1993 book *Eastern Sun, Winter Moon: An Autobiographical Odyssey.* Among the events chronicled are Paulsen's journey by car across the country to meet his long-absent father, his family's unsettling life in the Philippines, and the dissolution of his parents' marriage. While noting that the memoir lacks introspective depth, Tim Winton in the *Los Angeles Times Book Review* nevertheless found the book to be "no less powerful and dignified for its painful silences." Paulsen recounts more colorful episodes from his own life in *How Angel Peterson Got His Name: And Other Outrageous Tales about Extreme Sports, Caught by the Sea: My Life on Boats,* and *The Beet Fields: Memories of a Sixteenth Summer.* Many of the events described in *The Beet Fields,* while fictionalized in Paulsen's novels, in their original state are more "memorable and powerful," stated Vicki Reutter in a *School Library Journal* review of *The Beet Fields.* "Paulsen's simple but hard-edged prose strengthens this addition to his autobiographical odyssey."

Gary M. Salvner commented in *Writers for Young Adults*: "Whether angry or happy, whether writing about survival or growing up, Gary Paulsen is always a hopeful writer, for he believes that young people must be respected as they are guided into adulthood. And he continues to write enthusiastically, commenting that he has 'fallen in love with writing, with the dance of it.' Taken together, Gary Paulsen's sense of purpose and love of writing ensure that he will continue to write enjoyable and effective books for young adults for years to come."

BIOGRAPHICAL AND CRITICAL SOURCES:

BOOKS

Paulsen, Gary, *The Beet Fields: Memories of a Sixteenth Summer,* Delacorte Press (New York, NY), 2000.

Paulsen, Gary, *Caught by the Sea: My Life on Boats,* Delacorte (New York, NY), 2001.

Paulsen, Gary, *How Angel Peterson Got His Name: And Other Outrageous Tales about Extreme Sports,* Wendy Lamb Books (New York, NY), 2003.

Paulsen, Gary, *Pilgrimage on a Steelride: A Memoir about Men and Motorcycles,* Harcourt (New York, NY), 1997.

Paulsen Gary, *Puppies, Dogs, and Blue Northers: Reflections on Being Raised by a Pack of Sled Dogs,* Harcourt (New York, NY), 1996.

St. James Guide to Young Adult Readers, 2nd edition, St. James Press (Detroit, MI), 1999.

Salvner, Gary, M., *Presenting Gary Paulsen,* Twayne (New York, NY), 1996.

Twentieth-Century Children's Writers, 4th edition, St. James Press (Detroit, MI), 1995.

Twentieth-Century Western Writers, 2nd edition, St. James Press (Detroit, MI), 1991.

Writers for Young Adults, Scribner (New York, NY), 1997.

PERIODICALS

ALAN Review, fall, 1994, James A. Schmitz, "Gary Paulsen: A Writer of His Time."

Best Sellers, July, 1985.

Book, May-June, 2002, review of *Guts: The True Stories behind "Hatchet" and the "Brian" Books,* p. 29.

*Booklist,*December 15, 1997, Jeanette Larson, review of *Tucket's Ride* (audio version), p. 711; January 1, 1998, Stephanie Zvirin, review of *My Life in Dog Years,* p. 799; May 15, 1998, Roger Leslie, review of *The Transall Saga,* p. 1623; June 1, 1998, Carolyn Phelan, review of *Soldier's Heart: A Novel of the Civil War,* p. 1750; January 1, 1999, review of *My Life in Dog Years* and *Soldier's Heart,* p. 782, and Stephanie Zvirin, interview with Paulsen, p. 864; February 1, 1999, review of *Brian's Return,* p. 975, and Kay Weisman, review of *Canoe Days,* p. 982; February 15, 1999, Karen Harris, review of *Sarney: A Life Remembered,* p. 1084; April 1, 1999, Stephanie Zvirin, review of *My Life in Dog Years,* p. 1382; June 1, 1999, Roger Leslie, review of *Alida's Song,* p. 1816; December 1, 1999, Kay Weisman, review of *Tucket's Gold,* p. 707; February 15, 2000, Pat Austin, review of *Soldier's Heart,* p. 1129; July, 2000, review of *The Beet Fields: Memories of a Sixteenth Summer,* p. 2033; August, 2000, Gillian Engberg, review of *The White Fox Chronicles,* p. 2131; September 1, 2000, Kay Weisman, review of *Tucket's Home,* p. 119; December 1, 2000, Stephanie Zvirin, review of *The Beet Fields,* p. 693; February 15, 2001, Kelly Milner Halls, review of *Guts,* p. 1128; August, 2001, Elaine Hanson, review of *Tucket's Home,* p. 2142; September 15, 2001, review of *Caught by the Sea,* p. 222; December 15, 2002, GraceAnne A. DeCandido, review of *How Angel Patterson Got His Name: And Other Outrageous Tales about Extreme Sports,* p. 754; August, 2003, Kathleen Odean, review of *Shelf Life: Stories by the Book,* p. 1983.

Book Report, September-October, 1999, Deb Den Herder, review of *Alida's Song,* and Susie Nightingale, review of *Brian's Return,* p. 61.

Buffalo News, April 7, 1998, review of *My Life in Dog Years,* p. N7.

Christian Science Monitor, November 6, 1987, p. B5.

Denver Post, November 15, 1998, Claire Martin, review of *Soldier's Heart,* p. H2.

English Journal, November, 1999, Chris Crowe, review of *Soldier's Heart,* p. 147; January, 2001, Susan Nelson Wood, "Bringing Us the Way to Know: The Novels of Gary Paulsen," p. 67; November, 2001, review of *The Beet Fields* p. 122.

Horn Book, August, 1983, pp. 446-447; review of *Guts,* p. 233; November, 1998, Nancy Vasilakis, review of *Soldier's Heart,* p. 737, and Kristi Beavin, review of *Sarny,* p. 768; January, 1999, review of *Brian's Return,* p. 69.

Houston Chronicle, June 14, 1998, Marvin Hoffman, reviews of *Puppies, Dogs, and Blue Northers* and *My Life in Dog Years,* p. 19.

Journal of Adolescent and Adult Literacy, October, 1999, review of *Soldier's Heart,* p. 204.
Kirkus Reviews, August 1, 1987, pp. 1161-1162; September 15, 1997, p. 1443.
Library Journal, February 15, 1993.
London Review of Books, May 23, 1996, p. 28.
Los Angeles Times, December 12, 1987.
Los Angeles Times Book Review, March 21, 1993, pp. 1, 11; February 27, 1994, pp. 2, 13.
New York Times Book Review, June 29, 1986, p. 30; May 22, 1988; May 5, 1991, pp. 22-23; November 10, 1996, p. 46; November 15, 1998, Henry Mayer, review of *Soldier's Heart,* p. 40; June 17, 2001, review of *Guts,* p. 24.
*Publishers Weekly,*December 1, 1997, review of *My Life in Dog Years,* p. 55; May 25, 1998, review of *The Transall Saga,* p. 91; July 20, 1998, review of *Soldier's Heart,* p. 221; December 21, 1998, review of *Brian's Return,* p. 69; January 11, 1999, review of *Brian's Return,* p. 26; March 1, 1999, review of *Canoe Days,* p. 68; May 31, 1999, review of *Alida's Song,* p. 94; September 6, 1999, review of *Sarny,* p. 106; February 14, 2000, Leonard S. Marcus, interview with Paulsen, p. 98; June 26, 2000, review of *The White Fox Chronicles,* p. 75; September 4, 2000, review of *The Beet Fields,* p. 109; June 25, 2001, review of *Canoe Days,* p. 75; November 18, 2002, review of *Guts,* p. 63; January 20, 2003, review of *How Angel Peterson Got His Name,* p. 83; March 17, 2003, "The Perfect Book Tour," p. 34; June 30, 2003, reviews of *Shelf Life: Stories by the Book,* p. 79, and *The Glass Café; or, The Stripper and the State: How My Mother Started a War with the System That Made Us Kind of Rich and a Little Bit Famous,* p. 81.
Reading Teacher, September, 1998, Patricia L. Scharer, review of *Worksong,* p. 58.
San Francisco, October 25, 1998, Susan Faust, review of *Soldier's Heart,* p. 8.
School Library Journal, May, 1983, p. 84; May, 1994, pp. 131-32; July, 1995, p. 50; June, 1997, p. 24; March, 1998, Carol Kolb Phillips, review of *My Life in Dog Years,* p. 238; May, 1998, John Peters, review of *The Transall Saga,* p. 147; September, 1998, Steven Engelfried, review of *Soldier's Heart,* p. 206; February, 1999, Miriam Lang Budin, review of *Brian's Return,* p. 111; March, 1999, review of *Canoe Days,* p. 183; July, 1999, Barbara Auerbach, review of *Alida's Song,* p. 99; August, 1999, Suzette Kragenbrink, review of *The Transall Saga,* p. 70; October, 1999, Coop Renner, review of *Tucket's Gold,* p. 156; January, 2000, Barbara S. Wysocki, review of *Soldier's Heart,* p. 74; August, 2000, Trish Anderson, review of *The White Fox Chronicles,* p. 188; September, 2000, Vicki Reutter, review of *The Beet Fields,* and Victoria Kidd, review of *Tucket's Home,* p. 235; October, 2001, Vicki Reutter, review of *Caught by the Sea,* p. 190; February, 2003, Vicki Reutter, review of *How Angel Peterson Got His Name,* p. 168; August, 2003, Edward Sullivan, review of *Shelf Life,* p. 164.
Seattle Times, February 28, 1999, Kari Wergeland, "Award-winning Stories of Hope, Survival," p. M9.
Voice of Youth Advocates, October, 1986, p. 148; June, 1994; February, 1996, p. 375; February, 1997, p. 332.
Writer's Digest, January, 1980.

ONLINE

Gary Paulsen Web site, http://www.randomhouse.com/features/garypaulsen/ (January 23, 2004).*

* * *

PHILP, Richard B(lain) 1934-

PERSONAL: Born January 19, 1934, in Guelph, Ontario, Canada; son of Norman Lewis (a musician) and Minnie (maiden name, Humphries; later surname, Carter) Philp; married, wife's name Moira Shirley, November, 1955 (marriage ended, May, 1987); married Joan Taylor Whiteford, November 14, 1987; children: Robert Bruce, Erica Margaret Philp Gatten, Michael John, Anne Louise. *Ethnicity:* "British." *Education:* Earned D.V.M. and Ph.D. *Hobbies and other interests:* Painting, music, boating, cycling.

ADDRESSES: *Agent*—c/o Author Mail, Lewis Publishers, 2000 Corporate Blvd. NW, Boca Raton, FL 33431. *E-mail*—rphilp@uwo.ca.

CAREER: Practiced veterinary medicine, 1957-63; University of Western Ontario, London, Ontario, Canada, professor of pharmacology and toxicology, 1965—. Consultant to the pharmaceutical industry.

MEMBER: International Society for the Study of Xenobiotics, Pharmacological Society of Canada, Canadian Toxicological Society.

WRITINGS:

Methods of Testing Proposed Antithrombotic Drugs, CRC Press (Boca Raton, FL), 1981.

Environmental Hazards and Human Health, Lewis Publishers (Boca Raton, FL), 1995.

Ecosystems and Human Health: Toxicology and Environmental Hazards, 2nd edition, Lewis Publishers (Boca Raton, FL), 2001.

Contributor to books, including *Integrated Medicine,* Van Nostrand (New York, NY), 1981; *Atheroembolism,* CRC Press (Boca Raton, FL), 1986; and *Basic and Applied High Pressure Biology,* University of Rochester Press (Rochester, NY), 1994. Contributor of more than ninety articles to scientific journals.

WORK IN PROGRESS: Several scientific manuscripts.

SIDELIGHTS: Richard B. Philp once told *CA:* "Writing is an intrinsic part of the scientific process. The effective communication of research data and conclusions legitimizes the research and contributes to the ongoing process of each scientist building on the work of others. After a few years in veterinary practice, I decided to further my education and opted for a research career. I enjoy writing, and my recent teaching text on toxicology allowed me greater latitude in writing style and an opportunity to address some social aspects that are not usually available in conventional scientific writing."

Recently Philp added: "Now in semiretirement, I am especially enjoying pursuing one of my hobbies as a jazz drummer and playing with some very good musicians. I have also returned to riding a motorcycle and enjoy country rambles on less traveled roads. I am also reading *Zen and the Art of Motorcycle Maintenance* by R. M. Pirsig, something I've been meaning to do for years!"

Terry Pratchett

* * *

PRATCHETT, Terry 1948-

PERSONAL: Born April 28, 1948, in Beaconsfield, England; son of David (an engineer) and Eileen (a secretary; maiden name, Kearns) Pratchett; married; wife's name Lyn; children: Rhianna. *Hobbies and other interests:* Growing carnivorous plants.

ADDRESSES: *Agent*—Colin Smythe, Ltd., P.O. Box 6, Gerrards Cross, Buckinghamshire SL9 8XA, England.

CAREER: Novelist. Journalist in Buckinghamshire, Bristol, and Bath, England, 1965-80; press officer, Central Electricity Board, Western Region, 1980-87.

AWARDS, HONORS: British Science-Fiction Award, 1989, for "Discworld" series, and 1990, for *Good Omens;* Writers Guild of Great Britain best children's book award, 1993, for *Johnny and the Dead;* British Book Award citation, 1993, as Fantasy and Science Fiction Author of the Year; awarded Order of the British Empire, 1998; Carnegie Medal, and *Guardian* Children's Fiction Prize, both 2002, both for *The Amazing Maurice and His Educated Rodents;* honorary doctor of letters, University of Warwick, 1999.

WRITINGS:

"DISCWORLD" FANTASY SERIES

The Colour of Magic (also see below), St. Martin's Press (New York, NY), 1983, published as *The Color of Magic,* 2000.
The Light Fantastic, St. Martin's Press (New York, NY), 1986.
Equal Rites, Gollancz (London, England), 1986, New American Library (New York, NY), 1987.
Mort, New American Library (New York, NY), 1987.
Sourcery, Gollancz (London, England), 1988, New American Library (New York, NY), 1989.
Wyrd Sisters, Gollancz (London, England), 1988, Roc (New York, NY), 1990.
Pyramids, Penguin (New York, NY), 1989.
Eric, Gollancz (London, England), 1989.
Guards! Guards!, Gollancz (London, England), 1989, Roc (New York, NY), 1991.
Moving Pictures, Gollancz (London, England), 1990, Roc (New York, NY), 1992.
Reaper Man, Gollancz (London, England), 1991, Roc (New York, NY), 1992.
Witches Abroad, Gollancz (London, England), 1991, New American Library (New York, NY), 1993.
Small Gods, Gollancz (London, England), 1992, HarperCollins (New York, NY), 1994.
(With Stephen Briggs) *The Streets of Ankh Morpork,* Corgi (London, England), 1993, Bantam (New York, NY), 1994.
Mort: A Discworld Big Comic (graphic novel), illustrated by Graham Higgins, Gollancz (London, England), 1994.
(With Stephen Briggs) *The Discworld Companion,* Gollancz (London, England), 1994.
Lords and Ladies, Gollancz (London, England), 1993, HarperCollins (New York, NY), 1995.
(With Stephen Briggs) *The Discworld Mapp,* Corgi (London, England), 1995.
Men at Arms, Gollancz (London, England), 1993, HarperCollins (New York, NY), 1996.
Terry Pratchett's Discworld Quizbook: The Unseen University Challenge, Vista, 1996.
Interesting Times, HarperPrism (New York, NY), 1994.
Soul Music, HarperPrism (New York, NY), 1995.
Feet of Clay, HarperPrism (New York, NY), 1996.
Maskerade, HarperPrism (New York, NY), 1997.
Hogfather, HarperPrism (New York, NY), 1998.
Jingo, HarperPrism (New York, NY), 1998.
Carpe Jugulum, HarperPrism (New York, NY), 1999.
The Last Continent, HarperPrism (New York, NY), 1999.
(With Ian Stewart and Jack Cohen) *The First Discworld Novels* (contains *The Colour of Magic* and *The Light Fantastic*), Dufour Editions (Chester Springs, PA), 1999.
The Fifth Elephant, HarperCollins (New York, NY), 2000.
The Truth, Corgi (London, England), 2001.
The Last Hero: A Discworld Fable, illustrated by Paul Kidby, HarperCollins (New York, NY), 2001.
Night Watch, HarperCollins (New York, NY), 2003.
The Science of Discworld II: The Globe, Ebury (London, England), 2002.
Monstrous Regiment, HarperCollins (New York, NY), 2003.
The Wee Free Men, HarperCollins (New York, NY), 2003.
A Hat Full of Sky, HarperCollins (New York, NY), 2004.

"BROMELIAD" TRILOGY; JUVENILE FANTASY

Truckers (also see below), Doubleday (New York, NY), 1989.
Diggers (also see below), Delacorte (New York, NY), 1990.
Wings (also see below), Doubleday (New York, NY), 1990.
The Bromeliad Trilogy (contains *Truckers, Diggers,* and *Wings*), HarperCollins (New York, NY), 2003.

OTHER

The Carpet People (juvenile fantasy), Smythe, 1971, revised edition, Doubleday (New York, NY), 1992.
The Dark Side of the Sun (science fiction), St. Martin's Press (New York, NY), 1976.
Strata (science fiction), St. Martin's Press (New York, NY), 1981.

The Unadulterated Cat, illustrated by Gray Jolliffe, Gollancz (London, England), 1989.

(With Neil Gaiman) *Good Omens: The Nice and Accurate Predictions of Agnes Nutter, Witch,* Workman (New York, NY), 1990.

Only You Can Save Mankind (for young adults), Doubleday (New York, NY), 1992.

Johnny and the Dead (juvenile), Doubleday (New York, NY), 1993.

Johnny and the Bomb, Acacia, 1997.

Thief of Time, Doubleday (New York, NY), 2001.

The Amazing Maurice and His Educated Rodents, HarperCollins (New York, NY), 2001.

Nancy Ogg's Cookbook, Corgi (New York, NY), 2003.

ADAPTATIONS: Truckers was adapted into a television series by Cosgrove Hall, Thames Video, 1992; *Music from the Discworld,* based on Pratchett's series, was composed and performed by Dave Greenslade, Virgin Records, 1994; the video games "Discworld" and "Discworld II: Missing Presumed . . ." were developed by Sony/Psygnosis, 1994, 1996; *Johnny and the Dead* was adapted as a television series, London Weekend Television, 1995, and for the stage by Stephen Briggs, Oxford University Press, 1996; *Wyrd Sisters* was adapted for the stage by Briggs, Corgi (London, England), 1996; *Mort* was adapted for the stage by Briggs, Corgi (London, England), 1996; *Guards! Guards!* was adapted for the stage by Briggs, Corgi (London, England), 1997; *Men at Arms* was adapted for the stage by Briggs, Corgi (London, England), 1997; *Wyrd Sisters* was adapted as a television series, Cosgrove Hall Films, 1997; *Soul Music* was adapted as a television series, Cosgrove Hall Films, 1997.

SIDELIGHTS: British author Terry Pratchett is best known for his popular "Discworld" series, a humorous fantasy set in a world that rests upon a giant turtle's back. With more than thirty "Discworld" books to his credit, Pratchett is one of Great Britain's most recognizable and popular authors. "Pratchett's texts are woven from the stuff of fantasy," wrote Nicolas Tredell in *Contemporary Novelists.* "His fiction is both a hilarious parody of the fantasy genre and a genuine contribution to it, in that it creates a rich, imaginative 'multiverse' that absorbs and intrigues the reader. It shares with the strongest fantasy a concern with fundamental issues such as death, and it incorporates aspects of contemporary culture such as fast food and rock music." The "Discworld" novels do not build upon one another, but instead can be read in any order—a fact that has contributed to their popularity. Tredell noted: "Taken together these novels create an imaginative zone that is rich and strange, offering the reader both the pleasures of discovery, as new aspects are revealed, and of recognition, as familiar figures recur." David Langford concluded in the *St. James Guide to Fantasy Writers:* "Pratchett's achievement in the Discworld series is slightly frightening: so many books since 1983, and so consistently funny with scarcely a wobble." "Discworld"—as well as most of Pratchett's other works—offers parodies of the creations of other famous science-fiction and fantasy writers, such as J. R. R. Tolkien and Larry Niven, while it spoofs such modern trends as New Age philosophy and universal concerns like death, religion, and politics. "Nevertheless, buried amongst the slapstick comedy and witty word-play are serious considerations of humanity and its foibles. In a genre assailed by shoddiness, mediocrity, and . . . the endless series," asserted *Locus* reviewer Faren Miller, "Pratchett is never shoddy, and under the laughter there's a far from mediocre mind at work." Indeed, to quote Tredell, "The Discworld is full of stories that bear on our social and metaphysical concerns."

Pratchett wrote his first full-length work of fiction at the age of seventeen and published it as *The Carpet People,* in 1971. Aimed at young readers, the book describes a whole world set in a carpet, populated by creatures called deftmenes, mouls, and wights. The novel's protagonist, Snibril the Munrung, travels with his brother, Glurk, through the many Carpet regions—which are set off by different colors—to do battle against the evil concept of Fray. A *Times Literary Supplement* reviewer recommended *The Carpet People* and further noted that "the Tolkienian echoes may draw in some older readers."

The Dark Side of the Sun and *Strata,* both science-fiction novels by Pratchett, appear to spoof aspects of Larry Niven's "Ringworld," a huge, flat world that completely circles a star, according to Don D'Ammassa in *Twentieth-Century Science Fiction Writers. The Dark Side of the Sun,* in D'Ammassa's words, features "manipulation of the laws of chance"—a subject also prominent in Niven's *Ringworld; Strata* discusses the construction of artificial planets and resembles *Ringworld* "in many superficial ways." Edward Dickey, reviewing *The Dark Side of the Sun* in *Best Sellers,* observed that "it should have strong appeal for science fiction fans" and called the novel "entertaining fiction lightened by occasional touches of whimsy." Allan Jenoff, critiquing *Strata* in *Science Fiction and Fantasy Book Review,* found it "amusing and readable."

Pratchett used the concept of a flat world again when he embarked upon his first "Discworld" novel, *The Colour of Magic.* This time, however, he took an approach more suitable to the fantasy genre than to science fiction. As Philippa Toomey reported in the London *Times:* "A great turtle swims through space. On its back are four giant elephants, on whose shoulders the disc of the world rests. We know this only because the extremely inquisitive inhabitants of the small kingdom of Krull lowered some early astrozoologists over the edge to have a quick look." Pratchett has pointed out that many mythologies across the world espouse the notion that the world is a flat place being carried on the back of a great turtle.

The protagonist of the first "Discworld" novel, *The Colour of Magic,* is a hapless wizard named Rincewind; he teams up with a tourist from a remote portion of the disc for a series of precarious adventures. The resulting tale, according to W. D. Stevens in *Science Fiction and Fantasy Review,* is "one of the funniest, and cleverest, [sword and sorcery] satires to be written." Rincewind returns in Pratchett's second "Discworld" novel, *The Light Fantastic.* This time he must try to prevent Discworld from colliding with a red star that has recently appeared in its sky. The next book in the series, *Equal Rites,* puts the emphasis on the character of Granny Weatherwax, whom Tom Hutchinson in the London *Times* hailed as "one of my favorite fantasy heroines." Granny Weatherwax returns in *Wyrd Sisters,* this time accompanied by two fellow witches, one of whom, Magrat Garlick, likes to indulge in "New Age fripperies," according to Miller in *Locus.* In *Wyrd Sisters* Granny and her companions form a trio of witches reminiscent of those in William Shakespeare's play *Macbeth* and attempt to foil the plot of the evil Lord Felmet and his wife, who have usurped the rightful king. *Wyrd Sisters* led Miller to express his amazement at Pratchett for creating "an open-ended series that just keeps getting better."

Subsequent "Discworld" novels have introduced other compelling characters, including Death and his apprentice, Mort, as well as a bungling set of night watchmen who save the capital city of Ankh-Morpork from an invading dragon. The series does not shrink from addressing controversial topics, exploring issues such as immortality, dogmatic religion, oppressive politics, and the influential power of fairy tales. Langford observed: "Once established, the astrophysics of Discworld receded into the background, fleetingly mentioned in later books as 'series glue'. Discworld is a place where any story can be told, and its geography is fluid. But (and this is a major strength) it is not just another of those realms where anything can happen. Events are governed by a steely commonsense which may only be overruled by the important need to insert another joke or demented footnote. Nevertheless," the critic continued, "the surface hilarity glitters all the more for having such solid, uncompromising bones: in the best of the series the silly footnotes and mirthful throwaway lines are ornaments on a structure of steel."

The "Discworld" novel *The Fifth Elephant* revolves around some valuable natural deposits of minerals and high-quality fat, left behind when a cosmic elephant crashed and burned in the Uberwald region at the beginning of time. Policeman Sam Vimes, traveling to Uberwald to find the valuable Scone of Stone, becomes involved in what a reviewer for *Publishers Weekly* called "an exuberant tale of mystery and invention" in which Pratchett "skewers everything" including political, religious, and economic systems, to achieve a book that is "a heavyweight of lightness." *Booklist* reviewer Roland Green praised the author's humor and also his effective writing style, commenting: "He never lets a proper tone flag; thus, in the midst of all the satire, Vimes' death struggle with the werewolves is as grim as any thriller's climax, and the growing love between Captain Carrot and Corporal Angua the werewolf is handled straight. Pratchett is now inviting comparison with Kurt Vonnegut, but if he ends up with a reputation equivalent only to that of P. G. Wodehouse, the world will be the better for his having written."

In *Night Watch* Vimes has been made a duke and is living the good life with his wife, who is expecting their child. Still, he can't forget his days on duty, and finds himself going on patrol even when he is not required to do so. A surge of occult power sends him back to the past, but with some differences: He is now in charge of the future and required to remember everything correctly. "Discworld remains a place of punning, entertaining footnotes, and farce, in which Ankh-Morpork is still a great city," commented Regina Schroeder in *Booklist.*

Monstrous Regiment gave eager readers still more tales of Discworld. In this novel Pratchett introduces readers to the region of Borogravia, whose religion forbids chocolate, cats, dwarfs, the color blue, babies, and cheese, among other things. The story concerns Polly Perks, a determined barmaid who disguises herself as a man to more easily search for her brother in the infantry. To Polly's surprise, most of her fellow conscripts are similarly disguised. *New York Times* reviewer Kerry Fried noted that while the story is full of puns and humor, Pratchett's real subject is "the pity of war." Noting that the plot "can move from farce to sadness in seconds," Fried concluded that while *Monstrous Regiment* "is most often spirited and shambolic . . . it has some serious heft."

In 1989 Pratchett published the first of his "Bromeliad" fantasy trilogy for children. *Truckers* introduces young readers to the nomes, four-inch-high people from another planet who have crashed on Earth and who have made a new world for themselves under the floorboards of a department store. Other nomes, however, have also found their way to Earth and live on the outside; the fun begins when one of these, Masklin, meets with the nomes of the store. When they learn that the store is going out of business and will be torn down, together the nomes must cooperate to find a new home and to escape their old one in a human-sized truck. "A wild and hilarious chase sequence follows, with the baffled police doubting their sanity," observed a *Horn Book* reviewer. Elizabeth Ward in the *Washington Post Book World* summed up *Truckers* as "a delightful surprise" and a "benevolent little satire."

Diggers, the second "Bromeliad" installment, takes Masklin and his fellow nomes to their new home in an abandoned quarry. However, problems ensue when humans attempt to reactivate the quarry. "In the book's funniest scene," according to Patrick Jones in *Voice of Youth Advocates,* "a group of nomes 'attacks' one of the humans, ties him to his desk chair, and stuffs a note in his hand proclaiming: 'leave us alone.'" "Satire and allegory abound," a *Horn Book* reviewer concluded of *Diggers,* but the critic also noted that the nomes' "trials and emotions are both moving and amusing." In *Wings* Masklin and his friends attempt to return to their home planet by placing the Thing—a "magic" box which in *Truckers* had warned them of the store's demise—aboard a communications satellite so that it can summon their mother ship, which has been waiting for them throughout their earthly exile. Margaret A. Chang lauded this last book of the series in the *School Library Journal* as a "cheerful, unpretentious tale." A *Junior Bookshelf* correspondent wrote of *Wings:* "Here is a real effort of creativity, and a criticism of society no less forceful for being clothed in the garb of comedy."

Pratchett has also penned books outside his two famed series. With Neil Gaiman, author of the popular "Sandman" comic books and several highly praised graphic novels, Pratchett wrote *Good Omens: The Nice and Accurate Predictions of Agnes Nutter, Witch.* The story, which met with mixed reviews when it was published in 1990, spoofs the Bible's Book of Revelation and concerns the efforts of both an angel and a demon to prevent the end of the world because they have grown fond of mankind and life on Earth. Their tactics include such strategies as deliberately misplacing the Antichrist, who resides in an English suburb. Joe Queenan, critiquing the book in the *New York Times Book Review,* complained of "schoolboy wisecracks about Good, Evil, the Meaning of Life and people who drink Perrier." But Howard Waldrop in the *Washington Post* praised *Good Omens:* "When the book is talking about the big questions, it's a wow. It leaves room in both the plot and the readers' reactions for the characters to move around in and do unexpected but very human things."

In 1992 Pratchett penned the young-adult novel *Only You Can Save Mankind,* which, with its computer-game-playing protagonist, spoofs, among other things, the 1991 Persian Gulf War. Johnny, the book's hero, finds the tables turned upon him when the aliens he is fighting in his computer game suddenly surrender and enlist his aid. This humorous but ultimately serious tale has led to more "Johnny" titles, including *Johnny and the Dead* and *Johnny and the Bomb.* "Pratchett's philosophy is based on a humorous view of life and humanity," stated a reviewer in *Junior Bookshelf,* "and the fact that most of the characters in *Johnny and the Dead* are indeed dead does not mean that they are the less funny. The comedy and the philosophy are inseparable."

Pratchett won Great Britain's top award for children's literature with his book *The Amazing Maurice and His Educated Rodents.* In this tale, a cat named Maurice is behind a money-making scheme that involves rats and a piper named Keith. Trouble arises when the rats consume some magical trash and subsequently begin to develop moral scruples, questioning their way of life. "Pratchett's absorbing, suspenseful adventure is speeded along by the characters' wisecracking patter and deepened . . . by a willingness to tackle the questions of existence," stated Anita L. Burkham in *Horn Book*. Miranda Doyle commented in her *School Library Journal* review that *The Amazing Maurice and His Educated Rodents* is "laugh-out-loud" funny, but also added, "Despite the humorous tone of the novel, there are some genuinely frightening moments."

Pratchett once told *CA:* "I've been a journalist of some sort all my working life, and I suppose I tend to think of the books as a kind of journalism—although writing them is as much fun as anyone can have by themselves sitting down with all their clothes on.

"I can't speak for the United States—three thousand miles is a great barrier to casual feedback—but what does gratify me in the United Kingdom is that the 'Discworld' books, which are not intended for children, have a big following among kids who, in the words of one librarian, 'don't normally read.'

"I got my education from books. The official schooling system merely prevented me from reading as many books as I would have liked. So from personal experience I know that getting children to read is *important.* Civilization depends on it."

BIOGRAPHICAL AND CRITICAL SOURCES:

BOOKS

Contemporary Novelists, 6th edition, St. James Press (Detroit, MI), 1996.

St. James Guide to Children's Writers, 5th edition, St. James Press (Detroit, MI), 1999.

St. James Guide to Fantasy Writers, St. James Press (Detroit, MI), 1996.

Twentieth-Century Science Fiction Writers, St. James Press (Chicago, IL), 1991.

PERIODICALS

Analog Science Fiction & Fact, November, 2000, Tom Easton, review of *The Fifth Elephant,* p. 132.

Best Sellers, November, 1976, pp. 249-250.

Book, November-December, 2002, Chris Barsanti, "Terry Pratchett's Flat-out Success," p. 26; March-April, 2003, review of *Night Watch,* p. 39; May-June, 2003, review of *The Wee Free Men,* p. 30.

Booklist, April 15, 1998, Wilma Longstreet, review of *Johnny and the Dead,* p. 1460; June 1, 1998, Roland Green, review of *Jingo,* p. 1736; January 1, 2000, Roland Green, review of *The Fifth Elephant,* p. 834; August, 2000, Ray Olson, review of *The Truth,* p. 2075; September 15, 2001, Ray Olson, review of *The Last Hero,* p. 164; January 1, 2002, Sally Estes, review of *The Amazing Maurice and His Educated Rodents,* p. 842; September 1, 2002, Regina Schroeder, review of *Night Watch,* p. 7; April 15, 2003, Sally Estes, review of *The Wee Free Men,* p. 1465; August, 2003, Regina Schroeder, review of *Monstrous Regiment,* p. 1927.

Courier-Mail (Brisbane, Australia), July 5, 2003, Jason Nahrung, review of *The Wee Free Men,* p. M8.

Denver Post, May 27, 2001, Candace Horgan, review of *Thief of Time,* p. I6.

Fantasy Review, November, 1986, pp. 31-32.

Financial Times, June 13, 2002, Neil Gaiman, review of *The Amazing Maurice and his Educated Rodents,* p. 4.

Guardian, November 19, 1997, p. T14; November 9, 2002, A. S. Byatt, review of *Night Watch,* p. 27.

Horn Book, March-April, 1990, p. 202; May-June, 1991, p. 332; March-April, 2002, Anita L. Burkam, review of *The Amazing Maurice and His Educated Rodents,* p. 217; May-June, 2003, Anita L. Burkam, review of *The Wee Free Men,* p. 355.

Independent, May 19, 1998, p. 20.

Junior Bookshelf, December, 1990, p. 300; August, 1993, p. 157.

Library Journal, March 15, 2000, Jackie Cassada, review of *The Fifth Elephant,* p. 132; October 1, 2000, Douglas C. Lord, review of *Feet of Clay* and *Guards! Guards! Guards!* (audio versions), p. 165; October 15, 2000, Jackie Cassada, review of *The Truth,* p. 108; March 15, 2001, Douglas C. Lord, reviews of *Hogfather* and *Jingo* (audio versions), p. 126; November 15, 2001, Jackie Cassada, reviews of *The Last Hero,* p. 100, and *Thief of Time,* p. 166; November 15, 2002, Jackie Cassada, review of *Night Watch,* p. 106.

Locus, January 1989, p. 17; October, 1991, pp. 15, 17; June, 1992, p. 17; September, 1992, p. 66; February, 1993, p. 58.

Magazine of Fantasy and Science Fiction, March, 1998, Michelle West, review of *Maskerade,* p. 31;

April, 1999, Michelle West, review of *Hogfather,* p. 36; October, 2000, Michelle West, review of *The Fifth Elephant,* p. 44; March, 2002, review of *The Last Hero,* p. 34.

New Scientist, May 18, 2002, Roger Bridgman, "Narrative Drive: What Makes Us Human?," p. 56; February, 2004, Michelle West, review of *Monstrous Regiment,* p. 35.

New Statesman, August 29, 1986, p. 26; January 29, 1988, p. 30; January 3, 1992, p. 33.

New York Times, September 28, 2003, Kerry Fried, review of *Monstrous Regiment,* p. 21.

New York Times Book Review, October 7, 1990, p. 27; December 15, 2002, Therese Littleton, review of *Night Watch,* p. 28; June 22, 2003, J. D. Biersdorfer, review of *The Wee Free Men,* p. 23; September 28, 2003, Kerry Fried, review of *Monstrous Regiment,* p. 21.

Observer (London, England), August 18, 2002, Rachel Redford, review of *The Amazing Maurice and His Educated Rodents* (audio version), p. 19.

*Publishers Weekly,*October 26, 1998, review of *Hogfather,* p. 47; September 27, 1999, review of *Carpe Jugulum,* p. 77; March 6, 2000, review of *The Fifth Elephant,* p. 87; October 30, 2000, review of *The Truth,* p. 52; April 9, 2001, review of *Thief of Time,* p. 55; October 15, 2001, review of *The Last Hero,* p. 51; November 5, 2001, review of *The Amazing Maurice and His Educated Rodents,* p. 70; September 30, 2002, review of *Night Watch,* p. 54; May 12, 2003, review of *The Wee Free Men,* p. 68; September 8, 2003, review of *Monstrous Regiment,* p. 61.

School Library Journal, September, 1991, pp. 258-259; August, 1998, Susan Salpini, review of *Jingo,* p. 197; April, 2000, review of *Carpe Jugulum,* p. 162; July, 2000, review of *The Fifth Elephant,* p. 130; August, 2000, Ray Olson, review of *The Truth,* p. 2075; December, 2001, Miranda Doyle, review of *The Amazing Maurice and His Educated Rodents,* p. 142; May, 2003, Sue Giffard, review of *The Wee Free Men,* p. 158.

Science Fiction and Fantasy Book Review, April, 1982, p. 20; March, 1984, p. 35.

Times (London, England), February 12, 1987; August 9, 1990; November 21, 1991, p. 16; December 21, 1997, p. N3; February 4, 1998, p. S6.

Times Literary Supplement, April 28, 1972, p. 475.

Voice of Youth Advocates, February, 1991, p. 366.

Washington Post, December 20, 1990.

Washington Post Book World, February 11, 1990, p. 6; March 27, 1994, p. 11.

ONLINE

Terry Pratchett Books, http://www.terrypratchettbooks.com/ (January 7, 2004).*

Q

QUINDLEN, Anna 1953-

PERSONAL: Born July 8, 1953, Philadelphia, PA; daughter of Robert V. (a management consultant) and Prudence Quindlen; married Gerald Krovatin (a lawyer), 1978; children: Quin, Christopher, Maria. *Education:* Barnard College, B.A., 1974. *Religion:* Roman Catholic.

ADDRESSES: Home—New York, NY; Hoboken, NJ; Cherry Valley, PA. *Office*—c/o *New York Times,* 229 West 43rd St., New York, NY 10036. *Agent*—Amanda Urban, International Creative Management, 40 West 57th St., New York, NY 10019.

CAREER: New York Post, New York, NY, reporter, 1974-77; *New York Times,* New York, NY, general assignment and city hall reporter, 1977-81, author of biweekly column "About New York," 1981-83, deputy metropolitan editor, 1983-85, author of weekly column, "Life in the 30s" (syndicated), 1986-88, author of biweekly column "Public & Private" (syndicated), 1990-95; *Newsweek,* author of biweekly column "Last Word," 1999—. Member, Barnard College Board of Trustees, Board of St. Luke's School, Planned Parenthood Federation of America board of advocates, and NARAL Foundation board.

MEMBER: Author's Guild (member of council).

AWARDS, HONORS: Mike Berger Award for distinguished reporting, 1983, for best writing about New York City; named woman of the year, *Glamour,* 1991;

Anna Quindlen

Pulitzer Prize for Commentary, Columbia University Graduate School of Journalism, 1992, for "Public & Private" columns; fellow of Academy of Arts and Sciences, 1996; honors from Women in Communications, Associated Press, and Society of Silurians; Poynter journalism fellow, Yale University; Victoria fellow in contemporary issues, Rutgers University; University Medal of Excellence, Columbia University; honorary doctorates from Dartmouth College, Denison University, Moravian College, Mount Holyoke College, Smith College, and Stevens Institute of Technology.

WRITINGS:

Living Out Loud (columns), Random House (New York, NY), 1988.

Object Lessons (novel), Random House (New York, NY), 1991.

The Tree That Came to Stay (children's book), illustrated by Nancy Carpenter, Crown (New York, NY), 1992.

Thinking Out Loud: On the Personal, the Political, the Public, and the Private (columns), Fawcett (New York, NY), 1994.

Poems for Life: Famous People Select Their Favorite Poem and Say Why It Inspires Them, Arcade (New York, NY), 1995.

One True Thing (novel), Dell (New York, NY), 1995.

(With Nick Kelsh) *Naked Babies,* Penguin (New York, NY), 1996.

Happily Ever After (children's book), Viking (New York, NY), 1997.

Black and Blue (novel), Random House (New York, NY), 1998.

A Short Guide to a Happy Life, Random House (New York, NY), 2000.

Blessings, Random House (New York, NY), 2002.

ADAPTATIONS: One True Thing was adapted as a film starring Rene Zellweger and Meryl Streep, Universal, 1998.

SIDELIGHTS: Anna Quindlen, author of best-selling novels *Object Lessons, Black and Blue,* and *A Short Guide to a Happy Life* and the recipient of the 1992 Pulitzer Prize for Commentary, gained national attention and a loyal following as a syndicated newspaper columnist at the *New York Times* and as a contributor to *Newsweek* magazine's "Last Word" column. Marked by their unaffected style, Quindlen's essays are rooted at a domestic level, but address universal concerns. Toronto *Globe and Mail* contributor John Allemang noted that Quindlen "is the unofficial voice that news most obviously lacks, the personal columnist who finds her truths in the little things." Sybil Steinberg, writing in *Publishers Weekly,* further lauded Quindlen's style, remarking that in her work the author "tackles the basic questions of life with trenchant and sensitive insight; she has a gift for turning the quotidian into the existential, the mundane into the meaningful."

Another distinguishing characteristic of Quindlen's prose is her proud and outspoken expression of her feminist leanings. In the *New Republic,* Karen Lehrman observed that in her columns "Quindlen seem[s] at times to be trying to shock *New York Times* readers with her 'femaleness,' her daring intimacy." The author defended her approach in an interview with *Commonweal*'s Alexander M. Santora: "I write for me. . . . I tend to write about what we have come, unfortunately, to call women's issues. Those are issues that directly affect my life and those are issues that are historically underreported."

Although fiction was her first love, Quindlen pursued a journalism career as the most viable, stable outlet for her writing activity. She landed a job as a reporter before college graduation and, three years later, was offered a position at one of the nation's most venerable newspapers, the *New York Times.* Quindlen worked as a general-assignment reporter, periodically reminding her superiors of her interest in writing the paper's "About New York" column, a coveted post which she was eventually granted. In an interview with Chris Lamb of *Editor & Publisher,* the author explained how this assignment improved her writing skills: "I developed a voice of my own without using the first person and I developed the ability to come up with column ideas." In her next career step, Quindlen advanced in the editorial ranks, becoming deputy metropolitan editor. When her first child was born, however, she left the hectic newsroom to care for him and write a novel. During this time she agreed to write a freelance column targeted at female readers that would run in the *Times*'s "Home" section. She held no lofty expectations for this venture. As Quindlen told Steinberg, "I thought of the column as a way to make a little bit of money while writing my novel. I was just trying hard not to disgrace myself."

Quindlen's weekly columns proved so successful, though, that other newspapers approached her with job offers. Executive editor Abe Rosenthal kept Quindlen at the *New York Times* with a permanent slot as the author of a weekly column called "Life in the 30s." In "Life in the 30s" Quindlen wrote about her own life during the mid- to late-1980s, earning praise for her honesty and accessible writing style, while drawing readers with astute observations of family life. She also became an unintended voice for the baby-boom generation. *Newsweek* contributor Melinda Beck observed that the author "occasionally tackles news issues, but she is more at home in the rocky emotional terrain of marriage, parenthood, secret desires and self-doubts." Her candor generated substantial mail from readers eager to share their own stories. Beck quoted Quindlen's editor as saying, "It's as if, by revealing so much of herself, she gives readers permission to explore their innermost selves."

While Quindlen was writing biweekly opinion pieces, her novel *Object Lessons* was published in 1991. Explaining the work's focal point, she told Steinberg, "I can't think of anything to write about except families. They are a metaphor for every other part of society." *Object Lessons* serves as both a coming-of-age account and the story of a family growing apart but eventually reconciling during the course of a summer in the mid-1960s. Told through the eyes of twelve-year-old Maggie Scanlan, the work follows the events of a large Irish-Catholic family living in suburban New York. Brash and domineering patriarch John Scanlan runs a construction company, controlling his sons with his financial power. Only Maggie's father, Tommy, has rebelled against this manipulation by marrying Connie, a lower-class Italian girl, and refusing to work directly for his father.

During this summer, however, the family's well-being is threatened by a housing development behind Tommy's house. Built by a rival construction company, the project signals the Scanlan construction company's waning influence. Connie's daily interactions with the foreman, an old friend, strain her relationship with Tommy. Other family ties are tested after John suffers a stroke and exerts more pressure on Tommy to run the business and buys him a new house. As Maggie observes her parents trying to cope with their problems, her own world unravels when her best friend rejects her, her mean-spirited cousin Monica gets pregnant, and local boys begin noticing her on a romantic level. Noting the author's successful rendering of adolescent confusion, *Time* contributor Martha Duffy noted, "Quindlen is at her best writing about the dislocations of growing up, the blows a child does not see coming." In her appraisal of *Object Lessons* for the *New York Times Book Review,* Anne Tyler deemed the novel "intelligent, highly entertaining, and laced with acute perceptions about the nature of day-to-day family life."

While *Object Lessons* sat atop the bestseller lists, Quindlen continued writing her "Public & Private" columns. Her contributions to journalism were recognized in 1992 when she received the Pulitzer Prize for Commentary. Expressing her appreciation for the honor, she remarked in the *New York Times,* "I think of a column as having a conversation with a person that it just so happens I can't see. . . . It's nice to know that my end of the conversation was heard." Her second collection of *New York Times* columns, *Thinking Out Loud: On the Personal, the Political, the Public, and the Private,* covers topics as diverse as the Persian Gulf War, absentee fathers, and abortion. A *Kirkus Reviews* writer complimented Quindlen for writing with greater maturity and depth than in her previous collection. The book, Quindlen later explained, was her attempt to comment on world events from an "underrepresented and valuable female viewpoint."

Quindlen's second novel, *One True Thing,* deals with a person's right to die. The narrator, a twenty-four-year-old woman jailed for killing her dying mother, describes her story. Ellen had been asked by her father to return home after her college graduation to help nurse her dying mother. Always a "daddy's girl" and having previously dismissed her mother as an anachronism, Ellen was unprepared for the world she entered. A *Booklist* reviewer described the book as not an "easy read about how cancer ravages Ellen's once radiant and ever-nurturing mother, but it is eminently satisfying to witness Ellen's transformation from an often glib, emotionally suppressed overachiever into a woman who begins to fathom the meaning of love." A *Kirkus Reviews* writer described the novel as "wrenching, albeit flawed." In explaining Quindlen's handling of reestablishing the relationship between mother and daughter, the writer went on to say that "Quindlen shines, capturing perfectly the casual intimacy that mothers and daughters share, as well as the friction between women of two very different generations." The story has a mystery-like ending, which the *Kirkus* reviewer applauded, saying that when Quindlen "gets it right—which is often—she places herself in the league of Mary Gordon and Sue Miller."

Quindlen's third novel, *Black and Blue,* tells a story of spousal abuse. Frannie Benedetto, an abused woman, takes herself and her nine-year-old son Robert away from their violent home to start anew in a distant state, but things go awry. *Literary Guild* reviewer Miranda de Ray wrote, "Just when things seem like they're going well, they go terribly wrong. The pages leading up to that heart-stopping climax are turned with lightning-quick speed." Maggie Paley of the *New York Times Book Review* believed that Quindlen's attempt to "dramatize the gravity of domestic violence . . . is nowhere near as convincing as the news reports all of us have seen," but concedes that the book is a page-turner. Jill Smolowe in *People* complimented Quindlen for "demonstrating the same winning qualities that inform her journalism: close observation, well-reasoned argument and appealing economy of language." A *Time* magazine reviewer took this sentiment a step further, adding that Quindlen "has caught the evil essence," and described *Black and Blue* as being "to domestic violence what *Uncle Tom's Cabin* was to slavery—a morally crystallizing act of propaganda that works because it has the ring of truth."

The stately house in *Blessings,* which bears the novel's name, is modeled after the Quindlen's family home in Pennsylvania. When the story begins, the novel's main character, Lydia, is eighty years old and haunted by memories. When a baby is left on the doorstep of the house a young, lovable, ex-con caretaker discovers it and tries to persuade Lydia to help him keep the young infant. While the initial setting of the novel is intriguing, reviewer Nancy Pate concluded in the *Orlando Sentinel* that "what eventually hooks readers is the story of Lydia Blessings and her secret history." Nothing in Lydia's life has been the way it appeared: Lydia's husband was really in love with her late brother, Sunny, and Lydia became pregnant, but the child was not her husband's. Lydia's mother proclaimed to be Episcopalian, but was really Jewish. As Lydia reminiscences, shocking revelations unfold. "Quindlen drops clues to the past throughout the book," Pate added. "Some are like pebbles barely rippling the surface. . . . But others are like rocks—the flaming red of a child's hair, of ashes scattered across a pond—that plop into the narrative so loudly that subsequent revelations become anticlimatic." Critics praised the characterization in the book—including the characterization of the house itself. "The grand old house in *Blessings* is a force of safety, home and family," remarked Susannah Meadows in a review for *Newsweek International.* "There is a reassuring, steady feel to the writing and an intriguing spikeness to the characters," contended *Miami Herald* reviewer Amy Driscoll. A *Kirkus Reviews* contributor enjoyed the book's message about life and marriage, but concluded that *Blessings* does not measure up to Quindlen's prior works. The reviewer ultimately described the book as "comfortable, not Quindlen's best."

Quindlen's bestselling *A Short Guide to a Happy Life* is a brief but poignant compilation of Quindlen's advice on enjoying life. The book offers pointers, such as: "Don't ever confuse the two, your life and your work"; and "think of life as a terminal illness, because if you do, you will live it with joy and passion, as it ought to be lived." Writing for *Spirituality and Health Online,* reviewers Frederic and Mary Ann Brusset described the book as "a brief but snappy treasure trove of advice that sounds like it was given as a commencement address for college students." Many of Quindlen's inspirations stem from her grief over the death of her mother when Quindlen was nineteen. The tragedy caused Quindlen to appreciate life and view it in a different way. "So much of her writing deals with her life before and after her mother's death; she speaks honestly about how much her life changed as a result of that loss. I admire her writing style, and her ability to tell it like it is—as she does in this little book, a reminder to all to appreciate the wonder," praised Maria Shriver in *O: The Oprah Magazine.*

In 1999, after a break from column-writing, Quindlen assumed the role of biweekly columnist for *Newsweek*'s "Last Word," succeeding the late Meg Greenfield and alternating with George F. Will. *Newsweek* chairman and editor-in-chief Richard M. Smith praised Quindlen in a press release posted on the *Writenews* Web site, saying "Anna's wonderfully creative mind, her no-nonsense thinking and her unerring sense of justice and injustice have made her one of the most powerful voices of her generation."

BIOGRAPHICAL AND CRITICAL SOURCES:

PERIODICALS

Booklist, August 18, 1994; November 1, 1996; June 1, 1999, review of *Black and Blue,* p. 1797; September 15, 2002, Donna Seaman, review of *Blessings,* p. 180.

Chicago Tribune, October 17, 1988.

Christian Science Monitor, December 5, 1996, p. B1; February 11, 1998.

Commonweal, February 14, 1992, pp. 9-13.

Editor & Publisher, November 30, 1991, pp. 32-34.

Entertainment Weekly, March 12, 1999, review of *Black and Blue,* p. 63.
Globe and Mail (Toronto, Ontario, Canada), June 1, 1991; June 12, 1999, review of *Black and Blue,* p. D4.
Journal of Adolescent and Adult Literacy, March, 1999, review of *How Reading Changed My Life,* p. 504.
Kirkus Reviews, March 1, 1993; July 15, 1994; October 1, 1996; September 1, 2002, review of *Blessings.*
Library Journal, February 15, 1999, review of *Black and Blue,* p. 126; October 15, 2002, Nancy Pearl, review of *Blessings.*
Literary Guild, March, 1998, p. 15.
Miami Herald, September 18, 2001, Amy Driscoll, review of *Blessings.*
Ms., September, 1988, p. 88; January-February, 1998, p. 83.
New Republic, June 10, 1991, pp. 38-41.
Newsweek, April 4, 1988, p. 65.
Newsweek International, October 14, 2002, Susannah Meadows, review of *Blessings.*
New York, December 24, 1990, p. 100.
New York Times, December 1, 1988; April 18, 1991; April 8, 1992; May 11, 1997, p. 35; June 22, 1997, p. 6; February 6, 1998, p. E43.
New York Times Book Review, April 14, 1991, pp. 7, 9; December 29, 1996, p. 15; October 19, 1997, p. 7; November 16, 1997, p. 52; February 8, 1998; March 21, 1999, review of *Black and Blue,* p. 32.
O: The Oprah Magazine, December, 2001, Maria Shriver, review of *A Short Guide to a Happy Life,* p. 132.
Off Our Backs, December, 2001, review of *Black and Blue,* p. 34.
Orlando Sentinel, September 18, 2001, Nancy Pate, review of *Blessings.*
People, June 3, 1991, pp. 26-27; October 17, 1994.
Publishers Weekly, March 15, 1991, pp. 40-41; July 1, 1996; December 2, 2002, review of *Blessings,* p. 21.
School Library Journal, May, 1999, review of *Siblings,* p. 162.
Time, April 8, 1991, p. 76; February 23, 1998, Lance Morrow, review of *Black and Blue* p. 84.
USA Today, November 14, 1996.

ONLINE

Book Reporter, http://www.bookreporter.com/ (March 19, 2003), "Anna Quindlen, Bio."
Houston Chronicle Online, http://chron.com/ (September 20, 2002), Sharan Gibson, review of *Blessings.*
Royce Carlton Incorporated Web site, http://www.roycecarlton.com/ (November 24, 2003), "Anna Quindlen."
Spirituality and Health Online, http://www.spiritualityhealth.com/ (March 19, 2003), Frederic and Mary Ann Brusset, review of *A Short Guide to a Happy Life.*
Writenews, http://www.writenews.com/ (June 16, 1999), *Newsweek* press release.*

* * *

QUINNEY, Richard 1934-

PERSONAL: Born May 16, 1934, in Elkhorn, WI; son of Floyd and Alice (Holloway) Quinney; married Valerie Yow (a professor of history), 1958 (divorced, 1989); married Solveig Schavland, May 3, 1991; children: Laura, Anne. *Education:* Carroll College, B.S., 1956; Northwestern University, M.S., 1957; University of Wisconsin, Ph.D., 1962.

ADDRESSES: Home and office—345 Rolfe Rd., De Kalb, IL 60115-3149.

CAREER: St. Lawrence University, Canton, NY, instructor in anthropology and sociology, 1960-62; University of Kentucky, Lexington, assistant professor of sociology, 1962-65; New York University, New York, NY, associate professor, 1965-67, professor of sociology, 1967-72, on leave for research and writing at University of North Carolina, 1972-74; Brown University, Providence, RI, visiting professor, 1975-78, adjunct professor of sociology, 1978-83; Boston College, Chestnut Hill, MA, distinguished visiting professor, 1978-79, adjunct professor of sociology, 1980-83; Northern Illinois University, De Kalb, professor of sociology, 1983-97, professor emeritus, 1998—. Visiting professor, Brooklyn College and the Graduate Center of the City University of New York, 1974-75, and University of Wisconsin—Milwaukee, 1980. Has given numerous guest lectures. Has been research director and chairperson of numerous grants and studies. Has presented papers at numerous annual meetings; photography has been exhibited in North Carolina, New York, and Rhode Island.

MEMBER: American Sociological Association (member of executive council of criminology section, 1972-

74, chairperson, 1977-78; member of committee on committees, 1974-76), Society for the Study of Social Problems (chairperson of Crime and Juvenile Delinquency Division, 1975-77), American Academy of Religion, Midwest Sociological Society, Eastern Sociological Society, Rhode Island Historical Society, State Historical Society of Wisconsin.

WRITINGS:

Social and Cultural Profile of Lexington and Fayette County, Kentucky (pamphlet), City-County Planning Commission of Lexington and Fayette County, 1963.

(With Marshall Clinard) *Criminal Behavior Systems: A Typology,* Holt (New York, NY), 1967, 2nd edition, 1973.

(Editor) *Crime and Justice in Society,* Little, Brown (Boston, MA), 1969.

The Social Reality of Crime, Little, Brown (Boston, MA), 1970; Transaction (New Brunswick, NJ), 2001.

(With Marshall Clinard) *The Problem of Crime,* Dodd (New York, NY), 1970, 2nd edition (with John Wildeman) published as *The Problem of Crime: A Critical Introduction to Criminology,* Harper (New York, NY), 1977, also published as *The Problem of Crime: A Peace and Social Justice Perspective,* Mayfield (Mountain View, CA), 1991.

(Author of introduction) Nicholas M. Regush, *The Drug Addiction Business: A Denunciation of the Dehumanizing Politics and Practices of the So-Called Experts,* Dial (New York, NY), 1971.

Critique of Legal Order: Crime Control in Capitalist Society, Little, Brown (Boston, MA), 1974, new edition, with introduction by Randall G. Shelden, Transaction (New Brunswick, NJ), 2002.

(Editor) *Criminal Justice in America: A Critical Understanding,* Little, Brown (Boston, MA), 1974.

Criminology: Analysis and Critique of Crime in America, Little, Brown (Boston, MA), 1975, 2nd edition, 1979.

(Author of foreword) James A. Inciardi, *Careers in Crime,* Rand McNally (Chicago, IL), 1975.

Class, State, and Crime: On the Theory and Practice of Criminal Justice, Longman (New York, NY), 1977, 2nd edition, 1980.

Capitalist Society: Readings for a Critical Sociology, Dorsey Press (Homewood, IL), 1979.

Providence: The Reconstruction of Social and Moral Order, Longman (New York, NY), 1980.

Social Existence: Metaphysics, Marxism and the Social Sciences, Sage (Beverly Hills, CA), 1982.

(Editor, with Piers Beirne) *Marxism and Law,* Wiley (New York, NY), 1982.

Journey to a Far Place: Autobiographical Reflections, Temple University Press (Philadelphia, PA), 1990.

(Editor, with Harold E. Pepinsky) *Criminology As Peacemaking,* Indiana University Press (Bloomington, IN), 1991.

For the Time Being: Ethnography of Everyday Life, State University of New York Press (Albany, NY), 1998.

Bearing Witness to Crime and Social Justice, State University of New York Press (Albany, NY), 2000.

(With Kevin Anderson) *Erich Fromm and Critical Criminology: Beyond the Punitive Society,* University of Illinois Press (Urbana, IL), 2000.

Borderland: A Midwest Journal, University of Wisconsin Press (Madison, WI), 2001.

CONTRIBUTOR

Walter C. Reckless, *The Crime Problem,* Appleton-Century-Crofts, 1967.

Walter C. Reckless and Simon Dinitz, *Critical Issues in the Study of Crime,* Little, Brown (Boston, MA), 1968.

Harwin L. Voss, editor, *Society, Delinquency, and Delinquent Behavior,* Little, Brown (Boston, MA), 1970.

Anthony L. Guenther, editor, *Criminal Behavior and Social Systems: Contributions of American Sociology,* Rand McNally (Chicago, IL), 1970, 2nd edition, 1976.

Bernard Haring, *The Church on the Move,* Alba House, 1970.

Harwin L. Voss and David M. Petersen, *Ecology, Crime and Delinquency,* Appleton-Century-Crofts, 1971.

Jack D. Douglas, editor, *Crime and Justice in American Society,* Bobbs-Merrill (Indianapolis, IN), 1971.

Erwin O. Smigel, editor, *Handbook on the Study of Social Problems,* Rand McNally (Chicago, IL), 1971.

Jack D. Douglas and Robert A. Scott, editors, *Theoretical Perspectives on Deviance,* Basic Books (New York, NY), 1972.

Peter Woll, editor, *American Government: Readings and Cases,* Little, Brown (Boston, MA), 1972, new edition, 1978.

Erich Goode and Harvey A. Faberman, editors, *Social Reality,* Prentice-Hall (Englewood Cliffs, NJ), 1973.

Charles M. McCaghey and R. Serge Denisoff, editors, *Deviance, Conflict, and Criminality,* Rand McNally (Chicago, IL), 1973.

Nicholas N. Regush, editor, *Visibles and Invisibles: A Primer for a New Sociological Imagination,* Little, Brown (Boston, MA), 1973.

Jack Sussman, *Crime and Justice,* AMS Press, 1974.

Israel Drapkin and Emilio Viano, editors, *Victimology,* Lexington Books (New York, NY), 1974.

Ronald L. Akers and Richard Hawkins, editors, *Law and Control in Society,* Prentice-Hall (Englewood Cliffs, NJ), 1974.

Charles E. Reasons, editor, *The Criminologist: Crime and the Criminal,* Goodyear Publishing, 1974.

Abraham S. Blomberg, editor, *Current Perspectives on Criminal Behavior: Original Essays in Criminology,* Knopf (New York, NY), 1974, 2nd edition published as *Current Perspectives on Criminal Behavior: Essays on Criminology,* 1981.

James A. Inciardi, Jr., and Harvey A. Segal, *Emerging Social Issues,* Praeger (New York, NY), 1975.

Richard L. Hensel and Robert A. Silverman, editors, *Perception in Criminology,* Columbia University Press (New York, NY), 1975.

Stuart H. Traub and Craig B. Little, editors, *Theories of Deviance,* F. E. Peacock, 1975, 2nd edition, 1980.

Robert A. Silverman and James J. Teevan, Jr., *Crime in Canadian Society,* Butterworth, 1975.

F. James Davis and Richard Stivers, editors, *The Collective Definition of Deviance,* Free Press (New York, NY), 1975.

Klaus Lunderssen and Fritz Sack, *I Die selektiven Normen der Gesellschaft,* Suhrkamp Verlag (Frankfurt, Germany), 1975.

Joe Hudson and Burt Galaway, editors, *Considering the Victim,* Charles C Thomas, 1975.

Ian Taylor, Paul Walton, and Jock Young, editors, *Critical Criminology,* Routledge & Kegan Paul (London, England), 1975.

Derrall Cheatwood and Therold Lindquist, *The Human Image: Sociology and Photography,* State University of New York Press (Albany, NY), 1976.

Leon Radizinowicz and Marvin E. Wolfgang, editors, *Crime and Justice,* Volume I, Basic Books (New York, NY), 1977.

Timothy J. Curry and Alfred C. Clarke, *Introducing Visual Sociology,* Kendall/Hunt, 1977.

Arthur B. Shostak, editor, *Our Sociological Eye: Personal Essays on Society and Culture,* Alfred Publishing, 1977.

Leonard D. Savitz and Norman Johnson, editors, *Crime in Society,* Wiley (New York, NY), 1978.

M. David Ermann and Richard Lundman, editors, *Corporate and Governmental Deviance,* Oxford University Press (Oxford, England), 1978.

Saul D. Feldman, editor, *Deciphering Deviance,* Little, Brown (Boston, MA), 1978.

Ronald A. Farrell and Victoria Lynn Swigert, editors, *The Substance of Social Deviance,* Alfred Publishing, 1978.

Delos H. Kelly, editor, *Deviant Behavior: Readings in the Sociology of Deviance,* St. Martin's Press (New York, NY), 1979.

Lord Lloyd of Hampstead, *Introduction to Jurisprudence,* 4th edition, Stevens & Sons, 1979.

Scott G. McNall and Gary N. Howe, editors, *Current Perspectives in Social Theory: A Research Annual,* Volume II, JAI Press, 1981.

William E. Thornton, Jr., Jennifer James, and William G. Doerner, editors, *Delinquency and Justice,* Scott, Foresman, 1982.

Contributor of articles, book reviews, and photography to numerous periodicals, including *Social Forces, American Journal of Sociology, Infinity, Rural Sociology, Mirror, American Sociological Review, Social Problems, Contemporary Crises,* and *American Behavioral Scientist.* Associate editor, *Victimology,* 1976—, (and member of board of directors) *The Insurgent Sociologist,* 1977—, *Contemporary Crises,* 1977—, and *California Sociologist,* 1977—; advisory editor, *Offender Rehabilitation,* 1976—, and *Qualitative Sociology,* 1978—; contributing editor, *Crime and Social Justice: A Journal of Radical Criminology,* 1974-78; corresponding editor, *Theory and Society,* 1974-77; member of editorial board, *Criminology,* 1978-81.

SIDELIGHTS: About the body of Richard Quinney's work, David O. Friedrichs commented in *Radical Criminology: The Coming Crisis:* "Quinney's contributions to criminology to date might be classified, theoretically and chronologically, as conventional, conflict oriented, critical, neo-Marxist, and most recently prophetic. This singular intellectual career over a period of approximately two decades may be virtually without parallel in the discipline. But whatever direction his work now takes, Quinney has undeniably made a fundamental contribution to the development of radical criminology." Friedrichs concluded: "With rare intellectual courage, immense scholarly erudition, awesome imagination, and remarkable productiveness, Quinney has explored the outer reaches of the criminological frontier. Even if Quinney is 'wrong' or 'one-sided' in many instances, the conviction remains that his work and thought will continue to be discussed, will continue to inspire and provoke, long after his more timid if technically more 'correct' criminological brethren are forgotten or relegated to obscure footnotes."

As Friedrichs pointed out, Quinney's more recent work is thought-provoking and prophetic. In the prologue to *Providence: The Reconstruction of Social and Moral Order,* Quinney expresses his belief that the advanced capitalist society is rapidly approaching its demise, primarily because its attendant secularism alienates humanity from itself by extinguishing the spiritual dimension of existence. "Now in these days," he writes, "the word of God is seldom heard, and visions are not often granted. We are reaching the end of an age; the advanced capitalist society with its highly secular and utilitarian sensibility is coming to an end. The contradictions of the existing social and moral order and the personal and collective struggle are bringing about a new human history."

"The task ahead," Quinney suggests in *Social Existence: Metaphysics, Marxism and the Social Sciences,* "is to create the symbols that will allow us as human social beings to find our place in the world. The contemporary crisis is both material and symbolic: a social existence cannot be constructed without attending to both the conditions of material existence and the symbols for social and spiritual existence. Our hope is for a social existence filled with a meaning that relates to an order in the universe. Our immediate work is in the reconstruction of symbols in the struggle for social existence."

Since becoming a professor emeritus, Quinney's publications have frequently focused on personal matters. *For the Time Being: Ethnography of Everyday Life,* which saw print in 1998, discusses aspects of his own life and family history in the way an anthropologist might relate an ethnography of a foreigner. Though Roger Chapman in the *Journal of Popular Culture* questioned the relevance of a sociologist's personal reflections in general, he felt that *For the Time Being* "is . . . a very beautifully written work." He went on to conclude that "seldom does one find such warmth and introspection coming from an academic." Quinney continued in this vein with 2001's *Borderland: A Midwest Journal.* This volume discusses his return to his boyhood hometown in Wisconsin, and includes photographs Quinney took of the landscape surrounding his home. The book also deals with what the author feels it means to be a Midwesterner. Lori D. Kranz, discussing *Borderland* in the *Bloomsbury Review,* praised the "reflective tone of the prose" and labeled its bibliography, which contains all the writers Quinney quotes from, a "treasure trove."

BIOGRAPHICAL AND CRITICAL SOURCES:

BOOKS

Clinard, Marshall B., and Robert F. Meier, *Sociology of Deviant Behavior,* 5th edition, Holt (New York, NY), 1979.

Inciardi, James A., editor, *Radical Criminology: The Coming Crisis,* Sage (Thousand Oaks, CA), 1980.

Liska, Allen E., *Perspectives on Deviance,* Prentice-Hall (Englewood Cliffs, NJ), 1981.

Quinney, Richard, *Providence: The Reconstruction of Social and Moral Order,* Longman (New York, NY), 1980.

Quinney, Richard, *Social Existence: Metaphysics, Marxism and the Social Sciences,* Sage (Thousand Oaks, CA), 1982.

PERIODICALS

Bloomsbury Review, March-April, 2002, Lori D. Kranz, review of *Borderland: A Midwest Journal.*

Issues in Criminology, spring, 1971.

Journal of Popular Culture, summer, 2001, Roger Chapman, review of *For the Time Being: Ethnography of Everyday Life,* pp. 240-241.*

R

REICHARDT, Mary R. 1956-

PERSONAL: Born October 16, 1956, in Berwyn, IL; daughter of Howard Edward and Rita (Petrik) Reichardt. *Education:* Aquinas College, Grand Rapids, MI, B.A., 1978; University of Illinois—Urbana-Champaign, M.A., 1980; University of Wisconsin—Madison, Ph.D., 1987.

ADDRESSES: *Office*—Department of Catholic Studies, University of St. Thomas, 2115 Summit, St. Paul, MN 55105. *E-mail*—mrreichardt@stthomas.edu.

CAREER: University of St. Thomas, St. Paul, MN, began as associate professor, became professor of Catholic studies and English, 1988—, and director of Master's Degree Program in Catholic Studies. Editor and consultant for business and professional communi cations.

MEMBER: American Literature Association, Midwest Modern Language Association.

AWARDS, HONORS: Fellow, National Endowment for the Humanities, 1992.

WRITINGS:

The Uncollected Stories of Mary Wilkins Freeman, University Press of Mississippi (Jackson, MS), 1992.

A Web of Relationship: Women in the Short Stories of Mary Wilkins Freeman, University Press of Mississippi (Jackson, MS), 1992.

A Mary Wilkins Freeman Reader, University of Nebraska Press (Lincoln, NE), 1997.

Mary Wilkins Freeman: A Study of the Short Fiction, Twayne (Boston, MA), 1997.

(Editor) *Catholic Women Writers: A Bio-Bibliographical Sourcebook,* Greenwood Press (Westport, CT), 2001.

Reading Catholic Literature: A Study and Resource Guide, Sheed & Ward, 2003.

WORK IN PROGRESS: Editing *An Encyclopedia of Catholic Literature,* publication by Greenwood Press (Westport, CT).

* * *

RODRIGUEZ, Clara E. 1944-

PERSONAL: Born March 29, 1944, in New York, NY; daughter of Angelo M. and Clara G.(maiden name, Perez); married Gelvin Stevenson, (an economist/ writer) June 7, 1969; children: Gelvina, Jose Angel Stevenson-Rodriguez. *Ethnicity:* "Puerto Rican." *Education:* City College of the City University of New York, B.A.; Cornell University, M.A.; Washington University, St. Louis, MO, Ph.D. *Religion:* Roman Catholic.

ADDRESSES: *Home*—2160 Bolton St., No. 3-B, Bronx, NY 10462. *Office*—Department of Sociology and Anthropology, Fordham College at Lincoln Center, Fordham University, 113 West 60th St., New York, NY 10023. *E-mail*—crodriguez@fordham.edu.

CAREER: Centro Colombo-Americano, Cali, Colombia, instructor in English as a second language, 1965; New York Urban Coalition, New York, NY, staff associate in housing, 1969; Washington University, St. Louis, MO, instructor, 1970-71; Graduate Center of the City University of New York, New York, NY, research associate at Centro de Estudios Puertorriqueños, 1973; Herbert H. Lehman College of the City University of New York, Bronx, NY, head of department of Puerto Rican studies and associate of sociology department, 1974-76; Fordham University, Bronx, NY, dean of general studies and project director for Pre-Health Professions Program, 1976-81; Fordham University, Fordham College at Lincoln Center, New York, NY, professor of social sciences, 1981—, member of university executive board, 1981, member of executive committee of Latin American and Latino Studies Institute, 1997—, founder of Angelo Rodriguez Memorial Trust Fund, 1990. Massachusetts Institute of Technology, visiting scholar in urban studies and planning, 1987-88; Yale University, visiting fellow in American studies, 1992; Russell Sage Foundation, visiting scholar, 1993-94; Smithsonian Institution, senior fellow at National Museum of American History, 1998. Columbia University, guest lecturer, 1992, visiting professor, 1999; Rollins College, Alfred J. Hanna Distinguished Lecturer, 1993; guest lecturer at numerous colleges and universities, including Queens College of the City University of New York and John Jay College of Criminal Justice of the City University of New York, 1991, Harvard University, 1991 and 1992, Swarthmore College, Haverford College, and Bryn Mawr College, all 1993, and Universidad de Talca, Simmons College, University of Massachusetts—Boston, University of Groningen, University of Tübingen, and Wesleyan University, all 1998. Cornell University, founding member of Puerto Rican Research Exchange, School of Industrial Labor Relations, 1984— . Coordinator of an illiteracy program in Cali, 1965-66; Grass Roots Organization, founding member and member of board of directors of Youth Program and Summer Day Care Center, 1973-77; Aspira of America, member of educational advisory board, 1975-79; Puerto Rican Migration Consortium, founding member and member of board of directors, 1977-80; Center for Latino Family Policy, member of advisory council of Committee for Hispanic Children and Families, 1993—; New York State Economic Policy Research Council, member of coordinating committee; consultant to National Council of La Raza, Children's Television Workshop, Prescriptives Cosmetic Co., and National Puerto Rican Coalition. Bronx Museum of the Arts, member of board of trustees, 1977-80. Tremont Towers Tenants Association, organizer and president, 1973-80; Five Borough Institute, member of advisors, 1998—.

MEMBER: American Sociological Association (member of council, section on racial and ethnic minorities, 1988-91), American Anthropological Association, American Association for the Advancement of Science, American Public Health Association, Association for Public Policy and Management, Latin American Studies Association, Population Association of America, Sociologists for Women in Society, Union for Radical Political Economics, Eastern Sociological Society.

AWARDS, HONORS: Grants from National Institutes of Health, 1978-81, and Calder Foundation, 1979; Rockefeller fellow, 1988-89; grants from Ford Foundation, 1987, and Social Science Research Council 1988; American Sociological Association, grant, 1988, award for distinguished contribution to research, 2001; Star Award, New York Women's Agenda, 1992; Leadership in Educational Excellence Award, National Society of Hispanic M.B.A.s, 1995; Distinguished Prize in Social Sciences, Instituto de Puerto Rico, New York City, 1997; designated Centennial Historian of the City of New York, 1999.

WRITINGS:

The Ethnic Queue in the United States: The Case of Puerto Ricans, R & E Research Associates (San Francisco, CA), 1974.

(Editor, with Virginia Sanchez Korrol and Oscar Alers) *The Puerto Rican Struggle: Essays on Survival in the United States,* Puerto Rican Migration Consortium, 1979.

Puerto Ricans: Born in the USA, Unwin & Hyman (Boston, MA), 1989.

(Editor, with Edwin Melendez and Janice Barry-Figueroa, and contributor) *Hispanics in the Labor Force: Issues and Policies,* Plenum (New York, NY), 1991.

(Editor, with Virginia Sanchez Korrol) *Historical Perspectives on Puerto Rican Survival in the United States,* Markus Wiener (Princeton, NJ), 1996.

Latin Looks: Latina and Latino Images in the Media, Westview Press (Boulder, CO), 1997.

Changing Race: The Latinos, the Census, and the History of Ethnicity in the United States, New York University Press (New York, NY), 2000.

Also author of a book on Latinos in Hollywood, published by Smithsonian Institution (Washington, DC), 2003. Contributor to books, including *From Different Shores,* edited by Ronald Takaki, Oxford University Press (New York, NY), 1994; *Boricuas: Influential Puerto Rican Writings—An Anthology,* edited by Roberto Santiago, Ballantine (New York, NY), 1995; *Latinos in New York: Communities in Transition,* edited by G. Haslip-Viera and S. Baver, University of Notre Dame Press (Notre Dame, IN), 1996; *The Latino Experience in the United States,* edited by Mary Romero, Pierette Hondagneu-Sotelo, and Vilma Ortiz, Routledge (New York, NY), 1997; and *"Adiós, Borinquen querida": The Puerto Rican Diaspora,* CELAC, State University of New York—Albany (Albany, NY), 2000. Contributor of articles and reviews to academic journals and newspapers, including *Social Science Quarterly, American Quarterly, Women's Studies Quarterly, Ethnicity, Urban Review,* and *Ethnic and Racial Studies.* Coeditor of special issue, *Hispanic Journal of Behavioral Sciences,* 1992; founding member of editorial board, *Latino Studies Journal;* advisory editor, *Gender and Society.*

SIDELIGHTS: Clara E. Rodriguez once told *CA:* "I write because I feel there are stories to be told and views to be expressed that are not present when I read what I read. I write so that those who are 'missing' can connect with my work and create the bridges that others will follow and cross many times in many different directions.

"I am influenced by my experiences in life. These include my experiences of others' experiences, whether they are personal and direct or mediated through art, media, writing, or 'history telling.' Sometimes I feel strongly and begin to write. This is often when I write my best. At other times, I think and then write. Still other times, I write because this is what is needed. Usually, though, I feel strongly about what I write regardless of how I got there."

ROSENTHAL, Ken S. 1951-

PERSONAL: Born July 23, 1951, in Brooklyn, NY; son of Joseph (a high school mathematics teacher and department head) and Muriel (a teacher; maiden name, Tirschler) Rosenthal; married Judy Lindner, December 27, 1975; children: Joshua, Rachel. *Education:* University of Delaware, B.S., 1973; University of Illinois—Urbana-Champaign, M.S., 1975, Ph.D., 1977; Harvard University, postdoctoral study, 1977-79.

ADDRESSES: Home—320 Harvest Dr., Akron, OH 44333. *Office*—Northeastern Ohio Universities College of Medicine, Box 95, Rootstown, OH 44272-0095; fax: 330-325-5914. *E-mail*—ksr@neoucom.edu.

CAREER: Northeastern Ohio Universities College of Medicine, Rootstown, OH, professor of microbiology and immunology, 1979—.

MEMBER: American Association for the Advancement of Science, American Society for Microbiology, American Society of Biochemists and Molecular Biologists, New York Academy of Sciences, Sigma Xi, Phi Lambda Upsilon.

WRITINGS:

Ace the Boards Microbiology, Mosby (St. Louis, MO), 1996.

Medical Microbiology, Mosby (St. Louis, MO), 4th edition, 2001.

Rapid Reviews Microbiology and Immunology, Mosby (Philadelphia, PA), 2002.

Contributor to research journals.

WORK IN PROGRESS: A study of Herpes simplex virulence and anti-HSV vaccines.

SIDELIGHTS: Ken S. Rosenthal once told *CA:* "Writing and editing textbooks provides me with the opportunity to reach, teach, and enlighten a large number of students. As a professor in a medical school, one does not always get the opportunity to teach and, when one does get that opportunity, it is within a large lecture hall, where I present a large amount of material in a short period of time to large numbers of students. A textbook provides the opportunity to present the insights that I have gathered over the years and the excitement that I feel toward science in an intimate, one-to-one manner and still reach a large number of students.

"In developing the material for the book, I try to put myself in the reader's or student's perspective. A student is interested in learning first and then filling in the details. I try to teach, rather than just expound the facts. Difficult concepts must be described simply, with examples, illustrations, and analogies. I have the most fun with analogies because they translate uncommon concepts into common knowledge. In the end, for a student to learn from a book, the book has to be opened and used. Seeing a well-worn copy of one of my textbooks provides me with great satisfaction."

* * *

ROY, Arundhati 1960(?)-

Arundhati Roy

PERSONAL: Born c. 1960, in Kerala, India; daughter of Rajib (a tea plantation manager) and Mary (a teacher) Roy; married Pradip Krishen (a filmmaker), c. 1993. *Education:* Attended architectural school.

ADDRESSES: *Home*—New Delhi, India. *Agent*—c/o Author Mail, Random House, 201 East 50th St., New York, NY 10022.

CAREER: Actor, screenwriter, and novelist. Worked as an architect; sold cakes on a beach in Goa, India.

AWARDS, HONORS: Booker Prize, 1997, for *The God of Small Things;* Grand Prize of the World Academy of Culture (Paris, France), 2002; Lannan Award for Cultural Freedom.

WRITINGS:

The God of Small Things (novel), Random House (New York, NY), 1997.

The End of Imagination (essay; also see below), D.C. Books (Kottayam, India), 1998.

The Greater Common Good (essay; also see below), India Book Distributor (Bombay, India), 1999.

The Cost of Living (contains *The End of Imagination* and *The Greater Common Good*), Modern Library (New York, NY), 1999.

Power Politics (essays), South End Press (Cambridge, MA), 2001, published as *Power Politics: The Reincarnation of Rumpelstiltskin,* D.C. Books (Kottayam, India), 2001.

The Algebra of Infinite Justice (essays), Flamingo (London, England), 2002.

War Talk, South End Press (Cambridge, MA), 2003.

(With David Barsamian) *Globalization Dissent: Conversations with Arundhati Roy,* South End Press (Cambridge, MA), 2004.

Also author of screenplays; author of television series about India's nationalist movement.

WORK IN PROGRESS: A novel about nuclear power.

SIDELIGHTS: Arundhati Roy created an international sensation with her debut novel, *The God of Small Things,* which first earned its author a million-dollar publishing advance. The novel garnered Roy Britain's most prestigious literary award, the Booker Prize; she was the first citizen of India to win that award. Following the success of her first novel, Roy remained in the public eye due to her social activism, as well to as her outspoken criticism of globalization and the negative influence exerted by the United States on global culture. She has even been imprisoned for her activities and opinions, which she has expressed in many essays, including those collected in *The Cost of Living* and *Power Politics.*

Roy grew up in Kerala, India, a child of Syrian Christian and Hindu parents. When her parents divorced, Roy's mother fought for and won an inheritance, despite the bias of Indian laws favoring male heirs. The victory was perhaps more significant ethically than financially, for Roy still found it necessary to live in a slum area in order to save enough money to attend school in New Delhi. She began by studying architecture, but eventually drifted from that and took up an acting career. This led to success as a screenwriter, which put the writer in a good position to negotiate the contract for her first book. After first appearing in 1997, *The God of Small Things* has been translated into more than forty languages and has sold several million copies internationally.

The God of Small Things focuses on themes of history and the individual, as experienced by twin siblings. The novel's title, according to Meenakshi Ganguly in *Time* magazine, refers to the deity that rules over "social propriety." The novel tells the story of Ammu, a divorced mother of twin children. Rahel, Ammu's daughter, eventually ends up in the United States, while her son, Estha, becomes mute, but despite their physical separation the twins retain an empathic bond. The novel also explores Ammu's forbidden love with the carpenter Velutha who belongs to the class of untouchables, and portrays family relatives who have come back to visit their homeland from Great Britain. One of the visitors ends up dead, and Ammu's affair comes to a tragic end.

Ganguly noted that *The God of Small Things* is "infused with endless, cinematic fast-forwards that telegraph the tragedy ahead." The critic cautioned that "Indian readers may be put off by the incessantly brutal depiction of their country. . . . Buildings are in near-rot and roads are graced with squashed animals." Michiko Kakutani of the *New York Times* praised the novel, hailing it as "dazzling" and "a richly layered story of familial betrayal and thwarted romantic passion." Kakutani compared Roy to British Victorian novelist Charles Dickens and twentieth-century American novelist William Faulkner for her handling of issues pertaining to race, class, society, and character, and reported that critics in the author's native India have compared her to South American novelist Gabriel García Márquez. The critic also asserted that "Roy does a marvelous job of conjuring the anomalous world of childhood, its sense of privilege and frustration, its fragility, innocence and unsentimental wisdom."

Roy used her newfound fame and money to further her work as an activist, and also attracted additional attention with her essay *The Greater Common Good,* which has been published in book form. In this essay she denounces the multimillion dollar Sardar Sarovar Dam project on the Narmada river in western India. Although promoters have touted the dam as a solution to India's power and water shortages, opponents of the project believe that it will cause widespread social and environmental chaos, as it would submerge 245 villages and displace some forty million people. In another essay, *The End of Imagination,* Roy decries the nuclear bomb tests conducted by India in May of 1998. Why, she asks, did India spend the massive amounts of money it took to build and test the bomb when the country has 400 million citizens living in complete poverty and illiteracy? Both essays have been reprinted in the volume *The Cost of Living.* While a *Publishers Weekly* writer stated that "Roy surely has meaningful things to say about India," the critic added that "she is not yet nearly as accomplished a political critic as she is a novelist." *The Cost of Living* is, in the reviewer's opinion, "marred by general attacks on 'the system' and personal digressions that distract a reader from the substantive issues at hand." In *Library Journal,* Ravi Shenoy allowed that Roy's "polemical tract" is "not a dispassionate inquiry," but added that nonetheless it "raises some important questions about the real price of 'development,' whether in the form of big dams or bombs."

Power Politics presents more of Roy's essays, as she criticizes the political elite of India and that group's participation in globalization despite enormous social and environmental costs. The essays are "pithy and elegant," according to a writer in the *New Internationalist.* James Gerein urged in his *World Literature Today* review that readers of this book should "set aside prejudgments, follow her arguments, and try to empathize with what it would be like to lose one's land, village, job, income, way of life, and perhaps life itself to the imperatives of globalization. Her thesis is not some bleedingheart fantasy but a largely unreported consequence of big business pounding the voiceless down to compost level."

War Talk likewise presents Roy's views and her passion for them, as she explores the connections between violence, poverty, and globalization. Judy Coode reported in *Sojourners,* "Roy is an incisive, infuriated citizen of the world, and she is determined not to allow the powers that thrive on imbalance and inequity to silence her. The essays are fairly easy to read, though at times their subject matter is difficult to stomach. Roy barely restrains herself from screaming in frustration at humans and their inability to recognize the connection between inequality and the lack of peace. She exposes herself fully, writing with such emotion and articulation that the reader can almost see her expression of righteous fury and hear her . . . strong voice choked with tears." Despite the seemingly unrelieved seriousness of Roy's writing, Donna Seaman noted in a *Booklist* review of *War Talk* that, "So fluent is her prose, so keen her understanding of global politics, and so resonant her objections to nuclear weapons, assaults against the environment, and the endless suffering of the poor that her essays are as uplifting as they are galvanizing."

Roy has spoken of her unconventional, independent mother as an influence she is very thankful for. She told David Barsamian in an interview for *Progressive:* "I thank God that I had none of the conditioning that a normal, middle-class Indian girl would have. I had no father, no presence of this man telling us that he would look after us and beat us occasionally in exchange. I didn't have a caste, and I didn't have a class, and I had no religion, no traditional blinkers, no traditional lenses on my spectacles, which are very hard to shrug off." She further commented to Barsamian: "I don't see a great difference between *The God of Small Things* and my works of nonfiction. As I keep saying, fiction is truth. I think fiction is the truest thing there ever was. My whole effort now is to remove that distinction. The writer is the midwife of understanding."

BIOGRAPHICAL AND CRITICAL SOURCES:

BOOKS

Contemporary Literary Criticism, Volume 109, Gale (Detroit, MI), 1998.

Contemporary Novelists, 7th edition, St. James Press (Detroit, MI), 2001.

The Critical Studies of Arundhati Roy's "The God of Small Things," Atlantic Publishers & Distributors (New Delhi, India), 1999.

Dictionary of Literary Biography Yearbook: 1997, Gale (Detroit, MI), 1998.

PERIODICALS

Booklist, May 1, 1997, Donna Seaman, review of *The God of Small Things,* p. 1480; April 15, 2003, Donna Seaman, review of *War Talk,* p. 1433.

Christian Science Monitor, November 24, 1997, Merle Rubin, review of *The God of Small Things,* p. 11.

Ecologist, September, 2000, "I Wish I Had the Guts to Shut Up," p. 29.

Entertainment Weekly, May 16, 1997, Suzanne Ruta, review of *The God of Small Things,* p. 109.

Guardian, September 29, 2001, review of *The Algebra of Infinite Justice,* p. 1; November 30, 2002, Natasha Walter, review of *The Algebra of Infinite Justice,* p. 11.

Harper's Bazaar, May, 1997, p. 117.

Herizons, spring, 2001, Subbalakshmi Subramanian, review of *The Cost of Living,* p. 33.

Journal of Contemporary Asia, May, 2003, Zaheer Baber, review of *The Cost of Living,* p. 284.

Kirkus Reviews, review of *The God of Small Things,* p. 412.

Library Journal, April 15, 1997, Barbara Hoffert, review of *The God of Small Things,* p. 120; July, 1997, Eric Bryant, review of *The God of Small Things,* p. 102; October 15, 1999, Ravi Shenoy, review of *The Cost of Living,* p. 90.

Los Angeles Times Book Review, June 1, 1997, Richard Eder, "As the World Turns," p. 2.

Maclean's, October 27, 1997, "A Literary Queen," p. 64.

Mother Jones, January-February, 2002, Arlie Russell Hochschild, interview with Roy, p. 74.

Nation, September 29, 1997, Amitava Kumar, "Rushdie's Children," pp. 36-38.

National Review, February 7, 2000, Kanchan Limaye, review of *The Cost of Living,* p. 50.

New Internationalist, October, 2002, review of *Power Politics,* p. 31.

New Republic, December 29, 1997, James Wood, review of *The God of Small Things,* p. 32; April 29, 2002, Ian Buruma, review of *Power Politics,* p. 25.

New Statesman, June 27, 1997, Amanda Craig, "But What about This Year's Barbados Novel?," p. 49; April 30, 2001, Salil Tripathi, "The Goddess against Big Things," p. 22.

Newsweek, May 26, 1997, Laura Shapiro, "Disaster in a Lush Land," p. 76.

Newsweek International, March 18, 2002, interview with Roy, p. 94.

New Yorker, June 23, 1997, John Updike, "Mother Tongues," pp. 156-159.

New York Review of Books, August 14, 1997, Rosemary Dinnage, review of *The God of Small Things,* p. 16.

New York Times, June 3, 1997, Michiko Kakutani, review of *The God of Small Things,* p. B4; July 29, 1997, Elisabeth Bumiller, "A Novelist Begins with a Splash," p. B1; October 15, 1997, Sarah Lyall, "Indian's First Novel Wins Booker Prize in Britain," p. A4; January 12, 2000, Celia W. Dugger, "Author Seized," p. A6; August 7, 2001, Salman Rushdie, "A Foolish Dam and a Writer's Freedom," p. A19; November 3, 2001, Celia W. Dugger, "An Indian Novelist Turns Her Wrath on the U.S.," p. A3; March 7, 2002, "India Jails Novelist for Criticizing a Court Ruling," p. A4.

New York Times Book Review, May 25, 1997, Alice Truax, "A Silver Thimble in Her Fist," p. 5; November 25, 2001, Alex Abramovich, review of *Power Politics,* p. 28.

Observer (London, England), November 17, 2002, review of *The Algebra of Infinite Justice,* p. 20.

People, July 14, 1997, Francine Prose, review of *The God of Small Things,* p. 30; November 3, 1997, Thomas Fields-Meyer, "No Small Thing: A Stunning Debut Novel Earns Arundhati Roy the Fruits of Stardom," p. 107; May 11, 1998, p. 161.

Progressive, April, 2001, David Barsamian, interview with Roy.

Publishers Weekly, March 3, 1997, review of *The God of Small Things,* p. 62; September 20, 1999, review of *The Cost of Living,* p. 61; May 14, 2001, John F. Baker, "Roy's Indian Wars," p. 20; July 30, 2001, review of *Power Politics,* p. 72.

Sojourners, July-August, 2003, Judy Coode, review of *War Talk,* p. 57.

Time, April 14, 1997.

Vogue, October, 2002, Daphne Beal, "Portrait of a Renegade," p. 244.

Washington Post, October 20, 1997, Kenneth J. Cooper, "For India, No Small Thing: Native Daughter Arundhati Roy Wins Coveted Booker Prize," p. C1.

Whole Earth, winter, 2001, "India Will Not Behave," p. 78, Paul Hawken, review of *Power Politics,* p. 81.

World Literature Today, winter, 1998, Ramlal Agarwal, review of *The God of Small Things,* p. 208; summer, 2002, James Gerein, review of *Power Politics,* p. 79.

World Press Review, January, 1997, John Zubrzycki, review of *The God of Small Things,* p. 39.

World Watch, May, 2002, Curtis Runyan, review of *Power Politics,* p. 17.

Writer, November, 1998, Lewis Burke Frumkes, "A Conversation with Arundhati Roy," p. 23.

ONLINE

Salon.com, http://www.salon.com/ (September 30, 1997), Reena Jana, interview with Roy.*

S

SCHAEFER, Lola M. 1950-

PERSONAL: Born July 23, 1950, in Fort Wayne, IN; daughter of Richard L. (in management) and Rosalyn M. (a homemaker; maiden name, Gale) Bennett; married Ted R. Schaefer (a woodworker), November 3, 1973; children: Adam R., Wyatt S. *Education:* Indiana University, B.S., 1972, M.S., 1984.

ADDRESSES: Home and office—4924 CR 7, Garrett, IN 46738.

CAREER: St. Jude Elementary, Fort Wayne, IN, seventh-grade teacher, 1973-76; J. E. Ober Elementary, Garrett, IN, kindergarten teacher, 1983-84; McKenney-Harrison, Auburn, IN, elementary teacher, 1984-88; McIntosh Elementary, Auburn, IN, elementary teacher, beginning 1988. Educational consultant in reading, writing, and integrated language arts programs in Indiana elementary schools; speaker at Young Author Conferences in Indiana.

MEMBER: International Reading Association, Society of Children's Book Writers and Illustrators (regional advisor for Indiana), Pokagon Reading Council (president, 1986-87).

AWARDS, HONORS: Maxine Huffman Excellence in Reading Education Award, Indiana University—Fort Wayne, 1991.

WRITINGS:

FOR CHILDREN

Out of the Night, illustrated by Roby Gilbert, Whispering Coyote Press (Boston, MA), 1995.

Lola M. Schaefer

Candlelight Service, illustrated by Michele Warner, Rigby (Crystal Lake, IL), 1995.

Turtle Nest, illustrated by Neesa Becker, Richard C. Owen (Katonah, NY), 1996.

Zap!, Seedlings Publications, 1998.

Models, Yellow Umbrella Books (Mankato, MN), 2000.

What Grows from a Tree?, Yellow Umbrella Books (Mankato, MN), 2000.
This Is the Sunflower, illustrated by Donald Crews, Greenwillow Books (New York, NY), 2000.
This Is the Rain, illustrated by Jane Wattenberg, Greenwillow Books (New York, NY), 2001.
Pick, Pull, Snap!: Where Once a Flower Bloomed, illustrated by Lindsay Barrett George, HarperCollins (New York, NY), 2001.
What's Up, What's Down?, HarperCollins (New York, NY), 2002.
Arrowhawk, illustrated by Gabi Swiatkowska, Holt (New York, NY), 2004.
Loose Tooth, illustrated by Sylvie Wickstrom, HarperCollins (New York, NY), 2004.
A River Flows, illustrated by Stephen Alcorn, Millbrook Press (Brookfield, CT), 2004.

"FAMILIES" SERIES

Fathers, Pebble Books (Mankato, MN), 1999.
Mothers, Pebble Books (Mankato, MN), 1999.
Grandfathers, Pebble Books (Mankato, MN), 1999.
Grandmothers, Pebble Books (Mankato, MN), 1999.
Sisters, Pebble Books (Mankato, MN), 1999.
Brothers, Pebble Books (Mankato, MN), 1999.
Cousins, Pebble Books (Mankato, MN), 1999.
Uncles, Pebble Books (Mankato, MN), 1999.
Aunts, Pebble Books (Mankato, MN), 1999.
Family Pets, Pebble Books (Mankato, MN), 1999.

"OCEAN LIFE" SERIES

Crabs, Pebble Books (Mankato, MN), 1999.
Corals, Pebble Books (Mankato, MN), 1999.
Octopuses, Pebble Books (Mankato, MN), 1999.
Parrotfish, Pebble Books (Mankato, MN), 1999.
Sea Anemones, Pebble Books (Mankato, MN), 1999.
Sea Horses, Pebble Books (Mankato, MN), 1999.
Sea Stars, Pebble Books (Mankato, MN), 1999.
Sea Urchins, Pebble Books (Mankato, MN), 1999.

"HONEY BEES" SERIES

Honey Bees, Pebble Books (Mankato, MN), 1999.
Honey Bees and Flowers, Pebble Books (Mankato, MN), 1999.
Honey Bees and Hives, Pebble Books (Mankato, MN), 1999.
Honey Bees and Honey, Pebble Books (Mankato, MN), 1999.

"FALL FUN" SERIES

Costumes, Pebble Books (Mankato, MN), 1999.
Jack-o-Lanterns, Pebble Books (Mankato, MN), 1999.
Scarecrows, Pebble Books (Mankato, MN), 1999.
Masks, Pebble Books (Mankato, MN), 1999.

"WHAT KIND OF DAY IS IT?" SERIES

A Snowy Day, Pebble Books (Mankato, MN), 2000.
A Rainy Day, Pebble Books (Mankato, MN), 2000.
A Windy Day, Pebble Books (Mankato, MN), 2000.
A Hot Day, Pebble Books (Mankato, MN), 2000.
A Cold Day, Pebble Books (Mankato, MN), 2000.
A Sunny Day, Pebble Books (Mankato, MN), 2000.

"TRANSPORTATION LIBRARY" SERIES

Airplanes, Bridgestone Books (Mankato, MN), 2000.
Tow Trucks, Bridgestone Books (Mankato, MN), 2000.
Tractor Trailers, Bridgestone Books (Mankato, MN), 2000.
Tugboats, Bridgestone Books (Mankato, MN), 2000.
Barges, Bridgestone Books (Mankato, MN), 2000.
Cable Cars, Bridgestone Books (Mankato, MN), 2000.
Ferries, Bridgestone Books (Mankato, MN), 2000.
Airplanes, Bridgestone Books (Mankato, MN), 2000.
Bicycles, Bridgestone Books (Mankato, MN), 2000.

"HELPERS IN OUR COMMUNITY" SERIES

We Need Dentists, Pebble Books (Mankato, MN), 2000.
We Need Doctors, Pebble Books (Mankato, MN), 2000.
We Need Farmers, Pebble Books (Mankato, MN), 2000.
We Need Fire Fighters, Pebble Books (Mankato, MN), 2000.
We Need Mail Carriers, Pebble Books (Mankato, MN), 2000.
We Need Nurses, Pebble Books (Mankato, MN), 2000.

We Need Police Officers, Pebble Books (Mankato, MN), 2000.

We Need Veterinarians, Pebble Books (Mankato, MN), 2000.

"WHO WORKS HERE?" SERIES

Hospital, Heinemann Library (Chicago, IL), 2000.

Dental Office, Heinemann Library (Chicago, IL), 2000.

Airport, Heinemann Library (Chicago, IL), 2000.

Construction Site, Heinemann Library (Chicago, IL), 2000.

Police Station, Heinemann Library (Chicago, IL), 2000.

Supermarket, Heinemann Library (Chicago, IL), 2000.

Car Dealership, Heinemann Library (Chicago, IL), 2001.

Courthouse, Heinemann Library (Chicago, IL), 2001.

Fast-Food Restaurant, Heinemann Library (Chicago, IL), 2001.

Fire Station, Heinemann Library (Chicago, IL), 2001.

Library, Heinemann Library (Chicago, IL), 2001.

Zoo, Heinemann Library (Chicago, IL), 2001.

"HOLIDAYS AND CELEBRATIONS" SERIES

Chinese New Year, Pebble Books (Mankato, MN), 2001.

Hanukkah, Pebble Books (Mankato, MN), 2001.

Kwanzaa, Pebble Books (Mankato, MN), 2001.

Cinco de Mayo, Pebble Books (Mankato, MN), 2001.

"UNDERSTANDING DIFFERENCES" SERIES

Some Kids Are Blind, Pebble Books (Mankato, MN), 2001.

Some Kids Are Deaf, Pebble Books (Mankato, MN), 2001.

Some Kids Use Wheelchairs, Pebble Books (Mankato, MN), 2001.

Some Kids Wear Leg Braces, Pebble Books (Mankato, MN), 2001.

"FAMOUS AMERICANS" SERIES

Abraham Lincoln, Pebble Books (Mankato, MN), 1998.

Martin Luther King, Jr., Pebble Books (Mankato, MN), 1999.

Cesar Chavez, Pebble Books (Mankato, MN), 1999.

George Washington, Pebble Books (Mankato, MN), 1999.

"THE WAY THINGS MOVE" SERIES

Back and Forth, Pebble Books (Mankato, MN), 2000.

Push and Pull, Pebble Books (Mankato, MN), 2000.

Zigzag Movement, Pebble Books (Mankato, MN), 2000.

Vibrations, Pebble Books (Mankato, MN), 2000.

Circular Movement, Pebble Books (Mankato, MN), 2000.

Start and Stop, Pebble Books (Mankato, MN), 2000.

"FAMOUS PEOPLE IN TRANSPORTATION" SERIES

The Wright Brothers, Pebble Books (Mankato, MN), 2000.

Henry Ford, Pebble Books (Mankato, MN), 2000.

Robert Fulton, Pebble Books (Mankato, MN), 2000.

Robert Goddard, Pebble Books (Mankato, MN), 2000.

"ANIMAL KINGDOM" SERIES

What Is a Mammal?, Pebble Books (Mankato, MN), 2001.

What Is a Reptile?, Pebble Books (Mankato, MN), 2001.

What Is an Amphibian?, Pebble Books (Mankato, MN), 2001.

What Is an Insect?, Pebble Books (Mankato, MN), 2001.

What Is a Fish?, Pebble Books (Mankato, MN), 2001.

What Is a Bird?, Pebble Books (Mankato, MN), 2001.

"WILD WORLD OF ANIMALS" SERIES

Frogs: Leaping Amphibians, Bridgestone Books (Mankato, MN), 2001.

Sharks: Hunters of the Deep, Bridgestone Books (Mankato, MN), 2001.

Spiders: Spinners and Trappers, Bridgestone Books (Mankato, MN), 2001.

Wolves: Life in the Pack, Bridgestone Books (Mankato, MN), 2001.
Rhinos: Horn-Faced Chargers, Capstone Press (Mankato, MN), 2002.
Zebras: Striped Grass-Grazers, Capstone Press (Mankato, MN), 2002.
Giraffes: Long-Necked Leaf Eaters, Capstone Press (Mankato, MN), 2002.
Leopards: Spotted Hunters, Capstone Press (Mankato, MN), 2002.

"FIRST BIOGRAPHIES" SERIES

Christopher Columbus, Pebble Books (Mankato, MN), 2002.
Frederick Douglass, Pebble Books (Mankato, MN), 2002.
Rosa Parks, Pebble Books (Mankato, MN), 2002.
Pocahontas, Pebble Books (Mankato, MN), 2002.
Thomas Edison, Pebble Books (Mankato, MN), 2003.
Clara Barton, Pebble Books (Mankato, MN), 2003.
Jackie Robinson, Pebble Books (Mankato, MN), 2003.
Amelia Earhart, Pebble Books (Mankato, MN), 2003.
Alexander Graham Bell, Pebble Books (Mankato, MN), 2003.
Johnny Appleseed, Pebble Books (Mankato, MN), 2003.
Booker T. Washington, Pebble Books (Mankato, MN), 2003.
Mother Teresa, Pebble Books (Mankato, MN), 2003.
(With son Wyatt Schaefer) *Albert Einstein,* Pebble Books (Mankato, MN), 2003.

"HOME FOR ME" SERIES

Apartment, Heinemann Library (Chicago, IL), 2002.
House, Heinemann Library (Chicago, IL), 2003.
Houseboat, Heinemann Library (Chicago, IL), 2003.
Mobile Home, Heinemann Library (Chicago, IL), 2003.
Homes ABC, Heinemann Library (Chicago, IL), 2003.

"OOEY-GOOEY ANIMALS" SERIES

Earthworms, Heinemann Library (Chicago, IL), 2002.
Jellyfish, Heinemann Library (Chicago, IL), 2002.
Leeches, Heinemann Library (Chicago, IL), 2002.
Newts, Heinemann Library (Chicago, IL), 2002.
Sea Anemones, Heinemann Library (Chicago, IL), 2002.
Slugs, Heinemann Library (Chicago, IL), 2002.
Ooey-Gooey Animals 123, Heinemann Library (Chicago, IL), 2002.
Ooey-Gooey Animals ABC, Heinemann Library (Chicago, IL), 2002.

"MUSTY-CRUSTY ANIMALS" SERIES

Lobsters, Heinemann Library (Chicago, IL), 2002.
Crayfish, Heinemann Library (Chicago, IL), 2002.
Barnacles, Heinemann Library (Chicago, IL), 2002.
Horseshoe Crabs, Heinemann Library (Chicago, IL), 2002.
Sea Horses, Heinemann Library (Chicago, IL), 2002.
Medusa, Heinemann Library (Chicago, IL), 2002.
Hermit Crabs, Heinemann Library (Chicago, IL), 2002.
Musty-Crusty Animals 123, Heinemann Library (Chicago, IL), 2002.
Musty-Crusty Animals ABC, Heinemann Library (Chicago, IL), 2002.

"SYMBOLS OF FREEDOM" SERIES

Mount Rushmore, Heinemann Library (Chicago, IL), 2002.
The U.S. Capitol, Heinemann Library (Chicago, IL), 2002.
The Washington Monument, Heinemann Library (Chicago, IL), 2002.
The Pledge of Allegiance, Heinemann Library (Chicago, IL), 2002.

"TINY-SPINY ANIMALS" SERIES

Tiny-Spiny Animals 123, Heinemann Library (Chicago, IL), 2003.
Tiny-Spiny Animals ABC, Heinemann Library (Chicago, IL), 2003.
Sea Urchins, Heinemann Library (Chicago, IL), 2003.
Horned Toad, Heinemann Library (Chicago, IL), 2003.
Porcupine, Heinemann Library (Chicago, IL), 2003.
Echidna, Heinemann Library (Chicago, IL), 2003.

"IT'S MY BODY" SERIES

It's My Body ABC, Heinemann Library (Chicago, IL), 2003.

My Head, Heinemann Library (Chicago, IL), 2003.
My Neck and Shoulders, Heinemann Library (Chicago, IL), 2003.
Body Pairs, Heinemann Library (Chicago, IL), 2003.
Arms, Elbows, Hands, and Fingers, Heinemann Library (Chicago, IL), 2003.
Legs, Knees, Feet, and Toes, Heinemann Library (Chicago, IL), 2003.
Hair, Heinemann Library (Chicago, IL), 2003.

"WHEELS, WINGS, AND WATER" SERIES

Wheels, Wings, and Water ABC, Heinemann Library (Chicago, IL), 2003.
Shapes to Go, Heinemann Library (Chicago, IL), 2003.
Trains, Heinemann Library (Chicago, IL), 2003.
Boats, Heinemann Library (Chicago, IL), 2003.
Aircraft, Heinemann Library (Chicago, IL), 2003.
Bicycles, Heinemann Library (Chicago, IL), 2003.

NONFICTION; FOR ADULTS

Teaching Young Writers, Scholastic (New York, NY), 2001.
Ten Writing Lessons for the Overhead, Scholastic (New York, NY), 2002.
Writing Lessons for the Overhead: Grades Five and Up, Scholastic (New York, NY), 2003.

Several of Schaefer's titles for Heinemann Library have been translated into Spanish.

SIDELIGHTS: Drawing on her enduring love of books and experience in the classroom as an elementary school teacher, Lola M. Schaefer began writing books for emergent readers in the mid-1990s. As she once told *CA:* "For years I have had the great pleasure of sharing the best of children's literature with students in my classroom. I have seen their joy of reading grow with each wonderful book. My love of writing stems from a desire to contribute to the vast wealth of excellent literature." And contribute she has, penning over one hundred titles in a matter of four years for the Bridgestone and Pebble Books imprints and for the Heinemann Library. She has contributed to series about animals, careers, holidays, machines, and notable Americans, as well as writing stand-alone nonfiction juvenile titles and teaching materials.

Among her works are volumes for different series about animals, including the "Wild World of Animals," the "Animal Kingdom," "Ocean Life," "Honey Bees," "Ooey-Gooey Animals," and "Musty-Crusty Animals." Because these are all books for very young readers, the texts are short and photo-driven. In contrast, her stand-alone picture book *This Is the Sunflower,* constructed as a rebus and recounting the life cycle of a flower familiar to many children, was illustrated by David Crews. Although a *Publishers Weekly* reviewer called the rhyme and momentum "lockstep," indicating an unpleasant mechanical quality, other reviewers offered different opinions, including *School Library Journal*'s Carolyn Jenks, who dubbed it a "simple, elegant book." Likewise, Gillian Engberg commented that it would be "perfect for story hours" in her *Booklist* review. Todd Morning, writing in the same periodical, praised Schaefer's similar title *This Is the Rain* for both its "quiet, rhymed text" and attractive illustrations by Jane Wattenberg. So too, a *Publishers Weekly* contributor found that Schaefer's "simple" text "conjures up vivid images."

Animals are not Schaefer's only topic; people figure prominently in a number of series, including "Families," about the relationships between family members, "Helpers in Our Community," about the importance of common professions, and "Who Works Here?," about a variety of occupations. "First Biographies," "Famous Americans," and "Famous People in Transportation" all deal with individuals of great accomplishment, while "Understanding Differences" tells of people with special challenges. Commenting on the "Helpers in Our Community" titles *We Need Doctors, We Need Nurses, We Need Dentists,* and *We Need Veterinarians,* a *Science Books and Films* reviewer predicted that children "will enjoy [the] accurate, simplified information" provided. The "Famous People in Transportation" series also caught the attention of critics, including *School Library Journal*'s Anne Chapman Callaghan, who praised Schaefer's "easy-to-understand and interesting accounts."

Reflecting on her aspirations, Schaefer once told *CA:* "I want to grow as a writer and be able to offer children stories that will tickle their funny bone, awaken a sense of wonder, or simply entertain. There are a lot of stories within all of us. I want to share many of mine with children through the power of written language."

BIOGRAPHICAL AND CRITICAL SOURCES:

PERIODICALS

Booklist, July, 2000, Gillian Engberg, review of *This Is the Sunflower,* p. 2042; December 15, 2001, Todd Morning, review of *This Is the Rain,* p. 741; December 1, 2002, Ilene Cooper, review of *What's Up, What's Down?,* p. 686.

Horn Book, July, 2000, Lolly Robinson, review of *This Is the Sunflower,* p. 445.

Horn Book Guide, spring, 2001, Jennifer Soalt, review of *Airport, Construction Site, Dental Office, Hospital, Police Station,* and *Supermarket,* p. 93; spring, 2001, review of *Chinese New Year, Cinco de Mayo, Hanukkah,* and *Kwanzaa,* p. 98; fall, 2001, Barbara Barstow, review of *Car Dealership, Courthouse, Fast-Food Restaurant, Fire Station, Library,* and *Zoo,* p. 335; fall, 2001, Nell Beram, review of *Some Kids Are Blind, Some Kids Are Deaf, Some Kids Use Wheelchairs,* and *Some Kids Wear Leg Braces,* p. 338; fall, 2001, Mary R. Holt, review of *What Is an Insect?,* and Kitty Flynn, review of *Spiders: Spinner and Trappers,* p. 366; fall, 2001, Mary R. Holt, review of *What Is an Amphibian?* and *What Is a Reptile?,* and Kitty Flynn, review of *Frogs: Leaping Amphibians,* p. 367; fall, 2001, Mary R. Holt, review of *What Is a Fish?* and *What Is a Bird?,* and Kitty Flynn, review of *Sharks: Hunters of the Deep,* p. 369; fall, 2001, Mary R. Holt, review of *What Is a Mammal?,* and Kitty Flynn, review of *Wolves: Life in the Pack,* p. 372; spring, 2002, Barbara Barstow, review of *Giraffes: Long-Necked Leaf-Eaters* and *Zebras: Striped Grass-Grazers,* p. 347.

Publishers Weekly, April 10, 2000, review of *This Is the Sunflower,* p. 97; July 23, 2001, review of *This Is the Rain,* p. 76.

School Library Journal, May, 2000, Carolyn Jenks, review of *This Is the Sunflower,* p. 154; August, 2000, Anne Chapman Callaghan, review of *Tugboats,* p. 175; September, 2000, Anne Chapman Callaghan, review of the "Famous People in Transportation" series, p. 222; October, 2000, review of *Hanukkah,* p. 65; December, 2000, Diane Olivo-Posner, review of *Chinese New Year,* p. 136; January, 2001, Pamela K. Bomboy, review of *Some Kids Are Blind,* p. 123; May, 2001, Elizabeth Maggio, review of *Courthouse, Library,* and *Zoo,* p. 146; September, 2001, Adele Greenlee, review of *This Is the Rain,* p. 205; January, 2003, Marlene Gawron, review of *What's Up, What's Down?,* p. 129.

Science Books & Films, July, 2001, Mary Nalbandian, review of *What Is a Mammal?, What Is a Reptile?,* and *What Is an Insect?,* pp. 172-173; November, 2001, review of *We Need Doctors, We Need Nurses, We Need Dentists,* and *We Need Veterinarians,* pp. 247-248; November, 2001, Frank M. Truesdale, review of *Frogs* and *Spiders,* p. 272.*

* * *

SELF, Will(iam) 1961-

PERSONAL: Born 1961, in London, England; son of Peter (a college professor) and Elaine (a publisher; maiden name, Rosenbloom) Self; married Kate Chancellor, June 13, 1990 (marriage ended); married Deborah Orr (an editor); children: Alexis, Madeleine. *Education:* Attended Oxford University, 1979-92, received M.A. (with honors).

ADDRESSES: *Agent*—Ed Victor, 6 Bayley St., Bedford Sq., London WC1B 3HB, England.

CAREER: Worked as a clerk and a laborer. Full-time writer.

AWARDS, HONORS: John Llewellyn Rhys Prize shortlist, 1991; Geoffrey Faber Memorial Prize, 1992, for *The Quantity Theory of Insanity;* voted one of twenty best young British writers in *Granta,* 1993; Booker Prize, 2002, for *An Imitation.*

WRITINGS:

The Quantity Theory of Insanity (short stories), Bloomsbury (London, England), 1991, Atlantic Monthly Press (New York, NY), 1995.

Cock and Bull (two novellas), Atlantic Monthly Press (London, England), 1992.

My Idea of Fun: A Cautionary Tale (novel), Bloomsbury (London, England), 1993, Atlantic Monthly Press (New York, NY), 1994.

Grey Area and Other Stories, Bloomsbury (London, England), 1994.

Junk Mail, Bloomsbury (London, England), 1995.

The Sweet Smell of Psychosis, illustrations by Martin Rowson, Bloomsbury (London, England), 1996, Grove Press (New York, NY), 1999.

Will Self

A Story for Europe, Bloomsbury (London, England), 1996.
Great Apes, Grove Press (New York, NY), 1997.
Tough, Tough Toys for Tough, Tough Boys, Grove Press (New York, NY), 1999.
How the Dead Live, Grove Press (New York, NY), 2000.
Perfidious Man, Viking (London, England), 2000.
(With Stephen Levinson) *Antony Gormley: Some of the Facts,* Tate Gallery (London, England), 2001.
Dorian: An Imitation, Grove Press (New York, NY), 2003.

Also author of *The Rock of Crack As Big As the Ritz,* 1995. Contributor of cartoons to periodicals, including *New Statesman* and *City Limits,* and of articles and reviews to periodicals, including *Esquire, Harper's,* and *Independent.*

SIDELIGHTS: The works of Will Self are distinguished by their black humor and uncompromising themes. Self is the author of short stories, such as those collected in *The Quantity Theory of Insanity* and *The Grey Area and Other Stories,* as well as longer works of fiction, among them the two novellas that comprise *Cock and Bull* and the novel *Dorian: An Imitation.* In *Vanity Fair* Zoë Heller observed that "the tone of *Quantity Theory*—both energetic and strangely lugubrious—was often profoundly discomfiting. And it was not difficult to guess that Self's thematic preoccupations—madness, altered states, the sinister authority of the psychiatric establishment—refracted a painful biography."

Madness is a topic that repeatedly appears within the stories included in Self's first collection, *The Quantity Theory of Insanity.* In "Ward 9," for example, an art therapist suffers a nervous breakdown and enters a mental asylum. The title story is based upon the proposition "that sanity is a finite quantity in any given social group," according to Nick Hornby in the *Times Literary Supplement.* Hornby pointed out that Self's stories are "full of dreary but threatening institutions," and added: "Though you wouldn't want to live in the Self universe . . . in the end, you are grateful that he has gone through the agonies necessary for its creation."

The novellas in *Cock and Bull* both concern an inexplicable metamorphosis which transforms the respective main characters into the opposite sex. In *Bull* one-time rugby player John Bull awakens one morning to discover that he has a vagina located behind his knee. "John Bull's behavior grows more and more feminine as he starts coping with premenstrual tension, water weight gain and hormonal ups and downs," Michiko Kakutani elaborated in the *New York Times.* Seeking help from his physician, Bull visits Dr. Alan Margoulies, but the doctor becomes obsessed with Bull's condition and attempts to seduce him. "Margoulies' infatuation with Bull—or, rather, his new plaything—is a witty satire on the kind of man who is obsessed with women's sex organs and ignores the rest of them," commented Rhoda Koenig in *New York.* Koenig also noted that "the doctor gets his comeuppance, and Bull, who also acquires feminine qualities of vulnerability, finds satisfaction in a unique homosexual relationship."

Like Bull, the protagonist of *Cock* also undergoes a sexual transformation. This time, Carol, a homemaker, grows a penis and develops increasingly masculine traits. She begins to dominate her alcoholic husband and eventually, according to Julie Wheelwright in the

New Statesman, "enacts a rape as revenge for her husband's sexual ineptitude." Kakutani pointed out the perceived "blatant sexism" of the novella, writing that, "In *Cock,* we learn that the woman who stands up for herself relinquishes her femininity and literally turns into a man, in Carol's case a particularly foul-minded man filled with homicidal rage." However, Wheelright maintained that the altered sex organs of Bull and Carol "appear as satirical metaphors of liberation." Self explained in *Vanity Fair* that he wrote *Cock and Bull* to voice his "anger at the way gender-based sexuality is so predetermined, the way we fit into our sex roles as surely as if we had cut them off the back of a cereal packet and pasted them onto ourselves."

In 1993 Self issued his first full-length novel, *My Idea of Fun: A Cautionary Tale.* The story is about Ian Wharton, who chooses people at random to kill and mutilate in grotesque ways. Except for his past mentor, Samuel Northcliffe, no one suspects Ian of committing such heinous crimes. The themes in *My Idea of Fun* include madness and sexual confusion. Will Blythe commented in *Esquire* that this "impressively deranged" book "belongs to a whole new genre devoted to the psycho killer and the severed limb." Blythe concluded, "Self's extraordinary novel is an allegory of diseased consciousness, a parable for a decade when what trickled down was not money but scorn for those without it." A reviewer for *Publishers Weekly* called Self a "master of the grotesque" whose book uses "vivid, jarringly unsavory imagery, richly erudite diction and a persuasive, engaging narrative voice."

In Self's *Great Apes* London artist Simon Dykes wakes up to a world inhabited by chimpanzees. Although he notices that he too seems to be turning into a chimpanzee, his denial lands him in a mental institution. Dykes' therapist is Dr. Zack Busner, a maverick researcher who takes his most intriguing cases onto talk shows. Barbara Hoffert in *Library Journal* noted that while Self "can be very funny," the novel as a whole is not persuasive, partly due to the author's extensive use of profanity and focus on sex. Although Gary Krist admitted in the *New York Times Book Review* that *Great Apes* is not "a book that will delight everyone," he deemed it Self's "most satisfying book so far." In *Booklist* a critic compared Self's satire to the work of Franz Kafka and Jonathan Swift, adding that this novel "hypnotizes with its comic romps, existential posturings, and Shakespearean intrigues." A *Kirkus Reviews* contributor described *Great Apes* as "vividly imagined, extraordinarily credible, provocative and entertaining in equal measure."

The Sweet Smell of Psychosis satirizes London's media establishment. Richard Hermes is a new arrival in that milieu, and he is quickly drawn into the cocaine-driven, oversexed heart of it all. It does not take long for Hermes to go "from media hack to media whore," as Veronica Scrol put it in *Booklist.* Although he is in love with a woman named Ursula Bently, he winds up sleeping with a hateful but powerful man named Bell, a newspaper columnist and talk-show host on radio and television. Critiquing the book for the *Review of Contemporary Fiction,* Brian Budzynski commented that "Self's body of work is perhaps best termed as idiosyncratic; its rendering of the unusual and perverted as familiar and attractive is wonderful. In this sense, *The Sweet Smell of Psychosis* is nothing short of incredible."

Self drew comparisons with the satirist Jonathan Swift upon publication of his novel *How the Dead Live.* Both authors share a "misanthropic side" and make use of "outlandish scenarios," noted Bonnie Smothers in *Booklist.* A *Publishers Weekly* writer commented of the book: "Running on a vatic rage that is almost Swiftian in the totality of its object—the damned human condition—it sweeps across the charnel-fields of contemporary existence."As the title suggests, Self concerns himself here with death. The main character, Lily Bloom, is shown in various states of death and dying throughout the tale. Self uses Lily's marginal position to offer unique perspective on a culture that is centered on desire. As Bonnie Smothers remarked in *Booklist,* "The satire is biting, even cruel, but like most well-conceived satire, it offers rich food for thought."

In *Dorian: An Imitation* Self updates the classic novel *The Picture of Dorian Gray,* by nineteenth-century Irish writer Oscar Wilde, bringing the story of London's decadent underworld into the late years of the twentieth century. In Self's version, Dorian is a young man whose naked body is featured on an art installation titled "Cathode Narcissus." As the years pass by, Dorian's image on the screens degrades, while he somehow seems to escape the HIV-AIDS epidemic, despite his risky sexual habits and intravenous drug use. Dorian's story is entwined with that of Princess Diana, from the time of her marriage until her death in an automobile accident in Paris. Helen Elliott, a reviewer for the *Weekend Australian,* found *Dorian* to be "a hurtling, fascinating and dangerously amusing novel"; the critic added that "there's an infuriating epilogue that makes you wonder at everything you've just read." Reflecting on the surprising twist at the book's end, Neil Bartlett remarked in a review for the *Guardian:* "Self's reincarnation of Dorian has taken the fag ends of both an English century and an English myth and given them new, troubling and hugely entertaining life."

Grey Area and Other Stories is a collection of nine short stories that depict the lives of people whose environments are so dull and meaningless that they escape into complex inner worlds. Self demonstrates that the distinctions between sanity and insanity are not always perfectly clear. A *Booklist* contributor called Self a "caustic yet competent critic of society," noting that in these stories, the "commonplace becomes awkward and surreal, allowing revelations and fresh insight to surface." In *New Statesman and Society* Mary Scott commented, "Self's talent, like that of the best crime writers, is to drop . . . the clues that would enable us to reach his conclusions for ourselves—if we had his gift."

BIOGRAPHICAL AND CRITICAL SOURCES:

BOOKS

Contemporary Novelists, 7th edition, St. James Press (Detroit, MI), 1997.

Dictionary of Literary Biography, Volume 207: *British Novelists since 1960, Third Series,* Gale (Detroit, MI), 1999.

PERIODICALS

Advocate, March 4, 2003, David Bahr, review of *Dorian: An Imitation,* p. 74.

Atlantic, March, 2003, review of *Dorian,* p. 111.

Booklist, December 1, 1995; August 19, 1997; April 1, 1999, Bonnie Smothers, review of *Tough, Tough Toys for Tough, Tough Boys,* p. 1387; August, 1999, Veronica Scrol, review of *The Sweet Smell of Psychosis,* p. 2029; August, 2000, Bonnie Smothers, review of *How the Dead Live,* p. 2113; December 1, 2002, Frank Caso, review of *Dorian,* p. 648.

Courier-Mail (Brisbane, Australia), December 21, 2002, Craig Boland, review of *Dorian,* p. 72.

Economist, July 15, 2000, review of *How the Dead Live,* p. 13.

Esquire, April, 1994, p. 164.

Gentleman's Quarterly, June, 1999, Thomas Mallon, "Self-made World," p. 134.

Granta 43, spring, 1993, p. 259.

Guardian, September 21, 2002, Neil Bartlett, review of *Dorian,* p. 26; July 5, 2003, Will Self, "It's a Wild, Wilde World," p. 31.

Kirkus Reviews, July 1, 1997.

Library Journal, October 1, 1997, p. 126; May 1, 1999, Joshua Cohen, review of *Tough, Tough Toys for Tough, Tough Boys,* p. 115; November 15, 2002, David W. Henderson, review of *Dorian,* p. 103.

London Review of Books, October 7, 1993, p. 20; June 19, 1997, p. 21.

Los Angeles Times Book Review, April 17, 1994, p. 4.

New Statesman, October 30, 1992, p. 35; November 25, 1994, p. 41; June 13, 1997, p. 44; May 1, 1998, p. 55; December 18, 2000, review of *Perfidious Man,* p. 54.

New York, May 17, 1993, p. 87; September 1, 1997, p. 49.

New Yorker, April 11, 1994, p. 89.

New York Times, May 31, 1993; June 3, 1994, p. C24; September 12, 1997, p. C31; January 5, 2003, Sophie Harrison, review of *Dorian,* p. 6.

New York Times Book Review, April 24, 1994, p. 27; February 26, 1995, p. 11; May 26, 1996, p. 9; September 21, 1997, p. 7; December 7, 1997, p. 62; September 21, 1997, Gary Krist, review of *Great Apes,* p. 7; June 20, 1999, Jonathan Lethem, review of *Tough, Tough Toys for Tough, Tough Boys,* p. 9; September 19, 1999, Laura Miller, review of *The Sweet Smell of Psychosis,* p. 11; October 8, 2000, review of *How the Dead Live,* p. 8; January 5, 2003, Sophie Harrison, review of *Dorian,* p. 6.

Observer (London, England), November 20, 1994, p. 19; January 12, 1997, p. 16; May 11, 1997, p. 16; September 29, 2002, Jonathan Heawood, review of *Dorian,* p. 15.

Publishers Weekly, February 7, 1994, p. 6; July 14, 1997, review of *Great Apes,* p. 63; September 8, 1997, Anna Henchman, "Will Self: An Enfant Terrible Comes of Age," p. 52; March 1, 1999, review of *Tough, Tough Toys for Tough, Tough Boys,* p. 58; July 19, 1999, review of *The Sweet Smell of Psychosis,* p. 182; July 31, 2000, review of *How*

the Dead Live, p. 69; September 29, 2002, Robert McCrum, interview with Self, p. 15; January 6, 2003, review of *Dorian,* p. 38.
Review of Contemporary Fiction, spring, 1998, Paul Maliszewski, review of *Great Apes,* p. 238; fall, 1999, Paul Maliszewski, review of *Tough, Tough Toys for Tough, Tough Boys,* p. 177; spring, 2000, Brian Budzynski, review of *The Sweet Smell of Psychosis,* p. 191.
Seattle Times, February 9, 2003, John Freeman, review of *Dorian,* p. L8.
Times Literary Supplement, December 20, 1991, p. 25; October 9, 1992, p. 22; November 18, 1994, p. 20; January 5, 1996, p. 32; December 20, 1996, p. 24; May 9, 1997, p. 19.
Tribune Books (Chicago, IL), May 29, 1994, p. 5; March 5, 1995, p. 6; April 7, 1996, p. 6.
Vanity Fair, June, 1993, pp. 125-127, 148-151.
Washington Post Book World, April 3, 1994, p. 3; April 28, 1996, p. 3.
Weekend Australian, January 11, 2003, Helen Elliott, review of *Dorian,* p. B9.*

* * *

Olive Senior

SENIOR, Olive (Marjorie) 1941-

PERSONAL: Born December 23, 1941, in Jamaica; immigrated to Canada, 1991. *Education:* Carleton University, B.S., 1967.

ADDRESSES: *Home*—Kingston, Jamaica, and Toronto, Ontario, Canada. *Agent*—Nicole Aragi, Watkins/Loomis Agency, 133 East 35th St., Ste. 1, New York, NY 10016.

CAREER: *Daily Gleaner* (newspaper), Jamaica, reporter and subeditor; Jamaica Information Service, information officer, 1967-69; Jamaica Chamber of Commerce, public relations officer, 1969-71; *JCC Journal,* editor, 1969-71; Institute of Social and Economic Research, University of the West Indies, Jamaica, publications editor, 1972-77; *Social and Economic Studies,* editor, 1972-77; freelance writer and researcher, beginning 1977; worked as part-time teacher in communications, publishing consultant, and speech writer, 1977-82; Institute of Jamaica Publications, managing editor, 1982-89; *Jamaica Journal,* editor, 1982-89; University of the West Indies, Cave Hill, Barbados, visiting lecturer/writer-in-residence, 1990; Caribbean Writers Summer Institute, University of Miami, Florida, director of fiction workshop, 1994, 1995; St. Lawrence University, Canton, NY, Dana Visiting Professor of creative writing, 1994-95.

AWARDS, HONORS: Commonwealth Writers' prize, 1967; Gold, Silver, and Bronze medals for poetry and fiction, Jamaica Festival Literary Competitions, 1968-70; winner in two categories, Longman International Year of the Child Short Story Competition, 1978; Institute of Jamaica Centenary medal for creative writing, 1979; UNESCO award for study in the Philippines, 1987; Jamaica Press Association award for editorial excellence, 1987; Commonwealth Writers Prize: Best Novel, 1987, for *Summer Lightning;* United States Information Service, International Visitor award, 1988; Institute of Jamaica, Silver Musgrave medal for literature, 1989; Hawthornden fellow, Scotland, 1990; International Writer-in-Residence, Arts Council of England, 1991; F. G. Bressani Literary prize for poetry, 1994, for *Gardening in the Tropics.*

WRITINGS:

POETRY

Talking of Trees, Calabash (Kingston, Jamaica), 1986.
Gardening in the Tropics, McClelland & Stewart (Toronto, Ontario, Canada), 1994.

SHORT STORIES

Summer Lightning and Other Stories, Longman (London, England), 1986.
Arrival of the Snake-Woman, Longman (London, England), 1989.
(With others) *Quartet,* Longman (London, England), 1994.
Discerner of Hearts, McClelland & Stewart (Toronto, Ontario, Canada), 1995.

EDITOR

The Journey Prize Anthology: Short Fiction from the Best of Canada's New Writers, McClelland & Stewart (Toronto, Ontario, Canada), 1996.
Maria La Yacona, *Jamaica: Portraits, 1955-1998,* Marco Press (Marco Island, FL), 1998.
James Baldwin, *Go Tell It on the Mountain: And Related Readings,* McDougal Littell (Evanston, IL), 1998.

OTHER

The Message Is Change: A Perspective on the 1972 General Elections, Kingston Publishers (Kingston, Jamaica), 1972.
Pop Story Gi Mi (four booklets on Jamaican heritage for schools), Ministry of Education (Kingston, Jamaica), 1973.
A-Z of Jamaican Heritage, Heinemann & Gleaner (Kingston, Jamaica), 1984.
Working Miracles: Women's Lives in the English-speaking Caribbean, Indiana University Press (Bloomington, IL), 1991.

SIDELIGHTS: Olive Senior is a contemporary Caribbean writer. A journalist who has won acclaim for her poetry and short stories, she has also written several important nonfiction books about Caribbean culture, among them *A-Z of Jamaican Heritage.* Her fiction and poetry frequently focus on social and racial issues in Jamaica. Senior "has also played a vital role in putting women's issues on the literary agenda of her region," commented Denise deCaires Narain in the *Dictionary of Literary Biography.*

Senior was raised in a rural district of Jamaica, and in Narain's opinion, a sense of "rural isolation" pervades her work. She later went to live with more well-to-do relatives, which, the writer told Lisa Allen-Agostini in the *Sunday Guardian,* "meant a shift. I grew up in two households, sort of two different Jamaicas, not just because of material things, but also how people behaved." At Montego Bay High School she excelled at writing, and even began a magazine to showcase her own and her peers' work. After school and during vacations she worked at Jamaica's most distinguished newspaper, the *Daily Gleaner.* In 1967 she earned a bachelor of journalism degree at Carleton University in Toronto. While she now spends much of her time in Canada, Senior told Allen-Agostini, "I would describe myself as a conscious Caribbean person, even though I'm based somewhere else; my primary area of interest is still the Caribbean." She added: "I'm so concerned about what's happening in the Caribbean with young people and the fact that we have become so caught up in the 'satellite culture' that our true indigenous cultures—which just began to be explored at the time of independence—are being swept away or ignored. And you wonder, who are we going to be down the road if we don't have something of our own to cling to?"

Senior's first published book was the poetry collection *Talking of Trees.* In it, Senior presents "serious and noisy poems about the natural world while little ignoring the horrors of Jamaica's colonial history," explained Susan M. Schultz in *Contemporary Woman Poets.* The book's first section focuses on personal themes, while the second half is more political in nature. "Taken as a whole, the volume offers a series of lovingly detailed portraits of Jamaica, testifying to the toughness of the landscape and cityscape and to the resilience of its people," declared Narain. In *Gardening in the Tropics,* Senior's next poetry collection, she pays tribute to the cultural heritage of Jamaica, particularly its blend of Indian, African, and European cultures. The poems range from the region's first contact with Europeans up to the present day, with speakers from a wide variety of cultural and socioeconomic groups. "The overall effect of the volume is enchanting and liberating," stated Adele S. Newson in *World Literature Today.*

Summer Lightning and Other Stories confirmed Senior's standing in the literary world by winning the 1987 Commonwealth Writer's Prize. Many reviewers praised *Summer Lightning* for its sensitive, many-layered evocation of Jamaican culture. "The total effect is of a particular world illuminated from every angle, and by the time we turn the final page, intimately known," Evelyn O'Callaghan wrote in *Journal of West Indian Literature.* "There is much the reader can learn from Olive Senior's short fiction—about the rich resources of Jamaican speech varieties, about superstitions and folk beliefs and the details of daily life in rural society. . . . *Summer Lightning* is a slim well-crafted and beautifully packaged offering of treats to be savoured and enjoyed."

Senior's second story collection, *Arrival of the Snake-Woman and Other Stories,* is "more somber" than *Summer Lightning,* according to Narain. The title story concerns a village woman, Miss Coolie, who is viewed with suspicion by her neighbors. It "evokes a complex composite picture of rural and urban Jamaica. Although as in her first collection Senior often uses binary oppositions to structure her stories, she problematizes these to point to the inadequacy of the binary paradigm for interrogating the complex . . . reality of Caribbean culture." In *Discerner of Hearts,* another story collection, Senior provides "a juxtaposition of lively voices, rigid class lines and competing societies" in Jamaica, noted Maggie Barb in the *New York Times Book Review.* "Spotlighting the multiple marks of class and racial difference on the tiny Caribbean island, Ms. Senior offers a luminous portrait of people struggling to find their own place in a changing world." The stories in this collection cover a wide sweep of Carribean history, and according to Michael Thorpe in *World Literature Today,* they portray "a constricted society whose relationships are overdetermined by class and color; caste-power, or the lack of it, is constantly felt."

"Senior's short stories and poetry are the work of a creative talent of great sensitivity that expresses tremendous understanding of the human condition, particularly that of poor people both rural and urban," affirmed Velma Pollard in *Callaloo.* "The work is knit together by a common landscape and a recurring concern for humanity." Senior commented to Charles H. Rowell in an interview for *Callaloo:* "For me, writing, literature, is inextricably fused with magic. Though most of my writing is in a realistic vein, I am conscious at all times of other possibilities lurking just beyond consciousness, of the great ineffable mystery that lies at the core of each life, at the heart of every story."

BIOGRAPHICAL AND CRITICAL SOURCES:

BOOKS

Bardolph, Jacqueline, editor, *Short Fiction in the New Literatures in English,* Facultie des Lettres & Sciences Humaines (Nice, France), 1989.

Chamberlin, J. E., *Come Back to Me My Language: Poetry and the West Indies,* University of Illinois Press (Champaign, IL), 1993.

Contemporary Black Biography, Volume 37, Gale (Detroit, MI), 2003.

Contemporary Novelists, 6th edition, St. James Press (Detroit, MI), 1996.

Contemporary Poets, 7th edition, St. James Press (Detroit, MI), 2001.

Contemporary Women Poets, St. James Press (Detroit, MI), 1998.

Cudje, Selwyn, editor, *Caribbean Women Writers,* Calaloux (Wellesley, MA), 1990.

Davies, Carole Boyce, and Elaine Savory Fido, *Out of the Kumbla: Caribbean Women and Literature,* Africa World Press (New York, NY), 1990.

Dictionary of Literary Biography, Volume 157: *Twentieth-Century Caribbean and Black African Writers, Third Series,* Gale (Detroit, MI), 1995.

Kinnery, Malcolm, and Michael Rose, *Critical Strategies,* Bedford Books (Boston, MA), 1989.

Nasta, Susheila, editor, *Motherlands: Black Women's Writing from Africa, the Caribbean and South Asia,* Women's Press (London, England), 1991.

O'Callaghan, Evelyn, *Woman Version: Theoretical Approaches to West Indian Fiction,* Macmillan (London, England), 1993.

PERIODICALS

Ariel, January, 1993, pp. 13-33.

Black Collegian, March-April, 1989, Kuumba Kazi-Ferrouillet, review of *Summer Lightning and Other Stories,* p. 173.
Callalloo, summer, 1988, pp. 480-90, 540-51; winter, 1993, pp. 34-43.
Commonwealth Essays and Studies, spring, 1991, pp. 42-48.
Everywoman, June, 1991, pp. 19-22.
Journal of Caribbean Studies, spring, 1988, pp. 143-162.
Journal of Development Studies, October, 1992, Sally Lloyd Evans, review of *Working Miracles: Women's Lives in the English-speaking Caribbean,* p. 193.
Journal of West Indian Literature, October, 1986, pp. 92-94.
Kunapipi, no. 2, 1986, pp. 11-20.
Ms., November-December, 1995, p. 88.
New Voices, September, 1986, pp. 31-34.
New York Times Book Review, April 17, 1988, p. 42; October 1, 1995, p. 32.
Sunday Guardian, March 12, 2000, Lisa Allen-Agostini, "An Embodiment of Conflict," p. 19.
Third World Quarterly, April, 1988, pp. 995-998.
Times Literary Supplement, April 1, 1988, p. 364.
Women's Review of Books, November, 1987, p. 13.
World Literature Today, summer, 1990, p. 514; autumn, 1995, Adele S. Newson, review of *Gardening in the Tropics,* p. 852; spring, 1996, Michael Thorpe, review of *Discerner of Hearts,* p. 455.*

* * *

SETTLE, Mary Lee 1918-

PERSONAL: Born July 29, 1918, in Charleston, WV; daughter of Joseph Edward (a civil engineer) and Rachel (Tompkins) Settle; married Rodney Weathersbee, 1939 (divorced, 1946); married Douglas Newton (a poet and journalist), 1946 (divorced, 1956); married William Littleton Tazewell (a columnist and historian), September 2, 1978; children: Christopher Weathersbee. *Education:* Attended Sweet Briar College, 1936-38. *Politics:* Democrat. *Religion:* Episcopalian.

ADDRESSES: Home—544 Pembroke Ave., Norfolk, VA 23507. *Agent*—Roberta Pryor, International Creative Management, 40 West 57th Street, New York, NY 10019.

CAREER: Novelist. Worked as a model and actress in New York, NY, 1938-39; *Harper's Bazaar,* New York, NY, assistant editor, 1945; freelance writer, 1945—. *Flair* magazine, English correspondent, 1950-51; American Heritage, New York, NY, editor, beginning 1961; Bard College, associate professor, 1965-76; visiting lecturer at Iowa Writer's Workshop, 1976, and University of Virginia, 1978. Founder of PEN-Faulkner Award, 1980. *Wartime service:* Women's Auxiliary Air Force, 1942-43; Office of War Information in England, writer, 1944-45.

AWARDS, HONORS: Guggenheim fellowships, 1958, 1960; award from Merrill Foundation, 1975; National Book Award, 1978, for *Blood Tie;* Janet Heidinger Kafka Prize, honorable mention, 1981, for *The Scapegoat,* and award, 1983, for *The Killing Ground;* American Academy of Arts and Literature award in literature, 1984; West Virginia Folklife Center Achievement Award, 2003.

WRITINGS:

NOVELS

The Love Eaters, Harper (New York, NY), 1954.
The Kiss of Kin, Harper (New York, NY), 1955.
Fight Night on a Sweet Saturday, Viking (New York, NY), 1964.
The Clam Shell, Delacorte (New York, NY), 1971.
Blood Tie, Houghton Mifflin (Boston, MA), 1977.
Celebration, Farrar, Straus (New York, NY), 1986.
The Search for Beulah Land, Scribner (New York, NY), 1988.
Charley Bland, Farrar, Straus (New York, NY), 1989.
Choices, Doubleday (New York, NY), 1995.
Addie, University of South Carolina Press (Columbia, SC), 1998.
I, Roger Williams: A Fragment of Autobiography, Norton (New York, NY), 2001.

"BEULAH QUINTET"; NOVELS

O Beulah Land, Viking (New York, NY), 1956, with a new introduction by the author, University of South Carolina Press (Columbia, SC), 1996.
Know Nothing, Viking (New York, NY), 1960, published as *Pride's Promise,* Pinnacle Books (New York, NY), 1976, published under original title with a new introduction by the author, University of South Carolina Press (Columbia, SC), 1996.

Prisons, Putnam (New York, NY), 1973, published as *The Long Road to Paradise,* Constable (London, England), 1974, new edition, with a new introduction by the author, University of South Carolina Press (Columbia, SC), 1996.

The Scapegoat, Random House (New York, NY), 1980, new edition, with a new introduction by the author, University of South Carolina Press (Columbia, SC), 1996.

The Killing Ground, Farrar, Straus (New York, NY), 1982, new edition, with a new introduction by the author, University of South Carolina Press (Columbia, SC), 1996.

OTHER

Juana La Loca (play), produced in New York, NY, 1965.

All the Brave Promises: Memories of Aircraft Woman Second Class 2146391 (autobiography), Delacorte (New York, NY), 1966, reprinted, University of South Carolina Press (Columbia, SC), 1995.

The Story of Flight (juvenile), Random House (New York, NY), 1967.

The Scopes Trial: The State of Tennessee vs. John Thomas Scopes (juvenile), F. Watts (New York, NY), 1972.

Water World (juvenile), Dutton (New York, NY), 1984.

Turkish Reflections: A Biography of a Place (autobiography), Prentice-Hall (New York, NY), 1991.

Spanish Recognitions: The Roads to the Present, Norton (New York, NY), 2004.

Also author of six unpublished plays and four unproduced film scripts, 1945-55. Contributor of short stories to anthologies, including *The Girl in a Black Raincoat: Variations on a Theme,* edited by George Garrett, Duell, Sloan & Pierce (New York, NY), 1966, and *Rediscoveries,* edited by David Madden, Crown (New York, NY), 1971; and to periodicals, including *Harper's, Paris Review,* and *Argosy.*

SIDELIGHTS: American novelist Mary Lee Settle is best known for her five-volume "Beulah Quintet." Spanning a three-hundred-year period, the novels in the quintet trace the development of American cultural and political identity through the histories of three fictional West Virginia families. These three families share a common ancestor, whose refusal to bow to Oliver Cromwell led to his execution during the English civil war of the mid-seventeenth century. Though Settle's works have led some to rate her as "one of the best American novelists," in the words of a *Seattle Post-Intelligencer* writer, she has received perhaps less recognition than she rightly deserves, in part due to being classified as a regional or Southern writer.

As the daughter of a Southern coal mine owner and civil engineer, Settle had a patrician upbringing. She attended Sweet Briar College for two years, then left for New York City, where she worked as a model and actress from 1938 until her marriage in 1939. When her English husband was called into military service at the beginning of World War II, Settle went to England and served in the British Women's Auxiliary Air Force for a year before transferring to the Office of War Information in London as a writer.

After the war she returned to New York, where she worked briefly as an assistant editor at *Harper's* before devoting herself wholly to writing. Her decision was precipitated, she would later recall in an essay for *Contemporary Authors Autobiography Series (CAAS),* by a copy of *Wuthering Heights.* "I realized that Emily Brontë had written it and was dead by the time she was twenty-eight. I had just turned twenty-seven. So I saw my two ways. Either I would still be sitting there, a well-paid fashion and arts editor at forty, still writing about other people's accomplishments, or I would plunge into the precarious world of writing myself." She returned to England, and "wrote from 1945 to 1954 without publishing anything but the journalistic pieces that I did to live on." Far from regretting her years as a journalist, however, Settle once told *CA* that journalism is "the best training in the world. During that time I learned how to meet deadlines; I grew up as a get-it-on-the-page journalist who could research enough to write 5,000 lively words about anything in a few days."

During these years Settle wrote six unproduced plays and four unproduced film scripts before finally turning her hand to a novel. Her first published novel, *The Love Eaters,* was actually the second she had written. That book, as well as her first novel, *The Kiss of Kin,* were initially rejected by several U.S. publishers, but after British publisher Heinemann accepted *The Love Eaters,* both novels quickly found publishers on both sides of the Atlantic. These and *O Beulah Land,* the first novel of the "Beulah Quintet" to be written—

although second in the storyline's chronology—reflect several years of research at the British Museum into the history of the West Virginia region where Settle grew up, and of the English immigrants who settled there. "I knew when I began that it would be more than one book," Settle later told *CA*, "but I didn't expect that it would keep me busy for twenty-five years." Her idea was to set forth "the sort of social and political impulses that formed America—the reasons many of our forebears came here." Out of any given 100,000 settlers who came to Virginia from 1675 to 1775, she noted, 80,000 were probably felons. "It's extraordinary that no Virginian ever seems to have been descended from any of them," she remarked. "They must all have been sterile."

O Beulah Land describes the founding of the fictional West Virginia community of Beulah by Hannah Bridewell, a transported London prostitute, and Jeremiah Catlett, a fugitive bondsman, in the years before the American Revolution. Perhaps because of widespread critical disdain for the historical novel, *O Beulah Land* initially drew little critical attention. Writing in the *New York Times Book Review*, however, Charlotte Capers described the novel as "head and shoulders above most of its contemporaries," and added, "The author's research in the British Museum has paid off in the realism with which she invests her characters."

Know Nothing, the second novel published in the "Beulah Quintet," takes place during the years leading to the U.S. Civil War. William Peden, writing in the *Saturday Review*, felt that the multiplicity of Settle's characters and her "floating point of view" detract from the effectiveness of the novel. Nonetheless, he praised the book's depiction of "the growing tensions between irreconcilable political, social, and moral forces" and the author's "literary integrity and admirable seriousness of purpose."

Publication of Settle's work did not assure her financial stability, and the next ten years were difficult ones. Settle had returned to Charleston in 1955 following the publication of her first two novels. Her second marriage had broken up—in large part, perhaps, because of her sudden literary success. "By 1961," she recalled in *CAAS*, "I had been left without help or enough money to live on." An editing job with American Heritage in New York City supported her while she wrote what she intended to be the final novel in the "Beulah" series, *Fight Night on a Sweet Saturday*. The book, which is now not generally counted as part of the quintet, was not a success. A reviewer in the *Times Literary Supplement* complained of Settle's "hectic, uneven" writing. "Eloquent in many passages it surely is, and interestingly, thoughtfully constructed," admitted Robert M. Adams in the *New York Review of Books*. The critic nonetheless concluded that *Fight Night on a Sweet Saturday* is "not focused or resourceful enough to keep the reader content."

"I realized that I had not, as I had hoped, finished the work I had set out to do in 1954," Settle recalled. "A sense of failure, the fatigue of having worked for so long under such circumstances, and the end of the happiness I had hoped for in my personal life, plunged me into despair." She pulled through, however, and in 1965 found a part-time teaching position at Bard College that allowed her to support herself and still have time for her writing.

In 1966 Settle published *All the Brave Promises*, her memoir of her years in the WAAF. She wrote it, she observed in *CAAS*, "almost as a protest against the romanticism about the Second World War. The state of war—what the daily deprivation, grayness, drain of loss, and boredom did to people—was being forgotten." Writing in *Commonweal*, Alan Pryce-Jones commented that "Settle's victory is to show that a nasty experience was not entirely pain; her book, for all its rawness, is the book of a sympathetic and understanding woman. It is also relived with stereoscopic sharpness of outline. I hope it has . . . the success it deserves, among the few really good books to come out of World War II."

Disenchanted with the political atmosphere in the United States, Settle lived in England from 1969 to 1971 and in Turkey from 1972 to 1974, returning to Bard only to teach one semester each year. She wrote her novel *Blood Tie* after her return to West Virginia in 1974. The story concerns a group of expatriates living in Turkey—"not the wide-eyed, excited expatriate of the '20s," observed Anatole Broyard in the *New York Times*, "but the culture dropout of the '70s, someone who puts an ocean between himself and his past, who visits a foreign country . . . as a crasher enters a party." He noted of Settle, "Even for an experienced novelist, even for a good writer, she has done a remarkable job of capturing the culture that is, in a sense, the most important character in her book."

"It is one of those rare books in which that which is foreign becomes familiar and ceases to be simply strange," George Garrett wrote in the *Dictionary of Literary Biography.* "Multiple in narration, *Blood Tie* was clearly a virtuoso work."

In 1977 Settle left her position at Bard and turned her attention once again to her "Beulah" series. She had written *Prisons,* the first book chronologically although the third to be published, during her time in Turkey. In that novel, she turns to the England of the seventeenth century in her search for the seeds of American democracy. *The Scapegoat,* published in 1980, is the fourth novel of the "Beulah Quintet." The plot revolves around a West Virginia coal miners' strike that occurred in 1912; its characters include the historical figure Mother Jones, the United Mine Workers organizer. A reviewer in the *Washington Post Book World* suggested that Settle's "rather predictable rhetoric is the principal weakness in what is otherwise a powerful, distinctive, novel." Robert Houston, in the *Nation,* praised the author's attention to the sound of her characters: "Settle makes *The Scapegoat* a symphony of her characters' voices, captured with an unfailingly attuned ear." He also suggested that the author's avoidance of the popular styles in fiction contributed to her lack of commercial success in her early works. Houston commended the way Settle "has continued to write about such things as justice, the human heart, right and wrong—things it became fashionable to forget." Reviewing *The Scapegoat* in the *Washington Post Book World,* Anne Tyler called it "a quiet masterpiece."

The Killing Ground, the concluding volume of the "Beulah Quintet," returns to some of the events of *Fight Night on a Sweet Saturday.* The narrator, Hannah McKarkle—descendant of the families who are the focus of the quintet—presents herself as the author of the preceding four volumes. The novel, which brings the series into the present, examines the reasons why Hannah traces her family's history: her desire to make sense of her elder brother Johnny's violent death in jail. Hannah's motivation has something in common with Settle's own description of how she conceived the idea for the quintet. "I had a picture of one man hitting another in a West Virginia drunk tank one Saturday night," she once told *CA,* "and the idea was to go all the way back to see what lay behind that blow. At first I went back all the way to 1755, then I realized that wasn't far enough, and I went back further still, to Cromwell's England, in *Prisons,* to trace the idea of liberty from which so much of the American experience sprang."

Describing *The Killing Ground* as "part slag but part good, sturdy, useful black gold," Aaron Latham, in the *New York Times Book Review,* found the first half of the novel to be dull and over-long, but had high praise for the second half, which explores Hannah's motivations for writing. Reviewing the novel in Chicago's *Tribune Books,* Alexandra Johnson admired the "ingenious narrative conceit . . . that Hannah's novels are Settle's, thus updating and consolidating the Beulah saga into one novel." Johnson predicted that *The Killing Ground,* "so richly told and quietly haunting, [will] undoubtedly send readers scrambling for the earlier novels." "If you know any literate young person whom you wish well," suggested J. D. O'Hara in the *Nation,* "you might buy him or her a copy of *The Killing Ground* when you buy your own."

Settle's first work of fiction published after the conclusion of the "Beulah" series was a very different novel. *Celebration* was described by *Publishers Weekly* reviewer Wendy Smith as a "joyful and serene novel about a group of expatriates in London." *New York Times* reviewer Michiko Kakutani found the book's large cast of characters overwhelming, writing that "unfortunately, . . . *Celebration* begins to feel, at times, like an overcrowded town meeting." Nonetheless, Kakutani affirmed that "Settle has a fine sense of detail, as well as an uncanny ear for verbal inflections."

In Settle's 1989 novel, *Charley Bland,* she takes a minor character from *The Killing Ground,* and delves into his life. She also explores the life of the narrator, a novelist who has remained in Europe after wartime service, then returns to her home in West Virginia and has an affair with Charley, whom she has known since childhood. David Leavitt, writing in the *New York Times Book Review,* said that the author "writes with an acute and occasionally overwhelming consciousness of herself as a Southern writer." Leavitt praised the novel's "precision and emotional power," but concluded that "Settle's haunted obsession with her homeland ultimately frustrates." Monroe K. Spears, in a *Washington Post Book World* review, called *Charley Bland* "a lyrical novel, songlike in brevity and emotional intensity, though also richly meditative. . . . The remarkable thing is that the novel manages, in its brief space, to do so many things successfully: to place all the characters precisely in the economy, class system and mythology of the small West Virginia town in 1960-66, to explain the psychological relations of all the main characters, and to set forth a deeply meditated account of the significance of the affair to the narrator."

Settle's novel *Choices* tells of the rising and falling fortunes of Melinda, a beautiful, intelligent debutante whose father commits suicide in order to ensure his family's financial security. The tragedy drives Melinda away from her protected world, and she sets out for a life far different from the one her father wished for her. Passionately involved in crusading for the oppressed, she joins in relief efforts for the families of coal miners, who are being mercilessly punished for their efforts to unionize and is eventually jailed for her efforts. She later goes to Spain to join in the war against Franco's fascist government, and is shocked by the carnage she witnesses there. Later in life, she serves as a spy in the South for the civil rights movement. The book is "an eyewitness sojourn through the history of our century, the book's artistic magic, typically of Settle, lies in its details, how vividly she gives that history local habitations and names. More than that, though, we grow enrapt by Settle's richly human tapestry woven of wisdom, experience, and compassion around a woman whose heart seems to beat in constant sympathy with the hearts of others," wrote an essayist in *Contemporary Novelists. Booklist* reviewer Brad Hooper congratulated the author for her "experienced, nimble, and gracious configuring a hero who, at the same time, is a very real person." *Choices* was also lauded by a *Publishers Weekly* reviewer who stated: "Written with urgency, conviction and grace, this keenly observed story of one woman's passage through the storms of the 20th century is Settle's best book since the novels in the Beulah Quintet."

Settle's nonfictional *Turkish Reflections: A Biography of a Place* is based on her experience of Turkey during her three-year sojourn there in the 1970s and a return visit in 1989. Writing in the *New York Times Book Review,* Roderick Conway Morris described the result as "a diverting mix of travelogue, history, polemic and contemporary portrait." Travel narratives, suggested Joseph Coates in Chicago's *Tribune Books,* are often too far removed from personal experience for readers to enjoy. But *Turkish Reflections* he wrote, "is a luminous exception, a fully inhabited travel book." Dennis Drabelle, a reviewer for the *Washington Post Book World,* commented that Settle's "style has a well-turned simplicity that complements the spare materials of Turkish aesthetics."

Settle seems always to have been writing about places from afar: she wrote of West Virginia while in London and Turkey, of Britain while in America, and of Turkey while in West Virginia. "It's difficult to write a book in the place where it's set," she once told *CA.* "You have to have relief from the pitch of concentration involved in the writing. If when you get up from your desk you simply go out into the same scenes you're writing about, it's too much. I wrote *Prisons* in Turkey. I went there simply because I wanted somewhere warm and cheap to write. Then while I was there I gradually became aware of the outsiders living there, and the effect they had on the natives. That gave me the idea for *Blood Tie.* I didn't write the book in Turkey, of course, but after I came back to Charlottesville." Settle's travels were also the basis of her book *Spanish Recognitions: The Roads to the Present.*

In *Addie: A Memoir,* Settle relates her own family's story in a novel-like narrative that is dominated by two very different women: the author's mother, a genteel, determined woman, and her grandmother Addie, an emotional, fiery woman who told Settle about ghosts, took her to a tent revival to heal her eye problems, and in general made a world of myth and poetry accessible to Settle. Numerous other characters, as well as the author's younger self, enliven the pages. "Her mellifluous prose and her novelist's gift for setting scenes and delineating characters keeps this memoir flowing like a clear mountain spring," reported a *Publishers Weekly* reviewer. "There are places in Settle's capacious book for passion and politics, for social comedy, for the follies and pain of old hatreds, for lasting resentments and enduring gratitudes. Every portrait is three-dimensional," wrote a contributor to the *Seattle Post-Intelligencer,* who went on to say that *Addie* "will stand as a classic American memoir. This reader finished, wept, turned back, and read it plumb through all over again, for *Addie* is a book to love as well as to read, a book to pass from hand to hand, generation to generation, like a talisman."

Settle goes far back in English history for her next book, *I, Roger Williams: A Fragment of Autobiography.* This imaginative fictional biography of the life of Roger Williams, the founder of Rhode

Island, is told from Williams's point of view in his old age. The story takes in his humble beginnings, his tutelage under Sir Edward Coke, an influential jurist, and the many political developments that took place in England during the 1600s. Williams became a clergyman in England, but his dissenting views spelled trouble for him and his family, and he removed to New England in 1630. In Massachusetts, he found the Puritan church of the New World just as corrupt as he had believed England's to be, and he was eventually banished from the colony in the dead of winter. Rescued by native Americans, he eventually went down to the Naragansett Bay and founded the small settlement of Providence. "Settle brilliantly catches the combustible ironies of Williams's character, and they give light to this unusual novel," remarked Ron Charles in *Christian Science Monitor.* Roger Harris, reviewing the book in the Newark, New Jersey, *Star-Ledger,* advised: "Williams comes to complex life as a passionate, vibrant figure. . . . The writing is magnificent as Settle captures the passion of the religious and political battles in which Williams was involved."

In an interview with Wendy Smith of *Publishers Weekly,* Settle commented that Joseph Conrad's preface to *The Nigger of the Narcissus* contains a fitting summary of her own goals in writing: "My task is, by the power of the written word, to make you hear, to make you feel—it is, before all, to make you *see.* That—and no more, and it is everything." Settle has clearly aimed for this result in her fiction and nonfiction alike. Noted Anatole Broyard in a *New York Times* review, "She writes so well that one sometimes feels lost between illusion and reality, or literature and life."

BIOGRAPHICAL AND CRITICAL SOURCES:

BOOKS

Contemporary Authors Autobiography Series, Volume 1, Gale (Detroit, MI), 1984.

Contemporary Literary Criticism, Gale (Detroit, MI), Volume 19, 1981, Volume 61, 1990.

Contemporary Novelists, St. James Press (Detroit, MI), 2001.

Dictionary of Literary Biography, Volume 6: *American Novelists since World War II,* Gale (Detroit, MI), 1980.

Garrett, George, *Understanding Mary Lee Settle,* University of South Carolina Press (Columbia, SC), 1988.

Rosenberg, Brian, *Mary Lee Settle's Beulah Quintet: The Price of Freedom,* Louisiana State University Press (Baton Rouge, LA), 1991.

PERIODICALS

America, November 4, 1989, Patrick H. Samway, review of *Charley Bland,* p. 302; August 31, 1991, Patrick H. Samway, review of *Turkish Reflections: A Biography of a Place,* p. 123; October 7, 1995, Gary M. Ciuba, review of *Choices,* p. 31.

Antioch Review, winter, 1997, Suzann Bick, review of *Choices,* p. 109.

Atlantic, October, 1980, p. 101.

Booklist, April 15, 1995, Brad Hooper, review of *Choices,* p. 1481; April 1, 2001, Mary Ellen Quinn, review of *I, Roger Williams: A Fragment of Autobiography,* p. 1454.

Christian Science Monitor, May 24, 2001, Ron Charles, review of *I, Roger Williams,* p. 18.

Commonweal, March 31, 1967, p. 58.

Library Journal, June 15, 1989, Barbara Hoffert, review of *Charley Bland,* p. 82; May 15, 1991, Harold M. Otness, review of *Turkish Reflections,* p. 101; June 1, 1995, Ann H. Fisher, review of *Choices,* p. 166.

Los Angeles Times, November 14, 1986; October 27, 1989.

Los Angeles Times Book Review, November 5, 1980, p. 1; July 11, 1982, p. 1; July 12, 1987, p. 14; June 23, 1991, p. 6.

Mississippi Quarterly, fall, 1985, pp. 391-413.

Nation, November 8, 1980, pp. 469-471; August 21-28, 1982, pp. 150-152; July 10, 1995, John Leonard, review of *Choices,* p. 67.

National Geographic Traveler, March-April, 1992, Anthony Weller, review of *Turkish Reflections,* p. 142.

New Republic, December 27, 1980, pp. 37-39; June 16, 1982, pp. 30-32.

Newsweek, November 10, 1986, p. 84.

New Yorker, September 16, 1991, review of *Turkish Reflections,* p. 96.

New York Times, August 18, 1977, p. 52; October 22, 1980; October 9, 1986.

New York Times Book Review, October 26, 1980, p. 1; July 11, 1982, p. 1; October 26, 1986, p. 14; October 22, 1989, p. 12; July 14, 1991, p. 1; June 25, 1995, Thomas Mallon, review of *Choices,* p. 23; October 25, 1998, Angeline Goreau, review of *Addie,* p. 27; April 22, 2001, Caleb Crain, review of *I, Roger Williams,* p. 16.

Publishers Weekly, October 10, 1986, Wendy Smith, interview with Settle, p. 73; June 23, 1989, Sybil Steinberg, review of *Charley Bland,* p. 50; April 10, 1995, review of *Choices,* p. 55; September 7, 1998, review of *Addie,* p. 74.

Seattle Post-Intelligencer, December 12, 1998, review of *Addie,* p. C2.

South Atlantic Quarterly, summer, 1987, pp. 229-243.

Southern Review, October, 1984, pp. 842-850; winter, 1988, pp. 13-26; spring, 1989, Brian Rosenberg, interview with Settle, p. 351.

Star-Ledger (Newark, NJ), April 8, 2001, Roger Harris, review of *I, Roger Williams,* p. 4.

Times (London, England), February 17, 1983.

Times Literary Supplement, April 20, 1967, p. 339; April 10, 1992, p. 28.

Tribune Books (Chicago, IL), November 23, 1980, p. 7; August 1, 1982, p. 3; November 23, 1986, p. 5; November 26, 1989, p. 6; June 30, 1991, p. 6; June 18, 1995, p. 6.

Virginian Pilot, December 6, 1998, "With Typical Ferocity, Mary Lee Settle Examines Her West Virginia Origins," p. J3.

Virginia Quarterly Review, summer, 1989, pp. 401-417.

Washington Post, January 15, 1987.

Washington Post Book World, September 28, 1980, p. 1; June 13, 1982, p. 3; November 9, 1986, p. 7; October 15, 1989, p. 4; May 26, 1991, p. 4.*

* * *

SHORT, Roger, Jr.
See EYEN, Tom

* * *

SIMMONS, Dan 1948-

PERSONAL: Born April 4, 1948, in Peoria, IL; son of Robert Simmons (a business manager); married; wife's name Karen; children: Jane Kathryn. *Education:* Wabash College, B.A. (English), 1970; Washington University, M.A. (education), 1971.

ADDRESSES: Home—Colorado. *Agent*—c/o William Morrow, 10 East 53rd St., 7th Floor, New York, NY 10022.

Dan Simmons

CAREER: Freelance writer, 1987—. Worked as an elementary school teacher in Missouri, New York, and Colorado, c. 1971-87. Occasionally teaches writing at universities.

AWARDS, HONORS: Fulbright scholarship, 1977; Rod Serling Memorial Award, *Twilight Zone* magazine, 1982, for short story "The River Styx Runs Upstream"; World Fantasy Award for Best First Novel, 1985, for *Song of Kali;* Hugo Award, 1989, for *Hyperion; Locus* Award for Best Science Fiction Novel, 1989, for *Hyperion,* 1990, for *The Fall of Hyperion; Locus* Award for Best Horror/Dark Fantasy Novel, 1991, for *Summer of Night;* Nebula Award nomination, 1990, for *The Fall of Hyperion;* Bram Stoker Awards, Horror Writers Association, for Best Horror Novel, 1990, for *Carrion Comfort,* for Best Horror Collection, 1991, for *Prayers to Broken Stones: A Collection,* and for Best Novelette, 1994, for *Dying in Bangkok;* British Science Fiction

Association award, 1990; August Derleth Award, British Fantasy Society, 1990; honorary Ph.D., Wabash College, 1995; Best Bet citation, *San Francisco Chronicle,* 1997, for *Rise of Endymion;* Colorado Book Award for Best Novel, 2000, for *Darwin's Blade;* award for teaching from Colorado Education Association.

WRITINGS:

Song of Kali (horror novel), Tor Books (New York, NY), 1985.

Phases of Gravity (novel), Bantam (New York, NY), 1989.

Hyperion (science-fiction novel; also see below), Doubleday (New York, NY), 1989.

Carrion Comfort (horror novel), Warner Books (New York, NY), 1989.

The Fall of Hyperion (science-fiction novel; also see below), Doubleday (New York, NY), 1990.

Banished Dreams (short stories), Roadkill Press (Arvada, CO), 1990.

Prayers to Broken Stones: A Collection (short stories; includes "Vanni Fucci Is Alive and Well and Living in Hell" and "The Death of the Centaur"), Dark Harvest (Arlington Heights, IL), 1990.

Entropy's Bed at Midnight (short-story chapbook), Lord John Press (Northridge, CA), 1990.

Hyperion Cantos (science fiction; contains *Hyperion* and *The Fall of Hyperion*), Guild America (New York, NY), 1990.

Summer of Night (horror novel), Putnam (New York, NY), 1991.

Children of the Night (horror novel), Putnam (New York, NY), 1992.

The Hollow Man (novel), Bantam (New York, NY), 1992.

Going after the Rubber Chicken, Lord John Press (Northridge, CA), 1991.

Summer Sketches, Lord John Press (Northridge, CA), 1992.

Lovedeath: Five Tales of Love and Death, Warner (New York, NY), 1993.

Pele's Fire (novel), Putnam (New York, NY), 1994.

Fires of Eden (horror novel), Putnam (New York, NY), 1994.

Endymion (science-fiction novel; sequel to *The Fall of Hyperion*), Bantam (New York, NY), 1996.

The Rise of Endymion (science-fiction novel; sequel to *Endymion*), Bantam (New York, NY), 1997.

The Crook Factory (novel), Avon (New York, NY), 1999.

Darwin's Blade (novel), Morrow (New York, NY), 2000.

Phases of Gravity (novel), Olmstead Press (Chicago, IL), 2001.

Hardcase (crime novel; "Joe Kurtz" series), St. Martin's Minotaur (New York, NY), 2001.

Worlds Enough and Time: Five Tales of Speculative Fiction (novellas; contains "Looking for Kelly Dahl," "On K2 with Kanakaredes," "The Ninth of Av," "Orphans of the Helix," and "The End of Gravity"), Eos (New York, NY), 2002.

Hard Freeze (crime novel; "Joe Kurtz" series), St. Martin's Minotaur (New York, NY), 2002.

A Winter Haunting (horror novel; sequel to *Summer of Night*), Morrow (New York, NY), 2002.

Hard As Nails, St. Martin's Minotaur (New York, NY), 2003.

Ilium (science-fiction novel), Eos (New York, NY), 2003.

Also author of unproduced screenplay *The End of Gravity,* a screenplay adaptation of his *Children of the Night,* and two teleplays broadcast on the series *Monsters.* Work represented in anthologies, including *Night Visions V,* edited by Stephen King, Dark Harvest, 1988; *The Further Adventures of the Joker,* 1990; *Prayers to Broken Stones,* 1990; *Obsessions,* 1991; *The Ultimate Dracula,* 1991; *Masques IV,* 1991; *Still Dead,* 1992; *Freak Show,* 1992; *Omni Best Science Fiction #2,* 1992; and *Destination: 3001,* 2000. Contributor to periodicals, including *Galaxy, Omni, Isaac Asimov's SF Magazine, Playboy, New York Review of Science Fiction, Gauntlet,* and *Twilight Zone.*

ADAPTATIONS: Several of Simmons's books have been optioned for film.

WORK IN PROGRESS: Olympos, a sequel to *Ilium,* for Eos, expected 2004.

SIDELIGHTS: Dan Simmons is an award-winning author who has written stories in a wide variety of genres, from fantasy and science fiction to horror and suspense to crime stories and mainstream novels. His works have been especially noted by critics for their accurate research and intellectual sophistication. In *Booklist* Elliott Swanson described Simmons as "one of the most gifted writers in the psychological horror field," adding that the author's themes "touch on the private fears that can erode the lives of individuals, as well as the public engines of fear that numb the humanity of entire cultures." Although Simmons started his career as an elementary school teacher, an occupation in which he remained for eighteen years while writing in his spare time, he proved his talent from the outset, winning the World Fantasy Award in 1986 for his first novel, *Song of Kali.*

"Ever since Harlan Ellison raved about 'The River Styx Runs Upstream' at a 1981 writers' workshop, everyone has agreed that Dan Simmons is a writer of remarkable talents," declared Gary Westfahl in the *St. James Guide to Horror, Ghost, and Gothic Writers.* "Yet this in itself does not ensure success as a horror writer. At least at times, horror fiction must be visceral and explicit, not allusive and subtle, and a writer primarily focused on displaying his own literary sophistication may enervate his story and alienate his readers. This is a problem that Simmons faced and, fortunately, eventually conquered."

For his first forays into fiction Simmons explored the horror genre. *Song of Kali* relates the gruesome action that ensues when the daughter of an American journalist is kidnaped in Calcutta, India, by deranged, bloodthirsty worshipers of the Hindu goddess Kali. Faren Miller, writing in *Locus,* described *Song of Kali* as "harrowing and ghoulish," adding that it "makes the stuff of nightmare very real indeed." In *Carrion Comfort* a Holocaust survivor attempts to track down a group of deadly "mind vampires" who control people through telepathy, and *Summer of Night* tells of a group of Midwestern children who pursue an evil force at work in their small town. Westfahl criticized Simmons's early novels for an "irritating tendency to show off his knowledge," resulting in works that "would have been equally powerful at half the length." The critic's complaints notwithstanding, it is these novels—and the early segments of the "Hyperion" saga—that have won Simmons many of his literary awards.

Simmons's next works to receive substantial critical attention, *Hyperion* and its sequels *The Fall of Hyperion, Endymion,* and *The Rise of Endymion,* together constitute a lengthy chronicle of the Hegemony, a galactic civilization of humans who have promised their souls to the machine-based Technocore in exchange for advanced cosmological knowledge. Redemption for the Hegemony seems likely only on the planet Hyperion, an organic world—similar to Earth—with ties to the inscrutable, fearful Shrike. Appropriating the structure of Geoffrey Chaucer's medieval classic, *The Canterbury Tales,* Simmons's first two novels in the series concern seven Hegemony pilgrims who journey to Hyperion hoping to realize salvation by confronting the Shrike. As in Chaucer's work, the pilgrims of *Hyperion* and *The Fall of Hyperion* pass time by relating stories. The Hegemony, meanwhile, are at war with the Ousters, a band of space wanderers. The pilgrims are thus compelled to accelerate their trek to the Time Tombs, mysterious lands dominated by the Shrike. Gerald Jones, in his assessment for the *New York Times Book Review,* noted that *Hyperion* and *The Fall of Hyperion* are "generously conceived and stylistically sure-handed books." The reviewer added that each of the pilgrims' stories "would make a superb novella on its own."

The story is carried forward in *Endymion* and *The Rise of Endymion,* books in which Technocore has allied itself with a resurgent Catholic Church that can literally resurrect people from the dead. This powerful alliance is threatened by the heroine Aenea, and her protector, Endymion, who seek spiritual bonds through empathy and shared consciousness. A *Kirkus Reviews* critic noted that in *The Rise of Endymion* "Simmons's scope is truly staggering, his inventiveness continues to impress, and the narrative offers something for everyone."

Westfahl found Simmons's novels of the later 1990s "leaner, less pretentious, and more impressive." Notable among the author's more recent works are *Children of the Night,* a tale of Romanian vampires and their offspring, and *Fires of Eden,* a multi-layered horror tale about the destruction of earth's resources. A *Kirkus Reviews* writer called *Fires of Eden* "the flip side of a Don Ho single, short on poi and ukuleles but long on elemental carnage, vengeful immortals, and nimble plotting." Westfahl concluded that in *Fires of Eden,* "Simmons displays a healthy sense of humor regarding his own work that augurs well for his future fiction."

The less pretentious nature of Simmons's more recent books is also evident in 2002's *A Winter Haunting,* a sequel to *Summer of Night* that picks up the story of Dale forty years after the tragic death of his friend Duane in the first book. Dale is now a professor whose marriage has failed, so he goes back to his friend's now-empty home to write a book and clear his head. However, Duane's spirit, still in the house, joins with other eerie happenings to conspire against Dale in a story that audiences from teen to adult can appreciate. For example, Carole DeAngelo, writing in *School Library Journal,* pointed out that *Winter Haunting* is appropriate reading for teens who will find it "good spooky fun." A *Publishers Weekly* contributor further commented that "Simmons orchestrates his story's weird events craftily, introducing them as unremarkable details that only gradually show their dark side."

Simmons returns to science fiction for another series, which begins in the 2003 novel *Ilium.* Inspired by Homer's *Iliad,* the book was characterized by a *Publishers Weekly* critic as an "elegant monster of a novel." Here Simmons draws readers into a future Earth where the population lives unchallenging lives. In a parallel story, Simmons recounts the ongoing Trojan War, and brings to life the Homeric exploits of Achilles and the Gods. Layering the action, Simmons also introduces classics professor Thomas Hockenberry, who is restored to life by the Gods and sent back into the past to follow and report on the progress at Troy; meanwhile, from the moons of Jupiter come the Moravecs, who have detected problems in the solar system and travel to the planet Mars to check things out. These diverse threads weave together into a novel that the *Publishers Weekly* contributor described as "chock full of literary references, grand scenery, and fascinating characters," in sort, "Simmons at his best." While admitting that the novel is "as unwieldy and pretentious as it sounds," a *Kirkus* reviewer commended the author, noting that Simmons "never lets the story get away from him, using copious amounts of wit to keep the action grounded—and utterly addictive."

Simmons has also explored the crime thriller and mystery genres, although the author's unwillingness to be pegged down to a specific genre makes his books somewhat difficult to categorize. *The Crook Factory,* for example, is part spy story, part mystery, and part historical novel. It is based on the true story of Ernest Hemingway's efforts after World War II to organize a league of spies in Cuba. The main character in the story, Joe Lucas, is based on a real FBI agent who is sent to keep tabs on the famous author's activities. Lucas soon finds himself in a kind of coterie of spies, actors, and authors—among them Ingrid Bergman and Marlene Dietrich—who surround Hemingway at dinner parties and are impressed by his incisive mind. However, Lucas knows that despite the novelist's earnestness, Hemingway is still a rank amateur at the spy game. "This fabulously compelling and humorous rendering of little-known war operations and secret agent skulduggery in the Caribbean in the summer of 1942 will surely charm readers who love history, suspense, and intrigue," asserted *Booklist* contributor Vanessa Bush. The story, however, is fascinating not only for its spy intrigue but for Simmons's characterization of Hemingway. As Michael Rogers noted in *Library Journal,* "Simmons offers one of the best fictional portraits of Hemingway available."

Simmons does not categorize *The Crook Factory* as a spy thriller, he told Dorman T. Shindler in a *Publishers Weekly* interview, because it does not fit the accepted formula. "That subgenre has demands, protocols and formulae of its own," he said, adding that "*The Crook Factory* might be called a 'biographical literary mystery' in the sense that at the heart of it is the question 'Just who the hell was Ernest Hemingway?' but its pace and pulse are all wrong for a thriller." The same is true, said the author, for his novel *Darwin's Blade,* the story of physicist Dr. Darwin Minor, who investigates automobile crashes for an insurance company. Many of these crashes are bizarre, and Darwin has made a reputation for himself as someone who can uncover cases of fraud and just plain stupidity, saving his company millions of dollars. Things become more dicey when he finds himself targeted by what one *Publishers Weekly* reviewer described as "a Russian mafia-type group that specializes in staging accidents to perpetrate insurance fraud."

Part of the fun in *Darwin's Blade* are the series of strange accidents, which Simmons based on actual cases his brother, Wayne Simmons, an insurance investigator, told him about. For example, a man once attached rockets to his car to make it go faster and consequently slammed into a cliff. "The accidents in *Darwin's Blade* weren't always exact re-creations of real accidents," Simmons admitted to Shindler, "but were often amalgams. . . . Usually, however, I had to tone down rather than exaggerate the details." The novel was positively received by critics. David Pitt, writing in *Booklist,* found it to be a "welcome relief from thrillers that offer nothing more than action scenes strung together." And *Library Journal* reviewer David Keymer called *Darwin's Blade* "a hair-raising adventure to satisfy the most discriminating reader."

With the creation of character Joe Kurtz, who appears in the crime novels *Hardcase, Hard Freeze,* and *Hard As Nails,* Simmons challenges readers further by creating a highly disagreeable protagonist as his hero. When the audience is introduced to former private investigator Kurtz, he is being released from an eleven-year sentence at Attica for throwing a man out a window to his death. Violating the terms of his parole, Kurtz accepts a job from a mafia don to look for a missing accountant. He consequently becomes enmeshed in the plottings of various mobsters, drug lords, crooked cops, and assassins. *Hardcase* met with mixed reviews. A *Publishers Weekly* critic called it "all sinew and bloody gristle, stripped of the deep reflection and lively character development that usually give . . . [Simmons's] books a plusher texture." On the other hand, David Keymer praised the book in *Library Journal,* writing that "there's no letdown from explosive start to hell-for-leather finish in this hard-as-nails detective story."

In *Hard Freeze* Kurtz learns that the man who killed his partner is still alive; at the same time, he is working on a case to find a serial killer who stalks children. Reviewers of *Hard Freeze* especially appreciated the moody atmosphere the author creates in the city of Buffalo, and the story's action is touched with "glints of dark humor that sparkle nicely," according to Bob Lunn in *Library Journal.* Simmons, attested *Booklist* critic Frank Sennett, "writes action scenes that'll leave your hands clammy on the page" and has created "the least likable protagonist you'll ever find yourself rooting for." Kurtz finds himself confronted by a hill of corpses in *Hard As Nails,* while he also tries to avoid a gunman out to get him. Romantic interests also enter the mix in a novel that *Booklist* contributor David Wright dubbed a "nice, dark, all-purpose thriller."

Simmons is also the author of several story collections, including *Prayers to Broken Stones* and *Lovedeath: Five Tales of Love and Death.* Critics identified the more notable stories in *Prayers to Broken Stones* as "Vanni Fucci Is Alive and Well and Living in Hell," a depiction of religious hypocrites, and "The Death of the Centaur," an offbeat portrait of children and a flawed educational system. *Locus* contributor Edward Bryant was impressed with the wide range of stories in *Prayers to Broken Stones* and noted that the book demonstrates "a marvelous range of intellectual concerns, passionate commitments, keenly honed artistic blades—and stretching exercises. . . . This book is an architectural plan for the construction of a major literary career." Similar praise met the publication of *Lovedeath.* "Simmons has never been more stylish than here, with the short novel form compressing his effects and squeezing a lurid glow from each page," wrote a *Kirkus Reviews* contributor.

Continuing to write in whatever genre—or mix of genres—he chooses, Simmons continues to defy publishers' efforts to fit his work neatly into one category. While the author understands the business reasons behind such practices, it has forced him to switch publishers several times to get his books printed. Nevertheless, Simmons would rather do this than be forced to confine himself to writing only one type of book. "What I'm drawn to," he explained to Shindler, "are the most interesting tropes and protocols available to the writer. Damn the genre boundaries and let the formula hacks take the hindmost. . . . All sufficiently ambitious writers are cuckoos in the sense that they'll lay their eggs in whatever nest offers the best chance for artistic survival. The absolute best writers transcend even the need for nests."

BIOGRAPHICAL AND CRITICAL SOURCES:

BOOKS

Contemporary Literary Criticism, Volume 44, Gale (Detroit, MI), 1987, pp. 273-275.

St. James Guide to Horror, Ghost, and Gothic Writers, St. James Press (Detroit, MI), 1998, pp. 535-537.

PERIODICALS

Analog Science Fiction/Science Fact, December 15, 1989, pp. 179-180.

Booklist, October 15, 1993; August 19, 1997, p. 1887; December 1, 1998, Vanessa Bush, review of *The Crook Factory,* p. 620; September 1, 2000, David Pitt, review of *Darwin's Blade,* p. 8; January 1, 2002, Regina Schroeder, review of *A Winter Haunting,* p. 825; May 1, 2002, Regina Schroeder, review of *Worlds Enough and Time,* p. 1514; August, 2002, Frank Sennett, review of *Hard Freeze,* p. 1933; April 15, 2003, Roland Green, review of *Ilium,* p. 1428; September 1, 2003, David Wright, review of *Hard As Nails,* p. 71.

Fantasy Review, October, 1986, review of *Song of Kali,* pp. 13-14.
Kirkus Reviews, May 1, 1992; July 15, 1992; September 1, 1993; August 15, 1994; June 15, 1997; May 1, 2003, review of *Ilium,* p. 650; September 1, 2003, review of *Hard As Nails,* p. 1104.
Library Journal, October 15, 1994, p. 88; September 15, 1997, p. 106; January, 1999, Michael Rogers, review of *The Crook Factory,* p. 158; October 15, 2000, David Keymer, review of *Darwin's Blade,* p. 104; June 15, 2001, David Keymer, review of *Hard Case,* p. 105; August, 2002, Bob Lunn, review of *Hard Freeze,* p. 151; May 15, 2003, Jackie Cassada, review of *Ilium,* p. 131.
Locus, February, 1986, Faren Miller, review of *Song of Kali,* p. 13; October, 1990, Edward Bryant, review of *Prayers to Broken Stones,* pp. 23-24.
Mile High Futures, December, 1985, pp. 19-20.
New York Times Book Review, March 25, 1990, p. 30; January 28, 1996, p. 26.
Publishers Weekly, December 14, 1990; September 13, 1993, p. 90; August 29, 1994, p. 60; June 16, 1997, p. 50; January 11, 1999, review of *The Crook Factory,* p. 57; October 23, 2000, review of *Darwin's Blade,* p. 59; November 6, 2000, Dorman T. Shindler, "Between Two Worlds," p. 65; June 4, 2001, review of *Hard Case,* p. 61; January 14, 2002, review of *A Winter Haunting,* p. 45; April 29, 2002, review of *Worlds Enough and Time,* p. 47; July 29, 2002, review of *Hard Freeze,* p. 57; May 26, 2003, Michael Levy, "*The Iliad* As Science Fiction" (interview), and review of *Ilium,* p. 53; September 15, 2003, review of *Hard As Nails,* p. 48.
School Library Journal, June, 2002, Carol DeAngelo, review of *A Winter Haunting,* p. 173.

ONLINE

Dan Simmons Home Page, http://www.dansimmons.com/ (January 15, 2004).*

* * *

SIMON, (Marvin) Neil 1927-

Neil Simon

PERSONAL: Born July 4, 1927, in Bronx, NY; son of Irving (a garment salesman) and Mamie Simon; married Joan Baim (a dancer), September 30, 1953 (died, 1973); married Marsha Mason (an actress), 1973 (divorced, 1982); married Diana Lander, 1987 (divorced, 1989; remarried, 1990; divorced, 1998); married Elaine Joyce, 1999; children: (first marriage) Ellen, Nancy; (third marriage) Bryn (adopted daughter). *Education:* Attended New York University, 1946, and University of Denver.

ADDRESSES: *Office*—c/o Gary N. Da Silva, 111 North Sepulveda Blvd., Suite 250, Manhattan Beach, CA 90266-6850.

CAREER: Playwright. Warner Brothers, Inc., New York, NY, mail room clerk, 1946; Columbia Broadcasting System, Inc. (CBS), New York, NY, comedy writer for Goodman Ace, late 1940s; comedy writer for Robert W. Lewis *The Little Show,* radio, late 1940s; comedy writer for *The Phil Silvers Arrow Show,* National Broadcasting Co., Inc. (NBC-TV), 1948, *The Tallulah Bankhead Show,* NBC-TV, 1951, Sid Caesar's *Your Show of Shows,* NBC-TV, 1956-57, *The Phil Silvers Show,* CBS-TV, 1958-59, *The Garry Moore Show,* CBS-TV, 1959-60, and *The Jackie Gleason Show* and *The Red Buttons Show,* both CBS-TV, and for television specials. Producer of motion pictures, including *Only When I Laugh,* Columbia, 1981, *I*

Ought to Be in Pictures, Twentieth Century-Fox, 1982, and *Max Dugan Returns,* Twentieth Century-Fox, 1983. Appearances on television programs, including *52nd Annual Academy Awards,* presenter, 1980; *Caesar's Writers,* as himself, Public Broadcasting Service, 1996; *Pitch,* as himself, Hollywood or Bust Productions, 1997; *Sid Caesar Collection,* as himself, Creative Light Entertainment, 2000-01. *Military service:* U.S. Army Air Force Reserve; sports editor of *Rev-Meter,* the base newspaper at Lowry Field, CO, 1946.

MEMBER: Dramatists Guild, Writers Guild of America.

AWARDS, HONORS: Academy of Television Arts and Sciences Award (Emmy), 1957, for Sid Caesar's *Your Show of Shows,* and 1959, for *The Phil Silvers Show;* Antoinette Perry Award (Tony) nomination, 1963, for *Little Me,* 1964, for best play for *The Odd Couple,* 1965, for *Barefoot in the Park,* 1966, for *Sweet Charity,* 1968, for *Plaza Suite,* 1969, for *Promises, Promises,* 1970, for *Last of the Red Hot Lovers,* 1972, for *The Prisoner of Second Avenue,* 1973, for *The Sunshine Boys,* 1978, for book of a musical for *They're Playing Our Song,* 1979, for *Chapter Two,* and 1987, for *Broadway Bound;* Tony Award for best playwright, 1965, for *The Odd Couple,* for best drama, 1985, for *Biloxi Blues,* and best play, 1991, for *Lost in Yonkers;* special Tony Award for overall contributions to the theater, 1975; Writers Guild Award nomination, 1967, for *Barefoot in the Park; Evening Standard* Drama Award, 1967, for *Sweet Charity;* Sam S. Shubert Foundation Award, 1968; Academy of Motion Picture Arts and Sciences Award (Oscar) nomination, 1968, for *The Odd Couple,* and 1978, for *California Suite;* Writers Guild Award, 1969, for *The Odd Couple,* 1970, for *Last of the Red Hot Lovers,* 1971, for *The Out-of-Towners,* and 1972, for *The Trouble with People;* named Entertainer of the Year, *Cue* magazine, 1972; Oscar nomination and Golden Globe Award nomination, 1975, for *The Sunshine Boys,* and 1977, for *The Goodbye Girl;* Writers Guild Award, 1975; Hollywood Foreign Press Association award, 1978, for *The Goodbye Girl;* Laurel Award, Writers Guild of America, 1979; L.H.D., Hofstra University, 1981; New York Drama Critics Circle Award, 1983, for *Brighton Beach Memoirs;* elected to the Theater Hall of Fame, Uris Theater, 1983; Lifetime Creative Achievement Award, American Comedy Awards, George Schlatter Productions, 1989; a Neil Simon tribute show was held at the Shubert Theatre, March 1, 1987; Pulitzer Prize for Drama, and Drama Desk Award, both 1991, both for *Lost in Yonkers;* the Neil Simon Endowment for the Dramatic Arts has been established at Duke University; Apple Award, Nederlander Company and Wayne State University, 2001.

WRITINGS:

PLAYS

(With William Friedberg) *Adventures of Marco Polo: A Musical Fantasy* (music by Clay Warnick and Mel Pahl), Samuel French (New York, NY), 1959.

(Adaptor with William Friedberg) *Heidi* (based on the novel by Johanna Spyri; music by Warnick), Samuel French (New York, NY), 1959.

(With brother, Danny Simon) *Come Blow Your Horn* (also see below; first produced in New Hope, PA, at the Bucks County Playhouse, August, 1960; produced on Broadway at the Brooks Atkinson Theatre, February 22, 1961; produced on London's West End at the Prince of Wales Theatre, February 17, 1962), Samuel French (New York, NY), 1961.

Barefoot in the Park (also see below; first produced, under title *Nobody Loves Me,* in New Hope, PA, at the Bucks County Playhouse, 1962; produced on Broadway at the Biltmore Theatre, October 23, 1963; produced on the West End, 1965), Random House (New York), 1964.

The Odd Couple (also see below; first produced on Broadway at the Plymouth Theatre, March 10, 1965; produced on the West End at the Queen's Theatre, October 12, 1966; revised version first produced in Los Angeles at the Ahmanson Theatre, April 6, 1985; produced on Broadway at the Broadhurst Theatre, June, 1985), Random House (New York, NY), 1966.

Sweet Charity (also see below; musical; based on the screenplay *The Nights of Cabiria* by Federico Fellini; music and lyrics by Cy Coleman and Dorothy Fields; first produced on Broadway at the Palace Theatre, January 29, 1966; produced on the West End at the Prince of Wales Theatre, October 11, 1967), Random House (New York, NY), 1966.

The Star-Spangled Girl (also see below; first produced on Broadway at the Plymouth Theatre, December 21, 1966), Random House (New York, NY), 1967.

Plaza Suite (also see below; three one-acts entitled *Visitor from Hollywood, Visitor from Mamaroneck,* and *Visitor from Forest Hills;* first produced on

Broadway at the Plymouth Theatre, February 14, 1968; produced on the West End at the Lyric Theatre, February 18, 1969), Random House (New York, NY), 1969.

Promises, Promises (also see below; musical; based on the screenplay *The Apartment* by Billy Wilder and I. A. L. Diamond; music by Burt Bacharach; lyrics by Hal David; first produced on Broadway at the Shubert Theatre, December 1, 1968; produced on the West End at the Prince of Wales Theatre, October 2, 1969), Random House (New York, NY), 1969.

Last of the Red Hot Lovers (also see below; three acts; first produced in New Haven, CT, at the Shubert Theatre, November 26, 1969; produced on Broadway at the Eugene O'Neill Theatre, December 28, 1969; produced in London, 1979), Random House (New York, NY), 1970.

The Gingerbread Lady (also see below; first produced in New Haven, CT, at the Shubert Theatre, November 4, 1970; produced on Broadway at the Plymouth Theatre, December 13, 1970; produced in London, 1974), Random House (New York, NY), 1971.

The Prisoner of Second Avenue (also see below; first produced in New Haven, CT, at the Shubert Theatre, October 12, 1971; produced on Broadway at the Eugene O'Neill Theatre, November 11, 1971; reprised on London's West End, 1999), Random House (New York, NY), 1972.

The Sunshine Boys (also see below; first produced in New Haven, CT, at the Shubert Theatre, November 21, 1972; produced on Broadway at the Broadhurst Theatre, December 20, 1972; produced in London, 1975), Random House (New York, NY), 1973.

The Good Doctor (also see below; musical; adapted from stories by Anton Chekhov; music by Peter Link; lyrics by Simon; first produced on Broadway at the Eugene O'Neill Theatre, November 27, 1973), Random House (New York, NY), 1974.

God's Favorite (also see below; first produced on Broadway at the Eugene O'Neill Theatre, December 11, 1974), Random House (New York, NY), 1975.

California Suite (also see below; first produced in Los Angeles, CA, April, 1976; produced on Broadway at the Eugene O'Neill Theatre, June 30, 1976; produced in London, 1976), Random House (New York, NY), 1977.

Chapter Two (also see below; first produced in Los Angeles, CA, 1977; produced on Broadway at the Imperial Theatre, December 4, 1977; produced in London, 1981), Random House (New York, NY), 1979.

They're Playing Our Song (also see below; musical; music by Marvin Hamlisch; lyrics by Carol Bayer Sager; first produced in Los Angeles, CA, 1978; produced on Broadway at the Imperial Theatre, February 11, 1979; produced in London, 1980), Random House (New York, NY), 1980.

I Ought to Be in Pictures (also see below; first produced in Los Angeles, CA, 1980; produced on Broadway at the Eugene O'Neill Theatre, April 3, 1980; produced in London at the Offstage Downstairs, December, 1986), Random House (New York, NY), 1981.

Fools (also see below; first produced on Broadway at the Eugene O'Neill Theatre, April, 1981), Random House (New York, NY), 1982.

Brighton Beach Memoirs (also see below; first produced in Los Angeles, CA, at the Ahmanson Theatre, December, 1982; produced on Broadway at the Alvin Theatre, March 27, 1983), Random House (New York, NY), 1984.

Biloxi Blues (also see below; first produced in Los Angeles, CA, at the Ahmanson Theatre, December, 1984; produced on Broadway at the Neil Simon Theatre, March, 1985), Random House (New York, NY), 1986.

Broadway Bound (also see below; first produced at Duke University, October, 1986; produced on Broadway at the Broadhurst Theatre, December, 1986), Random House (New York, NY), 1987.

Rumors (first produced in San Diego, CA, at the Old Globe Theater in 1988; produced on Broadway at the Broadhurst Theatre, November 17, 1988), Random House (New York, NY), 1990.

Lost in Yonkers (first produced on Broadway at the Richard Rodgers Theatre, 1991), Plume (New York, NY), 1991.

Jake's Women (produced on Broadway at the Neil Simon Theatre, March 24, 1992), Samuel French (New York, NY), 1993, Random House (New York, NY), 1994.

Laughter on the 23rd Floor (produced on Broadway at the Richard Rodgers Theatre, November 22, 1993; produced on the West End, 1996), Random House (New York, NY), 1995.

London Suite (produced Off-Broadway at the Union Square Theatre, April 9, 1995), Samuel French (New York, NY), 1996.

OMNIBUS COLLECTIONS

The Comedy of Neil Simon (contains *Come Blow Your Horn, Barefoot in the Park, The Odd Couple, The*

Star-Spangled Girl, Promises, Promises, Plaza Suite, and *Last of the Red Hot Lovers*), Random House (New York, NY), 1971, published as *The Collected Plays of Neil Simon,* Volume 1, New American Library (New York, NY), 1986.

The Collected Plays of Neil Simon, Volume 2 (contains *The Sunshine Boys, Little Me* [also see below], *The Gingerbread Lady, The Prisoner of Second Avenue, The Good Doctor, God's Favorite, California Suite,* and *Chapter Two*), Random House (New York, NY), 1979.

The Collected Plays of Neil Simon, Volume 3 (contains *Sweet Charity, They're Playing Our Song, I Ought to Be in Pictures, Fools, The Odd Couple—Female Version, Brighton Beach Memoirs, Biloxi Blues,* and *Broadway Bound*), Random House (New York, NY), 1992.

UNPUBLISHED PLAYS

(Contributor of sketches) *Tamiment Revue,* first produced in Tamiment, PA, 1952-53.

(Contributor of sketches, with Danny Simon) *Catch a Star!* (musical revue), first produced on Broadway at the Plymouth Theatre, November 6, 1955.

(Contributor of sketches, with Danny Simon) *New Faces of 1956,* first produced on Broadway at the Ethel Barrymore Theatre, June 14, 1956.

(Adaptor) *Little Me* (musical; based on the novel by Patrick Dennis), music by Coleman, first produced on Broadway at the Lunt-Fontanne Theatre, November 17, 1962, produced on the West End at the Cambridge Theatre, November 18, 1964, revised version produced in New York, 1981.

(Contributor of sketch) *Broadway Revue* (satirical musical revue), first produced in New York City at the Karmit Bloomgarden Theatre, November, 1968.

(Editor of book for musical) *Seesaw* (based on *Two for the Seesaw* by William Gibson), first produced on Broadway, March 18, 1973.

The Goodbye Girl (musical; based on Simon's screenplay), lyrics by David Zippel, music by Marvin Hamlisch, first produced on Broadway at the Marquis Theatre, March 4, 1993.

Forty-five Seconds from Broadway, produced on Broadway at the Richard Rogers Theatre, November 11, 2001.

The Dinner Party, produced at the Music Box Theatre, New York, NY, October 23, 2000.

Oscar and Felix: A New Look at the Odd Couple, produced in New York, NY, 2002.

Rose and Walsh, produced in Los Angeles, CA, at the Geffen Playhouse, January 28-February 9, 2003.

SCREENPLAYS

Come Blow Your Horn (based on Simon's play of the same title), Paramount, 1963.

(With Cesare Zavattini) *After the Fox* (also known as *Caccia alla volpe*), United Artists, 1966.

Barefoot in the Park (based on Simon's play of the same title), Paramount, 1967.

The Odd Couple (based on Simon's play of the same title), Paramount, 1968.

The Out-of-Towners, Paramount, 1970.

Plaza Suite (based on Simon's play of the same title), Paramount, 1971.

(With Arnold Margolin and Jim Parker) *Star Spangled Girl,* Paramount, 1971.

Last of the Red Hot Lovers (based on Simon's play of the same title), Paramount, 1972.

The Heartbreak Kid (based on short story by Bruce Jay Friedman), Twentieth Century-Fox, 1972.

The Prisoner of Second Avenue (based on Simon's play of the same title), Warner Bros., 1975.

The Sunshine Boys (based on Simon's play of the same title), Metro-Goldwyn-Mayer, 1975.

Murder by Death, Columbia, 1976.

The Goodbye Girl, Warner Bros., 1977.

The Cheap Detective, Columbia, 1978.

California Suite (based on Simon's play of the same title), Columbia, 1978.

Chapter Two (based on Simon's play of the same title), Columbia, 1979.

Seems Like Old Times, Columbia, 1980.

Only When I Laugh (based on Simon's play *The Gingerbread Lady*), Columbia, 1981.

I Ought to Be in Pictures (based on Simon's play of the same title), Twentieth Century-Fox, 1982.

Max Dugan Returns, Twentieth Century-Fox, 1983.

(With Edward Weinberger and Stan Daniels) *The Lonely Guy* (based on the novel *The Lonely Guy's Book of Life,* by Bruce Jay Friedman), Universal, 1984.

The Slugger's Wife, Columbia, 1985.

Brighton Beach Memoirs (based on Simon's play of the same title), Universal, 1986.

Biloxi Blues (based on Simon's play of the same title), Universal, 1988.

The Marrying Man, Hollywood Pictures, 1991.

Lost in Yonkers (based on Simon's play of the same title), Columbia, 1993, published as *Neil Simon's Lost in Yonkers: The Illustrated Screenplay of the Film,* Newmarket Press (New York, NY), 1993.

Neil Simon's The Odd Couple II, Paramount Pictures, 1998.

The Odd Couple I and II: The Original Screen Plays, Simon & Schuster (New York, NY), 2000.

TELEPLAYS

The Trouble with People, NBC-TV, 1972.

Plaza Suite (based on Simon's play of the same title), ABC-TV, 1987.

Broadway Bound (based on Simon's play of the same title), ABC-TV, 1992.

Jake's Women (based on Simon's play of the same title), CBS-TV, 1996.

London Suite (based on Simon's play of the same title), NBC-TV, 1996.

The Sunshine Boys (based on Simon's play of the same title), Hallmark Entertainment, 1997.

Laughter on the 23rd Floor (based on Simon's play of the same title), Paramount Television/Showtime Network, 2001.

The Goodbye Girl (based on Simon's play of the same title), Turner Network Television, 2004.

Also coauthor of teleplay *Happy Endings,* 1975.

OTHER

Rewrites: A Memoir (autobiography), Simon & Schuster (New York, NY), 1996.

(Contributor) *Hold Fast Your Dreams,* edited by Carrie Boyko and Kimberly Colen, Scholastic (New York, NY), 1996.

Neil Simon Monologues: Speeches from the Works of America's Foremost Playwright, edited by Roger Karshner, Dramaline (Rancho Mirage, CA), 1996.

Neil Simon's Proposals, Samuel French (New York, NY), 1998.

The Play Goes On: A Memoir, Simon & Schuster, 1999.

Neil Simon Scenes: Scenes from the Works of America's Foremost Playwright, edited by Roger Karshner, Dramaline (Rancho Mirage, CA), 2000.

ADAPTATIONS: Come Blow Your Horn was filmed by Paramount in 1963; *Sweet Charity* was filmed by Universal in 1969; *The Star-Spangled Girl* was filmed by Paramount in 1971; *Barefoot in the Park* was adapted as a television series by American Broadcasting Co. (ABC) in 1970; *The Odd Couple* was adapted as a television series by ABC in 1970-75, as another television series, *The Oddball Couple,* 1975, as *The New Odd Couple,* ABC, in 1982-83, and a television movie, *The Odd Couple: Together Again* (also known as *The Odd Couple: One More Time*), CBS, 1993.

SIDELIGHTS: Playwright Neil Simon "can look back on an incredibly productive career that shows no signs of faltering despite the usual diminution of energy brought about by advancing years," according to Jonathan Yardley, writing in the *Washington Post.* Since 1959 Simon's comedies have dominated the Broadway stage and have been adapted as popular Hollywood films as well. As David Richards explained in the *Washington Post,* Simon's comedies have run "forever on Broadway and made him pots of money, after which they were turned into movies that made him pots more." Such plays as *Barefoot in the Park, The Odd Couple, Plaza Suite, The Prisoner of Second Avenue, The Sunshine Boys,* and the autobiographical trilogy of *Brighton Beach Memoirs, Biloxi Blues,* and *Broadway Bound* have ensured Simon a position as "one of America's most popular and prolific playwrights" and "the most formidable comedy writer in American theatre," as Sheila Ennis Geitner reported in the *Dictionary of Literary Biography.* Yardley similarly noted that Simon's productions "have worked their way into the heart of twentiethth-century American culture."

Even though Simon's plays are often praised for their humor, in later years they have grown more serious, confronting issues of importance, the humor developing naturally from the characters and their interactions. With these plays, Simon has gained a new respect for his own work. "Simon's mature theatre work," Robert K. Johnson wrote in *Neil Simon,* "combines comedy with moments of poignance and insight." Speaking of the Tony Award-winning *Biloxi Blues,* Frank Rich of the *New York Times* argued that Simon "at last begins to examine himself honestly, without compromises, and the result is his most persuasively serious effort to date."

Simon began his career as a radio writer in the 1940s. He and his brother Danny Simon worked as a team, writing comedy sketches for radio personality Goodman Ace. In the 1950s the pair graduated to television, working with such popular entertainers as Sid Caesar, Phil Silvers, and Jackie Gleason, and with such other writers as Mel Brooks and Woody Allen. But after some ten years in the business, Simon wanted out. "I hated the idea of working in television and having conferences with network executives and advertising executives who told you what audiences wanted and in what region they wanted it," Simon told the *New York Times Magazine.* With the success of his play *Come Blow Your Horn,* written with Danny, Simon was finally able to leave television and devote his efforts to the stage. He has never regretted the move. As he told Richards, "I would rather spend my nights writing for an audience of 1,000 than an audience of 14 million."

Since the initial success of *Come Blow Your Horn,* which ran for eighty-four weeks on Broadway, Simon has seldom had a disappointing reception to his work. His second play, *Barefoot in the Park,* ran for over 1,500 performances on Broadway; *The Odd Couple* for over 900 performances; *Plaza Suite* for over 1,000 performances; and *Last of the Red Hot Lovers* and *The Prisoner of Second Avenue* ran for over 700 performances each. Richards noted that "all but a handful of Simon's plays" have made a profit, while Simon is reputedly "the richest playwright alive and arguably the richest ever in the history of the theater." "Most of Simon's plays," Richard Christiansen remarked in the *Chicago Tribune,* "have been good box office. [And] he still holds the record for having the most plays running simultaneously on Broadway (four)."

Although Simon's plays have dealt with a wide range of situations and characters, certain elements recur in all of them. The setting is usually Simon's hometown of New York, the characters are often native New Yorkers, and their problems are similar to those experienced by Simon himself. *Come Blow Your Horn,* for instance, is a thinly disguised version of Simon and brother Danny coming of age and leaving home, *The Odd Couple* stems from Danny's experience of sharing an apartment with a divorced friend, and *Chapter Two* concerns Simon's recovery following the death of his first wife in 1973. Simon explained to Leslie Bennetts of the *New York Times* about how he has incorporated events from his own life into his plays: "The theme is me, my outlook on life. If you spread [my career] out like a map, you can chart my emotional life: some of the growth, some of the changes, some of the side trips."

Critics often point out that Simon has an admirable ability to accurately depict American domestic life. Writing in the *Humanist,* Julius Novick claimed that Simon immerses "himself in the minutiae of modern American upper-middle-class existence, which no one conveys with more authority—or, anyhow, more assiduity— than he."

Simon's plays usually focus on the members of one family or on a small group of friends, and often concern the more disruptive problems of modern life: divorce, urban crime and congestion, conflicts between children and parents, infidelity. These conflicts occur in a closed environment: an apartment or the family home. "Many of my plays [deal] with people being dumped together in a confined space, physically and emotionally," Bennetts quoted Simon as explaining. He uses this confined space with expert skill. David Kehr of the *Chicago Tribune* noted that Simon has "a kind of genius—a genius for stagecraft, the art of getting characters on and off a stage as unobtrusively as possible and of finding plausible, natural excuses for restricting a whole range of dramatic action to the confines of a single set. As a master of logistics, Simon is without peer."

Although Simon's plays are often concerned with domestic troubles, they nonetheless find humor in these painful situations. In his critique of *The Odd Couple* for the *Saturday Review,* Henry Hewes explained that Simon "makes comic cadenzas out of our bleats of agony." Simon's characters, Hewes maintained, "are blissfully unhappy but the pain of what they do to each other and to themselves is exploded into fierce humor."

In her *Neil Simon: A Critical Study,* Edythe M. McGovern argued that in his early plays Simon also advocated compromise and moderation. In *Barefoot in the Park,* for instance, a newly married couple are opposites: she is spontaneous; he is overly careful. Their different outlooks on life threaten to pull them apart. But by play's end, they have moderated their behavior so that they can live comfortably together. "Simon," McGovern wrote, "has made a point here regarding the desirability of following a middle course in order to live pleasurably without boredom, but with a sensible regard for responsibility."

The same theme is returned to in *The Odd Couple,* in which two divorced male friends share an apartment, only to find that the disagreeable personality traits which led them to get divorces also make their living together impossible. They are "two rather nice human beings who will never be able to communicate with one another simply because each man has a completely different way of viewing the world and is committed to what amounts to an extreme position with no intention of compromise," as McGovern explained. Their unyielding attitudes lead to an angry confrontation and eventual break. In showing the consequences of their inability to compromise, Simon again argues for "a middle course rather than an extremely polarized position," McGovern further commented. Speaking of Simon's handling of such important themes in his comedies, McGovern claimed that "to Neil Simon, . . . the comic form provides a means to present serious subjects so that audiences may laugh to avoid weeping."

But not all critics have been kind to Simon. Some believe his long string of hit comedies are filled with funny one-liners and little else. Jack Kroll of *Newsweek* referred to Simon's image as "Gagman Laureate." Writing in his *Uneasy Stages: A Chronicle of the New York Theater, 1963-73,* John Simon felt that "the basic unit of [Simon's] playmaking is the joke. Not the word, the idea, the character, or even the situation, but the gag. It kills him if here and there a monosyllable resists funnying up, if now and then someone has to make a move that won't fracture the audience."

For many years, Simon was taken less than seriously even by critics who enjoyed his work. Geitner remarked that Simon's reputation as "the most formidable comedy writer in American theatre . . . prevented his being considered a serious dramatist by many critics."

Since the autobiographical trilogy *Brighton Beach Memoirs, Biloxi Blues,* and *Broadway Bound* in the 1980s, however, critical opinion about Simon's work has improved enormously. Speaking of the critical reception of *Brighton Beach Memoirs,* Richards explained that "the critics, who have sometimes begrudged the playwright his ability to coin more funny lines per minute than seems humanly possible, have now decided that he has a very warm heart." And *Biloxi Blues,* his twenty-first Broadway play, won Simon in 1985 his first Tony Award for best drama. (He had twenty years earlier won the Tony for best playwright.)

The trilogy is based on Simon's own childhood and youth in the 1930s and 1940s, although he told Charles Champlin of the *Los Angeles Times:* "I hate to call it autobiographical, because things didn't necessarily happen, or happen to me. It's an Impressionist painting of that era and that place. But there are bits and pieces of me in several of the characters." *Broadway Bound* is close enough to the truth, however, for William A. Henry III of *Time* to report that both Simon "and his brother Danny have wept openly while watching it in performance."

Brighton Beach Memoirs is set in the Brooklyn of 1937 and tells of a Jewish family, the Jeromes, and their financial troubles during the Depression. When an aunt loses her job, she and her son move in with the Jeromes, and the family, now seven people in a cramped house, must survive their financial crisis and the aggravatingly close proximity to each other. Rich explained that "Simon uses the family's miseries to raise such enduring issues as sibling resentments, guilt-ridden parent-child relationships and the hunger for dignity in a poverty-stricken world." Simon's alter ego is the family's teenage son, Eugene, who comments on his family's problems in asides to the audience. Eugene, Richards commented, "serves as the play's narrator and [his] cockeyed slant on the family's tribulations keeps the play in comic perspective."

The play earned Simon some of the best reviews of his career. Brown wrote that *Brighton Beach Memoirs* has "plenty of laughs," but "Simon avoids the glib, tenderly probing the often-awkward moments where confused emotions cause unconscious hurts. . . . Simon's at his best, finding the natural wit, wisecracking and hyperbole in the words and wisdom of everyday people."

Eugene Jerome joins the Army in *Biloxi Blues,* the second play of the trilogy. The story follows Eugene through his ten weeks of basic training in Biloxi, Mississippi. During this training, one recruit is jailed for his homosexuality; one comes into constant conflict with his superior officers; and Eugene faces anti-Semitic insults from another soldier. Eugene, an aspiring writer, records these events faithfully in his diary, learning to examine his life and the lives of his friends honestly, and developing personal values in the process. Eugene's dream of becoming a writer is greatly furthered when he is assigned to work on an Army newspaper instead of being sent to the front, a fortunate turn of events that nonetheless makes him feel guilty.

Eugene's Army career is virtually identical to Simon's own stint in the military, and this self-examination was well received by the critics, who found that Simon realistically presents life in the Army. "For all the familiarity of its set pieces," Dan Sullivan of the *Los Angeles Times* said of *Biloxi Blues,* "it feels like life, not 'Gomer Pyle.'" Critics have also been impressed with how Simon subordinates the play's humor to its more serious concerns. Richards claimed that *Biloxi Blues* "may be the most touching play ever written about the rigors of basic training."

The story of Eugene Jerome continues in *Broadway Bound,* in which Eugene and his older brother, Stan, become comedy writers, leave home, and take jobs with a major network radio show. The breakup of their parents' marriage, the family's resistance to their new profession, and Eugene's realization that life does not contain the happy endings found in art form the basis of the plot. Danny Simon told Nina Darnton of the *New York Times* that *Broadway Bound* "is the closest in accuracy" of the three autobiographical plays.

Eugene's mother is the primary character in *Broadway Bound.* "Through much of the comedy," Christiansen noted, "she has been the needling, nagging Jewish mother who gets the old, familiar laughs. But by the end of the play, with her personal life a shambles, she has turned into a creature of great sorrow and weariness, as well." After recounting to Eugene the story of how she once danced with actor George Raft—an exhilarating and romantic moment she still recalls fondly—Eugene asks his mother to dance with him. "In this," Kroll observed, "perhaps the most delicate and highly charged moment in any Simon play, we feel the waste of a woman's unlived life and the shock of a young man who feels in his arms the repressed rhythm of that life." Eugene "sees that behind his mother's depressed exterior," Mel Gussow commented in the *New York Times,* "is the heart of a once vibrant and hopeful young woman; she is someone who has been defeated by the limits she has imposed on her life." Although he saw some flaws in *Broadway Bound,* Rich admitted that it "contains some of its author's most accomplished writing to date—passages that dramatize the timeless, unresolvable bloodlettings of familial existence as well as the humorous conflicts one expects."

Simon finally received critical recognition of his status as one of America's major playwrights in 1991, when his play *Lost in Yonkers* won both a Pulitzer Prize for drama and a Tony Award for best drama. The play, which tells the story of a dysfunctional Jewish-American family during World War II, is "closer to pure surrealism than anything Mr. Simon has hitherto produced," wrote David Richards in the *New York Times,* "and take[s] him several bold steps beyond the autobiographical traumas he recorded in *Brighton Beach Memoirs* and *Broadway Bound.*" "No longer content to dramatize divisive arguments around the family table," the critic continued, "he has pulled the family itself out of shape and turned it into a grotesque version of itself. These characters are not oddballs, they're deeply disturbed creatures. Were it not for his ready wit and his appreciation for life's incongruities, *Lost in Yonkers* could pass for a nightmare."

Lost in Yonkers is the story of how Eddie Kurnitz is forced by his economic circumstances to leave his two young sons, Arty and Jay, in the care of his severe, overbearing German-born Jewish mother. Grandma Kurnitz has tried to encourage self-reliance among her children by exercising strict discipline in her home, but she has only succeeded in scarring them emotionally. She continues to exert her authority over her gangster son Louie and her mentally impaired daughter Bella. "The two children," Richards declared in his *New York Times* review of the show, "are our sole connection to a world of conventional relationships and values." "During the eight months Jay and Arty spend with their relatives," Richards continued, "Bella takes it into her addled head that she's going to leave home, marry the usher at the local movie house, open a restaurant and have babies—more or less in that order." Grandma opposes Bella's show of individuality, and, with Arty's and Jay's help, Bella stages her own defiance of the family matriarch. "We are relieved, at the end, when the father reappears," wrote James S. Torrens in *America.* "And the youngsters, who have made it through the same ordeals as their parents . . . can be seen as having survived. *Lost in Yonkers* touches all the chords."

Critics have remarked on how Simon's later plays—including *Lost in Yonkers* and his autobiographical trilogy—turn from straight comedy toward the depiction of suffering. "Over the last decade," Richards wrote in a *New York Times Magazine* piece about the playwright, "pain has slowly crept into the comic world of Neil Simon. Although his popularity remains undiminished, his increasing willingness to recognize that the uproariously funny can also be ineffably sad may be freeing him from the taint of craven commercialism." "He was already a past master at depicting the sundry ways people get on one another's nerves," the critic wrote in a *Washington Post* article on Simon's career. "What have surfaced increasingly in his mature works are the hurt, the sadness and the longings that possess his characters. In *Lost in Yonkers,* . . . the ache and the absurdity of living are inextricably interwoven." Richards further noted that the prestigious National Theater of Britain has performed *Brighton Beach Memoirs,* that *Time* magazine cited *Broadway Bound* as the "best American play of the 1980s," and that PBS had deemed him worthy of inclusion with luminaries such as Jasper Johns, Cole Porter, and Edward R. Murrow by profiling him in the *American Masters* television series. Summarizing the reasons for Simon's enduring popularity, Richards declared that he is "the least philosophical of playwrights and politics rarely intrudes upon his world. . . . What he returns to, time and again, are the dynamics and difficulties of personal relationships, as they transpire in an essentially middle-class society—a perspective that helps explain the loyalty of Broadway audiences."

After the high drama of *Lost in Yonkers,* Simon returned to straight comedy in two farces: *Rumors* (1988) and *Jake's Women* (1992). In both cases critics remarked that the plays seemed almost too lightweight after the successes of his autobiographical plays and *Lost in Yonkers. Rumors* is "a self-described farce," reported Frank Rich in the *New York Times,* "that has nothing on its mind except making the audience laugh. And not exactly in the Moliere manner. Maybe I've led a charmed life, but I can't recall hearing this many toilet jokes since the ninth grade." *Jake's Women* received "scathing" reviews in the *Los Angeles Times,* stated *New York Times* reporter Mervyn Rothstein, and "the San Diego critics said it needed a lot of work but had promise."

Jake's Women and Simon's next play, *Laughter on the 23rd Floor* (1993), both failed to make a profit, in part because of the expense of Broadway productions. When *Laughter on the 23rd Floor*—based on stories from Simon's life working on Sid Caesar's *Your Show of Shows*—met with good reviews and had a decent run but was less than a financial success, Simon declared his intention to open his next play Off-Broadway. *London Suite,* a series of four one-act plays, opened Off-Broadway in 1995 and later traveled successfully to Chicago.

With his year 2000 play *Dinner Party,* Simon is once again "simply out to have fun," according to Clifford A. Ridley in the *Knight Ridder/Tribune News Service.* Ridley thought even the set of the play was "funny," with dialogue "zestily peppered with insult and misunderstanding." Simon devises an intriguing dinner party: three men, unknown to one another, have been invited by a common acquaintance, the divorce lawyer who served each successfully. Three other places are also laid at the table; seats for these men's former wives. Ridley ultimately felt that Simon's "insights seldom have matched his obsessiveness," and that comedy is soon replaced by a "string of colloquies about love and marriage."

In his 2003 play about love and loss, *Rose and Walsh,* Simon "finally confronts the afterlife and its effects on loved ones left behind, creating his most rewarding play in years," wrote Phil Gallo in *Variety.* Rose is a hard-living, prize-winning writer facing not only the end of her career but life without Walsh, her husband and legendary writer, who died five years earlier. Walsh has, however, kept in contact in a ghostly manner with his wife, and now recommends that she finish one of his mystery novels and also that she bring in a ghost writer, Clancy, a seemingly washed-up writer, to do so. Added to this strange brew is Arlene, Rose's secret daughter from a fling many years ago, a young woman who has only been able to spend time with her mother since Walsh's death. Somewhat inspired by the real-life relationship between Dashiell Hammett and Lillian Hellman, *Rose and Walsh* "is ultimately about transitions," Gallo further commented. Diane Haithman, reviewing the play in the *Los Angeles Times,* found it a "quirky love story," but one very much still under construction. For Haithman, it was an "erratic effort that, despite a few bright moments, plot-twists slowly in the wind." Gallo, however, felt the play was "simple in its construction— an often-comical, eventually poignant ghost story—and refreshing in its logic." Gallo also felt that Simon managed to strike "that delicate balance between the comic . . . and the profound."

Although primarily known for his plays, Simon also has written a score of popular films. These include the screen adaptations of many of his own hit plays—including *Barefoot in the Park, The Odd Couple,* and *The Sunshine Boys*—as well as such original screenplays as *The Cheap Detective, Murder by Death,* and *The Goodbye Girl.* Simon's best screen work is found in films where he creates a desperate situation, Vincent Canby argued in the *New York Times.* Simon's "wisecracks define a world of mighty desperation," Canby wrote, "in which every confrontation, be it with a lover, a child, a husband, a friend or a taxi driver, becomes a last chance for survival. When he writes a work in which the desperation is built into the situations, Mr. Simon can be both immensely funny and surprisingly moving."

But not all critics appreciate Simon's film work. Simon's adaptations of his own plays, while often good box office, have sometimes been criticized for being too stagey, like "photographed plays," as Johnson put it. Yet, most of Simon's films, especially *The Heartbreak Kid* and *Only When I Laugh,* have been extremely popular with audiences and critics alike.

The Heartbreak Kid concerns a young couple who get divorced during their honeymoon in Florida after the husband meets another woman. Simon creates humor in this film, as Johnson allowed, "out of situations which are not basically surefire comedy material." It is this blend of the humorous and the essentially tragic—with the humor emerging naturally from the actions and speech of the characters—which makes *The Heartbreak Kid* "the best film created thus far from a Neil Simon script," Johnson believed.

Only When I Laugh was also a critical success for Simon. It tells the story of Georgia Hines, an alcoholic Broadway actress who, despite rehabilitation, cannot beat her dependence. Georgia "is one of the most interesting, complicated characters that Mr. Simon, the master of the sometimes self-defeating one-liner, has ever written," according to Canby. Johnson found *Only When I Laugh* "one of the most absorbing pieces of work that Simon has written."

Yet after all his film successes, Simon eventually came to feel "disenchantment with Hollywood," according to Richards. The movie-making industry, which used to "give him carte blanche . . . now subjects him to the same corporate humiliations as anyone else." After an unhappy alliance with Disney Studios for the film *The Marrying Man,* Simon observed to Richards: "With a play, I have only two people to please—myself and the director. . . . With this movie it was nineteen executives, plus a director who'd never done anything but animation before, and two stars who would tell you what lines they'd say and what lines they wouldn't say." Richards concluded that despite the troubles plaguing the New York theater scene, "Simon knows his place, and it's on Broadway. If he is not so sure what that means these days, he thinks it still denotes accessibility and craftsmanship. It has to do with refining every detail, every line, every moment, so that he can feel, as he rarely does on opening night, a momentary sense of completion, of coming in to land."

Simon did venture onto the screen again, however, with his 1998 update of the antics of his humorous couple, Oscar and Felix. *Odd Couple II* finds the unlikely duo long retired and en route to their children's wedding in California. "Getting there is all the fun," noted George Meyer in the *Sarasota Herald Tribune.* During the course of their journey, the two manage to lose their luggage, get lost and arrested, and "bicker and spat continuously," as Leah Rozen noted in *People.* Meyer felt that Simon came up with a "delightful comedy," and one that is "witty, insightful and some of the best Simon writing in years." Other critics were not so positive about the merits of the movie. Renee Graham, writing in the *Boston Globe,* thought the picture was a "time-worn mixture of road picture and buddy movie" with a "lousy" script. *Entertainment Weekly*'s Mike D'Angelo called the movie a "dire sequel" and a "feeble" comedy, and Rosen felt the adventures of Felix and Oscar were "more strained than amusing," making for "one mighty long, slow journey."

"Writing is an escape from a world that crowds me," Simon admitted to John Corry of the *New York Times.* "I like being alone in a room. It's almost a form of meditation—an investigation of my own life." He explained to William A. Henry how he begins a play: "There's no blueprint per se. You just go through the tunnels of your mind, and you come out someplace." Accepting his success as a writer has also been difficult. "I was depressed for a number of years," Simon told Corry. The opening of a new play filled him with guilt. It took psychoanalysis, and a consultation with his second wife's swami, before Simon learned to enjoy his accomplishments.

Simon explores his life in writing in two memoirs, *Rewrites,* which traces his first forty-six years of life, up to the death of his wife Joan in 1973, and *The Play Goes On,* which continues from that point through his marriages to Marsha Mason and Diane Lander and the successes of the 1980s. Along the way, he recounts numerous behind-the-scenes anecdotes about plays and play-making. Christopher Lehmann-Haupt, writing in the *New York Times,* found *Rewrites* a "pleasant memoir," but with "surprisingly flat prose." For Everett Evans, writing in the *Houston Chronicle,* the same memoir was "frequently funny, occasionally poignant and resolutely unaffected." Similarly, *Billboard's* Trudi Miller Rosenblum thought the first installment was a "fascinating and thoughtful autobiography." Reviewing the second portion of the memoir, 1999's *The Play Goes On,* Larry King noted in *USA Today* that "Simon writes books as well as he writes plays, and there aren't any better." Peter Marks, writing in the *New York Times Book Review,* however, felt that despite a few "entertaining anecdotes," the book as a whole "feels tossed off." It was "too bad," Marks concluded, "this master play doctor was not encouraged to perform a little more surgery on his own story." Celia Wren, writing in *American Theatre,* found more to like in the title. She praised Simon's "low-key wit . . . [and] insight into the creative process."

Simon writes on a daily basis, although much of his work is never completed. Richards reported that "Simon's desk overflows with the plays he's begun over the years. On an average, for every one he finishes, there are ten he abandons after fifteen or twenty pages." Generally, if Simon gets past page thirty-five he will finish the play, a process that takes four months for a first draft, longer for the final draft. *Come Blow Your Horn,* for example, was rewritten twenty times before Simon was satisfied with it. In *Broadway Bound,* Simon has his alter ego, Eugene, say: "I love *being* a writer. It's the writing that's hard."

Despite the difficulty involved in writing, Simon has managed to produce an impressive body of work. A new Simon comedy every theatrical season was a Broadway staple for well over three decades. Henry called him "America's foremost stage comedist" and placed Simon "in the top rank of American playwrights." Rich similarly called him "not just a show business success but an institution." After surveying Simon's many achievements during his long career as a writer for the stage and screen, Johnson concluded by dubbing him "one of the finest writers of comedy in American literary history."

BIOGRAPHICAL AND CRITICAL SOURCES:

BOOKS

Contemporary Literary Criticism, Gale (Detroit, MI), Volume 6, 1976, Volume 9, 1979, Volume 31, 1985, Volume 39, 1986, Volume 70, 1991.

Dictionary of Literary Biography, Volume 7: *Twentieth-Century American Dramatists,* Gale (Detroit, MI), 1981.

Johnson, Robert K., *Neil Simon,* Twayne (Boston, MA), 1983.

Kerr, Walter, *Thirty Plays Hath November,* Simon & Schuster (New York, NY), 1969.

Konas, Gary, *Neil Simon: A Casebook,* Garland (New York, NY), 1997.

McGovern, Edythe M., *Neil Simon: A Critical Study,* Ungar (New York, NY), 1979.

Monaco, James, *American Film Now,* Oxford University Press (New York, NY), 1979.

Simon, John, *Uneasy Stages: A Chronicle of the New York Theater, 1963-73,* Random House (New York, NY), 1975.

Simon, Neil, *Rewrites: A Memoir,* Simon & Schuster (New York, NY), 1996.

PERIODICALS

America, May 4, 1991, James S. Torrens, "Absent and Lost: Seasonal High Points," pp. 496-97.

American Theatre, December, 1999, Celia Wren, review of *The Play Goes On: A Memoir,* p. 80.

Billboard, January 11, 1997, Trudi Miller Rosenblum, review of *Rewrites: A Memoir,* p. 86.

Boston Globe, April 10, 1998, Renee Graham, review of *The Odd Couple II,* p. D7.

Chicago Sun Times, October 13, 1996, Bill Zwecker, "One on One with Bill Zwecker" p. 3NC.

Chicago Tribune, November 2, 1986, Richard Christiansen, "Neil Simon, Himself: *Broadway Bound* Bares Playwright's Heart and Soul," p. 4; December 13, 1992, Richard Christiansen, "The Goodbye Guy: You Can Make Book on Neil Simon's Musical Scripts," section 13, pp. 4-5; November 23, 1993, Richard Christiansen, "Laugh Factory Humor Flows from *23rd Floor,*" section 4, p. 20;

October 8, 1995, Richard Christiansen, "Rewrite Specialist Even after 28 Plays, Neil Simon Is Still Fine-Tuning His Craft," section 7, p. 8.

Entertainment Weekly, October 9, 1998, Mike D'Angelo, review of *The Odd Couple II,* p. 90; November 12, 1999, Charles Winecoff, review of *The Play Goes On,* p. 74.

Financial Times, April 1, 1999, "Simon Is Just Too Cute for Words," p. 15.

Hollywood Reporter, June 21, 2002, Jay Reiner, "Oscar and Felix," pp. 22-23.

Houston Chronicle, November 17, 1996, Everett Evans, review of *Rewrites,* p. 22.

Humanist, September-October, 1976, Julius Novick.

Knight Ridder, October 9, 1996, Pat Craig, review of *Rewrites,* p. 1009K5245.

Library Journal, December, 1996, Gordon Blackwell, review of *Rewrites,* p. 169.

Los Angeles Times, December 5, 1982, Charles Champlin, "Neil Simon Remembers When Times Were Tough," p. 1; December 15, 1984, Dan Sullivan, review of *Biloxi Blues,* p. 1; October 14, 1999, Jonathan Levi, review of *The Play Goes On,* p. 3; February 7, 2003, Diane Haithman, review of *Rose and Walsh,* p. E1.

Newsweek, April 14, 1980, Jack Kroll, "I Ought to Be in Pictures," p. 106; April 20, 1981, Jack Kroll, review of *Fools,* p. 104; December 15, 1986, Jack Kroll, review of *It Only Hurts When I Laugh,* p. 76; March 4, 1991, Jack Kroll, "Going Bonkers in Yonkers," p. 60; March 15, 1993, Jack Kroll, "This Goodbye Is a Bad Guy," p. 82; December 6, 1993, Jack Kroll, "When Laughter Wasn't Canned," p. 81; November 17, 1997, Jack Kroll, "The Forest of Simon," p. 94.

New York Times, April 5, 1981, John Corry, "Why Broadway's Fastest Writer Cannot Slow Down," p. 1; March 27, 1983, Leslie Bennetts, "Neil Simon Delves into His Past," p. H1; March 24, 1985, Nina Darnton, "From Neil Simon: A New Film, a New Play," p. H1; April 7, 1985, Frank Rich, review of *Biloxi Blues,* p. H1; December 5, 1986, Frank Rich, review of *Broadway Bound,* p. C3; December 26, 1986, Nina Darnton, "Danny Simon's View of Younger Brother Neil," p. C10; January 8, 1987, Frank Rich, "Neil Simon Takes On Neil Simon," p. C20; March 25, 1988, Vincent Canby, review of *Biloxi Blues,* p. C1; November 13, 1988, Mervyn Rothstein, "For Neil Simon, the Prescription Was Farce," pp. 13, 41; November 18, 1988, Frank Rich, review of *Rumors,* p. C3; March 3, 1991, David Richards, review of *Lost in Yonkers,* pp. 1, 7; April 5, 1992, David Richards, review of *Jake's Women,* pp. 5, 37; April 10, 1995, Vincent Canby, review of *London Suite,* pp. C9, C11; October 24, 1996, Christopher Lehmann-Haupt, review of *Rewrites,* p. C19.

New York Times Book Review, October 24, 1999, Peter Marks, review of *The Play Goes On,* p. 19.

New York Times Magazine, May 26, 1985, "The Craft of the Playwright: A Conversation between Neil Simon and David Rabe," p. 36; February 17, 1991, David Richards, "The Last of the Red Hot Playwrights," pp. 30-32, 36, 57, 64.

People, April 20, 1998, Leah Rozen, review of *The Odd Couple II,* p. 35.

Philippine Daily Inquirer, March 2, 2002, Noelani Torre, review of *Rewrites.*

Sarasota Herald Tribune (Sarasota, FL), April 10, 1998, George Meyer, review of *The Odd Couple II,* p. 15.

Saturday Review, March 27, 1965, Henry Hewes.

Time, December 15, 1986, William A. Henry III, "Reliving a Poignant Past," p. 72; November 28, 1988, William A. Henry III, "Theater: Falling Short," p. 94.

Times—Picayune (New Orleans, LA), November 15, 2002, David Cuthbert, review of *The Prisoner of Second Avenue,* p. L14.

USA Today, October 4, 1999, Larry King, review of *The Play Goes On,* p. D2; October 7, 1999, David Patrick Stearns, review of *The Play Goes On,* p. D8.

Variety, February 17-23, 2003, Phil Gallo, review of *Rose and Walsh,* p. 48.

Washington Post, April 9, 1995, David Richards, "Simon: Give My Regards to Broadway; Economics Force Him to Think Small with New Play," p. G1; October 10, 1999, Jonathan Yardley, review of *The Play Goes On,* p. X2.

ONLINE

Kennedy Center Web site, http://www.kennedy-center.org/ (November 12, 2003), *Kennedy Centers Honors Profile for 1995.**

* * *

SMITH, Arthur L.

See ASANTE, Molefi Kete

SMITH, Patricia Clark 1943-

PERSONAL: Born February 14, 1943, in Holyoke, MA; daughter of James Joseph (a project engineer) and Rita Mary (a homemaker; maiden name, Dunn) Clark; married Warren S. Smith, August 25, 1964 (divorced, 1976); married John F. Crawford (a college professor and publisher), November 26, 1988; children: (first marriage) Joshua Briggs, Caleb Michael. *Ethnicity:* "Irish-French-Canadian-Micmac." *Education:* Smith College, B.A., 1964; Yale University, M.A., 1965, Ph.D., 1970. *Politics:* "Leftist; registered Green Party." *Religion:* Roman Catholic.

ADDRESSES: Home—2309 Headingly NW, Albuquerque, NM 87107. *Office*—c/o Department of English, University of New Mexico, Albuquerque, NM 87131; fax: 505-345-5729.

CAREER: Smith College, Northampton, MA, lecturer in English, 1968-69; Luther College, Decorah, IA, assistant professor of English, 1969-71; University of New Mexico, Albuquerque, assistant professor, 1971-82, associate professor, 1982-96, professor of English, 1996-2002, professor emeritus, 2002—.

MEMBER: Phi Beta Kappa.

WRITINGS:

Talking to the Land (poetry), Blue Moon (Tucson, AZ), 1979.

Changing Your Story (poetry), West End (Albuquerque, NM), 1990.

(Editor, with Paul Davis, Gary Harrison, David Johnson, and husband, John F. Crawford) *Western Literature in a World Context* (anthology), two volumes, St. Martin's Press (New York, NY), 1995, 2nd edition published as *The Bedford Anthology of World Literature,* six volumes, 2003.

(With Paula Gunn Allen) *As Long As the Rivers Flow: The Stories of Nine Native Americans,* Scholastic (New York, NY), 1996.

(Reteller, with Michael B. Running Wolf) *On the Trail of Elder Brother: Glous'gap Stories of the Micmac Indians,* illustrated by Michael B. RunningWolf, Persea Books (New York, NY), 2000.

Weetamoo, Heart of the Pocassets (novel), Scholastic (New York, NY), 2003.

Contributor to books, including *The Sacred Hoop,* edited by Paula Gunn Allen; *Working Class Women in the Academy: Laborers in the Knowledge Factory; To Speak or Be Silent: The Paradox of Disobedience in the Lives of Women; This Is about Vision: Interviews with Southwestern Writers;* and *Western Women: Their Land, Their Lives.* Contributor of short stories and reviews to *New American Review, Tierra: Contemporary Short Fiction of New Mexico, American Indian Quarterly, Rio Grande Writers' Newsletter,* and *Western American Literature.*

WORK IN PROGRESS: The Road to White Tail, a young adult novel set on the Mescalero Apache reservation in 1915.

SIDELIGHTS: Patricia Clark Smith once commented: "I was born on Valentine's Day, 1943, in Holyoke, Massachusetts. My family on both sides is French-Canadian, Irish, and Micmac Indian. I'm a mixed-blood person, and the more diverse that places are (like New Mexico), the more I feel at home there.

"When I was growing up in Massachusetts and Maine, my family told me stories, taught me the names of the birds and plants that grew around our house, and talked to me about what was happening in the world. They read to me all the time, and I became a hungry reader of everything from *Little Women* to horror comics. I made my first book when I was seven, writing the story, drawing the pictures, and sewing the pages together.

"In 1964 I graduated from Smith College in Northampton, Massachusetts, where my maternal grandmother had worked as a maid. I was the first person in my family to go to college, and often it was scary because I knew so many people were counting on me to do well. I wanted to be a writer and English professor, so I went on to Yale University, where I specialized in American literature.

"In 1971 I was hired by the University of New Mexico. I was soon asked to teach some of my classes onsite at different places on the Navajo Reservation. A lot of wonderful books by American Indian novelists and poets were being published, and I began to teach those books and publish articles about them. There was no such thing as Native American studies when I was in school, but now it is a respected field. My Native American literature classes are crowded every semester.

"Some of my Native American students, like Paula Gunn Allen, have gone on to become well-known writers. Paula and I have worked on scholarly articles together before, but *As Long As the Rivers Flow: The Stories of Nine Native Americans* is the first young people's book for both of us. *Scholastic* asked Paula to do the book, and she invited me to join her. We loved telling those stories! It was very important, we thought, to make readers aware of the range of Native American achievement. Some of the people we wrote about in the book are barely known, even though they were very important. Weetamoo, the Pocasset woman sachem and warrior, is a good example. She avoided war when she could, but when it became plain to her in the 1670s that the English colonists were making native ways of life impossible, she fought bravely beside Metacom (or King Philip, as the English called him) and gave the colonists a run for their money. She's my personal heroine. Now I've done a whole novel about her life as an adolescent, *Weetamoo, Heart of the Pocassets.*

"When I am not teaching or writing, I love to hang out with our nine cats, to tend my little outdoor fish pond, to cook, and to garden. My husband and I enjoy driving around the southwest and seeking different historical sights that aren't in the guidebooks, like the site of the ranch of John Chisum, the cattle rancher who knew Billy the Kid.

"Michael RunningWolf, a Micmac storyteller, and I have recently published a collection of traditional Micmac stories about Glous'gap, the great hero of our people. It was very well received by Micmac elders.

"My next book is set on the Mescalero Apache Reservation in southern New Mexico in 1915. In it, my young heroine learns about native plant medicine from her grandmother. This means doing a lot of the kind of research I love best, and right now my desk is piled high with books of Apache history and ethnology and books about native plants and their medicinal uses."

More recently Smith added: "Since I 'retired' in May, 2002, I've taught in a summer Native studies institute in Brandon, Manitoba, Canada, learned how to make and preserve chutney, and helped to produce a production of *The Wizard of Oz* put on by differently-abled adults at an Albuquerque community center."

BIOGRAPHICAL AND CRITICAL SOURCES:

PERIODICALS

Booklist, December 1, 1996, p. 645.
Library Journal, December 1, 1979, p. 2575.

* * *

STEIN, Dan J(oseph) 1962-

PERSONAL: Born September 17, 1962, in South Africa. *Education:* University of Cape Town, B.Sc., 1983, M.B., Ch.B. (with distinction), 1986; attended Columbia University, 1987-93.

ADDRESSES: *Office*—P.O. Box 19063, Tygerberg 7505, South Africa; fax: 27-21-932-9570. *E-mail*—djs2@sun.ac.za.

CAREER: Columbia-Presbyterian Hospital, New York, NY, resident in psychiatry at the hospital and at New York State Psychiatric Institute, 1987-1991, fellow in psychiatric research, 1991-93; Mount Sinai School of Medicine, New York, NY, assistant professor of clinical psychiatry, 1993-94; University of Stellenbosch, Stellenbosch, South Africa, director of psychiatry research, 1994—, director of Research Unit on Anxiety and Stress Disorders, Medical Research Council, 1998—.

WRITINGS:

(Editor, with J. E. Young) *Cognitive Science and Clinical Disorders,* Academic Press (San Diego, CA), 1992.
(Editor, with E. Hollander) *Impulsivity and Aggression,* John Wiley (Chichester, England), 1995.

(With J. Van Kradenburg, C. Wessels, and R. A. Emsley) *Mental Health Resource Guide for South Africa,* University of Stellenbosch (Stellenbosch, South Africa), 1996.

(Editor, with M. H. Stone) *Essential Papers on Obsessive-Compulsive Disorders,* New York University Press (New York, NY), 1997.

(Editor) *Cognitive Science and the Unconscious,* American Psychiatric Press (Washington, DC), 1997.

(Editor, with E. Hollander) *Obsessive-Compulsive Disorders: Etiology, Diagnosis, Treatment,* Marcel Dekker (New York, NY), 1997.

(Editor, with S. Levenstein) *Posttraumatic Stress Disorder,* Continuing Medical Education (New York, NY), 1998.

(Coeditor) *Neural Networks and Psychopathology: Connectionist Models in Practice and Research,* Cambridge University Press (New York, NY), 1998.

(Editor, with E. Hollander and G. A. Christenson) *Trichotillomania,* American Psychiatric Press (Washington, DC), 1999.

(Editor, with E. Hollander) *The American Psychiatric Publishing Textbook of Anxiety Disorders,* American Psychiatric Press (Washington, DC), 2002.

Author of more than 200 medical papers and articles.

* * *

STYRON, William 1925-

PERSONAL: Born June 11, 1925, in Newport News, VA; son of William Clark (a shipyard engineer) and Pauline (Abraham) Styron; married Rose Burgunder, May 4, 1953; children: Susanna, Paola, Thomas, Alexandra. *Education:* Attended Christchurch School, Middlesex County, VA, and Davidson College, NC, 1942-43; Duke University, B.A., 1947; studied writing at New School for Social Research, 1947. *Politics:* Democrat.

ADDRESSES: *Home*—12 Rucum Road, Roxbury, CT 06783, and Vineyard Haven, MA (summer).

CAREER: Writer. McGraw-Hill Book Co. (publishers), New York, NY, associate editor, 1947. Fellow of Silliman College, Yale University, 1964—. Honorary

William Styron

consultant in American Letters to the Library of Congress. Cannes Film Festival, jury president, 1983. *American Scholar,* member of editorial board, 1970-76; advisory editor of *Paris Review. Military service:* U.S. Marine Corps, World War II, 1944-45; became first lieutenant; recalled briefly in 1951.

MEMBER: National Institute of Arts and Letters, American Academy of Arts and Sciences, American Academy of Arts and Letters (inducted, 1988), Society of American Historians, Signet Society of Harvard (honorary), Academie Goncourt, Phi Beta Kappa.

AWARDS, HONORS: American Academy of Arts and Letters Prix de Rome, 1952, for *Lie down in Darkness;* Litt.D., Duke University, 1968, and Davidson College (Davidson, NC), 1986; Pulitzer Prize, 1968, and Howells Medal of the American Academy of Arts and Letters, 1970, both for *The Confessions of Nat Turner;* American Book Award, and National Book Critics Circle Award nominee, both 1980, both for *Sophie's Choice;* Connecticut Arts Award, 1984; Cino del Duca prize, 1985; Commandeur, Ordre des Arts et des Lettres (France), 1987; Edward MacDowell Medal, 1988; Bobst Award, 1989; National Magazine award, 1990; National Medal of Arts, 1993; Medal of Honor, National Arts Club, 1995; Commonwealth Award, 1995.

WRITINGS:

Lie Down in Darkness, Bobbs-Merrill (Indianapolis, IN), 1951.

The Long March, Vintage (New York, NY), 1957.

Set This House on Fire, Random House (New York, NY), 1960.

The Confessions of Nat Turner, Random House (New York, NY), 1967.

Sophie's Choice, Random House (New York, NY), 1979.

PLAYS

In the Clap Shack (three-act play; first produced at Yale Repertory Theatre, 1972), Random House (New York, NY), 1973.

OTHER

The Four Seasons, illustrated by Harold Altman, Pennsylvania State University Press (University Park, PA), 1965.

Admiral Robert Penn Warren and the Snows of Winter: A Tribute, Palaemon Press (Winston-Salem, NC), 1978.

The Message of Auschwitz, Press de la Warr (Blacksburg, VA), 1979.

Against Fear, Palaemon Press (Winston-Salem, NC), 1981.

The Achievement of William Styron (autobiography), edited by Robert K. Morris with Irving Malin, University of Georgia Press (Athens, GA), 1981.

This Quiet Dust, and Other Writings (essays), Random House (New York, NY), 1982.

(Author of introduction) Robert Satter, *Doing Justice: A Trial Judge at Work,* American Lawyer Books/Simon & Schuster (New York, NY), 1990.

Darkness Visible: A Memoir of Madness, Random House (New York, NY), 1990.

A Tidewater Morning: Three Tales from Youth, Random House (New York, NY), 1993.

(With Mariana Ruth Cook) *Fathers and Daughters: In Their Own Words,* Chronicle Books (San Francisco, CA), 1994.

(With James L. W. West III) *William Styron, a Life,* Random House (New York, NY), 1998.

(With others) *Dead Run: The Untold Story of Dennis Stockton and America's Only Mass Escape from Death Row,* Times Books (New York, NY), 1999.

Also author of *Inheritance of the Night: Early Drafts of "Lie Down in Darkness,"* Duke University Press (Durham, NC), 1993. Editor of *Paris Review: Best Short Stories,* Dutton (New York, NY), 1959. Contributor to *Esquire, New York Review of Books,* and other publications.

Manuscript collections of Styron's work are held by the Library of Congress, Washington, DC, and Duke University, Durham, NC.

ADAPTATIONS: Sophie's Choice was adapted for film, Universal Pictures, 1982 featuring Meryl Streep in the title role.

SIDELIGHTS: William Styron's novels have brought him major literary awards, broad critical notice, and a reputation for raising controversial issues. Writtten in the style of the Southern Gothic tradition made familiar by author William Faulkner, Styron's work has been described as both reckless and poetic, and his subject matter has been the focus of debate. In *The Confessions of Nat Turner* and *Sophie's Choice,* he wrote about victims of oppression: a slave and a concentration camp survivor. Although some critics have questioned his approach and his ability to enter the mind of a black slave or a mother in the Holocaust, most have praised Styron for probing into difficult subjects. Reviewers often consider Styron's timing a positive factor in the success of these two books; *Sophie's Choice,* published during renewed concern about the Holocaust, and *The Confessions of Nat Turner,* published during the racially explosive late 1960s, each found large audiences. George Steiner commented in the *New Yorker:* "The crisis of civil rights, the new relationships to each other and to their own individual sensibilities that this crisis has forced on both whites and Negroes . . . give Mr. Styron's fable [*The Confessions of Nat Turner*] a special relevance."

Styron based *The Confessions of Nat Turner* on the transcript of testimony given by a slave, Nat Turner, who had led a brief revolt against slave owners in

Virginia's Tidewater district. Styron considered his book a "meditation on history" rather than a strict retelling of events. He explained in a letter to the *Nation* that "in writing *The Confessions of Nat Turner* I at no time pretended that my narrative was an exact transcription of historical events; had perfect accuracy been my aim I would have written a work of history rather than a novel." Philip Rahv asserted that Styron's viewpoint was more valuable than a historical perspective. Rav wrote in the *New York Review of Books:* "This narrative is something more than a novelistic counterpart of scholarly studies of slavery in America; it incarnates its theme, bringing home to us the monstrous reality of slavery in a psychodynamic manner that at the same time does not in the least neglect social or economic aspects."

Styron's subjective approach drew ire from critics who felt that his portrait of Nat is based on white stereotypes. A *Negro Digest* critic took particular issue with Styron's depiction of Nat's sexuality: "In the name of fiction, Mr. Styron can do whatever he likes with History. When his interpretation, however, duplicates what is white America's favorite fantasy (i. e., every black male—especially the leader—is motivated by a latent [?] desire to sleep with the Great White Woman), he is obligated to explain . . . this coincidental duplication—or to be criticized accordingly. Since there is no such explanation in the technique of the novel and since it offers no vision or new perspective, but rather reaffirms an old stale, shameful fantasy . . . it is at best a good commercial novel." Albert Murray concurred in the *New Leader:* "Alas, what Negroes will find in Styron's 'confessions' is much the same old failure of sensibility that plagues most other fiction about black people. That is to say, they will all find a Nat Turner whom many white people may accept at a safe distance, but hardly one with whom Negroes will easily identify."

Styron wrote about human suffering in a more contemporary setting—post-World War II Brooklyn—in *Sophie's Choice.* Sophie is a beautiful Polish gentile who survived Auschwitz but lost two of her children and much of her self-esteem there. Her lover, Nathan—mad, brilliant, and Jewish—is haunted by the atrocities of the Holocaust, although he personally escaped them, and he torments Sophie with reminders. Stingo, a young writer who lives downstairs from Sophie and Nathan, narrates. According to Geoffrey Wolff in *Esquire,* "Stingo is in the tradition of *The Great Gatsby*'s Nick Carraway. Like Nick, he bears witness to the passion of characters he chances upon and tries modestly to judge and pardon. Like Nick, he is a refugee from settled values—Virginia's Tidewater country—back from a great war to make his way in the great world."

David Caute in the *New Statesman* heard additional voices. For Caute, in Styron's prose the "neo-Biblical cadences of Southern prose, of Wolfe and Faulkner, jostle . . . with the cosmopolitan sensibility of an F. Scott Fitzgerald." Other critics agreed that the influence of other writers sometimes muffles Styron's own voice. Jack Beatty wrote in the *New Republic* that *Sophie's Choice* "is written in an unvaryingly mannered style—High Southern—that draws constant spell-destroying attention to itself." The High Southern style associated with Faulkner and Thomas Wolfe is characterized by elaborate, even Gothic descriptions, and although Styron is "a novelist hard to categorise," he shows his "allegiance to that style . . . in all . . . [his] writing," according to Caute, with "a reluctance to leave any noun uncaressed by an adjective." Paul Gray, reviewing *Sophie's Choice* in *Time,* agreed, noting that Styron "often let Stingo pile up adjectives in the manner of Thomas Wolfe: 'Brooklyn's greenly beautiful, homely, teeming, begrimed and incomprehensible vastness'. . . . True, Stingo is pictured as a beginning writer, heavily in debt to Faulkner, Wolfe and the Southern literary tradition, but Styron may have preserved more redundant oratory than the effect of Stingo's youth strictly required."

Robert Towers, writing in the *New York Review of Books,* also faulted Styron for verbosity. "'All my life, I have retained a strain of uncontrolled didacticism,' says Stingo at one point," Towers noted, "and *Sophie's Choice* bears him out. The novel is made to drag along an enormous burden of commentary, ranging all the way from the meaning of the Holocaust, the ineluctable nature of evil, the corrosive effects of guilt, the horrors of slavery, and the frailty of goodness and hope to such topics as the misunderstanding of the South by Northern liberals, Southern manners as opposed to those of New York taxi drivers, and the existence of prejudice and cruelty in even the best of us." But Wolff defended Styron, observing that "the book's narrative flow is suspenseful if languid, if sometimes even glacial," and that *Sophie's Choice* "achieved an almost palpable evocation of its place and time—Poland before and during the war, Brooklyn and Coney Island immediately after." Caute, despite his criticisms, contended that Styron's prose is "marked also by clarity, honesty and accessibility."

In response to critics who questioned the validity of *Confessions* and *Sophie's Choice* on the grounds of Styron's personal background, Towers argued that "it should not be necessary to defend the right of Styron—a non-Jew, a Southern Protestant in background—to this subject matter—any more than his right to assume, in the first person, the 'identity' of the leader of a slave rebellion in Virginia in 1831." Gray agreed. "The question," he wrote in *Time,* "is not whether Styron has a right to use alien experiences but whether his novel proves that he knows what he is writing about. In this instance, the overriding answer is yes."

It cannot be said of Styron's 1990 work *Darkness Visible: A Memoir of Madness* that the author was writing of "alien experiences," as he had first-hand knowledge of the book's focus. *Darkness Visible* is Styron's account of his slow fall into depression in 1985. Leading up to his experience was the loss of his mother when he was thirteen, his father's own battle with depression, and Styron's forty-year dependency on alcohol. According to an interview with Laurel Graeber in the *New York Times Book Review,* the catalyst for Styron's account of his depression was his defense of the writer Primo Levi, who committed suicide in 1987. "Styron found himself defending Levi . . . from statements that seemed to attribute his action to moral weakness," wrote Graeber. Following an essay he published on the subject, Styron spoke on it, wrote a longer article, and then produced *Darkness Visible.*

Styron was compelled, "in romantic confessional style, that he had to write it, and it is good to have it," stated Karl Miller in his review of *Darkness Visible* for the *London Review of Books.* Noting that the book contains "some tremendous writing," Victoria Glendinning added that "The rhythmic beat of some sentences demands that they be read aloud," in a review for the *New York Times Book Review.* Miller noted that "There are passages in the book which might have been written in the nineteenth century—some of them, give or take a word or two, by Poe. . . . Styron writes of the dungeons 'of his spirit,' of a 'long-beshrouded metaphysical truth'—language that belongs to the Gothic strain of certain of his fictions."

A Tidewater Morning: Three Tales from Youth was Styron's first work following his depression and recovery. The three stories are autobiographical in nature and are narrated by a man in his fifties. The title novella takes place in 1938, the year Styron's own mother died, and focuses on a thirteen-year-old boy who watches his mother die of cancer. In the story "Love Day" the narrator recalls his experience in the U.S. Marines as a young man of twenty. The third story tells of a ten-year-old's friendship with neighbors who are descended from a prominent Southern family but have fallen onto harder times. The story "Shadrach" portrays a ninety-year-old former slave who returns to the family's land to die. James L. W. West III in *Sewanee Review* compared the collection to Faulkner's *Go down, Moses* and Hemingway's *In Our Time,* due to the connectedness of the stories "in ways obvious and subtle: this arrangement gives them a cumulative weight and thematic resonance that they would not possess if read separately." According to West, "The strongest cords binding these stories together are thematic. Styron is working through familiar territory for him, contemplating the fearful mysteries of grief, remorse, memory, guilt, rebellion, warfare, and death. . . . At crucial points . . . [the narrator] lifts himself above his doubt or pain, and fashions an imaginative rendering of the moment. This, Styron seems to be telling us, is the only way finally to address some of the almost intolerable ambiguities and injustices of our time."

BIOGRAPHICAL AND CRITICAL SOURCES:

BOOKS

Bryer, Jackson R., and Mary B. Hatem, *William Styron: A Reference Guide,* G. K. Hall (Boston, MA), 1978.

Casciato, Arthur D., and James L. W. West III, editors, *Critical Essays on William Styron,* G. K. Hall (Boston, MA), 1982.

Cologne-Brookes, Gavin, *The Novels of William Styron: From Harmony to History,* Louisiana State University (Baton Rouge, LA), 1995.

Concise Dictionary of American Literary Biography: Broadening Views, 1968-1988, Gale (Detroit, MI), 1989.

Contemporary Literary Criticism, Gale (Detroit, MI), Volume 1, 1973, Volume 3, 1975, Volume 11, 1979, Volume 15, 1980, Volume 60, 1990.

Cowley, Malcolm, *Writers at Work: The "Paris Review" Interviews, First Series,* Viking (New York, NY), 1958.

Crane, John K., *The Root of All Evil: The Thematic Unity of William Styron's Fiction,* University of South Carolina Press (Columbia, SC), 1985.

Dictionary of Literary Biography, Volume 143: *American Novelists since World War II, Third Series,* Gale (Detroit, MI), 1994.

Dictionary of Literary Biography Yearbook: 1980, Gale (Detroit, MI), 1981.

Friedman, Melvin J., *William Styron,* Bowling Green University (Bowling Green, OH), 1974.

Geismar, Maxwell, *American Moderns,* Hill & Wang (New York, NY), 1958.

Hadaller, David, *Gynicide: Women in the Novels of William Styron,* Fairleigh Dickinson University Press (Madison, NJ), 1996.

Kostelanetz, Richard, editor, *On Contemporary Literature,* Avon (New York, NY), 1964.

Leon, Philip W., *William Styron: An Annotated Bibliography of Criticism,* Greenwood Press (Westport, CT), 1978.

Mackin, Cooper R., *William Styron,* Steck Vaughn (Austin, TX), 1969.

Malin, Irving, and Robert K. Morris, editors, *The Achievement of William Styron,* University of Georgia Press (Athens, GA), 1975, revised edition, 1981.

Pearce, Richard, *William Styron* ("Pamphlets on American Writers" series), University of Minnesota Press (Minneapolis, MN), 1971.

Ratner, Marc L., *William Styron,* Twayne (New York, NY), 1972.

Ross, Daniel William, *The Critical Response to William Styron,* Greenwood Press (Westport, CT), 1995.

Ruderman, Judith, *William Styron,* Ungar (New York, NY), 1989.

Short Story Criticism, Volume 25, Gale (Detroit, MI), 1997.

Waldmeir, Joseph J., editor, *Recent American Fiction,* Michigan State University Press (Lansing, MI), 1963.

West, James L. W., III, *William Styron: A Descriptive Bibliography,* G. K. Hall (Boston, MA), 1977.

West, James L. W., III, *William Styron: A Life,* Random House (New York, NY), 1998.

PERIODICALS

Chicago Tribune, July 3, 1989.

Chicago Tribune Book World, May 27, 1979; January 16, 1983.

College Literature, number 1, 1987, pp. 1-16.

Commonweal, December 22, 1967.

Critique, number 2, 1985, pp. 57-65.

Detroit News, June 24, 1979.

English Journal, April, 1996, p. 87.

Esquire, July 3, 1979; December 1, 1985.

Harper's, July, 1967.

Journal of the American Medical Association, March 6, 1991, pp. 1184-1185.

London Review of Books, March 21, 1991, p. 6.

Los Angeles Times, December 14, 1983.

Los Angeles Times Book Review, January 16, 1983.

Mississippi Quarterly, number 2, 1989, pp. 129-145.

Nation, October 16, 1967; April 22, 1968; July 7, 1979.

New Leader, December 4, 1967.

New Republic, June 30, 1979.

New Statesman, May 7, 1979; November 19, 1993, pp. 47-48.

New Statesman & Society, March 8, 1991, pp. 37-38.

Newsweek, October 16, 1967; May 28, 1979.

New Yorker, November 25, 1967; June 18, 1979.

New York Review of Books, October 26, 1967; September 12, 1968; July 19, 1979.

New York Times, August 5, 1967; October 3, 1967; May 29, 1979; November 27, 1982.

New York Times Book Review, October 8, 1967; August 11, 1968; May 27, 1979; June 6, 1982; November 21, 1982; December 12, 1982; August 19, 1990.

Observer Review, May 5, 1968.

Partisan Review, winter, 1968; summer, 1968.

Sewanee Review, spring, 1994.

Southern Literary Journal, fall, 2001, p. 56.

Southern Quarterly, winter, 2002, Edwin T. Arnold, "The William Styron-Donald Harington Letters," pp. 98-141.

Southern Review, autumn, 2001, Michael Mewshaw, "A Writer's Account," p. 790.
Spectator, October 13, 1979.
Time, October 13, 1967; June 11, 1979.
Times Literary Supplement, May 19, 1968; November 30, 1979; June 10, 1983; December 10, 1993, p. 19.
Twentieth Century Literature, fall, 2000, Abigail Cheever, "Prozac Americans: Depression, Identity, and Selfhood," p. 346; fall, 2001, Lis Carstens, "Sexual Politics and Confessional Testimony in *Sophie's Choice,*" p. 293.
Village Voice, December 14, 1967.
Voice of Youth Advocates, February, 1994, p. 374.
Washington Post, May 18, 1979; January 4, 1983.
Washington Post Book World, May 29, 1979; December 5, 1982.
Whole Earth Review, fall, 1995, p. 41.
Yale Review, winter, 1968.*

* * *

SULLIVAN, Otha Richard 1941-

PERSONAL: Born December 28, 1941, in Hattiesburg, MS; son of Benjamin Franklin (in business) and Iola Estella (a homemaker; maiden name, Booth) Sullivan. *Education:* University of Kansas, B.S., 1965; Wayne State University, M.S., 1969, Ed.D., 1973.

ADDRESSES: *Home*—2112 East Dr., Jackson, MS 39204. *Office*—Alcorn State University, 1000 Alcorn State University Dr., Alcorn State, MS 39096. *Agent*—Clausen, Mays & Tahan, 249 West 34th St., New York, NY 10001.

CAREER: Classroom teacher at public schools in Detroit, MI, 1965-69; high school counselor in Highland Park, MI, 1969-70; University of Detroit, Detroit, MI, administrator and director of special education for public schools of Highland Park, 1970-73; Howard University, Washington, DC, associate professor, 1977-79; ombudsman for public schools, Washington, DC, 1979-83; District of Columbia Department of Corrections, Washington, administrator, 1983-87; Highland Park Community College, Highland Park, MI, executive vice president, 1990-91; Alcorn State University, Lorman, MS, associate professor, 1987-90; Detroit Public Schools, counselor, 1990-2000; Alcorn State University, Alcorn State, MD, professor and director of ACHIEVE Mississippi, 2000—.

MEMBER: Council for Exceptional Children, Urban League, National Association for the Advancement of Colored People, Kappa Alpha Psi.

AWARDS, HONORS: Booker T. Washington Educator's Achievement Award, 1998.

WRITINGS:

African American Inventors and Discoverers, John Wiley (New York, NY), 1997.
African American Women Scientists and Inventors, John Wiley (New York, NY), 2001.
African American Millionaires and Inventors, John Wiley (New York, NY), in press.

Contributor to magazines and newspapers, including *Freedomways Journal, Black Collegian, Dollars and Sense, Journal of the International Association of Pupil Personnel Workers, Natchez Democrat,* and *About Time Journal.*

WORK IN PROGRESS: A book on affirmations; a book chronicling the life of a young man growing up in Mississippi, completion expected in 2004.

SIDELIGHTS: Otha Richard Sullivan once told *CA:* "My primary motivation for writing is to inform. As a teacher, I recognize that students are more involved in the educational process when they can look at individuals and their struggles and identify how these people were able to overcome adversities. Students are able to develop skills to overcome formidable challenges, and this helps them to approach and overcome other obstacles. Starting out as a teacher of social science, I immediately realized that many youths do not know their history. This lack of knowledge often leads to difficulties and wasted time before the young people come to an epiphany about how they will plan and direct their lives.

"My work is greatly influenced by my heroes, my mother and father, who taught me that education is the key that opens doors to opportunities. As a student in elementary school, I was influenced by my teachers, who introduced me to the brilliance and achievements of black Americans who were systematically missing from the pages of history, the textbooks we used, and the audiovisual materials. My favorite teacher, Mrs. M. W. Chambers, infused black history in her classes on a daily basis, and this served to motivate students to greater achievement. Consequently, I developed a mission to write books and articles on the achievements of black Americans.

"The seeds for *African American Inventors and Discoverers* were sown at a middle school in Detroit, where I taught science. One day I asked students to name two black inventors. Most of them were stumped, unable to name two. I realized then that I had a responsibility to teach them about the myriad contributions of black Americans. At the same time, I began to unearth research completed some years ago at the Howard University library. I made a vow that, at the end of the year, students would identify, discuss, share, and apply the ingredients of success of many black Americans.

* * *

SYRUC, J.
See MILOSZ, Czeslaw

T

TAPPLY, William G(eorge) 1940-

PERSONAL: Born July 16, 1940, in Waltham, MA; son of H. G. (an outdoor writer) and Muriel (a registered nurse; maiden name, Morgridge) Tapply; married Alice Sandra Knight, 1962 (divorced, 1966); married Cynthia Ehrgott (a secretary), March 7, 1970 (divorced, 1995); married Vicki Stiefel; children: Michael, Melissa, Sarah, Blake, Ben. *Ethnicity:* "Caucasian." *Education:* Amherst College, B.A., 1962; Harvard University, M.A.T., 1963; Tufts University, postgraduate study, 1966-68.

ADDRESSES: *Home*—75 Antrim Road, Hancock, NH 03449. *Agent*—Fred Morris, The Jed Mattes Agency, 2095 Broadway #302, New York, NY 10023.

CAREER: Lexington High School, Lexington, MA, history teacher, 1963-66; Tufts University, Medford, MA, director of economic studies, 1968-69; Lexington High School, housemaster and teacher, 1972-90. Writer's Digest School, editorial associate, 1992—. Clark University and Emerson College, writing instructor, 1995—.

MEMBER: Mystery Writers of America, Authors Guild, Private Eye Writers of America.

AWARDS, HONORS: Scribner Crime Novel award, 1984, for *Death at Charity's Point.*

WRITINGS:

"BRADY COYNE" MYSTERY SERIES

Death at Charity's Point, Scribner (New York, NY), 1984.
The Dutch Blue Error, Scribner (New York, NY), 1985.
Follow the Sharks, Scribner (New York, NY), 1985.
The Marine Corpse, Scribner (New York, NY), 1986.
Dead Meat, Scribner (New York, NY), 1987.
The Vulgar Boatman, Scribner (New York, NY), 1987.
A Void in Hearts, Scribner (New York, NY), 1988.
Dead Winter, Delacorte (New York, NY), 1989.
Client Privilege, Delacorte (New York, NY), 1989.
The Spotted Cats, Delacorte (New York, NY), 1991.
Tight Lines, Delacorte (New York, NY), 1992.
The Snake Eater, Otto Penzler (New York, NY), 1993.
The Seventh Enemy, Otto Penzler (New York, NY), 1995.
Close to the Bone, St. Martin's Press (New York, NY), 1996.
Cutter's Run, St. Martin's Press (New York, NY), 1998.
Muscle Memory, St. Martin's Press (New York, NY), 1999.
Scar Tissue, St. Martin's Press (New York, NY), 2000.
A Brady Coyne Omnibus, St. Martin's Press (New York, NY), 2000.
Past Tense, St. Martin's Press (New York, NY), 2001.
(With Philip R. Craig) *First Light,* St. Martin's Press (New York, NY), 2001.
A Fine Line, St. Martin's Press (New York, NY), 2002.
Shadow of Death, St. Martin's Press (New York, NY), 2003.

NONFICTION

Those Hours Spent Outdoors, Scribner (New York, NY), 1988.

Opening Day and Other Neuroses, Lyons & Burford (New York, NY), 1990.

Home Water Near and Far, Lyons & Burford (New York, NY), 1992.

Sportsman's Legacy, Lyons & Burford (New York, NY), 1993.

The Elements of Mystery Fiction, Writer, Inc. (Boston, MA), 1995.

A Fly-Fishing Life, Lyons & Burford (New York, NY), 1997.

Bass Bug Fishing, Lyons Press (New York, NY), 1999.

Upland Days, Lyons Press (New York, NY), 2000.

Pocket Water: Favorite Streams, Favorite Fish, Lyons Press (New York, NY), 2001.

The Orvis Pocket Guide to Fly Fishing for Bass, Lyons Press (Guilford, CT), 2002.

OTHER

(With Linda Barlow) *Thicker Than Water* (suspense novel), Signet (New York, NY), 1995.

Contributor of numerous articles and stories to periodicals, including *Sports Illustrated, Better Homes and Gardens, Organic Gardening, Scholastic Coach, Drummer, Writer, Fins and Feathers, Worcester,* and *Outdoor Life.* Contributing editor, *Field and Stream.* Special correspondent, *American Angler.* Contributing editor, *Upland Journal.*

WORK IN PROGRESS: "My yearly Brady Coyne novel, another collaboration with Philip R. Craig called *Second Sight,* a fishing book called *Gone Fishin',* a second edition of my writing book, *The Elements of Mystery Fiction.*"

SIDELIGHTS: William G. Tapply is the author of a number of mystery novels featuring Brady Coyne, a Boston attorney serving a wealthy clientele. In an essay for the *St. James Guide to Crime and Mystery Writers,* Jim Huang called Coyne "a skillful blend of amateur versus professional, serious versus frivolous, and intellectual versus physical." Coyne selects interesting clients to make his otherwise boring legal practice bearable. He also sees his career as a means to finance his avocation, fishing, which is Tapply's own great love and the subject of several of the author's nonfiction works. A critic for *Publishers Weekly* wrote that "Tapply consistently delivers well-written, well-constructed and thoroughly entertaining mysteries."

Over the course of the series, Coyne has dealt with a variety of cases. A murder takes place on what is believed to be sacred Indian land in *Dead Meat,* an author dies under mysterious circumstances in *The Marine Corpse,* and a Vietnam veteran's memoirs cause trouble for many people in *The Snake Eater.* The controversy over gun control is a key plot element in *The Seventh Enemy.* The "Brady Coyne" series has won Tapply plaudits for his narrative skills. Lauding Tapply for writing "quietly and perceptively" in *Death at Charity's Point,* the story of Coyne's investigation of an apparent suicide, London *Times* contributor Marcel Berlins assessed the book as a "superior" thriller. Marilyn Stasio, critiquing *The Seventh Enemy* for the *New York Times Book Review,* called Tapply "a smooth stylist"; in a piece on *The Snake Eater* for the same publication, she noted, "there's never a break in that practiced, flowing style he has mastered over a dozen books." Huang asserted that "Tapply is among the smoothest storytellers around—his books glide along quickly and effortlessly—but the plots tend towards the straightforward and they're not necessarily fair. He will introduce new elements in the closing chapters in order to facilitate a resolution. . . . But only rarely do Tapply's stories really disappoint."

While lauding the author's portrayal of Coyne's eccentric clients, Huang complained, "If Tapply has a significant flaw, it's in Brady Coyne's peculiar reticence about his own life and feelings. . . . The adventures leave no mark on Coyne." For instance, Huang observed, Coyne remains unperturbed after being nearly blown to bits in *Dead Meat,* and he is largely unaffected by pleas to help the homeless in *The Marine Corpse.* Stasio found *The Snake Eater* an exception to Coyne's usual stoicism. "Tapply wrings some rare passion from Brady Coyne," she remarked, adding "this time his theme of friendship has jagged edges of anger and pain that cut through Coyne's reserve and draw blood." Huang granted that the character's customary restraint has its uses in the series: "Brady Coyne's wry, good-humored narration reminds us not to take it all too seriously." Tapply explained to Peter Cannon in *Publishers Weekly* that "Brady is a Yankee, and I suppose we Yankees tend to be reticent about our feelings. Books I read where the first-person narrators are terribly forthcoming about their feelings don't ring true to me. My writing philosophy is show don't tell."

In *First Light,* Tapply teamed up his character Coyne with mystery writer Philip R. Craig's character J. W.

Jackson. Jackson is an ex-cop who lives in Martha's Vineyard with his wife and two small children. In alternating chapters told from the viewpoints of their respective characters, Tapply and Craig tell a story involving two missing women, clashes between real estate developers and environmentalists, and unexpected violence. A reviewer for *Publishers Weekly* called *First Light* an "ultimately satisfying crime drama" offering "an intriguing and evocative picture of this high-profile vacation spot." A *Kirkus Reviews* critic concluded that "lively banter and a narrative brimming with mischief make this maiden voyage entertaining from start to stop." Rex Klett of *Library Journal* described *First Light* as "a most captivating read."

Tapply once told *CA* that he is reluctant to call his books mystery novels. "I write novels that, like most worthwhile novels, contain mysteries," he said. "I try to avoid formulas, although I suppose with a series character like my attorney Brady Coyne I have conceded that much. I place great emphasis in my writing on characterization, motivation, suspense, and humor—all of which seem to me important in all fiction. I try to tell stories rather than truths, but I think my stories convey some small truths now and then. I have been asked on occasion when I intend to write a 'real novel.' I reply, of course, that I already have."

More recently, Tapply told *CA:* "My father wrote a monthly column for *Field & Stream* for thirty-five years. I watched him work, absorbed his perfectionism, understood how hard writing was. This postponed my itch to write until I was in my thirties. When I began writing, I was fully prepared for the difficulty and frustrations. This, more than any writing lesson, has enabled me to stick to it.

"I've learned some things about the business of writing. We have to be businessmen as well as artists. I never anticipated any of that."

When asked which book was his favorite, Tapply answered, "My current book is always my favorite, because it's the only one I really think about. Still, I am fond of *Sportsman's Legacy,* which I wrote more than ten years ago. It's about my relationship with my father, and was the hardest piece of writing I ever had to do." When asked what effect he hoped his books would have, Tapply said, "I hope they will keep people up all night turning the pages."

BIOGRAPHICAL AND CRITICAL SOURCES:

BOOKS

St. James Guide to Crime and Mystery Writers, 4th edition, St. James Press (Detroit, MI), 1996.

PERIODICALS

Booklist, September 15, 1996, Bill Ott, review of *Close to the Bone,* p. 225; August, 1997, John Rowen, review of *A Fly-Fishing Life,* p. 1868; June 1, 1998, Wes Lukowsky, review of *Cutter's Run,* p. 1735; August, 1999, Wes Lukowsky, review of *Muscle Memory,* p. 2036; August, 2000, Bill Ott, review of *Scar Tissue,* p. 2123; September 1, 2001, Bill Ott, review of *Past Tense,* p. 57; November 15, 2001, John Rowen, review of *Pocket Water: Favorite Streams, Favorite Fish,* p. 540; December 1, 2001, GraceAnne A. DeCandido, review of *First Light,* p. 632; October 15, 2002, Frank Sennett, review of *A Fine Line,* p. 393.

Chicago Tribune, September 25, 1988.

Kirkus Reviews, August 15, 2001, review of *Past Tense,* p. 1174; November 1, 2001, review of *First Light,* p. 1517; October 1, 2002, review of *A Fine Line,* p. 1432.

Library Journal, February 1, 1998, M. Anna Falbo, review of *Close to the Bone,* p. 130; July, 1999, Rex Klett, review of *Muscle Memory,* p. 141; September 1, 2001, Rex Klett, review of *Past Tense,* p. 239; January, 2002, Rex Klett, review of *First Light,* p. 158.

New York Times Book Review, April 18, 1984; December 8, 1985; December 26, 1993; January 22, 1995; November 5, 2000, Marilyn Stasio, review of *Scar Tissue,* p. 32.

Publishers Weekly, October 4, 1993, p. 66; August 19, 1996, p. 55; July 7, 1997, review of *A Fly-Fishing Life,* p. 58; June 28, 1999, review of *Muscle Memory,* p. 57; September 11, 2000, Peter Cannon, "PW Talks to William G. Tapply," p. 72, and review of *Scar Tissue,* p. 72; December 10, 2001, review of *First Light,* p. 54; October 28, 2002, review of *A Fine Line,* p. 55.

Times (London, England), January 31, 1985.

ONLINE

William G. Tapply Home Page, http://www.williamgtapply.com/ (December 18, 2002).

TEMPLE, William F(rederick) 1914-1989

PERSONAL: Born March 9, 1914, in Woolwich, London, England; died, July 15, 1989; son of William and Doris Temple; married Joan Streeton, September 16, 1939; children: Anne, Peter. *Education:* Gordon School, London, 1919-1927; Woolwich Polytechnic, London, 1928-30.

CAREER: Writer. London Stock Exchange, London, England, head clerk, 1930-50; worked for a bookseller in Folkestone, England. *Military service:* Served in the Royal Artillery, 1940-46.

MEMBER: Science Fiction Writers of America.

WRITINGS:

FICTION

Four-Sided Triangle: A Novel, Long (London, England), 1949, Fell (New York, NY), 1951.
The Dangerous Edge, Long (London, England), 1951.
Martin Magnus, Planet Rover (juvenile), Muller (London, England), 1955.
Martin Magnus on Venus (juvenile), Muller (London, England), 1955.
Martin Magnus on Mars (juvenile), Muller (London, England), 1956.
The Automated Goliath [and] *The Three Suns of Amara,* Ace (New York, NY), 1962.
Battle on Venus, Ace (New York, NY), 1963.
Shoot at the Moon, Simon & Schuster (New York, NY), 1966.
The Fleshpots of Sansato, Macdonald (London, England), 1968.

NONFICTION

The True Book about Space-Travel, Muller (London, England), 1954, published as *The Prentice-Hall Book about Space Travel,* Prentice-Hall (New York, NY), 1955.

Contributor to books, including *Thrills,* edited anonymously by Charles Birkin, Philip Allan (London, England), 1935; *Dan Dare's Space Book,* Hulton (London, England), 1952; *The Girl Book of Modern Adventurers,* Hulton (London, England), 1952; *The Authentic Book of Space,* edited by H. J. Campbell, Hamilton (London, England), 1954; *The World-Wide Book for Boys,* Beaver (London, England), 1957; *Gay Stories for Girls,* Beaver (London, England), 1957; *New Writings in SF 7,* edited by John Carnell, Dodson, 1966; *The Double Bill Symposium: Being 94 Replies to "A Questionnaire for Professional Science Fiction Writers and Editors,"* edited by Bill Bowers and Bill Mallardi, D:B Press (Akron, OH), 1969; *Androids, Time Machines, and Blue Giraffes: A Panorama of Science Fiction,* edited by Roger Elwood and Vic Ghidalia, Follett (Chicago, IL), 1973. Contributor of short stories to *Amazing Stories, Tales of Wonder, New Worlds, Super Science Stories, Thrilling Wonder Stories, Authentic Science Fiction Monthly, Reveille, Weird Tales, Other Worlds Science Stories, Science Fantasy, Fantastic Adventures, Startling Stories, Nebula Science Fiction, Fantastic Universe, Boy's Own Paper, Imagination, Heiress, Analog, Famous Science Fiction, Worlds of If, Vision of Tomorrow, Story and Stanza,* and *Interzone.* Editor, *British Interplanetary Society Bulletin.*

ADAPTATIONS: Four-Sided Triangle was adapted for film.

SIDELIGHTS: William F. Temple learned his craft amidst the science fiction boom of pre- and post-World War II England. Inspired by his companionship with writers such as Arthur C. Clarke, John Wyndham, and John Christopher, Temple persevered through an African stint with England's army during World War II to release *Four-Sided Triangle,* a novel toying with love and cloning and the extraordinary dynamics that occur when the two are mixed. Darren Harris-Fain in the *Dictionary of Literary Biography* noted: "Like most popular fiction of the period, *Four-Sided Triangle* was largely ignored in the mainstream press, although it was avidly discussed among science-fiction fans. In the field the story has become a minor classic—especially in its expanded novel form, which most critics agree is superior to the original magazine story."

Temple published nine science fiction books, including the "Martin Magnus" series of books for children. Still, his works never achieved a higher point of acclaim than with his debut novel. His distinctly British prose received an indifferent reception by American critics. As Robert H. Wilcox noted in the *St. James Guide to Science Fiction,* "Some readers . . . find Temple's work a bit stuffy at times."

Temple's imagination is especially on display in his many published short stories. Harris-Fain noted several examples, including "Conditioned Reflex," in which "a Martian robot that escapes to Earth tries to convince the humans it meets that human beings are also robots, the products of Martian exploration of Earth thousands of years ago. The people do not believe it, but when the Martian robot leaves behind a device that works in controlling other humans, the truth of the robot's claims is realized. Yet another example is 'The Lonely,' published in the July, 1955, issue of *Imagination.* The entire thrust of this story rests on its idea—namely, following a major catastrophe the last woman in London finds the last man in London, only to discover that he is homosexual." Harris-Fain also explained that in many of his stories, "Temple sympathizes with the alien or the outsider and critiques the tendency to judge others by one's own limited cultural standards."

Temple himself gave up science-fiction writing after 1968's *The Fleshpots of Sansato.* As he noted in an interview with the *St. James Guide to Science Fiction Writers:* "I've read [science fiction] since childhood. At first, uncritically: I didn't notice it was only two-dimensional, i.e., lacked depth, especially in characterization. Then critically: I decided to try to add that third dimension in my writing. Then despairingly: Nobody noticed that I had. Then cynically: Nobody wanted it anyway. They preferred their robots. Then uncaringly: I don't bother to write it any more."

"The work and career of William F. Temple," concluded Harris-Fain, "are representative of many science-fiction writers who attempt to earn their livings as professional writers: competent if not brilliant, imaginative if not always innovative, with a firmer grounding in scientific fact than literary fiction. Like many such writers, he never gained much of a reputation beyond the science-fiction community; this limited exposure may also be a result of Temple's distaste for self-promotion. Also, like several magazine writers in science fiction of the 1940s and 1950s, Temple did not change with the times, and in the 1960s and beyond, readers came to view his work as dated. Nor is it likely that he will ever be read by many uninterested in science fiction. However, one cannot fully understand the development of modern science fiction without understanding writers such as Temple, and a good part of his legacy lies in the role he played in the subgenre at an important stage of its development."

BIOGRAPHICAL AND CRITICAL SOURCES:

BOOKS

Ashley, Mike, *The Work of William F. Temple: An Annotated Bibliography and Guide,* Borgo Press (San Bernardino, CA), 1994.

Dictionary of Literary Biography, Volume 255: *British Fantasy and Science-Fiction Writers, 1918-1960,* Gale (Detroit, MI), 2002.

St. James Guide to Science Fiction Writers, St. James Press (Detroit, MI), 1996.

PERIODICALS

Foundation, summer, 1992, Mike Ashley, "Tell Them I Meant Well: A Tribute to William F. Temple," pp. 5-24.

Lan's Lantern, January, 1989, Larry Nowinski, "The Female Characters of William F. Temple: A Limited Study," pp. 30-32, and Timothy Nowinski, "Old Ideas with a Twist," pp. 53-55.

Magazine of Fantasy and Science Fiction, February, 1967, p. 28.

Punch, January 1, 1969, p. 35.

Times Literary Supplement, November 28, 1968, p. 1346.*

* * *

THOMPSON, Colin (Edward) 1942-

PERSONAL: Original name Colin Willment; name legally changed; born October 18, 1942, in Ealing, London, England; married second wife, Anne, April 9, 1999; children: (first marriage) Charlotte; (second marriage) Hannah, Alice. *Education:* Attended art school in London, England. *Hobbies and other interests:* Rock-and-roll music, blues music.

ADDRESSES: *Home*—Bellingen, Australia. *Agent*—c/o Author Mail, Hodder Headline Australia, Level 22, 201 Kent St., Sydney, New South Wales 2000 Australia. *E-mail*—colin@colinthompson.com.

CAREER: Writer and illustrator of children's books, 1990—. Worked as a silkscreen printer, graphic designer, stage manager, documentary filmmaker for British Broadcasting Corp., and ceramist.

AWARDS, HONORS: Primary English Best Picture Book Award, 1994, for *Ruby.*

WRITINGS:

SELF-ILLUSTRATED CHILDREN'S BOOKS

Ethel the Chicken, Hodder & Stoughton (London, England), 1991.

A Giant Called Norman Mary, Hodder & Stoughton (London, England), 1991.

The Paper Bag Prince, Knopf (New York, NY), 1992, published as *The Paperbag Prince,* MacRae (London, England), 1992.

Pictures of Home, MacRae (London, England), 1992, Green Tiger Press, 1993.

Looking for Atlantis, MacRae (London, England), 1993, Knopf (New York, NY), 1994.

Sid the Mosquito and Other Wild Stories, Knight (London, England), 1993.

Ruby, Knopf (New York, NY), 1994.

Attila the Bluebottle and More Wild Stories, Hodder (London, England), 1995.

How to Live Forever, MacRae (London, England), 1995, Knopf (New York, NY), 1996.

Venus the Caterpillar and Further Wild Stories, Hodder (London, England), 1996.

The Haunted Suitcase and Other Stories, Hodder Headline (Sydney, New South Wales, Australia), 1996.

The Tower to the Sun, MacRae (London, England), 1996, Knopf (New York, NY), 1997.

Castle Twilight and Other Stories, Hodder Headline (Sydney, New South Wales, Australia), 1997.

The Paradise Garden, Random House (New York, NY), 1998.

The Puzzle Duck, Random House (Sydney, New South Wales, Australia), 1999.

The Last Alchemist, Knopf (New York, NY), 1999.

Future Eden: A Brief History of Next Time, Simon & Schuster (New York, NY), 2000.

No Place Like Home, Hodder Headline (Sydney, New South Wales, Australia), 2001.

Falling Angels, Hutchinson (London, England), 2001.

One Big Happy Family, Hodder Headline (Sydney, New South Wales, Australia), 2002.

Round and Round and Round and Round, Hodder Headline (Sydney, New South Wales, Australia), 2002.

Pepper Dreams, Hodder Headline (Sydney, New South Wales, Australia), 2003.

The Violin Man, Hodder Headline (Sydney, New South Wales, Australia), 2003.

OTHER CHILDREN'S BOOKS

Sailing Home, illustrated by Matt Ottley, Hodder Headline (Sydney, New South Wales, Australia), 1996.

The Last Circus, illustrated by Kim Gamble, Hodder Headline (Sydney, New South Wales, Australia), 1997.

The Staircase Cat, illustrated by Anna Pignataro, Hodder Headline (Sydney, New South Wales, Australia), 1998.

The Dog's Just Been Sick in the Honda, illustrated by Peter Viska, Hodder Headline (Sydney, New South Wales, Australia), 1999.

My Brother Drinks Out of the Toilet, illustrated by Peter Viska, Hodder Headline (Sydney, New South Wales, Australia), 2000.

Unknown, illustrated by Anna Pignataro, Walker (New York, NY), 2000.

Laughing for Beginners, Hodder Headline (Sydney, New South Wales, Australia), 2002.

There's Something Really Nasty on the Bottom of My Shoe, illustrated by Peter Viska, Hodder Headline (Sydney, New South Wales, Australia), 2003.

SIDELIGHTS: Author and illustrator Colin Thompson is lauded as a particularly imaginative artist as well as a committed supporter of the environment. He is recognized for providing young readers with demanding, yet satisfying, books that are considered both thought-provoking and entertaining. As an illustrator, Thompson creates colorful, intricate pictures filled with both realistic and surrealistic images as well as visual jokes and intertextual references; his work has been compared to such artists as Graeme Base and M. C. Escher. According to Shelle Rosenfeld in *Booklist,* speaking of Thompson's drawings for *The Last Alchemist,* "each page is a treasure chest bursting with color, minute detail, wit, and surprise."

The author came relatively late to writing literature for young children and did not begin publishing his detailed and inventive picture books and fantasies until the early 1990s. Born in Ealing, England, in 1942, his early schooling in both Yorkshire and West London led to two years of art instruction in his hometown of Ealing and in Hammersmith. Employed for a period of time as a silkscreen painter and graphic designer, he later studied film and worked for the BBC creating documentaries. In the late 1960s Thompson moved to Scotland's Outer Hebrides Islands and in 1975 to Cumbria. During this time, he began specializing in ceramics while living in a remote farmhouse, and spent a good deal of his avocational time planting trees—an activity indicating his lifetime concern for the environment—raising his family, and caring for his numerous adopted pets. Thompson moved to Australia in 1995 and married his second wife, Anne, in 1999. The couple now live in the town of Bellingen, about eight hours north of Sydney.

Thompson's first children's book, the easy reader *Ethel the Chicken,* appeared in 1990. Its heroine, Ethel, lives in a box labeled First Class Oranges, and has been all but forgotten since the death of the old woman who used to feed her. A rat named Neville happens upon Ethel, and the two meet regularly until Neville's family moves away. Briefly overcome with loneliness, Thompson's talking chicken finds happiness and companionship once again when a human family moves into the old woman's house. Written with care and childlike simplicity, *Ethel the Chicken* is designed to teach young children how to read, to appeal to their sense of humor, and to address their particular anxieties about friendship, love, and loneliness. *Growing Point* reviewer Margery Fisher lauded the work, noting, "When words and illustrations consort perfectly together, expressing both the warmth of humor and the tinge of wit, the result is a masterpiece and I think *Ethel the Chicken* is a masterpiece."

Thompson published his second picture book, *The Paper Bag Prince,* in 1992. This tale, set in a town dump, expresses a simple yet strongly pro-environmental message. Its protagonist, an old man whose name has long since been forgotten, is now simply called the "Paper Bag Prince." He lives on the site, inhabiting a derelict railroad car and surviving off the town's refuse and junk. The arrival of Sarah from the city council, and her announcement that the dump is to be shut down proves a welcome harbinger to the prince; the land—once the possession of the old man—will again be his and nature can now begin to reclaim the soil so long abused by humans. A *Kirkus Reviews* contributor enthused, "In Thompson's lovely, intricate art . . . signs of life and renewal creep in everywhere. . . . More than just another ecological fantasy, this dump is a compelling symbol of the earth itself; it's to be hoped that, like the old man, humanity will be here to welcome nature back if the pollution ever abates." Writing in *School Library Journal,* Lori A. Janick commented that *The Paper Bag Prince* "effectively portrays the tenacity of nature as well as the resilience of the human spirit," while *Books for Keeps* critic Trevor Dickinson called the book one "which deserves to be widely popular through and beyond the school years."

Published in 1992, *Pictures of Home* represents something of a departure for Thompson. The work consists of many detailed illustrations of houses—which he originally produced for the Leeds Permanent Building Society—accompanying several short, poetic texts provided by British schoolchildren. These words describe each child's individual interpretation of home; for example, "Home is my parents. / You should have love in all homes. / Love is my parents." Although critics generally approved of Thompson's almost surreal paintings, many found the book to be uncohesive overall, noting that a true connection between text and illustration was lacking. However, a critic in *Kirkus Reviews* called *Pictures of Home* a "fascinating book, to pore over and share."

In his next picture book, *Looking for Atlantis,* Thompson returned to the precise joining of text and pictures that was so successful in his earlier works. A man looks back to his childhood and the return of his grandfather from an ocean voyage. Upon his arrival, the old man tells the boy of a sea chest that contains the secret of a path to Atlantis. The rest of the story is a celebration of the joys of observation, accompanied by Thompson's detailed and engrossing drawings. Reviewing *Looking for Atlantis* for *School Library Journal,* Barbara Peklo Abrahams wrote that Thompson's "watercolor masterpieces . . . contain myriad images that are striking, mysterious, dreamlike, witty, and eternal, and the simple, spare prose holds transcendental truth." *Booklist*'s Mary Harris Veeder concluded that "Kids of the *Where's Waldo?* generation will . . . want to pore over the combination of fine, realistic detailing and fantastical images inch by inch."

The picture book mystery *Ruby* recounts two interconnected stories involving a red 1934 Austin Seven automobile called Ruby. One tale evokes Ruby's travels around the world to exotic locations such as China's Great Wall and England's Stonehenge, while the other presents a tiny family lured from the safety of their tree-home by the arrival of the shiny red car. The miniature family members find themselves trapped in the vehicle, while their son Kevin is doubly so, having locked himself inside a briefcase. As Kevin's family attempts to find the combination to the case in order to free the boy, Thompson invites his readers to do the same, informing them that Ruby's license plate number and the combination are one and the same. Only by actively exploring the book's illustrations can the mystery be solved, a challenge made by Thompson at the beginning of the book, which includes a contest to win the real Ruby. A *Publishers Weekly* critic commented, "Once again Thompson breaks barriers of narrative space and time with an ornately crafted, multilevel picture book," and a writer for *Kirkus Reviews* called *Ruby* "two wonderful picture books in one." This work was honored with the Primary English Best Picture Book Award in 1994.

Thompson displays his cleverness and artistic virtuosity once again in *How to Live Forever.* The story's hero, Peter, finds himself in a vast library of a thousand rooms purported to contain every book ever written. Peter learns that one book, alluringly titled "How to Live Forever," is missing. Eventually he happens upon the Ancient Child, a creature suspended in time, apparently because he has read the elusive book, and Peter wisely decides to give up his search. A *Junior Bookshelf* commentator praised the control of "Thompson's brief sentences and still more precise and exquisite drawings." Meanwhile, a *Publishers Weekly* critic warned that "many of the visual puns are too sophisticated for younger readers but will delight adults," adding that *How to Live Forever* is "a multilayered book that excites interest on several levels."

Set in the not-too-distant future, *The Tower to the Sun* presents a planet cloaked in a yellow fog of pollutants that permanently obscure the sun. The story opens as the world's wealthiest man promises his grandson that he will one day show him a blue sky and the shining sun, saying, "What use is all my money if I can't build dreams?" The man institutes an ambitious plan to construct a magnificent tower to achieve his goal, incorporating into his edifice such famous structures as the Guggenheim museum, the Taj Mahal, the Chrysler Building, and the Leaning Tower of Pisa. A *Publishers Weekly* critic mused, "With its rich visual tapestry, a subtle message about what constitutes real wealth and an upbeat ending, this one's a crowd-pleaser," while a *Reading Time* commentator called *The Tower to the Sun* an "extraordinary fantasy" and concluded that it "challenges readers' moral insights and at the same time leaves those readers aesthetically satisfied."

In *The Paradise Garden* a young boy leaves his troubled home to spend the summer in a lush garden in the middle of the city. There he finds true peace and, when he decides to return home, he takes with him the seeds to start his own garden. A *Publishers Weekly* reviewer found that "Thompson's quiet text sets a reflective mood. . . . In the jam-packed artwork, however, color and fantasy collide and multiply. Wherever the eye rests there is something to entertain, to tease and to perplex."

Thompson's *The Last Alchemist* tells of an alchemist hired by a king to make gold, a difficult task and with an impossible deadline. His many desperate efforts ultimately lead both the alchemist and the king to realize that there are more important things in life than gold. "The instructive tale takes place within a fantastical visual framework," according to a critic for *Publishers Weekly,* who noted that the book "seethes with the kind of curious detail and odd visual juxtapositions that have become [Thompson's] trademark." Rosenfeld described *The Last Alchemist* as "an enlightening allegory on material wealth versus the joy of emotional riches."

Future Eden: A Brief History of Next Time is a full-length novel in which Thompson tells a far-future story set on an Earth with few people left. Jay and his pet chicken Ethel, from previous Thompson books, gather a few others together for a strange quest to discover just why things have gone so wrong and how they might be able to improve the situation. John Peters in *School Library Journal* called the book a "wickedly barbed low fantasy." Peters concluded that "following the characters as they stumble into one near-catastrophe after another, Douglas Adams fans will feel right at home."

In a comment posted on his Web site, Thompson explained: "I have always believed in the magic of childhood and think that if you get your life right that magic should never end. I feel that if a children's book cannot be enjoyed properly by adults there is something wrong with either the book or the adult reading it."

BIOGRAPHICAL AND CRITICAL SOURCES:

PERIODICALS

Booklist, December 1, 1992, p. 678; April 1, 1994, Mary Harris Veeder, review of *Looking for Atlantis,* p. 1441; July, 1999, Shelle Rosenfeld, review of *The Last Alchemist,* p. 1947; May 1, 2000, John Peters, review of *Unknown,* p. 1680.

Books for Keeps, May, 1992, Trevor Dickinson, review of *The Paper Bag Prince,* p. 28.

Growing Point, July, 1991, Margery Fisher, review of *Ethel the Chicken,* pp. 5537-5538.

Junior Bookshelf, April, 1996, review of *How to Live Forever,* p. 63.

Kirkus Reviews, July 15, 1992, review of *The Paper Bag Prince,* p. 926; April 1, 1993, p. 465; November 11, 1994, p. 1544; March 15, 1997, p. 469.

New York Times Book Review, October 23, 1994, p. 30; May 14, 2000, Adam Liptak, review of *Unknown,* p. 29.

Publishers Weekly, August 31, 1992, p. 79; April 19, 1993, p. 59; April 4, 1994, p. 77; October 24, 1994, p. 60; May 13, 1996, p. 74; March 10, 1997, review of *The Tower to the Sun,* p. 65; March 16, 1998, review of *The Paradise Garden,* p. 64; June 14, 1999, review of *The Last Alchemist,* p. 70; December 17, 2001, review of *Falling Angels,* p. 94.

Reading Time, February 17, 1997, review of *The Tower to the Sun,* p. 15.

School Librarian, February, 1997, p. 34.

School Library Journal, February, 1993, p. 80; July, 1993, p. 82; May, 1994, p. 118; December, 1994, Barbara Peklo Abrahams, review of *Looking for Atlantis,* p. 87; July, 1996, p. 74; May, 1998, Heide Piehler, review of *The Paradise Garden,* p. 127; September, 1999, Kate McClelland, review of *The Last Alchemist,* p. 207; July, 2000, Holly Belli, review of *Unknown,* p. 88; November, 2000, John Peters, review of *Future Eden: A Brief History of Next Time,* p. 162.

Wilson Library Bulletin, November, 1992, p. 75.

ONLINE

Colin Thompson's Home Page, http://www.colinthompson.com/ (December 11, 2002).*

TROUPE, Quincy (Thomas, Jr.) 1943-

PERSONAL: Born July 23, 1943, in St. Louis, MO; son of Quincy, Sr. (a baseball player), and Dorothy (Marshall Smith) Troupe; married Margaret Porter; children: Antoinette, Tymme, Quincy, Porter. *Education:* Attended Grambling College, 1959-60.

ADDRESSES: Home—La Jolla, CA. *Agent*—Marie Brown, 412 West 154th St., No. 2, New York, NY 10032.

CAREER: Watts Writers' Movement, Los Angeles, CA, creative writing teacher, 1966-68; *Shrewd* (magazine), Los Angeles, associate editor, beginning 1968; University of California, Los Angeles, instructor in creative writing and black literature, 1968; Ohio University, Athens, instructor in creative writing and Third World literature, 1969-71; Richmond College, Staten Island, NY, instructor in third world literature, associate professor of American and third world literatures and director of poetry center, 1971-90; Columbia University, New York, NY, member of faculty of Graduate Writing Program, beginning 1985; instructor at institutions, including University of California at Berkeley, California State University at Sacramento, and University of Ghana at Legon; University of California at San Diego, instructor in creative writing and American, African American, and Caribbean literature, 1991-2002. Director of Malcolm X Center and John Coltrane summer festivals in Los Angeles, summers, 1969 and 1970. Has given poetry readings at various institutions, including Harvard University, New York University, Howard University, Yale University, Princeton University, Louisiana State University, Dartmouth College, Oberlin College, Ohio State University, University of Michigan, and Michigan State University. Presenter of lecture and readings series "Life Forces: A Festival of Black Roots" at the Church of St. John the Divine in New York City. *Code* magazine, editorial director, beginning 2000. *Military service:* Served in U. S. Army, 1961, stationed in France.

MEMBER: Poetry Society of America.

AWARDS, HONORS: International Institute of Education grant for travel in Africa, 1972; National Endowment for the Arts Award in poetry, 1978; grant from

Quincy Troupe

New York State Council of the Arts, 1979; American Book Awards, Association of American Publishers, 1980, for *Snake-back Solos,* and 1990, for *Miles: The Autobiography;* New York Foundation for the Arts fellowship in poetry, 1987; Peabody Award, 1991, for *The Miles Davis Radio Project;* two-time winner, World Heavyweight Championship Poetry Bout, Taos Poetry Circus; named poet laureate of California, 2002 (resigned).

WRITINGS:

(Editor) *Watts Poets: A Book of New Poetry and Essays,* House of Respect, 1968.

Embryo Poems, 1967-1971 (includes "South African Bloodstone—For Hugh Masekela," "Chicago—For Howlin Wolf," "Profilin, A Rap/Poem—For Leon Damas," "The Scag Ballet," "Midtown Traffic," "Woke Up Crying the Blues," "The Earthquake of Peru; 1970; In 49 Seconds—For Cesar Vallejo, Great Peruvian Poet," "In the Manner of Rabearivello," "Poem from the Third Eye—For Eugene Redmond," and "Black Star, Black Woman"), Barlenmir (New York, NY), 1972, 2nd edition, 1974.

(Editor, with Rainer Schulte) *Giant Talk: An Anthology of Third World Writings,* Random House (New York, NY), 1975.

(Author of foreword) Arnold Adoff, editor, *Celebrations: A New Anthology of Black American Poetry,* Follet (Chicago, IL), 1977.

(With David L. Wolper) *The Inside Story of TV's "Roots,"* Warner Books (New York, NY), 1978.

Snake-back Solos: Selected Poems, 1969-1977 (includes "Springtime Ritual," "The Day Duke Raised," "La Marqueta," "For Miles Davis," "Up Sun South of Alaska," "Today's Subway Ride," "New York Streetwalker," "Steel Poles Give Back No Sweat," "Ghanaian Song—Image," and "Memory"), I. Reed Books (New York, NY), 1978.

Quincy Troupe Reading His Poems with Comment in the Recording Laboratory (sound recording), Library of Congress (Washington, DC), 1978.

Skulls along the River (poetry), I. Reed Books (New York, NY), 1984.

Soundings, Writers & Readers (New York, NY), 1988.

(Editor) *James Baldwin: The Legacy,* Simon & Schuster (New York, NY), 1989.

(With Miles Davis) *Miles: The Autobiography,* Simon & Schuster (New York, NY, 1989.

Weather Reports: New and Selected Poems, Writers & Readers (New York, NY, 1991.

(With Michael S. Harper) *Michael S. Harper and Quincy Troupe Reading Their Poems* (sound recording), Library of Congress (Washington, DC), 1994.

Avalanche: Poems, Coffee House Press (Minneapolis, MN), 1996.

Choruses: Poems, Coffee House Press (Minneapolis, MN), 1999.

Miles and Me, University of California Press (Berkeley, CA), 2000.

Take It to the Hoop, Magic Johnson (juvenile poetry), illustrated by Shane W. Evans/Jump at the Sun (New York, NY), 2000.

Transcircularities: New and Selected Poems, Coffee House Press (Minneapolis, MN), 2002.

Little Stevie Wonder (juvenile poetry), illustrated by Lisa Cohen, Houghton Mifflin (Boston, MA), 2004.

Also author of a screenplay, with Hugh Masekala; author of film script *Thelonious Monk: American Composer,* for Multiprises Film (New York, NY). Also founding editor of *Confrontation: A Journal of Third World Literature* and *American Rag;* guest editor of black poetry and black fiction issues of *Mundus Artium,* 1973; senior editor of *River Styx,* 1983—. Work represented in anthologies, including *The New Black Poetry,* 1969; *We Speak As Liberators,* 1970; *New Black Voices,* 1972; *Black Spirits,* 1972; *Poetry of Black America,* 1973; and *A Rock against the Wind,* 1973. Contributor to periodicals, including *New Directions, Mundus Artium, Iowa Review, Black World, Callaloo, Essence, Antioch Review, Black Creation, Negro American Literature Forum, Umbra, Mediterranean Review, Concerning Poetry, Sumac, Paris Match, Black Review, New York Quarterly,* and *Village Voice.*

ADAPTATIONS: Miles: The Autobiography is scheduled for production as a film directed by Spike Lee.

WORK IN PROGRESS: A memoir, a novel.

SIDELIGHTS: Quincy Troupe is best known for his poetry that is a "melding [of] rap, jazz and be-bop rhythms," as Tony Perry noted in the *Los Angeles Times.* Twice winner of the American Book Award and a respected professor at the University of California at San Diego, Quincy made headlines in 2002, not for his poetry, however, but for a scandal involving falsified academic credentials.

Throughout a career that began in the late 1960s, Troupe has written verse that celebrates "jazz, sports, and the streets of St. Louis," as Robin Wilson commented in the *Chronicle of Higher Education.* In such poetry, Troupe employs a "furious rush of images, sometimes jarring, arising from personal experience," as Perry further commented. Troupe is "a poet of great feeling and energy," according to Michael S. Harper, reviewing *Snake-back Solos: Selected Poems, 1969-1977* in the *New York Times Book Review.* Troupe has also founded and edited magazines such as *Confrontation: A Journal of Third World Literature* and *American Rag,* in addition to having a distinguished academic career. Born in St. Louis, Troupe grew up listening to jazz and playing baseball, influenced by his father, who was a catcher in the Negro baseball leagues. Troupe also began a lifelong love of reading; graduating from high school in 1959, he went to Grambling College on a baseball scholarship, but disputes with white southern athletes and required chapel soon sent him packing. In 1961 he enlisted in the army, but following a knee injury he began writing and discovered a new direction.

Moving to Los Angeles after leaving the army, he began teaching creative writing for the Watts Writers' Movement in 1966; his other teaching responsibilities have included courses in black literature and third world literature. Troupe was already an established poet, and his scholarly interests had led him to compile *Giant Talk: An Anthology of Third World Writings* with Rainer Schulte, when in 1978 he reached a wider audience with *The Inside Story of TV's "Roots."* The book, which Troupe wrote with David L. Wolper, chronicles the production of the highly successful television miniseries about slavery in America, *Roots,* which was based on Alex Haley's book of the same title. Troupe's *Inside Story* has sold over one million copies. Acclaim for his writing spread even further after he collaborated with jazz great Miles Davis on *Miles: The Autobiography,* which won the American Book Award.

Troupe's first poetic publication came in 1964 when *Paris Match* featured his "What Is a Black Man?" Since then he has contributed poetry to many periodicals in addition to having volumes of his poems published in book form. The first of these, *Embryo Poems,* includes poems that display Troupe's interests in the use of dialect, such as "Profilin, A Rap/Poem—For Leon Damas," and in the area of music, such as "The Scag Ballet." The latter poem depicts the actions of drug addicts as a strange form of dance; another piece likens traffic noises to "black jazz piano." Yet another, "Woke Up Crying the Blues," concerns the assassination of black civil rights leader Martin Luther King, Jr. The sadness the speaker of the poem feels at the loss of "the peaceful man from Atlanta" mingles with the happiness of the news that one of his poems has been accepted for publication, producing a mixture of emotion essential to the singing of a blues song.

Snake-back Solos, Troupe's second volume of poetry, takes its title from a local name—"Snakeback"—for the Mississippi River, recalled from the poet's childhood in St. Louis. Harper cited such poems as "Today's Subway Ride" in praising Troupe's descriptions of "the strange reality of familiar scenes." The subway is painted starkly, its unpleasant atmosphere displayed in "pee smells assaulting nostrils / blood breaking wine stains everywhere." Though Harper faulted the repetition of some of *Snake-back Solos,* including "Up Sun South of Alaska," he lauded "Ghanaian Song—Image" and "Memory" as "striking" and concluded that "the strength and economy" of the poet's "best insights . . . are about people and places he has internalized and often left behind."

Troupe's academic work has also garnered applause from critics. *Giant Talk* was declared "comprehensive" by Jack Slater in the *New York Times Book Review.* The book, which Troupe edited with Rainer Schulte, contains poems, folk tales, short stories, and novel excerpts by black Americans, native Americans, Hispanic Americans, black Africans, and Central and South Americans. According to Slater, the editors define third world writers as "those who identify with the historically exploited segment of mankind, and who confront the establishment on their behalf"; hence the inclusion of U.S.-born authors along with those native to areas more traditionally identified with the third world. Slater hailed the editors' decision to group the anthologized pieces by concept rather than by geographical area or genre. By using categories like "Oppression and Protest" and "Ritual and Magic," Troupe and Schulte "have managed to lessen the unwieldiness of *Giant Talk*'s scope. The uninitiated reader can, therefore, savor with as much ease as possible bits and pieces of longer works . . . as well as enjoy complete works by . . . short-story writers and poets."

James Baldwin: The Legacy, published after Baldwin's death in 1987, is "a sustained fond retrospect," Nicholas Delbanco remarked in a Chicago *Tribune Books* review. The book includes tributes and remembrances "studded with remarkable images that attest to the writer's continuing brilliance" from Maya Angelou, Amiri Baraka, Toni Morrison, Chinua Achebe, and others, Charles R. Larson commented in the *Washington Post Book World,* and ends with an interview with Baldwin, conducted by Troupe several weeks before the author's death, which is "spirited and funny at times," *Los Angeles Times Book Review* critic Clancy Sigal noted. Delbanco related Troupe's description of the book: "'It is a celebration of the life, the vision and, yes, the death of our good and great, passionate, genius witness of a brother, James Arthur Baldwin.'"

Troupe's work on the autobiography of Miles Davis earned him even more critical praise, along with the prestigious American Book Award. Commenting on the resounding success of his collaboration with the legendary musician, Troupe was quoted as saying by Nzadi Zimele Keita in *American Visions,* "He didn't scare me. I wasn't in awe or anything; I loved his music, and he was one of my early heroes, but I told him that that was where it stopped, that he was a human being. . . . So I guess he felt I could probably withstand his personality." Keita noted that the "long, gritty process of writing the book" yielded a genuine bonding between Davis and Troupe, resulting in "a candid, though controversial, best seller."

Troupe parlayed that relationship into yet another book, *Miles and Me,* a "book on interviewing Miles Davis for the autobiography on which they collaborated," according to Douglas Henry Daniels, writing in *African American Review.* Daniels also commented that the book "analyzes [Troupe's] discoveries of the music in his St. Louis homeboy." For Daniels, *Miles and Me* is an "invaluable work" not just for the personal material on Davis and his influence on music, but also for Troupe's examination of the jazz musician's power to affect "dress style, slang, and . . . the general demeanor of Black urban males." Reviewing the work in the *New York Times Book Review,* Gene Santoro noted that Troupe discovered through his collaboration with Davis "a complex, sometimes lonely, even shy man." But, according to Santoro, Troupe also reveals an artist with a "laser-like focus" as well as an inner "discipline and drive that helped push him out of replicating past achievements." Similarly, *Booklist*'s Bill Ott found Troupe's book to be a "revealing look at a musical genius and a tender, surprisingly sweet remembrance." *Library Journal*'s William Kenz also noted that Troupe's work "reveals Davis as profoundly, artistically sensitive yet maddeningly mean-spirited and rude," while a contributor for *Publishers Weekly* thought that the "most compelling" part of the remembrance was Troupe's reconstruction of Davis's influence on his (Troupe's) own coming of age.

Troupe continued to demonstrate his skill as a poet, even after his success with other genres. Reviewing *Avalanche,* a *Publishers Weekly* writer advised that in the collection, "Troupe . . . writes with unchecked expression, redundant and inclusive. If it were any more laden, *Avalanche* would be inchoate. Any less would be our loss." In the 1999 verse collection *Choruses,* Troupe covers "a wide cultural bandwidth," in the words of another *Publishers Weekly* reviewer. Musicians, sports stars, and artists are sketched in his poems, as are contemporary issues and events, in what the critic called a "varied and deftly sung" collection. In the 2002 collection *Transcircularities,* Troupe "demonstrates his ebullient and undimmed powers," according to yet another reviewer for *Publishers Weekly.* Gathering poems from eight previous books, Troupe also adds some new pieces, many of which honor jazz greats such as John Coltrane, Duke Ellington, and Bud Powell. In "9/11 Emergency Calls Coming into Manhattan," the poet also addresses the September 11, 2001, terrorist attacks on the United States. Reviewing the same work in *Black Issues Book Review,* Hoke S. Glover III felt it was a "comprehensive collection." Glover further called Troupe a "master of rhythm, repetition and song."

In 2002 Troupe was named California's first Poet Laureate, but the honor turned out to be double-edged. While doing a background check on the poet, the state discovered that Troupe did not have the bachelor's degree from Grambling College that he had claimed while teaching in New York. Put on leave by the university after admitting the lie, Troupe ultimately resigned his lucrative teaching position in December, 2002, despite protests from colleagues and students who wanted the popular and charismatic teacher to remain. As Wilson pointed out in the *Chronicle of Higher Education,* "Many . . . say the university overreacted and pushed Mr. Troupe out. As a poet, they believed, it was Mr. Troupe's writing, not his academic credentials, that had earned him his job." Others disagreed, including Martha C. Nussbaum, professor of law, divinity, and philosophy at the University of Chicago. As quoted by Wilson, Nussbaum claimed, "You don't want somebody there teaching students who gives that kind of moral example. It's a wrong that goes to the heart of the integrity of the academic enterprise." For his part, Troupe also quit his honorary position as Poet Laureate of California and apologized for his lie, but also protested the fact that he had been a good instructor, degree or no degree. "There was some kind of suggestion that I was not doing my job," Troupe—quoted by Wilson—said. "But I was publishing books, I was bringing honor to the school, and the students loved me. I didn't cheat anybody."

BIOGRAPHICAL AND CRITICAL SOURCES:

BOOKS

Dictionary of Literary Biography, Volume 41: *Afro-American Poets since 1955,* Gale (Detroit, MI), 1985.

PERIODICALS

African American Review, spring, 2001, Douglas Henry Daniels, review of *Miles and Me,* pp. 152-153.

American Visions, February-March, Nzadi Zimele Keita, "Quincy Troupe," 1993, p. 30.

Black Issues Book Review, November-December, 2002, Hoke S. Clover III, review of *Transcircularities,* p. 63.

Black Scholar, March-April, 1981; summer, 1990.

Booklist, March 15, 2000, Bill Ott, review of *Miles and Me,* p. 1311.

Chronicle of Higher Education, April 4, 2003, Robin Wilson, "Fall from Grace: One Lie, Retold over 26 Years, Undoes a Professor's Teaching Career," p. A10.

down beat, December, 1989, p. 69; November, 1990, p. 68.

Economist, March 17, 1990, p. 86.

Essence, September, 1989, p. 28.

Freedomways, Volume 10, number 2, 1980.

Library Journal, October 1, 1989, p. 97; February 15, 2000, William Kenz, review of *Miles and Me,* p. 165.

Los Angeles Times, December 4, 2002, Tony Perry, "Poet Resigns Post at UC San Diego over Resume Lie," p. B6.

Los Angeles Times Book Review, April 30, 1989, Clancy Sigal, review of *James Baldwin: The Legacy,* p. 1.

Mother Jones, December, 1989, p. 42.

Nation, January 29, 1990, p. 139.

New Republic, February 12, 1990, p. 30.

New Statesman, January 5, 1990, p. 34.

New York Times Book Review, November 30, 1975, Jack Slater, review of *Giant Talk;* October 21, 1979, Michael S. Harper, review of *Snake-black Solos;* October 15, 1989, p. 7; April 9, 2000, Gene Santoro, review of *Miles and Me,* p. 22.

Publishers Weekly, March 17, 1989, p. 88; September 1, 1989, p. 69; January 20, 1992, p. 58; August 2, 1993, p. 31; March 18, 1996, review of *Avalanche,* p. 66; August 30, 1999, review of *Choruses,* p. 78; February 7, 2000, review of *Miles and Me,* pp. 77-78; September 23, 2002, Michael Scharf, review of *Transcircularities,* p. 69.

St. Louis Post-Dispatch, January 23, 2000, Kevin C. Johnson, "Larry Flynt-Backed *Code* Gives Black Males a Voice," p. E1.

Tribune Books, (Chicago), March 19, 1989, Nicholas Delbanco, review of *James Baldwin.*
Variety, January 3, 1990, p. 46.
Washington Post Book World, April 16, 1989, Charles R. Larson, review of *James Baldwin,* p. 1.

ONLINE

Academy of American Poets Web site, http://www.poets.org/ (May 1, 2003).*

* * *

TURNBULL, Peter (John) 1950-

PERSONAL: Born October 23, 1950, in Rotherham, Yorkshire, England; son of John Colin (an engineer) and Patricia (a nurse; maiden name, O'Brien) Turnbull. *Education:* Attended Cambridge College of Arts and Technology, 1971-74; Cardiff University, Wales, diploma in social work, 1978; University of Huddersfield, M.A. *Religion:* Anglican.

ADDRESSES: *Agent*—Peters, Fraser & Dunlop, Drury House, 34-43 Russell St., London WC2B 5HA, England. *E-mail*—shroggs49@hotmail.com.

CAREER: Strathclyde Regional Council, Glasgow, Scotland, social worker, 1978-95; fulltime writer, 1995—. Worked as steelworker and crematorium assistant in Sheffield and London, and has done social work in Brooklyn, NY.

MEMBER: Workers Guild of Great Britain.

WRITINGS:

"'P' DIVISION" CRIME SERIES

Deep and Crisp and Even, Collins (London, England), 1981, St. Martin's Press (New York, NY), 1982.
Dead Knock, Collins (London, England), 1982, St. Martin's Press (New York, NY), 1983.
Fair Friday, St. Martin's Press (New York, NY), 1983.
Big Money, St. Martin's Press (New York, NY), 1984.
Two Way Cut, St. Martin's Press (New York, NY), 1988.
Condition Purple, St. Martin's Press (New York, NY), 1989.
And Did Murder Him, St. Martin's Press (New York, NY), 1991.
Long Day Monday, St. Martin's Press (New York, NY), 1993.
The Killing Floor, HarperCollins (New York, NY), 1995.
The Man With No Face, St. Martin's Press (New York, NY), 1998.

"HENNESSEY AND YELLICH" CRIME SERIES

Fear of Drowning, St. Martin's Press (New York, NY), 2000.
Deathtrap, Severn House (Sutton, Surrey, England), 2000.
Perils and Dangers, Severn House (Sutton, Surrey, England), 2001.
The Return, Severn House (Sutton, Surrey, England), 2001.
After the Flood, Severn House (Sutton, Surrey, England), 2002.

OTHER

The Claws of the Gryphon (thriller), St. Martin's Press (New York, NY), 1986.
The Justice Game: The Lady from Rome (novelization of television series), BBC Publications (London, England), 1990.
The Killer Who Never Was, Clark Lawrence (London, England), 1996.

Also author of *Embracing Skeletons,* 1996. Contributor of short stories to *Ellery Queen's Mystery Magazine.*

WORK IN PROGRESS: Another "Hennessey" crime novel.

SIDELIGHTS: "The crime novels of Peter Turnbull are reassuringly familiar in form, with satisfying surprises and twists in their plotting, and an interesting cast of characters," according to Ian A. Bell in the *St. James Guide to Crime and Mystery Writers.* His police procedural novels involving the "P" Division of Glasgow's police force are noted for their gritty realism as they depict the dogged persistence of detectives gathering and sorting through the evidence to solve crimes. In his novels set in the city of York, and featuring Chief Inspector George Hennessey and Sergeant Yellich, Turnbull spins tales of crime in an area of England usually known for its quiet lifestyle. "Turnbull regularly manages to carry off the difficult feat of balancing the demands of detailed characterization with the need for fast-paced and compelling narrative," Bell wrote. Emily Melton in *Booklist* commented, "Turnbull's police procedurals have received high praise from readers and critics alike for their gritty realism, deft prose, and riveting plots."

Many novels in Turnbull's "'P' Division" crime series have received critical praise, including *The Killing Floor,* in which a decapitated body is found in the suburbs of Glasgow. Police soon discover that the headless woman was a social worker who had recently claimed to have unearthed a thirty-year-old mystery. A *Publishers Weekly* reviewer noted that Turnbull's "knife edged characterization . . . is as incisive as ever." Marilyn Stasio stated in a *New York Times Book Review* assessment of *The Killing Floor* that Turnbull's "forensic procedures are flawless, and his character sketches cut quick and deep." A reviewer for the *Mystery Guide* Web site called *The Killing Floor* "an unremittingly grim, hyper-realistic, 'slice of life' procedural."

The Man with No Face tells of a small-time Glasgow thief who, just hours after being released from prison for setting fire to an antiques store, is found with his face shot away. Investigation of the strange murder leads police to an unsolved kidnapping several years earlier, possible insurance fraud, and money laundering. As Andy Plonka explained in a review posted at the *Mystery Reader* Web site, the plot consists of "various engaging detectives tracking down different leads which yield clues connected to the crime. In the end, these clues ingeniously fit together to provide a fascinating and satisfying solution." Harriet Klausner, writing in *BookBrowser,* claimed that *The Man with No Face* is "a fantastic Scottish police procedural that will imbue fans of the subgenre with an intense need to find the series' previous eight novels."

With his novel *Fear of Drowning,* Turnbull began a new police procedural series, this time set in the city of York in northern England. In this initial outing, Chief Inspector George Hennessey and Sergeant Yellich are called upon to solve the murder of a middle-aged husband and wife. While it seems at first that the couple had no enemies, Hennessey uncovers illicit sexual and financial problems beneath the tranquil surface. Brian Ritterspak, reviewing the book for the *Crime Time Web site,* wrote: "Retaining the salty authenticity of his 'P Division' novels, Turnbull ensures that his tightly-plotted narrative moves with considerable speed towards its satisfyingly astringent finale." A critic for *Publishers Weekly* explained that "Turnbull closes on a quietly chilling scene of confession, the perfect end to a subtle novel rich in character, as well as in Yorkshire wit and wisdom."

In *Deathtrap* Hennessey investigates the death of a local journalist and, in the process, finds links to an unsolved murder case from years before. Writing in *Booklist,* David Pitt explained that, while the novel's plot is well handled, it is "the least of this rich novel's attractions. There's something especially lifelike about its characters, especially vivid and true about its dialogue." Pitt concluded that *Deathtrap* was "an utterly charming mystery."

In *Perils and Dangers* Turnbull tells of a professional blackmailer who is found murdered in his study. Faced with a host of suspects who were being blackmailed by the deceased, and no one anxious to find the killer, Hennessey and Yellich find their investigation much more difficult than usual. "While Turnbull offers an intriguing puzzle and evokes the walled city of York and environs in all their glory," wrote a critic for *Publishers Weekly,* "it's his characterizations, particularly of Hennessey and Yellich, that make this novel memorable." Pitt remarked that "Hennessey and Yellich make a great crime-fighting team, and Turnbull is a snappy, entertaining writer."

A murder from the past is the focus of *The Return,* in which a skeleton with a broken skull is discovered in a field. The victim is a law student who went missing some twenty years before, and the prime suspects are fellow students who practice law in York today. A critic for *Kirkus Reviews* concluded that *The Return* is "a snappy formula procedural on which Turnbull . . . lavishes nary an extra detail, emotion, or word." A *Publishers Weekly* reviewer believed that "this understated novel will satisfy all those who appreciate traditional, well-made whodunits."

After the Flood concerns another body found in a field. This time, following a flood, a Yorkshire farmer finds the corpse of a woman who was apparently buried some ten years earlier. But the head does not match the rest of the body. Hennessey and Yellich must discover just why the head of a nurse, who was accused of mistreating her patients, was buried with the body of another woman. A *Publishers Weekly* reviewer explained that "the investigation proceeds clue by clue to a rational and satisfying conclusion. . . . This is first-rate traditional mystery entertainment." Melton concluded: "Skillful plotting, well-drawn characters, and some unexpected twists make this fine police procedural a pleasurable and entertaining read."

Speaking of the Hennessey and Yellich stories as a whole, Pitt declared that "every new entry in this excellent series is a cause for celebration."

In an evaluation of his entire career, Bell judged Turnbull to be "easily the most accomplished writer of the police procedural novel in Britain today." Melton concluded: "This low-key Scottish author writes refreshingly intelligent books that are an absorbing blend of gritty murder mystery, human-interest story, psychological profile, and wry social commentary."

BIOGRAPHICAL AND CRITICAL SOURCES:

BOOKS

St. James Guide to Crime and Mystery Writers, 4th edition, St. James Press (Detroit, MI), 1996.

PERIODICALS

Booklist, February 15, 1995, Emily Melton, review of *The Killing Floor,* p. 1063; September 15, 1998, Emily Melton, review of *The Man with No Face,* p. 204; April 15, 1999, review of *The Man with No Face,* p. 1459; July, 2000, David Pitt, review of *Fear of Drowning,* p. 2015; October 1, 2000, David Pitt, review of *Death Trap,* p. 327; May 1, 2001, David Pitt, review of *Perils and Dangers,* p. 1642; December 1, 2001, review of *The Return,* p. 634; June 1, 2002, Emily Melton, review of *After the Flood,* p. 1692.

Kirkus Reviews, November 15, 2001, review of *The Return,* p. 1586; June 1, 2002, review of *After the Flood,* p. 776.

Library Journal, January, 1995, Rex E. Klett, review of *The Killing Floor,* p. 142.

New York Times Book Review, March 19, 1995, Marilyn Stasio, review of *The Killing Floor.*

Publishers Weekly, January 11, 1993; January 9, 1995, review of *The Killing Floor,* p. 58; August 31, 1998, review of *The Man with No Face,* p. 51; July 3, 2000, review of *Fear of Drowning,* p. 51; May 21, 2001, review of *Perils and Dangers,* p. 85; November 26, 2001, review of *The Return,* p. 41; July 1, 2002, review of *After the Flood,* p. 58.

ONLINE

BookBrowser, http://www.bookbrowser.com/ (October 12, 1998), Harriet Klausner, review of *The Man with No Face.*

Crime Time, http://www.crimetime.co.uk/ (December 11, 2002), Brian Ritterspak, review of *Fear of Drowning.*

Mystery Guide, http://www.mysteryguide.com/ (December 11, 2002), review of *The Killing Floor.*

Mystery Reader, http://www.themysteryreader.com/ (December 11, 2002), Andy Plonka, review of *The Man with No Face.*

V

Van LAAN, Nancy 1939-

PERSONAL: Born November 18, 1939, in Baton Rouge, LA; daughter of Philip Johannes (a colonel, U.S. Air Force) and Sarah (Hawkins) Greven; twice divorced; children: Jennifer, David, Anna. *Education:* Sullins College, Bristol, VA, A.A., 1959; University of Alabama, B.A., 1961; Rutgers University, M.F.A., 1979. *Politics:* Democrat. *Religion:* Protestant. *Hobbies and other interests:* Biking, kayaking.

ADDRESSES: Home—Doylestown, PA. *Agent*—Gail Hochman, Brandt and Brandt, 1501 Broadway, New York, NY 10036. *E-mail*—nvanlaan@aol.com.

CAREER: Writer, 1987—. *Children's Quiet Time* (weekly educational TV show), Birmingham, AL, producer, 1957; J. Walter Thompson Advertising Agency, New York, NY, assistant, 1961-62; ABC-TV, New York, NY, network censor, 1962-66; Solebury School, New Hope, PA, English teacher, 1984-89; Rutgers University, New Brunswick, NJ, creative writing instructor, 1986-89.

MEMBER: Society of Children's Book Writers and Illustrators; National Storytelling Association.

AWARDS, HONORS: New Jersey State "Best Play of the Year" Award, for *Park Place* and *The Disintegration of Daphne;* Notable Book, American Library Association (ALA), 1990, Parents' Choice Picture Book Award, 1990, Honor Book, Florida Reading Association, 1991, all for *Possum Come A-Knockin';* Reading Rainbow selection, Keystone State Reading Book Award, and Alabama Library Association Author's Award, all 1991, all for *Rainbow Crow: A Lenape Tale;* Notable Book, ALA, and ABC Choice Award, both 1996, both for *In a Circle Long Ago: A Treasury of Native Lore from North America;* Notable Book, ALA, 1997, and Carolyn Field Honor Award, Pennsylvania Library Association, 1998, both for *Shingebiss: An Ojibwe Legend;* Editors' Choice, *Booklist,* 1998, and Notable Book, ALA, 1999, both for *With a Whoop and a Holler: A Bushel of Lore from Way down South;* Blue Ribbon designation, *Bulletin of the Center for Children's Books,* Best Books, *School Library Journal,* and Pick of the Lists, American Booksellers Association, all 1998, all for *So Say the Little Monkeys;* Charlotte Zolowtow Award, Highly Commended Book, 2001, for *When Winter Comes.*

WRITINGS:

The Big Fat Worm, illustrated by Marisabina Russo, Knopf (New York, NY), 1987.

(Reteller) *Rainbow Crow: A Lenape Tale,* illustrated by Beatriz Vidal, Knopf (New York, NY), 1989.

Possum Come A-Knockin', illustrated by George Booth, Knopf (New York, NY), 1990.

A Mouse in My House, illustrated by Marjorie Priceman, Knopf (New York, NY), 1990.

(Adaptor) *The Legend of El Dorado: A Latin American Tale,* illustrated by Beatriz Vidal, Knopf (New York, NY), 1991.

People, People Everywhere, illustrated by Nadine Bernard Westcott, Knopf (New York, NY), 1992.

This Is the Hat: A Story in Rhyme, illustrated by Holly Meade, Joy Street Books, 1992.

The Tiny, Tiny Boy and the Big, Big Cow, illustrated by Marjorie Priceman, Knopf (New York, NY), 1993.

(Reteller) *Buffalo Dance: A Blackfoot Legend,* foreword by Bill Moyers, illustrated by Beatriz Vidal, Little, Brown (Boston, MA), 1993.

Round and Round Again, illustrated by Natalie Bernard Westcott, Hyperion (New York, NY), 1994.

Sleep, Sleep, Sleep: A Lullaby for Little Ones around the World, illustrated by Holly Meade, Little, Brown (Boston, MA), 1995.

Mama Rocks, Papa Sings, illustrated by Roberta Smith, Knopf (New York, NY), 1995.

In a Circle Long Ago: A Treasury of Native Lore from North America, illustrated by Lisa Desimini, Apple Soup Books, 1995.

La Boda: A Mexican Wedding Celebration, illustrated by Andrea Arroyo, Little, Brown (Boston, MA), 1996.

(Reteller) *Shingebiss: An Ojibwe Legend,* illustrated by Betsy Bowen, Houghton Mifflin (Boston, MA), 1997.

Little Baby Bobby, illustrated by Laura Cornell, Knopf (New York, NY), 1997.

With a Whoop and a Holler: A Bushel of Lore from Way down South, illustrated by Scott Cook, Atheneum (New York, NY), 1998.

Little Fish, Lost, illustrated by Jane Conteh-Morgan, Simon & Schuster (New York, NY), 1998.

(Reteller) *The Magic Bean Tree: A Legend from Argentina,* illustrated by Beatriz Vidal, Houghton Mifflin (Boston, MA), 1998.

So Say the Little Monkeys, illustrated by Yumi Heo, Atheneum (New York, NY), 1998.

Moose Tales, illustrated by Amy Rusch, Houghton Mifflin (Boston, MA), 1999.

A Tree for Me, Knopf (New York, NY), 2000.

When Winter Comes: A Lullaby, illustrated by Susan Gaber, Atheneum (New York, NY), 2000.

The Laughing Man, illustrated by Lisa Desimini, Simon & Schuster (New York, NY), 2001.

Tickle Tum, illustrated by Bernadette Pons Fudym, Atheneum (New York, NY), 2001.

Teeny Tiny Tingly Tales, illustrated by Victoria Chess, Atheneum (New York, NY), 2001.

Busy, Busy Moose, illustrated by Amy Rusch, Houghton Mifflin (Boston, MA), 2001.

Scrubba Dub, illustrated by Bernadette Pons, Atheneum (New York, NY), 2003.

Also author of the plays *Park Place* and *The Disintegration of Daphne.*

SIDELIGHTS: Nancy Van Laan is the author of numerous picture books for young readers, including the popular and award-winning *Possum Come A-Knockin'* and *Rainbow Crow.* Many of her read-aloud books feature animal protagonists and utilize rhythm and rhyme to introduce young listeners and readers to the world of words. Additionally, Van Laan often uses folktales and legends from around the world as the story line for her books.

"As soon as I was able to hold a pencil, I scribbled poetry and drew," Van Laan once recalled. "I still have poems and plays that I wrote when I was in elementary school. It was my favorite thing to do besides read. I loved books, especially those with lots of illustrations." Yet Van Laan would ultimately come to professional writing in a roundabout way—through dance, television, theater, and teaching—publishing her first book at age forty-eight.

The daughter of an Air Force colonel, Van Laan traveled a great deal when she was a child; in the eighth grade she attended schools in Canada, England, and the United States. Her avid reading continued throughout these years, her favorite books coming from the "My Book House" series originally published in the 1930s. "To this day I can quote most of the poetry found in those wonderful books which, unfortunately, are long out of print," Van Laan once commented. But when she was a teenager, dance took priority over books, and by age seventeen she had her own dance company and later choreographed *The Wizard of Oz* ballet for the Alabama Public Television network. Her dance career came to an abrupt end, however, when she sledded down a snowy hill on a cafeteria tray and broke the base of her spine. Subsequently Van Laan studied television and radio production at the University of Alabama, and after graduation worked for a time in New York as a censor for ABC-TV.

In 1965 and 1966 she had the first two of her three children, and domestic affairs occupied her time for several years thereafter. She also began painting, eventually doing murals for schools and private homes. Returning to college in 1976, she studied theater and playwriting; two of her plays were produced in regional productions in New Jersey and won Best Play of the Year awards. Her third child was born in 1980, and throughout much of the 1980s Van Laan headed the English department at a private boarding school in Pennsylvania. Then came the publication of her first children's book in 1987, *The Big Fat Worm,* and two years later she was able to give up teaching to write full time.

With her initial title, much of Van Laan's style and content were already in place. A circular tale, featuring repetitive and easy-to-read text, *The Big Fat Worm* features the first of her familiar animals as the protagonist. A *School Library Journal* reviewer noted that the simplicity of text and pictures "makes it extremely versatile, for it may be read as part of a program on animals, farms, or funny stories," or even for inventive dramatics. An earlier review by Lee Bock from that same journal declared that Van Laan's first book "provides an almost textbook example of what a good book for the very young can look like." Bock also drew attention to the rhythm and repetition of the tale and the bold colors employed for illustrations.

"Most of my picture books are full of rhythm and sometimes rhyme," Van Laan related. "This is because each story is like music to me. Sometimes I hear a certain beat before I actually put words to it." Additionally, Van Laan's years of teaching came in handy when she turned to writing children's books. "I taught for many years, so I usually try to incorporate hidden lesson plans in many of my books for young children. . . . Books for young children should teach as well as entertain, I think."

More animal protagonists were featured in Van Laan's next three books, *Rainbow Crow, Possum Come A-Knockin',* and *A Mouse in My House.* These three books also set the tone for her future output: books of legend, folktales, and simple rhythm and rhyme. Her *Rainbow Crow* retells a Lenape Indian legend and was the result of a lifelong interest in Native American folklore. She consulted with a Lenape elder for the book and gathered tales from many tribes. The result was "a fine read-aloud because of the smooth text and songs with repetitive chants," according to Kathleen Riley in *School Library Journal.* Rainbow Crow brings fire to the woodland creatures; his voice turns to a "caw" because of the smoke. Other woodland animals are also featured in this book that a contributor to *Kirkus Reviews* called "a good story for all ages."

Rhyming and animals are at the center of both *Possum Come A-Knockin'* and *A Mouse in My House,* as well. Possum, dressed in a top hat and vest, comes knocking at Granny's house, setting the house in a tizzy. "Practically begging to be read aloud, Van Laan's cumulative rhyme is a real toe-tapper," commented a reviewer for *Publishers Weekly,* while *Horn Book* contributor Elizabeth S. Watson dubbed the book a "raucous romp." With *A Mouse in My House,* Van Laan created the more traditional, cuddly-animal style of picture book, featuring a cookie-nibbling mouse and a rather greedy pig, among other animals. In this story, a little boy compares his own behavior to several such animals. The "text's rollicking rhythm, rhyme, and repetition will encourage young listeners to join in," remarked Danita Nichols writing in *School Library Journal.* Leone McDermott concluded in *Booklist,* "Bouncy rhymes are quick and fun to read aloud, and children will enjoy knowing that others share their difficulty with self-restraint."

With the success of these first titles, Van Laan was able to give up full-time teaching for full-time writing, but she had to allow for her own "undisciplined" work habits. "I do not sit down each day and write," she related. "In fact, I might stew for months about an idea before actually writing it down in a notebook. I always create my stories in longhand first, then, much later, transfer the final draft to computer. If I get what I think is a really good idea, then I work and work until it is finished. I write very quickly, so sometimes a story is finished in a few days. Not always, though. I once spent several months trying to think of how to write the last line of one tale, so it really depends on my muse, I suppose." One of her books, *In a Circle Long Ago,* took her three years to complete; another was written on the tablecloth in a restaurant where she was dining.

Van Laan's writing has followed the three directions set out in her earliest books: retellings of legends from Native American and other cultures, folktales, and contemporary stories that employ rhyme and rhythm to entice young listeners and readers. Van Laan recreated the Mayan legend of the Gold Man in *The Legend of El Dorado,* a book that a contributor to *Booklist* found to be "moving." Blackfoot legend was mined for *Buffalo Dance,* the story of the capture of a buffalo for winter food. "The universal themes of courage, love, self-sacrifice, and loyalty are movingly conveyed," commented Carolyn Polese in *School Library Journal.* Maeve Visser Knoth, writing in *Horn Book,* called *Buffalo Dance* "a graceful and attractive retelling of a Native American myth." An Ojibwe legend was retold in *Shingebiss,* in which the eponymous duck defies Winter Maker and will not be cold during the bleak months. Janice M. Del Negro noted in *Bulletin of the Center for Children's Books* that Van Laan "communicates the irreverent joy of Shingebiss as he happily overcomes winter's cold." With *In a Circle Long Ago,* Van Laan collected native lore from across North America in twenty-five legends and poems. In another *Horn Book* review, Knoth dubbed the collection "a true smorgasbord" and noted that "readers will get a taste of the richness of Native American folklore and will be tempted to search other books for a closer look at individual peoples." Wedding rituals of Mexico take center stage in Van Laan's *La Boda,* and the author has ranged as far afield as South America to gather other legends in her *The Magic Bean Tree,* from Argentina, and *So Say the Little Monkeys,* a Brazilian folktale that pokes fun at procrastinators.

Van Laan also employs folktales from closer to home to create focus for her rhythmic tales. Adapting a Scottish folktale for *The Tiny, Tiny Boy and the Big, Big Cow,* Van Laan told about the difficulties a little boy has trying to milk a large cow. Patricia Pearl Dole, writing in *School Library Journal,* called the book a "pleasing, culturally neutral romp," while *Horn Book* reviewer Knoth concluded that the "story begs to be shared aloud and will have children chanting" along with the text. Van Laan rummaged through the cultural history of her native South for various trickster tales, African folktales, and Appalachian tall tales for her compilation, *With a Whoop and a Holler,* a book that was, according to a *Publishers Weekly* reviewer, "presented . . . in the kind of slide-off-the-tongue colloquialisms guaranteed to make a sure-fire storyteller of the most shrinking violets." A critic for *Kirkus Reviews* concurred, noting that the book "crackles with vernacular humor."

More cumulative rhyming and rhythmic fun is presented in Van Laan's books about everyday objects, faces, sleep time, and even ecology. For the latter, Van Laan created a recycling mother in *Round and Round Again* who is such an ardent recycler that she has built a house from other people's discarded objects. Lullabies come in *Sleep, Sleep, Sleep* and *When Winter Comes.* The world of a Haitian family is presented in *Mama Rocks, Papa Sings,* a story told partly in Creole. The adventures of a hat, blown away on a rainy day, are recounted in more cumulative rhyme in *This Is the Hat,* which *Booklist*'s Jim Jaske called "clever" and a "fine book to use with preschoolers." A *Kirkus Reviews* contributor noted that *This Is the Hat* "tells another story with a rambunctious lilt."

In *Teeny Tiny Tingly Tales* Van Laan uses rhyme to tell three fun, creepy stories. In the story "Old Doctor Whango Tango," a mean doctor takes his malnourished animals to the top of a craggy hill where they all blow away in a sudden gust of wind. "It" tells of a strange creature who comes downstairs a piece at a time, assembling himself into a demented old man. And in "The Hairy Toe," an old woman finds a hairy toe in her garden, buries it, and is then haunted by a "Something" who wants his toe given back. A reviewer for *Horn Book* believed that the stories were "attuned to the silly sense of humor that allows kids to delight in the 'something's gonna get you' sequence that begins with an approaching imaginary monster and ends with a tickle." John Peters in *Booklist* admitted that the stories will "illicit giggles rather than gasps," while the *Kirkus Reviews* critic found that "children will enjoy Van Laan's storytelling cadence and the sheer fun of the language."

Lilting rhymes and shoe-tapping rhythms are Van Laan's stock in trade, one that she was a long time in coming to, but one in which she is very much at home now. "Today, writing is as much a part of me as going to sleep, waking up, singing, laughing, dancing, talking, baking pies, listening to music, and taking long walks down country roads," Van Laan explained. "I could not imagine *not* writing. It would make me sad and grumpy if I was told never to do it again. . . . The nicest part of writing is that I can take it with me wherever I go. I can also continue to do it for as long as I would like. And, my goal is to do it for a long, long time!" Speaking of how she gets her story ideas, Van Laan explained in an article posted on the *Teachers at Random House* Web site: "Ideas are sly critters. By listening quietly, sometimes I can catch them. Some come from deep inside myself, from a special place I have no control over. Other times, ideas are hiding in the shadows, somewhere outside myself. But by using all my senses, I can coax them out. If I don't pounce on them right away, they tend to disappear."

BIOGRAPHICAL AND CRITICAL SOURCES:

PERIODICALS

Booklist, October 1, 1990, p. 342; October 15, 1991, p. 378; November 15, 1992, p. 611; October 1, 1994, p. 225; January 15, 1995, p. 940; November

15, 1995, p. 558; December 15, 1995, p. 718; October 1, 1997, p. 339; April, 1998, p. 1328; October 15, 2001, John Peters, review of *Teeny Tiny Tingly Tales,* p. 402; July, 2003, review of *Busy Busy Moose,* p. 1370; February 15, 2003, Diane Foote, review of *Scrubba Dub,* p. 1078.

Bulletin of the Center for Children's Books, February, 1995, p. 217; September, 1997, p. 29; January, 1998, p. 103.

Horn Book, July-August, 1990, pp. 448-449; November-December, 1990, p. 734; May-June, 1993, pp. 325-326; September-October, 1993, pp. 612-613; November-December, 1995, p. 739; January-February, 1996, p. 84; November-December, 1997, pp. 691-692; September, 2001, review of *Teeny Tiny Tingly Tales,* p. 578.

Kirkus Reviews, April 1, 1989, p. 555; October, 1992, p. 1261; March 15, 1993, p. 381; August 15, 1995, p. 1195; April 15, 1996, p. 608; January 15, 1998, pp. 119-120; September 15, 2001, review of *Teeny Tiny Tingly Tales,* p. 1370; February 15, 2003, review of *Scrubba Dub,* p. 317.

Publishers Weekly, March 30, 1990, p. 61; November 6, 1995, p. 93; January 5, 1998, p. 66; January 26, 1998, p. 92; August 17, 1998, p. 70; October 23, 2000, review of *When Winter Comes,* p. 74; August 13, 2001, review of *Teeny Tiny Tingly Tales,* p. 311; November 25, 2002, Lisa Smith, review of *Scrubba Dub,* p. 66.

School Library Journal, December, 1987, p. 78; July, 1989, p. 81; July, 1990, pp. 64-65; December, 1990, p. 89; February, 1992, p. 41; October, 1992, p. 98; September, 1993, pp. 221, 227; December, 1994, p. 103; May, 1996, p. 101; April, 1998, p. 111; June, 1998, p. 136; September, 1998, pp. 198-199; September, 2003, Lisa Smith, review of *Busy Busy Moose,* p. 193; April, 2003, Bina Williams, review of *Scrubba Dub,* p. 140.

ONLINE

Nancy Van Laan Home Page, http://www.nancyvanlaan.com/ (November 14, 2002).

Teachers at Random House, http://www.randomhouse.com/teachers/ (November 14, 2002), Nancy Van Laan, "How I Write."*

VIGÉE, Claude (Andre Strauss) 1921-

PERSONAL: Born January 3, 1921, in Bischwiller, France; son of Robert (in business) and Germaine (a homemaker; maiden name, Meyer) Strauss; married Evelyne Meyer (a homemaker), November 29, 1947; children: Claudine, Daniel-Francois. *Education:* University of Strasbourg, France, B.A. 1938; Ohio State University, M.A., 1945, Ph.D. (Romance languages), 1947. *Religion:* Jewish. *Hobbies and other interests:* Classical music, sculpture, archaeology.

ADDRESSES: *Home*—21 Radak St., Jerusalem 92187, Israel; and 12 bis, rue des Marronniers, Paris 75016, France.

CAREER: Poet, essayist, translator. Professor of French and comparative literature, Ohio State University, Columbus, OH, 1947-49, Wellesley College, Wellesley, MA, 1949-50, Brandeis University, Waltham, MA, 1949-60, and The Hebrew University, Jerusalem, Israel, 1960-84.

MEMBER: Writers' Union (Israel), Societe des Gens de Lettres, Academie Mallarme, Academie d'Alsace, Societe des Ecrivains d'Alsace et de Lorraine, Deutsche, Akadamie fur Sprache und Dichtung.

AWARDS, HONORS: Pierre de Regnier prize, Academie Francaise, 1972, for body of work; Jacob- Burckhardt prize, University of Bale (Switzerland), 1977, for body of work; Femina-Vacaresco prize for criticism (Paris), 1979; Johann-Peter Hebel prize, 1984, for body of work; Rockefeller Foundation scholar, 1986; Grand Prix de la poesie de la Societe des Gens de Lettres, Paris 1987; Chevalier de la Legion d'honneur, Palmes academiques.

WRITINGS:

La Lutte avec l'ange (poems), Les Lettres (Paris, France), 1950.

L'Aurore souterraine, Pierre Seghers (Paris, France), 1952.

La Come du Grand Pardon, Pierre Seghers (Paris, France), 1954.
L'Ete indien (poems and journal), Gallimard (Paris, France), 1957.
Les Artistes de la faim (criticism), Calmann-Levy (Paris, France), 1960.
Revolte et louanges (criticism), Jose Corti (Paris, France), 1962.
Moisson de Canaan, Flammarion (Paris, France), 1967.
La Lune d'hiver, Flammarion (Paris, France), 1970.
Le Soleil sous la mer (poems), Flammarion (Paris, France), 1972.
Delivrance du souffle Flammarion (Paris, France), 1977.
Du bec a l'oreille, Editions de la Nuee-Bleue (Strasbourg, Fance), 1977.
L'Art et le demonique (essays), Flammarion (Paris, France), 1978.
L'Extase et l'errance (essay), Grasset (Paris, France), 1982.
Paque de la parole, Flammarion (Paris, France), 1983.
Le Parfum et la cendre (autobiography), Grasset (Paris, France), 1984.
Les Orties noires (poems and prose), Flammarion (Paris, France), 1984.
Heimat des Hauches, Elster Verlag (Baden-Baden, Germany), 1985.
(With Luc Balbont) *Une Voix dans le defile* (autobiography), Nouvelle Cite (Paris, France), 1985.
La Manne et la Rosee (essay), Descelee de Brouwer (Paris, France), 1986.
La Faille du regard (essays and interviews), Flammarion (Paris, France), 1987.
Wenderowefir, Association Jean-Baptiste Weckerlin (Strasbourg, France), 1988.
La Manna e la rugiada, Editiones Borla (Rome, Italy), 1988.
Aux Sources de la litterature moderne I, (essays), Entailles-Philippe Nadal (Bourg-en-Bresse, France), 1989.
Le Feu d'une nuit d'hiver (poems), Flammarion (Paris, France), 1989.
Leben in Jerusalem, Elster Verlag, 1990.
Apprendre la nuit (poems), Arfuyen (Paris, France), 1991.
La Terre el le Souffle, Claude Vigée, Albin Michel (Paris, France), 1992.
Dans le silence de l'Aleph (essays), Albin Michel (Paris, France), 1992.
Flow Tide: Selected Poetry and Prose, edited and translated by Anthony Rudolf, Menard-King's College Press (London, England), 1992.
L'Heritage du feu (essays, poems, and interviews), Mame (Paris, France), 1992.
Les Cinq rouleaux (Bible studies), Albin Michel (Paris, France), 1993.
Un Panier de Houblon (memoirs), Albin Michel (Paris, France), Volume 1, 1994, Volume 2, 1995.
Treize inconnus de la Bible, Albin Michel (Paris, France), 1996.
La Maison des Vivants, Editions de la Nuee Bleue (Strasbourg, France), 1996.
Aux portes du labyrinthe (poems), Flammarion (Paris, France), 1996.
Demain la seule demeure (essays), L'Harmattan (Paris, France), 1997.
La Lucarne aux etoiles: Dix cahiers de Jerusalem, 1967-1997, Cerf (Paris, France), 1998.
Vision et silence dans la poetique juive: Demain la seule demeure: Essais et entretiens, 1983-1996, Harmattan (Paris, France), 1999.

Contributor of poems and essays to journals, including *PMLA, Partisan Review, Comparative Literature, Webster Review, Southern Review, Poesie 42,* and *Chelsea Review.* Contributor of poetry to anthologies, including *Modern European Poetry,* Bantam Classics, 1966; *Jewish Frontier Anthology,* 1967; and *Voices within the Ark,* Avon Books, 1978. Translator into French of poems by R. M. Rilke, D. Seter, David Rokeah, Yvan Goll, and T. S. Eliot.

SIDELIGHTS: A poet, essayist, and professor, Claude Vigée was born into a Jewish family in the Alsace region of France along the Rhine River. In 1939, Vigée and his family were expelled from the area by the Nazis, and they took up residence in southern France. While studying medicine in Toulouse, from 1940 to 1942 Vigée helped organize the Jewish resistance against the German occupiers and the collaborating Vichy government of France. Because his family had been residents of the Alsace region for ten generations, Vigée, though a Jew, was allowed to travel freely, and he used this freedom to recruit others into the resistance movement. Vigée's first poems were published in *Poesie 42,* a resistance magazine. During this time he met the poet and novelist Louis Aragon, as well as poet Pierre Emmanuel, who became his lifelong friend.

When his life was endangered by his resistance activities, Vigée and his mother used forged travel papers to escape to Spain and eventually to immigrate to the

United States in 1943. He earned a doctorate degree in Romance languages and literatures from Ohio State University and married his longtime sweetheart, his cousin Evelyne. An illustrious teaching and writing career followed, in the United States and later in Israel, where Vigée and his family immigrated in 1960. Since the publication of his first collection of poetry *La Lutte avec l'ange,* in 1950, Vigée has published a steady stream of poetry, narratives, journal entries, essays, and translations. He has known and corresponded with many famous literary contemporaries, including Andre Gide, Albert Camus, Saint-Jean Perse, and T. S. Eliot, whose *Four Quartets* Vigée translated.

While his writings are varied, Vigée prefers to be described as a poet, "because narratives and essays constitute attempts at elaboration of the thematic cores of my poems," he wrote in *Le Parfum et la cendre.* "These throbbing cores are the primary elements of my sensibility. I am a storyteller but in no way a novelist. I am not gifted with the ability to invent characters or situations. But those that I live, those that I note around me, I seize them with my gaze, I garner them, I make them my own, and I know how to make them live in the eyes of others because I love to recount them. From mouth to ear first of all; in the secret of the thing written down, finally."

According to Freema Gottlieb in an article published in *Flow Tide: Selected Poetry and Prose,* it was in the United States that Vigée "first tasted true exile which, together with the longing for 'origins,' was to be the driving force in his writing." In the United States, Vigée felt deprived of a native land, a family, and a personal landscape. "In a sense, Vigée's whole oeuvre amounts to a yearning for lost origins, a perennial nostalgia transcended through return to Jerusalem, the 'origin of origins.' And yet, there remains the ache of betrayal that he tried to overcome," Gottlieb remarked.

Since retiring from teaching in 1984, Vigée has divided his time between France and Jerusalem, visiting Germany, Italy, and Greece.

BIOGRAPHICAL AND CRITICAL SOURCES:

BOOKS

Lartichaux, Jean-Yves, *Claude Vigée,* Seghers (Paris, France), 1978.

Vigée, Claude, *Flow Tide: Selected Poetry and Prose,* edited and translated by Anthony Rudolf, Menard-King's College Press (London, England), 1992.

WALDROP, Howard 1946-

PERSONAL: Born September 15, 1946, in Houston, MS; son of Raymond Evans (an aircraft worker) and Zora Vee (a waitress; maiden name, Morris) Waldrop. *Education:* Attended University of Texas at Arlington, 1965-70 and 1972-74.

ADDRESSES: Office—P.O. Box 49335, Austin, TX 78765. *Agent*—Joseph Elder, Joseph Elder Agency, P.O. Box 298, Warwick, NY 10990.

CAREER: Freelance writer, 1972—. Dynastat, Inc., Austin, TX, auditory researcher, 1975-80. *Military service:* U.S. Army, 1970-72.

MEMBER: Science Fiction Writers of America, Trout Unlimited.

AWARDS, HONORS: Nebula Award from Science Fiction Writers of America, 1980, and World Fantasy Award from World Fantasy Society, 1981, both for "The Ugly Chickens."

WRITINGS:

(With Jake Saunders) *The Texas-Israeli War: 1999* (science fiction novel), Ballantine (New York, NY), 1974.

Them Bones (science fiction novel), Ace Books (New York, NY), 1984, reprinted in hardcover, Mark V. Zeising (Willimantic, CT), 1989.

Howard Who? (stories; includes "The Ugly Chickens"; also see below), Doubleday (New York, NY), 1986.

All about Strange Monsters of the Recent Past: Neat Stories (also see below), Ursus, 1987, expanded edition published as *Strange Monsters of the Recent Past* (contains *All about Strange Monsters of the Recent Past: Neat Stories* and *A Dozen Tough Jobs*), Ace Books (New York, NY), 1991.

Strange Things in Close-Up: The Nearly Complete Howard Waldrop (contains *Howard Who?* and *All about Strange Monsters of the Recent Past*), Legends (London, England), 1989.

A Dozen Tough Jobs (novella; also see below), Mark V. Zeising (Willimantic, CT), 1989.

Night of the Cooters: More Neat Stories (stories), Mark V. Zeising (Willimantic, CT), 1991, revised edition (includes *A Dozen Tough Jobs*), Ace Books (New York, NY), 1993.

You Could Go Home Again (novella), Cheap Street (New Castle, VA), 1993.

Going Home Again (stories), St. Martin's Press (New York, NY), 1998.

Flying Saucer Rock and Roll, Cheap Street (New Castle, VA), 2001.

(With Leigh Kennedy and others) *Custer's Last Jump and Other Collaborations,* Golden Gryphon Press (Urbana, IL), 2003.

Contributor of stories to anthologies and periodicals, including *Omni, Amazing Stories, Isaac Asimov's Science Fiction Magazine, Playboy, Shayol, Galaxy, Eternity SF,* and *Haunt of Horror.*

SIDELIGHTS: "Howard Waldrop is one of science fiction's most distinctive stylists, one of the very few who might truly be called unique," according to an essayist for *Contemporary Southern Writers.* "Working predominantly in the shorter forms Waldrop has amassed an acclaimed body of work which consistently surprises, enlightens, and entertains. It isn't possible to define a typical Waldrop story in terms more precise than 'odd.'" Although he is a science fiction writer, Waldrop more often explores the possible past than the distant future. Many of Waldrop's most popular stories are tales of what would have happened if history had turned out differently. In his award-winning "The Ugly Chickens," for example, a scientist discovers that dodo birds, long thought extinct, were being raised for food on a Mississippi farm. In "You Could Go Home Again," novelist Tom Wolfe and musician Fats Waller are returning from the 1940 Japanese Olympics via dirigible. Jed Hartman, writing in *Strange Horizons Magazine,* claimed that "Waldrop is one of the most unusual writers in the speculative fiction field."

The believability of Waldrop's alternate histories is a reflection of the exhaustive research the author puts into each story, enabling him to layer his fables with rich detail. This same detail, however, has made some of Waldrop's stories somewhat intimidating. For the reader to find the clues and get the jokes planted within the narrative, he often must have working knowledge of the time period. As Richard Gehr pointed out in the *Voice Literary Supplement,* "Interdisciplinarianism isn't required, but it sure helps." The story "Thirty Minutes over Broadway," for example, runs thirty-seven pages and comes with a twelve-page appendix in which all the allusions from comic books and pulp fiction are explained. "Waldrop's densely imagined and erudite stories have rather oddly gotten the reputation of being caviar for the general. . . . ," claimed the *Washington Post Book World*'s Gregory Feeley. "In fact he is caviar for the masses, and deserves a wider audience than he has hitherto found."

It is not surprising that Waldrop's name goes largely unrecognized, even among science fiction enthusiasts—after all, he has produced only a handful of books since 1974, and most of those in limited editions. Still, Gehr explained that as "a free agent, Waldrop writes with the unconstricted pleasure of the nonaligned autodidact, and as such he steadily, weirdly, and affectionately breaks and remakes the promises inscribed in the history of ideas." This freedom has consistently paid off, for, as Karen Joy Fowler wrote in the *Washington Post Book World,* "Waldrop is one of sf's most dependably surprising writers."

In his collection *Going Home Again,* Waldrop rewrites "The Musicians of Brementon" as a 1920s gangster story, creates a different version of Charles Dickens's classic "A Christmas Carol," and imagines how Peter Lorre's career may have been different had Nazi Germany won World War II. Doris Lynch in *Library Journal* called the stories "clever, humorous, idiosyncratic, oddball, personal, wild, and crazy." A critic for *Publishers Weekly* stated: "The fantastic inventions and whimsical nostalgia in these nine stories suggest that Waldrop is either a pulp writer born out of his time or an autodidact from another world."

Waldrop once told *CA:* "I fish and help my friends move to new apartments. I am interested in books, movies, dancing, rock and roll (what's left of it), and all the stuff my stories are about. If it were possible to make a living writing short stories, that's all I would do."

BIOGRAPHICAL AND CRITICAL SOURCES:

BOOKS

Contemporary Southern Writers, St. James Press (Detroit, MI), 1999.

Lane, Daryl, William Vernon, and David Carson, editors, *The Sounds of Wonder: Interviews from the Science Fiction Radio Show,* Volume I, Oryx, 1985.

St. James Guide to Science Fiction Writers, 4th edition, St. James Press (Detroit, MI), 1996.

PERIODICALS

Analog Science Fiction and Fact, May, 1985, Tom Easton, review of *Them Bones,* p. 135; February, 1987, Tom Easton, review of *Howard Who?,* p. 186; October, 1991, Tom Easton, review of *Night of the Cooters,* p. 165; November, 1998, Tom Easton, review of *Going Home Again,* p. 135.

Booklist, July, 1998, Mary Carroll, review of *Going Home Again,* p. 1868; April 1, 2003, Roland Green, review of *Custer's Last Jump and Other Collaborations,* p. 1384.

Library Journal, June 1, 1998, Doris Lynch, review of *Going Home Again,* p. 165.
Magazine of Fantasy and Science Fiction, September, 1989, Orson Scott Card, review of *A Dozen Tough Jobs,* p. 43; September, 1998, p. 49; September, 2003, Charles De Lint, review of *Custer's Last Jump and Other Collaborations,* p. 39.
Nova Express, Volume 1, number 3, 1988, interview with Howard Waldrop.
Observer, December 17, 1989, p. 46.
Publishers Weekly, June 20, 1986, Sybil Steinberg, review of *Howard Who?,* p. 93; May 4, 1998, review of *Going Home Again,* p. 201; April 14, 2003, review of *Custer's Last Jump and Other Collaborations,* p. 54.
SF Eye, Volume 1, number 5, July, 1989, interview with Howard Waldrop.
Voice Literary Supplement, August, 1989, p. 19.
Washington Post Book World, February 24, 1991, p. 8; October 29, 1991, p. 8.

ONLINE

Howard Waldrop's Home Page, http://www.sff.net/people/Waldrop/ (April 8, 2003).
Mississippi Writers and Musicians Project of Starkville High School, http://www.shs.starkville.k12.ms.us/mswm/MSWritersAndMusicians/writers/waldrop.html/ (April 8, 2003), Bjorn E. Lundin, "Howard Waldrop: A Biography" and review of *Them Bones.*
Strange Horizons Magazine, http://www.strangehorizons.com/ (January 29, 2001), Jed Hartman, "Three Ways of Looking at Howard Waldrop (and Then Some)," George R. R. Martin, "Introduction to *Howard Who?,*" Gardner Dozois, "Introduction to *All about Strange Monsters of the Recent Past,*" and Eileen Gunn, "Alternate Waldrops."*

* * *

WATKINS, Gloria Jean 1952-
(bell hooks)

PERSONAL: Born September 25, 1952, in Hopkinsville, KY; daughter of Veodis (a custodian) and Rosa Bell (a homemaker) Watkins. *Education:* Stanford University, B.A. (English), 1973; University of Wisconsin, Madison, M.A. (English), 1976; University of California at Santa Cruz, Ph.D., 1983.

ADDRESSES: Home—New York, NY. *Office*—Department of Afro-American Studies, Yale University, New Haven, CT 06520.

CAREER: Social critic, educator, and writer. University of Southern California, Los Angeles, English instructor and senior lecturer in ethnic studies, 1976-79; taught various subjects at institutions, including San Francisco State University, during the early 1980s; Yale University, New Haven, CT, assistant professor of Afro-American studies and English, beginning c. 1985; Oberlin College, Oberlin, OH, associate professor of women's studies and American literature, 1988-94; City College of the City University of New York, distinguished professor of English, beginning 1994.

AWARDS, HONORS: American Book Award, Before Columbus Foundation, 1991, for *Yearning: Race, Gender, and Cultural Politics;* Writer's Award, Lila Wallace-*Reader's Digest,* 1994.

WRITINGS:

UNDER NAME BELL HOOKS

Ain't I a Woman: Black Women and Feminism, South End Press (Boston, MA), 1981.
Feminist Theory: From Margin to Center, South End Press (Boston, MA), 1984, 2nd edition, 1999.
Talking Back: Thinking Feminist, Thinking Black (essays), South End Press (Boston, MA), 1989.
Yearning: Race, Gender, and Cultural Politics, South End Press (Boston, MA), 1990.
(With Cornell West) *Breaking Bread: Insurgent Black Intellectual Life,* South End Press (Boston, MA), 1991.
A Woman's Mourning Song (poetry), Writers and Readers, 1992.
Black Looks: Race and Representation, South End Press (Boston, MA), 1992.
Sisters of the Yam: Black Women and Self Recovery, South End Press (Boston, MA), 1993.
Outlaw Culture: Resisting Representations (essays), Routledge (New York, NY), 1994.
Emma Amos: Changing the Subject: Paintings and Prints (catalog essay), Art in General (New York, NY), 1994.
Teaching to Transgress: Education As the Practice of Freedom, Routledge (New York, NY), 1994.

Killing Rage: Ending Racism, Holt (New York, NY), 1995.

Art on My Mind: Visual Politics (essays), Norton (New York, NY), 1995.

(Editor) *Gumbo YA YA: Anthology of Contemporary African-American Women Artists,* Midmarch Arts, 1995.

Bone Black: Memories of Girlhood, Holt (New York, NY), 1996.

Happy to Be Nappy (juvenile), illustrated by Chris Raschka, Hyperion (New York, NY), 1996.

Reel to Real: Race, Sex, and Class at the Movies, Routledge (New York, NY), 1996.

Wounds of Passion: A Writing Life, Holt (New York, NY), 1997.

Remembered Rapture: The Writer at Work, Holt (New York, NY), 1999.

All about Love: New Visions, Morrow (New York, NY), 2000.

Feminism Is for Everybody: Passionate Politics, South End Press (Cambridge, MA), 2000.

Where We Stand: Class Matters, Routledge (New York, NY), 2000.

Homemade Love (juvenile), Hyperion (New York, NY), 2001.

Salvation: Black People and Love, Morrow (New York, NY), 2001.

Be Boy Buzz (juvenile), Hyperion (New York, NY), 2002.

Communion: Female Search for Love, Morrow (New York, NY), 2002.

Rock My Soul: Black People and Self-Esteem, Atria Books (New York, NY), 2003.

We Real Cool: Black Men and Masculinity, Routledge (New York, NY), 2003.

Teaching Community: A Pedagogy of Hope, Routledge (New York, NY), 2003.

Also author of *And There We Wept* (chapbook of poems), 1978; *Black Is a Woman's Color* (part 1 of memoirs), c. 1996; and *Cat Island Woman* (part 2 of memoirs), c. 1996. Contributor to *Double Stitch: Black Women Write about Mothers and Daughters,*1992; *Daughters of the Dust: The Making of an African-American Woman's Film,* 1992; *Felix Gonzales-Torres: Traveling,* 1994; and *Spoils of War: Women of Color, Culture, and Revolution,*1998. Contributor of essays to periodicals, including *Utne Reader, Catalyst, Callaloo, Emerge,* and *Essence.*

SIDELIGHTS: Gloria Jean Watkins, who writes under the name bell hooks (cited in lowercase), has written prolifically about many social issues. Her work takes an approach that is at once analytical yet also impassioned and personal. She explores the ways that African-American culture, womanhood, feminism, the civil rights movement, and critical theory both clash and complement each other, in the world at large and in her personal life. She has challenged the feminist movement with being largely racist, and has frequently voiced her concern over the negative images of blacks perpetuated in the popular media. She has also written children's books and poetry, memoirs, and books dealing with the need for love and increased self-esteem among the members of the African-American community. "At her best she exhibits a command of various voices that range from subtle overlays of the personal and historical to a refreshing public forthrightness that stings," wrote P. Gabrielle Foreman in the *Women's Review of Books.* "Inevitably, a reader will cheer through one essay and scowl through another."

Watkins grew up in rural Kentucky, in a small, segregated community with five sisters and one brother. Her father worked as a custodian for the U.S. Postal Service, and her mother worked as a domestic. Watkins has said that growing up in a family of strong women was extremely important to her, and she took her great-grandmother's name as a way of paying homage to the legacy of her female ancestors. She recalled in *Talking Back: Thinking Feminist, Thinking Black,* "I was a young girl buying bubble gum at the corner store when I first really heard the name bell hooks. I had just talked back to a grown person. Even now I can recall the surprised look, the mocking tones that informed me I must be kin to bell hooks, a sharp-tongued woman, a woman who spoke her mind, a woman who was not afraid to talk back. I claimed this legacy of defiance, of will, of courage, affirming my link to female ancestors who were bold and daring in their speech."

Watkins was drawn to literature and writing from an early age. Her scholastic achievement was such that she was able to attend Stanford University on scholarships. It was in college that she became aware of class differences and racism in a way she never had before. She found the campus environment much less liberal and open than she expected, and was surprised at the lack of attention paid to black women by the fledgling feminist movement. She perceived a lack of material about African-American women at the library, as well, which spurred her to begin writing her own books. Her first publication was the poetry chapbook *And There We Wept,* published in 1978.

After several years and numerous revisions, Watkins published *Ain't I a Woman: Black Women and Feminism,* her first book of theory. In *Ain't I a Woman* she explains how racism pervades mainstream feminism and chides white women for ignoring blacks, while discussing how black women can find their place in feminism anyway. Using a feminist perspective, Watkins chronicles the history of black women in America, from the slavery era through the 1970s, and posits the theory that African-American women were more strongly feminist in the nineteenth century than the twentieth. The work got a chilly reception, as many critics questioned Watkins's methods of analysis and some of her assertions, such as her opinion that slavery was worse for women than for men. She has continued to develop similar themes in *Feminism, Feminist Theory: From Margin to Center,* and *Talking Back: Thinking Feminist, Thinking Black.*

In *Feminist Theory* Watkins clearly states that the basic ills of the three "isms"—racism, classism, and sexism—have at their root the notion of domination. This kind of organization is opposed to a consensual/collectivist model which would eradicate the existing forces of control, manipulation, and domination, and thus redefine power throughout society. Being at the bottom of such a power structure, black women are naturally in the vanguard of liberation from the existing structure, by their very efforts at individual self-determination. They are not, however, recognized as such by mainstream feminist organizations, who see the world with the same hierarchical eyes as do white males, wanting merely to be in their positions. Real feminism, says Watkins, should attack the whole hierarchical system. The paradigm is played out in Watkins's book *Talking Back,* which contains twenty-three essays on different aspects of the black/feminist connection, varying from "writing autobiography, teaching women's literature, black homophobia, intimate violence, racist feminists, black porn, and politics at Yale," noted Beverly Miller in *Library Journal.*

Watkins's first three works have sometimes been seen as taking on too many voices to deal with their complex, inflammatory issues. A reviewer for *Publishers Weekly,* for example, noted that "although the author makes perceptive and provocative observations, they are diminished by redundancy and weakened by her doctrinaire Marxist rhetoric." Patricia Bell-Scott, in the *Women's Review of Books,* admitted to reacting defensively to some arguments that run against the feminist grain, and pointed to the Marxist flavor as possibly irritating. "However," Bell-Scott continued, "we must keep in mind the author's goal, to enrich feminist discourse and 'to share in the work of making a liberatory ideology,' as we struggle with the uncomfortable issues she raises."

Although all of Watkins's work contains self-examination, her fourth book, *Yearning: Race, Gender, and Cultural Politics,* seems to reassess all her efforts, as well as her various voices. In it she continues to broaden her cultural criticism, using more and more of the theoretical tools available to—and expected from—a cutting-edge, post-modern academic. Critics like P. Gabrielle Foreman find that central to this effort is the essay "Homeplace: A Site of Resistance," in which Watkins once more returns home to find her "location" of strength, a sense of community in the households set up by black women. This "location" helps her to solidify her base point of view, even as she sets out to examine more of her overall culture, and a black woman's part in it, from more varied and theoretical perspectives. This might be the reason that critics, among them Foreman, see her often contradicting herself and taking on the white feminists' point of view. For Foreman, though, it is her "'intervention' into the politics of post-modern theory and practice that makes *Yearning* so timely and valuable." She tries, for example, to untangle the theories of "Otherness"—the position of outsiders within a culture—that have been primarily produced by insiders or white scholars. This includes their theorizing on "essentialism"—in this case the reality of racial groupings, and the politics of identity based on those groupings. This is a complicated question for Watkins, since blacks can be affected by both sides of this dilemma.

The reassessment of Watkins's "locations" as an African-American intellectual continue in *Breaking Bread: Insurgent Black Intellectual Life,* a dialogue with social critic and professor Cornel West. Their discussion ranges over the various crises of the black community, and how marketing to blacks, and depictions of blacks in the media, have contributed to those problems. This theme, which has threaded its way through her earlier work, is enlarged upon in *Black Looks: Race and Representation.* In its twelve chapters, she explores the implicit meaning of black images in phenomena such as advertising, Madonna's music videos, and the Anita Hill-Clarence Thomas hearings. Her most serious indictment of the media is that it further threatens the position of the black woman by selling black males a macho self-image. Widely greeted with approval for its groundbreaking breadth and theoretical rigor, *Black Looks* caused a *Library Journal* critic to remark, "hooks continues to produce some of the most challenging, insightful, and provocative writing on race and gender in the United States today."

In 1994 Watkins published both *Teaching to Transgress: Education As the Practice of Freedom* and *Outlaw Culture: Resisting Representations.* Reviewing these books in the *New York Times Book Review,* Jerome Karabel noted that *Teaching to Transgress* is "often marred by a disconcerting reliance on pop psychology." However, Karabel concluded, each book allows readers "to confront the political undercurrents of life in America." "*Outlaw Culture: Resisting Representations* continues the investigation of the depiction of African Americans in modern culture that Watkins explored in *Breaking Bread,*" noted Melissa L. Evans in *Feminist Writers.* "*Outlaw Culture* specifically focuses on cinematic, artistic, and musical representations of race, and is particularly interesting due to Watkins's commentary on figures such as Madonna and gangster rap. Aside from cultural commentary, Watkins also offers her commentary, critical as it is, on the 'new feminism' of figures such as Camille Paglia."

Watkins recalls her own life in the books *Bone Black: Memories of Girlhood, Wounds of Passion: A Writing Life,* and *Remembered Rapture: The Writer at Work.* In *Bone Black* she relates the story of her youth in a traditional Southern working-class family. It is significant "both as a documentation of one black woman's girlhood and as a beautifully crafted narrative," decided Evelyn E. Shockley in her *African American Review* appraisal of the book. *Bone Black* was praised as "vivid" and "extraordinary" by Catherine Burt in *American Visions,* the critic adding that the book "reveals the events and experiences as well as the feelings, thoughts and dreams of a wise and sensitive girl as she sifts through the magical world around her and shapes her identity." *Bone Black* reveals much about the source of Watkins's "forcefulness and candor," mused Donna Seaman in *Booklist,* and it does so in a book that is "lyrical, deeply moving, and brilliantly structured."

In *Wounds of Passion: A Writing Life* the author moves on to subjects such as poetry, feminism, sexuality, and a fifteen-year romantic relationship, telling her stories in a "consistently fresh and bravely honest voice," according to a *Publishers Weekly* writer. *Remembered Rapture: The Writer at Work* is a collection of twenty-two essays discussing spirituality and writing. The styles range from personal, reflective life memories to more highly structured, formal essays that reflect the author's experience as a university lecturer. As usual, Watkins "emphasizes the importance of personal and political identity to writing," found a *Publishers Weekly* writer. "Her prose is clear and she presents her arguments with a confident passion. If her politics are predictable, hooks infuses the best of these essays with a personal tone that sheds warm light on this one particular writer's writing life."

Watkins turns her attention to various aspects of love in books such as *All about Love: New Visions, Salvation: Black People and Love,* and *Communion: Female Search for Love.* In *All about Love* she suggests that the hatred encountered in the experience of racism and other oppressive relationships can be negated by the experience of profound love. She notes with distress the lack of belief in real love that is expressed by even very young children in contemporary times. Aleta Richards in the *Civil Rights Journal* stated that this book "teaches us how to find and keep love in a culture full of hatred." Richards remarked that while at first glace the book might seem to be a rather superficial pop-psychology manual, in fact, "it's an important book about the sociological implications of oppression and why it's hard to give and receive love in our highly individualized, Western culture."

In *Salvation* Watkins again advocates for the increase of unselfish love. She identifies lack of love and trust as the root of many other social problems, particularly the collapse of communities. "Readers of every hue will benefit from hooks' piercing insights into the troubled state of our collective soul and find solace in her belief that 'love is our hope and salvation,'" commented Seaman in *Booklist. Communion* tackles problems unique to women, who are made to feel that their lovableness is based on their attractiveness and their service to others. Women have made great strides in becoming socially empowered, but they are still questing for satisfying love, because society has conditioned men to think that withholding their emotions is a validation of their manhood. The author suggests that women may have to be creative in looking for love, pointing out the possibilities of same-sex love, romantic friendships, and "circles of love."

Low self-esteem, rooted in generations of slavery, has negatively affected the African-American spirit for years, Watkins argues in *Rock My Soul: Black People and Self-Esteem.* She reflects on the successes and failures of efforts to build black pride in the past, and suggests pathways to a future in which African Americans can replace chronic emotional pain with healthy ways of thought. "To read her is to set out on the path toward healing," claimed Seaman in a *Booklist* review, while a *Publishers Weekly* writer concluded: "With each new book, hooks is deeply exploring the inner terrain of the black community, calling for a return to sound values, self-love and commonsense solutions while seeking new ways to cope with a modern world gone slightly mad."

BIOGRAPHICAL AND CRITICAL SOURCES:

BOOKS

Black Literature Criticism Supplement, Gale (Detroit, MI), 1999.

Black Writers, 2nd edition, Gale (Detroit, MI), 1994.

Contemporary Black Biography, Volume 5, Gale (Detroit, MI), 1994.

Contemporary Literary Criticism, Volume 94, Gale (Detroit, MI), 1996.

Dictionary of Literary Biography, Volume 246: *Twentieth-Century American Cultural Theorists,* Gale (Detroit, MI), 2001.

Encyclopedia of World Biography, 2nd edition, Gale (Detroit, MI), 1998.

Feminist Writers, St. James Press (Detroit, MI), 1996.

Newsmakers 2000, Gale (Detroit, MI), 2000.

Notable Black American Women, Book II, Gale (Detroit, MI), 1996.

The Schomburg Center Guide to Black Literature, Gale (Detroit, MI), 1996.

PERIODICALS

African American Review, fall, 1997, Evelyn E. Shockley, review of *Bone Black: Memories of Girlhood,* p. 552.

American Visions, April-May, 1997, Catherine Burt, review of *Bone Black,* p. 28.

Black Collegian, February, 1996, Mamie Webb Hixon, review of *Killing Rage: Ending Racism,* p. 11; October, 2002, Corinne Nelson, review of *Rock My Soul: Black People and Self-Esteem,* p. 126.

Black Enterprise, June, 1992, p. 23.

Black Issues Book Review, March, 2001, Angela Dodson, review of *Salvation: Black People and Love,* p. 64; March-April, 2002, Gary Dauphin, interview with Watkins, p. 50; November-December, 2002, Evette Porter, review of *Be Boy Buzz,* p. 42.

Black Scholar, January, 1983, pp. 38, 46.

Booklist, June 1, 1995, Donna Seaman, review of *Art on My Mind: Visual Politics,* p. 1715; September 15, 1995, Bonnie Smothers, review of *Killing Rage,* p. 118; September 15, 1996, Donna Seaman, review of *Bone Black,* p. 189; September 15, 1997, Donna Seaman, review of *Wounds of Passion: A Writing Life,* p. 185; December 15, 1998, Donna Seaman, review of *Remembered Rapture: The Writer at Work,* p. 721; August, 1999, Hazel Rochman, review of *Happy to Be Nappy,* p. 2064; January 1, 2000, Donna Seaman, review of *All about Love,* p. 839; February 15, 2001, Donna Seaman, review of *Salvation,* p. 1098; February 15, 2002, Donna Seaman, review of *Communion: The Female Search for Love,* p. 1002; November 1, 2002, Hazel Rochman, review of *Be Boy Buzz,* p. 508; February 1, 2003, Donna Seaman, review of *Rock My Soul,* p. 814, Gillian Engberg, review of *Homemade Love,* p. 1001.

Bookwatch, July 1989, p. 4; September, 1992, p. 10.

Choice, April, 1982, p. 1141; July, 1985, p. 1703.

Chronicle of Higher Education, May 19, 1995.

Civil Rights Journal, fall, 2000, Aleta Richards, review of *All about Love,* p. 58.

Emerge, November, 1995, Lori S. Robinson, review of *Killing Rage,* p. 92; February, 2000, Meri Nana-Ama Danquah, review of *All about Love,* p. 108.

Essence, December, 1997, Martha Southgate, "Do We Need Kwanzaa?," p. 68; July, 1989, p. 20.

Interview, October, 1995, Ingrid Sischy, interview with Watkins, p. 122.

Library Journal, July, 1995, Ann Burns, review of *Killing Rage,* p. 107; October 1, 1997, Ann Burns, review of *Wounds of Passion,* p. 94; December 1, 1981, p. 178; March 15, 1985, p. 68; November 1, 1998, Ann Burns, review of *Remembered Rapture,* p. 81; December, 1988, p. 126; July, 1992, p. 109; July, 1993; November 1, 1999, Ann Burns, review of *All about Love,* p. 107; November 1, 2000, Ann

Burns, review of *Where We Stand: Class Matters, and Salvation,* p. 104; February 15, 2002, Deborah Bigelow, review of *Communion,* p. 166; November 1, 2002, Ann Burns, review of *Rock My Soul,* p. 115; October 1, 2003, Scott Walter, review of *Teaching Community: A Pedagogy of Hope,* p. 92.

Ms., July, 1983, p. 24; October, 1985, p. 25; February-March, 2000, Pearl Cleage, review of *All about Love,* p. 84; December, 2000, Jocelyn L. Womac, review of *Feminism Is for Everybody: Passionate Politics,* p. 88.

Multicultural Review, April, 1992; March, 1993.

National Review, January 22, 2001, Maggie Gallagher, review of *Feminism Is for Everybody.*

New Directions for Women, January, 1992, p. 22.

New Statesman, October 22, 1982, p. 31; November 30, 1990, p. 39.

New York Review of Books, April 18, 1996, George M. Fredrickson, review of *Killing Rage,* p. 16.

New York Times Book Review, February 28, 1993; December 18, 1994; November 21, 1999, p. 58; January 30, 2000, Elise Harris, review of *All about Love,* p. 21.

Phylon, March, 1983, p. 85.

Political Science Quarterly, spring, 1983, p. 84.

Progressive, March, 1991, p. 42.

Publishers Weekly, June 26, 1995, review of *Art on My Mind,* p. 104; November 18, 1988, p. 72; November 22, 1991, p. 49; June 15, 1992, p. 95; July 17, 1995, review of *Killing Rage,* p. 211; August 5, 1996, review of *Bone Black,* p. 421; September 22, 1997, review of *Wounds of Passion,* p. 64; November 23, 1998, review of *Remembered Rapture,* p. 29; July 19, 1999, review of *Happy to Be Nappy,* p. 194; November 29, 1999, review of *All about Love,* p. 60; December 4, 2000, review of *Salvation,* p. 60; September 30, 2002, review of *Be Boy Buzz,* p. 71; November 18, 2002, review of *Homemade Love,* p. 59; November 25, 2002, Robert Fleming, interview with Watkins, and review of *Rock My Soul,* p. 54; September 1, 2003, review of *Teaching Community,* p. 77.

Queen's Quarterly, summer, 1990, p. 318.

Savoy, March, 2002, Catherine Kelly, review of *Communion,* p. 36.

School Library Journal, March, 1997, Dottie Kraft, review of *Bone Black,* p. 217; November, 1999, Karen James, review of *Happy to Be Nappy,* p. 120; December, 2002, Anna DeWind Walls, review of *Be Boy Buzz,* and Amy Lilien-Harper, review of *Homemade Love,* p. 97.

Sight and Sound, June, 1991, p. 36.

Signs, autumn, 1994.

Village Voice Literary Supplement, June, 1982, p. 10.

West Coast Review of Books, April, 1982, p. 51.

Women's Review of Books, February, 1985, p. 3; September, 1991, p. 12.*

* * *

WHITE, John H(oxland), Jr. 1933-

PERSONAL: Born November 10, 1933, in Cincinnati, OH; son of John Hoxland (an accountant) and Christine (Seebaun) White. *Education:* Miami University, Oxford, OH, B.A., 1958.

ADDRESSES: Home—101 Beechpoint Dr., Oxford, OH 45056. *Office*—Department of History, Miami University, Oxford, OH 45056. *E-mail*—jwengine@hotmail.com.

CAREER: Smithsonian Institution, National Museum of American History, Washington, DC, began as museum aide, became associate curator, 1958-67, curator of transportation, 1967-90, chair of Department of Industries in the 1970s, and senior historian; Miami University, Oxford, OH, member of history faculty, 1996—. Lecturer at University of Pennsylvania, 1966, University of California, 1970, and University of Moscow, 1973; Science Museum, London, England, fellow, 1983, 1984. Consultant, Pennsylvania State Railroad Museum, 1968-90, and California State Railroad Museum, 1970-90. Also worked as a mechanic and drafter.

MEMBER: Railway and Locomotive Historical Society, Society for the History of Technology, Cincinnati Historical Society.

AWARDS, HONORS: National Book Award nomination, 1979, for *The American Railroad Passenger Car;* Lifetime Achievement Award, Railroad and Locomotive Historical Society, 1982; Dexter Book Prize, Society for the History of Technology, 1994; D.Letters, Miami University, 1996.

WRITINGS:

Cincinnati Locomotive Builders, 1845-1868, Smithsonian Institution Press (Washington, DC), 1965.

American Locomotives: An Engineering History, 1830-1880, Johns Hopkins University Press (Baltimore, MD), 1968, published as *A History of the American Locomotive: Its Development, 1830-1880,* Dover (New York, NY), 1979, revised edition published as *American Locomotives: An Engineering History, 1830-1880,* Johns Hopkins University Press (Baltimore, MD), 1997.

(Editor) *Development of the Locomotive Engine,* MIT Press (Cambridge, MA), 1970.

Early American Locomotives, Dover (New York, NY), 1972.

Horsecars, Cable Cars and Omnibuses, Dover (New York, NY), 1974.

The American Railroad Passenger Car, Johns Hopkins University Press (Baltimore, MD), 1978.

The John Bull: 150 Years a Locomotive, Smithsonian Institution Press (Washington, DC), 1981.

A Short History of American Locomotive Builders in the Steam Era, Bass, 1982.

The Great Yellow Fleet, Golden West Books (San Marino, CA), 1986.

American Railroad Freight Cars, Johns Hopkins University Press (Baltimore, MD), 1993.

(With Robert J. White) *The Island Queen: Cincinnati's Excursion Steamer,* University of Akron Press (Akron, OH), 1995.

Cincinnati: City of Seven Hills and Five Inclines, Cincinnati Railroad Club (Cincinnati, OH), 2001.

Cincinnati Railroads: A Selective History, Cincinnati Railroad Club (Cincinnati, OH), 2003.

Contributor of more than 130 articles and reviews to museum bulletins and transportation journals. Editor, *Railroad History,* 1970-79.

SIDELIGHTS: John H. White, Jr. told *CA:*"My primary motivation for writing is to make a record of my research and thinking on the history of technology available to others, particularly future historians. My work has been influenced by Louis Hunter and Howard I. Chapelle, both able researchers who presented their ideas in clear and detailed texts."

BIOGRAPHICAL AND CRITICAL SOURCES:

PERIODICALS

Invention and Technology, fall, 1990.

New Republic, December 9, 1978.

New York Times Book Review, June 4, 1978; April 13, 1980.

Village Voice, December 3, 1980.

* * *

WILLARD, Fred 1939

PERSONAL: Born September 18, 1939, in Shaker Heights, OH. *Education:* Graduated from the Virginia Military Institute.

ADDRESSES: *Agent*—Cunningham, Escott, Dipene and Associates, 257 Park Ave. S, Suite 900, New York, NY 10010.

CAREER: Actor, comedian, and comedy writer. Member of the improvisational comedy troupes Second City, Chicago, IL; Ace Trucking Company, San Francisco, CA; and The Committee, all during the late 1960s. Appeared in television series as a regular performer in *The Burns and Schreiber Comedy Hour,* ABC, 1973; as assistant district attorney H. R. "Bud" Nugent in *Sirota's Court,* NBC, 1976-77; as Jerry Hubbard in *Fernwood 2-Night,* syndicated, 1977, renamed *America 2-Night,* syndicated, 1978; as a host of *Real People,* NBC, 1979, then 1981-83; as Fred the bartender in *D.C. Follies,* syndicated, 1987-89; as Scott in *Roseanne,* ABC, c. 1995-96; and as President Garner, *Lois and Clark: The New Adventures of Superman* (also known as *Lois and Clark* and *The New Adventures of Superman*), ABC, 1995-96.-

Appeared in pilots for television series, and appeared as Bower in *Operation Greasepaint,* CBS, 1968; as Captain Thomas Woods in *Space Force,* NBC, 1978; as Jack LaRosa in *Flatbed Annie and Sweetiepie: Lady Truckers* (also known as *Flatbed Annie*), CBS, 1979; and as Ralph in *Pen 'n' Inc.,* CBS, 1981. Appeared as Larry Crockett in the television production *Salem's Lot* (also known as *Blood Thirst, Salem's Lot: The Miniseries,* and *Salem's Lot: The Movie*), CBS, 1979. Appeared in made-for-television movies as Lance Colson in *How to Break Up a Happy Divorce,* NBC, 1976; as Pearson in *Escape from Bogen County,* CBS, 1977; as A. J. Foley in *Lots of Luck,* The Disney Channel, 1985; as Hal Harrison in *Martin Mull in Portrait of a White Marriage* (also known as *Scenes from a White Marriage*), Cinemax, 1988; as master of ceremonies

Fred Willard

Georgie Porgie in *Mother Goose Rock 'n' Rhyme,* The Disney Channel, 1990; in "Hart to Hart: Old Friends Never Die" (also known as "Hart to Hart: Hart Attack"), *NBC Friday Night Mystery,* NBC, 1994; as Clarence Gentry in *Sodbusters,* Showtime, 1994; as a loan officer in *Back to Back: American Yakusa II* (also known as *Back to Back*), HBO, 1996; made an uncredited appearance as a talk-show host in *Breast Men,* HBO, 1997; as Howard Cosell in *When Billie Beat Bobby,* ABC, 2001. Appeared in television specials, including *Madhouse 90,* 1972; *The Paul Lynde Comedy Hour,* 1975; *Gabriel Kaplan Presents the Small Event,* ABC, 1977; *The Second City Comedy Special,* 1979; as an NBC team member in *Battle of the Network Stars,* ABC, 1981; as a host of *Getting the Last Laugh,* 1985; *The History of White People in America: Volume I,* Cinemax, 1985; *The Second City 25th Anniversary Special,* HBO, 1985; as a host of *What's Hot, What's Not,* 1985; *The History of White People in America: Volume II,* Cinemax, 1986; *Martin Mull Live! from North Ridgeville, Ohio,* HBO, 1987; *This Week Indoors,* 1987; *Merrill Markoe's Guide to Glamorous Living,* Cinemax, 1988; *Superman's 50th Anniversary: A Celebration of the Man of Steel,* 1988; *The 14th Annual Circus of the Stars,* CBS, 1989; *The Third Annual American Comedy Awards,* 1989; as a host of *Access America,* 1990; *Candid Camera . . . Funny Money,* CBS, 1990; *Candid Camera . . . Smile, You're on Vacation!,* CBS, 1990; as himself in *Comics Only,* 1991; *The Fifth Annual American Comedy Awards,* 1991; *Louise DuArt: The Secret Life of Barry's Wife,* Showtime, 1991; as a host of *Real People Reunion Special,* NBC, 1991; "Rodney Dangerfield's The Really Big Show," *HBO Comedy Hour,* HBO, 1991; *Tom Arnold: The Naked Truth,* HBO, 1991; *A Spinal Tap Reunion,* NBC, 1992; *Subaru Presents Fair Enough: Martin Mull at the Iowa State Fair,* Comedy Central, 1994; and *Steve.Oedekerk.Com,* NBC, 1997.

Actor in episodes of television series, and appeared as John Emil Tobin in "Tobin's Back in Town," *The Bob Newhart Show,* CBS, 1975; as Jerry Hubbard in *Forever Fernwood,* syndicated, 1977; "The Bonanza," *We've Got Each Other,* CBS, 1977; as the guest host of *Saturday Night Live* (also known as *NBC's Saturday Night, Saturday Night,* and *SNL*), NBC, 1978; as himself in *Thicke of the Night,* syndicated, 1983 and 1984; "No More Alimony," *The Love Boat,* ABC, 1984; as Willie Potts in "Mama Buys a Car," *Mama's Family,* NBC, 1984; as Larry in "The Three Little Pigs," *Faerie Tale Theatre,* Showtime, 1985; "Home for Dinner," *George Burns Comedy Week,* CBS, 1985; *Life's Most Embarrassing Moments,* ABC, 1985; "Couples," *The Love Boat,* ABC, 1985; "A Friendly Christmas," *The New Love, American Style,* ABC, 1985; "Secret Romance," *Fast Times,* CBS, 1986; "Love and the Lambergenni," *The New Love, American Style,* ABC, 1986; "CPR," *Punky Brewster,* NBC, 1986; as Al Stefano in "Best Buddies," *Fame,* syndicated, c. 1987; "For Old Time's Sake," *My Secret Identity,* syndicated, 1988; "The Box Is Missing," *Out of This World,* syndicated, 1988; as Bob in "Dateline: Miami," *The Golden Girls,* NBC, 1991; as a guest performer in *The Ben Stiller Show,* Fox, 1992; as Fenton Harley in "Up All Night," *Dream On,* HBO, 1992; as Stan in "My Dinner with Anthrax," *Married . . . with Children,* Fox, 1992; as Bud Long in *Dave's World,* CBS, 1993; as Hatfield Walker in "Stand Up for Bastards," *The Jackie Thomas Show,* ABC, 1993; as Vice Principal Mallet in "The Looney Bin," *Family Matters,* ABC, 1994; as Dick in "Dick and Dottie," *Murphy Brown,* CBS, 1995; as Mr. Mitushka in *Sister, Sister,* ABC and The WB, 1995; as Joe Pasadine in *Clueless,* ABC, 1996; as Mr. Lipson in "The One after the Superbowl, Part I," *Friends,* NBC, 1996; as himself in "Needledrop," *Space Ghost Coast,* The

Cartoon Network, 1997; as an award-show host in "The Competition," *The Weird Al Show,* CBS, 1997; as Henry Vincent in "Fire at Riff's," "The Finale," and "The Thanksgiving Show," all episodes of *Mad about You* (also known as *Loved by You*), NBC, 1998; as himself in "Conner Family Reunion," *The Roseanne Show,* syndicated, 1998; as Calzone in "Rumor Mill," *Sabrina, the Teenage Witch,* ABC, 1998; as Willard J. Fredrick in *The Tonight Show with Jay Leno,* NBC, 1998; as Larry in "Hostess to Murder," *Just Shoot Me,* NBC, 1999; as a voice characterization in "Sunday, Cruddy Sunday," *The Simpsons* (animated), Fox, 1999; as Hank MacDougal in numerous episodes of *Everybody Loves Raymond,* 2003; as Charlie in "Battle of Evermore," *That '70s Show,* 2003; and as voice characterizations in the animated series *Kim Possible,* and *Dexter's Laboratory, Hey Arnold!,* and *King of the Hill;* also appeared in episodes of *SCTV Network 90* (also known as *SCTV Comedy Network* and *SCTV Network*), NBC and Cinemax; and *Skip TV,* Continental Cable System (Los Angeles, CA).

Appeared in films, including *Teenage Mother,* Cinemation, 1967; *Jenny* (also known as *And Jenny Makes Three*), Cinerama, 1969; as a gas station attendant in *The Model Shop,* Columbia, 1969; as a member of the Ace Trucking Company in *The Harrad Experiment,* Cinerama, 1973; *Harrad Summer* (also known as *Student Union*), Cinerama, 1974; as an interrogator in *Hustle,* Paramount, 1975; as F.B.I. agent Peter in *Chesty Anderson, U.S. Navy* (also known as *Anderson's Angels* and *Chesty Anderson, U.S.N.*), Atlas, 1976; as Jerry Jarvis in *Silver Streak,* Twentieth Century-Fox, 1976; *Cracking Up,* American International Pictures, 1977; as Bob in *Fun with Dick and Jane,* Columbia, 1977; as Vincent Vanderhoff in *Americathon,* United Artists, 1979, rereleased as *Americathon 1998;* as presidential assistant Feebleman in *First Family,* Warner Bros., 1980; as Robert in *How to Beat the High Co$t of Living,* American International Pictures, 1980; as President Fogarty in "Success Wanters," *National Lampoon Goes to the Movies* (also known as *National Lampoon's Movie Madness*), United Artists, 1981; as himself in *Second City Insanity,* Lorimar Home Video, 1981; as Lieutenant Hookstratten in *This Is Spinal Tap* (also known as *Spinal Tap*), Embassy, 1984; as Terrence "Doc" Williams in *Moving Violations,* Twentieth Century-Fox, 1985; as himself in *Big City Comedy,* LIVE Home Video, 1986; as Tom Osborne in *Ray's Male Heterosexual Dance Hall,* Chanticleer Films, 1987; as Mayor Deebs in *Roxanne,* Columbia, 1987; as an insurance salesman in *High Strung,* Rocket Pictures, 1991; as Thomas MacGregor in *Prehistoria! 3* (also known as *Prehysteria 3*), Paramount Home Video, 1995; as Ron Albertson in *Waiting for Guffman* (also known as *The Christopher Guest Project*), Sony Pictures Classics, 1996; as Craig Ziffer in *Permanent Midnight,* Artisan Entertainment, 1998; as Chester in *Can't Stop Dancing,* Stoneridge Entertainment/PM Entertainment Group, 1999; *McClintock's Peach,* West Wind Entertainment, 1999; as the president in *The Pooch and the Pauper,* 1999; as broadcaster Buck Laughlin in *Best in Show,* 2000; as Roger Dickey in *Teddy Bears' Picnic,* 2002, and as Chancellor Huntley in *How High,* 2002. Also appeared in *The Perfect Woman,* 1978, *Kid-A-Littles,* 1987, and *Poker with the Joker.* Appeared in stage productions, including *The Return of the Second City in "20,000 Frozen Grenadiers,"* Square East Theatre, New York City, 1966; *Arf,* Stage 73, New York, NY, 1969; *Little Murders,* Circle in the Square Theatre, New York City, 1969; *Elvis and Juliet,* Theatre at the Improv, Los Angeles, CA, 1994; and *Anything Goes,* UCLA, 2002. Also appeared in advertisements with Martin Mull.

WRITINGS:

TELEPLAYS; SPECIALS

Getting the Last Laugh, 1985.

SCREENPLAYS

(Contributor of improvisational material based on a script outline by Christopher Guest and Eugene Levy) *Waiting for Guffman* (also known as *The Christopher Guest Project*), Sony Pictures Classics, 1996.

(Contributor of improvisational material based on a script outline by Christopher Guest) *Best in Show,* 2000.

(Contributor of improvisational material based on historic commentary by Howard Cosell) *When Billie Beat Bobby,* ABC, 2001.

Has also written improvisational material for the stage.

SIDELIGHTS: Comedian and actor Fred Willard began his performing career with the comedy improvisational groups Second City, The Committee, and Ace Trucking Company during the late 1960s. He has appeared regularly in film and television roles since the 1960s in addition to writing and hosting the 1985 comedy special *Getting the Last Laugh.* Willard starred in the syndicated television series *Fernwood 2-Night,* a show later renamed *America 2-Night.* Willard played Jerry Hubbard, the dimwitted but affable cohost of a fictional late night talk show hosted by Barth Gimble, a character played by Martin Mull. *Fernwood 2-Night* "constitutes the first serious attempt to poke fun at the television talk show" and was distinguished by a "delightful sense of wicked satire" noted Walter J. Podrazik and Harry Castleman in *Harry and Wally's Favorite TV Shows.* Although Podrazik and Castleman admitted that *Fernwood 2-Night* "is probably too weird for many viewers," it did become a cult favorite.

Following *Fernwood 2-Night,* Willard appeared in several television productions. He appeared in the series *Real People, D.C. Follies,* and *Lois and Clark: The New Adventures of Superman.* Willard also made guest appearances in episodes of several popular television shows, including *The Bob Newhart Show, The Love Boat, Married . . . with Children,* and *Murphy Brown.* On the series *Roseanne,* he once again worked with Martin Mull. Willard and Mull have enjoyed a long working relationship, appearing together in the aforementioned television series as well as specials such as *The History of White People in America, Volume I* and *The History of White People in America, Volume II,* the made-for-television movie *Martin Mull in Portrait of a White Marriage,* and even advertisements.

Willard has also acted in several films. He appeared with Richard Pryor and Gene Wilder in *Silver Streak,* played Lieutenant Hookstratten in the fake "rockumentary" *This Is Spinal Tap,* and appeared in the 1987 film *Roxanne,* actor-comedian Steve Martin's adaptation of the play *Cyrano de Bergerac.* Willard portrays travel agent Ron Albertson in the 1996 film *Waiting for Guffman,* a comedy about the efforts of the townspeople of Blaine, Missouri, to stage a show commemorating the town's sesquicentennial (150th) anniversary. The cast also includes Christopher Guest, Catherine O'Hara, Eugene Levy, and Parker Posey. The cast members improvised from a basic script outline developed by Guest and Levy, and critics admired the results. *Newsweek* contributor David Ansen praised "the terrific cast" and commented that "*Guffman* is both a savvy satire of smalltown boosterism and an affectionate salute to the performing spirit," noting that "the movie is, from start to finish, a hoot." Writing in *People,* Tom Gliatto found the spoof "wonderfully silly." Much like *This Is Spinal Tap,* another fake documentary, *Waiting for Guffman* became a cult favorite.

A versatile performer, Willard can also be counted on to flesh out a script idea or change dialogue to suit his character. In the made-for-television film *When Billie Beat Bobby,* Willard was faced with the task of paraphrasing the commentary of the late Howard Cosell, because Cosell's historic comments were under copyright. In the comic send-up of fancy dog shows, *Best in Show,* Willard romped as a clueless American broadcaster providing television commentary while knowing nothing at all about competitive dog breeding. In *Entertainment Weekly* Willard said that he developed his style of improvisation by watching his mother and grandmother "say stupid things" when he was young. He concluded: "Everyone has a little trapdoor in their mind where you go to say something and then you think no, you shouldn't say this. I just open that door."

BIOGRAPHICAL AND CRITICAL SOURCES:

BOOKS

Podrazik, Walter J., and Harry Castleman, *Harry and Wally's Favorite TV Shows,* Prentice Hall Press (New York, NY), 1989.

PERIODICALS

Entertainment Weekly, August 15, 1997, p. 84; October 6, 2000, Owen Gleiberman, "Arfhouse Cinema," p. 58; October 13, 2000, Fred Schruers, "Bark Victory," p. 24; April 20, 2001, "Triumph of the Willard: The 'Best in Show' Scene Stealer Apes Howard Cosell in 'When Billie Beat Bobby,'" p. 57.

Insight on the News, April 22, 2002, Rex Roberts, "It's No Picnic," p. 27.

Newsweek, February 10, 1997, p. 66.

People, September 12, 1988, p. 11; March 17, 1997, pp. 21-22; September 12, 1998, p. 11.

Variety, September 1, 1997, p. 30; April 1, 2002, Scott Foundas, review of *Teddy Bears' Picnic,* p. 33.

Video Business, April 15, 2002, review of *How High,* p. 13.*

* * *

WOODY, Elizabeth (Ann) 1959-

PERSONAL: Born December 26, 1959, in Ganado, AZ; daughter of Guy Woody and Charlotte Pitt (counselor). *Ethnicity:* "Native American." *Education:* Evergreen State College, B.A., 1991; attended Institute of American Indian Arts, 1980-1983. *Hobbies and other interests:* Beadwork, basketweaving, mixed media fine arts.

ADDRESSES: *Office*—Ecotrust, 1200 Northwest Front Ave., Portland, OR 97209.

CAREER: Institute of of American Indian Arts, Santa Fe, NM, program assistant.

MEMBER: Soapstone, Inc., Women Writer's Retreat (Board of Directors), Wordcraft Circle, Native American Mentor-Apprenticeship (mentor and Advisory Caucus member), Northwest Native American Writer's Association (cofounder).

AWARDS, HONORS: Brandywine Visiting Artists Fellowship, Brandywine Workshop, 1988; American Book Award, Before Columbus Foundation, for *Hand into Stone,* 1990; Traditional Arts Master/Apprenticeship Fellowship, Oregon Folk Arts Program, 1992-93; "Medicine Pathways for the Future" Fellowship/ Kellogg Fellowship, American Indian Ambassadors Program, 1993; William Stafford Memorial Poetry Award, Pacific Northwest Booksellers Association, 1995; one of 80 artists nominated for Artist's Fellowship, Flintridge Foundation, 1996.

WRITINGS:

Hand into Stone (poetry), Contact II Press (New York, NY), 1988.

(Designer) Andrea Lerner, editor, *Dancing on the Rim of the Earth: An Anthology of Contemporary Northwest Native American Writings,* University of Arizona Press (Tucson, AZ), 1990.

Luminaries of the Humble (poetry), University of Arizona Press, 1994.

Seven Hands, Seven Hearts (prose and poetry), Eighth Mountain Press (Portland, OR), 1994.

(With others) *Salmon Nation: People and Fish at the Edge* (essays), original maps by Dorie Brownell, Edward C. Wolf and Seth Zuckerman, editors, Ecotrust (Portland, OR), 1999.

Work represented in anthologies, including *The Songs from This Earth on Turtle's Back: Contemporary American Indian Poetry,* edited by Joseph Bruchac, Greenfield Review Press (Greenfield Center, NY), 1983; *The Clouds Threw This Light: Contemporary Native American Poetry,* edited by Phillip Foss, Institute of American Indian Arts Press (Santa Fe, NM), 1983; *Talking Leaves: Contemporary Native American Fiction,* edited by Craig Lesley, Laurel (New York, NY), 1991; *Durable Breath: Contemporary Native American Poetry,* edited by John E. Smelcer and D. L. Birchfield, Salmon Run Press/American Indian Press (Anchorage, AK/San Francisco, CA), 1994; *Oregon Literature Series,* five volumes, University of Oregon Press (Corvallis, OR), 1994; *Returning the Gift: Poetry and Prose from the First North American Native Writers Festival,* University of Arizona Press, 1994.

Contributor of essays to books, including *Between Species: Women and Animals* (prose), Ballantine, 1997; *Home Places: Contemporry Native American Writing from "Sun Tracks,"* University of Arizona Press, 1995; *Reinventing the Enemies Language* (prose), edited by Joy Horjo and Gloria Bird, W. W. Norton (New York, NY), 1996. Contributor of photographs to magazines, including *Reflex.* Illustrator of *Old Shirts and New Skins,* a collection of poems by Sherman Alexie, University of California Press, 1993.

WORK IN PROGRESS: *Twentieth-Century Native American Art: Essays on History and Criticism,* for Routledge; *Elenco Racconti Raccolta Scrittrici Indianoamericane* (poetry and fiction), for Giunti Gruppo Editoriale; *Speaking For The Generations* (essay), for University of Arizona Press; *The Writer's Journal* (essay), for Dell Publishing.

SIDELIGHTS: In a language foreign to her Navajo/ Warm Springs/Wasco/Yakama ancestors, writer Elizabeth Woody has developed a strong but gentle voice that has found expression in poetry, short stories, and essays. With several books and contributions to numerous anthologies, she has explored topics that are firmly rooted in her tribal culture and history. Woody told *CA:* "I am pleased to be a part of an American literary tradition informed by a native aesthetic and legacy, honed by a specific environment with natural law for millennia. The stories, songs, artifacts are connected to a specific family and these legacies thrive in our communities. As a writer, I hope to never stop listening."

Woody's first book of poetry, *Hand into Stone,* was published in 1988 and received the American Book Award in 1990. The book's themes include changes to the Columbia River and the political crisis in tribal fishing rights; the dangers of nuclear energy and other environmental issues; the oppression of Native peoples; and the importance of the oral tradition.

The nature of Woody's work creates a tension that few writers have to deal with, the difficulty of writing in what is essentially a foreign language. Although Woody grew up speaking English, her maternal grandfather knew six native dialects. *Notable Native Americans* quoted Woody regarding this loss: "Eradication of the native languages through colonization . . . has impacted massive stores of knowledge. Losing the indigenous language meant that I had to become proficient in a language entirely different from that of my Sahaptin-Wasco Dine ancestors." However, Woody has made great strides in closing this language gap. Critic C. L. Rawlins wrote in the *Bloomsbury Review,* "English is hers, spoken and written, and she brings to it a supple unpredictability like the Irish poets who not only adopted the invader's tongue, but made it shiver and thunder and burn."

Woody's second book of poetry, *Luminaries of the Humble,* was published in 1994. Critical response identified her as a talented practitioner, whose work was both subtle and multifaceted. Elaine A. Jahner commented in *Parabola,* "Elizabeth Woody's *Luminaries of the Humble* shows an extraordinarily versatile poetic voice in the making. Each of the book's three sections . . . has an integrity and identity such that one is astonished that they are all the work of the same poet." Richard Dauenhauer praised Woody's thematic approach in *World Literature Today.* He described the book as "a collection of quiet and powerful poems exploring the integration of the specifics of one's life with the abstractions of eternity. . . . In poetry that reaches out and reaches back, that looks around, looks forward and back—and especially looks inward—the individual is called on to examine one's personal present and society, and one's own history and future."

Also published in 1994, *Seven Hands, Seven Hearts,* is a collection of Woody's poetry and prose. The book includes all of the work from *Hand into Stone* plus new poems, short fiction, and essays. The collection elicited this response from C. L. Rawlins: "*Seven Hands, Seven Hearts* is not only about building a durable self. There is also profound anger in it, as Woody wrestles with the invasion of her homeland: the changing of the her known place into one possessed by strangers. Yet the emotion in these passages is transparent, something like flame. And like flame, it is the source of both pain and power."

Woody credits her writing professors and colleagues at the Institute of American Indian Arts as important sources of support and inspiration. Through her connection with the Northwest Native American Writers Association and Wordcraft Circle, she assumed the role of mentor to the growing ranks of native writers. "While my work is beginning to reach a wider audience, I know that there are many aspiring native writers who have not found the opportunity. I hope to be able to provide encouragement and mentorship within my community at the Reservation of Warm Springs, Oregon, someday. In the Native Writer's community there are many individuals who have given me encouragement," Woody told *CA.* The poet also credits her grandmother and other Native American women who have taught her how to do beadwork and weave root bags with helping her find inspiration, as well as a sense of belonging, through the work and through their stories.

BIOGRAPHICAL AND CRITICAL SOURCES:

PERIODICALS

Bloomsbury Review, July-August,1995, p. 15.
Parabola, fall, 1995, pp. 92-96.
School Library Journal, July, 1993, p. 112.
World Literature Today, spring, 1995, p. 411.

Y

YOLEN, Jane (Hyatt) 1939-

PERSONAL: Born February 11, 1939, in New York, NY; daughter of Will Hyatt (an author and publicist) and Isabelle (a social worker, puzzle-maker, and homemaker; maiden name, Berlin) Yolen; married David W. Stemple (a retired professor of computer science and ornithologist), September 2, 1962; children: Heidi Elisabet, Adam Douglas, Jason Frederic. *Education:* Smith College, B.A., 1960; University of Massachusetts, M.Ed., 1976; also completed course work for doctorate in children's literature at the University of Massachusetts. *Politics:* Liberal Democrat. *Religion:* Jewish/Quaker. *Hobbies and other interests:* "Folk music and dancing, reading, camping, politics, all things Scottish."

ADDRESSES: Home—Phoenix Farm, 31 School St., Box 27, Hatfield, MA 01038, and Wayside, 96 Hepburn Gardens, St. Andrews, Fife, Scotland KY16 9LN. *Agent*—Elizabeth Harding, Curtis Brown, Ltd., 10 Astor Place, New York, NY 10003. *E-mail*—JaneYolen@aol.com.

Jane Yolen

CAREER: Saturday Review, New York, NY, production assistant, 1960-61; Gold Medal Books (publishers), New York, NY, assistant editor, 1961-62; Rutledge Books (publishers), New York, NY, associate editor, 1962-63; Alfred A. Knopf, Inc. (publishers), New York, NY, assistant juvenile editor, 1963-65; full-time professional writer, 1965—. Editor of imprint, Jane Yolen Books, for Harcourt Brace Jovanovich, 1988-98. Teacher of writing and lecturer, 1966—; has taught children's literature at Smith College. Chairman of board of library trustees, Hatfield, MA, 1976-83; member of Arts Council, Hatfield.

MEMBER: Society of Children's Book Writers (member of board of directors, 1974—), Science Fiction Writers of America (president, 1986-88), Children's Literature Association (member of board of directors, 1977-79), Science Fiction Poetry Association, National Association for the Preservation and Perpetuation of Storytelling, Western New England Storyteller's Guild (founder), Bay State Writers Guild, Western Massachusetts Illustrators Guild (founder), International Kitefliers Association, Smith College Alumnae Association.

AWARDS, HONORS: Boys' Club of America Junior Book Award, 1968, for *The Minstrel and the Mountain;* Lewis Carroll Shelf Award, 1968, for *The Emperor and the Kite,* and 1973, for *The Girl Who Loved the Wind;* Best Books of the Year selection, *New York Times,* 1968, for *The Emperor Flies a Kite; World on a String: The Story of Kites* was named an American Library Association (ALA) Notable Book, 1968; Chandler Book Talk Reward of Merit, 1970; Children's Book Showcase of the Children's Book Council citations, 1973, for *The Girl Who Loved the Wind,* and 1976, for *The Little Spotted Fish;* Golden Kite Award, Society of Children's Book Writers, 1974, ALA Notable Book, 1975, and National Book Award nomination, 1975, all for *The Girl Who Cried Flowers and Other Tales;* Golden Kite Honor Book, 1975, for *The Transfigured Hart,* and 1976, for *The Moon Ribbon and Other Tales;* Christopher Medal, 1978, for *The Seeing Stick,* and 2000, for *How Do Dinosaurs Say Goodnight?*; Children's Choice from the International Reading Association and the Children's Book Council, 1980, for *Mice on Ice,* and 1983, for *Dragon's Blood;* LL.D., College of Our Lady of the Elms, 1981; Parents' Choice Awards, Parents' Choice Foundation, 1982, for *Dragon's Blood,* 1984, for *The Stone Silenus,* and 1989, for *Piggins* and *The Three Bears Rhyme Book; School Library Journal* Best Books for Young Adults citations, 1982, for *The Gift of Sarah Barker,* and 1985, for *Heart's Blood;* Garden State Children's Book Award, New Jersey Library Association, 1983, for *Commander Toad in Space;* CRABbery Award from Acton Public Library (MD), 1983, for *Dragon's Blood; Heart's Blood* was selected one of ALA's Best Books for Young Adults, 1984; Mythopoeic Society's Fantasy Award, Adult Novel, 1985, for *Cards of Grief,* 1993 for *Briar Rose,* and 1998 for children's novels *The Young Merlin Trilogy: Passager, Hobby, Merlin;* Daedelus Award, 1986, for fantasy and short fiction; *The Lullaby Songbook* and *The Sleeping Beauty* were each selected one of Child Study Association of America's Children's Books of the Year, 1987; World Fantasy Award, 1988, for *Favorite Folktales from around the World;* Kerlan Award for "singular achievements in the creation of children's literature," 1988; Parents' Choice Silver Seal Award, Jewish Book Council Award, and Sydney Taylor Award, all 1988, Golden Sower Award from the Nebraska Library Association, 1989, and Charlotte Award from New York State Reading Association, all for *Piggins;* Smith College Medal, 1990; Skylark Award, New England Science Fiction Association, 1990; Regina Medal for body of writing in children's literature, 1992; Mythopoetic Fantasy Award, Adult, 1993, for *Briar Rose;* Keene State College Children's Literature Festival Award, 1995 and Children's Book Award, 1998; Maud Hart Lovelace Award, 1996, for *The Devil's Arithmetic;* Nebula Award, Best Short Story, 1997, for *Sister Emily's Lightship,* and 1998, for *Lost Girls;* Literary Lights for Children Award, Boston Library, 1998; H.D. L., Keene State College, 1998; Anna V. Zarrow Award, 1999; Remarkable Women Award, 1999; California Young Reader Medal, young adult category, 2001, for *Armageddon Summer;* National Outdoor Book Awards, children's category, 2002, for *Wild Wings;* Network 2003 ORACLE Award for outstanding contributions to the literary body of storytelling, 2003; honorary doctorate, Smith College, 2003; Parents' Choice Gold Medal for *Sword of the Rightful King,* 2004; honorary doctorate, Bay Path College, 2004. Fifteen of Yolen's books have been selected by the Junior Literary Guild. In addition, *The Emperor and the Kite* was named a Caldecott Medal Honor Book, 1968, for its illustrations by Ed Young, and *Owl Moon* received the Caldecott Medal, 1988, for its illustrations by John Schoenherr.

WRITINGS:

FOR CHILDREN; PICTURE BOOKS AND FICTION

The Witch Who Wasn't, illustrated by Arnold Roth, Macmillan (New York, NY), 1964.

Gwinellen, the Princess Who Could Not Sleep, illustrated by Ed Renfro, Macmillan (New York, NY), 1965.

The Emperor and the Kite, illustrated by Ed Young, World Publishing (Cleveland, OH), 1967, Philomel Books (New York, NY), 1988.

The Minstrel and the Mountain: A Tale of Peace, illustrated by Anne Rockwell, World Publishing (Cleveland, OH), 1967.

Isabel's Noel, illustrated by Arnold Roth, Funk & Wagnalls (New York, NY), 1967.

Greyling: A Picture Story from the Islands of Shetland, illustrated by William Stobbs, World Publishing (Cleveland, OH), 1968, new edition, illustrated by David Ray; Philomel Books (New York, NY), 1991.

The Longest Name on the Block, illustrated by Peter Madden, Funk & Wagnalls (New York, NY), 1968.

The Wizard of Washington Square, illustrated by Ray Cruz, World Publishing (Cleveland, OH), 1969.

The Inway Investigators; or, The Mystery at McCracken's Place, illustrated by Allan Eitzen, Seabury (New York, NY), 1969.

Hobo Toad and the Motorcycle Gang, illustrated by Emily McCully, World Publishing (Cleveland, OH), 1970.

The Seventh Mandarin, illustrated by Ed Young, Seabury (New York, NY), 1970.

The Bird of Time, illustrated by Mercer Mayer, Crowell (New York, NY), 1971.

The Girl Who Loved the Wind, illustrated by Ed Young, Crowell (New York, NY), 1972.

The Girl Who Cried Flowers and Other Tales, illustrated by David Palladini, Crowell (New York, NY), 1974.

The Boy Who Had Wings, illustrated by Helga Aichinger, Crowell (New York, NY), 1974.

The Adventures of Eeka Mouse, illustrated by Myra McKee, Xerox Education Publications (Middletown, CT), 1974.

The Rainbow Rider, illustrated by Michael Foreman, Crowell (New York, NY), 1974.

The Little Spotted Fish, illustrated by Friso Henstra, Seabury (New York, NY), 1975.

The Transfigured Hart, illustrated by Donna Diamond, Crowell (New York, NY), 1975, Magic Carpet Books/Harcourt Brace (San Diego, CA), 1997.

Milkweed Days, photographs by Gabriel Amadeus Cooney, Crowell (New York, NY), 1976.

The Moon Ribbon and Other Tales, illustrated by David Palladini, Crowell (New York, NY), 1976.

The Seeing Stick, illustrated by Remy Charlip and Demetra Maraslis, Crowell (New York, NY), 1977.

The Sultan's Perfect Tree, illustrated by Barbara Garrison, Parents' Magazine Press (New York, NY), 1977.

The Hundredth Dove and Other Tales, illustrated by David Palladini, Crowell (New York, NY), 1977.

Hannah Dreaming, photographs by Alan R. Epstein, Museum of Fine Art (Springfield, MA), 1977.

The Lady and the Merman, illustrated by Barry Moser, Pennyroyal, 1977.

Spider Jane, illustrated by Stefan Bernath, Coward (New York, NY), 1978.

The Simple Prince, illustrated by Jack Kent, Parents' Magazine Press (New York, NY), 1978.

No Bath Tonight, illustrated by Nancy Winslow Parker, Crowell (New York, NY), 1978.

The Mermaid's Three Wisdoms, illustrated by Laura Rader, Collins (New York, NY), 1978.

Dream Weaver and Other Tales, illustrated by Michael Hague, Collins (New York, NY), 1979, reissued as *Dream Weaver,* 1989.

Spider Jane on the Move, illustrated by Stefan Bernath, Coward (New York, NY), 1980.

Mice on Ice, illustrated by Lawrence DiFiori, Dutton's Children's Books (New York, NY), 1980.

Shirlick Holmes and the Case of the Wandering Wardrobe, illustrated by Anthony Rao, Coward (New York, NY), 1981.

The Acorn Quest, illustrated by Susanna Natti, Harper (New York, NY), 1981.

Brothers of the Wind, illustrated by Barbara Berger, Philomel Books (New York, NY), 1981.

Sleeping Ugly, illustrated by Diane Stanley, Coward (New York, NY), 1981.

The Boy Who Spoke Chimp, illustrated by David Wiesner, Knopf (New York, NY), 1981.

Uncle Lemon's Spring, illustrated by Glen Rounds, Dutton's Children's Books (New York, NY), 1981.

Owl Moon, illustrated by John Schoenherr, Philomel Books (New York, NY), 1987.

(Reteller) *The Sleeping Beauty,* illustrated by Ruth Sanderson, Knopf (New York, NY), 1986.

Dove Isabeau, illustrated by Dennis Nolan, Harcourt Brace (San Diego, CA), 1989.

Baby Bear's Bedtime Book, illustrated by Jane Dyer, Harcourt Brace (San Diego, CA), 1990.

Sky Dogs, illustrated by Barry Moser, Harcourt Brace (San Diego, CA), 1990.

(Reteller) *Tam Lin: An Old Ballad,* illustrated by Charles Mikolaycak, Harcourt Brace (San Diego, CA), 1990.

Elfabet: An ABC of Elves, illustrated by Lauren Mills, Little, Brown (Boston, MA), 1990.

Letting Swift River Go, illustrated by Barbara Cooney, Little, Brown (Boston, MA), 1990.

The Dragon's Boy, Harper (New York, NY), 1990.

Wizard's Hall, Harcourt Brace (San Diego, CA), 1991.

Hark! A Christmas Sampler, illustrated by Tomie dePaola, music by Adam Stemple, Putnam (New York, NY), 1991.

(Reteller) *Wings,* Harcourt Brace (San Diego, CA), 1991.

All Those Secrets of the World (autobiographical fiction), illustrated by Leslie Baker, Little, Brown (Boston, MA), 1991.

Encounter, illustrated by David Shannon, Harcourt Brace (San Diego, CA), 1992.

Eeny, Meeny, Miney Mole, illustrated by Kathryn Brown, published by Harcourt Brace (San Diego, CA), 1992.

Mouse's Birthday, illustrated by Bruce Degen, Putnam (New York, NY), 1993.

Hands, illustrated by Chi Chung, Sundance Publishing (White Plains, NY), 1993, also published as *Hands: Big Book,* 1993.

Beneath the Ghost Moon, illustrated by Laurel Molk, Little, Brown (Boston, MA), 1994.

Honkers, illustrated by Leslie Baker, Little, Brown (Boston, MA), 1993.

Travelers Rose, Putnam (New York, NY), 1993.

Grandad Bill's Song, illustrated by Melissa Bay Mathis, Philomel Books (New York, NY), 1994.

And Twelve Chinese Acrobats (autobiographical fiction), illustrated by Jean Gralley, Philomel Books (New York, NY), 1994.

Good Griselle, illustrated by David Christiana, Harcourt Brace (San Diego, CA), 1994.

The Girl in the Golden Bower, illustrated by Jane Dyer, Little, Brown (Boston, MA), 1994.

Old Dame Counterpane, illustrated by Ruth Tietjen Councell, Putnam (New York, NY), 1994.

(Reteller) *Little Mouse and Elephant: A Tale from Turkey,* illustrated by John Segal, Simon & Schuster (New York, NY), 1994.

(Reteller) *The Musicians of Bremen: A Tale from Germany,* illustrated by John Segal, Simon & Schuster (New York, NY), 1994.

The Ballad of the Pirate Queen, illustrated by David Shannon, Harcourt Brace (San Diego, CA), 1995.

Before the Storm, illustrated by Georgia Pugh, Boyds Mills Press (Honesdale, PA), 1995.

(Reteller) *A Sip of Aesop,* illustrated by Karen Barbour, Blue Sky Press (New York, NY), 1995.

Merlin and the Dragons, illustrated by Ming Li, Dutton's Children's Books (New York, NY), 1995.

The Wild Hunt, illustrated by Francisco Mora, Harcourt Brace (San Diego, CA), 1995.

(With daughter, Heidi Elisabet Yolen Stemple) *Meet the Monsters,* illustrated by Patricia Ludlow, Walker (New York, NY), 1996.

Nocturne, illustrated by Anne Hunter, Harcourt Brace (San Diego, CA), 1997.

Child of Faerie, Child of Earth, illustrated by Jane Dyer, Little, Brown (Boston, MA), 1997.

Miz Berlin Walks, illustrated by Floyd Cooper, Philomel Books (New York, NY), 1997.

(Reteller) *Once upon a Bedtime Story: Classic Tales,* illustrated by Ruth Tietjen Councell, 1997.

The Sea Man, illustrated by Christopher Denise, Putnam (New York, NY), 1997.

Twelve Impossible Things before Breakfast (short stories), Harcourt Brace (San Diego, CA), 1997.

House, House, illustrated with photographs by the Howes Brothers and Jason Stemple, Marshall Cavendish (New York, NY), 1998.

King Long Shanks, illustrated by Victoria Chess, Harcourt Brace (San Diego, CA), 1998.

(Reteller) *Pegasus, the Flying Horse,* illustrated by Ming Li, Dutton's Children's Books (New York, NY), 1998.

The Book of Fairy Holidays, illustrated by David Christiana, Blue Sky Press (New York, NY), 1998.

Raising Yoder's Barn, illustrated by Bernie Fuchs, Little, Brown (Boston, MA), 1998.

(Reteller) *Prince of Egypt,* Dutton's Children's Books (New York, NY), 1998.

(Compiler with Linda Mannheim) *The Liars' Book,* illustrated by Kevin Hawkes, Blue Sky Press, 1998.

(With Heidi E. Y. Stemple) *Mary Celeste: An Unsolved Mystery from History,* illustrated by Roger Roth, Simon & Schuster (New York, NY), 1999.

Moonball, illustrated by Greg Couch, Simon & Schuster (New York, NY), 1999.

How Do Dinosaurs Say Goodnight?, illustrated by Mark Teague, Blue Sky Press (New York, NY), 2000.

Off We Go!, illustrated by Laurel Molk, Little, Brown (Boston, MA), 2000.

Harvest Home, illustrated by Greg Shed, Harcourt Brace (San Diego, CA), 2000.

Where Have the Unicorns Gone?, illustrated by Ruth Sanderson, Simon & Schuser (New York, NY), 2000.

Welcome to the River of Grass, illustrated by Laura Regan, Putnam (New York, NY), 2000.

The Hurrying Child, illustrated by Stephen T. Johnson, Silver Whistle Books (San Diego, CA), 2001.

Firebird, illustrated by Vladimir Vagin, HarperCollins (New York, NY), 2002.

The Sea King, illustrated by Stefan Czernecki, Crocodile Books (Brooklyn, NY), 2003.

My Brothers' Flying Machine: Wilbur, Orville, and Me, paintings by Jim Burke, Little, Brown (New York, NY), 2003.

How Do Dinosaurs Get Well Soon?, illustrated by Mark Teague, Blue Sky Press (New York, Ny), 2003.

Hoptoad, illustrated by Karen Lee Schmidt, Silver Whistle Books, (San Diego, CA), 2003.

The Flying Witch, illustrated by Vladimir Vagin, HarperCollins (New York, NY), 2003.

Meow: Cat Stories from around the World, illustrated by Hala Wittwer, HarperCollins (New York, NY), 2004.

How Do Dinosaurs Count to Ten?, illustrated by Mark Teague, Blue Sky Press (New York, NY), 2004.

"GIANTS" SERIES; ILLUSTRATED BY TOMIE DEPAOLA

The Giants' Farm, Seabury (New York, NY), 1977.

The Giants Go Camping, Seabury (New York, NY), 1979.

"COMMANDER TOAD" SERIES; ILLUSTRATED BY BRUCE DEGEN

Commander Toad in Space, Coward (New York, NY), 1980.

Commander Toad and the Planet of the Grapes, Coward (New York, NY), 1982.

Commander Toad and the Big Black Hole, Coward (New York, NY), 1983.

Commander Toad and the Dis-Asteroid, Coward (New York, NY), 1985.

Commander Toad and the Intergalactic Spy, Coward (New York, NY), 1986.

Commander Toad and the Space Pirates, Putnam (New York, NY), 1987.

Commander Toad and the Voyage Home, Putnam (New York, NY), 1998.

"ROBOT AND REBECCA" SERIES

The Robot and Rebecca: The Mystery of the Code-Carrying Kids, illustrated by Jurg Obrist, Knopf (New York, NY), 1980, student book club edition illustrated by Catherine Deeter, Random House (New York, NY), 1980.

The Robot and Rebecca and the Missing Owser, illustrated by Lady McCrady, Knopf (New York, NY), 1981.

"PIGGINS" SERIES; ILLUSTRATED BY JANE DYER

Piggins, Harcourt Brace (San Diego, CA), 1987.

Picnic with Piggins, Harcourt Brace (San Diego, CA), 1988.

Piggins and the Royal Wedding, Harcourt Brace (San Diego, CA), 1988.

"YOUNG MERLIN" TRILOGY

Passager, Harcourt Brace (San Diego, CA), 1996.

Hobby, Harcourt Brace (San Diego, CA), 1996.

Merlin, Harcourt Brace (San Diego, CA), 1997.

"TARTAN MAGIC" SERIES

The Wizard's Map, Harcourt Brace (San Diego, CA), 1998.

The Pictish Child, Harcourt Brace (San Diego, CA), 1999.

The Bagpiper's Ghost, Harcourt Brace (San Diego, CA), 2002.

FOR CHILDREN; NONFICTION

Pirates in Petticoats, illustrated by Leonard Vosburgh, McKay (New York, NY), 1963.

World on a String: The Story of Kites, World Publishing (Cleveland, OH), 1968.

Friend: The Story of George Fox and the Quakers, Seabury (New York, NY), 1972.

(Editor, with Barbara Green) *The Fireside Song Book of Birds and Beasts,* illustrated by Peter Parnall, Simon & Schuster (New York, NY), 1972.

The Wizard Islands, illustrated by Robert Quackenbush, Crowell (New York, NY), 1973.

Ring Out! A Book of Bells, illustrated by Richard Cuffari, Seabury (New York, NY), 1974.

Simple Gifts: The Story of the Shakers, illustrated by Betty Fraser, Viking (New York, NY), 1976.

(Compiler) *Rounds about Rounds,* music by Barbara Green, illustrated by Gail Gibbons, Watts (New York, NY), 1977.

The Lap-Time Song and Play Book, musical arrangements by son Adam Stemple, illustrated by Margot Tomes, Harcourt Brace (San Diego, CA), 1989.

A Letter from Phoenix Farm (autobiography), illustrated with photographs by son Jason Stemple, Richard C. Owen (Katonah, NY), 1992.

Jane Yolen's Songs of Summer, musical arrangements by Adam Stemple, illustrated by Cyd Moore, Boyds Mills Press (Honesdale, PA), 1993.

Welcome to the Green House, illustrated by Laura Regan, Putnam (New York, NY), 1993.

Jane Yolen's Old MacDonald Songbook, illustrated by Rosekrans Hoffman, Boyds Mills Press (Honesdale, PA), 1994.

Sing Noel, musical arrangements by Adam Stemple, illustrated by Nancy Carpenter, Boyds Mills Press (Honesdale, PA), 1996.

Milk and Honey: A Year of Jewish Holidays, illustrated by Louise August, musical arrangements by Adam Stemple, Putnam (New York, NY), 1996.

Welcome to the Sea of Sand, illustrated by Laura Regan, Putnam (New York, NY), 1996.

Welcome to the Ice House, illustrated by Laura Regan, Putnam (New York, NY), 1998.

Tea with an Old Dragon: A Story of Sophia Smith, Founder of Smith College, illustrated by Monica Vachula, Boyds Mills Press (Honesdale, PA), 1998.

(With Heidi E. Y. Stemple) *The Wolf Girls: An Unsolved Mystery from History,* illustrated by Roger Roth, Simon & Schuster (New York, NY), 2000.

(With Heidi E. Y. Stemple) *Roanoke: The Lost Colony: An Unsolved Mystery from History,* illustrated by Roger Roth, Simon & Schuster (New York, NY), 2003.

The Perfect Wizard: Hans Christian Andersen, illustrated by Denis Nolan, Dutton's Children's Books (New York, NY), 2004.

FOR CHILDREN; POETRY

See This Little Line?, illustrated by Kathleen Elgin, McKay (New York, NY), 1963.

It All Depends, illustrated by Don Bolognese, Funk & Wagnalls (New York, NY), 1970.

An Invitation to the Butterfly Ball: A Counting Rhyme, illustrated by Jane Breskin Zalben, Parents' Magazine Press (New York, NY), 1976, Caroline House (Honesdale, PA), 1991.

All in the Woodland Early: An ABC Book, illustrated by Jane Breskin Zalben, Collins, 1979, Caroline House (Honesdale, PA), 1991.

How Beastly! A Menagerie of Nonsense Poems, illustrated by James Marshall, Philomel Books (New York, NY), 1980.

Dragon Night and Other Lullabies, illustrated by Demi, Methuen (New York, NY), 1980.

(Editor) *The Lullaby Songbook,* musical arrangements by Adam Stemple, illustrated by Charles Mikolaycak, Harcourt Brace (San Diego, CA), 1986.

Ring of Earth: A Child's Book of Seasons, illustrated by John Wallner, Harcourt Brace (San Diego, CA), 1986.

The Three Bears Rhyme Book, illustrated by Jane Dyer, Harcourt Brace (San Diego, CA), 1987.

Best Witches: Poems for Halloween, illustrated by Elise Primavera, Putnam (New York, NY), 1989.

Bird Watch, illustrated by Ted Lewin, Philomel Books (New York, NY), 1990.

Dinosaur Dances, illustrated by Bruce Degen, Putnam (New York, NY), 1990.

(Compiler) *Street Rhymes around the World,* illustrated by seventeen artists, Wordsong (Honesdale, PA), 1992.

Jane Yolen's Mother Goose Songbook, musical arrangements by Jason Stemple, illustrated by Rosekrans Hoffman, Boyds Mill Press, 1992.

(Compiler) *Weather Report,* illustrated by Annie Gusman, Boyds Mills Press (Honesdale, PA), 1993.

Mouse's Birthday, illustrated by Bruce Degen, Putnam (New York, NY), 1993.

Raining Cats and Dogs, illustrated by Janet Street, Harcourt Brace (San Diego, CA), 1993.

What Rhymes with Moon?, illustrated by Ruth Tietjen Councell, Philomel Books (New York, NY), 1993.

(Compiler and contributor) *Alphabestiary: Animal Poems from A to Z,* illustrated by Allan Eitzen, Boyds Mills Press (Honesdale, PA), 1994.

Sacred Places, illustrated by David Shannon, Harcourt Brace (San Diego, CA), 1994.

Animal Fare: Zoological Nonsense Poems, illustrated by Janet Street, Harcourt Brace (San Diego, CA), 1994.

The Three Bears Holiday Rhyme Book, illustrated by Jane Dyer, Harcourt Brace (San Diego, CA), 1995.

Water Music: Poems for Children, illustrated with photographs by Jason Stemple, Boyds Mills Press (Honesdale, PA), 1995.

(Compiler) *Mother Earth, Father Sky: Poems of Our Planet,* illustrated by Jennifer Hewitson, Boyds Mills Press (Honesdale, PA), 1996.

O Jerusalem, illustrated by John Thompson, Scholastic Books (New York, NY), 1996.

Sea Watch: A Book of Poetry, illustrated by Ted Lewin, Putnam (New York, NY), 1996.

(Compiler and contributor) *Sky Scrape/City Scape: Poems of City Life,* illustrated by Ken Condon, Boyds Mills Press (Honesdale, PA), 1996.

(Compiler) *Once upon Ice and Other Frozen Poems,* illustrated with photographs by Jason Stemple, Boyds Mills Press (Honesdale, PA), 1997.

Snow, Snow: Winter Poems for Children, illustrated with photographs by Jason Stemple, Wordsong (Honesdale, PA), 1998.

The Originals: Animals That Time Forgot, illustrated by Ted Lewin, Philomel Books (New York, NY), 1998.

Color Me a Rhyme: Nature Poems for Young People, photographs by Jason Stemple, Wordsong/Boyds Mills Press (Honesdale, PA), 2000.

(With Heidi E. Y. Stemple) *Dear Mother, Dear Daughter: Poems for Young People,* illustrated by Gil Ashby, Wordsong/Boyds Mills Press (Honesdale, PA), 2001.

Wild Wings: Poems for Young People, photographs by Jason Stemple, Wordsong/Boyds Mills Press (Honesdale, PA), 2002.

Horizons: Poems As Far As the Eye Can See, photographs by Jason Stemple, Wordsong/Boyds Mills Press (Honesdale, PA), 2002.

Least Things: Poems about Small Natures, photographs by Jason Stemple, Wordsong/Boyds Mills Press (Honesdale, PA), 2003.

FOR YOUNG ADULTS; FICTION

(With Anne Huston) *Trust a City Kid,* illustrated by J. C. Kocsis, Lothrop, 1966.

(Editor) *Zoo 2000: Twelve Stories of Science Fiction and Fantasy Beasts,* Seabury (New York, NY), 1973.

The Magic Three of Solatia, illustrated by Julia Noonan, Crowell (New York, NY), 1974.

(Editor and contributor) *Shape Shifters: Fantasy and Science Fiction Tales about Humans Who Can Change Their Shape,* Seabury (New York, NY), 1978.

The Gift of Sarah Barker, Viking (New York, NY), 1981.

Neptune Rising: Songs and Tales of the Undersea Folk (story collection), illustrated by David Wiesner, Philomel Books (New York, NY), 1982.

The Stone Silenus, Philomel Books (New York, NY), 1984.

Children of the Wolf, Viking (New York, NY), 1984.

(Editor and contributor, with Martin H. Greenberg and Charles G. Waugh) *Dragons and Dreams,* Harper (New York, NY), 1986.

(Editor and contributor, with Martin H. Greenberg and Charles G. Waugh) *Spaceships and Spells,* Harper (New York, NY), 1987.

The Devil's Arithmetic, Viking (New York, NY), 1988.

(Editor and contributor, with Martin H. Greenberg) *Werewolves: A Collection of Original Stories,* Harper (New York, NY), 1988.

The Faery Flag: Stories and Poems of Fantasy and the Supernatural, Orchard Books (New York, NY), 1989.

(Editor and contributor, with Martin H. Greenberg) *Things That Go Bump in the Night,* Harper (New York, NY), 1989.

(Editor and contributor) *2041 AD: Twelve Stories about the Future by Top Science Fiction Writers* (anthology), Delacorte Press (New York, NY), 1990, reprinted as *2041,* Delacorte Press (New York, NY), 1991.

(Editor and contributor, with Martin H. Greenberg) *Vampires,* HarperCollins (New York, NY), 1991.

Here There Be Dragons (original stories and poetry), illustrated by David Wilgus, Harcourt Brace (San Diego, CA), 1993.

Here There Be Unicorns (stories and poetry), illustrated by David Wilgus, Harcourt Brace (San Diego, CA), 1994.

Here There Be Witches (stories and poetry), illustrated by David Wilgus, Harcourt Brace (San Diego, CA), 1995.

(Editor and contributor) *Camelot: A Collection of Original Arthurian Tales,* illustrated by Winslow Pels, Putnam (New York, NY), 1995.

(Editor, with Martin H. Greenberg, and contributor) *The Haunted House: A Collection of Original Stories,* illustrated by Doron Ben-Ami, HarperCollins (New York, NY), 1995.

Here There Be Angels (stories and poetry), illustrated by David Wilgus, Harcourt Brace (San Diego, CA), 1996.

Here There Be Ghosts (stories and poetry), illustrated by David Wilgus, Harcourt Brace (San Diego, CA), 1998.

(With Bruce Coville) *Armageddon Summer,* Harcourt Brace (San Diego, CA), 1998.

Not One Damsel in Distress: World Folktales for Strong Girls, Silver Whistle Books (San Diego, CA), 2000.

Boots and the Seven Leaguers: A Rock-and-Troll Novel, Harcourt Brace (San Diego, CA), 2000.

(Editor and contributor) *Sherwood: A Collection of Original Robin Hood Stories,* illustrated by Dennis Nolan, Philomel Books (New York, NY), 2000.

Sword of the Rightful King: A Novel of King Arthur, Harcourt Brace (San Diego, CA), 2003.

Mightier Than the Sword: World Folktales for Strong Boys, illustrated by Paul Colón, Harcourt Brace (San Diego, CA), 2003.

"YOUNG HEROES" SERIES; FICTION

(With Robert J. Harris) *Odysseus in the Serpent Maze,* HarperCollins (New York, NY), 2001.

(With Robert J. Harris) *Hippolyta and the Curse of the Amazons,* HarperCollins (New York, NY), 2002.

(With Robert J. Harris) *Atalanta and the Arcadian Beast,* HarperCollins (New York, NY), 2003.

(With Robert J. Harris) *Jason and the Gorgon's Blood,* HarperCollins (New York, NY), 2004.

"STUART" QUARTET; FICTION

Queen's Own Fool, Philomel Books (New York, NY), 2001.

(With Robert J. Harris) *Girl in a Cage,* Philomel Books (New York, NY), 2002.

Prince across the Water, Philomel Books (New York, NY), 2004.

"PIT DRAGON" SERIES; FICTION

Dragon's Blood: A Fantasy, Delacorte Press (New York, NY), 1982, Harcourt Brace (Orlando, FL), 2004.

Heart's Blood, Delacorte Press (New York, NY), 1984, Harcourt Brace (Orlando, FL), 2004.

A Sending of Dragons, illustrated by Tom McKeveny, Delacorte Press (New York, NY), 1987, Harcourt Brace (Orlando, FL) 2004.

FOR ADULTS; FICTION

Cards of Grief (science fiction), Ace Books (New York, NY), 1984.

Sword and the Stone, Pulphouse (Eugene, OR), 1991.

Briar Rose, Tor Books (New York, NY), 1992.

The Books of Great Alta (includes *Sister Light, Sister Dark, White Jenna,* and *The One Armed Queen*) Tor (New York, NY), 1997.

COLLECTIONS

Merlin's Booke (short stories), illustrated by Thomas Canty, Ace Books (New York, NY), 1982.

Tales of Wonder (short stories), Schocken (New York, NY), 1983.

Dragonfield and Other Stories (story collection), Ace Books (New York, NY), 1985.

Storyteller, New England Science Fiction Association Press (Cambridge, MA), boxed edition illustrated by Merle Insinga, 1992

(With Nancy Willard) *Among Angels* (poetry), illustrated by S. Saelig Gallagher, Harcourt Brace (San Diego, CA), 1995.

Sister Emily's Lightship and Other Stories, (science fiction), Tor Books (New York, NY), 2000.

The Radiation Sonnets (poetry collection) Algonquin Books (Chapel Hill, NC), 2003.

ANTHOLOGIES

(Editor) *Favorite Folktales from around the World,* Pantheon Books (New York, NY), 1986.

(Editor and contributor, with Martin H. Greenberg) *Xanadu,* Tor Books (New York, NY), 1993.

(Editor and contributor, with Martin H. Greenberg) *Xanadu Two,* Tor Books (New York, NY), 1994.

(Editor and contributor, with Martin H. Greenberg) *Xanadu Three,* Tor Books (New York, NY), 1995.

(Editor) *Gray Heroes: Elder Tales from around the World,* Penguin Books (New York, NY), 1998.

(With Heidi E. Y. Stemple) *Mirror, Mirror,* Viking (New York, NY), 2000.

(With Shulamith Oppenheim) *The Fish Prince and Other Stories: Mermen Folk Tales,* illustrated by Paul Hoffman, Interlink Books (New York, NY), 2001.

NOVELTY

Time for Naps, illustrated by Hiroe Nakata, Little Simon (New York, NY), 2002.

Animal Train, illustrated by Hiroe Nakata, Little Simon (New York, NY), 2002.

Bedtime for Bunny: A Book to Touch and Feel, illustrated by Norton Parker, Little Simon (New York, NY), 2002.

"WHITE JENNA" SERIES; FICTION

Sister Light, Sister Dark, Tor Books (New York, NY), 1988.

White Jenna, Tor Books (New York, NY), 1989.

The One-armed Queen, with music by son Adam Stemple, Tor Books (New York, NY), 1998.

FOR ADULTS; NONFICTION

Writing Books for Children, The Writer (Boston, MA), 1973, revised edition, 1983.

Touch Magic: Fantasy, Faerie and Folklore in the Literature of Childhood, Philomel Books (New York, NY), 1981, revised edition, August House, 2000.

Guide to Writing for Children, The Writer (Boston, MA), 1989.

Take Joy: A Book for Writers, Kalmbach Trade Press (Waukesha, WI), 2003.

Also author of the play *Robin Hood,* a musical with music by Barbara Greene first produced in Boston, MA, 1967, and of the chapbook *The Whitethorn Wood.* Ghostwriter of a number of books for Rutledge Press that were distributed by other publishing houses, including *One, Two, Buckle My Shoe,* a counting rhyme book published by Doubleday, and a series of activity books. Editor of books, including *A Plague of Sorcerers* by Mary Frances Zambreno, *Appleblossom* by Shulamith L. Oppenheim, *Jeremy Thatcher, Dragon Hatcher* by Bruce Coville, *The Jewel of Life* by Anna Kirwan-Vogel, *The Patchwork Lady* by Mary K. Whittington, and *The Red Ball* by Joanna Yardley, all Harcourt Brace, 1991. Contributor to many books, including *Dragons of Light,* edited by Orson Scott Card, Ace Books, 1981; *Elsewhere,* edited by Terri Windling and Mark Alan Arnold, Ace Books, Volume 1, 1981, Volume 2, 1982; *Hecate's Cauldron,* edited by Susan Schwartz, DAW Books, 1982; *Heroic Visions,* edited by Jessica Amanda Salmonson, Ace Books, 1983; *Faery!,* edited by Windling, Ace Books, 1985; *Liavek,* edited by Will Shetterly and Emma Bull, Ace Books, 1985; *Moonsinger's Friends,* edited by Susan Schwartz, Bluejay, 1985; *Imaginary Lands,* edited by Robin McKinley, Greenwillow, 1985; *Don't Bet on the Prince: Contemporary Feminist Fairy Tales in North America and England,* by Jack Zipes, Methuen, 1986; *Liavek: Players of Luck,* edited by Will Shetterly and Emma Bull, Ace Books, 1986; *Liavek: Wizard's Row,* edited by Will Shetterly and Emma Bull, Ace Books, 1987; *Visions,* by Donald R. Gallo, Delacorte, 1987; *Liavek: Spells of Binding,* edited by Will Shetterly and Emma Bull, Ace Books, 1988; *Invitation to Camelot,* by Parke Godwin, Ace Books, 1988; and *The Unicorn Treasury,* by Bruce Coville, Doubleday, 1988, and dozens more. Author of introduction for *Cut from the Same Cloth: American Women of Myth, Legend, and Tall Tale,* collected and told by Robert D. San Souci, Philomel Books, 1993; *Best-Loved Stories Told at the National Storytelling Festival,* National Storytelling Association, 1996; and *Fearless Girls, Wise Women, and Beloved Sisters: Heroines in Folktales from around the World* by Kathleen Ragan, Norton, 1998. Yolen has also written songs and lyrics for folksingers, some of which have been recorded. Her papers are housed at the Kerlan Collection, University of Minnesota.

Author of column "Children's Bookfare" for *Daily Hampshire Gazette* during the 1970s. Contributor of articles, reviews, poems, and short stories to periodicals, including *Chicago Jewish Forum, Horn Book, Isaac Asimov's Science Fiction Magazine, Language Arts, Los Angeles Times, Magazine of Fantasy and Science Fiction, New Advocate, New York Times, Parabola, Parents' Choice, Washington Post Book World, Wilson Library Bulletin,* and *Writer.* Member of editorial board, *Advocate* (now *New Advocate*) and *National Storytelling Journal,* until 1989. Some of Yolen's books have been translated into twenty-one languages, including Afrikaans and Xhosa, and have been published in many countries, including Australia, Austria, Brazil, Denmark, England, France, Germany, Japan, South Africa, Spain, and Sweden. She also writes as Jane H. Yolen.

ADAPTATIONS: The Seventh Mandarin was produced as a motion picture by Xerox Films, 1973; *The Emperor and the Kite* was produced as a filmstrip with cassette by Listening Library, 1976; *The Bird of Time* was adapted as a play and first produced in Northampton, MA, 1982; *The Girl Who Cried Flowers and Other Tales* was released on audio cassette by Weston

Woods, 1983; *Dragon's Blood* was produced as an animated television movie by Columbia Broadcasting System (CBS), 1985, and shown on *CBS Storybreak; Commander Toad in Space* was released on audio cassette by Listening Library, 1986; *Touch Magic . . . Pass It On,* a selection of Yolen's short stories, was released on audio cassette by Weston Woods, 1987; *Owl Moon* was produced as a filmstrip with cassette by Weston Woods, 1988, and as both a read-along cassette, 1990, and a video; *Owl Moon* was also adapted as part of the video *Owl Moon and Other Stories* produced by Children's Circle; *Piggins and Picnic with Piggins* was released on audio cassette by Caedmon, 1988; *Best of Science Fiction and Fantasy* was released on audio cassette by NewStar Media, 1991; *Merlin and the Dragons* was released on audio cassette by Lightyear Entertainment, 1991, was produced as a video by Coronet, 1991, and was released as *What's a Good Story? Merlin and the Dragon* with commentary by Yolen; *Greyling* was released on audio cassette by Spoken Arts, 1993; *Hands* was released on audio cassette by Sundance Publishing, 1993; *Beneath the Ghost Moon* was produced as a video by Spoken Arts, 1996; *Wizard's Hall* was released on audio cassette by "Words Take Wines," narrated by Yolen, 1997. Recorded Books has also issued audio cassettes of three of Yolen's books: *Briar Rose,The Devil's Arithmetic,* and *Good Griselle.* Yolen is the subject of the audio cassette *The Children's Writer at Work—Jane Yolen,* produced by Real Life Productions; in addition, she is the subject of the videos *Good Conversation: A Talk with Jane Yolen,* produced by Weston Woods, and *The Children's Writer at Work,* produced by Reel Life, 1997. *The Devil's Arithmetic* was the inspiration for a TV movie broadcast on Showtime, which won two Emmys.

WORK IN PROGRESS: As of May, 2003, thirty books under contract.

SIDELIGHTS: Dubbed "the American Hans Christian Andersen" by editor/publisher Ann K. Beneduce and "a modern equivalent of Aesop" by Noel Perrin in the *New York Times Book Review,* Jane Yolen is considered a gifted, versatile author who has developed a stellar reputation as a fantasist while contributing successfully to many other genres. An exceptionally prolific writer, she is the creator of approximately three hundred books for children and young adults and approximately twenty-five for adults. Yolen has written fiction for young adults and adults as well as poetry, criticism, and books on the art of writing and the genre of fantasy for an adult audience. She has also edited and compiled a number of works for both younger and older readers and has also contributed to several collections and anthologies. As a writer of juvenile literature, Yolen addresses her books to an audience ranging from preschool through high school and has written works ranging from picture books and easy readers to young adult novels. She is the creator of realistic fiction, mysteries, verse, animal tales, concept books, historical fiction, humorous stories, and lyrical prose poems, as well as informational books on such subjects as kites, bells, the Shakers, the Quakers, and the environment. Several of Yolen's books have been published in series, and she is particularly well known for the "Pit Dragon" series of young adult fantasy novels in which she created a mythological world based around cockfighting dragons on an arid planet. A folksinger and storyteller, Yolen has created several works that reflect her love of music and oral folklore, including compilations of international songs, rhymes, and stories. Several of the author's books are autobiographical or incorporate elements from her life or the lives of her family, and her three children all contribute to her works—daughter Heidi Elisabet as a writer and sons Adam and Jason as a musical arranger and photographer, respectively.

Yolen is perhaps best known as a writer of original folk and fairy tales and fables with a strong moral core. She has received special recognition for her literary fairy tales, works in the tradition of Oscar Wilde and Laurence Housman that combine familiar fantasy motifs with contemporary elements and philosophical themes. As a fantasist, Yolen is noted for creating elegant, eloquent tales with deep psychological insights that evoke a timeless sense of wonder while having relevance to contemporary life. She includes figures such as dragons, unicorns, witches, and mermaids as characters, and her stories often revolve around shape-shifters, animals who have the ability to transform into humans or humans into animals. As a writer, Yolen invests her works with images, symbols, and allusions as well as with wordplay—especially puns—and metaphors. She is considered an exceptional prose stylist whose fluid, musical writing is both polished and easy to read aloud.

As a writer of nonfiction, the author is credited for capturing the spirit of her subjects as well as for the enthusiasm with which she invests her books. Although her fiction is occasionally criticized for unlikely plots and sketchy characterizations and her fairy tales are sometimes considered too mannered, Yolen is generally praised as a writer of consistent quality whose books are evocative, moving, and enjoyable. Peter D. Sieruta of *Children's Books and Their Creators* stated: "With a confident writing style and inexhaustible imagination, Jane Yolen has proven herself one of the most prolific and diverse creators in the field of children's literature." In Yolen's entry in *Twentieth-Century Children's Writers,* Marcia G. Fuchs commented: "Faerie, fiction, fact, or horrible fantasy, Yolen's lyrical and magical tales are indeed tales to read and to listen to, to share, to remember, and to pass on." Jane Langton, herself a noted writer of fantasy, stated in the *New York Times Book Review* that Yolen's fables "are told with sober strength and native wit. They are simple and perfect, without a word too much." Writing in *Teaching and Learning Literature,* Lee Bennett Hopkins toasted the author: "May the pen of Yolen never run dry. The world of children's literature has been, and will continue to be, richer for her vast talents."

Writing in the *Fourth Book of Junior Authors and Illustrators (FBJAI),* Yolen said, "I come from a long line of storytellers. My great-grandfather was the Reb, the storyteller in a small village in Finno-Russia, my father an author, my mother a mostly unpublished writer." Yolen once remarked for *CA:* "My father's family were merchants and storytellers (some called them well-off liars!). My mother's family were intellectuals. I seem to have gotten a bit of both, though not enough of either." Yolen's father publicized the sport of kite flying so successfully that, according to his daughter in *CA,* he "forced a renaissance in kiting that is still going on"; in 1968 Yolen published *World on a String: The Story of Kites,* a well-received informational book about the subject. The author's mother quit her job as a social worker in order to raise Jane and her younger brother, Steven; in her free time, Isabelle Yolen wrote short stories and created crossword puzzles and double acrostics. Jane spent most of her childhood in New York City. She also spent summers in Virginia, the birthplace of her mother, and lived for a year and a half in California, where her father did publicity for Warner Brothers.

Yolen told *CA,* "I was a writer from the time I learned to write." An early reader as well as a tomboy, Yolen played games in Central Park while being encouraged in her reading and writing by her teachers. "I was," she recalled "the gold star star. And I was also pretty impossibly full of myself. In first or second grade, I wrote the school musical, lyrics and music, in which everyone was some kind of vegetable. I played the lead carrot. Our finale was a salad. Another gold star." Yolen wrote in *FBJAI,* "If I had to point to my primary source of inspiration, it would be to the folk culture. My earliest readings were the folk tales and fairy stories I took home from the library by the dozens. Even when I was old enough to make the trip across Central Park by myself, I was still not too old for those folk fantasies." Yolen once told *CA* that she read "all the Andrew Lang fairy books as a child and any kind of fairy stories I could get my hands on. I vividly remember *Treasure Island* and the Louisa May Alcott books. All of the Alcott books, *Jo's Boys,* and even the Alcott books that nobody else had heard of, became part of my adolescent reading. I read *The Wind in the Willows* and the Mowgli stories. We didn't have 'young adult' fiction, so I skipped right into adult books which tended to be very morose Russian novels—my Dostoevsky phase—then I got hooked on Joseph Conrad. Adventure novels or lugubrious emotional books are what I preferred. Then I went back into my fairy tale and fantasy stage. Tolkien and C. S. Lewis, metaphysical and folkloric fantasy." In a transcript of a speech in *Judaica Librarianship,* Yolen commented that she was raised "on tales of King Arthur and Robin Hood. I was a fanatical reader of fantasy and magic, history and adventure." She also began to develop her musical abilities, singing with a friend and earning enough money by passing the hat to buy sodas and ice cream. In sixth grade, Yolen was accepted by Hunter, a girls' school for what were called "intelligently gifted" students. The author said: "With my gold stars and my writing ability, I expected to be a superior gift to Hunter. To my surprise—and horror—I was barely in the middle of my class and managed to stay there by studying extremely hard."

While at Hunter, Yolen wrote in *CA,* "Music became a mainstay in my life." Her father, who sang and played the guitar, introduced Yolen to folk songs. She wrote in *FBJAI,* "I went him some better in learning every old English, Scottish, Irish, and Appalachian love song and ballad I ever heard." Yolen starred as Hansel in the school production of Engelbert Humperdinck's opera *Hansel and Gretel,* played the piano, and wrote songs; in addition, she studied at Balanchine's American School of Ballet. She also developed her interest in writing. In eighth grade, Yolen wrote her first two books, a nonfiction book on pirates, and a novel about a trip across the West by covered wagon. She described this work, which is seventeen pages long and includes a plague of locusts, death by snake bite, and the birth of a baby on the trail, as "a masterpiece of economy." Her experience writing the novel helped Yolen to develop an appreciation for the short form. She wrote in *CA* that short stories and poetry "have remained my first loves." During her twelfth and thirteenth summers, Yolen attended Indianbrook (now Farm and Wilderness), a Quaker camp in Vermont. Here, she said, "I learned about pacifism, swimming, storytelling, mucking out horse stalls, planting a garden, and kissing, not necessarily in that order."

After returning from her second summer at Indianbrook, Yolen moved with her family to Westport, Connecticut. As a student at Staples High School, she became captain of the girls' basketball team; news editor of the school paper; head of the Jewish Youth Group; vice president of the Spanish, Latin, and jazz clubs; a member of the school's top singing group; and a contributor to the school literary magazine. She also won a Scholastic Writing Award for one of her poems, a contest called "I Speak for Democracy," and her school's English prize. Before graduation, her class named Yolen "Best Voice for The Perfect Senior." A high school friend, Stella Colandrea, introduced Yolen to the Catholic Mass. "It was because of Stella's influence that I became enamored of different religions. My own Judaism and camp-discovered Quakerism were the most morally appealing, but the panoply of Catholic rites seem to have taken hold of my imagination and wind in and out of many of the elaborate religious rituals I write about in my fantasy tales. And, since I am an Arthurian buff and a lover of things medieval, knowing a bit about the church helps," Yolen wrote in *CA*. However, Yolen's greatest influence in high school was her cousin-in-law Honey Knopp, a pacifist and peace activist who held hootenannies at her home and gave Yolen a copy of *Journal* by George Fox, the founder of the Quaker faith. Fox later became the subject of Yolen's biography *Friend: The Story of George Fox and the Quakers.* The home that Honey Knopp shared with her husband, Burt, according to Yolen, "became my haven. Oh, I still went to basketball games and dances and parties, wisecracking with my friends and being outrageous. But Honey called out another side of me." Honey's influence is present in many of Yolen's most well-known books, such as *The Gift of Sarah Barker* and *The Transfigured Hart.*

After graduating from high school, Yolen attended Smith College, a prestigious institution for women in western Massachusetts. Going to Smith, Yolen wrote in *CA,* "was a choice that would, all unknowingly, change my life. It made me aware of friendships possible—and impossible—with women. It created in me a longing for a particular countryside, that of New England. It charged me with a sense of leftsidedness, of an alien or changeling awareness. And it taught me, really, about poetry and literature and the written word." At Smith, Yolen majored in English and Russian literature and minored in religion. She ran several campus organizations, authored and performed in the class musicals, and wrote her final exam in American intellectual history in verse, receiving an A+ as her grade. She also wrote poetry: between her junior and senior year, one of Yolen's poems was published in *Poetry Digest,* and her verse was also published in other small literary magazines.

Although poetry was in her soul, Yolen decided to become a journalist. During the summer between her freshman and sophomore years, Yolen worked as a cub reporter for the *Bridgeport Sunday Herald.* "It was there," Yolen recalled in *CA,* "I wrote my first signed pieces for a newspaper. My very first byline read 'by Joan Yolen.' I did not take it as a sign." Other vacations were spent as a junior counselor in New Jersey and working for *Newsweek* magazine as an intern; she also contributed to the *New Haven Register* and published an article on kites in *Popular Mechanics.* Yolen dismissed the idea of being a journalist when she found herself making up facts and writing stories off the top of her head; she also found that she was emotional when it came to interviewing the poor. "It became clear," she told *CA,* "that I was a fiction writer." However, Yolen did continue her musical pursuits, writing in *FBJAI* that she "made an unhappy college career bearable by singing with a guitar-playing boyfriend at fraternity parties and mixers. We made a little money, a lot of friends, and imprinted hundreds of folk tunes on our hungry minds." After graduating from Smith, Yolen moved to New York City and worked briefly for *This Week* magazine and *Saturday Review* before launching her career as a freelance writer. She helped her father write his book *The Young Sportsman's Guide to Kite Flying* and did a number of small freelance jobs. Yolen took an apartment in Greenwich Village with two roommates. At a wild party there in the summer of 1960, she met her future husband, David Stemple, who was a friend of one of her roommates; the couple were married in

1962. Yolen has noted that one of her most popular books, *The Girl Who Loved the Wind,* is about her meeting with David, a computer expert and photographer who is Yolen's chief advisor on her books. "In it," she stated in *CA,* "a Persian girl is kept in a walled-in palace by an overprotective father until the day the wind leaps over the garden wall and sweeps her away into the wide, everchanging world."

Approached by an editor from the publisher Alfred A. Knopf, Yolen fibbed and said that she had a book-length manuscript ready for review. She recalled in *CA:* "Caught in the web of this deceit, I, who always prided myself on my honesty, realized there was nothing to do but sit down at my typewriter and get something done quickly. Children's books! I thought. They'd be quickest and easiest." Yolen soon learned that writing books for children was not as quick and easy as she first thought. She collaborated with a high school friend, illustrator Susan Purdy, on several manuscripts, none of which were accepted by the editor at Knopf. Then, Yolen and Purdy sent their manuscripts to other publishers, but with no success. In 1961, Yolen became an assistant editor at Gold Medal Books, a paperback house known for its western novels and spy thrillers. She wrote in *CA:* "I was famous for about a moment in publishing as the one who coined 'she was all things to two men' for some Gothic novel." Her father introduced Yolen to Eleanor Rawson, the vice president of David McKay Publishing Company. In turn, Rawson introduced the fledgling author to Rose Dobbs, the editor in charge of children's books. Yolen's first book, the nonfiction title *Pirates in Petticoats,* was followed by *See This Little Line?,* a picture book in rhyme that was published the same year.

After leaving Gold Medal Books, where she got to know such authors as Kurt Vonnegut and Harlan Ellison, Yolen became an associate editor at Rutledge Press, a small packaging house that created books and then sold them to larger publishing companies for distribution. Yolen became a ghostwriter for Rutledge, authoring several books—often concept and activity books—that were published under different names. While at Rutledge, Yolen met Frances Keene, an editor who became head of the children's book department at Macmillan. Writing in *CA,* Yolen called Keene, who was to publish five of her books, "a great teacher as well as a fine editor. She taught me to trust my storytelling ability and to work against being too quick. . . . She also pushed me into delving deeply into folklore while at the same time recognizing my comedic talents." Yolen described her association with Keene as the "beginning of an editorial relationship that I *really* count as the start of my writing career." In 1963 Yolen became an assistant editor in the children's department at Knopf, where she met authors and illustrators such as Roald Dahl and Roger Duvoisin and learned about children's literature. She formed a writers' group with such aspiring authors and editors as Jean van Leeuwen, Alice Bach, and James Cross Giblin; one of the members of the group, Anne Huston, collaborated with Yolen on the realistic young adult novel *Trust a City Kid.*

In 1965 the Stemples decided to spend a year traveling. For nine months, they trekked across Europe and then sailed for Israel and Greece. Yolen wrote in *CA* that bits and pieces "of our wanderings have already found their way into my stories." She added that "places and people we met were stored away in my memory, and months, even years, later were transformed into the magical landscape of my tales." While they were traveling, Yolen discovered that she was pregnant; Heidi Stemple arrived in 1966, shortly after her parents returned to America. David Stemple took a job at the University of Massachusetts Computer Center in Amherst, so he and Jane relocated to western Massachusetts. Adam Stemple was born in 1968 and Jason Stemple in 1970. During the late 1960s, Yolen met editor Ann K. Beneduce, whom the author described in *CA* as "another seminal influence in my writing life." Yolen and Beneduce, who, according to the author, "produced book after book in the handsomest way possible," worked on approximately thirty books together.

The Emperor and the Kite, a picture book that was among the first of Yolen's works to be edited by Beneduce, is the first of the author's titles to receive major awards. The story outlines how Djeow Seow, the youngest and smallest daughter of an ancient Chinese emperor, saves her father after he is kidnapped by sending him a kite to which is attached a rope made of grass, vines, and strands of her hair. Writing in the *Dictionary of Literary Biography (DLB),* William E. Krueger noted that the story "is simply told in the folk tradition, with traditional motifs which provide an aura both of antiquity and of familiarity to the tale." The critic also observed the theme—"that those whom society considers deficient are capable and perhaps more proficient than others—recurs in subsequent tales." A critic in *Publishers Weekly* said that *The Emperor and the Kite* "is easily one of the most distinguished [books with Oriental backgrounds]—and distinguished proof that extravagance, intelligence, premeditated extravagance, always justifies itself." A reviewer in *Children's Book News* commented: "Here is a writer who delights in words and can use them in a controlled way to beautiful effect." In *The Girl Who Loved the Wind,* a picture book, again illustrated by Ed Young, a widowed merchant tries to protect his beautiful daughter from unhappiness but ends up making her a virtual prisoner. The wind visits her and sings to her about life, how it is always full of change and challenges. Finally, the merchant's daughter escapes with the wind into the world. Writing in *School Library Journal,* Marilyn R. Singer stated that Yolen "produced a treasure. The story has the grace and wisdom of a folk tale, the polish that usually comes from centuries of telling." Eleanor Von Schweinitz of *Children's Book Review* added that the author "has an especial gift for the invention of traditional-type tales and this is complemented by her rare ability to use language creatively. Here she has used the simple rhythms of the storyteller to conjure up the distinctive flavour of an Eastern tale." Writing in *CA,* Yolen said that she wrote *The Girl Who Loved the Wind* "for myself, out of my own history. But recently I received a letter from a nurse who told me that she had read the story to a dying child, and the story had eased the little girl through her final pain. The story did that—not me. But if I can continue to write with as much honesty and love as I can muster, I will truly have touched magic—and passed it on."

When Yolen was sixteen, her aunt's sister by marriage, Honey Knopp, gave her a copy of the journal of George Fox, the founder of the Quakers. "Since then," Yolen told *CA,* "I've been interested in the Quakers." Yolen became a member of the Religious Society of Friends (Quakers) in 1971. The next year, she published another of her most well-received titles, *Friend: The Story of George Fox and the Quakers.* A biography of the seventeenth-century Englishman who founded the movement that came to be known as Quakerism as part of his own quest for religious freedom, the book is noted for portraying Fox—with his long hair and pronouncements in favor of women's rights and against war and slavery—as a kindred spirit to the young radicals of today. William E. Krueger of *DLB* called *Friend* "a quite readable biography, interesting and, in places, quite touching, without fictionalization." Writing in *Library Journal,* Janet G. Polacheck noted: "Even where the subject is not in great demand, this beautifully written, valuable biography is an essential purchase."

The Girl Who Cried Flowers and Other Tales, is a collection of five stories that, according to a reviewer in *Publishers Weekly,* "could be called modern folk- or fairy tales, since they boast all the usual ingredients—supernatural beings, inexplicable happenings, the struggle between good and evil forces." The critic concluded that Yolen's "artistry with words . . . makes a striking book." A critic in *Kirkus Reviews* called *The Girl Who Cried Flowers* a "showpiece, for those who can forego the tough wisdom of traditional fairy tales for a masterful imitation of the manner." Reflective of a clear moral tone, *The Girl Who Cried Flowers* is also considered notable for suggesting the close relationship of humanity and nature. William E. Krueger of *DLB* called the book "haunting in its mythic implications" and stated that "the tone and poetic elements are Yolen's unique contributions."

All in the Woodland Early is a concept book that teaches the alphabet through the author's verses and musical score. The book outlines a little boy's hunting expedition in the woods; each letter represents the animal, bird, or insect—both familiar and unfamiliar—for which he is searching. At the end of the last verse, readers discover that the boy is gathering the animals to play with him and a little girl. Yolen also provides music to go with her words. Writing in the *Washington Post Book World,* Jerome Beatty, Jr. said: "Count on versatile Jane Yolen to invent something special and intriguing." He summed up his review by saying: "So clever! It adds another dimension to a lesson in the ABCs, does it not?" A reviewer in *Publishers Weekly* called *All in the Woodland Early* "an outstanding alphabet book," while William E. Krueger of *DLB* called it a "beautifully composed book, reminiscent of cumulative nursery rhymes. . . . This work exhibits Yolen's delightful handling of image, verse, and music."

Commander Toad in Space is the first of her popular "Commander Toad" series for beginning readers that pokes fun at the popular "Star Wars" films—for example, Commander Toad's ship is called the *Star Warts*—and the "Star Trek" television series. Yolen's series is usually considered a humorous and entertaining way of introducing children to literature. In *Com-*

mander Toad in Space, the brave captain and his frog crew discover a watery planet and an evil monster, Deep Wader, who is defeated by being engaged in a sing-along. Judith Goldberger of *Booklist* stated: "Any beginning-to-read book with brave space explorers, a ship named the *Star Warts,* and a monster who calls himself Deep Wader would be popular almost by definition. The bonus here is that the adventure of Commander Toad and his colleagues is a clever spoof and really funny reading." A reviewer in *School Library Journal* called the book a "hoppy combination of good story and clever media exploitation" before concluding: "This one holds water."

Simple Gifts: The Story of the Shakers is an informational book about the history of Shakerism, a millennium religion that grew out of Quakerism but has different beliefs. *The Gift of Sarah Barker* is a historical novel for young adults that is set in a Shaker community. The story features two teenagers, Abel and Sarah, who have grown up in the Society of Believers, a celibate religious community, and now find that they are sexually attracted to each other. As the young people struggle with their feelings, Yolen depicts the contradiction between the religious ecstasy of the Shakers—whose dances and celebrations gave the group their nickname—and the repressive quality of their lifestyle. Sarah and Abel decide to leave the community, but not before Sister Agatha, Sarah's abusive mother, commits suicide. Writing in *Children's Book Review Service,* Barbara Baker called *The Gift of Sarah Barker* "an absorbing tale" and a "jewel of a historical novel," while Stephanie Zvirin of *Booklist* stated: "Into the fabric of a teenage romance [Yolen] weaves complicated and disturbing—at times violent—undercurrents that add a dimension both powerful and provocative." Before writing *Sarah Barker,* Yolen interviewed some of the few remaining Shakers for background information. She also used her daughter, Heidi, who was becoming interested in boys, as the prototype for Sarah. Yolen told *CA,* "I kept wondering how, in a Shaker community, you could keep the boys away from a girl like Heidi or keep Heidi away from the boys. I imagined a Romeo and Juliet story within the Shaker setting."

Dragon's Blood: A Fantasy, is the first volume in her "Pit Dragon" series. High fantasy for young adults that incorporates elements of science fiction and is often compared favorably to the "Pern" books by Anne McCaffrey, the "Pit Dragon" series is acknowledged for Yolen's imaginative creation of a completely realized world. *Dragon's Blood* features Jakkin, a fifteen-year-old slave boy whose master is the best dragon breeder on the planet Austar IV, a former penal colony where inhabitants train and fight dragons domesticated by the early colonists. Jakkin steals a female dragon hatchling to train in secret for the gaming pits, a cockfighting ritual that contributes largely to the planet's economy. Hoping to win his freedom by raising a superior fighting dragon, Jakkin establishes an amazing mental link with his "snatchling," which he names Heart's Blood. The story ends with the dragon's first win; Jakkin—now free—learns that his master knew about his theft and that Akki, a bond girl training in medicine whom Jakkin loves, is his master's illegitimate daughter. Writing in *Horn Book,* Ann A. Flowers called *Dragon's Blood* an "original and engrossing fantasy," while Patricia Manning of *School Library Journal* said that the novel provides a "fascinating glimpse of a brand new world." Pauline Thomas of the *School Librarian* called the book "splendid entertainment," adding, "the author explains little, letting the reader work out the details of geography, natural history, social structure, and sexual mores. The result is remarkably convincing. Austar IV is a world as real as [Ursula K. Le Guin's] Earthsea."

In the second volume of the series, *Heart's Blood,* Jakkin is the new Dragon Master and Heart's Blood has given birth to five hatchlings. Jakkin becomes involved in Austar politics when he is asked to infiltrate rebel forces and rescue Akki. Becoming the pawns in a deadly game, Jakkin and Akki flee with Heart's Blood into the freezing cold of night, called Dark After. Cornered by the authorities after inadvertently blowing up a major arena, the trio fight for their lives. In the battle, Heart's Blood is killed. In order to survive the freezing temperatures, Jakkin and Akki enter her carcass; when they emerge, they have been given the gift of dragon's sight—telepathy—and the ability to withstand the cold. Charlotte W. Draper of *Horn Book* stated: "Rich in symbolism, eloquent in the evocation of a culture which carries within it the seeds of its own destruction, the book stretches the reader's conception of human capability." In *A Sending of Dragons,* the third volume in the series, Jakkin and Akki avoid capture by running into the wilderness with Heart's Blood's five babies. When they enter a hidden tunnel, the group encounter an underground tribe of primitives who have discovered the way to extract metals on Austar IV. Jakkin and Akki also learn that these people, who, like them, are bonded to dragons, have developed a bloody, terrifying ritual of dragon sacrifice. At the end of the novel, Akki, Jakkin, and Heart's Blood's fledglings escape with two of the primitive community's dragons. Confronted by their pursuers from above ground, they decide to return to the city and use their new knowledge to bring about an end to the feudalism and enslavement on Austar IV. A reviewer in *Publishers Weekly* stated: "Yolen's tightly plotted, adventurous trilogy constitutes superb storytelling. She incorporates elements of freedom and rebellion, power and control, love and friendship in a masterfully crafted context of a society sick with perversion." Writing in *School Library Journal,* Michael Cart said that, like the two volumes preceding it, the particular strengths of *A Sending of Dragons* are in "the almost encyclopedic detail which Yolen has lavished upon her fully realized alternative world of Austar IV, in her sympathetic portrayal of the dragons as both victims and telepathic partners, and in the symbolic sub-text which enriches her narrative and reinforces her universal theme of the inter-dependency and unique value of all life forms."

One of Yolen's most highly acclaimed books is *The Devil's Arithmetic,* a young adult time-travel fantasy that is rooted in one of the darkest episodes of history. The novel features Hannah Stern, a twelve-year-old Jewish girl who is transported from contemporary New York to rural Poland in 1942 when she opens the door for Elijah during her family's Seder celebration. Captured by the Nazis, Hannah—now called Chaya—is taken to a death camp, where she meets Rivka, a spirited young girl who teaches her to fight against the dehumanization of the camp and tells her that some must live to bear witness. When Rivka is chosen to be taken to the gas chamber, Chaya, in an act of self-sacrifice, goes in her place; as the doors of the gas chamber close, Chaya—now Hannah again—is returned to the door of her grandparents' apartment, waiting for Elijah. Hannah realizes that her Aunt Eva is her friend Rivka and that she also knew her grandfather in the camp. A critic in *Kirkus Reviews* wrote of *The Devil's Arithmetic:* "Yolen is the author of a hundred books, many of which have been praised for their originality, humor, or poetic vision, but this thoughtful, compelling novel is unique among them." Writing in *Bulletin of the Center for Children's Books,* Roger Sutton noted that Yolen's depiction of the horrors in the camp "is more graphic than any we've seen in holocaust fiction for children before." Confirming that Yolen has brought the "time travel convention to a new and ambitious level," Cynthia Samuels of the *New York Times Book Review* concluded that "sooner or later, all our children must know what happened in the days of the Holocaust. *The Devil's Arithmetic* offers an affecting way to begin." Yolen, who has said that she wrote *The Devil's Arithmetic* for her own children, stated in her acceptance speech for the Sydney Taylor Book Award: "There are books one writes because they are a delight. There are books one writes because one is asked to. There are books one writes because . . . they are there. And there are books one writes simply because the book has to be written. *The Devil's Arithmetic* is this last kind of book. I did not just write it. The book itself was a mitzvah."

With *Encounter,* a picture book published to coincide with the five-hundredth anniversary of the discovery of America, Yolen created what is perhaps her most controversial work. Written as the remembrance of an elderly Taino Indian man, the story, which describes the first encounter of Native Americans with Columbus, depicts the man's experience as a small boy. The narrator awakens from a terrifying dream about three predatory birds riding the waves to see three anchored ships. Frightened yet fascinated by the strangers who come ashore, the boy tells his chief not to welcome the men, but he is ignored. The boy and several other Indians are taken aboard the ships as slaves. After he escapes by jumping overboard, the boy tries to warn other tribes, but to no avail; the Taino are wiped out. Calling *Encounter* an "unusual picture book," Carolyn Phelan of *Booklist* noted that "while the portrayal of Columbus as evil may strike traditionalists as heresy, he did hunger for gold, abduct native people, and ultimately (though unintentionally), destroy the Taino. This book effectively presents their point of view." Writing in the *New Advocate,* James C. Junhke called *Encounter* "among the most powerful and disturbing publications of the Columbus Quincentennial." Noting the "pioneering brilliance" of the book, the critic called Yolen's greatest achievement "the reversal of perspective. This book forces us to confront what a disaster it was for the Taino people to be discovered and destroyed by Europeans. Readers young and old will fervently wish never to be encountered by such 'strangers from the sky.'" Writing in response to Junhke's review in the same publication, Yolen said, "If my book becomes a first step towards the exploration of the meeting between Columbus and the indigenous peoples—and its tragic aftermath—then it has done its work, whatever its flaws, perceived or real." The author concluded, "We cannot change history. But we—and most especially our children—

can learn from it so that the next encounters, be they at home, abroad, or in space, may be gentler and mutually respectful. It is a large hope but it is, perhaps, all that we have."

Yolen has a penchant for viewing popular versions of stories from a new perspective. Of *Sword of the Rightful King,* Kelly Milner Halls wrote in the *Denver Post:* "Master storyteller Jane Yolen deftly turns the popular myth upside down in this vibrant new look at Arthur's dubious destiny and the cast of characters who helped deliver it." In the book, Yolen ponders such questions as what if pulling the sword from the stone did not entitle the young Arthur to become king? Maybe the fable was created after the boy was crowned king as a public relations effort to gain the people's devotion? Maybe Merlin (Merlinnus, in the book) was simply manipulating Arthur for his own political gain? What if the brave knights of the round table were easily deceived? "The theme of power and belief becoming reality, while not new, is used to good effect here to properly explore the Authurian myths in a new light," commented Mike Jones in *SF.*

Companion book to *Not One Damsel in Distress: World Folktales for Strong Girls, Mightier Than the Sword* begins with a letter from Yolen to the "boys" in her life—her sons and grandsons. She writes, "being a hero [is] more than whomping and stomping the bad guy" and comments on the truth "that brains trump brawn almost every time; that being smart makes the battle shorter, the kingdom nearer, the victory brighter, and the triumph greater." The book consists of fourteen folktales in which, according to Susan Dove Lempke in *Horn Book* magazine, "boys solve their seemingly impossible problems not with force but with wit, trust, kindness and other virtues." Writing in the *Bulletin of the Center for Children's Books,* Janice M. Del Negro said that even so, there is still plenty of action in the tales, and the similarity many of them bear to already classic fables—such as "The Bremen Town Musicians" and "Puss in Boots"—"make this title valuable for comparative folktale curricula and collections."

Throughout her career, Yolen has woven bits and pieces of her personal history—and that of her family and friends—into her works. She was quoted in *DLB* as saying that she uses "these scraps the way a bird makes a nest and a mouse makes a house—snippet by snippet, leaf and bough and cotton batting and all." Several of the author's books are directly autobiographical. For example, *All Those Secrets of the World* is set during the two years that her father was away at war. Yolen recalls how, as a four-year-old, she watched her father depart by ship. The next day, Janie and her five-year-old cousin Michael see some tiny specks on the horizon while they are playing on the beach; the specks are ships. Michael teaches Janie a secret of the world, that as he moves farther away, he gets smaller. Two years later, when her father returns, Janie whispers Michael's secret after he tells her that she seems bigger: that when he was so far away, everything seemed smaller, but now that he is here, she is big. A reviewer in *Publishers Weekly* wrote: "Yolen here relates a bittersweet memory from an important period in her childhood. . . . This timely nostalgic story is told with simple grace, and Janie's thoughts and experiences are believably childlike." Phyllis G. Sidorsky of *School Library Journal* called *All Those Secrets of the World* an "affecting piece without an extraneous word and one that is particularly timely today."

And Twelve Chinese Acrobat is based on family stories about her father's older brother. Set in a Russian village in 1910, the book features Lou the Rascal, a charming troublemaker who keeps getting into scrapes. When Lou is sent to a military school in Kiev, the family—especially narrator Wolf, Lou's youngest brother (and Yolen's father)—is sad. Lou is expelled from military school. Months later, he surprises everyone by bringing home a troupe of twelve Chinese acrobats he met while working in a Moscow circus. The acrobats fascinate the locals with their descriptions of an exotic world far removed from the little village. When the acrobats leave the *shtel* in the spring, Lou's father, recognizing his son's managerial ability, sends him to America to find a place for the family. Writing in the *Bulletin of the Center for Children's Books,* Betsy Hearne said: "The relationship between the two brothers, Lou and Wolf, lends an immediate dynamic to the historical setting." The critic concluded that the compressed narrative, brief chapters, spacious format, large print, and "vivaciously detailed pen-and-ink illustrations dancing across almost every page [by Jean Gralley] make this a prime choice for young readers venturing into historical fiction for the first time, or, for that matter, considering a probe into their own family stories." A critic in *Kirkus Reviews* called *And Twelve Chinese Acrobats* a book "radiating family warmth, in words, art, and remembrance."

Yolen again drew on personal experience when her husband was diagnosed with an inoperable brain tumor in 2003. Suddenly finding her life spinning out of control, she attempted to combat the helpless sensation by each night retiring to her attic office to compose a sonnet. "It is such a rigid form that it imposes structure; it empowered me because then I had control," she told Eric Goldscheider of the *Boston Globe.* The result: forty-three sonnets written over the course of her husband's forty-three-day radiation regimen and released as *The Radiation Sonnets.* "Some of the poems are funny and some of the poems are just a cry for help," she told Goldscheider.

In an article for *Horn Book,* Yolen stated: "As a writer I am the empress of thieves, taking characters like gargoyles off Parisian churches, the *ki-lin* (or unicorn) from China, swords in stones from the Celts, landscapes from the Taino people. I have pulled threads from magic tapestries to weave my own new cloth." The author concluded, "Children's literature is about growth. Just as we do not put heavy weights on our children's heads to stunt their growth, we should not put weights on our writers' heads. To do so is to stunt story forever. Stories go beyond race, beyond religion—even when they are about race and religion. The book speaks to individuals in an individual voice. But then it is taken into the reader's life and recreated, re-invigorated, re-visioned. That is what literature is about."

Writing in *CA,* Yolen mused that her life, "like anyone else's is a patchwork of past and present. . . . I can also see a pattern that might tell me my future—as long as I remain consistent. I consider myself a poet and a storyteller. Being 'America's Hans Christian Andersen' means trying to walk in much-too-large seven-league boots. I just want to go on writing and discovering my stories for the rest of my life because I know that in my tales I make public what is private, transforming my own joy and sadness into tales for the people. The folk."

During an interview for *Bookbird* with Eva-Maria Metcalf, Yolen discussed the relevance of folklore in her work. She commented: "Only in America do we seem to want to throw away the past and constantly rebuild afresh. We seem to think that there is no need to stand on the shoulders of giants. That we ARE the giants. Give me a moment of metaphor here. In Scotland, where I live half the year, the old stones from houses and churches, and cathedrals, become incorporated into new buildings. Harled over and whitewashed, they are still a reminder of how close to their own ghosts the Scots dwell. I believe that is a better way."

BIOGRAPHICAL AND CRITICAL SOURCES:

BOOKS

Authors and Artists for Young Adults, Volume 4, Gale (Detroit, MI), 1990, pp. 229-241.

Children's Literature Review, Volume 4, Gale (Detroit, MI), 1982, pp. 255-269; Volume 44, 1997, pp. 167-211.

de Montreville, Doris, and Elizabeth D. Crawford, editors, *Dictionary of Literary Biography,* Volume 52: *American Writers for Children since 1960: Fiction,* Gale (Detroit, MI), 1986, pp. 398-405.

Drew, Bernard A., *The One Hundred Most Popular Young Adult Authors,* Libraries Unlimited (Englewood, CO), 1996.

Roginski, Jim, *Behind the Covers: Interviews with Authors and Illustrators of Books for Children and Young Adults,* Libraries Unlimited (Englewood, CO), 1985.

St. James Guide to Fantasy Writers, St. James Press (Detroit, MI), 1996.

St. James Guide to Young Adult Writers, St. James Press (Detroit, MI), 1999.

Silvey, Anita, editor, *Children's Books and Their Creators,* Houghton Mifflin (Boston, MA), 1995, pp. 700-701.

Twentieth-Century Children's Writers, St. James Press (Detroit, MI), 1989, pp. 1075-1078.

Yolen, Jane, *Guide to Writing for Children,* The Writer (Boston, MA), 1989.

Yolen, Jane, *Touch Magic: Fantasy, Faerie, and Folktale in the Literature of Childhood,* Philomel Books (New York, NY), 1981.

Yolen, Jane, *Writing Books for Children,* The Writer (Boston, MA), 1973, revised edition, 1983.

PERIODICALS

Bookbird, May, 2003, Eva-Maria Metcalf, interview with Jane Yolen, pp. 52-55.

Booklist, November 15, 1980, Judith Goldberger, review of *Commander Toad in Space,* p. 464; May 15, 1981, Stephanie Zvirin, review of *The Gift of Sarah Barker,* p. 1250; March 1, 1992, Carolyn Phelan, review of *Encounter,* p. 1281.

Boston Globe, May 22, 2003, Eric Goldscheider, interview, "At Home with Jane Yolen," p. H2; June 8, 2003, Liz Rosenberg, "High-Flying Youths and Brave Patriots," review of *My Brothers' Flying Machine: Wilbur, Orville, and Me,* p. H.9.

Bulletin of the Center for Children's Books, October, 1988, Roger Sutton, review of *The Devil's Arithmetic,* pp. 23-24; June, 1995, Betsy Hearne, review of *And Twelve Chinese Acrobats,* p. 365; May 2003, Elizabeth Bush, review of *My Brothers' Flying Machine,* p. 379-380; July-August 2003, Janice M. Del Negro, review of *Mightier Than the Sword: World Folktales for Strong Boys,* p. 466; September 2003, Janice M. Del Negro, review of *Sword of the Rightful King: A Novel of King Arthur,* p. 41; September 2003, Elizabeth Bush, review of *Roanoke: The Lost Colony: An Unsolved Mystery from History,* p. 40-41.

Childhood Education, summer, 2003, Heather J. B. Arbuckle, review of *Wild Wings: Poems for Young People,* pp. 244-245.

Children's Book News, January-February, 1970, review of *The Emperor and the Kite,* pp. 23-24.

Children's Book Review, December, 1973, Eleanor Von Schweinitz, review of *The Girl Who Loved the Wind,* pp. 172-173.

Children's Book Review Service, June, 1981, Barbara Baker, review of *The Gift of Sarah Barker,* p. 100.

Denver Post, August 3, 2003, Kelly Milner Halls, review of *Sword of the Rightful King,* p. H2.

Horn Book, August, 1982, Ann A. Flowers, review of *Dragon's Blood,* pp. 418-419; April, 1984, Charlotte W. Draper, review of *Heart's Blood,* p. 206; November-December, 1994, Jane Yolen, "An Empress of Thieves," pp. 702-705; May-June 2003, Susan Dove Lempke, review of *Mightier than the Sword,* p. 362-363.

Judaica Librarianship, spring, 1989-winter, 1990, transcript of Yolen's acceptance speech for the Sydney Taylor Book Award, pp. 52-53.

Kirkus Reviews, July 15, 1974, review of *The Girl Who Cried Flowers and Other Tales,* p. 741; August 15, 1988, review of *The Devil's Arithmetic,* p. 1248; April 15, 1995, review of *And Twelve Chinese Acrobats,* p. 564.

Library Journal, June 15, 1972, Janet G. Polacheck, review of *Friend: The Story of George Fox and the Quakers,* p. 2245.

New Advocate, spring, 1993, James C. Juhnke and Jane Yolen, "An Exchange on *Encounter,*" pp. 94-96.

New York Times Book Review, November 20, 1977, Jane Langton, review of *The Hundredth Dove and Other Tales,* p. 30; November 13, 1988, Cynthia Samuels, "Hannah Learns to Remember," p. 62; November 8, 1992, Noel Perrin, "Bulldozer Blues," p. 54; August 10, 2003, Eric Nagourney, review of *How Do Dinosaurs Get Well Soon?,* p. 19.

Publishers Weekly, August 14, 1967, review of *The Emperor and the Kite,* p. 50; July 22, 1974, review of *The Girl Who Cried Flowers and Other Tales,* p. 70; January 11, 1980, review of *All in the Woodland Early,* p. 88; October 9, 1987, review of *A Sending of Dragons,* p. 90; March 22, 1991, review of *All Those Secrets of the World,* p. 80; April 14, 2003, Diane Robak, review of *Sword of the Rightful King;* August 4, 2003, review of *The Flying Witch,* p. 78.

School Librarian, December, 1983, Pauline Thomas, review of *Dragon's Blood,* p. 384.

School Library Journal, March, 1973, Marilyn R. Singer, review of *The Girl Who Loved the Wind,* p. 102; December, 1980, review of *Commander Toad in Space,* p. 66; September, 1982, Patricia Manning, review of *Dragon's Blood,* p. 146; January, 1988, Michael Cart, review of *A Sending of Dragons,* pp. 87-88; July, 1991, Phyllis G. Sidorsky, review of *All Those Secrets of the World,* p. 66.

SF, August, 2003, Mike Jones, review of *Sword of the Rightful King,* pp. 66-68.

Teaching and Learning Literature (TALL), November-December, 1996, Lee Bennett Hopkins, "O Yolen: A Look at the Poetry of Jane Yolen," pp. 66-68.

USA Today, April 24, 2003, Ayesha Court, review of *Mightier Than the Sword,* p. D.06.

Washington Post Book World, April 13, 1980, Jerome Beatty, Jr., "Herds of Hungry Hogs Hurrying Home," p. 10; July 13, 2003, review of *Sword of the Rightful King.*

ONLINE

Jane Yolen Home Page, http://www.janeyolen.com/.

OTHER

The Children's Writer: Jane Yolen (video), ReelLife Productions, produced 1996.

Good Conversations: A Talk with Jane Yolen (video), Tom Podell Productions, produced 1998.

SCHEELE MEMORIAL LIBRARY
3 6655 00114376 6

REF Z 1224 .C6 NRS v.126
Contemporary authors
Contemporary authors
LIMITED CIRCULATION

DATE DUE

REF Z 1224 .C6 NRS v.126
Contemporary authors
Contemporary authors
LIMITED CIRCULATION

DATE DUE	BORROWER'S NAME

Concordia College Library
Bronxville, NY 10708